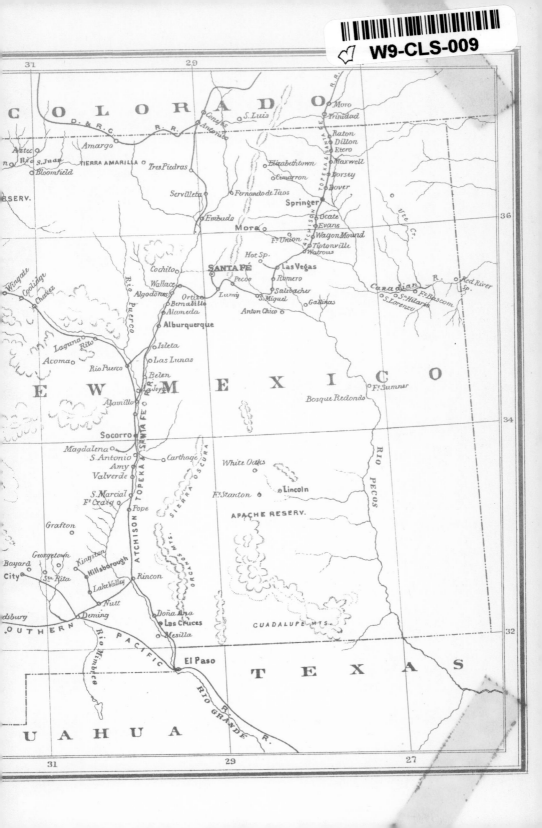

BANCROFT'S
HISTORY OF
ARIZONA & NEW MEXICO

HUBERT HOWE BANCROFT

HISTORY OF

ARIZONA AND

A facsimile of
the 1889 Edition
published coincident to
the 50th Anniversary of
New Mexico & Arizona Statehood

NEW MEXICO
1530-1888

NEW MEXICO FOREWORD
by Senator Clinton P. Anderson

ARIZONA FOREWORD
by Senator Barry Goldwater

HORN & WALLACE, Publishers
Albuquerque   1962

NEW MEXICO FOREWORD

Nearly thirty years ago, in writing a foreword to a guide to New Mexico, I expressed the belief that in this state, time becomes visible.

That can be true because we see the blending of the glories of the past with the marks of progress. We cling tenaciously to the traditions of the past. Yet progress, by its very nature, is disruptive of the past.

If man could have his choice, there would be two worlds: one in which his brand new inventions serve him with splendid convenience; another in which the rustic, charming past feeds his sense of reverence for tradition. Few places on earth provide an opportunity to live in both worlds at the same time, but one of them is close at hand in the form of New Mexico: a combination of Twentieth Century values and Fifteenth Century rusticity and charm.

New Mexico in the present era represents a blend of three cultures—Indian, Spanish and modern—each of which, at one time or another, provided a dominant influence. Yet today they exist side by side: new office buildings in the contemporary manner with great expanses of glass stretching into the sky, complete with every modern convenience known to man; remote Spanish-American villages reminiscent of Sixteenth Century culture, in which the language of the people is more in keeping with that of the Spaniards of that period than with those in Spain today;

Indian communities, maintaining traditions inaugurated back in the time when Coronado came searching for the cities of gold and found instead corn shining in the sun of the roofs of Zuñi adobe dwellings.

Visitors to New Mexico today invariably are entranced by this complex mixture of past and present, of progress and tradition. Moreover, the mixture is not a new development, for indeed it has captured the fancy of observers since the close of the Civil War, at which point the great American migration to the Southwest began in earnest.

Hubert Howe Bancroft, one of the first to note and record the treasures of New Mexico, undertook to state his conclusions as a part of an extraordinary historical series dealing with the Spanish-American West.

Of Puritan stock, Bancroft was a product of early Nineteenth Century New England, where the "West" was thought to begin somewhere in the vicinity of Pittsburgh, and where it was generally assumed that anything occurring west of that point was of little consequence to the fate of the "real" world of the Eastern seaboard.

Yet in Bancroft, as in many New Englanders of his time, there was the suspicion that maybe the general assumption was not quite exact; that perhaps there was something of value out there in what the map makers labeled "The Great American Desert." He would take a look, just to make sure. His look carried him to San Francisco where, in 1858, he founded a publishing and mercantile firm, and promptly became wealthy.

Bancroft was not, however, exclusively concerned with wealth. Far from it. He was primarily concerned with books and what they had to offer. If what they offered included wealth, he was willing to accept it. But if, in turn, the production of books entailed the expenditure of great sums —and if he thought the product worthy of the cost—he was by no means hesitant to empty his personal treasury in the interest of literary accomplishment.

Moreover, as one concerned with ideas, Bancroft became

obsessed with the ideas underlying the development of the West. And as one concerned with history, he was chagrined to note the unimportant role given to the West in the average American history text. He therefore conceived a plan—gargantuan in nature—of telling in detail the history of the Pacific Coast; a plan ultimately expanded to include the western half of North America, from Alaska to Panama.

So immense an undertaking would have been impossible to produce alone in the manner conceived by the author and the time at his disposal. Tired of the standard political approach to history, he envisaged a chronicle in which the ways, the customs, the hopes, dreams, and aspirations of the common people were allotted a position of major importance.

To go so deeply into small detail on a one-man or lone-scholar basis would have taken forever. Therefore, Bancroft hired a staff and with the assistance of its members inaugurated one of the first co-operative histories on record. As editor-in-chief, Bancroft was to set the tone of the work and to determine all policy, with the result that every book in the series bears the stamp of his style and basic beliefs.

It is to be observed, in the reading of this volume, The History of Arizona and New Mexico, that Bancroft was no mere sentimentalist; nor was he a mere propagandist beating the tub for the cause of American progress alone. Here in New Mexico when the first white settlers arrived, was an Indian civilization surpassing that of any other part of what would ultimately become the United States; a civilization shaken by the first appearance of the white man—tragically shaken, as Bancroft so well describes—and shaken again, repeatedly, as warring foreigners appeared to fight over the land ruled for so many centuries by the Indian gods. The tale, as told by Bancroft, is not of New Mexico as related to the political progress of the United States, but of New Mexico as related to the lives, the hopes, and aspirations of its inhabitants, from the earliest historical times, through to the date of publication.

In an essay on "History Writing" (Bancroft, Works, Vol. xxxviii (pp. 84-85), Bancroft once remarked that great men deserve their place in history, but not in the foreground. He urged historians to note the way in which nations begin and grow; to pay attention to the operations of ecclesiastical as well as civil government, to family relationships and to every species of social phenomena, including labor, industry, the arts, the intellect—"in short the progress of man's domination over nature."

The formula set forth above is the basis of every paragraph recorded in *The History of Arizona and New Mexico*. Notwithstanding the temptation to retell in standard detail the exciting political struggles of the region, Bancroft was inclined to direct his efforts into other, untraveled channels.

Among other things, he was dealing with the oldest European settlements in the western United States—so old that ten years before the Pilgrims landed at Plymouth Rock, a history of New Mexico was already in publication. Also to be dealt with was an Indian civilization of high accomplishments, which had persisted through centuries with the least modification. In addition to these, there was the American culture, wheeling in from the East toward the middle of the Nineteenth Century. With every culture, Bancroft deals in the manner of a combined sociologist, economist, religionist, political analyst, and psychologist. He seeks out justice and courage wherever it is to be found or by whomever displayed, and takes no sides between the vying cultures, except to applaud the just and the courageous in every culture. He describes the battles between contending armies in a manner doing justice to everyone involved.

Consequently, in reading this work, one is enabled to come away with a picture of the grandeur, the degradation, the accomplishment, and the shortcomings of everyone involved in the creation of first a territory and then a state, and to realize better the complexity of its conflicting traditions.

Throughout the narrative runs a theme which, in a certain respect, exemplifies New Mexico. This concerns the mineral wealth of the region, which, like a beacon, brought the white man here originally, opening up to civilization the beauties and advantages of the Southwest, without, except to a limited extent, supplying the sought-for wealth. It is one of the ironies of the State that it should have been founded on the zeal of gold-hungry adventurers, with little appreciation for the many other wonders they discovered. To this theme, Bancroft directs considerable attention, both from the point of view of the Indian culture (upset by the appearance of the Spanish), and of the Spanish and later the Anglo cultures, founded on the ruins of lost hopes and dreams of financial wealth.

It is interesting to note, in connection with the great size of the volume, that the author devoted a decade to collecting his materials on the West before setting pen to paper. Much of the specialized literature that Bancroft was able to utilize in the production of *The History of Arizona and New Mexico* was of superior quality, including Zebulon Pike's narrative, Pedro Bautista Pino's *Exposicion Sucinta*, the Benavides memorial, Siguenza y Gongora's *Mercurio Volante*, and many official reports on the Mexican War, boundary surveys and railroad surveys. The extent of the research put into the volume renders it important enough to reproduce today, notwithstanding the passage of seventy years since the date of original publication.

Naturally as I grow older and a little more crochety, I see things in the New Mexico portions of the huge volume that annoy me.

Bancroft spells the name of my hometown ALBURQUERQUE. I know that the town is named for the Duke of Alburquerque, and that there was an early "r" in his name, but the people in our community have called it ALBUQUERQUE for a hundred years—and that it will remain. It is a little like the capital of my native state of South Dakota—Pierre. The people who have an appreciation of French would like to call it P-AIR, but the people of South Dakota pronounce it as if it were a structure out in the ocean—PIER. Likewise, the folks of my hometown hold fast to ALBUQUERQUE.

The Bancroft cooperative writings are a little laborious with the long lists of legislators, governors, justices, and the laws that they wrote, administered and interpreted. There are footnotes ad nauseam. I often wonder what fun the staff got out of their writing. Nor do they always talk with authority. Repeatedly we find something like "I cannot claim to have made any original research in this phase of the matter."

But when I have said these things, I must admit that every time I read Bancroft, I wish I had time to read his work slowly—every page and every footnote. I long for time to trace the families that he mentions and to see how seats in the New Mexico Legislature went from father to son among the leading New Mexico families.

Each time I dip into the material on New Mexico, I thrill with the prospectors who search out the mineral wealth. I rejoice with them that by 1884 ore to the value of $3,660,000 was being taken from the earth of New Mexico in a single year. But today I know that in searching for the gold and silver, the lead and zinc, they walked over a yellow dust which an atomic age would require that industry mine and mill in New Mexico at an annual rate that makes insignificant all the silver of the Bridal Chamber near Lake Valley, all the gold in the Ortiz placer,—yes, even the copper below the Kneeling Nun at Santa Rita.

Time had to run, and each oncoming generation had to wait patiently for its hour to strike. Perhaps that is one of the lessons to be learned in a careful reading of this reprint.

CLINTON P. ANDERSON

Albuquerque, New Mexico
January 1962

ARIZONA FOREWORD

Three-fourths of a century has passed since the last type was proofread for Volume XVII of *The Works of Hubert Howe Bancroft*. This was distributed in 1889 as *History of Arizona and New Mexico 1530-1888*. Nothing so orderly and detailed had been attempted before, nor has any single work about this region since come close to matching the exacting research and preparation of this careful but not faultless volume.

This was a key edition in the third distinct step of Bancroft's monumental achievement in compiling a *History of the Pacific States*. His first unit was five books given to a study of the *Native Races*. Next came a generally orderly chronological pattern that began with the *History of Central America* in three volumes, that of *Mexico* in six, and a two-volume history of *North Mexican States and Texas* immediately preceding the Arizona–New Mexico book.

This was followed by the *History of California* in seven volumes, after which Bancroft discarded the chronological scheme in devoting nine other volumes to remaining territory in the West, including British Columbia and Alaska. In all, thirty-nine volumes were published, of which some 6,000 sets were sold by subscription.

Time has not diminished the value of the *Works* as a whole and actually has doubled or tripled the value of an individual copy of *Arizona and New Mexico*. No public or institutional library with any serious thought toward presentation of the history of Western America could be without the *Works*, and no private shelf of Western reference books in these two states can properly overlook the regional volume.

Treated jointly with the Texas–Northern Mexico edition, this Arizona–New Mexico work provides a path by which Bancroft traced the transition from Spanish to Anglo-American influence, in the settlement of the West. The evolution is nowhere better demonstrated than in this one volume.

Thus, nearly thirty years before Dr. Herbert E. Bolton assumed the directorship of the Bancroft Library in Berkeley and became the leading exponent of the Spanish influence in American development, Bancroft already had blocked out the pattern of Southwestern growth. Bolton himself was to bring it to recognition as a mainstream of American historical evolution. His epic essay, "The Mission As a Frontier Institution in the Spanish-American Colonies," found nourishment in Bancroft's pioneering studies of Mexican archives, which became part of his unexcelled collection of Western Americana. Bolton's inspiration for enlargement and synthesis of this area of study certainly was stimulated by Bancroft's writings and was projected in the library Bancroft created.

Yet, to speak of *Arizona and New Mexico* as a history "written" by the relentless Bancroft is to expose a controversy that raged about him a few years after its publication.

Critics of Bancroft, who were numerous fifty years ago and are very scarce today, built their animosity toward him upon two elements: a delayed public reaction to the hardnosed aggressiveness of his commission salesmen, in the first instance; and, secondly, upon his egocentric failure to give his fellow workers and employees credit for their authorship with him of the *Works*.

In *Arizona and New Mexico* he acknowledged on page 25 that he utilized a co-operative system of authorship, noting that a contemporary historian, Dr. Justin Winsor of Harvard, "employs a corps of authors, who write under their own names." He said Winsor was, like himself, an editor, but "also to a great extent the author."

With some ambiguity Bancroft withheld final judgment on whether Winsor's system of sharing credit with his co-authors was superior or had more defects than the publication of the *Works* without identification of the staff of writers who assisted him.

The credit that Bancroft would not share for this work soon was claimed by the man who had been librarian of the Bancroft collection for eighteen years, Bancroft's chief collaborator, and within a limited sphere a recognized expert on the Spanish borderlands. This was Henry L. Oak, who in bitterness later presented to his alma mater, Dartmouth College, a set of ten of the thirty-nine volumes of the *Works* in which he had written his name as author. Bancroft never publicly denied the assertion that Oak had written *Arizona and New Mexico*, based in turn upon a preliminary draft by a young Englishman, T. Arundel Harcourt, who died in 1884 before its completion. There were many others, researchers and compilers both in the field and in Bancroft's "Literary Workshop" in San Francisco, whom Oak also neglected to identify.

John Walton Caughey, in his sympathetic biography, *Hubert Howe Bancroft: Historian of the West*, stipulated that "omission of [author] credits was a serious mistake, probably the most serious of Bancroft's entire career."

In this facsimile publication of one volume can be rectified one of the errors of a man to whom history in the West owes a great deal. Mr. Oak cannot possibly know of this belated credit. He resigned his association with Bancroft in 1887, upon completion of the basic manuscript, and before the addition of a note added "just as these pages go into print" in which Bancroft's pride took precedence over his recognition of Oak's talents.

Bancroft's personal retort to Oak's demand for public

recognition had been a callous reference to the good pay and pleasant associations Oak had enjoyed throughout their eighteen years of collaboration. Despite this quarrel over the honors of authorship, Oak defended Bancroft publicly from less privileged attacks by others. He stoutly upheld the quality of the *Works*—and thereby his own craftsmanship —in saying, "While the defects are superficial, the merits go deeper. . . ." His only serious criticism of the *Works*, aside from the personal consideration, was the failure of Bancroft to make full use of manuscript material available in Mexican and Spanish depositories.

Oak did not detract from Bancroft's masterfulness as editor and writer; in the last instance he "hailed his chief as the worst compiler but the best writer of the entire staff," Caughey has commented.

Nevertheless it was Bancroft who conceived the *Works*, planned them, devised the technique followed by his staff, financed and profited from the success of the venture, and who usually polished and often enlarged upon final manuscripts. His personal touch must also have been added to *Arizona and New Mexico*.

To Oak's criticism of failure to use manuscript material in Mexico and Spain may be added a like neglect on the part of the "Literary Workshop" to utilize the vast store of government documents accumulated in various Washington departments. The Bancroft effort was essentially a Western undertaking, operated from the library of 40,000 books and thousands of pamphlets, manuscripts, dictations, and newspapers which in 1905 Bancroft sold to the University of California. While his staff made exhaustive handwritten copies of vital California and Western records, they did not penetrate the maze of bureaus in the national capital. Federal records had not yet been centralized. The National Archives was established in 1934.

Bancroft directed his staff to a meticulous condensation of the annals of each area. "His duty, as he envisioned it, was to assemble and present the facts about the course of development in this vast and little-studied area, to measure their meaning as far as possible, but without obscuring or beclouding the basic record," Caughey has noted.

Thus the text of the *Works* was printed in legible 12-point type and in a style of subjective narrative that was acceptable to the average subscription purchaser. Below, in much smaller type, footnotes that often consumed the majority of space on a page promised more absorbing study of supplemental detail. Here his staff had digested into notes a remarkable mass of pertinent facts supporting and enlarging upon the subjects generally treated in narrative form above.

The bibliography provided for *Arizona and New Mexico* on fourteen pages in the front of the book does not encompass all the references in following footnotes, yet it includes a scope of source material on the region that no library in either of the states is privileged to own. Many of these materials are held in the splendid Bancroft Library, and are there available for further study.

The thoroughness of Bancroft's footnotes presented a challenge to the users of the *History* that as yet has gone unanswered in Arizona and New Mexico. Here were direct leads that suggested that this single, condensed volume should be supplemented with more specific and detailed annals of historical development such as Bancroft's staff had produced in the several volumes of the *History of California*. Evidently he anticipated or expected that others would follow him with equal scholarship and care to round out the regional history. For the scholar and research worker these footnotes have incomparable value. A lifetime of joyful study awaits any student of the region with the patience and desire to investigate the materials outlined in these notes.

To a certain extent this has been done by Ralph Emerson Twitchell's *Leading Facts of New Mexican History*, and by Thomas E. Farish with his eight volumes of *History of Arizona* published from 1915 to 1918, and James E. McClintock in 1916 with his two-volume history, *Arizona:*

Prehistoric — Aboriginal — Pioneer — Modern. New Mexico history has been studiously enlarged in the *New Mexico Historical Review* by the extensive and erudite writings of its editors, Lansing B. Bloom and Frank D. Reeve, and by brilliant elaboration of early Spanish history by George P. Hammond who now is director of the Bancroft Library.

By comparison with New Mexican achievements, Arizona suffered irreparable interruptions in the publication of the *Arizona Historical Review,* but the emergence of *Arizona and the West* under the editorship of John Alexander Carroll promises a resumption of penetration into historical annals long neglected in my own state.

Bancroft grouped Arizona and New Mexico together in one book, since they had a common birth through Spanish exploration, but used separate chapters to delineate the diverse development of the neighbors. New Mexico developed a strong and continuous Hispanic culture, while most of Arizona remained unsettled until after the Civil War. Arizona history in the Bancroft treatment virtually covers a forty-year period, with the greatest concentration upon the formative years from 1863 to 1886. Little of major importance was unmentioned in that period. He admitted to gaps in Spanish and Mexican colonial periods of New Mexican history that since have been provided by the research of Bolton, Hammond, and France V. Scholes, in particular.

Arizona and New Mexico, as Texas had been, were presented as a bridge between Mexico and the United States. Bancroft spoke of them as "states" in his text, anticipating a maturity that was delayed longer than he might have expected. He did recognize the differences in their cultures, but these were distinctions that were not to be finalized until 1906 when a plebiscite in the territories determined that they would enter the Union, if at all, apart. Even then New Mexico, with a dominant Mexican-derived population, stood for joint statehood, while Arizona, composed largely of Anglo-Americans, voted for separation.

While Bancroft produced a classic in historical condensation without losing touch with the broad concept of regional development, he was sometimes intolerant of the problem of the Indians, despite his great sympathy for their mistreatment from white hands. His conclusion on the future of the Apache cannot be markedly disputed even seventy-five years after he succinctly closed this episode thus: "Serious outbreaks are probably at an end. The problem of ultimate improvement remains unsolved."

Bancroft inserted details of historical achievement into *Arizona and New Mexico* within a few months of press-time. But he left the territories on the brink of development with completion of two transcontinental railroads, a promise of peace in the air with cessation of Indian warfare, and, except for mining, the whole gamut of industrial development not developed and hence not defined.

In the intervening three-fourths of a century there has been an unfortunate lag in historical scholarship and elaboration to match that of Bancroft. *Arizona and New Mexico* remains a classic at the elbow of every serious student of our regional history. Revival of interest in such studies with the population explosion in the Southwest and greater emphasis upon Western Americana have led to the well-devised facsimile. Bancroft's commendable work continues to be a "first reliance," as Caughey has said, awaiting a new synthesis of our regional history to incorporate the new discoveries, facts, and developments of the long span of years since 1889.

BARRY GOLDWATER

Phoenix, Arizona
January 1962

BANCROFT'S
HISTORY OF
ARIZONA & NEW MEXICO

THE WORKS

HUBERT HOWE BANCROFT

HISTORY OF

ARIZONA AND NEW MEXICO

1530—1888

SAN FRANCISCO
THE HISTORY COMPANY, PUBLISHERS
1889

PREFACE.

FOR several reasons, the history of Arizona and New Mexico, particularly in the early times, is not surpassed in interest by that of any portion of the Pacific United States, or perhaps of the whole republic. Notable among these reasons are the antiquity of these territories as Spanish provinces—for they were the first to be occupied by Europeans, and ten years before the Pilgrims landed at Plymouth Rock, a *Historia de la Nueva Mexico* was published; the peculiar Pueblo civilization, second only to that of the Aztecs and Mayas in the south, found among the aborigines of this land, and maintaining itself more nearly in its original conditions than elsewhere down to the present day; the air of romance pervading the country's early annals in connection with the Northern Mystery, quaint cosmographic theories, and the search for fabulous empires in Cíbola, Teguayo, and Quivira; the ancient belief in the existence of immense mineral treasures as supplemented by the actual discovery of such treasures in modern times; the long and bloody struggle against raiding Apaches, the Ishmaelites of American aborigines; the peculiar circumstances under which this broad region fell into the hands of the United States; the fact that the eastern portion, unlike any

other territory of the republic, is still inhabited mainly
by a Spanish-speaking people; its position on the
national frontier; its peculiarities of physical config-
uration and climate; and finally, the marvellous strides
towards prosperity in the last decade, of a country
formerly regarded as an unpromising section of the
Great American Desert.

That the annals of these countries, so extensive both
chronologically and territorially, are compressed into
one volume of this *History of the Pacific States*, while
seven volumes are devoted to the record of a sister
province, California, is a fact that may seem to require
a word of explanation, though it is in accordance with
a plan deliberately formed and announced at the outset.   All Spanish-American provinces are in certain
respects so similar in their annals one to another that
it was and is believed sufficient and best in a comprehensive work like this to present the minutiæ of local
and personal happenings of but one.   California was
chosen for this purpose, not only because of its modern
prominence, but because its records are remarkably
perfect, and because its position on the coast, facilitat-
ing intercourse with Mexico and foreign nations, its
mission system, its trading and smuggling experience,
its Russian complications, its political vicissitudes, and
its immigrant and other foreign elements gave to its
history, as compared with that of interior provinces, a
notable variety, tending greatly to mitigate the inevitable monotony of all provincial annals, even before
the knowledge of its golden treasure came to startle
the world.   The history of New Mexico written on the
same scale as that of the Pacific province would not
only fill many volumes, but from the lack of continuous archive evidence, and from the fact that the

story goes back beyond the aid of memory, it would be at the best fragmentary and irregular; and by reason of the country's isolation and non-intercourse with the outer world, as well as on account of the peculiar nature of its petty events, it would also be most tedious reading. Not only is this true of the first and most important period of the country's history—that of Spanish rule to 1821—but of the second period, embracing the Mexican rule of 1822–46, the growth of the Santa Fé trade, the change of flag, the Indian wars, and the early territorial days down to 1875 or later. The Mexican archive record is more meagre even than the Spanish, the early enthusiasm of conquest and exploration had died out, nothing more monotonous in detail than the endless succession of Indian wars can be imagined, and of the more important events and developments several are more conveniently and satisfactorily treated in the annals of other adjoining regions. And as to the third and last period, that of railroads, Indian reservations, mining development, industrial progress, and American immigration, a valid reason for condensation is found in the fact that this grand unfolding of resources has but just begun, that all is in a transitory, changeable condition, so that the result of the most minute treatment would probably become antiquated and of comparatively little value within a few years. Thus there are good reasons for the plan and scale I have adopted. The omission of personal and local details, moreover, adds greatly to the interest of this volume; and so far as the general course of events and developments is concerned, no volume of the series has been founded on more careful or exhaustive research.

My sources of information for this volume are shown

in the list of authorities prefixed, in the fine-print appendix to the first chapter, and in the notes scattered profusely throughout the work. In no section of the field have my resources of original data been richer or more varied. Besides many rare works in print consulted only imperfectly or not at all by previous writers, I have consulted the Santa Fé archives, and have had access to rich stores of the most important documentary records from Spain and Mexico in my own and other private collections; and I have been especially fortunate in being able to utilize, practically for the first time, the work of Villagrá and several important documents bearing on Oñate's conquest, never before correctly recorded. For later events of territorial history I have studied all the publications extant, including government reports and newspapers; and have besides, here as in the other parts of my field, taken the testimony of many prominent citizens and officials who have thrown new light on many phases of the subject. Here as elsewhere I give full credit to the sources on every point.

Several praiseworthy works on the history of these territories have been published; but they are of very uneven quality, with not a few errors, and more omissions—defects due in most cases not so much to the incompetence of the author as to the inaccessibility of original authorities. Nowhere in my work have I been able to correct more erroneous statements, fill more historical gaps, or, except in the matter of minute details as already explained, to supply in comparison with preceding writers more new matter. Yet experience leads me to expect that the old inaccurate and thread-bare sources will still be consulted to a considerable extent in preference to better and original authorities at second-hand. Doubtless writers will continue to give inaccurate dates and details for Oñate's conquest; to seek new locations for Coronado's Cíbola and Tiguex; to name Cabeza de Vaca as the discoverer of New Mexico, and speak of his descendants as still living in the country; to talk of the Aztecs and of Montezuma in this northern region; to describe Santa Fé as the oldest town in the United States, dating its foundation back to the sixteenth or fifteenth century, or that of Tucson to the sixteenth; to chronicle the expedition of Peñalosa to Quivira; to name the duke of Alburquerque and other viceroys among the governors of New Mexico; to derive the name of Arizona from 'arid zone,' or 'narizona,' the big-nosed woman; to accept the current traditions of rich mines of gold and silver discovered and worked by the Jesuits and conquerors, or by enslaved Indians under their cruel direction; and to repeat various other errors that have found place in the legendary annals of these provinces. However, I have presented the facts and the evidence on which they rest. My statements should be accepted or disproved.

Arizona and New Mexico are properly presented together in one volume, as they have historically and physically much in common. In Spanish and Mexican times they were practically or to a great extent one country, and their annals are accordingly somewhat intermingled; but the chapters devoted to each, though mixed in the order of presentment, are kept distinct in substance, so that the record of each province may be read continuously. Since their organization as territories of the United States the history of each is given separately in consecutive chapters. As between the two there is no difference in scale or treat-

ment, though I have been able slightly to condense
the earlier Arizona record because of Pimería having
been covered by the history of Sonora in another
volume, and though New Mexican history is much
more voluminous in the aggregate by reason of its
greater chronologic extent.

Though first among the Pacific States to be settled
by Europeans, Arizona and New Mexico have been
last to feel the impulse of progressive civilization; yet
they have felt it, and as a result must assume good
rank among their sister states. In natural conditions
of healthful climate, fertile soil, and mineral wealth,
the two territories closely resemble each other; and
while Arizona has the advantage of a less apathetic
and ignorant population, and thus far takes the lead in
mining and agricultural industry, their aspirations and
possibilities are similar, and ultimate precedence is by
no means assured to the western territory. Both, as
it has proved, are fortunate in their mid-continental
position, which has given them railroad communication
with the east and west and south long before they
could have expected it otherwise. Both have made a
good start in the race, and in each the spirit of progress is actively working. Ultimate success is not
doubtful. The danger of serious Indian troubles is
believed to be past; the old and absurdly inaccurate
ideas of the east respecting this country and its people
are rapidly disappearing; and the present invasion of
the farther west by climate-seekers cannot fail to benefit the interior. When the mining industry shall have
been more fully systematized, workings being directed
somewhat more to mineral lodes and somewhat less to
the pockets of outside speculators; when the senseless
national raid against bimetallic currency shall be at

an end; when systematic irrigation works shall make available the water resources; when the government shall provide for the sale of the mesa lands in tracts of convenient size for stock-raising; when the population of Mexican race shall adopt improved methods of tillage or make way for others who have adopted them; when the immense deposits of iron and coal shall be utilized—then will come the day of great and permanent prosperity for this land of old-time mystery. All this will not be done in a year or in ten; but it will be done. Then the historic records of this volume will have a new and ever-increasing interest.

CONTENTS OF THIS VOLUME.

CHAPTER I.

INTRODUCTORY REMARKS AND RÉSUMÉ.

CHAPTER II.

NIZA AND CORONADO IN ARIZONA.

1539–1540.

CHAPTER VI.

OÑATE'S CONQUEST OF NEW MEXICO.

1595–1598.

CHAPTER VII.

OÑATE'S CONQUEST, CONTINUED.

1598–1599.

CHAPTER VIII.

EIGHTY YEARS OF NEW MEXICAN ANNALS.

1599–1679.

CHAPTER IX.

A DECADE OF FREEDOM.

1680-1691.

CHAPTER X.

RECONQUEST BY DON DIEGO DE VARGAS.

1692-1700.

CHAPTER XI.

FIRST HALF OF THE EIGHTEENTH CENTURY.

1701-1750.

CHAPTER XII.

LAST HALF OF THE EIGHTEENTH CENTURY.

1751–1800.

CHAPTER XIII.

LAST YEARS OF SPANISH RULE.

1801–1822.

CHAPTER XIV.

A MEXICAN TERRITORY.

1823–1845.

CHAPTER XV.

PIMERÍA ALTA AND THE MOQUI PROVINCE.

1543–1767.

CHAPTER XVI.

PIMERÍA ALTA, OR ARIZONA.

1768–1845.

CHAPTER XVII.

CHAPTER XIX.

CHAPTER XX.

CHAPTER XXIV.

COUNTIES AND TOWNS OF ARIZONA.

1864-1887.

CHAPTER XXV.

TERRITORY OF NEW MEXICO.

1851-1863.

CHAPTER XXVI.

INDIAN AND MILITARY AFFAIRS.

1851-1863.

CHAPTER XXVII.

CONFEDERATE INVASION OF NEW MEXICO.

1861–1862.

CHAPTER XXVIII.

CHRONOLOGIC AND OFFICIAL.

1864–1886.

CHAPTER XXIX.

INDIAN AND MILITARY AFFAIRS.

1864–1887.

CHAPTER XXX.

INDUSTRIES AND INSTITUTIONS.

1864–1887.

CHAPTER XXXI.

COUNTIES AND TOWNS OF NEW MEXICO.

1887.

AUTHORITIES QUOTED

IN THE

HISTORY OF ARIZONA AND NEW MEXICO.

Abert (J. W.), Report of his Examination of New Mexico, 1846–7. Washington, 1848.

Alaman (Lúcas), Disertaciones. Mexico, 1844–9. 3 vol.

Alarcon (Hernando), Relatione della Navigatione. In Ramusio, iii. 363; Hakluyt, iii. 425; Ternaux-Compans, série i. tom. ix. 299.

Alarcon (Hernando) and Ulloa, Relacion del Armada. In Col. Doc. Inéd., iv. 218.

Alburquerque Academy, Annual Reports, 1879–80 et seq. Alb., 1880 et seq.

Alcedo (Antonio), Diccionario Geográfico Histórico. Madrid, 1786–9. 5 vol.

Alegre (Francisco Jav.), Historia de la Compañía de Jesus. Mex., 1841. 3 vol.

Alvarado (Hernando) and Fr. Juan de Padilla, Relacion de lo que descubrieron (1540). In Florida, Col. Doc., 65.

Álvarez (Ignacio), Estudios sobre la Historia General de Mexico. Zacatecas, 1875. 5 vol.

American Almanac. Boston, 1830–61. 32 vol.

American Ethnological Society, Transactions. 1845 et seq.

American Quarterly Register. Phil., 1848–51. 5 vol.

American Review. Phil., 1827 et seq.

American State Papers. Boston, 1817 et seq.

Ancient Santa Fé, MS., extracts from N. Mex. newspapers.

Amigo del Pueblo, newspaper. Mex.

Anderson (Alex. D.), The Silver Country. N. Y., 1877.

Annals of Congress. 1st–18th Cong. Wash., 1834–56. 42 vol.

Anquetil, Universal History. Lond., 1809. 9 vol.

Anza (Juan B.), Carta de 1766. In Sin. y Son., Cartas, 108; Descubrimiento de Sonora á Californias, 1774. MS.; Diario de la Expedicion á Moqui, 1780. MS.; Diario de una Exped. desde Sonora á S. Francisco Cal., 1775–6. MS.; Diario de la Exped. contra la nacion Comanche, 1779. MS. In N. Mex., Doc., 861; Expedicion de Anza y muerte de 'Cuerno Verde,' 1779. MS.

Aparicio (Manuel R.), Los Conventos Suprimidos en Mexico. Mex., 1861.

Apostólicos Afanes de la Compañía de Jesus. Barcelona, 1754.

Appleton's Journal. N. Y.

Archæological Institute of America, Papers. Boston, 1883.

Archivo de California. MS. 273 vol.

Archivo de Nuevo Mexico. In Doc. Hist. Mex., 3d series, pt iv., 127 et seq.
Archivo de Santa Fé. Unbound MSS. preserved at Sta Fé.
Archivo General de Mexico. MSS. 32 vol. Copies in Bancroft Library;
 also printed in part in Doc. Hist. Mex.
Arco Iris, newspaper. Mex.
Arizona, Acts of the Legislature, 1864 et seq. Prescott and Tucson; Consti-
 tution of the Provisional Government. Tucson, 1860 (1st book printed in
 Ariz.); History of (Elliott & Co.). S. F., 1884. Fol.; Howell Code. Pres-
 cott, 1865; Journals of Legislature, 1864 et seq. Prescott and Tucson;
 Memorial and Affidavits showing outrages by Apache Ind. S. F., 1871;
 Message of the Governor, 1864 et seq. Prescott and Tucson; Mining
 Law. Prescott, 1864; Newspapers (see names of towns where published,
 also list in chap. xxv.); Reports on Indian Tribes, 1874. MS. 2 vol.;
 Reports of Surveyor-general, in U. S. Land Office Reports; Resources.
 S. F., 1871; Scraps, a col. of newspaper clippings classified.
Arizpe Restaurador Federal, newspaper. 1838.
Arlegui (Joseph), Chrónica de la Provincia de S. Francisco de Zacatecas.
 Mex., 1737.
Armijo (Manuel), Libro de Ordenes, 1843. MS. In Arch. Sta Fé.
Arny (W. F. M.), Centennial Historic Oration. Sta Fé, 1876. See also N.
 Mex., Mess. of Gov.
Arricivita (J. D.), Crónica Seráfica y Apostólica. Madrid, 1792.
Arrillaga (Basilio), Recopilacion de Leyes. Mex., 1838–50. 22 vol.
Atlantic and Pacific R. R., Prospectus.
Autos contra los Indios Jenízaros del pueblo de Abiquiú, 1763. MS. of Pinart
 Col.
Avery (A.), Hand-Book and Travellers' Guide of N. Mex. Denver, 1881.
Ayers (John), A Soldier's Experience in N. Mex. MS. 1884.
Ayeta (Francisco), Memorial al Virey, 1676. MS. In N. Mex. Doc., 481.

Balch (Wm R.), Mines, Miners, and Mining Interests of the U. S. Phil.,
 1882. Fol.
Bancroft (George), History of the U. S. Boston, 1870.
Bancroft (Hubert H.), History of California, vol. i.–v.; History of Mexico,
 vol. i.–v.; History of the North Mexican States, vol. i.; History of the
 Northwest Coast, 2 vol.; Native Races of the Pacific States, 5 vol.—all
 included in Bancroft's Works. S. F., 1883 et seq.
Bancroft (M. G.), New Mexico Miscellany. MS.
Bandelier (Ad. F.), Historical Introduction. Boston, 1881.
Barber (John W.) and Henry Howe, History of the Western States. Cin-
 cinnati, 1867.
Barreiro (Antonio), Ojeada sobre Nuevo Mexico. Puebla, 1832.
Barter (D. W.), Directory of Tucson. S. F., 1881.
Bartlett (John R.), Personal Narrative of Explorations, 1850–3. N. Y., 1854.
 2 vol.
Beadle (J. H.), Undeveloped West. Phil. (1873); Western Wilds. Cin., etc.,
 1879.
Beale (Edward F.), Wagon Road from Fort Defiance to the Colorado River.
 1857. (35th cong. 1st sess., H. Ex. Doc. 124.)
Beaumont (Pablo de la P. C.), Crónica de la Provincia de Michoacan. Mex.,
 1873–4. 5 vol.; also MS.
Beltrami (J. C.), Le Mexique. Paris, 1830. 2 vol.
Benavides (Alonso), Memorial. Madrid, 1630; Reqveste Remonstrative.
 Bruxelles, 1631.
Benton (Thos H.), Abridgment of Debates in Congress. N. Y., 1857–63. 16
 vol.; Thirty Years' View. N. Y., 1854. 2 vol.
Benzoni (Girolamo), Historio del Mondo Nuovo. Venitia, 1572.
Berger (Wm M.), Tourists' Guide to N. Mex. Kansas City, 1883.
Bernal (Cristóbal M.), Relacion del Estado de la Pimería, 1687. In Doc. Hist.
 Mex., 3d ser. iv.; also MS.
Bernalillo News, newspaper.

Bernardez (J. de R.), Descripcion Breve de Zacatecas. Mex., 1732.
Bigelow (John), Memoir of Life and Services of John C. Frémont. N. Y., 1856.
Bigler (Henry W.), Diary of a Mormon, 1846–8. MS.
Bingley (Wm), Travels in North America. Lond., 1821.
Boggs (Thomas O.), Dictation, 1885. MS.
Bonilla (Antonio), Apuntes sobre N. Mex., 1776. MS. In N. Mex., Cédulas.
Borbon, Parecer del Fiscal sobre el proyecto.... Presidio en el Rio Colorado, 1801. MS. In Arch., Cal.
Borica (Diego), Informe sobre communicacion con N. Mex., 1796. MS. In Arch., Cal.
Botulph, San Miguel College, Sta Fé, by the president. MS.
Bourke (John G.), Apache Campaign, 1883. N. Y., 1886; The Snake dance of the Moquis. N. Y., 1884.
Brackenbridge (B. H. M.), Mexican Letters. Wash. 1850; Early Discoverers. Pittsburg, 1857.
Brackett (Albert G.), History of the U. S. Cavalry. N. Y., 1865.
Brevoort (Elias), New Mexico. Sta Fé, 1874; Sta Fé Trail. MS.
Brown (D.), Advertising Agency. S. F., 1884.
Browne (J. Ross), Adventures in the Apache Country. N. Y., 1871; Mineral Resources of the Pacific States. Wash. and S. F., 1868; Resources of the Pacific States. S. F., 1869; Sketch of the Settlement of L. California. S. F., 1869.
Browne (J. Ross), and James W. Taylor, Reports upon the Mineral Resources of the U. S. Wash., 1867.
Bryan (R. W. D.), Alburquerque Indian School. MS., 1884.
Buchanan (James), Confidential Circular, May 13, 1846. In Larkin's Doc., iv. 121.
Buelna (Eustaquio), Compendio Histórico de Sinaloa. Mex., 1878.
Burchard (H. C.), Report of the Director of the Mint. Wash., 1881 et seq.
Burney (James), Chronological History of Discovery. Lond., 1803– 7. 4to, 5 vol.
Bustamante (Carlos M.), Apuntes para la Historia de Santa Ana. Mex., 1845; Diario de Mexico, 1841–3; El Gabinete Mexicano. Mex., 1839–41. MS. 4 vol.; Mex., 1842. 2 vol.; Invasion de los Anglo-Americanos. MS.; El Nuevo Bernal Diaz. Mex., 1847. 2 vol.
Bustamante (Juan D.), Residencia del Gobernador de N. Mex., 1731. MS.

Cabeza de Vaca (Alvar Nuñez), Relation. Wash., 1851; also in Ramusio, iii. 310; Ternaux-Compans, série i. tom. vii.
Calhoun (James S.), Reports of an Indian Agent, 1849–51. In U. S. Govt Doc.
California Agriculturist, magazine.
California and New Mexico, Message and Documents, 1850.
Californian. S. F., 1880 et seq.
Calle (Juan Diaz), Memorial y Noticias Sacras. n. p., 1646.
Camp (David W.), American Year-Book and National Register. Hartford, 1869.
Campbell (Albert W.), Report upon Pacific Wagon-roads, 1859. (35 cong. 2d sess., H. Ex. Doc. 108.)
Cano (Francisco), Testimonio del descubrimiento de la laguna del N. Mex. In Pacheco, Col. Doc., xix. 535.
Carleton (James H.), Correspondence of 1862-5. In U. S. Ind. Aff., Rept Joint Spec. Com., 1867, p. 98 et seq.
Carson (Christopher), Papers of the Carson family, furnished by Thos O. Boggs, 1886. MS.
Castañeda (Pedro), Relation du Voyage de Cíbola, 1540. In Ternaux-Compans, Voy., 1st series, ix.
Castaño de Sosa (Gaspar), Memoria del Descubrimiento, 1590. In Pacheco, Doc., xv. 191.
Catlin. The Maxwell Dynasty. MS.

Cavo (Andrés), Tres Siglos de Mexico. Mex., 1836–8. 3 vol.
Ceballos (Ramon), Vindicacion de Mejico. Madrid, 1856.
Cedulario, Col. of MSS. 3 vol.
Chacon (Fernando), Informe del Gobr sobre Industrias del N. Mex., 1803.
    MS. In Arch., Sta Fé.
Chivington (J. M.), First Colorado Regiment. MS.
Cincinnatus, Travels on the Western Slope. S. F., 1857.
Clavigero (Francisco S.), Storia della California. Venegia, 1789. 2 vol.
Clifford (Josephine), Overland Tales. S. F., 1877.
Clifton Clarion, newspaper.
Clusky (M. W.), Political Text-book. Phil., 1860.
Coast Review, S. F. magazine.
Codallos y Rabal (Joaquin), Reduccion de los indios de Navajó, 1745. MS.;
    Testimonio á la letra sobre Camanches, 1748. MS. In Arch., Sta Fé.
Coleccion de Documentos Inéditos. See Pacheco.
Colorado, House Journal. 3d Session.
Coombs (Franklin), Narrative. In Mexico in 1842.
Compañia de Jesus, Catálogo de Sugetos. Mex., 1871.
Congressional Debates. 18–25th Congress. Wash., 1824 et seq. 14 vol.
Congressional Globe (and Record). Wash., 1836 et seq.
Conklin (E.), Picturesque Arizona. N. Y., 1878.
Cooke (Philip St George), Conquest of N. Mex. and Cal. N. Y., 1878; Jour-
    nal of the March of the Mormon Battalion. (30th cong. spec. sess., Sen.
    Doc. 2); Report of his March, 1846. With Emory's Notes.
Córdoba (Luis C.), Historia de Felipe II. Madrid, 1619.
Coronado (Francisco Vasquez), Relacion del Suceso de la Jornada de Cíbola.
    In Pacheco, Doc., xiv. 318, and Florida, Col. Doc., i. 147; Letter to the
    Emperor, Oct. 20, 1541. In Pacheco, Doc., iii., xiii.; Ternaux-Compans,
    Voy., 1st ser., ix.; Letter to the Viceroy, Aug. 3, 1540. In Ramusio, iii.;
    Hakluyt, iii.
Correo de España, newspaper. Mexico, 1854 et seq.
Correo de la Federacion, newspaper. Mex., 1826 et seq.
Cortés (Hernan), Escritos Sueltos. Mex., 1871.
Coutts (Cave J.), Diary of a March to California, 1848. MS.
Coyner (David H.), The Lost Trappers. Cincinnati, 1859.
Cozzens (Samuel W.), The Marvellous Country. Boston (1874).
Cremony (John C.), Life among the Apaches. S. F., 1868.
Crespo (Benito), Memorial Ajustado. Madrid, 1738.
Crespo (Francisco Ant.), Informe que hizo al virey...Descub. de N. Mex.
    para Monterey (1774). MS. In N. Mex., Doc. Hist., 802.
Creuzbauer (Robert), Route from Gulf of Mexico to Cal. N. Y., 1849.
Cronise (Titus F.), Natural Wealth of Cal. S. F., 1868.
Crook (George), Annual Reports, 1883–4.
Cutts (James M.), The Conquest of Cal. and N. Mexico. Phil., 1847.

Dale (Frank W.), Dictation. MS. 1885.
Dampier (Wm), A New Voyage round the World. Lond., 1699–1709. 3 vol.
Dávila (Julian Gutierrez), Memorias Históricas. Mex., 1736.
Davis (W. W. H.), El Gringo. N. Y., 1856; Spanish Conquest of N. Mex-
    ico. Doylestown, 1869.
Dawson (J. B.), Dictation. MS. 1885.
Dead Man's Gulch. MS.
DeBow (J. D. B.), Encyclopedia of Trade. Lond., 1854. 2 vol.
DeCourcy (Henry), The Catholic Church in the U. S. N. Y., 1857.
Delgado (Cárlos), Informe sobre las Execrables hostilidades y tiranías de los
    Gobernadores, 1750. MS. In N. Mex., Doc., 128; Relacion de la Sierra
    Azul. MS. In Id., 769; Noticia del Gran Teguayo. MS. In Id., 790.
Del Mar (Alex.), History of the Precious Metals. Lond., 1880.
Denver, History of (Baskin & Co.). Denver, 1880.
Derby (Geo. H.), Reconnoisance of the Gulf of Cal. and the Colorado. Wash.,
    1852.

Dewees (W. B.), Letters. Louisville, 1852.
Diario de Mexico. Mex., 1805–10. 13 vol.
Diaz del Castillo (Bernal), Historia Verdadera de la Conquista. Mad., 1632.
Dinkel (Geo. J.), Statement, 1885. MS.
Disposiciones Varias, Col. of Doc. MSS. and print. 6 vol.
Disturnell's Business Directory, 1881.
Dixon (Hepworth), White Conquest. Lond., 1876. 2 vol.
Dobbs (Arthur), Account of the countries adjoining to Hudson's Bay. Lond., 1744.
Documentos para la Historia de Mexico. Mex., 1853–7. 4 series, 20 vol. Most of the doc. also in MS.
Dold (Henry), Dictation, 1885. MS.
Domenech (Emmanuel), Deserts of North America. Lond., 1860. 2 vol.; Histoire du Mexique. Paris, 1868. 3 vol.
Dominguez (Atanasio) and Silvestre V. Escalante, Diario y Derrotero, 1776. In Doc. Hist. Mex., 2d ser., i. 377.
Dorsey (S. W.), Dictation of a Cattle-raiser. MS. 1885.
Downs (Francis), Dictation, 1884. MS.
Dublan (Manuel) and J. M. Lozano, Legislacion Mejicana. Mex., 1856–80. 11 vol.
Dunbar (E. E.), American Pioneering. (N. Y.), 1863.
Dunlop (James), Digest of General Laws of the U. S. Phil., 1856.
Dunn (J. P.), Massacres of the Mountains. N. Y., 1886.
Durango Registro Oficial, newspaper.
Durango, Informe del Obispo sobre Misiones, 1789. MS. of Pinart Col.
Dwyer (Joseph W.), Dictation, 1885. MS.

Eckhoff and Riecker's Official Map of Arizona, 1880.
Edwards (Frank S.), Campaign in New Mexico. Phil., 1847.
Ellison (Samuel), History of New Mexico, 1884. MS.
Emory (Wm H.), Journal, 1846–7. In Niles' Reg., lxxi.; Notes of a Military Reconnoissance. Wash., 1848.
Escalante (Silvestre Velez), Carta. In Arch., N. Mex.; Carta de 1776 sobre Moqui. MS. In N. Mex., Doc., 985; Informe y Diario...Moqui, 1775. MS. In Id., 1022.
Escalona, Carta de Relacion, 1601. In Torquemada, i. 673.
Escalona and Barrundo, Relacion, 1582. In Pacheco, Doc., 146; Cartas de Indias, 230.
Escudero (José A.), Noticias Estadísticas de Chihuahua. Mex., 1834; Id. de Sonora y Sinaloa. Mex., 1849.
Espejo (Antonio), Expediente y Relacion, 1584. In Pacheco, Doc., xv. 151; Relacion. In Id., 100; Viaie que hizo. In Hakluyt's Voy., iii. 383.
Espinosa (Isidro F.), Crónica Apostólica. n. p., 1746. 2 vol.
Estrella de Occidente, Sonora newspaper.

Falconer (Thomas), Notes. In Lond. Geog. Soc., Jour., xiii.
Farmer (L. J.), Resources of the Rocky Mountains. Cleveland, 1883.
Farnham (Thos J.), Life and Adventures. N. Y., 1846, 1857; Mexico. N. Y., 1846.
Fédix (P. A.), L'Orégon. Paris, 1846.
Fergusson (David), Report on the Country, Route between Tucson and Lobos Bay. 1862. (37th cong. spec. sess., Sen. Ex. Doc. 1.)
Fernandez Duro (Cesáreo), Don Diego de Peñalosa. Madrid, 1882; Noticias de Expediciones, 1523–1783. In Id.
Figueroa (Francisco), Becerro General. MS. 1764.
Fischer (M.) and A. A. Abeitia, Report as to Socorro Co. Socorro, 1881.
Fisher (L. P.), Newspaper Agency. S. F., 1884.
Florence Territorial Enterprise, newspaper.
Florida, Coleccion de Documentos. Lond. (1857).
Font (Pedro), Journal of a Journey, Sonora to Monterey, 1775. MS.
Foster (Stephen C.), Los Angeles in '47. MS.

Fountain (A. J.), Report on Doña Ana Co. Mesilla, 1882.
Frejes (Francisco), Historia Breve de la Conquista. Mex., 1839.
Frémont (Jessie B.), A Year of American Travel. N. Y., 1878.
Freytas (Nicolás), Relacion del descubrimiento de Quivira. In Shea's Exped.; also in Fernandez Duro, Don Diego de Peñalosa.
Frignet (Ernest), La Californie. Paris, 1867.
Fröbel (Julius), Aus Amerika. Leipzig, 1856. 2 vol.
Frost (John), Indian Wars of the U. S. Auburn, 1852; Mexican War. New Haven, 1850; Pictorial History of Mexico. Phil., 1862.
Furber (George C.), Twelve Months' Volunteer. Cin., 1850.

Gaceta de Gobierno de Mexico. 1722, et seq.
Gaceta Imperial de Mexico. Mex., 1821-3.
Gallatin (Albert), Sur l'ancienne civilization du N. Mexique. In Nouv. An. des Voy., cxxi. 237; articles in Amer. Ethnol. Soc., Trans., i. ii.
Galvano (Antonio), Discoveries of the World. Lond., 1601, 1862.
Galvez (Conde de), Instruccion á Ugarte, 1786. Mex., 1786.
Garcés (Francisco), Diario y Derrotero, 1775-6. In Doc. Hist. Mex., 2d ser., i. 226.
Garrett (Pat F.), Authentic Life of Billy the Kid. Sta Fé, 1882.
Gilpin (Wm), Mission of the North American People. Phil., 1878.
Gleeson (W.), History of the Catholic Church in Cal. S. F., 1872. 2 vol.
Globe Arizona Silver Belt, newspaper.
Goddard (F. B.), Where to Emigrate and Why. N. Y., 1869.
Gomara (Francisco Lopez), Historia de Mexico. Anvers, 1554; Historia General de las Indias. Anvers, 1554.
Gomez (José), Diario. In Doc. Hist. Mex., 2d ser., vii.
Gordon (J. B.), Historical and Geographical Memoir. Dublin, 1820.
Gorman (Samuel), Address before Hist. Soc. of N. Mex. N. Y., 1860.
Gottfriedt (J. L.), Neue Welt. Francfurt, 1665.
Graham (J. D.), Report on Boundary, 1852. (32d cong. 1st sess., Sen. Ex. Doc. 121.)
Greenhow (Robert), History of Oregon and California. N. Y., 1845.
Gregg (Josiah), Commerce of the Prairies. N. Y., 1844. 2 vol.; Scenes and Incidents. Phil., 1858. 2 vol.
Griffin (John S.), Journal, 1846. MS.
Guadalupe Mountains. n. p., n. d.
Guëmes y Horcasitas, Medios para la pacificacion de los Camanches. 1746. MS.
Guijo (G. M.), Diario, 1648-64. In Doc. Hist. Mex., 1st ser., i.

Hakluyt (Richard), Divers Voyages. Lond., 1850; Principal Navigations (Voy.). Lond., 1599-1600. 3 vol.
Hall, Sonora. MS.
Hall (Edward H.), The Great West. N. Y., 1865.
Hamilton (Patrick), The Resources of Arizona. S. F., 1884.
Harper's New Monthly Magazine.
Harrison (H. W.), Battlefields of the Republic. Phil., 1857.
Henshaw Arizona Bullion, newspaper.
Hayden (F. V.), The Great West. N. Y., 1870. See also U. S. Geol. Survey.
Hayes (A. A., Jr), New Colorado and the Sta Fé Trail. N. Y., 1880; The New Mex. Campaign of 1862. In Mag. of Amer. Hist., Feb. 1886.
Hayes (Benj.), Diary of a journey overland, 1849. MS.; Scrap-books.
Hayward (J. L.), The Los Cerrillos Mines. South Framingham, 1880.
Hazledine (Wm C.), Report on Bernalillo Co. New Alburquerque, 1881.
Head (Lafayette), Dictation, 1885. MS.
Henriques (E. C.), Statement, 1885. MS.
Herrera (Antonio), Historia General. Mad., 1601. 4 vol.
Heylin (Peter), Cosmography. Lond., 1701. Fol.
Hickox (Geo. W.), Dictation, 1885. MS.
Hinton (Richard J.), Hand-Book of Arizona. S. F., 1878.

Historical Magazine and Notes and Queries. Boston, etc., 1857–69. 15 vol.
Hittell (John S.), Article in the Californian, i. 130; Wash. Ter. Scrapbook.
Hobbs (James), Wild Life in the Far West. Hartford, 1875.
Hodge (Hiram C.), Arizona as it is. N. Y., 1877.
Hollister (Ovando J.), First Regiment of Col. Volunteers. Denver, 1863.
Holmes (Abiel), Annals of America. Cambridge, 1829. 2 vol.
Honolulu Polynesian, newspaper.
Hoyt (John P.), Arizona, Leading Events. MS., 1878.
Hughes (J. T.), Doniphan's Expedition. Cin., 1850.
Hughes (Samuel), Pima Co. and Tucson. MS.
Humboldt (Alex.), Essai Politique. Paris, 1811. Fol. 2 vol. and atlas.
Hunt's Merchants' Magazine.
Hurtado (Juan Paez), Campaña contra los Apaches, 1715. MS. in Pinart Col.
Hutton (N. H.), Report El Paso and Ft Yuma Wagon-road. (35th cong. 2d sess., H. Ex. Doc. 108.)

Ibarra (Francisco), Relacion de los Descubrimientos. In Pacheco, Doc., xiv. 453.
Icazbalceta (Joaquin García), Coleccion de Documentos. Mex., 1858–66. 2 vol.
Ilzarbe (Joaquin), Estado de las Misiones, 1788. MS. of Pinart Col.; Informe del P. Provincial, 1787. Ditto.
Indian Affairs. See U. S. Ind. Aff.
Ingersoll (Ernest), Crest of the Continent. Chicago, 1855; Knocking Round the Rockies. N. Y., 1883.
Instruccion formada en virtud de Real Orden. Mex., 1786.
Iris de España, Mex. newspaper.
Ives (Joseph C.), Report upon the Colorado River, 1857–8. Wash., 1861. 4to.

Jaramillo (Juan), Relacion que dió. In Pacheco, Doc., xiv. 304; Florida, Col. Doc., 154; Ternaux, 1st ser., ix. 364.
Jenkins (John S.), History of the Mexican War. Auburn, 1851.
Johnson (C. Granville), History of Arizona. S. F., 1869.
Johnston (Abraham R.), Journal, 1846. In Emory's Notes.
Julian (Geo. W.), Land-claims acted on in 1882–6. MS., 1887.

Kendall (Geo. W.), Narrative of the Texan Santa Fé Exped. N. Y., 1844. 2 vol.
Kendrick (H. L.), Table of Marches, 1849. In Cal. and N. Mex., Mess., 1850, p. 91.
Kerr (Robert), General History and Collection of Voyages. Edin., 1824. 18 vol.
Kino (Ensebio), Cartas. In Sonora, Materiales.
Krönig (Wm), Report as to Mora Co. Las Vegas, 1881.

Lacunza (José M.), Discursos Históricos. Mex., 1845.
Lacy (Mrs S. C.), Statement, 1885. MS.
Ladd (S. G.), Little Colorado Settlements. MS.
Laet (Joannis de), Novus Orbis. Lvgd. Batav., 1633. Fol.
Lafond (Gabriel), Voyages. Paris, 1844. 8 vol.
Lafora (Nicolás), Viaje á Sta Fé, 1766. MS.
Laramie Sentinel. Aug. 1872.
Lardner (Dionysius), History of Maritime and Inland Discov. Lond., 1830. 3 vol.
Larenaudière, Mexique et Guatemala. Paris, 1843.
Las Casas (Bartolomé), Historia de Indias. Mad., 1875. 5 vol.
Las Vegas Jesuit College, Prospectus. Las V., 1882, 1884.
Las Vegas Mining World, 1880–4.
Las Vegas Optic Annual. Las V., 1884.
Lawrence (Wm E.), Dictation on the Cattle Business. 1885. MS.

Leary (James C.), Statement. 1885. MS.
Lezaun (Juan S.), Noticias lamentables acaecidas en la N. Mex., 1760. MS.
    In N. Mex., Doc., 128.
Liceo Mexicano. Mex., 1844. 2 vol.
Lizasoin (Tomás I.), Informe sobre las Prov. de Sonora y N. Vizcaya, 1763.
    In Sonora, Materiales, iv. 683; also MS.
Lockman, Travels of the Jesuits. Lond., 1743. 2 vol.
Lomas (Juan B.), Asiento y Capitulacion. In Pacheco, Doc., xv. 54.
Lopez (Francisco), Dictation, 1885. MS.
Lopez de Haro, Nobilario.
Loring (L. Y.), Report on the Coyotero Apaches, 1875. MS.
Lossing (Benson J.), History of the U. S. N. Y., 1860; Pictorial History of
    the Civil War. Hartford, 1868. 2 vol.
Love (John), Statement, 1885. MS.
Low (F. F.) and J. H. Carleton, Correspondence, 1865-6. In Cal., Jour.
    Legisl., Appen., 16th sess.

McBroom (W. H.), Items, 1885. MS.
McCabe (James D.), Comprehensive View   Phil., 1876.
McCall (Geo. A.), Letters from the Frontier.   Phil., 1868.
McCormick (Rich. C.), Arizona, its Resources.   N. Y., 1865; Oration.   Pres-
    cott, 1864.
McCroham (Geoffrey), Dictation, 1885. MS.
McFarlane (James), The Coal Regions of America.   N. Y., 1873.
McKee (W. H.), Territory of N. Mex.   N. Y., 1866.
McKenney, Business Directory.   Oakland and S. F. (1883).
Macomb (J. N.), Report of Explor. Exped. from Sta Fé, 1859.   Wash.,
    1876.
Magazine of American History.   N. Y., 1883-6.
Magdalena, Prospectus of New Town.   Sta Fé, 1885.
Magin, Histoire Universelle des Indes.
Magliano, St Francis.
Mange (Juan M.), Historia de la Pimería Alta.   In Doc. Hist. Mex., 4th ser.,
    i. 226.   MS.
Marchand (Étienne), Voyage autour du Monde, 1790-3.   Paris.   6 vol.
Marcy (Russell), Statement of a Cattle Man and Banker, 1885.   MS.
Marcy (R. B.), Thirty Years of Army Life.   N. Y., 1866.
Marcy (R. B.) and Geo. B. McClellan, Exploration of the Red River.   Wash.,
    1853.
Mariana (Juan), Historia General de España.   Mad., 1780. 2 vol.; 1794. 10
    vol.
Marmier (Xavier), Les Voyageurs Nouveaux.   Paris, n. d.   3 vol.
Martin (Cristóbal), Asiento....Descubrimiento de N. Mex., 1583.   In Pa-
    checo, Doc., xvi. 277.
Martineau (James H.) Settlements in Arizona.   MS.
Martinez (Damian), Carta al P. Morfi 1792.   MS.   In N. Mex., Doc., 450.
Matthews, Navajo Silversmiths.   Wash., 1883.
Maulding (L. F.), Statement, 1885.   MS.
Mayer (Brantz), Mexico.   Aztec, etc.   Hartford, 1853. 2 vol.
Medina (Baltasar), Chrónica de S. Diego de Mex.   Mex., 1682.
Melgares (Facundo), Demostraciones....Independencia, 1822.   In Gaceta
    Imp., Mar. 22, 26, 1822, ii. 85-93.
Meline (James F.), 2,000 Miles on Horseback,   N. Y., 1867.
Mendieta (Gerónimo), Historia Eclesiástica Indiana.   Mex., 1870.
Mendoza (Gaspar D.), Residencia Contra el Gobernador, 1744.   MS.
Mendoza (Juan), Carta del Gobernador de Sonora, 1757.   In Sonora, Mat.,
    i. 84.
Menchero (Juan M.), Declaracion del P. Procurador, 1744.   MS.; Informe,
    1749.   MS.; Peticion sobre Navajóes.   MS.
Mercantile Agency Annual.   N. Y., 1871.
Mesilla Times, newspaper, 1861.

Mexico, Coleccion de Constituciones. Mex., 1828. 3 vol.; Coleccion de Órdenes y Decretos. Mex., 1829. 3 vol.; Correspondencia Diplomática. Mex., 1882. 2 vol.; Leyes (Palacio Col.); Legislacion Mejicana. Mex., 1855–6. 12 vol.; Memorias de Agricultura, Fomento, etc.
Mexico in 1842. Mad., 1842.
Mexico and U. S., Boundary Survey, Report 1852. (32d cong. 1st sess., Sen. Ex. Doc. 119.)
Miller (David J.), Historical Sketch of Sta Fé. In Sta Fé, Centennial Sketch, 1876.
Mills (T. B.), Hand-Book of Mining Laws and Guide. Las Vegas, n. d.; San Miguel Co. Las V., 1885.
Miner, The, a magazine.
Mineral Park Mojave Miner, newspaper.
Mining Industry. Denver, 1881.
Mining Magazine. N. Y., 1853 et seq.
Mining Review.
Miscellaneous Historical Papers. MS. Cal. Collection.
Modern Traveller, Mexico and Guatemala. Lond., 1825. 2 vol.
Mofras (Eugène D.), Exploration de l'Orégon. Paris, 1844; 2 vol., atlas.
Möllhausen (Baldwin), Reisen. Leipzig, 1861. 2 vol.; Tagebuch. Leipzig, 1858. 4to.
Montanus (Arnoldus), De Nieuwe en Oube-Kende Weereld. Amsterdam, 1671.
Monteros (Espinosa), Exposicion sobre Sonora y Sinaloa. Mex., 1823.
Moqui, Juntas de Guerra, 1713–15. MS.; Providencias tomadas, 1779. MS. In N. Mex., Doc., 922.
Morelli (Ciriacus), Fasti Novi Orbis. Venetüs, 1776.
Morfi (Juan A.), Viaje de Indios y Diario de N. Mex., 1777. In Doc. Hist. Mex., 3d ser., iv. 305; Desórdenes que se advierten en N. Mex., 1792. MS.
Morgan (L. B.), Article in N. Amer. Review. April 1869.
Morris (Wm G.), Address before Soc. of Cal. Volunteers. S. F., 1866.
Mota Padilla (Matias), Historia de la Conquista de N. Galicia. Mex., 1870; also MS.
Mountains and Mines of New Mexico, 1884. MS.
Mowry (Silvester), Arizona and Sonora. N. Y., 1864; Geography and Resources of Arizona and Sonora. Wash., 1859; S. F. and N. Y., 1863; Memoir of the proposed Territory of Ariz. Wash., 1857; Mines of the West. N. Y., 1864.
Müller (J. W.), Reisen. Leipzig, 1864. 3 vol.
Murray (Hugh), Historical Account of Discoveries. Lond., 1829. 2 vol.; Pictorial History of the U. S. Edin., 1844.

National Almanac. Phil., 1863–4. 2 vol.
National Convention of Cattlemen, Proceedings.
Nava (Pedro), Informe, 1801. In Arch., Cal.
Navarrete (Martin F.), Coleccion de Viajes. Mad., 1825–37. 5 vol.
New Mexico (or Nuevo Mejico), Acts of the Legislative Assembly. 1851 et seq.; Bureau of Immigration, Reports on Counties. 10 vol. 1881–2 (see authors' names); Bureau of Immig., Report 1883; Cédulas, MS. Collection; Compiled Laws. Sta Fé, 1885; Complete Business Directory and Gazeteer. Sta Fé (1882); Constitution, n. p., n. d. 16mo; Correspondence on Civil Affairs, 1850. (31st cong. 2d sess., Sen. Ex. Doc. 1); Defensas de Misioneros, 1818. MS. In Arch. Sta Fé; Destruction of Spanish and Mex. Archives. (S. F., 1871); Discurso y Proposiciones. In Pacheco, Doc., xvi. 38; Documentos para la Historia. MS. 3 vol.; Exposition and Driving Park Assoc., Premium List. Alburquerque, 1883; Informe del P. Provincial al Virey, 1750. MS. In N. Mex., Doc., 1–99; Historical Society, Inaugural Address. Sta Fé, 1881; Journal of the Convention of 1849. (31st cong. 1st sess., H. Ex. Doc. 17, p. 93); Journals of the Legislative Assembly, 1851 et seq.; Laws of the

Territory. Sta Fé, 1852 et seq.; Memorial sobre el N. Mex, 1595-1602. In Pacheco, Doc., xvi. 188; Message of Governor, 1851 et seq.; Mining Company, Preliminary Report. N. Y., 1864; and the N. Mexicans, a Political Problem, 1876; Newspapers (see names of towns and list in chap. xxx.); Pointers on the South-west. Topeka, 1883; Railroad Laws, Catron and Thornton. Sta Fé, 1881; Real Estate in Sta Fé, 1883; Reports of the Governor to Sec. of the Interior, 1879 et seq. In U. S. Govt Doc.; Its Resources and Advantages. Sta Fé, n. d.; Rules of the House of Representatives. Sta Fé, 1877; Rules of the Legislative Council. Sta Fé, 1877; Schedule of Distances. Ft Union, 1867; Scraps, a col. of newspaper clippings; Statutes (revised). St Louis, 1865; Stockgrowers' Assoc., By-laws. Sta Fé, 1884; Supreme Court Reports. S. F., 1881; Testimonio Dado en Mejico sobre el Descubrimiento, 1582-3. In Pacheco, Doc., xv. 80-150; Tourist's Shrine. Sta Fé (1882); Traslado de una Cédula, 1621. MS. In Arch., Sta Fé; Traslado de Posesion, 1598. In Pacheco, Doc., xvi. 88-141; Voice from, on Private Land Claims Wash., 1874; Ytinerario (1597-9), or Discurso de las Jornadas In Pacheco, Doc., xvi. 228-76.

New Mexico and California, Message and Documents, 1848. (30th cong. 1st sess., H. Ex. Doc. 70.)

Newlin (J. W.), Proposed Indian Policy. Phil., 1881.

Niel (Juan A.), Apuntamientos. In Doc. Hist. Mex., 3d ser., iv. 56.

Niles' Register. Baltimore, etc., 1811-49. 76 vol.

Nims (F. C.), Across the Continent. Chicago, n. d.

Niza (Marcos), Descubrimiento de las Siete Ciudades. In Pacheco, Doc., iii. 325; Ramusio, iii. 356; Hakluyt, iii. 362; Ternaux, 1st ser., ix. 256.

North American Review. Boston, 1819 et seq.

Noticia de Expediciones, 1744. In Sonora, Materiales, iv. 667; also MS.

Northern New Mexico Stock Growers' Assoc., Brand Book. 1883, Las Vegas; 1884, Raton.

Noticioso General. Mex. newspaper.

Nouvelles Annales des Voyages. Paris, 1819-60. 168 vol.

Nueva España, Breve Resumen del Descubrimiento. MS. 1767. 2 vol.

Nuevo Mexico (or Mejico). See New Mexico.

Obediencia y Vasallaje á su Magestad por los Indios de Sto Domingo, 1598. In Pacheco, Doc., xvi. 101.

Ogilby (John), America. Lond., 1671. Fol.

Olavide y Michelena (Henrique), Autos de Visita, 1738. MS.; Autos de Residencia del Gobernador, 1739. MS.

Oñate (Alonso), Pide se Confirme la Capitulacion, 1600. In Pacheco, Doc., xvi. 316.

Oñate (Juan), Copia de Carta, 1599. In Pacheco, Doc., xvi. 302.

Oswald (Fr.), Californien. Leipzig, 1849.

Otermin (Antonio), Consulta al Virey, 1682. MS.; Extractos de Doc. Hist. N. Mex. sobre levantamiento de 1680. MS.

Overland Mail Co., Observations, 1860; Memorial, 1860; Services (1857).

Oviedo y Valdés (Gonzalo F.), Historia General de las Indias. Mad., 1851-5. 4 vol.

Owen (Rich. F.) and E. T. Cox, Report on the Mines of N. Mex. Wash., 1865.

Pacheco (Joaquin F.) et al., Coleccion de Documentos Inéditos. Mad., 1864 -81. 34 vol. (Cited as Pacheco, Doc.)

Pacific Coast Directory, 1871-3.

Pacific Railroad Reports. Wash., 13 vol.

Palafox y Mendoza (Juan), Informe al Conde de Salvatierra, 1642. MS.

Palmer (Wm T.), Colonisation du Colorado. Paris, 1874.

Palou (Francisco), Relacion Historica, Vida de Junípero Serra. Mex., 1787.

Papeles de Jesuitas. MS. Collection.

Paredes (Alonso). See Posadas.

Parke (John G.), Report of Explorations, 1854. In Pac. R. R. Repts, ii.; Id., 1855. In Id., vii.

Pattie (James O.), Personal Narrative. Cincinnati, 1833.
Patton (J. H.), History of the U. S. N. Y., 1860; 1867.
Peralta (Juan Suarez), Noticias Históricas. Mad., 1878.
Peterson (Charles J.), Military Heroes of the Mex. War. Phil., 1858.
Peto (Morton), Resources of America. N. Y., 1866.
Pettingill's Newspaper Directory. N. Y., 1878.
Phœnix Gazette; Herald; newspapers.
Pike (Zeb. M.), Account of Travels. Phil., 1810; Exploratory Travels.
    Lond., 1811; Voyage au N. Mexique. Paris, 1812. 2 vol.
Pinal Drill, newspaper.
Pinart (Alphonse), Coleccion de Pimería Alta. MS.; Col. de Doc. sobre N.
    Mexico. MS.; Documents for the History of Sonora. MS. 5 vol.;
    Voyage dans l'Arizona. Paris, 1877.
Pino (Pedro B.), Exposicion Sucinta. Cádiz, 1812; Noticias Históricas. Mex.,
    1849.
Pixlee (P. C.), Dictation, Fond du Lac Cattle Co., 1885. MS.
Pope (John), Report of Exploration of a route for Pac. R. R., 1854. In Pac.
    R. R. Repts, ii.
Popular Science Monthly.
Porter (Gay E.), City Directory of Las Vegas. Las V., 1882.
Posadas (Alonso), Informe. In Fernandez Duro, Don Diego de Peñalosa;
    also in Doc. Hist. Mex., 3d ser., iv. 211 (under name of Paredes).
Poston (Charles D.), Apache-land. S. F., 1868; Arizona. In Prescott Miner,
    May 7, 1875; Narrative. In Browne's Apache Country, chap. xxiv.;
    Reminiscences. In Tucson Citizen, Apr. 15, 1884; Speech in H. of R. on
    Ind. Affairs. N. Y., 1865; Sun-worshipers. S. F., 1877.
Poussin (G. T.), De la Puissance Américaine. Paris, 1848, 2 vol.; Question de
    l'Orégon. Paris, 1846; The United States. Phil., 1877.
Powell (J. W.), Exploration of the Colorado, 1869-72. Wash., 1875.
Presidios, Reglamento i Instruccion, 1872-3. Mad., 1772-3.
Prescott Arizona Gazette; Arizona Miner; Arizonian; Journal; newspapers.
Prieto (Guillermo), Indicaciones; Rentas Generales. Mex., 1850.
Prince (L. Bradford), Historical Sketches of N. Mex. N. Y., 1883; Pamphlets,
    a collection of 5 by this author.
Pumpelly (Raphael), Across America. N. Y., 1870.
Purchas, His Pilgrimes. Lond., 1625-6. 5 vol.

Ramusio (Giov. B.), Navigationi et Viaggi. Venitia, 1554, 1583, 1565. 3 vol.
Rand, McNally, & Co., Guide to Colorado and N. Mex. Chicago, 1879; Over-
    land Guide. Chicago, 1883.
Raymond (Rossiter W.), Statistics of Mines. Wash., 1869-77.
Razonador, El, Mex. newspaper.
Reavis (James A.), El Caudal de Hidalgo (Peralta Grant). S. F., 1884; Coro-
    nado's Route. MS.
Relacion del Suceso. See Coronado, Rel.
Remesal (Antonio), Historia de la Provincia de S. Vicente de Chyapa. Mad.,
    1619.
Revilla Gigedo (Virey), Carta de 27 Dic., 1793. In Dicc. Univ., v. 426; also
    MS.
Reyes (Francisco A.), Noticia del Estado Actual de las Misiones. In Sonora,
    Mat., iv. 724; also MS.
Ribas (Andrés Perez), Historia de los Trivmphos de Nvestra Santa Fé. Mad.,
    1645.
Rideing (Wm H.), A-saddle in the Wild West. N. Y., 1879.
Riesgo and Valdés, Memoria Estadística, MS. In Pinart, Doc. Hist. Son., i.
    107.
Riley (B.), Report, Sta Fé Route, 1829. In Amer. St Pap., Mil. Aff., iv. 277.
Ripley (R. S.), War with Mexico. N. Y., 1849. 2 vol.
Ritch (Wm G.), Aztlan. Boston, 1855; Chronologic Annals. In Id., Legisl.
    Blue-Book; History of N. Mex. MS.; Illustrated N. Mex. (Sta Fé) 1883;
    Legislative Blue-Book. Sta Fé, 1882.

Rivera (Manuel), Los Gobernantes de Mexico. Mex., 1872. 2 vol.; Historia Antigua y Moderna de Jalapa. Mex., 1869–71. 5 vol.
Rivera (Pedro), Diario y Derrotero, 1724–8. Guathemala, 1736.
Robert (H. M.), Itineraries of routes in Ariz. S. F., 1869.
Roberts (Edwards), With the Invader. S. F., 1885.
Robertson (Wm), History of America. Lond., 1777. 2 vol.
Robles (Antonio), Diario de los Años 1665 y 1703. In Doc. Hist. Mex., 1st ser., ii.
Robson (Charles J.), The Maricopa Stake. MS.
Rodenbough (Theo. F.), From Everglade to Cañon. N. Y., 1875.
Romero, Documentos, Expedicion de 1823–6. MS. In Arch., Cal.
Romero (Benigno), Dictation, 1885. MS.
Rowell & Co., Gazeteer. N. Y., 1873.
Royce (Josiah), California. Boston, 1886.
Ruiz (Joaquin J.), Gobierno de las Misiones, 1773. MS. In N. Mex., Doc., 1059.
Rusling (James F.), Across America. N. Y., 1874.
Ruxton (Fred.), Sur la Migration. In Nouv. An. Voy., cxxvi. 37.
Ruxton (Geo. F.), Adventures in Mexico. N. Y., 1848.

Sacramento Bee; Union; and other newspapers.
Safford (A. K. P.), Arizona. MS.; Arizona. In S. F. Spirit of the Times, Dec. 25, 1877.
Saint Francis of Assisi, Life. N. Y., 1867.
St John Apache Chief; Orion Era, newspapers.
Salazar de Mendoza (Pedro), Monarquia de España. Mad., 1770–1. 3 vol.
Salmeron (Gerónimo de Z.), Relaciones de N. Mex. In Doc. Hist. Mex., 3d ser., iv.
Salt Lake Herald, 1877, newspaper.
Salvatierra (Juan M.), Relaciones 1697–1709. In Doc. Hist. Mex., 4th ser., v.
San Diego Union, newspaper.
San Francisco Alta; Bulletin; Californian; Cal. Star; Call; Chronicle; Examiner; Herald; Post; Scientific Press; Times; and other newspapers.
San Luis Potosí, Relacion Circumstanciada, 1733. MS.
San Miguel (Juan Rod.), Fondo Piadoso. Mex., 1845; La República Mexicana. Mex., 1845.
Sanchez (Bartolomé), Informe al Virey, 1785. MS.; Carta de 1751. In Sonora, Mat., i. 94.
Santa Anna (Antonio L.), A sus compatriotas. Apr. 12, 1858.
Santa Fé, Centennial Celebration. Sta Fé, 1876; Conquest of. Phil., 1847; Inundaciones de 1767. MS. In Pinart Col.; Message from the President. ... Arrest of Amer. citizens. Wash., 1818.
Santa Fé Gazette; N. Mex. Review; Post; Republican; Trail; and other newspapers.
Scenes in the Rocky Mountains. Phil., 1846.
Schoolcraft (Henry R.), Archives of Aboriginal Knowledge. Phil., 1860. 6 vol.
Schott (Charles A.), Distribution and Variation. Wash., 1876; Precipitation. Wash., 1872.
Scribner's Monthly Magazine.
Sedelmair (Jacobo), Entrada á la Nacion de Yumas, 1749. In Sonora, Mat., i. 18; also MS.
Semblanzas de los Miembros ...Cámara de Diputados. N. Y., 1828.
Serrano (Pedro), Informe del Provincial sobre Males de N. Mex., 1761. MS. In N. Mex., Doc., 173
Shakespeare Mining Journal. (St Louis, 1880.)
Shea (John G.), Expedition of Don Diego de Peñalosa. N. Y., 1882.
Sheldon (Lionel A.), Administration in N. Mex. MS. 1885.
Shinn (Charles H.), Mining Camps. N. Y., 1885.
Sigüenza y Góngora (Cárlos), Carta al Almirante. MS.; Mercurio Volante, Recuperacion del N. Mex. Mex., 1693. (MS. copy.)
Silliman's Journal of Science. N. Haven, 1819 et seq.
Silver King Mining Co. Report. S. F., 1880.

Simpson (James H.), Coronado's March.   In Smithsonian Rept, 1869; Journal
  of a Military Reconnoissance, 1849.   Phil., 1852.
Sinaloa, Memorias para la Historia.   MS.
Sinaloa y Sonora, Cartas.   In Doc. Hist. Mex., 4th ser., ii.
Sitgreaves (L.), Report of an Expedition down the Zuñi and Colorado (1851).
  Wash., 1853.
Slattery (Michael), Stock-raising.   1885.   MS.
Smitch (G. C.), Original Papers on Arizona.   MS.
Smith (Hugh N.), Address to the People of N. Mex.   Wash., 1850.
Smithsonian Institution, Annual Reports.   Wash., 1853 et seq.
Smyth (John H.), Law of Homestead.   S. F., 1875.
Sociedad Mexicana de Geografía, Boletin.   Mex., 1861 et seq.   (Includes
  Instituto Nacional.)
Sonora, Descripcion Geográfica, 1764.   In Id., Mat., iv. 493; also MS.; Ma-
  teriales para la Historia.   In Doc. Hist. Mex., 3d ser., iv.; 4th ser., i.;
  also MS.
Sonorense, El, newspaper.
Spaniards in N. Mex., Anonymous Notes.   MS.
Spanish Empire in America.   Lond., 1847.
Spiegelberg (Lehman), Commerce of Sta Fé.   MS.
Spitz (S.), Mexican Filigree.   Sta Fé, 1884.
Squier (E. G.), Article in Amer. Review.   Nov. 1848.
Stone (Wilbur F.), General View of Colorado.   MS.
Stoneroad (N. B.), Dictation, 1885.   MS.
Storrs (Augustus), Santa Fé Trade, 1824.   In U. S. Govt Doc.
Stratton (R. B.), Captivity of the Oatman Girls.   S. F., 1857; N. Y. (1858).
Sturenburg (R.), Report on N. Mex. Mines.   In U. S. Land Off. Repts, 1867.

Tamaron (Pedro), Visita del Obispado de Durango (1765).   MS.
Taos County Herald, newspaper.
Taos (Fernandez de), Review of the Boundary Question.   Sta Fé, 1853.
Temple (James E.), Statement.   MS.
Ternaux-Compans (Henri), Voyages, Relations et Mémoires.   Paris, 1837–41.
  2 series, 10 and 8 vol.
Thesaurus Geographicus.   Lond., 1709.
Thompson (A. W.), Law of the Farm.   S. F., 1876.
Thompson (Waddy), Recollections.   N. Y., 1844.
Thrall (H. S.), History of Texas.   St Louis, 1879.
Thrümmell (A. R.), Mexiko.   Erlanger, 1848.
Tiempo, El, Mex. newspaper.
Tombstone Epitaph; Nugget; newspapers.
Torquemada (Juan), Monarquia Indiana.   Mad., 1723.   3 vol.
Torre (Mariano R.), Entrada en la prov. de los Moquinos, 1755.   MS.   In N.
  Mex., Doc., 842.
Trigo (Manuel de S. J. N.), Informe sobre Misiones de Cebolleta y Encinal,
  1750.   MS.   In N. Mex., Doc., 1090; Informe sobre Misiones de N.
  Mex., 1754.   In Id., 283.
Troy (Jerome), Dictation of a Sheep-raiser, 1885.   MS.
Tubac Arizonian, newspaper.
Tubac, Libro de Mision.   MS.
Tubutama, Libro de Mision.   MS.
Tucson Arizonian; Citizen; Dos Repúplicas; Star; newspapers.
Tumacácori, Libro de Mision.   MS.
Tuthill (Franklin), History of California.
Tyler's Posts and Stations.
Tyler (Daniel), Concise History of the Mormon Battalion.   Salt Lake City, 1881.

United States Government Documents (Agriculture, Census, Chief of Engi-
  neers, Commerce and Navigation, Education, Indian Affairs, Land Office,
  Monetary Commission, Official Register, Secretary of Interior, War, etc.,
  Statutes, Surgeon-general, etc.) cited by titles alphabetically and dates.

United States Government Documents (House, Senate, Miscellaneous; documents and reports, etc.) cited by congress, session, number, and page.
United States Geographical Survey, Annual Reports (Geo. M. Wheeler), 1871-8. Wash., 8vo and 4to, with atlases.
United States Geological Survey (Hayden).
United States and Mexican Boundary Survey, 1854-5, Report of Wm H. Emory. Wash., 1857. 3 vol.
University of New Mexico, 1st Annual Catalogue. (Sta Fé) 1882.

Vallejo (Mariano G.), Documentos para la Historia de Mexico. MS. 2 vol.
Valverde y Cosío (Antonio), Diario y Derrotero del Norte, 1719. MS. of Pinart Col.; Expedicion á la prov. de Moqui, 1730. MS.
Van Tramp (John C.), Prairie and Rocky Mountain Adventures. St Louis, 1860.
Vargas (Diego), Acusacion del Cabildo de Sta Fé, 1697-8. MS. In Arch., Sta Fé; Campañas de 1694. MS. Ditto; Reconquista de N. Mex. MS. Ditto.
Vega (Plácido), Documentos. MS. 15 vol.
Velarde (Luis), Descripcion de la Pimería. In Sonora, Mat., i. 344; also MS.
Velasco, Historia du Royaume de Quito. In Ternaux, Voy.
Velasco (José F.), Noticias Estadísticas de Sonora. Mex., 1850.
Velasco (Virey), Relacion de lo que descubrió Diego de Ibarra. In Pacheco, Doc., xiv. 553.
Venegas (Miguel), Noticia de la California. Mad., 1757. 3 vol.
Vetancurt (Augustin), Chrónica de la Prov. del Sto Evangelio de Mexico. Mex., 1697, 1871; Menologio Franciscano. n. p., n. d.; Mex., 1871.
Victor (Frances F.), The River of the West. Hartford, 1870.
Viagero Universal. Mad., 1796-1801. 43 vol.
Vigil (Apolonio), Biographical Dictation, 1885. MS.
Vildosola (Agustin), Cartas del Padre Provincial, 1742. In Sonora, Mat., i. 1-17; iv. 721; also MS.
Vildosola (Gabriel), Cartas del Capitan. In Sonora, Mat., i. 186.
Villagrá (Gaspar), Historia de la Nueva Mexico. Alcalá, 1610.
Villaseñor y Sanchez (José A.), Theatro Americano. Mex., 1746. 2 vol.
Voto de Sonora, newspaper.
Voyages, A Selection. Lond., 1812.

Walker (Joel P.), Narrative of a Pioneer of '41. MS.
Warner (J. J.), Reminiscences. MS.
Warren (G. K.), Memoir of R. R. routes. In Pac. R. R. Repts, ix.
Washington (John M.), Reports of the Military Governor, 1849. (31st cong. 1st sess., H. Ex. Doc. 5.)
Watts (J. H.), Santa Fé Affairs, 1878. MS.
Whipple (A. W.), Report of Explorations, 1853-4. Wash., 1856; Pac. R. R. Repts, iii.
Whitney (J. D.), Metallic Wealth of the U. S. Phil., 1854.
Wilhelm (Thomas), History of the Eighth U. S. Infantry. Headquarters, 1873.
Willard, Inland Trade with Mexico. In Pattie's Narrative.
Wilson (Benj. D.), Observations. MS.
Wilson (H. T.), Historical Sketch of Las Vegas. Chicago, n. d.
Wingfield (Ed. H.) (Defence of his Acts as Indian Agent.) Wash., 1854.
Wizlizenus (A.), Denkschrift über ein Reise. Braunschweig, 1850; Memoir of a Tour to Northern Mexico. Wash., 1848.
Wood Brothers, Live-stock Movement. 1880-4.
Worthington, Woman in Battle.

Young (Philip), History of Mexico. Cin., 1850.
Yuma Arizona Sentinel, newspaper.

Zabriskie (J. C.), Public Land Laws of the U. S. S. F., 1870; Supplement S. F., 1877.
Zamacois (Niceto), Historia de Méjico. Barcelona, 1877-85. 16 vol.
Zúñiga (Ignacio), Rápida Ojeada al Estado de Sonora. Mex., 1835.

HISTORY

OF

ARIZONA AND NEW MEXICO.

CHAPTER I.

INTRODUCTORY REMARKS AND RÉSUMÉ.

THE ABORIGINES—NEW MEXICO AS A FIELD OF ANTIQUARIAN RESEARCH—
CONCLUSIONS IN THE 'NATIVE RACES'—THE PUEBLO TOWNS AND PEOPLE
—PRIMITIVE HISTORY—NO PREHISTORIC RELICS—NO AZTECS IN ARI-
ZONA AND NEW MEXICO—A PROTEST—RÉSUMÉ OF NORTH MEXICAN HIS-
TORY—EARLY IDEAS OF GEOGRAPHY—THE STRAIT—CORTÉS ON THE PA-
CIFIC—NUÑO DE GUZMAN—SAN MIGUEL DE CULIACAN—CALIFORNIA—
EBB AND FLOW OF ENTHUSIASM FOR NORTHERN EXPLORATION—MEAGRE
RESULTS—NUEVA GALICIA AND NUEVA VIZCAYA—OUTLINE OF NORTHERN
ANNALS FOR THREE CENTURIES—THE NORTHERN MYSTERY—CONJEC-
TURE AND FALSEHOOD—CABEZA DE VACA'S REMARKABLE JOURNEY
ACROSS THE CONTINENT—HE DID NOT ENTER NEW MEXICO OR SEE THE
PUEBLO TOWNS—BIBLIOGRAPHIC NOTES.

IT was in the sixteenth century that the Spaniards
first explored the region that forms the territorial
basis of this volume. The discoverers and early
explorers found there the home, not only of several
wild and roving tribes of the class generally denominated savages, but of an aboriginal people much further
advanced in progress toward civilization than any other
north of Anáhuac, or the region of Central Mexico.
This people, though composed of nations, or tribes,
speaking distinct languages, was practically one in the
arts and institutions constituting the general features
of its emergence from savagism. It was an agricul-

HIST. ARIZ. AND N. MEX. 1

tural people, dwelling in several-storied buildings of
stone or adobes. All that pertains to this most interesting people, or to the other native inhabitants of
Arizona and New Mexico, has been put before the
reader in an earlier work of this series. My present
purpose requires but the briefest repetition or résumé
of matters thus presented in their proper place, and
even that only in certain peculiar phases.[1]

This region offers for antiquarian research a field
not surpassed, in several respects, by any in America;
for here only we find a people, far in advance of the
savage tribes if far behind the highest types, retaining
many of their original characteristics, and living on
the same sites, in buildings similar to, or in several
instances perhaps identical with, those occupied by
their ancestors at the coming of the Europeans, and
for centuries before. These are the oldest continuously inhabited structures on the continent; and these
Pueblo Indians—so called from the Spanish term
applied to their community-houses, or towns, in the
absence of any general aboriginal name—are probably
more nearly in their original condition than any other
American tribes. It is therefore hardly possible to
overestimate the importance of these tribes for ethno-
logic study, unless, indeed, we adopt the extreme
views of those who refuse to credit testimony to the
effect that the most advanced Nahua and Maya nations possessed any trait or custom or institution or
degree of culture different from or superior to those
found among these Pueblos, or even inferior tribes of
the north.

In my *Native Races*, after describing the monuments
of this peculiar people, I expressed a hope that the
work might encourage further research and the publication of much additional information on the subject,

[1] See *Native Races of the Pacific States;* tribal relations, manners and customs, institutions, general description, etc., vol. i., p. 422, 465–6, 471–556;
mythology or religious customs, iii. 75–83, 135–6, 170–5, 521–8; language, iii.
568–9, 593–603, 671–4, 680–6; antiquities, ruins, relics, and historic traditions,
iv. 615–86; v. 537–8.

at the same time predicting with confidence—founded
on the uniformity of data already accessible—that
newly discovered relics would not differ materially in
type from those I was able to study, and that they
would require no essential modification of my conclusions respecting the primitive New Mexicans. This
hope and prediction have proved well founded. During the decade and more that has passed since my
work appeared, able investigators have directed their
efforts to this field, with results in the form of accurate
knowledge of the people, and their traditions, languages, and material relics that probably surpass in
many respects all that was known before; yet these
results, so far as I am familiar with them, are confirmatory of the general views which had been taken
by me, and which it seems proper to embody briefly
here, aboriginal annals being a fitting preface to the
record of foreign invaders' deeds to follow.

In their sixteenth-century explorations, the Spaniards found from seventy to a hundred of the Pueblo
towns still inhabited, there being much confusion of
names in the different narratives of successive visits.
Most of the towns cannot be definitely identified or
located; but as groups they present but slight difficulties; and they covered substantially the same territory then as now. South of this territory, in
southern Arizona and northern Chihuahua, and probably north of it, in southern Colorado and Utah,
though there may have been exceptions, similar wide-
spread structures were then as now in ruins. In the
next century, chiefly during the wars following successful revolt against the Spaniards, many of the
towns were destroyed or abandoned, the number being
reduced in that period or a little later to about twenty-
five, the dates and circumstances of the few later
changes being for the most part known.

It is only in the broadest outline that the history
of this people is known by their material relics, tradition affording but slight aid. Clearly the whole region,

extending somewhat farther north and south than the bounds of Arizona and New Mexico, was in the past occupied by semi-civilized tribes, not differing among themselves or from the Pueblos more than do the latter as known since the sixteenth century, and occupying the most fertile valleys with their stone and adobe town houses, similar, but often vastly superior, to the later well-known dwellings of the Pueblos. Long, perhaps centuries, before the Spaniards came, began the decline of this numerous and powerful people. The cause of their misfortunes must be traced to wars with savage predatory tribes like the Apaches, and with each other, drought and pestilence contributing to the same end. All the ruined structures and other relics of the long past were so evidently the work of the Pueblos or cognate tribes that there exists no plausible reason for indulging in conjectural theories respecting the agency of extinct races. Yet nothing is more common than to read of the discovery of prehistoric relics of the long-lost race that once peopled this land. My work has had but slight effect to check this popular tendency to the marvellous.

It is also still the custom of most writers to refer to the ruins and relics of this region as undoubtedly of Aztec origin, and to adopt more or less fully the theory that the ancestors of the Pueblo tribes were Aztecs left in Arizona during the famous migration from the north-west to Mexico. As the reader of my *Native Races* is aware, it is my belief that no such general migration occurred, at least not within any period reached by tradition; but whether this belief is well founded or not, I have found no reason to modify my position that the New Mexican people and culture were not Aztec.[2] The Montezuma myth of

[2] 'I can hardly conceive of structures reared by human hands differing more essentially than the two classes in question' (New Mexican and those of Cent. Am. and Mex.) 'In the common use of adobes for building material; in the plain walls rising to a height of several stories; in the terrace structure, absence of doors in the lower story, and the entrance by ladders; in the absence of arched ceilings of overlapping blocks, of all pyramidal structures,

the Pueblo communities, so far at least as the name is concerned if not altogether, was certainly of Spanish origin. Monumental and institutional resemblances are hardly sufficient to suggest even contact with the Nahua nations, yet such contact at one time or another is not improbable, and is indeed indicated by the dialects of some of the tribes. Linguistic affinities, however, like institutional and architectural resemblances, if any exist, do not indicate an Aztec base for the New Mexican culture at the beginning, but rather a superstructural element of later introduction. I offer no positive assertion that the northern advancement was indigenous or independent of the spirit that actuated the mound-builders or the architects of Palenque and Uxmal; but I claim that any possible connection is but vaguely supported by the evidence, and may at least be regarded as antedating the period of traditional annals. The origin of this most interesting aboriginal people is a legitimate subject of investigation, and there are many more competent than myself to form an opinion; yet I feel justified in protesting against the too prevalent tendency of most writers to accept in this matter as fact what is at the best but vague conjecture.

This chapter is intended to include all that it is necessary to say in a preliminary way, respecting the history of this territory, before beginning the chronologic narrative with the first coming of the Spaniards. An obviously important and necessary feature of this introductory matter is the annals of Spanish progress

of sculptured blocks, of all architectural decorations, of idols, temples, and every trace of buildings evidently designed for religious rite, of burial-mounds and human remains; and in the character of the rock-inscriptions and miscellaneous relics, not to go further into details—the N. Mex. monuments present no analogies to any of the southern remains. I do not mean to express a decided opinion that the Aztecs were not, some hundreds or thousands of centuries ago, or even at a somewhat less remote period, identical with the natives of N. Mex., for I have great faith in the power of time and environment to work unlimited changes in any people; I simply claim that it is a manifest absurdity to suppose that the monuments described were the work of the Aztecs during a migration southward since the 11th century, or of any people nearly allied in blood and institutions to the Aztecs as they were found in Anáhuac.' *Nat. Races*, iv. 683.

from Mexico northward, of the successive steps by which the broad regions south of this distant province were discovered, explored, and to some extent settled before the army of invasion secured a foothold in Arizona and New Mexico. But this is a subject that has been presented with all desirable detail in the first volume of my *History of the North Mexican States*, to which the reader is referred, not only for events preceding the discovery of New Mexico, but for later happenings in the southern regions, an acquaintance with which will greatly stimulate interest in and facilitate the study of the accompanying northern developments. Because this matter is fully treated in the volume alluded to, and because it is also presented in various outline-combinations as a necessary introduction to volumes on other northern Pacific states, I may properly restrict its treatment here to narrow limits; but cannot, consistently with my general plan of making each work of the series complete in itself, omit it altogether.[3]

As soon as the Spaniards had made themselves masters of the valley of Mexico, their attention was attracted in large degree to the north as presenting new and promising fields for conquest. This was natural from their comparatively complete knowledge of southern geography and ignorance of the north, with its probably vast extent, its prospectively rich and powerful nations of aborigines, and its correspondingly attractive mysteries. But there was another and more potent incentive in the current theories respecting geographical relations of the new regions to Asia and the Indies. These theories, legitimately founded on the slight data accessible, furnish the key to all that might otherwise be mysterious in the annals of

[3] In like manner the record in *Hist. North Mex. States*, i., is made complete by brief résumés, in the proper places, of northern events. Thus not only are the successive expeditions that extended beyond Sonora and Chihuahua into Ariz. and N. Mex. recorded in outline, but on pp. 127–9, 373–5, 642–4, is a sketch of N. Mex. history in 1540–1800; and in the chapters devoted to Sonora may be found the annals of Pimería Alta, which included southern Arizona. Chap. 1 of *Hist. Cal.*, i., is a résumé of the *North Mex. States*, including New Mexico.

north-western exploration.   So fully have they been
explained by me elsewhere in various connections that
mere mention may suffice here.   At first it was supposed that Columbus had reached the main Asiatic
coast, which might be followed south-westward to the
Indies.   Then a great island—really South America—
was found, which did not seriously conflict with the
original idea, but was of course separated from the
main by a strait, through which voyagers to and from
India by the new route must pass.   Further exploration failed to find this strait, but revealed instead an
isthmus effectually impeding south-western progress in
ships; and when Balboa in 1513 crossed the Isthmus
to find a broad expanse of ocean beyond, and others a
little later explored the western coast for many leagues
northward, it became apparent that the old geographic
idea must be modified, that the new regions, instead
of being the Asiatic main, were a great south-eastern
projection of that main.   The idea of the 'strait,' however, had become too deeply rooted to be easily abandoned; accordingly, it was located in the north, always
to be sought just beyond the limit of actual exploration in that direction.   Of course, this cosmographic
ignis fatuus did not obstruct but rather stimulated the
quest for new kingdoms to conquer, new riches for
Spanish coffers, and new souls to be saved by spiritual
conquest.

   Fully imbued, not only with the desire to extend
his fame as a conqueror, but with the prevalent geographic theories, Hernan Cortés, within a year or two
after the fall of Anáhuac, convinced himself, through
reports of the natives and of his lieutenants sent to
plant the Spanish flag on South Sea shores, that the
great westward trend of the Pacific coast that was to
connect the new regions with Asia must be sought
farther north than the latitude of Tenochtitlan.   The
plan conceived by him was to build ships on the Pacific, and in them to follow the coast northward, then
westward, and finally southward to India.   In this

voyage, he would either discover the 'strait,' or prove
all to be one continent; discover for his sovereign rich
coast and island regions; perhaps find great kingdoms
to conquer; and at the least explore a new route to
the famous Spice Islands.   His ship-yard was established at Zacatula in 1522, but through a series of
misfortunes, which need not be catalogued here, his
maritime exploration in 1530 had not extended above
Colima.   Meanwhile, however, various land expeditions had explored the regions of Michoacan and
southern Jalisco up to the latitude of San Blas, or
about 21° 30'.   In the interior at the same date the
advance of northern exploration had reached Querétaro, and possibly San Luis Potosí, in latitude
22°.   On the east a settlement had been founded at
Pánuco, and the gulf coast vaguely outlined by several expeditions, the last of which was that of Pánfilo
de Narvaez, whose large force landed in 1828 in
Florida, and with few exceptions perished in the
attempt to coast the gulf by land and water to
Pánuco.

In 1531 the first great movement northward was
made, not by Cortés, but by his rival Nuño de Guzman, who, with a large army of Spaniards and Indians,
marched from Mexico up the west coast to Sinaloa.
His northern limit was the Yaqui River in about
latitude 28°; and branches of his expedition also
crossed the mountains eastward into Durango, and
perhaps Chihuahua; but the only practical result of
this grand expedition, except a most diabolic oppression and slaughter of the natives, was the founding of
the little villa of San Miguel in about latitude 25°,
corresponding nearly with Culiacan, an establishment
which was permanent, and for many a long year maintained a precarious existence as the isolated frontier
of Spanish settlement.   Guzman returned to Jalisco,
whose permanent occupation dates from this period;
and the province or 'kingdom' of Nueva Galicia was
ushered into existence with jurisdiction extending

over all the far north, and with its capital soon fixed at Guadalajara.

But Cortés, though opposed at every step by his enemy, Guzman, and involved in other vexatious difficulties, continued his efforts, and despatched several expeditions by water, one of which was wrecked on the Sinaloa coast in latitude 26°, and another in 1533 discovered what was supposed to be an island in about latitude 24°. Here, in 1535, Cortés in person attempted to found a colony, but the enterprise was a disastrous failure; the settlement at Santa Cruz—really on the peninsula—was abandoned the next year, and the place was named, probably by the settlers in their disgust, California, from an Amazon isle "on the right hand of the Indies very near the terrestrial paradise," as described in a popular novel. Meanwhile nothing had been accomplished farther east that demands notice in this connection; and the great northern bubble seemed to have burst.

Yet little was needed to renew the old excitement, and the incentive was supplied even before Cortés' ill-fated colony had left California. In April 1536, there arrived at San Miguel de Culiacan Álvar Nuñez and three companions, survivors of Narvaez' expedition of 1528, who had wandered across the continent through Texas, Chihuahua, and Sonora, and who brought reports of rich towns situated north of their route. They carried the news to Mexico, and the result was a series of more brilliant and far-reaching explorations by sea and land than any that had been undertaken before. Soto's wanderings of 1538-43 in the Mississippi Valley may be connected, chronologically at least, with this revival of interest. Cortés despatched a fleet under Ulloa, who in 1539 explored the gulf to its head, and followed the outer coast of the peninsula up to Cedros Island in latitude 28°. Viceroy Mendoza took the fever, and not only sent Alarcon to the head of the gulf and up the Rio Colorado, and a little later Cabrillo to the region of Cape Mendocino on the outer coast, but also despatched Niza as a pioneer, and presently Vasquez de Coronado with his grand army of explorers, who in 1540–2 traversed Sonora, Arizona, New Mexico, and the plains north-eastward to perhaps latitude 40°, and whose adventures will be narrated in the following chapters. The explorers, however, returned without having achieved any final conquest, or established any permanent settlement; and again interest in the far north died out—a result partly due, however, to the great revolt of native tribes in Nueva Galicia, known as the Mixton war of 1540–2.

With the suppression of this revolt, the final conquest of Nueva Galicia was effected; and before 1550 the rich mines of Zacatecas were discovered, and the town of that name founded. Exploration of the northern interior was mainly the work of miners, though the missionaries were always in the front rank. Francisco de Ibarra was the great military explorer from 1554, his entradas covering the region corresponding to the Durango, Sinaloa, and southern Chihuahua of modern maps, besides one vaguely recorded expedition that may have extended into Arizona or New Mexico. About 1562 the new province of Nueva Vizcaya, with Ibarra as governor and capital at Durango, was created, to include all territory above what is now the line of Jalisco and Zacatecas, theoretically restricted to the region east of the mountains, but practically including the coast provinces as well; yet the audiencia of Guadalajara retained its judicial jurisdiction over all the north. Before 1565 there were mining settlements in the San Bartolomé Valley of southern Chihuahua, corresponding to the region of the later Parral, Allende, and Jimenez. These settlements on the east, with San Felipe de Sinaloa on the west, may be regarded as the frontier of Spanish occupation in 1600; yet, as we shall presently see, several expeditions had penetrated the country north-eastward even to New Mexico, the conquest of which province at this date was thus far in advance of the general progress northward. South of the frontier line as noted, the regions of Sinaloa, Durango, and southern Coahuila were occupied by many flourishing missions under the Jesuits and Franciscans; and there were numerous mining settlements, with a few military posts; though the general Spanish population was yet very small.

Seventeenth-century annals of the north may be briefly outlined for present purposes. In the beginning, Vizcaino, on the outer coast, repeated Cabrillo's explorations to or beyond the 40th parallel; while pearlfishers and others made many trips to the gulf waters. In Sinaloa, the Jesuits prospered; in Sonora, beginning with the Yaqui treaty of 1610, and the conversion of the Mayos in 1613, the missionaries made constant progress until a large part of the province was occupied; and in the last decade, not only did Baja California become a mission field, but Pimería Alta, where Padre Kino pushed forward his explorations northward to the Gila. East of the mountains, Nueva Vizcaya was for the most part a land of war during this century; eight Jesuits and two hundred Spaniards lost their lives in the Tepehuane revolt of 1616 in Durango; but the missionaries not only regained lost ground, but pushed forward their work among the Tarahumares of Chihuahua, where also there were many revolts. North-eastern Durango and eastern and northern Chihuahua formed the mission field of the Franciscans, whose establishments, exposed to the frequent raids of savage foes, maintained but a precarious existence, yet were extended before 1700 to the Casas Grandes, to the site of the later city of Chihuahua, and to El Paso on the Rio Grande. Meanwhile the mines in all directions yielded rich results; and a small military force under the governor's management strove more or less ineffectually to protect missions and mining camps, and to repel the endless and ubiquitous incursions of marauding tribes.

Northern Coahuila was occupied by the Franciscans, and several settlements were founded in the last quarter of this century. Texan annals of the period are divided into three distinct parts: first, the various expeditions from New Mexico to the east in 1601- 80; second, the disastrous attempts at colonization by the French under La Salle in 1682–7; and third, efforts of the Spaniards from 1686, resulting in several exploring expeditions from Coahuila, and in the foundation of several Franciscan missions on the branches of the rivers Trinidad and Neches, which were abandoned in 1693.

In the eighteenth century, but for the conquest of Nayarit in 1721–2, the provinces of Sinaloa and Durango relapsed into the monotonous, uneventful condition of Nueva Galicia, that of a *tierra de paz;* but Sonora and Chihuahua were more than ever a *tierra de guerra,* the victim of murderous raids of Apaches and other warlike and predatory tribes. A line of presidios was early established along the northern frontier, which, with occasional changes of site as demanded by circumstances, served to prevent the abandonment of the whole region. There was hardly a settlement of any kind that was not more than once abandoned temporarily. New mines were constantly discovered and worked under occasional military protection; the famous mining excitement of the Bolas de Plata, at Arizonac, occurred in 1737–41; rich placers of gold were found in Sonora; and the Real de San Felipe, or city of Chihuahua, sprang into existence near the mines of Santa Eulalia early in the century. The missions showed a constant decline, which was not materially affected by the expulsion of the Jesuits and substitution of the Franciscans in 1767. Many new missions were founded, but more were abandoned, and most became but petty communities of women, children, and invalids, or convenient resorts of the able-bodied from time to time, the friars retaining no practical control. There was but slight gain of new territory, though in Pimería Alta the missions and presidios were extended northward to San Javier del Bac and Tubac, in what was later Arizona. On the west coast, however, in 1769–1800, the Spanish occupation was extended to latitude 37°, and exploration to the 60th parallel, while the Franciscans founded a series of nineteen new and flourishing missions in Alta California; and in the extreme east Texas was reoccupied in 1716–22 with missions and presidios, the country remaining permanently under Spanish dominion, though the establishments were never prosperous.

There is yet another introduction or accompaniment, pertaining appropriately enough to the early history of New Mexico, to which I may call attention here, at the same time suggesting that a perusal of its details as recorded in another volume of this series may yield more of pleasure and profit if undertaken a little later, after the reader shall have made himself familiar with the record of the earliest expeditions as presented in the opening chapters of this volume. I allude to the mass of more or less absurd conjectural theories respecting northern geography, which, plentifully leavened with falsehood, were dominant among writers and map-makers for two centuries, and which —belonging as much and as little to New Mexico as to any part of my territory—under the title of the Northern Mystery I have chosen to treat in my *History of the Northwest Coast*.[4] The earliest theories respecting the geographic relations of America to Asia were in a sense, as we have seen, reasonable and consistent; but after the explorations of 1539–43, this element of consistency for the most part disappeared, as the Spanish government lost much of its interest in the far north, with its faith in the existence of new and wealthy realms to be conquered there. There remained, however, a firm belief in the interoceanic strait, and an ever-present fear that some other nation

[4] Vol. i., chap. i.–iv., with copies of many old maps.

would find and utilize it to the disadvantage of Spain. Meanwhile, there were many explorers legitimately desirous of clearing up all that was mysterious in the north, conquerors bent on emulating in that direction the grand achievements of Cortés and Pizarro, friars eager to undertake as missionaries the spiritual conquest of new realms for God and their king; and their only difficulty was to gain access to the royal treasury in behalf of their respective schemes. The fear of foreign encroachment was a strong basis of argument, and in their memorials they did not hesitate to supplement this basis with anything that might tend to reawaken the old faith in northern wealth and wonders. These interested parties, and the host of theorists who embraced and exaggerated their views, generally succeeded in convincing themselves that their views were for the most part founded in fact. The old theories were brought to light, and variously distorted; the actual discoveries of 1539–43, as the years passed on, became semi-mythical, and were located anywhere to suit the writer's views, Indian villages being magnified without scruple into great cities; each new discovery on the frontier was described to meet requirements, and located where it would do the most good; and even the aborigines, as soon as they learned what kind of traditions pleased the white men most, did excellent service for the cause. It must be understood that much of all this was honest conjecture respecting a region of which little or nothing was known;[5] but theory became

[5] A late writer says, somewhat in this connection: 'It is difficult for persons in our generation to realize the circumstances under which the various expeditions connected with N. Mex. were made during the 16th, and indeed the 17th, century. We have been so accustomed to the general geog. contour of the Amer. continent from our earliest youth, we know so well the distance from ocean to ocean, and from the gulf to the Artic region, that it seems difficult to remember that the intrepid explorers who penetrated to the north after the fall of the Montezumas had no idea at all of the extent of the mainland, and were never sure as they ascended a mountain but that its summit would bring to view the South Sea to the west, the North Sea, or Atlantic, to the east, or the great Arctic Ocean toward the pole....The explorer of those days was travelling entirely in the dark. Nothing in more modern times has been similar to, or can again resemble, the uncertainty and romance

rapidly and inextricably mingled with pure fiction; and there were few of the reported wonders of the north that had not been actually seen by some bold navigator, some ship-wrecked mariner wandering inland, or some imaginative prospector or Indian-fighter. Not only did the strait exist, but many voyagers had found its entrance on the east or west, and not a few had either sailed through it from ocean to ocean, or reached it from the interior by land. The kingdoms and cities on its banks were described, though with discrepancies, which, indeed, threw no doubt on its existence, but rather suggested that the whole northern interior might be a great network of canals, among which the adventurer—would the king but fit out a fleet for him—might choose his route. Only a small portion of the current speculations and falsehoods found their way into print, or have been preserved for our reading; but quite enough to show the spirit of the time. The resulting complication of geographic absurdities, known as the Northern Mystery, has had a strange fascination for me, and its close connection with the early annals of New Mexico, as with those of the other Pacific United States, will doubtless be apparent to all.

of those early expeditions. For the recent explorers of Africa, for example, had a perfect knowledge of the shape of the exterior of the continent, and knew exactly what tribes lived on each shore, and what rivers emptied into each ocean. All that was left as a *terra incognita* was a certain area in the centre, and that of known length and breadth. But the early explorers of America literally knew nothing of the land they entered. It was absolutely virgin soil. They might find impassable mountains or enormous lakes; they might have to traverse almost interminable deserts, or discover rivers whose width would forbid their crossing; they might chance upon gigantic volcanoes, or find themselves on the shore of the ultimate ocean. And as to the inhabitants and products, they were equally ignorant. We are sometimes induced to smile at the marvellous stories related by some of the older explorers, at their still more extravagant expectations, and the credulity with which everything (however exaggerated or unnatural) relating to the new continent was believed. But we must remember that it was a day of real marvels, and that nothing could well be imagined more extraordinary and unexpected than those things which had already been discovered as realities. An entire new world had been opened to the enterprise, the curiosity, the cupidity, and the benevolence of mankind. It is as if to-day a ready mode of access to the moon were discovered, and the first adventurers to the lunar regions had returned laden with diamonds, and bearing tidings of riches and wonders far beyond the wildest imagination of former generations.' *Prince's Hist. Sketches of New Mexico*, 16–18.

The wanderings of Cabeza de Vaca, including, as most or all writers on the subject have agreed, the first visit of Europeans to New Mexico, have been recorded somewhat in detail in another volume of this series.[6] For that reason, but chiefly because it is my opinion that Cabeza de Vaca never entered New Mexico, I devote in this volume comparatively little space to the subject; and for the latter reason, what I have to say is given in this introductory chapter instead of being attached to the record of actual explorations in the next. Álvar Nuñez, or Cabeza de Vaca, Andrés Dorantes, Alonso del Castillo Maldonado, and a negro slave called Estevanico were the only known survivors of the expedition of Narvaez to the gulf coast in 1528. After years of captivity among different native tribes, they finally escaped from servitude on the Texas coast, crossed the continent in a journey that lasted nearly a year, and arrived at San Miguel de Culiacan in April 1536. The success of so remarkable a trip resulted from the leader's wonderful good luck in establishing his reputation as a great medicine-man among the natives, who escorted the strangers from tribe to tribe along the way with full faith in their supernatural powers; or perchance the wanderers were, as they believed, under the miraculous protection of their god.

Naturally no journal was kept; but a report was made on arrival in Mexico, and a narrative was written by Alvar Nuñez after he went to Spain in 1537.[7] There is no reason to question the good faith of either report or narrative as written from memory; but there is much discrepancy and confusion, not only between the two versions, but between different statements in each. Moreover the narrative informs us

---

[6] See *Hist. North Mex. States*, i. 60–70.
[7] *Relacion que dió Álvar Nuñez*, etc., 1st pub. in 1542, with later ed. as *Relacion y Comentarios* and as *Naufragios*, also Italian and French translations. The report made in Mex. 1536 is known only by the version in *Oviedo, Hist. Ind.*, iii. 582. Buckingham Smith, in his carefully annotated *Cabeza de Vaca's Relation*, a translation of the narrative, made use also of the report through Oviedo. For further bibliog. details, see ref. of note 6.

that they passed through so many peoples that "the
memory fails to recall them," and the report disposes of
an important part of the journey by the remark that
they went forward "many days." There are, however,
allusions to two or three large rivers, which, if the
record has any significance, can hardly have been other
than the Pecos, Rio Grande, and Conchos; and the
route—shown on the annexed map without any attempt to give details—may be plausibly traced in
general terms from the Texan coast near Galveston

CABEZA DE VACA'S ROUTE.

north-westward, following the course of the rivers,
then south-west to the region of the Conchos junction,
then westward to the upper Sonora and Yaqui valleys
in Sonora, and finally south to San Miguel in Sinaloa.[8]

The belief that Cabeza de Vaca passed through
New Mexico and visited the Pueblo towns is not supported by the general purport of the narrative, or
of what followed. Not only is it wellnigh certain

[8] 'It is not possible to follow, and to trace geographically, the erratic course
of Cabeza de Vaca with any degree of certainty. His own tale, however
authentic, is so confused that it becomes utterly impossible to establish any
details of location.' *Bandelier's Hist. Introd.*, 6. This writer of 1881 seems
to imply at least a doubt that N. Mex. was discovered at this time. Prince,
however, in '83, *Hist. Sk.*, 80, 91-2, has no doubt of the discovery.

that had he seen those wonderful structures, they
would have figured largely in his reports in Mexico,
but we know that the effective part of his statement
was the report, obtained from Indians, of populous
towns with large houses and plenty of turquoises and
emeralds, situated to the north of his route.   There
are but two bits of testimony that might seem to conflict with my conclusion, and both, when examined,
seem rather to confirm it.   One of the relations of
Coronado's later expedition indicated that traces of
Cabeza de Vaca's presence were found on the plains
far to the north-east of the Santa Fé region; but in
another it is explained that they simply met an old
Indian, who said he had seen four Spaniards in the
direction of New Spain, that is, in the south.   Again,
according to the narrative, the wanderers, long before
they heard of the great houses of the north, came to
"fixed dwellings of civilization;" and indeed, it is implied that they travelled for long distances in the regions of such dwellings; but that these were not the
Pueblo structures is clear, not only from the lack of
description, but from the fact that the natives built
new houses for the accommodation of their guests.   I
suppose these fixed dwellings were simply ranchería
huts of a somewhat more permanent nature than those
that had been seen farther east on the plains; and indeed, the Jumanas were found before the end of the
century living in such houses, some of them built of
stone.   Again, it is to be noted that Espejo in 1582
found among the Jumanas, not far above the Conchos
junction, a tradition that the Spaniards had passed
that way.   Even Davis, who has no doubt that the
party visited New Mexico, has to suggest that that
country then extended much farther south than now,
thus somewhat plausibly proving that if Alvar Nuñez
did not come to New Mexico, a convenient lack of
boundaries enabled the province to go to Cabeza de
Vaca.   It seems to me that the most positive assertion that can be made in connection with the whole

matter, except that the wanderers arrived at San
Miguel, is that they did not see the Pueblo towns;
yet it can never be quite definitely proved that their
route did not cut off a small south-eastern corner of
what is now New Mexico. While Cabeza de Vaca is
not to be credited with the discovery of the country,
he was the first to approach and hear of it; his reports were the direct incentive to its discovery and exploration; and thus, after all, his wonderful journey
may still be regarded as the beginning of New Mexican annals.

BIBLIOGRAPHY OF EARLY NEW MEXICAN HISTORY.

An alphabetic list of works consulted in the preparation of this volume is
given as usual at its beginning. By far the most important authorities for
the Spanish and Mexican periods are of a documentary nature; but documents and books relating to special events, topics, or epochs of the history
will be noticed bibliographically, as my custom is, when their subjects in
succession present themselves for treatment. Besides these, there are, however,
some archive collections and general works in manuscript and print covering
the whole ground of Spanish and Mexican annals, or a considerable portion
of it, which, having no specially appropriate chronologic place, may be most
conveniently noticed here. This note may also properly include a mention,
not only of general works on the history of Arizona and New Mexico, but of
others devoted mainly to other subjects, yet containing scattered information
on points treated in this volume, and also of various collections of voyages or
documents rich in New Mexican matter, the separate items of which will
require more detailed attention elsewhere. Mention of works devoted to the
modern history of these countries as territories of the United States, even if
they include a superficial outline of earlier events, will, as a rule, be reserved
for later chapters.

Naturally, archive records are here as elsewhere to be regarded as the
foundation of history; but in this case these records must be sought from a
variety of sources, of which the archives proper—that is, the documents preserved in government keeping at Santa Fé, and cited by me as *Archivo de
Sta Fe*, MS.—are not the most fruitful or important. The earliest records,
those preceding 1680, were almost entirely destroyed in the revolt of that
and the following years. The bulky accumulations of 160 later years, never
adequately cared for in Spanish and Mexican times, were most shamefully
neglected under U. S. rule. Hundreds of documents were lost or destroyed
from time to time, until about 1870, during the rule of Governor Pile, when
the remaining archives were removed from the *palacio* and sold for wrapping-
paper, only about one fourth being recovered. See N. Mex. newspapers of
1870, extracts from which were published in pamphlet form as *N. Mex.,
Destruction of Spanish and Mexican Archives in New Mexico, by United States
Officials*, n. p. (1870), 8vo, 4 p. After several years more of neglect and
ruin, the fragments were at last gathered up, properly cared for, and roughly
classified in 135 pasteboard boxes, by Judge Samuel Ellison, who has been
their keeper as territorial librarian since 1881, and who has kindly afforded
me every facility for consulting the treasures in his care. Thus it will be
seen that the *Arch. Sta Fé*, though immensely valuable in the aggregate,
and containing many important documents, is very imperfect, fragmentary,
and utterly inadequate to the forming of a complete record of the country's
annals in any phase. It is vastly inferior to the *Archivo de California*, so ex-

tensively cited in another work of this series; and it should also be noted
that the scale on which this volume is written by no means calls for or permits so detailed a reproduction of the archive record as is given in my work
on California. In the papers at Sta Fé, the fragmentary mission books and
other documents preserved at some of the old pueblos, and the private archives of New Mexican families, there is still ample field for the research of
historical societies or individuals who may delve for data on local and personal
minutiæ of the old times. Many documents of the *Arch. Sta Fé* are given
separate titles in my list, and are noticed under their proper dates in these
pages. It should also be noted that a few documents of the archives before
their destruction were consulted by different writers, who have thus preserved
matter not without value.

Fortunately, a formal search of the Sta Fé archives for historical purposes
was made in the 18th century, while the records were still comparatively in-
tact. This search, made in part by Padre Escalante in 1778, and completed
by him or some other Franciscan in the following years, covered the period
from 1681 to 1717; the result, very much more complete than any that could
be reached by an examination of the original records in their present condition—though I have found many of the fragments by which to test parts of
the work—was sent to Mexico and Spain, and it is still extant, though I believe I am the first in modern times to consult it. It is cited by me under
two titles: 1st, *Escalante, Carta del P. Fr. Silvestre Velez de Escalante, Escrita
en 2 de Abril de 1778 años* (Sta Fé), fol., p. 113–26. The author had, it seems,
been requested by his superior, P. Juan A. Morfi, to search the N. Mex. archives. This letter contains an epitome of such information as he has found
from 1680 to 1692, all papers of earlier date than 1680 having been lost in the
revolts of '80 or '97. He hopes to complete the search in a month or two;
therefore he was probably the author of the following: 2d, *Archivo de Nuevo
Mexico*, fol., p. 127–208, which is a continuation of the preceding, covering
the period of 1692–1717. It contains many copies or extracts of original
papers, some of which still exist with the paging as here given. At the beginning it is divided into *cuadernos*, and later into paragraphs corresponding
to the administrations of successive governors. Its value as an historical
authority of course requires no explanation. These invaluable records are
found in MS., in the *Archivo General de Mexico*, tomo ii.–iii., the Andrade-
Maximilian copies of which are in my Library; and they were also printed,
1856, in the *Doc. Hist. Mex.*, 3d series, pt iv. p. 113–208, which is the form
in which I cite the *Escalante, Carta*, and the *Arch. N. Mex.*, though I have
introduced some corrections from the MSS.

There are several other valuable collections of archive material, each containing important papers not found in any other, and all constituting for some
periods a very perfect record. Vol. xxv. of the *Arch. Gen. Mex.*, MS., is entitled *Documentos para la Historia de Nuevo Mexico*, of which a copy in my
Library filling 1,756 pages is cited in this volume as *N. Mex. Doc.*, MS. These
documents are official reports of friars and secular authorities covering a large
part of the 18th century, but also including some very important papers of
the 17th. The original copies seem to have been made both at Sta Fé and in
Mexico, and very few of the records have been consulted by any earlier
writer. M. Alphonse Pinart has a *Coleccion de Documentos sobre Nuevo Mexico*, composed of a large number of unbound original MSS., collected by himself from various sources and kindly furnished for my use. It is particularly
rich in official communications between the rulers of N. Mex. and the superior authorities in Chihuahua and Mexico; and it has enabled me to fill
many a gap in the country's annals. Still another collection of original and
not previously used matter in my Library is the *Nuevo Mexico, Cédulas*, MS.,
60 fol., which contains 18th-century copies of some 35 royal orders, of various
dates from 1631 to 1762, selected for their importance in connection with New
Mexican events. I think this collection was also made by or for Padre Morfi.
It is preceded by *Bonilla (Antonio), Apuntes sobre Nuevo Mexico*, 1776, MS., 31
fol., a valuable outline of provincial annals to date; and is followed by collections of *Cédulas* on Baja Cal., and other provinces.

The 32 volumes of MSS. which make up the *Archivo General of Mexico*, or which rather form an introduction or beginning for the hundreds of volumes of records preserved there—collected from all parts of the country by order of Cárlos IV., dated Feb. 21, 1790, are rich in matter on our present subject. In tom. ii.-iii., printed in *Doc. Hist. Mex.*, 3d series, pt iv., p. 1–225—besides the *Escalante, Carta*, and the *Arch. N. Mex.*, already noted, are found three other important documents as follows: (1st) *Salmeron, Relaciones de todas las cosas que en el Nuevo-Mexico se han visto y Sabido, así por mar como por tierra, desde el año de 1538 hasta el de 1626, por el Padre Gerónimo de Zárate Salmeron, predicador de la órden de los menores de la provincia del Santo Evangelio. Dirigidas á N. Rmo P. Fr. Francisco de Apodaca, padre de la provincia de Cantabria y comisario general de todas las de esta Nueva-España* (printed in 1856), fol., p. 1–55. For more about the author, see chap. viii. of this vol. The work was approved by Fr. Francisco Velasco of the Franciscan convent in Mexico on Aug. 18, 1629. It is a very interesting and complete résumé—the best extant, when taken in connection with the following work—of the earliest northern explorations, being by no means confined to N. Mex.; yet the writer is so fully imbued with the spirit of his time, and so eager to promote new entradas, that he considerably exaggerates reports of gold, silver, great cities, and other northern wonders, and somewhat to the neglect unfortunately of events of his own time on which he might have thrown much light. (2d) *Niel, Apuntamientos que á las memorias del P. Fr. Gerónimo de Zárate hizo el P. Juan Amando Niel de la Compañia de Jesus, no tan solo estando práctico del terreno que se cita, si no es que llevaba en la mano las memorias para cotejar las con él*, p. 56–112. The author was a missionary in Sin., Son., and Chih. from 1697 to 1710, and was evidently well acquainted with all that had been accomplished in the north, though it does not appear that he ever visited N. Mex. His work is more valuable in a sense than that of Salmeron, since it includes literally or in substance all the latter's statements, corrects many of his errors, and makes considerable additions from the author's more extended knowledge. Niel wrote a century later than Salmeron, but knowledge of northern geography had in the mean time made but little progress. I have used both works extensively in my study of the Northern Mystery in another work of this series. (3d) *Paredes, Utiles y curiosas noticias del Nuevo-Mexico; Cíbola, y otras naciones confinantes; La antigua tradicion de Copala, cuna no solo de los Indios Mexicanos, sino generalmente de todas las naciones indianas que en diversos tiempos salieron á poblar los vastos paises de este Nuevo-Mundo*, p. 211–25. This title, cited by me in earlier volumes as *Paredes, Noticias*, was probably intended to include other documents besides this, the special title of which is *Copia de un informe hecho á Su Magestad sobre las tierras del Nuevo Mexico (por el P. Fr. Alonso de Paredes)*. But the author's name, though written and printed Paredes, and so used by me as above stated in earlier volumes, was really Posadas; and the report has been recently republished from a MS. of the Acad. de Hist. as *Posadas (Fr. Alonso), Informe á S. M. sobre las tierras de Nuevo Mejico, Quivira y Teguayo*, in *Fernandez Duro, Don Diego de Peña loza*, 53–67. Therefore, I correct the error (not mine), and cite it in this vol. as *Posadas, Informe*. The writer was custodio of N. Mex. in 1660–4, and a missionary there for 10 years before. This report was written about 1686, in reply to a royal order of 1678. It refers more to the regions north and east than to N. Mex. proper, but is immensely important on a few points of N. Mex. history, as will be noted later. It is most unfortunate that Posadas, like Salmeron, did not write more fully of his own observations.

Of the old standard chronicles in Spanish, relating for the most part to the country's earliest annals down to 1700, by far the most important for purposes of this volume are *Torquemada, Monarquia Indiana*, bringing the record down to 1608, and *Vetancurt, Crónica* and *Menologio*, of 1691; but some valuable matter is also found in *Mendieta, Historia Eclesiástica; Oviedo, Hist. Gen.; Herrera, Hist. Gen.; Gomara, Hist. Ind.; Medina, Chrónica; Beaumont, Cron. de Michoacan; Mota Padilla, Conq. N. Galicia;* and especially *Villaseñor, Theatro*, of 1748. Other useful Spanish works of similar nature are *Calle, Noticias; Cavo, Tres Siglos; Revilla Gigedo, Carta de 1793; Alegre, Hist. Comp.*

Jesus; Frejes, Hist. Breve; Aparicio, Conventos; Velasco, Not. Sonora; and *Escudero, Not. Chihuahua.* All the works of this paragraph relate mainly to other regions, but contain more or less original and useful material on our territory.

Collections of manuscript or archive material have been named; but there are equally important collections of original documents in print. Of these, two are especially valuable: 1st, the *Documentos para la Historia de Mexico,* Mex., 1853–7, 20 vol. in 4 series, of which the 8 volumes of the 3d and 4th series relate particularly to northern regions, and contain vast quantities of indispensable matter on N. Mexico and Arizona, a large portion of the documents being from the *Arch. Gen. de Mex.* already mentioned; and 2d, the *Coleccion de Documentos Inéditos relativos al descubrimiento, conquista, y colonizacion de las posesiones Españolas en America y Oceania, sacados, en su mayor parte, del Real Archivo de Indias.* Madrid, 1864–80, 8vo, 35 vol. This collection, from the name of its first editor, I have cited as *Pacheco, Col. Doc.* Vols. xv., xvi., are of greatest value as containing original records of Oñate's conquest; but vols. ii., iii., iv., and xix. also contain useful documents. *Ternaux-Compans, Voyages, Relations et Mémoires Originaux pour servir á l'histoire de la découverte de l'Amérique,* Paris, 1837–41, série i. tom. ix.–x., is a collection containing translations of the chief original authorities on the expeditions of Niza and Coronado; while the old standard voyage collections, *Hakluyt's Voyages, Ramusio, Navigationi,* and *Purchas his Pilgrimes,* contain documents whose value was originally very great, though somewhat impaired now by their appearance elsewhere in better form. See also *Florida, Col. Doc.; Navarrete, Col. Viajes;* and *Burney's Chron. Hist. Voy.*

Of the MSS. contained in the collections cited, or existing separately in my Library, each of which is duly noticed in its place in the following chapters, there may be named here the following: *Otermin, Extractos,* 1680–2; *Ayeta, Memorial,* 1676; *Vargas, Reconquista,* 1692; *Id., Campañas de '94; Moqui, Noticias; Id., Juntas de Guerra,* 1713–15; *Id., Providencias,* 1779; *Hurtado, Campaña,* 1715; *Bustamante, Residencia,* 1731; *Olavide y Michelena, Autos,* 1738–9; *Mendoza, Residencia,* 1744; *Delgado, Relacion de la Sierra Azul,* 1743; *Id., Noticias del gran Teguayo,* 1743; *Id., Informe,* 1750; *Menchero, Declaracion,* 1744; *Id., Peticion sobre Navajóes,* 1749; *Id., Informe,* 1749; *Codallos y Rabal, Reduccion del Navajó,* 1745; *Id., Testimonio sobre Comanches,* 1718; *Trigo, Informe,* 1750; *Id., Informe,* 1754; *Güemes y Horcasitas, Medios,* 1745; *N. Mex., Informe del P. Provincial,* 1750; *Id., Defensas de Misioneros,* 1818; *Rodriguez de la Torre, Entrada,* 1755; *Tamaron, Visita del Obispo,* 1760; *Lafora, Viaje a Sta Fé,* 1766; *Sta Fé, Inundaciones de 1767: Crespo, Informe* (1776); *Escalante, Informe y Diario,* 1775; *Id., Carta de 1776; Anza, Diarios,* 1779–80; *Morfi, Desórdenes en N. Mex.* (1792); *Ruiz, Gobierno de Misiones,* 1773; *Serrano, Informe,* 1761; *Ilzarbe, Informe,* 1787; *Id., Estado de Misiones,* 1788; *Durango, Informe del Obispo,* 1789; *Lezaun, Noticias,* 1760; *Chacon, Informe sobre Industrias,* 1803.

And among the most important of similar documents in print the following: *Niza, Descubrimiento,* 1539; *Castañeda, Relacion,* 1540–2; *Coronado, Relacion del Suceso,* 1540–2; *Jaramillo, Relacion,* 1540–2; *Espejo, Relacion,* 1582; *Id., Expediente,* 1582; *N. Mex., Testimonio,* 1582–3; *Id., Memorial,* 1595–1602; *Id., Ytinerario,* 1547–9; *Id., Traslado de Posesion,* 1598; *Id., Discurso y Proposicion,* 1602; *Martin, Asiento,* 1583; *Lomas, Asiento,* 1589; *Castaño de Sosa, Memoria,* 1590; *Oñate, Copia de Carta,* 1599; *Freytas, Relacion,* 1661; *Dominguez and Escalante, Diario,* 1776; *Garcés, Diario,* 1776; *Melgares, Demostraciones,* 1822.

Of separately printed books on special topics, incomparably the most noteworthy is *Villagrá, Hist. N. Mex.;* but there may also be mentioned *Benavides, Memorial* and *Requeste,* 1630–1; *Sigüenza y Góngora, Mercurio Volante,* 1693; *Crespo, Memorial Ajustado,* 1738; *Presidios, Reglamento,* 1772–3; *Pino, Exposicion* and *Noticias Históricas,* 1812; *Pike's Acct. of Exped.,* 1806–7; *Coyner's Lost Trappers,* 1807–10; *Sta Fé, Mess. of President,* 1818.

Most of the matter cited relates to the Spanish period. For the Mexican annals the records are not only much less complete, but of a different nature in some respects; that is, the narrative has to be eked out with fragments from many sources, which are indicated in my notes, and need not be catalogued here. Among the chief sources of information, however, may be mentioned the *Mexico, Memorias,* of the different departments; the *U. S. Govt Doc.;* various Mexican newspapers; *Niles' Register; Arrillaga, Recop.,* and other collections of laws; fragments from the *Arch. Sta Fé,* MS.; *Barreiro, Ojeada; Abert's Report; San Miguel, Repub. Mex.; Bustamante, Gabinete Mex.; Id., Apuntes; Gregg's Commerce of the Prairies; Kendall's Narr. of the Texan Sta Fé Exped.; Falconer's Notes; Prieto, Rentas; Storrs' Sta Fé Trade; Willard's Inland Trade; Riley's Report; Pattie's Narr.; Wilson's Observ.,* MS.

Much of what precedes relates mainly to New Mexico, but also in part to Arizona. Standard authorities for the early annals of Arizona proper, or Pimería Alta, include *Apostólicos Afanes de la Comp. de Jesus; Sonora, Materiales,* MS. (tom. xvi.–ii. of the *Arch. Gen.,* and printed in *Doc. Hist. Mex.,* 3d series, tom. iv. pp. 489–520, 4th series, tom. i. pp. 1–408, which is the most valuable of all, separate titles being given to many documents as mentioned in chap. xv. et seq.); *Mange, Historia de la Pimería; Velarde, Descripcion; Alegre, Hist. Comp. Jesus; Venegas, Noticias de Cal.; Salvatierra, Relaciones; Pinart, Coleccion de Pimería Alta,* MS.; *Tamaron, Visita,* MS.; *Arricivita, Crónica Seráfica; Reyes, Noticia.*

Thus formidable being the array of original authorities, it becomes necessary to consider the use of them that has been made by modern writers. The first place among such writers belongs without question to W. W. H. Davis, who was U. S. attorney in New Mexico in 1853–5, and whose work was *The Spanish Conquest of New Mexico, by W. W. H. Davis, A. M., member of the 'Historical Society of Pennsylvania,' and the 'New York Genealogical and Biographical Society,' author of 'El Gringo, or New Mexico and her People,' 'History of the 104th Penn. Regiment,' 'History of the Hart Family,' and 'The Life of General John Lacey.'* Doylestown, Pa., 1869, 8vo, 425 p., portrait and map. This work is little more than a slightly condensed version or translation from the English, French, and Spanish, of the narratives of successive expeditions, from that of Cabeza de Vaca down nearly to 1700. The author writes in a clear and pleasing style, and has added to his work not only a map, but some useful notes drawn from his own knowledge of the country. His translations from the French are better than those from the Spanish. Down to the end of Coronado's expedition, his work, from the well-known printed narratives, is careful and accurate enough, but after that period irregular and sometimes inexplicably careless. This, however, doubtless results to a large extent from the condition in which he found his originals. His authorities for the later chapters were MSS. of the *Arch. Sta Fé,* or fragments of a few of the documents that I have cited from the same and other sources. He also obtained from Texas a copy of a portion of what he calls Oñate's journal, perhaps a fragment of Salmeron; and he attaches more importance than they deserve to the works of Frejes and Larenaudière. Mr Davis falls into some radical errors; notwithstanding the title of his book, he really knows very little of the 'conquest' proper, even putting its date seven years too early; and he has the faulty method of not clearly indicating his sources for many points— apparently sometimes with a view of concealing their poverty. Yet the work has received and merits high praise, indicating much intelligence, and considerable research under unfavorable circumstances on the part of the writer. His earlier book, *El Gringo* (N. Y., 1856), contained also much historical information, with a narrative of personal adventure and a description of the country and its people.

There has been but one other formal attempt to write the history of New Mexico, and that has resulted in the work called *Historical Sketches of New Mexico from the Earliest Records to the American Occupation, by L. Bradford Prince, President of the Historical Society of New Mexico, Late Chief Justice of New Mexico, etc.* Second edition. N. Y. and Kansas City, 1883, 12mo, 330 p. This unpretentious and excellent little work covers the same ground as that of Davis, but continues the story to 1847. So far as the Spanish period is concerned, it is not a work of original research, but for the most part a condensation of the story as told by Davis, though some of the well-known printed originals are named in the preface; the Peñalosa hoax is accepted as authority for a chapter, and a few of Davis' errors are corrected, while others —like the introduction of several viceroys in the list of governors—are repeated. The fact that in so small a volume 40 pages are devoted to the wanderings of Álvar Nuñez in Florida and Texas, and 20 pages to those of Niza in Sonora and Arizona, while six pages suffice for Oñate's conquest, illustrates probably not so much the author's idea of symmetry as the nature of his authorities. Indeed, wellnigh all the faults of the book are attributable to the authorities rather than to the author. He gives an excellent introduction, nowhere makes an effort to conceal the paucity of his sources, and writes throughout in an admirable and interesting style. His conclusions always command respect; his narrative of 19th-century annals could hardly be improved in matter or manner; and the work as a whole merits higher praise than the preceding remarks might seem to indicate.

In this connection should be noticed the *Historical Introduction to studies among the Sedentary Indians of New Mexico, Part i., by Ad. F. Bandelier.* Boston, 1881, 8vo, 33 p. This is an introduction to the *Papers of the Archæological Institute of America, American Series i.*, and relates mainly to Coronado's expedition, with particular reference to the original pueblo sites, but with notes bearing on later entradas. A continuation, bringing the annals of exploration down to 1605, is promised, but so far as I know has not appeared. Bandelier, a writer of high standing on archæological topics, shows an acquaintance with the most important of the original authorities; namely, the *Col. Doc. Ined.*, and the *Doc. Hist. Mex.;* and within the narrow limits which he has thus far assigned himself in history proper, his work merits nothing but the highest praise. John Gilmary Shea's *The Expedition of Don Diego Dionisio de Peñalosa, etc.*, N. Y., 1882, including *Freytas, Relacion del descubrimiento del pais y ciudad de Quivira echo por D. Diego Dionisio de Peñalosa*, and an English translation of the same, *Freytas, Relation*, etc., merits mention here, by reason of its introductory and supplementary notes, though the main narrative relates to a single expedition, and one that in reality was never made. Much more important—though perhaps it should be properly named earlier in this note as a collection of original material—is the *Don Diego de Peñalosa y su descubrimiento del reino de Quivira. Informe presentado á la Real Academia de Historia por el capitan de navío Cesáreo Fernandez Duro, individuo de número.* Madrid, 1882, large 8vo, 160 p. Fernandez Duro not only presents the *Freytas, Relation*, and all other matter given by Shea, but in his comments proving that narration to be a hoax he introduces much original information, including the *N. Mex., Discurso y Proposicion; Posadas, Informe;* and *Lopez, Memorial*, entire. He also appends a *Noticia de algunas expediciones organizadas en Nueva España para descubrir los territorios del Norte y señaladamente los reinos de Cíbola, Quivira y Teguayo*, arranged chronologically from 1523 to 1783; and concludes with a résumé of Villagrá's history of the conquest. Thus the whole work is one of the most valuable of modern times on our subject.

Miller's Historical Sketch of Santa Fé formed a part of the *Sta Fé Centennial Celebration* of 1776, and deserves mention from the fact that the author, David J. Miller, was translator and chief clerk in the U. S. surveyor-general's office, being well acquainted with the archives. Wm G. Ritch, for many years territorial secretary and sometime governor, and president of the Historical Society, has given much attention to the early as well as modern history of the country, as shown in his *Aztlan., The History, Resources, and Attractions of New Mexico*, 6th ed., Boston, 1885; and by the *Chronological Annals of New Mexico*, at the end of *Ritch's Legislative Blue-book of the Territory of New Mexico*, Sta Fé, 1887. It may be added that Gregg, *Commerce of the Prairies*, and Meline, *Two Thousand Miles on Horseback*, included in their works a sketch of early history; and quite a number of modern books, pamphlets, and newspaper and magazine articles might be named as containing similar and more or less accurate résumés not resulting from actual research. So far as Arizona proper is concerned, there are no modern works which merit notice so far as early history is concerned. I should not, however, forget to allude to a large number of valuable antiquarian essays on the location of Cíbola, Tiguex, Chichilticale, etc., containing a considerable amount of geographic and historic data. Simpson's *Coronado's March* is one of the best of these.

Just as these pages go into print, I have received *The Narrative and Critical History of America, edited by Justin Winsor, librarian of Harvard University*, etc. Vol. ii., Boston and N. Y., large 8vo, 640 p., with many maps, portraits, and other illustrations. Volumes i. and iii.–viii. are to be published later. Mr Winsor's volume covers a considerable part of the field, both geographic and chronologic, that I have treated in this and earlier works of the present series; the author has honored my work by citing it constantly with occasional comments of praise or condemnation, but always in a spirit of fairness; and with his treatment of my researches, on the whole, I am content. Had I occasion to go over the field again with Winsor's work before me, I should find it helpful, cite it often with commendation, and doubtless have occasion to criticise some of its details. The latest writer in the light of new evidence and special research on certain points has and always will have this advantage. This is obviously not the place for a critical estimate of the new work, even if I had the time for such a study as its claims and merits deserve. Mr Winsor as editor employs a corps of authors, who write under their own names; and an effort is made to draw a sharp distinction for the benefit of different classes of readers between the narrative, critical, and bibliographic portions of the work. This plan has its obvious advantages, and probably its defects as well. Whether Mr Winsor's system of coöperation is or not on the whole superior to my own for the production of a continuous, symmetrical, and accurate historic record of a broad territory, with all its geographic and chronologic complications, it is yet too early to decide. When the work is completed, we may see if all the gaps have been filled. In this volume the editor is also to a great extent the author; he is an expert in bibliography, with exceptional resources; and in the result the bibliographic element predominates in space and in value. Occasionally, if I mistake not, this predominance is somewhat too marked, as where in the case of radically opposing views and arguments on the part of different authorities, the author is content to simply note the conflict without so clear an opinion of his own as a 'critical history' should contain. Sometimes, indeed, the author implies a preference for the view that apparently is not supported by the critical notes. As a rule, the various narratives show a high order of literary merit, notable fairness of treatment, and as much unity as could be expected in the productions of different writers. The work is a noble contribution to American history, a monument of conscientious and laborious research, as well as of great literary skill on the part of editor and authors, and mechanically a magnificent specimen of bookmaking.

One chapter of Winsor's work demands particular notice here, as being devoted to a subject treated in this volume. This is chapter vii., p. 473–504, on *Early Explorations of New Mexico. By Henry W. Haynes, Archæological Institute of America*. The author has also written on the same subject in the *Amer. Antiq. Soc., Proceedings*, Oct. 1881, and cites also some writings of Haie and Savage in the same publication on the identity of Cíbola, Quivira, etc., which have not been used by me. Mr Haynes' treatise should be classed with those of Simpson, Davis, Prince, Bandelier, and others, as mentioned in this note. It is a clear statement of the earlier expeditions, with pertinent and judicious if not very elaborate notes. If it adds nothing important in the way of theory or evidence, it is because Simpson and Davis and the rest had left little to be added either by Haynes or myself. I think the author has not sufficiently considered my argument to the effect that Cabeza de Vaca did not enter New Mexico (p. 474); while agreeing for the most part with his praise of Davis, I cannot accept his conclusion that Davis is 'likely to remain always the leading authority' on Coronado's route (p. 402), in view of the fact that the author in question has fallen into several radical errors; I know not why 'Tiguex should be placed west of the Rio Grande, between Acoma and Quirex' (p. 485), when the writer seems to favor Bandelier's view; and

I deem it not hypercritical to object, in a work of this character, to the use of antiquated forms, confusion of Spanish, Italian, English, and French forms, and the careless use and non-use of accents, as exemplified in the following names: Compostella, Guadalaxara, Pamphilo, Nizza, New Gallicia, Melchior, d'Arellano, d'Alvarado, Roderigo, Garcia, García Lopez de Cardenas, Cicuyé, and Cíbola (for Compostela, Guadalajara, Pánfilo, Niza, Nueva Galicia or New Galicia, Melchor, Arellano or de Arellano, Alvarado, Rodrigo, García, García Lopez de Cárdenas, Cicuye, and Cíbola). The author's conclusions agree for the most part with my own, which is not a radical defect, in my opinion. It is noticeable that the record extends only to Coronado's expedition, or 1542, except that the editor adds a note on the late works of Fernandez Duro and Shea, giving a list of the later expeditions mentioned by the former, very briefly noting without comment his exposure of the Peñalosa hoax, not noticing my own remarks on the same subject, and rather strangely ignoring the most important work of Villagrá. It would naturally be expected that the later explorations, conquest, and settlement of New Mexico should find place in a volume entitled *Spanish Explorations and Settlements in America from the Fifteenth to the Seventeenth Century.* Presumably, however, this record will be given in another volume; in which case, time of publication permitting, I hope Mr Winsor may find these chapters of mine helpful.

CHAPTER II.

NIZA AND CORONADO IN ARIZONA.

1539–1540.

THE DISCOVERERS—VICEROY MENDOZA'S PLANS—FRAY MARCOS DE NIZA AND
THE NEGRO—JOURNEY TO THE NORTH—WONDERFUL REPORTS OF THE
SEVEN CITIES—FATE OF ESTEVANICO, THE FIRST PIONEER OF ARIZONA
—FRAY MARCOS IN SIGHT OF CÍBOLA—NEW KINGDOM OF SAN FRANCISCO
—NIZA'S REPORT—DISCUSSION OF THE ROUTE FROM SINALOA TO ZUÑI—A
NEW FUROR—CORTÉS AND ULLOA—ALARCON ON THE RIO COLORADO, OR
BUENA GUIA—FRANCISCO VASQUEZ DE CORONADO—A GRAND ARMY
—DIAZ AND ZALDÍVAR—BIBLIOGRAPHY OF THE EXPEDITION—THE SO-
NORA SETTLEMENT—MELCHOR DIAZ—FROM SONORA TO CÍBOLA—THE
ROUTE—CHICHILTICALE—MAP—IDENTITY OF CÍBOLA AND ZUÑI—CON-
QUEST OF GRANADA—THE FRIAR CURSED AND SENT HOME—TOBAR'S EX-
PEDITION TO TUSAYAN, OR THE MOQUI PUEBLOS—CÁRDENAS VISITS THE
CAÑON OF THE COLORADO.

THE glory of discovering this territory must be given
to a negro and a Franciscan friar, who crossed the
line into Arizona in 1539. So great was the interest
taken by Viceroy Mendoza in the statements of Cabeza de Vaca respecting the populous towns of which he
had heard on his way across the continent, that he at
once planned an expedition, in 1537, buying the slave
Estevanico and obtaining the services of his master
Dorantes, as guides; but the project was temporarily
abandoned, and no more is heard of Dorantes or Maldonado, Álvar Nuñez having gone to Europe.[1]

Late in 1538, however, with a view to exploration
and conquest on a grander scale, and under a new policy, so far as treatment of the natives was concerned,
it was arranged that Francisco Vasquez de Coronado,

---

[1] Mendoza's letters to the king, 1537–40, in *Pacheco, Col. Doc.*, ii. 206–7;
Florida, Col. Doc., 136, 139; *Ternaux-Compans, Voy.*, série i. tom. ix. p. 287.

the newly appointed governor of Nueva Galicia, should make a tour of inspection to the northern parts of his province, and there set on foot certain preliminary investigations by the aid of friars and liberated Indian slaves, subsequently devoting himself, should the results prove satisfactory, to the organization of a force for the proposed military expedition. Not much is known of several preparatory tours, intended mainly to inspire confidence in Spanish good faith and reform among the natives of northern Sinaloa;[2] but one had a broader scope, and is fully recorded, being the one that involves the discovery of Arizona.

Fray Marcos de Niza, chief of the Franciscan band destined for the northern field, was an Italian, who had come to America in 1531, had gone with Pizarro to Peru in 1532, served in Nicaragua, and come north with Pedro de Alvarado, being a man of prominence in his order, of ardent zeal for all new enterprises, and withal of lively imagination.[3] Having received special instructions from the viceroy through Coronado in November 1538, Fray Marcos set out from San Miguel on the 7th of March, 1539, accompanied by another friar named Onorato, the negro Estevanico, and a band of natives from Culiacan. On the Petatlan[4] Onorato fell ill, and was left behind; but Niza went on "as the holy spirit did guide" him, always kindly welcomed by the natives, but with no notable occurrence for some 25 or 30 leagues, except that he met Indians from the island where Cortés had been—

[2] See *Hist. North Mex. St.*, i. 72–3, note 3, for a few details.

[3] For biog., see *Vetancurt, Menologio Franciscano*, 37 (p. 117–19 of ed. of 1871); *Mendieta, Hist. Ecles.*, 674; *Torquemada, Monarq. Ind.*, iii. 499–500; and *Figueroa, Becerro General*, MS., 41, where Fr. Marcos is said to have been the founder of the Fran. provincia of Lima. In the introd. to *Velasco, Hist. Royaume de Quito*, as pub. by Ternaux, also preface to *Castañeda, Rel.*, v., he is said to have been the author of several works on the conquest and native races of Quito and Peru. In '40–3 he was provincial of his order in Mexico, though most of the time absent in the north, where he lost his health. He lived later in Jalapa, and died at Mexico in 1558. Niza is the proper Span. form of his name, that of the town Nice, the Italian form being Nizza. For a portrait—not stated to have been taken from an Arizona photograph of 1539—see *Frost's Pict. Hist. Mex.*, 135.

[4] Pueblo de Petatean in the original, as printed; possibly not on the Rio Petatlan (the Sinaloa).

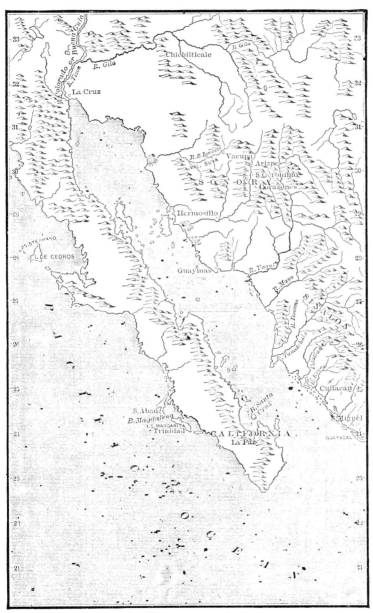

THE NORTHWEST IN 1539.

California—half a league from the main, and they
told him of 30 other inhabited islands beyond, and of
pearls. Then after four days' journey through an uninhabited tract, he came to a people who had never
heard of Christians, who called him Sayota, or 'man
from heaven,' and who knew of large settlements in a
valley four or five days inland, where cotton was used
for clothing, and gold for implements and ornaments.
For three days his way led him through the country
of this people, till he came to Vacapa, a settlement of
good size and plenty of food, 40 leagues from the sea.

At Vacapa Niza remained some nine days, sending
messengers to the coast, who brought back tidings of
the pearl islands—now 34 in number—and cowhide
shields. Here he met natives from the east, known as
'pintados,' who had something to say of the 'seven
cities.' And from here he sent the negro ahead to
explore the way, and after four days Estevanico sent
back such glowing reports of what he had heard about
Cíbola, with its seven great towns and stone buildings
and turquoises, that even the credulous fraile hesitated
to credit them. About the 6th of April, with two
islanders and three 'pintados' added to his company,
he left Vacapa, and in three days came to the people
who had given the negro his information about Cíbola,
and who now gave the good friar his fill of marvels.
Pressing on for five days—possibly including the previous three—through a well-settled country, they came
to a pleasant and well-watered settlement near the
borders of a desert. Between Vacapa and this place
without much doubt they had crossed what is now the
southern bound of Arizona.[5]

<hr />

[5] Vacapa, or S. Luis, was a ranchería from 12 to 19 l. southward of Sonoita,
or S. Marcelo, visited by Kino and Mange in 1699–1701, and shown on Kino's
map. See *Hist. North Mex. St.*, i. 72–5, 271, 495, 499; *Mange, Hist. Pimeria*,
327; *Apost. Afanes*, 273–4, 282–5. Mange notes the place as the one passed
by Coronado's (Niza's) exped., as described by Herrera. Padre Garcés, *Diario
y Derrotero*, 365, in 1777 says: ' El pueblo de Bacapá que cita se halla hoy en la
Papaguería con nombre de *Quitobapcapa*, en lengua pima quiere decir; en *Bac*
quiere decir *tule*, conque en Quitobapc dice *tule chiquito*.' Evidently there is
typographic confusion here; but Vacapa may have been Quitobac. This name
of Vacapa is, of course, an important point in following Niza's route. The

The desert having been crossed in four days, the route lay for five days through a fertile, irrigated valley, with many settlements of superior and friendly Indians. This may be reasonably regarded as the Gila valley in the region of the Pima villages. Here the friar understood that the coast turned abruptly westward, which means simply that the natives described the ocean as much farther off than the gulf coast had been in the south; but he says he went in person and saw that such was the case, which was hardly possible.[6] These people knew of Cíbola, wore turquoises, and in some cases cotton, and they told of woollen garments woven in Totonteac from the fur of a small animal. In one of the rancherías was met a native of Cíbola, who gave much information about its seven towns, Ahacus being the largest—exaggerated though in a sense tolerably accurate descriptions of the since well-known Pueblo towns. He also told of other towns and provinces.[7] Many others confirmed and supplemented the reports all along the way; turquoises and hides and other articles from Cíbola were plentiful; and the negro, whose zeal kept him far in advance with his native attendants, sent back the most encouraging messages. For three days more they travelled in this valley or a similar one; and then, on the 9th

identity is not certain, as these rancherías were sometimes moved long distances. If Niza went so far west he must have turned eastward later, for from that Vacapa he could not have travelled 5 or 8 days northward in a settled country to the borders of a desert. Whipple's location, *Pac. R. R. Repts*, iii. 104, of V. in the region of Magdalena, as hitherto favored by me, *Hist. North Mex. St.*, i. 72–5, making the pleasant, well-watered settlement near the desert in the Tucson region, would be much more convenient; but the general features are clear enough, and nothing more can be hoped for.

[6] 'Y así fui en demanda della y ví claramente que en los 35° vuelve al Oueste, de que no menos alegría tuve que de la buena nueva de la tierra.' *Niza, Descub.*, 339. Of course the lat. 35° was all wrong. We shall find a similar statement about the westward trend in Coronado's narrative, but more clearly explained by the statement that here the gulf ended. If Niza continued N. W. from the Sonoita region to the Gila, and thence up that river, a visit to the head of the gulf, if possible, must still be regarded as very improbable.

[7] South-east of Cíbola was the kingdom of Marata, with many large towns, though weakened by wars with Cíbola; another in the same direction was Totonteac, the most populous and richest of all; and another, Acus (distinct from Ahacus, which was only a town), in a direction not stated. These references were clearly to the N. Mex. Pueblo towns toward or on the Rio Grande.

of May, they entered the final *despoblado;* that is, from the region of the modern Phœnix or Florence they entered the mountainous uninhabited tract, their course lying north-eastward, toward Zuñi.

For twelve days Fray Marcos pressed on, following the negro's route, and well supplied with food by the natives accompanying him, until, on the 21st of May, he met one of Estevanico's men returning with the worst of news. On reaching Cíbola, instead of the usual welcome, the negro had received an order not to enter the town, on pain of death, being forced to remain with his company in a house outside, without food, and being deprived of all the presents he had received on the journey. Next day, one of the men, going to a stream for water, looked back, and saw the negro running away from pursuers, who killed some of his companions. Then he made haste to inform the friar. Niza's companions were greatly terrified, but went forward at his solicitation; and one day's journey before reaching Cíbola, two more of Estevanico's men were met, wounded, and stating that the negro had been killed.[8] Thus perished black Stephen, the discoverer of Arizona.

There were threats among Niza's followers of holding him responsible for the killing of their friends, and the friar said he was willing to die; but through the agency of gifts and threats the excitement was calmed. He then went forward with two chiefs, and from a hill got a glimpse of Cíbola, on a plain at the foot of a round hill, just as the natives had described it, and apparently more populous than Mexico, though said

---

[8] Castañeda, *Relation*, 12–13, tells us that Stephen had a weakness for rich gifts, including handsome women; that he made a demand on the Cibolans for their wealth and women; that his claim of being the predecessor of white men who were coming to teach them seemed suspicious, on account of his color; and that they put him to death as a spy sent by enemies coming to subjugate them, releasing his 60 companions, though retaining a few boys. Coronado, *Hakluyt*, iii. 380, says the Cíbolans claimed to have killed him because he killed and violated their women, and was reported to be a 'wicked villain.' One of his comrades, a boy from Petatlan, remained at Cíbola, and was found by Coronado. News of Estévan's death was also given to Alarcon, on the Colorado.

to be the smallest of the seven in a province far excelled by others beyond.   A cross being erected on a heap of stones, formal possession was taken in Mendoza's name, for the king, of all that region, as the new kingdom of San Francisco.   Then Fray Marcos hastened homeward, "con harto mas temor que comida," at the rate of eight or ten leagues per day.   In a valley stretching eastward below Vacapa, he saw far off seven 'poblaciones razonables,' and heard that gold was plentiful there, but deemed it best to postpone a closer examination.   At Compostela, perhaps in June or July, he reported to the governor, to whom he had before sent messengers from various points; and in August went with Coronado to Mexico, where, on the 2d of September, he formally certified the accuracy of his report.[9]

Cortés claimed that Niza's narrative was fiction, his pretended discoveries resting only on reports of the natives and information derived from Cortés himself; but Don Hernan was not in this instance an impartial critic.[10]   Coronado and his companions, in their expedition of the next year, disappointed in their expectations, applied some plain terms to certain phases of the friar's misrepresentations.   Padre Kino seems to have thought that the Gila ruins might have been Niza's seven cities, and Humboldt partially

[9] *Niza, Descubrimiento de las Siete Ciudades*, in *Pacheco, Doc.*, iii. 325–51, including Mendoza's instructions of Nov. '38, and a certificate of P. Ciudad-Rodrigo, the provincial, dated Aug. 26, '39; Ital. transl. in *Ramusio, Navig.*, iii. 356–9; Engl., in *Hakluyt's Voy.*, iii. 366–73; French, in *Ternaux-Compans, Voy.*, série i. tom. ix. 256–84.   For a long list of additional references, see *Hist. North Mex. St.*, i. 74–5.   A few others are *Peralta, Not. Hist.*, 143–5, 148–9, 341–3; *Mendieta, Hist. Ecles.*, 398–400; *Remesal, Hist. Chyapa*, 160–1; *Purchas his Pilgrimes*, iv. 1560–1; *Bandelier's Hist. Introd.*, 7–9; *Prince's Hist. Sk.*, 96–115; *Zamacois, Hist. Mej.*, iv. 606–9, 652–9; *Liceo Mex.*, ii. 153–6; *Burney's Chron. Hist.*, i. 189–92; *Hinton's Handbook*, 385–6; *Magliano's St Francis*, 573–4; *Hittell*, in *Californian*, i. 130–5; *Poussin, Puissance Amér.*, i. 340–1; *Id., Question de l'Orégon*, 18; *Id., The U. S.*, 234; *Voyages, Selection*, 43; *Graham's Discov.*, 207; *Lafond, Voy.*, i. bk i. 200–1; *Cozzens' Marvellous Country*, 32; *Arizona Hist.* (Elliott & Co.), 35–6.

[10] *Icazbalceta, Col. Doc.*, ii. xxviii.–ix.; *Cortés, Escritos*, 299–304; *Navarrete, Col. Viages*, iv. 209.   Cortés says he had tried to enlist the friar's services, imparting with that view what he had learned in the north.   He also accused N. of similar treachery in Central and South America.

accepts that view.[11]   And most later writers have
had occasion to dwell on his gross exaggerations,
sometimes indulging in harsher terms.   Yet the fact
that Coronado, accompanied by Niza to Cíbola in
1540, with all his criticism does not seem to doubt
that the friar actually made the trip as he claimed, is,
of course, the best possible evidence against the theory
that he visited northern Sonora, and imagined the rest.
A close examination shows that nearly all the statements most liable to criticism rest solely on the
reports of the natives, and only a few, like the visit
to the coast, and the actual view of a great city at
Cíbola, can be properly regarded as worse than exaggeration.   My space does not permit the reproduction
of descriptive matter with sufficient fulness to illus-
trate the author's inaccuracies.   Fray Marcos was
an imaginative and credulous man, full of faith in
northern wonders, zealous for spiritual conquest in a
new field, fearful that the great enterprise might be
abandoned; hence the general couleur de rose of his
statements; hence perhaps a few close approximations
to falsehood; but there is no good reason to doubt
that he really crossed Sonora and Arizona to the
region of Zuñi.

As to his route, so far as details are concerned, the
narrative furnishes no foundation for positive theories,
though possibly by a reproduction of all the data with
carefully prepared topographic maps, obviously impracticable here, approximately accurate results might
be reached.   As far as the Gila valley, Niza's route
was possibly farther west, in part at least, than that
of Coronado, to be noticed presently; I have no doubt
that it crossed the region between the Pima villages
and Florence; and beyond that point the two routes
were perhaps nearly identical.   I refer the reader also
to the map given later in this chapter.

[11] *Apost. Afanes,* 253.   'On est tenté de croire que les ruines des Casas
Grandes du Gila....pourraient avoir donné occasion aux contes débitées par
le bon père Marcos de Nizza.' *Essai Pol.,* 310.   Heylyn, *Cosmog.,* 967–8, says,
'so disguised in Lyes and wrapped up in fictions that the light was little
more than Darkness.'   Coronado 'found the Fryer to be a Fryer; nothing of
moment true in all his Relations.'

Preliminary reports of Niza's progress, sent south
by the friar and reaching Mexico before July 1539—
possibly including an outline of what he said of his
discoveries after his return to San Miguel or Compostela—moved Cortés to renewed effort, lest perchance
the great northern prize should elude his grasp; for
he claimed the exclusive right of conquest in that
direction, and had strenuously but vainly opposed
Mendoza's act in preparing for an expedition; though
he denied that the friar's pretended discoveries had
any foundation in truth.   He had a fleet ready, and
he made haste to despatch three vessels, under the
command of Francisco de Ulloa, from Acapulco in
July.   As this expedition did not reach the territory
now under consideration, its results being confined to
a survey of the gulf and peninsula coasts, and especially as the voyage has been fully recorded in another
volume,[12] I do not deem it necessary to say more on
the subject here.   The viceroy also entered into a
contract with Pedro de Alvarado, with a view to northern exploration, but the Mixton war and Alvarado's
death prevented any practical results.   After protesting and struggling against the new expeditions of
1540, Cortés went to Spain, and appears no more in
northern annals.

Another expedition by sea, fitted out by Mendoza
to coöperate with that of Coronado on the land, was
that of Hernando de Alarcon.   This also has been
described elsewhere,[13] and as an exploration of the
gulf requires no further notice in this connection; but
in August and September Alarcon made two trips in
boats up the Colorado River, which he named the
Buena Guia.   He possibly passed the mouth of the
Gila, though he mentions no such branch; and it may
be regarded as probable that he at least passed the
Arizona line.   This party also heard reports of Cíbola,
and of Niza's adventures; and near the mouth of the

[12] See *Hist. North Mex. St.*, i. 77–82; and on the Alvarado contract, p. 96.
[13] *Id.*, i. 90–5.

Colorado they left letters, found a little later by a branch of Coronado's expedition under Melchor Diaz.

Governor Coronado, as we have seen, came to Mexico with Niza, to consult the viceroy and make final arrangements for the conquest of Cíbola and its seven cities. The conditions were most favorable; Mendoza was an enthusiastic supporter of the scheme; the friar's tales were eagerly listened to, and often repeated with the usual distortions; an air of secrecy and mystery on the part of Coronado served still further to excite the popular interest; and never since the time of Nuño de Guzman had the response to a call for volunteers been so satisfactory. There was a fever of exploring zeal, and it seemed as if the whole population of Mexico might be easily induced to migrate northward.[14] Niza was made provincial of his order, and the Franciscans became zealous in the cause. A force of 300 Spaniards and 800 Indian allies was easily enlisted. Many of the former were gentlemen of good family and high rank, some of them bound to serve Coronado, who was made captain-general of the expedition, only by their promises as gentlemen. The names of those bearing by actual rank or courtesy the title of captain are given in the appended note.[15] In February 1540, the army was at

---

[14] Says Suarez de Peralta, in his *Noticias*, 143, 148–9: 'Fué de manera la grita, que no se trataba ya de otra cosa...Era tanta la cudiçia que á todos puso la nueva de las *Siete Ciudades* que no solo el virrey y marqués levantaron los pies para yr á ella, sino á toda la tierra, y tanto, que por favor se negociaba el yr los soldados, y sacar liçençia; y era de manera que se vendian, y no pensaba el que la tenia, sino que ya era título por lo menos, porque lo encareçia el frayle que habia venido de allá, de suerte, que dezia ser la mejor cosa que habia en el mundo...Segun el lo pintaba, debia ser el parayso terrenal...En todo esto dijo verdad.'

[15] Pedro de Tobar, standard-bearer; Lope de Samaniego, maestro de campo (killed at Chametla); Tristan de Arellano, Pedro de Quevara, Garci-Lopez de Cárdenas, Juan de Zaldívar, Francisco de Obando, Alonso Manrique de Lara, Gomez Suarez de Sigueroa, Juan de Sotomayor, Juan de Jaramillo, Rodrigo Maldonado, Diego Lopez, Diego Gutierrez; Pablo Melgosa de Búrgos, com. of the infantry; Hernando de Alvarado, com. of the artillery; Francisco de Barrio-nuevo, Melchor Diaz, Juan Gallegos, Lope de Urrea, Luis Ramirez de Vargas, Francisco Garbolan; —— Ribero, factor; Viliega. Castañeda gives some information respecting the family and rank of several of these officers.

Compostela, whither went Viceroy Mendoza to deliver
a parting address of encouragement; and in April the
general with an advance party set out from San
Miguel de Culiacan.

Before leaving the north for Mexico, Coronado had
despatched Diaz and Zaldívar, with fifteen men, to
verify as far as possible Niza's reports.   This party
started in November 1539, and perhaps reached the
Gila valley, but on account of the excessive cold
decided not to attempt a crossing of the country
beyond.   From the natives they obtained information
about Cíbola and the other provinces, similar to that
given by the friar, but considerably less attractive
and highly colored; and they also learned that the
Cíbolans had requested the south-western tribes not
to permit the Christians to pass, but to kill them.
This report was brought south by Zaldívar and three
men, who met Coronado at Chametla; and while the
news was kept secret, it was generally understood to
be bad, and Fray Marcos had to exert his eloquence
to the utmost to prevent discouragement.[16]

I append a note on the bibliography of Coronado's
expedition.[17]   As I have said, the general left San

[16] Mendoza's letter to the king, of April 17, 1540, with quotations from
Diaz' report. *Pacheco, Doc.*, ii. 356–62; *Castañeda, Rel.*, 29–30.

[17] The most complete narrative is that of Pedro Castañeda de Nágera,
known to the world only through the French translation, *Castañeda, Relation
du Voyage de Cíbola*, in *Ternaux-Compans, Voy.*, série i. tom. ix. 246 p., with
an appendix of various doc. pertaining to the subject.   The author accompanied the expedition in a capacity not stated; wrote about 20 years after
the occurrence of the events described, and acc. to M. Ternaux was a resident of Culiacan.   He was a man of ability and education, being a most
entertaining chronicler, and apparently a faithful historian.   There is a degree of inaccuracy in dates, but otherwise the record is remarkably clear and
satisfactory.   Fernandez Duro, in his *Noticias de Algunas Expediciones*, 125,
represents the Spanish original as pub. in *Pacheco, Doc.*, ix. or xiv. 373; but
this is an error.   If it is pub. in some other vol. or p. of that col., I have
not found it.   A copy of the Span. original is said to have existed in the
Lenox collection in '54, when an effort was made to have it printed by the
Smithsonian Inst.

There are two other accounts written by officers connected with the expedition.   The first is the *Relacion del Suceso de la Jornada que Fran. Vasquez
de Coronado hizo en el Descubrimiento de Cíbola*, in *Florida, Col. Doc.*, i. 147–54;
also in *Pacheco, Doc.*, xiv. 318–29, from an original at Simancas.   The writer's name is unknown.   The second is the *Relacion que dió el Capitan Juan
Jaramillo*, in *Florida, Col. Doc.*, i. 154–63; *Pacheco, Doc.*, xix. 304–18; and

Miguel about the middle of April, taking with him 50
horsemen, a few foot-soldiers, a body of native allies,

transl. in *Ternaux*, i. ix. 364–82. These narratives, though less extensive
than that of Castañeda, are hardly less important in several respects, both
authors having accompanied Coronado throughout the march to Quivira. A
letter of Coronado to the viceroy, dated Aug. 3, 1540, and describing the
events of the campaign down to date, is found translated in *Ramusio, Navig.*,
iii. 359–63; and *Hakluyt's Voy.*, iii. 373–9. His letter of April 20, '41, to the
emperor is not, so far as I know, extant; but a later letter, of Oct. 20, '41, describing the exped. to Quivira, is found in *Pacheco, Doc.*, iii. 362–9; repeated
in xiii. 261–8; and in *Ternaux*, i. ix. 355–63. In *Pacheco, Doc.*, xix. 529–32,
is the *Traslado de las Nuevas*, a letter or report from Cíbola, dated July 20,
'40, giving an account of the march and of the taking of Cíbola, the writer's
name not appearing.

Among the early standard writers, Mota Padilla, *Conq. N. Gal.*, iii. 14,
158–69, seems to be the only one giving details not apparently not drawn from
the originals named above; but his additions are for the most part of slight
importance and of unknown origin. Other references to authorities of this
class are as follows: *Torquemada, Monarq. Ind.*, i. 609–10; iii. 358–9, 610–12;
Herrera, Hist. Gen., dec. vi. lib. ix. cap. 11–12; *Oviedo, Hist. Gen.*, iii. 168;
iv. 19; *Gomara, Hist. Ind.*, 272–4; *Mendieta, Hist. Ecles.*, 400; *Beaumont, Cron.
Mich.*, iv. 213–34, 378–86; *Benzoni, Hist. Mondo Nuovo*, 107; *Bernal Diaz,
Hist. Conq. Mex.*, 235; *Las Casas, Hist. Apol.*, nos. 32–7, 127–9; *Ribas, Trium-
phos*, 26–7; *Venegas, Not. Cal.*, i. 167–9; *Clavigero, Stor. Cal.*, 153; *Alegre,
Hist. Comp. J.*, i. 237–8; *Salmeron, Relaciones*, 7–9; *Cavo, Tres Siglos*, i. 127–9;
Lorenzano, in *Cortés, Hist. Mex.*, 325; *Galvano's Discov.*, 226–7; *Noticias de
Exped.*, MS., 241–2; *Sinaloa, Mem. Hist.*, MS., 10–12.

Among modern writers who have added to their version of the narrative
useful comments on the route, etc., the first place should be given to Gen. J.
H. Simpson, *Coronado's March*, in *Smithsonian Rept*, '69, p. 308–40, who has
discussed the question of route, localities, etc., in a manner that left little or
nothing to be desired. Davis, *Span. Conq. of N. Mex.*, 141–233, has given a
condensed translation of Castañeda, with notes and remarks from his own
knowledge of the country. The results of Bandelier's, *Hist. Introd.*, 9–29,
investigations on the identity of the pueblo groups visited by Coronado have
been most satisfactory, this writer having access to documents and books not
known to the others. In the same connection may be named the following
works: *Prince's Hist. Sk.*, 116–48; *Gallatin*, in *Amer. Ethnol. Soc., Trans.*, ii.;
Squier, in *Amer. Review*, Nov. '48; *Whipple*, in *Pac. R. R. Repts*, iii. 108–12;
Morgan, in *N. Am. Rev.*, April '69; *Möllhausen, Reisen*, ii. 211–12, 403; *Emory's
Notes*, 129, 134; *Abert's Rept*, 30th Cong. 1st Sess., Ex. Doc. 41; *Ives' Col.
Riv.*, 19–20; *Davis' El Gringo*, 61–70; *Schoolcraft's Arch.*, iv. 23–39; vi. 67–71;
Miller's Centen. Sk., 13.

See also the following general references: *Payno*, in *Soc. Mex. Geog.*, 2d
ep., ii. 138–40; *Escudero, Not. Son.*, 9, 27–9; *Gottfriedt, N. Welt*, 560–1; *Laet,
Novus Orbis*, 299–305; *Magin, Hist. Univ. Ind.*, 91–2; *Burney's Chron. Hist.*,
i. 216–17; *Gil*, in *Soc. Mex. Geog.*, viii. 481–2; *Montanus, N. Weereld*, 209–15;
Purchas his Pilgrimes, v. 853; *Gallatin*, in *Amer. Ethnog. Soc.*, i. 201; *Id.*, in
Nouv. An. Voy., cxxxi. 247–74; *Ruxton*, in *Id.*, cxxvi. 44; *De Courcy's Cath.
Ch.*, 14; *Mayer's Mex. Aztec*, i. 145; *Domenech's Deserts*, i. 174–9, 182; *Green-
how's Or. and Cal.*, 60–1; *Ind. Aff. Rept*, '63, p. 388; *Murray's Hist. Trav.*,
ii. 73–9; *Brackenbridge's Mex. Letters*, 81; *Id., Early Discov.*, 7–15; *Dobb's Acct
Hud. Bay*, 162; *Fedix, l'Orégon*, 68–9; *Lardner's Hist. Mar. Discov.*, ii. 98–9;
Cronise's Nat. Wealth, 31; *Browne's L. Cal.*, 16–17; *Gleeson's Hist. Cath. Ch.*,
i. 66–8; *Tuthill's Hist. Cal.*, 10–11; *Frignet, La Cal.*, 7; *Marchand, Voy.*, i.
viii.; *Barber's Hist. West. St.*, 547; *Farnham's Life in Cal.*, 125–6; *Larenaudière, Mex. Guat.*, 145; *Taylor*, in *Cal. Farmer*, Feb. 21, Mar. 14, Aug. 25,

and all the friars, including Marcos de Niza. His route was across the Yaqui to Corazones and the Sonora valley, thence continuing his way northward. At the end of April the main army under Arellano also left San Miguel for Sonora, where the Spaniards founded a settlement at San Gerónimo and remained till October, then joining the general in the far north, except a garrison left at the new town. With the fortunes of this Sonora settlement of San Gerónimo, abandoned after a change of site before the return of Coronado, we are not directly concerned here. It should be stated, however, that Melchor Diaz, sent back from Cíbola to command the garrison of 80 men, made, in 1540, an expedition to the gulf shore, and thence up the Colorado, which he crossed to make explorations southward on the western bank. He did not, apparently, reach the Gila, but he may possibly have passed the Arizona line. He gave the name Rio del Tizon, from the fire-brands with which the natives warmed themselves, to the Colorado, which Alarcon had called Buena Guia; and in this enterprise he lost his life.[18]

The march of Coronado's party from Sonora to Cíbola in June and July, and that of the main army under Arellano in November and December, presented nothing of special importance or interest for the chroniclers, who have given us but few particulars of adventure or hardship. For us the chief interest centres upon the route followed, which, in its general features, is by no means so vaguely recorded as has often been supposed, though in the absence of the original diary the narratives are naturally confusing, incomplete, or

'62; *Hinton's Handbook*, 386–91; *Hittell*, in *Californian*, i. 130–6; *Poussin, Puissance Amér.*, i. 340–3; *Id., Question de l'Orégon*, 18–20; *Id., The U. S.*, 234–5; *Voyages, Selection of Curious*, 46–8; *Frejes, Hist. Breve*, 191–5; *Arizona Hist.* (Elliott), 37–42; *McKenny's Direct.*, 307; *Zamacois, Hist. Mej.*, iv. 605, 654–7; *Mofras, Explor.*, i. 95; *Bancroft's Hist. U. S.*, i. 40; *Marcy's Thirty Years*, 78–9; *Kerr's Col. Voy.*, ii. 110–11; *Buelna, Compendio*, 10–11; *Johnson's Hist. Ariz.*, 6; *Hodges' Ariz.*, 17.

[18] For Diaz' exped. and the annals of S. Gerónimo, see *Hist. North Mex. St.*, i. 87–90.

perhaps erroneous as to details, for some of which **I**
refer the reader to the appended note.[19]

[19] Jaramillo, *Rel.*, who was with Coronado's advance, gives most details.
The route to Sonora was as follows: Culiacan; 4 days to Rio Petatlan; 3 days
to Rio Sinaloa; 5 days to Arroyo de Cedros; 3 days to Rio Yaqui; 3 days to
an arroyo where were straw huts; 2 days to the village of Corazones; time
not given, distance perhaps 6 or 7 l. (10 l. acc. to *Rel. del Suceso*, 318), apparently on the same stream, to Sonora; and 1 day crossing the stream to a village called (doubtfully) Ispa (clearly regarded as in the Sonora valley). From
Sonora about 4 days over the desert (or unoccupied country), to the arroyo
called Nexpa (probably the Sta Cruz, but possibly the S. Pedro); 2 days down
this stream; thence turning to the right at (or to) the foot of a mountain
range, which was followed for 2 days, and which was said to be called Chichil-
tic-calli, crossing which range they came to a deep stream, with steep banks
(Gila or S. Pedro?). How much they turned to the right (perhaps only keeping on N. while the stream turned to the left) of the Nexpa, or how near their
route was to the mts followed, is not shown; but that they were between the
Sta Cruz and S. Pedro seems clear enough. Elsewhere J. says they gave the
name Chichilte Calli to the place where they passed, because they had learned
from Ind. farther back that they called it so. What precedes is from the
French version; the Span. original (which may be imperfectly printed) differs
somewhat, as follows: 2 days down the Nexpa, then leaving the stream, 'we
went to the right to the foot of the cordillera in a journey of 2 days, where
we learned that it was called Chichiltie. There (clearly "Chichiltie Alli" is a
misprint for Chichilte Calli) the cordillera being passed, we went to a deep
arroyo and cañada, where we found water and grass for the horses;' or elsewhere, 'which (the cordillera de sierras 300 l. from Mex., correcting an evident error of punctuation) we named Chichitté Calli, etc.' J. says that from
this place they turned to the N. E., thus implying that the previous course
had been N., which, with the general tenor of all the narratives, is fatal to the
theory—slightly favored by Bandelier—that Coronado may have crossed the
main sierra to the Chihuahua Casas Grandes, and then turned N. (or N. W.)
to Zuñi. J. does not mention any ruin.

Castañeda, p. 40-1 (who was with the main army), tells us simply that
Coronado crossed the inhabited country till he came to Chichilticale, 'where
the desert begins.' 'He was especially afflicted to see that this Chichilticale,
of which so much had been said, was reduced to a house in ruins, and without roof, but which, nevertheless, seemed to have been fortified. It was
clearly seen that this house, built of red earth, was the work of civilized
people come from afar. They left this place and entered the desert.' The
last village toward the desert, visited by Niza (p. 12). Beginning of the
desert, 200 l. from Culiacan, reached by Diaz and Zaldívar (p. 29). The main
army passed a province called Nacapan, where grew tunas, or Ind. figs, and
reached Chichilticale, near which they saw a flock of horned sheep, and then
entered the desert (p. 53-4). Name of Chichilticale given formerly to the
place, because the friars found in that region a house which had long been
inhabited by a people from Cibola. Here the country ceases to be covered
with *arbres épineux*, and changes its aspect; here the gulf ends and the coast
turns. (This identifies the place with Niza's fertile valley, supposed by him
to be in 35°.) The mts follow the same direction (that is, they trend westward), and must be crossed in order to enter again into the plains (p. 160-1).
The mt chain is that of the South Sea (that is, the main sierra and its
branches), and from Chichilticale, where the mts begin, to Cíbola is 80 leagues
(p. 188). The general course from Culiacan to Cíbola is a little E. of N. (p.
181).

Says Coronado, *Hakluyt*, iii. 375: 'I departed from the Caracones, and
always kept by the Sea coast, as neere as I could iudge, and in very deed I
still found my selfe the farther off; in such sort, that when I arrived at Chi-

In the map the reader will find the general limits of the route indicated, with no attempt to show details, by the dotted lines on the right, and Niza's route by those on the left. The location of Sonora, in the region of Arizpe, though there are difficulties respecting the exact sites of Corazones, San Gerónimo, and the village of Sonora, may be regarded as unquestionable. That Coronado's route was via the Santa Cruz, and the site of the later Tucson, or that Chichilticale, the place where he changed his course to the north-east, was in the region where the Gila emerges from the mountains, is hardly less certain. Chichil-

chilticale I found myselfe tenne dayes iourney from the Sea; and the father provinciall sayd that it was onely but five leagues distance, and that he had seene the same. Wee all conceived great griefe, and were not a little confounded when we saw that wee found euery thing contrary to the information which he had given your Lordship,' and more to the same purport. He says that the coast turns west opposite Corazones 10 or 12 l., and he had heard of the ships passing. He remained 2 days at Chichilticale, and on June 21st entered the desert or mts beyond. In the *Relacion del Suceso* there is no information about the route from Sonora to Cíbola; and the same is true of the anon. letter in *Pacheco, Doc.*, xix. 529.

On the route beyond Chichilticale, Jaramillo says: 3 days N. E. (from the cañada reached by crossing the mts) to a river named S. Juan, from the day; 2 days more to N., to river called Balsas, because it had to be crossed on rafts; 2 short days to Arroyo de la Barranca, nearly N. E.; 1 day to Rio Frio; 1 day through a pine wood to an arroyo, where 3 men died of poison; 2 days to the Arroyo Vermejo, N. E.; and 2 days to the first town of Cíbola. James A. Reavis, a man well acquainted with this region, where he has a large land claim, in *Coronado's Route*, a MS. kindly furnished for my use, identifies the streams as follows: the deep arroyo, perhaps Pinal Creek; S. Juan, south fork of the Rio Salado; Rio de las Balsas, White Mt River; Arroyo de la Barranca, Summit Spring; Rio Frio, Colorado Chiquito; next arroyo, Carrizo; and Rio Vermejo, Zuñi River. Castañeda (p. 41) says that in 15 days they arrived within 8 l. of Cíbola, on a river called Vermejo (red), on account of its soily and red waters; and (p. 55) that the main army, 3 days into the desert, on a river in a deep ravine found a large horn that Coronado had seen and left as a guide. One day before reaching Cíbola they had a gale and snow storm. From Chichilticale to Cíbola 80 l. (p. 162). Cíbola was in a narrow valley between steep mts. The largest town was called Muzaque (p. 163-4). Coronado (*Hakluyt*, iii. 375) says that after 30 l. they found fresh rivers and grass; also flax, especially on a river called Rio del Lino (prob. Colorado Chiquito); then they came to the city of Granada; and (p. 377) there were 7 towns within 4 l., all called Cíbola, but no one of them so named. Only one was larger than that called by C. Granada, which had some 200 houses within the walls, and perhaps 300 others. Jaramillo says there were 5 towns within 6 l. Castañeda (p. 42) says that Cíbola was the village called Granada. In the *Relacion del Suceso*, 319-20, the author says that Niza had understood all the 7 towns—which really had from 150 to 300 houses each—to be one city, called Cíbola. The route from Culiacan is 240 l. N. to 34° 30′ (at Chichilticale), and thence N. E. to Cíbola in about 36° (really about 35°). Niza had understood the largest town to be called Ahacus, as will be remembered.

ticale, the 'red house,' a ruin which gave name to the
place, has been generally identified with the famous
Casa Grande of the Gila, and I find no reason to question the identity.   The ruin in itself would not suffice
to fix the route, but it goes far to confirm the general
purport of all the evidence.   It is not necessary to
suppose that Coronado's Chichilticale was the casa
grande itself, but rather a place named for that remarkable structure, not far away.   Niza had probably
received his impressions of the Gila valley from the
Pima villages; Diaz had noted rather the adobe ruin;
and Coronado may have passed to the right of it, or
merely gone with a small party westward to examine
it.   Nothing short of a minute diary of each day's
journey could be expected to give a clearer idea of
the course followed.   I make no attempt to identify
the streams crossed on the march north-eastward
from the Gila between Florence and the San Pedro
mouth to Cíbola.

   The identity of Cíbola and the Pueblo towns of
Zuñi is so clearly established by all the evidence, and
has been so generally confirmed by such investigators
as Simpson, Davis, Prince, Bandelier, and others, that
I do not deem it necessary even to fully recapitulate
the proofs.   No other group of towns will at all meet
the requirements of the narratives.   The difficulties
and objections hardly merit notice.   The few who
have favored other groups have been led mainly by a
desire to justify some exaggerations of the discoverers,
by finding ruins to represent a grander Cíbola; and in
support of their conclusions have found little more
than the presence of ruins in most directions from
most groups.   The position of Cíbola as the first Pueblo province found in coming north-east, or left on
going south-west; its geographical relations to Moqui
in the north-west and Acoma on the east; the definite
statement of Castañeda that as far as Cíbola, and a
day or two beyond, the streams flowed into the South
Sea, but later into the North Sea; the correspondence

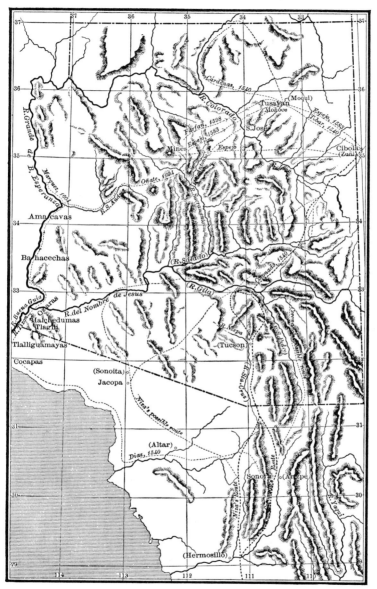

CORONADO AND NIZA IN ARIZONA.

of one of its towns on a rock to the ruins of Old Zuñi,
and of the rest to the still existing town and ruins in
the vicinity; and the agreement from the time of Espejo of all the early Spanish authorities who wrote
intelligently on the subject—appear to me conclusive.[20]

Thus about the 10th of July—I give only approximate dates, without pointing out minor discrepancies
in the different narratives—Coronado and his men
came in sight of the famous Cíbola. The town first
approached, and named by the Spaniards Granada,
stood on a rocky mesa corresponding to the ruins of
Old Zuñi; the one seen by Niza, if he saw any, was
in the valley, like the pueblo still standing but perhaps built later; while the others are still represented
by heaps of ruins.[21]   The people of Granada, not
appreciating the benefits to be gained by submission
to the Spaniards' king and Christians' God, came out
in warlike array to annihilate the little band of invaders, their arrows killing a horse and piercing a friar's
gown; but with the battle-cry of 'Santiago' the sol-

---

[20] A résumé of reasons for the identity is given in my *Native Races*, iv.
673–4. Bandelier, *Hist. Introd.*, 12–16, gives an excellent analysis of the evidence. Espejo, *Relacion*, 117–20, 180, found at Zuñi some Mex. Ind. whom
Coronado left at Cíbola, and therefore his testimony to the identity should
be in itself conclusive. True, there are two copies of E.'s *Relacion*, one of
which gives the name Amé or Amí instead of Zuñi, thus suggesting the suspicion that the latter name in the other, and Hakluyt's version from it, may
possibly have been an interpolation; but I think it more likely that Amé is
a misprint; at any rate, the proof is more than sufficient without this. Salmeron, *Relaciones*, 7–9, writing in 1628, speaks of Cíbola as the capital of the
Zuñi province. Davis, *Span. Conq.*, 120, found in a MS. of 1688 a reference
to Zuñi as the buffalo province, which he regards as conclusive.

About the origin of the word Cíbola there seems to be no certainty. It is
the Spanish name in modern dictionaries of the American bison, or buffalo
(feminine of *cíbolo*), and was, I suppose, of American origin. I learn from
Gatschet, through Bandelier, *Hist. Introd.*, 9, that *Sihulodá* in the Isleta dia-
lect means 'buffalo.' We may suppose either that the Spaniards, finding a
strange animal during their trip to the much talked of seven cities of Cíbola,
formed a needed name from that of the towns; or that the towns had previously received the native name of the buffalo. I think it not unlikely, however, that the name was never applied to the towns till after the Spaniards
came; but that the latter, far in the s. w., hearing the name—that of the
buffalo or buffalo country—often used by the natives, took it for granted
that it belonged to the cities or province, the Ind. gradually adopting the
usage. But all is mere conjecture, so far as I am concerned. In a note to a
doc. in *Pacheco, Doc.*, iv. 299, Cíbola is said to be the name of a province or
its capital in Peru, noted for its hides.

[21] See descrip. of these and other ruins in *Nat. Races*, iv. 641–74.

diers charged, and drove them within the walls, killing several.   The town was taken by assault, after a
struggle in which the general was knocked down by
stones thrown from the roofs, and had his foot pierced
by an arrow.[22]   Submitting, the natives forthwith
abandoned their town.   A few days later the other
villages sent in their formal submission, with some
gifts; but on being urged to become Christians and
Spanish subjects, they fled to the hills.   Some of them
came back as the weeks passed by; and relations between the two races during the conqueror's stay were
friendly, though marked by caution on the part of the
natives.

   And now that Coronado was at last master of the
famous 'seven cities,' both he and his companions were
grievously disappointed.   They had found, indeed, an
agricultural people, living in stone and adobe houses
of several stories, dressed to some extent in cotton,
skilled in the preparation of buffalo hides, and various
other petty arts, and even having a few turquoises.
Yet the kingdom of rich cities had dwindled to a
small province of small and poor villages, and the
conquest seemed a small achievement for so grand and
costly an expedition.   Doubtless, however, the Pueblo
towns as they were found would have excited much
admiration but for the contrast between the reality
and the brilliant magnificence of the invaders' expectations.   On making inquiries respecting Niza's three
grand kingdoms outside of Cíbola, they learned that of
Marata the natives had no knowledge whatever; that
Totonteac was said to be a hot lake, with four or five
houses and other ruined ones on its shores; and that
Acus, a name that had no existence 'with an aspira-
tion nor without,' was probably Acuco, a small town
and not a province.   Right heartily was the padre
provincial cursed by the army for his gross exaggerations, to which a much harsher term was freely applied.

---

[22] According to the *Rel. del Suceso*, the Spaniards were repulsed in the
assault, and had to withdraw to a short distance and use their fire-arms.

What Fray Marcos had to say in his own defence
does not appear; but Cíbola was soon made too hot
for the good friar, who was sent back to Sonora, and
thence farther south, to appear no more in northern
annals.[23]   He probably departed with captains Diaz
and Gallego, who in August were despatched with
orders for the main army under Arellano, who was to
join the general, leaving Diaz in command at Sonora,
while Gallego should go on to Mexico, carrying Coronado's report of August 3d, as already cited.

Coronado remained at Zuñi from July to November.   Notwithstanding his disappointment, he had no
thought of returning without making additional explorations; and, indeed, there were reports of more
distant provinces, where fame and wealth might yet
be successfully sought.   The most brilliant indications pointed to the east, whither we shall follow the
invaders in the next chapter; but information was
also obtained about a province of Tusayan, with seven
towns, situated some 25 leagues toward the north-
west, doubtless the Moqui villages.[24]   Before August
3d Captain Tobar, with a small force including seventeen horsemen and Fray Juan Padilla, was sent to
explore.   Marching for five days through an uninhabited country, this party entered the province by
stealth, and approached one of the towns at night.
In the morning the surprised inhabitants came out,
and after listening to what the strangers had to say,
they drew on the ground a line which must not be
passed.   Then Fray Juan, who had been a soldier in
his youth, lost his patience, and said to the captain,
"Indeed, I know not for what we have come here."
The Spaniards made a charge; and the natives after

---

[23] *Castañeda, Rel.*, 48.

[24] The name is also written Tucayan, Tuzan, Tusan, Tucano, and in Castañeda's chapter-heading Tutaliaco.   Castañeda in one place (p. 165) gives
the distance as 20 l.   In the *Rel. del Suceso* the distance is given as 35 l.
westward; Jaramillo says it was 5 days.   The real distance to Moqui in a
straight line is over 40 l.   Whipple, *Pac. R. R. Repts*, iii. 108–12, thinks
Tusayan was not Moqui, but perhaps identical with the Rio Verde ruins;
which, however, are still farther from Zuñi.

losing many lives were defeated, and sued for peace, bringing gifts of food, cotton stuffs, leather, and a few turquoises. They, too, admitted the invaders to their towns, similar to those of Cíbola but somewhat larger, and became for the time submissive vassals of the king of Spain. They had their tales to tell of marvellous things beyond, and mentioned a great river, several days' journey down the course of which lived a nation of very tall men. Thereupon Don Pedro returned and reported to the general.

Then Captain Cárdenas, who had succeeded Samaniego as maestro de campo, was sent, with twelve men, to seek the great river and the tall men. Being kindly received by the people of Tusayan, who furnished guides, Cárdenas marched for twenty days, or fifty leagues as one narrative has it, westward over a desert country, and at last reached the river. But so high were its banks, that though deemed as large as the river that flows past Seville in Spain, and said by the Indians to be over half a league wide, it looked like a mere rivulet flowing three or four leagues below; and so precipitous that in five or six days' journey the Spaniards could find no place where they could get to the water. At the most favorable spot, three men spent a day in the attempt, but only succeeded in descending about one third of the distance. Being advised by the guides that it would be impossible to penetrate farther for want of water, Cárdenas returned to Cíbola. This was the first visit of Europeans to the great cañon of the Colorado, a region but rarely penetrated even in modern times. It was clearly understood by the chroniclers of the expedition that this river, flowing from the north-east to south-south-west, was the Rio del Tizon, discovered by Melchor Diaz near its mouth. No further explorations were attempted in this direction, and the Moqui towns were not revisited by Europeans for more than forty years.[25]

[25] Pedro de Sotomayor was the chronicler of this branch expedition, according to Castañeda; and the three men who tried to reach the bottom of the great

cañon were Capt. Melgosa, Juan Galeras, and an unnamed soldier.   On the way
back, at a cascade, they found crystals of salt.   A westward course from Moqui
would have led to the Colorado at the junction of the Colorado Chiquito,
where the main river turns abruptly to N. of W.   As no crossing of the
branch is mentioned, and as the course of the river is given as N. E. to S. S.
W., it would be much more convenient to suppose that Cárdenas went N. W.
to the river, and followed it southward, but not much importance can be attached to this matter.   Gomara, *Hist. Ind.*, 272, and some other writers,
speak of Cárdenas' trip as having extended to the sea, perhaps confounding
it with that of Diaz to the gulf.   This may partially account for the subsequent curious transfer of Coronado's discoveries from the N. E. interior to the
N. W. coast on many early maps.

CHAPTER III.

CORONADO IN NEW MEXICO.

1540–1542.

At Cíbola, or Zuñi—Alvarado's Tour in the East—Tales of the Turk—Buffalo Plains—Acuco, Tiguex, and Cicuye—Map—Arrival of Arellano and the Army—In Winter Quarters—Spanish Outrages —A Winter of Snow and Warfare — Expedition to the North-east —Coronado in Quivira — Wigwam Villages and No Gold—Back at Tiguex—The Rio Grande Valley—Pueblo Names —Second Winter in New Mexico—Plans for a New Conquest—Orders to Return—Dissensions—Fray Juan de Padilla—March to Sonora—A Demoralized Army—Remarks on Results—Northern Mystery and Early Maps—Ibarra's Entradas, 1563-5—The Name of New Mexico.

THE discovery of New Mexico dates from the 7th to the 10th of July, 1540, when General Francisco Vasquez de Coronado arrived from the south-west at the province of Cíbola, or the Zuñi towns, as related in the last chapter. On the 14th the general visited a peñol four leagues distant, where the natives were said to be fortifying their position, and returned the same day.[1] During the absence of Cárdenas on his trip to the Moqui towns and Rio Colorado, there came to Cíbola a party of natives from the eastern province of Cicuye, with gifts of various leathern articles and offers of tribal friendship and alliance. Their chief and spokesman was Bigotes, so named by the Spaniards for his long mustaches, and he had much to say of the 'cows,' that is, the buffaloes, of his country.

---

[1] *Coronado, Traslado de las Nuevas,* 532. Nothing is said of results or of the direction. The fortified peñol suggests the well-known Inscription Rock east of Zuñi, though the distance as given is too small.

Accordingly, Captain Alvarado was ordered with twenty men to accompany the natives on their return, and to report within eighty days respecting their country and its wonderful animals.

In a journey of five days[2] Alvarado came to a town named Acuco, supposed to be Niza's Acus, built like Granada of Cíbola on a rock, and accessible only by a narrow stairway, terminating in mere holes for the hands and feet. The inhabitants were hostile at first, but on threats of battle made peace and furnished food. Three days more brought the party, in a distance of twenty leagues toward the east, according to one of the narratives, to the province of Tiguex, with its twelve towns in a broad valley, on a large river flowing from north to south, said to be well settled for fifty leagues or more, and to have villages for fifteen or twenty leagues from the river on either side. This province became the centre of subsequent operations; and indeed, Alvarado at this time recognized its advantages, sending back a recommendation to the general to come on and establish here his winter quarters. Then he went on with Bigotes for five days to Cicuye, on the border of the plains. The natives in respect of friendliness fulfilled the promises that had been made by their ambassadors, and, besides their specialty of hides, their gifts included some cloth and

---

[2] Thirty leagues acc. to *Coronado, Rel. del Suceso.* In the *Florida Col. Doc.*, 65–6, is found the *Relacion de lo que Hernando de Alvarado y Fray Juan de Padilla descubrieron en demanda de la mar del Sur* (Norte?), of which the substance is as follows: Left Granada Aug. 29, 1540, toward Coco (Acuco); 2 l. to an old edifice like a fort; 1 l. to another, and a little farther to a third; then a pretty large city, all in ruins 6 stories high; 1 l. to another city in ruins. Here is the separation of two roads, one to Chia (to left or N.), and the other (to S. and right) to Coco (Acoma), which town is briefly described; thence to a 'very good laguna' (perhaps that where the pueblo of Laguna stands in modern times); and thence to a river called Nuestra Señora, from the day (Sept. 8th, the arrival being on the 7th, making the whole journey 9 d. instead of 8, as in Castañeda). Then follows a description of the 12 pueblos of this prov. (Tiguex, not named) in the broad valley. It is also stated that there are 7 pueblos abandoned and destroyed by the wild tribes of the plains, prob. referring to those in the direction of Pecos; also, that in the whole country are 80 towns. There is no record of the journey beyond the river. Some descriptive matter on a large town, 3 stories of tapia and 3 of wood, with 15,000 inhab., apparently Taos. As we shall see, Castañeda states later that Alvarado had visited Braba (Taos) on his journey to Cicuye.

even turquoises. But what particularly attracted the captain's attention here was the statements of an Indian, who claimed to be a native of Hurall, or Harale, some 300 leagues farther east toward Florida. From something in his appearance this man was named by the Spaniards El Turco, or the Turk. He spoke, 'tout autrement qu'il n'aurait dû le faire,' of great cities in his country, and of what was yet more enticing, gold and silver in large quantities; and his tales were sent back by special messengers to the general. After such news, buffaloes seemed of slight importance; yet Alvarado, in compliance with his instructions, made a trip out into the plains in search of them, with the Turk as a guide, and he found the animals in great numbers.

In this tour he followed a river for some 100 leagues south-eastward. Then he returned to Tiguex, where he found that Cárdenas had arrived from Cíbola to prepare winter quarters for the army, and where Alvarado now remained to await the general.

From the preceding narrative of Alvarado's expedition, the reader familiar with the country, or having a map before him, will naturally identify Acuco with the since famous and still existing pueblo of Acoma, the province and river of Tiguex with the valley of New Mexico's 'great river,' the Rio Grande del Norte, and Cicuye at the edge of the buffalo plains, from the vicinity of which a river flowed south-eastward, with the now ruined pueblo of Pecos. The record of subsequent happenings will, I think, confirm these first conclusions beyond all doubt; and I append some descriptive and other matter from the different narratives which point irresistibly in the same direction.[3] So far as Acuco is concerned, the identity has

---

[3] Acuco 5 days E. of Cíbola and 3 days w. of Tiguex, Castañeda, 69, 71; 30 l. and 20 l. substituted for the 5 and 3 days in Rel. del Suceso. On the march of the main army, Acuco was passed, but no distances are given by Castañeda, 82. Jaramillo, 309, places this village about midway—1 day more or less—of the 9 days' journey from Cíbola to Tiguex; but this author, by an evident blunder, calls the village Tutahaco, which, as will be seen, was another place. Eaton, as cited by Schoolcraft, Simpson, and others, gives Hah-koo-kee-ah as the Zuñi name of Acoma. Bandelier, 14, gives the Queres name as Ágo.

never been questioned, I believe; yet there will be
found in most of the early narratives, indications that

Tiguex—also printed Tihuex and Tihueq—is 40 l. N. (E.?) of Cíbola. *Castañeda*, 165-6.   3 d. (eastward) of Acuco. *Id.*, 71.   It has 12 vil. on a great
river; the val. is about 2 l. wide, and bounded on the w. by high snowy mts;
4 vil. at the foot of the mts; 3 others on the heights. *Id.*, 167-8.   Tiguex is
the central point of all the pueblos; 4 vil. on the river below T. are S. E., because the river makes a bend to the E. (no such bend appears on modern
maps); up and down the val. the region explored extends about 130 l., all
inhabited. *Id.*, 182.   20 l. E. of the peñol of Acuco, a river flowing from N. to
s., well settled, with 70 pueblos, large and small, in its whole extent (and
branches?); the settled region extends 50 l. N. and s., and there are some vil.
15 or 20 l. away on either side. *Rel. del Suceso*, 323.   On the river are 15 vil.
within 20 l., and others on the branches. *Jaramillo*, 309.   Coronado, *Pacheco,
Doc.*, iii. 368, says T. was the best province found; yet not desirable for Span.
occupation.   Gallatin, 73, followed by Davis, 185, and Prince, 128, put Tiguex
on the Puerco.   The reasons are the N. E. direction of Jemez from T., and the
great river crossed after passing Cicuye, which these authors identify with
the Rio Grande.   In my opinion, these points are of slight weight in opposition to the general tenor of all the narratives.   It seems incredible that the
Spaniards should have described the valley of the Puerco as the broad valley
of a large river on which and on its branches for over 100 l. on the right and
left were situated most of the pueblos.   Davis admits that the Puerco was
but a small stream, but suggests that it may have been full or flooded at the
time; yet in a year and more the Span. had ample time to learn its comparative size.   They went in their explorations far below the junction, and if the
Rio Tiguex had been the Puerco, its junction with a larger river would naturally have been noted.   See also what is said below on Cicuye.   If, however, any further proof is needed, we have the fact that Espejo, ascending the
Rio Grande 40 years later, found the province of Tiguas with reports of Coronado's visit and fights with the natives. *Espejo, Rel.*, 112-13.   This province
of the Tiguas, distinct from the Teguas, or Tehuas, was well known at the
end of the 16th and in the 17th centuries, being on the Rio Grande and
almost certainly in the region of Sandía.   Bandelier, *Hist. Introd.*, 18-20,
after a study of documentary evidence which he cites, and which I shall have
occasion to use later, has no hesitation in locating Tiguex at or near Bernalillo.   Squier, Kern, and Morgan had previously located Tiguex on the Rio
Grande, above the Puerco junction.   Simpson, *Coronado's March*, 334-5,
while admitting that some of the evidence points to the northern location,
yet chooses to find Tiguex below the mouth of the Puerco, because only there
is the valley bounded on the west by snowy mts, the Socorro Range, citing
also *Jeffery's Atlas* of 1773, which puts Tigua at the foot of those mts.
Simpson's view of this matter would remove some of the difficulties in connection with Espejo's trip, as we shall see; but it would also create other and
greater difficulties.

Cicuye (printed also Cicuic, Cicuique, Ticuique, Tienique, and Acuique),
reported to be about 70 l. east of Cíbola, *Castañeda*, 67, 5 d. from Tiguex,
strongly fortified, with houses of 4 stories. *Id.*, 71.   On the way back from
Quivira, Coronado reached the Rio de Cicuye 30 l. below where he crossed it
on the way from C., and followed it up to C.   The Ind. said it flowed into
the Rio Tiguex 20 d. below. *Id.*, 134.   Built on the summit of a rock, forming a square, with houses of 4 stories; 500 warriors. *Id.*, 176.   In a narrow
valley between pine-covered mts, on a little river, *Id.*, 179   70 l. from Cíbola
and 30 l. from the edge of the plains; the last village toward the east. *Id.*,
188.   Between Cicuye and Quirix there is a small, well-fortified village called
by the Span. Ximera or Ximena (S. Cristóbal acc. to Bandelier), and another
larger one, nearly abandoned, called by the Span. Silos, and a 3d, entirely
ruined, as was said, by an irruption of the Teyas savages 5 or 6 years before,

the original Acoma may have been farther north than
the modern peñol pueblo, and more nearly in a line
between Zuñi and Tiguex. As to Tiguex and Cicuye,
Gallatin, followed by Davis and Prince, has located
the former on the Rio Puerco, and the latter west of
the Rio Grande. These authors thus escape from a
few slight difficulties, to become involved, as it seems
to me, in many greater ones, ignoring several clear
points in the testimony and the general tenor of the
records. While Tiguex, however, was certainly in the
Rio Grande valley, there remains a slight doubt as to
its latitude, such excellent authorities as Simpson and
Bandelier differing in their conclusions. The latter
puts the pueblo and province in the region of Bernalillo and Sandía, while the former prefers a site below
the mouth of the Puerco. Although Simpson makes
one or two strong points in favor of his position, yet
the preponderance of evidence is overwhelming—
amounting, I think, to proof—in support of the
northern site of Tiguex. Much that may seem vague

they having attacked Cicuye, but without success. There are 7 vil. bet. C.
and the Sierra Nevada, one of them subject to C. and half destroyed by the
savages (possibly the one called Silos above). *Id.*, 177–9. The largest of the
ordinary pueblos, with houses 4 and 5 stories high; 15 l. east of the Rio de
Tiguex, on the border of the buffalo plains. *Rel. del Suceso.* Four days (eastward) from Tiguex, past 2 vil. not named; then 3 d. a little more N. E. to
the Rio de Ticuique (Cicuye); then N. E. into the plains. *Jaramillo*, 309.
Simpson, 336, shows that the way from Pecos to the Rio Gallinas (the main
branch of the R. Pecos) leads N. E. about 50 miles over rough mts, and may
have taken 4 days (only 3 acc. to Jaramillo); also that the Gallinas, being
flooded, might require a bridge and be called a large river in May and June.
He might have added that Alvarado's earlier trip down what may have been
this stream for 100 l. may have had something to do with its being called a
large stream. S. also notes the place called Sayaqué, resembling Cicuye, on
Jeffrey's atlas. It must, however, be admitted that if the great river was the
Gallinas, the omission of any mention of the Canadian, so large and so near,
is remarkable. Davis, 198–9, and Prince, 128, put Cicuye on the Rio Jemes
or on or near the Rio Grande and west of that river, in the region of Sta Ana.
This is to fit the location of Tiguex on the Puerco, and the only merit of this
theory, so far as I can see, is to provide a great river to be bridged—though
hardly three days from Cicuye—and D. has even heard of some traces of a
bridge in this region! The theory of D. and the others would completely
ignore all the pueblos E. of the Rio Grande. Bandelier's confirmation of the
identity of Pecos and Cicuye derives especial weight from his personal examination of Pecos and the adjoining region. 111–17. He tells us that the aboriginal name of Pecos was Aqui or Agin (Agiu?), 20; and he suggests that
the original Spanish of Castañeda may possibly have been Acuye instead of
Cicuye, especially as the name is in one narrative (*Rel. del Suceso*) written
Acuique.

to the reader of this chapter will become perfectly
clear from later records.

Meanwhile Coronado, having despatched Alvarado
to the east, and having sent Cárdenas, after his return
from the north-west, to prepare winter quarters at Tiguex as already related, awaited at Cíbola the arrival
of the main army under Arellano, who came late in

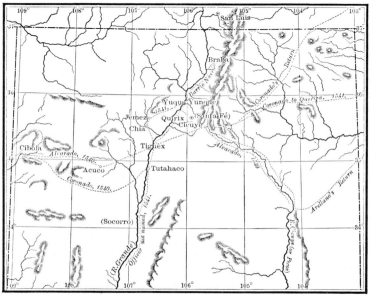

CORONADO IN NEW MEXICO.

November or early in December, without having had
any noteworthy adventures on the march from Sonora.[4]   Then the general, ordering the army to rest
for twenty days before following him, started for Tiguex with thirty men.   Instead of the direct route by
way of Acuco, or Acoma, he went farther to the right,
or south, bent on new discoveries, as he had heard of

[4] Castañeda is clearly in error when he says the army left Sonora in the
middle of Sept., and that Arellano remained behind.

other towns in that direction. His party suffered severely on the way for want of water, which had to be
sought in the mountains, where the intense cold was
as oppressive as the thirst had been before; yet in
eleven days they reached the Rio Grande at the province of Tutahaco with its eight villages,[5] hearing of
others farther south, and then following the river for
four leagues up to Tiguex.

Here Coronado found Cárdenas and Alvarado awaiting him, together with the Turk, to whose tales of
eastern wealth he listened with the greatest pleasure
and credulity, all his companions becoming presently
most enthusiastic in their hopes of a grand conquest
in the near future.[6] These hopes doubtless made them
less careful than they might otherwise have been to
conciliate the natives of Tiguex. Unmindful of the
viceroy's instructions, and of the new Indian policy of
which Coronado was to be the exponent, the invaders
did not hesitate to take such houses as they desired
for their own uses, turning out the inhabitants without ceremony, and otherwise disregarding the property
rights of the people who had given them so kind a reception. The friendly folks of Cicuye received no
better treatment, except that as yet they had not the
army to support. Alvarado, being sent to obtain certain golden bracelets which the Turk falsely claimed
to have left at that pueblo, arrested Bigotes and an-

[5] Tutahaco with 8 vil. 4 l. down the river s. e. from Tiguex. *Castañeda,*
76, 168, 182. Not named in the *Rel. del Suceso.* By Jaramillo, 309, it is
confounded with Acuco. Simpson does not attempt to identify it. Davis,
180-1, and Prince, 130, entirely misunderstand the route, and mistranslate
the original of Castañeda to identify this province with the Laguna group n.
of Acoma. Bandelier, 21-3, identifies Tutahaco with the region of Isleta, a
comparatively modern pueblo (that is, modern in its actual site; the original Isleta was, however, as we shall see, in the same region, though possibly a little farther south). This conclusion, which of course cannot be
questioned in view of the distance from Tiguex, makes Tutahaco practically
one of the Tigua towns. There is something suggestive of possible error in
the existence of a province of 8 towns only 4 l. below the other 12, and about
which so little is said; still the record is clear enough.

[6] By Mota Padilla, *Conq. N. Gal.,* 160 et seq., and by some other writers,
Copala Lake is mentioned as one of the regions respecting which the Spaniards at this time heard from El Turco and others. The same author states
on authority not known that the town where the Spaniards were lodged was
called Coofer.

other chief because the ornaments were not produced, and brought his prisoners in chains back to Tiguex. The general called upon the natives for a large quantity of clothing for the army soon expected to arrive, refused them time to call a council to apportion the tax among the towns as was their custom, and sent soldiers to take the clothing by force, the Indians being obliged in many cases to take the garments off their backs. A Spanish officer, coolly calling to an Indian to hold his horse, ascended by a ladder to an upper apartment, where he violated the Indian's wife, and the wronged husband could get no justice. One pueblo was burned for some offence of the inhabitants not clearly specified; and many other outrages were committed. It is fair, however, to state that Castañeda, on whom we have to depend for particulars of this winter's bloody deeds, was not very friendly to Coronado; and in the other brief narrative it is implied that the troubles began with the killing of horses by the natives. Whatever may have been the truth—and I have no doubt that these haughty caballeros were as usual utterly disregardful of the Indians' rights—the result was, that civilization and christianity were soon in bad odor; and when Arellano arrived with the main army from Cíbola in December,[7] the whole province was in open revolt.

The winter was spent, so far as the heavy snowfall and intense cold—to which neither men nor animals were accustomed—would permit, in efforts to conquer or conciliate the revolted pueblos. Captain Cárdenas marched against the town where the woman had been outraged, gained the roofs by assault, and there fought constantly for two days and one night. Meanwhile the Mexican allies, by introducing inflammable material through subterranean passages, forced the defenders to sue for peace. Captains Melgosa and

---

[7] The 1st night out from Cíbola the army was lodged at the largest town of the province, named Muzaque, some of whose houses are said to have been 7 stories high. Their later route was via Acuco, where they were kindly received, and where many climbed to the top of that famous peñol. *Castañeda*, 79-83, 163.

Lopez responded to their signs by crossing their arms, whereupon the Indians threw down their arms and surrendered. Being conducted to the tent of Captain Cárdenas, the latter ordered them to be burned alive; and on seeing the preparations the prisoners, about 100 in number, resisted desperately and were slaughtered. Cárdenas alleged that he had no knowledge of the capitulation, and had followed his general's orders.[8] A few escaped to tell their countrymen how the Spaniards kept their promises; and from this time to the final departure of the army the people of this province refused to listen to any propositions of peace from a race they could not trust. They defended themselves by barricading their towns, or ran away to the mountains, but to every offer of pardon and conciliation they simply pointed to past acts of bad faith. Captain Cárdenas going with thirty men to the pueblo of Tiguex to propose terms was required to advance alone and unarmed; and being knocked down, was with difficulty rescued, several others being seriously wounded. Nearly all the natives of the province had taken refuge in this pueblo and another three or four miles distant.

Then Coronado advanced with his army to attack Tiguex, but was repulsed in the first assault by the stones and arrows of the defenders with twenty men wounded, several of them fatally. Then followed a siege of 50 days, with many assaults and sorties, in which were killed some 200 of the natives and a number of Spaniards, including Captain Obando and a gentleman named Francisco de Pobares.[9] The besieged, suffering for want of water, dug a well inside the town, which caved in and buried thirty of their

[8] Mota Padilla, *Hist. Conq. N. Gal.*, 161, says that Cárdenas was afterward imprisoned in Spain for this act. Frejes, acc. to *Escudero, Not. Son.*, 27–9, says C. was sentenced and imprisoned in Mex. Bustamante, in *Gomara, Hist. Mex.* (ed. 1826), 184, says that C. died at Chametla. As we shall see presently, C. left N. Mex. for Spain via Mex., in advance of the army.

[9] Castañeda, 97–8, says that Obando or Cárdenas—it is not clear which—was captured and carried alive into a pueblo during one of the expeditions; perhaps C., since it is said that O. was maestro de campo in C.'s absence.

number. A little later they were allowed to send away women and children, about 100 of whom departed; and after two weeks more of resistance they all attempted to escape by night. The movement being discovered, the fugitives bravely attacked the foe, and were either cut down or driven to perish in the icy waters of the Rio Grande. A similar fate befell those who had taken refuge in the other town; and all the villages were taken and plundered, the inhabitants being killed, enslaved, or driven from the province. Not one submitted, or would accept the conquerors' permission to return to his home.

The natives of some of the other provinces, however, proved more tractable. The pueblo of Chia, a large and populous one, four leagues west of the river,[10] sent in its submission voluntarily, and was visited by a captain, the inhabitants being intrusted as a mark of especial confidence with the care of four useless bronze cannon. Another party was sent to the province of Quirix, or of the Queres, situated north of Tiguex, and including seven pueblos.[11] The people of the first were timid and ran away, but being overtaken and reassured as to the strangers' intentions, they not only became friendly, but aided in tranquillizing the whole province. During the winter, also, Coronado found occasion to visit Cicuye, or Pecos, where, to conciliate the people with a view to his proposed expedition eastward, he liberated one of the captive chieftains, and promised the early release of the other.

[10] The pueblo of Cia, Zia, or Silla still stands in about the place indicated. It is mentioned by Castañeda and without location or description in *Rel. del Suceso*. The name Silla is probably a corruption, as the Mexicans pronounce it Siya or Ciya. This direction of Cia is of course a point in favor of the northern location of Tiguex, and against that on the Puerco, though there is no certainty that the modern site corresponds exactly to the ancient. This is a pueblo, however, which we shall find often mentioned in the 17th-century annals. Davis, 202, mistranslates '4 l. distant on the river' to suit his theory.

[11] The province was later called S. Felipe de Queres. Its pueblos of S. Felipe, Sto Domingo, Sta Ana, Cochití, and Cia still stand in the same region, though as we have seen Cia in 1540 was named by Castañeda as a distinct pueblo. Quirix is also printed Quivix. There seems to be no reason to doubt its identity with Queres, a well-known name of later annals.

It was not until May 1541 that the ice in the Rio Grande was sufficiently thawed to make the stream fordable;[12] and on the 5th of that month the general marched with his entire force in search of the reported wealth of the regions beyond Tiguex, having previously sent Captain Tobar back to Sonora to bring up half the force left there. At Cicuye, Bigotes having been released in accordance with an earlier promise, the Spaniards were received as friends, and a guide was obtained, who claimed to be a native of Quivira. The Turk had before this time rendered himself liable to suspicion in respect of his veracity, being also detected in divers conversations with the devil; but as the new guide, named Xabe, confirmed to some extent his reports of gold and silver, the Spaniards were much elated at their prospective conquest. A march of three or four days over a mountainous country brought them to "a great and very deep river which flows also near Cicuye, and was therefore named Rio de Cicuye," where it took them four days to construct a bridge. This river would seem to have been the Gallinas, the eastern and larger branch of the Pecos.[13]

A little later they entered the great buffalo plains, and in ten days came to the first habitations of the wandering tribes. Details of Coronado's long march over these vast plains have but little intrinsic interest, and still less importance so far as the history of New Mexico is concerned; moreover the records, as might naturally be expected, are far from being sufficiently

---

[12] It must have been a most extraordinary winter; but probably the floods following the breaking-up of the ice may have been as formidable obstacles to fording as the ice, and a month of floods should perhaps be included in the delay. Coronado, however, gives the date of starting as April 23d.

[13] As we have seen, the size of this stream has to be explained by the season of flood, with the possible addition of earlier exploration by Alvarado. To thus explain away the difficulty is a very different matter from Davis' similar theory about the Rio Puerco, because on the Puerco the army spent, if D. and the others are right, two winters, and had ample time to learn its size and its connection with the Rio Grande; while the Cicuye was merely crossed at this point once in May, and was once or twice explored below and shown to be really a large river. D.'s position that the Cicuye was the Rio Grande is wholly untenable. Yet, as I have said, it is strange that the Canadian fails to figure in these narratives.

minute to enable us to fix the exact route followed. About the expedition in general, however, there is little or nothing of mystery or confusion. According to Castañeda, the army marched in 37 days to a point 250 leagues from Tiguex, on a north-north-east course for the larger part of the way, and perhaps all, though the most enticing reports pointed to the east, and the statements respecting the direction are at the last not quite clear.[14] Jaramillo implies that more than half the journey was directed eastward. I think it clear that east-north-east is nearer the general route followed than north-east. Two tribes of Indians, the Querechos and Teyas, both migratory, dwelling in skin tents and living chiefly on buffalo meat, were passed on the way; and their reports, though contradictory, seemed to confirm the idea of a rich country farther on. The explorers also visited a ranchería, where an old native explained by signs that he had seen Cabeza de Vaca's party in the south.

Besides Xabe, there was another Quivira Indian named Sopete or Isopete, accompanying the army, who had declared the Turk a liar, without gaining much credit, as the Querechos had partially confirmed the latter's testimony; but what the Teyas said favored Sopete's version, and indicated that the Turk, perhaps from a desire to reach his own country, had led the Spaniards much too far east, Quivira being in the north. Finally, in a valley which formed the extreme eastern limit of the exploration, it was decided at a council of war held about the middle of June that the general should go with thirty-six picked men

[14] Castañeda's statements from time to time seem to foot up 23 days from Cicuye, exclusive of the 4 d. detention in bridge-building and others, 16 d. at least being N. N. E.; then in summarizing he says they had marched 37 d. at the rate of 6 or 7 l. per day, or a total of 250 l. from Tiguex. The *Rel. del Suceso*, on the contrary, gives the march as 150 l. E. and then 50 l. s. Jaramillo agrees with Castañeda that the route was N. N. E. for about 10 d. from the crossing of the Cicuye to the country of the Querechos; but he says that for 20 d. or more from that point they turned east, or at least more toward the east. Coronado in his letter says the march was 9 d. to the great plains (from Tiguex), then 17 d. to the Querechos, and 5 d. to the Teyas without any definite indication of the direction.

in search of Quivira, while the main army under
Arellano should return to Tiguex. The chief reason
for this decision was the lack of other food than buffalo meat; but Coronado states also that the guides
had already confessed that they had deceived him
respecting the buildings of Quivira, which were really
of straw.[15] Arellano's force, after remaining fifteen
days to hunt buffalo, returned in twenty-five days by
a shorter and more southern route—in itself a proof
that they had gone far to the east rather than the
north—to Tiguex. On the way they passed many salt-
marshes, noticed multitudes of prairie-dogs, reached
the Rio Cicuye, or Pecos, thirty leagues below the
former crossing, following it up to the pueblo, and
learning that that river flowed into the Tiguex, or
Rio Grande, some twenty days' journey below. The
arrival at Tiguex was before the end of July.[16]

After leaving the main army Coronado went northward for about forty days over the plains till he
reached Quivira late in July, remained there twenty-
five days, and arrived at Tiguex on his return in
August or September.[17] Quivira proved to be one of
several Indian villages of straw huts, or wigwams, on
or near a large river. The inhabitants resembled the
roving Querechos and Teyas in most respects, but
were somewhat superior, raising a small quantity of
maize. The country was an excellent one in respect

[15] *Pacheco, Doc.*, iii. 365.

[16] On this return an Ind. woman, slave of Zaldívar, escaped, and afterward
within 9 days she fell into the hands of Spaniards in Florida, who, however,
claimed to have been at the time over 200 l. in the interior. So Castañeda,
135, heard from these Span. in Mexico.

[17] Coronado, in his letter of Oct. 20th, says he travelled 42 d., making 67
in all from Tiguex (apparently 73 by computation), or over 300 l., to Quivira
950 l. from Mex., and in 40°. Castañeda, who was not with the general, says
the journey out was 48 days, and the return 40 d.; and that all was over
the plains, though at Quivira some mts began to be in sight. The author of the
Rel. del Suceso, who accompanied the party, says they travelled 30 d. N. to the
Rio de Quivira, and 30 l. more to the settlements, 330 l. out (from Tiguex),
and 200 back; also putting Q. in 40°. Jaramillo, also with Coronado, says
about 30 d. N. (short days and irregular acc. to the water); named the Rio
de S. Pedro y S. Pablo for the day of arrival (June 29th); then to R. Quivira
(possibly the same, as the text is not clear), and down that river N. E., 7 or 8
d. to Q., where they were after the middle of Aug. (?). A cross was set up
bearing the general's name at Q.

of soil, climate, and natural productions; but the people had no knowledge of the precious metals; and even in their reports of large tribes beyond, there was but slight indication of either wealth or civilization. Moreover, El Turco now confessed that all his tales had been lies; but he claimed to have told them at the instigation of the people of Cicuye that the Spaniards might be led far out into the plains, to perish or to be so reduced in strength that on their return they might be easily vanquished. Having put the Turk to death, the general returned by a more direct route to Cicuye, where Arellano came to meet him, and thence to Tiguex.

Coronado and his associates believed Quivira to be in latitude 40°, and about 200 leagues north-east of Tiguex. There is nothing in the Spaniards' descriptions of the region, or of the journey, to shake confidence in Simpson's conclusion that it was in the modern Kansas, between the Arkansas and Missouri rivers; yet on the other hand, it is quite possible that, as Bandelier is inclined to think, Coronado travelled more in a circle, and did not go so far to the north; and elsewhere in recording Texan annals of the next century, I have said that "it is to the east and southeast of Santa Fé, to the Indian Territory and Texas of modern maps, that we must look for the scene of Spanish explorations in this century, and that there is no need of placing Quivira in the far north-east or beyond the Missouri, as many writers are fond of doing."[18] It is not, however, of much importance in connection with the history of New Mexico to fix definitely the location of this wigwam province, even if it were possible. Several writers, misled by the name—including rather strangely Davis, who was

[18] *Hist. North Mex. St.*, i. 391, and preceding pages. In the earliest editions of the *Native Races*, iv. 672, I carelessly said, 'Quivira, if not one of the Pueblo towns of the Rio Grande, was at least not more distant than the region of the S. Juan or its tributaries,' having then in mind the popular idea of Q. as a great town, and not the statements of the original records. In later issues the statement has been changed.

well acquainted with the geography of the country—have fallen into the blunder of identifying Quivira with the ruins of Gran Quivira of mixed Spanish and native origin at a much later date, and situated only two or three days' journey south of east from Tiguex.[19]

Meanwhile Captain Arellano made preparations for passing a second winter at Tiguex, meeting with many difficulties on account of the continued hostility of the people, who still refused to occupy their towns. Arellano also caused some further explorations to be made. Captain Barrio-nuevo was sent up the valley northward. First he visited the province of Hemes, or Jemes, with seven towns, one of which in the same region still retains the name.[20] The inhabitants of this province submitted, and furnished supplies; but not so those of another province of Yuque-Yunque, who abandoned their two fine towns on the river and fled to the mountains, where they had four others strongly fortified in places difficult of access;[21] yet a store of food was left in the deserted villages, with fine earthen-ware, and glazing that indicated the probable existence of silver mines. Twenty leagues farther up the river this party came to a large town built on both banks of the stream, with wooden bridges connecting the two parts, and with the largest *estufas* yet seen. Its name was Braba; the Spaniards called it

[19] Prince, 138–40, does not follow Davis in this instance, believing that the army reached the cañons of the Canadian branches, and that Coronado reached Kansas.

[20] Castañeda, 138, says that B. went up the river northward and visited Hemes; but on p. 168 he says that Hemes was 7 l. N. E. of Tiguex (or perhaps from Quirix). This is the chief support of those who put Tiguex on the Puerco, but I have no doubt it is an error for N. W. According to Bandelier, 23, 109–10, the Pecos language was spoken at Jemes, and the original pueblo was at the S. Diego ruins, 13 miles N. of the present site. This author also includes in this Jemes group the prov. of Aguas Calientes, with 3 pueblos mentioned but not located by Castañeda, 182. I know of no special reason for or against this latter identification, except that Ojos Calientes, or Aguas Cal., is applied on some modern maps to ruins N. of Jemes.

[21] Yuque-Yunque is identified by Bandelier, 18, 23–4, with the Tehua group N. of Sta Fé, including S. Ildefonso, S. Juan, Sta Clara, Pujuaque, Nambé, and Tesuque. In strong confirmation of this, I note that S. Juan, or S. Gabriel, the capital of N. Mex. in the early years of the 17th century, is called in *Escalante, Carta*, 116, S. Gabriel del Yunque. The later Cuyamunque may also have some connection with this name.

Valladolid; and its identity with Taos can hardly be questioned.[22] Leaving the northern country in peace, Barrio-nuevo returned down the valley to Tiguex. Another officer was despatched down the river to explore its lower branches, as mentioned by the people of Tutahaco. He advanced eighty leagues southward, to a place where the river disappeared underground, to appear again below, as the natives said, larger than ever.[23] Somewhere on the way, but not necessarily at the southern limit of the exploration, they found four large villages, whose people offered no resistance. These were the southernmost pueblos, and may be identified with those of the Piros in the Socorro region, abandoned during the wars of the next century.[24] This concludes the list of the New Mexican pueblos visited by Coronado or his officers, most of which, as we have seen, can be identified, in groups at least, with reasonable accuracy. It is noticeable, however, that the group between Zuñi and Tiguex, represented by Laguna, Cebolleta, Moquino, and Pujuaque, is not mentioned,[25] and as a matter of fact, these pueblos did not exist till much later.

After these explorations had been accomplished,

[22] Braba is written also Yuraba. Castañeda, 139, says that Alvarado had visited this town on his 1st trip to Cicuye, which hardly seems probable. On p. 182 he says Braba was the last province toward the N. E., up the valley, and had but one town. In the *Rel. del Suceso*, Yuraba is mentioned as the northern limit of exploration, the largest pueblo in the country, with some 15,000 inhab., and differing somewhat from the others in its construction. The distance of 20 l. from the Tehua towns is sufficiently accurate. Castañeda, 168, mentions a province of Acha, 40 l. N. E. of Tiguex; but in his summary, 182, this prov. is not named. This leaves us to suppose either that Acha and Braba were the same, or to follow Bandelier, 23, in identifying Acha with Picuríes. B. also notes, 109–10, 120, that from Taos in the N. to Isleta in the south, including Picuríes, S. Cristóbal, Sandía, and Galisteo, the same language was spoken, that of the Tanos.

[23] The distance would carry the party nearly down to lat. 33°, and below the limit of the pueblo-town region. Of course this distance would be absurd if applied to the Puerco. The sinking of the river has not been very satisfactorily explained, except as nearly all streams in this region are swallowed up in the sand at certain dry seasons. See *Simpson's Coronado's March*, 323, with quot. from Gallatin and Humboldt on this subject.

[24] Bandelier, 24, who notes that Senecú, farther s., was a Piros pueblo founded under Span. auspices in 1630.

[25] In his summary, Castañeda, 179–82, mentions 6 pueblos in the snowy mountains; but the reference would seem to be to the Cicuye, or Pecos, region.

Captain Arellano set out with forty horsemen to meet the general on his return from Quivira, having a fight with the natives of Cicuye, where Coronado soon joined him. The report from Quivira was a bitter disappointment. For some unexplained reason, the guide Xabe had remained with the army, and he maintained to the last the truth of what had been said of gold and silver in his country, rejoicing at the approach of Coronado to confirm his statements, and correspondingly disappointed at the actual result. His words and manner had great influence on the army, which had unwillingly parted from the general in the east. Many of the officers and soldiers did not believe that he had made so long a march, or so thorough a search as he pretended; even the commander and his companions evidently still retained some hope of eventual success in the north-east; and these circumstances partially account for the grand rôle subsequently played by Quivira in the imagination of explorers, writers, and map-makers. The plan was to undertake a new expedition out into the plains in the spring of 1542, as the rainy season had already begun. Just as the army was going into winter quarters at Tiguex, Captain Tobar returned from Sonora with half the force that had been stationed at San Gerónimo. By this party Captain Cárdenas, who had broken an arm, received news that called him to Spain, and soon started with a few others, carrying Coronado's letter of October 20th to the king.

The winter was for the most part an uneventful one; but there was considerable suffering, especially for want of clothing, as the natives were still hostile and refused to reoccupy their towns or to furnish supplies. Therefore the soldiers became discontented, and there was much disagreement between the general, officers, and gentlemen about the distribution of such food and clothing as remained. At the approach of spring, when preparations for a new expedition had been far advanced, Coronado, while engaged in a tournament

on a day of festival, was thrown by the breaking of a
girth, and received from Maldonado's horse a kick on
the head.   He was seriously injured and long confined
to his bed.   After partial recovery he had a dangerous
relapse, caused by the return of Cárdenas with news
that the Sonora colonists had been massacred by
Indians.   Superstition also had its influence on his
weakened mind; for a necromancer in Spain had long
ago predicted for him a brilliant career in a distant
land, to be terminated by a fall that would cause his
death.   The prevailing discontent among officers and
men tended greatly to increase the leader's despon-
dency and his desire to return that he might die near
his wife and children.[26]   The soldiers at last presented,
or were induced to present, a petition for return; it
was decided in a council of officers to grant the petition, abandoning further attemps at conquest; and
the corresponding orders were issued; some of the
gentlemen officers opposed this resolution, and others
soon repented of their vote; but apparently a majority,
including the general, though willing to shirk responsibility, were not really desirous of remaining; and
notwithstanding the alleged protests of many, and
their demands to be allowed to continue the enterprise
with a part of the army, Coronado refused to modify
his plans, and even remained in his tent, pretending
to be in worse health than he really was, in order to
escape the importunities of his associates.

Fray Juan de Padilla and Padre Luis, a lay brother,
resolved to remain in the country and make an attempt
to convert the natives of Cicuye and Quivira.   An
escort was furnished as far as Cicuye, where Padre
Luis remained; while Fray Juan, accompanied by a
Portuguese named Campo, a negro, a mestizo, and a
few Mexican Indians, pressed on to Quivira.   Subsequently some sheep were sent to Brother Luis, and
the messengers reported him as saying that he had

---

[26] He had shortly before married a daughter of the treasurer, Alonso de
Estrada.   Mendoza's letter of '37 in *Florida, Col. Doc.*, i. 128-9; *Bernal Diaz,
Hist. Conq. Mex.*, 235.

been well received by the masses, though the old men
hated him, and would probably bring about his death.
After the departure of the army nothing was ever
known respecting the fate of this pioneer missionary
of Pecos. But the Portuguese, with some of his
companions, is said to have found his way later by the
gulf coast to Mexico, bringing the report that Padilla
had received the crown of martyrdom at the hands of
the Quivirans, who killed him because he insisted on
going to attempt the conversion of a hostile tribe.
This is substantially the version of Castañeda; but
there are several others; and respecting the number,
names, and nationality of the padres and their attendants, the place and manner of their death, or the circumstances of their escape, hardly two writers agree.
This shows that little was really known on the subject.[27]

[27] Jaramillo, 316–17, says that he left with P. Luis de Escalona a slave boy
named Cristóbal; also that several Indians, one of them a Tarascan named
Andrés, and two negroes, one named Sebastian belonging to J. and another
the slave of Melchor Perez, remained behind; also that P. Padilla took to
Quivira a Portuguese, a negro who was a kind of subordinate friar, a mestizo,
and 2 Ind. of Zapotlan, all dressed as friars, taking also sheep, mules, and a
horse.   After Padilla was killed, the Portuguese and Sebastian the Indian (?)
escaped to Pánuco.   J. suggests that Sebastian might give useful information
about the route to Q. from the east.   Torquemada, *Monarq. Ind.*, iii. 610–12,
tells us that Padilla was an Andalusian who had been guardian at Tulancingo
and Zapotlan.   He was one of 5 friars who went with Coronado, another
being Fr. Juan de la Cruz, and the two remaining in the far north with Andrés
del Campo, the Portuguese, and 2 Ind. of Michoacan.   P. went with the 3 attendants in quest of new tribes to convert.   Seeing that he was to be killed
he sent the Portuguese away; and the two Ind., Lúcas and Sebastian, managed
by the aid of miracles to escape, though the latter soon died.   Fr. Juan de la
Cruz remained at Tiguex, and nothing was ever known of his fate.   Same
version in *Mendieta, Hist. Ecles.*, 742–5, and *Vetancurt, Menologio*, 121–2.
Gomara, *Hist. Ind.*, 274, calls Padilla's companion Fr. Francisco (or prob.
Franciscan), and there were 12 Michoacan Ind.   Both friars were killed.
Beaumont, *Cron. de Mich.*, iv. 378–86, represents Fr. Marcos de Niza and Fr.
Daniel as having returned with the army, leaving in the N. Fr. Juan de Pa-
dilla, Fr. Luis de Escalona, and the lay brothers Fr. Luis de Ubeda and Fr.
Juan de la Cruz, with the two Michoacan *donados*, Lúcas and Sebastian, besides some other Ind. and the Portuguese and negro (who later became a friar
in Mich.).   It is stated that Padilla and Cruz were killed, and implied that
the others were also; but the Portuguese and 2 Mich. donados crossed the
Missouri and reached Pánuco, and later Mich.   Herrera, dec. vi. lib. ix. cap.
12, seems to follow Jaramillo.   Mota Padilla, *Hist. Conq. N. Gal.*, 167–9,
gives about the same version as Beaumont, but does not name Escalona; and
he adds that Fr. Juan de la Cruz and Fr. Luis de Ubeda remained at Coquite
(Cicuye?), while Padilla went to Quivira and was killed.   Cruz was shot soon,
but Ubeda lived in a hut and did good deeds, and nothing was known of his
death.   'The first martyrs of the church in the U. S.' *De Courcey's Cath. Ch.*,
14.

The return march of Coronado's army was begun in April 1542. All natives of Tiguex and other provinces of the north who had been enslaved were now released, for fear that if they were carried to Mexico their fate would be avenged on the friars who remained; but a number of Mexican Indians, besides those who went with the missionaries to Cicuye and Quivira, remained at Cíbola, where they were found, as we shall see, many years later. Between Tiguex and Cíbola over thirty horses died, though apparently in good condition. It should be noted that from horses left in the country during this expedition may have originated the immense droves that in later times ranged the plains northward, though I have found no positive evidence of so early an origin; also that sheep were introduced by Coronado. The march from Cíbola south-eastward was uneventful. At Chichilticale, on the Gila, they met Captain Gallegos with reënforcements and supplies. The members of this party were greatly disappointed at meeting a retreating army, instead of joining the conquerors in the enjoyment of Quiviran spoils. The gentlemen officers thus reënforced renewed their efforts for a renewal of the conquest, or at least for a halt until the viceroy could be consulted; but the soldiers would listen to nothing of the kind. Gallegos' men and others were insubordinate, but Coronado-had lost all control, his authority both as general and governor being disregarded. Most of the force disbanded at Culiacan in June; and Coronado finally reached Mexico with barely 100 men. Though at first coldly received by Mendoza, he gave explanations which were satisfactory, was honorably relieved of his command, and as soon as his health was restored resumed his duties as governor of Nueva Galicia.

Thus ended the grandest exploring expedition of the period, in which the Spaniards learned in a sense all that was to be known of Arizona and New Mexico, though they did not find the wonders they had sought, and though they neither remembered nor made any use of their discoveries. The great Mixton revolt prevented any immediate resumption of northern enterprises, which, however, would very likely not have been prosecuted in any event. Castañeda, writing twenty years later, expresses the opinion that in order to find any of the great things believed to be connected in some way with the Indies, they should have directed their course to the north-west instead of the north-east; and he suggests that Quivira and the adjoining regions might be reached by a better route through the interior, or from the gulf coast, with aid of the guides who had escaped in that direction after the friar's death.

The narratives of Coronado's expedition we have found remarkably accurate in a general sense, and quite as satisfactory as any records except an original detailed diary with maps could be expected to be. The general route has been easily traced, and several principal points on the journey have been identified with reasonable accuracy. There is a notable absence of exaggeration and mystery; indeed, the country, its people and its towns, are represented as they actually existed. Yet it is no less remarkable, after making allowance for the stories scattered broadcast in Mexico and Spain by the returning soldiers of Coronado's army, how little effect this exploration had on geographical knowledge. For two centuries, though the narratives were extant and occasionally repeated with approximate accuracy, and though now and then an official report showed a fair knowledge of the facts in certain circles, no map within my knowledge—except Padre Kino's and a few others on the regions of Pimería Alta up to the Gila—throws any light on the geography of Arizona and New Mexico, or makes any considerable approach to the general cartographic results that might have been reached by a fairly intelligent use of the Coronado narratives alone.

The historian Gomara before 1554 represented Coronado as having reached the coast, where he saw ships from Cathay with decorations in gold and silver; thus laying the foundation for endless confusion.[28] Espejo, visiting New Mexico in 1582, as will be related in the next chapter, while he found traces of Coronado's visit, had no definite idea of that officer's explorations. Benavides, writing in 1630, though custodian of the Franciscans in New Mexico for years, giving a good account of the country, and even describing Coronado's journey, seems not to have had the slightest idea that New Mexico had been the region explored.[29] Mota Padilla about 1740 gravely tells us that if Coronado had gone farther north and somewhat westwardly he would probably have discovered what is now New Mexico.[30] Many more accounts might be cited of similiar nature, with others much more and much less inaccurate; and I may add that most modern writers—that is, those who allude in a general way without special investigation to this expedition—have evidently regarded it as mysterious in most of its geographic phases, and have had a vague idea that almost any place from California across to Florida may have been visited by Coronado, if indeed the exploration was not altogether mythical. I think it time that the mysterious elements of the subject should be eliminated.

And here I may suggest to the reader a perusal of the chapters devoted to the Northern Mystery, as already referred to.[31] There will be found, besides the curious complication of inaccuracies, exaggerations, and falsehoods, current for two centuries or more and resting on the expeditions of Niza and Coronado as well as on others real and fictitious, a reproduction of many old maps, which, while includ-

---

[28] *Gomara, Hist. Ind.*, 274.
[29] *Benavides, Reqveste Remonstrative*, 108-17.
[30] *Mota Padilla, Conq. N. Galicia*, 169.
[31] See *Hist. Northwest Coast.* i., chap. i.–iv., this series, especially maps on p. 49, 54, 65, 68, 82–4, 104, 108, 110, 114, 128, 131.

ing in a sense the territory now under consideration,
cannot be repeated conveniently here, except one of
1597, which explains itself. On the others will be
seen on the South Sea coast, or on tributaries of the
gulf of California, between latitudes 35° and 45° for
the most part, scattered with but slight regard to any
kind of order, the names, variously spelled, of Seven
Cities, Quivira, Sierra Nevada, Cicuic, Axa, Tiguex,
Cucho, Cíbola, Tuchano, Totonteac, Granada, Marata,
Chichuco, Rio Tizon, Laguna de Oro, New Mexico,

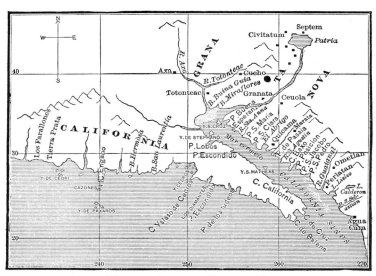

WYTFLIET-PTOLEMY MAP OF 1597.

Rio del Norte, Rio Bravo, Rio Buena Guia, Moqui,
Ameies, Zuny, and finally after 1700 Santa Fé on a
river flowing into the Mexican gulf. Of these, Quivira, Marata, New Mexico, and Granada transformed
into New Granada are made prominent often as provinces, while the province or kingdom of Tolm is added.
At last in 1752–68 the maps of De L'Isle and Jefferys,
with all their absurdities in other parts, give a tolerably accurate idea of Arizona and New Mexico in their

rivers and other general features, details being largely
and wisely omitted.

While Coronado's was the last of the grand military expeditions for half a century, and while for
much longer the far north was left almost exclusively to the theorists, yet toward the north there
was a constant progress in the interior through the
efforts of miners and missionaries in Nueva Galicia
and Nueva Vizcaya, destined in time to cross the line
of our territory.   It was forty years before the line
was again passed, unless there may have been one
exception in the expeditions of Francisco de Ibarra
in 1563–5.   From a point not very definitely fixed
in the sierra between Sinaloa and Durango, Ibarra
marched for eight days to a point from which he
saw a large town of several-storied buildings; and
later, having gone to Sinaloa, he says he " went 300
leagues from Chametla, in which entrada he found
large settlements of natives clothed and well provided
with maize and other things for their support; and
they also had many houses of several stories.   But
because it was so far from New Spain and the Spanish settlements, and because the governor had not
people enough for settlement, and the natives were
hostile, using poisoned arrows, he was obliged to return."   " Beaumont, deriving his information from unknown sources," as I have written elsewhere,[32] "adds
that Ibarra was accompanied by fifty soldiers, by
Pedro de Tobar"—of Coronado's expedition—"and
by Padre Acebedo and other friars.   His course was
to the right of that followed by Coronado and nearer
New Mexico.   He reached some great plains adjoining those of the *vacas*—the buffalo plains—and there
found an abandoned pueblo whose houses were of several stories, which was called Paguemi, and where
there were traces of metals having been smelted.   A

[32] See *Hist. North Mex. St.*, i. 105–10; also *Ibarra, Relacion*, 482–3; *Velasco,
Relacion*, 553–61; *Beaumont, Cron. Mich.*, v. 538–41.   Vargas, *N. Mex. Testim.*,
129 (about 1583), tells us that Ibarra 'revolvió sobre la parte del norte hasta
que dió en los Valles de las Vacas.'

few days later, as this wiiter seems to say, Ibarra reached the great city of Pagme, a most beautiful city adorned with very sumptuous edifices, extending over three leagues, with houses of three stories, very grand, with various and extensive plazas, and the houses surrounded with walls that appear to be of masonry." This town was also abandoned, and the people were said to have gone eastward. It is difficult to determine what reliance should be placed on Beaumont's narrative; and there appear to be no grounds for more than the vaguest conjecture as to what region was thus explored by Ibarra. He may have visited some of the abandoned pueblos of the Gila valley; or may, as Beaumont seems to think, have gone farther to the region of the Moqui towns; or perhaps he went more to the east and reached the Casas Grandes of Chihuahua.

There is nothing that can be added to throw new light on this subject, and I simply leave the record of what was possibly a new crossing of the Arizona line. It is perhaps worthy of notice, however, that in connection with Ibarra's entrada of 1563 the province of Copala is mentioned, a name that—though here applied apparently to Topia or an adjoining region in the sierra—figured later in the mythic northern geography; and especially that on his return Governor Ibarra boasted that he had discovered a 'new Mexico' as well as a new Vizcaya. It is not unlikely that from this circumstance the name New Mexico came to be applied in later years to a country that Don Francisco had probably never seen. Another noteworthy circumstance in this connection was the discovery in 1568 by a party of mining prospectors from Mazapil, in northern Zacatecas, of a lake which was formally named Laguna del Nuevo Mexico. This lake was apparently one of those in the modern Coahuila, but the tendency to find a 'new Mexico' in the north is noticeable.[33]

[33] *Testimonio del descub. y posesion de la Laguna del Nuevo Mexico, hecho por Fran. Cano, ten. de alcalde mayor de las Minas de Mascipil en la Nueva Galicia,* in *Pacheco, Doc.,* xix. 535.

CHAPTER IV.

ENTRADAS OF RODRIGUEZ AND ESPEJO.

1581–1583.

The Franciscans in Nueva Vizcaya—Fray Agustin Rodriguez—Province of San Felipe—Details of Wanderings—Chamuscado's Return—Testimony in Mexico—Bibliography of the Entrada—The Friars Killed—Antonio Espejo and Fray Bernardino Beltran—Up the Rio del Norte—The Jumanas—Traces of Cabeza de Vaca—The Pueblos—News of Coronado—Map—To Acoma and Zuñi—Moqui Towns—Silver Mines—Return of Beltran and Part of the Company—Espejo Visits the Quires, Ubates, and Tanos—Pecos or Cicuique—A Hostile Province—Down the Rio de Vacas and Home—The Name New Mexico.

Forty years had passed away, and in that time the achievements of Fray Marcos and Francisco Vasquez had been wellnigh forgotten, or at least had taken the form of vague and semi-mythic traditions, so mingled with baseless geographic conjectures as to retain but the frailest foundation of historic fact. But in those years Spanish occupation had gradually extended over a broad field northward from Nueva Galicia to the latitude of southern Chihuahua. Here, in the region corresponding to the later Allende and Jimenez, known then by the various names of San Bartolomé, Santa Bárbara, Santa Bárbola, and San Gregorio, rich mines had been discovered, a flourishing settlement had sprung into existence, the Franciscan friars were striving with their accustomed zeal, and a small military force was maintained for the protection of miners, missionaries, and a few settlers from the ever-impending raids of savage tribes of the north and east.[1]

[1] For the annals of this region in the 16th and 17th centuries, see *Hist. North Mex. States.*

One of the missionary band stationed at this frontier outpost of the San Bartolomé valley was Fray
Agustin Rodriguez.[2] In the wanderings to which
he was called by duty and by his ardent desire for
martyrdom, the good friar came in contact with the
Conchos, who lived on the river so called, and from
them he heard rumors of a superior people dressed in
cotton, whose home was in the north. Padre Agustin chanced to have read Cabeza de Vaca's narrative,
and this gave the new reports additional interest in
his eyes, though he appears to have known nothing of
Coronado's entrada. If, while winning his coveted
crown of martyrdom, he could also achieve the glory
of a new conquista espiritual, so much the better for
himself and his order. Therefore, in November 1580,
he applied to Viceroy Coruña for a license to undertake the enterprise, apparently visiting Mexico for
that purpose. The king had forbidden new entradas
except with royal license; yet the viceroy took the
liberty of authorizing the organization of a volunteer
escort not exceeding twenty men, who might also
carry along some articles for barter; the padre provincial gave the required permission; and the friar returned to San Bartolomé to fit out his party.

Two other Franciscans, padres Juan de Santa María
and Francisco Lopez, were assigned by the provincial
to the new field; eight or nine soldiers of the twenty
allowed were induced, in the hope of finding mines, to
volunteer their services, one of the number, Francisco
Sanchez Chamuscado, being made their leader;[3] and
from eight to fifteen Indian servants, besides a mestizo named Juan Bautista, were engaged for the trip.

[2] In the narrative attached to Espejo's relation, more widely circulated
than any other, he is called Agustin Ruiz, and by this name he is known to
modern writers; but the original records to be cited presently leave no doubt
on the matter; and he is also called Rodriguez by Torquemada, Arlegui, Mota
Padilla, Aparicio, and others. Vargas, in *Pacheco, Doc.*, xv. 131, calls him
Ayamonte.

[3] Their names were Pedro Bustamante, Hernan Gallegos, Felipe Escalante,
Hernando Barrundo, and (according to Villagrá) Pedro Sanchez de Chavez,
Juan Sanchez, Herrera, and Fuensalida. There were perhaps 8 men besides
the leader.

This party, some twenty strong, set out from San
Bartolomé on the 6th of June, 1581, and followed the
Rio Concha, or Conchos, down to its junction with a
very large river which they named the Guadalquivir,
really the Rio Grande, or Bravo del Norte.   Up this

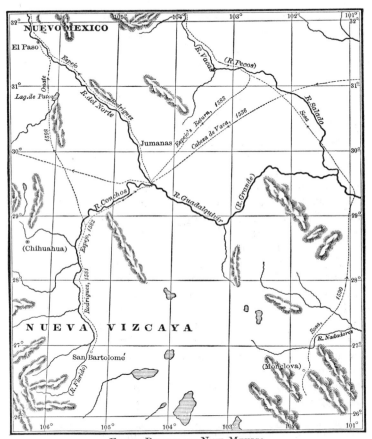

EARLY ROUTES TO NEW MEXICO.

river they marched for 20 days, or 80 leagues, as they
overestimated the distance, to the first group of pueblos, to which province, or rather to the whole region
of the pueblos, they gave the name of San Felipe,

arriving in August.[4] This first group was in the Socorro region, being the same visited by Coronado's officers. From this point they continued their journey up the valley, and visited most of the groups on the main river and its branches. I append an outline of their movements,[5] from which it will be apparent that the towns visited cannot be accurately identified from the meagre details of the testimony, the good faith of which, however, there is no reason to question. A pueblo of Puaray was made the centre of operations, and from later records it is reasonably clear that this place was in the Tigua province, or Coronado's Tiguex. Here the friars remained while the soldiers made all or part of their exploring trips; and here they were finally left with their Indian attendants and the mestizo, by Chamuscado and his men, who set out on their return in December or

[4] Barrundo and Escalante in their *Relacíon* state that from S. Bartolomé they travelled 31 days among tribes of wild Ind., then 19 days through a desert, uninhabited country, and on Aug. 15th found an Ind. who told of a maize-producing people ahead, the pueblos being reached on Aug. 21st; but there is some confusion, as 31 and 19 d. from June 6th would not be Aug. 15th.

[5] The statement of B. and E. as cited in note 4 is that the 1st pueblo had 45 houses, and half a league farther were found 5 more towns; and in all the province for a space of 50 l. there were 61 towns with a pop. of over 130,000. The following is the narrative of Bustamante and Gallegos: Heard of many pueblos on both sides of the river; went on up the river, visiting many and seeing more; reached a province of different language and dress; and still another with better houses, a good descrip. of the towns being given. (This may be supposed to have been the Tigua prov., or Coronado's Tiguex.) Then they left the river, but still went N. one day to a large pueblo of 400 or 500 houses of 4 or 5 stories, which they called Tlascala (possibly Cia); and heard of a large settlement 10 d. farther N.; but turned back, and from one of the pueblos previously visited and named Castildavid crossed the river to the S. (?), and by a small branch river went to 3 fine pueblos, where they heard of 11 more of a different nation farther up not visited, this valley (not clear if it was the one with 3 or that with 11) being named Valleviciosa. Then they went 30 l. in dif. directions in quest of buffalo, finding many, especially at certain springs and plains which they called Llanos de S. Francisco y Aguas Zarcas; saw also a ranchería of wild Ind. with dogs carrying burdens. Thence they returned to the pueblo (one of the 3), and from that point went down the river to a pueblo called Puaray, or Puara (near Tiguex). Here they heard of a valley of Camé in the s., which they visited, finding 6 pueblos of a dif. nation, hearing also of a valley of Asay, or Osay, with 5 pueblos and much cotton, but the snow prevented their going farther. Back at Puaray they went 14 l. across the Sierra Morena to visit some fine salinas, where they obtained specimens of salt for Mexico, and where they saw and heard of other towns. Returning again to Puaray, where the friars had remained, Chamuscado and his soldiers started back for S. Bartolomé.

January. The natives had been everywhere friendly, and no trouble was anticipated; or at least there is no evidence that the missionaries objected to the departure of the escort.

On his return to San Bartolomé, Chamuscado and some of his men started for Mexico to report, particularly on some mining prospects they had found in the far north; but the leader died on the way. In May 1582 the testimony of two of the men was taken before the viceroy, and this, as supplemented by other evidence a little later, constitutes our best authority on the expedition of Padre Rodriguez.[6] This supplementary investigation was occasioned by rumors that the friars left in the north had been killed; and Barrundo, one of Chamuscado's men, testified that among the southern Indians who had voluntarily remained at Puaray were three named Andrés, Francisco, and Gerónimo, the latter a servant of the witness. Francisco had made his appearance at San Bartolomé, and had stated that Padre Lopez, the guardian or chief of the friars, had been killed by the natives of Puaray, whereupon the three Indians had taken flight, believ-

---

[6] (*Nuevo Mexico*), *Testimonio dado en Méjico sobre el Descubrimiento de doscientas leguas adelante de las minas de Santa Bárbola, gobernacion de Diego de Ibarra; cuyo descubrimiento se hizo en virtud de cierta licencia que pidió Fr. Agustin Rodriguez y otros religiosos Franciscanos. Acompañan relaciones de este descubrimiento y otros documentos. Años 1582–3.* In *Pacheco, Doc.*, xv. 80–150. First we have the testimony of Bustamante and Gallegos, given May 16th, the day after their arrival, pp. 80–95; 2d, testimony of Hern. Barrundo, taken Oct. 20th, pp. 95–7; 3d, report of the viceroy to king, Nov. 1st, with other corresp. of later date, pp. 97–101; 4th, *Espejo, Relacion*, as noted elsewhere, including a brief preliminary account of Rodriguez' trip, pp. 101–26; 5th, an undated résumé of the N. Mex. expeditions, including those of Rodriguez and Espejo, by Francisco Diaz de Vargas, pp. 126–37; 6th, views of Rodrigo Rio de Losa on the preparations necessary for a new entrada, resulting in that of Espejo, pp. 137–46; 7th (*Escalante* and *Barrundo*), *Relacion Breve y verdadera del descubrimiento del Nuevo Mexico*, a statement by two of Chamuscado's men, made after the return of part of Espejo's force, pp. 146–50. (Also given in *Cartas de Indias*, 230–3.) A repetition of Espejo's relation follows in another expediente. For other authorities, see the following note.

All the witnesses speak of the discovery of mines, and E. and B., *Rel.*, 149, give the following details: ' Así mismo descubrimos en la dicha tierra once descubrimientos de minas con vetas muy poderosas, todas ellas de metales de plata, que de los tres déllos se truxo el metal á esta ciudad, y se dió a Su Excelencia; él lo mandó ensayar al ensayador de la casa de la moneda, el cual los ensayó y les halló, al un metal déllos á la mitad de plata; al otro halló á veinte marcos por quintal, y al otro cinco marcos.'

ing from the tumult they heard that Rodriguez and Santa María were also killed. Andrés was killed on the return, but Gerónimo was found in the Zacatecas mines, and confirmed what Francisco had said, coming to Mexico with the witness, but subsequently disappearing. This may be regarded as practically all that was ever known respecting the circumstances of the friars' death. It would appear, however, that Santa María was the first to die instead of Lopez, and that he was killed at some distance from Puaray, where the others met their fate. Some variations of the story, possibly resting to a slight extent on additional information, are appended.[7]

[7] Espejo, *Rel.*, 164, 175-7 (112-15), represents Sta María as the first victim at a distance from Puaray, and even states that he was killed before Chamuscado's departure; but this last would seem unlikely, since it would involve the witnesses in direct falsehood. E. may have confounded C.'s return with that of the 3 Indians a little later. In *Hakluyt's Voy.*, iii. 383, 389-90, is given a version of Rodriguez' (called Ruiz, as already noted) expedition with that of Espejo, in Span. and Engl., taken from Gonzalez de Mendoza's *Hist. China*, ed. of Madrid, 1586, which I have not seen. Laet, *Novus Orbis*, 300, took the account from the ed. of 1589. I have the Ital. ed. of '86 and the Span. of '96, neither of which contains this matter. Neither does Brunet or any other bibliographer that I have consulted note any such difference in editions; though of course I do not doubt that such a curious difference exists. This version is the one followed by most modern writers, as *Whipple*, in *Pac. R. R. Repts*, iii. 113-15. It is given substantially in *Montanus, N. Weereld*, 215-16; and *Dapper, N. Welt*, 242-3; *Ogilby's Amer.*, 292-5; *Holmes' Annals of Amer.*, i. 95.

P. Zárate de Salmeron, *Relaciones*, 9-10, and P. Niel, *Apunt.*, 87-8, followed by Davis, *Span. Conq.*, 234-9, Prince, *Hist. Sk.*, 149-52, and others, tell us that at Puara (located by Davis 8 miles above Alburquerque) the soldiers refused to go on, and in spite of the friars' persuasions abandoned them and returned to the south. The padres went on to Galisteo, of the Tanos nation, where P. Sta María volunteered to go on to Mexico for a missionary reënforcement, while the others returned to Puara. Sta María crossed the Sandía Mts, and on the 3d day at S. Pablo (S. Pedro acc. to Niel, perhaps S. Pedro y S. Pablo), of the Teguas (Tiguas) nation, when he stopped to rest under a tree, the natives killed him and burned his remains. After a season of spiritual prosperity at Puara, P. Lopez, while engaged in his devotions about a league from the pueblo, was killed by an Ind., and his body was brought for burial to the town. P. Ruiz (Rodriguez) was now alone, but even the protection of the Tigua chief, who removed him to Santiago a league and a half up the river, could not save his life; and his dead body was soon thrown into the river. The remains of Lopez were disinterred in 1614, and reburied in the church at Sandía. Of course the statements of Salmeron and Niel command respect, even though the source of their information is not definitely known. Davis seems to have translated Salmeron's text—which on p. 278 he says he was unable to find—without knowing it, having probably seen a MS. copy which he may have mistaken for an original doc. in the archives.

Torquemada's version, *Monarq. Ind.*, iii. 459, 626-8, is similar to that just

It seemed to the viceroy and his advisers in Mexico altogether proper and even necessary that something should be done, not only to ascertain the fate of the two friars, and succor them if still alive, but to investigate the truth of Chamuscado's reports respecting silver mines, and the general desirability of the northern province for Spanish occupation. But long before the red-tape processes in vogue at the capital could be concluded, the expediente completed, the king consulted, and any practical result reached, a new expedition was planned and carried out independently of the national authorities.

The Franciscans of Nueva Vizcaya were naturally much troubled about the fate of Padre Rodriguez and his companion, after the return of their native attendants with reports that one of the three friars had been killed; and Padre Bernardino Beltran was eager to represent his order in a new entrada. Don Antonio Espejo, a rich citizen of Mexico who chanced to be sojourning temporarily at the Santa Bárbara mines, and who had a taste for adventure, was willing to pay the expenses of the expedition, and serve as commander. There was no time to consult the viceroy, but the alcalde mayor of Cuatro Ciénegas took it upon

noticed. He gives some biographic matter about the three martyrs. Rodriguez was a lay friar, a native of Niebla in Spain, who had penetrated some distance northward before he went to Mex. to get a license for the expedition. Lopez was an Andalusian, and superior of the band. Sta María was a Catalan, versed in astrology, which peculiarity led him to try a new route of return. The friars went on 150 l. after the soldiers left them, to N. Mex.—so named by this party. His meaning is perhaps that the escort turned back somewhere in the El Paso region, and did not reach the pueblos. This author is followed literally or in substance by Vetancur, *Cron.*, 95; *Id., Menologio*, 57–8, 130; Mendieta, *Hist. Ecles.*, 732–5; and Fernandez, *Hist. Ecles.*, 57–8. Arlegui, *Chron. de Zac.*, 227–32, gives a similar version, but tells us that the soldiers turned back at S. Bartolomé, and the friars kept on to a spring called Sta María de las Canetas (in northern Chihuahua), where two were killed, after the other had started to return, by a tribe hostile to the one with whom they worked. Aparicio, *Conventos*, 281, makes the date 1551, and the distance to the Tiguas 400 l. Mota Padilla, *Conq. N. Gal.*, 167–9, tells us they went beyond the Tiguas and were killed in the prov. of Marata! Alegre, *Hist. Comp. Jesus*, i. 326–7, seems to have no idea that they went so far north as N. Mex. Alcedo, *Dicc.*, iii. 183–4, implies that Ruiz accompanied Espejo. Villagrá, *Hist. N. Mex.*, 35, gives a poetical version, and, as we have seen, names the members of Chamuscado's party. See also *Calle, Noticias*, 101–2; *Salazar, Monarquía de España*, ii. 258–9; *Frejes, Hist. Breve*, 145; *Pino, N. Mex.*, 5; *St Francis' Life*, 575.

himself to issue the needed license and commission; fourteen soldiers volunteered for the service;[8] a number of native servants were obtained; Espejo fitted out the party with the necessary arms and supplies, including 115 horses and mules; and the start was made from San Bartolomé on the 10th of November, 1582. The route as before was down the Rio Conchos to the junction of the Bravo, a distance of 59 leagues, accomplished in fifteen days, as is somewhat vaguely indicated in the narrative.[9] On the way Espejo found

[8] The soldiers were Juan Lopez de Ibarra, Diego Perez de Lujan, Gaspar de Lujan, Cristóbal Sanchez, Gregorio Hernandez, Juan Hernandez, Miguel Sanchez Valenciano, with wife and two sons, Lázaro Sanchez and Miguel Sanchez Nevado, Pedro Hernandez de Almansa, Francisco Barreto (Barrero or Barroto), Bernardo de Luna (or Cuna), Juan de Frias, and Alonso Miranda. The *Hakluyt* version does not give the force. Aparicio says there were 100 horsemen. Vargas, 131–2, says there were 17 men and a woman; and he names the padre Pedro de Heredia. Espejo, himself, in one letter, *Expediente*, 151, says he had 15 men. Arlegui and Mota Padilla tell us there were two friars, the latter naming the 2d Juan de la Cruz.

[9] *Espejo, Relacion del Viage que yo Antonio Espejo, ciudadano de la ciudad de México, natural de la ciudad de Córdoba, hize con catorce soldados y un religioso de la orden de San Francisco, á las provincias y poblaciones de la Nueva Andalucía, á quien puse por nombre la Nueva Andalucía, á contemplacion de mi patria, en fin del año 1582*, in *N. Mex. Testim.*, 101–26; repeated with a few verbal variations on pp. 163 et seq. of the same vol. *Pacheco, Doc.*, xv. This is of course the best authority for the expedition, being written at S. Bartolomé in Oct. 1583, just after the author's return. There are also some items of information in Espejo's letters and other doc., in the *N. Mex. Testim.*, and *Espejo, Expediente*, in the same vol.

The best known authority, and indeed in substance the only one consulted by modern writers, is that in *Hakluyt's Voy.*, iii. 383–96, in Spanish and English, under the following title: *El Viaie que hizo Antonio de Espeio en el anno de ochenta y tres; el qual con sus companneros desubrieron vna tierra en que hallaron quinze Prouincias todas llenas de pueblos, y de casas de quatro y cinco altos, á quien pusieron por nombre El nueuo Mexico, por parecerse en muchas cosas al viejo*, etc., taken from Gonzalez Mendoza's *Hist. China*, as mentioned in note 7 of this chap. This narrative, written in the third person, is in parts identical with the *Relacion*, but in other parts differs widely; and it does not appear on what the variations rest. The original *Relacion* clears up some of the difficulties found in connection with the *Viaje*, but also creates some new ones. I shall follow the former, but indicate the principal variations in my notes.

Salmeron, *Relaciones*, 11, Niel, *Apuntaciones*, 88, and Villagrá, *Hist. N. Mex.*, 35, barely mention Espejo's entrada; Davis, *Span. Conq.*, 240–61, follows mainly Hakluyt's translation, introducing a few verbal and other changes from a source not mentioned, some of them being evidently errors; and nothing is added to the Hakluyt version by any of the following: *Torquemada, Monarq. Ind.*, iii. 359; *Mendieta, Hist. Ecles.*, 400–1; *Descrip. de America*, 113–16; *Morelli, Fast. Nov. Orbis*, 28; *Purchas his Pilgrimes*, iv. 1561–2; *Alegre, Hist. Comp. J.*, i. 327; *Calle, Noticias*, 102; *Aparicio, Conventos*, 281–2; *Mota Padilla, Conq. N. Gal.*, 167–9; *Laet, Nov. Orbis*, 309–14; *Montanus, N. Weereld*, 243–6; *Gottfriedt, N. Welt*, 561–5; *Otermin*, in *N. Mex. Doc.*, ii. 1135–43; *Prince's Hist. Sk.*, 153–60; *Whipple*, in *Pac. R. R. Repts*, iii. 113–15; *Brackenridge's Early Discov.*, 17–21; *Ariz. Hist.* (Elliott), 43; *Hinton's Handbook*, 387–8.

silver prospects, and passed through the country of
the Conchos, Pazaguates, and Tobosos successively,
all being friendly, though the Tobosos—in later years
rivalling the Apaches in their savage raids—at first
fled, because, as they said, they had formerly been ill
treated by a party of Spaniards.

About the junction of the rivers, and extending
twelve days' journey up the Rio Grande, were the
Jumanas—the name being written also Jumanos and
Humanos—or Patarabueyes, who like the Tobosos
were hostile at first, attacking the camp at night, killing a few horses, and fleeing to the mountains; but
like the rest they finally listened to explanations, gave
and took gifts, furnished guides and escorts, and became altogether friendly. These Jumanas in several
respects were superior to the southern tribes, and
especially in their buildings, many of which were flat-
roofed, and probably built of stone or adobes,[10] being
doubtless Cabeza de Vaca's "fixed dwellings of civilization;" for indeed, these natives had a smattering of
christianity, obtained, as they explained, from "three
christians and a negro" who had passed that way in
former years.[11]

From the Jumana province, which must have terminated I think some distance below the modern
boundary of New Mexico, the Spaniards went on up
the river, but nothing definite is recorded of time or
distance. Two populous provinces of inferior but
friendly natives were traversed, eight days' journey
apart, about which little could be learned for want of
an interpreter, not even the names of these nations. In
the first the people had some cotton cloth and feather-
work, which they were understood to have obtained
by bartering buffalo and deer skins with a western

---

[10] 'Casas de Azotea, bajas y con buena traza de pueblos.' The Hakluyt version has it de calicanto, that is, of masonry, but this is not in the original.
Many of the dwellings, however, were mere straw huts. There were 5
towns and 10,000 inhabitants.

[11] See p. 18 of this vol. This is almost positive proof that Cabeza de Vaca
did not enter N. Mex.

people; and they also on being shown samples of silver indicated that plenty of that metal could be found five days westward. In the second province, where the rancherías were near lagoons on both sides of the Rio del Norte—so called here probably for the first time— was found a Concho who told of a large lake fifteen days westward, on the borders of which were many towns of houses several stories high.[12] He offered to guide the Spaniards thither, but their duty called them to the north.

Still up the valley of the Rio Grande, through forests of mezquite, pine, cottonwood, and other trees, journeyed Espejo's company for fifteen days, or 80 leagues, without meeting any inhabitants; and then, twelve leagues beyond a ranchería of straw huts, they reached the first group, or province, of the pueblos, where the houses were from two to four stories high, and where ten towns were visited on both banks of the river in two days' journey, and apparently others were seen in the distance, all containing a population of some 12,000 friendly natives, whose manners and customs are described with tolerable accuracy. This southernmost group must be identified with those visited by Coronado and Rodriguez, beginning apparently in the region of latitude 34°, and certainly between Fra Cristóbal and the mouth of the Puerco.[13]

Half a league beyond the limits of this first district they entered another, that of the Tiguas, or Coronado's Tiguex, and soon came to the pueblo of Puara— also written Puala, Pualas, and Poala—near the site of the modern Bernalillo, as we have seen, and one of 16 towns constituting the province. It was at Puara, as

[12] It is idle to speculate on the possible meaning of these reports. There was no such lake with its towns, unless possibly the reference was to Laguna and its adjoining group in the N. W.—which group almost certainly was not in existence at that time.

[13] Davis and Prince think it was in the region of Isleta; and indeed, the two days' journey from Socorro might well include Isleta, or Coronado's Tutahaco. In the N. Mex., Traslado de Pos, 116, the southernmost pueblo is named Trenaquil. The 4 days spent in this prov. may or may not have included the two days mentioned as the extent of the prov.

was now definitely ascertained, that padres Rodriguez
and Lopez with their attendants had been killed;[14] and
the natives, fearing that vengeance was Espejo's object,
fled to the mountains, and nothing could induce them to
return; but fortunately they left in the towns—or possibly the town, for it is not quite clear that any but
Puara was abandoned—a plentiful store of food.[15] Not
only was information here obtained about the friars,
but, writes Espejo, "we found very truthful statements
that Francisco Vasquez Coronado was in this province,
and that they killed here nine of his soldiers and forty
horses, and that for that reason he had destroyed a
pueblo of the province; and of this the natives of these
pueblos gave us an account." This clear statement,
omitted in the Hakluyt version of the narrative hitherto followed, would have saved Gallatin, Davis, and
others from the error of locating Coronado's Tiguex
on the Rio Puerco.

The main object of the entrada had now been accomplished, and the return was talked of; but it
seemed to the leader that as there were reports of
other friendly provinces farther on, especially in the
east and not far off, the opportunity was good to do
his Majesty good service at comparatively slight cost
by additional exploration; and this view, being discussed in council at Puara, was approved by Padre
Beltran and the rest. Accordingly, with two companions, the captain went in two days eastward to a
province of the Maguas, or Magrias, on the borders
of the buffalo plains, where he found eleven pueblos
of some 40,000 inhabitants, and where, as he learned,
Padre Santa María had been killed. It was a country
of pine woods, without running streams, and with
good indications of metals in the mountains on the

---

[14] There is nothing to show that the remains were found as Davis states.

[15] Salmeron, *Rel.*, 11, says the town was sacked by Espejo in vengeance;
Niel, *Apunt.*, 88, that the guilty ones were brought to justice; and Arlegui,
Cron. Zac., 221, that several thousand Ind. were killed; but nothing of this is
in the original, and it is improbable, considering E.'s small force and his am-
bitious views for the future. Yet it is stated by Zaldívar, in *N. Mex.
Memorial*, that E. on his return burned Puara and garroted 16 Ind.

way.[16]   Thence he returned to Puara on the Rio del
Norte.

The next move, and of the whole company, was one
day's journey of about six leagues up the river to the
province of the Quires, or Coronado's Quirix, with

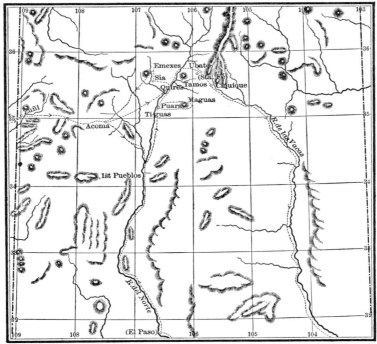

ESPEJO IN NEW MEXICO.

its five pueblos, and 15,000 people, where the strangers were given a most friendly reception, and where
observations showed a latitude of 37° 30', at least two
degrees too far north.   Then they went two days, or

[16] In *Espejo, Exped.*, 156, the prov. of Magrias is said to adjoin that of the
Tiguas on the N. E.   Thus it would seem to have been in the Galisteo region
though I know of no ruins to indicate so large a prov., and some other difficulties will appear in connection with later wanderings.   Davis and Prince, misled probably by the word cíbola ('esta provincia confina con las vacas que
llaman de Civola') or 'buffalo,' represent this exped. as having been directed to
the west.

some 14 leagues, to a province of the Punames—also
written Pumames and Cunames—with five towns,
the capital being Sia, or Siay, of eight plazas, and
houses plastered and painted. This pueblo was on a
small tributary of the Rio Grande flowing from the
north; but clearly the distance is much exaggerated
if it is to be in any way identified with the Cia of
modern times.[17] The next province, six leagues to
the north-west, and doubtless up the branch river, was
that of the Emexes—Emeges or Amejes—clearly
that of Jemes, with seven pueblos and some 30,000
souls, one of the towns, a large one in the mountains,
not being visited. From Jemes Espejo gives his
course as to the west for 15 leagues—really over 20
leagues south-west—to Acoma, on a peñol 50 yards
high, accessible only by steps cut in the solid rock.
Its population was estimated at over 6,000.[18] The
next stage of the journey was four days, or 24 leagues,
westward to Zuñi, or Cíbola,[19] with its six pueblos,
and over 20,000 people.

At Zuñi the Spaniards found, not only crosses
standing near the towns, but three christian Indians
still living, who had come with Coronado 40 years
before. These were Andrés, Gaspar, and Anton,
natives of Culiacan, Mexico, and Guadalajara, respect-

[17] There were over 20,000 inhab. in the province; mines were reported in
the sierra, and even rich ores were shown. In the Hakluyt version the
pueblo is called Cia. There can be no doubt of the general identity of this
region with the valley of Cia and Jemes, though besides Espejo's careless
distances, both pueblo sites have probably been changed in later times.

[18] Acc. to *N. Mex., Memorial*, 206-7, crosses were found here as at other
points in the west. Espejo tells us that the Acomans had their cultivated and
irrigated fields 2 l. from the peñol, where the stream was dammed. The
mountain tribes are numerous and warlike; they are called Querechos (the
name, it will be noted, that Coronado applies to a nation on the eastern plains),
and work for the pueblo, besides bringing salt, game, and skins to trade for
cotton and other articles. It is noticeable that Espejo elsewhere, *Expediente*,
157, puts Acoma N. w. of Quires. Here, as in other earlier narratives, it
would be more convenient to locate Acoma farther north than the peñol
pueblo of later years.

[19] The Hakluyt version has it, 'que se nombra en lengua de los naturales
Zuny, y la llaman los Espannoles Cibola;' but the original reads, 'que la provincia llaman Zuni, y por otro nombre Cibola,' or in the other copy, 'y le
llaman Amé (or Amí) y por otro nombre Cibola.' One of the 6 pueblos is called
Aquico, p. 118.

ively; and they told of the explorations in the west made by Coronado's captains, Don Pedro de Tobar being named. What was still more interesting, they asserted that 60 days' journey in the west, far beyond where Coronado's men had been forced to turn back for want of water, there was a great lake with many settlements on its banks, where the people had gold in abundance, wearing that metal in the form of bracelets and ear-rings. This fabulous lake, as we have seen, was destined to play an important rôle in annals of the Northern Mystery. Here at Zuñi, Padre Beltran and four or five of the soldiers announced their desire to return to Nueva Vizcaya, believing it useless to search for gold and silver where Coronado had failed to find them, and also that their force was too small for a further advance. These men were accordingly left at Zuñi with permission to return; but the leader resolved to visit another province reported to be not far distant.

With nine soldiers, the three Mexican Indians, and 150 friendly Cíbolans, Espejo marched westward from Zuñi, and in a journey of four days, or 28 leagues, reached the province of Mohoce, or Mohace, with five large pueblos and over 50,000 inhabitants. One of the towns was Aguato, or Zaguato.[20] There can be little doubt that the Mohoce province was identical with the Moqui towns. The people, though they sent messengers to warn the strangers not to approach on pain of death, were easily convinced of the visitor's friendly intentions, and gave them a most enthusiastic welcome, loading them with cotton *mantas* and food, besides delighting their ears with confirmation of the tales respecting wealth in the far west. The horses inspired more fear than the men, and Espejo humored the terror of the natives by admitting the animals' ferocity, thus inducing the chief to build a

[20] The name Mohoce, suggestive of Moquí, is not given in the Hakluyt version, only the pueblo Zagnato being named. In the later *N. Mex.*, *Memorial*, 206-7, the following pueblos, in connection with E.'s trip, are named as being apparently in the western region: Deziaquabos, Gaspé, Comupaví, Majananí, and Olalla.

kind of stone fort to hold the monsters—a fort which, in case of trouble, might be useful to the small Spanish force. Hakluyt notes this as "a witty policie to be used by the English in like cases." Here they remained six days, visiting all the pueblos, and becoming so firmly convinced of the natives' friendship that the leader left in the province five of his men to return to Zuñi with the luggage.

With four of his soldiers and some Moqui guides, Espejo set out to find rich mines reported in the west; and after a journey of 45 leagues over a mountainous country he found the mines, and with his own hands obtained rich samples of silver ore. On the streams he found large quantities of wild grapes, walnut-trees, flax, magueyes, and Indian figs. Several settlements of mountain tribes were visited, where the people raised maize and were uniformly friendly. These natives also told of a great river beyond the mountains—clearly the Colorado; and drew liberally on their imagination for the additional information that the river was eight leagues wide, with great towns on its banks, in comparison with which towns all the other provinces were nothing. The river flowed into the north sea, and the natives used canoes to cross it. From the mines the explorers returned by a more direct route of 60 leagues to Zuñi. It will be remembered that Coronado had reached the Colorado by a westerly or north-westwardly course from Moqui; and it is probable that Espejo's route was rather to the south-west, as he only heard of the great river beyond the mountains. Taking his distances of 45 leagues from Moqui and 60 leagues from Zuñi, we might locate his mine in the region of Bill Williams Mountain 40 or 50 miles north of Prescott. The record hardly justifies any more definite location.[21]

[21] The Hakluyt version speaks more definitely of 'dos rios razonables,' on the banks of which was found flax, etc. One of these streams was doubtless the Colorado Chiquito, sometimes called Rio de Lino from the flax. Davis on his map locates the mines in about lat. 36°, long. 112°, or considerably farther north than the site I have indicated; but between the two I venture no positive opinion, the data being too meagre. The origin of Davis' name Tubirans, applied to the western tribes, I do not know.

Back at Zuñi Espejo found not only the five men he had left at Moqui, but Padre Beltran and his companions, who had not yet started on their return, but soon did so, by the same route, perhaps, that they had come, or more likely crossing directly from Acoma south-eastward to the Rio Grande, and thence down the river.[22] The commander with his eight remaining companions, with a view of making further explorations up the Rio del Norte, marched in ten days, or about 60 leagues, to the Quires province,[23] and thence eastward in two days, or 12 leagues, to the province of the Ubates, or Hubates, with some 20,000 people in five pueblos. From this province, having spent two days in visiting some mines, they went in one day to the province of Tamos with its three large pueblos and 40,000 inhabitants. One of these pueblos was Cicuique, that is, Pecos, situated half a league from the Rio de las Vacas. I think it most likely that Espejo on quitting the Quires went up the river as he had intended—north-east instead of east, as his relation has it—and that the Ubates were the Tehua pueblos north of Santa Fé. The name Tamos, or Tanos, as applied to pueblos in the Galisteo region, was well known in later years; and Pecos is clearly indicated by Espejo as one of the three towns, though we are left in doubt as to the other two, as we were before respecting the province of Maguas between this group and the Tiguas.[24]

[22] In the statement of Escalante and Barrundo in *N. Mex. Testim.*, 148-9, made before Espejo's return, but at a date not given, allusion is made to the return of Beltran, leaving E. in the north. B.'s report, if he made any, I have not found. The returning party at first consisted of Miguel Sanchez and his two sons, Greg. Hernandez, Cris. Sanchez, and Frias, or 6 in all, leaving Espejo 9 for the Moqui trip; later, on E.'s return, the alférez Gregorio Hernandez, or Fernandez, is said to have joined Beltran's party, leaving E. 8 men. There is some confusion in these names and numbers.

[23] Not 'towards' the Quires, as in the Hakluyt version.

[24] Bandelier, *Hist. Introd.*, 116, thinks there can be no doubt that Pecos was one of the Ubates towns; but he seems not to have noticed Espejo's direct statement, or the name Cicuique, not occurring in the Hakluyt version. In the *N. Mex. Ytinerario*, 258, it is positively stated that Pecos was identical with Espejo's Tamos. There can be no foundation for Davis' identification of Tamos and Taos on his map.

The Tanos, unlike the other nations visited, were not friendly to the Spaniards, refusing admission to their towns and furnishing no food. It was therefore deemed unwise to remain longer in the country with so small a company, some of the soldiers being also ill. It was now July 1583. A Pecos Indian was employed to show a shorter route for departure than that by which they had entered the country. In half a league they reached the Rio de las Vacas, or Cow River, later known as the Pecos; and down this river, seeing many buffaloes in the first part of the journey, they travelled 120 leagues, eastward as the narrative has it—but Espejo's directions are often inaccurate—until they found three natives of the Jumana nation, who directed them across to the Rio Concho in 12 days, or some 40 leagues. Thence Espejo went to San Bartolomé, where he arrived on the 20th of September, and where he dated his report at the end of October. Padre Beltran and his party had arrived long before, and had gone to Durango. A map accompanied Espejo's report, but is not known to be extant.

Thus Espejo, a private citizen, accompanied by only a friar and fourteen soldiers, peacefully wandering from province to province, had accomplished substantially as great results as had Coronado with his grand army, his winter's warfare on the Rio Grande, and his barbarous oppression of the unoffending natives. Espejo visited 74 pueblos, the population of which, exclusive of the Tiguas, he estimated at 253,000 souls, doubtless a gross exaggeration. It is evident also that he overrated, from motives that will presently appear, the general resources and advantages of the country as a field for Spanish enterprise. Yet there is no reason to question the truthfulness of his narrative, nor is there much difficulty in satisfactorily tracing his route or identifying most of the pueblo groups visited. The expeditions of Rodriguez and Espejo must be regarded as most remarkable ones,

modestly and accurately recorded, and in their practical results vastly more important than the earlier
efforts which gave such fame to Niza and Coronado.

At the end of the last chapter I have shown how the
name Nuevo Mexico—in the early times as often Nueva
Mexico, in the feminine—had been in a sense invented
and held in readiness for future grand discoveries.
The application of the name to the country that was
to bear it permanently has been attributed by good
authorities, early and modern, both to Rodriguez and
to Espejo, though the former really called it San
Felipe and the latter Nueva Andalucía.   The truth
would seem to be, that the name was applied in
Mexico, under circumstances not fully recorded, after
Chamuscado's return, and during Espejo's absence.
Its first occurrence, as far as I know, is in Rio de
Losa's essay written about this time.   San Felipe de
Nuevo Mexico appears occasionally in early documents.   It was obviously natural that such a name
should have suggested itself as appropriate for any
newly discovered province whose people and buildings
resembled in a general way—that is, in comparison
with the wild tribes and their huts—those of the valley of Mexico.[25]

[25] *Espejo, Rel.,* 101, 164; *N. Mex. Testimonio,* 83, 90, 137, 142; *M. Mex.,
Memorial,* 204.   Name applied by the early Span. to all their possessions
along the N. W. coast (!), but later referred to the intendency on the Rio
Grande.   *Cutts' Conq. Cal.,* 28; name prob. derived from the resemblance of
its inhab. to those of the city of Mex. and its environs. *Gregg's Com. of the
Prairies,* i. 116.   Because of the great number of inhab. *Arlegui,* 229.   At
first called Nueva Granada (!). *Barreiro, Ojeada,* 7; *Davis' El Gringo,* 74.
Bartlett, *Pers. Narr.,* i. 184, incorrectly says there was a mission at El Paso
before 1600.   Davis, *El Gringo,* 79–1, speaks of a P. Marcos de Niza, not the
original, but perhaps his son (!), who penetrated to Zuñi before 1598.   Hosta,
native governor of Jemes, related to Simpson, *Journal,* 22, the tradition of a
priest who mysteriously appeared before the conquest.   His custom of taking anything he wanted at last enraged the Ind., who planned to kill him;
but he disappeared as mysteriously as he had come.

CHAPTER V.

It was in November 1582, before anything was
known in Mexico of Espejo's proposed expedition from
Nueva Vizcaya, that Viceroy Coruña reported to the
king the result of his investigation respecting the entrada and probable fate of Rodriguez and his companion friars.[1] In this report he enclosed for the royal
guidance a communication from Don Rodrigo del Rio
de Losa, lieutenant captain-general of Nueva Galicia,
who had been consulted as a man "de mucha experiencia en entradas," having served with Arellano in
Florida and with Ibarra in Nueva Vizcaya. Don
Rodrigo wrote on the supposition that the people of
New Mexico were now hostile, and urged that a sufficient force should be sent to punish the murderers of
the friars, and to inspire such respect for Spanish
arms as would prevent future outrages and revolts.
The number of soldiers should not be less than 300,

[1] Nov. 1, '82, viceroy to king. *N. Mex. Testim.*, 97–9.

with seven mules and horses for each man. For after the recent murders had been avenged, and the country reduced to a state of peace, a few settlers being left, it should be the main object of the expedition to continue its march across the buffalo plains to Quivira and beyond, even to the shores of the north or south sea, or to the "strait which is near China, in latitude 57°," the occupation of which by the French or English might thus be prevented. With this view, material for building two small ships should be carried, for the crossing of rivers or straits, or perhaps the sending back of news respecting any great discovery. Details of the necessary outfit are suggested; friars must of course be sent with the explorers; and it would be well to encourage the officers and men by release from taxation, offers of titles, and liberal encomiendas of New Mexican Indians.[2] The result was a royal order of March 1583, in which the viceroy was instructed to make a contract with some suitable person to undertake the expedition in accordance with the laws and regulations, without cost to the royal treasury; but the contract must be submitted to the consejo for approval before anything was actually done.[3]

Then came Beltran and Espejo, bringing reports calculated to increase the growing interest in New Mexico and the regions beyond. The people were not hostile, but well disposed to welcome Spanish visitors; the country in its climate and products presented many attractions for settlers from the south; though the natives made no use of the precious metals, ores rich in silver had been found at several points, and the development of profitable mines might with confidence be hoped for. The spiritual prospects were even more brilliant than the mineral, for 250,000 natives of superior intelligence were awaiting conversion; and es-

---

[2] No date. Rio de Losa to viceroy. *N. Mex. Testim.*, 137–46.
[3] March 29 and April 19, '83. *Pacheco, Doc.*, xv. 100; xvi. 297. The order was received in Mex. in August.

pecially, to say nothing of the long-coveted wealth of Quivira in the north-east easily accessible from New Mexico as a base, a great lake and broad river, with populous towns and plenty of gold, afforded a new incentive to exploring effort in the north-west. And moreover, it would seem to have been about this time that fears of foreign encroachment in these regions were renewed by the statement of Padre Diego Marquez, who had fallen into the hands of 'gente luterana,' and had been closely questioned at the English court respecting his knowledge of the north. This he made known to the authorities in Mexico, who felt that something must be done to prevent this fair land from falling into the hands of impious Lutherans.[4]

The first to take advantage of the king's order was Cristóbal Martin, a vecino of Mexico, who in October 1583, probably with knowledge of Padre Beltran's return, applied to the audiencia for a contract to undertake the conquest and settlement of New Mexico in accordance with the late cédula and earlier ordinances. He was willing to fit out an expedition of 200 or 300 men, and to spend $50,000 in the enterprise. He desired a missionary force of six Franciscans, besides two secular clergymen; and asked to be supplied with certain arms and ammunition; but otherwise the entrada was to be at his own cost. There was, however, nothing small about Don Cristóbal's demands. Though full of faith and loyalty, he could not afford to save souls and win for his king new provinces at his own cost for nothing. He must have the position of captain-general and governor of the new reino for himself and family during three lives; the right to distribute as encomiendas to his men all the natives of the conquered towns and provinces for ten lives; the authority to appoint and remove all officials, and to grant lands; a reduction of the king's fifth to one twentieth of the

___

[4] *Villagrá, Hist. N. Mex.*, 36. Rio de Loza, 139, had declared the importance of occupying N. Mex., to prevent ' que otras naciones de franceses ó ingleses luteranos no la ocupen.'

product of mines for 100 years; the privileges of *hijos-dalgo* for the conquistadores and their descendants; exemption from taxation on all products for 100 years; free use of the salinas for the three lives; the chief judicial authority as governor; the right to discover and settle for 1,000 leagues beyond the first New Mexican towns, to occupy ports on either ocean, and to trade with two ships from one of these ports without paying duties; the right to call on the viceroy for additional men and supplies by paying the costs; the right to found a *mayorazgo*, or entail, for his heirs, with sufficient revenue to perpetuate the family name and glory; and many other things which need not be catalogued here. These conquerors of the sixteenth century took great risks, regulating their demands accordingly; and as the burden was to fall on the Indians mainly, the king was often most liberal in his concessions. From October to December, Martin several times renewed his petition, and it would appear that his contract was finally approved by the Mexican authorities and sent to the consejo de Indias for confirmation.[5]

Espejo himself was next in the field as an aspirant for New Mexican glory, plausibly claiming that his recent service, experience, and success clearly pointed to him as above all others entitled to preference. But Don Antonio proposed no contract with the Mexican authorities. From motives of pride or policy[6] he chose to apply directly to the king; indeed, he urged most earnestly that the viceroy should have nothing

---

[5] *Martin, Asiento con Cripstobal Martin por el que se ofrece á ir en persona al descubrimiento, pacificacion, y poblacion del Nuevo Mexico, bajo las condiciones que expone.— Mexico á 26 de Octubre de 1583.* In *Pacheco, Doc.*, xvi. 277–301. This is the testimonio, or expediente, of the Mexican proceedings sent to Spain at a date not given, but soon after Dec. 24th, when the transcript is certified. It does not appear in these doc. that the contract was signed; but at the beginning M. says that 'él fué el primero que capituló é asentó en virtud de una Real Cédula de V. A., el negocio de la poblacion y descobrimiento del N. Mex., y fué remitido a Vuestra Real Consejo de Yndias.'

[6] Perhaps he had reason to suppose that the viceroy would not favor him. Indeed, there is a slight reference in one of his letters to a part of his estate as *embargada*, or attached, which may indicate troubles with the authorities of Nueva España.

to do with the enterprise. This, in the empresario's opinion, was absolutely essential to prevent ruinous wrangles and delays, wars and outrages on the natives, or dissensions and desertions among officers and men; and to insure the safe, speedy, and economical transformation of New Mexico into a flourishing community of tribute-paying subjects of Spain. In his original report of October 1583, summing up what he had accomplished, Espejo expressed his desire to spend his life and fortune in the king's service, at the same time announcing that he had brought from the north a native of Mohoce, and another of the Tanos, who might be trained for useful service as interpreters. In a letter to the archbishop he also made known his intention to apply for a royal commission to conquer and settle the country he had visited, and to explore the regions beyond, even to the ocean coasts on either side.[7] Accordingly in April 1584, he authorized his son-in-law, Pedro Gonzalez de Mendoza, about to start for Spain, with Bonilla and Barbadillo already at Madrid, to represent him at court, and obtain in his name the "conquista y pacificacion y gobernacion" of the provinces of New Mexico, or Nueva Andalucía, "which provinces I have discovered and taken possession of in the name of his Majesty." At the same time were forwarded a copy of his *Relacion*, and his formal petition, including a plan of his proposed operations. The expedition was to consist of 400 men, for the most part recruited in Spain, 100 of them with wives and children, to be organized in four companies. The men were to be well supplied with all they could need,

---

[7] *Espejo, Relacion,* 124–6; *Id., Expediente y Relacion,* 162–3, 186–9. This latter collection, in *Pacheco, Doc.,* xv. 151–91, is a continuation of the *N. Mex., Testimonio,* and might as well be included in it, though in print it has a separate title—indeed, two of them, the first being *Expediente sobre el ofrecimiento que hace Fran. Diaz de Vargas,* etc., though it contains nothing about V. The contents are: 1st, three undated communications (1584) of Espejo to the king, the last being his formal petition, p. 151–63; 2d, a copy of the *Espejo, Relacion* (as sent to the king with the petition), p. 163–89; 3d, April 23, '84, appointment of an agent, p. 189–91. There is another letter of E. to the king (April 23, '89), in *N. Mex., Testim.,* 100–1.

either as soldiers or settlers; and besides the cavalry horses required, large droves of mares, cattle, and sheep were to be provided. Spiritual interests of the new *reino* would be intrusted to twenty-four Franciscans. The entry would be made in two divisions, one going by the Rio del Norte, and the other, with the live-stock and wagons, by the Rio de Vacas. The garrison and families would at first be stationed in the vicinity of Acoma. In dealing with the natives, a conciliatory policy of justice and peace was to be strictly followed. In carrying out the scheme, Espejo was ready to expend over 100,000 ducats, besides the 10,000 he had already spent; he had twenty associates of considerable wealth; and he would give bonds in the sum of $200,000. The reward claimed for his devotion to the royal interests—"much less than what your Majesty promises in the ordenanzas," yet doubtless including the capitanía general and governorship, with privileges, titles, land-grants, encomiendas, and other emoluments for himself and associates—was to be made known in a supplementary memorial, which, as far as I know, is not extant. There are some indications that Don Antonio went in person to Spain to urge his claims.[8]

It does not clearly appear that anything was known in Mexico of Espejo's proposed conquest; but it is probable that respecting this project or that of Martin, some additional investigation was ordered, and Francisco Diaz de Vargas—alguacil mayor and regidor of Puebla—called upon for his views. At any rate, Don Francisco found occasion about this time to address the king on this subject.[9] He began by presenting a brief résumé of northern exploration from the time of Cortés down to the date of writing; and from that résumé he concluded that where so many able explorers had failed to find anything worth retaining,

---

[8] (April 1584.) Espejo's petition to the king, in *Espejo, Exped. y Rel.*, 152–63.

[9] No date (1584–5). Vargas to king, in *N. Mex. Testim.*, 126–37. Espejo's entrada is mentioned, but not his new project.

the presumption was, that the country was poor and undesirable. Doubtless the New Mexicans were a superior people; yet notwithstanding their agriculture, cotton, buffalo-skins, and many-storied stone and adobe dwellings, they were a distant, isolated community, surrounded for hundreds of leagues by wild and warlike tribes, and their country therefore offered at present but slight inducements for Spanish settlers. As the latest reports, however, were more favorable than earlier ones, as there was a prospect of rich mines, and since it was desirable to learn what foundation there might be for the reports of wealth beyond New Mexico, and especially what connection the great lake and river might have with the strait of Anian, it seemed advisable to send out an expedition —not of colonization and conquest, but simply of exploration. For this purpose a force of 50 or 60 men would suffice to verify the recent reports, push investigation 200 leagues farther north, and report results. These were sensible views, and Diaz de Vargas had the courage of his convictions; for in his patriotic zeal, mindful, not only of his own past services in high positions, but of those of his father, who was one of the old conquistadores, he even offered—and here we have at last the true inwardness of the document—to command the exploring party in person! And later, should the preliminary survey prove satisfactory, Don Francisco, accepting the titles and emoluments in such cases provided, would himself take charge of the great work of conquering and colonizing New Mexico.

Thus we have three empresarios in the field; and it is not unlikely that there were others. But respecting the fate of the different projects, or rather the circumstances that prevented their acceptance and execution, we know absolutely nothing; or at least I have found no document relating to either of the propositions after they were sent to the king and council. Perhaps the empresarios' demands were deemed excessive, or they could give no satisfactory

assurances of their ability to comply with the conditions of the contracts, or were not willing to accept
the conditions, or perhaps died; at any rate, nothing more is heard of Martin, or Espejo, or Diaz de
Vargas; and for five years nothing is heard of New
Mexico.

At the beginning of 1589 Juan Bautista de Lomas
y Colmenares, resident at the Nieves mines, and reputed to be the richest man in Nueva Galicia, presented to Viceroy Villamanrique a memorial of 37
articles, in which he proposed to undertake the conquest of New Mexico.   He was much more exacting
in his conditions than even Martin had been, demanding, besides all that the latter had claimed and much
more that cannot be specified in the space at my
command, the office of captain-general and governor,
with almost unlimited authority for six lives, at a salary of 8,000 ducats; jurisdiction over all territory
beyond the Rio Conchos, with the exclusion of all
other conquerors from the territory beyond what he
might choose to conquer; the title of count or marqués
for himself and descendants, with 40,000 vassals; the
privilege of granting three pueblos as an entailed en-
comienda, and another for the descendants of conquistadores not otherwise provided for; and the right to
fortify ports and build ships on either ocean.   His
sons were associated with him in the enterprise, and
Don Juan Bautista evidently had no intention of sac-
rificing the family prestige and wealth.   He claimed
to have rendered most important services at his own
expense on the northern frontier.[10]

Lomas' contract was approved by the viceroy on
the 11th of March, 1589; but the latter, though it
appears that by a cédula of 1586 he had full powers to
authorize entradas, deemed it best to consult the king

[10] *Lomas, Asiento y capitulaciones que el virey de la Nueva España, marqués
de Villamanrique, hizo con Joan Bautista de Lomas Colmenares, sobre el descubrimiento y Poblacion de las provincias del Nuevo México á 15 de Febrero de 1589*, in
Pacheco, Doc., xv. 54–80.   This is a copy of the expediente sent from Mexico
in 1592, and attached to Lomas' renewed petition of 1595.

in so important a matter; and at court the project received no attention whatever, or at least it drew out from the king no order or response. In 1592, Velasco, having succeeded Villamanrique as viceroy, Lomas attempted to revive the matter, but could obtain nothing more than a certified copy of the preceding documents. For it seems that Velasco favored another claimant, and made a new contract with Francisco de Urdiñola.[11] Before the latter could begin operations, however, he was arrested by order of the audiencia of Guadalajara on a charge of poisoning his wife—a charge which Villagrá in a burst of poetic indignation declares to have been founded only on *invidia venenosa;* and during subsequent legal complications New Mexican affairs were naturally neglected. Once more in 1595 Don Juan Bautista made an effort to obtain from the king an order to Viceroy Monterey to renew his contract with such modifications as might be deemed desirable; but nothing more is heard of his project or its author.[12]

While the several empresarios named were vainly striving to obtain from the king legal authority to win fame and wealth in the north, another determined to take a short cut to glory by undertaking an entrada without the royal license. This was Gaspar Castaño de Sosa, who had been alcalde mayor at San Luis Potosí in 1575, and in 1590 was acting as lieutenant-governor of Nuevo Leon. He claimed some kind of authority for his expedition; but it is evident from subsequent events that his acts were regarded as irregular and illegal. I suspect that he may have been duly authorized to explore and colonize the Nuevo Leon region, and that he was led by Espejo's

[11] About this time Urdiñola seems to have been sent with a Tlascaltec colony to Coahuila. *Hist. North Mex. St.*, i. 126-7. He was later gov. of N. Galicia, according to Villagrá.

[12] Villagrá, *Hist. N. Mex.*, 36-8, briefly mentions Lomas' project and Urdiñola's contract. Modern writers do not mention this or the preceding ones of Vargas, Espejo, and Martin.

reports to transfer, without special license from king or viceroy, his efforts to a more promising field. The name of Cristóbal Martin among his associates is also suggestive. Respecting the preliminaries of the expedition, little or nothing is known; but the original diary has fortunately been preserved.[13]

The start was on the 27th of July, 1590, from the villa de Almaden, wherever that may have been— probably somewhere in Nuevo Leon—and the force was over 170 persons including women and children.[14] A wagon train was laden with supplies deemed needful for a new settlement. In two days the company reached the Rio de Nadadores, remaining ten days; and, mentioning also the Sabinas and several streams not found on any modern map, they arrived on the 9th of September at the Rio Bravo, where they spent the rest of the month, awaiting the return of messen-

---

[13] *Castaño de Sosa, Memoria del descubrimiento que Gaspar Castaño de Sosa, teniente de gobernador y capitan general del nuevo reino de Leon por el rey D. Felipe nuestro señor, va a hacer, al cumplimiento de las provisiones que el dicho gobernador les han concedido, y á él como su lugar teniente, como mas largamente se verá por la dicha provision é cédulas reales y libro de nuevas leyes de pobladores concedidas á todos los vecinos del dicho reino, etc.,* etc., in *Pacheco, Doc.,* iv. 283–354; *Id.,* xv. 191–261. From the Muñoz collection, and at the end, was a note as follows: 'Hizose relacion dello, y vióse por los Señores del Consejo en 10 de Noviembre de 1592—Sant Andrés.' It would seem to be a copy of the original diary made in some official book of records, probably in connection with legal difficulties in which the leader became involved.

It is a somewhat perplexing narrative; long, verbose, and complicated; requiring close study, but rewarding that study with only the most meagre general results. If a man lost his way, we have all the details of his wandering back to camp; we know exactly the day and hour when the dog of Juan Perez was killed by the kick of an ox; we have all the discussions and diplomatic manœuvres resulting from a difference of opinion as to whether a bushel of corn might safely be distributed as rations; but we rarely find the course or distance of a day's journey. Were it not for the vicinity of two great rivers, the reader might be in doubt whether the travellers were going northwest in Guatemala or south-east in New England.

[14] The following names appear scattered in the narrative, evidently those of leading men in the company: Cris. de Heredia (captain and maestro de campo), Andrés Perez (secretary), Manuel de Medreras, Fran. Lopez de Recalde, Juan de Carbajal, Juan de Contreras, Domingo de Santistévan, Diego Diaz de Verlanda, Alonso Jaimes y Ponce, Fran. de Mancha, Fran. Salado, Juan Perez de los Rios, Martin de Salazar, Juan Rodriguez de Nieto, Pedro Flores, Blas Martinez de Mederos, Cris. Martin, Jusepe Rodriguez, Juan de Estrada, Gonzalo de Lares, Diego de Biruega, Cris. de Biruega, Pedro de Iñigo, Juan Rodriguez de Ávalos, Hernan Ponce de Leon, Pedro Pinto, Juan de Vega, Alonso Lúcas, Domingo Hernandez, Fran. de Bascones, and Juan Sanchez.

gers who had been sent to Mexico,[15] and making some explorations for a later advance. It was decided to go forward by way of the Rio Salado, a stream whose existence seems to have been known, though just how it was known or what was the origin of the name does not appear.

Here on the Rio Bravo their troubles began. After receiving conflicting reports from several exploring parties they started on the 1st of October for the Rio Salado. To find a way for the wagons over a rough country and across intermediate streams—the principal one being called the Rio de Lajas—to the river which was the object of their search, and to get out of the mountains into the plains, consumed most of the month; and only at the end of October did they start up the valley of the Salado to their land of promise. I make no attempt to trace their wanderings of this month in Coahuila and Texas, or even to determine where they crossed the Bravo, or Rio Grande; but content myself with the conclusion that the Salado was without doubt Espejo's Cow River, or the Pecos.[16]

Slowly the caravan crept up the valley and over

[15] They were sent about Aug. 21st with letters to the viceroy, but they did not return. Probably this corresp. with the viceroy would throw much light on Castaño's enterprise. Possibly he wrote to obtain authority for a change of plans involving the trip to N. Mex.

[16] The narrative is too long and complicated for a study of details here, especially as the travellers were not yet in N. Mex. territory. The most definite statement is on p. 289, while they were on the Bravo. One explor. party had found a stream which it could not cross; then Capt. Heredia was sent out 'el cual salió en demanda del dicho rio Salado, y llegó al rio que estaba descubierto [that is, by the earlier party] y halló paso en el dicho rio para poder pasar las carretas, porque hasta entonces no se habia hallado. Y descubierto el dicho paso, fué atravesando aquella lomería que habia hasta el rio Bravo, y llegó al dicho rio Bravo; y se volvió al dicho real, diciendo que por alli podiamos pasar y ir atravesando al rio Salado.' But they found many difficulties in following this road; the fording the Bravo is not clearly recorded; and after they reached the region of the Salado it took many days to get down to its banks. The Sabinas of Coahuila is called the Salado on many maps, but of course the idea of following this river up to N. Mex. is absurd. That Castaño did not go up the Bravo is shown by his efforts while on that river to find the other; by the broad *sabanas*, or plains, over which the route lay; and by the statement that a spring far up the Salado, p. 306, was the first since leaving the Bravo. Perhaps they crossed in the region of Fort Duncan, and the Lajas was the S. Pedro in Texas.

the broad Texan plains, at first on the eastern bank of
the river, but later crossing and recrossing it often,
with no incident calling for mention, meeting a few
roaming Indians, and passing no settlements.   The
1st of December an unfordable branch stream forced
them to cross to the eastern bank of the main river.
On the 7th was noticed the first grove of cottonwoods.
On the 23d a small advance party returned to meet
the main body with exciting news.   They had entered
a pueblo farther up the river, eastward, where they
had been kindly received, and had spent the night
there; but the next morning while engaged in peaceful efforts—if we take their word for it—to collect a
supply of maize, they were suddenly attacked and
driven away, losing a part of their arms and luggage,
and having three of their number wounded.

Leaving the women and children with the wagons
properly guarded at a place called Urraca, Castaño
set out on the 27th with the larger part of his force,
and on the last day of the month and year arrived at
the pueblo, which was situated about half a league
from the river, being a large town with buildings of
four and five stories—evidently identical with Pecos.
The inhabitants were on the roofs in hostile attitude,
armed with stones and bows and slings.   After a great
part of the day had been spent in vain attempts to
conciliate them, an attack was made late in the afternoon, and the town was taken after a fight which seems
to have been attended with no very serious casualties
on either side.   Great care was taken to prevent
outrages, and to gain the people's confidence; but
though they submitted, it was impossible to overcome
their suspicion and timidity.   During the second night
they all left the pueblo and fled.   The Spaniards remained five or six days, admiring the many-storied
houses, the five *plazas*, the sixteen *estufas*, the immense stores of maize, amounting to 30,000 fanegas,
the garments of the men and women, the beautiful
pottery, and many other curious things.

Having sent back much needed supplies of food to
the camp at Urraca, the teniente de gobernador started
on the 6th of January, 1591, in quest of new discoveries. Two days over a mountainous snow-covered
country and across a frozen stream brought him to
the second pueblo, a small one whose inhabitants
were well disposed, and readily submitted to the
appointment of governor, alcaldes, and other officials,
thus rendering allegiance to the Spanish crown.
Four other pueblos, all of the same type, differing
only in size, and apparently not far apart or far from
the second, were now visited successively, submitting
without resistance or serious objection to the required
formalities. In each a cross was set up with all possible ceremony and solemnity.[17] The seventh pueblo
was a large one in another valley two leagues distant,
with adobe houses of two and three stories, and in the
plaza a large structure half under ground which seemed
to serve as a kind of temple. The eighth and ninth
pueblos were a day's march up a large river northward;
but the tenth, a very large one with buildings from
seven to nine stories high, situated five leagues beyond
the last, where the inhabitants wore chalchihuites for
ornaments, though seen was not entered, because the
people were not altogether friendly, and on account of
the cold, and lack of forage for the horses, the necessary time for conciliation could not now be spared.[18]
Returning through the snow to the southern towns,
Castaño next received the submission of pueblos eleven
and twelve across the river westward, a league apart,
and then of number thirteen after recrossing to the
eastern bank. The next move was over a snowy
route to another valley in two days; and here
were found, all in sight of each, four towns of the

[17] It would seem that Castaño continued his journey N. W. from Pecos, and
reached the Tehua pueblos N. of Sta Fé. The next 3 towns may have been
of the same group, or farther up the river, possibly to Picuries; but all is
mere conjecture.
[18] Though the distance given is too small, this pueblo from its size and description should be Taos in the extreme north.

Quereses, the only aboriginal name applied in this narrative, apparently identical with Coronado's Quirix, Espejo's Quires, and the later well-known Queres about the junction of the Galisteo and Rio Grande. The eighteenth, nineteenth, and twentieth pueblos, about a league apart, the first and perhaps the others being also of the Queres nation, graciously submitting to the strangers' god and king, were named respectively San Márcos, San Lúcas, and San Cristóbal.[19]

On the 24th of January, after a heavy fall of snow, the little army started eastward from San Cristóbal with native guides to bring up the rest of the colony, and the wagon-train from Urraca. Passing through pine forests and melting snow to get water for men and horses, they crossed the Rio Salado, or Pecos, on the 26th, and next day reached the camp at Urraca, most opportunely, for the store of food was wellnigh exhausted. Four days later the whole company started on the return; but progress being slow, on account of excessive cold and occasional accidents to the wagons, it was not till February 8th that they left the Pecos, reaching San Cristóbal on the 15th, and San Márcos on the 18th. This town for a time was made a centre of operations. A few days after the return a new pueblo, the twenty-first, two leagues away, was visited and peaceably reduced to Spanish allegiance. In the first days of March Castaño with a small party made a trip apparently to pueblo number one, or Pecos, but possibly to number ten, finding the people recovered from their fears, and ready for the formalities of submission. Next he went by way of a place and stream named Iñigo to the twenty-second pueblo, named Santo Domingo, on a 'rio caudaloso' called also Rio

---

[19] These names are not mentioned in the diary till a little later on the return from the east. There is little probability that these names or that of Sto Domingo, given later, were permanent; nor is it possible to identify them accurately; still there is little doubt that they were in the region of Sta Ana, S. Felipe, and Sto Domingo. Near S. Márcos promising mines were discovered. It is somewhat remarkable that saints' names are not applied to the other pueblos.

Grande, to which point the main camp was soon transferred.[20]

In these days was brought to light a plot of certain
men to desert their leader, perhaps even to kill him,
and to quit the country. Their cause of complaint, if
we may credit the perhaps not impartial chronicler,
was the kindness shown the natives by the teniente de
gobernador, and the consequent lack of opportunities
for plunder. All implicated, however, were pardoned
by the kind-hearted Castaño at the intercession of all
the camp; and the only punishment inflicted was on
Alonso Jaimez whose commission to go to Zacatecas
for reënforcements was revoked. Permission was even
given to such as might desire it to abandon the enterprise and go home, but none took advantage of the
offer. This was about the 11th of March; and in his
search for mines Castaño found in the mountains two
pueblos, twenty-three and twenty-four, which had been
abandoned recently because of Indian wars. No more
dates are given; but the final tour of exploration was
to the province where the padres were said to have been
killed years before. This is the only allusion in the
diary to any knowledge on Castaño's part that New
Mexico had ever been visited before. In this province
there were fourteen pueblos in sight on the river bank,
nine of which—numbers twenty-five to thirty-three—
were visited. Most of them were temporarily deserted
by the inhabitants, in the fear that the invaders came to
avenge the death of the friars; but the rest submitted
without resistance. We must suppose that in this last
expedition Don Gaspar went from Santo Domingo
down the Rio Grande to the province of the Tiguas.[21]

On his return from this tour, with a few men Castaño met Indians who reported the arrival of a new
party of Spaniards. A little later he met some of his

---

[20] It seems most likely that this was not the Sto Domingo of later years,
but a pueblo farther south, or down the river.

[21] There is nothing to show the direction, and that little is confusing, as,
for instance, the statement that he went 'up the river' in visiting the towns.

own men, who said that Captain Juan Morlete[22] had arrived from the south with 50 men. Hoping to learn that reënforcements had been sent to him, though the names were not familiar, the teniente de gobernador hastened to the camp, only to learn that Morlete had come with orders from the king and viceroy for his arrest. He quietly submitted, and here the diary ends abruptly, after Don Gaspar had been put in shackles. Apparently the whole company returned south with their unfortunate chief. Lomas in 1592 tells us that Morlete was accompanied by Padre Juan Gomez, and arrested Castaño "for having entered the said country without license from Vuestra Señoría." Oñate in 1598 found traces of the wagons, showing the return route to have been down the Rio Grande. Salmeron says of this expedition "and those of Captain Nemorcete and of Humaña I do not write, because they all saw the same things, and one telling suffices"— an unfortunate resolution of the venerable Franciscan, since he probably had at his command information that would have thrown desirable light on all these entradas. Father Niel adds nothing to the statement of his predecessor except in correcting Nemorcete's name to Morlete; and the poet Villagrá supplies no details.[23]

Of the expedition attributed by Salmeron and other writers to Humaña, as it was an illegal one— *contra bando*, as the Spaniards put it—no diary could

[22] The diary has it Morlote, which may be correct.
[23] *Lomas, Asiente*, 58; *N. Mex., Ytinerario*, 245; *Salmeron, Rel.*, 11; *Niel, Apunt.*, 88. Villagrá's version, *Hist. N. Mex.*, 36-7, is as follows:
‘ Y por el de nouenta entró Castaño,
Por ser allá teniente mas antiguo,
Del Reyno de Leon á quien siguieron
Muchos nobles soldados valerosos,
Cuio Maese de campo se llamaua
Christoual de heredia bien prouado
En cosas de la guerra y de buen tino,
Para correr muy grandes despoblados,
A los quales mandó el Virey prendiese
El Capitan Morlete, y sin tardarse,
Socorrido de mucha soldadesca;
Braba, dispuesta, y bien exercitada,
A todos los prendió, y bolvio del puesto.’

have been expected to be written, even had the unfortunate adventurers lived to return and report their
discoveries. Francisco Leiva Bonilla, a Portuguese,
was the veritable chief, and Juan de Humaña one of
his companions. The party was sent out on a raid
against rebellious Indians by the governor of Nueva
Vizcaya at a date not exactly known, but apparently
in 1594–6. Captain Bonilla, moved by the current
reports of north-eastern wealth, determined to extend
his operations to New Mexico and Quivira. The governor sent Pedro de Cazorla to overtake the party and
forbid such an expedition, declaring Bonilla a traitor
if he disobeyed; but all in vain, though six of the
party refused to follow the leader, and returned. The
adventurers' progress to and through New Mexico has
no record. They are next heard from far out on the
buffalo plains in search of Quivira. Here in a quarrel
Humaña killed his chief and assumed command. A
little later, when the party had passed through an
immense settlement and reached a broad river which
was to be crossed on balsas, three Mexican Indians
deserted, one of whom, José, survived to tell the tale
to Oñate in 1598. Once more we hear of the gold-
seekers. Farther toward Quivira, or Tindan, or perhaps returning gold-laden from those fabulous lands,
they encamp on the plain at the place since called
Matanza. The Indians set fire to the grass, and rush,
thousands strong, upon the Spaniards just before
dawn. Only Alonso Sanchez and a mulatto girl
escape the massacre. Sanchez became a great chief
among the natives, and from him comes the story,
just how is not very clear, since there is no definite
record that he was ever seen later by any white man.
When we take into consideration their sources, it is
not surprising that the records of Humaña's achievements are not very complete.[24]

[24] Villagrá, *Hist. N. Mex.*, 37, 142, is the authority for the first part of
this expedition; and he also as an eye-witness speaks of the Ind. deserter
José, or Jusepe, at S. Juan. Oñate, *Carta de 1599*, 303, 309, says that he

was instructed to free the province from traitors by arresting Humaña and his men; also that one of H.'s Indians (José) joined his force. Gregg, *Com. Prairies*, i. 117, seems to have seen a copy of this communication or another containing similar statements at Sta Fé. Niel, *Apunt.*, 89–95, calls Humaña adelantado and governor; says that he killed Capt. Leiva, his bravest officer, and that the Indian José was found by Oñate among the Picuríes. Davis, *Span. Conq.*, 260, seems to follow Niel for the most part, without naming that author. He says Humaña was killed three days after leaving Quivira, which D., as before stated, persists in identifying with the ruins of that name far south of Sta Fé.

CHAPTER VI.

HAVING chronicled in the preceding chapters all the
various explorations of New Mexican territory from
1540 to 1596, together with several unsuccessful projects of colonization, I now come to the final success
of another similar undertaking, to the actual conquest
and occupation of the country accomplished by Don
Juan de Oñate for the king of Spain, in 1598–9.
While this achievement may properly be regarded as
the most important in New Mexican annals, the cor-
ner-stone of the historic structure, its record has
hitherto been left almost a blank.   The early standard
writers somewhat unaccountably gave but a brief and
generally inaccurate outline of the conquest.   Nearly
all gave the date as 1595–6, fixing it by that of Oñate's
preparations, and greatly underestimating the delays
that ensued; and only Mariana, the historian of Spain,
seems to have given a correct date.   The sum and
substance of all these versions, rejecting errors, would

be hardly more than a statement that in 1595 Oñate undertook the enterprise, and soon with the aid of Franciscan friars succeeded in occupying the province, and even made a tour to the Quivira region in the north-eastern plains.[1]

That later writers, consulting only a part of these earlier authorities, should not have materially improved the accuracy and completeness of the record is not surprising. They have made a few slight additions from documentary sources; but they have retained for the most part the erroneous dates, and have introduced some new errors, the latest and best of them, Davis and Prince, having copied the blunder of some faulty document consulted, and moved the conquest backward to 1591.[2] The real and original authorities

[1] Torquemada, *Monarq. Ind.*, i. 670 et seq., mentions the confirmations of O.'s contract in 1595 by Viceroy Monterey, the enlistment of men in Mex., and the appointment of a comisario of the Franciscan band; but gives no further details or dates until after N. Mex. was occupied, that is, after 1600. ' Pasaron todos, hasta llegar á las poblaciones que llaman N. Mexico, y allí asentaron Real, y oi Dia permanece, y de la que ha ido sucediendo se dirá en sus lugares.' This is virtually Torquemada's history of the conquest. Mendieta, *Hist. Ecles.*, 402, writing in 1596, merely notes that the viceroy is now fitting out O.'s expedition. Vetancur, *Chrónica*, 95, notes the contract made by Velasco and confirmed by Monterey, the appointment of friars, as in Torquemada, and then says: ' Llegaron con facilidad, y entre los dos rios fundaron una Villa á S. Gabriel dedicada.' Calle, *Noticias*, 102, after noting the contract ratified Sept. 30, 1595, the Franciscans, etc., like the rest, thus records the conquest: ' Llegó al Nuevo Mexico y hizo asiento, tomo possession del por la Magestad Católica del Rey N. Señor, y puso su Real en el pueblo que se intituló San Gabriel cuyo sitio está en 37° de altura al Norte, situado entre dos rios, donde fundaron Convento luego los Religiosos, y hasta el año de 1608 bautizaron 8,000 almas.' Salmeron, *Relaciones*, 23–4, recording the start in 1596, the names of friars, number of soldiers, etc., tells us, ' dejadas largas historias, que no hacen á mi intento,' that Oñate with over 400 men went 400 miles N., pitched his camp in lat. 37° 30', and went on to make further entradas and explorations. But he adds an account of the Quivira exped., pp. 26 et seq. Niel, *Apunt.*, 89–94, cannot be said to add anything to Salmeron's version, and neither implies that the entrada was delayed more than a few months, in 1596. Ludovicus Tribaldus, in a letter to Richard Hakluyt, printed in *Purchas his Pilgrimes*, iv. 1565–6 (see also descrip., v. 853–6), and in Laet, *Novus Orbis*, 314, mentions certain early troubles at Acoma. Alegre, *Hist. Comp. J.*, i. 310–11, mentions the exped. as of 1596. See also *Mariana, Hist. España*, ii. 527; *Morelli, Fast. Nov. Orb.*, 31; *Thesaurus, Geog.*, ii. 252–3; *Cavo, Tres Siglos*, i. 225–9; *Arlegui, Cron. Zac.*, 56–7; *Aparicio, Conventos*, 282; *Alcedo, Dicc.*, iii. 189; *Bernardez, Zac.*, 31–4; *Revilla Gigedo*, in *Dicc. Univ.*, v. 441, who makes the date 1600.

[2] Barreiro, *Ojeada*, 5, thus records the conquest, writing before 1832: ' Pero lo cierto es que en el año de 1595 con cédula de Felipe segundo dirigida al Virrey de México Zuñiga y Acevedo, conde de Monterey, entró al Nuevo-México Juan de Oñate con los primeros españoles que lo poblaron, trayendo

—a book published in 1610, and documents obtained
in modern times from the Spanish archives—are now
utilized practically for the first time in writing the
history of New Mexico.   I say practically, because in
the long interval between the writing and final revision
of this chapter, a Spanish investigator has given to
the public a résumé of the book referred to, and another in America has made known his acquaintance
with the volumes containing the confirmatory documents.[3]

The veritable authority for the events presented in
this chapter is to be found in the shape of an epic poem,
written by Captain Gaspar de Villagrá, one of Oñate's
companion conquistadores, and published only eleven
years after the occurrence of the events narrated.[4]

consijo 65 religiosos franciscanos.' Pino, *Exposicion*, 35–6, of 1812, and *Id.*,
Noticias, 2–8, a new ed. of '49, gives the king's cédula of July 8, 1602, in
Oñate's favor, which is copied by Davis and others.   The latter edition also
contains Barreiro's statement and that of Calle as already quoted, and in
addition that of Frejes, *Hist. Breve.*, 243, which is to the effect that Espejo
having been sent by the viceroy to protect the missions of N. Mex., and
some trouble having arisen with adjoining tribes, presidios were needed and
Oñate was therefore sent, arriving in 1595! Zamacois, *Hist. Méj.*, v. 206–10,
implies that the conquest was effected in 1596–7, and tells us that two years
later was founded the 1st city named Monterey.   Rivera, *Gobernantes de Mex.*,
i. 71–2, gives no exact dates and few details, but he adds a little genuine information about the troubles before N. Mex. was reached.   Gregg, *Com. of
the Prairies*, i. 117 et seq., found at Sta Fé a very important document, the
memorial of Oñate dated Sept. 21, 1595, which is not known to have been
seen since, and of which the author gives a résumé.   Davis, *Span. Conq.*,
263–78, as I have stated, gives the date as 1591, but adds a note on the confusion of dates.   He seems to have used a MS. copy of part of Salmeron's
work, regarding it as Oñate's diary.   He also copies the cédula of 1602 as
given by Barreiro, has evidently consulted Gregg, and also cites Larenaudière (*Mexique*, 147, who gives the date as 1600, not 1599).   See also—none of
them containing original or additional material—*Prince's Hist. Sk.*, 161–6;
Viagero Univ, xxvii. 144–5; *Mayer's Mex. Aztec*, i. 174; *Meline's 2,000 Miles*,
135–6; *Domenech's Deserts*, 185; *Murray's Cath. Ch.*, 74–6; *Nouv. Ann. Voy.*,
cxxxi. 255; *Farnham's Mex.*, 23; *Modern Traveller*, ii. 71–2; *Hinton's Hand-
book*, 388–9; *Müller, Reisen*, iii. 188; *Magliano's St. Francis*, 575–7; *Davis'
El Gringo*, 73.

[3] I allude to Fernandez Duro (1882) and Bandelier (1881), whose works are
elsewhere noticed.   In the same interval, 1877–86, I have also discovered
that the book was used in 1619 in a blundering sketch by Córdoba.   My surprise in this matter has been for 10 years that the *Doc. Hist. Mex.*, the *Col.
Doc. Inéd.*, and the work of Villagrá have not been utilized by historical
students.

[4] *Villagrá, Historia de la Nueva Mexico, del Capitan Gaspar de Villagrá.
Dirigida al Rey D. Felipe nuestro señor Tercero deste nombre. Ano 1610. Con
privilegio, en Alcala, por Luys Martinez Grande.   A costa de Baptista Lopez
mercader de libros.* 16mo, 24, 287 leaves.   The preliminary leaves contain a

This work, though by no means unknown to bibliographers, is very rare; and its historic value seems to

quaint wood-cut portrait of the author; the usual certificates of secular license and ecclesiastic approval; dedication to the king; prologue; a series of numerous short *canciones* and *sonetos* by different writers, full of flattery addressed for the most part to Villagrá or Oñate, the longest being by Luis Tribaldos, the same who wrote to Hakluyt on the conquest; and finally a table of contents of the 33 cantos which make up the book. The 1st begins as follows:

HISTORIA DE LA NUEVA MEXICO.
DEL CAPITAN GASPAR DE VILLAGRÁ.
Canto Primero.
Que declara el argumento
de la historia, y sitio de la nueva Mexico, y noticia
q della se tuvo, en quanto la antigualla de
los Indios, y de la salida y decen-
dencia de los verdaderos
Mexicanos.

Las armas y el varon heroico canto,
El ser, valor, prudencia, y alto esfuerço,
De aquel cuya paciencia no rendida,
Por un mar de disgustos arrojada,
A pesar de la inuidia ponçoñosa,
Los hechos y prohesas va encumbrando.
De aquellos Españoles valerosos,
Que en la Occidental India remontados,
Descubriendo del mundo lo que esconde,
Plus vltra con braueza van diziendo,
A fuerça de valor y braços fuertes,
En armas y quebrantos tan sufridos,
Quanto de tosca pluma celebrados;
Suplicoos Christianissimo Filipo,
Que pues de nueva Mexico soys fenix,
Nueuamente salido y producido,
De aquellas viuas llamas y cenizas,
De ardentísima fee, en cuyas brasas,
A vuestro sacro Padre, y señor nuestro,
Todo deshecho y abrasado vimos,
Suspendais algun tanto de los hombres (hombros),
El grande y graue peso que os impide,
De aquese inmenso globo que en justicia,
Por solo vuestro braço se sustenta,
Y prestando gran Rey atento oido,
Vereis aqui la fuerça de trabajos,
Calumnias y afliciones con que planta,
El Euangelio santo y Fé de Christo,
Aquel Christiano Achiles que quisistes,
Que en obra tan heroica se ocupase,
Y si por qual que buena suerte alcanço,
A teneros Monarca por oiente,
Quien duda que con admirable espanto,
La redondez del mundo todo escuche,
Lo que a tan alto Rey atento tiene,
Pues siendo assi de vos fauorecido,
No siendo menos escriuir los hechos,
Dignos de que la pluma los leuante,
Que empréder los q no son menos dignos
De que la misma pluma los escriua,

have been concealed from the public until 1883.   When
I had occasion to consult its pages in 1877, I did so

> Solo resta que aquellos valerosos,
> Por quien este cuydado yo he tomado,
> Alienten con su gran valor heroico,
> El atreuido buelo de mi pluma,
> Porque desta vez pienso que veremos,
> Yguales las palabras con las obras.
> Escuchadme gran Rey que soi testigo,
> De todo quanto aqui señor os digo.

Or, rendering the same in English as literally as possible, with an exact reproduction of the measure, and with a remarkably successful effort not to be
a better poet than Don Gaspar, we have:

HISTORY OF NEW MEXICO.

BY CAPTAIN GASPAR DE VILLAGRÁ.

First Canto.

Which makes known the argument
of the history, and the situation of New Mexico, and
knowledge had of it from ancient monuments
of the Indians, and of the departure
and origin of the
Mexicans.

Of arms I sing and of the man heroic;
The being, valor, prudence, and high effort
Of him whose endless, never-tiring patience,
Over an ocean of annoyance stretching,
Despite the fangs of foul, envenomed envy
Brave deeds of prowess ever is achieving;
Of those brave men of Spain, conquistadores,
Who, in the Western India nobly striving,
And searching out all of the world yet hidden,
Still onward press their glorious achievements,
By their strong arms and deeds of daring valor,
In strife of arms and hardships as enduring
As, with rude pen, worthy of being honored.
And thee I supplicate, most Christian Philip,
Since of New Mexico thou art the Phœnix
Of late sprung forth and in thy grandeur risen
From out the mass of living flame and ashes
Of faith most ardent, in whose glowing embers
Thy own most holy father and our master
We saw inwrapped, devoured by sacred fervor—
To move some little time from off thy shoulders
The great and heavy weight, that thee oppresses,
Of that terrestrial globe which in all justice
Is by thine own strong arm alone supported;
And giving, gracious king, attentive hearing,
Thou here wilt see the weight of weary labors,
And grievous calumnies with which is planted
The holy gospel and the faith of Jesus
By that Achilles who by royal order
Devotes himself to such heroic service.
And if I may by rare access of fortune
Have thee, most noble Philip, for a hearer,
Who doubts that with a universal impulse
The whole wide world will hold its breath to listen
To that which holds so great a king's attention?

with an idea that it might furnish material for a brief note as a literary curiosity; but I found it a most complete narrative, very little if at all the less useful for being in verse. The subject is well enough adapted to epic narration, and in the generally smooth-flowing endecasyllabic lines of Villagrá loses nothing of its intrinsic fascination. Occasionally the author quits the realm of poesy to give us a document in plain prose; and while enthusiastic in praise of his leader and his companions, our New Mexican Homer is modest in recounting his own exploits. Of all the territories of America—or of the world, so far as my knowledge goes—New Mexico alone may point to a poem as the original authority for its early annals. Not less remarkable is the historic accuracy of the muse in this production, or the long concealment of the book from the eye of students.[5]

> Then, being thus by thee so highly favored,
> Since it is nothing less to write the story
> Of deeds that worthy are of the pen's record,
> Than to achieve deeds that no less are worthy
> Of being put by the same pen in writing,
> Nothing remains but that those men heroic,
> For whose sake I this task have undertaken,
> Should still encourage by their acts of valor
> The flight ambitious of a pen so humble,
> For in this case I think we shall see equalled
> Deeds by the words in which they are recorded.
> Listen to me, great king, for I was witness
> Of all that here, my lord, I have to tell thee.

[5] In the prose documents V.'s name is generally written Villagran and sometimes Perez de V. He was procurador general in the expedition, as well as captain. Cesáreo Fernandez Duro, *Don Diego de Peñalosa*, 148–60, gives in 1883 an excellent summary of V.'s work, which is as I have said the first announcement to the world in modern times of its historic value. He quotes from *Lopez de Haro, Nobilario*, some slight biog. matter, from which it appears that Don Gaspar was of the illustrious family of the Perez of Villagrá, a town in the province of Campos, Spain, a family which included several valiant captains, among them Don Francisco de Villagrá, well known in connection with the conquest of the Araucanos in S. America. Luis Cabrera de Córdoba, *Historia de Felipe*, ii., Madrid, 1619, gave a trashy account of the early explorations of N. Mex., and also a brief account of the conquest, in which he follows Villagrá. This is the only instance known to me in which V.'s work has been consulted. The extract on N. Mex. is translated in *Ternaux-Compans, Voyages*, ser. i. tom. x. p. 429–50.

Fernandez Duro, *Noticia de Exped.*, 131, part of the work noticed above, cites under date of 1604 *Figueredo, Relacion del viaje al Nuevo Méjico que hizo el Capitan general D. Juan de Oñate, por Fr. Roque Figueredo, misionero franciscano en la expedicion*, as a MS. mentioned by Beristain; also *Oñate, Diario y relacion de la entrada que hizo D. Juan de Oñate en el Nuevo México, hacia el reino de Tolan, enviada al Rey*, MS., cited by Barcia. From the date those MSS. may refer exclusively to O.'s expeditions from rather than to N. Mex.

Viceroy Velasco on the failure of Urdiñola's project, not favoring as we have seen that of Lomas, accepted the propositions of Juan de Oñate in the autumn of 1595.[6] Don Juan was a rich and prominent resident of Zacatecas, son of the brave and popular conquistador Don Cristóbal; married to Doña Isabel, daughter of Juan de Tolosa, granddaughter of Hernan Cortés, and great-granddaughter of Montezuma;[7] and was backed by the wealth, nobility, and power of Nueva Galicia. Oñate's petition and contract are not extant; but the former with marginal notes of approval and dissent was seen by Gregg at Santa Fé; and his brief résumé, confirmed by incidental allusions in other documents, shows that the contract did not differ materially from the earlier ones that have been described.   The empresario agreed to raise a force of 200 men or more at his own expense; but seems to have been furnished by the king with a considerable quantity of arms and ammunition, and even a sum of money, being also authorized to confiscate the property of Bonilla and other adventurers if he could catch them. He was made governor, adelantado, and captain-general of the territories to be colonized; and his somewhat extravagant claims for honors, titles, lands, and other emoluments were freely granted by Velasco so far as the royal instructions would permit.[8]

[6] Villagrá says the capitulations were concluded on Aug. 24th. In the *N. Mex., Mem.*, 188–9, it is stated that O.'s petition was dated Sept. 25th, and the contract approved Dec. (clearly a misprint for Oct.) 15th. Gregg saw the memorial at Sta Fé, and gives the date as Sept. 21st, which may be an error for 25th, or vice versa. Villagrá's Aug. 24th may be the date of some preliminary agreement. I have no doubt the final approval by Velasco was in Oct. It was at least before the new viceroy's arrival on Nov. 5th. Torquemada, i. 670–3, makes the date Sept. 30th; and Alaman, *Disert.*, iii. apen. 18, says it was in '94. Velasco's instructions were issued Oct. 21, '95.

[7] Fernandez Duro, 130, says Don Juan married Doña Isabel Cortés Montezuma, daughter of Cortés. Arlegui, *Chron. Zac.*, 56–7, makes Doña Isabel the wife of Cristóbal de Oñate and the mother of Don Juan. Bernardez, *Zac.*, 31–4; confirms the statement of Villagrá as in my text. The *S. Luis Potosí, Relacion Circuns.*, 1, calls O. 'descubridor, conquistador, y poblador' of S. Luis 1583, and son of Doña Isabel acc. to Haro's *Nobilario*.

[8] According to Gregg's résumé of the memorial, O. offered to raise 200 men, and to supply at his own expense live-stock, implements, merchandise, and one year's provisions for the colony. In return, he asked for himself the titles of gov., etc., for 5 lives; 30 leagues of land with all the vassals thereon;

The contract once signed, Don Juan, securing the support of the highest officials and most influential men of Mexico, Nueva Galicia, and Nueva Vizcaya, invoking the aid of his four brothers, and the four brothers Zaldívar, his nephews, and of other active friends,[9] set about the task of recruiting an army, by no means a long or difficult one.   The sargento mayor, Captain Vicente Zaldívar, unfurled his enlistment banner in the grand plaza of Mexico with a salute of artillery; the scenes of '30 and '40 under Guzman and Coronado were repeated; recruits came in from all directions, attracted by the favorable terms offered and the hope of wealth and fame in the north, and the ranks were soon full.[10]

All was enthusiasm; success seemed assured; and preparations for an early departure were wellnigh completed, when a change of viceroys occurred in November, the count of Monterey succeeding Velasco. This in itself naturally caused some delay; but more serious causes were at work.   Oñate's brilliant pros-

a salary of 8,000 ducats, and exemption from the crown tax for working mines; for his family; hereditary nobility and liberal encomiendas; for his army, arms and ammunition; for his officers, repartimientos of native laborers; for his colony, a loan of 20,000 pesos from the royal treasury; and for the spiritual well-being of all, 6 friars and the fitting church accoutrements.   He also asked for instructions respecting the forcible conversion of gentiles and the collection of tribute.   Gregg does not indicate what demands were granted or declined in the marginal notes; nor is it apparent whether this was the original arrangement or the final one as modified by a new viceroy. It is stated in the *N. Mex., Mem.*, 188–9, that Velasco accepted the offer by indorsing the several articles of the petition in marginal notes.   Villagrá says O. got $4,000 in money; Torquemada and Calle add also $6,000 as a loan.

In *Pino, Not. Hist.*, 2–3, and more complete in Davis, *Span. Conq.*, 264–5, is the royal order of July 8, 1602, confirming the title of hijosdalgo to Oñate's associates for 5 years in the conquest, according to an article of the original contract.

[9] There are named Gov. Diego Velasco of N. Vizcaya, Rodrigo del Rio de Loza, Santiago del Riego and Maldonado of the audiencia, Lequetio, Antonio de Figueroa, the Bañuelos, Ruy Blas de Mendoza, Juan Cortés—great-grandson of Hernan—Juan de Guevara, and Salas, the alcalde of Zacatecas.   Oñate's brothers were Fernando, Cristóbal, Alonso, and Luis Nuñez Perez.   The Zaldívar brothers, whose mother seems to have an Oñate, were Cristóbal, Francisco, Juan, and Vicente, who were apparently the sons of the Juan Z. who was a captain of Coronado's army in '40.   Villagrá and some others imply that the Zaldívars were O.'s cousins; but O. calls them *sobrinos*.   Vicente also married a daughter of Juan Oñate.

[10] Salmeron and Niel say that 600 or 700 men were enlisted, though this seems doubtful, as there was no known authority to enlist more than 200.

pects, and the unusual prerogatives granted him, had
created jealousy; and his rivals and foes appear to
have had more influence with the new viceroy than
with the old one. Even before he reached the capital, Monterey asked for a delay; but after Velasco had
explained the matter by letter, he consented to a completion of the arrangements. Arriving the 5th of
November and taking possession of his office, he proceeded to investigate somewhat at his leisure the adelantado's fitness for his position, and the truth of
certain charges against him. The exact nature of
the accusations is not revealed; but soon everybody
seems to have had something to say against Don Juan
and his enterprise; virtue, if we may credit the poet
companion and eulogist, being in this instance wellnigh overpowered by calumny. A prominent element, however, in the new viceroy's policy was his
favor to one Pedro Ponce de Leon, who wished to
undertake the conquista himself; at any rate, he wrote
to the king on December 20th, asking that ratification
of Oñate's project be delayed until new information
could be obtained. The poet's narrative of these and
latter complications is confirmed by documents from
the Spanish archives.[11]

[11] These documents on Oñate's conquest are published in the *Pacheco, Doc.*
xvi., and are of the greatest importance, as follows: *N. Mex., Memorial sobre
el Nuevo México y sus acontecimientos*, 1595–1602, p. 188–227. This is a documentary résumé of Oñate's negotiations, contracts, and acts, made by or for
Vicente Zaldívar in 1602, in connection with his efforts to obtain further aid
from the govt. It contains not only a résumé of documents, corresp., etc.,
but much testimony taken in Mexico on O.'s achievements and the importance
of continuing the conquest, alluding incidentally to the results of earlier
explorations. *Ytinerario de las minas del Caxco, de la gobernacion de la Nueva
Vizcaya . . . con los aguages y leguas de su distancia, camino todo de carretas
. . . Fecho por testigo de vista y experiencia, y que trata verdad, y es sacerdote.*
Another title of the same is *Discurso de las Jornadas que hizo el campo de su
Magestad desde la Nueva España á la provincia de la Nueva Mexico. Año de
1526* (1597–9), p. 228–76. This is a diary, or *derrotero* from the Caxco mines
Aug. 1, '97, to the fall of Acoma, Jan. 24, '99. It bears indications, how-
ever, of having been prepared in Mex. from memory, notes, doc., etc.,
and not a copy of an original diary as written from day to day. It, like all
the other doc., is a part of the Zaldívar expediente of 1602. *Traslado de la
posesion que en nombre de su Magestad tomó Don Joan de Oñate, de los Reynos y
Provincias de la Nueva Mexico; y de las obediencias y vasallaje que los Judios de
algunos pueblos de los dichos Reynos y provincias le dieron en el dicho nombre.
Año de 1598*, p. 98–141. The formal acts of taking possession of N. Mex.

At last the viceroy was induced to approve his predecessor's contract with certain modifications, insisting particularly that Oñate should not, as he demanded, be independent of the audiencia in the administration of justice, or of the viceroy in war and finance. Preparations were now actively renewed for the march; but when the modifications alluded to became known to some members of the colony, whose privileges were more or less curtailed, a new storm of complaints and curses burst upon the leader's head; and his foes took advantage of the occasion to renew their attacks. Oñate deemed it wiser to flee from than resist such foes; accordingly he made haste to begin his march northward.[12] In Zacatecas a halt was made for final preparations. In June 1596, Lope de Ulloa y Lemos was commissioned by Monterey to make a *visita general*, or inspection and inventory. Ulloa was also instructed to remove the army from the settlements on account of certain complaints of disorderly conduct; and he began his inspection in July, appointing Francisco de Esquivel as assistant or comisario.[13] This caused an annoying and seemingly needless delay from the poet's point of view; but as the viceroy

for Spain followed by the acts of submission of the pueblos and native chieftains, with dates and witnesses, especially valuable by reason of the many pueblo names. *Oñate, Copia de Carta escripta al Virrey Conde de Monterrey (por) Don Joan de Oñate, de la Nueva Mexico, á dos de Marzo de 1599 años*, p. 302–15. A letter written at S. Juan, describing briefly what has been done, and dwelling particularly on the brilliant prospects—all to solicit further aid. *N. Mex., Discurso y Proposicion que se hace á Vuestra Magestad de lo tocante á los Descubrimientos del Nuevo Mexico por sus capitulos de puntos diferentes*, p. 38–66. A letter of Viceroy Monterey to the king, probably of 1602, containing a résumé of what had been done in the Oñate matter, and the viceroy's ideas of what more should be done. It is also given in *Fernandez Duro, Don Diego de Peñalosa*, 13–27. *Oñate (Alonso de), Pide se confirme la capitulacion que hizo el Virey con Don Juan de Oñate*, p. 316–22. Dated May 4, 1600, at Madrid, and addressed to the king. There follows a letter of May 5th of like purport and addressed to the consejo.

[12] With him at this time went several Franciscans under P. Rodrigo Duran as comisario. Those named are Baltasar, Cristóbal de Salazar, and Diego Marquez, or Martinez—he who had formerly been captured by 'gente luterana'—who went as confessor or representative of the Inquisition.

[13] *N. Mex., Mem.*, 191; *Id., Dis. y Prop.*, 43–4. Villagrá says nothing of any complaint of disorders. Rivera, *Gob. de Mex.*, tells us that O.'s men mutinied at Taxco, refusing to go on unless the force was increased, and certain promises were fulfilled. The viceroy sent Ulloa to punish the malecontents and make them go on!

had already sent a friendly letter, assuring the governor that the visita was a mere formality, not based on any suspicion, no serious discontent resulted at this time, and soon the force moved on, a part to the Caxco, or Taxco, mines in Durango,[14] and the rest still farther to the San Bartolomé valley.

About a year had now passed since the contract was signed, and the military colony had been considerably reduced during the delay.[15]   A courier was daily expected with marching orders, and at last he came, the 9th of September, with a sealed packet for Ulloa, which contained, as the general and all the army thought, the welcome order.   Bitter was Oñate's disappointment when the packet was found to be, instead, a royal order of May 8th, directing a suspension of the entrada until the receipt of further instructions, in consequence of the viceroy's letter of the past December and the pending negotiations with Ponce de Leon. Enclosed was the viceroy's letter of August 12th to Ulloa, instructing that officer to make known the king's will, and to order Oñate, under the severest penalties, including a revocation of all past concessions, to make no further advance.[16]   In October came from

---

[14] I do not find this place on the maps, but I have a note, of forgotten origin, to the effect that it was on the Rio Nazas in central Durango.   This is confirmed by the later route which led through Zarca and Cerro Gordo, and is probably correct.   They reached Caxco, via Avino and S. Juan del Rio, on Nov. 1, '96.   *N. Mex., Ytin.,* 229.

[15] Villagrá says reduced to 500 men; and we have noted that some authorities give the original force as 600 or 700; but only about 200 besides negroes, Indians, etc., are mentioned in any of the original doc. or corresp.

[16] Llegó luego un correo con gran priessa
Pidiendo albricias por el buen despacho,
De las nueuas alegres que traia,
De Vuestro Visorey, en que mandaua,
Que luego todo el campo se aprestase,
Y que la noble entrada prosiguiesse,
Y como está mas cerca del engaño,
Aquel que esta mas fuera de sospecha,
Assí fué que el correo assegurado,
Con gran contento entró y dio su pliego,
El qual se abrio en secreto, y con recato,
Que ninguno supiesse ni entendiesse,
Lo que el cerrado pliego allí traia,
Y como no ay secreto tan oculto,
Que al fin no se reuele y se nos muestre,

Mexico a repetition of the order. The governor with a heavy heart thought of his past efforts, and of the 500,000 ducats already spent; but kissed the unwelcome *pliego* and promised to obey. He concealed the bad news from his army for a time, and joined in their festivities. He had no thought of giving up his enterprise; and Juan Guerra generously offered to bear a portion of the heavy expense to be entailed by this new delay, which was destined to last over a year.

It seems unnecessary to narrate in detail the history of this gloomy period. Soldiers were constantly deserting, and more than once utter failure seemed inevitable. One visita after another was ordered; but Oñate was able on each occasion to keep his force and supplies up to the standard of his contract.[17] To his protests against the delay, and those of his brothers and friends, the viceroy, although professing the most friendly disposition, replied always that he could not act without royal orders. The adelantado's foes wished of course to break up the expedition altogether, and at times such was the policy of the government as well; but at other times there seemed to be a desire to keep the force together until Ponce de Leon or some other royally favored individual could be in some way given the command. Padre Duran became discouraged and left the company with most of his friars in spite of all remonstrances.[18] But amid all troubles. Oñate, if we may credit his somewhat

El que en aqueste pliego se encerraua,
Contra las buenas nueuas que el correo,
Con inocencia á todos quiso darnos.
Sin quitar una letra ni añidirla,
Quiero con atencion aqui escriuirla.

And accordingly the poet dismounts from Pegasus and gives us these doc. in prose. *Villagrá*, 54–60. They are reproduced in Fernandez Duro's summary; and the dates of reception are found in *N. Mex.*, *Mem.*, 192.

[17] From Nov. '96 to Feb. '97 many communications between Ulloa and Oñate, in relation to the visitas, are given in *N. Mex.*, *Mem.*, 192–7. Part of the force at this period was at Caxco and the rest at Sta Bárbara. There were a few over 200 soldier-colonists, besides negro slaves and Indians. It is implied that O. had contracted to pay expenses of his colony only until N. Mex. was reached, so that the delay was ruinous. O. seems to have visited Mex. in the interval.

[18] Torquemada and others also mention this fact.

partial biographer, stood firm as a rock, sustained by his friends, and by the influence of Doña Eufemia, the beautiful wife of Alférez Peñalosa, who publicly harangued the men, urging them to imitate the fortitude of their leader. Some were mutinous, and bent on going to New Mexico in spite of the king's prohibition; but cutting off the head of their leader checked the ardor of this party.

Late in 1597 came orders to get ready, to submit to a final visita, and to start. The royal cédula of April 2d, on which these orders were founded, I have not seen. In September Juan Frias de Salazar was commissioned as visitador, Esquivel retaining his position as comisario, and in December, when the army had been reunited at the Santa Bárbara mines, the final inspection began.[19] If we follow Villagrá's version, the expectation was that Oñate could not pass the inspection; and the viceroy even advised him not to attempt it but to disband his force. The general's reply was that he would submit, not only to this visita, but to as many more as the government might choose to order; and he did submit, and successfully passed the ordeal. The viceroy states, however, that Salazar was secretly instructed to deal as leniently as possible with Oñate, disregarding small deficiencies; and the records show that there was a deficiency in both

[19] Villagrá does not name Salazar, but calls the successor of Ulloa—who was sent to China—Capt Guerrero, with Jaime Fernandez as secretary. This may be an error, or Guerrero may have been intermediate between Ulloa and Salazar. The new visitador acc. to V. was a bitter foe of Oñate, and the quarrel between the two waxed very hot. As a sample of the obstacles thrown in the way of the colony, I note the following: Instead of permitting a halt while the inspection was being conducted, as was usual and expected, the *visitador* ordered an immediate march. Then in some most unsuitable place he would order a halt, forbid the men for several days to leave their tents to look after the live-stock, forbid the purchase of any animals, and then suddenly order the goats or some other class to be presented immediately at his office for inspection! *Villagrá, Hist. N. Mex.*, 72–4.

The rear division of the army had left Caxco Aug. 1st, and marched via Carrizal, Zarca, Los Patos, Cerro Gordo, La Parida, Bauz, Rio Florido, and Rio Bunuelos to Sta Bárbara in S. Bartolomé valley, where they arrived Aug. 19th, and remained till Dec. 17th. Then they pitched the camp a few leagues farther on, at the arroyo de S. Gerónimo, where the visita began Dec. 22d, and where they remained a month. *N. Mex., Ytinerario*, 229–32; *Id., Mem.*, 197–5; *Id., Discurso*, 44.

supplies and men, of whom only 130 remained. It was decided that the viceroy should raise 80 men at Oñate's expense—Juan Guerra and his wife, Ana de Mendoza, becoming sureties—and about this number were indeed sent north the next year.[20]

OÑATE'S ROUTE, 1598.

[20] *N. Mex., Mem.*, 197–8; *Id., Discurso*, 44. As we have seen, most authorities speak of only short delays, and imply that the exped. started for N. Mex. in the summer of '96. The delays are attributed by Salmeron and Niel to the devil, who trembled at the prospect of losing his grasp on so many thousands of souls. Cavo, *Tres Siglos*, i. 225–9, like Rivera, tells us the delay was caused by a mutiny at Caxco, which Ulloa succeeded in quelling.

The final inspection having been concluded the 20th
of January, 1598, the army started northward six days
later, and on the 30th reached the Conchos. Spanish
travellers in America never encamped if it were possible to avoid it, on the near, but always on the farther, side of a stream; therefore haste was made to
cross; and the bustle and incidents of bridging and
fording the river are vividly portrayed by our poet
chronicler. They remained in camp on the Conchos
for a week, getting rid of the visitador, who is said to
have departed without bidding the colonists good-by,
but also having to part with Padre Marquez, their
confessor. Arrangements had, however, been made
for a new band of ten Franciscans; and these friars,
under Padre Alonso Martinez, as comisario, came north
with Captain Farfan and his party, who had escorted
Padre Marquez on his return, and joined the army
soon after the start.[21]

The force that left the Conchos on the 7th of February is given by Salmeron and Niel, and implied by
Villagrá, as 400 men, 130 of whom were accompanied
by their families. The documentary records indicate
only the 130 soldier colonists, besides a large number
of servants and Indians; and it is difficult to understand how there could have been more whom Oñate
could not utilize to make up the 200 of his contract.
Don Cristóbal de Oñate, son of Don Juan, accompanied
the expedition as teniente de gobernador y capitan
general, at the age of ten years! Juan de Zaldívar
was maestro de campo; Don Vicente, his brother, sargento mayor; Captain Villagrá, procurador general;
Captain Bartolomé Romeros, contador; Zubia, or
Cubia, proveedor; and Juan Velarde and Juan Perez
Donis, secretaries. I append a list of such names as

[21] They arrived March 3d.   Their names were Alonso Martinez, Francisco
de Zamora, Juan Rosas, Alonso Lugo, Francisco de San Miguel, Andrés Corchado, Cristóbal Salazar (a cousin of Oñate), Juan Claros, Pedro Vergara, and
Juan de San Buenaventura—the last 2 lay friars; also brothers Martin, Francisco, and Juan de Dios are named.   Barreiro, *Ojeada*, 5, says Oñate had 65
Franciscans with him !

I have found in the various records, well worth preserving, as including the first settlers of New Mexico; though unfortunately the full names and titles of all could not be made to fit the metre of the poetic version.[22]   There were 83 wagons in the train, and 7,000 head of cattle.

[22] Alphabetic list of Oñate's associates in the conquest of N. Mex.

Capt. Pablo de Aguilar
Araujo
Ascencio de Archuleta
Ayarde
Alf. Dionisio de Bañuelos
Bartol
Juan Benitez
Bibero
Capt. Juan Gutierrez de Bocanegra
Juan Perez de Bustillo
César Ortiz Cadimo
Juan Camacho
Estévan Carabajal
Carrera
Juan de Caso
Alf. (Capt.) Bernabé de las Casas
Castillo
Juan Catalan
Cavanillas
Capt. Gregorio César
Cordero
Alf. Juan Cortés
Márcos Cortés
Pedro Sanchez Damiero
Juan Diaz
Sec. Juan Perez de Donis
Capt. Felipe Escalante
Juan Escarramal
Capt. Marcelo de Espinosa
Capt. Márcos Farfan de los Godos
Juan Fernandez
Manuel Francisco
Álvaro García
Francisco García
Márcos García
Simon García
Luis Gascon
Bartolomé Gonzalez
Juan Gonzalez
Juan Griego
Guevara
Francisco Guillen
Antonio Gutierrez
Alf. Gerón. de Heredia
Antonio Hernandez
Francisco Hernandez
Gonzalo Hernandez
Pedro Hernandez

Antonio Conde de Herrera
Cristóbal de Herrera
Juan de Herrera
Alonzo Nuñez de Hinojosa
Leon de Isasti
Jimenez
Capt. Diego Landin
Francisco de Ledesma
Alf. Juan de Leon
Domingo de Lizana
Cristóbal Lopez
Juan Lopez
Alonso Lúcas
Lucío
Mallea
Francisco Marquez
Capt. Gerónimo Marquez
Hernan Martin
Juan Martinez
Juan Medel
Medina
Monroi
Alonso Gomez Montesinos
Baltasar de Monzon
Morales
Juan Moran
Munuera
Naranjo
Capt. Diego Nuñez
Juan de Olague
Ten. Gen. Cristóbal de Oñate
Capt. Gen. Juan de Oñate
Juan de Ortega
Ortiz
Regundo Paladin
Simon de Paz
Juan de Pedraza
Alf. Pereyra
Simon Perez
Capt. Juan Piñero
Alf. Fran. de Posa y Peñalosa
Capt. Alonso de Quesada
Fran. Guillen de Quesada
Martin Ramirez
Juan Rangel
Rascon
Pedro de los Reyes
Pedro de Ribera

Instead of descending the Conchos as earlier explorers had done, Oñate seems to have taken a northward course to the Rio Bravo. Two exploring parties were sent out in advance to find a way for the wagons, and Villagrá, who accompanied the sargento mayor, devotes more than two cantos of his work to a description of their adventures; and in the *Ytinerario* the dates, distances, and names of successive points reached by the main army are given; but though this was the first exploration of northern Chihuahua, the details have no special interest in connection with our present subject except as appended in a note.[23]   Progress with the wagons was naturally slow, but there

Alonso del Rio	Sosa
Diego Robledo	Capt. Tabora
Francisco Robledo	Capt. Francisco Vaca
Pedro Robledo	Varela
Pedro Rodriguez	Francisco Vasquez
Sebastian Rodriguez	Jorge de la Vega
Bartolomé Romeros	Sec. Juan Velarde
Capt. Moreno de la Rua	Francisco Vido
Capt. Ruiz	Juan de Victoria Vido
Juan Ruiz	Capt. Gaspar de Villagrá
Lorenzo Salado	Villalba
Juan de Salas	Villaviciosa
Alonso Sanchez	Capt. Juan de Zaldívar
Cristóbal Sanchez	Capt. Vicente de Zaldívar
Francisco Sanchez	Alf. Leon Zapata
Antonio Sariñana	Prov. Zubia
Juan de Segura	Zumaia.
Serrano	

[22] Feb. 7th, left the Conchos; 3 l. to La Tentacion. 8th, 2 l. to Agua del Incendio.   9th, 3 l. to barrancas.   10th, 3 l. to Rio S. Pedro, forded in 28° 45′, remaining a month, and the padres arriving March 3d.   March 11th, 3 l. to Charcos.   12th, 5 l. to Rio de Nombre de Dios.   14th, back to S. Buenaventura a short distance, whence Landin started for Mex.   18th, 3 l. to Sierrazuela de las Hogueras.   19th, 1 l. to S. José, or Sacramento, where holy Thursday was celebrated with great ceremonies.   20th, 3 l. to Sta Cruz.   22d, 3 l. to Encinar de la Resurreccion.   24th, 2 l. to Alameda de la Asumpcion.   25th, 1 l. to Laguna de S. Benito y Ojuelos del Norte, a lake 2 l. in circum.   26th, 3 l. to Aguage de la Cruz.   27th, 1 l. to Peñol de Velez in lat. 30°.   30th, 2 l. to Ancon del Recelo.   31st, 2 l. to fuente de S. Fran. de Paula.   April 1st–2d, 3 l. to Socorro del Cielo.   3d–5th, 6 l. to Rio de la Mentira and Ciénega de S. Isidro in about 30° 30′.   7th, 2 l. to Alchicubite de S. Vicente.   8th–9th, 3 l. to Ciénega de la Concepcion, and beginning of the sand dunes.   10th, 1½ l. to fuente de S. Leon in lat. 31°.   11th, spring of S. Emenegildo.   12th, 3 l. to Bocas de los Médanos.   19th–20th, 6 l. to the Rio del Norte in 31° 30′, river called Rio Bravo farther s. E.   April 28th–May 3d, 8½ l. up the river.   May 4th, forded the river in exactly 31° (not a typog. error, for the writer notes that they had lost 30′ in going 8½ l.!); they called the ford Vado de los Puertos; in many leagues there is no other way for wagons.

were no adventures or calamities. Captain Landin was despatched for Mexico with letters in the middle of March. On the 20th of April they reached the Rio Grande. On the last day of the month, a few leagues up the river on the western bank, Oñate proceeded with all the complicated and curious ceremonial deemed essential in such cases, to take formal possession for God, the king, and himself, of New Mexico "and all the adjoining provinces," as appears from the long and verbose act of possession duly certified by Juan Perez, the royal escribano, in the presence of the friars and all the army.[24] There were also imposing religious ceremonies, including mass in a chapel built for the occasion, and a sermon by the padre comisario; and finally in the evening the performance of an original comedy written by Captain Farfan on a subject connected with the conquest of New Mexico—early days of the drama, indeed.[25]

[24] This *acta* is given in full by Villagrá, p. 129–32; and also in *N. Mex. Traslado*, 88–101. In this doc. Oñate alludes to the king's order of April 2, '97, approving his appointment; and also names all the friars of his company. Space does not permit the translation of this paper as a curiosity.

[25] 'Hobo sermon, gran solemnidad eclesiástica y seglar, gran salva y alegría, y á la tarde comedia.' *N. Mex., Ytin.*, 242.

CHAPTER VII.

OÑATE'S CONQUEST CONTINUED.

1598-1599.

El Paso del Norte—Up the Rio Grande—The First Pueblo Group at Socorro—A Miracle at Puarai—From Pueblo to Pueblo—Obedience and Vassalage—San Juan de los Caballeros, San Gabriel, and City of San Francisco—Universal Junta—Distribution of Missionaries—List of Towns—Zaldívar's Trip to the Plains—Oñate's South-eastern Tour—The Captain-general Starts for the Mar del Sur—Submission of Acoma, Zuñi, and the Moqui Towns—Visit to Mines in Arizona—Villagrá's Adventures, Acoma to Zuñi—Revolt of Acoma—Death of Zaldívar and Fifteen Companions—Vengeance of the Spaniards—Battle of the Peñol—Destruction of Acoma and Slaughter of the Natives—End of the Epic and Other Records.

On the 4th of May, 1598, only twenty-five miles above the point where they first reached the Rio Grande, the Spaniards were shown by natives a convenient ford, and the army crossed to the eastern bank. The latitude is confusedly given as 31° or 31° 30'; and I have no doubt that this "ford of the river of the north" was the original El Paso del Norte, a name that has been retained ever since for the locality where the river leaves the territory which is now New Mexico. From the 5th to the 20th the army marched slowly up the river on the eastern side for fifteen and a half leagues, with none but trivial incidents, if we except the death of several persons of the colony, and without applying names to localities. Here Captain Aguilar returned from an advance exploration, having reached the first pueblos and entered one of them against the orders of his chief, who, however, pardoned him at the intercession of his men. Fearing that the natives might be alarmed and run away with their food supplies, Oñate with the Zaldívars, Villagrá, padres Salazar and Martinez, and fifty men,[1] started on the 22d, and in six days, 26 or 22 leagues, reached the first group of pueblos, a storm with thunder, lightning, and perhaps an earthquake marking the approach, and drawing from the padres all the prayers of the litany.

It is noticeable that the distance of 41 or 38 leagues from El Paso confirms our identification, from the reports of earlier explorers, of the southernmost group of pueblos with the Socorro region in latitude 34°; and indeed, the pueblo of Teipana, three leagues above Qualacú of the first two, was now named Socorro. Besides these three which are mentioned as occupied, there were others abandoned, but only these two names are given. The natives gave a kind welcome to the strangers, entertained the governor in their towns, and furnished supplies of maize, which desirable 'socorro' was sent back to the main camp. It was the middle of June when Oñate and his advance party left what may be regarded as the first group of towns.[2]

The next advance up the river was to a small pueblo named Nueva Sevilla, seven leagues above Socorro, the first in which the soldiers slept, and where they remained a week while the Zaldívars went to explore the Abó pueblos,[3] and Villagrá made a tour in search of maize. Then on the 22d of June they went on for four leagues to a new but abandoned pueblo, which they

[1] Oñate, *Cop. de Carta*, 303, says there were 70 men; and that one of his objects was to find and arrest Humaña. The force is not given in the *Ytinerario*.

[2] The purport of Oñate's narrative, however, indicates less clearly than those of earlier explorers a grouping of the towns; but rather makes a continuous line of pueblos at intervals of 3 or 4 l. The text of the *Ytinerario* leaves it slightly doubtful whether the next town was not four instead of 7 l. above Socorro.

[3] This is the first mention of this name. The ruins of Abó are in about lat. 34° 30', 25 or 30 miles east of the river, and agreeing very well with the indications of this record. Sevilla was not far from the junction of the Rio Puerco. The *Ytinerario*, 242–53, is chiefly followed for this part of the journey, as Villagrá disposes of it somewhat briefly.

named San Juan Bautista, as they were there on the 24th, or Saint John's day.[4] Here the general heard of two Mexican Indians left by Castaño, and started northward on the 25th in search of them, reaching Puruai, named San Antonio, in a journey of sixteen leagues. Here the friars were lodged in a newly painted room, and in the morning they beheld on the walls life-like portraits of the martyred Rodriguez and Lopez of seventeen years ago, which the natives had vainly tried to conceal with the paint! The two Mexicans, Tomás and Cristóbal, were presently brought in from another pueblo, and they proved as interpreters a most valuable acquisition to the Spaniards. Before the end of June they visited the pueblo of Tria—possibly Cia—which they named San Pedro y San Pablo; and moved on three leagues from Puruai to San Felipe, and thence four leagues to Guipui, or Santo Domingo.[5] This town was made a kind of headquarters or capital for a time, all of Oñate's advance party coming up apparently; and in this province we are told was chosen[6] a convent named Asumpcion, though nothing appears later about such an institution. On the 4th of July Captain Juan de Zaldívar was sent back to bring up the rest of the wagons and colonists who had reached the first pueblos on June 26th, but who did not join the advance army till August.

At Santo Domingo on the 7th of July seven chieftains representing some thirty-four pueblos assembled to acknowledge the supremacy of new masters temporal and spiritual. Tomás and Cristóbal, serving as interpreters, explained at great length the material prosperity and eternal happiness that must result from

[4] S. Juan must have been some distance below Isleta, and must not be confounded with S. Juan de los Caballeros.

[5] Perhaps S. Felipe was 3 l. beyond S. Pedro y S. Pablo instead of Puruai; or Sto Domingo 4 l. from P. instead of from S. Felipe. Elsewhere in the *Ytinerario* Sto Domingo is said to be 6 l. from P. Not much importance can be attached to exact distances in these records. Clearly S. Felipe and Sto Domingo correspond with those still so called, though it is not certain that the sites were not slightly changed in the next century.

[6] 'Se elixió convento de la advocacion de Nra Sra de la Asumpcion.' *Ytin.*, 254. Perhaps it should be 'se erigió,' or was built instead of chosen.

being 'good,' and submitting cheerfully to Felipe II.
and God, as contrasted with present disaster and future damnation inseparably connected with refusal;
and the chiefs, disposed to be friendly or fearing the
strangers' guns and horses, even if they had some lin-
gering doubts respecting the political and doctrinal
theories presented, humbly kneeled and swore the required allegiance, as was duly recorded in a ponderous
document.[7]   On July 9th the army left the pueblo of
Bove, or San Ildefonso,[8] and in two days, or ten
leagues—the wagons going by a longer route of sixteen leagues via San Márcos—to Caypa, or San Juan,
doubtless identical, or nearly so, with the pueblo still
bearing the name near the junction of the Rio Grande
and Rio Chama just above latitude 36°.   From the
courtesy of the people—especially after much-needed
rain had been produced by the padres' prayers—this
town was soon called San Juan de los Caballeros, and
for several years was the Spanish capital, or centre of
operations.   The name San Gabriel was also applied
by the friars to their establishment here, or more probably to another pueblo not far distant.[9]

[7] *Obediencia y Vasallaje á Su Magestad por los indios de Santo Domingo* (July
7, 1598), in *N. Mex. Traslado*, 101-8.   As there were several similar acts a
little later, it will be more convenient to name the pueblos together in a subsequent note.

[8] Of their going from Sto Dom. to S. Ild. nothing is said, nor is the distance mentioned; but it would seem that S. Ild. may have been much nearer
to Sto Dom. than the pueblo now called S. Ild., else the distance of 10 l. to
S. Juan would be inexplicable.

[9] Both in the *Ytinerario* and in *Oñate, Cop. de Carta*, 304, the distance is
given as 61 l. from the point where O. originally left the wagons far south of
Socorro, and this corresponds nearly enough with the actual distance from a
point just above lat. 33° to one just above 36°.   The place is often called S.
Juan Bautista, but must be distinct from the southern pueblo originally so
named.   Davis' statement, *Span. Conq.*, 289, that the name 'de los Caballeros'
originated from the gentlemanly conduct of the natives during the great revolt of the next century, though founded on several early statements, is an
error.   Several early writers speak of the villa de San Gabriel, and indeed
Zaldívar so calls the Span. headquarters in 1602. *N. Mex., Mem.*, 198.   Torquemada and others cited earlier in this chapter state that the Spaniards established themselves at S. Gabriel between the Rio Grande and a smaller
stream.   Salmeron and Niel locate it between the Zama, or Chama, and Rio
Grande.   In the *Arch. N. Mex.*, 158, the ruins of S. Gabriel are mentioned
as on the Chama 6 l. above its mouth.   S. Gabriel del Yunque, in *Escalante
Carta*, 116, recalls Coronado's Yunque Yunque.   It will be noted that in the
subsequent distrib. of friars in Sept., S. Gabriel is named as distinct from S.
Juan.

From San Juan on the 13th Oñate went to Picuríes, or San Buenaventura, six leagues; and thence
six leagues farther to Taos, or San Miguel, or Tayberon, the northern limit. Returning to San Juan
he went to San Ildefonso on the 20th, and thence five
leagues east to San Márcos next day, and the next to
San Cristóbal.[10] On the 24th and 26th he went to
Pecos, or Santiago,[11] by way of Glisteo, or Santa Ana;
returning to San Cristóbal and San Márcos on the
26th, and next day going down to Santo Domingo,
where the main company from below under Saldívar
arrived the same day. From the 2d to the 7th of
August Oñate made a tour by way of the great pueblo
of Tria—probably Cia—to the great one of the Emenes
or Jemes, visiting also some others of the eleven
pueblos in that province, and finding some hot sulphur
springs. Having returned to Santo Domingo, he
went up to San Ildefonso on the 9th, and next day
probably arrived at San Juan.[12]

It was the next day after this arrival, or the 11th
of August, that work was begun on the ditches required to bring water for the city of San Francisco
which it was determined to found, some 1,500 Indians
assembling to aid in the labor. I believe that the site
of this intended city was at or in the immediate vicinity of San Juan, and not at Santa Fé, where the city
was really built in later years. For a long time
nothing more is heard of it, and it is probable that
the progress of the work was soon interrupted by
troubles presently to be noticed; or the water-works

[10] S. Cristóbal and S. Márcos belonged apparently to the Nambé and Tesuque group north of Sta Fé, yet in later years they seem to have been south
and again north of Sta Fé. They may be the pueblos so named by Castaño,
as Oñate had an Ind. girl of S. Cristóbal carried away by C.; and near S.
Márcos certain mines, called de Escalante, are mentioned as by C.

[11] Pedro Orez, a native of Pecos carried away by Espejo, had died; but
Brother Juan de Dios of O.'s band had learned the language, and he later
settled here.

[12] The diary is not clear for the 10th, there being apparently an omission
of the doings of that day. Except for what follows about the new city this
would have no importance, and I think there can be no doubt that they went
to S. Juan.

may have been completed for San Juan, and the building of the city postponed to a more convenient season when a change of site was found desirable. I find not the slightest reason to date the founding of Santa Fé from 1598.[13] While San Francisco was to be the name of the new city, San Pablo was chosen by the Indians as the general patron of the territory. The last of the colonists and wagons arrived on the 18th, and thus all were reunited at San Juan de los Caballeros. A few days later a mutinous plot of certain soldiers, including apparently Captain Aguilar, was revealed, but the governor was moved by tears and supplications to grant a general pardon.[14] From August 23d to September 7th a church was built, and dedicated on the 8th with great ceremonies terminating with a sham battle between Christians and Moors. There was a week of general sports at this time which brought in a large number of natives from all directions, some of them coming, as the poet tells us, as spies to study the invaders' strength.

A 'universal junta de toda la tierra' was held at San Juan on the 9th of September, on which occasion the native chiefs, including representatives of pueblos

[13] 'Se empezó la saca del agua para la ciudad de nuestro Padre Sant Francisco.' N. Mex., Ytin., 262. In Id., Traslado, 116, 'la cibdad de Sant Francisco de los Españoles que al presente se edifican' is included with S. Juan in the missionary field of P. Salazar in the distribution of Sept. 9th; and this is cited by Bandelier, Hist. Introd., 19, as 'documentary evidence regarding the establishment of Sta Fé,' though it does not follow that B. really opposes my view of the matter. That the writer of the Ytinerario, after carefully noting Oñate's tour through the Sta Fé region and return to S. Juan, should have referred to the beginning of work on the new city the next day, having in mind a site 25 or 30 miles away, with no preliminary record of choosing the site, etc., is as improbable as that a city at Sta Fé in process of construction should have escaped all mention for 10 years or more; but there is nothing at all strange in the record if the meaning is that the city was to be at S. Juan, since the work may have gone on slowly for years or its suspension during the later troubles have left no record. Since writing what precedes I find in Vetancur, Chron., 101, the following, which settles the question: From S. Juan de los Caballeros are in sight (1680–91) the 'edificios de la villa de S. Gabriel, primera fundacion que se pasó á Sta Fé á la otra parte del rio.'

[14] Over 45 men were concerned, acc. to Oñate, Cop. Carta, 304. Four men subsequently ran away for the 'tierra de paz,' with a band of horses; but Villagrá and Marquez went in pursuit, hanged two of the men, and recovered the animals, going as V. claims in 14 days to Sta Bárbara; and indeed Oñate, 305, says that they wrote to the viceroy from Sta B. They started Sept. 12th, and returned early in Nov.

and provinces that had before submitted and many
others, renewed their formal submission, after listening to a new explanation of the system by which
the Almighty was represented in New Mexico *en lo
temporal* through the king by Oñate, and *en lo espiritual* through the pope by the padre comisario Martinez.
They also expressed the joy with which they would
receive the friars at their pueblos as spiritual teachers
and masters, after listening to the cheering assurance
that if they refused or disobeyed the padres they
would all be burned alive, besides burning later in
hell. Villagrá tells us, however, that while they
readily submitted to the king, they very sensibly told
the padre comisario that so far as the new faith was
concerned they had no objection to adopting it, if after
proper instruction they found it desirable, adding
naïvely that of course he would not wish them to embrace a faith they did not fully understand! Thereupon Martinez proceeded to apportion the pueblos
among his co-laborers.[15]

In my narrative of earlier entradas I have given in
text or notes all the pueblo names mentioned by the
successive explorers, with such comments as seemed
necessary to show their identity. In the records of
Oñate's conquest, and especially in the acts of *obediencia y vasallaje* and distribution of friars, these names
are very numerous, and doubtless in many instances
very inaccurate as written or printed; yet I have
deemed it desirable to preserve them; and for the convenience of reader and student I append them in compact form, adding all the names that appear in earlier
narratives. Identification is in most cases, so far as
individual pueblos are concerned, impossible; indeed,
there is nothing left with which to identify them, and
I make no attempt at arbitrary location on my maps,
though all existing data of distance, direction, etc.,
will be found in these chapters. Fortunately, the

---

[15] *Obediencia y Vasallaje á Su Magestad por los indios del Pueblo de San Juan
Bautista* (Sept. 9, '98), in *N. Mex.*, *Traslado*, 108–17, including the distribution of the missionaries. Also *Villagrá, Hist. N. Mex.*, 152–5, with less details.

identity by groups or leading pueblos presents few difficulties, and in nearly every group a few names have survived to modern times. The towns in the sixteenth century occupied the same general range of territory as in the nineteenth; but most of them were destroyed in the seventeenth, and many of those remaining were moved from their original sites.[16] I

[16] The body of what follows is from the *Obediencias* of the *N. Mex.*, *Traslado*, items in parentheses being from the *Ytinerario*, Villagrá's narrative, and other doc. relating to Oñate's expedition; while notes from earlier expeditions and comments are enclosed in brackets.

Under care of Fr. Francisco de S. Miguel, prov. of the Pecos (Santiago) with the 7 pueblos of the eastern Ciénega, and the Vaquero, or wild tribes, of that region to the Sierra Nevada, and the pueblos of the 'gran salina' behind the sierra of Puruay; and besides the pueblos of Quanquiz, Hohotá, Xonalús, Xatol, Xaiméla, Aggéy, Cuzá, Cizentetpi, Acoli, Abbo (Abó), Apena, Axauti, Amaxa, Couna, Dhiu, Alle, Atuyama, and Chein; and the 3 great pueblos of the Jumanas, or 'rayados' called in their language Atripuy, Genobey, Quelotetrey, and Pataotrey. In the *Obediencia* of Oct. 12th we have also in this s. e. region the prov. of Cheálo with the pueblos of Acolocú, Cuzayá [Cuzá above], Junetre, and Paáco; and in the *Obed.* of Oct. 17th those of Cuelóce, Xenopué, Patasce, and Abo. [Coronado calls Pecos Cicuye, Cicuio, Cicuique, Ticuique, Tienique, or Acuique, not naming others in the region. Rodriguez mentions prov., or valleys, of Camé with 6 pueblos, and Asay, or Osay, with 5, somewhere in the s. e. Espejo names the prov. of Tamos—Tanos—one of its pueblos being called Ciquique, or Pecos; and also the prov. of Maguas, or Magrias, of 11 pueblos n. e. of the Tiguas. Sayaqué appears on Jeffery's atlas.] Glisteo, or Sta Ana, is named in the *Ytin.* [In all this eastern region of about 40 pueblos alluded to we have in modern times only the ruins Pecos, Galisteo, Abó, Gran Quivira, and various scattered heaps of nameless ruins.]

Fr. Juan Claros, prov. of the Chiguas, or Tiguas, and pueblos of Napeya and Tuchiamas, and that of Pura with the 4 'consecutive' down the river, that of Poxen, Puaráy (S. Antonio), Trimati, Guayotrí, Acacafuí, Henicohio, Vareato 'with all its subjects to Puaráy up and down the Rio del Norte'(?); also the prov. of Xalay, the prov. of Mohoqui (?), and the prov. of the Atripuy down the river with its pueblos which are Preguey, Tuzahe, Aponitre, Vumahein, Quiápo, Trelaquepú, Cunquilipinoy, Calciati, Aquicato, Encaquiagualcaca, Quialpo, Trelagú, Pesquis, Ayquí, Yancomo, Teyaxa, Qualacú (2d pueblo coming from s., acc. to *Ytin.*), Texa, Amo, on 'this side' [west?] of the river; and on the other, Pencoana, Quiomaquí, Peixolóe, Zumaque, Teeytraan, Preguey [see above, repeated], Canocan, Peytre, Qui-Ubaco, Tohol, Cantensapué, Tercao, Poloocá, Treyéy, Queelquelú, Átepíra, Trula, Treypual, Tecahanqualahámo, Pilopué, Penjeacú, Teypamá (Teipana, or Socorro, 3 l. above Qualacú), and Trenaquel 'de la mesilla' which is the 1st pueblo coming from Mexico. (Which of these were the ones called Nueva Sevilla and S. Juan Bautista in the *Ytin.* does not appear.) In the *Obed.* of July 7th the Chigua pueblos named are Paniete, Piaqui, Axoytre, Piamato, Quioyaco, and Camitre, or at least these were under the captain of the Chiguas. [Niza's Totonteac may possibly have been the Tigua prov. Coronado wintered in Tiguex, Tihuex, or Tihueq, a prov. of 12 or 15 pueblos; and visited Tutahaco, a prov. of 8 pueblos down the river in the Isleta region; also 4 towns in the Socorro region not named, which were also mentioned without being named by Rodriguez and Espejo. R.'s visit 1st shows the name Puaray or Puara; and E. names the pueblo of Puara, Puala, or Poalas, one of 16 in the prov. of Tiguas. It is not probable that a single one of these 60 pueblos of the southern section of the Rio Grande valley is still standing, though there are a few of later origin].

have no doubt that the number of pueblos, about 170,
is greatly exaggerated through a confounding of
names pertaining to towns, tribes, and chieftains.

Fr. Juan de Rosas, prov. of the Cheres, or Cherechos (Hores) [Queres.
The name Querechos is applied by Coronado and Espejo to wild tribes in the
east and west] with the pueblos of the Castixes, or S. Felipe and Comitre,
Sto Domingo or Guipui, Alipoti, Chochití or Cochití; that of the Ciénega de
Carabajal; S. Márcos, S. Cristóbal, Sta Ana, Ojana, Quipana, del Puerto, and
Pueblo Quemado. In the *Obed.* of July 7th are also named Tamy, Acogiya,
Cachichi, Yates, and Tipotí. (Villagrá gives the Queres prov. to P. Zamora,
omitting Rosas.) [Coronado names Quirix, or Quivix, a prov. of 7 pueblos.
Espejo calls it Quires with 5 pueblos   Castaño called it Quereses, naming
one of the towns Sto Domingo, perhaps the same so called by Oñate, and also
S. Márcos, S. Lúcas, and S. Cristóbal.   Pueblos still standing in this region,
the Rio Grande valley, in about lat. 35° 30′, retain the names of Sta Ana, S.
Felipe, Sto Domingo, and Cochití, some of them perhaps identical with those
of the 16th century.]
     Fr. Cristóbal de Salazar, prov. of the Tepúas (Téguas, acc. to Villagrá)
[Tehuas], with the pueblos of Triapí, Triaque, S. Ildefonso or Bove, Sta
Clara, San Juan [de los Caballeros] or Caypa, S. Gabriel, Trovmaxiaquino,
Xiomato, Axol, Camitria, Quiotráco, and the city of S. Francisco 'que se
edifican.'   [Coronado calls the prov. Yuque-Yunque with 6 towns; and his
Ximera, or Ximena, with Silos and other abandoned villages may have been
in this region.   Espejo calls the province or the eastern part of it Ubates or
Hubates.   Of the 10 or 11 Tehua pueblos, the names of S. Juan, Sta Clara,
and S. Ildefonso still remain in this district, and of the same prov. are the
towns of Nambé, Pujuaque, and Tesuque.]
     Fr. Francisco de Zamora, prov. of the Picuríes, with all the Apaches N.
and w. of the Sierra Nevada; also prov. of the Taos with pueblos in that
region and upper valley of the Rio Grande.   Taos was also called Tayberon
and S. Miguel; and Picuríes was S. Buenaventura.   [Coronado called Taos
Braba, Uraba, or Yuraba; and his Acha prov. in this region was possibly
Picuríes.]
     Fr. Alonso de Lugo, prov. of the Emmes (Emés) [Jemes], and the pueblos
of Yjar, Guayoguía, Mecastría, Quiustá, Ceca, Potre, Trea [Cia?], Guatitruti,
Catróo; and the Apades [Apaches] and Cocoyes of the sierra and region.   In
the *Obed.* of July 7th, the Emmes pueblos are called Yxcaguayo, Quiamera,
Fía, Quinsta, Leeca, Poze, Fiapuze, Friyti, and Caatri.   [If, as seems likely,
these are different spellings of the same 9 pueblos, our confidence in the
accuracy of these doc. is considerably shaken.   Coronado mentions the prov.
of Hemes with 7 towns, and that of Aguas Calientes with 3.   Espejo calls
the prov. that of the Emexes, Emeges, or Amejes.   The pueblo of Jemes
still stands, but not on its original site.]
     Fr. Andrés Corchado, prov. of Trias, or Trios, with pueblos of Tamaya,
Yacco, Toajgua, and Pelchin.   In the *Obed.* of July 7th are named Comitre
and Ayquiyu, with Triati and Pequen, perhaps in this region.   Corchado's
district lay westward from the 'gran pueblo' of Tria or S. Pedro y S. Pablo
(Zia, *Villagrá.*)   [Cia, called Chia by Coronado.   Perhaps the Tlascala of Rodriguez.   Sia, or Siay, of Espejo, the capital of the prov. of Punames, Pumames, or Cunames of 5 pueblos.]   Also Acoma, *Obed.* of Oct. 27th.   [Possibly
Niza's prov. of Acus or Marata.   Coronado's Acuco, or Coco.   Espejo's
Acoma.   If this pueblo could be located in the early times farther N. than its
present site, say on the Puerco about lat. 35° 30′, it would agree better with
the records; but I find no evidence of a change, and the peculiarities of the
peñol site render a change improbable, though not impossible.]   Also Zuñi,
or Truni—*Obed.* of Nov. 9th—a prov. of 6 pueblos, Aguicobi or Aguscobi,
Canabi, Coaqueria, Halonagu, Macaqui, and Aguinsa.   *Obed.* of Nov. 9th.
[Niza's prov. of Cíbola with 7 pueblos, one of them Ahacus.   Coronado's
Cíbola, with 2 of the 7 towns named Granada and Muzaque, perhaps the

After the general assembly and its attendant festivities, Vicente Zaldívar was sent with fifty men to

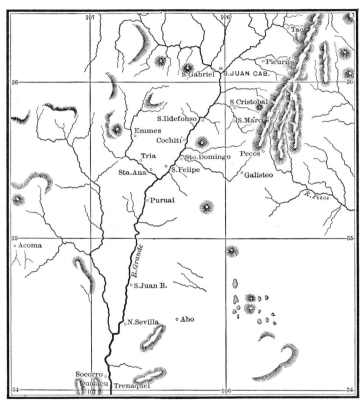

NEW MEXICO IN THE SIXTEENTH CENTURY.

Macaqui above. Espejo's Zuni, Zuny, Amé, or Amí, one of the towns being
Aquico.] Also the prov. of Mohoce or Mohoqui—*Obed.* of Nov. 15th—with its
pueblos of Mohoqui, Naybé, Xumupamí, Cuanrabí, and Esperiez; the captains
of which, perhaps confused with the pueblo names, were Pananmá, Hoynigua,
Xuynuxá, Patiguá, and Aguatuybá. *Obed.* of Nov. 15th. [The modern
names of the 7 Moqui towns—*Nat. Races*, i. 528—are Oraibe, Shumuthpa,
Mushaiina, Ahlela, Gualpi, Siwinna, and Tegua; or acc. to Garcés in the 18th
century, Sesepaulabá, Masagneve, Janogualpa, Muqui, Concabe, and Muca
or Oraive. Coronado's Tusayan, Tucayan, Tuzan, Tusan, or Tucano with 7
towns. Espejo's Mohoce, or Mohace, with 5 towns, one of them Aguato, or
Zaguato; other pueblos of Deziaguabos, Gaspé, Comupaví, Majananí, and
Olalla being mentioned in connection with his exped.]

Other pueblos named in the *Obed.* of July 7th with no indication of locality,
and not named in the distribution of friars, are Aychini, Baguacat, Xutis,
Yucaopi, Acacagua, Ytriza, and Atica.

explore the buffalo plains of the east, with no results
of a geographic or historic nature worth noticing here.
Some petty adventures among the roving bands of
natives, the shooting of the first bull by the valiant
major, and a grand buffalo hunt with brilliant but not
very successful efforts to capture some of the *cíbolos*
alive, claim, however, at the hands of our poet chronicler more space than the annalist can devote to them.
Zaldívar's absence was from September 10th to November 8th, and he found traces of the expedition of
Bonilla and Humaña. His course was probably north-
east. In October Oñate made a tour to the salinas
eastward of Pecos, and thence south to Abó and
the Jumana territory, the formal submission of the
pueblo groups being on the 12th and 17th, and he
returned about the 20th to the Rio Grande.

On the 23d of October the general started from
Puarai on a western tour, accompanied by Padre
Martinez; and four days later received the *obediencia*
of Acoma. Here according to Villagrá he had a narrow escape without knowing it at the time. Zutucapan, a chief who had not been invited to the conference
at San Juan, had harangued the people from the house-
tops, and urged them not to yield to the haughty
Castillos.[17] He had some success at first, but wiser
counsels prevailed when his son Zutancalpo and the
venerable Chumpo—120 years of age—had made the
people understand how very difficult it would be to
defeat the valiant strangers, and the utter ruin that
must result to Acoma in the case of failure. Still
Zutucapan gained a following, and a secret plan was
made by twelve conspirators to kill Oñate in an estufa,
which on one pretence or another he was to be induced
to visit. The adelantado with his small force arrived,
was satisfied with his friendly reception, and was
filled with admiration at sight of the peñol town with
its wonderful natural strength and defensive works.

---

[17] So the Span. were generally called by the N. Mexicans. The name is a
corruption of Castellanos.

One of the twelve invited Oñate to see something very curious, but he cautiously and fortunately declined to enter the fatal estufa. The formal submission of the pueblo having been received, the little army continued its march westward to Zuñi and to Mohoqui, where formal submission was rendered by the native chieftains on the 9th and 15th of November.[18]

Of Oñate's western explorations in what is now Arizona we know but little. He was everywhere hospitably entertained by the natives, who held grand hunts to furnish diversion and game for their guests. A party under captains Farfan and Quesada were sent out from Moqui in search of mines, which were found in a pleasant, well-watered country some thirty leagues westward, perhaps in the same region previously explored by Espejo.[19] There were also salt deposits, and according to Villagrá pearl-oyster shells, which caused a belief that the coast was not far distant. The general had intended to reach the ocean on this tour, and soon after starting had sent orders to Juan Zaldívar to turn over the command at San Juan to his brother Vicente as soon as the latter should arrive from the plains, and to join his general in the

[18] *N. Mex., Traslado*, 132–41. In the *Ytin.* it is stated that O. like Espejo found at the Zuñi towns, not only crosses, but Mex. Ind. left by Coronado.

[19] It may be well to give the *Ytin.* from Puarai (near Bernalillo or Sandía) to Acoma, Zuñi, Moqui, and the mines as follows: w. 4 l. to Torrente de los Alamos, half-way between being the Arroyo de los Mimbres; 7 l. to Manantial de la Barranca, and 2 l. (apparently, for the text is confusing) to Acoma. (It is difficult to make this agree with the present location of Acoma with respect to Sandía; and here, as in many earlier statements, we are tempted to locate A. much farther north.

From the Peñol de Acoma 4 l. to source of the Rio de Mala Nueva; 8 l. to Agua de la Peña; 4 l. to 'agua que va a Juni' (source of Zuñi River?), where are 3 ruined pueblos; 3 l. to 1st Zuñi pueblo, there being 6 within a space of 3 l., and a famous Salina de Grano 9 l. east (?).

From Zuñi, 6 l. to Cienguilla; 6 l. to Manantialejos; 5 l. to 1st Moqui town; 3 l. to 2d pueblo; 4 l. to 4th, via 3d. These towns are the eastern (western?) limit of settlements found down to Dec. 20, '98 (which may mean that O. remained here till that date, or some of his party).

From Moqui, 6 l. w. to Fuentecilla de los Médanos; 3 l. to Rio de la Alameda; 3 l. to foot of the Sierra sin Agua; 2 l. to Estanque del Pinal; 2½ l. to ranchería de los Gandules; 6 l. in the mts to Agua del Valle; 2 l. to rancheria de los Cruzados; 3 l. to the valley of partridges, magueys, with a fine river; 4 l. to 3d river, and 2 l. to 4th, both large streams; thence to the mines and hot springs, no distance given. Here the *Ytin.* terminates abruptly with p. 276; but later events at Acoma are given on previous pages. This western derrotero is an addition without dates.

west with thirty men.   But trouble occurred, as we
shall see, in connection with the carrying-out of these
orders, and the Mar del Sur had to wait.

We have seen that captains Villagrá and Marquez
had in September been sent south in pursuit of deserters.   They returned at the beginning of November, and the former started alone with his horse and
dog to join his leader and report the success of his
mission.   At Acoma he was so closely questioned by
Zutucapan that his suspicions were aroused, and he
refused to dismount.   Stating that a large Spanish
force was not far behind, and pleading urgent haste to
overtake the general, he hurried on; and sleeping that
night by the wayside he awoke in a snow-storm.   Soon
he fell into a pitfall that the treacherous natives had
prepared for him, left his horse dead therein,[20] and
plodded on through the snow on foot, taking the precaution to reverse his boots, with a view to mislead
pursuers.   After suffering intensely from hunger for
several days, at last he killed his dog for food, but as
the faithful animal with the life-torrent pouring from
his side turned to lick the hand of his slayer, Villagrá
had no heart to eat the food obtained at such a cost.[21]
Soon after, when just ready to perish, he was rescued
by three of Oñate's men who were searching for lost
horses in the Zuñi region.   At the same time his
pursuers—possibly imaginary—came up, but thinking
the main force near at hand dared not attack.[22]

---

[20] The best of historians, even poets, leave now and then a point obscure.
Perhaps the author, if he were still living, might reconcile the death of his
horse in the pitfall with an earlier statement that at the time of writing he
still had the noble charger that bore him on this journey ! A small woodcut
in connection with V.'s portrait on the frontispiece is intended, as close examination leads me to believe, to represent this adventure in the pit.   It certainly represents nothing else.

[21] In the interests of history, and to the sacrifice of sentiment, I must add
that the want of a fire to cook the dog was not without influence on the poet's
decision.   He had not thought of this when he did the cruel deed !

[22] It must be noted that acc. to the *Ytinerario*, 267, 275, Capt. Marquez
was the man who made this trip, leaving Puarai Nov. 4th, and reaching Zuñi
half dead with cold and hunger; but I think it more likely that this is a slip
of the pen than that Don Gaspar should have appropriated the achievements
of another; especially as V. was at Zuñi on Nov. 9th, as is shown in the *Obediencia*.

Don Vicente Zaldívar returned from the plains on
the 8th of November, and on the 18th Don Juan set
out as ordered to join Oñate.   Meanwhile the wily
and patriot Zutucapan—if we are to credit the poet
chronicler, who may have drawn on his imagination
largely for his facts, or may on the other hand have
obtained accurate information from the natives later—
had renewed his efforts at Acoma, and this time successfully; for after the orators of the former occasion
had spoken and others had added their eloquence on
both sides, it was determined to test the boasted in-
vulnerability of the Spaniards by attacking them on
their arrival, having first taken the precaution to scatter
them where they would fall an easy prey.   Such was
the situation when Zaldívar and his companions approached the peñol.   The natives came out to meet
them with gifts and every demonstration of friendly feeling.   They offered all the supplies that were needed, and
next day the soldiers, no treachery being suspected,
were sent in small parties to bring the provisions from
different parts of the pueblo.   A loud shout from the
Indians first warned the maestro de campo of his peril;
he wished to order a retreat, and thus in his leader's
absence avoid the responsibility of open war; but another officer not named—severely blamed by Villagrá
and accused of subsequent cowardice—opposed him
until it was too late, and retreat was impossible.

A desperate hand-to-hand fight of three hours ensued; Zutucapan, Pilco, Amulco, Cotumbo, and Tem-
pol were the native chieftains most prominent in the
battle; the Spaniards performed prodigies of valor in
single combats; but the odds were too great, and one
by one the little force melted away.   At last the brave
Zaldívar fell under the club of Zutucapan; the native
warriors set up a cry of victory; five surviving Spaniards fled to the edge of the mesa and leaped down
the cliff, four of them reaching the plain alive.   Three
others had escaped from the peñol, and all joined
Alférez Casas, who was guarding the horses.   Captain

Tabora was sent to overtake Oñate; others went to warn the padres at their different stations, while the rest bore the sad tidings back to San Juan.[23]

The scene in camp when the disaster was announced to the wives, children, and friends of the slaughtered company may be left to the imagination of the reader. Solemn funeral rites for the dead were hardly completed when Tabora returned, saying that he had not been able to find the governor; whereupon Alférez Casas with three companions volunteered for the service; and after many difficulties met Oñate beyond Acoma, near where Villagrá had been succored a month before. The adelantado retired to his tent and spent the night in prayer before a rude cross, if we may believe his eulogist, and in the morning made a speech of consolation to his men. Having with the least possible delay called in the several bands of explorers, he marched his army carefully and sadly back to San Juan, where his safe arrival on December 21st was celebrated by a te deum.

Formal proceedings were now instituted before Juan Gutierrez Bocanegra, appointed alcalde for the occasion, against the rebels; and after the friars had given a written opinion respecting the elements of a just war and the rights of victors over a vanquished people, it was decided that Captain Vicente de Zaldívar be sent against Acoma; that the inhabitants of that town must be forced to give up the arms of the murdered soldiers, to leave their peñol, and to settle on the plains; that the fortress must be burned; and that all who might resist must be captured and enslaved. Seventy brave men were selected for the

---

[23] The fight took place on Dec. 4th. **Acc.** to Villagrá and *N. Mex.*, *Mem.*, 213, 223, the killed were 11, but only Spaniards were included. The list as given in the *Ytin.*, 268, is as follows: Captains Diego Nuñez and Felipe de Escalante, Alf. Pereyra, Araujo, Juan Camacho, Martin Ramirez, Juan de Segura, Pedro Robledo, Martin de Riveros, Sebastian Rodriguez, two mozos, a mulatto, and an Indian, besides Capt. Juan de Zaldívar. The wounded were Leon Zapata, Juan de Olague, Cavanillas, and the alguacil real, Las Casas, who was struck twice with stones. If the no. of survivors is correctly indicated, Z. could not have taken 30 men as ordered.

service, under officers including captains Zubia, Romero, Aguilar, Farfan, Villagrá, and Marquez, Alférez Juan Cortés, and Juan Velarde as secretary.   This army started on the 12th of January, 1599, and on the 21st arrived at Acoma, Villagrá with twelve men visiting Cia on the way for supplies.   After Zaldívar's departure there seems to have been an alarm of threatened attack on San Juan, which, although it proved unfounded, gave our chronicler an opportunity to describe the preparations for defence, and to record the heroic offer of Doña Eufemia to lead the women to combat.

At Acoma the followers of Zutucapan were exultant, and succeeded in creating a popular belief that their past victory was but the prelude to a greater success which was to annihilate the invaders and free the whole country.   Gicombo, a prominent chieftain who had neither taken part in nor approved the first attack, and had many misgivings for the future, called a general assembly of chiefs, to which were invited certain leaders not belonging to Acoma.   It seems to have been tacitly understood that after what had happened war could not be averted, and all were ready for the struggle; but Gicombo, Zutancalpo, and Chumpo urged the necessity of removing women and children, and of other extraordinary precautions.   Zutucapan and his party, however, ridiculed all fears, and boastingly proclaimed their ability to hold the peñol against the armies of the universe.   When Zaldívar drew near, crowds of men and women were seen upon the walls dancing stark naked in an orgy of defiance and insult.

The sargento mayor, through Tomás the interpreter, sent the rulers of Acoma a summons to come down and answer for the murder they had done; but they only replied with taunts, while the Spaniards pitched their tents on the plain and prepared for an assault.   There were two points at which the ascent could be effected; and the summit plateau was divided

by a ravine into two parts connected by a narrow pass.
Zaldívar's strategy was to assault one of the peñoles
with his main force, while a small and chosen party
should hold themselves in readiness to scale the other.
The night was spent in revelry by the natives; by the
Spaniards in preparations and rest.   On the morning
of San Vicente, the 22d of January, the Indians began
the battle by a discharge of arrows, and the Spanish
leader sent what seemed to be his entire army to assault one of the entrances, where he soon concentrated
the whole strength of the foe to oppose his ascent.
Meanwhile, with twelve chosen men who had been
concealed during the night, he mounted the other
peñol, and gained the summit without serious resistance.   The twelve were speedily reënforced, and all
day long the battle raged fiercely, both at the pass
between the two plateaux and at the entrance to that
not yet gained.

For two days, and perhaps part of the third, the
battle raged, and in five cantos of our epic are the
details recounted of personal combats, desperate
charges, individual acts of prowess on the part of
Castilians and natives, religious services in the Christian camp, juntas and discussions and dissensions in
the fortress on the cliff, the death-struggles of nearly
all the Acoma chieftains and of several of Oñate's
men, hair-breadth escapes of Villagrá and his comrades—details which may not be followed here, but
in which the poet fairly revels.   The Spanish loss
seems to have been very small—perhaps only one
man—and that of the natives very large, as was natural considering the difference in weapons and armor.
Zutucapan's only chance of a successful resistance was
lost when the invaders gained a footing on the plateau.
It was only by desperate valor, by immense superiority of numbers, and by the advantages of defence
offered by the summit pass, that the fated people
were able to prolong the combat for three days.   During the last day's battle the buildings of the pueblo

were in flames, and hundreds killed each other in their desperation, or threw themselves down the cliff and perished rather than yield.   Santiago or San Pablo was clearly seen by the natives during the conflict fighting for the Christians.

Finally, on the 24th the Spaniards gained full possession of the peñol pueblo, which they proceeded to destroy, at the same time slaughtering the inhabitants as a punishment for their sin of rebellion; though a remnant—600 in number, out of an estimated population of 6,000, under the venerable Chumpo, according to Villagrá—was permitted to surrender, and came down to settle on the plain.[24] The pride and strength of the valiant Acomenses were broken forever; and it must have seemed hopeless for the other New Mexican communities to attempt what this cliff town, with all its natural advantages, had failed to accomplish.   There is no record that any other pueblo became involved in open hostility to the Spaniards; indeed, of definite events for the rest of 1599 we have no record at all.   With the fall of Acoma all the regular chronologic records end, including the *Ytinerario* and Villagrá's epic.   The poet promised his sovereign to continue the narration of New World adventures when the duties of his lance should give leisure to his pen; but so far as I know the opportunity never came.

[24] The two authorities do not agree about the termination of the battle. Villagrá implies that it lasted three days, when Chumpo and his 600 survivors surrendered, after which the town was burned.   The *Ytin.* seems to say that the fight lasted from the evening (prob. a misprint for morning) of the 22d to the evening of the 23d, when the foe surrendered; but the Span. did not occupy the pueblo till the 24th, when the surviving inhabitants made further resistance in their estufas and minas; whereupon 'hizose la matanza y castigo de los mas dellos, á fuego y sangre; y de todo punto se asoló y quemó el pueblo.'   Oñate, *Cop. Carta,* 309, says Acoma had about 3,000 Indians 'al qual en castigo de su maldad y traicion....y para escarmiento á los demas, lo asolé y abrasé todo.'   The description of Acoma, with its plateau divided by a ravine into two parts, does not agree with the present pueblo site, and adds to our doubt about the identity.   It agrees much better with El Moro, or Inscription Rock; but the distance of 6 l. E. from the head of Zuñi Cr. in the *Ytinerario*, as well as the distances given in earlier narratives, seem to make this identification difficult.   There may be a similar cliff farther east than El Moro and farther north than Acoma.

CHAPTER VIII.

THE history of this province, from the fall of Acoma in 1599 to the great revolt of 1680, can never be made complete, for lack of data. The home archives were destroyed in the revolt, and we must depend on such fragments as found their way out into the world before that outbreak. I can do no more than simply bring together in this chapter more of these fragments than have ever been presented before. There were several writers of the period—notably Salmeron, Benavides, and Posadas—who might have left a satisfactory record, at least in the aggregate; but unfortunately the past and future had more charms for them than the present, and New Mexico less than the half-mythic regions beyond.

On the 2d of March, 1599, the governor wrote to the viceroy an outline record of what he had accomplished, painting in bright colors the land he had conquered, and sending samples of its products.   The western region since known as Arizona was most highly praised by him in respect of fertility and mineral promise; but perhaps the idea of South Sea glories in that direction was prominent in his mind.   What he wanted was an increase of force with which to win for Spain the rich realms that must lie just beyond; and the couleur de rose of his epistle, so far as New Mexico was concerned, was intended for effect on the viceroy and king, since ultimate success began to seem dependent on an increase of resources.[1]   Captains Villagrá, Farfan, and Pinero were sent to Mexico to carry this letter and make personal explanations; while at the same time, with an escort under Alférez Casas, padres Martinez, Salazar, and Vergara went south to obtain a reënforcement of friars.   Both missions were moderately successful.   Salazar died on the journey, Martinez was retained in Mexico, but Padre Juan de Escalona as comisario was sent to the north with Vergara and six or eight friars not named.   Casas also returned with the 71 men who, as will be remembered, had been provided for to complete Oñate's force of 200 in 1598.[2]   The viceroy wrote to the king, who by a cédula of May 31, 1600, ordered him to render all possible support and encouragement to the New Mexican enterprise.   It is possible that some additional reënforcement was sent in consequence of this order, but there is no positive evidence to that effect.[3]

[1] *Oñate, Cop. de Carta*, 302-15.   Five hundred men would not be too many to send to such a country, where he is sure to gain for his Majesty ' nuevos mundos pacíficos, mayores que el buen Marqués le dió. '   He alludes to his past misfortunes, and most earnestly entreats that aid be not withheld now when success is almost within his grasp.   He wishes his daughter Mariquita to come to N. Mex.

[2] See p. 123, this volume.

[3] Torquemada, *Monarq. Ind.*, i. 671-3, is the best authority on movements of the friars; see also *Vetancur, Chron.*, 95; *Aparicio, Conventos*, 282.   On the sending of the 71 men under Casas at Juan Guerra's expense—to inspect which force Juan Gordejuela was appointed Oct. 1, 1599—see *N. Mex., Mem.*, 197-8; *Id., Discurso*, 38-9.

In May 1600, before the date of the cédula of May 31st (which is copied in *N. Mex., Doc. Hist.*, MS., 492-4), we have two petitions of Don Alonso de Oñate in Madrid in behalf of Don Juan, directed to the king and council, in which he demands a ratification of the original contract with Velasco, on the

After the lesson taught at Acoma, the natives were not likely to attempt further resistance; and Oñate in his capital at San Juan was left in undisputed possession of New Mexico. The colonists were well content with the country as a home, and the friars as a field of missionary labor. Don Juan was also satisfied in a sense with his achievement; that is, as a basis for other and greater ones. True, the pueblo province was but a small affair in the conquistador's eyes; it did not once occur to him that it was in itself his final possession, the goal of all his efforts, the best the north had to offer; but it would serve as a convenient base of supplies for further conquests, and its possession would give weight to his demands for aid from the king. At present his force of little more than 100 men was insufficient for the realization of his schemes; and for some two years he contented himself with preparations, with the search for mines, and with minor explorations of regions near at hand, respecting which no record remains. The reënforcement of soldiers and friars may be supposed to have arrived early in 1600, but possibly later.

Trouble was soon developed between the two opposing elements in the Spanish camp. The colonists favored the most conciliatory measures toward the natives, and the encouragement of agriculture and stock-raising with a view to permanent residence; they were in favor of letting well enough alone. Oñate on the other hand, with such of the soldiers as had not brought their families, thought mainly of holding the natives in subjection, of reducing new pueblos, of collecting the largest possible amount of food and clothing, and of preparing for new entradas. The friars regarded the conversion of gentiles as the

ground that the modifications introduced by Monterey were accepted only by Don Cristóbal, who had no such authority from his brother. He asks that the title of adelantado, now fully earned, be given at once; and he wishes that other orders as well as the Franciscans be allowed a share in the spiritual conquest. *Pacheco, Doc.*, xv. 316–22. The immediate result, as we have seen, was merely a royal order of encouragement, the main issues being held in abeyance. More of this in 1602.

great object of the occupation, and were disposed to think the military element desirable or useful only as a protection to the missions. Of course the governor had his way, and how bitter became the quarrel will presently appear. It was unfortunate for the country, especially as no golden empire was ever found in the north—at least not by Spanish conquerors.

In June 1601, the general was ready for active operations. Accompanied by padres Velasco and Vergara, and guided by the Mexican survivor of Humaña's band, he left San Juan with 80 men and marched north-eastward over the plains.[4] The route in general terms, no details being known, was similar to that of Coronado in 1541, for 200 leagues in a winding course to an estimated latitude of 39° or 40°. Probably the northern trend is greatly exaggerated.[5] The Spaniards had a battle with the Escanjaques, and killed a thousand of them on the Matanza plain, scene of Humaña's defeat. The battle was caused by Padre Velasco's efforts to prevent the Escanjaques from destroying the property of the Quiviras who had fled from their towns at the approach of the Spaniards

[4] On Oñate's exped. to Quivira, see *N. Mex.*, *Mem.*, 198–8, 209–25; *Id.*, *Discurso*, 53–8; *Salmeron*, *Rel.*, 26–30; *Niel*, *Apunt.*, 91–4; *Torquemada*, *Monarq. Ind.*, i. 671–3; *Purchas his Pilgrimes*, iv. 1565–6; *Posadas*, *Noticias*, 216–17; *Davis' Span. Conq.*, 273–5; *Prince's Hist. Sk.*, 165–6. Salmeron and most other authorities give the date erroneously as 1599; and S. speaks of a fight on May 8th. Posadas says O. marched from Sta Fé in 1606; and Salmeron, followed by Davis, calls the place Villa de N. Mexico. The viceroy says half the 80 men were not *gente de servicio*, and were of no use. Don Diego de Peñalosa, as we shall see later in this chapter, fitted the narrative of this exped. to a fictitious one of his own in 1662 for use in France.

[5] Posadas, a good authority, says that O. went nearly 300 l. east in search of the ocean, reaching the country of the Aijados s. of Quivira and w. of the Tejas. The natives guided him to Quivira, but knew nothing of the ocean. Tribaldo, in *Purchas*—also quoted in a fragment, chap. 22–6, of a MS. history, vaguely accredited to Otermin in 1680, in *N. Mex.*, *Doc. Hist.*, iii. 1145-7, of no apparent value—says they went to the River of the North and to the great lake of Conibas (which figures in mythic geog. of the northern region), on the bank of which was seen 'afarre off a city 7 l. long and above 2 l. broad,' the market-place being so strongly fortified that the Span. dared not attack. Salmeron says the way was winding, 200 l. N. E. to a fertile land of fruits; the natives saying that a shorter way was N. by Taos and the land of Capt. Quivira. The viceroy says it was estimated by able men at over 40° and about 300 l. from either ocean. O. went N. E., while Coronado had gone N. w.(!) 39° or 40°. *N. Mex.*, *Mem.* See *Hist. North Mex. St.*, i. 383. Details concern the history of Texas more than that of N. Mex.

and their allies.   Large villages were seen, and advance parties claimed to have found utensils of gold, which was said to be plentiful in the country of the Aijados not far away; and a native captive sent south is said to have caused a sensation in Mexico and Spain by his skill in detecting the presence of gold.   It is not quite clear that Quivira was actually visited, but ambassadors from that people—also called Tindanes— were met, who wished to join the Spaniards in a raid on the gold country.   Oñate, however, deemed it unwise to go on with so small a force, or perhaps was forced to turn back by the clamors of his men.   He returned to San Juan probably in October.[6]

Back at the pueblos Oñate found New Mexico almost deserted.   Colonists and friars with few exceptions had gone south to Santa Bárbara, on the plea of absolute destitution, leaving them only a choice between death and desertion.   Padre Escalona, who remained with Alférez Casas to await the governor's return, explained the situation in a letter to the comisario general, dated October 1st, and carried south by the fugitives.   In this letter he stated that Oñate and his captains had sacked the towns, taking the whole reserve store of six years' crops saved by the natives, as was their custom for a possible year of famine.   He had not allowed any community planting for the support of the garrison; the season had been one of drought; and the Indians were forced to live on wild seeds.   Fortunately, several settlers had planted and irrigated corn-fields on their own account, thus saving the colony from starvation.   Therefore they decided to retire to Nueva Vizcaya, report to the viceroy, and await orders whether to settle in the south or return with a new outfit to New Mexico. The friars went with them at their earnest request and the order of the padre comisario, who deemed it his

[6] Davis' narrative of O.'s exped. ends abruptly with the arrival at Quivira, the author not finding the rest of Salmeron's relation, which he calls O.'s diary.

own duty to remain at the risk of his life, but who begged for a speedy decision. There were said to be good spots for settlement in Nueva Vizcaya, he wrote, but it seemed a pity to abandon New Mexico after such efforts, expense, and something of success.[7]

Don Juan, returning from an unsuccessful tour, with much discontent in his own ranks, was naturally furious on learning the state of affairs at San Juan. Finding men to testify against their absent comrades, he at once began legal proceedings against the so-called traitors, condemned some of them to death, prepared reports to the viceroy and king to offset those of the friars, who now and later reiterated their charges, and sent Vicente de Zaldívar to carry his reports to Mexico and Spain, to arrest and send back the recalcitrant colonists, and to urge the importance of completing the conquest. A little later Padre Escalona wrote to his provincial that he and Padre Velasco, Oñate's cousin, were resolved to quit the country; that they were of no use as missionaries, serving merely as chaplains to the raiders; that the governor's charges were false; and that no real progress could be hoped for until the king should take the government from Oñate's hands.[8]

Zaldívar seems to have forced the colonists to return, acting with great cruelty, if the friars may be credited. Early in 1602 he appeared before the audiencia in Mexico to urge the importance of continuing the conquest from New Mexico as a base. The *expediente* of papers presented by him related wholly to past achievements, and has been one of our main authorities for the two preceding chapters.[9] The

---

[7] *Escalona, Carta de Relacion 1601*, in *Torquemada*, i. 673–4. Written at S. Gabriel. The retiring padres included San Miguel and Zamora of the original party; and Lope Izquierdo and Gaston de Peralta, presumably, of the new. Velasco and Vergara were with Oñate; the others, Rosas, Lugo, Corchado, Claros, and San Buenaventura are not named, but may be supposed to have gone to Sta B. and returned later. The last appears again in N. Mex.

[8] *Torquemada*, i. 675–7. P. San Miguel wrote from Sta B. on Feb. 2, 1602, protesting still more bitterly against O.'s tyranny, falsehood, and general unfitness for his position.

[9] In *Pacheco, Doc.*, xvi. See p. 118 of this vol.

quarrel with friars and settlers did not figure at all in these proceedings; and the documents bearing on that matter are not extant. The fiscal in May threw cold water on the scheme by an opinion that the encouragement to spend money was much less, now that the country's poverty was known, than formerly when New Mexico was reputed rich.

From Mexico Zaldívar went to Spain to lay the matter before the king. The viceroy also wrote the king a long letter, giving an outline of Oñate's enterprise from the beginning. Respecting the merits of the recent controversy, he and the audiencia had not been able to decide from the various memorials of interested and prejudiced parties on both sides, all of which documents had been forwarded to Spain; but it is clear that he was not friendly to Oñate. He strongly urged that his amendments to the original contract should be enforced, and that Don Juan's extravagant demands, especially that of independence from the audiencia, should not be granted. While the new province had been overpraised, yet it had many attractions in the way of climate, soil, products, and docile inhabitants; and it should not be abandoned. The number of settlers should be increased to at least 100, to live in one or two small villas so as to protect the padres and not annoy the Indians. The natives might be 'encommended' as tribute-payers among the settlers by the governor and comisario acting together This report includes a somewhat extended, and in comparison with other documents of the time sensible, view of the Northern Mystery; and the writer, after exploding many of the absurd theories of northern wonders, and showing that there was small hope of finding great and wealthy kingdoms for conquests, admits that further exploration toward Anian and Labrador is desirable, and thinks that if the king is willing to pay the cost it might be well to furnish a force of 100 men and six officers for a year and a half. Oñate might properly be put in command and re-

quired to help support the men; but he would have
no claim whatever to authority over the regions discovered.   The animus of this report is evident, though
the wisdom of many of the views expressed cannot be
questioned.[10]
   Such records as are extant fail to show exactly the
results of Zaldívar's efforts in his uncle's behalf.[11]
Calle tells us that Oñate was made adelantado by
cédula of February 7, 1602, the title being extended
to his son.   We have also a cédula of July 8th, confirming the *hidalguía*, or nobility, originally conferred
on conquistadores to Oñate's associates, and overruling
some of the modifications introduced by Monterey.[12]
Salmeron states that the king authorized the raising
of 1,000 men if Zaldívar could raise half of them for
the northern conquest, but on Zaldívar's failure nothing was accomplished.[13]   The truth would seem to be,
though the evidence is meagre, that while Oñate was
confirmed in his office and prerogatives so far as New
Mexico was concerned, receiving some aid from the
king, with reënforcements of colonists and missionaries, he had not the means himself, nor could he in-

[10] *N. Mex., Discurso*, 38–66; not dated, but evidently of 1602, corresponding to Z.'s departure for Spain.
[11] Fernandez Duro, *Don Diego de Peña losa*, 145, cites a MS. *Relacion dirigida al Rey Nro Sr. de la expedicion y pacificacion del Nuevo Méjico, por D.
Vicente de Zaldívar*, as cited by Barcia and Beristain; and also the following
MSS. which I have not seen: *Noticias del N. Méjico por el P. Rodrigo Vivero;
Diario de las exped. al N. Méjico por El Capitan D. Fernando Rivera; Hist. de la
introd. del Evangelio desde el Parral hasta el N. Méj. por Fr. Juan Espinosa;
Relacion de lo que habian visto y oido de la tierra adentro de Mex. los religiosos
misioneros franciscanos.   Por D. Fran. Nieto de Silva, gob. del N. Méj.;* and
*Diario de la entrada en el N. Méj., dirigido á los prelados de su órden, por Fr.
Pedro Salmeron.*   None have dates; and some prob. never existed; but the
last is mentioned also in *Vetancur, Chron.*, 118, and apparently belongs to
1604.
[12] *Calle, Not.*, 103; *Pino, Expos.*, 35–6; *Id., Not.*, 2–3; *Davis' Span. Conq.*,
264–5.   The audiencia acquiesced in this order by act of June 20, 1604, on
Zaldívar's return to Mex.   It appears that O.'s original demand for the governorship, etc., for four lives instead of two was not finally granted; and as
we shall see, he did not transmit it even to his son.
[13] 'Como no cumplió, porque no pudo, tampoco el rey.' *Salmeron, Rel.*, 28;
Davis' Span. Conq., 276.   *Cavo, Tres Siglos*, i. 229, tells us that O. took the
country without resistance, asked for more men, who were sent with permission for the discontented to return, as they did, abusing a country that had
yielded no treasure.

duce the government to furnish men and supplies for
northern conquests on a scale commensurate with his
ambitious views.   Zaldívar returned from Spain in or
before 1604, and perhaps to New Mexico.

Though he had failed in his north-eastern expedition, there remained the Mar del Sur, which Oñate
was determined to reach; and as soon as he had recovered from the troubles just recorded, having most
of his original 200 men reunited at San Juan, with
possibly a small reënforcement brought by Zaldívar,
the governor started on October 7, 1604, for the west
with thirty men, accompanied by padres Francisco
Escobar and San Buenaventura, the former the new
comisario.[14] Visiting the Zuñi province "more thickly
settled by hares and rabbits than by Indians," where
the chief town of the six is now called Cíbola, or in
the native tongue Havico, or Ha Huico, the explorers
went on to the five Moqui towns with their 450 houses
and people clad in cotton.   Ten leagues to the westward they crossed a river flowing from the south-east
to the north-west, named Rio Colorado from the color
of its water, and said to flow into the sea of California after a turn to the west, and a course of 200
leagues through a country of pines.   This was the
stream still known as the Colorado Chiquito, and it
is not unlikely that this was the origin of the name
Colorado applied later to the main river.   The place
of crossing was named San José, and farther west, or
south-west, they crossed two other rivers flowing south
and south-east, and named San Antonio and Sacramento—really branches of the Rio Verde in the
region north of Prescott, near where Espejo had been

---

[14] According to *Torquemada*, i. 678, Padre Velasco was comisario after
Escalona and before Escobar.   Both the E.'s died in N. Mex. *Id.*, iii. 598.
Vetancur, *Chron.*, 95–6, as well as Torquemada, says that Escobar brought 6
friars, though his statement about the date is confusing.   Among Escobar's
party were perhaps PP. Pedro Salmeron and Pedro Carrascal, the latter
being later guardian in Mex. and dying in 1622. *Id., Menol.*, 92.   Escalona
died at Sto Domingo in 1607.   P. Cristóbal Quiñones, skilled in the language
of the Queres, estab. church, convent, and hospital at S. Felipe, where he
died in 1609.   P. Vergara of the original band died in Mex. 1646.

twenty-three years before.[15] It was a fertile, attractive country, whose people wore little crosses hanging
from the hair on the forehead, and were therefore
called Cruzados.[16]

The Cruzados said the sea was 20 days or 100
leagues distant, and was reached by going in two
days to a small river flowing into a larger one, which
itself flowed into the sea. And indeed, fifteen leagues
brought them to the small stream, named San Andrés,
where the tierra caliente began to produce the pita-
haya; and twenty-four leagues down its course the
general came to the large stream, and named it Rio
Grande de Buena Esperanza; that is, he followed the
Santa María, or Bill Williams fork, down to its junction with the Colorado. The explorers seem to have
had no idea that there was any connection between
this great river of Good Hope and the one they had
named Rio Colorado; but they knew it was the one
long ago named Rio del Tizon farther down; indeed,
one of the men had been with Vizcaino in the gulf,
and said this was the stream for which his commander
had searched.[17]

For some distance above and below the junction
lived the Amacava nation, or Mojaves.[18] Captain
Marquez went up the river a short distance; then the

[15] One version reads, 'from this stream [the Col. Chiquito] they went w.,
crossing a piny range 8 l. wide, at whose southern base runs the river S.
Antonio; it is 17 l. from S. José, which is the Colorado, runs N. to S. through
a mountain region, has little water but much good fish. From this river it
is a tierra templada. 5 l. w. is Rio Sacramento, like the S. Ant. in water
and fish, rising 11 l. farther w., runs N. w. to S. E. at foot of lofty sierras,
where the Span. got good metals.' The other speaks of the S. Antonio as
being '17 l. from the Colorado, here called S. José.'

[16] It was afterwards learned, so say the chroniclers, that a Franciscan had
visited this people before, and taught them the efficacy of the cross in making friends, not only of God, but of white and bearded men who might one
day appear.

[17] This is not the place to go into details of Cal. geography as represented
or thought to be represented by the Indians. The ocean was near, in all
directions from w. to N. E., the brazo de mar extending round to Florida;
Aztec was still spoken, and gold bracelets were worn at Lake Copala; and the
island with giant queen was not wanting. Information here obtained had
considerable influence indirectly on the Northern Mystery from this time.

[18] The form in the 18th century as occurring in Cal. annals was Amajava,
which later became Mojave. Possibly in this narrative it should also be
Amajava, the 'c' being a misprint.

whole party followed its banks southward, the natives being friendly, and interviews respecting the Northern Mystery taking the place of adventures.   Below the Amacavas were the Bahacechas, and next the Ozaras, a somewhat ruder people living on a large river flowing from the south-east, and named the Rio del Nombre de Jesus.   This was the Gila, and the valley was said to be occupied by the same nation in twenty towns. Below the junction for twenty leagues to the sea the country was thickly inhabited by tribes similar in manners and language to the Bahacechas.   First were the Halchedumas in eight towns or rancherías; then nine settlements of the Coahuanas, five of the Tlaglli, or Haglli, six of the Tlalliguamayas, and nine of the Cocapas at the head of tide-water, five leagues from the river's mouth.   The population on the eastern bank alone was not less than 20,000.[19]

Oñate reached tide-water on January 23, 1605, and on the 25th, with the friars and nine men, went down to the mouth.   Here he found a fine harbor, formed by an island in the centre, in which he thought 1,000 ships might ride at anchor.   That the sea extended indefinitely north-westward behind a range of hills, the Spaniards believed on the authority of the Indians; and this belief had much to do later with the opinion that California was an island.   The port was formally christened, from the day, Puerto de la Conversion de San Pablo.   The rest of the company came down to see the port, and then the explorers began their return march by the same route to New Mexico.   There were ten different languages spoken on the way, and Padre Escobar on the return could speak them all (!), thus gathering new items of fable respecting western and northern wonders.   They had to eat their horses, but arrived safe and sound at San Gabriel on the 25th

[19] Vetancur, *Chron.*, 95–6, says he has seen the doc. dated Jan. 15, 1605, by which Oñate in the king's name gave to Escobar, or to the faith in his person, possession (assignment as a future missionary field?) of the region from the Rio del Norte 200 l. s. to the Puerto (Rio?) de Buena Esperanza.

of April. This important exploration of Arizona has been entirely unknown to modern writers.[20] There seems to have been a preceding expedition in 1604, directed to the north, with padres Velasco and Salmeron as chaplains.[21] The expedition accredited by Peñalosa to Zaldívar in 1618—with forty-seven soldiers and Padre Lázaro Jimenez, who went fifteen leagues from Moq to the Rio de Buena Esperanza, but were driven back by tales of giants—is merely, as I suppose, a confused reference to that of Oñate just described.[22]

Nothing is definitely known of Oñate's acts in New Mexico after his return from the west in 1605; nor have I seen any record of his later career,[23] except that a new expedition out into the eastern plains is rather doubtfully attributed to him in 1611.[24] He may indeed have been still in the country at that date and later, engaged as captain of explorers in a vain search for northern wealth; but there is evidence that he ceased to rule as governor in 1608, and was per-

[20] *Salmeron, Rel.*, 30-8; *Niel, Apunt.*, 81-6. Cardona, *Relacion*, 32-3, had heard from capt. Marquez and Vaca that they struck the Tizon in 36° 30'; that the famous port was in 35°; that the giant queen took powdered pearls in her drink; and that south of the Tizon was a large Rio del Coral. Casanate, *Mem.*, 24, gives a similar report with less of detail. P. Garcés, *Diario*, 364, in 1776, says that Oñate heard of a Rio Turon, probably identical with one of which he himself heard while crossing from Cal. to the Colorado, and with that mentioned by P. Escalante in 1775. The fact that Davis does not mention this exped. shows that he had but a fragment of Salmeron.

[21] *Vetancur, Chron.*, 118. The author has seen P. Pedro Salmeron's report of the entrada; and the same doc. is cited in *Fernandez Duro*, 145, without date.

[22] The story is given in the works of Shea and Fernandez Duro; also from Shea, in *Prince's Hist. Sk.*, 176-8.

[23] Lopez de Haro, *Nobilario*, as cited by Fernandez Duro, 130, implies that O. was still serving the king in 1620, but says nothing of his having left N. Mex.

[24] Barreiro, *Ojeada*, 7, says O. went E. in 1611, and discovered the Canibar lakes and a Rio Colorado, or Palizade, prob. Los Cadauchos, thus gaining a right to the eastern country. Davis, *El Gringo*, 73-4, *Span. Conq.*, 276-7, tells the same story, taking it perhaps from Barreiro, changing *Canibares* to 'Cannibal,' and giving the opinion that the Rio Palizada was prob. the Canadian. He credits the exped. to O. in 1611, though by his own reckoning O. must have ceased to rule some years before. Posadas, as we have seen, dates O.'s exped. to Quivira in 1606, doubtless by error. Zaldívar's exped. of 1618, as we have also seen, is only a confused ref. to that of 1604.

haps succeeded by Don Pedro de Peralta.[25] About the same time, when 8,000 natives had been converted, Padre Alonso Peinado came to succeed Escobar as comisario, accompanied by eight or nine friars, being in turn succeeded by Padre Estévan Perea in 1614.[26] The names of Governor Peralta's successors for a dozen years or more are not known, and the history of the whole period is wellnigh a blank.

Yet within this period, or rather between 1605 and 1616, was founded the villa of Santa Fé, or San Francisco de la Santa Fé. The modern claim that this is the oldest town in the United States rests entirely on its imaginary annals as an Indian pueblo before the Spanish conquest. There are but slight indications, if any, that Santa Fé was built on the site of a pueblo; and its identification with Cicuye, Tiguex, or any other particular or prominent pueblo, has no foundation whatever.[27] We have seen that San Juan was Oñate's

[25] Calle, *Not.*, 103, a good authority, says a new gov. was appointed in 1608 with a salary of $2,000. Vetancur, *Chron.*, 96, says that in 1608 the king assumed the support of both soldiers and padres; that it probably put an end to the Oñate contract. Davis, *Span. Conq.*, 420, or Miller, found evidence in the archives at Sta Fé that Peralta ruled 9 years after Oñate's coming, that is, in 1607 or 1608, and not 1600 as D. makes it by dating O.'s entry in 1591. Prince suggests that P. ruled in 1600, but O. was reinstated later!

[26] *Vetancur, Chron.*, 96; *Id., Menol.*, 65; *Torquemada*, ii. 678. V. says P. succeeded Escalona, clearly a slip of the pen. See also *Barriero, Ojeada*, 7; *Villagrá, Hist.*, 177; and *Salmeron, Rel.*, 11. The latter says that in 1614 the remains of the martyred Padre Lopez of 1581 were found by P. Perea, the com., and buried at Sandía. Yet Vetancur implies that Perea came in '28.

[27] In the pamphlet *Sta Fé, Centennial Sketch*, of 1876, the title bears the inscription 'Santa Fé, the oldest city in North America'! Ex-gov. Arny in his address, *Id.*, pp. 6–8, informs us that Cabeza de Vaca and Coronado found the Indians living in cities, and 'especially the pueblo city, with its many thousand inhab.', where we now stand '; that the governor's palace in full view of the audience was built before 1581, from the material of the old Indian town; that the Indians revolted before 1583, driving out the settlers and priests; but that Espejo reconquered the province and forced the natives to toil in the mines! Fortunately, the imaginative orator committed the preparation of his historic sketch proper to David J. Miller, who knew more of his subject; yet even M. thinks Sta Fé identical with Cicuye. Bandelier, *Hist. Introd.*, 19, to correct the popular impression at Sta Fé, notes that the town stood on the site of Tiguex. But in *Ritch's Aztlan*, 201, the same writer seems to think there was at Sta Fé a pueblo whose aboriginal name was Po-o-ge. A few years ago, since 1880, a grand celebration was held of the 300th (or 350th or 400th, it matters not which) anniversary of the founding! Similar errors might be cited in no end of newspaper and pamphlet sketches. Prince, *Hist. Sk.*, 168, thinks Sta Fé may have been built at El Teguayo, one of the chief pueblos, where the first missionary station after S. Ildefonso was established.

capital from 1598, and that preparations were made for building a city of San Francisco in that vicinity. Naturally, in the troubles that ensued, little if any progress was made; and after the controversies were past—not during Oñate's rule, I think[28]—it was deemed best to build the new villa on another site. I have been able to find no record of the date; but the first definite mention is in 1617, on January 3d of which year the cabildo of Santa Fé petitioned the king to aid the "nueva poblacion."[29]

In 1617, as appears from the document just cited, though the friars had built eleven churches, converted 14,000 natives, and prepared as many more for conversion, there were only forty-eight soldiers and settlers in the province. Among the inscriptions copied by Simpson from El Moro is one to the effect that the governor passed that way on July 29, 1620, returning from a successful tour of pacification to Zuñi.[30] In 1620, or possibly a little earlier, controversies arose between the political and ecclesiastical authorities, the custodio assuming the right to issue excommunication against the governor, the latter claiming authority to appoint petty Indian officials at the missions, and both being charged with oppressive exactions of labor and tribute from the natives. This matter was referred to the audiencia, and drew out reprimand and warning against both parties.[31]

It was about this time that Padre Gerónimo de Zárate Salmeron entered this missionary field, where

[28] See p. 132–3 of this vol. Calle, *Not.*, 103, says that the new gov. in 1608 was ordered to live at Sta Fé; and one or two authorities say that Oñate left Sta Fé for his western tour of 1604–5; but I suppose these are careless references to what was the capital at the time of writing.

[29] *N. Mex., Doc.*, MS., i. 494–6. In reply, the king, by cédula of May 20, 1620, ordered the viceroy to render all possible aid to the cabildo and settlers.

[30] *Simpson's Jour.*, 105, pl. 67. Under the inscription are the names of Diego Nuñez Bellido, Joseph Ramos (?) Diego, Zapata, and Bartolomé Naranjo, or Narrso; one of which may be that of the gov. Domenech, *Deserts*, i. 416–17, makes Naranjo the gov.; and Prince, *Hist. Sk.*, 174, misquotes the inscription to add Narrso to his list of governors. It will be noticed that Capt. Diego Nuñez, Alf. Leon Zapata, and Naranjo are among the names in the list of Oñate's original company of 1598.

[31] *N. Mex. Traslado de una Cédula*, Jan. 9, 1621, in *Arch. Sta Fé*, MS. The Zuñis and Moquis were exempt from tribute.

for eight years he "sacrificed himself to the Lord among the pagans," toiling chiefly among the Jemes, of whom he baptized 6,566, and in whose language he wrote a *doctrina*.   He also served at Cia and Sandía among the Queres, and once pacified Acoma after a revolt.[32]   Above all things he was eager to convert new tribes; and it was with a view to overcome obstacles in this direction that in 1626 he came to Mexico with his *Relaciones*.   In this most valuable work, elsewhere fully noticed, he unfortunately for our present purpose dealt chiefly with the past and future, saying little of events in his own time, partly perhaps because there was not much to say.   The padre was delighted with the country, its climate, people, and products, agricultural and mineral;[33] but disgusted with the apathy of the Spaniards "content if they have a good crop of tobacco to smoke, caring for no more riches, apparently under a vow of poverty, which is saying much for men who in their thirst for gold would enter hell itself to get it."

In 1621 the missions, with over 16,000 converts, were formed into a 'custodia de la conversion de San Pablo.'[34]   Padre Alonso Benavides came as the first custodio, and brought with him twenty-seven friars.[35] Yet in 1626, when according to Salmeron and Bena-

---

[32] It did not remain pacified, since in '29 Acoma was again reduced to peace and Christianity by the miraculous recovery on baptism of a dying child. *Benavides, Reqveste*, 39. Also in *Laet, Novus Orbis*, 361.

[33] He is careful to note the existence of rich mines, many of them discovered by himself.   When Oñate had passed through Tula on his way N. Padre Diego had prophesied, 'By the life of Fray Diego there are great riches in the remote parts of N. Mex.; but by the life of Fray Diego it is not for the present settler that God holds them in reserve.' Gregg, *Com. Prairies*, i. 121, 162-3, speaks of many rich mines having been worked traditionally before 1680, later lost or concealed by the natives to prevent a repetition of brutal outrages, the elders still lecturing the young men on the danger of divulging the secret.   Yet I have no faith in extensive mining operations in N. Mex. during this century, or anything more than prospecting.

[34] *Revilla Gigedo, Carta de 1793*, p. 441; *Calle, Not.*, 103.   Yet Vetancur often speaks of the chief of the friars as custodio as well as comisario in the earlier years.   Aparicio, *Conventos*, 282, says there were seven monasteries in '23.

[35] P. Martin de Arvide seems to have been one of them.   He served at Picuríes and at Zuñi, but was killed by the Zipias in '32.   *Vetancur, Menol.*, 16, 24.

vides over 34,000 Indians had been baptized and forty-three churches built—so effectually had the soil been fructified by the early martyrs' blood—only sixteen friars and three laymen were left in the field, the cause of the decrease not being explained.[36] The lack of workmen and the promise of the field having been reported by the custodio to the comisario general, the king in 1627 ordered thirty new friars and a number of laymen to be sent immediately, and all needed aid to be rendered in future. This reënforcement came from the provincia del Santo Evangelio in Mexico in 1628–9.[37]

In these years we have the names of two governors, Felipe Zotylo at some time during Benavides' term as custodio, that is, 1621–9, and Manuel de Silva in 1629.[38] In 1630 the Franciscan comisario general represented to the king the necessity of erecting a bishopric in New Mexico, where 500,000 gentiles had been converted and 86,000 baptized, where over 100 friars were at work in 150 pueblos, where there were

[36] Salmeron gives the no. of baptisms as 34,650; Benavides as 34,320, from a royal cédula of '26. Acc. to *St Francis' Life*, 575, the Socorro mission estab. 30 years after the 1st was the 37th. Laet, *Nov. Orb.*, 315, says three churches were built in the Socorro district, at Senecú, Pilabo, and Sevilleta in 1626.

[37] Under P. Estévan de Perea—already mentioned, perhaps erroneously, as comisario in '14. *Vetancur, Chron.*, 96. The same writer names P. Tomás Manso as custodio in 1629, possession being given by a doc. of March 6th, of the region from Rio Sacramento N. toward Quivira. This P. Manso was procurador of N. Mex. for 25 years; provincial in Mex. '55; and later bishop of Nicaragua, where he died. *Id., Menol.*, 135. Other friars apparently of this party were García de San Francisco y Zúñiga, who founded Socorro and a pueblo of Mansos in '59, died '73, buried at Senecú; Antonio de Arteaga, companion of García and founder of Senecú' 30; Fran. Letrado, who toiled among the Jumanas and later at Zuñi, killed by gentiles in '32; Fran. Acebedo, who built churches at S. Greg. de Abó, Tenabo, and Tabira, dying in '44; Fran. Porras, who with PP. Andrés Gutierrez and Cris. de la Concepcion went to Moqui, where God worked many miracles through him, but he was poisoned on June 28, '33; Gerón. de la Llana, who died at Quarac pueblo in '59; Tomás de S. Diego, who died in Oajaca '59; Juan Ramirez, who went to Acoma, where the arrows failed to touch him, and he worked many years, dying in Mex. '64; and Juan de la Torre, who become comisario gen. of New Spain, and bishop of Nicaragua, where he died in '63. *Vetancur, Menol.*, 7–8, 16, 66, 75, 77, 82, 135–6; *Medina, Chron.*, 162–3, 168–70, 175–6.

[38] Incidentally mentioned in *Vetancur, Menol.*, 24; *Id., Chron.*, 96. Fernandez Duro, 146, cites an undated MS. report by Francisco Nieto de Silva, gov. of N. Mex. He also cites under date of 1628 an *Expedicion del P. Fr. Antonio (Alonso?) Peinado á la provincia de Moqui*, a MS. in the *Acad. de Hist.*

no clergymen and none authorized to administer the right of confirmation. A bishop would save much expense, and would easily be supported by tithes, especially as rich mines had been found and the population was rapidly increasing. The viceroy was ordered to investigate and report on the desirability of this change; but long delays ensued and nothing was accomplished.[39]

Padre Benavides went in person to Spain, and his report to the king, dated Madrid, 1630, although meagre and superficial in comparison with what it might have been, is the most important authority extant on these times.[40] It shows that there were about 50 friars, serving over 60,000 christianized natives in over 90 pueblos, grouped in 25 missions, or conventos, as they were called, each pueblo having its own church. The Indians as a rule were easily controlled, and paid tribute in corn and cotton to support the garrison of 250 Spaniards at Santa Fé, where a church had recently been completed. The outlying gentile tribes—all known as Apaches and classified as Apaches de Xila, Apaches de Navajó, and Apaches Vaqueros—had as yet caused no serious troubles; in fact, in the Xila province and among the Navajos peace had been

[39] Royal order of May 19, '31, citing the demand of Com. Gen. Sosa. *N. Mex., Cédulas*, MS., 1–2; also order of June 23, '36, on the same subject, and adds that the pope has been asked to grant to some friar authority to confirm pending the election of a bishop. *Id.*, 3–6; see also *Bonilla, Apuntes*, MS., 1; *Revilla Gigedo, Carta de 1793*, MS.; *Calle, Not.*, 103. As early as 1596 the bishop of Guadalajara set up a claim to N. Mex. as within his bishopric. *N. Mex., Mem.*, 227. The statistics of the com. gen. as given in my text would seem to be greatly exaggerated.

[40] *Benavides, Memorial que Fray Juan de Santander...presentó á Felipe IV.* Madrid, 1630, 4°, 109 p. P. Santander was the Franciscan com. gen., and presented B.'s memorial with some introd. remarks of his own. I have not seen the original, but use *Benavides, Reqveste remonstrative av Roy d'Espagne svr la conversion du Nouveau Mexico.* Bruxelles, 1631, 16mo, 10 l., 120 p., in the library of M. Alphonse Pinart. I regard this as a translation of the *Memorial.* Fernandez Duro, 132–3, says 'P. Benavides published in 1632 another memorial, proposing the opening of the rivers of the bay of Espíritu Santo, acc. to a reference of P. Posadas. Juan Laet made an extract of the *Descrip. Novisima* of N. Mex. in his work, the *Novus Orbis.* Fr. Juan Gravenden translated it (the original *Mem.*, I suppose) into Latin; and in French it was pub. in 1631.' Extracts in *N. Mex. Doc.*, MS., iii. 1147–52; *Nouv. Ann. Voy.*, cxxxi. 303–9. P. Benavides did not return to N. Mex., but became archbishop of Goa in Asia.

made; and in the former, where Benavides had been, a missionary was now working with much success.[41] The author recounts the miraculous conversion of the Jumanas, living 112 leagues east of Santa Fé, through the supernatural visits of Sister Luisa de la Ascension, an old nun of Carrion, Spain, who had the power of becoming young and beautiful, and of transporting herself in a state of trance to any part of the world where were souls to be saved.[42] The padre has something to say of Quivira and the Aijaos east of the Jumanas; and concludes with a brief account of Coronado's expedition and the countries by him discovered, without suspicion that those countries were identical with his own custodia of New Mexico. The work is mainly descriptive, and has some special value as giving more definitely than any other authority the territorial locations of the pueblo groups in the 17th century, and thus throwing light on earlier explorations. It is to be regretted that the writer did not, as he might easily have done, give more fully the pueblo names and locations, and thus clear up a subject which it is to be feared must always remain in confusion and obscurity.[43]

[41] The Xila prov. was 30 l. from Senecú, and I suppose this to be the 1st use of the name later applied to the Rio Gila, which rises in this region. Navajó is said to mean *grande semaille* or 'great sowing.' The author has much to say of the manners and customs of these wild tribes.

[42] Details pertain to Texas rather than N. Mex. In Spain B. learned that he was wrong about the woman; for he had an interview with María de Jesus, abbess of the convent of Agreda, who often since 1620 had been carried by the heavenly hosts to N. Mex. to preach the faith. Sometimes she made the round trip several times in 24 hours. She described events that had occurred in B.'s presence when she had been invisible to all but Ind. eyes. She spoke of the kingdoms of Chillescas, Cambujos, and Titlas east of Quivira. She could easily speak the native dialects when on the ground, but not in Spain! She enclosed a letter of encouragement to the padres in 1631. *Palou, Vida de Junip. Serra*, 331–41. The conversion of the Jumanas in 1629 is also noted by *Vetancur, Chron.*, 96, who says that P. Juan de Salas and Diego Lopez went from S. Antonio Isleta after the miraculous operations of the lady.

[43] Benavides' classification and statistics are as follows: See also Vetancur's at end of this chap.

Piros, or Picos, nation, southernmost of N. Mex., on both sides the Rio Grande for 15 l., from Senecú to Sevilleta; 15 pueblos, 6,000 Ind., all baptized; 3 missions, Nra Sra del Socorro at Pilabo, S. Ant. Senecú, and S. Luis Obispo Sevilleta.

Toas (doubtless Tiguas), nation 7 l. above Piros, 15 or 16 pueblos, 7,000

A half-century's history from 1630 is made up of a probably incomplete list of governors, a few references to explorations on the eastern or Texan frontier, a few uncertain records of troubles with the Indians, and an occasional item of mission progress or politico-ecclesiastical controversy. While making considerable additions in every phase of the subject to the results of previous investigations, I can present nothing like a continuous and complete narrative; and I do not propose to waste space by a pretence of so doing.

Fernando de Argüello is named as governor in 1640.[44] Luis de Rosas next held the office, being murdered in 1641 or 1642, and succeeded by Valdés, and he by Alonzo Pacheco de Heredia.[45] Argüello

Ind., all baptized; 2 missions, S. Antonio Sandía and S. Antonio Isleta. (It will be remembered that Puruai had also been called S. Antonio.)

Queres nation, 4 l. above Tiguas, extending 10 l. from S. Felipe and including Sta Ana on the w.; 7 pueblos, 4,000 Ind., all bapt.; 3 missions.

Tompiros nation, 10 l. E. of Queres (prob. should be Tiguas and Piros), extending 15 l. from Chilili; 14 or 15 pueblos, over 10,000 Ind., all converted and most baptized; 6 missions, one called S. Isidoro Numanas (Jumanas?); Ind. also called Salmeros (Salineros) living near the Salinas.

Tanos nation, 10 l. N. of Tompiros, extending 10 l.; 5 pueblos; one mission; 4,000 Ind., all baptized.

Pecos, pueblo of Jemes nation and lang., 4 l. N. of Tanos; 2,000 Ind.; mission.

Sta Fé, villa; 7 l. w. of Pecos; capital; 250 Span. and 700 Ind.; mission church nearly completed.

Toas or Tevas (Tehuas) nation, w. of Sta Fé toward the river, extending 10 or 12 l.; 8 pueblos, including Sta Clara; 6,000 Ind.; 3 missions, including S. Ildefonso. These were the first natives baptized.

Picuríes pueblo of Toas (Tehuas) nation, 10 l. up the river from S. Ildefonso; 2,000 Ind. baptized, the most savage in the province, and often miraculously restrained from killing the padres.

Taos pueblo of same nation as Picuríes, but differing a little in language; 7 l. N. of P.; 1,500 Ind. converted to Christian ideas of marriage by lightning sent to kill a woman who opposed it; mission and 2 padres.

Acoma pueblo, 12 l. w. of Sta Ana (same discrepancy as so often noted before); 2,000 Ind., reduced in 1629; one friar.

Zuñi nation, 30 l. w. of Acoma, extending 9 or 10 l.; 11 or 12 pueblos· 10,000 converted Ind.; 2 missions.

Moqui nation, 30 l. w. of Zuñi; 10,000 Ind., who are being rapidly converted.

[44] Davis' list, originally prepared by Miller for the surv.-gen. (U. S. Land Off. Rept, '62, p. 102), completed by D. and revised by M. The orig. had but one gov. before '80. The names and dates are taken from ref. in later doc. of the Arch. Sta Fé. I shall make important additions of names and dates from various sources. I think Argüello's rule of '40 may be doubtful. Davis' list to '80 is Peralta 1600 (1608 et seq.), Argüello '40, Concha '50, Ávila y Pacheco '56, Villanueva, Frecinio '75, Otermin '80-3.

[45] Valdés is named in a royal order. In '81 Capt. Juan Dominguez de Men-

is named again in 1645.[46] Luis de Guzman held the
office before 1650,[47] and Hernando de Ugarte y la
Concha in 1650.   Juan de Samaniego was the newly
appointed ruler in 1653.[48]   In 1656 Enrique de Ávila
y Pacheco had succeeded to the place.[49]   Bernardo
Lopez de Mendizábal is named as having become involved in troubles with the inquisition, and surrendered
his office in 1660 or the next year; while the more or
less famous Don Diego de Peñalosa Briceño ruled
in 1661–4.[50]   Next came Fernando de Villanueva,[51]
Juan de Medrano, and Juan de Miranda, the dates
of whose rule are not known.   Juan Francisco Treviño
seems to have ruled in 1675;[52] and Antonio Otermin
was governor in 1679–83.   Captain Dominguez testified in 1681 that he had known fourteen governors,
from Pacheco to Otermin, in the past thirty-eight
years, and my list with thirteen names may therefore
be regarded as nearly complete for that period.[53]

The eastern entradas, as far as their meagre results
are concerned, belong to the annals of Texas rather
than of New Mexico, and have been noticed elsewhere.[54]
They include missionary tours of padres Salas, Perea,
Lopez, and Diego Ortega to the country of the Jumanas, in the far east or south-east, on a river named
the Nueces, in 1629–32; an expedition of Captain

doza testified that, being now 50 years old, he had come at the age of 12 with
Gov. Pacheco (that is, in '43); and Gov. Otermin in '82 stated that Gov. P.
punished the murderers of Gov. Rosas; this is soon after '41–2. *Otermin, Extractos*, MS., 1395–6, 1600.

[46] Escalante's list: Argüello '45, Concha '50, Villanueva, Medrano, Miranda, Treviño, and Otermin.   The 3 names preceding O. rest on a statement
of P. Farfan that they ruled successively before O. *Carta*, 115–16.

[47] At least such a man, called ex-gov. of N. Mex., was killed in a duel at
Mex. in Nov. '50. *Guijo, Diario*, 154–5.

[48] Viceroy's letter to king, March 20, '53, in *N. Mex., Cédulas*, MS., 8–9.
Posadas, Not., 211–16, calls him Samiego, in ruling '54.

[49] Miller's list; name found in a doc. of '83.

[50] More of his rule later in this chapter.   Mendizábal is barely mentioned
in the Peñalosa papers. *Shea's Exped.*, 10–11.

[51] Perhaps earlier.   He was between Concha and Treviño. Davis' list.

[52] Called Frecenio by Davis and Frenio by Miller. *Sta Fé Cent.*, 14.

[53] Most authors begin Otermin's rule in '80; but Escalante says the great
revolt was in the 2d year of his rule.   Dominguez' testimony is found in
Otermin, Extractos, MS., 1395–6.   Davis and Miller found the allusion to 14
rulers, but make the date '40 instead of '43.

[54] See *Hist. North Mex. St.*, i. 382–7.

Alonso Vaca in 1634, eastward 300 leagues to the great river across which was Quivira; another of captains Hernan, Martin, and Diego del Castillo in 1650 to the Nueces, and far beyond to the country of the Tejas, where they found pearls; another similar one of Diego de Guadalajara in 1654, resulting in a fight with the Cuitoas; a backsliding about the middle of the century of certain families of Taos, who went out into the eastern plains, fortified a place called Cuartalejo, and remained there until the governor sent Juan de Archuleta to bring them back;[55] and finally the fictitious entrada of Governor Peñalosa to Quivira in 1662, of which I shall have more to say a little later. A royal order of 1678 alluded to projects of exploring Quivira and Teguayo, and to conflicting reports on the geography and wealth of these and other distant provinces, calling for an investigation; and it was in reply that Padre Posadas made his later report, which is the best authority on the outside regions, but contains very little on the history proper of New Mexico, of which the author was custodio in 1660–4, and a missionary from 1650.

In February 1632, padres Arvide and Letrado were killed by the gentile Zipias somewhere beyond the Zuñi region; and the next year Padre Porras was poisoned by the Moquis.[56] In 1640–2 there were serious difficulties between the governor and the friars, the latter being accused of assuming, as jueces eclesiásticos and officials of the inquisition, extraordinary and absolute powers, and of having even gone so far as to encourage a revolt, in connection with which Governor Rosas lost his life. We know but little of the controversy, which was deemed in Mexico very

[55] *Posadas, Not.*, 214–18; *Escalante, Carta*, 125. Simpson, *Jour.*, pl. 65–70, reproduces inscriptions on El Moro, including the names of Capt. Juan Archuleta in 1636, Agustin Hinojos and Bartolomé Romelo in '41, and Ant. Gonzalez in '67. This was, however, in the west.

[56] *Vetancur, Menol.*, 16, 24, 66. Fernandez Duro, 133, cites the *Verdadera relacion de la grandiosa conversion que ha habido en el N. Mex., enviada por el P. Fr. Estévan de Perea, custodio de las provincias . . . . daudole cuenta del estado de aquellas conversiones*, etc. Sevilla, 1632, fol., 4 l. This report I have not seen.

serious, and which seems to have been the beginning of a series of troubles that terminated in the great revolt of 1680. The padres were blamed, and special efforts were ordered to avoid a costly war, which it was thought could not be afforded in a province that yielded no return for an annual expenditure of 60,000 pesos.[57]

Several writers mention a revolt of 1644, in which the governor and many friars were killed;[58] but I suppose this is but a confused reference to the troubles of 1642 and 1680. In the time of Governor Argüello, probably about 1645 or later, there was a rising in consequence of the flogging, imprisonment, and hanging of 40 natives who refused to give up their faith; but the rebels were easily overpowered. In another revolt of the Jemes, aided by Apaches, a Spaniard named Naranjo fell, and in return the governor hanged 29, imprisoning many more for idolatry.[59] In 1650 or thereabouts it is evident that, partly as a result of the preceding quarrels, troubles with both converts and gentiles began to assume a serious aspect. At the same time complaints of oppression on the governor's part were sent to Mexico and Spain.[60]

During Concha's rule, or in 1650, there was a plot

[57] *Palafox, Informe al Conde de Salvatierra*, 1642, MS.; letter of same to king, July 25, '42, and royal order of July 14, '43, in *N. Mex., Ced.* MS. 7–8; *Bonilla, Apuntes*, MS., 1; *Revilla Gigedo, Carta de 1793*, p. 441. The latter says the matter was reported to the king in 1640, including an Ind. revolt, as well as scandalous quarrels between the friars and secular authorities. It appears that Rosas was stabbed—perhaps while under arrest awaiting his residencia—by a man who accused him of intimacy with his wife; but the woman had been put in his way that an excuse for killing him might be found. Antonio Vaca is named as a leader in this movement.

[58] *Calle, Not.*, 103; *Pino, Expos.*, 5; *Id., Not.*, 2; *Alcedo, Dicc.*, iii. 184; *Barreiro, Ojeada*, 5–6; *Alegre, Hist. Comp. J.*, i. 327. In the general chapter of the Franciscans at Toledo, 1645, the plan of changing the New Mex. custodia to a provincia independent of the Sto Evangelio in Mex. was discussed, but abandoned. *Ylzarbe, Informe*, in *Pinart, Col. Doc. Mex.*, 347.

[59] *Otermin, Extractos*, MS., 1301, 1395–6. This is the testimony of Dominguez in '81; consulted also by Davis, 279 et seq. D. says the 29 were only imprisoned.

[60] *Bonilla, Apuntes*, MS., 1; *N. Mex., Céd.*, MS., 6, 8–9. The king in his cédula of Sept. 22, '50, notes these complaints and the popular discontent and strife leading to raids by the gentiles, and orders viceroy to investigate and remedy. The viceroy replied March 20, '53, that he had given strict orders to the new gov.; the king approves and orders continued vigilance June 20, '54.

of the Tehuas and Apaches to kill the soldiers and friars on Thursday night of passion week, when all would be in church; but by chance the plot was discovered by Captain Vaca, nine leaders were hanged, and many more were sold into slavery for ten years. A like result followed an uprising of the Piros, who ran away during Governor Villanueva's time and joined the Apaches, killing five Spaniards before they could be overpowered. Several of the same nation now or a little later were put to death for sorcery. Estévan Clemente, governor of the Salineros towns, was at the head of the next conspiracy for killing the tyrants, after stealing their horses to prevent escape; but Don Estévan was hanged. The Taos drew up on two deer-skins a plan for a general movement, but it was abandoned because the Moquis refused their aid. No dates are given for these happenings.[61]

Diego Dionisio de Peñalosa y Briceño ruled New Mexico in 1661–4, having been appointed in 1660. He was a native of Peru, an adventurer and *embustero*, bent on achieving fame and fortune with the aid of his unlimited assurance and his attractive person and manners, by which alone presumably he obtained his appointment from the viceroy. Of Don Diego's rule and acts, as in the case of other rulers of the period, almost nothing is known. It appears, however, that he visited Zuñi and the Moqui towns, heard of the great kingdom of Teguay through a Jemes Indian who had been captive there, and also of Quivira and Tejas, and the Cerro Azul, rich in gold and silver ores; and that he planned an expedition to some of these wonderful regions.[62] I have seen an order dated at Santa Fé in 1664 which bears his autograph.[63] Like

[61] *Otermin, Extractos*, MS., followed by Davis. Zamacois, *Hist. Mej.*, v. 376, says that Alburquerque was founded in 1658, which is an error. The 1st duke of A. was viceroy in 1653–60; but the 2d duke of A., for whom the town was named, ruled in 1701–10. In the *Arch. Sta Fé*, MS., it is stated that the Pueblo del Paso del Rio del Norte was founded in 1659. The allusion is to the mission of Guadalupe del Paso, not to town or presidio.

[62] Juan Dominguez de Mendoza, maestre de campo in Peñalosa's time, report of later years as cited by Fernandez Duro, 49, 75.

[63] Jan. 20, '64, order that the Indians be not employed in spinning and

his predecessor, Mendizábal, he became involved in troubles with the padre custodio representing the inquisition; or more probably, as I think, he went to Mexico in 1664 or later to urge his scheme of northern conquest, and there came in conflict with the holy tribunal, by which he was perhaps kept long in prison; and at any rate, in February 1668 he was forced to march bareheaded through the streets carrying a green candle, for having talked against the santo oficio and said things bordering on blasphemy.[64] Unable to interest the viceroy and king in his project, he went to London and Paris in 1671–3, and there attempted to organize a grand filibustering enterprise of conquest against his former sovereign, freely resorting to falsehood, and claiming for himself the title of Conde de Santa Fé, with half a dozen others to which he had no claim. He died in 1687, and his efforts are closely connected with the expedition of La Salle of 1682–7; but these matters pertain to the annals of Texas, and not of New Mexico.[65]

In France Peñalosa presented to the government what purported to be a narrative of an expedition to Quivira made by himself in 1662, written by Padre Freitas, one of the friars of his company, and sent to the Spanish king. He never made any such entrada or rendered any such report. The narrative was that of Oñate's expedition of 1601, slightly changed to suit his purposes in Paris. I made known this fraud in an earlier volume of this series, but have since received the work of Fernandez Duro, published two years before my volume, in which that investigator, by

weaving without the gov.'s license; that friendly Indians be well treated, but that wild tribes coming to trade be not admitted to the towns, but obliged to lodge outside. Signed Diego de Peñalosa Briceño. *Arch. Sta Fé*, MS. This is the only orig. doc. I have seen at Sta Fé that dates back of the revolt of '80.

[64] *Robles, Diario*, 56–7; *Alaman, Disert.*, iii. appen. 35–6; *Zamacois, Hist Mej.*, v. 412–13. Z. tells us, p. 387, that 24 missions or pueblos were established in 1660–4.

[65] See *Hist. North Mex. St.*, i. In *N. Mex., Céd.*, MS., 56–60, are two royal orders, of 1675 and 1678, on the conq. of Quivira, growing out of P.'s efforts. Padre Posadas' report of about 1686 was also drawn out in the same connection.

similar arguments, reached the same conclusions.[66]
I suppose that it is to Don Diego's statements in
Europe that we must look for the origin of the famous
hoax of Admiral Fonte's voyage on the north-west
coast in 1640, the story having first appeared in 1708,
and Peñalosa being represented as vice-admiral of the
fleet.[67]

From about 1672 the various Apache tribes became
troublesome, destroying in their raids one of the Zuñi
towns and six of the pueblos farther east.[68]   Several
friars lost their lives.   In 1675 we are told that four
natives were hanged, 43 or 47 whipped and enslaved,
and many more imprisoned for having killed several
missionaries and other Spaniards, besides bewitching
the padre visitador, Andrés Duran; whereupon a
force of warriors marched to Governor Treviño's house
to demand the release of the prisoners for a ransom,
retiring on a favorable promise, but declaring they
would kill all the Spaniards or flee to the sierra and
risk annihilation at the hands of Apaches rather than
see their sorcerers punished.   Pope, prominent in a

[66] See *Hist. North Mex. St.*, i. 386, pub. in 1884.   The fictitious narrative,
Freytas, Relacion del Descub. del Pais y Ciudad de Quivira, given to the French
minister in 1675, and claimed to have been sent to the king of Spain in 1663,
was printed in *Shea's Exped. of Don Diego de Peñalosa*, N. Y., 1882, with
Span. and Engl. text, and valuable notes and extracts from Margry and other
authors respecting Peñalosa.   Later in 1882 appeared *Fernandez Duro, Don
Diego de Peñalosa y su descub. del reino de Quivira*, a report to the Royal Acad.
of Hist.   This author reproduces all of Shea's matter and adds much more on
the same and kindred subjects.   For his conclusion that the story was a
fraud he relies largely, as I did, on the report of Padre Posadas (erroneously
called Paredes by me from the printed ed., apparently not known to F. D.),
who was custodio during Peñalosa's term of office and who mentions no such
expedition.   I did not see the Madrid work of '82 or know of its existence till
after the publication of my volume.   Prince devotes a chapter to this exped.,
not recognizing its fictitious character.

[67] See *Hist. N. W. Coast*, i. 115 et seq.

[68] *Escalante, Carta*, 115–16.   The Zuñi town was Jahuicu (or Ajuico, where,
acc. to *N. Mex., Doc.*, MS., i. 502, P. Pedro de Ayala was killed by the
gentiles on Oct. 7, 1672); those of the Tehuas were Chilili (which Benavides
represents as a Tompiro town), Tafique, and Quarac; and those of the Tompiros, Abó, Jumancas, and Tabira.   One of these was very likely the famous
Gran Quivira.   Escalante says that before '80 there were 46 pueblos of
Christian Ind., one Span. villa, and several small Span. settlements.   Calle,
Not., 103–4, says that in '45 there were 25 doctrinas, with 60 friars, receiving
from the king 42,000 pesos per year.   Cavo, *Tres Siglos*, ii. 42, 46, tells us
that 24 Ind. towns were formed by the Span. in (before?) 1660; and that
Alburquerque was founded earlier with 100 Span. families.   See note 61.

later trouble, was now a leader either of the imprisoned offenders or of the band of rescuers.[69] All the tribes were known as Apaches, except the Yutas, occupying a part of the northern plains, and with whom Governor Otermin was the first to open communication. The Comanches did not make their appearance in the records of this century; but the Apaches del Navajó are mentioned. In 1676 the condition of affairs was reported to be serious. Towns and churches had been destroyed and many Christians killed by the Apache raiders; while the defensive force was only five men for each frontier station, and these were sadly in lack of arms and horses. A reënforcement of 40 or 50 men was needed at once if the province was to be saved. Padre Francisco Ayeta, the custodio, having come from New Mexico for succor, was preparing to start with a wagon train of supplies for the missionaries; and he made an earnest appeal for the 50 men and 1,000 horses to accompany the train, at an expense of 14,700 pesos to the royal treasury. The junta approved the measure on September 9th, perhaps of 1677; the viceroy reported to the king his resolution to send succor on January 13, 1678; the king approved on June 18th; and finally, after an unaccountable delay, the train started from the city of Mexico on the 29th or 30th of September, 1679. The relief arrived too late, as we shall see, to prevent the abandonment of the province; but it prevented still more serious disaster among the fugitive settlers and missionaries.[70]

---

[69] *Otermin, Extractos*, MS., 1441-3, 1459-66, 1480-1, being the testimony in '81 of Dominguez, Lopez, Quintana, and P. Ayeta. Escalante, *Carta*, 116, says nothing of this affair, but states that Pope and 46 others were arrested for various crimes. On March 28, '74, there died at Sta Fé Doña Juana Arias, wife of the visitador Gonzalo Suarez. *Robles, Diario*, 159. On Jan 23, '75, P. Alonso Gil de Ávila, minister of Renecuey (Senecú?), was killed by the Ind. *N. Mex., Doc.*, MS., i. 502. Other friars named in different records as serving in '80 or earlier are Antonio Acebedo, Lorenzo Analiza, Francisco de Ayeta, Antonio de Aranda (apparently custodio in '50), Juan Bernal (cust. in '80), Fran Gomez de la Cadena, Sebastian Calzada, Andrés Duran, Juan de Jesus Espinosa. Fran. Farfan, Cris. Figueroa, Alonso Gil, Ant. Guerra, Juan de Jesus, Simon de Jesus, Jesus de Lombarde, Albino Maldonado, Juan Mora, Jesus Morador, Juan de Vallada, Fernando de Velasco, and Juan Zavaleta.

[70] *Ayeta, Memorial al Virey*, 1676, including various docs. on the subject, in *N. Mex., Doc.*, MS., i. 481-513. Viceroy's rept to king and royal order

I close this chapter with a note from Vetancur's standard chronicle of the Franciscans, written about 1691, but showing the missions as they existed just before the great revolt of 1680. A padron of 1660 is said by this author to have shown a population of 24,000 Spaniards and Christian Indians, of whom it would seem the former must have numbered about 2,400 in 1680. Padre Francisco de Ayeta came as custodio, with a reënforcement of friars, in 1674, but, as we have seen, went back to Mexico for succor two years later.[71]

in reply, 1678, in *N. Mex., Cédulas*, MS., 9–10. Starting of the train and troops, the viceroy going to Guadalupe to see them off, Sept. 29 or 30, '79. *Robles, Diario*, 290; *Rivera, Diario*, 14.

[71] *Vetancur, Chron.*, 98 et seq. Missions of N. Mex. in 1680. See similar statement for 1630, p. 164 of this chapter.

Senecú (S. Antonio), 70 l. above Guadalupe del Paso, founded in 1630 by P. Ant. Arteaga, suc. by P. García de Zúñiga, or San Francisco, who is buried there; Piros nation; convento of S. Antonio; vineyard; fish-stream.

Socorro (Nra Sra), 7 l. above Senecú, of Piros nation; 600 inhab.; founded by P. García.

Alamillo (Sta Ana), 3 l. above Socorro; 300 Piros.

Sevilleta, 5 l. from Alamillo across river; Piros.

Isleta (S. Antonio), no distance given; where a small stream with the Rio del Norte encloses a fertile tract with 7 Span. ranchos; convent built by P. Juan de Salas; 2,000 inhab. of Tiguas nation. Here is the *paso* for Acoma, Zuñi, etc.

Alameda (Sta Ana), 8 l. above Isleta; 300 inhab. of Tiguas nation; named for the *álamos* which shade the road for 4 l.

Puray, or Puruay (S. Bartolomé), 1 l. from Sandía (Alameda ?); 200 Tiguas; the name means 'gusanos,' or worms.

Sandía (S. Francisco), 1 l. (from Puaray); 3,000 Tiguas; convent, where P. Estévan de Perea, the founder, is buried; also the skull of P. Rodriguez, the 1st martyr, is venerated.

S. Felipe, on the river on a height (apparently on E. bank); 600 inhab. with the little pueblo of Sta Ana; of Zures (Queres) nation; convent founded by P. Cris. Quiñones, who, with P. Gerón. Pedraza, is buried here.

Sto Domingo, 2 l. above S. Felipe; 150 inhab.; one of the best convents, where the archives are kept, and where, in '61, was celebrated an auto-de-fé, by order of the inquisition; P. Juan de Escalona buried here; padres in '80, Talaban (once custodio), Lorenzana, and Montesdeoca.

Sta Fé, villa, 8 l. from Sto Domingo; residence of the gov. and soldiers, with 4 padres.

Tesuque (S. Lorenzo), 2 l. from Sta Fé, in a forest; 200 Tiguas (Tehuas); P. Juan Bautista Pio.

Nambé (S. Francisco), 3 l. E. of Tesuque, 5 l. from Rio del Norte; 2 little settlements of Jacona and Cuya Mangue; 600 inhab.; P. Tomás de Torres.

S. Ildefonso, near the river, and 2 l. from Jacona, in a fertile tract, with 20 farms; 800 inhab.; PP. Morales, Sanchez de Pro, and Fr. Luis.

Sta Clara, convento, on a height by the river; 300 inhab.; a visita of S. Ildefonso.

S. Juan de los Caballeros, 300 inhab.; visita of S. Ildefonso. In sight are the buildings of the villa de S. Gabriel, the 1st Span. capital.

Picuríes (S. Lorenzo), 6 l. (from S. Juan), on a height; 3,000 inhab.; Fr. Ascensio de Zárate served and is buried here; P. Matías Rendon in '80.

Tahos (S. Gerónimo de Taos), 3 l. (?) from Picuríes and 5 l. from the river, in a fine valley; 2,000 inhab. and some Spaniards; in 1631, P. Pedro Miranda de Ávila was killed here; PP. Juan de Pedrosa and Antonio de Mora in '80.

Acoma (S. Estévan), east (?) of Cia on a peñol 1 l. in circum. and 30 *estados* high; 1,500 inhab., converted by P. Juan Ramirez; in '80, P. Lúcas Maldonado.

Hemes (S. Diego de Jemes), a large pueblo formed of 5 smaller ones, with 5,000 inhab.; in charge of P. Juan de Jesus.

Alona (Purísima), 24 l. from Acoma, with 2 visitas, called Mazquía and Caquima; 1,500 inhab.; P. Juan de Bal. (Zuñi prov.)

Aguico (Concepcion), 3 l. w. of Alona, with other small pueblos; 1,000 inhab; they revolted in '32, and killed P. Fran. Letrado; in '80 the padre escaped.

Aguatobi (S. Bernardino), in Moqui prov., 26 l. from Zuñi; 800 inhab. converted by P. Fran. de Porras; much pumice stone; P. José de Figueroa, or Concepcion, in '80.

Xongo pabi (S. Bartolomé), 7 l. from A., with a visita called Moxainabi; 500 inhab.; P. José Trujillo in '80.

Oraybi (S. Fran.; others say S. Miguel), farthest w. of the Moqui towns, over 70 l. from Sta Fé; had 14,000 gentiles, but a pestilence consumed them; 1,200 in a visita called Gualpi; PP. José de Espeleta and Agustin de Sta María.

Cochití, 3 l. from Sto Domingo; 300 inhab. of Queres nation; the padre escaped in '80.

Galisteo (Sta Cruz), 6 l. (from Cochití?), with S. Cristóbal as a visita; 800 inhab. of Tanos nation; here once served P. Antonio de Aranda; in '80 PP. Juan Bernal, custodio, and Domingo de Vera.

Pecos (Porciúncula), on the eastern or Quivira frontier, in a finely wooded country; has a magnificent church with six towers; pop. not given; P. Fern. de Velasco.

S. Márcos, 'on the right toward the N., 5 l. from Sto Domingo;' 600 inhab. of Queres nation; 2 visitas, S. Lázaro and Ciénega; P. Manuel Tinoco.

Chilili (Natividad), 3 l. from S. Lázaro; 500 Piros. converted by P. Alonso Peinado, who is buried here; this is the 1st pueblo of the Salinas valley.

Quarac (Concepcion), 3 l. from Chilili; 600 Tiguas speaking Piros lang.; converted by P. Perea; here is buried P. Gerónimo de la Llana.

Taxique (S. Miguel), 2 l. from Quarac; 300 inhab.; the padre escaped in '80.

Abbo (S. Gregorio), in the Salinas valley, which is 10 l. in circum., and produces much excellent salt; 800 inhab.; 2 visitas, Tenabo and Tabira (Gran Quivira?); 15 l. farther east are some Christian Jumanas served by the padre of Quarac; P. Fran. de Acebedo is buried at Abbo.

All the padres named above as serving in '80 were killed in the revolt of that year; the survivors are named in note 5 of the next chapter. See also map in next chapter.

CHAPTER IX.

A DECADE OF FREEDOM.

1680-1691.

Causes of the Revolt—Religious Tyranny—The Patriot Leaders—Pope, Catiti, Tupatú, and Jaca—The Knotted Cord—The Plot Revealed — Massacre of 400 Spaniards — Twenty-one Martyr Friars—Names—Siege of Santa Fé—The Governor's Victory and Retreat—Down the Rio del Norte to El Paso—Presidio del Paso del Norte—Pope's Rule in New Mexico—Liberty and Anarchy—Fruitless Entrada of 1681—Destruction of the Pueblos — The Faithful Tiguas of Isleta — Otermin Censured — Events at El Paso—Mission Items—Rule of Cruzat and Reneros —Huerta's Project—Battle at Cia—A New Governor.

THE pueblo communities were now to rid themselves for a time of their Spanish masters, whom they regarded as tyrants. Past efforts to shake off their fetters had only shown how tightly they were riveted. They were required to render implicit obedience, and to pay heavy tribute of pueblo products and personal service. Their complaints, however, in this direction are not definitely known. The Spaniards in their later gathering of testimony ignored this element of secular oppression, if, as can hardly be doubted, it existed, and represented the revolt to be founded exclusively, as it was indeed largely, on religious grounds. The New Mexicans seem to have been more strongly attached than most American tribes to their aboriginal faith, and they had secretly continued so far as possible the practice of the old forms of worship. The friars had worked zealously to stamp out every vestige of the native rites; and the authorities had enforced the strictest compliance with Christian regulations, not

(174)

hesitating to punish the slightest neglect, unbelief, relapse into paganism, so-called witchcraft, or chafing under missionary rule, with flogging, imprisonment, slavery, or even death. During the past thirty years large numbers of natives had been hanged for alleged sorcery, or communion with the devil, though generally accused also of projected rebellion or plotting with the Apaches. The influence of the native old men, or priests—sorcerers, the Spaniards called them —was still potent; the very superiority of the pueblo organization gave the patriotic conspirators an advantage; past failures had taught caution; and so skilfully was the movement managed that the premature outbreak a few days before the time agreed upon was hardly less successful and deadly than would have been the revolt as planned.[1]

Pope, connected with a former disturbance and accused of many crimes, was the moving spirit now. He was a San Juan Indian, but made Taos the centre of his efforts. Appealing to the popular superstition as well as patriotism, he claimed to have formed an alliance with the Great Spirit, or El Demonio of the Spaniards; and personally or through his agents and associates —chief among whom were Catiti of Santo Domingo, Tupatú of Picurí, and Jaca of Taos—Pope brought into his scheme all the pueblos except those of the Piros in the south, who for some unexplained reason were not invited. The Tanos and the Queres of Ciénega are doubtfully said to have shown some reluctance. A knotted cord was the mysterious calen-

[1] Testimony on the causes and methods of the plot was taken from many natives in the next 15 years, and is somewhat voluminously recorded; but I shall make no attempt to present details. There is a general agreement in the evidence, whether it comes from secular or ecclesiastical sources. Notwithstanding past quarrels, the friars seem to have had no charges to make against the gov. and his officers in this matter, all attributing the revolt to demoniac influences on a superstitious and idolatrous people. Sigüenza, *Mercurio Volante*, 589, tells us that the plot had been brewing for fourteen years. Vetancur, *Chron.*, 103–4, *Id.*, *Menol.*, 119, says it was foretold 6 years in advance by a girl miraculously raised from the dead, who said it was to be due to prevalent lack of respect for the padres. All suits against the friars were thereupon dropped in terror, but it was too late. A friar abroad also foretold the event.

dar sent by swift runners to all the pueblos to make
known the date of rising, which seems to have been
fixed for the 13th of August, 1680.[2]

Despite the utmost precautions, however—no
woman being intrusted with the secret, and Pope
killing his own son-in-law on suspicion of treachery—

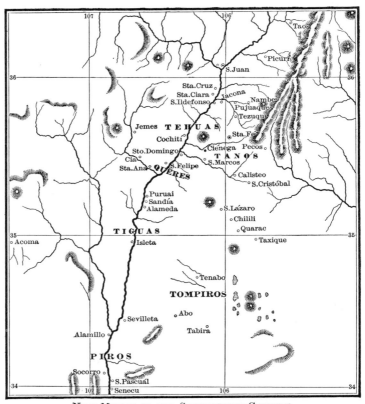

NEW MEXICO IN THE SEVENTEENTH CENTURY.

[2] Escalante in print makes the date the 18th, but my MS. copy has it 13th,
as does Gregg. Davis and Miller, and some of the orig. corresp., make it
Aug. 10th, the plot being revealed on the 8th. Otermin's narrative begins
abruptly with the 10th, and says nothing of preceding revelations. The
knotted cord is mentioned by the original authorities. Davis' explanation,
that the knots represented days before the rising, and that each pueblo consenting untied one knot, is not very clear.

the influence of the friars over certain converts was
so strong that the plot was revealed, perhaps as early
as the 9th, from several different sources.[3]
The Tanos of San Lázaro and San Cristóbal revealed
Pope's plot to Padre Bernal, the custodio. Padre
Velasco of Pecos received a like confession from one
of his neophytes. The alcalde of Taos sent a warning
which caused the governor to arrest two Tesuque
Indians who had been sent by the Tehuas to consult
with the Tanos and Queres. Otermin sent messengers in all haste to warn padres and settlers south of
San Felipe to flee to Isleta, while those of the north

[3] The original authority on the revolt of 1680 is *Otermin, Extractos de Doc.
Hist. N. Mex., sacados de los autos existentes en el oficio del Supremo gobierno de
esta corte, que sobre el Levantamiento del año de 1680 formó Don Antonio de Otermin, gobernador y capitan general del mismo reino,* copy from the Mexican archives, in *N. Mex., Doc. Hist.,* MS., 1153–1728. This record, equivalent to a
journal of the governor's movements, expanded by various corresp. and autos,
extends from Aug. 10, 1680, to the spring of 1682. It is very voluminous, and
tediously verbose, most of the record being repeated several times in various
forms, and a report by the fiscal in Mex. being a résumé that is more satisfactory to the reader than the bulky original. In the same col. of *N. Mex., Doc.,*
MS., 514–81, are several important letters written at El Paso in Aug.–Dec.
1680 by the friars. In *Vetancur, Chronica,* 94–104, and *Id., Menologio, passim,*
the standard chronicle of the Franciscan provincia del Santo Evangelio, pub.
in 1697, but written about 1691, before the reconquest of N. Mex., we find
much valuable information about the missions just before the revolt, and the
friars who lost their lives. Escalante, *Carta,* 116 et seq., is also one of the
best authorities on the subject, the author having searched the archives by
order of his superior in 1778, and thus consulted doubtless much missionary
corresp. in addition to Otermin's record. Davis, *Span. Conq.,* 287–335, gives
a very satisfactory narrative from the archives—that is, following Otermin, a
copy of whose *Extractos* was found at Sta Fé. The same authority was consulted by Gregg, *Com. Prairies,* i. 121–7, and Miller, in *Sta Fé Centennial.*
Otermin, Vetancur, and Escalante may be regarded as the standard authorities on this subject. Other works, to some of which I shall have occasion to
refer on special points, are as follows: *Niel, Apunt.,* 103 et seq.; *Villagutierre,
Hist. Conq. Itza,* 204–9; *Dávila, Mem. Hist.,* pt ii. 1–2; *Cavo, Tres Siglos,* ii.
57–60; *Villaseñor, Teatro,* ii. 419; *Mange, Hist. Pimería,* 227–8; *Arch. N.
Mex.,* 129; *Lezaun, Noticias,* MS., 129 et seq.; *Arricivita, Cron. Seráf.,* 199; *Arlegui, Cron. Zac.,* 249–50; *Rivera, Gob. de Mex.,* i. 252–3; *Id., Hist. Jalapa,* i.
98, 102; *Sigüenza y Góngora, Mercurio Volante,* MS., 589 et seq.; *Zamacois,
Hist. Mej.,* v. 429–37; *Bustamante, Gabinete Mex.,* i. 35–6; *Alvarez, Estudios,*
iii. 224–6, 264–5; *Lacunza, Discursos,* no. xxxv. 503; *Escudero, Not. Chih.,*
231; *Espinosa, Cron.,* 35; *Prince's Hist. Sk.,* 190–205; *Carleton,* in *Smith. Inst.
Rept,* 1854; *Brevoort's N. Mex.,* 83; *Dampier's Voy.,* i. 272; *Mayer's Mex. Aztec,*
i. 213–14; *St Francis, Life,* 557; *Davis' El Gringo,* 75–80, 134–7; *Meline's 2000
Miles,* 136; *Beltrami, Mex.,* i. 280–1; *Nouv. Ann. Voy.,* cxxxi. 255; *Domenech's
Des.,* 180–3; *Modern Trav., Mex.,* ii. 72; *Hinton's Handbook,* 388. The matter
thus referred to varies from accurate narrative to worthless mention, but contains no original information of value. The pages cited or the following ones
in most cases include the reconquest in 1692.

were to start for the capital or Santa Cruz de la
Cañada. Pope saw that his only hope of success
was in immediate action, and by his orders the Taos,
Picuríes, and Tehuas attacked the missions and farms
of the northern pueblos before dawn on the 10th,
"llevandolo todo á sangre y fuego." Apparently,
hostilities had been committed at Santa Clara a day
or two earlier, and some of the more distant pueblos
rose a day or two later, as soon as they heard of the
premature outbreak. I follow Escalante's version for
what is not found in Otermin's journal; but little reliance can be put in the accuracy of details. All agree
that the outbreak was on the 10th, day of San Lorenzo, and that it was premature. On that day Alférez Lucero and a soldier arrived at Santa Fé with
news of the rising of the Tehuas, reporting that the
alcalde mayor had collected the people at La Cañada,
and that the rebels were in force at Santa Clara.
Captain Francisco Gomez was sent out to reconnoitre, and returned on the 12th with confirmation
and a few details of the disaster. The governor on
the 13th ordered the alcalde and sargento mayor, Luis
Quintana, to bring in the people from La Cañada to
Santa Fé, which was probably accomplished.[4] He
sent out native scouts, despatched an order to Lieutenant-general Alonso García to send aid from Isleta,
and prepared to defend the capital.

It was the plan of the New Mexicans to utterly ex-
terminate the Spaniards; and in the massacre none
was spared—neither soldier, priest, or settler, personal
friend or foe, young or old, man or woman—except that
a few beautiful women and girls were kept as captives.
From San Felipe south all were warned in time
to make their escape. Many settlers of the valley
farther north took refuge at La Cañada and were
saved; but in all the missions of the north and east

---

[4] Otermin is not clear about this, but I find no foundation for Davis' inter-
pretation to the effect that all at La Cañada perished. Escalante says they
reached Sta Fé safely; and it is certain that Quintana himself did so.

and west only the friar at Cochití, those at Santa Fé, and one in the Zuñi province—who was perhaps absent—escaped death. The number of victims was slightly over 400, including 21 missionaries and 73 men capable of bearing arms; those who escaped were about 1,950, including 11 missionaries and 155 capable of bearing arms.[5] It will be noticed that the friars with few exceptions were new-comers, and that the whole number in the province was less than might have been expected from preceding annals.

On August 14th the scouts returned and reported that 500 Indians from Pecos and the eastern pueblos were approaching; and next morning the foe appeared at San Miguel in the suburbs of the villa.[6] One of the number was induced to enter the town and hold a conference; but he said that nothing could change the determination of his countrymen, who had brought two crosses, one red, as a token of war, the other white, indicating peace; but if the Spaniards should choose the white flag they must immediately quit the country. They said they had killed God and Santa María, and the king must yield. The governor sent out a force to attack the enemy before reënforcements could arrive, and soon went out in person. The battle lasted nearly all day, but when the Spaniards seemed

[5] The friars who perished are named, with some biog. information, by P. Ayeta in a letter of Sept. 11th, and also by Vetancur as follows: P. Juan de Bal, Spaniard, came to N. Mex. in '71; Juan Bernal, custodio, Mexican, came in '74; José Espeleta, Span., before '50; José Figueroa, Mex., '74; Juan Bautista, Span., '77; Juan de Jesus, Span., '67; Fran. Ant. Lorenzana, Span., '74; Lúcas Maldonado, Span., '67; Juan Montesdeoca, Mex., '67; Ant. Mora, Mex., '71; Luis Morales, Mex., '64; Juan Pedrosa, Mex., '64; Matias Rendon, Mex., '74; Antonio Sanchez, Mex., '77; Agust. Sta María, Mex., '74; Juan Talaban, Span., '62; Manuel Tinoco, ——, '74; Tomás Torres, Mex., '77; José Trujillo, Span., '67; Fern. Velasco, Span., before '50; Juan Dom. Vera, Mex., '74. For distribution, see end of the preceding chapter. The surviving friars named in a letter of P. Sierra of Sept. 4th were PP. José (or Ant.) Bonilla, Fran. Gomez de la Cadena, Andrés Duran, Fran. Farfan, Nicolás Hurtado, Diego Mendoza, Fran. Muñoz, Diego Parraga, Ant. Sierra, Tomás Tobalina, and Juan Zavaleta. Five captains are named as having been killed: Fran. Jimenez, Agustin Carbajal, Cris. de Anaya, José Nieto, and Andrés Gomez.

[6] Davis, Miller, and Gregg imply that it was on the 12th or 13th; but Otermin's record is clear. Escalante speaks of the Tlascaltec suburb or ward of Analco, which is not unlikely, though I have found no earlier mention of such a Tlascaltec colony in N. Mex.

on the point of victory, the northern army of Taos,
Picuríes, and Tehuas appeared on the field, and Otermin was obliged to retire with his men to protect the
palacio, where women and children had taken refuge.
The siege of Santa Fé lasted five days.[7] The natives
were about 3,000 strong. They soon took and destroyed the suburbs, and indeed all but the plaza and
casas reales. The church and convent were burned,
and the water supply was cut off. Out of a population of 1,000, Otermin had less than 150 men, many
of them servants utterly unfit for military service;
but the situation was critical, and finally on the 20th
with 100 men he made a desperate sortie. Invoking
"the sweet name of María," this forlorn hope threw
itself against the besiegers and drove them back,
killing 300 and bringing 47 captives into the villa,
who, after their testimony had been taken, were shot
in the plaza.[8] During the whole siege and battles
only five Spaniards were killed, though the governor
and many others were wounded.

It was decided on the 21st to abandon Santa Fé,
or, as the original record puts it, to march to the relief
of Isleta; clothing to the value of $8,000 was dis-
tributed; and the governor, garrison, women and
and children, and three friars—Cadena, Duran, and
Farfan—about 1,000 persons in all, began their march
on foot, each carrying his own luggage, as the horses
were barely sufficient for the sick and wounded. The
natives, though watching the fugitives from the hills
and sometimes being seen at a distance, made no
attack. Perhaps they had not yet the courage to
face the desperate valor of Otermin's little band, or

---

[7] From the 16th to 19th, or 7 days, 15th to 20th. Most writers make it
9 days, that is, from the 1st alarm on the 10th to the 19th.

[8] Miller says nothing of this affair, representing the Spaniards as having
cut their way out. Cavo.says they escaped by stealth when hunger and the
stench of dead bodies became intolerable. Villagutierre tells us that Gov.
O. cut off the water to drive the Indians out of the fort they had seized.
The captives said the plot had been made long ago at Tesuque; but that the
real leader was a man in the north whom Montezuma had left behind as
lieutenant on his departure for Mexico.

they waited for the hardships of the march to render their deadly task less difficult; but it is more likely that they were content to avoid further bloodshed, now that their chief object had been effected in the invaders' retreat.

The route was by Santo Domingo, where were found the bodies of three padres and five other Spaniards who had been murdered, and thence to San Felipe and Sandía, whose Spanish inhabitants had escaped, though all these pueblos had been sacked and partially ruined, all vestiges of Christianity having been destroyed. Several haciendas on the way were found in ruins, with evidence that the occupants had been killed. Isleta was reached on the 27th; but the refugees under Captain García had left this pueblo thirteen days before and gone south to Fra Cristóbal.[9] At Alamillo, in the region of Socorro, the governor met García, who had been overtaken by his messengers and returned. Legal proceedings were begun against him for having left Isleta without orders; but he claimed to have acted from necessity, having neither force nor supplies, and believing that all in the north were dead. Here also, on September 6th, was met Pedro de Leiva with thirty men, part of the escort of Padre Ayeta's supply train, sent up from El Paso by the procurador to aid the fugitives. All went south to Fra Cristóbal, where on the 16th a council determined that under the circumstances it

---

[9] Sept. 4th García writes from Fra Cristóbal to P. Ayeta at El Paso, having just received news from the gov. *N. Mex., Doc.*, MS., 514–20; also P. Sierra to same on same date, giving names of surviving padres. *Id.*, 570–5. It appears that capt. Seb. Herrera and Fern. Chavez, returning from the Yuta country, were at Taos when the revolt occurred, but escaped, reached Sta Fé while the siege was in progress, and passed on to join García at Isleta. Aug. 31st, letter of Ayeta to viceroy when he had heard of the revolt, but supposed Otermin and all in the N. to have perished. *Id.*, 559–81. He says Leiva has started N. on the 30th with 27 men and supplies; thinks a stand must be made at El Paso or all the north will be lost to Spain; urges that Leiva be made gov. if Otermin is dead; thinks 27 padres have perished. It is a long, rambling letter, showing the writer's natural anxiety at such a time; and referring to the *autos* for more details. On Sept. 11th he writes again, when he has heard of succor having reached both parties of fugitives. He gives names and brief biog. of the murdered friars. *Id.*, 525–41.

was impracticable to return to Santa Fé; and before
the end of September the whole force was encamped
in the region of El Paso del Norte, where for twenty
years or more the Franciscans had had a mission of
Guadalupe.[10]

[10] Sept. 18th, Otermin writes from Salineta, 41. from Guadalupe, and speaks
of a great flood which makes it difficult to cross the river; but he apparently
crosses on the 22d to inspect Ayeta's supplies. *Otermin, Extractos,* 1183–4.
Dec. 20th, P. Ayeta writes to the com. gen., chiefly on details of supplies. He
says the army is now encamped in three divisions on the river, 2 l. apart; 1st
the gov., cabildo, and 5 friars at S. Lorenzo, so named for the day of the
great revolt; 2d, the camp of S. Pedro de Alcántara with 4 padres; and 3d,
the camp of Sacramento, under P. Alvaro Zavaleta as prelate. The rest of
the padres are at the convent of Guadalupe, P. Nicolás Hurtado having been
appointed custodio. *N. Mex., Doc.,* MS., 541–58. Vetancur, *Chron.,* 98, tells
us that Guadalupe was founded by P. García de Zúñiga among the Mansos
in 1659, and the church was dedicated in '68 by P. Juan Talaban. In about
1691 it has 1,000 neophytes, or 2,000 with the fugitives from N. Mex. Twelve
l. away is a mission station of S. Francisco, with one padre; and 1½ l. from
here (S. Fran. or Guadalupe?) is the Real de S. Lorenzo.
   The following items about the revolt, collected by Davis and others, but
not noted by Escalante, may in a few instances have some slight foundation
in fact.   P. Jesus Morador, of Jemes, was taken from bed, bound naked on a
hog's back, and thus with blows and yells paraded through the town, being
afterwards himself ridden and spurred till he fell dead. (Gregg tells the
same story, but of a padre at Cia, on the authority of a captive named Ojeda.
Vetancur says there was a dispute at Jemes, some of the people wishing to
save Padre Juan de Jesus, who was finally killed kneeling in the plaza and
embracing the Christ.)   At Acoma PP. Maldonado, Figueroa, and Mora
(only Maldonado was really at Acoma) were tied together and marched naked
through the streets with abuse and insult of every kind, till Figueroa, by
open defiance and predicting the tormentors' downfall in 3 years, provoked
them to kill all three with clubs and stones.   At Zuñi PP. Analiza, Espinosa,
and Calzada (no such padres were in the country at this date) were shot by
A.'s servant, who was forced to do the deed.   Here the victims were buried
in the church, but elsewhere thrown outside the pueblo limits. (There may
be some vague ref. to an earlier event. D., in *El Gringo,* 75–9, mentions a
trad. that the Zuñi padre was not killed—which was true—but abjured his
faith.)   The Moqui padres Vallada and Lombarde (names incorrect) were
stoned to death after the usual insults; and the P. procurador on his way
from Acoma to Zuñi was killed while kneeling in prayer. Gregg preserves
the tradition that S. Felipe remained faithful and saved also the padre of
another pueblo, who when water failed and all were about to perish, prayer-
fully opened a vein in each arm, from which flowed water in copious streams.
Arlegui, *Cron. Zac.,* 249–50, mentions a P. Alonzo Gil who, in this revolt of
some other, appeared at the window of the church where the Christians had
taken refuge, and was shot while trying to appease the rebels.   At S. Juan,
acc. to *Arch. N. Mex.,* 129, three Span. women were kept alive and bore
children during their captivity.   Villaseñor and others state that S. Juan de
los Caballeros was so named for the gentlemanly conduct of its people in this
revolt, but the name had really been given 81 years before. Pino, *Expos.,* 5,
and Frejes say that S. Juan and Pecos remained faithful to the Span.; and
Bandelier thinks this may be true of Pecos, but it does not agree with the
original records.   Carleton, *Smiths. Inst.,* '54, p. 313, preserves the story that
the 70 padres of Quivira, only 2 of whom escaped, buried immense treasure,
the existence of which was revealed later by one of the last survivors of the

Father Ayeta's wagon-train of supplies, the departure of which from Mexico has been noted in the preceding chapter, was a veritable godsend to the refugees, without which many must have perished, and no stand could have been made at El Paso. As it was, with all the padre procurador's energy and liberality, distributing from his store—most of which had been sent for the friars—ten head of cattle and ten fanegas of corn daily, and with some aid from the Nueva Vizcayan authorities at Parral and Casas Grandes, there was much suffering among the exiles. Many abandoned the company and were scattered in the Chihuahua settlements. At the end of the year Ayeta went to Mexico with a full report of misfortunes and a petition for relief, and his mission was successful;[11] for the viceroy not only took steps to relieve present necessities, but ordered preparations to be made for the reconquest of the lost province. Ayeta came back early in 1681, still in charge of the royal interests, bringing cheering news, supplies, and reënforcements. Then—or possibly not till 1682—El Paso was founded, at or near the temporary camp of San Lorenzo, as a kind of presidio and supply station for the reconquest and protection of New Mexico.[12]

extinct race; hence the holes made by treasure-seekers among the ruins. Dampier, *Voy.*, i. 272, who heard of the revolt when cruising off the Jalisco coast in 1686, learned that some of the Span. from N. Mex. had fled to the gulf of Cal. and escaped in canoes.

[11] In *Otermin, Extractos*, MS., 1185–1205, is a documentary record of Ayeta's proceedings, largely filled with unimportant details. He had spent $29,250, of which $9,625 was from the royal coffers. He had an appointment as procurador gen. of New Spain, and was ordered to Spain; but the audiencia in Feb. '81 authorized him to suspend his departure in order to go on with his N. Mex. enterprise. On March 20th there was a religious service at the convent of S. Francisco in memory of the 21 martyrs. Dr Sariñana preached. *Robles, Diario*, 319.

[12] Davis and others seem to labor under the impression that El Paso was already an old and flourishing town, which idea leads them into some confusion. As to exact localities I make no attempt to clear up the matter. As we have seen, there was an old mission of Guadalupe in the vicinity. El Paso was 'the ford' of Oñate's men in 1598, and not, as Gregg suggests, 'the passage from the north' of the fugitive Spaniards, or as others have thought, 'the passage' of the river from the mts into the broad valley. Niel, *Apunt.*, 103, tells us that Otermin having crossed the river a flood occurred that prevented the pursuing Ind. from crossing, ahd as for two years the river did not *cuajar* (that is, I suppose, return to its normal condition) the gov. had time to fortify El Paso!

The New Mexicans were again masters in their
own country, free to use or abuse the liberty they had
won.   Unfortunately, they had a leader who, like the
governor he had deposed, claimed supreme authority.
Willing to restore the old faith, or estufa-sorcery,
Pope had no idea of surrendering his newly acquired
power or of granting independent government to the
pueblos.   Therefore, or because of other remnants of
Spanish influence, perhaps from the wrath of native
dieties or retribution sent by the Christian god, aboriginal prosperity was at an end.   Civil war, drought,
famine, and pestilence devastated the province for a
decade.   Naturally, we know but little of what happened during this period save the final result; and to
the reconquest itself must be attributed a large share
of the devastation.   Moreover, the Spaniards, who
tell the story, are disposed to exaggerate the ruin
that followed apostasy from the faith.

Pope's first task was to obliterate Christianity with
all its tokens.   He ordered the destruction of all
crosses and church implements; forbade the naming
of Jesus or María; decreed that men should put away
their wives and take others to their liking; that all be
cleansed of baptism by water and soap-weed, baptismal names being dropped; that churches be destroyed
and estufas reopened; that the Spanish language be
abandoned for native dialects; and that none but native
crops be raised.   The new sovereign travelled from pueblo to pueblo to superintend the execution of his decrees.   Assuming supernatural powers, he proclaimed
that the Christian god was dead, having been made of
rotten wood, and powerless, while the native gods
were still potent to make the New Mexicans a prosperous people.   The Castillos were not to be feared,
for he had built walls up to the skies to keep them
away.   On his tour Pope dressed in full Indian costume, and wore a bull's horn on his forehead.   Everywhere he was received with honors similar to those
formerly exacted by the governor and custodio, scat-

tering corn-meal upon the people as a token of his blessing. The destruction of Christian relics was attended by noisy demonstrations, processions, dances, offerings to heathen deities, and every conceivable profanation of all that the missionaries had held most sacred.

All this was good fun during the insane excitement of victory and freedom from restraint; but Pope's rule became oppressive. He not only threatened vengeance of the gods on all who refused to obey his orders, but proceeded to execute that vengeance, often inflicting the death penalty. The most beautiful women were taken for himself and his captains. Excessive tribute was imposed for the support of the central government. Civil discords and wars followed, supplemented by drought, which was less adequately provided against than of old. The pagan deities seem to have abandoned their worshippers, and caused some very strange phenomena. The Apaches and Yutas took advantage of the situation to renew their raids for plunder. Many pueblos were abandoned, sites of others were changed, and tribes were scattered. Barbarism darker than that of aboriginal times settled down upon this northern land.[13]

[13] Says Escalante, *Carta*, 122–3: 'The rebel pueblos began to quarrel and wage bitter war. The Queres, Taos, and Pecos fought against the Tehuas and Tanos; and the latter deposed Pope—on account of his despotism, etc.— electing Luis Tupatú in his place.' He ruled the Tehuas and Tanos till 1688, when Pope was again elected; but died soon, and Tupatú was again chosen. Alonso Catiti died earlier; entering an estufa to sacrifice, he suddenly burst, all his intestines coming out in sight of many Ind. Later each pueblo of the Queres governed itself. The Apaches were at peace with some of the pueblos, but in others did all the damage they could. The Yutas, as soon as they learned the misfortune of the Span., waged ceaseless war on the Jemes, Taos, and Picuríes, and especially on the Tehuas, on whom they committed great ravages. Not only thus and with civil wars were the apostates afflicted, but also with hunger and pestilence. The Queres and Jemes destroyed the Tiguas and Piros remaining after Otermin's entrada (of '81, to be described presently), because they deemed them inclined to favor the Span. Of the Tiguas only a few families escaped and retired to the province of Aloqui (Moqui?); of the Piros none escaped.' Davis and Prince give a good account of the developments of this period. Niel, *Apunt.*, 103–6, says that for seven years it 'rained ashes,' while for nine years no water fell, and the streams all dried up. The Tompiros were exterminated; very few Tiguas and Jemes survived; somewhat more of the Tehuas, Taos, and Pecos were left; and the Queres, protected by the walls of Sta Fé, suffered least of all. Finally, by

It was not until the autumn of 1681 that Governor Otermin was ready; or, if not ready, was required by the viceroy's orders to attempt the recovery of the lost province.   While the record is meagre, it is clear enough that there was much opposition to this attempt, there being two parties among the soldiers, officers, colonists, and even the friars.   Many believed that the opportunities for missionary work and colonization were better in the south than in the north; they had lost their property and their families or friends, and had not yet recovered from the terror of the massacre; they were in favor of utilizing the funds and forces lately received to strengthen their position at El Paso, and of putting off the conquest to a more convenient season.   Otermin himself may have been lukewarm in the cause, but if so the viceroy's instructions left him no choice.   Captain Juan Dominguez de Mendoza, who had served in New Mexico from his boyhood, had retreated from Isleta with García, and had succeeded the latter as lieutenant-general, was leader of the opposition, and legal proceedings had on that account been begun against him and others.[14]   Most if not all the friars favored an experimental entrada at least, hoping that the natives,

the sacrifice of a virgin, water was restored to the bed of the Rio Grande, and thus life was saved, and their 'stubborn, insolent apostasy' was confirmed. Niel also tells a curious story to the effect that of the Tanos after the revolt only half remained to quarrel with other nations for supremacy, while the rest—4,000 men, women, and children—went away with their Spanish plunder to preserve themselves and let their cattle increase.   They went via Zuñi to Moqui, and having induced that people to give them a home, gradually gained possession of the country and towns, reducing the original Moquis to complete subjection, extending their conquests far to the s. w., and seating their young king, Trasquillo, on the throne at Oraibe.   They brought with them many who had served the Span., and learned from them all they could, instead of avoiding everything Spanish like the other nations.   Certain linguistic and other peculiarities of the different pueblos are sufficient, if not to give plausibility to this story, at least to make it worth preserving here. Arricivita, *Cron. Seráf.*, 199, tells us that the Tanos of Galisteo intrenched themselves at Sta Fé.   Acc. to *Arch. N. Mex.*, 129, a good authority, the Tanos of S. Cristóbal and S. Lázaro, south of Sta Fé, were forced by hostilities of Apaches, Queres, and Pecos to transfer their pueblos to the region of S. Juan, where the towns were rebuilt under the same names.

[14] This is shown in the fiscal's report of '82. *N. Mex., Doc.*, MS., 1623–1704.   Most writers say nothing of these troubles.   Escalante says 'hubo algunas dificultades que causaron una dilacion muy nociva.'

prompted to revolt and apostasy by the devil and a few sorcerers, had now seen the error of their ways, and would be eager for peace and pardon.

Otermin's army consisted of 146 soldiers, with 112 Indian allies, 975 horses, and a supply train of ox-carts and pack-mules.[15] Juan Dominguez de Mendoza was lieutenant-general and maestre de campo; Francisco Javier was civil and military secretary; and Padre Ayeta, the procurador general, accompanied the expedition with Padre Antonio Guerra, and perhaps one or two other friars.[16]

The start from Paso del Norte was on the 5th of November, and the march up the river past Estero Largo, Robledo, Perrillo, Cruz de Anaya, Fra Cristóbal, and Contadero, presents nothing of interest except these names.[17] From November 26th to the 4th of December, Otermin visited the southern group of pueblos, Senecú, San Pascual, Socorro, Alamillo, and Sevilleta. All these towns had been abandoned by the native Piros, and all ranchos along the route had been pillaged. Everywhere there were clear traces of revolt against Christianity in burned churches and broken images, of a revival of pagan rites in rebuilt estufas, and of later devastation, perhaps by

[15] Davis, 308, notes a petition of the old residents of Sta Fé that during their absence on the campaign their families be supported with the garrison at S. Lorenzo. This was dated Sept. 18th and was granted. An original MS. of the Pinart collection shows that on March 9, 1681, at 'Paso del Rio del Norte, conversion de Nra Sra de Guadalupe,' Gov. O. took testimony of 4 Ind. lately arrived from N. Mex., who said the Tiguas, Piros, and Apaches had formed a plot to attack El Paso. In an orig. doc. of the *Arch. Sta Fé,* the ayuntamiento of Paso del Rio del Norte is named, consisting of Fran. de Anaya Almazan, Cris. B. de Villanueva, J. Javier de Noriega, Fran. Romero de Pedraza, and Ant. de Monroy; escribano mayor, Ant. Lucero de Godoy.

[16] The sargentos mayores amd captains named in *N. Mex., Doc.,* MS., 1500, are Juan Dominguez, Pedro Leiva, Nicolás Rodriguez, Juan and Diego Lucero de Godoy, Luis de Granillo, Alonso del Rio, Sebastian de Herrera, Diego Lopez Zambrano, Luis de Quintana, Pedro de Marquez, Roque de Madrid, Diego Dominguez, Ignacio and Cristóbal Vaca, Felipe Romero, José Narvaez, Fran. Anaya, Fran. Madrid, Antonio Marquez, Gonzalo Paredes, Salvador Olguin, Antonio Dominguez, Ant. de Ávalos, Don José Chavez, and José Padilla. Escalante is the only authority for the exact force.

[17] Diary in *Otermin, Extractos,* 1207 et seq., followed by Davis, *Span. Conq.,* 308 et seq., with some slight errors. Escalante, 120, gives but a brief outline. The stretch of 32 l. without water, from Robledo to Fra Cristóbal, is noted; since known as La Jornada del Muerto.

northern rebels but probably by Apache raiders. The Spaniards completely destroyed all that was left.

Isleta, in the Tiguas province, was the first pueblo whose inhabitants had remained, and it was taken by assault on the 6th of December, after a slight resistance. Next day, the 1,511 inhabitants formally renewed their allegiance, received pardon with much advice, and offered many children for baptism. Here the walls of the burned church served as a corral for cattle; but the people had plenty of excuses to offer, attributing all that was unchristian to the northern apostates, who had come to attack their town and force these faithful subjects of the Spanish king to feign a relapse to idolatry. Indeed, they regarded Otermin's arrival as a most fortunate event, for they had plenty of corn, and were expecting an attack from the famine-stricken rebels of the north. A few Indians had escaped before the town was taken, and had gone north with news of the Spaniards' arrival; and now others were sent out by the governor to notify the rebels of his friendly intentions if they would return to their allegiance.

From Isleta on the 8th, Dominguez was despatched with seventy men to make a reconnoissance of the northern pueblos; and a few days later the governor and his army followed up the river, in a snow-storm, encamping from the 16th to the 23d at a point in sight of Alameda, Puaray, and Sandía.[18] These pueblos, whose inhabitants had fled, were found in the same condition as those below Isleta, except that they contained large stores of maize, all of which, with the towns themselves, was burned by the governor's orders. Dominguez rejoined Otermin on the 18th,

[18] Alameda seems to be represented as 6 l. above Isleta, with the Etsancia de Dominguez (not far from Alburquerque) half-way between. The 3 pueblos in the order named were near together. This is the best possible proof that Coronado's Tiguex, Rodriguez' Puara, and Espejo's Tiguas prov. have been correctly located in the region of the still standing Sandía, and Alameda above Alburquerque, though of course it is not certain that either Isleta, Alameda, or Sandía stands exactly on its original site. Everything indicates, however, that they all stood in the same district as now.

having visited San Felipe, Santo Domingo, and Cochití, which he had found abandoned, like the rest
with stores of maize, but which he had not burned.
At Cochití he met a large force of Indians, who approached in hostile array, but finally consented to
parley. Catiti, their chief, professed deep penitence
for his sins, shedding tears, and promising in a day
and a half to bring in all the rebels of the three
towns to accept pardon and renew their allegiance.
He failed to keep his agreement; the hostages held
were strangely allowed to depart; and much evidence
was obtained to show that Catiti's penitence was but
a ruse, to gain time for the Moquis and other distant
tribes to join the rebel force at Cieneguilla for a combined attack on the Spaniards. Accordingly, Dominguez returned south to rejoin the governor, who
severely criticised his management of the expedition,
blaming him for not having burned the pueblos, for
not having sent reports, and for various other shortcomings.

Otermin spent the week of his stay near Sandía,
chiefly in examining witnesses on the details of Dominguez' expedition, and on the causes of the original
revolt, the acts of the Indians during the past year,
and their present disposition. Among the witnesses
were two half-breeds, who claimed to have been forced
into the rebellion, and who gave themselves up voluntarily. The record is very voluminous,[19] and many
pages might be filled with details that would have
more interest than real importance. On the 23d a
junta de guerra was held, and radical differences of
opinion were expressed; but the decision was that in
view of the natives' bitter hostility, the inadequacy of
the force for a military conquest, the bad condition of
the men, and especially of the horses, the snow and
intense cold of midwinter, and finally the news that
the hostile natives under Tupatú were threatening

[19] *Otermin, Extractos*, MS., 1227-1580. Davis, *Span. Conq.*, 318-35, reproduces many particulars.

the faithful Tiguas—it was best to retire to a point opposite Isleta, which was done on the 24th or 25th. Here other witnesses were examined, and evidence accumulated to the effect that the rebels were preparing to run off the horses and massacre the enfeebled Spaniards. Matters were still further complicated by the defection of a large part of the Isletas, who fled to join the rebel army. Though some were nominally in favor of remaining, it is clear that none, not even Otermin or Ayeta, was zealous in the cause; and that the chief anxiety was to fill the autos with evidence that should justify a retreat. Yet it must be admitted that this evidence, if somewhat highly colored, had much real force.

The final junta began on the last day of the year, and on January 1, 1682, it was decided to march southward. There were 385 Indians at Isleta who still remained faithful, and who could not fairly be left to the vengeance of the apostates; therefore they accompanied the army. The pueblo having been burned, with all the grain and other property that could not be carried, the retreat down the valley began on the 2d; and on the 11th of February Otermin reached Estero Largo, only a few leagues from El Paso.[20] From this point the governor sent a general report to the viceroy, accompanied by the autos, to which he referred for details. In this document he made known his plans for settlement and missionary work in the El Paso region, asked for more stringent regulations to keep the colony together and bring back fugitives of the past few years, and also for leave of absence to visit Parral for medical treatment.[21] On the 25th of June the fiscal of the audiencia in Mexico

[20] On Jan. 15th they were opposite Socorro; on the 18th at Qualacu (one of Oñate's names, as will be remembered) and S. Pascual; 19th, Senecú; 21st, Fra Cristóbal; Feb. 1st, Robledo; 4th, Doña Ana; 11th, Estero Largo. *Otermin, Extractos,* MS., 1596–1612.

[21] *Otermin, Consulta at Virey,* 11 de Feb., 1682, in *Id., Extractos,* MS., 1612–23.

made a report, in which, after a careful résumé of the entrada from the autos, he commented in severe terms on the acts of Dominguez de Mendoza, recommending criminal prosecution of that officer; and he also blamed Otermin for not having made a stand at Sandía or some other convenient point, since the large stores of maize destroyed in the southern pueblos and left undestroyed in the north would have sufficed to restore the horses and support the army until help or new orders could be received. The fiscal favored, however, the proposed settlement and presidio at El Paso, though the New Mexican soldiers should not be permitted to enlist in the southern presidial company; and he also approved strict measures to collect and keep together all fugitives of the colony, whether Spaniards or Indians. The governor's leave of absence was not granted.[22]

With the termination of Otermin's journal in the spring of 1682, the record again becomes fragmentary and meagre. We have, however, some items of mission work in the El Paso region, the succession of governors, and a few attempts to regain lost ground in the north.[23] With the 385 natives that had come with Otermin from Isleta, a few who had accompanied the original refugees of 1680, and some who came later, the padres proceeded to found three new mission pueblos in the south. These were Senecú, Socorro, and Isleta.[24] Not much is known of what was

---

[22] Fiscal's report of June 25, 1682, in *Otermin, Extractos*, MS., 1623–1704. The copy consulted by Davis did not apparently include the two final documents. On Jan. 1, 1682, news had reached Mex. that a civil war had broken out among the troops in N. Mex., the commander being killed, but P. Ayeta escaping. *Robles, Diario*, 334.

[23] Brevoort, *N. Mex.*, 83, adds a discovery by the Franciscans of the Mina de los Padres, all traces of which they obliterated later when forced to give way to the Jesuits!

[24] S. Ant. de Senecú, of Piros and Tompiros, 2 l. below El Paso (or Guadalupe); Corpus Christi de Isleta (Bonilla, *Apuntes*, MS., 2, calls it S. Lorenzo del Realito), of Tiguas 1½ l. E. of Senecú; and Nra del Socorro, of Piros, Tanos, and Jemes, on the Rio del Norte 7 l. from Isleta and 12 l. from El Paso. In '83 the Ind. of Socorro attempted to kill P. Antonio Guerra and a few Span. families. The plot was discovered, and those involved fled to N. Mex., the

accomplished in the following years, and that little belongs mainly to the annals of Chihuahua and Texas; but there were many troubles with converts and gentiles, and most of those who came from New Mexico gradually disappeared from their new homes.   During most of the decade Padre Nicolás Lopez, perhaps the same as Hurtado, held the office of custodio and procurador general.[25]   In 1687 there was a royal order that twenty new missionaries should be sent to the Rio del Norte.[26]

The rule of Governor Otermin ended in 1683, and he was succeeded the same year by Domingo Jironza Petriz Cruzat, though Bartolomé de Estrada Ramirez is named as an intermediate ruler.[27]   Cruzat, or Cruzate as the name is also written, held the office four years, though involved in controversies with the governor of Nueva Vizcaya, and perhaps temporarily suspended in 1684–5.[28]   Captain Mange, the explorer

others being moved to a site nearer Isleta, where the pueblo still stood in 1778.   In '83 also a mission of the Sumas was estab. at Ojito de Samalayuca, 8 l. below El Paso, but next year the converts apostatized and fled, the revolt including Sumas, Janos, and the Mansos of Guadalupe, who killed P. Manuel Beltran and were not reduced till '86.   It was also in '83–4 that the padres made a visit to the Tejas, and also founded the ill-fated mission at the junction of the Conchos. *Escalante, Carta*, 120–2. See also *Hist. North Mex. St.*, i. 364–6.

[25] *N. Mex., Céd.*, MS., 14; *Fernandez Duro*, 48, 67–74. In '85 the vice-custudio and juez ecles. was P. Juan Muñoz de Castro, and the guardian of the convent of Guadalupe del Paso was P. Fran. de Vargas. *Arch. Sta Fé*, MS. Papers of indulgence for N. Mex. friars in '85. *Robertson's Hist. Amer.*, ii. 1017. The Jumanas ask for padres in '84. *Vetancur, Chrón.*, 96–7. By Fernandez Duro, 134, is cited from Barcia a MS. *Relacion que envió el gobr. de N. Mex. al virey de N. España de los Ind. Xumanas que pedian religiosos*, in '84. The same year, acc. to *Espinosa, Chrón.*, 92, the friars of the college of Sta Cruz de Querétaro wished to enter the N. Mex. field but did not succeed.

[26] Cédula of Sept. 26, '87, in *N. Mex., Céd.*, MS., 14–16. It was in reply to a request from P. Lopez.

[27] Davis' list. 'Knight of the order of Santiago, gov. and capt. gen. of N. Mex.' 1683.   Estrada may have ruled for a short time ad int., or may have been appointed and never have come.   I am not certain that Otermin ruled after '82.

[28] *Escalante, Carta*, 115, 121, says that Cruzat succeeded in Aug. '83.   In the col. of M. Pinart is an original order signed by Gov. C. on Nov. 29th, giving instructions for an entrada about to be undertaken among the Jumanas and adjoining nations.   Davis' earliest date is '84.   Vigil, in *Simpson's Jour.*, 108, tells us that Garbaceo de Cruzat y Góngora succeeded Otermin in '81, retook Sta Fé the next year, extended his conquest till '83, and then returned to Sta Fé!   The troubles with the gov. of N. Vizcaya are indicated by an original order of the viceroy on Nov. 28, '85, that Cruzat be restored

and writer, nephew and eulogist of Don Domingo, tells us that he ruled *con aplauso*, chastised the apostates, routed a combination of ten nations, reduced some of them to pueblo life, made fifteen campaigns, ruled more as a father than as a governor, and in his final *residencia* was pronounced a "bueno, recto, y limpio juez," and thanked in the king's name;[29] and indeed, much of this praise seems to have been well deserved.

In September 1683 the king approved all that had been done by the viceroy, including the establishment of a presidio of 50 men at El Paso; and he ordered that every effort should be made, with the slightest possible expense, to regain the lost province.[30] In August 1684 a force of 50 Spaniards and 100 Indians was sent against a ranchería of apostate and gentile Apaches to kill the men and capture the women and children.[31] In September 1685 the governor issued strict orders for the arrest and return of all fugitives. It was perhaps in connection with this order that the troubles with Governor José de Neiva of Nueva Vizcaya occurred; and it is to be noted that in the same month the maestre de campo, Juan Dominguez de Mendoza—before involved, as will be remembered, in serious charges—ran away from El Paso with the intention of going to Mexico, accompanied by several other officers.[32] Alonso García succeeded Dominguez as maestre de campo and lieutenant-governor.

and maintained in his office, with all its titles as held by his predecessor; while the gov. of N. Vizcaya must keep within the bounds of his own govt and not interfere with the gov. of N. Mex. *Doc.*, in *Pinart Col.*

[29] *Mange, Hist. Pimería*, 228. Jironza had been sent by Cárlos II. from Cádiz in '80 as visitador of the Leaward Isles, with a force of 50 men, rank of infantry capt., and instruc. to the viceroy to give him an office in reward for his services in the wars against Portugal. He was made alcalde mayor of Mestitlan, and soon promoted to be gov. of N. Mex.

[30] *N. Mex., Cédulas*, MS., 11–14. Orders of Sept. 4th. There had been a junta in Mex. on July 28, '82, and the viceroy had reported to king on Dec. 22d.

[31] Aug. 16th. *Arch. Sta Fé*, MS. Sargt. Mayor Roque de Madrid was in com. Other officers named are Luis Granillo, Diego Copoz, Ign. Vaca, Felipe Romero, Sebastian Gonzalez, H. Dominguez, Alonso Garcia, and Fran. de Anaya. Pedro Ladron de Guevara is named as sec. in '84–7, at dif. times.

[32] *Arch. Sta Fé*, MS. The *proceso* shows many charges against Dominguez, but no result. The others were Sargt. Mayor Juan Lucero de Godoy, Regidor Lázaro de Mirquía, Baltasar Dominguez, Juan de Anaya, and the govt sec.,

In 1686, under circumstances that are not explained, but on which the despatches carried by Dominguez and his companions to Mexico would probably throw much light, Cruzat was succeeded by Don Pedro Reneros de Posada, who ruled till 1689.[33] Of his rule nothing appears except that he seems to have made an entrada to the towns of the Queres, and that according to Mange there were complaints of his inefficiency, resulting in the reappointment of Jironza de Cruzat.[34] The latter in 1688 or 1689 renewed the entrada and fought the Queres, with other tribes fortified at Cia, killing 600 of the apostates and capturing over 70, who, except a few old men who were shot in the plaza, were with the king's license sold into slavery for 10 years, many of the natives having been burned to death in their dwellings rather than submit to capture.[35] Next year, or in 1690, the governor had his

Alfonso Rael de Aguilar. As the latter was again sec. in '94, it seems that the consequences of the desertion were not very serious. The deserters are said to have carried despatches from the padres, which may indicate a controversy between them and the gov. Davis, 337, found a doc. showing the presence of Gov. C. at S. Ant. Sinolu (Senecú) on Nov. 26, '85.

[33] In *Arch. Sta Fé*, MS., is an order signed by Reneros on Sept. 17, '86; also in the *Pinart Col.* a doc. showing Cruzat to be gov. in '86. Escalante, *Carta*, 115, says that R. succeeded in '88. Davis does not include R. in his list of gov., though he names him as having come to N. Mex. with Cruzat. There is another order signed by him on Feb. 11, '87, in the *Arch. Sta Fé*.

[34] *Mange, Hist. Pim.*, 228. On Oct. 8, '87, a town of the Queres (perhaps Cia) was attacked and fire set to the huts, many perishing in the flames; 10 were captured and sentenced to 10 years in the mines of N. Viz. *Arch. Sta Fé*, MS. Escalante, *Carta*, 123, says R.'s entrada was to Cia in '88, nothing being accomplished except the taking of a few horses and cattle. R.'s exped. to Sta Ana and Cia is also noted in *Sigüenza, Mercurio Volante*, MS., 595. In 1695 Reneros was alguacil mayor of the inquisition in Mex. *Arch. Sta Fé*, MS.

[35] Davis and others give the date as '88, as do apparently certain doc. in the *Arch. Sta Fé*. Mange, who says that 90 captives were formed into a new pueblo, gives no date. Escalante says it was in Sept. '89. Sigüenza, *Mercurio*, MS., 595–6, says the battle was on Aug. 29, '89. The viceroy reported the entrada to the king Feb. 9, '90, and the king's cédulas of July 16 and 21, '91, expressed thanks, etc., also permitting the enslavement of the 70 captives, but not their children or any Ind. under 14 years of age; also other matters, as in my text. *N. Mex., Cédulas*, MS., 23–8.

In the *U. S. Land Off. Rept*, '56, p. 307–26, is printed a series of doc. from the arch., with translations, which are regarded as the original titles to the pueblo lands of several pueblos, the others having lost their papers. The papers are dated Sept. 20–5, '89. Each one consists of the formal statement under oath of Bartolomé Ojeda, one of the Ind. captured at Cia, and who had taken a prominent part in the fight, to the effect that the natives of Jemes— also S. Juan, Picuríes, S. Felipe, Pecos, Cochití, and Sto Domingo—were so ter-

preparations made for another effort in the north; but a revolt of the Sumas demanded his attention.

In 1689 Toribio de Huerta, claiming to have been one of the original conquerors of New Mexico, applied to the king for authority to undertake the reconquest, with the title of marqués, and other emoluments as usually demanded for such service. Of course, his chief aim was the saving of apostate souls; but he also reminded the monarch that between Zuñi and Moqui was the Sierra Azul, a region immensely rich in silver, and made all the more desirable by the well-known existence of a quicksilver mine near at hand. This picture seems to have struck the fancy of the king and his counsellors, for he instructed the viceroy to give the subject particular attention, investigating the feasibility of the scheme, and Don Toribio's means for accomplishing it. As we hear no more of the matter, we may suspect that the empresario could not support all his allegations about northern wealth.[36]

rified by the event of 'last year,' that is, the defeat at Cia, that they would not revolt again or refuse to render allegiance; whereupon the gov. proceeds to assign the pueblo boundaries, generally 4 sq. l., with the church in the centre, but sometimes by fixed landmarks. In the case of Acoma and Laguna, Ojeda's testimony is as to the bounds of the pueblos, and the reasons why Acoma has moved to the peñol (from which it had been removed in 1599), and why Laguna had moved near to Acoma. It also is implied that the gov. had in his entrada visited other pueblos besides Cia. I confess that these doc. are very mysterious to me; and I cannot imagine why the gov. on such an occasion at El Paso, on the testimony of a captive that the rebels were disposed to submit, should have troubled himself to fix the town limits.

Davis, 336, found in the archives the foundation for a very unintelligible story, to the effect that Cruzat was accompanied by Reneros and Juan de Oñate· 'O. took with him 70 Franciscan friars, among whom was one Marcos de Niza (!), a native of the province. The latter said he had made a visit to Zuñi, called the buffalo prov., during the reign of Philip II. At the first arrival of himself and people in N. Mex. the inhab. were much surprised, being astonished at seeing white men, and at first believed them to be gods, and reported them as such. After the surprise had worn off, a cruel war broke out, the gov. and most of the priests being killed, a few only escaping to the pueblo of El Paso. Among those who escaped was a Fran. friar, who went to Mex. and carried with him an image of our lady of Macana, which was preserved for a long time in the convent of that city.' On this image of Nra Sra de la Macana we have a MS. in *Papeles de Jesuitas*, no. 10, written in 1754, which tells us that in the great N. Mex. revolt of '83 ('80) a chief raised his macana and cut off the head of an image of Our Lady. Blood flowed from the wound; the devil (?) hanged the impious wretch to a tree; but the image was venerated in Mex. for many years.

[36] *N. Mex., Céd.,* MS., 16–23. Order of Sept. 13, '89.

Before the king heard of Cruzat's zeal and success, he had appointed as his successor Diego de Vargas Zapata Lujan Ponce de Leon. In later orders of July 1691, he instructed the viceroy that if Vargas had not taken possession of the office, or if he was not ruling successfully, he was to be given another good place and Cruzat retained as governor; but Vargas had begun to rule early in 1691, and Cruzat was a few years later made governor of Sonora.[37] In the orders to which I have alluded, the king consented to raise the pay of the presidio soldiers from 315 to 450 pesos per year, declined to sanction the abandonment of the El Paso garrison, and suggested that Cia might be a better site than Santa Fé for the proposed restoration of the Spanish villa.

[37] *N. Mex., Cédulas*, MS., 23–8; *Mange, Hist. Pim.*, 228–9.

CHAPTER X.

RECONQUEST BY DON DIEGO DE VARGAS.

1692–1700.

RECORDS of the reconquest, with its various entradas and complications down to the end of the century, are comparatively complete and satisfactory, containing naturally a large mass of petty though not uninteresting detail that cannot be compressed within the limits of a chapter.[1]   The new governor and captain-

---

[1] The printed *Archivo de N. Mex.* (see bibliog. note on p. 20 of this vol.) is the most complete authority; but of the MS. *Archivo de Sta Fé*, from which the former was drawn in the last century, large fragments still exist and have been consulted by me. They were also consulted, when probably less imperfect than now, but with too little care in some matters, by Davis, *Span. Conq.*, 336 et seq., whose record ends practically with '96, and who has been followed more or less closely by Prince and other late writers. Another excellent and contemporary version, founded of course on the same doc., or Vargas' reports to Mexico, is *Sigüenza y Góngora, Mercurio Volante, con la de la recuperacion de las provincias del Nuevo Mexico, conseguida por Don Diego de Vargas*, etc., written by order of the viceroy Conde de Galve, and printed at Mexico 1693. It contains a brief summary, of no special value, of the discovery, conquest, and revolt of N. Mex. I have not seen the original print, but have a MS. copy in *N. Mex., Doc. Hist.*, 581–661. Escalante, in his *Carta*, 123–4, brings the record, with few details, down to the end of Sept. 1692. Sigüenza, *Carta al Almirante*, MS., 6–7, mentions the subject. As to miscellaneous references on the reconquest, except such as I may have occa-

general had been selected with special reference to the regaining of New Mexico; but on account of troubles with the Sumas and other tribes nearer El Paso, over a year passed away before Vargas could give his attention to the far north. Then so great was his impatience that he did not await the arrival of a reënforcement of fifty men from Parral assigned to this campaign by the viceroy, but leaving a note, in which he informed the conde de Galve that he preferred "antes incurrir en la nota de osado que en la de receloso," he set out from El Paso on August 21, 1692, with a force of 60 soldiers and 100 Indian auxiliaries, accompanied also by padres Francisco Corvera, Miguel Muñiz, and Cristóbal Alonso Barroso.[2]

The march up the valley of the Rio Grande was uneventful; all the pueblos up to Sandía, as we have seen, had been destroyed years before; and no Indians were seen. On the 9th of September the baggage was left at the Hacienda de Mejía, with a small guard under Captain Rafael Tellez; Santo Domingo and Cochití were found entirely abandoned; and at dawn on the 13th Don Diego's little army appeared before Santa Fé, surrounding the town and cutting off both the water supply and all communication with the outside. Here the Tanos of Galisteo were strongly fortified, but were apparently taken by surprise. At first they were defiant, and declared they would perish rather than yield to the invaders, or rather, that they would kill all the Spaniards, with any cowardly natives who might join their country's foes. But Vargas and the friars, while preparing "like brave men and zealous Christians for battle," also renewed their offers of pardon for past offences and their entreaties for peaceful submission; and before night

sion to cite on special topics in the following pages, there is no occasion to say more than that many of the works cited in the preceding chapter on the revolt contain also brief mention of succeeding events to 1700.

[2] Vargas in a letter says he started Aug. 21st, his force at Sta Fé being 40 Span. and 50 Ind.; while Sigüenza notes that 14 Span. and 50 Ind. were left with the baggage at Mejía. Davis says the force was 200 Span. and less than 100 Ind.

the natives yielded without a blow. Next day they were properly lectured and formally absolved from their apostasy; children were presented for baptism; and thus Santa Fé became once more a loyal Spanish villa.[3]

Don Luis Tupatú, the most powerful of the rebel chieftains since the death of Pope and Catiti, presently made his appearance on horseback, clad in Spanish costume, to tender his allegiance and that of the Tehuas. He said the Pecos, Queres, Jemes, and Taos had refused to recognize his authority and might resist the Spaniards; but he offered to accompany the governor on his tour, and aid him to the best of his ability. The fifty soldiers from Parral arrived on the 21st, and joined Vargas at Galisteo. Pecos was abandoned by the inhabitants, who in five days could not be induced to return, though a few were captured, and released bearing offers of peace and pardon. Returning to Santa Fé, Vargas started for the north on the 29th, visiting all the pueblos in that direction.[4] The people took their dose of absolution with a good grace. Those of Taos ran away at first, but were soon induced by Tupatú to return; and they soon revealed a plot of the hostile nations to attack the Spaniards from an ambush; but also joined the governor's force in considerable numbers, as did those of other pueblos, to act as warriors or messengers of peace, as occasion might demand. Returning to Santa Fé on October 15th, Vargas wrote next day a report to the viceroy, announcing that he had "conquered for the human and divine majesties" all the pueblos for 36 leagues, baptizing nearly 1,000 children born

---

[3] There is no foundation whatever for the bloody battle lasting all day, or the allied rebels gathering for the defence of Sta Fé, as narrated by Davis and Prince. There was no blood shed during all this campaign of 1692.

[4] S. Cristóbal, S. Lázaro, Tesuque, Nambé, Cuyammique (?), Jacona, Pujuaque, S. Ildefonso, Sta Clara, S. Juan, Picuríes, and Taos are named. A fragment of the original MS., *Vargas, Reconquista de N. Mex.*, 118–34, in the *Arch. Sta Fé*, records this northern tour, and on following pages later developments are recorded. As a rule I shall not refer to these original fragments unless they contain something not in the printed version.

in rebellion. To hold the province for the king he must have 100 soldiers and 50 families; and he recommended the sending of convict mechanics from Mexican jails to serve as teachers and search for metals [5]

Next Pecos submitted on the 17th; but Galisteo and San Márcos were found deserted. The people of Cochití, San Felipe, and San Márcos [6] were found together, and persuaded on the 20th to reoccupy their pueblos. Those of Cia and Santa Ana had built a new pueblo on the Cerro Colorado four leagues from the old Cia; and those of Jemes and Santo Domingo, with a few Apaches, were in another three leagues from the old Jemes. All submitted after some slight hostile demonstrations on the part of the Jemes. Cold weather and snow had now become troublesome; and on the 27th, from the Hacienda de Mejía, Vargas despatched for El Paso his artillery, disabled horses, Indian auxiliaries, ten settlers, and a party of rescued captives,[7] with an escort of soldiers. A junta voted to postpone the completion of the campaign to another year, but the leader refused his assent.

Marching on the 30th the army of 89 men reached Acoma on November 3d.[8] The people were ready for defence, slow to believe they would be pardoned,

[5] Vargas' letter of Oct. 16, 1892, in *Arch. N. Mex.*, 129; also in *Arch. Sta Fé.* The gov. is about to start to conquer the remaining pueblos and to look after the quicksilver mine. The messenger bearing the letter reached Mex. Nov. 21st, and next day there was a great celebration of the victory, the cathedral being illuminated by the viceroy's order. *Robles, Diario,* 117; *Zamacois, Hist. Mej.,* v. 468; *Sigüenza, Merc. Vol.,* MS., 631. Davis says that 500 families were demanded.

[6] S. Marcos was 3 l. from Galisteo.

[7] Acc. to *Arch. N. Mex.*, 132, there were 43 of these captives. In the *Arch. Sta Fé* it is stated that they numbered 17 males and 40 females. Sigüenza gives the number as 66 at this time, but in all 77. They were persons—mostly half-breed or Ind. servants, and including no Span. except a few women, with the children they had borne in captivity—that had been held by the rebels since 1680. Davis gives a list of some of the women and children, 28 in all, whom he calls prisoners, but cannot understand for what offence.

[8] Route from Hac. de Mejía: Isleta 5 l.; Rio Puerco (perhaps the earliest mention of this name in *Arch. Sta Fé*, MS.); the Laguna and Arroyo de S. Felipe are named between the Puerco and El Pozo) 7 l.; El Pozo 11 l.; Acoma 1 l.; R. Nacimiento or Cubero 5 l.; Ojo del Nacimiento 3 l.; El Morro 14 l.; Ojito de Zuñi 6 l.; Mesa de Galisteo 4 l. (Zuñi). Sigüenza calls the cliff Caquima.

and fearful of being killed for past offences; they wished Vargas to pass on to Zuñi, and give them time for deliberation; but finally they yielded to persuasion, and the governor, padres, and fifteen men were admitted to the peñol summit, where the ceremonies of submission were performed, and 87 children baptized on the 4th. At Zuñi the inhabitants were found to have left their old pueblo and built a new one on a lofty mesa.[9] Here the Apaches made a dash, and drove off a band of the Spaniards' cattle; but Zuñi was restored to loyalty and faith on the 11th, about 300 children being baptized. Here the sacred vessels and all the property of the martyr missionaries had been carefully preserved, and in one room were found candles burning on a kind of altar, this being the only pueblo that for the past twelve years had shown the slightest respect for Christianity.

Finally, having left a guard at Zuñi, Vargas went on to the Moqui towns, arriving at Aguatuvi on the 19th.[10] The Moquis, having been advised by the Navajos not to trust the Spaniards, came out in hostile attitude 700 or 800 strong, but the chief Miguel was well disposed, his people required but little persuasion, and the invaders were ceremoniously welcomed on the 20th. Miguel said the other pueblos were hostile, yet they all submitted without resistance except Oraibe, which was not visited. These people had a kind of metallic substance, which was said to come from a Cerro Colorado across the great river. The indications seemed to point to a quicksilver mine, and specimens were brought away for the viceroy.

[9] This may throw some doubt on the antiquity of the ruins known as Old Zuñi. On the Morro, or Inscription Rock, is inscribed: 'Here was Gen. D. Diego de Vargas, who conquered for our Holy Faith and for the royal crown all New Mexico at his own cost in the year 1692.' Copied in *Simpson's Jour.*, pl. 71; but S.'s translation is inaccurate, and that of Domenech, *Deserts*, i. 416, is still more so.

[10] Route: Zuñi, Flia Hinin, to a waterless *monte*, 6 l., 15th; Aguage del Entretenimiento, 6 l., 16th; Chupaderos, 9 l., 17th; Magdalena (only in MS.), 18th; S. Bernardo de Aguatuvi, 10 l., 19th; S. Bernardino Gualpi, 22d; S. Buen. de Mossaquavi (or Moxionavi), 22d; S. Bernabé Jongopavi (or Xommapavi), 23d.

The horses were in bad condition, some alarming reports of Apache raids came from Captain Tellez, and Vargas returned to Zuñi, whence the whole army soon started for the east and south.[11] On the way there occurred two attacks by Apaches, who wounded a soldier and secured some horses; but one of the gentiles was caught, exhorted, baptized, and shot; Vargas reached El Paso on December 20th; and Captain Roque de Madrid two days later with the rear-guard of the army. Thus ended Vargas' first entrada, in which, without shedding a drop of blood except in conflicts with Apaches, he had received the nominal submission of all the rebel pueblos, while the friars had baptized 2,214 children.[12]

New Mexican submission was as yet but a formality, as no Spaniards had remained in the north. On receipt of Vargas' letter of October 1692, the viceroy and his advisers decided to supply the soldiers and families asked for;[13] but a little time was required to fit out the colony, and the governor, as before, started before the reënforcement came. With about 100 soldiers, having collected all the volunteer settlers and families he could at El Paso and in Nueva Vizcaya— 70 families with over 800 persons in all—he set out on the 13th of October, 1693,[14] accompanied by seventeen

[11] The deserted pueblo of Alona was left on Nov. 29th. The route from the Morro to Socorro seems to have been a new and direct one to the s. of Acoma. The itinerary is given. On the Sierra de Magdalena the ruins of an ancient pueblo were found. The sierras of Sandía, Salinas, and Ladrones are named as seen. The whole distance was 156 l. This ends the 2d cuaderno of Vargas in the *Arch. N. Mex.*, 137. Of the original in the *Arch. Sta Fé* there is fol. 118–238 of the *Reconquista de Vargas*, with some gaps.

[12] Simpson, *Jour.*, 22, gives a tradition of the Jemes about a fight with the Span., an apparition of Our Lady of Guadalupe and a dispersion of the tribe. Frejes, *Hist. Breve*, 146, and Pino, *Expos.*, 5, *Noticias*, 2, 6, relate that S. Juan and Pecos remained faithful and greatly aided Vargas. This idea reappears in various forms and places, but has apparently no foundation in fact. On Dec. 27th Gov. V. formally delivered to the president of the missionaries the Christian relics found at Zuñi. *Arch. Sta Fé*, MS. P. Joaquin de Hinojosa was now vice-custodio.

[13] Letter of viceroy to Gov. V. Sept. 4, 1693, stating that he had obtained 66½ families, aggregating 235 persons, whom well supplied for the journey, he had sent to El Paso. Orig. MS. of the *Pinart Col.*

[14] Sept. 20th V. issues a bando, making known the viceroy's order that

friars under Padre Salvador de San Antonio as custodio. Preparations being inadequate, progress was slow, and 30 persons died on the way from hunger and exposure. The start was in three divisions. Lieutenant-general Luis Granillo was second in command, and Captain Juan Paez Hurtado had special charge of the colonists.[15] From the deserted hacienda of Lopez, near Socorro, Vargas had to press on in advance with his soldiers, leaving the colonists to struggle forward as best they could. Details of the march present little of interest.[16] At the pueblos the Spaniards were received without opposition, but with more or less coolness. Some leading men said the people were afraid of being killed, founding their fears on a pretended statement of an interpreter during the preceding visit. There were signs of trouble,[17] but the army was joined by the lagging immigrants, and on December 16th, under Oñate's original banner, made a triumphal entry into Santa Fé.

The Tanos inhabitants of the villa were polite but not enthusiastic; and the army encamped outside to avoid a rupture. San Felipe, Santa Ana, and Cia were reported friendly, but the rest only awaited an opportunity for hostility—except Pecos, which kept its promise of the year before, revealed the plans of the malecontents, and even offered aid. Vargas sent

the 100 soldiers recruited by V. for the Sta Fé presidio, and all the original vecinos of Sta Fé now at El Paso, should go to the north. *Arch. Sta Fé*, MS. In the later proceedings against V. in 1698 in the same *Arch.*, it appears that he enlisted the men without expense to the treasury, by advancing $150 to each, to be deducted from his later pay. It is also stated that he obtained at Zacatecas, Sombrerete, and Fresnillo about 27 families of 'viudas viejas, negras, coyotas, y lobas.' Acc. to the *Arch. N. Mex.*, 13, Davis, 373–85, makes the start on Oct. 11th, and the force 1,300.

[15] Other prominent officers were captains Roque de Madrid, José Arias, Antonio Jorge, Lázaro de Misquía, Rafael Tellez Jiron, Juan de Dios Lucero de Godoy, Fernando Duran y Chavez, Adj.-gen. Diego Varela, Adj. Fran. de Anaya Almazan, sergt. and sec. Juan Ruiz. Alfonso Rael de Aguilar and Antonio Valverde figure as civil and mil. sec. in 1693.

[16] The authority is the 3d and following cuadernos of Vargas in the *Arch. N. Mex.*; also fragments of each cuaderno and a few detached doc. in the *Arch. Sta Fé*, MS., the latter followed as before, sometimes closely and accurately, sometimes carelessly, by Davis.

[17] There was also some discontent in the ranks. A corporal and several soldiers deserted and started for El Paso on Dec. 3d. *Arch. Sta Fé*, MS.

out many parties to reconnoitre, but the Indians,
though not very liberal with their corn, professed
friendship, and in turn sent their chiefs to Santa Fé.
During their visit, Captain Arias of the rear-guard
arriving, the governor announced the receipt of news
that 200 soldiers were on the way to New Mexico.
This made a good impression, and a quantity of food
was obtained. But the Tanos soon began to show
their independence by declining to furnish corn or to
bring timber with which to repair the San Miguel
chapel. They offered, however, an estufa—quite
good enough they said for divine service until warm
weather should come.

Then the Picuríes and others bethought them of a
device to scatter the Spanish force, becoming much
concerned for their own spiritual welfare, and asking
for an immediate distribution of the padres. On
December 18th, Padre San Antonio and his companions presented a formal protest against the distribution. While ready to sacrifice their lives for the faith,
they were not willing to go rashly and needlessly to
sure death.[18] The governor acceded to their views.
Another petition of the colonists, through their cabildo,
represented that they were suffering from cold by
reason of insufficient shelter, twenty-two children
having died within a few days, and asked that the
Tanos be persuaded or forced to vacate the casas reales
and dwellings of the villa in favor of the rightful owners. Though dreading a conflict, the governor was

[18] Dec. 18th, petition of the friars in *Arch. N. Mex.*, 142–3. It is fol. 87
of the original MS.; but only fol. 37–79 of this cuaderno still exist in the
Arch. Sta Fé, MS. The friars who signed were as follows: Salv. de S. Antonio,
Juan Zavaleta, Francisco Corvera (the name seems to be Cervera in MS. records of the entrada of '92), Juan Alpuente, Juan Ant. del Corral, Juan Muñoz
de Castro, Antonio Obregon, Juan Daza, Buenaventura Contreras, Antonio
Carbonel, José Narvaez Valverde, Diego Zeinos (sec.), Fran. de Jesus María
Casañes, Gerónimo Prieto, Antonio Bahamonde, Domingo de Jesus María,
and José Diez. The last 5—with 3 others, Miguel Tricio (or Tirso), José
García, and Blas Navarro, who perhaps arrived a little later—were from the
college of Sta Cruz de Querétaro (the rest being of the Prov. del Sto Evangelio, Mex.), who came to N. Mex. in '93 and departed about '96, all but one,
who 'rubricó con su sangre la fé que predicaba.' *Espinosa, Chron.*, 92, 282–4;
Arricivita, Cron. Seráf., 176, 199–200.

obliged to call a junta de guerra, which decided that the Tanos must be transferred to their old pueblo of Galisteo. The natives had attributed Spanish forbearance to fear; speakers in their juntas had urged war, claiming that the invaders were few and weak, their governor an *embustero*, and the story of approaching reënforcements a lie. The order to quit the villa brought matters to a crisis. On December 28th the Tanos closed the entrance to the plaza and prepared for defence. Summoned to surrender, they demanded a day for deliberation, and then, with shouts of insult, proclaimed their purpose to resist. El Demonio they said could do more for them than God or María; the Christians would be defeated, reduced to servitude, and finally killed.

Don Diego caused prayers to be read for his kneeling soldiers, raised the virgin's picture on the battle flag, and then the army, shouting praises to the Santo Sacramento, rushed in two divisions upon the capital. This was on the 29th, and the conflict lasted all day. Arrows, stones, and boiling water rained upon the assailants from defensive works erected by the Spaniards years ago. At last the plaza gate was burned and the new estufa captured; but Tehua reënforcements appeared. Twice did the cavalry charge and scatter this new foe, but night had come and Vargas could do no more than prevent the interference of the enemy from abroad. Next morning the besieged surrendered, their losses being severe and their wounded governor having hanged himself. Seventy surviving warriors—only nine having been killed in the fight— including Antonio Bolsas, their leading spirit, were immediately shot, after an exhortation to penitence by Father Alpuente. The women and children, 400 in number, were distributed as 'hostages,' to serve until the viceroy should decide their fate—that is, they were made slaves.[19] This ended the year 1693 in New Mexico.

[19] The Pecos aided the Spaniards, having 5 killed, and this is the foundation of the current rumor that they were faithful from '80. Davis says noth-

The Spaniards had now better protection from the
cold and from the foe in the dwellings and fortifications of the villa; moreover, they had acquired slaves
and a large quantity of corn; yet their prospects as
colonists were gloomy, as their occupation was limited
to Santa Fé; all beyond was hostile, raids on the
cattle were frequent, arms were broken, and ammunition was scarce. The season was not favorable for
offensive operations with so small a force. Pecos,
Cia, Santa Ana, and San Felipe remained friendly,
but had all they could do to defend themselves against
their angry neighbors. Early in January Juan Ye,
chief of the Pecos, applied for aid against the rebels
and Apaches, and Captain Madrid was sent out with
thirty men; but it proved to be a false alarm invented
to test the sincerity of Spanish promises. On the 9th
Vargas marched with ninety men to the abandoned
pueblos of Tesuque and Nambé, and thence to the
mesa of San Ildefonso, where the Tehuas of these
three towns and of Pujuaque, Cuyamanque, Santa
Clara, and Jacona, with the Tanos of San Cristóbal
and San Lázaro, were encamped. They promised to
come to the villa and make peace, but this was only
a device to gain time for a junction with the Jemes,
Picuríes, Taos, and others.

On the 23d there came the viceroy's letter, already
mentioned, sent from Cerro Gordo by Padre Farfan,
the procurador, who asked for an escort under which
to send up his colony of seventy families from El Paso.
Vargas in reply explained the impossibility of sparing
an escort, and urged Farfan to come on to Santa Fé
with the party, at the same time sending for ammunition.[20] On the 28th he marched again to the mesa
with offers of peace and pardon. The natives professed

ing of the friars' petition, gives the date of assault as Dec. 26th, says the native
gov. was hanged by the Ind., and puts the loss at 160. Arricivita, *Cron.*,
199-200, gives 60 as the no. executed, and says that 60 of the women and
children died a little later from an epidemic.

[20] In an orig. MS. of the *Pinart Col.*, V. seems to say that he did send a
guard, and that they had a fight with the Apaches, killing two and capturing three, who were shot.

repentance, but wished the governor and padre to come alone and receive their submission, believing that if they could kill the leader the rest of the Spaniards would leave the country. Failing in this, they paid no heed to entreaties or threats, and Vargas returned to Santa Fé. Captain Madrid attempted to get material for balls from a lead mine that had been worked by his father near San Marcos; but the Indians had filled it up. Hostilities now became frequent, and through messengers sent from the friendly pueblos, as from occasional captives, always questioned and shot, news was often received of what the rebels were doing. It seems there was a small element among the enemy favoring surrender, but their arguments were always answered by a reference to the seventy Tanos shot after the taking of Santa Fé. Meanwhile, efforts were made by the hostiles to get aid from Acoma, Zuñi, and Moqui, and to form alliances with Apache bands. Raids on the Spaniards' live-stock were frequent, and sometimes slightly successful in February; while Vargas, on the other hand, had sent out various raiding parties, taking a few captives and obtaining large quantities of maize before the 24th, when the natives began to destroy all the supplies they could not remove.[21]

Late in February the governor, resolving on a vigorous offensive policy, marched with about 100 soldiers and many settlers and Indians for the mesa of San Ildefonso.[22] Encamping at the pueblo of that name, he sent Captain Madrid across to the west bank of the Rio Grande to reconnoitre and recover stolen animals, and finally began the attack on the 4th of March, his two pieces of artillery bursting at the first discharge. Charging up the hill in two divisions, the

[21] *Arch. N. Mex.*, 149-52; *Vargas, Campañas de '94*, MS.; *Arch. Sta Fé*, MS. Davis has nothing of events in Jan.-Feb.

[22] Acc. to *Arch. N. Mex.*, 152, and *Arch. Sta Fé* (a fragment of 64 p. of a kind of diary of events), the start was on the 27th, and the force 110 Span., besides Ind. In his *Campañas de '94*—an orig. MS. report to the viceroy of events from Feb. 15th, dated June 2d in the *Pinart Col.*—the date is Feb. 25th and the force 90. Davis, 386 et seq., makes the start in March, and is inaccurate in what follows. Most details are omitted by me.

Spaniards were met and repulsed in a fight of five hours, fifteen Indians being killed and twenty Spaniards wounded, eight of them seriously. Obtaining reënforcements and sending his disabled back to the villa, Vargas repeated the assault on the 11th, fighting six hours, without gaining any advantage. Next night the Indians came down and made an attack, but were repulsed. The siege was continued till the 19th, and then abandoned on account of bad weather, disabled horses, and lack of ammunition. The army returned to Santa Fé, having killed about thirty Indians, recovered 100 horses and mules, and taken a large store of maize, of which 100 fanegas were sent south for the approaching families.[23]

The friendly Queres now asked for help against the rebels of Cochití, who were said to be intrenched with others on the mesa of Cieneguilla, and to be plotting an attack on the Spaniards and their allies. Accordingly, Vargas marched on April 12th, joined the Queres under Ojeda of Santa Ana—the man already named as one of Governor Cruzat's captives of 1689, now a firm friend of the invaders[24]—and on the 17th defeated the foe at their new pueblo, capturing and shooting thirteen warriors, besides the seven killed in battle, taking 342 women and children, with 70 horses and 900 sheep, and next day sending a provision train with a guard of twenty soldiers to the villa, where on the 17th a band of raiding Tehuas had been repulsed by Lieutenant-general Granillo. The governor remained at Cieneguilla with 36 men; and the natives were now very penitent, desiring the release of their women and children; but Vargas insisted on their burning the new pueblo, and returning to their old home

---

[23] March 30th, V. rec'd a letter from Farfan, and the supplies started April 3d. On April 3d F. wrote again from Los Patos, not apparently having reached El Paso. P. Buen. Contreras was with F. *Arch. Sta Fé.*

[24] A Zuñi chief also joined V. at S. Felipe on the 15th, and served in the exped. He was friendly, and desired aid for his people against their foes. V. wished the Zuñis to move to some of the abandoned pueblos on the Rio Grande, and the chief promised to consult his people on this change. *Arch. Sta Fé,* MS.

at Cochití. On the 20th or 21st the Spanish camp was suddenly attacked, and 150 of the captives were lost, two soldiers being killed, one of them accidentally, and Adjutant Francisco de Anaya Almazan being drowned a few days later in crossing the river. The mesa pueblo was burned, and the army returned to Santa Fé in two divisions on the 25th and 27th.[25]

Back at the capital, Don Diego gave his attention to the distribution of slaves and live-stock, to the apportionment of lands, and to the posting of guards, and other measures to protect the settlers and friendly natives while putting in their crops.[26]

On the 21st of May the hostiles of fourteen towns, or six nations, made a raid on the real de caballada, or grazing camp, but were repulsed by the guard;[27] whereupon Vargas marched to the mesa of San Ildefonso, where he had several skirmishes, taking 48 animals and a few captives, and returning to Santa Fé. The Queres had also sent in five Jemes prisoners, two of whom were not shot—one because he promised to show the grave of a martyred friar, and the other at the intercession of the Pecos chief Juan Ye.[28] The families from Mexico under Padre Farfan arrived on June 23d, and were lodged in the villa until on the close of the war lands could be assigned elsewhere. With the colonists or a little later came new stores of ammunition and other needed articles.

The Queres had again applied for aid, but the river was so high it could not be crossed. On June 30th

[25] The three original authorities are clear enough on this campaign, but Davis, 389 et seq., confuses it most inextricably.

[26] April 28th, Gov. V. gives 200 sheep to the vice-custodio for the two missions (proposed) at Pecos and Cia; also 100 to the padres for their support. Same date, V. sends a letter to the Zuñis and Moquis, urging the people to submit and resume friendly relations. The letters were sent by the Zuñi chief already mentioned. *Arch. Sta Fé*, MS. Davis mentions the coming of a party of Apaches from the eastern plains, with tales of silver to be found in their country.

[27] It is not quite clear whether this was at Sta Fé, or during an exped. of the gov. to Tesuque and beyond.

[28] One of our authorities, *Vargas, Campañas de '94*, ends with June 2d, when V. was confident of breaking up the alliance of rebel pueblos, which, with the coming of reënforcements, would end the war.

Vargas marched northward, killing eleven Tehuas of Cuyamanque the first day, finding Picurí abandoned, and reaching Taos on the 3d of July. This pueblo was also deserted, but the people had left their property protected by crosses, which they supposed the Spaniards would respect, as they did for a time. The Taos were in a cañon not far off, but after a complicated series of negotiations, carried on chiefly through Juan Ye and a band of friendly Apaches, nothing could be effected, and the pueblo was sacked, a large amount of maize being taken. To reach Santa Fé the governor took a roundabout way northward into the Yuta country, across the river, and thence southward to Ojo Caliente, Rio Chama, and San Juan. On the way he had several skirmishes, and spent some days hunting buffalo for meat. In the night of the 12th he was attacked by the Yutas on a stream called San Antonio, losing eight soldiers killed. The savages were repulsed, pardoned on the plea that they mistook the Spaniards for hostile Indians who had often invaded their country in Spanish dress, and became very friendly. Finally, having reconnoitred the mesa of San Ildefonso, where the rebels were still strongly posted, he returned by way of Pujuaque and Tesuque to Santa Fé, arriving on July 16th.[29]

Governor Vargas marched on July 21st with 120 men to join the Queres under Ojeda in an attack on the Jemes, who after his start assaulted Cia and killed five men, but whose new pueblo on the mesa Don Diego carried by assault on the 24th, after a hard fight, in which the allies of Santa Ana and Cia fought bravely, Don Eusebio de Vargas—perhaps a brother of the governor—greatly distinguished himself, and the enemy lost 84 killed and 361 or 371 prisoners. The pueblo was sacked and burned, after 300 fanegas

[29] There is much confusion in details, both in the printed *archivo*, which is most complete, and in the MS., which contains two separate but similar reports, as also of the following campaign. V. visited what were supposed to be the ruins of Oñate s S. Gabriel, near the stream of Ojo Caliente and 6 l. N. of the mouth of the Rio Chama, which is not very intelligible.

of maize had been sent to the villa, the rest of the plunder being distributed among the native allies, except 106 animals given to Padre Alpuente for his proposed mission at Cia. Before returning, Vargas went to the old pueblo of Jemes, where he recovered the remains of Padre Juan de Jesus, killed in the revolt of 1680, deposited with appropriate ceremonies in the chapel at Santa Fé on the 11th of August.[30] Six days later messengers came in to ask pardon for the Jemes, attributing all their bad actions to the influence of the chief Diego, whom they were willing to give up; also promising to return to their old pueblo and to render aid against the common foe. Their offer was accepted, and Diego was brought in on the 26th to be sentenced to death—a sentence which at the last moment, on the intercession of his people, was commuted to ten years' labor in the mines of Nueva Vizcaya. The Jemes were given some implements, promised their *chusma* when they should have proven their good faith, ordered to be ready for a march against the mesa, and sent home to rebuild their old town.

Vargas now felt the importance of striking a decisive blow against the Tehuas and Tanos before the winter should set in. With all his available force, including 150 Queres and Jemes, he marched on the 4th of September, assaulted the mesa of San Ildefonso, and was driven back with a loss of 11 men wounded, including Captain Antonio Jorge of the Santa Fé presidio. On the 5th the native allies with three soldiers and an arriero marched up the slope, challenged the foe and were put to flight, the muleteer and

[30] *Arch. N. Mex.*, 158–62, includ. V.'s letter describing the finding of the padre's remains; also two records in *Arch. Sta Fé*, MS. Many details of the battle are given. With this campaign Davis' record practically ends, though, as the Sta Fé documents show many later details, it is not easy to understand why. The Jemes campaign is also mentioned in a brief report in the *Pinart Col.* In the *Arch. Sta Fé*, MS., Fr. Francisco Farfan is named as procurador general, Diego Varela as adjutant-gen., Fr. Juan Muñoz de Castro as vice-custodio; and Vargas signs as New Mexico's 'nuevo restaurador, conquistador á su costa, y reconquistador y poblador en él, y castellano de sus fuerzas y presidios por su majestad,' besides being gov. and capt.-gen.

one soldier being killed. For several days Vargas now gave his attention to the cutting-off of supplies. At sight, however, of their fields of corn in the milk trampled by the Spaniards, and of their native foes dancing round the scalp of a fallen warrior, the Tehuas several times came down and engaged in desperate conflict; but they were repulsed, soon became discouraged, and on the 8th began to treat for peace, sending trifling gifts to appease the governor's wrath. Peace and pardon were granted on condition of return to their pueblos. Thus New Mexico at last, except the towns of the extreme north and west—those of the south being annihilated—became once more a Spanish province.[31]

The Jemes, having proved faithful allies in the last campaign, were now given their women and children at the politic intercession of their destined missionary. On the 13th of September the chiefs of San Juan, San Cristóbal, San Lázaro, and Santa Clara came in with some mules which they had taken from the Apaches, reporting that all the Tehuas and Tanos were hard at work rebuilding their pueblos. Vargas now appointed the regular pueblo officials, and on the 17th he started on a tour of inspection, which satisfied him that the natives had submitted in good faith. Other tours followed, during which occurred the formal submission and pardon of other pueblos. The vice-custodio was notified that the missions were ready for their respective padres, and by the end of 1694 the friars were distributed and at work, though obliged to content themselves with very humble quarters while the Indians were rebuilding churches and houses.[32]

[31] The *Arch. N. Mex.*, 162 et seq., is the only authority for this final campaign, and for what followed to the end of 1694. Davis has nothing on this period; nor for the rest of 1694 is there anything left in the *Arch. Sta Fé*, MS.

[32] The distribution was as follows: P. Fran. Corvera at S. Ildefonso and Jacona; P. Gerón. Prieto at S. Juan and (temporarily) Sta Clara; P. Ant. Obregon at S. Cristóbal and S. Lorenzo (Lázaro?); P. Diego Zeinos at Pecos; P. Juan Alpuente at Cía; P. Fran. J. M. Casañes at Jemes; P. Juan Muñoz de Castro, vice-custodio and com. de la inquisicion, at Sta Fé; P. José Diez at Tesuque; P. José García Marin at Sta Clara; P. Ant. Carbonel at S. Felipe,

The several tours of the governor and custodian to inspect the pueblos and settle the missionaries need not be described, though some particulars are preserved in the records. The natives had made up their minds to submit to the inevitable, and not to revolt again until a favorable opportunity should present itself. The women and children taken from the different towns and distributed as servants among the colonists and soldiers were now gradually given up, not without much regret and opposition on the part of their masters. Of the Tanos chusma taken at Santa Fé 45 ran away, whereat the vecinos complained bitterly; but the chieftains were ordered to bring back the fugitives, and did so, which so pleased Vargas that he released the 45 and promised to free the rest soon, proposing to settle with them the village of Cieneguilla, five leagues west of the capital. This policy naturally pleased the natives, but it made for the governor many bitter foes among the colonists. Padre San Antonio, who had gone to El Paso, resigned his office, and Padre Francisco Vargas arrived as custodio on the 1st of November with four new friars. Meanwhile the governor sent south an order to a friend to purchase and forward 3,000 fanegas of maize, wishing to relieve the Indians of excessive taxation for a time until the old prosperity should return.[33]

In 1695 the seventy Mexican families who had come up with Padre Farfan were settled in the new villa of Santa Cruz de la Cañada, founded on the 12th of April,[34] under an alcalde mayor and capitan a

Cochití, and later Taos: P. Miguel Tirso at Sto Domingo; P. José Arbizu at S. Cristóbal; P. Ant. Moreno at Sta Fé (temporarily), La Cañada, and later Nambé; P. Ant. Acebedo at Nambé; P. Fran. Vargas, custodio. This leaves some of the original friars unaccounted for, and also one of the 4 who came in Nov.

[33] *Arch. N. Mex.*, 162–7. On Jan. 10, '95, V. wrote to the viceroy, thanking him for the provision made of 3,000 fan. of corn; and again, May 9th, on the trouble he had had in transporting that corn. *Arch. Sta Fé*, MS. This, however, may not indicate that it was not purchased on V.'s account. It was charged later that only about 580 fan. ever reached N. Mex., and much of that was wasted in the distribution.

[34] Yet we have seen indications that already in 1680 there was a settle-

guerra, sergeant, four corporals, and alguacil, with
Padre Moreno as the first minister. The new villa
and the lands assigned to the vecinos included the
sites of San Cristóbal and San Lázaro, the Tanos of
those pueblos being deprived of their homes and
lands, very injudiciously as the friars claimed later
and perhaps now. Some of the exiles were attached
to San Juan, and others, after being scattered in different Tehua pueblos, were later united and sent to
repeople Galisteo. This year the Picuríes and Taos
were peaceably reduced to submission and put in
charge of missionaries; but hardly had the friars
begun work when rumors of new troubles began to
circulate. The Indians had lost little of their hatred
for the invaders, and now that the padres were again
at their stations and the military force somewhat scattered, there were chiefs, especially among the implac-
able Tehuas, who began to dream of a new revolt and
massacre like those of 1680, by which once more to rid
their country of the tyrant foreigners. The threatened dangers, however, took no definite shape this year;
although the natives of San Cristóbal and San Lázaro,
chafing under the loss of their lands, ran away to the
sierra in December. As the other pueblos did not
join the movement, the Tanos were persuaded without
much difficulty to come back and be pardoned.[35]

It appears that in 1695-6 there was a failure of
crops, resulting in serious privations,[36] or even in a

ment at La Cañada under an alcalde mayor, Luis Quintana. At this founding of 1695 this villa was given the 'preeminencia de antigüedad' over all the
settlements of N. Mex. except Sta Fé. The poblaciones of Cerrillo and Bernalillo are also mentioned in records of this year.

[35] *Arch. N. Mex.*, 168-9. May 31st, the settlers had been selling arms to
the Ind., which Vargas forbids by a bando of this date. Padre Zeinos shot and
killed an Ind. at Pecos; but it was accidental and he was not blamed. The
padre's full name was Diego de la Cassa Zeinos, and he was sec. of the custodia, definidor, com. del santo oficio, and guardian. Luis Granillo was still
lieut.-general. *Arch. Sta Fé*, MS.

[36] In Nov. 1695, Gov. V. sent to the viceroy a petition of the cabildo and
vecinos for relief, as all that they had sown had been consumed by the worms.
The viceroy and junta in Feb. 1696 decided to send them 200 cattle from
Parral, with some arms and ammunition, at the same time warning them that
they must learn to rely on themselves and not on the govt for succor. *Arch.
Sta Fé*, MS.

terrible famine, if we credit the highly colored and partisan statement made in later legal proceedings against Vargas. According to this authority, the people were forced to live on dogs, cats, horses, mules, bull-hides, 'foul herbs,' and old bones; finally roaming over the fields like wild animals, and many of them hiring themselves to the Indians to carry wood and water, and grind corn, over 200 dying from the effects of insufficient and noxious food. Of course, the governor's failure to distribute properly the stores of maize was noted as one cause of the famine; and it is also stated that four settlers, driven by their sufferings to desert, were brought back and hanged without the last consolations of religion. To what extent these statements were founded in fact it is difficult to determine, but though doubtless exaggerated, they were supported by the sworn testimony of many a few years later, as we shall see.[37]

In the spring of 1696 the missionaries, who had the best opportunities for knowing the real sentiments of the natives, found the indications so alarming in various quarters that the custodio on March 7th made known to Vargas in writing the imminent danger of a revolt, the defenceless condition of the missions, the risks taken by the padres, and the incalculable damage that must result from a new disaster like that of 1680. He concluded by begging for a guard of soldiers for each mission. Two other petitions of like tenor were written on the 13th and 22d, and from different directions came reports that the Indians had already committed outrages in the new temples; but the governor, believing that the natives had submitted in good faith, and that the complaints and fears had no better foundation than idle rumor, either would not or could not furnish the desired escoltas. He permitted the friars, if they were afraid, to retire to Santa

---

[37] *Vargas, Acusacion del Cabildo de Sta Fé contra el ex-gobernador*, in *Arch. Sta Fé*, MS.; followed by Davis, *Span. Conq.*, 412-13. The padre cronista who prepared the printed *Arch. N. Mex.* rather strangely says nothing of this famine.

Fé, as some of them did. In his report of March
28th to the viceroy he not only stated that all was
quiet, and the danger imaginary, but used language
which the padres regarded as an imputation of cowardice. Their pride was touched, and they returned
to their stations quietly to await the crisis. It came
on the 4th of June, when the Taos, Picuríes, Tehuas,
Queres of Santo Domingo and Cochití, and the Jemes
rose, killed five missionaries and 21 other Spaniards,
in most cases immediately abandoning their pueblos
and fleeing to the mountains.[38]

The governor started on the 7th for a tour among
the deserted towns, and "saw to regret what he ought
to have believed to remedy." Pecos, Tesuque, San
Felipe, Santa Ana, and Cia had remained faithful,
but the Acomas, Zuñis, and Moquis had aided the
rebels, or at least were sheltering the fugitives, and
were said to be planning new attacks. The chief of
Santo Domingo, a leading spirit in the revolt, was
captured and shot on the 14th; and several revolutionary agents were also put to death at Pecos, with
the governor's consent. On the 23d of July, a body
of rebels was attacked and 10 of the number killed.[39]

[38] *Arch. N. Mex.*, 168–71, and several records in the *Arch. Sta Fé*, MS.,
including the gov.'s report of July 27th. In the *Acusacion* already referred
to, followed by Davis, the no. of killed is given as 34 instead of 21, and the
famine is given as one of the chief causes of the revolt; that is, the Ind. took
advantage of the enfeebled and scattered condition of the Span.

The padres killed were Arbizu of S. Cristóbal, Carbonel of Taos, Corvera
of S. Ildefonso, Moreno of Nambé, and Casañes of Jemes. Corvera and
Moreno were shut up in a cell at S. Ildefonso, and burned with the convent.
P. Cisneros of Cochití had a narrow escape. P. Navarro of S. Juan succeeded
in escaping to La Cañada with the sacred vessels, etc. Acc. to *Espinosa*,
Cron. Seráf., 260–86, P. Casañes at Jemes had foreseen his fate, and asked
the Ind. to let him die at the foot of a certain cross. Summoned to attend a
sick person, he was led into an ambush of Apaches, who killed him with clubs
and stones at the chosen spot. He was the first martyr of the Querétaro college, and Espinosa gives an account of his life, including his miraculous
transportation by an angel on mule-back to visit unknown Texan tribes.
Capt Lázaro Mizquía, with Alf. José Dominguez and 12 soldiers, escaped from
Taos and reached Sta Fé in 9 days after in a sorry condition. Gregg, *Com.
Prairies*, i. 128, dates this revolt in '98.

[39] July 27th the cabildo asked for an escort for a bearer of despatches to
El Paso and Mex., to ask the viceroy for aid. V. replied that he was expecting 200 cattle to arrive shortly. On Sept. 24th the viceroy replied to V.'s
letter of July 27th, promising aid and his influence in obtaining rewards from
the king. *Arch. Sta Fé*, MS.

At the beginning of August an expedition was made to Cia, with a view to operate either against the Acomas or Jemes; but Don Diego was recalled to the capital to distribute 200 cattle, which now arrived from the south.[40] On the 8th he marched for Acoma, and attacked that pueblo on the 15th, capturing five natives, one of them the chief, but failing to reach the peñol summit. Then he released the chief and resorted to persuasion, without success, finally shooting the captives, ravaging the corn-fields, and retiring.[41] Subsequently, Adjutant Juan Ruiz was sent against the Jemes In September Don Diego attacked the Taos in a cañon not far from their town, and after several skirmishes they surrendered on the 8th of October, returning to live in the pueblo. The Picuríes and the Tehuas of San Juan feigned a desire for peace in order to save their crops; but Vargas discovered their plans, and attacked them on October 26th, capturing 84 of their women and children, to be distributed as servants among the soldiers on his return to the capital, early in November. There were other campaigns, productive of but slight results, as it was difficult to find any considerable number of the rebels together. On the 24th of November, the date of the governor's report to the viceroy, all had been reduced to nominal submission except those of Acoma and the west, Pujuaque, Cuyamanque, and Santa Clara, with perhaps Santo Domingo and Cochití. Yet many of the pueblos contained but a few families each. The rest of the population was scattered in the mountains, among the gentile tribes, or in the western pueblos.[42] The surviving Querétaro Franciscans left the country in 1696. A few officials of the year are named in a note.[43]

[40] *Arch Sta Fé*, MS.
[41] Padres Juan de Mata and Diego Chavarría, new names, are mentioned as chaplains of this expedition.
[42] *Arch. N. Mex.*, 171–4; gov.'s report of Nov. 24th, in *Arch. Sta Fé*, MS. The alcalde of La Cañada in an inspection found at S. Ildefonso 17 men and 36 women and children; at Jacona 10 and 19; at Nambé 4 and 10. Davis says that 'during the rebellion more than 2,000 Ind. perished in the mountains, while as many more deserted their villages and joined the wild tribes.'
[43] *Espinosa, Crón. Apostól.*, 92, 284–6; *Escudero, Not. Son.*, 43–7. Capt.

The governor's term of five years expired in 1696, and Pedro Rodriguez Cubero had been appointed by the king to succeed him. Vargas had asked for re-appointment, but though the king was favorably disposed, the application came too late. Overruling Don Diego's objections, the viceroy sustained Cubero, who came to New Mexico and took possession of the office on the 2d of July, 1697.[44] The king approved when after long delay the matter reached him in 1699, but at the same time he thanked Vargas for his services, gave him the choice of titles between marqués and conde, and granted a reappointment, to take effect on the expiration of Cubero's term in 1702, or sooner if the office should become vacant.[45] In the same cédula was approved all that the viceroy had done in connection with the reconquest; and it was ordered that the presidial force of Santa Fé should be raised to 100 men, the Parral force retiring; that the force at El Paso should not be reduced, as had been proposed;[46] and that additional families should be sent, not from Nueva Vizcaya, but from Mexico.

Meanwhile Vargas was involved in serious troubles; and indeed, at the date of being thus highly honored by the king he had been two years in the Santa Fé prison. There had been more or less misunderstanding between him and the cabildo from the first. En-

Fern. Duran de Chavez was alcalde mayor of S. Felipe and the 'puesto de Españoles de Bernalillo;' Capt. Roque Madrid, lieut.-gen. of cavalry and alcalde mayor of 'la villa nueva de los Mexicanos de Sta Cruz (de la Cañada);' Domingo de la Barreda, sec. de gobierno y guerra; Capt. Alonso Rael de Aguilar, lieut.-gov. and capt.-gen. in place of Granillo. The cabildo of Sta Fé was Alcalde Lorenzo de Madrid, Fran. Romero de Pedraja, Lázaro de Mizquía, Diego Montoya, José García Jurado; clerk, Capt. Lucero de Godoy. *Arch. Sta Fé*, MS.

[44] This date from a royal cédula of Jan. 26th, approving the viceroy's act, as it preceded the reappointment which it had been intended to grant to V., and V. therefore had no right to object. *N. Mex. Cédulas*, MS., 28–9. Acc. to *Arch. N. Mex.*, 174, the date was July 4th. Cubero's accession had been made known in the viceroy's letter of April 18, 1698.

[45] June 15, 1699, in *N. Mex. Cédulas*, MS., 29–33. I find no foundation for Davis' statement that Vargas was removed from office in consequence of complaint from the cabildo. These complaints and charges were of later date.

[46] In March 1699, Don Antonio de Valverde y Cosío, later gov., was appointed capt. of the El Paso presidio. *Id.*, 34.

joying the confidence of the viceroy, he had been given entire control of the expedition, and attending in person or through his agents to all details financial as well as military, he had ignored and offended the colony officials. Moreover, there had been much dissatisfaction, as we have seen, at his policy in depriving the settlers of their Indian slaves by restoring these captives to their pueblos as a means of gaining the good-will of the natives. Cubero had a commission as juez de residencia, and though Vargas is understood to have passed the ordeal successfully, he gave up his office unwillingly and made of his successor a bitter foe; and the cabildo, with the additional incentive of gaining favor with the new ruler, renewed the quarrel in earnest.

Formal charges were presented before the governor, whose authority to consider them was very doubtful. The ex-governor was accused of having embezzled large sums of money furnished him for the recruiting and support of the colonists; of having provoked, by shooting the Tanos captives at Santa Fé, and by other oppressive acts, all the hostilities of 1694–6; of having caused, by his mismanagement and failure to properly distribute the small remaining portion of the food supply, which had been paid for by the king but sold by Vargas in the south for his own profit, the deadly famine of 1695–6; and of having driven away by his oppression the families likely to testify against him in his residencia. Juan Paez Hurtado was also involved in the accusations, as Vargas' accomplice, and as principal in other serious charges.[47] Cubero gratified his

[47] The charges in detail are recited in the original documents, still preserved, though not complete, in the *Arch. Sta Fé*. The accusation of the cabildo is not dated, but was apparently written in Oct. 1697. Oct. 20, 1697, Gov. C. orders Capt. Granillo at El Paso to arrest Paez Hurtado and send him to Sta Fé. At the same time Capt. Ant. Valverde, Alf. Martin Uriosto, and Adj. Félix Martinez were exiled from N. Mex., probably in connection with the same affair. Hurtado was accused of having defrauded the colonists of half the allowance by the crown, of collecting $100 each for 38 settlers who did not come; of hiring vicious persons for $4 or $6 each to personate colonists, for each of whom he collected $100, subsequently filling their places in part with negro and mixed-breed tramps; of collecting the $100 several times

personal enmity and that of the cabildo by treating
Vargas in a most harsh and unjust manner.   He was
fined 4,000 pesos for costs of the suit, all his property
was confiscated, and he was kept in prison for nearly
three years.   Few even of his own family were allowed to see him, and every precaution was taken to
prevent the sending of any written communication to
Mexico or Spain.   Padre Vargas, the custodian, visited Mexico and obtained an order for the prisoner's
release under bonds to defend himself before the viceroy; but Don Diego refused to accept liberty on such
conditions, claiming that to give bonds would be de-
grading to a man of his rank and services, especially
in view of the king's recent orders in his favor.   At
last came an order for his release without conditions,
and he started for Mexico in July 1700.   Here the
charges against him are said to have been fully investigated by royal order; at any rate, he was exonerated
from all blame, and his reappointment as governor, as
we shall see, remained valid.   As we have no original
records in the case except the partisan charges, it would
perhaps be going too far to declare Don Diego entirely innocent; the cabildo, however, later retracted
its accusations, attributing all the blame to Cubero;
and the chronicler, a Franciscan who can hardly be
suspected of prejudice in Vargas' favor, states—doubtless reflecting the views of his order—that Don Diego,
while somewhat over-enthusiastic, disposed to promise
more than he could perform, and to ignore in his reports many of the difficulties and dangers in New
Mexico, never gave the Spaniards any just cause of
enmity, but rather merited their love as a protector.[48]

of one person under different names; of stealing a box containing $7,000; of
aiding Gov. V. in his rascalities, etc.   All his property was confiscated, but
the arresting officers seem not to have found him, at least not at first.   H.
was later gov. ad. int.
    [48] *Arch. N. Mex.*, 174–7.   The cabildo, hearing of V.'s reappointment on
Dec. 16, 1700, petitioned the king against permitting him to return and
avenge himself; but the king, by a cédula of Oct. 10, 1701, ordered an investigation; and the cabildo soon began to make excuses, etc.   Davis in his list,
like Meline, Prince, and others, names several viceroys of Mex. as governors
of N. Mex.!   Viceroy Mendoza, conde de Galve, figures in 1694–5 and in 1722.

Of Cubero's rule, within and beyond the limits of this chapter, there is little to be said. Father Vargas resigning the office of custodio was succeeded by padres Diego de Chavarría, Juan Muñoz de Castro, and Antonio Guerra. A document of May 1697 indicates that the number of settlers, heads of families, in the province, including new-comers, was 313. This did not include the soldiers; and the total of so-called Spanish population was probably not less than 1,500.[49] Early in the same year Santa Cruz de Galisteo was resettled with Tanos; and later the rebel Queres of Cieneguilla, Santo Domingo, and Cochití formed a new pueblo four leagues north of Acoma, on the stream called Cubero.[50] In July 1698, it was decided in a junta de hacienda at Mexico that the New Mexican colonists must in future depend on their own exertions, since the aid then furnished would be the last; yet this regulation was not strictly enforced, as agricultural implements at least were afterward supplied. In July 1699, the governor Cubero made a tour in the west. On the 4th the new pueblo of the Queres submitted, being named San José de la Laguna; two days later Acoma, now called San Pedro instead of San Estévan, renewed its allegiance; and on the 12th La Purísima de Zuñi, formerly Asuncion and later Guadalupe, followed the example of its eastern neighbors.[51]

The Moquis, noting the submission of other nations, and dreading war more than they feared or loved Christians, sent ambassadors in May 1700 to treat with the governor, professing their readiness to rebuild churches and receive missionaries. At the same time

[49] *Arch. Sta Fé*, MS. Distrib. on May 1st of a large quantity of cloth and live-stock, including 600 cows, 260 bulls, 3,300 sheep and rams, 2,200 goats; some of which, however, had been left at El Paso. On Dec. 10th Gov. C. orders the auth. of El Paso to permit no maize or other grain to be carried out of the province, as there had been a failure of crops.

[50] Named for the gov., probably; and this may be the origin of the name Covero still applied to a pueblo in that vicinity.

[51] Niel, *Apunt.*, 108–9, says that Moqui was also visited at this time. A doc. in the *Arch. Sta Fe*, MS., shows that during the gov.'s absence the friends of Vargas made an effort to cause a disturbance and make V. gov. No details.

Espeleta, chief of Oraibe, sent for Padre Juan Garaicoechea to come and baptize children. The friar set
out at once with Alcalde José Lopez Naranjo,[52] and
went to Aguatuvi, where he baptized 73 young Moquis. On account of a pretended rumor that the
messengers to Santa Fé had been killed, he was not
permitted to visit Oraibe or the other pueblos at this
time; but Espeleta promised to notify him soon when
they were ready for another visit, Garaicoechea returning to Zuñi and reporting to the governor on
June 9th.[53]   In October the Moquis were again heard
from, when Espeleta came in person to Santa Fé with
20 companions, and with somewhat modified views.
He now proposed a simple treaty of peace, his nation,
like Spain, to retain its own religion! Cubero could
offer peace only on condition of conversion to Christianity. Then the Moqui chief proposed as an ulti-
matum that the padres should visit one pueblo each
year for six years to baptize, but postponed permanent residence till the end of that period. This scheme
was likewise rejected, and Espeleta went home for
further deliberation.[54]

There were in those days fears of French invasion.
Padre Niel tells us that among the captives whom
the Navajos were accustomed to bring to New Mexico
each year for Christian ransom, he rescued two little
French girls. In 1698 the French had almost annihilated a Navajo force of 4,000 men; and in 1700 the
Apaches reported that a town of the Jumanas had
been destroyed by the same foe. Toward the Spaniards the Navajos were friendly down to 1700, but in

[52] P. Antonio Miranda is also named as his companion in *Fernandez Duro,
Noticias,* 137.
[53] In the *Moqui, Noticias,* MS., 669, it is stated that the other Moquis,
angry that Aguatuvi had received the padres, came and attacked the pueblo,
killed all the men, and carried off all the women and children, leaving the
place for many years deserted. I think this must be an error.
[54] *Arch. N. Mex.,* 177–9; *Moqui, Noticias,* MS., 664–70. P. Garaicoechea
was in charge of Zuñi and P. Miranda of Acoma and Laguna. In June 1700
one Miguel Gutierrez was sentenced to be shot and his head stuck on a pole,
to show the Jicarillas and other gentile nations that they must not harbor
fugitive Span. *Arch. Sta Fé,* MS.

that year they committed some depredations, and the governor started on an expedition against them, making peace, however, with the Navajo chief at Taos. There was also a campaign against the Faraon Apaches, but of it we know only that nothing was accomplished. This same year there was trouble at Pecos, resulting from the execution by Don Felipe, the chief, of five rebels in the war of 1596. There was an attempt to raise a revolt against that chief, but the ringleaders were imprisoned at Santa Fé until they escaped and joined the Jicarilla Apaches. The pueblo became divided into two factions, which often came to blows, until at last, Don Felipe's party having the best of it, the other asked permission to live at Pujuaque. It is not recorded that the change was actually made.

CHAPTER XI.

FIRST HALF OF THE EIGHTEENTH CENTURY.

1701–1750.

Permanent Submission—Cubero's Rule—Revolt at Zuñi—Rule and
Death of Governor Vargas—Founding of Alburquerque—Moquis
and Apaches—Marqués de la Peñuela—Navajo War—Refounding of Isleta—Rule of Flores—The Yutas—Governor Martinez
—The Comanches—A Controversy—Valverde in Command—Entrada to the North—Bustamante's Rule—Smuggling—French
Encroachments—Padres versus Bishop—Cruzat Governor—Olavide's Rule—Mendoza—Frenchmen—Converts from Moqui—Governors Codallos and Cachupin — Moqui — Jesuits Defeated—
Navajo Missions—A Quarrel— Statistics—List of Governors to
1846.

The submission of New Mexico in the last years of
the seventeenth century may be regarded as permanent; the natives were now too few and weak, and
the Spanish power too firmly established, for any
general movement of revolt. Petty local troubles or
rumors of troubles in the different pueblos were of
not infrequent occurrence, some of which will be
noted in these pages, as will occasional raids of the
gentile tribes. These, with the succession of governors, now and then a political controversy, periodical
renewals of efforts to make Christians of the Moquis,
a few reports of mission progress or decadence, some
not very important expeditions out into the plains or
mountains, feeble revivals of the old interest in mysterious regions of the north, rare intercourse with
the Texan establishments, fears of French and English encroachment—make up the annals of the eighteenth century. The archive record is meagre and
fragmentary, yet in respect of local and personal de-

tails much too bulky to be fully utilized within the scope of my work. From 1700 New Mexico settled down into that monotonously uneventful career of inert and non-progressive existence, which sooner or later is to be noted in the history of every Hispano-American province. The necessity of extreme condensation may not, therefore, prove an unmixed evil.

The Moqui chief did not decide to accept the Spaniards' terms; and it appears that the people of Aguatuvi were even punished for past kindness shown to visiting friars. Governor Cubero therefore marched in 1701 to the province, killing a few Moquis and capturing many; but it was deemed good policy to release the captives, and Cubero returned without having accomplished anything, unless to make the natives more obstinate in their apostasy, as the not impartial Vargas declared later.[1] In the spring of 1702 there were alarming rumors from various quarters, resting largely on statements of Apaches, who seem in these times to have been willing witnesses against the town Indians. Cubero made a tour among the pueblos to investigate and administer warnings, but he found slight ground for alarm. It appeared, however, that the Moquis, or perhaps Tehua fugitives in the Moqui towns, were trying to incite the Zuñis and others to revolt; and it was decided to send Captain Juan de Uribarri with a force to make investigations, and to leave Captain Medina and nineteen men as a garrison at Zuñi.[2] This was probably done, but, all being

[1] *Arch. N. Mex.*, 179; *Moqui, Not.*, MS., 669. In *Arch. Sta Fé*, MS., is a petition of the cabildo to Gov. C. when about to start on this exped., asking him not to go, referring to the affair of '99, and expressing fears that in his absence Vargas' friends would succeed in creating a revolt; or perhaps would go to El Paso en masse to represent that by C.'s harsh treatment they had been forced to flee. In *Heylin's Cosmog.*, 1701-2, is a mention of N. Mex. and its supposed boundaries in 1701.

[2] Full record of investigations, etc., in Feb.-Mar. 1702, an orig. MS. of 74 p. in the Pinart collection. P. Ant. Guerra is named as custodio; P. Martin Hurtado took part in the councils; also Adj. José Dominguez. Uribarri was capt. of the Sta Fé company. Among the measures ordered was the transfer of the Sta Clara Ind. to S. Ildefonso, where lands confiscated from former rebels were assigned them.

quiet, the escolta was soon reduced. The remaining soldiers behaved badly, and three Spanish exiles from Santa Fé much worse, treating the Indians harshly, and living publicly with native women. The padre complained; the governor failed to provide any remedy; and on March 4, 1703, the Indians killed the three Spaniards, Valdés, Palomino, and Lucero, fleeing, some to the peñol, others to Moqui. The soldiers seem to have run away. Padre Garaicoechea was not molested, and wrote that only seven Indians were concerned in the affair; but evidently in his missionary zeal and sympathy for the natives he underrated the danger. The governor, justifying his course by the viceroy's orders to use gentle means, sent Captain Madrid to bring away the friar, and Zuñi, like the Moqui towns, was left to the aborigines.[3]

In August 1703, Cubero, learning that Vargas— whose exoneration and reappointment have been recorded—was on the way to succeed him, and fearing retaliation for past acts, though as a matter of fact Vargas brought no authority to investigate his acts, left the country without waiting to meet his rival. He claimed to have retired by permission of the viceroy; it was said he feigned an Indian campaign as an excuse for quitting the capital; and his successor charged that he ran away for fear of the natives, whose hatred he had excited. Cubero was appointed governor of Maracaibo and given other honors, but died in Mexico in 1704. Don Diego, now marqués de la Nava de Brazinas, assumed the office of governor and captain-general at Santa Fé, on November 10, 1703.[4] He was urged by Padre Garaicoechea to re-

[3] *Arch. N. Mex.*, 180–6, with letters of P. Garaicoechea and Miranda. The latter wrote from Acoma that all the Zuñi property had been stolen, the missionary's life in danger, and that the Ind. of Acoma and Cia wished to go to the padre's rescue, which he did not permit, fearing that the hostiles on hearing of the approach of a force would kill the padre. He thought the Zuñis might be easily subdued, having no water on the peñol; but if they were not conquered the whole western country was lost, as the Moquis were at the bottom of the movement.
[4] Davis, Prince, and others name the duke of Alburquerque as gov. in 1703–10, another viceroy of Mexico!

establish a mission among the Zuñis, with whom the
padre had kept in communication; but the governor
lacked faith in the good-will of that people, or at least
found no time to attend to the matter during his brief
rule, and that of Padre Juan Álvarez as custodio.
At the beginning of 1704 there were more rumors of
revolt, but nothing could be proved except against the
ever-hostile Moquis. In March Vargas started on a
campaign against the Apaches, but was taken suddenly ill in the sierra of Sandía, died at Bernalillo on
the 4th of April, and was buried at Santa Fé in the
parish church.[5]

Juan Paez Hurtado, lieutenant-general of the province and an old friend of Don Diego, served as acting
governor till the 10th of March, 1705, when Don
Francisco Cuervo y Valdés assumed the office of
governor ad interim, that is, by the viceroy's appointment.[6] The condition of affairs was not very encouraging. Depredations by Apaches and Navajos were
frequent, the Moquis were defiant, the Zuñi rebels
still on their peñol, and the presidial soldiers in great
need of clothing, arms, and horses, their pay having
been cut down about five per cent in support of the
Chihuahua mission of Junta de los Rios. Cuervo's
rule was marked by a series of appeals for aid; but
except a few arms and implements—and plenty of
censure for complaining that his predecessors had
given more attention to their quarrels than to the
country's needs—nothing was obtained. On his way
north he had to stop at El Paso to fight Apaches;
and on arrival at the capital he stationed his garrison
in seven detachments at exposed points.[7] Early in

---

[5] *Arch. N. Mex.*, 187.

[6] In a letter of Oct. 11, 1704, the viceroy notified the king of Cuervo's appointment on account of his distinguished services and merits. On June 25,
1705, the king acknowledges receipt of the letter, and announces the appointment of Chacon as proprietary gov. *N. Mex., Cédulas*, MS., 35. The month
of Cuervo's arrival is omitted in the printed *Arch. N. Mex.*, 188, but given in
my MS. copy, p. 345. It is noticeable that he is here called Cubero, and
that Cubero in the royal cédulas (or at least in my copies) is called Cuervo.
C. was a knight of Santiago, and had been a treasury official at Guadalajara.
His rule was fro n March 10, 1705, to July 31, 1707.

[7] The vecinos by order of the gov. presented themselves for inspection of

1705 Padre Garaicoechea went back to Zuñi, and brought the rebels down to the plain to submit on April 6th to Captain Madrid. In July Don Roque marched against the Navajos, who were incited and aided by refugee Jemes. During this campaign the horses' thirst was miraculously assuaged in answer to the chaplain's prayers, whereupon the foe was so terrified as to surrender, and the army turned back to Cia in August. In September the finding of a knotted cord at Zuñi recalled the dread days of 1680, but nothing came of it.

In 1706 Governo Cuervo informed the viceroy that he had founded with 30 families the new villa of Alburquerque, named in honor of the viceroy;[8] with 18 Tanos families from Tesuque, he had resettled Santa María—formerly Santa Cruz—de Galisteo; transferred some Tehua families to the old pueblo of Pujuaque, now called Guadalupe; and refounded with 29 families the old villa of old La Cañada, long abandoned, renaming it Santa María de Grado, a name that did not last. He asked for church ornaments, which were supplied; but he was blamed for founding the new villa without authority, and its name was changed from San Francisco to San Felipe de Alburquerque, in honor of the king. It was ascertained later that in all these reports Cuervo had considerably overstated his own achievements. Captain Uribarri

arms in April—74 at Sta Fé, 37 at Bernalillo, and 82 at La Cañada. *Arch. Sta Fé*, MS. Sta Clara, Cochití, Jemes, and Laguna were among the points where guards were stationed. It was decided to bring up the cavalry at El Paso to Sta Fé. P. Juan Álvarez was still custodio; P. Juan de Zavaleta com. del sto oficio. Capt. Valverde was lieut.-gen. and com. at El Paso; Juan Paez Hurtado and Juan de Uribarri are named as generals; Lorenzo de Madrid maestro de campo; captains Félix Martinez, Juan Lucero Godoy, Diego de Medina, and Alf. Juan Roque Gutierrez; alcalde Capt. Diego Arías de Quirós; alguacil mayor Ant. Aguilar; regidores Capt. Antonio Montoya, Capt. Ant. Lucero, Fran. Romero de Pedraza, Alf. Martin Hurtado; escribano Cristóbal Góngora, all at Sta Fé. At Bernalillo, captains Fern. Chavez, Diego Montoya, Manuel Vaca, Alf. Cris. Jaramillo, sergt Juan Gonzalez. At Villanueva de Sta Cruz (La Cañada), captains Silvestre Pacheco, Miguel Tenorio, José de Atienzía, Nic. Ortiz, and sergt Bartolo Melabato.

[8] The name is commonly but inaccurately written Albuquerque in N. Mex. Davis and others erroneously derive the name from a governor. Some authors have dated the founding back to the time of the 1st duke of A. who served as viceroy.

marched this year out into the Cíbolo plains; and at
Jicarilla, 37 leagues north-east of Taos, was kindly
received by the Apaches, who conducted him to Cuartalejo, of which he took possession, naming the province
San Luis and the Indian ranchería Santo Domingo.

The Moquis often attacked the Zuñis, who were
now for the time good Christians, and to protect whom
Captain Juan Roque Gutierrez was sent in April 1706
with eight men. With this aid the Zuñis went to
Moqui in May, killed two of the foe, and recovered
70 animals. Captain Tomás Holguin was sent with
a new reënforcement, and in September surrounded
the Tehua pueblo between Gualpi and Oraibe, forcing
the Indians after a fight to sue for peace and give hostages; but the Tanos and other reënforcements arrived, attacked the Spaniards and allies as they
retired, and drove them back to Zuñi, the hostages
being shot. Presently the Zuñis—now under Padre
Miranda, who came occasionally from Acoma—asked
to have their escolta removed, a request which aroused
fears of a general rising in the west. A junta at Cia
in April 1707 resolved to withdraw the frontier escoltas to Santa Fé for recuperation of the horses, and
thus the west was again abandoned.[9]

It was on the 1st of August, 1707, that the governor ad interim was succeeded by the admiral Don
José Chacon Medina Salazar y Villaseñor, marqués de
la Peñuela, who had been appointed by the king in
1705, and who ruled till 1712. The new ruler turned
his attention like others to the Moquis, toward whom
his predecessors, according to his theory, had acted
harshly, shooting captives and exasperating the natives. He sent an embassy of Zuñis[10] with an exhortation to peace and submission; but the only reply

---

[9] *Arch. N. Mex.*, 194–5. There is some confusion of dates. P. Juan Minguez is named as a member of these exped. *Moqui, Not.*, 670; *Fernandez Duro,
Not.*, 137.

[10] Notwithstanding the abandonment before noted, P. Fran. de Irazábal
seems to have been now in charge of Alona, one of the Zuñi pueblos.

was a raid of refugee Tanos and Tehuas on Zuñi.
Nothing more important is recorded in 1708 than the
building of a parish church on the site of the one
destroyed in 1680. It was built by the marqués governor at his own cost, though permission was obtained
to employ Indians on the work, and was completed
within two years.[11] The year 1709 was marked by a
war with the Navajos, who had become very bold in
their depredations, sacking the pueblos of Jemes in
June, but who were defeated by the governor in a
vigorous campaign, and forced to make a treaty of
peace. This year, also, the custodio, Padre Juan de
la Peña, collected some scattered families of Tiguas,[12]
and with them refounded the old pueblo of San Agustin Isleta. Padre Peña engaged moreover in a spiritual campaign against estufa-rites and scalp-dances;
and complaints sent to Mexico of abuses on the part
of the governor and alcaldes brought from the viceroy
stringent orders against forcing the Indians to work
without compensation.[13]

Padre Peña died, and was succeeded as custodio by
Padre Juan de Tagle, after Padre Lopez de Haro as
vice-president had been for a time in charge of the
office. There was a quarrel in progress, of which we
know little or nothing, between the marqués and his
predecessor Cuervo; and Tagle with other friars favored the latter, and were the objects of Peñuela's
complaints in Mexico.[14] In 1711 and the two follow-

[11] Prince, *Hist. Sk.*, 223–4, notes an inscription on the church, ' El señor
marqués de la Peñuela hizo esta fábrica; el alférez real Don Agustin Flores
Vergara su criado año de 1710.' Peñuela was not, as Prince says, later viceroy of N. Spain.
[12] Called Tehuas in *Arch. N. Mex.*, 197–8; but they were more likely, I
think, Tiguas, the original occupants of the town, some of whom, it will be
remembered, had been settled by Gov. Otermin near El Paso. The P. Cronista
seems confused himself on the subject.
[13] Revilla Gigedo, *Carta de 1793*, 441, says there were 20,110 tax-payers
registered in 1710, the garrison of Sta Fé being 120. Events of these years
in *Arch. N. Mex.*, 197–9.
[14] *Arch. N. Mex.*, 198–9. The gov. not only complained of Tagle's being
kept in office through Cuervo's influence, but that he had done great harm by
removing P. José Lopez Tello from his ministry. He also charged that P.
Fran. Brotoni of Taos had ordered his Ind. to rebuild their estufas. His
complaining report was on May 20, '12, and it was referred on Aug. 13th to
the com. gen. of the Franciscans.

ing years, we find several royal orders on New Mexican affairs; but none of them has any historic importance. The soldiers had asked for an increase of pay, the friars for reënforcements, and Governor Cuervo had reported his great achievements in town founding; the cédulas were routine replies, ordering the viceroy to investigate and report, but always to look out for the welfare of the northern province. The sum total of information seems to be that there were 34 padres in the field, which number the viceroy deemed sufficient, though he was authorized by the king to increase the missionary force whenever it might be deemed best.[15]

Juan Ignacio Flores Mogollon, formerly governor of Nuevo Leon, had the royal appointment as governor and captain-general; and the marqués de la Peñuela retiring at the expiration of his term of five years, Governor Flores assumed the office on October 5, 1712, ruling until 1715.[16] The Sumas of the south revolted in 1712, but were reduced by Captain Valverde, and settled at Realito de San Lorenzo, a league and a half from El Paso, probably at Otermin's old camp of 1681. In May 1713 the natives of Acoma and Laguna, offended by the anti-pagan zeal of Padre Cárlos Delgado, thought favorably of a proposition to kill him at the instigation of a Zuñi Indian—at least so Padre Irazábal reported; but nothing could be

[15] *N. Mex.*, *Cédulas*, MS., 35–42, orders of Feb. 9, 13, Jan. 17, March 2, 1711; Dec. 10, 1712; Aug. 4, Sept. 27, 1713. Gov. Peñuela had written direct to the king, Oct. 28, 1707, on Apache troubles; on Nov. 25th, had forwarded a petition of the soldiers for a restoration of the old pay, and that it might be paid at Mex. instead of Guadalajara. Gov. Cuervo, on April 15, 1706, had forwarded a complaint of P. Álvarez on neglect of the missions; on Aug. 18, 1706, had asked for more friars; and on June 13, 18, 23, 1706, had reported his founding of Alburquerque, etc. The cédula of Dec. 10, '12, asks for information on the pay of Capt. Félix Martinez of the Sta Fé company. The order of Aug. 4, '13, relates to the soldiers' petition, but does not clearly show whether it was granted or not.

[16] *Arch. N. Mex.*, 199. Davis, Prince, and the rest find room for another viceroy, the duke of Linares, as gov. in 1712. Prince, *Hist. Sk.*, 224, tells us, and accurately so far as I know, that Flores was commissioned at Madrid Sept. 27, 1707, for 5 years; qualified Oct. 9th; did not come to Mex. for a long time; was recommissioned (?) by the viceroy Feb. 9, '12; and installed at Sta Fé Oct. 5th. His salary was $2,000.

proved. In October of the same year Captain Serna
with 400 soldiers and allies defeated the Navajos in
their own country; and besides this achievement the
Faraon Apaches were warned to desist from their depredations! In 1714 the Yutas and Taos had many
fights, but the governor restored harmony by an enforced restitution of stolen property. Navajo raids on
the Jemes had again to be checked by a campaign of
Captain Madrid, while Captain Valverde marched
against the Apache hoards of Pharaoh, as did also the
French from Louisiana.

A junta of civil, military, and missionary authorities was held to deliberate on two questions deemed
momentous: First, should the Christian Indians be
deprived of fire-arms? The military favored such a
policy, but the friars opposed it, both to avoid offence
and afford the converts protection; and the governor
at last ordered the arms taken away except in the case
of natives especially trustworthy. Second, should
the converts be allowed to paint themselves and wear
skin caps, thus causing themselves to be suspected of
crimes committed by gentiles, or enabling them to
commit offences attributed to gentiles? Governor
Flores and his officers, with some of the padres, were in
favor of forbidding the custom; but the rest of the friars
took an opposite view, holding that no Christian Indian
had ever been known to use his paint for a disguise to
cover crime, that it was impolitic to accuse them of
so doing, that painting was the native idea of adorn-
ment, and in that light no worse than Spanish methods;
and finally, that the custom was objectionable only in
connection with superstition, in which respect it must
be removed gradually by Christian teachings. The
decision is not recorded.[17] Like other years of this

---

[17] *Arch. N. Mex.*, 201–4, including a letter of P. Miranda, who made himself
the champion of the Ind.   On the other side are named PP. Lúcas Arévalo
of Taos and José Ant. Guerrero of Sta Fé.   The junta was on July 6, 1714.
In M. Pinart's col. is an original order of Gov. F. this year, that a new estufa
at Pecos be suppressed and great care taken by all alcaldes to prevent anything of the kind.

and most other periods, 1715 had its vague rumors of an impending revolt, ever dreaded by the New Mexicans, not traceable to any definite foundation. I find also the record of one of the typical campaigns against Apaches on or toward the Colorado River, made by Juan Paez Hurtado, with no results of importance.[18]

It must not be supposed that nothing was heard from the Moquis, for I find original records of five juntas de guerra at Santa Fé on their account.[19] In June 1713 an Indian named Naranjo was refused permission to visit the Moquis, but in December two natives of Zuñi, through Padre Irazábal, obtained the license and were given letters. They found the Moquis eager for peace and alliance with the Zuñis, but the controlling element under the chief of Oraibe had no desire for the Spaniards' friendship. In March 1715 a Moqui appeared at the capital with favorable reports, and was sent back with assurances of goodwill. Next, in May a chief from Oraibe came to make further investigations, reporting that a grand junta of all the towns had decided on peace and Christianity. This chief was sent back with gifts, and in July eight Moquis came to announce that after harvest the formal arrangements for submission would be completed. Thus all went well so long as the Moquis were the ambassadors; but when the governor sent messengers of his own choosing, the truth came out that the pretended ambassadors were traders, who had invented all their reports to account for their visits and insure their own safety, the Moqui authorities being as hostile as ever!

Governor Flores was an old man in feeble health, who resigned on account of his infirmities. He was succeeded by Captain Félix Martinez, who assumed

---

[18] *Hurtado, Campaña contra los Apaches Agosto–Set. 1715*, MS., in *Pinart Col.*, including diario, junta de guerra, corresp., etc. The force was 250 soldiers and allies.

[19] *Moqui, Juntas de Guerra, 1713–15*, orig. MS. of the *Pinart Col.* The juntas were on Dec. 26, '13, March 12, May 3, July 5, Nov. 2, '15.

the office as acting governor, or perhaps governor ad
interim by the viceroy's appointment, on October 30,
1715, and who, instead of permitting his predecessor
to depart with an escort for Mexico as ordered,
engaged in quarrels and lawsuits with him, keeping
him under arrest for two years.[20] During Martinez'
rule of two years two campaigns are recorded. In
August 1716 the governor marched in person against
the Moquis with 68 soldiers, accompanied by the custodio, Padre Antonio Camargo, the cabildo of Santa
Fé, and a force of vecinos from Alburquerque and
La Cañada. Commissioners were sent forward from
Alona, and some of the Moquis seemed willing to
submit, but the people of Gualpi and the Tanos pueblo
refused. Two fights occurred in September, the Indians being defeated, if we may credit the diary, with
many killed and wounded; but the army, after destroying corn-fields, retreated to Santa Fé, and the
pretended victories may be regarded as very doubtful.[21]

[20] *Arch. N. Mex.*, 105–6. Martinez had come with Vargas, enlisted as a
soldier, became capt. of the Sta Fé company in Peñuela's time, was forced to
resign on account of his somewhat quarrelsome character in '12, but in '15
had got a new appointment from the king as captain for life and regidor per-
petuo of the villa. Flores Mogollon was a native of Sevilla. A sierra in N.
Mex. preserves his name. Davis, Prince, and others make Capt. Valverde
gov. in '14, and so he may have been acting gov. at some time during Flores'
illness. These writers also state, to quote from Prince, that Flores 'was accused of malefeasance in office, but the case did not come on for trial until
after a delay of some years. By the king's command he was relieved from
his position Oct. 5, 1715, after serving exactly 3 years. His trial was had at
Sta Fé in 1721, long after he had left N. Mex.; and his sentence was sent to
the viceroy for confirmation, the costs being adjudged against him. The officer reported that neither the accused nor any of his property could be
found.' I suppose that these statements rest on some doc. of 1721 in the
Arch. Sta Fé, MS., which I have not found.

[21] Certified copy of Martinez' diary, in *Arch. Sta Fé*, MS., the original
having been carried by M. to Mex. The return to Sta Fé was on Oct. 8th.
Acc. to *Arch. N. Mex.*, 206–7, the gov. accomplished nothing, and the truth
which he concealed in his diary came out in his later residencia. The padre
cronista is apparently wrong in naming P. José Lopez Tello as custodio.at this
time and P. Miranda as his predecessor. He also tells us that the gov.
decided to wage war on the Moquis after consulting the viceroy, but before
awaiting his reply. In *Moqui, Noticias*, MS., 671–4, P. Domingo Araos is
named as a companion of P. Camargo; and an account is given of the preliminary negotiations, but not of the fights that followed. It seems that the
Moquis at first pretended to be well disposed but required time to deliberate, spending the 5 days allowed in preparations for war. The exped. is
mentioned in *Fernandez Duro, Noticias*, 137. On this trip Gov. M. left his
name inscribed on El Morro, Aug. 26th, with a record that he was on the

During the governor's absence in the west the
Yutas and Comanches—perhaps the first definite appearance in history of the latter nation—attacked
Taos, the Tehua towns, and even some of the Spanish
settlements.   On his return Martinez sent Captain
Serna, who attacked the foe at the Cerro de San
Antonio, thirty leagues north of Santa Fé, killing
many Indians and capturing their chusma.   It subsequently came out in the governor's residencia that
the captives were divided between Don Félix and his
brother, and sold on joint account in Nueva Vizcaya,
the Yutas being told later that their chusma had died
of small-pox![22]

In September 1716, the new viceroy, marqués de
Valero, informed secretly of how things were going in
New Mexico, ordered Governor Martinez to present
himself in Mexico, at the same time directing Captain
Antonio Valverde y Cosío to go up from El Paso, assume the governorship ad interim, and investigate
certain charges.   Valverde arrived at Santa Fé the 9th
of December; but Martinez, supported by the cabildo,
refused to give up the office or presidio books.   He
could not, however, disobey the viceroy's summons,
and having appointed Juan Paez Hurtado to act as
governor in his absence, he started on the 20th of
January, 1717, taking with him apparently Flores
Mogollon, his predecessor.   Valverde was ordered to
accompany him to El Paso, but feigned illness, and
took refuge with his friend, Padre Tagle, at the convent of San Ildefonso.   As to resulting complications
between Hurtado and Valverde, I have found no record, but suppose that the former ruled but a few
months, and that before the end of 1717, as soon as
orders could be returned from Mexico, Valverde

way to reduce the Moquis with the custodio, P. Camargo, and Juan García
de Rivas, alcalde of Sta Fé. *Simpson's Jour.*, 104–5, pl. 65, 67.

[22] In a memorial of 1722, *Arch. Sta Fé*, MS., all the officers and soldiers
stated that N. Mex. was in great peril during M.'s rule.   'Con su insaciable
y voraz codicia, robos y engaños manifiestos, estuvo pendiente de un cabello
para una total asolacion.'

assumed the office, which he held for four or five years.[23]

A leading event of Valverde's rule was his expedition of 1719, with 105 Spaniards and 30 Indians, being joined also on the way by the Apaches under Captain Carlarna, against the Yutas and Comanches, who had been committing many depredations. His route was north, east, south-east, and finally south-west back to Santa Fé. He thus explored the regions since known as Colorado and Kansas, going farther north, as he believed, than any of his predecessors. He did not overtake the foe, encountering nothing more formidable than poison-oak, which attacked the officers as well as the privates of his command.[24] On the Rio Napestle, apparently the Arkansas, Valverde met the Apaches of Cuartelejo, and found men with gunshot wounds received from the French and their allies, the Pananas and Jumanas.[25] An order came from the

[23] *Arch. N. Mex.*, 207–8. This invaluable authority comes to an end here, and its absence will be felt in the remainder of this chapter. Davis and the others name no ruler in '19–20. The *Arch. Sta Fé*, MS., shows V. as gov. in '18–20, and he probably held the office in '17–21. I find no original record of how the troubles of Martinez and Flores were settled in Mexico, but there are some indications that a juez de residencia was sent to Sta Fé in '21 to take testimony.

[24] P. Juan Pino was the chaplain, and the start was on Sept. 15th. The men, suffering terribly from poison-oak, found the best remedy to be chewing chocolate and applying the saliva to the parts affected. The route was N. with the sierra on the left to Oct. 10th, the names given being Rio S. José at Rosario, Rio Colorado (an arroyo) or Soledad, Sacramento, Rio S. Miguel (poison-oak experience), Rio Sto Domingo, S. Lorenzo at junction of two streams, Rio S. Antonio, Rio S. Francisco 4 l., S. Onofre, Dolores Spr. 4 l., Cármen Spr. 6 l., Sta Rosa in sand dunes, S. Ignacio more eastward, Sta Etigenia 5 l., S. Felipe de Jesus Cr. 6 l. Thence Oct. 11th–20th down the river Sta María Magdalena E. and S. E. to S. Nicolás Obispo 4 l., Pilar 6 l., La Cruz 4 l., Sta Teresa, Rio Napestle 10 l. Here they met the Apaches Calchufines, and sent P. Pino and a party to Taos for supplies. Soon they met the Apaches of Cuartelejo. The diary ends abruptly when they started back for Sta Fé. *Valverde y Cosío (Antonio), Diario y Derrotero,* 1719; orig. MS. written by Sec. Alonso Rael de Aguilar, in the *Pinart Col.*

[25] It was said the French had given these Ind. fire-arms, and that they had formed two large towns. I suppose the Pananas may have been Pauanas, or Pawnees. Escalante, *Carta,* 125, tells us that in this year, 1719, a company under Capt. Villasur was sent (perhaps after the gov.'s return) to find the Pananas, 300 l. N. E. of Sta Fé. He reached the river on which their towns stood, but the Pananas—who, he thinks, may have been the Quiviras—attacked Villasur in the night with guns, killing V., P. Juan Mingües, and

viceroy to establish a presidio of 25 men at Cuartelejo, some 130 leagues from Santa Fé, in the heart of the Apache region; but a council of war decided this to be impossible, believing the viceroy had meant Jicarilla, some 40 leagues from the capital, as the site, and that even there 25 men would not suffice. In 1719–20 the governor made a tour of inspection, visiting every pueblo and settlement in the province.[26] He also sent information on the Moquis for which he was thanked by the viceroy; and the same persistent apostates were mentioned in a royal order, from which it appears that the Jesuits were trying to be put in charge of the Moqui conversion, a phase of the matter that belongs to the annals of Arizona in another chapter of this volume.[27] From the same document it appears that there was a dispute between the bishop

most of the party, including the French guide. Ritch, *Aztlan*, 244, mentions this Pawnee massacre as having been on the Missouri.

In a letter of Feb. 1886, Dr J. F. Snyder of Virginia, Cass Co., Ill., informs me that a massacre of Spaniards by the Missouris, mistaken for Pawnees by the victims, in 1720, is mentioned in all the early histories of the region. He cites the narrative as given in *Reynolds' Pioneer Hist. of Illinois*, 34, and also cites *Charlevoix, Journal*, that author having obtained some Spanish relics in the north, said to have been obtained at a great massacre of the New Mexicans. There is much variation as to details, but the general version is that the Spaniards came to drive out the French and met disaster by confiding their hostile plans to a tribe that was friendly to the French and led them into an ambush. Dr S. has been shown the spot in Saline Co., Mo., where the affair occurred. It would seem that the expedition must have been that of Villasur, or one sent out after Valverde's return, and in consequence of his reports about the French. It is unfortunate that no original records have been found. It is possible that Villasur reached the Missouri; but it is strange that such a disaster has left no more definite trace in the archives.

[26] *Arch. Sta Fé*, MS. In these years Mig. Tenorio de Alba, Mig. Enriquez de Cabrera, and Alonso Rael de Aguilar appear as govt secretary. Capt. Pedro de Villasur was lieut.-gen. The alcaldes mayores were Alf. Cris. Torres, Sta Cruz de la Cañada; Capt. Luis García, Alburquerque, Bernalillo, Sta Ana, Cia, and Jemes; Capt. Alonso García, Isleta; Capt. Ant. de Uribarri, Laguna, Acoma, Alona, or the Zuñi region; Capt. Alonso Rael de Aguilar, Pecos and Galisteo; and Capt. Mig. Tenorio de Alba at S. Gerón. de Taos. In 1718 there were complaints from Cochití against the alcalde mayor, Miguel de Vaca, for beating and otherwise abusing the Ind. They led to an investigation and an order of the gov. for more care in Ind. treatment. The bulky record is in *Arch. Sta Fé*, MS.

[27] *N. Mex., Cédulas*, MS., 42–4, order of Feb. 11, '19. *Arch. Sta Fé*, MS. At the end of '18 Gov. V. sent some Tanos to assure the fugitive Tanos, Tehuas, and Tiguas of Moqui that they might return without fear to their pueblos. He was ordered by the viceroy to use only gentle measures. A royal cédula of March 7, '19, ordered investigation of past management of Capt. Félix Martinez and other presidio com., especially in financial matters. *N. Mex., Céd.*, MS., 44–5.

of Durango and the archbishop of Mexico on the ecclesiastic jurisdiction of New Mexico.

Don Juan de Estrada y Austria seems to have come in 1721 as juez de residencia to investigate the still pending charges against and controversies between ex-governors Flores and Martinez; and he may have held, as was sometimes customary, the position of acting governor during the performance of his duties as judge;[28] if so, he turned over the office before the end of the year or early in the next; and on March 2, 1722, the regularly appointed governor, Don Juan Domingo de Bustamante, succeeded;[29] ruling two full terms, or until 1731. A visitador general, in the person of Captain Antonio Cobian Busto, came in 1722 to investigate the condition of provincial affairs.[30] Some Spaniards engaged in illicit trade with the French inhabitants of Louisiana, which brought out

[28] Davis, Prince, and others represent him as 'his Majesty's residuary (!) judge, acting gov., etc.,' in 1721. I have seen no original record of his presence.

[29] The date of B.'s assuming office at Sta Fé is given in a doc. of '22 in Arch. Sta Fé, MS. On March 15, '22, the officers and soldiers of Sta Fé sign a memorial of praise in favor of ex.-gov. V., who had been relieved by B. (no ref. to Estrada). They accredit V. with all kinds of good conduct. He had built at his own cost a church and chapel at the capital, and a chapel at S. Ildefonso; paid his men regularly and treated them well. V. was capitan vitalicio of the presidio of El Paso, and now returned to his post.

[30] Arch. Sta Fé, MS. In Oct. a junta was held at Sta Fé to explain to Busto for the king's edification why the country from Chihuahua up to N. Mex. was not fully settled by prosperous and tribute-paying Spaniards. The reason was found in the small number and poverty of the settlers, and the fear of gentile raiders. The remedies proposed were a presidio of 50 men and a settlement of 200 families at Socorro, and another presidio of 50 men at Aguatuvi. The country was rich in metals and well adapted to agriculture and stock-raising; and any expenditure of money by the govt would be a good investment.

Mig. Enriquez was now sec. Paez Hurtado and Ant. Becerro Nieto are named as generals, the latter of Janos, in N. Mex. temporarily. Capt. Fran. Bueno de Bohorques y Corcuera was alcalde mayor of Sta Fé; Aguilar was a sargento mayor. Captains Ignacio de Roybal and Diego Arias de Quirós and Lieut. Fran. Montes Vijil are named. Hurtado was lieut.-gen. in '24.

Padres named in '22 are: Juan de Tagle, comisario del sto oficio and visitador, Juan de la Cruz, custodio and juez ecles., Juan Sanchez, Diego Espinosa de los Monteros, Juan de Mirabal, Juan Ant. de Celi, Manuel de Sopena, Cárlos Delgado, Juan del Pino, Fran. Irazábal, Domingo de Araos, Fran. Ant. Perez, com. sto oficio, José Ant. Guerrero, guardian of the Sta Fé convent. These were all at the Sta Fé junta. P. José Diez, who left N. Mex. in 1696, died at Querétaro in '22, age 65. Arricivita, Cron. Seráf., i. 189–206.

prohibitory orders from the king in 1723; and orders regulating the trade with gentile tribes were issued by Governor Bustamante the same year.[31] Early in 1724 the Yutas committed depredations at Jemes; and the Comanches attacked the Apaches at Jicarilla, forced them to give up half their women and children to save their lives and town, burned the place, and killed all but 69 men, two women, and three boys— all mortally wounded.[32] In 1727 Bustamante notified the viceroy that the French had settled at Cuartelejo and Chinali, 160 leagues from Santa Fé, proposing an expedition to find out what was being done, and asking for troops for that purpose; but it was decided that such an entrada was not necessary, though all possible information should be obtained from the Indians.[33] The Jesuits still desired to convert the Moquis, and obtained in 1726 favorable orders from king and viceroy, of which they made no practical use. Padres Miranda and Irazábal visited the province in 1724, obtaining what they considered favorable assurances for the future; and in 1730-1 padres Francisco Archundi and José Narvaez Valverde seem to have had a like experience. The Moquis had no objections to an occasional interview so long as they could put off their submission to a convenient time not the present.[34]

[31] *N. Mex., Céd.*, MS., 45-6, orders of March 10, '23, and March 7, '24. It was charged that N. Mex. traders went to La and bought $12,000 worth of goods. Gov. B.'s order about trade with gentiles, Apr. 3, '23, in *Arch. Sta Fé*, MS. The people were allowed to trade with gentiles who came to Taos and Pecos, but some were accustomed to go out in the plains to meet them.

[32] Letters of PP. Mirabal and Irazábal, in *Arch. Sta Fé*, MS. The padres thought as the Jicarillas were Christians and the Comanches had been notified of it war on the latter was justifiable acc. to scripture. Paez Hurtado was ordered in Feb. to make an exped. with 100 men, but I have not found any report of results. In '26, Rivera, *Diario y Derrotero*, 28-9, mentions Alburquerque as a villa of mixed Span., mestizos, and mulattoes, mostly scattered on the ranchos. Bonilla, *Apuntes*, MS., says that in '26 a reënforcement of troops was ordered; also that Brig. Pedro de Rivera visited N. Mex. to reorganize the presidio, the force being consequently fixed at 80 men with $400 each. P. Niel, *Apunt.*, 96-100, gives some geographic notes of '29 for the N. Mex. settlements that seem to be confused references to earlier records, and are so faulty that I do not deem them worth reproduction.

[33] Orig. MS. in Pinart collection.

[34] *N. Mex., Céd.*, MS., 46-8, order of March 20, '26, and viceroy's report of May 14, '25. See later chap. on Ariz.; *N. Mex., Doc.*, MS., 674-8, state-

There was a complicated controversy in these and later years between the missionary and episcopal authorities. The bishop of Durango claimed New Mexico as part of his bishopric, insisting on his right to appoint a vicar and control ecclesiastic matters in the province, which the friars refused to recognize. Bishop Crespo, in his *visita* of 1725, reached El Paso, and exercised his functions without much opposition; but in August 1730, when he extended his tour to Santa Fé, though he administered the rite of confirmation there and at a few other towns, at some of the missions he was not permitted to do so, the friars objecting by instruction of the custodio, Padre Andrés Varo, and he, of course, obeying the instructions of his superior in Mexico. The bishop also appointed Don Santiago Roybal as juez eclesiástico, whose authority was only partially recognized. Crespo began legal proceedings against the Franciscan authorities in Mexico, and besides demanding recognition of his episcopal rights, he made serious charges against the New Mexican friars, alleging that they did not properly administer the sacraments; that they did not learn the native language; that the neophytes, rather than confess through an interpreter, who might reveal their secrets, did not confess at all, except *in articulo mortis;* that of 30 padres provided for, only 24 were serving; that the failure to reduce the Moquis was their fault; that some of them neglected their duties, and others by their conduct caused scandal; and that tithes were not properly collected or expended. These charges, especially those connected with ignorance of the native language, were supported by the formal testimony of 24 prominent officials and residents, taken by the governor at Santa Fé in June 1731.

ments of PP. Miranda, Irazábal, Archundi, and Valverde. The latter had served in N. Mex. since '92. It does not clearly appear here that he had visited Moqui; but Fernandez Duro, *Noticias*, 137, cites a MS. of 120 pp. in the Acad. de Hist., entitled *Valverde, Exped. á la prov. de Moqui*, 1730. On Archundi's entrada, see also *Crespo, Mem. Ajust.*, 51, where it is said that in an entrada of '31 a padre sacrificed his life (?). Some time before Nov. '32, P. Fran. Techungui entered Moqui and brought away 5 Tiguas to Isleta. *Id.*, 54.

Details of the suit are too bulky and complicated for notice here. There was a royal order of 1729 favorable to the bishop, and another of 1731 to some extent sustaining the position of the Franciscans; but the decision in 1733 was in substance that, pending a final decision on the great principles involved, the bishop had, and might exercise, jurisdiction in New Mexico; and as we shall see, he did make a *visita* in 1737. In Spain, the case came up on appeal in 1736, and a main feature of the friars' plea was the claim that the testimony against them was false, having been given by bad men, moved by prejudice against the padres, who had opposed their sinful customs. To prove this, they produced the evidence, taken by the vice-custodio, Padre José Antonio Guerrero, in July 1731, of another set of officials and citizens, to the effect that the missionaries had performed every duty in the most exemplary and zealous manner, though it was not pretended that they knew the native dialects. Counter-charges were also made that the governor and his officials abused the Indians, forcing them to work without pay. The record from which I take this information was printed in 1738, when no permanent decision had been reached.[35]

[35] *Crespo, Memorial ajustado que de órden del consejo supremo de Indias se ha hecho del pleyto, que siguió el Illmo. Sor Don Benito Crespo, obispo que fué de Durango, y lo continua el Illmo. Sor Don Martin de Elizacoechea, su successor en dicho obispado. Con la religion de N. P. S. Francisco, de la Regular Observencia, y su procurador general de las Indias. Sobre visitar, y exercer los actos de la jurisdiccion diocesana en la custodia del Nuevo Mexico en la Nueva España, poner vicario foraneo, y otras cosas.* Madrid, 1738, fol., 64 l. The padres accused of neglect, so far as named, were PP. Ant. Gabaldon of Nambé, Juan de la Cruz of S. Juan, Cárlos Delgado of Isleta, Manuel Sopena of Sta Clara, José Yrigoyen of S. Ildefonso, Domingo Araos of Sta Ana, Ant. Miranda of Cia, Pedro Montano of Jemes, Juan Mirabal of Taos, and Juan Ant. Hereiza of Picuríes. Some of the witnesses against the padres were Capt. Juan Gonzalez, alc. mayor of Alburquerque; Diego de Torres, lieut.-alc. m. of Sta Clara; Juan Paez Hurtado; Ramon García, alc. m. of Bernalillo; and Miguel Vega, alc. m. of Taos. Witnesses in favor of the padres included Capt. Tomás Nuñez de Haro, Capt. Ant. de Uribarri, Capt. Sebastian Martin, Capt. Alonso Rael de Aguilar, Andrés Montoya, alc. m. of S. Felipe, Capt. Nicolás Ortiz Niño, and some of the opposing witnesses on certain points. P. Juan Mig. Menchero was in N. Mex. as visitador, and took some part in this affair. The bishop's visits, both in '25 and '30, are said to have produced copious rains, and thus greatly benefited the province. The marriage of Manuel Armijo and María Francisca Vaca, which the juez ecles. tried to prevent, figured largely in the testimony.

Governor Bustamante's rule ended in 1731, and the result of his residencia was favorable, though on one charge—that of illegal trade, admitted to be for the benefit of the country—he was found guilty and forced to pay the costs of trial.[36]   His successor was Gervasio Cruzat y Góngora, who ruled for a full term of five years.   The period was a most uneventful one so far as we may judge by the meagre record in the shape of detached items.   A mission of Jicarilla Apaches was founded on the Rio Trampas, three or five leagues from Taos, in 1733, prospering for a time under Padre Mirabal; no Indian campaigns or troubles are recorded, and nothing is heard even of the apostate Moquis.[37] From the governor's part in taking evidence for the bishop in the great controversy already noticed, it may be presumed that he was not regarded as a friend by the friars.

A successor was appointed—ad interim, by the viceroy—on May 17, 1736, in the person of Enrique de Olavide y Michelena, who, however, may not have assumed the office till 1737.   This year Bishop Elizacoechea visited the province, without opposition so far as is known, and extended his tour to the Zuñi towns. In 1738 Governor Olavide visited all the pueblos, at each publicly announcing his presence and calling upon all who had grievances against the alcaldes or individuals to make them known; but nothing more serious was submitted than a few petty debts of a horse, cow,

[36] *Bustamante (Juan Dom.), Residencia del gobernador y Capitan general que fué de N. Mexico. Tomada por D. Fran. de la Sierra y Castillo, 1731.* Orig. MS. of 177 l., in Pinart col.   One witness for making malicious charges was fined $100.

[37] Founding of the Apache mission. *Villaseñor, Teatro,* ii. 420; *Crespo, Mem. Ajust.,* 61.   There were 130 Ind. at this mission in '34; but few or none were left in '48.   In '33 an Ind. greatly excited the wrath of P. Montaño at Alburquerque by presenting himself during service without a cloak and with braided hair, being sustained in the ensuing quarrel by his grandfather. The padre complained through the custodio, P. José Ant. Guerrero, to the gov., and declared that the grandfather should be shut up in a dungeon with shackles for his impious conduct. *Arch. Sta Fé,* MS.   May 20, '35, Gov. C. strictly forbids the sale of arms to gentiles, under severe penalties—a fine of 10,000 maravedís for Span., and 100 lashes and 50 days in prison for Ind. *Id.*   July 14, '36, Gen. Juan Paez Hurtado, inspector, left his name on El Morro. *Simpson's Jour.,* pl. 67.   P. José Ortiz Velasco was custodio in '33-5.

or pair of drawers. Let us hope that Don Enrique's orders for payment were promptly obeyed. The governor's residencia was prosecuted in January 1739, by Juan José Moreno as juez; and as the answers to the twenty-eight routine questions by twenty-four witnesses, half of them Indians, were uniformly favorable, the decision was most flattering to a ruler respecting the occurrences of whose rule little is known.[38]

The new governor, appointed by the king on May 12, 1737, and assuming office in January 1739, was Gaspar Domingo de Mendoza, who ruled till 1743. About 1740 a small party of Frenchmen came by way of Jicarilla and Taos, two of them remaining, and the rest departing by another route; and this occurrence is rather vaguely connected by certain writers with a plan of the French to take possession of the Rio Colorado region.[39] In 1742 padres Delgado and Ignacio Pino went to the Moqui towns and succeeded in bringing away 441 Tiguas, who before the great revolt had lived in the pueblos of Sandía, Alameda, and Pajarito, which the friars now wished to reëstablish, though the governor declined to act without special instructions. Meanwhile the recovered neo-

[38] Feb. 1, '37, gov. issues a bando forbidding trade with the Ind. except by permission of the proper authority, under penalty of fine, forfeiture of goods, and flogging in the case of a native offender. *Arch. Sta Fé*, MS. On the governor's tour of inspection, *Olavide y Michelena (Henrique), Autos de visita hechos por el gobr, 1738*, MS., 38 l., in the Pinart col. The bishop's *visita* is recorded in an inscription on El Morro of Dec. 28–9th, when he started for Zuñi. *Simpson's Jour.* Prince, *Hist. Sk.*, 226, is in error when he says this was the 1st episcopal visit. On the final trial of Gov. O., I have *Olavide y Michelena, Autos de residencia, 1739*, an orig. MS. of 178 l. in the Pinart col.

[39] Mention of the arrival of 9 Frenchmen, in *Arch. Sta Fé*, MS. Of the 2 who remained, one, Jean d' Alay, married and became a good citizen (and barber) of Sta Fé; the other, Louis Marie, became involved in troubles, and was shot in the plaza in Mendoza's time. *Codallos y Rabal, Testimonio*, etc., in *Id.* The French criminal sentenced to death, 'sacado el corazon por las espaldas,' is mentioned by the gov. in a letter of '43. *N. Mex., Doc.*, MS., 691. Acc. to this, the Frenchmen came in '39. They are also mentioned in *Menchero, Declaracion*, MS., 726, who says that for their country a settlement near Isleta was named Canadá. Salvador, *Consulta*, 662–3, says they were on the way to settle in the west; and Villaseñor, *Teatro*, ii. 416, tells us that they settled at a place near Alburquerque called Cañada, and later Limpia Concepcion, or Fuenclara. Acc. to records of land grants, published with transl. in *U. S. Land Off. Repts*, '56, p. 291–8, it appears that the settlement of Tomé Dominguez was founded in 1739, by some 30 settlers who received lands.

phytes were distributed in different missions.[40]   Mota
Padilla, the historian of Nueva Galicia, devotes some
attention to New Mexico, and gives its population of
Spaniards in 1742, not including the soldiers and their
families, as 9,747, living in 24 towns.[41]   Mendoza's rule
ended late in 1743, and his residencia, conducted by
his successor, brought to light no complaints or unfavorable testimony.[42]

Joaquin Codallos y Rabal was the next governor,
ruling for a little more than a full term, from the end
of 1743 to 1749.[43]   Colonel Francisco de la Rocha
was appointed in 1747 or earlier to succeed Codallos
on the expiration of his term; but Rocha declined on
account of his age and infirmities.   The viceroy wished
to appoint a substitute, but the king would not permit
it, appointing to the office Tomás Velez Cachupin, who
took command as early as May 1749, and ruled to and
beyond the end of the half-century covered by this
chapter.   New Mexican affairs in these years, somewhat more fully recorded than for the preceding, may
be most conveniently grouped—except a few detached
items given in a note[44]—in four or five topics, to each
of which I devote a paragraph.

[40] Letters of gov. M., and PP. Delgado, Pino, and Cris. Yraeta (at El
Paso) in '42–3. *Moqui, Noticias*, MS., 678–92.   P. Gabriel Hoyuela is named
as custodio (still holding the office in '45 with P. Juan García as sec.), and P.
Fran. Bruno de la Peña is mentioned, and P. José M. Lopez.   P. Yraeta
blames the gov. for not aiding the missionary projects, and says twice as
many might have been rescued from Moqui with proper aid.   It was proposed to try again the next year.   The gov. unintelligibly mentions missions
called Viní and Sargarría.   Villaseñor, *Teatro*, ii. 416, mentions the entry of
the 2 padres, and notes that in Oct. 440 Moquis came to Sta Fé to ask for
protection and friars.   They were settled in different pueblos and given
$2,000 in live-stock, etc.
[41] *Mota Padilla, Conq. N. Gal.*, 319, 515–16.   He calls Alburquerque the
capital, with a garrison of 80 men.   The Apaches and Comanches are constant
in their raids; the presidios are expensive and of little use.   The estimate of
pop. is more than twice too large.
[42] *Mendoza (Gaspar Domingo), Residencia....contra el teniente coronel....del
tiempo que fué gobr y cap.-gen. de este reino....1744*, MS. of 133 l., in the Pinart
col.
[43] That is of course excepting 1747, when acc. to Davis, Prince, and others
another viceroy, Güemes y Horcasitas ruled ad interim! Gov. C. was a
major in the army.
[44] The viceroy in a report of Nov. 8, '47, notified the king of Rocha's inability to serve, and the king in an order of Jan. 20, '49, forbids the appoint-

But for the route from El Paso up the Rio del Norte, the region between Santa Fé and Zuñi on the north and the frontier presidios of Janos, Corodeguachi, and Guevavi on the south was a tierra incognita occupied by savage tribes. In 1747 the viceroy ordered a combined movement or campaign in this country. Thirty soldiers and as many settlers and friendly Indians were to march north by separate routes from each of the four southern presidios to meet a corresponding force sent south-westward from Santa Fé. They executed the movement and reached the Acoma region late in the year; but Governor Codallos was unable to coöperate, on account of a Comanche raid, not reaching Cubero until the others had departed. Therefore nothing was effected against the Indians, at which the viceroy was angry, and deducted $8,000 from the New Mexican *situado*, though he later accepted the governor's excuses. We have, unfortunately, no details of the explorations, except that Padre Menchero was with the El Paso company, turning to the west from the Jornada del Muerto, reached the upper Gila, and thence went north to Acoma through an entirely new region.[45]

The prospect of having to surrender the Moqui field

ment of a substitute. *N. Mex., Céd.*, MS., 54–5. The king in this cédula says nothing of a new appointment, and if at that time he had appointed Cachupin the latter could not have been at Sta Fé so early as May '49; so that after all C. may have been the substitute confirmed by the king.

Dec. 24, '44, order of the viceroy to suppress 5 plazas of the Sta Fé presidio, reducing the force to 80 men, its former number. MS. of Pinart col. In '44 a Frenchman named Velo arrived at Pecos. He was arrested and sent to Mex. *Arch. Sta Fé*, MS. In *Id.*, for this and following years there are various orders of the gov. against gambling, maltreating Ind., etc.; also appeals to Mex. for arms, etc. In '47 P. Mig. Menchero made another tour as visitador; and coming from El Paso with a large party, they turned west from the Jornada del Muerto, reached the upper Gila, and thence went N. to Acoma, thus exploring a new region. *Tamaron, Visita*, MS., 97–8. In '48 citizens called to serve against gentiles and failing to obey had to pay a fine. *Arch. Sta Fé*, MS. This year 33 Frenchmen visited the Comanches at the Rio de Jicarilla and sold them muskets. The gov. thought that in this party must have been some of those who visited N. Mex. before, and that the French had hostile designs. *Id.* The gov. recommended a presidio of 50 men at J., but the viceroy declined to authorize it now. *Id.* Taking of a census ordered by viceroy. *Id.* Royal order against gambling and other excesses pub. by Gov. C. in '49. MS. of Pinart col.

[45] Original corresp. of gov., viceroy, etc., in *Arch. Sta Fé*, MS.; *Tamaron, Visita*, MS., 97–8.

to the Jesuits was a thorn in the flesh of the Franciscans.   Their great achievement to prevent the change was the entrada of 1742, in which 441 apostates were recovered, as already related; but they continued their efforts, mainly with the pen, the venerable Delgado being the leading spirit.   In 1743, and again in 1744, they wished to make a new entrada, but, as they claimed, could not get the governor's permission and aid.   In 1745, however, padres Delgado, Irigoyen, and Juan José Toledo got the required license, with an escort of 80 Indians under an ex-soldier, and visited all the Moqui towns, counting 10,846 Indians, who listened gladly to their preaching.   Of course they made the most of their success, ridiculed the idea that the natives had expressed a preference for the *padres prietos* instead of the *padres azules*, and they even sent in glowing reports on the wealth of the Sierra Azul and grandeur of the great city or empire of Teguayo, with a view to reawaken interest in the Northern Mystery.   Meanwhile the king was induced to change his mind and to believe that he had been grossly deceived respecting the geographical situation of Moqui, the hostility and power of its people, and the vain efforts of the soldiers and friars to reduce them.   Surely, if two missionaries could go alone, without a cent of expense to the royal treasury, and bring out 441 converts, the Moquinos could neither be so far off from New Mexico, nor so confirmed in their apostasy, as had been represented.   So reasoned the king; and in a royal cédula of November 23, 1745, he explained his views, took back all he had said in favor of the Jesuits, and ordered the viceroy to support the Franciscans in every possible way.   Thus the *azules* won the fight, though the Moquis were not much nearer salvation than before.   In 1748, however, the rescued Tiguas of 1742, or some of them, were united at Sandía, and their old pueblo was rebuilt at or near its original site.[46]

[46] In '43 P. Delgado not allowed to visit Moqui; sends a *Relacion de la Sierra Azul*, as gathered from 4 Ind. *Menchero, Declaracion*, MS., 769-73.

The Navajos attracted still more attention than the Moquinos. Padres Delgado and Irigoyen started in March 1744 by way of Jemes for the Navajo country, and found the Indians apparently eager to become Christians and receive missionaries, 4,000 of them being 'interviewed.' They promised to come the next full moon to see the governor, and did so, being received with flattery, gifts, and promises of protection, as well as salvation. The padres wrote of this in June; the governor advised the sending of several new missionaries, and prospects were deemed excellent, though as usual there were vexatious delays. The viceroy ordered a complete investigation; and in 1745 a dozen witnesses formally told the governor all they knew about the Navajos, which was not much. The king heard of the 'conversion' of 5,000 gentiles, and ordered the viceroy to sustain the friars and help along the good work. The viceroy authorized the founding of four missions in the Navajo country, with a garrison of thirty men for their protection. This was in 1746, and Padre Menchero, the visitador, took up the enterprise with much zeal, visiting the gentiles in person, and inducing some 500 or 600 to return with him and settle temporarily at Cebolleta in the Acoma region. The hostile Apache bands in various directions made it impossible, in Governor Codallos' opinion, to spare the mission guard required; and a year or two later a bitter war between the Navajos and

'44, D. intends to go in July to bring out the remains of the martyred padres. *Moqui, Noticias*, MS., 700. June 18, D. writes to his superior on the risks the Jesuits will run in entering Moqui. If they go with soldiers and bluster, all will be lost. *N. Mex., Doc.*, MS., 779–83. Sept. 14, '45, Gov. Codallos at Zuñi permits an entrada, but has no soldiers to spare. *Arch. Sta Fé*, MS. Visit of the 3 padres in Sept. '45. The Ind. told of Jesuit efforts from Sonora, in which they had been driven back by another tribe (see later chap. on Ariz.). *N. Mex., Doc.*, MS., 786–90. P. Delgado's *Noticia del Gran Teguayo*, 200 l. N. w. of N. Mex., where the padre proposes to go the next year. *Id.*, 790–5. Royal cédula of Nov. 23, '45, in *N. Mex., Céd.*, MS., 49–54. It is a long doc., in which the king gives a long account of preceding orders, etc. Refounding of Sandía (Dolores) in '48, at the petition of P. Menchero. *Arch. Sta Fé*, MS.; *Prince's Hist. Sk.*, 38; *Meline's 2,000 Miles*, 214–20. In *Menchero, Informe 1749*, MS., the writer says he had not yet been able to visit Moqui, as he had intended; but that the natives had 3 times come to Sandía to ask him when he was coming to bring them away from their apostasy.

their foes, the Yutas and Chaguaguas, interfered with the conversion of the former. Accordingly, in 1749, in response to Menchero's petitions, a new governor advised, what a new viceroy approved, the founding of the missions, not in the far north or Navajo country proper, but in the Acoma district; and this was done, some additions being made to the converts already there, and two missions of Cebolleta and Encinal being established, under padres Juan de Lezaun and Manuel Bermejo. All went well for a very brief time; but in the spring of 1750 there was trouble, which Lieutenant-governor Bernardo Antonio de Bustamante, with the vice-custodio, Padre Manuel de San Juan Nepomuceno de Trigo, went to investigate. Then the real state of affairs became apparent. Padre Menchero had been liberal with his gifts, and still more so with promises of more; hence his success in bringing the Navajos to Cebolleta. But they said they had not received half the gifts promised, and their present padres—against whom they had no other complaint—were too poor to make any gifts at all. What, then, had they gained by the change? At any rate, pueblo life and Christianity had no charms for them, and they were determined not to remain. They would still be friends of the Spaniards and trade with them, and would always welcome the friars, who might even baptize and teach their children; perhaps the little ones might grow up to like a different life, but as for themselves, they had been born free, like the deer, to go where they pleased, and they were too old to learn new ways. Indeed, they took a very sensible view of the situation. Thus stood the matter in 1750, and the Navajo conversion was a failure.[47]

[47] In '43 a Christian Apache reported a mountain of silver in the Navajo country, and a large party went to find it, without success; indeed, the Navajos had never heard of it. *Codallos, Reduccion,* MS. Entrada of '44. *Arch. Sta Fé,* MS.; also letters of PP. Delgado and Irigoyen, in *N. Mex., Doc.,* MS., 692-704, 777, etc. Delgado gave away his clothes, and begs his superior for more—old ones, not new—so that he may with decency meet people. He thinks his late achievements will shut the mouths of the bishop and Jesuits

Of the Yutas and Apaches during this period we know nothing definitely, except that in most years they gave trouble in one way or another; but respecting the Comanches our information is somewhat less incomplete. In June 1746 they made a raid on Pecos, killing 12 inhabitants of that pueblo, and also committed hostilities at Galisteo and elsewhere. The popular clamor for a campaign against them was great, and the governor asked for increased powers. The auditor in Mexico made a long report in October on the preliminary efforts that must be made before war could be legally waged, and corresponding instructions were sent by the viceroy. In October 1747 Codallos, with over 500 soldiers and allies, overtook the Comanches with some Yuta allies beyond Abiquiú, and killed 107 of them, capturing 206, with nearly 1,000 horses. Four Yuta captives were shot. In January 1748, with a smaller force, he repulsed the foe at Pecos, though with some loss of Indian allies; yet a month or two later he gave a friendly reception to 600 Comanches at Taos, on their assurance that they had taken no part in the war. Later in the year, by the viceroy's orders, a junta was held at Santa Fé to determine whether the Comanches should be permitted to attend the fairs at Taos for purposes of trade. All admitted the unreliable and treacherous character of the tribe; but a majority favored a continuance of trade because the skins, meats, and horses they brought for sale were much needed in the province; and moreover, their presence at the fairs would bring them within Christian in-

at least. Taking of testimony in '45. *Codallos y Rabal (Joaquin), Reduccion de los Indios gentiles de la Provincia de Navajo, 1745. Testimonio á la letra de los Autos*, etc., MS., in the Pinart col. Royal order of Nov. 23, '45, in *N. Mex., Céd.*, MS., 48–9. Viceroy's order of June 28, '46, and record of later developments, in *Arch. Sta Fé*, MS. Letters of PP. Mirabal, Irigoyen, and Toledo to their superior on Menchero's efforts. *N. Mex., Doc.*, MS., 795–802. Record of '49, petition of P. Menchero, and orders of gov. and viceroy. *Menchero (Juan Miguel), Peticion sobre Conversion de los Navajóes, con otros papeles*, MSS., in the Pinart col. Troubles of '50, with official record of the investigations and report of P. Trigo to Mex. *Trigo (Manuel de S. J. N.), Informe sobre las Misiones de la Cebolleta y Encinal y sus acaecimientos en este Año de 1750*, MS., in *N. Mex., Doc.*, 1090–1134.

fluences, especially the captives they brought for sale, who might otherwise be killed.   The governor decided accordingly, against the views of the padre custodio.[48]

The bishop, who had practically won his case, does not appear to have attempted in these years any exercise of his episcopal authority; but the quarrel started by Crespo's charges was still in progress, as appears from two long reports of 1750.   Juan Antonio de Ordenal y Maza in some secular capacity visited New Mexico in 1748–9, and made a report to the viceroy, in which in a general way he represented the padres as neglectful of their duties, oppressive to the Indians, often absent from their posts to engage in trade, neither learning the native dialects nor teaching Spanish to the natives.   Don Juan advised that the number of missions should be reduced by consolidation, and that some of the Spanish settlements should be put under curates.   This being referred to the Franciscan provincial brought out from him a long reply, in which he denies the truth of all the charges, defends his friars, and impugns Ordenal's motives, accusing him of being merely the mouth-piece through which Governor Cachupin expressed his well-known hatred of the padres.[49]   The other report was one written by Padre Delgado, who had served 40 years at Isleta, and was now in Mexico, being called upon probably to write something that would counterbalance current charges against the friars; and the veteran missionary did so with a vengeance.   He

[48] *Güemes y Horcasitas, Medios para la pacificacion de los gentiles Cumanches. Decreto del virey 26 de Oct. 1746*, MS., in the Pinart col.   *Codallos y Rabal, Testimonio á la letra sobre Camanches, 1748*, MS., in *Arch. Sta Fé.*
[49] *N. Mex., Informe del R. P. Provincial al virey impugnando el que dió contra los misioneros de N. Mex. Don Juan de Ordenal y Maza, 1750*, in *N. Mex., Doc.*, MS., 1–99.   I have not seen Ordenal's report, but its substance is given in this.   There is not much of value in the reply; indeed, the writer's main position is that O.'s charges are general, vague, unsupported by evidence, and evidently the work of a man who had no authority, facilities, or ability to make an investigation—in fact, a superficial partisan report worthy of no reply, though he writes a long one.   It appears that there had been a controversy with the gov., who had claimed the right as vice-patrono to direct charges of friars from mission to mission.   Later, in the California missions, the right was recognized, and changes could not be made without the governor's consent.

represented the governors and alcaldes mayores of
New Mexico as brutal tyrants, who treated the natives
as slaves, forcing them to work without compensation,
or accomplishing the same result by appropriating the
products of their corn-fields, obliging the friars to keep
silent by refusing otherwise to sign the warrants by
which their sínodos were collected, and thus driving
the converts into apostasy, and effectually preventing
the conversion of gentiles. There are indications in
other correspondence that Delgado was more or less a
'crank'; and it is certain that in this instance he
overshot the mark; for, if true, his charges were in
reality almost as damning to the padres who submitted to these atrocities as to the officials who committed them. I have no doubt that the natives here
as elsewhere, and to a greater extent than in many
provinces, were the victims of oppression from Spanish officials, many of whom were bent on pecuniary
gain, and were favored by their isolated position; but
I find in the records nothing to support, and much to
contradict, the supposition that the rulers were for the
most part blood-thirsty brutes, practically sustained in
their rascalities by the Franciscans.[50]

[50] *Delgado (Cárlos), Informe que hizo el R. P. á N. R. P. Jimeno sobre las
execrables hostilidades y tiranías de los gobernadores y alcaldes mayores contra los
indios en consternacion de la custodia, año de 1750,* in *N. Mex., Doc.,* MS.,
99–128, dated March 27, '50, at Tlatelolco. The alcaldes are creatures of the
gov., appointed on condition of making all they can and dividing with the
gov. From each pueblo they take a squad of 30 or 40 Ind. to do all their
work of tilling the soil, making adobes, building, etc.; others are employed
to trade with gentiles and drive live-stock to Chihuahua, none receiving other
pay than an occasional handful of tobacco or glass beads. Those left at the
pueblos have to weave each year for their oppressors 400 *mantas* and 400
sábanas, besides tilling their own *milpas.* When harvest time comes they are
forced to transport nearly all their maize to the villas and sell it on credit,
the payment of worthless trinkets being in three instalments *tarde, mal, y
nunca.* The Ind. women are used for the gratification of lust. Once, in the
padre's presence, a woman came to upbraid the gov. for taking her daughter,
whereupon he gave her a buffalo-skin to make it all right. Any slight disobedience is punished by the stocks and flogging. In his visits to the gentiles
the padre has found apostates generally covered with scars and refusing to be
Christians again at such cost. On an unsupported charge of stealing 3 ears of
corn an Ind. was shot by orders of a capt. On a march 3 Ind. who were
footsore and could not keep up were killed and their children sold as slaves
for the commander's profit. For a somewhat similar and famous report from
Cal. in 1796, see *Hist. Cal.,* i. 587–97. P. Andrés Varo, who had been twice
custodio, came to Mex. in '49 and made a report. He was sent back for a 3d

The standard work of Villaseñor, published in 1748, and the manuscript report of Padre Menchero in 1744, contain some statistics and other general information on the condition of New Mexico about the middle of the century. Descriptive matter cannot be presented in the space at my command, but I append a statistical note. On population Villaseñor and Menchero agree in some points, but differ widely in others. Bonilla, however, gives a table of 1749 which agrees tolerably well with the general conclusions of the others. The Spanish population was 3,779—too small a figure, I think—and the number of Christian Indians 12,142, besides about 1,400 Spaniards and the same number of Indians at El Paso. This is Bonilla's statement. Villaseñor and Menchero give the population as 536 to 660 families of Spaniards, and 1,428 to 1,570 families of neophytes, besides 220 and 330 families in the district of El Paso. Mota Padilla's estimate of about 9,500 Spaniards in 1742 was an exaggeration. Of course, many of the so-called Spaniards were of mixed breed. I attach to the statistical note a chronologic list of governors from the beginning down to 1846.[51]

term, and was still living in '61, having come from Spain in '18. *Serrano, Informe*, MS., 176-7.

[51] *Menchero (Juan Miguel), Declaracion, 1744*, in *N. Mex., Doc.*, MS., 704-73; *Bonilla, Apuntes*, MS., 376-81; *Villaseñor, Teatro*, ii. 409-23. In *Span. Empire in America*, 89-94, is a slight descrip. of N. Mex. in '47. In what follows the figures in brackets are from Bonilla; those in parentheses from Menchero; the rest chiefly from Villaseñor.

Sta Fé, villa [965 Span., 570 Ind.], 300 (127) Span. fam. and a few Ind. under a curate (2 PP., *M.*). Sta Cruz de la Cañada, villa [1,205 Span., 580 Ind., including mission and ranchos], 260 (100) fam.; 1 padre; new church being built in '44. Alburquerque, villa, with suburb of Atrisco and mission [500 Span., 200 Ind.], 100 fam.; 1 padre. Concepcion, or Fuenclara, Span. settlement of 50 fam., under padre of Isleta. M. calls it Gracia Real or later Canadá, from the Canadians who settled here in '40; not mentioned by B. It was prob. the Tomé of '39. The following ranchos are named by M. and V., their pop. being included in B.'s figures: Chama, 17 fam., and Sta Rosa Abiquiú, or Rosa Hawicuii, 20 fam., under padre of S. Ildefonso; Ojo Caliente, 46 fam., and 4 other ranchos 10 fam., under padre of Taos; Soldedad, 40 fam., under padre of S. Juan, 7 l.; Embudo, 8 fam., under padre of Picuríes; Bocas, 10 fam., under padre of Sta Ana; and Alameda, 8 fam., under padre of Alburquerque. Few of these are named by V.

Missions, each with one padre, including some ranchos of Span.: Taos [125 Span., 541 Ind.], 80 (170) fam.; with an alcalde mayor; the mission of Jicarilla, 5 l. N., being abandoned in '44. Picuríes [64, 322], 80 fam. S. Juan [346, 404], 60 fam. Sta Cruz, included in La Cañada. S. Ildefonso and its

visita, Sta Clara [89, 631], 100 fam.   Tesuque and Pujuaque [507 Ind.], 50 and
18 (30) fam., both visitas of Sta Fé.   Nambé [100, 350], 50 fam.   Pecos (1,000
Ind.), 125 fam.; curate, *V.;* 2 padres, *M.;* fine church and convent.   Galisteo
[350 Ind.], 50 fam.; ranchos.   Cochití [25, 400], 85 (80) fam.; ranchos.   Sto
Domingo [300 Ind.], 50 (40) fam.   S. Felipe [70, 400]. 60 (70) fam.; ranchos.
Jemes [574 Ind.], 100 fam.   Sta Ana [100, 606], 50 fam.; on Rio Bernalillo.
Cia [100, 606], 50 fam.; 2 ranchos.   Laguna [401 Ind.], 60 fam.; 3 ranchos.
Acoma [750 Ind.], 110 fam.   Zuñi [2,000 Ind.], 150 fam.; 2 padres.   Isleta
[100, 250], 80 fam.   Sandía, not founded till '48, and not mentioned by M. or
N.   B. gives it a pop. of 400 Ind. in '49.

Tomé, or Valencia—called by V. Genízaros, made up of ill-treated neophytes—·is mentioned by M. as a settlement of 40 Ind. fam., who were captives of the Apaches and Comanches, sold to the Span., and released from
servitude by the gov. in '40 to form this visita of Isleta, being 2 l. s. of that
mission.   See note 39 of this chap. for origin of another Tomé.   The El Paso
establishments, presidio, and 5 missions, not included in the figures of my
text, included about 220 Span. fam. and 330 Ind. fam. [1,428 Span., 1,431
Ind. in '49. *Bonilla*].   Villaseñor tells us there were a few unprofitable and
abandoned mines in the country; the Ind. rode horseback and saluted the
Span. with 'Ave María'; the route up the river to Alburquerque was infested
with savages; and there was some trade via El Paso, where fairs were held.

In '48 P. Juan José Perez Mirabal was custodio; Man. Zambrano vice-cus-
todio and ex-visitador; Man. Sopeña discreto and min. of Sta Clara; Ant.
Gabaldon ex-visitador, discreto, and min. of Sta Cruz; Juan Ant. Ereiza
ex-vice-cust. at S. Ildefonso; Ant. Zamora at Nambé; Juan Martinez, sec.;
Toledo at Zuñi; Irigoyen at Alburquerque; and Delgado at Isleta. *Arch.
Sta Fé.*   Additional padres named by Menchero in the reports of '50, some
of them doubtful, were Andrés Varo, cust., Pedro Pino, Man. Bermejo, Mig.
Colluela, José Urquiros, José Tello, Marcelino Alburn, Ant. Roa, Fran. Con-
cepcion Gonzalez, Trigo, Guzman.

List of Span. and Mex. governors and captain-generals of N. Mex.:

Juan de Oñate, 1598–1608.

Pedro de Peralta, 1608–

Felipe Zotylo, (1621–8).

Manuel de Silva, 1629.

Fern. de Argüello, 1640 (?).

Luis de Rosas, 1641.

—— Valdés, (1642).

Alonso Pacheco de Heredia, 1643.

Fern. de Argüello, 1645.

Luis de Guzman, (1647).

Hernando de Ugarte y la Concha,
1650.

Juan de Samaniego, 1653–4.

Enrique de Ávila y Pacheco, 1656.

Bernardo Lcpez de Mendizábal, to
1661.

Diego de Peñalosa Briceño, 1661–4.

Fern. de Villanueva.

Juan de Medrano.

Juan de Miranda.

Juan Francisco de Treviño, 1675.

Antonio Otermin, 1679–83.

Domingo Jironza Petriz Cruzat, 1683
–6.

Pedro Reneros de Posada, 1686–9.

Domingo Jironza Petriz Cruzat, 1689
–91.

Diego de Vargas Zapata Lujan Ponce
de Leon, 1691–7.

Pedro Rodriguez Cubero, 1697–1703.

Diego de Vargas, etc., marqués de la
Nava de Brazinas, 1703–4.

Juan Paez Hurtado, acting, 1704–5.

Francisco Cuervo y Valdés, ad int.,
1705–7.

José Chacon Medina Salazar y Villaseñor, marqués de la Peñuela, 1707
–12.

Juan Ignacio Flores Mogollon, 1712–
15.

Félix Martinez, ad int., 1715–17.

Juan Paez Hurtado, acting, 1717.

Antonio Valverde y Cosío, ad int.,
1717–22.

Juan de Estrada y Austria (?), ad int.,
1721 (?).

Juan Domingo de Bustamante, 1722–
31.

Gervasio Cruzat y Góngora, 1731–6.

Enrique de Olavide y Michelena, ad
int., 1736–9.

Gaspar Domingo de Mendoza, 1739–
43.

Joaquin Codallos y Rabal. 1743–9.

Francisco de la Rocha (appt'd), 1747.

Tomás Velez Cachupin, 1749–54.

Francisco Antonio Marin del Valle,
1754–60.

Mateo Antonio de Mendoza, acting, 1760.
Manuel Portillo Urrisola, acting, 1761 –2.
Tomás Velez Cachupin, 1762–7.
Pedro Fermin de Mendinueta, 1767–78.
Francisco Trebol Navarro, acting, 1778.
Juan Bautista de Anza, 1778–89.
Manuel Flon (appt'd), 1785.
Fernando de la Concha, 1789–94.
Fernando Chacon, 1794–1805.
Joaquin del Real Alencaster, 1805–8.
Alberto Mainez, acting, 1807–8.
José Manrique, 1810–14.
Alberto Mainez, 1815–17.
Pedro María de Allande, 1816–18.
Facundo Melgares, 1818–22.
Francisco Javier Chavez, 1822–3.
Antonio Vizcarra, 1822–3.

Bartolomé Vaca, 1823–5.
Antonio Narbona, 1825–7.
Manuel Armijo, 1827–8.
Antonio Vizcarra, acting, 1828.
José Ant. Chavez, 1828–31.
Santiago Abreu, 1831–3.
Francisco Sarracino, 1833–5.
Juan Rafael Ortiz, acting, 1834.
Mariano Chavez, acting, 1835.
Albino Perez, 1835–7.
Pedro Muñoz, acting, 1837–8.
José Gonzalez, revolutionary gov., 1837–8.
Manuel Armijo, 1838–46.
Antonio Sandoval, acting, 1841.
Mariano Martinez de Lejanza, acting, 1844–5.
José Chavez, acting, 1845.
Juan Bautista Vigil y Alarid, acting, 1846.

CHAPTER XII.

SEQUENCE OF EVENTS—RULE OF CACHUPIN AND MARIN DEL VALLE—INDIAN CAMPAIGNS—MENDOZA AND URRISOLA—COMANCHES—CACHUPIN AGAIN—VISIT OF RUBÍ—FLOOD AT SANTA FÉ—REGLAMENTO DE PRESIDIOS—MOQUIS—ESCALANTE'S WRITINGS AND EXPLORATIONS—TOUR OF PADRE GARCÉS—BONILLA'S REPORT—PROVINCIAS INTERNAS—GOVERNOR ANZA—COMANCHE CAMPAIGN OF '79—THE MOQUI FAMINE AND PESTILENCE—FLON, CONCHA, AND CHACON—MORFI ON REFORM—FRIARS VERSUS GOVERNOR—THE MISSION SYSTEM—CONSOLIDATION OF MISSIONS—SECULARIZATION—COLLEGE—LIST OF PADRES—INDUSTRIES OF THE PROVINCE—AGRICULTURE — STOCK-RAISING— TRADE OR BARTER — ANNUAL FAIRS AT TAOS AND CHIHUAHUA—IMAGINARY MONEY—COMMERCIAL EVILS—STATISTICS OF POPULATION AND LOCAL ITEMS.

EXISTING records for these fifty years are much more voluminous, and in several important respects more satisfactory, than for the preceding half-century. They include several general reports of secular and missionary authorities, with statistical information that is comparatively complete. They throw much light on the mission system, on the condition of the pueblo Indians, on the Franciscan friars and their controversy with governor and alcaldes mayores, on the commerce and other industries of the province; but these and other general topics will be detached from the chronologic narrative and presented in a later part of this chapter. As to the series of happenings from year to year—the succession of rulers, campaigns against the various gentile tribes, the never-ending question of Moqui conversion, and occasional complaints of impending ruin, with corresponding projects by which it might be averted—both events and the record are as before somewhat fragmentary and meagre, though there is little reason to fear that any momentous occurrence has been buried in oblivion.

Governor Cachupin marched against the Comanches in 1751, setting fire to a *tular* into which he had driven 145 of the foe, killing 101 and capturing the rest.[1] This elicited commendation from the viceroy and was reported to the king. It may be well, however, to bear in mind that according to the friars, who were particularly bitter against Cachupin, the governor's reports of Indian campaigns had often no foundation in fact. At the end of his five years' term in 1754, Don Tomás was succeeded by Don Francisco Antonio Marin del Valle, who perhaps served ad interim by the viceroy's appointment,[2] and who was also cordially hated by the padres. In 1755 Padre Rodriguez de la Torre, with a small party of neophytes, visited the Moqui towns, being well received and permitted to preach; but whenever the masses showed any sign of yielding to his persuasions a 'cacique endemoniado' would rise to talk on the other side. The padres were good men, he said, but his people were too sensible and strong to become slaves of the alcaldes.[3]

[1] *Arch. Sta Fé*, MS. The Comanches had raided Galisteo. Gov. C. had 164 men, of whom only one was killed. Forty of the captives were released with the women and children, but 4 were held as hostages for the return of earlier prisoners. In 1752 the Cosninas, 30 l. from Moqui, 10,000 souls in 11 rancherías are said to have asked through P. Menchero for Christian instruction. *Id.*

[2] He signs a doc. as 'gobernador político y militar' on Nov. 26, 1754. *Arch. Sta Fé.* I think he was regularly appointed by the king. Davis and Prince name him as acting gov. in 1761–2, which I think is an error. Acc. to Prince, Gov. Marin and wife presented the great carved stone reredos, or altar screen, in the Sta Fé cathedral.

[3] *Rodriguez de la Torre (Mariano), Entrada en la prov. de los Moquinos 1755*, MS., written in '70. In *N. Mex., Doc.*, MS., 842–53. He remained 14 days. A curious story heard by him was that the Moquis had a board on which they had made one mark each year since the revolt of 1680; when the board was covered with marks, then would they submit to Christianity. A MS., *Dominguez (Atanasio), Exped. lá a Prov. de Moqui* in '55 is cited in *Fernandez Duro, Not.*, 138, as in the Acad. de Hist.; but I suppose the date should be '75. In '56–7 Bernardo Miera y Pacheco obtained permission to remelt the old useless cannon and make new ones. It was not his trade, but he thought he could do no harm by trying. He was then alcalde mayor of Pecos and Galisteo. The result is not recorded. MS. in Pinart col.

The leading event of Valle's rule was the visit of Bishop Tamaron of Durango, who at the different settlements confirmed 11,271 persons, besides 2,973 in the district of El Paso. The visita was from April to July of 1760, and met no opposition on the part of the missionaries.[4] Later in the same year Mateo Antonio de Mendoza acted as governor for a few months, and in 1761–2 the position was held by Manuel Portillo Urrisola.[5] Don Manuel distinguished himself, if we take his word for it, by killing 400 Comanches in a fight at Taos in December 1761.[6] The governor had hoped that this victory would settle the Comanche question and strike terror to all gentile raiders; but was disappointed at finding his successor averse to energetic and warlike methods, and the country consequently not yet saved.

That successor, who took command on the 1st of February, 1762, was no other that Cachupin, who, despite the bitter opposition of the Franciscans, had been appointed by the king for a new term.[7] During

[4] *Tamaron (Pedro), Visita del Obispo de Durango 1759–63*, MS., p. 123–53, 160–1. There were 64 in the party from El Paso in Apr., including the P. custodio and a guard of 22 men. The bishop's carriage was once overturned, but he fell on top of the custodio and was not hurt! At Pecos, as elsewhere, there was a grand ceremonial reception, which an Indian a little later proceeded to burlesque, playing himself the part of bishop; whereupon to punish his impious conduct a bear came down from the mountains and chewed up his head in a fatally effective manner. On the return the season was so wet that water was found even in the Jornarda del Muerto.

[5] Mendoza is named only by P. Serrano, *Informe*, MS., 266, 269, writing in '61, who says he ceased to rule in Dec. '60 or Jan. '61. His successor in a MS. of the Pinart col. is called Francisco Portilla. Serrano, 276, notes the almost complete dispersion of mission Ind. of the El Paso estab. in '60–1.

[6] In Aug. '60 the Comanches made a raid on Taos, and attacking the people who had taken refuge in the house of one Villalpando, killed all the men and carried off 50 women, though losing 49 of their own force. Gov. Valle pursued them 200 l. in 40 days, but accomplished nothing. *Tamaron, Visita,* MS., 141. The sequel is told in a letter of Urrisola to the bishop, dated Feb. 24, '62, in *Id.*, 141–4. In Aug. '61 the Ind. came back to trade as if nothing unusual had occurred, but were not admitted. They returned again in Dec. in large force to insist on the privilege of trading, even offering to give up 7 of their captives. Gov. U. with 80 men hastened to Taos, and engaged in complicated negotiations and wrangles with the warlike traders, whose independence and insolence soon resulted in a fight, with the result as given in my text. During the battle, however, the Yutas took advantage of the opportunity to drive off 1,000 horses! I have not much faith in the accuracy of this report, and suspect that the gov. may have been an embustero.

[7] Appointment March 5, 1761, with orders to the viceroy to put C. in pos-

this second rule of five years Don Tomás sent a party to search for mines in the San Juan and Gunnison regions of what was later Colorado,[8] attended to the routine duties of his position,[9] and waged legal warfare on certain Indians accused of witchcraft at Abiquiú, the whole affair presenting a striking picture of silly superstition—on the part of the Spaniards.[10] In 1766 the Marqués de Rubí visited New Mexico in his tour as inspector of frontier presidios.[11]

Colonel Pedro Fermin de Mendinueta succeeded Cachupin as governor and captain-general—being the last to hold the latter title—in 1767.[12] In that year

session of the office without delay, 'con pretexto ni motivo alguno.' On Aug. 30, '62, the king has rec'd viceroy's report of Dec. 17, '61, with copy of secret instructions to Gov. C. *N. Mex., Céd.*, MS., 56. At the time of Urrisola's Comanche campaign an escort of 22 soldiers had been sent to El Paso for the new gov. *Tamaron, Visita*, MS., 141–4.

[8] *Dominguez* and *Escalante, Diario*, 388–9, 409–10. Acc. to this printed diary of an entrada of 1776, Juan María Rivera visited the region (about the junction of the Gunnison and Uncompahgre) in 1761; it was visited by a party sent by Gov. C., and the name of La Plata given to a sierra and river, from silver discovered at that time; and perhaps a 3d visit made in 1775. But Fernandez Duro, *Noticias*, 139, 142, who consulted a MS. copy of the diary in the Acad. Hist., makes the date of Rivera's tour 1765. Dominguez saw Rivera's *derrotero*.

[9] In '62 some 50 citizens of Alburquerque protest their inability to comply with the gov.'s orders to keep horses, etc., in readiness for Ind. service; and in May are chided by the gov. for their lack of patriotism. They must obey and stop selling their arms and animals to avoid service. In 1763, 40 citizens of the same town petitioned for the removal of their alcalde mayor, Ant. Vaca, and 33 other citizens protested that V. was a good official, though the object of the enmity of a few. To keep the peace Mig. Lucero was appointed temporarily to fill the office. MSS. of Pinart col.

[10] *Autos contra unos Indios Jenízaros del pueblo de Abiquiú sobre ser acusados de hechiceros maléficos por su ministro el R. P. Fr. Juan Joseph de Toledo y el indio Juachinillo.* MS. of the Pinart col. The case dated in 1760–6, but the trial was chiefly in 1763. One effect of the alleged sorcery was a sad condition of the padre's stomach. The trial was before the alc. mayor of La Cañada, Cárlos Fernandez, and over 100 pp. are filled with testimony. The result was that 7 or 8 Ind. were condemned to 'become the servants' of certain Span. families. A detachment of troops was sent to Abiquiú to destroy relics of supposed idolatrous worship, including a stone with hieroglyphics, etc.

[11] *Lafora (Nicolás), Viage del ingeniero á Sta Fé, 1766.* MS. in Pinart col. L. accompanied Rubí and kept the diary, which contains little or nothing of interest except statistics utilized later. L. also made a map, which so far as I know is not extant.

[12] Morfi, *Desórdenes*, MS., 407, writes the full name Lara y Mendinueta, and calls him brigadier. Davis and Prince represent him as ruling also in 1759 and 1762, and Cachupin in 1773, all of which must, I think, be wrong. They mention the fact of his being the last capt.-gen.; and certainly no one had that title after him; but I am not quite sure that all his predecessors held it, and I have seen no doc. in which he uses that title. M. was a knight of Santiago.

there was a great flood at Santa Fé in October, the course of the river being turned into the Rio Chiquito and threatening the safety of the public buildings.[13] Against this ruler and his successors I have found no complaints from the missionaries. In 1771 he announced the conclusion of a treaty with the Comanches on the 3d of February;[14] and the viceroy, replying with thanks, called for a report on the condition and needs of the province, which was furnished in March 1772. Mendinueta declared that the force of 80 soldiers at Santa Fé was not sufficient to protect so broad a territory, raided by savage foes from every side. True, there were about 250 men capable of bearing arms among the settlers, besides the pueblo Indians; but these were poorly supplied with weapons, and could not leave their homes unprotected to engage in distant campaigns. The governor's proposed remedy was a new presidio at Taos, and an enforced law requiring the Spaniards to live in compact pueblos like the Indians.[15]

The subject of northern frontier defences received much attention in these years, and in 1772–3 the new *reglamento de presidios* was published. The only change ordered in New Mexico proper was the detachment of thirty soldiers from Santa Fé to join thirty citizen auxiliaries from El Paso, forming a garrison at Robledo, which was to protect the route up the river and serve as a base for reëstablishing the ruined pueblos of Senecú, Socorro, Alamillo, and Sevilleta. For the protection of El Paso the militia was to be organized, the presidial company being transferred to Carrizal on the frontier of Nueva Viz-

---

[13] *Sta Fé, Inundaciones de 1767*. MS. of Pinart col. The gov. in decree of Nov. 7th orders all citizens to turn out by list under certain superintendents and work to restore the river to its original bed. Fran. Guerrero was alcalde mayor. July 15, '69, orders of viceroy to gov. M. about a projected campaign against the Apaches. MS. in *Id.*

[14] April 25, '71, Gov. M. to the people, announcing the treaty, and urging all to use the utmost care to treat the Ind. in exact conformity with the conditions. MS. in Pinart col.

[15] March 26, 1772, Gov. M. to Viceroy Bucareli, in *Doc. Hist. Mex.*, 3d ser., iv. 720–3; *Bonilla, Apuntes*, MS., 352–6.

caya.[16]   Nothing of all this was carried into effect, except the transfer of the presidio—or of the main force, a detachment being always or generally stationed at El Paso—the governor very properly protesting against the division of the force at Santa Fé, and some convenient excuse being always ready for failure to organize the militia.

The conquest or conversion of the Moquis was a matter still kept in view, though for about twenty years no practical efforts in that direction are recorded, down to 1774–6, when the project was revived in connection with the California expeditions from Sonora. Captain Juan Bautista de Anza made an experimental or exploring trip by way of the Gila to California in 1774; and it was desired that in connection with his second expedition the region between the Gila and Moqui towns should be explored. This region had not been traversed since the time of Coronado in 1540–3, except by Oñate, whose journey was practically forgotten. The country and its people were wrapped in mystery, and were the objects of much curiosity and theorizing. To find a way to Moqui was deemed important, especially as it was proposed, if possible, to occupy the Gila valley and some of its branches.[17]   The New Mexican friars were called

[16] *Presidios, Reglamento é Instruccion 1772-3*, p. 11, 16–18, 118–22; given also in whole or in part in several works. See *Hist. North Mex. St.*, i. 646, 668. The Sta Fé presidio as reorganized was to have 1 capt. (the gov.) at a salary of $4,000, 2 lieut. at $700, 2 sergt. at $350, 6 corp. at $300, and 68 sold. at $290; there was to be a lieut.-gov. at El Paso, with a salary of $1,000, and the 30 vecinos auxiliaries at Robledo were to receive $15 per month for 10 years, to be armed like soldiers, to be free from cuartel duty, and finally to have land-grants. Bonilla, *Apuntes*, MS., gives some particulars about the non-execution of the reglamento and the orders following it. Antonio María Daroca was made lieut.-gov., but died soon from wounds received in an Apache campaign; and was succeeded by Manuel Arrieta, and he by Narciso Muñiz.

[17] *Crespo* (*Fran. Ant.*), *Informe que hizo al virey el gobr. de Sonora acerca del descubrimiento de N. Mex. para Monterey*, in *N. Mex., Doc.*, MS., 802–23. The details pertain to Ariz. rather than N. Mex. The writer proposes a branch exped., after Anza's return from Cal., to the Colorado, that is, from the Mojave region to Moqui and N. Mex. This doc. is cited under a different title by Fernandez Duro, *Not.*, 141, as in the Acad. Hist. He also cites *Garcés, Diario desde N. Mej., á la Cal.*, which may be a ref. to Garcés' journal of Anza's 1st trip, or of G.'s trip of '76 to N. Mex., to be noticed later. On Anza's exped. of '74 and '76, see *Hist. Cal.*, i. 220–4, 257–78.

upon for their views, and Padre Escalante developed much enthusiasm on the subject. In June 1775, or possibly 1774, he spent eight days in the Moqui towns, trying in vain to reach the Rio Grande de Cosninas beyond. In a report to the governor he gave a description of the pueblos—where he found 7,494 souls, two thirds of them at Oraibe, in seven pueblos on three separate mesas—and his ideas of what should be done. He earnestly recommended—subsequently writing to his superior a long argument in support of his position —that the Moquis should be reduced by force of arms and a presidio established there. The Moquinos, he said, were well disposed, but their chiefs had determined not to give up their power, not only keeping their own people from submission, but the Cosninas as well, who were eager to be Christians. As to the routes, Escalante thought from what he could learn by Indian reports that the way from Terrenate by the Gila and thence north to Zuñi would not be very difficult; that the central route from the Colorado to Moqui would probably be found impracticable; but that the best of all was one leading from Monterey eastward in a nearly direct line to Santa Fé.[18]

Alas for the good padre's geographic theories! In 1776, with a party of nine, including Padre Francisco Atanasio Dominguez, he attempted to reach Monterey from Santa Fé by the northern route. This tour belongs mainly to the annals of Utah and Colorado, as recorded in other volumes. The explorers reached Utah Lake and thus accomplished results that should make their names famous; but fortunately—else they would not have lived to tell the story—when on the approach of winter provisions became scarce and the

[18] *Escalante (Silvestre Velez), Informe y Diario de la Entrada que en junio de 1775 hizo en la prov. de Moqui.* MS., in *N. Mex., Doc.*, 1022–57; also without title in *Id.*, 951–84. It is dated Oct. 28, 1775. The author has heard of some white men in the west before the founding of Monterey, and thus introduces the Northern Mystery, shipwrecked Spaniards, etc. Garcés, *Diario*, 362–4, alludes to a similar report—perhaps the same—written by Escalante on Aug. 18, 1775. *Escalante, Carta de '76 sobre Moqui*, in *N. Mex., Doc.*, MS., 985–1013, is the argument alluded to in my text to prove the justice and policy of using force.

natives showed no knowledge of Spaniards in the west, lots were cast, and fate decided that the journey to Monterey should be postponed. Accordingly, they returned south-eastward, forded the Colorado, came to the Moqui towns, and returned to Santa Fé. The Moquinos, though furnishing food and shelter, would not receive presents. A meeting was held to discuss submission, but while willing to be friends of the Spaniards, the people proudly refused to be subjects or Christians, preferring to 'go with the majority' and be gentiles, as the traditions of their fathers directed them.[19]   Not only did Escalante fail to demonstrate the merits of his favorite northern route, but earlier in the same year the central one was proved to be practicable; and this, so far as the Moqui question was concerned, was the only result of Anza's California expedition. Padre Francisco Garcés, leaving Anza at the Gila junction, went up the Colorado to the Mojave region with a few Indian servants, and after making important explorations in California started eastward for Moqui, which he reached without any special difficulty in July. The Moquis, however, would not admit him to their houses or receive his gifts, cared not for his painting of heaven and hell, and refused to kiss the image of Christ. After passing two nights in the court-yard he wrote a letter for the padre at Zuñi, returned in sorrow to the Yamajabs, or Mojaves, and went down the Colorado, finding his way to Bac in September. His was a wonderful trip, though not very effective in respect of Moqui salvation.[20]

[19] *Dominguez* and *Escalante, Diario y Derrotero,* 1776; also incomplete MS. copy in *N. Mex., Doc.,* 1729–56; and in *Id.,* 831–42, a letter of Dominguez in '80, giving a résumé of the trip.   See also *Hist. Utah* and *Hist. Colorado,* this series, with map.   The start was on July 29th, the arrival at Moqui Nov. 16th, and the return to Sta Fé Jan. 3, '77.   The Colorado was forded about on the Utah and Ariz. line, or at the corner of the four territories.

[20] *Garcés (Francisco), Diario y Derrotero que siguió...á los pueblos del Moqui de N. Mex., 1776.*   In *Doc. Hist. Mex.,* 2d ser., i. 225 et seq., the Moqui trip being described on pp. 309–37.   For some additional details, see chap. xvi. of this vol. on Ariz. history.   The padre visited Oraibe, or Muca, and one other pueblo, and he gives a good descrip. of the towns and people.   He found a

It was in 1776 that Lieutenant-colonel Antonio Bonilla, of Coahuila, embodied in a formal report, not only a résumé of New Mexico's past history, but his views as to what should be done to avert impending ruin. He believed that as a frontier outpost among gentile tribes who had now lost all the fear and respect inspired by the first conquerors, and who themselves used fire-arms and horses, the holding of the province had an importance far beyond its direct value as a Spanish possession, since if it were lost the savage hordes would direct their whole force against Nueva Vizcaya and Sonora. Therefore a vigorous warfare should be waged by veteran troops from New Mexico as a centre.[21]

It was also in 1776–7 that the northern provinces of Mexico were organized as the Provincias Internas, under the Caballero de Croix as comandante general, independent of the viceroy. This change and the following complications of the military and civil status of the various districts have but slight direct bearing on New Mexico, simply depriving the governor of his title of captain-general, and making him subordinate at times to the comandante general instead of the viceroy, and they cannot be properly presented here in the

Zuñi Ind. who could speak Spanish, as could some of the Moquis. His letter to the Zuñi padre of July 3d is copied in *N. Mex., Doc.*, MS., 828–30. It does not appear that Escalante received it before starting on his northern trip. In *Fernandez Duro, Not.*, 141, is cited a letter. *Garcés, Exped. desde Sta Fé á Cal.*, etc., in the Acad. Hist.

[21] *Bonilla (Antonio), Apuntes Históricos sobre el N. Mex., 1776*, MS. in *N. Mex., Doc.*, 327–81; also as a preface to *N. Mex., Cédulas*, MS. Besides the sending of veteran troops, B. recommends as necessary measures the reformation of Span. settlements in compact form, the organization of the militia, a garrison at Robledo without reducing the Sta Fé force, the execution of existing orders respecting the Paso del Norte district, and more careful treatment of the Christian Ind., perhaps including measures of secularization to get rid of the friars. B. did not favor the presidio at Taos, because he thought it better to spend money at present on active measures rather than on permanent establishments.

Morfi, Viaje de Indios y Diario del N. Mex., is misleading in its title. It is a diary of the visita of the Caballero de Croix in '77, but does not include N. Mex., at least as printed in *Doc. Hist. Mex.*, 3d ser., iv. 305. In Nov. '77 there was a fight with the Comanches and Apaches, who in one of their raids had killed 11 persons, and who now lost 30 killed and 40 horses. The gov. was ordered to make peace, if possible, with the Comanches, so as to use them against the Apaches. *Arch. Sta Fé*, MS.; MSS. in Pinart col.

space at my command; yet, as they are in a general
sense an essential part of the history of all the northern
regions, I refer the reader to the annals of Nueva Vizcaya and Sonora in the last quarter of the century, as
compactly presented in another volume of this series.[22]

Governor Mendinueta retired in March 1778, leaving Francisco Trebol Navarro in command as acting
governor;[23] but before the end of the year a successor
came, in the person of Lieutenant-colonel Juan Bautista
de Anza, as political and military governor.[24] Anza,
whose Californian expeditions have been noticed, was
a native of Sonora, a man of excellent ability and
character, and of wide experience in Indian warfare.
He seems to have proved in every way worthy of the
Caballero de Croix's high esteem; yet with all his
energy he effected but slight change for the better in
New Mexican affairs.   His first recorded enterprise
was a campaign against the Comanches with a force
of 645 men, including 85 soldiers and 259 Indians.
His course was north and north-east for some 95
leagues, and the result was the killing of Cuerno Verde,
the famous Comanche chieftain, with four of his leading sub-chiefs, his high-priest, his eldest son and heir,
and 32 of his warriors.[25]

[22] See *Hist. North Mex. States*, i. 636–91.

[23] March 14, '78, Gov. Mendinueta's instruc. to his successor. MS. in the
Pinart col.   Ind. affairs and care of the presidio horses demand chief attention.   There is no use in pursuing Ind., unless there is a possibility of catching them.   Pecos and Galisteo as frontier posts require special care.   The
Yutas have been at peace, and pains should be taken to keep them so, no attention being paid to petty offences.   The Navajos are at peace, but are said
to join the Gileño Apaches in raids.   No peace should be made with the
Apaches, but always war.   The Comanches should be drawn to peace, but
never trusted, for their custom is to be at peace with Taos and at war with
other parts.   In the *Arch. Sta Fé*, MS., and Pinart col. are several minor
commun. of Croix and Rubio to the gov. on details of Ind. policy.   In the
same year P. Escalante writes very sensibly on Teguayo, which is the Yuta
country, shown by ruins and pottery to have been once the home of pueblo
Ind., the stories of white bearded men in the N. w. being proven false by E.'s
late trip; also on Quivira, which is nothing more wonderful than the Panana,
or Pawnee villages. *Doc. Hist. Mex.*, 3d ser., iv. 124–6; *Fernandez Duro, Not.*,
146–7.

[24] Anza was appointed in June '77. *Cédulario*, MS., iii. 9.   The date of his
arrival does not appear; but he signs orders in Jan. and Feb. '79. *Arch. Sta
Fé*, MS.   One doc. seems to show him in com. in June '78.   Davis and Prince
make his rule begin in '80.

[25] *Anza (Juan B.), Diario de la Expedicion que sale á practicar contra la na-*

Back from this campaign, Governor Anza gave his attention to the Moquis. A failure of crops had reduced that people to such straits that the time was deemed most favorable for their conversion, even Christianity being perhaps preferable to starvation. Many of them were said to have abandoned their towns to seek food in the mountains and among the Navajos, and these fugitives were reported as disposed to submit, though the others still preferred death. It was feared that if something were not done now all the Moquis might quit pueblo life and join the hostile gentiles. Anza wrote repeatedly to Croix on the prospects, enclosing letters from the padres, and advising that an effort should be made either to establish missionaries at the towns, which would require some additional force, or to induce the natives to migrate en masse and settle in new pueblos nearer the Spanish centres.[26] In reply, the comandante general did not favor the use of force, but advised that Anza on some pretext, as of an Apache campaign, should visit the Moquis, give them some food, and persuade them, if possible, to settle in New Mexico; otherwise the foundation might be laid for future conversion. The governor continued his efforts, and in August 1780 a message came that 40 families were ready to migrate if he would come in person to bring them. He started in September with padres Fernandez and García, vis-

cion Comancha, 1779, MS. In N. Mex., Doc., 861–922, preceded by Anza's letter of Nov. 1st and Croix's letter of thanks Jan. 1, '80. The campaign was in Aug.–Sept. '79; 200 Yutas and Apaches joined the army as allies on the way; 30 women and children with 500 horses were captured. Names on the way and return above Taos, are Paso de S. Bartolomé on the Rio del Norte, 15 l. from its source, Ciénega de S. Luis, Arroyo de S. Ginés, Aguage de Yutas, Rio S. Agustin, Lomas Perdidas, Rio Sta Rosa, Sierra de Almagre, Arr. de Cristo, Rio Dolores, Rio Culebra, and Rio Ductil.

[26] Moqui, Providencias tomadas á consecuencia de los avisos comunicados por Anza, 1779, in N. Mex., Doc., MS., 922–1022. Letters of Anza to Croix, Nov. 1st, 13th, with a letter of P. Andrés García, who had made some vain efforts to find the Moqui fugitives among the Navajos; also Escalante's letters, already noticed, and Croix's reply of Dec. 31st.

In connection with Anza's operations, Bernardo Miera y Pacheco, the same who had tried to manufacture cannon, and a member of the exploring party of Dominguez and Escalante, made two maps, covering all the settlements of N. Mex. in '79, which are preserved in the Acad. Hist. at Madrid, but which I have not seen. Fernandez Duro, Not., 143.

iting all the towns, two of which were completely abandoned. The 40 families had been forced by hunger 15 days ago to go to the Navajo country, where the men had been killed and the women and children seized as slaves. Moqui affairs were indeed in a sad condition. Escalante in 1775 had found 7,494 souls; now there were but 798; no rain had fallen in three years, and in that time deaths had numbered 6,698. Of 30,000 sheep 300 remained, and there were but five horses and no cattle. Only 500 fanegas of maize and beans could be expected from the coming crop. Pestilence had aided famine in the deadly work; raids from the Yutas and Navajos had never ceased. There were those who believed their misfortunes a judgment for their treatment of Padre Garcés in 1776. The chief at Oraibe was offered a load of provisions to relieve immediate wants, but he proudly declined the gift, as he had nothing to offer in return. He refused to listen to the friars, and in reply to Anza's exhortations declared that as his nation was apparently doomed to annihilation, the few who remained were resolved to die in their homes and in their own faith. Yet his subjects were free to go and become Christians if they chose to do so; and finally 30 families were induced to depart with the Spaniards, including the chief of Gualpi.[27] I find no record as to what became of these converts, but I have an idea that with them and others, a little later, the pueblo of Moquino, in the Laguna region, may have been founded.

Not only among the Moquis did pestilence rage, but small-pox carried off 5,025 Indians of the mission pueblos in 1780–1; and in consequence of this loss of population, Governor Anza, by consolidation, reduced the number of missions, or of sínodos, to 20, a change which for the next decade provoked much protest on

---

[27] *Anza, Diario de la expedicion que hace á la provincia de Moqui, 1780.* Orig. MS. in the Pinart col. The start was on Sept. 10th from Sta Fé, Zuñi 17th, Moqui 20–4th, back at Sta Fé Oct. 1st.

the part of the friars.[28] Pino, followed by other authors, gives 1783 as the date of a long effective treaty with the Comanches; but as he mentions the defeat of Cuerno Verde in the same connection, this may be a reference to an earlier event.[29] In 1786 Viceroy Galvez, in his instructions to General Ugarte, introduced a new Indian policy in the north, a policy of extermination, the main features of which were to be unrelenting warfare on all tribes to secure treaties, free trade and gifts to tribes at peace, the creation among the savages of needs that could be supplied only by the Spaniards, the distribution of guns and powder of inferior quality, the liberal use of spirituous liquors to demoralize the Apaches, and constant efforts to promote a war of extermination between the different tribes. Little or nothing appears respecting the carrying-out of this policy in New Mexico; but the instructions in some parts had special reference to that province.[30]

[28] Anza's report of May 6, '81. *Arch. Sta Fé*, MS.; *Revilla Gigedo, Carta de 1793*, p. 443.

[29] *Pino, Exposicion*, 39, 43; *Id., Noticias*, 87–8; *Velasco, Not. Estad. de Son.*, 262; *Davis' El Gringo*, 82. Yet a mention of the campaign appears in the *Gaceta de Mex.*, i. 131–2. It may be that a treaty was made in '83 in consequence of the victory of '79. Davis, *El Gringo*, 82–3, also describes a later battle of '85 with the Comanches at Rabbit Ear, the Span. leader being Lieut. Guerrero, and the foe being so effectually defeated that they sued for peace and made a permanent treaty. I have found no original record of this affair.

[30] *Instruccion formada en virtud de real órden, 1786*. See also *Hist. North Mex. States*, i. 648. The N. Mex. troops were to be aided by settlers and Ind.; movements were to be made, when possible, in conjunction with forces of N. Viz. and Sonora; all to be directed by the gov.; hostilities between Apaches and Navajos to be promoted; the peace with Yutas to be scrupulously observed, and they to be used against the others; also peace with the Jicarillas; Comanche offers of peace at Taos not to be rejected, but encouraged by trade; a report on the Moqui condition to be made. Oct. 6th, Gen. Ugarte to Anza, will devote $6,000 a year to the task of defeating the Gileños and keeping peace with the Comanches, Yutas, and Navajos. Four hundred horses and a large amount of stores were sent at the beginning of the year. A salary to be paid the Com. chiefs for their services. Oct. 25th, he complains that certain Navajos aided the Gileños in an attack on Arizpe. Jan. 17, 1787, Anza says that gentle measures with the Moquis have been successful and should be continued. Over 200 are content in their new homes. June 13, 1789, Ugarte orders active operations against the Apaches during the rest of the year, with Comanche aid. July 4th, gov. reports a campaign in May, in which he killed 6 Apaches. Against orders he has consented to a truce with the Apaches at Tecolote who promise well, and will be watched, MSS. in Pinart col. Navajos reduced to peace in '88. *Escudero, Not. Chih.*, 227. Ind. of N. Mex. at peace June '88, acc. to viceroy's report. *Cavo.*

Lieutenant-colonel Manuel Flon came from Spain in 1785 with a commission as governor, and started for New Mexico; but there are no indications that he ever assumed the office.[31]   Anza's successor was Fernando de la Concha, who arrived after the middle of 1789, and ruled for a full term of five years.[32]   Concha was succeeded in 1794 by Lieutenant-colonel Fernando Chacon, whose rule continued to the end of the century and later.[33]   For the last years of the period I find many items in the archives; but nearly all are of so trivial and unimportant a nature that they are not worth reproduction.   They relate almost exclusively to Indian affairs, and seem to indicate that all the tribes were behaving tolerably well, except the Apaches, against whom constant warfare was waged, with results not clearly shown by the records.[34]

Evidently not much had been effected in the way of general reform; for in the last decade we have from the pen of Padre Juan Agustin Morfi, not one of the

Tres Siglos, iii. 77.   About '90 a Comanche chief, Maya, put his son at school in Sta Fé under Lieut. Troncoso.   The son later became chief and a firm friend of the Spans. *Pino, Expo.*, 38.

[31] *Gomez, Diario*, 214–16; *Arch. Cal., Prov. St. Pap.*, MS., v. 181.   Flon's wife was a sister of the vireina; and he was later prominent in Mex.

[32] Aug. 10, '89, Gen. Rengel notifies Anza from El Paso that Concha is on the way to succeed him. *Arch. Sta Fé*, MS.   Davis and Prince make his rule '88–93, and again in 1800.   He was prob. appointed in '88.

[33] July 21, 1794, Gen. Nava notified the lieut.-gov. at El Paso of Chacon's appointment and coming. *Arch. Sta Fé*, MS.

[34] In May 1793 there was a suspicious meeting of the Ind. at S. Ildefonso, leading to some arrests and long investigations.   Nothing definite was proven, though half a dozen Ind. were flogged or condemned to several months in chains. *Arch. Sta Fé*, MS.   Lieut. Fran. Javier de Uranga is named as lieut.-gov. at El Paso in 1794. *Id.*   In Aug. 1795 Gen. Nava ordered a gen. movement from Chih., Coahuila, and N. Mex. against the Apaches, to be made in Sept.–Nov. and again in the spring; no *gandules* to be spared.   MS. of Pinart col.   In July 1795 Gov. Chacon reports the Navajos as friendly to Span., foes to the Apaches, occupied in agric., fond of wearing jewelry and speaking Span.—yet a spy is always kept among them to watch and report their plans. *Arch. Sta Fé*, MS.   In Aug. Gen. Nava complains that of five Ind. killed the ears were not brought in as proofs, 'que es la práctica que se observa en esta provincia.' *Id.*   Lieut. Cañuelas sent with 160 men against Apaches, who had raided Alburquerque. *Id.*   In '96 the gov.'s inspection of Abiquiú and Sandía is preserved, mere formality, nothing of importance. *Id.*   In May 1800 the gov. and 500 men made a campaign against the Apaches Navajos (?), 20 chiefs appearing to make peace, giving up 28 animals.   Another exped. of Lieut. José Manrique with 250 men to the sierras of S. Mateo and Magdalena recovered two animals.   Gen. Nava in July complains that so little has been effected. MS. of Pinart col.

New Mexican friars, an able presentment of the country's ills similar to those alluded to by earlier writers. Chief among the evils to be remedied were the lack of order in Spanish settlements, the houses being scattered, and the settlers beyond the reach of law and religion, besides being exposed to Indian raids; a vicious system of trade, and absence of money, of which more will be said presently; the free admission of Spaniards and *castas* to live in the Indian pueblos, these penniless intruders generally succeeding in making the industrious native proprietors practically slaves through debt, or in driving them away to live among the gentiles, the remedy being to forbid the Spaniards to live in the pueblos or own property in them except by marriage;[35] the oppressive tyranny of the alcaldes mayores, more fully noticed elsewhere in this chapter; and finally the unsettled and unfortunate status of the Genízaros, or rescued Indian captives.[36]

Before 1750, as recorded in the preceding chapter, the padres were charged by secular and ecclesiastic authorities with culpable neglect of their duties as missionaries, notably in their failure to acquire the native languages, or to speak Spanish to the Indians, the result being that their preaching and religious instruction had no real effect, that the neophytes were Christians only in name, and that confession of sins through interpreters was generally postponed until the approach of death. While this matter did not in this half-century assume a controversial aspect, yet the charges are sustained by such evidence as exists. Bishop Tamaron in his visit of 1760 had occasion at many points to administer severe reproof; and the

[35] A mulatto felt insulted because a pueblo Ind. wished to marry his daughter! This absurd pride of the castas and their assumed superiority over the natives should be discouraged. Ind. should not be allowed to sell or mortgage their lands. The laws on these matters are not observed.

[36] *Morfi* (*Juan Agustin*), *Desórdenes que se advierten en el N. Mex. y medios que se juzgan oportunos para mejorar su constitucion* (*1792*). MS. in *N. Mex., Doc.*, 381–450. P. Morfi declares that the New Mexicans are much worse off than before the coming of the Span. or than the Moquis who have retained their independence.

friars, while making various excuses for their remissness, denying some of its worst results, and even promising reforms, did not claim the ability to communicate with their neophytes, except through interpreters. Charges of neglect in other matters, of oppressing the natives, of being frequently absent from their posts, and of undue fondness for trade are not supported by any evidence of this period.[37]

It should be noted that the New Mexican missions were radically different from the Californian establishments of later years. Practically, except in being subject to their provincial and paid by the king, instead of being under the bishop and supported by parochial fees, these friars were mere parish priests in charge of Indian pueblos. There were no mission estates, no temporalities managed by the padres, and except in petty matters of religious observance the latter had no authority over the neophytes. At each pueblo the padre had a church, where he preached, and taught, and said mass. With the performance of these routine duties, and of those connected with baptism, marriage, and burials, he was generally content. The Indians, for the most part willingly, tilled a little piece of land for him, furnishing also a few servants from week to week for his household service and that of the church. He was in most instances a kindhearted man, a friend of his Indians, spending much of his salary on them or on the church. If sometimes reproved by conscience for having lost something of the true Franciscan spirit, he redoubled his zeal in petty parish duties for a time, bethought him of ad-

[37] *Tamaron, Visita,* MS., passim. The bishop offered to print *confesionarios* in native lang. if the friars would write them. Some promises were made, and some later corresp. had, but nothing effected down to 1763. Nov. 13, 1764, the viceroy orders Gov. Cachupin to see to it that the Ind. learn Span., and that the padres attend zealously to their duties. Recent reports indicated that the friars were not careful enough to destroy idols and heathen temples, or to study the native character. MS. of Pinart col. Bonilla, *Apuntes,* MS., 368–9, in 1776 advises a careful investigation of the friars' treatment of Ind., with a view to learn if the missions should not be secularized. In 1784 Gov. Anza was ordered to see to it that the Ind. were protected in all their rights. *Arch. Sta Fé,* MS.

verse circumstances and of the 'custumbre del país,' and relapsed into the customary inertia. If reproved by the governor or bishop or provincial—for even the latter occasionally complained that the New Mexican friars were beyond his control—he had stored up in his memory no end of plausible excuses and counter-charges. The Indians were in no sense Christians, but they liked the padres in comparison with other Spaniards, and were willing to comply with certain harmless church formalities, which they neither under-stood nor cared to understand. They had lost all hope of successful revolt, but were devotedly attached to their homes and their ancestral ways of pueblo life; dreaded apostasy, because it involved a precarious existence among hostile tribes of savages; and thus, as a choice of evils, they lived and died as nominal Chris-tians and Spanish subjects, or perhaps more properly slaves.[38]

[38] *Trigo (Manuel de S. J. N.), Informe sobre las Misiones del N. Mex., 1754,* MS., in *N. Mex. Doc.,* 283–326, is devoted mainly to unimportant descrip. matter on each mission, with particular ref. to the personal service rendered by the Ind. to the padres instead of *obvenciones,* fees, or taxes. Many details of the mission routine are found in *Ruiz (Joaquin de J.), Gobierno de las Mi-siones, 1773,* MS., in *N. Mex., Doc.,* 1059–76; and also in *Serrano, Informe,* of '61. Humboldt, *Ess. Pol.,* 305–6, gives some attention to the condition of the N. Mex. missions. Davis, *Span. Conq.,* 416, notes a decree of the audien-cia of Mex in '81, prohibiting the Ind. from selling or otherwise disposing of their lands. Ilzarbe, *Informe del P. Provincial, 1787,* MS., in Pinart col., complains somewhat of the difficulty of getting reports from the N. Mex. friars, but praises the efficiency with which they perform their duties as mis-sionaries and teachers. At Sta Fé the padre was supported by fees, elsewhere by the sínodos of $330 per year. I. says the reduction of the number of mis-sions or of salaries is a wrong to the friars, and interferes considerably with mission discipline. His complaints are more strongly urged in his *Estado* of 1788; and the bishop, *Durango, Informe del Obispo sobre Misiones, 1789,* MS. of Pinart col., declares it has been impossible to get satisfactory reports from the N. Mex. custodio. Viceroy Revilla Gigedo, in his *Carta de 1793,* 443, etc., gives much information on the condition and management of the missions. The pueblo is ruled in local matters by a native gov., or alcalde, war captain, and various subordinates elected each year under the supervision of the alcalde mayor, with approval of the gov. These officials also render aid against the gentile foe. In internal affairs they often act arbitrarily. There is no community property or formal distribution of lands, each fam. regarding as its own the land held by its ancestors, cultivating it acc. to needs or fancies; yet as the pueblo lands are the best, the Ind. got a living more easily than the Span., the latter having sometimes to rent land of the Ind., or even to work for them in bad years. Good crops and much live-stock. The Ind. do not generally dress in Span. style or speak Spanish, though many of them under-stand it. They hunt deer and buffalo, or barter for them with the gentiles. No brotherhoods or *cofradías;* churches generally in a state of decadence;

Countercharges of the friars against the governors and alcaldes mayores, as embodied in Padre Delgado's letter of 1750, were repeated in this period, especially in an exhaustive report of the provincial, Padre Pedro Serrano, in 1761, which included long quotations from a letter of Padre Varo, the custodio, and from statements of other friars. The last governors, Cachupin, Marin del Valle, and Mendoza, are represented as the worst, but all as speculating tyrants, without skill or experience in matters of Indian warfare or government, habitually sending to Mexico reports of campaigns never performed, bent only on enriching themselves, treating the pueblo Indians most inhumanly as slaves, using their women and all female captives for the gratification of their lusts, cheating the gentiles, and by outrageous treatment keeping alive their hostility. The alcaldes are mere tools or accomplices of the governors, and jueces de residencia are also in the ring of oppressors. The Indians are the chief victims of these rascals; but the Spanish settlers are hardly less unfortunate, and even the soldiers are cheated out of half their pay. The padres are the objects of hatred, and if they open their mouths in protest are by perjured and suborned testimony made the victims of outrageous calumnies, their reports to Mexico being intercepted on the way. The partisan bitterness and prejudice of the writers, with their allusions to offences, terrible only in the eyes of friars, and the sickening cant and priestly verbiage in which they clothe their charges, indicate clearly enough that the accusations are too sweeping, and often grossly over-colored; yet enough of candor and honest evidence remains to

Ind. ignorant of the faith. The child is baptized, but does not keep his baptismal name; he attends doctrina from the age of 6 or 7 years, but soon forgets after marriage the little he has learned, and dies for the most part like the pagans. The Span. are but little better. The *Arch. Sta Fé*, MS., contains records of various formal inspections of the missions by the gov., who finds affairs in tolerable condition, though the Ind. are much too fond of their old ways. Gov. Chacon, in his report of '99, says each pueblo has 1 league of land assigned, though at some pueblos more is cultivated. We have seen, however, that in the preceding century 4 sq. l. had been assigned to some of the pueblos.

justify the conclusion that New Mexican affairs were
in a sad plight, and that the pueblo Indians were little
better than slaves.   With all their shortcomings, the
padres were better men than their enemies.   After
1761 not much is heard against the governors, though
the friars were not able to prevent the reappointment
of Cachupin.   Probably there were reforms in some
directions under the later rulers; but if we may credit
Padre Morfi's statements, the condition of the Indians
was but slightly bettered, since the alcaldes mayores,
through the creation of debts, a vicious commercial
system, and various abuses of their official authority,
still kept the natives in their power as before.[39]

[39] *Serrano (Pedro), Informe del P. Provincial sobre los males de N. Mex.,
1761*, MS., in *N. Mex., Doc.*, 173–283, addressed to the viceroy and founded
on various reports in the archives.   One of these reports is *Lezaun (Juan Sans),
Noticias lamentables acaecidas en la N. Mex., y atrasos que cada dia se experi-
mentan así en lo espiritual como en lo temporal, 1760*, MS. in *Id.*, 128–73.   A
somewhat more temperate and later statement of the case is *Morfi (Juan
Agustin), Desórdenes que se advierten en el N. Mex., 1792*, MS. in *Id.*, 381–450.
I give a few details of the accusations, but have no space for most.   Eighty
padres have lost their lives in N. Mex.; yet, by the governor's fault, little has
been accomplished.   At Zuñi 4,000 Ind. live without religion, the single padre
expecting death, and the gov. refuses an escort.   The gov. and his friends
interrupt padres during divine service, declaring the king to be the pope's
equal, entering church on horseback after accused persons or even friars,
often threatening to put padres in chains.   In '50 the gov. forbade the issu-
ance of any certificates to friars, so that they can send no reports; before that
time reports were doubtless stolen on the way, except a few sent by returning
padres.   The gov. had threatened to turn out all the padres and substitute
Jesuits or Franciscans of Zacatecas.   The gov. collects all the wool he can,
and divides it among the pueblos for spinning and weaving, and the Ind. have
to transport the product to Sta Fé.   All agric. work, shelling and grinding
corn, building, tending stock, etc., must be done by the Ind. without pay;
and the slight product of his own fields must be sold on credit, to be paid for
at half-price in gimcracks.   The cream of all barter with the gentiles is taken
by the gov., and the people have to live on what is left.   Girl captives are
resold after a time, with the recommendation, 'que ya estan buenas;' the best-
looking women are selected for service at the *palacio*, and usually return to
their pueblo enceinte.   Many Ind. refuse to marry because ashamed of their
wives having children of light color.   When anything is accomplished against
the gentiles it is by vecinos, not the soldiers.   Militiamen are selected, not for
military service, but as cheap servants of the gov.   Once the gov. sold all the
powder and left the militia without any.   The artillery at Galisteo was dis-
mounted, and the iron made into implements for trade with the Ind.   Morfi
tells us that the alcaldes mayores are rarely of Span. blood, the most ignorant
and vicious of all the inhabitants.   They rarely visit the towns under their
charge, requiring all they need to be brought to them.   They are the only
ones who trade with the pueblo Ind., and get all their property for little or
nothing.   Few girls escape infamy.   The worst of the gang have been Clemente Gutierrez, Fran. Trebol (once acting gov.), Baltasar Vaca, Pedro Pino,
Nerio Montoya, Manuel Vigil, Cris. Vigil, and José Mig. de la Peña.   *Mar-*

The population of pueblo Indians decreased by about 2,400 during these 50 years, local particulars and approximately exact figures being presented in the final note of this chapter. Of mission history proper in addition to what has been given in other connections, there is little to be said. In 1767 the four establishments of Santa Fé, La Cañada, Alburquerque, and El Paso were ordered to be put under secular curates, and this was perhaps done, though later records seem to indicate that friars were still stationed at those places. The founding of a missionary college was ordered by the king and pope in 1777–9, but nothing was accomplished. In consequence of the small-pox epidemic of 1780–1, as we have seen, the number of missions was reduced by consolidation in 1782, Jemes, Santa Ana, Acoma, Nambé, Tesuque, Pecos,· San Felipe, and San Ildefonso being reduced to the condition of visitas, a saving of about $4,000 in sínodos being thus effected. The friars were naturally displeased, and down to the end of the century were constant in their efforts to obtain an increase of missionaries, or of salaries, or the privilege of collecting parochial taxes, but without success. In addition to some references and particulars of these and other matters, I give in the appended note a list of friars serving in 1751–1800, including all the names I have found in the various documents consulted, but doubtless far from being complete.[40]

tinez (Damian), Carta al P. Morfi, 1792, MS., in N. Mex., Doc., 450–83, contains many of the items on which Morfi's report rests, and also considerable information on minerals, etc., of the province.

[40] Santiago Roybal was still vicar and juez ecles. in '56, and apparently in '60. MS. of Pinart col.; Tamaron Visita, MS. Acc. to an article in the Soc. Mex. Geog., Boletin, 2da ep., i. 571–2, the 6 doctrinas of the El Paso district were secularized in '56, but the curates were replaced by friars again in '71. The secularization orders of '67 for the 3 villas and El Paso appear in original communications of the viceroy and com. gen. de Indias in July of that year. MS. of Pinart col. The expense of supporting the friars in '76 was 10,473 pesos per year. Revilla Gigedo, Carta, 442. Pino, Exposicion, 35–6, cites a royal order of June 30, '77, and a pope's brief of Nov. 17, '79, for the missionary college. He says a convent was built and lands were assigned, but nothing more done down to 1812. Croix in '77 or '78 asked the king to employ Zacatecan friars in N. Mex., acc. to the bishop's statement of '91. MS. of

New Mexican industries were agriculture, stock-raising, and barter. There was no mining, though occasional indications of mineral wealth were found. Manufactures, beyond the preparation of skins for home use or a southern market, the weaving of cotton in small quantities at a few pueblos, and the making of pottery at others, were confined to the fabrication of coarse woollen blankets by the pueblo Indians. Agricultural products, chiefly from irrigated

Pinart col. In '81 Gov. Anza by Croix's order distributed to the other estab. the sacred vessels, etc., that had been provided for the Navajo missions. *Arch. Sta Fé*, MS. Revilla Gigedo, *Carta de '93*, p. 443, gives most particulars about the dissatisfaction of the padres with the reduction of missions for '82; but in the *Arch. Sta Fé*, MS., is a record of troubles at Sta Clara and S. Ildefonso, where the padre objected to serving both places because the river flowing between them was often not fordable, and because Sto Domingo and Cochití, though nearer together and on the same side of the river, had not been united, on account of the gov.'s unfair favoritism to the padre there. There was more controversy in '86. 1790, petition for a vicario castrense and juez ecles. in N. Mex. *Id.* In '91 there was an order for an examin. of all doctrineros for the position of curate; but the bishop writes that in N. Mex. there are no examiners but the padres to be examined; besides, the order is contrary to law. MS. of Pinart col.

Alphabetical list of friars serving in N. Mex. in 1750–1800: PP. Manuel Isidoro Abadiano before '61. Rafael Benavides at Zuñi '88. Blas Benitez at Alburquerque '88. Juan Bermejo Nuñez, chaplain at Sta Fé and cust. from '82. (Andrés B. before '61 and José B. at Abiquiú in '88 may be different men.) Cayetano José Ign. Bernal at Isleta '82, at Senecú '88. José Bilchis at Taos '88. Francisco Bueno at Cañada '88. Fran. de Búrgos at Sandía '88. (Manuel de B. of '65–70, perhaps the same.) Ant. Caballero at Cochití '82, Alburquerque '88. Cris. Calvo before '61. Ant. Campos at El Paso '88. Jacobo Castro, custodio '55. Ant. Cenizo at Cochití '88. José Corral at Laguna '88. Patricio Cuellar '65–70. Fran. Javier Dávila at Picuries '82. Fran. Atanasio Dominguez, visitador '70–6, at Cia '88. Fran. Dueñas at Sta Clara '88. Silvestre Velez Escalante at Zuñi '74–8. Ign. Estarrona before '61. Sebastian Fernandez '80, at Cochití '88. Tomás Salv. Fernandez at Acoma '82. Ant. Galfarzozo at Sta Fé '88. Andrés García '65–70, at Zuñi '79–80. (Angel García perhaps the same.) Fernando Ant. Gomez, sec. '75. Ramon Ant. Gonzalez at Sta Clara '82, at S. Juan '88. Ambrosio Guerra at Pujuaque '88. Juan José Hernandez before '61. Hezio, see 'Osio.' Agustin Ant. Iniestra '65–70. Juan José Inojosa, cust. '71. Joaquin Jerez. José Junguera at S. Juan '62. Diego Muñoz Jurado at Abiquiú' 82, at Sta Clara '88. Juan Labora before '61. Gabriel Lago at Pujuaque '88. Juan Sans de Lezaun '61. Fran. Mariño. Dan. Martinez at Zuñi and El Paso before '92. José Medrano at Sto Domingo '82. Juan Miguel Menchero '52–71. Diego Muñoz at Picuries '88. Tomás Murciano. Fran. Osio at Sta Fé '82, Taos '88, custodio '88 (called also Orontaro). José Paez before '61. José Palacios at Laguna '82. Pedro Ign. Pino at Acoma '60. José Prado El Paso dist. '88. Gabriel Quintana '65–70. Manuel Rojo at Alburquerque '60. Joaquin Rodriguez. Mariano Rosete at Isleta '88. Fran. Sanchez before '61. Santiago Fernandez de la Sierra at Sta Clara and S. Juan '82–8. Juan José Toledo at Abiquiú '60–6. Mariano Rodriguez de la Torre '55–70, vice-cust. '70–1, '76, cust. '75. Manuel de S. Juan N. Trigo, vice-cust. '51–61. Tomás Valencia at S. Felipe '60. Manuel Vega at Zuñi '88.

lands, were maize, wheat, and beans in the north, or New Mexico proper, with a little cotton, fruits for home consumption, and an inferior species of tobacco known as *punche;* while the southern district of El Paso was famous for its fruit orchards, vineyards, wine, and aguardiente. Of live-stock, sheep formed the chief element, these animals being raised in large numbers, both for their wool and meat, though there are no reliable statistics extant. Horses and cattle were also raised, but the former were always scarce in the province on account of the numbers sold to and stolen by the wild Indians. I find no definite indications that cattle were raised to any great extent for their hides and tallow.

But all was subordinate to the commercial industry,[41] and all trade was *cambalache,* or barter. Each

[41] Nov. '54, Gov. Valle orders that the price of a horse be fixed at 12 to 15 skins; or a piece of cotton cloth weighing 10 arrobas for 2 pack-horses, or an iron knife for a skin. *Arch. Sta Fé,* MS. No mares, mules, asses, or offensive weapons to be sold the Ind. *Id.* Bishop Tamaron, *Visita,* MS., 99–100, 151, gives some account of the annual caravans, and notes that the one of '60 was attacked by Ind. between El Paso and Chih., losing their horses. Martinez, *Carta,* MS., 473–7, gives many details of trade. He notes that in Gov. Cachupin's time fine gold was assayed, but no mines worked; also silver, copper, and quicksilver. In Gov. Mendinueta's time a ball of fine silver was found. In '67 the gov. objected to the viceroy's proposition to enforce the tobacco *estanco,* as very little real tobacco was used in N. Mex., only *punche,* and by the Ind. a leaf called *mata;* yet in '76 the *estanco* was ordered to be enforced, and the planting of *punche* prohibited. MS. of Pinart col. In *Domenech's Deserts,* i. 182–3, *Wizlizenus' Tour,* 25, are found more or less absurd rumors of an earlier exportation of gold and silver to Spain, with reports that the Gran Quivira ruins represented a former mining city, where the people, being attacked by Ind., buried an immense amount of treasure, to find which some expeditions were made later. This is all humbug. Oct. 14, '75, gov. forbids citizens of any class to visit the Yutas for trade. MS. in Pinart col. *Bonilla, Apuntes,* MS., contains some commercial matter. Sept. '77, Gen. Croix refuses to abolish the 2 per cent tax on exports, on the ground that it is simply added to prices, and is therefore borne by the Chih. traders. *Arch. Sta Fé,* MS. Oct. 25, '88, Gen. Ugarte makes a long report on N. Mex. trade, recommending the encouragement of Chih. industries, now being abandoned on account of the decadence of mining; also the sending of artisan instructors to N. Mex., exemption from taxes, etc., so as to increase manuf. and give the prov. a balance of money. *Id.* In Aug. '89 M. Louis Blanc, com. at Natchidoches, writes to Gen. Ugarte, urging the opening of trade bet. N. Mex. and Louisiana, by establishing a presidio among the Jumanas. This would prevent smuggling and tend to keep the peace with Ind. tribes like the Osages. The journey with freight was only 40 days, through a fertile country. Pierre Vial and a party had recently made the trip. Gen. U. sends the letter to Gov. Concha for his consideration and report. *Id.* A little money after '98. *Pino, Not.,* 64. Slight ment. of N. Mex. resources in *Anquetil's Univ. Hist.,* ix. 566. *Morfi, Desórdenes,* MS., contains the best

year in July or August the people met the Comanches and other tribes of the plains at Taos, where a grand fair was held. Some trade was done at other frontier points, and also by citizens and pueblo Indians, who went out in various directions to meet customers, but this was discouraged and at times forbidden. To this fair the wandering gentiles brought skins of deer and buffalo, with Indian captives to barter for knives and other iron implements, horses, beads, and trinkets, and to some extent blankets. At the end of the year the New Mexicans went in caravans, sometimes of 500 men, to attend the January fair at Chihuahua, where they exchanged the skins, Indian servants, blankets, and to slight extent other products of the province for cloths, groceries, and various articles for the year's Indian trade. The value of each year's exports was estimated by the comandante general in 1788 at $30,000. The departure and return of the caravan were the great events of the year. In 1776 the governor delayed the publication of an important bando till the people had returned from their 'ordinaria anual salida;' and the provincial in 1788 explains the impossibility of obtaining reports from New Mexico until the people come down to the January fair. There was no trade as yet with the French in Louisiana, or with the Spaniards in Texas. There was no coin or other money in New Mexico, but the traders for their accounts invented a system of imaginary currency, including four kinds of dollars—*pesos de plata*, worth eight reales; *pesos de proyecto*, six reales; *pesos antiguos*, four reales; and *pesos de la tierra*, two reales.

general presentment of the country's commercial condition and needs, explaining the system of imaginary money, and giving instances of enormous profits. Revilla Gigedo, *Carta de '93*, 444, gives this picture of the general condition: 'No son mejores [in comp. with the Ind.] respectivamente las costumbres de los vecinos españoles y demas castas, cuyas poblaciones consisten en casas ó ranchos dispersos, donde no tienen testigos que descubran los vicios y la disolucion en que se prostituyen, imitando á los indios en la vida ociosa, y reduciéndose todos sus afanes y comercio á la permuta usuraria de semillas y frutos, y á la venta que hacen ellos en la villa de Chihuahua, adonde bajan en cordon cada año y se proveen de los géneros, efectos, y utensilios para sus vestuarios, atenciones domisticas, y labores del campo.'

The beauty of this system was that the traders always bought for the cheap pesos and sold for the dearer kinds, all being 'dollars' to the Indians. Profits were enormous, a trader by two or three barters in a year often getting $64 for a piece of cloth which cost him six. Advantage was also taken of the Indians' weakness for baubles and ignorance of their real value. Señor Trebol bought a *guacamaya*, or macaw, for eight dollars, and sold the gay feathers for $492. Another system of swindling commerce was the habitual selling of goods to be paid for in future products. Thus, for a little seed grain six fanegas at harvest were promised; or for a bottle of brandy in holy week a barrel was exacted. The natives through debt became practically slaves, besides losing their land, and the poor settlers were hardly less the victims of commercial oppression. While the settlers and pueblo Indians were always in debt to the traders, the latter in turn were debtors to or agents for Chihuahua merchants, who thus monopolized all the profits, and nothing was left for New Mexico, except for certain traders, who as alcaldes mayores utilized their political authority for private gain. Padre Morfi's proposed remedy for these evils was the encouragement of home manufactures by sending artisan teachers and machinery to the province, with a view to render the inhabitants independent of Chihuahua. His plan was to send criminals of the better class, whose offences were chiefly due to drink and the temptations of a city, from Mexico to the far north, and through them to reform the New Mexican industrial system. This expedient was tried in California later without any brilliant success.

The population in 1750 has been given as 3,779 Spaniards and 12,142 pueblo Indians, a total of 15,921 in New Mexico proper, or 18,721 including the district of El Paso. In 1760 official reports show that the number of Spaniards had increased to 7,666, that of Indians decreased to 9,104, and the total was 16,770, or 21,752 including El Paso.   Down to 1788 there was slight change in the figures, but in the final decade there was an inexplicable doubling of the Spanish population; and at the end of the century the figures stood as follows: Spaniards, including of course the *castas* or negroes and mixed breeds, 18,826, Indians 9,732, total 28,558, or, including El Paso, 34,138.   Details are shown to best advantage in the appended table, though some of the figures are confusing, in consequence of varied groupings of the pueblos in the different reports.   I also add some local items not given in the table.[42]

[42] Table of population in N. Mex., 1750–1800:

Settlements.	1760. Span.	1760. Ind.	1788. Total.	1793. Span.	1793. Ind.	1798. Span.	1798. Ind.	1799. Span.	1799. Ind.
Alburquerque....	1,814	....	2,146	1,650	.....	2,279	.....	4,020	603
Santa Fé.	1,285	.....	2,244	2,419	.....	.....	.....	4,194	314
La Cañada.	1,515	316	1,076	1,650	.....	2,594	.....	7,351	1,079
Abiquiú	617	166	1,181	1,147	216	1,573	176		
Taos...	160	505	578	403	518	789	531	1,351	782
Picuríes	208	328	212	1,310	254	566	251		
San Juan.	575	316	1,566	2,173	260	1,971	202		
Santa Clara.	277	257	452	635	139	1,840	1.3		
San Ildefonso	30	484	.....	.....	240	225	251		
Pujuaque.	.....	99	368	308	53	229	79		
Nambé	118	204	.....	.....	155	20	178		
Tesuque.	.....	232	.....	200	138	148	155		
Pecos and Galisteo.	.....	539	.....	.....	152	150	180		
Cochití.	140	450	.....	400	720	425	505		
Santo Domingo.	....	424	608	.....	650	257	1,488		
San Felipe.	.....	458	.....	.....	532	424	282		
Jemes.	.....	373	.....	375	485	314	272	308	1,166
Cia.	.....	568	1,035	.....	275	.....	262		
Santa Ana	.....	404	.....	.....	356	84	634		
Sandía (Alameda).	222	291	596	810	304	384	236	1,490	1,513
Isleta, Tomé, Belen.	620	304	2,103	2,680	410	1,771	603		
Acoma...	.....	1,052	.....	10	820	.....	757		
Laguna.	85	600	1,368	6	668	15	802	15	1,559
Zuñi.	.....	664	1,617	10	1,935	7	2,716	7	2,716
Total.	7,666	9,104	17,153	16,156	9,275	16,065	10,762	18,826	9,732
El Paso district.	3,588	1,394	4,927	3,622	1,900	.....	.....	4,943	637
Grand Total.	11,254	10,498	22,080	19,778	11,175	.....	.....	23,769	10,369

The 5 reports embodied in the table are as follows: *Tamaron, Visita, 1760*, MS., in which the bishop expresses the opinion that the padron of Sta Fé does not show more than half the real pop.; *Ilzarbe (Joaquin), Estado de las Misiones, 1788*, MS., in Pinart col., the writer—provincial of the Sto Evangelio province—stating that there were 18 missions (the omissions in his list as per table showing the consolidation effected by Anza), 11 annexes, 24 padres (who are named), 5,508 fam., and for the year 1,254 baptisms, 438 marriages, and 647 deaths, this author making no distinction of races; *Revilla Gijedo, Carta de 1793, sobre misiones*, 441–2, also MS., the viceroy giving the latitude of each settlement and the tribe inhabiting it, and being followed in his statistics by Humboldt, *Essai Pol.*, 57, and through H. by several others; the report of the custodio, P. Fran. Osio (called Hezio), for '98, as given in *Meline's 2,000 Miles*, 208–9, the totals as printed and followed by Prince, *Hist. Sk.*, 227, being apparently erroneous, the report including also the totals for '96, Span. 14,167, Ind. 9,453; also baptisms for '96–8, Ind. 708, Span. 1,283; marriages, Ind. 170, Span. 226; deaths, Ind. 469, Span. 522; and finally, Gov. Chacon's report of '99, in *Meline's 2,000 Miles*, 220, this doc. giving only the totals for each jurisdiction.

A doc. of '90, *Arch. Sta Fé*, MS., gives the total pop. as 30,955, and adds 'que por los enlaces que han tenido unos con otros, á penas se hallan individuos que no sean parientes.' In '94 Gov. Chacon gave the pop. as follows:

	Men.	Women.	Boys.	Girls.	Total.
Span.	7,502	5,912	2,153	1,763	17,330
Ind.	4,343	4,267	1,539	1,219	11,368
Castas	1,941	1,601	792	1,224	5,558
	13,786	11,780	4,484	4,206	34,256

In '93 a similar statement is given, the figures varying but slightly from the above, and the grand total being 34,201. The *castas*, I think, cannot here include the mixed Span. and Ind., but perhaps negro mixtures. There were but very few full-blooded Span. *Arch. Sta Fé*, MS. In *Lafora, Viage*, the pop. for '66 in 37 settlements of 15 nations is given as 10,524 Span. and 9,580 Ind., including El Paso. The extent of N. Mex. is given by Lafora as lat. 32° to 38°; long. 258° to 264° from Teneriffe; and by Revilla Gigedo as lat. 34° to 37½°; long. 268° to 274°. The jurisdictions, or districts, as given in the *Arch. Sta Fé*, MS., in '93–4, were Sta Fé, Cañada, Alburquerque, Queres; Zuñi, Laguna, and Acoma; and El Paso. No. 1, 2, 3, and 6 are the same in all reports, but the others vary. Revilla Gigedo gives Taos, S. Felipe, Queres, Sandía, Laguna, and Zuñi. Gov. Chacon in '99 gives Alameda (Sandía), Taos, Jemes (Queres?), Laguna, and Zuñi. In *N. España, Breve Resúmen*, MS., ii. 321–2; and in *Viagero Univ.*, xxvii. 144–52, are brief descrip. and historic sketches of N. Mex. for '67 and '99 respectively.

Local items in addition to pop. as given in the table: Abiquiú (Sto Tomás), a pueblo of genízaros, or rescued captives, yet having a large Span. pop. It was in the jurisd. of La Cáñada. In 1771 the citizens wished to abandon the place, but Gov. Mendinueta, through the alcalde mayor, Marcos Sanchez, forbade it, as all danger from the Comanches was past. The pop. of this and other settlements includes that of scattered ranchos in the vicinity. In '88 there were 54 baptisms, 10 marriages, and 17 deaths.

Acoma (S. Estévan), pueblo of Queres Ind., but with a few Span. in the last decade; a visita of Laguna in '88, and prob. had no padre later.

Alburquerque (S. Felipe Neri), villa of Span., with a friar acting as curate, and a vicar appointed by the bishop in '60. Militia force 80 in '66. Though nominally a villa, it was scattered many leagues up and down the valley, the people living on their ranchos, chiefly at the Alameda, and only coming to the town on Sundays. Two padres in '88; bapt. 89, marr. 21, deaths 26. In '60 the bishop confirmed 732.

Belen, Span. settlement of 38 fam. in '66, included in pop. with Isleta. A considerable number of genízaro fam. lived here also, and at the settlement of Tomé, near by, 60 in all in '92, having much trouble with the Span., who, like the Christian Ind., looked down upon these sons of gentiles. They wished to form a pueblo at Sabinal, but did not succeed.

Cañada (Sta Cruz de la), largest of the Span. villas, 1,517 confirmations in '60, and a vicar appointed; 97 bapt., 23 marr., 35 deaths in '88, when P. Fran. Bueno was in charge.

Cebolleta, in the Laguna region, abandoned Navajo mission; a few Navajos and Apaches were still living in a ranchería in the vicinity.

Cia (Asuncion), mission of Queres, with Jemes and Sta Ana as visitas after '82; 99 bapt., 32 marr., 56 deaths in '88.

Cochití (S. Buenaventura), pueblo of Queres, visita of Sto Domingo after '82.

Cubero, or Covero, pueblo in the Laguna region, not mentioned in this half-century; prob. abandoned.

Galisteo, visita of Pecos, with 255 Ind. in '60; not mentioned in later reports; prob. abandoned.

Isleta (S. Agustin), mission pueblo of Tehuas(?), whose padre had charge of Belen and Tomé; bapt. 74, marr. 25, deaths 31 in '88.

Jemes (S. Diego), pueblo of Jemes, Pecos lang., a visita of Cia after '82.

Laguna (S. José), mission of Queres, with some fam. of half-converted Navajos and Apaches in vicinity; had Acoma as a visita after '82; bapt. 33, marr. 24, deaths 12 in '88.

Moquino, pueblo of the Laguna region, not mentioned in this period, but perhaps estab. with Moqui fam. now or a little later.

Nambé (S. Fran.), pueblo of Tehuas, visita of Pujuaque after '82.

Pecos (Los Angeles), visita of Sta Fé, and rapidly declining in pop.

Picuríes (S. Lorenzo), mission with many Span. settlers in the vicinity; bapt. 15, marr. 6, deaths 8 in '88.

Pujuaque (Guadalupe), pueblo of Tehuas, visita of Nambé in '60, but after '82 mission with visitas of N. and Tesuque; 2 padres in '88; bapt. 42, marr. 13, deaths 14.

S. Felipe, mission of Queres; visita of Sto Domingo after '82.

S. Ildefonso, mission of Tehuas; visita of Sta Ana after '82.

S. Juan de los Caballeros, mission of Tehuas, with many Span. in the vicinity; 2 padres in '88; bapt. 16, marr. 19, deaths 25.

S. Rafael de los Gentiles, 15 settlers of this place, location not given, petitioned for and obtained in '65 arms to defend themselves.

Sandía (Asumpcion or Dolores), mission of 96 Tehuas (?) and 196 Moquis in '60; bapt. 57, marr. 27, deaths 18 in '88.

Sta Ana, pueblo of Queres, had a padre in '60; visita of Cia after '82.

Sta Clara, mission of Tehuas, with S. Ildefonso as visita after '82; bapt. 66, marr. 22, deaths 98 in '88.

Sto Domingo, mission of Queres, called Sto Dom. de Cochití after '82; with S. Felipe and S. Buen. (Cochití) as visitas; bapt. 124, marr. 25, deaths 31 in '88, having 2 padres.

Sta Fé, capital villa, with garrison of 80 soldiers, but no fortifications; 2 padres, 1 acting as vice-custodio (the custodio generally living at El Paso), and a secular priest paid by tithes; 2 churches and another almost completed in '60, built by Gov. Marin del Valle. Pop. 2,324 in '66. *Lafora.* In '88 Gen. Ugarte approved Gov. Concha's project of reforming the villa and building a cuartel, or presidio, $2,000 being assigned for the work. There had been some talk of building the cuartel at the suburb of Analco, and even of moving the villa to Sto Domingo, though both vecinos and Ind. objected. The gov. was authorized to use his judgment, and the villa was not moved. *Arch. Sta Fé,* MS.

Taos (S. Gerónimo), mission pueblo, with a large Span. pop. on ranchos in the vicinity; 2 padres in '88; bapt. 65, marr. 43, deaths 41. Taos was the great trading rendezvous for the tribes of the plains; and, as we have seen, several bloody fights took place in that region during the half-century.

Tesuque (S. Diego), pueblo of Tehuas; visita of Sta Fé in '60, and of Pujuaque after '82.

Tomé (Concepcion), settlement of Span. and genízaros; 70 vecinos in '66; 402 confirm. in '60; had a good church under padre of Isleta or Alburquerque.

Zuñi (Guadalupe), mission pueblo of many Ind., though a large part of the pop. was usually scattered; 2 padres in '88, bapt. 35, marr. 23, deaths 47. In '90, with its 5 ranches, had a pop. of 1,121. *Arch. Sta Fé,* MS.

El Paso (Nra Sra del Pilar y S. José), presidio and later town, with 2 friars and 2 priests; captain and alcalde mayor, later lieut.-gov. El Paso was famous for its vineyards and orchards; and except the raids of hostile gentiles, its chief concern was about its irrigating ditches and the dam of the Rio del Norte, which supplied them. This dam was usually carried away by the floods of May–July.   A doc. in the Pinart col. shows the constant but futile efforts of the authorities in '54–62 to collect a special tax of 50 cents on each 100 vines to build a solid dam.   There were 250,000 vines, but the owners declared they were too poor to pay the tax either in money or work.   In this district were S. Lorenzo, Senecú, Isleta, and Socorro, respectively 1, 3, 5, and 6 l. eastward down the river; also Carrizal, 36 l. toward Chihuahua, founded in '58; pop. 161 Span. in '60, with a guard of 20 soldiers from El Paso; later site of the presidio.

CHAPTER XIII.

LAST YEARS OF SPANISH RULE.

1801–1822.

Two Books—Succession of Governors—Chacon, Alencaster, Mainez, Manrique, Allande, Melgares, Chavez, and Vizcarra—Indian Affairs—Comanches, Navajos, and Moquis—Melgares in the North-east—Election of a Delegate to the Córtes—Pedro Bautista Pino Goes to Spain—The Louisiana Purchase and Boundary Question—Lalande and Pursely—Zebulon M. Pike—Attempts at Trade—McKnight—Choteau and De Mun—Glenn, Bucknell, and Cooper—Population—Local Items—Trade—Agriculture—Manufactures—Mining—Institutions—Government—Military—Missions and Bishopric—Charges against the Friars—War of Independence—Viva Iturbide!

The same kind providence that causes rivers to flow near large towns, the moon and stars to shine at night, when their feeble light is of some use, sends snow only in the winter, when there is no hot sun to melt it, and performs other beneficent acts, is not always unmindful of the annalist's needs. Thus, when the history of the last years of Spanish rule in New Mexico seemed likely to resemble the famous chapter on snakes in Ireland, not only was it put into the head of the United States government to send an explorer to this far-off province, and of the people to send a delegate to the córtes of Spain, but both explorer and delegate were inspired with the idea of writing a book, as the friar Benavides and the conqueror Villagrá had been in earlier times; and the result was a mass of information which goes far to make this chapter as long and as interesting as those that have preceded it.

For this, as for earlier periods, I do not deem it necessary to consider here the complications of military and civil government in the Provincias Internas of northern Mexico, a subject that is as fully treated as the meagre records permit in another work of this series.[1] There was always a governor or acting governor in New Mexico, subordinate to the comandante general of the Provincias, a state of things which has led modern writers into some confusion, causing them to include some of the southern officials in their lists of governors, just as they brought sever l viceroys of New Spain to rule the province in earlier times. Governor Chacon ruled until the spring of 1805, when he was succeeded by Colonel Joaquin del Real Alencaster.[2] The latter's name does not appear after 1808, and Alberto Mainez is named as acting governor in 1807–8, and next in the list is Lieutenant-colonel José Manrique, ruling in 1810–14, perhaps ad interim for part of that period. Mainez ruled again in 1815–17,[3] Pedro María de Allande in 1816–18, and Facundo Melgares—who as a lieutenant serving in Chihuahua had visited New Mexico before—in 1818–22. Melgares was the last governor under Spain, and was succeeded on July 5, 1822, by Francisco Javier Chavez as jefe político, ruling in 1822–3, though Antonio Vizcarra also held the office for a time in 1822.[4]

[1] *Hist. North Mex. States*, i., ii.

[2] I find in the *Arch. Sta Fé*, MS., an order of Chacon in March, and of Alencaster in May 1805. The latter name is a form of the English Lancaster, more often written, except in N. Mex., Alencastre, as in the case of the viceroy of that name. Pino, *Expos.*, 40, seems to say that A. was gov. from 1805 to 1812, and this may indicate that his successor in 1808–12 was only acting gov.

[3] Also in '14, acc. to Davis, *El Gringo*, 83, who says that in that year a conspiracy was formed by Corp. Antonio Armijo and Dionisio Valdés, who were exiled for 10 years to Chihuahua.

[4] In the *Gaceta de Mex.* of March 7, '19, the governorship of N. Mex. is declared vacant, and aspirants are notified to send in their petitions. Melgares, in the documents of '19–20, is called gov. ad interim. I regret that I am not able in this period, as I have been in earlier ones, to correct from original sources the list of governors, and an obliged to follow Davis, Meline, Ritch, Prince, etc., though there is evidently a little confusion of dates. They take their information from land-grants, etc., in the archives, and in the *U. S. Land Reports*, and my original notes add nothing of importance.

Troubles with the Indians were much less serious and constant than in former years, the combined efforts of the frontier garrisons, with a consistent system of treaties and gifts, producing apparently excellent results. The Comanches, in particular, were friendly, being zealous in bringing information and rumors respecting the movements of Americans in the north-east, and even eager to aid Spain in crushing the insurgents under Hidalgo; and the other tribes were often in the same mood.[5] The Navajos were hostile, however, in 1803–5, having intrenched themselves in the cañon de Chelly —since famous for its ruined pueblos—where they deemed their position impregnable. Governor Chacon led several expeditions against them, as did Lieutenant Antonio Narbona after Alencaster's accession, and in 1805 they were reduced to submission and friendship.[6] In 1806 Lieutenant Melgares was sent up from Chihuahua with 100 dragoons to join a force of 500 militia in an

[5] *Pino, Expos.*, 42–4. This author says the Ind., by gifts, etc., had been kept friendly for the most part since Anza's time down to 1811.

[6] Jan. 25, 1805, Narbona to gov. reports from Zuñi a fight in Chelly cañon, where he killed 90 bucks, with 25 women and children, besides capturing 36, with 30 women and children; also 30 horses and 350 sheep. He had only one Ind. chief killed and 64 wounded. Chelly is a very strong position, and a larger force will be required for further movements. *Arch. Sta Fé*, MS. In 1804 the com. gen. refuses to grant a request of the Navajos to settle at Cebolleta. MS. of Pinart col. March 25, 1805, Gov. C. announces the terms to be granted the Navajos. They shall have no claim to Cebolleta or to livestock in possession of the Span.; for their 2 captives 4 women might be released; they must not go with their live-stock beyond the cañon de Juan Tafoya, Rio del Oso, and S. Mateo; whenever they commit any robbery or aggression they are to be punished by force of arms, unless they return stolen property and surrender the aggressors; when visiting Sta Fé they must expect no gifts except sustenance; and they must give up 4,000 sheep, 150 cattle, and 60 horses which they have stolen. *Arch. Sta Fé*, MS. Pino, *Expos.*, 40–1, *Not.*, 85–6, narrates in general terms the final efforts and success, the fall of Chelly, and the treaty of 1805. It seems that Lieut. Narbona was sent up from Chih. to join Gutierrez, Vaca, and others. Lieut. Vicente Lopez also defeated the foe at Chacá, but was suspended for some intrigue in 1808. April 1806 the Navajo chief complains that he receives no gifts from the king, as do other friendly tribes; but is informed by Gen. Salcedo that they must depend on their own industries for sustenance, though later, when they shall have shown their good faith by abstaining from petty robberies, etc., they may obtain some gifts. *Arch. Sta Fé*, MS. I think that Prince, *Hist. Sk.*, 232, exaggerates the magnitude and constancy of Navajo troubles in this and later periods, though they doubtless gave more trouble than other tribes.

expedition out into the north-eastern plains.   This was
not a campaign against the Indians, but a tour of exploration, undertaken with a view to conciliate the
natives and to look out for American explorers and
filibusters; for the intention of the United States to explore their newly acquired Louisiana territory had been
announced, and there were also reports of Burr's conspiracy as likely to affect the Spanish frontier.   Melgares went down the Red River, held a council with
the Comanches, crossed northward to the Arkansas,
made a visit to the Pawnee nation on the Kansas,
distributing medals and flags, and thence perhaps
went up the Arkansas to the mountains, returning to
Santa Fé in October.   He did not find any Americans, of whose doings in that region I shall have something to say presently.[7]

Pino, in his report of 1812, declares the system of
treaties and gifts as a feature of the new Indian policy
to have been a grand success in every way.   He also
relates that in 1811 José Rafael Sarracino made an
expedition to the Yuta country to investigate the
truth of their reports respecting a Spanish people
dwelling in the far north-west.   In three months he
reached a region where the natives had knives and
other implements of European manufacture, obtained,
as they said, from a people living beyond a great river,
which Sarracino could not or did not cross.[8]   In 1818
–19 the Navajos renewed their hostilities.   It was

[7] *Pike's Acct. of Exped.*, 142–3, 206; *Prince's Hist. Sk.*, 231, and other
works.   I have found no information of this exped. except that originating
from Pike's book.   A treaty with the Mescalero and Gileño Apaches is noted
in 1810, no rations being granted, and their hunting-grounds being clearly
designated. MS. of '32 in Pinart col.

[8] *Pino, Expos.*, 41–4; *Not.*, 84–8.   P. notes that the Comanche chief at this
time was a son of the old chief Maya, educated at Sta Fé, and a firm friend
of the Span.   He also says the Americans had established gun factories (?)
among the Jumanas and Cahiguas, and muskets and powder from this source
were obtained for N. Mex.   (This is in a note, which may possibly be of later
date.)   In connection with Sarracino's exped., respecting the date of which
Pino may be in error, it is well to note that in Aug. 1808 an Ind. from the
Tulares arrived at S. Fernando, Cal., with a flag that had been sent through
a cordillera of 10 tribes by a captain who wished to know if it were true that
there were padres and *gente de razon* west of the sierra. *Hist. Cal.*, ii. 85.   I
may notice also that in 1801 a project for opening commun. bet. Cal. and N.
Mex. by land was discussed and dismissed in Mex. *Id.*, 3–4.

reported in Mexico in January 1819, that Governor
Melgares had in December forced them to sue for
peace; but it appears that they had to be defeated
twice more in February and March, and that the
treaty was finally signed on August 21st.[9]　A notable
feature of this affair is the fact that the Navajos, being
hard pressed, settled near the Moqui towns, and the
Moquis sent five of their number to ask aid from the
Spaniards.　This was deemed a most fortunate occurrence, opening the way to the submission of this nation
after an apostasy of 139 years.　It was resolved to
take advantage of the opportunity, but of the practical
result nothing is known, since this is the only mention
of this remnant of a valiant and independent people
that I have been able to find in the records of the
period.

Under the decree of the 'junta central de las Es-
pañas,' dated February 14, 1810, New Mexico was
entitled to a diputado in the Spanish córtes.　Accordingly, on the 11th of August the alcaldes and
leading men of the province—there being no ayuntamientos—assembled at Santa Fé, Governor Manrique
presiding, to select a delegate.[10]　From the three can-

[9] *Gaceta de Mex.*, x. (xxxix.-xl.) 186, 559–62, 1127–30; *Noticioso Gen.*, June
14, Oct. 29, '19.　In the 2d exped. 33 were killed and 14 captured, with
460 sheep and 24 horses.　The treaty is given in 18 articles, being signed by
5 Navajo chiefs.　A native general was to be appointed and to live as near
Jemes as possible, being held responsible for his nation; 4 youths or one chief
were to be held as hostages; the N. were granted all their old territory to
cañon Largo, boca del cañon de Chacá, and Agua Azul; and they bound
themselves to respect the rights of the Moquis.　Notwithstanding this treaty,
we are told by Davis and Prince, *Hist. Sk.*, 232, *El Gringo*, 83–4, that in 1820
a party of Navajos coming into Jemes to make a treaty were foully murdered
by the inhab., under their alcalde, Juan Ant. Vaca.　The ringleaders were
arrested, but the proceedings dragged along till '24, when they were released,
only to be killed by the Navajos 10 years later.　I am disposed to question
the accuracy of this statement.

[10] These representative men were José Pino, capt. of militia and ex-alcalde
of Alburquerque; Ant. Ortiz, alférez real; Diego Montoya 1st alc. of Sta Fé;
José García de Mora, retired lieut., representing Sta Cruz de la Cañada; José
Miguel Tafoya, 2d alc. of Sta Fé, for 29 years corp. in the *compañia veterana;*
José Ant. Chavez, 1st alc. of Alburquerque; Manuel García, for 24 years alc.
of La Cañada and partido; Mig. Ant. Vaca, 2d alc. of Alburquerque; Cleto
Miera y Pacheco, alc. of S. Cárlos de la Alameda; and Tomás Ortiz, alc. of
Taos.

didates receiving the highest number of votes the
delegate was chosen by lot, and the honor fell to Pedro Bautista Pino, an old and influential resident.
Provided with instructions, not only from the junta
that elected him, but from several prominent men,
Don Pedro started on his mission in October 1811,
being, as he believed, the first native-born New Mexican to visit Spain. He had to pay the expenses of
his journey; but the patriotic people contributed
$9,000 as a donativo to the cause of Fernando VII.[11]

Of Pino's labors in Spain we have no other record
than his report of November 1812 to the córtes, published at Cádiz the same year, and 37 years later at
Mexico. This report is by far the best source of information respecting New Mexico for the period
covered by this chapter, being a very complete description of the province, with its institutions, condition, and needs. Of course, much of its contents is
only confirmatory of what appears from other original
sources in earlier chapters, but the rest is utilized in
different parts of this chapter. The author was an
enthusiastic admirer of his country and its people,
praising in high terms their purity of blood,[12] their
loyalty to Spain, and their bravery in defending their
homes against the savage tribes. He exaggerated—
and perhaps intentionally, as the best means of arous-
ing the attention of the government—the danger of
aggression from the Americans in union with the Indian tribes of the plains.[13] The military defence of the

---

[11] The other two candidates were Antonio and Juan Rafael Ortiz. Pino
took with him his grandson Juan de los Reyes Vaca y Pino, aged 11, Bartolomé Fernandez as clerk, who died on the voyage, and the retired soldier Salvador Leiva y Chavez. Padre Fran. Osio (Hocio), for 26 years chaplain at
Sta Fé, furnished a *Prospecto ó plan sobre diferentes solicitudes;* also written
suggestions from Mariano de la Peña, Ignacio Sanchez Vergara, alc. of Jemes,
José Gutierrez, Capt. Bart. Vaca, and Juan José Silva. To raise the $9,000
some of the citizens are said to have 'sacrificed the liberty of their sons.'

[12] He says there were absolutely no negro *castas* in N. Mex., only Span.
and Ind. blood. This, I think, is not strictly true, as in earlier times there
had been complaints of mixed-breed colonists and a vicious mulatto element in
the population.

[13] Pino states that the Amer., noting how N. Mex is neglected by Spain,
have tried in various ways, by offers of liberal and protecting laws, advan-

country was naturally held out as the great object to be kept in view, and accordingly Pino demanded, not only a reorganization of the military service, including the payment of citizens doing duty as soldiers, but the founding of five new presidios, or rather the transfer to the north of frontier presidios no longer needed in the Provincias Internas. Other demands were for a separate bishopric, with a college and system of schools to be supported by the tithes; and for a civil and criminal audiencia at Chihuahua, that of Guadalajara being too distant for any practical benefit to New Mexico.[14] Except that the establishment of a bishopric was ordered the next year, no special attention was paid to the delegate's demands. Don Pedro Bautista came home and was reëlected for 1820-1. The sum of $6,000 was sent to Mexico to pay his expenses, but on reaching Vera Cruz he could only obtain of this sum enough to pay for his journey to that point; and as his arrival in Spain would be late in any event, he

tageous commerce, etc., to attract the people, with a view of joining N. Mex. to their Louisiana purchase; they have also tried with much success to convince the Ind. that the Span. are by no means invincible, but that with Amer. weapons, etc., they may hope to conquer the province; yet the people of N. Mex. have never yielded to the temptation.

[14] Pino (Pedro Bautista), Exposicion sucinta y sencilla de la provincia del N. Mex.; hecha por su diputado en córtes...con arreglo á sus instrucciones. Cádiz, 1812, 8vo, 48 p., 2 l. Also republished with various additions by José Agustin de Escudero, at Mex., 1849, as Noticias históricas y estadísticas de la antigua provincia del Nuevo-Mexico, presentadas por su diputado en córtes D. Pedro Bautista Pino en Cádiz el año de 1812. Adicionadas por el Lic. D. Antonio Barreiro en 1839; y ultimamente anotadas por el Lic. Don José Agustin de Escudero, para la comision estadística militar de la República Mexicana. Mex., 1849, 8vo, 98 p., 2 l. The work of Barreiro alluded to I have not seen, but have his Ojeada sobre Nuevo-Mexico, of 1832, in which there is no allusion to Pino, though his work may have been used as a base. Juan Lopez Cancelada is said to have been the writer of the Exposicion, using information supplied by Pino; and it is to be noticed that in the paragraph entitled Regalos que se hacen á los gentiles (Noticias, p. 87-8), the initial capitals of the sentences spell C.'s name. The five presidios asked for were to be at El Paso, Rio de Pecos, Socorro, Taos, and (as a depot of supplies, etc.) at S. Cristóbal. The term of service for settlers should be reduced. Through Pino the people also asked that the province should be divided into 3, each with a gov. These positions should be of 3 grades, in respect of salary and rank, and each gov. should begin with the lowest grade, being promoted for good conduct and experience. The salaries should be $25,000, $35,000, and $45,000, respectively, which in the aggregate would not be much more than the govt now costs, and besides much larger savings might be effected by suppressing useless positions in Mexico, such as that of viceroy! Clearly Don Pedro was a man of some cheek.

decided to return home, 'no obstante sus descos de servir á la patria.'[15]

All of the old Louisiana territory west of the Mississippi, ceded by France to Spain in 1762–3 and returned to France in 1800, was finally ceded to the United States in 1803. From this date to 1819 the question of boundary between United States territory and Spanish possessions was an open one. Negotiations on the subject belong properly to the history of Texas, and are treated in another work of this series.[16] Near the coast the line between Louisiana and Texas had by long occupation been practically settled for many years to the satisfaction of all but partisan theorists; but in the interior no boundary had ever been fixed or needed, and indeed, little was known geographically of that region. An equitable line would have been one from a point on Red River above the settlements extending north-westward to the Rocky Mountains at a long distance from the New Mexican outposts. By way of bluster, the Americans, without a shadow of right, sometimes claimed all to the Rio Grande, and the Spaniards, with but slightly better reasons, all to the Missouri; but the real ideas of the two nations did not differ materially. The Americans thought that Red River might rise in the mountains and flow southeastward, so as to constitute in itself the proper boundary;[17] the Spaniards of New Mexico in a sense regarded the Arkansas, or Napestle, as the practical limit of the territory explored by them in their Indian campaigns; and thus the territory that might plausibly

---

[15] *Diario de Córtes Estraordinarias*, Oct. 21, 1821, vol. ii., MS., 10; *Arizpe, Idea general*, 50. In Pino's letter to the Córtes explaining his non-attendance, he complains that the decrees of that body in response to his *Exposicion*, though confirmed by royal order of May 9, '13 (probably on the bishopic, etc.), had not been carried into effect.

[16] See *Hist. North Mex. States*, ii., with references to the original correspondence.

[17] Pike's narrative, to be noted presently, shows this general idea; yet some earlier maps—see, for instance, that of Le Page du Pratz, 1757, in *Hist. N. W. Coast*, i. 601—represent, not only the Red River, but the Arkansas, as too far south in the interior to serve the purpose, having their sources south of Santa Fé.

be the subject of dispute was of slight extent and value, and would disappear when on exploration Red River should be found not to have its source in the mountains, but far south of the legitimate Spanish boundary. And indeed, in the final settlement of 1819, the Spanish proposition was accepted, and the Arkansas from the mountains down to longitude 23° became, and most equitably, the permanent dividing line.

Between Louisiana and New Mexico there had been no trade or habitual communication before 1800, though some slight efforts had been made to open such intercourse. From both directions, however, a flourishing trade with the Indians had grown up. In 1804 William Morrison of Kaskaskia, despatching the creole trader Baptiste Lalande up the Platte, instructed him to carry his goods to Santa Fé, with a view to test the commercial prospects in that direction. Obeying his instructions, Lalande succeeded in being arrested by the Spaniards and carried to the capital. The New Mexicans liked the goods, and Baptiste liked the country so well that he resolved to settle there, and even omitted the formality of accounting to Morrison for the consignment.[18] In 1805 James Pursley, a Kentuckian who left St Louis three years before, after many adventures among the Indians, was sent by the latter to negotiate for Spanish trade, and after succeeding in this mission he also settled at Santa Fé, working as a carpenter.[19]

Zebulon M. Pike, a lieutenant of the sixth United States infantry, after an exploration of the Upper Mississippi while Lewis and Clarke were engaged in their famous expedition to the far west, was sent with twenty-two men in 1806 to explore the country of the Red and Arkansas rivers, and to establish a good

[18] *Pike's Acct. of Exped.*, 195, 210. P. found L. at Sta Fé in reduced circumstances in 1807. Escudero, in *Pino, Not.*, 74, says L. died in N. Mex., leaving a large family and great wealth.

[19] *Pike's Acct. Exped.*, app. iii. 16–17. Pike seems to be the source of all that is known of Pursley and Lalande, being followed by Gregg, Prince, and others who have written on the Sta Fé trade. Prince, however, has a few elaborations of petty items that may possibly come from other sources.

understanding with the Indians, especially with the Comanches. His mission was in many respects similar to that of Melgares from the opposite direction, though his force was much less imposing. His preliminary and successful negotiations with the Osages, Pawnees, and other nations, from the start in July from the Missouri River at Belle Fontaine, have no special connection with the annals of New Mexico. In October he was on the Arkansas, where, as before reaching that stream, he found frequent traces of the Spaniards' recent visit. At the end of the month Lieutenant Wilkinson, with a part of the men, embarked in boats on the river to follow it down to the Missouri junction; while Pike, with the rest of the party, started up the river for the mountains, intending, according to his instructions, to return by the Red River to Natchitoches.[20]

Pike had no serious troubles with the Indians; neither did he accomplish anything in his mission of conciliating their good-will. Late in November he was at the base of the lofty peak which has since borne his name. Then followed two months of winter wanderings in the snows and mountains and parks of what is now Colorado,[21] marked by the most terrible sufferings from cold and hunger. The only wonder is that all did not perish. Crossing the range in the vicinity of the modern Leadville, Pike thought himself on the Red River; but after a perilous descent though the cañon, found himself back at his old camp on the Arkansas. Again he struggled on, over another series of ranges, and at the end of January 1807 succeeded with part of his companious—the rest being left behind with frozen feet—on reaching another large river,

[20] The company after the separation consisted of Capt. Z. M. Pike, Dr John H. Robinson, Sergt. Wm E. Meek,* Corp. Jeremiah Jackson,* private Henry Kennerman, John Brown, Jacob Carter,* Thos Dougherty,* Wm Gorden, Theodore Miller,* Hugh Menaugh, Jacob Mountjoy, Alex. Roy, John Sparks,* Fat. Smith,* Freegift Stoute, and Baroney Vasquez* as interpreter. Those marked with a star did not reach Sta Fé and Chihuahua with Pike, as explained later.

[21] See *Hist. Colorado*, this series.

which must, he thought, be the Red at last. His plan was to descend the stream in boats or rafts to Natchitoches; therefore he sought a suitable spot for a fortified camp, where the necessary preparations might be made, and to which the rest of the party might be brought, as a few of them soon were.[22] I give a copy of the western portion of Pike's map, showing his route in Colorado and New Mexico.

The lieutenant's instructions required him to be very cautious as he approached the Spanish frontier.[23] His idea of the boundary, however, seems to have been peculiar, for he built his fort, not on the eastern or American side of his Red River, but five miles up a western branch! Here he raised the stars and stripes. He desired to extend his exploration into Spanish territory, or at least to learn the geographic relation of his fort to Santa Fé; and he had a pretext ready, for he had brought William Morrison's bill against Lalande, and with this document Dr Robinson started alone on February 7th for the city of Holy Faith. Ten days later a Spanish dragoon and an Indian made their appearance, regarded by Pike as spies, who said they had come from Santa Fé in four days, and that Robinson had arrived in safety; learned the location of the fort, and Pike's intention to descend the river to Natchitoches; and departed. Another ten days passed, and then came a force of 50 dragoons and 50 militia under lieutenants called in the narrative Ignacio Saltelo and Bartolomé Fernandez. Now Pike was informed that he was not on

[22] The 8 names marked with a star in note 20 are those who did not come to the camp before Pike's departure. They were brought into Sta Fé a little later, but I find no definite record of what became of them. P. had 8 men with him. The map is taken from the French edition.

[23] 'As your interview with the Comanches will probably lead you to the head branches of the Arkansaw and Red rivers, you may find yourself approximated to the settlements of N. Mex., and there it will be necessary you should move with great circumspection, to keep clear of any hunting or reconnoitring parties from that province, and to prevent alarm or offence; because the affairs of Spain and the U. S. appear to be on the point of amicable adjustment, and moreover it is the desire of the president to cultivate the friendship and harmonious intercourse of all the nations of the earth, and particularly our near neighbors, the Spaniards.' *Pike's Acct. Exped.*, 108. The instruc. were given by Gen. James Wilkinson.

Red River, but on the Rio del Norte, his camp being on the Conejos just above the junction; whereupon he at once lowered his flag, for he could but admit—

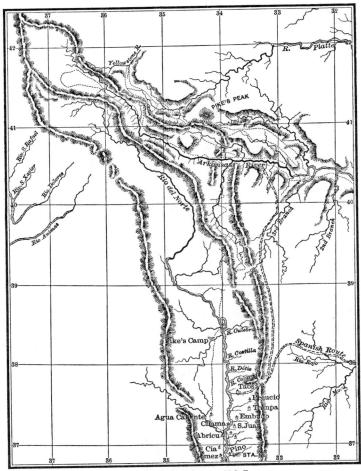

PIKE'S EXPEDITION, 1806–7.

especially in the presence of 100 soldiers—that the Spaniards might have some legitimate claim to territory occupied by them for over two centuries. The Spaniards were most courteous and kind, supplying the half-starved and half-naked explorers with food and blankets; but the officers presently admitted, what Pike had supposed from the first, that the Americans must go to Santa Fé. Accordingly, they started on the 27th, part of the Spanish force remaining behind to bring in the eight explorers who had not yet reached the fort.[24]

The route from the Conejos was across to the Chama and down that stream past Ojo Caliente and San Juan. The people were uniformly kind and hospitable in their treatment of the strangers, though their nondescript and ragged apparel, consisting of overalls, breech-cloths, and leather coats, without covering for the head, prompted the inquiry if the Americans were a tribe living in houses or wearing hats. Baptiste Lalande and another Frenchman tried to gain Pike's confidence, but were regarded by him as spies. Solomon Colly, one of the Nolan party, was living in New Mexico, and served as interpreter.[25] The arrival at Santa Fé was on the 3d of March, and the adventurers were questioned by Governor Alencaster, whose conduct was courteous and dignified, but who said that Pike and his men must appear before General Salcedo at Chihuahua. Pike denied that Dr

[24] Pike accuses the Spanish lieut. of deceiving him, by claiming at first to have come from Gov. Alencaster simply to aid the unfortunate explorers and to escort them via Sta Fé to the real Red River. Possibly there was some foundation for the charge, but it is also probable that Pike, full of the prejudices of his time and race, regarding himself as the victim of outrage on account of an innocent blunder, exaggerates the matter. The fact is, that orders from the com. gen. of Provincias Internas required the gov., and very properly, to arrest and send to Chihuahua any Amer. who might be found in Span. territory, always avoiding, if possible, any violent measures. Pike's entry may have been, as he claims, an innocent error, yet the location of his fort, as already noted, even on the Red River theory, and Robinson's coming alone to Sta Fé as to a place not far off or very difficult to find, were suspicious circumstances strengthened by minor details of Pike's later conduct. We are told that, while the leader recognized the necessity of submitting, some of the men were disappointed at not being allowed to test the strength of their fort against the foe—or having a *dust* with the Spaniards. Communication was chiefly in French, Pike knowing but few words of Spanish.

[25] See *Hist. North Mex. States and Texas* for Nolan's adventures in Texas and Chih.

Robinson was a member of his party; attempted by a ruse to prevent the examination of his papers, deeming himself sadly 'deceived' when the governor shrewdly prevented the success of his trick;[26] and occasionally deemed it his duty as a free-born American to be suspicious, independent, and disagreeable to the verge of insolence. It was never quite clear to any of Anglo-Saxon blood that a Spanish official might rightfully interfere with his personal freedom to do as he pleased. Yet Pike frankly admits the kindness with which he was treated, and says much in praise of the Spaniards in New Mexico. As men, he and his party were well treated; as Americans, they must needs have a grievance. Though assured he was not a prisoner, Pike insisted on receiving a certificate that he was obliged to go to Chihuahua.

They left the capital on March 4th, after a dinner given by the governor in their honor, Alencaster taking Pike in his coach drawn by six mules for three miles. Captain Antonio Almansa commanded the escort, and the route was by way of Santo Domingo and Alburquerque to a point below Isleta,[27] where

[26] Pike distributed the important papers among his men, showing his trunk containing the rest to the gov., who seemed satisfied and returned the trunk. Then P. collected the papers, fearing the men, who were drinking pretty freely, might lose them or give them up. But next morning the gov. called for the trunk again, and Zebulon was outwitted!

[27] The places named by P. below Alburquerque are Tousac, S. Fernandez, Sabinez (Sabinal), Jacales, and Sibilleta (Sevilleta, or Cebolleta, acc. to Prince). These may be supposed to include Isleta, Tomé, and Belen, Sabinal being the only name which may be approximately correct. Sibilleta, on the east side of the river, is described as a fine and regular village, and such a place is mentioned in several Span. records as the starting-point of the caravans, sometimes garrisoned by 7 men. Of its founding I find no record, nor is it mentioned in statistical lists of '20-1.

At Sto Domingo rich paintings and images were noted in the church; at S. Felipe a fine bridge across the river. Here Padre Rubí was found to be a liberal and educated man, showing a valuable statistical table. Sandía is called St Dies. At Alburquerque P. Ambrosio Guerra was hospitable, though sadly disappointed that he could not make a Christian of Pike. Here a party of beautiful girls contributed to the entertainment, including two of English parentage, who had been rescued from Ind. captivity. Apparently at Isleta (not named) Dr Robinson was added to the party, and told the story of his adventures. They were welcomed with a dance at Tousac (Tomé?); and at S. Fernandez met Melgares, who sent out an order for the handsomest girls of the region to be sent in for a fandango, 'which portrays more clearly than a chapter of observations the degraded state of the common people.

Lieutenant Facundo Melgares, returning southward with his dragoons, took charge of the party. For Almansa and Melgares Pike has nothing but words of praise. Starting on March 11th, they reached El Paso on the 21st and Chihuahua on April 2d. Here General Salcedo treated them much as Governor Alencaster had done, but insisted on retaining Pike's papers. The Americans were finally sent home through Coahuila and Texas under an escort, leaving Chihuahua at the end of April, and reaching Natchitoches in July. Pike's book was published in 1810; he was promoted to brigadier-general, and lost his life at the taking of Toronto in 1813. His narrative was interesting, and at the time of its publication of much value. Naturally, it adds but little if anything to information derived from Pino and the archive records, yet I shall have occasion to cite it on several points.[28]

Moved by Pike's account of the New Mexican country, and entertaining an idea, perhaps, that Hidalgo's revolution had removed the old restrictions on trade, Robert McKnight, with a party of nine or ten, crossed the plains in 1812, and reached Santa Fé. The result was that their goods were confiscated, and they were arrested, being held in Chihuahua and Durango as prisoners until 1822, when they were re-

---

[28] *Pike (Zebulon Montgomery). An account of expeditions to the sources of the Mississippi, and through the western parts of Louisiana to the sources of the Arkansaw, Kans, La Platte, and Pierre Jaun, rivers; performed by order of the government of the United States, during the years 1805, 1806, and 1807. And a tour through the interior parts of New Spain, when conducted through these provinces, by order of the captain-general, in the year 1807. By Major Z. M. Pike. Illustrated by maps and charts.* Phil., 1810, 8vo, with portrait. Parts ii., iii., contain the exped. to N. Mex. and Chih., from p. 107; also descriptive and documentary appendices to parts ii., iii., separately paged. Also an English edition, from a copy of the MS., with a few verbal corrections and notes by the editor, Thomas Rees, under the title *Pike's Exploratory Travels, etc.*, London, 1811, 4to; and the French translation of M. Breton, *Pike, Voyage au Nouveau Mexique.* Paris, 1812, 8vo, 2 vol. See also *Warren's Memoir*, 20-1; *Prince's Hist. Sk.*, 246-65; *Pino, Expos.*, 14-15; *Barreiro, Ojeada*, 30 (Pike being 'Paykie' to the Span.); *Sta Fé Conquest*, 9; instructions in *Annals of Conq.*, 1808-9, app. 1789-94; *Sta Fé, N. Mex. Review*, July 29, '83; *Bingley's Travels*, 228-39; also Meline, Gregg, and all the well-known writers on N. Mex. subjects. There is no other source of real information than Pike's original narrative.

leased by Iturbide's order. Efforts had been made in 1817 in their behalf, at the intercession of John Scott, the Missouri congressman, by Secretary Adams, through the Spanish minister Onis; but though the latter wrote on the subject both to king and viceroy nothing could be effected.[29]

In 1815 Auguste P. Choteau and Julius de Mun formed a partnership, and went with a large party to the upper Arkansas to hunt and trade with the Indians. They claim to have confined their operations to American territory, which was perhaps somewhat elastic in their eyes; at any rate, we have only their version. Visiting Taos and Santa Fé in 1816 they were most favorably received by Governor Mainez, a very polite old gentleman, who said there would be no objection to their trapping and trading east of the mountains and north of Red River. He even thought he might get from the general for them a license to hunt beaver on the branches of the Rio Grande. Retiring to the north to await the desired permission, they were often visited by parties from the settlements, who came to trade. But early in 1817, after Governor Allande's accession, there was a decided change of Spanish policy. A force of 200 men under Lieutenant Francisco Salazar, marched out to search for an American fort, said to exist on the Rio de las Ánimas, with cannon and 20,000 men! This fort was not found, but in June Sergeant Mariano Bernal was sent out to arrest the Americans, and not only did he bring in Choteau, De Mun, and 24 men as prisoners, but opened their caches on the upper Arkansas, and

[29] *Sta Fé, Message from the president of the U. S., transmitting... information relative to the arrest and imprisonment of certain American citizens at Sta Fé.* Wash., April 15, '18, 8vo, 23 p.; also *Amer. St. Pap.*, xii. 435–52; *U. S. Govt Doc.*, 15th Cong. 1st Sess., 319, 471; *Id.*, 18th Cong. 2d Sess., Sen. Doc. 7, p. 3; *Annals of Congress*, 1817–18, ii. 1954–66; *Gregg's Com. of the Prairies*, i. 19–20; and other works on the Sta Fé trade. The names as given by Scott were Robert McKnight, Benj. Shrive, James Baird, Alfred Allen, Michael M'Donough, Wm Mines, Samuel Chambers, Peter Baum, Thomas Cook, and Miers, an interpreter, with perhaps others. It is said that 2 of them escaped in a canoe down the Canadian in '21. Foster, *Los Ang. in '47*, MS., 3–4, says that in '45 McKnight was one of the owners of the Sta Rita copper mines.

took goods to the value of $30,380.74½. At Santa Fé the prisoners were tried by court-martial, kept for 48 hours in jail, and then dismissed without their property. In September they were back at St Louis appealing to congress for relief. In 1825–6 their claim for $50,000 damages was still being urged; and in 1836 the committee of foreign relations reported "that the demand ought to be made and pressed with an earnestness proportionate to the magnitude of the injury and the unreasonable delay which has arisen in making satisfaction for it." Ex parte testimony in such claims for damages must of course be taken with due allowances.[30]

With the independence of 1821–2 the Santa Fé trade proper—legitimate but for some liberties taken with Mexican custom-house regulations, and unobstructed except by difficulties and dangers of the journey across the plains—may be said to have begun; and it will be a prominent topic of later annals. Captains Glenn, Becknell, and Stephen Cooper were the men who in 1821–2 visited Sante Fé with small parties, making large profits on the limited quantities of goods they succeeded in bringing to market, and laying the foundations of future success. About these earliest trips we have but little information, except that the traders, uncertain as to the best route, endured terrible sufferings from thirst. Becknell made two trips. Major Cooper still lives in California, as I write in 1886; and from Joel P. Walker, one of his companions, I have an original narrative of their adventures.[31]

[30] *Sta Fé, Mess.*, etc., as in note 29, a larger part of the pamphlet being devoted to the Choteau claim than to the McKnight affair. The doc. include a long narrative by Julius de Mun, at St Louis, Nov. 25, '17, and a sworn statement of 11 members of the party—French Canadians all signing with a 'X'—dated Sept. 25, '17. On the claim in 1825–36, see *U. S. Govt Doc.*, 24th Cong. 1st Sess., Sen. Doc. nos. 400, 424. Mention in *Niles' Reg.*, xiv. 47; xvi. 272; xxvii. 312. There was another claim, for the imprisonment of J. Farro, but no particulars are given.

[31] *Walker (J. P.), Narrative of a Pioneer of '41*, MS. For details of their adventures with Ind. and sufferings for want of water, I have no space. Capt. Joe Walker, brother of Joel, with a party of trappers, joined Cooper on the way and accompanied him to Taos. See also, on these exped., *Gregg's Com. Prairies*, i. 20–4; *Escudero*, in *Pino, Not.*, 75; *Niles' Reg.*, xxiii. 16, 177; xxvii. 315; xxviii. 299; *Prince's Hist. Sk.*, 271–3.

The general subject of early exploration, hunting
and trapping, and Indian trade and warfare, in the
great interior, though one that is closely connected
with the history of each of these Pacific States, cannot, of course, be fully treated in any one of my volumes. In each I note those expeditions that directly
concern its territory, and refer the reader to the annals
of other territories, as given in different volumes of
this series. Some chapters on Colorado and the regions
farther north will be found useful in connection with
New Mexican history; and matter that is especially
interesting may be found in my volumes on the *North-
west Coast*.[32]

During these 22 years the population of *gente de
razon* may be said to have increased from 19,000 to
30,000 in New Mexico proper, excluding the El Paso
district; while the number of pueblo Indians remained
practically unchanged, between 9,500 and 10,000. Official reports establish these figures with tolerable accuracy, but afford no satisfactory basis for more detailed
classification.[33] The capital villa of Santa Fé reached,

[32] *Coyner's Lost Trappers*, Cin., 1859, is a little work containing many interesting and valuable details of the early trappers' experiences; but in the
part concerning N. Mex. there is evidently a serious error in dates. Workman and Spencer in 1807-9 are represented as having crossed from the upper
Arkansas, south of Pike Peak, to the Colorado, descended that river to the
ford, started on the Span. trail for Sta Fé, met a caravan from that town,
accompanied it to Cal., and returned with it to Sta Fé in 1810, and lived
there for 15 years, until the traders came often from the east. But no caravans crossed from N. Mex. to Cal. in Span. times, or before '22, so that the
date must be wrong, and much doubt is thrown on the general accuracy of
this part of the narrative. The northern Sta Fé trail to Cal. was first followed by Wolfskill, in '31, and the trading caravans were of later date.
[33] A report of Gov. Alencaster in 1805, given in *Meline's 2,000 Miles*, 212,
gives a total pop. of 20,626 Span. and 8,152 Ind., besides 6,209 Span. at El
Paso; and reports of Gov. Melgares in '19-20 give Span. 27,214 and 28,436;
Ind. 8,626 and 9,923. *Arch. Sta Fé*, MS. Reports of the custodio, P. José
Pedro Rubin de Célis, for '20-1, not including the large towns, gives, Span.
17,401 and 19,174; Ind. 7,840 and 9,034. *Id.* These are the only exact reports that are reliable. There are general estimates, for the most part including El Paso and Ind., as follows: 1803, pop. 40,200, acc. to Humboldt, *Essai
Pol.*, 155, and other works, followed by a dozen or more writers; 1804, Gov.
Chacon, in *Arch. Sta Fé*, followed by Pino; 28,798 in 1801. *Prince's Hist.
Sk.*, 230-1; 39,797. *Soc. Mex. Geog.*, ii. 20. About 30,000, half Ind. *Pike.*
34,205 in 1810. *Soc. Mex. Geog.*, vii. 138; 2da ép., i. 291. 40,000, perhaps
50,000, in 1811. *Pino, Expos.*, 44-5; *Not.*, 14-17. 30,825. *Humboldt.*

perhaps, a population of 6,000 in its immediate vicinity; but on account of the meagre records, frequent discrepancies, and irregular grouping of the settlements in partidos, local items of population have little significance. In number, location, and in all respects except an increase of Spanish population at certain points, the settlements remained as before, and I refer to the final note of the preceding chapter.[34]

Commercial methods continued as before. Presumably, fairs were still held at Taos for trade with the Indians, though I find no direct indication of the fact in this period;[35] each autumn the great caravan departed for the south; at El Paso, to a greater extent than before, the company was divided, small parties seeking different markets; and large flocks of sheep were now driven from the province. In 1805 the viceroy decreed that all goods bartered by New Mexicans at the annual fair in San Bartolomé valley from the 18th to the 23d of December should be free from the payment of taxes or duties.[36] Down to about 1798

[34] According to the official reports cited in note 33, the Span. pop. of the leading towns, most or all including outlying ranchos, in 1805 and 1820 was as follows: Sta Fé, 3,741, 6,038; La Cañada, 2,188, 2,633; Alburquerque, 4,294, 2,564; S. Juan de los Caballeros, 1,888, 2,125; Abiquiú, 1,218, 2182 (3,029 in '21); Belen, 1,588, 2,103 (1,756 in '21); Taos, 1,337, 1,252; Sta Clara, 967, 1,116; Isleta, 378, 2,324; Picuríes, 17, 1,041. In the report of '21 Socorro is given with a pop. of 1,580. The largest Ind. pueblos in '20–1 were: Taos, 751; S. Ildefonso, 527; Cochití, 653; Sta Ana, 527; Laguna, 950; Acoma, 829; Zuñi, 1,597; and Isleta, 513. Humboldt for 1803 gives Sta Fé a pop. of 3,600, Alburquerque, 6,000, Taos, 8,900; Pike in 1807, with a good descrip., gives Sta Fé 4,500 souls, and Pino in 1811 a pop. of 5,000. Pecos, acc. to Pino, was on its last legs, having but 30 fighting men in '11, and in '20 its pop. was 58. An official report of the ayuntamiento gives the pop. of El Paso in '22 as 8,384 souls, of which married couples 161, single men 2,267, single women 3,173, widowers 305, widows 417, farmers 2,072, artisans 681, laborers 269, teachers 8, priests 2, merchants 5, manuf. 6, retired soldiers 6, students 3, treasury officials 2; total value of property $234,018. *Arch. Sta Fé*, MS. Pike describes Ojo Caliente as a town of 500 inhab. and a mill; and his mention of several unknown names in the south has been noticed.

[35] April 24, 1806, Gen. Salcedo orders the trade with Ind. at the settlements to be encouraged. *Arch. Sta Fé*, MS. Possibly the Taos trade declined, or was more scattered to other points.

[36] Dec. 18, 1805, original decree of the viceroy in behalf of N. Mex. trade. *Dispos. Varias*, i. 131; *Diario de Mex.*, i. 353. All duties were paid in the south, there being no custom-house in N. Mex. In 1803 Gov. Chacon made a report on the industries of N. Mex. *Arch. Sta Fé*, MS. He notes the division of the caravans, and the export of 25,000 sheep per year (Pike makes it 30,000). Interior trade is carried on by 12 or 14 merchants, only 2 or 3 of

no coin was known, but later the salaries of officers and
soldiers were paid in money, furnishing a supply by
no means adequate to provincial needs. The government *estanco* on tobacco, powder, and playing-cards,
especially the first, was a great burden for the people.
The total value of imports, as given by Pino from an
official report of the Vera Cruz *consulado* in 1804, was
$112,000 in a year; while the exports, chiefly wool,
wine, and peltries, were only $60,000, leaving a bal-
ance of trade of $52,000 against New Mexico. Ex-
ports might easily be tripled, as Pino thought, by
proper encouragement, including the opening of ports
on the Texas and Sonora coasts.[37]

There were no new developments in agricultural
industries. Products in New Mexico proper were
wholly consumed at home, and irrigation generally
protected the inhabitants against drought, as in 1803
and 1820–2; and the Indians, as far as possible, tried
to follow their old custom of storing the products of
plentiful harvests, though the improvident settlers
were sometimes caught napping and suffered from
scarcity. All reports praise the agricultural, and
especially the stock-raising, advantages of the province, under proper encouragement.[38]   Spanish artisans

them using their own capital. Everybody trades in his own way, often a
very bad way. Pino describes the preparations and outfit of the caravans,
starting 500 strong from La Joya de Sevilleta in Nov.; and he notes that a
smaller force starting in 1809 was attacked by Ind., losing several killed and
300 horses. For Pike's statement that two caravans left N. Mex., one in the
spring and the other in autumn, I find no foundation; and the same remark
may be made of his assertion that 30,000 sheep are driven each year from the
province. Pike gives some current prices as follows: flour, $2 per 100 lbs.;
salt, $5 per mule-load; sheep, $1 each; pork, 25 cts per lb.; beeves, $5 each;
wine del Paso, $15 per bbl.; horses, $11 each; mules, $30 each; superfine
cloths, $25 per yd; fine do, $20; linen, $4; and other dry goods in proportion.
And Pino: native tobacco, 4 reales per lb.; wheat and maize, $1 per fanega;
cotton, $3 per fanega (!).

[37] The imports included $61,000 of European goods, $7,000 Asiatic, $34,000
American, and—though N. Mex. was a stock-raising country—$10,000 of
horses and mules. Yet the gov. in 1803 says that 600 horses and mules were
annually sent away.

[38] *Chacon (Fernando), Informe del gobernador sobre Industrias del N. Mex.*,
1803, in *Arch. Sta Fé*, MS., dated Aug. 28th. Tobacco raised for home consumption even by the padres, and but for the estanco on cigars, snuff, etc., the
product might be vastly increased. Books on agric. and stock-raising much
needed. Wool, sheep, and a little cotton exported. No use made of timber.

included a few carpenters and blacksmiths, but nearly all mechanical and other work was done by the Indians, who still made pottery for home use, tanned leather, from which bridles were made, and wove large quantities of coarse blankets. They also made some progress in weaving cotton textures of low grade under an instructor from Mexico.[39] Governor Chacon, in 1803, says that copper is abundant, and apparently rich, but no mines are worked, though there is much coal of good quality. Pino, in 1812, also notes the existence of rich deposits of copper, gold, and silver, of which no use is made; but Pike, in 1807, states that a copper mine west of the river, in latitude 34°, yields 20,000 mule-loads of metal annually, while vessels of wrought copper were among the country's exports. Bartlett tells us that the Santa Rita mine—really just below 33°—was worked from 1804; and Prince gives more details, to the effect that the mine was discovered in 1800 by Lieutenant-colonel Carrisco, who sold it in 1804 to Francisco Manuel Elguea of Chihuahua, by whom work was at once begun, 100 mules being constantly employed to transport the metal to Mexico for use in the mint.[40] I think there is room for some doubt as to the early working of this mine, though a beginning was probably made before 1822. Pino says that old silver mines were found closed up, with the tools inside, and doubtless the prospect-holes made by the Spaniards before 1680 were thus found occasionally; but there is little or

Pino tells us that maize yields 50 to 100 fold. Tithes amount to about $10,000, and are distributed as follows, giving an idea of the country's products: maize 3,000 fanegas, wheat 2,000 fan., vegetables 1,000 fan., wool 1,000 arrobas, cotton 40 arr., wine 400 arr., sheep 5,000, calves 200, goats 500. As we have seen, there are some slight indications that each pueblo, in earlier times, had 4 sq. leagues of land assigned; but Pino states that in 1811 a pueblo has but 1 league, and for this should properly have 500 Ind. As few have over 300, there is much land not used, on which Span. should be allowed to settle. See mention of agric. topics in *Nouv. Ann. Voy.*, xxvi. 409; *Gordon's Hist. and Geog. Mem.*, 85–6; *Niles' Reg.*, xxiii. 16.

[39] *Pino, Expos.*, 13; *Id., Not.*, 19–20; *Pike's Explor. Trav.*, 335.

[40] *Bartlett's Pers. Narr.*, i. 227–9; *Prince's Hist. Sk.*, 241; *Sta Fé, N. Mex. Review*, July 29, '83. In 1804 a Comanche reported a gold mine in a cerro 15 d. from Pecos, and was ordered to bring in some of the ore. *Arch. Sta Fé*, MS. Coal ment. in *Soc. Mex. Geog.*, ii. 20, in 1805.

nothing to show that any practical mining was ever done in New Mexico under Spanish rule. Stone was not used for building, but only adobes; yet a semi-transparent *yeso*, or gypsum, was quarried near Santa Fé and used for window-panes. Pike calls it a flexible talc.[41] Pino tells us that roads in the province were good, but he did not allude to artificial improvements.

There were no colleges or public schools, and no professional man—except of the military profession—or priest had been produced in New Mexico. There were a few private teachers in the larger towns, and at El Paso from 1806-7 a school seems to have been maintained.[42] The only medical man in the country was the presidial surgeon at Santa Fé. Of social manners and customs we have nothing pertaining especially to this period, except the somewhat superficial observations of Pike. He represents the New Mexicans, however, as brave, industrious, and above all hospitable, but somewhat loose in their ideas of morality, implying that on this point he could say much more than would be in good taste, considering the kindness with which he had been treated. In most social respects this province closely resembled California, where the condition of affairs is well known to readers of other volumes in this series.

The government and administration of justice were still essentially military, as they had always been, the governor being also military chief. There were no ayuntamientos or other municipal bodies, no courts, no taxes, no treasuries or municipal funds. Each of the eight alcaldes attended to all local matters in his own *alcaldia*, being responsible to the governor, from whose decision the only appeal was to the audiencia of Guadalajara. An audiencia at Chihuahua was deemed an urgent necessity. The governor, with a salary of $4,000, had no legal adviser or notary, but

[41] The yeso is mentioned by Chacon and Pino.
[42] Five hundred and eighty-four children in attendance in 1806; 460 in 1807. *Arch. Sta Fé*, MS. Pino says there were no beggars or vagrants.

was aided by two lieutenants and two alfereces. The alcaldes were vecinos, who got no pay. A lieutenant of the governor in his military capacity ruled at El Paso for a salary of $2,000.[43]

The regular military force supported by the royal treasury was 121 men, forming the presidial or veteran company of Santa Fé.[44] But Pino states that an average force of 1,500 men had been required to defend the province, which the settlers had furnished without pay, and even armed and equipped at their own cost, thus saving the king $43,090,000 in the past 118 years.[45] There was probably a degree of exaggeration in this, but the deputy complained, with reason, that this system was an intolerable burden, urging that New Mexico should be put in this respect on the same basis as other provinces; that the militia should be properly organized, paid, and armed; and that five presidios should be established or transferred from the south. In January 1813 Pino urged this part of his scheme anew in the córtes; it was referred to the *comision ultra marina;* and in May some kind of an order had been issued by the regency to the viceroy, probably one to investigate and report.[46] A year later Don Simon Elias, being called upon for his opinion, reported against the transfer of the southern presidios to New Mexico, but favored the establishment of two new ones on the Rio Grande between Sevilleta and El Paso.[47] So nothing was done. At this time

[43] Davis, *El Gringo*, 83, notes the execution of a soldier in '15 for a petty theft 'as an evidence of the iron rule that prevailed in those days.' By the constitution a prov. of less than 60,000 pop. was to be joined to the adjoining prov. for the election of a diputado. Sto Domingo was an exception, and Pino argued that N. Mex. should be another.

[44] Distrib. as follows, acc. to Pino: 39 in the real de caballada, or movable detachment, 12 on guard at the capital, 7 at Sevilleta on the southern frontier, and the rest scattered at various points with the militia. The pay of a soldier was $240. Pike, *Explor. Trav.*, 344, talks of a force of 1,000 dragoons at Sta Fé.

[45] *Pino, Expos.*, 14–20; *Id., Not.*, 41 -4. In 1808, 3 companies of militia were organized under captains Lorenzo Gutierrez, José Fran. Pino, and Bartolomé Vaca, 61 men in each comp.; but down to 1812 they had received no pay.

[46] *Diario de Córtes*, 1813, xvii. 50; xix. 307.

[47] May 20, '14, report of Elias, in *Pinart, Doc. Hist. Chih.*, MS., 15–24. Cost of Sta Fé comp., 127 men, in '14, $36,644. MS. of *Pinart Col.*

HIST. ARIZ. AND N. MEX. 20

the presidio of Carrizal, formerly at El Paso, was no longer considered as belonging to New Mexico.

We have seen that the number of christianized pueblo Indians neither increased nor diminished perceptibly in these 22 years; nor were there any changes in the system of mission management. There were from 19 to 22 Franciscan friars in charge of the missions; but they lived chiefly at the places having a large Spanish population. Pino states that in 1811 in 19 purely Indian pueblos there were but five missionaries. There was one secular priest at Santa Fé, and there, as at Alburquerque and Santa Cruz, the friars were supported by fees; the rest by their sínodos of $330 from the royal treasury.[48]   On one phase of the earlier controversy—complaints of the padres against the governor and alcaldes for ill-treating the Indians— I find nothing new, though there is little reason to suppose that any practical reform had been effected. Lieutenant Pike found the natives virtually slaves, and cruelly treated by the Spanish officers. On the other hand, the friars' shortcomings were still a current topic of dispute. In consequence of a petition from the natives, the exact purport of which is unknown to me, Protector-general Andrade at Guadalajara in 1810 appointed Felipe Sandoval 'protector partidario' of the New Mexican Indians. Sandoval in his report stated that the padres were content with simply saying mass, and the neophytes were in reality deprived of spiritual instruction. This brought out a reprimand from the bishop of Durango; and the vice-custodio, Padre Sebastian Álvarez, called upon the friars for a defence in 1818. They indignantly denied the truth of the charges, declaring that the 'protector' was not

---

[48] *Pino, Not.*, 15–16, 88; *Expos.*, 7–8. He notes that an Ind. woman will not bear more than 4 children, taking preventive drinks. In '20–1, there were 19–21 padres, with 11 sínodos, amounting to $3,289 or $3,900. *Chacon, Informe*, MS. I make no attempt to record the names of padres serving during this and later periods, though many of them might probably be obtained from old mission registers and other records still existing.

only influenced by evil motives but was a thief.[49]   No bishop visited the province after 1760, and therefore there were no confirmations.   Delegate Pino, a New Mexican 50 years of age, had never seen a bishop until he came to Spain in 1812.   He urgently demanded the erection of his province into a separate bishopric, and the carrying-out of the royal order and papal bull of 1777–9 in favor of a college.   His idea was that the tithes, yielding $9–10,000, as disadvantageously rented, were ample to pay the episcopal salary and all other necessary expenses; besides, the sínodos of six missions might justly be added, since the fees at Belen, Isleta, Abiquiú, Santa Clara, San Juan, and Taos would suffice for the friars' support.   Accordingly, on January 26, 1813, the erection of a bishopric and establishment of the college were decreed by the córtes; and some supplementary instructions were issued in May; but practically nothing was done under Spanish rule.[50]

It is to be regretted that nothing is known of political events and sentiments in New Mexico during the war of independence in 1811–21.   There is no indication that the great national struggle sent even a ripple of excitement to the northern interior; and we may reasonably conclude that officials and people here, as in California, were content to await the issue, in which

[49] Appointment of Sandoval Aug. 20, 1810, in *Arch. Sta Fé*, MS.   Developments of 1818. *N. Mex., Defensas de Misioneros*, in *Id*.   On March 26, '18, the gov. and bishop were asked by the audiencia to see that the Ind. of Jemes should receive proper Christian instruction in Spanish. *Id*.   The friars who signed the *Defensas* were Mariano Peñon, Laguna; José Pedro Rubí, Belen; José Ign. Sanchez, Isleta; Diego Martinez de Arellano, Sandía; Gerónimo Riego, S. Felipe.   In 1805 Padre Prada asks the gov. for relief for Zuñi, where the position of the padre in time of peace was intolerable, and in war most perilous.   The Zuñis have no inclination to Christianity, and only a few pay any attention to its rites.   They were friendly to the hostile Navajos, who, on their visits to Zuñi, were always furnished women with whom to sleep; and similar privileges were offered to Lieut. Narbona and his men. *Arch. Sta Fé*, MS.

[50] *Pino, Not.*, 19, 22, 31–3, 90–2; *Id., Expos.*, 7–8, 25–7; *Diario de Córtes*, 1812, xvi. 160; 1813, xx. 141–2; *Córtes, Col. de Decretos*, iii. 200; *Arrillaga, Recop.*, 1830, p. 95–6.   In his *Adiciones* to Pino, p. 34 of *Noticias*, Barreiro speaks of a decree of Jan. 26, '18, in favor of the bishopric and colegio.   Something was also attempted in '23.

they took but slight interest, and of which in its details they were to a great extent kept in ignorance.
In New Mexico, the element of private correspondence, so important an aid in tracing the annals of
this period in California, is entirely lacking in the
records within my reach.   We have seen that in 1822
Governor Melgares was succeeded by Chavez, and
also that Vizcarra ruled for a time in the same year.
Besides this brief record, we have one important document ⸫ 1821, which shows how news of Iturbide's
accession was received, and which may indicate that
New Mexicans were not behind Californians in the ver-
satility displayed in accepting the successive changes
of government, with prodigious and suddenly acquired
enthusiasm for each.

It was on September 11th that the 'dulce voz de
libertad' was first heard, and lovers of the country and
religion swore to the independence at Santa Fé; and on
December 26th—¡dia glorioso! ¡Dia de admiracion,
y dia tan eternal para los Nuevos Méxicos, que de padres á hijos se ira trasmitiendo hasta la mas remota
posteridad!—came news of Iturbide's entry into Mexico.   Dozens of citizens received communications in
writing and print by the mail of that day, which they
read aloud to the crowd at the post-office, the governor reading a patriotic address from the city of
Tepic, with a poetic effusion of that 'liberalísimo
europeo' Don Pedro Negrete, on listening to which
all, from the 'tierno parvulito' to the 'trémulo an-
ciano,' were beside themselves with joy, and filled the
air with *vivas*, as Melgares shouted, "New Mexicans,
this is the occasion for showing the heroic patriotism
that inflames you; let your sentiments of liberty and
gratitude be published abroad, and let us show tyrants that although we live at the very extremity of
North America we love the holy religion of our
fathers; that we cherish and protect the desired
union between Spaniards of both hemispheres; and
that, with our last drop of blood, we will sustain the

sacred independence of the Mexican empire!" The
6th of January, 1822, was set apart for a formal celebration, which should, if possible, excel that of Tepic.
At dawn the salutes of artillery and the marching of
processions began; and with dawn of the next day,
ended the grand *baile* at the palacio.   Never did
Santa Fé behold such a splendid display.   The *inde-
pendientisimo* postmaster, Juan Bautista Vigil, excelled himself in painting decorations; the *excesivo
independiente* alcalde, Pedro Armendaris, led a tri-
umphant *paseo;* and a grand *loa de las tres garantias*
was performed, by Alférez Santiago Abreu representing independence, Curate and Vicar Juan Tomás
Terrazas religion, and Chaplain Francisco Osio the
union.   All through the day and night the villa was
painted red with independence or death, and Governor Melgares wrote a flaming account of the whole
affair for the *Gaceta Imperial.*[51]   Doubtless Don Facundo, realizing the side on which his bread was but-
tered, saw to it that nothing was lost in telling the
story; and presumably the fall of Iturbide a little
later was celebrated with equal enthusiasm.   There
was nothing mean or one-sided in New Mexican
patriotism.

[51] *Melgares (Facundo), Demostraciones que para soleminzar la Independencia del
Imperio hizo la ciudad de Sta Fé, 1822.*   In *Gaceta Imp.*, March 23, 26, '22, ii.
85–93.   Proclamation of the plan de Iguala in N. Mex., 1821, mentioned in
Alaman, Hist. Mej., v. 237–9, from the same source.   It is noticeable that in
the celebration the gov. is called *jefe político*, and an *ayuntamiento* is mentioned.   Sept. 10, '22, N. Mex. was made one of the 5 Provincias Internas
under a com. gen. at Chih., corres. to the earlier intendencia; that is, there
was practically no change in N. Mex. *Mex., Mem. Guerra,* 1823, p. 25.

CHAPTER XIV.

A MEXICAN TERRITORY.

1823-1845.

THE ruler at Santa Fé during the Mexican republican régime of 1823–46 was known as jefe político until 1837, and later bore the title of gobernador. The list, as made up from those of Prince, Meline, Ritch, and the United States land-office reports, with slight corrections from original sources, is given in a note.[1] As a rule, nothing is definitely known respecting the acts of these officials or the circumstances of their accession to power.

Until 1824 New Mexico was a province, one of the Provincias Internas, until, by the acta constitutiva of January 31st, it was joined to the provinces of Chi-

[1] List of governors of N. Mex., 1823–46: Antonio Vizcarra to June 1823; Francisco Javier Chavez, June and July, acting; Bartolomé Vaca, 1823 to Sept. 1825; Antonio Narbona, Sept. 1825 to May 1827; Manuel Armijo, 1827–8; Antonio Vizcarra, acting in 1828; José Antonio Chavez, 1828–31; Santiago Abreu, 1831-2, or perhaps to 1833; Francisco Sarracino, 1833 to May 1835, though Juan Rafael Ortiz seems to be named in the archives in Oct. 1834; Mariano Chavez, acting, May to July 1835; Albino Perez, 1835-7; Pedro Muñoz, acting, 1837-8; José Gonzalez, pretendant or revolutionary gov., 1837-8; Manuel Armijo, Jan. 1838 to 1846; Antonio Sandoval, acting, 1841; Mariano Martinez de Lejanza, acting, 1844-5; José Chavez, acting, Sept. to Dec. 1845; and Juan Bautista Vigil y Alarid, acting, in Aug. 1846.

huahua and Durango, to form the Estado Interno del Norte. Durango, however, protesting against this arrangement, because the capital was fixed at Chihuahua, the two southern provinces were made states, and from July 6th New Mexico became a territory of the republic. At the same time the El Paso district was joined to Chihuahua, but no eastern or western bounds were assigned to New Mexico, it being understood that the territory extended in those directions far out beyond the settlements, and in the north to the Arkansas, the limit of Mexican possessions since 1819. Under the new constitution of December 1836 the territory became a department, and was so called to the end of Mexican rule.[2]

Under the new forms of the republican régime there was practically no change in the government, all branches being controlled somewhat arbitrarily by the governor. There was a kind of legislature, or executive council, of four or six members, known as the diputacion provincial, or territorial, from 1824, junta departamental from 1837, and sometimes asamblea in 1844–5; but this body is stated by Barreiro and others to have been a nullity, and very little is known of its acts.[3] Instead of the alcaldes mayores of Spanish times, there were ayuntamientos at a few of the larger towns, with ordinary alcaldes at the smaller settlements.[4] In 1844, by a decree of the assembly,

[2] July 19, 1823, decree alluding to N. Mex. as one of the Provincias Int. de Occidente, and providing that the civil and military command be separated. *Mex., Col. Ord. y Decretos*, ii. 147–8. Acta const. of Jan. 1824. *Mex., Col. Constit.*, i. 3. Decree of Feb. 4, 1824, N. Mex. to send one diputado to the diputacion provincial of Chih. *Mex., Col. Ord. y Dec.*, iii. 25. July 6th, 'La prov. de N. Mex. queda de territorio de la federacion.' *Id.*, 55. July 27th, bounds of Chih., including El Paso. *Id.*, 59. Protest of Durango against estado del norte, with capital at Chih. *Pinart, Doc. Hist. Chih.*, MS., ii. 1. Law of Dec. 30, 1836, 'N. Mex. será departamento.' *Arrillaga, Recop.*, 1836, p. 379. Jan. 18, 1845, N. Mex. declared one of the departamentos fronterizos, as per art. 134, pt 17, of the constitution. *Mex., Leyes (Palacio)*, 1344–6, p. 81.

[3] *Barreiro, Ojeada*, 27–8. In 1831 the members are named, Ant. J. Martinez being the first. *Arch. Sta Fé*, MS. In 1844 Jesus María Gallegos was pres. and J. B. Vigil sec. *Abert's Rept*, 479. In 1845 the asamblea had four members, and one suplente not named. *S. Miguel, Rep. Mex.*, 60.

[4] In 1827–32, acc. to *Barreiro, Ojeada*, 42, and a table by Narbona, in *Pino, Not.*, 27–30, only Sta Fé, Cañada, and Taos had ayuntamientos. The parti-

published in a bando by the governor, the department
was divided into three districts and seven partidos;
and presumably prefecturas were organized, since one
or two prefects are incidentally named. Of New
Mexican representatives in congress, I have found no
record.[5]

dos were Sta Fé, including S. Miguel del Vado, Cochití, Jemes, Sandía, and
Alameda under alcaldes, and also Tesuque, Pecos, Sto Domingo, Cia, Sta
Ana, and S. Felipe; Alburquerque, including Isleta, Tomé, Belen, Socorro,
and Laguna as alcaldías, and also Sabinal, Acoma, and Zuñi; and Cañada, including S. Juan, Taos, and Abiquiú under alcaldes, with Sta Clara, S. Ildefonso, Pujuaque, Nambé, and Picuríes. The division into districts and
partidos on June 17, 1844, was as follows: Central district, cabecera Sta Fé,
which is also capital of the department, with three partidos: 1st, Sta Fé, in-
cluding S. Ildefonso, Pujuaque, Nambé, Cuyamanque, Tesuque, Rio Tesuque,
Ciénega, Cieneguilla, Agua Fria, Galisteo, Real del Oro, and Tuerto; 2d,
Algodones, including Rayada, Cochití, Peña Blanca, Chilili, Sto Domingo,
Cubero, S. Felipe, Jemes, Cia, Sta Ana, and Angostura; 3d, S. Miguel del
Vado, including Pecos, Gusano, Rio de la Vaca, Mula, Estramosa, S. José,
Pueblo, Puertecito, Cuosto, Cerrito, Anton Chico, 1ecolote, Las Vegas, and
Cepillo. Northern district, cabecera Los Luceros, with two partidos: 1st,
Rio Arriba, capital Luceros, including Sta Cruz de la Cañada, Chimayo,
Truchas, Sta Clara, Vegas, Chama, Cuchillo, Abiquiú, Rito, Colorado, Ojo
Caliente, Ranchitos, Chamita, S. Juan, Rio Arriba, Joya, and Embudo;
2d, Taos, capital Don Fernandez (S. Fernando de Taos?), including S.
Francisco, Arroyo Hondo, Arroyo Seco, Desmontes (Dos Montes?), Ciene-
guilla, Picuríes, Sta Bárbara, Zampas, Chemisal, Llano Peñasco, Moro,
Huérfano, and Cimarron. South-eastern district, cabecera Valencia, with
two partidos: 1st, Valencia, including S. Fernando, Tomé, Socorro, Limitar,
Polvaderas, Sabinal, Elames, Casa Colorado, Cibolleta (Sevilleta), Sabino,
Parida, Luis Lopez, Belen, Lunas, Lentes, Zuñi, Acoma, and Rito; 2d,
Bernalillo, including Isleta, Padilla, Pajarito, Atrisco, Placeres, Alburquerque, Alameda, Corrales, and Sandía. Doc. from the Arch. Sta Fé, translated
in Abert's Rept., 477–9. Abert and Prince choose to call the partidos 'counties.'

[5] Except of José A. Chavez, in 1827–8, described in the Semblanzas de Diputados as 'consigned' to Francisco Tagle.

Gregg, Com. Prairies, i. 222, 233–8, and Davis, El Gringo, 105–7, give an
account of the administration of justice by the alcaldes, or through the arbitration of hombres buenos, appeals to the governor, penalties of fine and imprisonment, not very impartially awarded, absence of all the legal forms of
court routine, exemptions under the military and ecclesiastical fueros, the
impossibility of obtaining justice, and the consequent prevalence of thefts and
other petty offences. In these matters N. Mexico was like all the distant Mexican territories, and much light will be thrown on them by a perusal of the annals of California, where the records are more complete. In Mex., Mem.
Justicia, 1826, p. 6, it is said there was no juez de letras nor lawyer in N. Mex.,
and litigation had to be carried on at enormous cost in Durango, Zacatecas, etc.
In Id., 1828, no. 2, p. 14, there is said to be a juzgado de distrito at Sta Fé;
also that the circuit court of Parral has jurisdiction in N. Mex. In Id.,
1831, p. 7. 18, $3,000 has been assigned for a lawyer to serve as juez de letras.
Yet in 1832 Barreiro, Ojeada, 38–9, who has served two years as asesor, or
legal adviser, complains that 'jamas se castigan los delitos, porque no hay en
lo absoluto quien sepa formar una sumaria, evacuar una defensa, ni llevar la
voz fiscal; that few are able to carry their cases to Mex.; and that he de-
spairs of being able to introduce order into the administration of justice in

Down to 1839 the territory was under the military rule of a commandant, called militar, principal, or de armas, who was subordinate to the comandante general of Chihuahua. At times the civil and military commands were held by the same and at others by different men. In 1824 the presidial company at Santa Fé had 119 men, including officers, at a total cost of $35,488. A Mexican law of 1826 provided for three permanent cavalry companies of 100 rank and file, each at a cost of $87,882; and for two companies of active militia, each of 100 men. Barreiro, however, writing in 1832, states that the territory had still only its one company, urging an increase of force and a transfer of the presidio to Valverde. In 1835, on the coming of Governor Perez, who was also comandante principal, some slight effort seems to have been made to reorganize the forces, without definite results. In 1839 New Mexico was separated from Chihuahua, and made a comandancia, Governor Armijo having later the title of comandante general. From this time, also, in Mexican reports the existence of the three companies is noted, though with only men enough for one. The truth seems to be that here, as in California during the larger part of Mexican rule, the military organization hardly existed except on paper.[6]

N. Mex. He urges the 'reëstablishment' of a juzgado de letras. In the estimates of 1838, *Mex.*, *Mem. Hac.*, 2d pt, the ministros and fiscales are to receive $4,000 each. Prince, 229, names Ex-gov. Abreu as chief justice down to 1837. All is very confusing, and it is hard to determine whether the territory ever had any courts except those of the ordinary alcaldes.

[6] Company report of Dec. 1824, showing that the captain was jefe político, with $4,000 pay. MS. of the *Pinart Col.* Law of March 21, 1826, establishing presidial and militia companies. *Arrillaga, Recop.*, Jan–June 1836, p. 193–204; *Riesgo* and *Valdés, Mem. Estad.*, 26. In 1824 Juan José Arocha was com. de armas. *Arch. Sta Fé*, MS., 1832; Barreiro, *Ojeada*, 30–6, on military matters. He urges the necessity of an increased force to hold the Americans as well as the Indians in check, separation from the Chihuahua comandancia, and especially a transfer of the presidio to Valverde, it being of no use at Sta Fé. He advises selling the old wall of the capital for building material; also the establishing of a military school, and organization of the militia. On Aug. 1, 1834, Blas Hinojos was capt. of the company and comandante principal of N. Mex., signing a proclamation in favor of Sta Anna, which is also signed by sergeants and corporals of Sta Fé, Taos, and S. Miguel del Vado, indicating either a distribution of the company at 3 points or an attempt to

Of events in their order from year to year, there are but few which require more extended notice than is given in the appended summary, or chronologic list.[7]

partially organize the three companies. *El Tiempo*, Sept. 28, 1834. Gov. Perez, in 1835, brought money and arms. *Doc. Hist. Cal.*, MS., i. 166; *Arrillaga, Recop.*, 1835, p. 23–4. Support of powder manufactory in N. Mex. *Id.*, Jan.–June 1836, p. 404–5. Law of April 22, 1839, establishing a comandancia gen. *Id.*, 1839, p. 104–5; *Vallejo, Doc. Hist. Mex.*, i. 179; *Mex., Col. Leyes y Dec.*, 1839, p. 129. A presidial comp. at Vado in 1841. *Arch. Sta Fé*, MS. Some vague records of the regular and militia companies 1843–5, in *Mex., Mem. Guerra*, 1844, docs. 3, 22–3; *Id.*, 1845, docs. 1, 4, 6, 8; *Id.*, 1846, doc. 11, 15–16. In 1845 Col Rafael Archuleta is named as comandante militar. *S. Miguel, Rep. Mex.*, 85.

[7] 1823. Vizcarra, Chavez, and Vaca, gov. Treaty of peace with the Navajos.

1824. Vaca, gov. N. Mexico a province of the Estado del Norte, and a territory from July. Beginning of the regular Sta Fé trade and first use of wagons. U. S. overtures to N. Mexico, according to *Ritch*. Pattie's visit.

1825. Vaca and Narbona, gov. Survey of a U. S. road for the Sta Fé trade begun. Navajos again troublesome.

1826. Narbona, gov. Mexican decree for increase of military force.

1827. Narbona and Armijo, gov.

1828. Armijo, Vizcarra, and Chavez, gov. Under the Mex. law expelling Spaniards, according to Prince, all the friars were forced to depart, except two, Albino and Castro, who, by reason of their extreme age, and by the payment of $500 each, were permitted to remain. In *Niles' Reg.*, xxxvii. 230, it is recorded that many of the expelled Spaniards came to the U. S. with the Sta Fé caravans of 1828–9. Discovery of the 'old' gold placers.

1829. Chavez, gov. Proposition of John D. Bradburn to navigate the Rio Grande and colonize N. Mex. declined by Mex. govt. *Bustamante, Voz de la Patria*, i. no. 7, p. 9–10. Bent's fort on the Arkansas built.

1830. Chavez, gov. New decree for the establishment of a bishopric, but nothing done. Communication with California opened by Vaca and Ewing Young.

1831. Chavez and Abreu, gov. Wolfskill, Jackson, and Young visit Cal.

1832. Abreu, gov. Publication of the *Ojeada sobre Nuevo-Mexico. Que da una idea de sus producciones naturales, y de algunas otras cosas que se consideran oportunas para mejorar su estado, é ir proporcionando su futura felicidad. Formada por el Lic. Antonio Barreiro, asesor de dicho territorio. A peticion del escmo. señor ministro que fué de justicia Don José Ignacio Espinosa. Y dedicada al escmo. señor vice-presidente de los Estados Unidos Mexicanos Don Anastacio Bustamante*. Puebla, 1832, 8vo, 42 p., 2 l., 10 p. This somewhat meritorious little work was also embodied in a later edition of Pino's *Noticias Históricas*. Fr. Juan Felipe Ortiz, vicar-general of N. Mexico.

1833. Sarracino, gov. Visit of the bishop of Durango, whose reception is described by Prince as very enthusiastic.

1834. Sarracino and Ortiz, gov. Grand demonstration of civil and military authorities on Aug. 1st in favor of Santa Anna and the pronunciamiento of Cuernavaca. *El Tiempo*, Sept. 28, 1834.

1835. Serracino, Chavez, and Perez, gov. First newspaper of N. Mexico, *El Crepúsculo*, published at Taos by Padre Martinez for four weeks. Founding of Las Vegas. Mora grant. War with the Navajos.

1836. Perez, gov. Under the new central system N. Mexico was to be a department, and the ruler a governor instead of political chief.

1837. Perez, Gonzalez, and Muñoz, gov. Revolution, as narrated elsewhere in this chapter. Fatal typhoid epidemic, which, with the following small-pox, according to Gregg, carried off one tenth of the inhabitants in 1840. Custom-house opened at Taos.

Troubles with the Indians were not very serious or frequent, so far as can be determined from scanty and indefinite records, the most startling occurrences in this connection resting on authority that is somewhat doubtful. The system of treaties and bribes was still in vogue, and, as a rule, the tribes found it to their interest to be nominally at peace. Still, the Navajos made trouble occasionally, and one band or another of the Apaches was generally on the war-path. There are but few items of interest or value in the record of Indian affairs for this period, though it is probable that local and personal details, if known, would furnish material for many an episode of adventure.[8]

1838. Armijo, gov. to 1844. Trouble between the Americans and gov. in 1838-9 on account of the murder of a man named Daley. *Kendall's Nar.*, i. 352-3.

1839. N. Mexico made a separate comandancia general. Discovery of the 'new' gold placers.

1840. Foreigners in trouble on account of the 'accidental' murder of a Mexican. *Kendall*, i. 353.

1841. Sandoval, acting gov. Texan Santa Fé invasion of 1841-2, as elsewhere recorded.

1842. Settlement of La Junta. Treaty with Mescalero Apaches.

1843-5. Continued troubles with the Texans.

1844. Martinez, acting gov. Destructive fire at Sta Fé. *Defensor de la Integridad Nacional*, Sept. 25th.

1845. Chavez and Armijo, gov. Pronunciamiento of the gov. in favor of Santa Anna. *Amigo del Pueblo*, Aug. 19th, p. 99.

1846. Armijo and Vigil, gov. Occupation of N. Mexico by the U. S.

[8] 1823. Indians constantly making raids. *Mex., Mem. Rel.*, 1823, p. 57. Treaty made by Gov. Vizcarra in Feb. with Navajos, who restored captives, but claimed to be dying of hunger and unable to pay for past robberies. They were given 4 months to decide about conversion and settlement. *Arch. Sta Fé*, MS. More threatened dangers in Aug. 1825, but averted by the governor's activity. *Mex., Mem. Rel.*, 1826, p. 10. Steck, in *Ind. Aff. Rept*, 1863, p. 109-10, and Thümmel, *Mexiko*, 349-50, tell us that with the independence the Mexicans became cruel and faithless, and the Ind. consequently hostile after a long peace. Once a party of Navajos invited to Cochití to make peace were massacred. Bartlett, *Pers. Narr.*, i. 174, says that in an amphitheatre in the Waco mts 150 Apaches were surprised and put to death. Nidever, *Life and Adven.*, MS., 33, who was in N. Mex. in 1830, says the Arapahoes made frequent raids and never spared a Mexican. By Cooke, *Conq. N. Mex. and Cal.*, 48, we are told that Span. protection of the Navajos having ceased about 1832, they later suffered much from attacks of other tribes. Pattie, *Pers. Narr.*, passim, has much to say of Ind. hostilities against the Mexicans during his residence and wanderings of several years in N. Mex. 1832. Jicarillas peaceful since they were driven by Comanches from their old strongholds. *Escudero, Not. Chih.*, 227. Comanches allies of the Mexicans in 1833. *Id.*, 229-30. Lipanes long friendly, but bitter foes of the Comanches. *Id.*, 226. 1835. Comanches faithful; Apaches committing murders in the Socorro region. *Arch. Sta Fé*, MS. Gregg, *Com. Prairies*, i. 288-9, and Thümmel, *Mex.*, 350-1, narrate that late in 1835, in a campaign against the Navajos, the

In 1837–8 New Mexico had its revolutionary movement, corresponding in many respects with Alvarado's revolt of 1836–7 in California. It was nominally, and to a slight extent really, a rising against centralism and the new constitution of Mexico; that is, direct taxation—unknown in the territory under the jefes políticos, but introduced in the department by the governor—caused much popular discontent, affording at least a pretext for revolt. Several other motives, however, were in the aggregate more potent, though in the absence of original contemporary evidence it is not possible to ascertain their relative importance. Thus, there is said to have existed a prejudice against Governor Perez, an excellent man, because he was a stranger sent from Mexico, and not a native or old resident like most rulers of earlier years. Some of his special acts besides the imposition of taxes created discontent.[9] Manuel Armijo, formerly governor, moved chiefly by ambition, but also by dissatisfaction at having been removed from his place as custom-house officer, is accused by Gregg and Kendall of having secretly fomented the revolt, which he hoped to control, and which by a counter-pronunciamiento he finally turned to his own advantage.[10]

Mexicans were ambushed and defeated, Capt. Hinojos being one of the killed. It was one of H.'s sergeants who opened a keg of powder with a red hot poker. Roberts, *With the Invader*, 40–1, notes Starvation Peak, between Las Vegas and Sta Fé, as a spot where the Mexicans in 1837, being invited to a council without arms, were treacherously attacked, and the survivors starved to death. In 1839 an Apache chief came to El Paso to demand the release of his wife and other captives, which was promised; but the gov. summoned troops, who killed the chief and 20 of his men, but not before the chief had slain the gov. *Gregg*, i. 297–8. 1840–1. Navajos still hostile; two exped. sent out by the com. gen. *Mex., Mem. Guerra*, 1841, p. 36. 1842. Com. Gen. Armijo reports the Mescalero Apaches as desiring to make a treaty, on condition of receiving $5,000 a year and monthly rations. A. approves the terms. *Pinart, Doc. Hist. Chih.*, MS., ii. 32; *Voto de Sonora*, April 15, 1842.

[9] According to Davis and Prince the revenue officials were arrested for peculation in 1836, and brought to trial before the district court. Two of the judges, Abreu and Nafero, were accused as accomplices, and not allowed to sit, but the other judge, Juan Estévan Pino, found the accused guilty, whereupon Gov. Perez took the case out of court and restored the administrador de rentas to his place, which had been temporarily filled by Manuél Armijo.

[10] Juan Estévan Pino and Juan Rafael Ortiz were his leading associates in the plot, as Davis says. Gregg claims to have heard Armijo's own brother intimate that A. hoped to be made gov. by the rebels.

Again, it was believed by the Mexicans, and not altogether without reason, as I suspect, that the revolt was 'another Texan affair,' instigated more or less directly by the Americans, with a view of fomenting, by revolutionary troubles, the discontent already believed to be prevalent among New Mexicans.[11]

On the 1st of August a mob released an alcalde of a northern town, who had been imprisoned on some unpopular charge,[12] this serving as a beginning of the insurrection; and a great crowd, largely composed of pueblo Indians, soon assembled at La Cañada, where, on the 3d, the rebel 'plan' was issued, the only tangible part of which was 'not to admit the departmental plan,' and 'not to admit any tax,' three out of five articles being devoted to platitudes on God, country, and liberty, including, as a matter of course, the resolve to 'spill every drop of blood' in the sacred cause.[13] Governor Perez, with all the force he could raise, about 150 militia, including the friendly warriors of San Juan and Santo Domingo—the whereabouts of the presidial company not appearing—marched northward and met the foe at the mesa of San Ildefonso; but most of his men passed over to the rebels, and he was obliged to flee with about 25 companions, returning first to Santa Fé, but soon abandoning the capital. Within a few days, and at different points, the party

[11] Bustamante says: 'La causa de la revolucion la habia dado la entrada de una porcion de carros del Norte-América que trajeron muchas mercaderías, cuyos derechos no querian pagar los anglo-americanos, y tratando de estrecharlos á la exhibicion el gobernador, le suscitaron el alzamiento.' This was probably not true of the traders. Gregg tells us that they even furnished means for quelling the revolt. He also says: 'Some time before these tragic events took place, it was prophesied among them [the pueblo Indians] that a new race was about to appear from the east, to redeem them from the Spanish yoke. I heard this spoken of several months before the subject of the insurrection had been seriously agitated. It is probable that the pueblos built their hopes upon the Americans, as they seemed as yet to have no knowledge of the Texans.' He also says the rebels proposed sending to Texas for protection, though there had been no previous understanding. While there is no documentary proof, it is wellnigh impossible, considering the date and circumstances, to believe that the Texans had no influence directly or indirectly in the affair.

[12] The alcalde was arrested at the governor's orders by Ramon Abreu, who is called prefect.

[13] Davis gives a translation from an original MS. copy in his possession.

breaking up for self-preservation, the governor and a dozen or more of his associates were killed, the head of Perez being carried as a trophy to the insurgent headquarters, and the bodies of Santiago Abreu and others being barbarously mutilated.[14]

It was on August 9th or 10th that the rebels took possession of Santa Fé, where they committed no excesses beyond confiscating the property of the victims; and having elected as governor José Gonzalez, a pueblo Indian of Taos, they for the most part disbanded. Gonzalez summoned an assembly of alcaldes and influential citizens from the north, which body on the 27th confirmed all that had been done.[15] Now Manuel Armijo, formerly jefe político and customs officer, either as a part of his original plot, or perhaps disappointed because Gonzalez was preferred to himself as rebel governor, or possibly moved by patriotic devotion to the legitimate government—for the exact truth eludes all search—'pronounced' at Tomé, the 8th of September, raised a force with the aid of Curate Madariaga, and marched to the capital to 'suffocate the rebellion.' Gonzalez retired up the river, and Armijo had little difficulty in making himself recognized as acting governor and commandant-general. Possibly, also, he marched north and induced the rebels to submit to his authority and give up the leaders of the movement.[16] At any rate, he reported

[14] Those named as killed, all on or before Aug. 9th, were Col Albino Perez, gov.; Santiago Abreu, chief justice and ex-gov.; Jesus María Alarid, sec. state; Ramon Abreu, prefect of Rio Arriba; lieut. Miguel Serna, Joaquin Hurtado, and Madrigal; Sergt. Diego Sais, or Saenz; Marcelino Abreu, Loreto Romero, Escoto, and Ortega.

[15] Ritch tells us that 'according to the original MS. of the proceedings, a committee was appointed to prepare an address, and to proceed in person to present the same to the supreme govt. In the mean time, as resolved, all were to yield obedience to Gov. Gonzalez until such time as the com. could report.' Armijo was a member of this committee.

[16] So says Bustamante, who seems to follow Armijo's reports, as published in the *Diario del Gobierno*. Thus A. claimed to have prevented the 'pérdida total' of the country, since the rebels had resolved to join the savage tribes against the province. Most writers imply that he was recognized only at Sta Fé, the rebels keeping up their organization in the north. Davis, however, says the rebels were 'kept in a state of comparative peace by the authorities, under the pretext of desiring to treat with them' until the troops arrived; and Miller tells us that A. marched on Sept. 13th against Gonzalez

his patriotic achievement to the Mexican government, and asked for reënforcements. These, to the number of 300 or more, of the Escuadron de Vera Cruz and presidial troops of Chihuahua, under Colonel Justiniani, arrived before the end of the year. The rebels had again assembled at or near La Cañada, and were defeated in battle on January 27, 1838. Gonzalez and several of his associates were captured and shot. Armijo, in recognition of his services, was given the rank of colonel, and confirmed for eight years in his assumed positions of governor and comandante general.[17]

Besides the revolution of 1837, the only notable event of New Mexican history in this period, though one that in most of its phases belongs properly to the annals of another territory,[18] was the capture of the Texan Santa Fé expedition of 1841. Hitherto there had been little or no direct intercourse between the New Mexicans and their neighbors of the adjoining

and his lieut.-gov., Antonio Domingo Lopez, at Pujuaque, inducing them through the influence of a priest to negotiate for peace, but finally insisting on an unconditional surrender. But Miller speaks of no later troubles.

[17] Bustamante gives most particulars of the battle, or rather of the two battles, the first at the Pujuaque pass, and the other nearer Cañada. The troops numbered 582, Justiniani giving the chief command to Armijo. Four dragoons were killed and others wounded in an ambush. The rebels were over 1,300, and lost 20 killed, many wounded, and 8 prisoners. Antonio Vigil, their commander, was killed in the 1st fight. Davis says that Gonzalez, the brothers Desiderio and Antonio A. Montoya, and Alcalde Esquibel were shot by sentence of a court-martial at Sta Fé. Others imply that there was no formal trial. Gregg and others accuse Armijo of cowardice in the fight, attributing the victory to Capt. Muñoz, of the Vera Cruz troops. Miller mentions no fight; but says Gonzalez, with Lopez, his second in command, was hanged at Sta Cruz on Jan. 25th. Prince tells us that the Montoyas, Esquibel, and Gen. 'Chopon' were shot near the garita in Sta Fé; Juan Antonio Vigil 'executed' near Cuyamanque; and Gonzalez killed by the immediate command of Armijo.

Bustamante, *Gabinete, Mex.*, i. 33–6, gives a narrative in 1842, founded mainly on Armijo's report published in the *Diario del Gobierno*, Nov. 30, 1837. Gregg, *Com. of the Prairies*, i., writing in 1844, was at Sta Fé during the revolt. Kendall, *Narr. Texan Santa Fé Exped.*, i. 348–51, also of 1844, includes an account of the revolt in a very abusive biog. sketch of Armijo. Davis, *El Gringo*, 86–92, as we have seen, claims to have had a copy of the rebel plan, and his account is as complete as any. Ritch, *Aztlan*, 248, also alludes to a MS. record of the assembly at Sta Fé. Later narratives are those of Miller, *Hist. Sketch of Sta Fé*, 22–4, and Prince, *Hist. Sketches*, 285–9. There is a notable absence of original documentary evidence.

[18] See *Hist. North Mex. St. and Texas*, vol. ii.

but distant Texas; yet the comparative success of the eastern rebels was not unknown to the less fortunate agitators of the west. Texan influences, probably not inactive in the troubles of 1837–8, had certainly been potent in fomenting later discontent. Santa Fé traders from the United States seem as a class to have feared a revolution, which might for a time imperil their commercial interests; but among them, especially those who had become residents, there was an element fully in sympathy with the filibusters. These sympathizers reported that the New Mexicans awaited only an opportunity to rise and declare their independence, and that even the authorities were not disposed to offer much resistance.[19]

Besides crediting these exaggerated reports, the Texans had a theory, without foundation in fact or justice, that their territory extended to the Rio Grande, and that it was therefore their duty to release from tyranny all inhabitants of that territory, including, of course, the New Mexicans living east of the river. They had, moreover, a strong desire to divert through Texan channels the Santa Fé trade that had proved so lucrative to merchants of the United States. Under these circumstances, in the spring of 1841 President Lamar fitted out an expedition of about 300 men, in six companies, under the command of Hugh McLeod as brevet brigadier-general. Three commissioners were sent to establish Texan authority in the west, well provided with proclamations explaining the advantages of the proffered freedom; and a number of traders and travellers joined the expedition in quest of gain or adventure, some of them possibly not fully understanding its real purpose.[20] It was not proposed

[19] In *Niles' Reg.*, lxi. 61, 100, is a letter from Sta Fé, which represents all the pueblo Indians and Americans, with two thirds of the Mexicans, as anxious for the Texans to come. The gov. tells the writer that he neither can nor will resist. That such reports were circulated and believed in Texas and the U. S. is shown by the general tenor of all records of the period.

[20] The commissioners were Wm G. Cooke, José Antonio Navarro, and Richard F. Brenham. The captains were Wm P. Lewis, J. S. Sutton, W. D. Houghton, Ratcliff Hudson, Matthew Caldwell, and J. H. Strain. The purport of the proclamation, according to Kendall, was 'that the exped. was sent

exactly—at least, such was the explanation offered later—to undertake with 300 men the conquest of New Mexico against the will of the inhabitants; but if the people were found not favoring or ready for revolt the expedition would be content with trade, and would retire to await a more favorable opportunity. This, however, has no real bearing on the character of the party. They were simply armed invaders, who might expect to be attacked, and if defeated, to be treated by the Mexicans as rebels, or at best—since Texan belligerency and independence had been recognized by several nations—as prisoners of war. They left Austin in June, and in September, after a tedious march by the worst routes over an unknown country, they arrived ragged, worn out, and half starved on the New Mexican frontier.

Meanwhile, the Mexican authorities had long expected an invasion from Texas, and special warnings, with promise of reënforcements, had recently been received from the national capital. While there was no lack of disaffection in certain quarters, the masses of the people were far from ready to accept the so-called freedom offered by filibusters, and the rulers still further from any intention to permit a change of government. Every possible effort, on the contrary, was made to prepare for defence, and to foment the current popular idea of the Texans as valiant but reckless desperadoes, from whom might be expected, not liberty, but pillage, murder, and outrage. All foreigners were closely watched, and several were arrested on suspicion of complicity in schemes of invasion.[21] Satisfied

for the purpose of trading, and that if the inhabitants were not disposed to join peacefully the Texan standard, the exped. was to retire immediately (!). These procl. were printed in both Spanish and English, and not a doubt existed that the liberal terms offered would be at once acceded to by a population living within the limits of Texas, and who had long been groaning under a misrule the most tyrannical.' *Narr.*, 270. See also 365–7.

[21] According to an account followed by Bustamante, 'En julio de 1839 los estrangeros del Norte en Sta Fé, so pretesto de pedir justicia atentaron descaradamente contra el gobierno, de quien exigian por la fuerza de las armas que se fusilaron por el mismo gobernador, ó se les entregasen unos reos que en 1837 mataron á un estrangero, Regentaban este atentado Guillermo Driden y Santiago Querqu? [James Kirker] que comandaba una gavilla de

that danger was near, Governor Armijo sent southward an appeal for aid, ordered a close watch of foreigners, who were forbidden to leave their places of
residence, and sent Captain Dámaso Salazar to reconnoitre the eastern frontier. On September 4th Salazar sent in as captives three men, who were regarded
as spies from the invading army. They were forbidden to leave the capital, but escaped a week later, and
on being recaptured, were put to death.[22] On the
15th a Mexican named Cárlos and an Italian, Brig-
noli, who had been with the Texans in August, were
found, and induced to tell what they knew of the invasion. Meanwhile, every effort had been made for effective defence; the rurales, or militia, called into
service and sent to the frontier under Lieutenant-
colonel Juan Andrés Archuleta; Prefect Antonio
Sandoval summoned to the capital to act as governor;
while Armijo set out on the 16th with the presidial
troops. On the same day five men, sent on in advance
of the foremost division of Texans, were captured,
disarmed, and put in jail at San Miguel del Vado.[23]
Next day Colonel Cooke and Captain Sutton, with
94 Texans, surrendered to Armijo and Salazar at
Anton Chico. The governor established his headquarters at Las Vegas, distributed among the captors

indios sahuanos; mas se resistió á ello el gobernador. Desde aquella época
hasta último de agosto de 1841 se suscitaron conspiraciones por diferentes
puntos del departamento contra el gobierno, y si en todas no han sido los estrangeros los principales motores, á lo ménos han tenido parte. La de agosto
la dirigia el Americano Julian Werkeman, á quien los Tejanos tenian apode-
rado en este departamento, con el solo objeto de que formara la revolucion,
para lo que vino desde Taos á Sta Fé, acompañados de otros paisanos suyos
decididos á asesinar al gobernador Armijo.' Gregg also mentions the act of
the Americans, though not admitting that it had any political aspect. Kendall notes the arrest of Thomas Rowland. Suspicions against Workman and
John Rowland in this connection had something to do with their migration to
Cal. in 1841. Kirker, named above, died in Cal. about 1853. Dryden was a
prisoner in Chih. in 1841–2. B. D. Wilson, *Observations*, MS., who had lived
in N. Mex. since 1833, tells us that not only Rowland and Workman, but
about 20 more, including himself, joined the Cal. party because, on account
of Texan complications, they did not deem it safe to remain.

   [22] They were Howland, Baker, and Rosenburg. The latter was killed in
resisting recapture, and the others were executed later. This is called murder by Kendall, but the act seems to have been justifiable.

   [23] These were Capt. Lewis, Van Ness, Howard, Fitzgerald, and Kendall.
The Spanish account makes the number 6.

the property taken from the Texans, made a bonfire in the plaza of Lamar's proclamations, sent off Cooke and his fellow-prisoners under a guard of 200 men for Mexico, and sent out explorers to find the rest of the invaders. These, under McLeod, about 200 in number, finally surrendered to Archuleta, at a place called Laguna Colorada, on the 5th of October; on the 16th Armijo was given a public and most enthusiastic reception at the capital, and next day the last of the prisoners left San Miguel on their tedious march to Mexico, where they arrived in several divisions at the beginning of 1842. A few were released in April, or earlier, at the intercession of foreign ministers, on the plea that they were not Texans, and had joined the expedition without knowing its real objects. The rest, after confinement at different Mexican prisons, some of them being compelled to work in chains on the roads, were finally released by President Santa Anna on his saint's day, the 13th of June. The only exception was in the case of Navarro, who was at one time condemned to death, but finally escaped and returned to Texas.[24]

[24] The best narrative of these events, from a Mexican stand-point, is that in *Bustamante, Gabinete Mexicano*, ii. 216–25, entitled 'Espedicion de los Tejanos rendida á las fuerzas del General Don Manuel Armijo en 5 de Octubre de 1841,' or 'una memoria que se me ha remitido de Santa Fé de Nuevo-México de la que he copiado lo siguiente.' The writer closes his narrative with an extract from an address of John Quincy Adams, in which he denounced this invasion of adventurers, or pirates, from the U. S., rejoicing at their failure, and ridiculing their pretensions as traders and travellers. In the *Arch. Sta Fé*, MS., is a fragmentary diary of Lieut.-col Archuleta's operations from Sept. 30th to Oct. 9th, including the capture of McLeod's party. In *Bustamante, Diario*, MS., xliii. 253–5, 327, is an account of the celebration of the news in Mex. on Nov. 16th, including an extra of the *Fanal*, and letters from García Conde at Chihuahua. The *Diario del Gob.*, Feb. 20, 1842, has a translation of an article in a N. Orleans paper, ridiculing the idea that the Texans had been captured by the New Mexicans. In *Mex., Mem. Guerra*, 1844, p. 37–8, is a brief notice of the affair; and in *Id., Mem. Rel.*, 1844, doc. i.–xl., appears the diplomatic correspondence in Mex. on the case of Kendall and others, who claimed the protection of the U. S. See also *Ceballos, Vindic. Mej.*, 69–72.

On the other side, the leading authority is the *Narrative of the Texan Santa Fé Expedition, comprising a description of a tour through Texas and across the great south-western prairies, the Camanche and Caygüa hunting-grounds, with an account of the sufferings from want of food, losses from hostile Indians, and final capture of the Texans, and their march as prisoners to the city of Mexico. With illustrations and a map. By Geo. Wilkins Kendall.* N. Y., 1844, 12mo, 2

There can be no doubt that Governor Armijo was
fully justified in seizing the Texan invaders, disarming
them, confiscating their property, and sending them to
Mexico as prisoners of war. He and his officers are
accused, however, of having induced their victims to
surrender by false assurances of friendship and false
promises of welcome as traders, the giving-up of their

vols; also later editions. The author was one of the editors of the New
Orleans *Picayune*, in quest of adventure and material for a book, both of
which he found. He was one of those who claimed to have joined the expedition in ignorance of its filibustering purpose, and after much correspondence
he was liberated at the request of U. S. representatives. His narrative is a
most fascinating one, and is full of valuable information respecting the countries through which he passed. No effort is made to conceal his intensely
bitter hatred of the New Mexicans, though he speaks well of the women and
of a few men who were kind to the Texans in their misfortunes. Gov.
Armijo is described not only as a tyrant, but as an inhuman and bloodthirsty
wretch, an unprincipled libertine, and a boastful coward, whose fortune was
founded on early success as a sheep-thief, and whose only good quality was a
fine personal appearance. Captain Salazar and other officers are described as
worthy followers of such a chief. The author's views of Armijo are supported
to a considerable extent by Gregg and other Americans who knew the governor, and they have been adopted more or less fully by later writers. Kendall narrates minutely the capture and treatment of his own little party, and
he gives particular attention to Capt. Lewis, who had lived in Spanish-American provinces, knew the language, and was implicitly trusted by the Texans.
Lewis is accused of having betrayed his comrades, revealed all their plans,
and induced Cooke and McLeod to surrender, by false assurances of kind
treatment and false representations of the enemy's force. Of course, the subject of Lewis' treachery and that of Kendall's wrongs, real or pretended, as
an innocent citizen of the U. S., have very little importance as part of the
annals of N. Mex.

Franklin Combs, another of the prisoners, wrote a *Narrative*, which was
published in the newspapers, and may be consulted with other matter, including a list of the members of the expedition in *Mexico in 1842*, p. 232–50. An
account of some parts of the affair by Lieut. Lubbock is quoted by Kendall
and others. Thomas Falconer, an Englishman, who was set at liberty immediately on reaching Mexico, wrote *Notes of a Journey through Texas and New
Mexico in the years 1841 and 1842*, published in the *Lond. Geog. Soc., Jour.*,
xiii. 199–226. His notes are chiefly devoted to a description of the country.
He claims to have joined the expedition without any knowledge of its real
character. Of McLeod's capture he says: 'A surrender was agreed upon, and
the terms, securing to the party the treatment of prisoners of war, were
signed by the officers on both sides;' but he confirms Kendall's statement
that on the march several men were shot and their ears cut off. In *U. S.
Govt Doc.*, 27th cong. 2d sess., Sen. Ex. Doc. 325, H. Ex. Doc. 266, is
found the bulky correspondence between the Mex. and U. S. representatives,
as above referred to in Spanish. See also same sess. *House Jour.*, 183, 234,
1480; and *Cong. Globe*, 1841–2, p. 131, 977–8. Waddy Thompson, U. S. minister in Mex., in his *Recollections*, 5, 50, 92–3, 155–6, mentions this affair, and
states, what indeed is practically admitted by all, that the prisoners were
well enough treated in Mexico. Gregg, *Com. Prairies*, i. 227–32, relates some
instances of outrages on Amer. residents in 1841. See also many articles and
items in *Niles' Reg.*, lxi.–ii., as per index; *Prince's Hist. Sk.*, 236–9; *Dewees'
Letters*, 238–41; *Wilson's Amer. Hist.*, 665–7; *Young's Hist. Mex.*, 285–6, and
most works relating to the annals of Texas.

arms being represented as a mere formality imposed on all visitors to Santa Fé. Their arms once secured, it is said the lives of one party were saved only by the intervention and protest of Gregorio Vigil, and of another by a majority of one in a vote on the proposition to shoot them. And after their surrender, particularly on the march to El Paso, it is claimed they were starved and otherwise inhumanly maltreated, some five or six of their number, because of their illness and inability to keep up, having been deliberately shot down, and their ears cut off, to be carried to Chihuahua as proof that they had not escaped. There is, of course, nothing to be said in justification of such acts, if the charges are true. My knowledge of Armijo does not lead me to say in his defence much more than that he was certainly not so bad a man as he is represented; nor am I prepared to say that Salazar was not a brute, or that some barbarous acts may not have been committed by irresponsible and unmanageable subordinates. The Mexicans claim to have offered but life as a condition of surrender, and to have treated their captives with all the courtesy due to prisoners of war. It is well to consider the ex parte nature of the evidence against them, and the evident bias, amounting to hatred, of Kendall and other witnesses, leading to many obvious exaggerations. The Texans, if technically but soldiers of a belligerent nation, were in Mexican eyes rebel desperadoes, entering a peaceful province under false pretences, to stir up bloody strife. Let it be remembered that the capture and transportation of 300 Texan filibusters by the miserably organized soldiery of New Mexico was no slight undertaking, and small wonder if in such a struggle some of the kid-glove niceties of regular warfare were not observed; moreover, the march to Mexico was necessarily attended with much hardship and suffering, and some doubt is thrown on the charges of murder by the statement of Powhatan Ellis to Webster, that one, involving the shooting of three pris-

oners, was a 'fabrication' transferred from a northern
newspaper to the columns of the *Siglo Diez y Nueve*.
Again, if the promises alleged to have been broken
were given in good faith to the Texans as peaceful
traders, Armijo was fully justified in breaking them
on learning, through Lewis' treachery and Lamar's
proclamation, how he had been deceived; if, on the
contrary, the Mexicans, knowing the real character
of the expedition, made the promises, intending to
break them, as a device to get possession of the enemy's weapons, the trick was at the least not more dis-
honorable than that attempted by McLeod and Cooke.
The Texan adventurers were, at best, engaged in a
risky invasion of an enemy's territory; fortune was
against them, and disaster resulted, for which they
deserve but little sympathy. Armijo and his men,
on the contrary, had the most wonderful good luck in
defending their country, and merit but little of the
obloquy that has been heaped upon them.[25]

Naturally, the Texans were grievously disappointed
at the utter failure of their grand filibustering expedition, and loud in their threats of vengeance for what
they chose to regard as the treachery and barbarity of
the New Mexicans. Active preparations began as
soon as the captives of 1841 had returned. The retaliatory enterprise, as talked about in advance through
the press and otherwise, had a wide scope. Not only
was New Mexico to be invaded and brought under
Texan sway, but probably the banner of freedom
would be unfurled in Chihuahua, and all of Northern
Mexico revolutionized; and at the very least, Armijo
and Salazar, with the traitor Lewis, were to be taken,
dead or alive. For these purposes a force of 500 or

[25] There is a notable similarity in several respects between the rule of Armijo in N. Mex. and that of Alvarado in Cal.—see *Hist. Cal.*, iii., iv.—the
revolts against centralism in 1836-8, and the following troubles with foreigners in 1841, as represented by the Texan expedition and the Graham
affair. Both rulers were grossly abused by foreign critics, Kendall's ravings
bearing a marked resemblance to those of Farnham. Charges against Alvarado were for the most part false; of Armijo and his acts much less is known.

800 men, under Colonel Jacob Snively, was to be raised, the only difficulty being to keep the number down, such was the popular enthusiasm at home and across the line in the United States. The project was made known by traders at Santa Fé—American spies, the Texans called them—and considerable alarm was felt in Mexico, especially because of the belief that the movement was to be in reality under the auspices of the northern republic. Accordingly, a large force was sent north from Chihuahua, under General José M. Monterde, to support Armijo, who, as the result proved, had little need of reënforcements.

This grand scheme of vengeance, invasion, and revolution reduced itself in the execution to a raid for plunder on the Santa Fé caravans; for this trade, of which much more is said in this chapter, was now to a considerable extent in the hands of Mexicans. First, John McDaniel, a Texan captain, or calling himself so, enlisted in Missouri fifteen vagabonds, and with them in April 1843 attacked and plundered the caravan of José Antonio Chavez on the Little Arkansas, in United States territory. Seven of the number, with their share of the booty, at once started back for the Missouri settlements; and the other eight did likewise, after murdering Chavez for the gold about his person. This outrage was a little more than even the Texan sympathy or anti-Mexican prejudice of the south-western frontier could justify; ten of the party were captured and condemned to death or imprisonment, according as their crime was murder or simply robbery. About the same time, Colonel Warfield, with a similar party of twenty-four adventurers, attempted a raid on the little New Mexican settlement of Mora. By a surprise he killed five Mexicans of a party of hunters, and took a few horses, which he presently lost, with all his own, when the foe turned on him, and he was forced to retreat on foot. Warfield, with a few of the fugitives, succeeded in joining Snively; another party disbanded and found their way northward; while still another of five men was captured and apparently taken to Santa Fé.

Meanwhile, Colonel Snively, with his grand army of not 800 or 500, but about 180 men, reached the Arkansas late in May, to lie in wait for the traders. The caravan of the year, composed of both Mexicans and Americans, bound to Santa Fé from Independence, was approaching, escorted by two companies of United States dragoons under Captain Cook; and Governor Armijo, with 500 men or more, marched out of his capital on May 1st to meet the caravan at the Arkansas. On June 19th the Texans succeeded in cutting off an advance party of Armijo's force, about 100 militiamen and Indians under Ventura Lobato, killing some twenty, and making prisoners of the rest, except one or two who escaped to the governor's camp.[26] Ten days later, as the force was deemed too small to attack Armijo, and as it was thought the caravan might have turned back through fear, about 80 of the Texans started homeward; but Captain Cook soon came up, and forced one detachment of the rest, greatly to their disgust, to give up their arms, claiming that they were on United States soil. About 50 now started for Missouri, while the remainder—part of whom, under Captain Chandler, had been absent at the disarming, and another part are said to have deceived Cook by giving up only captured Mexican weapons, concealing their own rifles—could not agree on any course of action until the caravan had crossed the river and gone on their way unmolested. Then the renowned 'Texian Invincibles' went home, losing some men in fights with the Indians on the way.

In July and August the Mexican minister complained to Waddy Thompson that the United States government was responsible for the so-called Texan

---

[26] Bustamante's statement that Snively 'á todos los pasó á cuchillas deis pues de rendidas las armas' is probably unfounded. Some other authorites say that the prisoners were released. The Texans and Americans state that Armijo, on learning of the disaster, retreated in great haste, without waiting for the caravan.

invasion; but the reply denied such responsibility, even if there had been any invasion, which was declared doubtful. Meanwhile, General Monterde marched northward to New Mexico with some 700 men; and he and Armijo flattered themselves that they had saved their country. Good luck and a broad desert frontier had done more to defeat Texan schemes than the zeal of Mexican patriots.[27]

We have noted the adventurous beginnings before 1822 of the trade between Santa Fé and the Missouri River. With the end of Spanish rule ceased all opposition to the traffic on the part of Mexican authorities, and a profitable market was assured for goods from the United States. The eastern rendezvous was Franklin, Missouri, down to 1831, and later Independence. From this point in May of each year set out the trains, or caravans, of pack-animals in 1823, but subsequently of wagons, drawn at first by horses and mules, but later by mules or oxen, four pairs usually to each wagon, but sometimes five or six pairs, with

[27] In the *Arch. Sta Fé*, MS., is Armijo's *Libro de Ordenes*, showing something of his operations from May 1st to July 1st, including the capture of 5 Texans on June 6th or 7th. *Niles' Reg.*, lxiv. 195, 210, 280, 290, 323, 327, 354, and especially 234-5, 406, contains a large amount of information on details of the affair. Bustamante, *Apuntes Hist. Santa Anna*, 206-9, tells us of the 'nueva invasion de Nuevo-Mexico por los Anglo-Americanos.' The diplomatic correspondence in Mex. is given in *Mex., Mem. Rel.*, 1844, doc. lxiii.-ix., and the affair is also noted in *Id., Mem. Guerra*, 1844, p. 37-8, where we are told that on June 17, 1843, the Mex. govt had been obliged to decree death to all foreigners entering the country as bandits, or fighting under a flag not recognized by Mex. The *Voto de Sonora* of Sept. 14, 1843, contains a report of Armijo, forwarded by Monterde Aug. 9th, on the successful effect of defensive measures. M. was about to return, leaving 300 men under Lieut.-col Mauricio Ugarte. Gregg, *Com. Prairies*, ii. 166-77, gives an excellent account of the expedition, and though his sympathies are not wholly against the Texans he shows that they acted very unwisely, even from their own point of view, in killing Chavez, whose family was not friendly to Armijo, and whose brother and sister-in-law did much in 1841 to aid the Texan prisoners; in planning to attack a caravan which contained many Americans, who could not honorably desert their Mex. friends; in attacking Mora, whose inhabitants had always been friendly to foreigners; and in butchering the pueblo Indians of Armijo's vanguard, who had always been bitter against the governor, and who were now incensed beyond measure at Taos, forcing several naturalized foreigners to flee for their lives. *Scenes in the Rocky Mts*, 244-70, also contains a good narrative; and *Beadle's Western Wilds*, 60-80, a fantastic one, purporting to be by one of Warfield's men, and evidently founded on fact in the earlier parts.

a load of 5,000 pounds.   Cotton goods were the staple
article of traffic, but there was also carried a miscellaneous assortment of dry goods and hardware.   The
route of over 800 miles lay in an almost direct line
west-south-west to San Miguel del Vado, and thence
north-west to Santa Fé; but this route, with some of
the most common variations, is best shown by the
map.   Midway of the journey was the crossing of the
Arkansas, the boundary between United States and
Mexican territory; and the route corresponds nearly,
in a general way, with that of the Atchison, Topeka,
and Santa Fé railroad of later times.   The arrival
was generally in July, and the return departure in
August.   The selling price of goods was on an average about double the cost, and at this rate was, for a
time, sufficiently low to control the market as against
foreign goods imported by way of Vera Cruz or Chihuahua; and indeed, a large proportion of the Missouri
goods were sent from Santa Fé to the south by the
regular autumn caravans.   Duties, after an 'understanding' with custom-house officers—for very slight
attention was paid to the national *arancel de derechos*
—were from 25 to 50 per cent of cost, and the traders' net profit was as a rule from 20 to 40 per cent,
though some cargoes were sold at a loss.   The goods
were paid for mainly in gold and silver coin, though
a considerable quantity of furs and blankets was taken,
and the wagons were sometimes partly laden with
wool, there being no duty on exported products.[28]   I

[28] The tax on exports was remitted in favor of N. Mex. by a decree of July
19, 1823, for 7 years; and the privilege was renewed in 1830, 1838, and 1845.
Arrillaga, Recop., 1829–30, p. 100; 1830, p. 131; 1838, p. 143; 1845–6, p. 95–6;
also other collections of laws.   The receipts of the N. Mex. custom-house, as
reported to the Mex. govt, were as follows, according to *Prieto, Rentas*, 204,
doc. 3—the sums in parentheses being from the govt *memorias*, and differing
somewhat: 1825, 8 months, $2,053 (12 mo., $3,595); 1826, 10 mo., $10,391;
1826–7, $8,607; 1827–8, $5,938; 1828–9, $27,008 ($27,907); 1829–30, $12,691;
1830–1, $10,581 ($31,882); 1831–2, $31,314; 1833–4, $29,297; 1836–7, $21,219;
1841, ($1,195); 1842, ($27,921); 1843, ($81,400).   Gregg mentions a custom,
said to prevail, of dividing the legal duties into three equal parts, one for the
officers, one for the trader, and one for the govt.   He also says that of the
$50,000 to $80,000 annually collected, nearly half has been embezzled.   It
was believed at first that the N. Mex. authorities were collecting much
more than the Mex. law permitted; but such was not the case.   There was
a prohibitory duty of $4 per pound on tobacco.

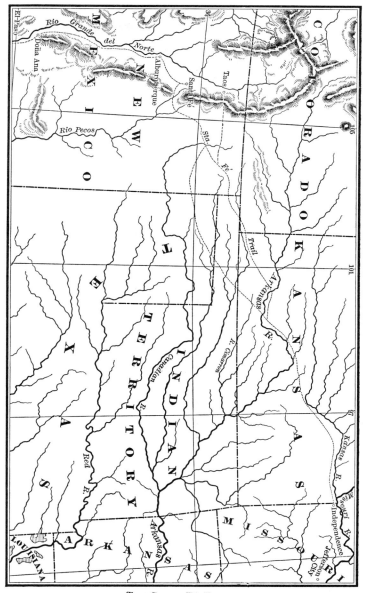

THE SANTA FÉ TRAIL.

make no attempt here to picture the pleasures and
perils connected with this 'commerce of the prairies,'
or to present details of commercial methods, referring
the reader for such matter, to the standard and often-
cited work of Gregg, from which, however, before
proceeding to notice the Santa Fé trade in some of
its chronologic aspects, I append a table showing the
growth of the trade from year to year.[29]   It should

[29] Table showing approximate amounts of merchandise, number of wagons,
hired men, proprietors, and the amount of goods sent south, chiefly to
Chihuahua.

Year.	Mdse.	Wagons.	Men.	Traders.	To Chih.
1822	$15,000	...	70	60	
1823	12,000	...	50	30	
1824	35,000	26	100	80	$3,000
1825	65,000	37	130	90	5,000
1826	90,000	60	100	70	7,000
1827	85,000	55	90	50	8,000
1828	150,000	100	200	80	20,000
1829	60,000	30	50	20	5,000
1830	120,000	70	140	60	20,000
1831	250,000	130	320	80	80,000
1832	140,000	70	150	40	50,000
1833	180,000	105	185	60	80,000
1834	150,000	80	160	50	70,000
1835	140,000	75	140	40	70,000
1836	130,000	70	135	35	60,000
1837	150,000	80	160	35	80,000
1838	90,000	50	100	20	40,000
1839	250,000	130	250	40	100,000
1840	50,000	30	60	5	10,000
1841	150,000	60	100	12	80,000
1842	160,000	70	120	15	90,000
1843	450,000	230	350	30	300,000

In *Farnham's Mex.*, 33, is given the estimate of David Waldo, 30 years in
the trade, of the business of 1846, as follows: cost of goods, $937,500; cost of
outfit, insurance, wages, etc., $414,750; profit, $400,000.   There were 375
wagons, 1,700 mules, 2,000 oxen, and 500 men.
  *Commerce of the Prairies; or the journal of a Santa Fé trader, during eight
expeditions across the great western prairies, and a residence of nearly nine years
in Northern Mexico.   Illustrated with maps and engravings.   By Josiah Gregg.*
N. Y., 1844.   12mo, 2 vol.   I have also the 4th edition of Phil., 1850; and that
of Phil., 1857, under the title, *Scenes and Incidents in the Western Prairies.*
Gregg made his first trip with the caravan of 1831.   His work is the principal source of all that has been or can be written about the Sta Fé trade down
to 1843; and it also contains an excellent description of the country, people,
and customs of the northern states of Mexico, with many historic items of
value.   After Gregg's work I have found the extracts and correspondence in
Niles' Register, from year to year, the most useful source of information.   I
may also refer to *Prince's Hist. Sk.*, 266-84; *Ritch's Aztlan*, 247; *Mayer's
Mex. Aztec*, ii. 364; *Harper's Mag.*, July 1880, p. 187-90; *Nouv. Ann. Voy.*,
xciii. 308-13; *Escudero*, in *Pino, Noticias*, 75-9; *Barreiro, Ojeada*, 24-5; *Ban-

also be noted that before many years had passed Santa Fé merchants of Spanish race fitted out regular caravans and controlled a large portion of the trade.

Freight was carried by pack-animals till 1824, when wagons were introduced as an experiment, and making the trip without difficulty were used exclusively after 1825. These first wagons seem to have taken the Taos route.[30] By the success of this experiment was attracted the attention of wealthier men than any that had previously engaged in the trade; and these men lost no time in bringing the matter before the government. Memorials were sent to congress by the people and authorities of Missouri, demanding protection for the new industry, by treaties with Indian tribes, the marking-out of a road, establishing of a fort on the Arkansas, and the appointment of agents at Santa Fé and Chihuahua to prevent extortion in the collection of duties. Senator Benton took up the project with his customary zeal, and laid before the senate the statement of Augustus Storrs on the history and prospects of the prairie commerce. Finally, in January 1825, a bill was passed, authorizing the marking-out of a road, and appropriating $30,000 for this purpose and that of obtaining the Indians' consent to the road and its unmolested use.[31] The

croft's N. Mex. Miscel., MS., 1-2, 13-17; Hunt's Merch. Mag., xi. 475, 501-17; Marmier, Voyageurs Nouveaux, ii. 29-64. See also references of the following notes.

[30] Storrs' Santa Fé Trade in 1824. He gives the route as from Ft Osage w. s. w. to the Arkansas; up the Ark. N. of w. 240 miles; s. to the Cimarron; up the C. w. 100 miles; and s. w. to Taos. Gregg, i. 24-5, implies that the wagons reached Sta Fé, and his map shows no route to Taos. Storrs accompanied the caravan, and his narrative, or statement, drawn out in govt investigations, was published in Niles' Reg., xxvii. 312-16, as also in govt doc., as cited in the next note. It was the best account extant before that of Gregg, who consulted it, and who had also a diary of Marmaduke, later lieut.-gov. of Mo. The year's caravan consisted of 81 men, 156 horses and mules, and 23 wagons, making the round trip in 4 months and 10 days. Storrs, however, speaks of 4 parties starting in Feb., May, Aug., and Nov.; and gives the product of the year's trade as $180,000 in gold and silver, besides $10,000 in furs.

[31] The bill was approved on March 3d. The only objection urged in congress was to the survey of a road in Mex. territory. U. S. Govt Doc., 18th cong. 2d sess., Sen. Doc. 7, p. 1-14; Sen. Jour., same sess.; Cong. Debates, 1824-5, p. 109-10, 342-8, 356-61; Annals of Cong., 1824, p. 2703-4; Benton's Debates, viii. 106, 126-34; Niles' Reg., xxvi. 263-4; xxvii. 250-1, 301, 312-17, 348, 351.

New Mexicans were not less eager than the Americans for the protection and development of trade; and in June 1825 Manuel Simon Escudero of Chihuhua was commissioned by Governor Vaca to visit St Louis and Washington.[32] The same year a treaty was made with the Osages by the payment of a small sum; and the survey of the road was begun, to be completed— that is the route partially marked by a series of mounds—from Fort Osage to Taos two years later.[33] It does not appear, however, that the traders ever made use of the road as surveyed, preferring to follow the earlier trail, with such modifications as the condition of grass and water suggested.

Meanwhile, the trade grew in proportions, and the caravans made their yearly trips[34] without notable adventures, except that the Indians—probably not without fault on the part of the traders—became increas-

[32] *Escudero*, in *Pino, Not.*, 76–7. Not much is definitely stated as to the nature and results of this mission, but the assurances from U. S. authorities and Mex. minister were encouraging. E. arrived at St Louis in Oct. *Niles' Reg.*, xxix. 85. In 1824 the gov. of N. Mex. was said to have announced his intention of marching with 1,500 men to Council Bluffs to secure trade, pacify Ind., etc. *Id.*, xxvi. 252.

[33] The U. S. commissioners were Benj. Reeves, Geo. C. Sibley, and Thomas Mather; and the surveyor J. C. Brown. This road struck the Arkansas near Plum Buttes, and followed it up to Choteau Island; thence s. to the Cimarron; up the C. 87 miles; thence to Rabbit-Ear Creek, and continuing westward entered the mts near the source of Ocate River, terminating at Taos. *Warren's Memoir*, 26–7. Gregg and Prince, however, state that the road was never marked by mounds beyond the Arkansas, and only in part to that river.

[34] In 1825 a party left Sta Fé in June, and arrived at Franklin in Aug., with 500 mules and horses, being attacked by the Osage Ind. A caravan also left Franklin in May with 81 men, 200 horses, and $30,000 in goods; much suffering. There were already complaints that the trade was overdone. *Niles' Reg.*, xxix. 54, 100. 263. Another, of 105 men, 34 wagons, 240 mules. Money scarce, but mules and horses to be had for $10–20 to $20–30 cash, for goods at 100 per cent profit. *Id.*, xxviii. 309. In 1825–6, Dr Willard went with a caravan from St Charles to Sta Fé, and thence to Chih.; and his *Inland Trade with Mexico* was published in 1833, as an appendix to *Pattie's Narr.*, 255–300, being mostly occupied with descriptive matter. In 1827–43, Collins, later supt Ind. affairs in N. Mex., made several trips. *Ind. Aff. Rept Joint Com.*, 1867, p. 330. Brief account of caravan of 1827, in *Niles' Reg.*, xxxii. 292. There were 53 wagons, the largest number yet. The return cargo in 1829 was $240,000. *Id.*, xxxvii. 230, 274. In 1829, Capt. Austin was to go up the Rio Grande with a steamer and schooner, to open a new route for trade. *Id.*, xxxvi. 424. In a later memorial of the Mo. assembly—*U. S. Gov. Doc.*, 26th cong. 1st sess., Sen. Doc. 472, p. 8—it was stated that 1828, when 200 wagons carried $500,000 worth of goods, was the year of greatest prosperity, followed by a rapid decline; but this does not seem to agree with Gregg's figures. Acc. to Ritch, Bent's fort on the Arkansas was established in 1829.

ingly hostile, being ever on the watch for small detached
parties imperfectly armed or not sufficiently vigilant.
Thus a party in 1826 lost 500 horses and mules, and
one of 1828 over 1,000 animals, having, besides, three
men shot. This caused a renewal of demands for gov-
ernmental protection; and the committee on military
affairs having reported to congress in favor of a movable escort rather than a fixed garrison, Major Riley
was ordered to escort the caravan of 1829 to and from
the Arkansas, with four companies of the 6th infantry
from Fort Leavenworth. Soon after the traders left
the troops at the Arkansas, they were attacked by the
Indians, losing one man; whereupon, Riley came up
and guarded the caravan for a short distance into Mexican territory. The troops waited at Choteau's island
till October, and the returning caravan was escorted
to this point by a Mexican force under Colonel Vizcarra.
Though there was some further discussion of the matter in congress, the escort was not continued.[35]

In 1830 oxen were first used by the traders, the
experiment having been successfully tried the year
before by Riley's supply train. 1831 was the year of
Gregg's first trip, and of Jedediah Smith's death.[36]
There were also hostilities on the Canadian in 1832–3,
several men being killed; but in 1834 an escort of 60
dragoons under Captain Wharton was again furnished.
The revolt of 1837 did some injury to the American
traders, since the property of their richest customers
was confiscated; but they had no success in obtaining

[35] Rept of cong. committee, in *Amer. St. Pap.*, Mil. Aff., iii. 615. *Riley's
Report* of Nov. 22, 1829, in *Id.*, iv. 277–80. See also *Niles' Reg.*, xxxvi. 182,
199–200; xxxvii. 230, 274, 291, 405, 419; xxxviii. 57, 101. There was some
unfavorable criticism of the action of govt in furnishing 4 comp. of troops to
protect a trade of $200,000, as favoring commerce over other industries. In
1830 there was an investigation, and a bill was passed to 3d reading providing
10 comp. for this service. In 1827 there had been an effort to induce Mexico
to pay for robberies by Ind. in Mex. territory. *Id.*, xxxii. 79.
[36] See *Hist. Cal.*, iii., for Smith's Cal. adventures. He joined the caravan
of which Smith, Sublette, and Jackson were chief owners. He and a clerk
were shot by the Comanches, while separated from the main party in search
of water. J. J. Warner, still living in Cal., 1886, was a member of the same
caravan. *Remin.*, MS., 5–11. Chas Bent is named as capt of a caravan of 93
wagons in '33, escorted by a comp. of rangers; and Kerr as capt in '34, with
$200,000 in specie. *Niles' Reg.*, xliv. 374; xlxii. 147.

indemnity from Mexico. In 1837, however, the frontier custom-house of Taos was opened to foreign trade.[37] From 1838 the Missouri traders, through their assembly, governor, chambers of commerce, and senator, made earnest efforts to secure from congress a custom-house on the Missouri River, with privilege of drawback and debenture for foreign goods, claiming that the trade had constantly diminished since 1828, and could in no other way be restored. A bill in their favor was tabled in 1842, but in 1845 another was finally passed.[38] In 1839 an attempt was made by Mexicans, with the aid of H. Connelly, an American merchant, to divert the course of trade from Santa Fé to Chihuahua direct. A caravan of 100 men made the trip through Texas, and returned to Chihuahua in 1840 without any serious casualty; but the attempt was not repeated.[39] For a short time in these years Governor Armijo tried the experiment of collecting as duties $500 on each wagon-load of goods; but the size of the wagons that began to be used soon prompted a return to ad valorem duties.

We have seen that the Texan attempt of 1841 to wrest the Santa Fé trade from the United States was not successful;[40] and the troubles experienced by the caravans of 1843 at the hands of Texan robbers have also been recorded. Notwithstanding these outrages,

[37] Decree of Feb. 17, 1837. *Prieto, Rentas*, 204; *Arrillaga, Recop.*, 1838, p. 187.

[38] A memorial of '38 says that only 7 wagons started in '37, and the trade was surely ruined by competition with goods introduced with drawback privileges via Matamoros and Vera Cruz from U. S. ports. *U. S. Govt Doc.*, 26th cong. 1st sess., Sen. Doc. 472. See also *Id.*, H. Ex. Doc., 191; *Id.*, H. Jour., 27th cong. 2d sess., p. 877, 1478; *Id.*, 28th cong. 2d sess., H. Jour., pp. 361, 432, 576; *Cong. Globe*, 1841–2, Index. 'Chih.;' *Id.*, 1844–5, p. xi.; *Benton's Debates*, xiii. 752; *Niles' Reg.*, lxiii. 15; lxviii. 119. Mention of caravans of '39 and '41 in *Id.*, lvii. 133, lxi. 209, including a letter from one of the Cal. emigrants, perhaps Toomes or Given.

[39] *Gregg's Com. Praires*, ii. 163–4; *Niles' Reg.*, lvi. 261, 403; lvii. 216. A caravan under Pickett and Gregg is also named as leaving Van Buren, Ark., in May for Chih., with an escort of 40 U. S. dragoons.

[40] See p. 319 et seq. of this volume. The return of the caravan of '41 in Sept. is noted in *Niles' Reg.*, lxi. 100. A party of Mexicans came with it, bringing $80,000 to purchase goods. The caravan of '42, Mex. and Amer., started in May with 62 wagons, 800 mules, and $150,000 in goods. The expenditure of $5,000 by the Mex. for wagons and harness at Pittsburg gave the papers of that town a chance to puff its prospects. *Id.*, lxii. 19, 192.

the year's business was very large and profitable;[41] yet President Santa Anna, by a decree of August 7, 1843, closing the frontier custom-house of Taos, put an end to the Santa Fé trade, much to the disgust of New Mexicans as well as Missourians. "Should the obnoxious decree be repealed, the trade will doubtless be prosecuted with renewed vigor and enterprise," writes Gregg; and it was repealed almost before it had gone into effect, on March 31, 1844, so that the trade of 1844–6 was as large as ever, though selling prices, and therefore profits, had been constantly diminishing for fifteen years.[42]

Besides the regular traders of the caravans, there were others, who resided permanently or for years in New Mexico; also many fur-trading trappers and miscellaneous adventurers, whose experiences would fill a most fascinating volume, as, indeed, in one case —that of James O. Pattie—they have done. Pattie and his father, with others whose aim was Indian trade and trapping, came to Taos and Santa Fé with a caravan of 1824, and for four years engaged in a series of the most remarkable rovings within and beyond the limits of Arizona and New Mexico. Frequent encounters with hostile Indians and bears diversify the story of long journeys and the many perils of a hunter's life; while the claimed rescue of Jacoba, daughter of an ex-governor, from the savages, adds a slender thread of romance. Finally, in 1828, the Patties arrived in California, the elder to die, the younger to continue his exploits, as fully recorded in another work of this series. Probably in the east, as

[41] Many items in *Niles' Reg.*, lxiv.–v. It appears that after the Texan troubles of May–June, another caravan of 175 wagons left Independence in August, still escorted by Capt. Cook. There was some complaint against this use of troops. *U. S. Govt Doc.*, 28th cong. 1st sess., H. Ex. Doc. 2, p. 63.

[42] *Prieto, Rentas*, 204; *Greggs' Com.*, ii. 177; *Niles' Reg.*, lxv. 166; lxvi. 281, 352; lxvii. 133, 385; lxviii. 31, 148; lxix. 416. The custom-house had been only nominally at Taos, goods being really entered at Sta Fé. The business of '44 was estimated at $750,000, but this year and the next there was some loss of animals, and traders were also perplexed by rumors of impending war. A caravan left Chih., in Dec. '45, being at Sta Fé in Jan., and at Independence in Feb. '46.

certainly in the west, there is much of exaggeration, not to say falsehood, in the story of personal adventure; but there is sufficient groundwork of fact to make the story valuable as well as fascinating.[43] Benjamin D. Wilson was another of the pioneers who had a varied career as trader and trapper in Arizona, New Mexico, and Sonora, before coming to settle in California.[44]

Communication with California began in 1830, when José Antonio Vaca visited that country with a small party of his countrymen, and Ewing Young, with a company of foreign trappers, possibly including Kit Carson, made a fur-hunting tour in the western valleys.[45] In 1831–2 three trapping and trading parties made the journey under Wolfskill, Jackson, and Young, the first-named opening the long-followed trail from Taos north of the Colorado River. From this time the route was travelled every year, often by parties of only a few individuals. Trade between the two territories consisted of the exchange of New Mexican blankets for Californian mules and horses; and it

[43] *The Personal Narrative of James O. Pattie, of Kentucky, during an expedition from St Louis through the vast regions between that place and the Pacific Ocean,* etc., etc. *Edited by Timothy Flint.* Cincinnati, 1833, 12mo. For more bibliographic details, and a full account of Pattie's Cal. adventures, and his return by sea and land via Mexico, see *Hist. Cal.,* iii. 162–72. The following is a chronologic outline of P.'s movements in 1824–7; July 1824, left Council Bluffs; Nov., arr. at Sta Fé, via Taos; also engaging in Nov. in an Ind. campaign, for the rescue of Mex. prisoners. From Nov. to April 1825 he made a trapping trip down the Gila and up its different branches, returning to the copper mines, where his father remained. In May he made another trip down the Gila, to bring furs that had been cached; in June–July visited Sta Fé, and spent the rest of the year at the copper mines, acting as a guard, his father renting the mine and remaining there. In Jan.–July 1826 he went down the Gila to the Colorado junction, up the Colorado and across the Rocky mts, trapped on the Platte, Yellowstone, Clarke's fork of the Columbia, and Arkansas, returning down the Rio Grande to Sta Fé. In Sept.–Nov. 1826 he went to Janos, across Sonora to Guaymas, and back via Chihuahua and El Paso to the mines. From Nov. to April several minor Indian-fighting and hunting tours were made; and in May–July 1827 he went to Sta Fé, El Paso, and Chih., in a vain pursuit of an agent who had cheated his father at the mines out of all his wealth. Finally, in Sept. the two Patties organized another trapping party, and in Dec. were on the Colorado, whence they presently went west, and falling into the hands of the Mexican authorities, were carried as prisoners to S. Diego.

[44] *Wilson's Observations,* MS. *Coyner's Lost Trappers* probably narrates adventures of this period chiefly, rather than of the earlier dates given in the book.

[45] *Hist. Cal.,* iii. 173–5.

must be confessed that the traders soon earned a most unenviable reputation.   There were many honorable exceptions; but most of the trading parties were composed of New Mexican, foreign, and Indian vagabonds, whose object was to obtain mules, without scruple as to methods, often by simple theft, and oftener by connivance with hostile Californian tribes. In 1833, especially, they caused a great excitement, and some of them, including Villapando, their leader, were arrested at Sta Fé.[46]   In 1835–7 John A. Sutter, afterward famous in California, was engaged in trade at Santa Fé; in 1841 the Workman-Rowland party brought many foreign and native New Mexicans to California; in 1842 a large trading party under Vigil included some twenty families in quest of homes, most of whom came back to settle in the San Bernardino region; and down to the end of the Mexican rule the movement of traders and emigrants continued.[47] Among native New Mexican settlers in California were members of the Vaca, Peña, and Armijo families, while many well-known Californian pioneers had spent some years in New Mexico.[48]

Industrially, there was for the most part no change, except a slight deterioration in some branches, from the unprosperous conditions of former years.   Of home records on the subject I have found none of any value; and while Gregg and his followers, in connection with commercial annals, give excellent reviews of the country's industries or lack of them, their remarks would apply as well to the Spanish as to the Mexican

[46] *Hist. Cal.*, iii. 386–8, 395–6.   Charlefoux was a Canadian in command of 30 or 40 'Chaguanoso' or Shawnee 'traders,' who took some part in the sectional politics and warfare of Cal. in '37–8. *Id.*, iii. 495, 518–20.   About these matters I find nothing in N. Mex. records.

[47] *Hist. Cal.*, iv. 124–5, 276–8, 342–3, 387.

[48] Among these may be named Cyrus Alexander, D. W. Alexander, F. Z. Branch, Lewis Burton, Moses and 'Kit' Carson, Wm G. Chard, Job F. Dye, Wm Gordon, Isaac Graham, Wm Knight, J. P. Leese, J. L. Majors, Wm Pope, Antoine and Louis Robidoux, John Rowland, Isaac Sparks, J. J. Warner, Isaac Williams, B. D. Wilson, John R. and Wm Wolfskill, Wm Workman, Ewing Young, and Geo. C. Yount.   See *Hist. Cal.*, Pioneer Register, for biog. sketches of these and many more.

period, being confirmatory of what I have written in earlier chapters. It is possible, however, that the decadence noted, as in sheep-raising and the manufacture of blankets, was more apparent than real, being founded on an exaggerated idea of what had been accomplished in the past.[49]

In mining, though nothing appears respecting the famous copper mine of the south-west, except the somewhat doubtful statements of the trapper Pattie,[50] some progress was made, since placeres of gold were successfully worked in two districts some thirty miles south-west of Santa Fé. The 'Old Placers' were discovered in 1828, and the 'New Placers' in 1839. The former yielded from $60,000 to $80,000 per year in 1832-5, and later considerably less. At the latter sprang up the town of Tuerto, with 22 stores in 1845, when the yield of both districts is given as $250,000. The metal was very fine and pure, but water was scarce, the chief reliance being on the artificially melted snows of winter; apparatus was primitive, consisting of the *batea*, or bowl; and prejudice against foreigners prevented the introduction of improved methods. At various other points, as near Taos, Abiquiú, and Sangre de Cristo, gold was found, and mines were perhaps worked for a short time. No silver mines were worked in the Mexican period.[51]

[49] Gregg, *Com. Prairies*, i. 189, says that 10 or 20 years ago, that is, in 1824-34, about 200,000 sheep were annually driven to southern markets, and sometimes, perhaps, as many as 500,000; and sheep were still the principal article of exportation. Narbona, in *Pino, Not. Hist.*, 24, gives the live-stock of the country in 1827 as cattle 5,000, sheep and goats 240,000, horses and mules 3,000; total value $221,650.

[50] Pattie, *Narrative*, 71-81, 112, 115, 123, 129-32, says that the mine was worked by a Spanish superintendent, Juan Onis, for the Span. owner, Francisco Pablo Lagera. 'Within the circumference of three miles there is a mine of copper, gold, and silver, and besides, a cliff of load-stone. The silver mine is not worked, as not being so profitable as either the copper or gold mines.' The Ind. were very troublesome, and the trappers did good service in keeping them in order, by force and treaties. Finally, the Patties leased the mines for 5 years, at $1,000 per year, and the elder P. remained there, established a stock ranch on the Mimbres, and made money. But in 1827, when he thought of buying the property, a rascally Span. agent, intrusted with $30,000 in gold, ran away with the money, and ruined Pattie. At the same time the owner was exiled as a Spaniard, and it is implied that the mines were abandoned.

[51] *Gregg's Com. Prairies*, i. 162-77; *Prince's Hist. Sk.*, 241-3; *Meline's 2,000*

In educational matters a slight increase of interest is to be noted, though with very meagre results.   In 1826 the diputacion territorial was about to establish some kind of a college at the capital, under the protectorship of Agustin Fernandez de San Vicente; and from 1827 to 1832 archive records show the existence of primary schools at several of the principal towns; but in 1834 there was no school at Santa Fé, and probably none elsewhere, as the diputacion announced that there were no funds, and called upon the ayuntamientos to reopen the schools, if possible, by private contributions.[52]   About 1834 a printing-press was brought to the country, and with it in 1835 Padre Martinez issued for four weeks at Taos the *Crepúsculo*, the only New Mexican newspaper of pre-Gringo times.[53]

The missions continued as before, there being no formal secularization, but were missions only in name. The government still paid—or at least made appropriations for—the sínodos of from 23 to 27 Franciscan

Miles, 171–2. These and other writers cannot refrain from comparing the poor showing of mining industry at this time, not only with the developments of later years, but with those of the 17th century.   Gregg even attempts to make of Gran Quivira in the s. e. the ruins of an ancient mining city.   I have already expressed the opinion that nothing more than prospecting was done by the Spaniards.   The *salinas* of the south-east yielded an unlimited supply of salt.

[52] *Arch. Sta Fé*, MS., including 'estatutos para el régimen de la escuela general.'   Schools opened at 6 a. m. in summer and 7 in winter.   30 scholars at Cañada in 1828.   Marcelino Abreu teacher of a Lancasterian school at Sta Fé in 1829–30.   A report of Narbona, 1827, in *Pino, Not. Hist.*, 56–7, indicates 18 schools and 17 teachers at Sta Fé, Vado, Cochiti, Cia, Sandía, Alameda, Alburquerque, Tomé, Belen, Laguna, La Cañada, S. Juan, Taos, and Abiquiú; but very likely only 5 or 6 of these had any real existence; for Barreiro, *Ojeada*, 43, names for 1832 only Sta Fé, with $500 assigned for teachers' salary, S. Miguel, Cañada, Taos, Alburquerque, and Belen with from $250 to $300 each.   Prince, *Hist. Sk.*, 239, tells us that Gov. Martinez was a special friend of education, sending young men to Durango and Mexico to be educated, besides establishing govt schools at Sta Fé.   Ritch, *Aztlan*, 249, speaks of private schools established by Vicar Martinez at Taos, by Padre Leiva at S. Miguel, and by other priests.   All writers note the prevalent ignorance of the New Mexicans and the absence of books, also noting the facts that there were still no physicians or lawyers in the country.

[53] *Gregg's Com. Prairies*, i. 200–1; *Prince's Hist. Sk.*, 234.   Gregg says the editor's object was to get himself elected to congress, in which effort he succeeded.   He also states that some primers and catechisms were printed on this press before 1844; but I have never seen any of these early productions. In the newspapers of 1876 is noted the death of Jesus M. Vaca, who was a printer on the *Crepúsculo*.

friars; but these were for the most part acting curates
at the Mexican settlements, making occasional visits
to the Indian pueblos under their spiritual charge.
Only five of the latter had resident missionaries in
1832.[54] The Mexican congress in 1823, and again in
1830, decreed the carrying-out of the old Spanish order
for the establishing of a bishopric; but nothing was
effected in this direction. Among the vicars appears
in 1825–6 the name of Agustin Fernandez de San
Vicente, the famous canónigo who had visited California in 1822 as the commissioner of the emperor
Iturbide. In 1833 the bishop of Durango visited this
distant part of his diocese, and his reception is described by Gregg and Prince as having been marked
by great enthusiasm.[55]

The population has been given as 30,000 whites
and 10,000 pueblo Indians in 1822. In these 24 years
I suppose that the white population was somewhat
more than doubled, and that of Indians slightly diminished; or that the total in 1845–6 was not far from
80,000, though there is one official report that makes
this total much larger.[56]

[54] *Barreiro, Ojeada,* 15, 39–41; *Escudero, Not. Chih.,* 31.   Yearly appropriations for the stipends. *Correo de la Fed.,* Oct. 14,'1827; *Mex., Mem. Hac.,*
1826, doc. 15; *Id., Mem. Just.,* 1831, annex. 8; *Id., Mem. Hac.,* 1832, doc. N;
Id., 1837, annex. F; *Id,,* 1844, presupuesto 7. The no. of friars 27, with
$8,880 in stipends includes El Paso, Narbona in 1827 gives the number of
curates as 17. The statement of Ritch, *Aztlan,* 249–50, that before 1846 all
the padres from abroad had been supplanted by native-born New Mexicans
seems doubtful. Aug. 26, 1842, order of the president authorizing the gov.
and junta to grant lands of the Ind. pueblos where there were few Ind. and
many vecinos. *Pinart Col.*
[55] Decrees on bishopric. *S. Miguel, Mex.,* ii. 2; *Arrillaga, Recop.,* 1830, p.
94–6; *Mex., Col. Ord. y Dec.,* ii. 148. Tithes rented for $10,000 to $12,000 per
year, about one third of their value. *Barreiro,* 41.   Juan Felipe Ortiz is
named as vicar in '32–41; and Fr. José Pedro Rubin de Célis was custodio of
the missionaries in 1827. *Arch. Sta Fé,* MS.
[56] The census report of 1827 by Narbona, in *Pino, Not Hist.,* 56–7, is the
only detailed one extant. It makes the total 43,433, about evenly divided
between the sexes. Married couples 7,677. Farmers 6,588, artisans 1,237,
laborers 2,475, traders 93, teachers 17, curates 17, surgeon 1. There is no
separation of whites and Ind. The larger towns, most of them including one
or more small pueblos, are Sta Fé 5,759, S. Miguel del Vado 2,893, Alburquerque 2,547, Tomé 2,043, Cañada 6,508, S. Juan 2,915, Taos 3,606, and
Abiquiú 3,557. Pop. in 1831 estimated at 50,000. *Mex. Mem., Rel.,* 1832
annex. 1, p. 11; *Barreiro,* 17. Mayer, *Mex. Aztec,* ii. 369, gives the pop. of
the missions (?) in 1831 as 23,025. Pop. in 1833 52,360. *Wizlizenus, Mem.,*
26; *De Bow's Ency.,* 268. Cortina, in *Instituto Nac. Bol.,* no. 1, p. 18, gives a

pop. of 43,439 in 1829 and 57,176 in 1833. Pop. in '38, '39, or '42, 57,026. *Cortina*, in *Soc. Mex. Geog., Bol.*, vii. 139; *Mex., Mem. Rel.*, 1847, p. 112; *Wizlizenus* and *De Bow*. In 1840 Gov. Armijo, *Pino, Not. Hist.*, 55, gives 28,939 men and 26,464 women, or total 55,403. Pop. in 1841 about 60,000 Span. acc. to sec. state, as quoted by Gregg, who also alludes to a census of 32 as showing 72,000. Gregg, *Com. Prairies*, i. 148–9, estimates, however, the pop. in '44 at 70,000, of whom 10,000 Ind. An original report of pop. in connection with the division into districts, etc. makes a total in '44 of 99,204; or by partidos—Sta Fé 12,500, Sta Ana 10,500, S. Miguel 18,800, Rio Arriba 15,000, Taos 14,200, Valencia 20,000, and Bernalillo 8,204. The summing up of the printed doc. is 100,064; but I suppose the correct total of 99,204 is an exaggeration, though Hughes, *Doniphan's Exped.*, 38, gives the pop. as 160,000. Wizlizenus' gives 70,000 as the figure in 1846.

CHAPTER XV.

PIMERÍA ALTA AND THE MOQUI PROVINCE.

1543-1767.

Earliest Annals of a Non-existent and Nameless Province—A Century and a Half of Neglect—Entradas of Espejo and Oñate—Down the Colorado to the Gulf—Conversion and Revolt of the Moquis—Progress in Sonora—Pimería Alta—Maps—Labors of Father Kino—Explorations in Arizona—The Gila and Casa Grande—Mange's Diaries—Kino's Map—First Missions in 1732—Bac and Guevavi—Bolas de Plata—Revolt—Jesuit Efforts to Enter the Moqui Field—Triumph of the Franciscans—Explorations of Keller and Sedelmair—Up the Colorado—Last Years of the Jesuit Régime—Decadence of the Missions—Tubac Presidio—Ranchería of Tucson—Apache Raids and Military Expeditions.

Now that eastern annals have been brought down to the end of Mexican rule, it is time to turn again to the west, to that portion of our territory known later as Arizona. In Spanish and Mexican times there was no such province, under that or any other name, nor was the territory divided by any definite boundaries between adjoining provinces. That portion south of the Gila was part of Pimería Alta, the northern province of Sonora. Except a small district of this Pimería, the whole territory was uninhabited, so far as any but aborigines were concerned. A small tract in the north-east was generally regarded as belonging to New Mexico, because the Spaniards of that province sometimes visited, and had once for a brief period been recognized as masters of, the Moqui pueblos. Not only were no boundaries ever formally indicated, but I have found nothing to show how far in Spanish and Mexican opinion New Mexico was re-

(344)

garded as extending west or Sonora north.   Each was
deemed to stretch indefinitely out into the *despoblado*.
California, however, while no boundary was ever fixed
officially, was not generally considered to extend east
of the Rio Colorado.   The name Moqui province was
sometimes rather vaguely applied to the whole region
north of the Gila valley.   Arizona—probably Arizonac in its original form—was the name given by the
natives to a locality on the modern frontier of Sonora,
and was known from just before the middle of the
eighteenth century as the name of the mining camp,
or district, where the famous *bolas de plata* were
found.   It is still applied to a mountain range in that
vicinity.

Nearly all of what we now call Arizona has no
other history before 1846 than the record of exploring entradas from the south and east.   The exception
is the small tract, of not more than sixty miles square,
from Tucson southward, mainly in the Santa Cruz
valley, which contained all the Spanish establishments,
and whose annals are an inseparable part of those pertaining to Pimería Alta as a whole, or to Sonora,
which included Pimería.   Thus, the only history our
territory has in early times belongs to that of other
provinces, and is given elsewhere in this or other works
of this series.   To dispose of the matter here, however,
by a mere reference to scattered material to be found
elsewhere, would be by no means consistent with the
unity I have aimed to give to my work as a whole
and to each part.   The story must be told, but it may
be greatly condensed, reference sufficing for many details.   Neither the condensation nor the repetition
involved can properly be regarded as a defect, each
contributing, if I mistake not, to the completeness,
clearness, and interest of the record.

The negro slave Estévan, closely followed by the
Spanish friar Marcos de Niza, crossed Arizona from
south-west to north-east in 1539; and these earliest

explorers were followed in 1540 by Vasquez de Coronado, who, with an army of Spaniards, marched from Sonora to Zuñi, extended his exploration north-westward to the Moqui towns and the great cañon of the Colorado, and recrossed Arizona in 1542 on his return from eastern exploits and disasters among the New Mexican pueblos.   These expeditions, the beginning of Arizona annals, are fully recorded in the second and third chapters of this volume; and the map, showing also one or two later entradas, is here reproduced.   While Coronado's observations were recorded with tolerable accuracy, no practical use was made of the information gained, and all that was accurate in the reports was soon forgotten.   A century and a half was destined to pass before the Arizona line should again be crossed from the south.

But it was only forty years before the territory was again entered by Spaniards from the east.   Antonio Espejo, with a few companions, in 1583, coming from the Rio Grande valley by way of Zuñi, marched to the Moqui towns, and thence penetrated some fifty leagues farther west or south-west, listening to tales of great towns said to lie beyond the great river, visiting maize-producing tribes, obtaining samples of rich silver ore in the region forty or fifty miles north of the modern Prescott, and returning by a more direct route to Zuñi.[1]   Fifteen years later the eastern line was again crossed by Juan de Oñate, the conqueror of New Mexico, who, at the end of 1598, very nearly repeated Espejo's Arizona exploration, starting out to reach the South Sea, but called back in haste to Acoma by news that the peñol patriots were in arms to regain their independence.[2]   In 1604 Oñate resumed his search for the Mar del Sur, and found it. With thirty men he marched westward, still via Zuñi and Moqui; crossed the Rio Colorado—as he named the branch since known as the Colorado Chiquito;

[1] For Espejo's entrada, see p. 38-9 of this vol.
[2] See p. 139, this volume.

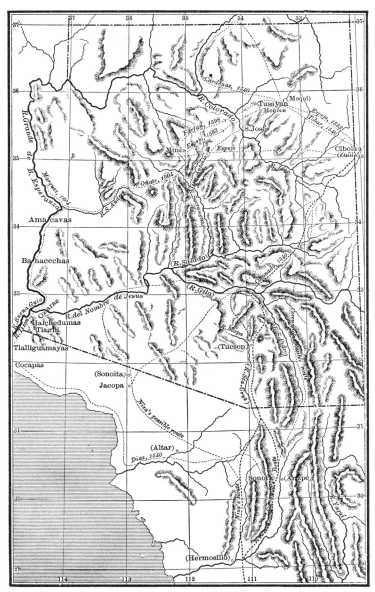

EARLIEST EXPLORATIONS OF ARIZONA.

gave the names San Antonio and Sacramento to two branches of the river later called Rio Verde in the region north of Prescott—a considerable portion of his route corresponding in a general way with the line of the Atlantic and Pacific railroad of more modern centuries; and kept on south-westward to and down the San Andrés—Santa María and Bill Williams fork—to its junction with the Rio Grande de Buena Esperanza, that is, the Colorado.   One of the captains went up this river a short distance; and then all followed its course southward, fully understanding its identity with the stream called Rio del Tizon in Coronado's time, to the head of the gulf.   The main eastern branch, or Gila, was named Rio del Nombre de Jesus.   In January 1605, they reached tide-water and named a fine harbor Puerto de la Conversion de San Pablo; and then they returned by the same route to New Mexico.   Nearly two centuries passed before the region between Moqui and Mojave was revisited by Spaniards.   Oñate's expedition to the South Sea, though of the greatest importance and accurately narrated, like that of Coronado had slight effect on real knowledge of geography, its chief effects being to complicate the vagaries of the Northern Mystery.[3]

There were no more explorations from any direction in the seventeenth century, and Arizona annals for the whole period are confined to a few meagre items about the Moqui district as gathered from earlier chapters of this volume.   It may be well to state here, however, that the name of Arizona's chief river is apparently used for the first time in a report of 1630, being applied to a New Mexican province of Gila, or

[3] For Oñate's exped. of 1604–5, see p. 154 of this vol.   Native tribes on the Colorado, from north to south, were, above the Gila, the Amacavas (later Yamajabs, Amajavas, or Mojaves), Bahacechas, and Ozaras; between the Gila and tide-water, the Halchedumas, Coahuanas, Tlaglli, Tlalliguamayas, and Cocapas.   Among the contributions of this expedition to the Northern Mystery was the existence, as reported by the natives, of Lake Copala, where Aztec was spoken and golden bracelets were worn.   The Spaniards also concluded, from their observations and statements of the natives, that the gulf extended indefinitely north-westward behind the mountains from the river's mouth, thus confirming the idea long entertained that Cal. was an island.

Xila, where the river has its source.[4] At the beginning of the century the Moquis, like the other pueblos,
accepted Christianity, were often visited by the friars
from the first, and probably were under resident missionaries almost continuously for eighty years; yet of
all this period we know only that Fray Francisco
Porras, who worked long in this field, converting some
800 souls at Aguatuvi, was killed by poison at his
post in 1633; that Governor Peñalosa is said to have
visited the pueblos in 1661–4; and that in 1680 four
Franciscans were serving the five towns, or three
missions. These were José Figueroa at San Bernardino de Aguatuvi, José Trujillo at San Bartolomé de
Jougopavi, with the visita of Moxainavi, and José
Espeleta, with Agustin de Santa María, at San Francisco de Oraibe and Gualpi, all of whom lost their lives
in the great revolt. From that time the valiant Moquis maintained their independence of all Spanish or
Christian control. It is not clear that they sent their
warriors to take part in the wars of 1680–96 in New
Mexico, but they probably did so, and certainly afforded protection to fugitives from the other pueblos,
the Tehuas and others even building a new town adjoining those of the Moquis, in which part of the tribe
lived from that period. In 1692 they had, like the
other nations, professed their willingness to submit to
Governor Vargas; but in the following years no attempt to compel their submission is recorded. In
1700, however, fearing an invasion, they affected penitence, permitted a friar to baptize a few children, and
negotiated in vain with the Spaniards for a treaty that
should permit each nation to retain its own religion![5]

Meanwhile, during this century and a half, though,
as I have said, the Arizona line was not crossed from
the south, the Spanish occupation was extended nearly
to that line. In Coronado's time the northern limit
of settlement was San Miguel de Culiacan. The

---

[4] *Benavides, Reqveste Remonst.* See p. 162–3 of this vol.
[5] On Moqui items of 1599–1700, see chap. vii.–x., this volume.

villa of San Felipe de Sinaloa was founded in 1584, after the failure of several attempts, a little farther north. It was in 1591 that the Jesuits began their missionary work in Sinaloa, but they had no permanent establishments north of that province before 1600.[6] The Fuerte de Montesclaros, giving name to the Rio del Fuerte, was built in 1610, and in the same year Captain Hurdaide, after a series of hard-fought battles and several reverses, made peace with the Yaqui Indians. In 1613 and 1617 respectively, missions were established among the Mayos and Yaquis, and a beginning was thus made of Jesuit work in Sonora. From 1621 eleven padres served 60,000 converts in the northern, or Sonora, mission district, called San Ignacio; in 1639 the spiritual conquest had extended to the Sonora valley proper, the region of Ures, among the Ópatas, where the district of San Francisco Javier was organized; by 1658 this district had been extended so as to include missions as far north as Arizpe and Cuquiarachi; and by 1688 these northern missions— beyond Batuco and Nacori, in Pimería Baja, eighteen pueblos in six missions partidos—had been formed into the new district, or rectorado, of Santos Mártires de Japon. The next advance of missionary work northward will bring us to the subject proper of this chapter. It should be noted here that in 1640–50 there was a temporary division of the province, northern Sonora above the Yaqui River being called Nueva Andalucía. In consequence of a quarrel with the Jesuits, the governor of the new province attempted to put the missions in charge of Franciscans; but, though a small party of friars came to the country, nothing was accomplished; and all trace of the change, secular and religious, disappeared about the middle of the century.[7]

[6] For particulars, see *Hist. North Mex. States*, i. 107–23. This reference includes Ibarra's expeditions of 1564–5, which may possibly furnish an exception to my statement that the Arizona line was not crossed till nearly the end of the next century.

[7] See annals of Sinaloa and Sonora, 1600–1700, in *Hist. North Mex. St.*, i. 202–50.

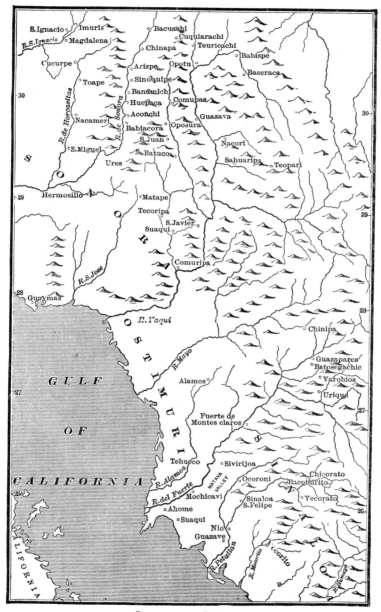

SINALOA AND SONORA.

Pimería Alta, home of the Pimas, but also including that of the Pápagos, Sobas, and Sobaipuris, besides other tribes in the north, was bounded on the south by the rivers Altar and San Ignacio with the latter's southern affluents, on the north in a general way by the Gila valley, on the west by the gulf and Rio Colorado, and on the east by the San Pedro, the country farther east being the home of Apaches and other savage tribes. This broad region was explored within a period of twenty years at the close of the seventeenth century and beginning of the eighteenth by the famous Jesuit, Father Eusebio Francisco Kino. Over and over again, often alone, sometimes with associates, guides, and a guard, this indefatigable missionary traversed the valleys bounding the region on the south, east, and north, and more than once crossed in different directions the comparatively desert interior, besides giving special attention to the gulf shore and Colorado mouth, for his original purpose was to reach and convert the Californians from this direction. He found the natives, grouped in a hundred or more rancherías, most docile and friendly, displaying from the first a childish eagerness to entertain the padre, to listen to his teachings, to have their names entered on his register, and to have their children baptized. They were, above all, desirous of being formed into regular mission communities, with resident padres of their own; and at many rancherías they built rude but neatly cared for churches, planted fields, and tended herds of live-stock in patient waiting for missionaries who, in most cases, never came. Kino's great work began in 1687, when he founded the frontier mission of Dolores, his home or headquarters for the rest of his life. For six years he toiled alone, till fathers Campos and Januske came in 1693 to take charge of San Ignacio and Tubutama; and only eight padres besides Kino worked in this field during the latter's life, there being rarely, if ever, more than four at the same time. Missions were, however, established, besides the three named, at Caborca, Suamca, and Cocóspera, with a dozen or more of the other rancherías as visitas. Those which became missions or visitas before 1800, with the presidios and other settlements, are best indicated on the appended map.

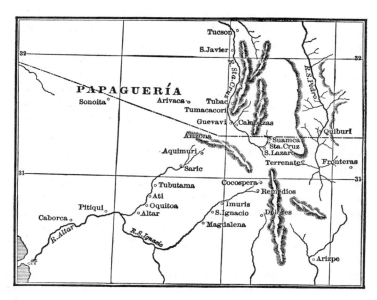

MISSIONS OF PIMERÍA ALTA.

The great difficulty, and one that caused Kino no end of anxiety and sorrow, but never discouragement, was that, besides the zealous padre himself, no one seemed really to believe in the docility and good faith of the Pimas, who were accused of being treacherous, hostile, and in league with the Apaches. Even Jesuit visitors, when once they were beyond the reach of Kino's magnetism and importunity, were disposed to regard the padre's projects as visionary and dangerous, thus furnishing the Spanish authorities a plausible pretext for withholding pecuniary support. There were no other establishments in these times except a garrison, or presidio, at Fronteras, or Corodeguachi; this and a *compania volante* being charged with resisting the almost constant raids of savage tribes in the north-east, and often requiring assistance from other presidios. All this region was under a comandante de armas, residing generally at San Juan Bautista, farther south, and there was no other government in the north. Captain Juan Mateo Mange was detailed with a part of the flying company from 1694 to protect the padres in their tours, and his excellent diaries constitute our best authority for events to 1702.[8] There was a revolt in 1695, in which Padre Saeta, of Caborca, lost his life, several servants were killed, and many of the churches were sacked or destroyed. Yet notwithstanding the oppressive acts of military men and Spanish employees, which, according to the Jesuits, provoked the revolt, and the murderous slaughter by which it was avenged and the natives were forced to sue for peace, the padres seem to have had no difficulty in regaining all their earlier influence in a year or two; and the Pimas and Sobaipuris soon proved their fidelity by aiding the Spaniards most effectually in warfare against the Apaches, who in turn often raided the Pima rancherías, destroying the mission of Cocóspera in 1698. Still, by a perplexing combination of satanic influences, missionaries could not be obtained for the far north; and the old prejudice against the Pimas was no sooner partially conquered than it was transferred in full force to the Gila tribes, where Padre Eusebio, with a view to his Californian projects, desired to establish missions. Kino died at his post in 1711.

---

[8] *Mange, Historia de la Pimería Alta.* MS. of the *Arch. Gen. de Mex.,* printed in *Doc. Hist. Mex.* Hardly inferior as an authority, and extending over a longer period, is the *Apostólicos Afanes,* made up mainly from Kino's letters; and *Alegre, Hist. Comp. Jesus,* is another standard work. Full details in *Hist. North Mex. States,* i.

Having thus presented a general view of the Pimería missions, it is necessary to notice somewhat more in detail explorations north of the Arizona line, where there was no mission with resident padre during Kino's life, though there were churches at several rancherías in the Santa Cruz valley. Kino may have crossed the line as far as Tumacácori with Salvatierra in 1691, and he is said to have reached Bac in 1692; but the records of these earliest entradas are vague, and doubtless some of his later tours in the Santa Cruz valley have left no trace. In 1694, however, he penetrated alone to the Gila valley in quest of ruins reported by the Indians, reaching and saying mass in the Casa Grande, an adobe structure that had probably been visited by Niza and Coronado in 1539–40, and still standing as I write in 1886. In 1696 another visit to Bac is mentioned. Thus far, however, we have no particulars.

In November 1697 was undertaken the first formal exploration in this direction of which any detailed record has survived. Lieutenant Cristóbal Martin Bernal, with Alférez Francisco Acuña, a sergeant, and twenty soldiers, marched from Fronteras via Terrenate and Suamca, while Kino and Mange with ten servants came from Dolores. The two parties united at Quiburi, not far from the site of the modern Tombstone; Coro, a Sobaipuri chief, with thirty warriors, joined the expedition; and all marched down the Rio Quiburi, since called the San Pedro, to its junction with the Gila, now so called in the records for the first time, though, as we have seen, the Gila province of New Mexico was named as early as 1630. Down the main river went the explorers to and a little beyond the Casa Grande, which is for the first time described and pictured by simple drawings in the diaries. From the Gila they returned southward up the river, since called the Santa Cruz, by way of Bac and Guevavi, reaching Dolores at the beginning of December. They had marched 260 leagues, had been warmly welcomed everywhere, had registered 4,700 natives and baptized 89, besides conferring badges of office on many chieftains. Some details of this the first of Arizona explorations definitely recorded are given in a note.[9]

² *Bernal, Relacion, 1697*, in *Doc. Hist. Mex.*, 3d series, pt iv., p. 797–809; *Mange, Hist. Pimeria*, 274–91; also both diaries in MS. Bernal left Corodeguachi Nov. 5th, and marched to Surratapani de Guachi, 8 l.; 6th, to Terrenate, 12 l.; 7th, to Sta María (Suamca), 12 l., where P. Contreras' mission was in a prosperous condition; 8th, to the valley and ranchería of S. Joaquin, 12 l.; and 9th, to the ranchería de Quiburis, 8 l., where Kino was met. Meanwhile Kino and Mange, leaving Dolores Nov. 2d, had marched to Remedios, 8 l. N.; 4th, to Cocóspera, 6 l. N., where was P. Contreras; 5th, to S. Lázaro, 6 l. N. on another stream, which rises near Suamca and makes a great circle (the Sta Cruz, see map); thence eastward up the river to Sta María (Suamca), 6 l.; 6th, over plains and rolling hills to S. Joaquin Basosuma, 14 l. N.; 7th, the Sta Cruz de Gaibanipitea, 6 l. E., on a hill on west bank of a river which rises in the plains of Terrenate (that is, the S. Pedro; there are ruins known as Sta Cruz a few miles w. of Tombstone on the river). Here they were received in a house of adobes and beams built for the padre. Here they joined Martin, and went 1 l. N. to Quiburi on the 9th, being entertained by Coro and his warriors, who were dancing round Apache scalps. (There is a slight difference between the two diaries as to date and place of meeting. Later I use both diaries together.)

Nov. 11th, from Quiburi down the river to Álamos, 10 l. N.; 12th, to Baicadeat, 13 l., passing some abandoned rancherías; 13th, past the farthest point ever reached by Spaniards—a narrow pass which had been visited by Capt. Fran. Ramirez—to Causac, 2 l., and Jiaspi, or Rosario, 2 l. (Bernal says the day's journey was 3 l.); 14th, past Muiva and other rancherías to Aribaiba, or Aribabia, 6 or 7 l.; 15th, past Zutoida and Comarsuta to the last ranchería of the river called Ojio or Victoria, 9 or 11 l. N. Two others, Busac and Tubo, were on a creek flowing into the river (perhaps the Arivaipa, though said to flow east). The valley is described as pleasant and fertile, with irrigating ditches and its rancherías—with 390 houses and 1,850 inhabitants counted—prosperous though much harassed by the Jocomes and Apaches of the east. 16th, to the Gila junction, 6 l., and 2 or 3 l. down the Gila to a place named Mange.

Nov. 17th, down the Gila at some distance from the river, to S. Gregorio spring, 8 l. w.; and to S. Fernando on the bank, 2 l.; 18th, over the plain 9 l. w. to Casa Grande, Sergt Escalante swimming the river with two companions about midway of the journey to examine some ruins on the north side. Besides describing the Casa Grande and other ruins, Mange gives a tradition of the natives respecting their origin, 1 l. to a ranchería on the river bank; 19th, to Tusonimon 4 l. w., over sterile plains; 20th, to S. Andrés, 7 l. w., whose chief had visited Baseraca, and had been baptized at Dolores, where rumors were heard of quicksilver mines in the N. w. and of white men who came to the Colorado armed with muskets and swords—perhaps English or shipwrecked Spaniards, but probably only the apostate Moquis with stolen fire-arms (!); 21st, back to Tusonimó, or Sta Isabel, 7 l. E., and 3 l. s. into the desert; 22d, to an artificial tank, or pond, 4 or 5 l. s.; and to ranchería of Sta Catalina Cuitciabaqui, 14 or 15 l. s.; 23d, up the dry bed of the river (Sta Cruz), to ranch. of the valley of Correa, 9 l. s.; and to S. Agustin Oiaur, 6 l. s.; 24th, to ranch. of Bac, Batosda, or S. Javier, 6 l. s. This was the largest ranchería of all Pimería, 830 persons living in 176 houses; and there was an adobe house ready for the padre, with a wheat-field and some live-stock well tended.   26th, to Tumacacori, or S. Cayetano, 18 or 20 l. s.; 27th, to Guevavi, 6 l. s.; and 7 l. to Bacuanos (Bacuancos), or S. Antonio (?); 28th, to S. Lázaro,

Again, in 1698, Kino returned by way of Bac to the
Gila; and from San Andrés, the limit of the previous
trip, or from the region of the Pima villages of modern maps, he crossed the country south-westwardly to
Sonoita and the gulf shore; but unfortunately, Mange's
place was taken by Captain Carrasco, and no particulars affecting Arizona are extant.[10] In the next tour
of 1699 with Mange, he went first to Sonoita via Saric;
and thence crossed north-westward to the Gila at a
point about ten miles above the Colorado junction.
The natives refused to guide him down the river where
he had intended to go; therefore he went up the river
eastward, cutting off the big bend, sighting and naming the Salado and Verde rivers, from a mountain top,
reaching San Andrés Coata where he had been before,
and returning home by the old route via Encarnacion,
San Clemente, San Agustin, and Bac. In this trip he
called the Colorado Rio de los Mártires, the Gila Rio
de los Apóstoles, and the four branches of the latter
—that is, the Salado, Verde, Santa Cruz, and San
Pedro—Los Evangelistas.[11] In October of the same

7 l.; and to Cocóspera, 6 l.; 29th, to Remedios; Dec. 1st, to Dolores. Kino's
party left Bernal on the 26th, and the latter by the same route arrived at
Dolores Dec. 2d.

[10] *Kino, Carta*, in *Sonora Mat.*, 817–19; *Apost. Afanes*, 272–4; *Alegre, Hist.*,
iii. 203–4; *Lockman's Trav. Jesuits*, i. 355. The details given affect only observations on the gulf shore, to which sufficient attention is given elsewhere.

[11] *Mange, Hist. Pimería*, 292–310. Route from S. Marcelo Sonoita: Feb.
17th, down the stream w. 10 l. to a carrizal; 18th, 6 l. N. w. and 14 l. N., by
moonlight over sterile plains to the watering-place of La Luna; 19th, 12 l.
N. w., and w. to a small ranchería not named; 20th, 15 l. over barren plains
and past mineral hills to Las Tinajas; 21st, 6 l. N. w. to the Gila, where were
600 Pimas and Yumas, the latter now visited and described for the first time.
Mange from a hill saw the junction of the Colorado, on which river the Alchedomas were said to live. M. also found some slight tradition of Oñate's visit
in 1605, and heard of white men who sometimes came from the north coast to
trade, the reports resembling those heard before at S. Andrés and Casa
Grande. Feb. 23d, 12 l. E. up the river; 24th, 16 l. E. up river; 25th, 4 l. to
ranch. S. Matias Tutum; 4 l. to ranch. S. Mateo Cant; 26th, 14 l. up the
river to ranch. Tádes Vaqui; 27th, 3 l. across a bend to a ranch. on the river;
to another S. Simon Tucsani; and to another of Cocomaricopas, 12 l. in all;
28th, 8 l. s. w. (s. E. ?), leaving the river on account of the big bend, past 5
rancherías, to one of Pimas, who welcomed them with triumphal arches, etc.,
a good place for a mission; March 1st, 11 l. E. over a rocky and sterile country
to a spring; 2d, 13 l. E. over a range of hills from which they saw the rivers
Verde and Salado—perhaps flowing from the famous Sierra Azul of N. Mex.
annals—to the river 3 l. below the junction, where was the ranch. of S. Bartolomé Comac; 3d, 10 l. up river to S. Andrés Coata, where they had been in

year, with Padres Leal and Gonzalez from abroad,
they went again to Bac.   Here the moving of a stone,
thought at first to be an idol, uncovered a hole on the
top of a hill, and produced a hurricane which lasted
till the stone was replaced over the entrance to this
home of the winds.   From Bac, they took a south-
west course to Sonoita, registering 1,800 Papabotes.[12]
Padre Francisco Gonzalez was delighted with Bac,
declaring it to be fit, not only for a mission of 3,000
converts, but for a city of 30,000 inhabitants; and he
promised to return as a missionary.   Mange states
that he did come 'mucho despues,' or much later, but
that he remained only till 1702, being driven away by
the hostilities of two rancherías not far away.   It
would seem that this must be an error.   In April
and May 1700, Kino went again to Bac and laid the
foundation of a large church, which the natives were
eager to build, but respecting the further progress of
which nothing is known.   In September he reached
the Gila, by a route for the most part new, striking

1697.   They had registered 1,800 men, Yumas and Cocomaricopas; 4th, E.
past Encarnacion 9 l. to a fertile tract; 5th, s. E. away from river, 9 l. to the
tank or cistern built by the people of Casa Grande, when they went south to
settle Mexico (!); 13 l. (or 4) s. to Sta Catarina; 6th, s. past S. Clemente to
S. Agustin Oiaur; 7th, up the river s. past 4 rancherías, 6 l. to S. Javier del
Bac, where 1,300 natives welcomed them with dances and songs, a magnificent
place for a large mission; 9th–10th, 7 l. s., Kino being very ill; 11th, 13 l. s.
to opposite S. Cayetano Tumagacori; 12th, 6 l. to Guevavi, 7 l. to Bacuancos;
13th, 16 l. to Cocóspera which had been destroyed and abandoned; 14th, to
Remedios 6 l., 8 l. to Dolores.

[12] *Mange, Hist. Pim.*, 311–20.   Route: left Dolores Oct. 24th, 8 l. to Remedios, where a fine new church was being built; 25th, 6 l. down one stream
and up another to Cocóspera; 4 l. to Rio Sta María at S. Lorenzo (S. Lázaro?);
26th, 11 l. down river to S. Luis Bacuancos, past Quiquiborica (one of which
may have been the later Buenavista); 27th, 6 l. to Guevavi, or Gusutaqui, at
the junction of a stream from the E.; 4 l. to S. Cayetano, Jumagacori (Tumacácori); 28th, 6 l. N.; 29th, 10 l. to Bac, west of which was a ranch. of Otean.
Nov. 1st, 2d, Mange and Kino went on down to Oiaur, 6 l., and 15 l. to Sta
Catarina Caituagaba and S. Clemente, and returned; near Bac two ranch. of
Juajona and Junostaca are mentioned as existing later; 5th, 10 l. w. to springs;
6th, 6 l. w. to Tups, where they were shown silver ore; 3 l. w. to Cops, or
Humo, of the nation Pima-Papabotas; 7th, 8 l. w. over plains to S. Serafin
Actum, where they were visited by natives from S. Fran. Atí; 8th, P. Leal
left the party for Tubutama in his carriage; while the rest went on N. w. and
w. 13 l. to S. Rafael; 9th, 9 l. more N., to Baguiburisac, N. 16 l. (or 7), to
Coat and Sibagoida; 10th, 33 l. s. w. and w. to Sonoita; 11th, 12th, 60 l. E.
and s. E. to Busanic, where they joined Leal; and 13–18th returned via Tubutama, Magdalena de Buvuibava, S. Ignacio, and Remedios to Dolores.

the river east of the bend, following it down to the
Yuma country, thence following the north bank to the
Colorado, and giving the name San Dionisio to a
Yuma ranchería at the junction.   The diaries are not
extant, and such details as we have relate mainly to
Californian geography, having little interest for our
present purpose.[13]

In 1701 Kino and Salvatierra went by way of
Sonoita to the coast, but could not carry out their intention of reaching the Colorado. On the return, however, parting from Salvatierra at Sonoita, Kino and
Mange crossed the country to Bac, and returned home
by the old route.[14]   Later in this year the venerable
explorer crossed from Sonoita to San Pedro on the
Gila, went down to San Dionisio, and thence down
the Colorado past Santa Isabel, the last Yuma ranchería, to the country of the Quiquimas, whence he
crossed into California; and on his return he may be
supposed to have made the map which I append.
Early in 1702, Father Kino made his last trip to the
Gila and Colorado, very nearly repeating the tour of
1701, but reaching the head of the gulf; and it was
also, so far as can be known, the last time he crossed
the Arizona line.   The rest of his life was devoted to
constant efforts, with the aid of padres Campos and
Velarde, to prevent the abandonment of the old establishments, and to obtain missionaries for new ones,
who, though sometimes promised, never came.   The
obstacles in his way seem to have been increased by
the unwise policy of a new commander of the flying
company, whose oppressive acts were a severe test,

---

[13] See *Hist. North Mex. States*, i. 270–1.   The route was Dolores, Remedios, S. Simon y S. Judas, Busanic, 28 l.; Tucubavia, Sta Eulalia, Merced,
12 l.; S. Gerónimo, 29 l.; Gila, 5, 12, 10 l.; down the Gila 50 l.; and return—
Trinidad, Agua Escondida, 12 l.; watering-place, 12 l.; creek, 18 l.; Sonoita,
8 l.; S. Luis Bacupa, 12 l.; S. Eduardo, 20 l.; Caborca, 16 l.; Tubutama 12
l.; S. Ignacio, 17 l.

[14] *Mange, Hist. Pim.*, 385–7.   The route from Sonoita was, Gubo 13 l. E.;
Guactum (Actum?), 18 l. E. past a pool of Vatqui and 5 rancherías; Tupo, 18
l. E.; 12 l. E. to Bac, the 1st pueblo of Sobaipuris; 20 l. s. to Tumagacori; 12
l. past Guevavi to Bacuancos, at both of which rancherías was an adobe house
for the padre, with much live-stock; 14 l. to Cocóspera; thence to Dolores.

KINO'S MAP OF 1701.

not only of the padre's patience, but of the Pimas' good faith and desire for mission life. As I have said, there is no satisfactory evidence that Arizona had either a regular mission or a resident Jesuit before Kino's death in 1711.[15]

After Kino's death, for more than twenty years no Spaniard is known to have entered Arizona. It is not unlikely that a padre may have visited the rancherías of the Santa Cruz valley,[16] or that parties of soldiers from Fronteras may have crossed the line in pursuit of Apache foes, but no such entradas are recorded. Padres Campos and Velarde were left for the most part alone in Pimería Alta, and though zealous workers, they had all they could do, and more, to maintain the prosperity of the old missions, without attempting new enterprises. They could not visit the northern rancherías, and they could not give much encouragement to visitors from distant tribes, who came to inquire why the padres did not come as promised. All communication gradually ceased, the Gila tribes forgot what Kino had taught them, and even the nearer Pimas and Sobaipuris lost much of their zeal for mission life. Only two or three other padres are known to have worked in the field before 1730. Yet there were spasms of interest in the north; the bishop became interested in the subject; some favorable orders were elicited from the king; a presidio was talked of on the Gila; and, as we shall presently see,

[15] A few rumors of padres stationed there can be traced to no definite source; and the whole tenor of such records as exist is against them. On the annals of Pimería down to 1711, see *Hist. North Mex. States*, i., chap. x., xviii.

[16] A writer in the *Tucson Dos Repúblicas*, Aug. 26, 1877, names padres Alejandro Rapmani and José de Torres Perea as having served at Bac in 1720-1. This article bears internal evidence of careful preparation and original authorities in some parts, and therefore merits notice in this part. Possibly the two padres named visited Bac in 1720-1, and left some kind of a record of their presence; but there are indications that this writer drew his information from fragments of mission registers in the south, taking it for granted in some cases that a padre who served in Pimería Alta must have served at S. Javier del Bac. His later list is Ildefonso de la Peña 1744, José Garrucho and Miguel Copetillo 1745, and Bartolomé Saens 1746-50, which names may be compared with those in my text.

there was a project for reaching the Moquis from this
direction.

In 1731, however, there came a small reënforcement
of missionaries, and two of them were in 1732 sent to
the north, effecting what may be regarded as the first
Spanish settlement of Arizona. Father Felipe Se-
gesser took charge of San Javier del Bac, and Juan
Bautista Grashoffer of San Miguel de Guevavi, which
from this time may be regarded as regular missions,
the other rancherías becoming visitas. It is probable
that during the rest of the Jesuit period the two missions were but rarely without padres, though annals
of the establishments are almost a blank. Grashoffer
soon died; Gaspar Steiger was at Bac in 1733–6, and
in 1750 the missionaries were Padre José Garrucho at
Guevavi and Francisco Paver at San Javier. In
1736–7 Padre Ignacio Javier Keller of Suamca made
two trips to the Gila, visiting the Casa Grande, seeing
from a hill the rivers Verde and Salado, which united
to form what he seems to have named the Asuncion,
and finding that many of the rancherías of Kino's time
had been broken up. It was also in 1736–41 that occurred the mining excitement of the famous and wonderful Bolas de Plata at Arizonac. The site was
between Guevavi and Saric, but apparently just south
of the Arizona line. The unparalleled richness of the
silver deposits brought a crowd of treasure-seekers,
and caused the king to claim it as his own, it being
not a mine, but a criadero de plata; but the supply of
nuggets was soon exhausted, and the place was in a
few years wellnigh forgotten. North of the line I
find no records of mining operations in these early
times, though prospecting may have been prosecuted
to some extent, and though popular but wholly unfounded traditions have been current of rich mines
worked by the Jesuits. In 1741 the presidio of Terrenate was founded, but the site was changed more
than once, and for a time before 1750 the garrison was
apparently stationed at or near Guevavi. In 1750

occurred the second revolt of the Pima tribes, in which two missionaries at Caborca and Sonoita were killed, as were about 100 Spaniards in all. Bac and Guevavi were plundered and abandoned, but the two padres escaped to Suamca, which, on account of the nearness of the presidio, was not attacked. Peace was restored in 1752, and the missions were reoccupied; but a bitter controversy between the Jesuits and their foes respecting the causes of the trouble did much to increase the demoralization arising from the revolt itself, and all semblance of real prosperity in the establishments of Pimería Alta was forever at an end.

Meanwhile the Moquis of the north-east maintained their independence of all Spanish or Christian control. The proud chieftains of the cliff towns were willing to make a treaty of peace with the king of Spain, but they would not become his subjects, and they would not give up their aboriginal faith. At intervals of a few years from 1700 there were visits of Franciscan friars, to explore the field for a spiritual reconquest, or of military detachments, with threats of war, but nothing could be effected. At the first town of Aguatuvi, the Spaniards generally received some encouragement; but Oraibe, the most distant and largest of the pueblos, was always closed to them. The refugee Tehuas, Tanos, and Tiguas of the new pueblo were even more hostile than the Moquis proper; and by reason of their intrigues even Zuñi had more than once to be abandoned by the Spaniards. In 1701 Governor Cubero in a raid killed and captured a few of the Moquis. In 1706 Captain Holguin attacked and defeated the Tehua pueblo, but was in turn attacked by the Moquis and driven out of the country. In 1715 several soi-disant ambassadors came to Santa Fé with offers of submission, and negotiations made most favorable progress until Spanish messengers were sent, and then the truth came out—that all had been a hoax, devised by cunning Moqui traders seeking only a safe pretext for commercial visits to New

Mexico. The governor thereupon made a campaign, but in two battles effected nothing. From about 1719 the Franciscans understood that the Jesuits were intriguing for the Moqui field, but beyond visiting Aguatuvi and obtaining some favorable assurances for the future, they did nothing—except, perhaps, with their pens in Europe—in self-defence until 1742, when, the danger becoming somewhat more imminent, two friars went to the far north-west and brought out 441 apostate Tiguas, with whom they shortly reëstablished the old pueblo of Sandía. Again, in 1745, three friars visited and preached to the Moquis, counting 10,846 natives, obtaining satisfactory indications of aversion to the Jesuits, and above all, reporting what had been achieved, with mention of the Sierra Azul and Teguayo, and the riches there to be found. Their efforts were entirely successful; and the king, convinced that he had been deceived—that a people from among whom two lone friars could bring out 441 converts could be neither so far away nor so hostile to the Franciscans as had been represented—revoked all he had conceded to the Jesuits. With the danger of rivalry ended the new-born zeal of the *padres azules*, and for 30 years no more attention was given to the Moquis![17]

The project of extending the Jesuit field from Pimería to the Moqui province was perhaps at first but a device for drawing the attention of the government to the northern missions, and securing a presidio in the Gila valley, with a view to the ultimate occupation of California. Kino and his associates moreover greatly underrated the distance of the Moquis from the Gila, and correspondingly distorted their geographical relations to New Mexico. From about 1711 various reports are said to have been received, through native messengers across the mountains, and also from New Mexican sources, that the Moquis desired Jesuit missionaries, and had a horror of the Franciscans. The project was greatly strengthened

[17] See chap. xi. of this volume, passim, for more particulars.

by the support of the bishop of Durango, whose quarrel with the Franciscans of New Mexico is recorded elsewhere in this volume, and who in 1716, with authority of the viceroy, attempted to put the Jesuits in charge, but failed. The king, however, in a cédula of 1719 approved the bishop's views, and ordered the viceroy to make the change, the viceregal orders to that effect being issued in 1725, and approved conditionally by the king the next year. There seems to be but little truth in the statement of Jesuit writers, that the company declined to interfere in territory claimed by another order; but delays ensued, which were largely due to various schemes for conquering the Moquis by force of arms, and also, perhaps, to a change of opinion on the bishop's part. The viceroy having in 1730 reported such conquest to be impracticable, and additional testimony having been obtained respecting different phases of the subject, the king by a cédula of 1741 positively repeated his orders of 1719. How this incited the New Mexican friars to renewed effort I have already told.

The king's order of 1741 also inspired an attempt on the part of the Jesuits to reach the Moqui towns from Pimería. Padre Keller went up to the Gila in 1743, and attempted to penetrate the country northward; but he was attacked by the Apaches, lost most of his horses and supplies, had one of his nine soldiers killed, and was forced to return. This disaster was known to the Moquis, and through them to the New Mexican friars. In the same year Padre Jacobo Sedelmair of Tubutama reached the Gila by way of Sonoita; and in 1744 the same explorer set out to visit the Moquis. He reached the Gila in the region of the Casa Grande, but the Indians could not be induced to guide him northward by a direct course, and therefore he went down the river on the north bank, for the first time exploring the big bend, and crossed over some forty leagues to the Colorado.[18] At the

[18] Unfortunately, the diaries of this and Keller's expedition are not extant; but in his *Relacion*, 849–50, Sedelmair names the rancherías, beginning 12 l.

point of departure from the Gila was a warm spring, probably that still known as Agua Caliente, and a fine spring, called San Rafael Otaigui, was found where the trail struck the Colorado, perhaps near the modern Ehrenberg. Sedelmair went on up the river to near the junction of "another *rio azul,* near the boundaries of the Moqui province," where the main river seemed to emerge from an opening in the sierra and turn to the south-west. The Moquis were understood to live not more than two or three days' journey away, having frequent commercial intercourse with the Colorado tribes; but for some reason not clearly set forth, perhaps the refusal of the natives to serve as guides, the padre had to return without reaching the object of his tour. His branch river was clearly the Bill Williams fork of modern maps.[19]

In a cédula of 1744, the king called for new information, Sedelmair was summoned to Mexico, and elaborate reports on the northern projects were prepared, both by the Jesuit provincial and the Franciscan procurador general. Without attaching much importance to the Jesuit claim that the company had no intention of interfering with Franciscan missionary work, I still find in the evidence strong indications that the principal aim was to secure the establishment of missions and a presidio in the lower Gila valley, with a view to a further advance to the north-west or north-east, as circumstances might decide. But the argument of Padre Oliva, representing the Franciscans, proved altogether conclusive so far as the Moquis

below the junction of the Salado (where he represents the big bend as beginning ?) as follows: Stue Cabitic, Norchean, Gohate, Noscaric, Guias, Cocoigui, Tuesapit, Comarchdut, Yayahaye, Tuburh, Caborh, Pipiaca, Oxitahibuis, Aicatum, Pitaya, Soenadut, Aopomue, Atiahigui, Cohate, S. Felipe Uparch, Aritutoc, Urchaoztac, Tubutavia, Tahapit, Amoque, Shobotarcham, Aqui, Tuburch, Tucsares, Cuaburidurch, Oitac, Toa, Caborica, Cudurimuitac, Sudac, Sasabac, Sibrepue, Aycate, Aquimundurech, Toaedut, Tuburch, and Dueztumac, near which is a warm spring, about 45 l. above the Colorado junction. These rancherías, all of Cocomaricopas, lie along the river for about 36 l. The author says the Colorado tribes were also kindred to the Gila Cocomaricopas. Rio Colorado, that is, 'red river,' or *buqui aquimuti,* was the original Pima name of the river.

[19] *Sedelmair, Relacion,* 846–54; *Id., Entrada,* 20; *Apost. Afanes,* 351–8; *Venegas, Not. Cal.,* ii. 530–6; *Alegre, Hist. Comp. Jesus,* ii. 283–4.

were concerned; for in a cédula of November 23, 1745, the king confessed that he had been deceived by false testimony respecting the geographical position, the hostile disposition, the strength, and the apostasy of the Moquis, as well as the lack of zeal and facilities for their reduction on the part of the friars; and he accordingly revoked the order of 1741, thus putting an end to the company's project.[20] As I have said before, the Moquis were now left to their own salvation by missionary orders for some thirty years. The Gila and Colorado field still remained open to Jesuit effort, but various obstacles prevented any notable success. An effort seems to have been made to reach Moqui in connection with the military movement of 1747, but nothing was effected. Sedelmair, however, made two more entradas in 1748 and 1750. In the first, from Tubutama, by a route not described, he reached the Gila at a point near the ranchería previously called San Felipe Uparch, and went down the river, noting the 'painted rocks,' to the point where in 1744 he had turned off to the north-west. Here he named the warm spring ranchería, in a fine site for a mission, Santa María del Agua Caliente.[21]

Thence he went on for the first time on the northern bank to the Yuma country, and finally crossed over to the Colorado at a point about two leagues above the junction, subsequently going down to the last Yuma ranchería below the Gila. But the Yumas were not very friendly, and it had been a year of drought for all the friendly Cocomaricopa tribes. The padre's return was by the same route.[22] His second and last tour was made at the end of 1750,

[20] N. Mexico, Cédulas, MS., 46–55; Hist. North Mex. States, i., chap. xviii.–xix. The latter version is here somewhat modified and extended by the former documents.

[21] He says the spring had never been seen before; but it, or another near by, is mentioned in his Relacion of 1745 or 1746. Above the 'piedras escritas' is named a sierra of Sibupue.

[22] Sedelmair, Entrada á la Nacion de los Yumas gentiles, 1749 (8), in Sonora, Mat., 18–25; Apost. Afanes, 360–1. A mission site on the Gila was called S. Júdas Tadeo; that near where he struck the Colorado, S. José; and that at the junction Nra Sra de Loreto.

and about it we known only that he went farther
down the Colorado to the Quiquima or Quimac rancherías, found the natives hostile, and returned across
the desert by way of Sonoita.[23]

During the remaining years of the Jesuit period,
1751–67, the missions of Pimería Alta barely maintained a precarious existence. The Spanish Jesuits
in many cases had been replaced by Germans, and all
were more or less discouraged and disgusted by the
complicated and fruitless controversies of earlier years.
There was no progress, but constant decadence. As
I have said in another volume, "a few neophytes were
induced, by the persuasions of the padres, and by the
hope of occasional protection from the presidios against
the Apaches, to remain faithful; the missions were,
moreover, convenient places for the Pimas, Sobas,
Pápagos, and Sobaipuris in which to leave their
women, children, old, and infirm, while living themselves in the mountains, or, perhaps, aiding the Seris
or Pimas Bajos in their ever-increasing depredations—
convenient resorts for food when other sources failed,
and even well enough to live in occasionally for brief
periods. The natives lived for the most part as they
pleased, not openly rebellious nor disposed to molest
the padres, so long as the latter attempted no control
of their actions, and were willing to take their part in
quarrels with settlers or soldiers. Missionary work
proper was at a standstill; the Jesuit establishments
had only a nominal existence; the mission period of
Sonora history was practically ended. But for the
hostility between Pimas and Apaches the Spanish
occupation of Pimería Alta would probably have been
confined to the four garrisons, with a few bands of
adventurous miners risking an occasional sortie beyond
the protection of the presidios."

These general remarks from the annals of Sonora
may be applied especially to the northern establish-

[23] *Apost. Afanes*, 362–4.

ments of the later Arizona; but particulars relating to the latter, which I would gladly present here in full, are extremely meagre. A presidio of fifty men was established in 1752 at Tubac, or San Ignacio; and under its protection the two missions of Guevavi and Bac with their half-dozen pueblos de visita were enabled to exist, as was Suamca, some of whose visitas were also north of the line. Exactly how long they had been abandoned after the revolt of 1750 is not known; but in 1763 Padre Alonso Espinosa was in charge of Bac, as he was still at the time of the Jesuit expulsion of 1767. At Guevavi the minister was Ignacio Pfefferkorn in 1763, Padre Jimeno in 1764, and Pedro Rafael Diez in 1767. At Suamca Padre José Barrera was in charge in 1760-7, while his predecessors from 1751, according to fragments of the mission register before me—some of them doubtless mere visitors—were Keller, Vega, Nentoig, Diaz, Álava, and Labora. The ranchería of Tucson was a visita of Bac in these years, and a few Spanish settlers seem to have lived there; but in 1763 it was, like the mission, abandoned by all but a few sick and infirm Indians. This state of things, especially on account of the gente de razon at Tucson, called out much correspondence and several plans for relief which brought no relief. There were also nearly 200 gente de razon at Guevavi, Santa Bárbara, and Buenavista. The visitas of Tumacácori and Calabazas were composed of Pima and Pápago neophytes, but the latter had run away in 1763. Respecting the expulsion of the Jesuits in 1767, nothing is known except the names of the three padres, Espinosa, Diez, and Barrera. The whole number of Arizona neophytes in 1764-7 seems to have been only about 1,250.[24]

[24] *Lizazoin, Informe,* 1763, p. 686; *Sonora, Materiales,* 124–38; *Tamaron, Visita,* MS., 112–16; *Sonora, Descrip. Geog.,* 176, p. 566–84; *Pinart, Col. Pimería Alta,* MS., passim; *Compañia de Jesus, Catálogo;* also *Hist. North Mex. States,* chap. xx., this series.

Tuscon, 5 l. N. of Bac, was its only visita, and there is no mention of white population in 1764–7. The visitas of S. Miguel Guevavi were Calabazas, 1½ l. N.; Sonoita, 7 l. E. N. E. (distinct from the western Sonoita); and

VENEGAS' MAP OF 1757.

The Apaches were continuously troublesome, and many campaigns were undertaken against them by forces from the presidios of Fronteras, Terrenate, and Tubac. One of these expeditions seems to have been almost exactly like another, but only a few are recorded at all, and those very meagrely. The only success achieved was the killing of a few warriors, and the capture of their women and children; but often while one band of savages ran away from the soldiers another band attacked some point near the presidios; and it finally came to be seriously questioned by many whether these campaigns were of the slightest advantage. If the diaries were extant, they would furnish some interesting items of early geographic knowledge and nomenclature; but as it is, the mere mention in fragmentary reports is of slight value. Several of these entradas in 1756–8 and 1765–6, directed to the upper Gila in the regions about the later boundary between New Mexico and Arizona, are somewhat fully reported, but so confusedly as to yield nothing more satisfactory than a mere list of names. These campaigns were made by forces under the captains of Fronteras and Janos, Captain Anza of Tubac, and Governor Mendoza. They had some success in killing and capturing Apaches, found several groups of ruins, and satisfied themselves that the Moqui towns might conveniently be reached by that route if deemed desirable.[25]

Tumacácori, 8 l. N. N. W. The visitas of Sta María Suamca, some of them north of the line, were: S. Juan Quiburi, Santiago Optuabo, S. Andrés Esqugbaag or Badz, S. Pablo Baibcat, S. Pedro Turisai, and Sta Cruz Babisi. The presidio of S. Felipe Gracia Real de Terrenate is described as 4 l. N. (E. ?) from Suamca, pop. 411 gente de razon, including the garrison of 50 men under Capt. Francisco Elías Gonzalez. The presidio of S. Ignacio de Tubac was 4 l. N. of Guevavi, pop. de razon 421, including 50 soldiers under Capt. Juan B. Anza, chaplain José Manuel Diaz del Carpio. Arizona is named as a visita of Saric, 5 l. N. E., where were the 'Bolas de Plata de Agua Caliente,' pop. 45 gente de razon.

[25] Hist. North Mex. States, i. chap. xx.; Sanchez, Carta, 1757, in Sonora Mat., i. 88–94; Id., Carta de 1758, in Id., 94–7; Mendoza (Juan), Carta del Gobernador de Son., 1757, in Id., 84–8; Vildosola, Cartás, 186–206; Anza, Carta de 1766, in Son. y Son., Cartas, 108–12. The places named seem to be chiefly in south-western N. Mexico.

CHAPTER XVI.

PIMERÍA ALTA, OR ARIZONA.

1768-1845.

A Meagre Record—Errors of Modern Works—Exaggerations of Early
Prosperity—Coming of the Franciscans—State of the Missions—
Military and Presidio Annals—A New Apache Policy—San Javier
del Bac—Presidio of Tucson—Tubac—Pima Company—Guevavi and
Tumacácori—Calabazas—Aribac—Explorations in the North—
Garcés, the Franciscan Kino—Tours to the Gila and Colorado—
Anza's Trips—Crespo's Views—Escalante—Font's Map—Garcés
Visits the Moquis—Colorado River Missions—The Moquis Perish—
The Peralta Land Grant—Mining Operations—Later Annals—Era
of Prosperity—Final Ruin—Apache Wars—End of the Missions—
American Trappers.

No chronologic narrative of early Arizona annals
can ever be formed with even approximate accuracy
and completeness, for lack of data. As already explained, the country so far as occupied by Spaniards
was but a small part of Pimería Alta, which in turn
was but a part of Sonora, the annals of which province
as a whole are but imperfectly recorded. From Sonora history we may get a general idea of progress in
Pimería, and on Pimería annals we must depend for
a similar general idea of events in Arizona, to which
may be added only a few scattered items of local happenings. It is not strange, then, that nothing like a
consecutive record can be presented; nor can anything
be reasonably expected from future research beyond
the bringing to light of new items. As we advance
from the Jesuit to the Franciscan period, and from
Spanish to Mexican rule, the state of things, from a
historic point of view, becomes worse rather than bet-

(372)

ter. There is much reason, however, to believe that complete original records, could they be restored, would affect only local, personal, and chronologic minutiæ, and would hardly modify the general purport of these chapters.

In this connection, also, it is proper to note that the few and brief presentments of early Arizona annals which are extant, as prefatory matter to modern works devoted chiefly to later history, and to a description of the country and its resources, are not only meagre and fragmentary in detail, as they like my own must necessarily be, but full of errors, and almost wholly misleading in their general scope; though it should be added that the works in question often merit high praise for their accurate treatment of the later topics that come more properly within their field.[1] In these works the tendency is to regard Padre Kino's wanderings as mission-founding expeditions, though, as a matter of fact, there were no missions in Arizona till long after his death. From the Spanish names on early maps—identical with or corresponding to those of Kino and Venegas, as presented in the preceding chapter—the conclusion has been drawn that up to the Gila valley Arizona was covered with prosperous Spanish missions and settlements, which had to be abandoned later in consequence of Apache raids; yet in truth, as the reader knows, there was no Spanish occupation beyond a narrow region of the Santa Cruz valley, and even there only two missions, Bac and

---

[1] Such works are Silvester Mowry's *Arizona and Sonora*, N. Y., 1864, 3d ed., in its original form an address delivered in 1859 before the Amer. Geog. and Stat. Soc.; Hiram C. Hodge's *Arizona as It is*, N. Y., 1877; Richard J. Hinton's *Hand-book to Arizona*, S. F., 1878; the *History of Arizona Territory*, published by Elliott & Co., S. F., 1884; Samuel W. Cozzens' *The Marvellous Country*, Boston, etc. (1874); Edwards Roberts' *With the Invader*, S. F., 1885; and Patrick Hamilton's *The Resources of Arizona*, S. F., 3d ed., 1884. Perhaps some injustice is done by naming these books in a group, since they differ greatly in their value so far as modern Arizona is concerned; but these differences to some extent will appear in later chapters. From all a very good sketch of modern condition and progress may be formed. In their treatment of early times they vary also—from bad to very bad. They contain some accurate statements drawn from well-known authorities on Niza's and Coronado's expeditions; and it should be added that Hinton reproduces for the first time a valuable early map.

Guevavi, with a few rancherías de visita, under resident padres from 1732, or possibly 1720, and protected in their precarious existence by the Tubac presidio from 1752. The misleading Spanish saint names were simply those applied by Kino and his associates to the rancherías visited on their exploring tours, whose inhabitants, in some instances, were induced to make preparations for the reception of missionaries promised, but who never came. The Arizona missions were never more than two, and they were never prosperous. So, also, the rich mines and prosperous haciendas, with which the country is pictured as having been dotted, are purely imaginary, resting only on vague traditions of the Planchas de Plata excitement, and on the well-known mineral wealth of later times. The Jesuits of course—though the contrary is often alleged —worked no mines, nor is there any evidence that in Jesuit times there were any mining operations in Arizona beyond an occasional prospecting raid; and even later, down to the end of the century, such operations were, on a small scale, confined to the vicinity of the presidios; and the same remark may be made of agricultural operations, all establishments being often abandoned, and oftener plundered by the savages. And finally, it has been the fashion to regard Tucson as a more or less prosperous town from a very early time. Some writers even date its foundation in the sixteenth century; though, as a matter of fact, it is not heard of even as an Indian ranchería till the middle of the eighteenth, and was not properly a Spanish settlement till the presidio was moved there in later years.[2]

[2] 'For extreme instances,' says Roberts, *With the Invader*, 116, 'Tucson is an ancient city. Antedating Jamestown and Plymouth, it was visited by Coronado in 1540, lived in by Europeans in 1560, and had its first missionaries in 1581. But long before 1540 there was an Indian village existing on the site of the present city, so that Tucsonians can, if they please, claim an age for their town as great as the Santa Féans claim for theirs. But for all practical purposes 1540 is a sufficiently early date.' And Hodge, *Arizona*, 17–18: 'About the year 1560 a permanent settlement was made by the Spanish explorers and Jesuit (!) fathers near where Tucson now is. It may be mentioned in this connection that Santa Fé was supposed to have been set-

On the expulsion of the Jesuits in 1767, all mission property, being regarded as belonging to the Jesuits and not to the natives, was confiscated by the Spanish government, and its care was intrusted temporarily to royal comisarios. Respecting the definite acts of these officials in Pimería Alta we have no information; but respecting the whole province, the viceroy wrote in 1793: "There is no reason to doubt that they either wasted or embezzled the rich temporalities of all or most of the missions, and that these funds being lost, decadence or ruin could not be prevented."[3] The southern Sonora establishments were secularized, but those of the Pimerías were put in charge of fourteen Franciscans of the college of Santa Cruz de Querétaro, who arrived and were distributed to their destinations in June 1768. Our chief authority for the ensuing period of mission history, though meagre in respect of most details, is the standard chronicle of the Santa Cruz college and the operations of its friars.[4] On the condition of affairs during the few following years, I quote from another volume of this series.

"The missions were found by the Franciscans in a sad state. Some of the establishments had been plundered by the Apaches, and were again plundered, as at Suamca and Bac, during the first year of Franciscan occupation. In some cases the comisarios had grossly neglected their duties. Everywhere the neophytes had been for a year free from all control, and had not been improved by their freedom. Not only had they relapsed to a great extent into their roving and improvident habits, but they had imbibed new ideas of independence, fostered largely by settlers and soldiers. They regarded themselves as entirely free

tled in 1555' (really about 1615), 'Tucson in 1560, and San Augustine, Fla, in 1565, thus making Sta Fé the first, Tucson the second, and San Augustine the third settled town within the present domain of the U. S.'

[3] *Revilla Gigedo, Carta de 1793*, p. 435.

[4] *Arricivita, Crónica Seráfica y Apostólica del Colegio de Propaganda Fide de la Santa Cruz de Querétaro.* Mexico, 1692, pp. 394 et seq. See also *Hist. North Mex. States*, i., chap. xxiv., this series.

from all control by the missionaries, whose whole duty
in these later times was to attend to religious matters.
The padres might not, so these independent aborigines
thought, give orders, but must prefer requests to
native officials; if they required work done for them
they must pay for it.   The friars at first had nothing
to do with the temporalities, but Galvez in 1770 "—it
was really in June 1769—" ordered the property
returned to their control, and the slight remnants
were thus restored.   They received a stipend of $300
each from the royal treasury, and spent it on their
churches and neophytes.   They worked faithfully,
though often discouraged, and presently the state of
affairs became, in all essential respects, similar to that
in Chihuahua, the padres keeping together the skele-
ton communities, instructing the children, caring for
the sick, and by gifts and persuasion exercising slight
and varying control over the masses of the Indians,
who were Christians only in name." [5]   All this applies
to Arizona as well as other parts of Pimería, and is all
that can be said on the subject.   Notwithstanding
these obstacles, and the martyrdom of some of their
number, the Queretaranos made some progress, especially in the building of churches; and they even
made some extensive explorations in the north with a

[5] And to continue: 'Officers intrusted with the expulsion of the Jesuits,
in order to reconcile the Indians to the change and prevent disturbances, had
taken pains to make them regard the measure as a release from bondage.
This had much to do with the independent spirit that proved so troublesome
to the new missionaries.   Yet it is to be noted that the Franciscans joined
more readily than was warranted by justice or good taste in the prevalent
habit of decrying the Jesuits and their system, as is shown in the correspondence cited, where it is often implied that the difficulties encountered were
largely due to the oppression and neglect of missionaries in former years.
Naturally, the friars were disposed to magnify their troubles and throw the
blame on others; but the only charge that was to some extent well founded
was that the natives had not been taught to speak Spanish; the systems followed by the two orders did not differ in any important respect, and the
Jesuits were by no means responsible for the evils that now beset the missions.'   'By no means all existing troubles,' however, 'arose from the natives'
new-born independence of missionary control.   Each establishment had a
large number of native officials who quarrelled among themselves; and the
few settlers of Spanish or mixed blood had their separate *jueces reales*, who
were not slow to interfere in matters that did not concern them.   There was
likewise confusion in ecclesiastical affairs, for the friars were forbidden to
exercise control over any but Indians.'

view to extend the mission field, as we shall presently
see. In 1769 the eight missions and sixteen visitas[6]
of Pimería Alta had 2,018 neophytes and 178 gente
de razon; in 1772 the two missions and three visitas
of Arizona had 607 neophytes; but all other statistics
of the later part of the century pertain to all the
Sonora establishments as a whole, and throw no light
on the north. It is probable, however, that there was
a marked gain before 1800; and Pimería Alta is also
said to have been somewhat less unprosperous than
more southern districts. It should be noted moreover
that from 1783 the Sonora missions were organized as
a *custodia* of San Cárlos, and thus removed from control of the college. The change seems to have had no
important bearing on our present subject; at any rate,
the friars were not pleased with it, and in 1791 the
old order of things was restored. Besides the work
of Arricivita, and the viceroy's report of 1793 already
cited, a leading authority for developments of the period,
is a report of the Padre Antonio de los Reyes in 1772.[7]

Military annals, so far as our special territory is concerned, are no more fully recorded than those of the
missions; yet in this case, as in the other, the general
situation of affairs is clear. The coast and island
tribes of Sonora had become even more troublesome
than the Apaches, and in 1767–71, while these tribes
were being reduced to submission, campaigns on the
northen frontier were for the most part suspended,
and attention was confined mainly, without notable
success, to the protection of the presidios and missions.
Then aggressive campaigns were resumed, though we
have no particulars. By the reglamento of 1772–3,
the service against Apaches was rendered more effective by certain reforms in military discipline and
Indian policy; and at the same time changes in

[6] Arricivita, 402, has it 8 visitas, but the larger number would seem more
likely to be correct.
[7] *Reyes, Noticias del estado actual de las misiones*, in *Doc. Hist. Mex.*, 3d
ser., pt iv., p. 724–65. Other references in *Hist. North Mex. States.* The
viceroy's report was founded largely on one by Bishop Reyes in 1784, not
extant.

the sites of the four frontier presidios at Altar, Tubac, Terrenate, and Fronteras were ordered.[8] These changes, except at Altar, were made, including a transfer of Tubac to Tucson, but the exact dates and other details are not known.[9] In 1774, or a little later, Hugo Oconor came as inspector to see that the reglamento had been properly enforced; General Croix from 1779 is credited with having effected useful reforms in the military service; before 1780 the garrison at each presidio was increased from fifty to seventy-five men; and in 1784 a company of Ópata allies was organized, which rendered efficient aid to the Spanish soldiers.[10] In the records which show these facts there is much information respecting the Apaches and their methods of warfare; and all records of the time contain a general complaint of never-ending depredations; but of campaigns, disasters, and other events from year to year, practically nothing is known. In 1786 General Ugarte, by the viceroy's order, introduced all along the frontier line of the Provincias Internas some radical changes in Indian policy. The Apaches were to be forced by unceasing campaigns, with the aid of friendly Pimas and Ópatas, to make treaties of peace, never before permitted with that nation; and so long as they observed such treaties, though closely watched, they were to be kindly treated, furnished with supplies, encouraged to form settlements near the presidios, taught to drink intoxicating liquors, and to depend as much as possible on Spanish friendship for the gratification of their needs. Hitherto war had been the business, as easier than

---

[8] *Presidios, Reglamento é Instrucciones.*

[9] A report of Gen. Elias in 1814 contains most that we know of these changes. *Pinart, Doc. Hist. Chih.*, MS., 17-19. The idea was to locate the presidios in a line, at intervals of about 40 leagues. Terrenate was to be moved to one of the valleys of S. Pedro, Nutrias, Guachuca, or Terrenate, and nearer Fronteras. It was moved to Sta Cruz, 40 l. from Tucson, then to Nutrias, and finally to the abandoned mission of Sta María (Suamca). Fronteras was moved, as ordered, to the valley of San Bernardino, nearer Janos, but was later restored to the former site, 35 l. from Terrenate.

[10] *Sonora, Resúmen,* 224; *Arch. Cal., Prov. St. Pap.*, MS., iv. 1-9, 12-14; *Pueblo de Sonora,* Feb. 4, 1868; *Pinart, Doc. Hist. Son.*, MS., i. 1-5; *Velasco, Not. Son.*, 152; *Zúñiga, Rápida Ojeada,* 4.

hunting, by which they had lived; now they were to be made to dread war, as sure to cut off their supplies. The plan seems to have been remarkably successful; at least for twenty years or more there are but slight indications of Apache depredations. They were still regarded as hostile and treacherous at heart, but they were gradually forced to form treaties, which in many instances it was made their interest to keep for years, many of them settling near the Spanish establishments, and being supported by the government at a cost of $18,000 to $30,000 a year. Detached bands sometimes made trouble, as did gentile and renegade Pimas and Pápagos, requiring constant vigilance and bloody chastisement; but in comparison with its condition in earlier and later times, the country in the last decade of the century and first of the next was at peace. Then it was that the Arizona establishments had their nearest approximation to prosperity, that new churches were built, that mines were worked to some extent, and haciendas. Unfortunately, we may not know the particulars.[11]

San Javier del Bac, known as a ranchería since the seventeenth century, and as a mission since 1732 or 1720, was, in June 1768, committed to the care of Padre Francisco Garcés, who was its minister for eight or ten years, but whose successors are not named in any record that I have seen.[12] The neophytes were scat-

[11] *Galvez, Instrucciones á Ugarte,* 1786; *Escudero, Not. Son.,* 69–70; *Soc. Mex. Geog., Bol.,* v. 312–13; xi. 89; *Revilla Gigedo, Carta,* 436; *Velasco, Not. Son.,* 240–1; *Monteros, Exposicion de Son.,* 21, 26; *Arricivita, Cron. Seráf.,* 457, 485–8, 524–9; *Ilustracion Mex.,* iv. 418; *Gaceta de Mex.,* i. 85.

[12] P. José del Rio is named by Arricivita, 417–18, as a *compañero* of Garcés, sent to Mex. on a mission in 1770–1, and he may have served at Bac, though his mission in 1768–9 was Tubutama. Fr. Pedro Arriqutbar was probably the minister in 1819, as he appears on the Tubac register as chaplain of Tucson. A writer in the *Tucson, Dos Repúblicas,* of Sept. 16, 1877, who has apparently examined some of the mission registers, names the following padres as having served in Arizona between 1768 and 1828: Francisco Garcés, Juan Diaz, José Matías Moreno, Juan Antonio Barreneche, *Bartolomé Jimenez, *Gaspar de Clemente, *Juan Carzoll, *Clemente Moreno, *Clemente Rijarch, Pedro Arriquibar, *Juan B. Nelderrain, Joaquin Antonio Velarde, Baltasar Carrillo, Narciso Gutierrez, Mariano Bordoy, Ramon Lopez, Ramon Liberós, Juan Maldonado, and Rafael Diaz, who was in charge of S. Agustin del Pueblito de Tucson in 1826. It is to be noted that this list does not include P. Gil de Bernave, the original minister of Guevavi. The 2d, 3d, and 4th on the list

tered and had forgotten their doctrina, so it is said, but they consented to return if not compelled to work. Before the end of the year the mission was destroyed by Apaches, who killed the native governor and captured two soldiers, the padre and most of the neophytes being absent at the time. In several subsequent raids the mission live-stock disappeared, but after 1772 lost ground was more than regained, though Padre Garcés, as we shall see, was for a large part of the time engaged in northern explorations.[13] The official report of 1772 shows a population of 270 on the registers, and describes the church as moderately capacious, but poorly supplied with furniture and vestments. All the churches of Pimería Alta at this period are described as of adobes, covered with wood, grass, and earth.[14] Arricivita, writing in 1791, mentions on one page that the Franciscans have built here adobe houses for the natives and walls for defence against the Apaches; but though specifying somewhat minutely the various churches that had been built or repaired, he says nothing of such work at Bac. In a similar statement on another page, however, he includes Bac, as well as Tucson, among the places where churches of brick had been built.[15] Yet I think the chronicler would not have dismissed with so slight a notice the magnificent structure still standing at San Javier, which has elicited many a description from modern visitors. The church is said to bear the date of 1797, which is presumably that of its completion.[16] The

were the padres killed at the Colorado missions in Cal., never serving in the Arizona establishments, where it is probable that their names and others of the list appear only as visitors. The 6 marked with a * I have not found elsewhere; but the rest appear on books of the Pimería Alta missions, south of Arizona. Only Garcés, Arriquibar, Gutierrez, Liberós, and Fr. Juan B. Estelric—the latter not named in the *Dos Repúblicas*—have I found in Arizona proper; but I have not seen the original registers, except a fragment at Tubac.

[13] *Arricivita*, passim.

[14] *Reyes, Noticia*, 754–6. Anza, *Descub.*, MS., found 74 Pima families at Bac. in 1774.

[15] *Arricivita*, 448, 488–9. 'Todas de ladrillo y bóvedas.'

[16] *Las Dos Repúblicas*, Sept. 15, 1877, as already cited. The author mentions traditions that it was built on the site of the old Jesuit church, that its construction occupied 14 years, and that two brothers Gaona were the

building, or rebuilding, was probably begun soon after
the date of the reports on which Arricivita based his
work, and completed in the final decade of the century,
during the epoch of comparative peace and prosperity
to which I have alluded.   Neither church nor mission
has any later recorded history.   The establishment
seems to have had no minister, and to have been
practically abandoned from about 1828, though the
Pápago ex-neophytes are said to have cared for the
building to some extent in later years.[17]

Tucson, as we have seen, is first mentioned in 1763
as a ranchería visita of Bac, which had been for the
most part abandoned.   In the last years of Jesuit control, however, it had 331 Indians, more or less, under
control of the missionaries.   Reyes, in his report of
1772, describes San José de Tucson as a visita of Bac,
without church or padre's house, on a fertile site where
a large number of gentile and Christian Indians—not
registered, but estimated at over 200 families—had
congregated.   Many of these seem to have been subsequently scattered; at least Anza found only eighty
families of Pimas in 1774.   Says Arricivita, the
Apaches "have always sought to destroy a small ranchería at Tugson, it being the point of entry for their
irruptions; but by the efforts of Padre Garcés, there
was built a pueblo, with a church, house for the padre,
and a wall for defence; and it is to-day a presidio of
Spaniards."   As we have seen, the presidio was transferred from Tubac, in accordance with the reglamento
and instructions of 1772.   The change was made in or

builders.   He thinks it was built during the ministry of PP. Carrillo and
Gutierrez.   It would serve no good purpose to refer to the many descriptions
extant, each with a few words of most inaccurate history.   Many writers regard the church as having been built by the Jesuits; and one tells us it was
built by the Spanish govt, under Jesuit direction, at a cost of $33,300!   An
original report of 1842 shows the friendly Pápagos to have been living at Bac
in considerable numbers.

[17] Brackett, in *Western Monthly*, 1869, p. 170, says the property was secularized in 1824; but there are no definite records on the subject.   In *Riesgo*
and *Valdes, Memoria Estad.* (*Pinart, Doc. Hist.*, MS., i. 107), Bac is named
as a pueblo belonging to the presidio of Tucson.   In 1834, Bac is also named
as a pueblo, in a decree forming a partido to which it belonged. *Pinart, Col.*.
Doc., print, no. 302.

before 1777, and probably by order of Inspector Hugo
Oconor, given during his visit of about 1775, so that
the date of the founding of Tucson as a Spanish settlement may be set down as probably 1776.[18]　The Indians were quartered in a little pueblo adjoining the
presidio, called from this time San Agustin del pueblito de Tucson, the presidio also being sometimes
called San Agustin.[19]　Annals of this place are a
blank for many years, and practically so down to
1846, since we know only by occasional mention that
the presidio maintained its existence; that the garrison numbered, in officers and men, about 106 men,
though the ranks were often not full; and that there
was frequent complaint of inadequate arms, ammunition, and other supplies.　We have no statistics, but
the population of Tucson and the adjoining districts,
in the last years of the period covered by this chapter,
may have been about 2,000, including the families of
the soldiers.[20]

Tubac is a name that first appears in 1752, when a
presidio was established there.　In 1764–7, and for
some years later, it was under the command of Captain
Juan B. Anza, and had a population of nearly 500.
Under orders following the reglamento of 1772, the

[18] *Arricivita*, 448, 449.　On the latter page he says the Tucson church,
like that of Bac, was of brick and ‘de bóvedas.’　This writer proves that the
presidio change was before 1791; but that it was before 1777 is shown by
a petition, dated S. Agustin de Tuson, Nov. 24, 1777, written in the interest
of Tubac, and asking for a restoration of the fort to the south.　Translation
in the *Yuma Sentinel*, April 13, 1878.　The change had not yet been made
in Oct. 1775, when Tuison, or Tuguison, is named as a pueblo by Anza.
Diario, MS., 9, and Font, *Journal*, 6.

[19] Some modern writers say that S. Agustin was founded in 1769; but the
ranchería, before 1772, was called S. José.

[20] F. Pedro Arriquibar, chaplain in 1819.　*Tubac, Lib. Mis.*, MS.　Cost of
the garrison of 4 officers and 101 men in 1824, $29,744. *Pinart, Doc. Hist.
Son.*, MS., i. 36.　Six officers and 94 men in 1828 cost $27,854.　Alcaldes
de policía.　Fine climate, but cold winters. *Riesgo* and *Valdés, Mem. Estad.*
In 1838 the comandante was José M. Martinez.　He had so few men and
horses that he had to hire Apaches to go and look after a party of Americans
25 l. away. *Restaurador Federal* (Arizpe), Jan. 16, 1838.　In 1842–3 Antonio
Comaduran was comandante.　The comp. had 89 men, or 11 less than required by the reglamento of 1826.　He writes complaining letters. *Pinart,
Col. Doc.*, MS., no. 40–1.　Velasco, *Not. Son.*, 113–14, tells us that Tucson
had but 60 cavalry, and the district had become so dangerous that the population was reduced to less than 1,000 men.

presidio was transferred, in 1776-7, to a site farther north, at Tucson. This left the few settlers of the region more exposed to the depredations of the Apaches, and they wished to quit the country, but were prevented from doing so by orders from the government to be enforced by severe penalties. They sent in, however, many petitions for a restoration of the presidio, or for an increase of troops;[21] and at a date not exactly recorded, but before 1784, a company of Pima allies was organized and stationed here. Subsequently Spanish soldiers seem to have been added to the garrison; and the law of 1826 provided for a presidial company at Tubac as well as Tucson, though in later years the company seems to have been one of infantry. The post has no other annals than an occasional mention of its existence and force. In 1828 a silver mine is spoken of as having been worked for several years. In 1834 all the Arizona establishments were organized as a partido with Tubac, or San Ignacio, as Cabecera. In 1842-3 a ranchería of friendly Apaches lived here. Spiritual interests were attended to by the padre of the adjoining mission.[22]

[21] The document of 1777 already cited. *Yuma Sentinel* contains the following: ' Daily experiencing more violence from the enemy because he is aware of the few troops that we possess, we have desired to break up our homes and sell our effects. . . . And now, finally, the last month the Apaches finished with the entire herd of horses and cattle which we guarded; and at the same time with boldness destroyed the fields and carried away as much corn as they were able. Since the fort was removed to Tucson these towns and missions have experienced some casualties; so much so that they have been obliged to burn the town of Calabazas—a calamity it never before experienced. Also, but few days ago the cavalcade, which the Apaches brought from the west, was grazing for three days in the vicinity, falling every day upon the fields to load with corn, and to run away with those whom they found there; and lastly, they not leaving the neighborhood, we momentarily expect that they may serve us and our families as they have served our property.' The document gives some description of the Tubac region, where over 600 fanegas of wheat and maize were produced each year, not one third of the land being occupied.

[22] For 1814-24 I have some fragments of the *Tubac Lib. Mis.*, MS. The place is denominated both presidio and 'pueblo y mision.' Capt. Nicolás Herrera is named in 1819; Alf. Juan B. Romero in 1821; and Lieut. Ignacio Elias Gonzalez as comandante in 1821. This same year the books were inspected by the bishop. The law of March 21, 1826, providing for two presidios, is mentioned in *Riesgo* and *Valdés, Mem. Estud.*, 26. In 1828 the Pima comp., called ' de Buenavista,' had 3 officers and 81 men, cost $13,373; silver mine worked. *Pinart, Doc. Hist. Son.*, MS., i. 37, 60-4, 109. July 1, 1834, order of Son. congress, organizing the partido of S. Ignacio. *Id., Col. Doc.*, print, no. 302. Nov. 1, 1842, the company, apparently regulars and not

Guevavi, in Jesuit times called San Miguel and also for a time San Rafael, but by the Franciscans termed Santos Angeles, was a mission which, like Bac, dated back to 1732, or perhaps 1720, and in 1764–7 had 111 neophytes, or with its three visitas, 517. Padre Juan Crisóstomo Gil de Bernave was its minister for several years from 1768. He became president of the missions, and in 1773 was killed by the Indians of his new mission of Carrizal, Sonora.

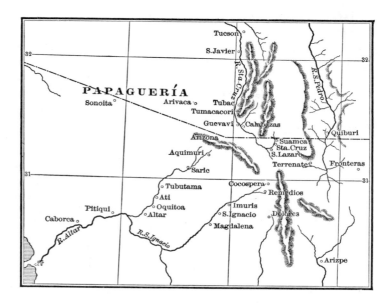

MISSIONS OF ARIZONA, 1768–1846.

Pimas, had 33 men, rank and file, under Lieut. Roque Ibarra of Pitic since 1840, when Lieut. Salvador Moraga had been retired. There was a capitan de indios, José Rosario. About half the garrison were absent at Cucurpe and Rayon. One soldier was a prisoner of the Apaches. A ranchería of Apaches, 169 souls under Francisco Coyotero, as chief, lived near the presidio. *Id.*, MS., no. 2. In 1843 the force remained as before. *Id.*, passim. In Dec. 1844, José Rosario, the captain of Indians, joined the pronunciamiento of the garrison at Ures in favor of Paredes. *Id., Doc. Hist. Son.*, MS., iii. 223–4.

In 1772 Guevavi had 86 Indians, and with its visitas, 337. The church was a poor affair, and the establishment was often raided by Apaches. Before 1784 it was abandoned, and Tumacácori became head of the mission. The visita of San Ignacio Sonoita, or Sonoitac, seems also to have been deserted before 1784.[23] The name of the latter is still retained, but that of Guevavi seems to have disappeared from modern maps.

Tumacácori, or San José, a visita of Guevavi from Jesuit times, with 199 Indians in 1764–7, and 39 in 1772, was almost in ruins in the latter year, having been attacked in 1769 by the Apaches at midday. But before 1791 a new roof had been put on the church, and from 1784, or earlier, San José had become a mission instead of a visita. Adobe houses for the neophytes and a wall for their protection were also built. After Padre Gil de Bernave, I have no records of missionaries in charge of this mission and the adjoining presidio in early times; but Fray Narciso Gutierrez was the minister in 1814–20, Juan B. Estelric in 1821–2, and Ramon Liberós in 1822–4.[24] The ruins of Tumacácori are still to be seen near Tubac, on the west bank of the river. San Cayetano de Calabazas, the only pueblo de visita that seems to have survived 1784, had 64 neophytes in 1772, but no church or house for the padre, though these were supplied before 1791. In 1828 Calabazas is mentioned as a rancho near which some poor people worked a gold mine.[25] Aribac, or Arivaca, in the west, appears on a doubtful map of 1733 as a pueblo. Anza, in 1774, says it had been deserted since the

[23] *Arricivita*, 518–22; *Reyes, Noticias*, 757; *Revilla Gigedo, Carta*.

[24] *Tubac, Lib. Mis.*, MS. In 1822 a new church was in process of construction or extension, but work was for a time suspended on account of trouble about the pay for 4,000 cattle that P. Estelric had sold to obtain funds. *Pinart, Doc. Hist. Son.*, MS., i. 30–1. In 1844, by a padre who admits he knows very little about it, Tumacácori is described as having an elegant church and being a visita of Bac! *Id.*, iii. 182. In the *Arizona Hist.* (Elliott & Co.), 52, the first church is described as having been built by the Jesuits in 1752, and destroyed by Apaches in 1820. The ruins are described here and in the *S. F. Bulletin*, March 19, 1879.

[25] *Riesgo* and *Valdés, Mem. Estad.*, MS., 60–4.

HIST. ARIZ. AND N. MEX. 25

Pima revolt of 1751, though mines were worked until
1767.   In 1777 it is noted as a place rich in mines,
and one Ortiz is said to have applied about this time
for a grant of the rancho.   Zúñiga, in 1835, mentions
it as a 'rancho despoblado.'[26]   It may also be noted
here that in the early part of the present century, if
not before, the old Terrenate presidio was located at
or near the abandoned mission of Suamca, just south
of the Arizona line, and was known as Santa Cruz.

The coming of a new order of missionaries to take
the place of the Jesuits, the natural desire of the friars
to do something more than simply fill the places of
their predecessors, their success on the coast in effecting the spiritual conquest of Alta California, and
above all the indefatigable zeal of Father Francisco
Garcés, the Kino of the Franciscans, caused renewed
interest to be felt in the northern interior, in the conversion of the Gila tribes, and of the apostate Moquis.
The result was a series of somewhat extensive explorations which must be recorded here, but with comparative brevity, because they were for the most part but
reëxplorations, and because, in certain phases, they are
presented elsewhere in this series of works.

As early as August 1768, Padre Garcés, moved by
favorable reports from visiting natives at Bac, set out
with one Indian of his mission and four Pápagos from
abroad and crossed the country west and north-west to
the Gila, visiting many rancherías, and explaining the
mysteries of the faith and the grand achievements of
the Spanish king.   The natives behaved much as in
Kino's time, eager to be converted, to have padres,
and to have their children baptized.   The friar could
do nothing but .promise great things for the future,
and on his return a severe illness interfered, for a time,
with his plans.   In 1770, however, a year in which
the measles raged among the northern tribes, he was

---

[26] Map in *Sonora Materiales*, MS.; *Anza, Descub. de 1774*, MS.; *Yuma Sentinel*, April 13, 1878, Oct. 18, 1879; *Zúñiga, Rápida Ojeada*, 33.

sent for by some of the sufferers, set out "equipped only with charity and apostolic zeal," and again reached the Gila, where he was as warmly welcomed as before, and from this time the project of founding missions in this region took firm possession of his mind.[27]

The project was approved in Mexico, both by Franciscan and secular authorities; five additional friars were sent to Sonora to be in readiness; and the early founding of the missions was regarded as a certainty, though a change of viceroys and of presidents caused some annoying delays. Meanwhile, Garcés deemed it necessary to make additional explorations for mission sites as well as to explain to the natives the slight delay, thus preventing dissatisfaction; and accordingly he started August 8, 1771, on a new tour, accompanied only by a single Pápago, with a horse to carry the apparatus for saying mass. He reached the Gila on the 22d by way of Papaguería, and for about two months he wandered in various directions over the region of the lower Colorado, possibly crossing that river to the California side. Though Arricivita gives a somewhat minute narrative with extracts from the explorer's diary, it is not possible for me to trace his route, though I attempt a résumé in the appended note.[28]

[27] *Arricivita, Crón. Seráf.*, 403–4, 416–17. There is nothing to indicate his exact route or even the region where he struck the Gila. A diary of the 2d trip was written but is not published. In the 1st he say he went west, north, and south-west through the country of the Pápagos. Of the 2d, more details are given. He left Bac Oct. 18th, through a new valley past the rancherías of Cuitoat, Oapars, and Tubasa; 19th, west, seeing ranchería of Aquitun; 20th, reached the ranch. of Pitac on the Gila; 21st, to the place where he had been in 1768, where he had to baptize 22 persons, the Indians almost detaining him by force. But he went down the river, saw many ranch., especially one very large one called Napeut on the other bank; thence past Sutaquison he went to a Salina and N. W. to the country of the Opas on the 23d. The Opas could speak Pima, had never seen padres, and desired to know if he was man or woman 'y otras impertinencias iguales á su rudeza.' At one ranch. they had seen white traders from Moqui. Here he turned south; on the 28th saw six Ind. from the Colorado; turned east and in three days across the desert reached the Pápago rancherías.

[28] *Arricivita*, 418–26. Aug. 8, 1771, west past several rancherías, including Atí, to Cubac on the 15th, and perhaps Sonoi (Sonoita?) on the 16th. Thence his course was by the sierra, or volcano, of Sta Clara and broad sand plains to the Gila at an unoccupied well-wooded spot, where he arrived on the 22d. Soon was seen a branch river conjectured to be the Rio Azul.

In this tour the padre was always well treated, though he had much difficulty in obtaining guides, each tribe being anxious that he should not risk his life in the territory of their foes. But the prospects for an early founding of the missions, deemed so encouraging just before, had now mysteriously disappeared, and no further movement was made for three years. In 1774, however, Captain Juan B. Anza

Indians came from across the Gila, some of them called Noraguas. 23d, among many others came the gov. of the Pimas from below and volunteered as a guide; but all refused to guide him to the Colorado and made every possible effort to prevent his going in that direction. At last he started apparently from Pima rancherías, went 2 days s. w., but had to return. On Sept. 8th he started again, was soon deserted by his guides, but kept on alone. At one ranchería he found houses burned and many wounded in a recent attack of the Quiquimas. His course was down the Gila to near the Colorado junction, thence turning south on Sept. 14th. This day and the next he wandered s., e., n., and w. among marshes, pools, lagunas, and tulares to the bank of a river which seemed larger than the Gila, but smaller than the Colorado. (Of course it was one of the two.) 16th, started s. to reach the mouth and see the Quiquimas, but turned back with some Ind. he met to Yuma rancherías, where he was well treated, but the best he could do was to persuade an old Ind. to go with him to the 'junction of the rivers;' but this old man soon left him, and the padre going on alone became involved in such a network of mud-holes that he returned to the Yuma town. 'Seeing himself on the other bank of the river (?), it seemed hard to return without seeing all he could;' so he went with some Ind. from the w. on the 20th, and on the 21st, still w., past well-peopled ranchos to a laguna many leagues long, which he crossed on a balsa, and came soon to another very large body of water which seemed to be the Colorado, whence he turned back to the rancherías. 22d, followed the 'current of that large laguna' past rancherías where there was some knowledge of Christianity, to some poor ranchos. He declined to cross (recross ?) the laguna as the Ind. wished; and the Ind. refused to accompany him west, but he went on alone on the 23d to the n. w., and 24th, n. e. and e. 25th, to west past a large pueblo and to the sierra, without finding the Colorado, and back to the pueblo, when he heard much of the padres in S. Diego and N. Mexico. 28th, n. w. all day and night to where he could see the Sierra Madre, and what seemed the pass or opening where the Colorado entered the sea. From this point he seems to have desired to take an eastern course (homeward ?); but the Pimas sent messengers, urging his return to their rancherías, else he would be lost and they would be blamed by the Spaniards. So on Oct. 3d he set out with the Ind. south (?), and presently north, and then eastwardly in quest of the Gila; thence up the river to the place where the Yumas had fought with Cocomaricopas, Opas, and Gileños, arriving on the 10th. On the 11th and 12th mourning ceremonies of the Yumas. 12th, the Yumas offered to guide the padre to the Ind. of Cujant or to Zúñiga in four days. He chose the former in order to go direct to Sonoitac; and so turned back and recrossed (?) the Gila on the 13th; and on the 15th started by the 'customary route' for Caborca, where he arrived on the 27th.

I am aware that this résumé is very unsatisfactory, but space does not permit the reproduction of the full narrative, which is even more confusing. On p. 450, 454, 459, Arricivita states that on this trip Garcés had crossed the Colorado and visited the rancherías farther west; from the narrative I am unable to determine whether such was the fact or not.

obtained permission to explore a route by land to
California, being influenced largely, as the Franciscan
chronicler states, by the arguments and diaries of
Garcés, who, still bent on carrying into execution his
mission project, was glad to serve as guide or chaplain
for the new expedition, being also accompanied by
Padre Juan Diaz. Anza's party of thirty-four men
left Tubac on January 8th, and marched by way of
Caborca and Sonoita to the junction of the Gila and
Colorado, fording the latter river the 9th of February.
Returning from California, this party went up the
Gila, and by way of Tucson and Bac to Tubac in
May.[29] The Yumas at the junction, under the chief
Captain Palma, whose residence was on the island of
Trinidad, formed by the two rivers, gave the Span-
iards a most friendly reception; and thus, not only was
the practicability of this route to California demon-
strated, but new interest was awakened in the pro-
posed missions. Garcés had instructions to investigate
the possibility of communicating with New Mexico,

[29] *Anza, Descubrimiento de Sonora á Californias en el año de 1774*, MS., in
the collection of M. Pinart; *Arricivita, Crón. Seráf.*, 450-6; see also *Hist.
Cal.*, i. 221-4, this series.
The route was as follows: Jan. 8, 1774, from Tubac 1 l, to ford of S. Ignacio; 9th, s. w. to Arivac valley; 10th, s. s. w. to Agua Escondida, 7 l.;
11th, 12th, ditto (?); 13th, to Saric, 7 l. 'From this mission it is 8 l. N. to
Arizona. The mother vein has not been found.' 14th, to La Estancia, 4 l.;
15th, s. w. to Atí, 5½ l.; 16th, w. to Oquitoa, 6 l.; 17th, to Altar presidio, 2
l.; 19th, w. N. w. to Pitic, 5 l.; 20th, to Caborca, 2 l.; 22d, N. w. to S.
Ildefonso, a new name, 4 l.; 23d, to Aribaipia or S. Eduardo, 9 l. in the
Papaguería, which extends 60 or 70 l. N. and s. by 30 or 40 l. E. and w., and
has 2,500 souls; 24th, to pool of S. Juan de Mata, 4 l.; 25th, 6 l.; 26th, w. N.
w. to ranchería of Quitobac or S. Luis Bacapa, 6 l.; 27th, N. to foot of a hill,
5½ l.; 28th, N. N. E. to Sonoita, 5 l.; 29th, w. to Carrizal, 9 l.; 30th, N. N. w.,
6 l.; 31st, w. N. w., 9 l.; Feb. 1st, N. w. to Purificacion, 3 l.; 4th, to springs,
5 l.; 5th, to Agua Escondida, 7 l.; 6th, s. w., 6¼ l.; 7th, to Trinidad isl. and
Palma's ranchería, 10½ l., called by the Jesuits S. Dionísio; 8th, forded the
Gila; 9th, forded the Colorado.
Return, May 10th, to the junction at S. Dionísio, lat. 32° 44'; 15th, up
the s. bank of the Gila, 3 l.; 16th, ditto, 9 l.; 17th, ditto, past the watering-
place of S. Pascual, 8 l.; 18th, to 1st, Cocomaricopa ranchería or S. Bernardino, 4 l.; 19th, up N. bank of Gila, 8 l.; 30th, up s. bank, 5 l. to within one
l. of Simon y Judas de Upasoitac; 21st, through Upasoitac, leaving river,
where it turns N., 8 l.; 22d, to the Pima ranchería of Sutaquison, where are
some old ruins at casas grandes, 6 l.; 23d, to Tutiritucar, or S. Juan Capistrano, a ranchería of 300 souls, 2 l.; 24th, along the Gila, 2 l. to within 2 l.
of the Casa Grande, thence s.; 25th, s. to Tucson, 24 l. from the Gila; 26th,
5 l. to Bac and 15 l. to Tubac, 103 l. from S. Dionísio.

and with this in view he remained behind at San Simon y Judás on the Gila, attempting to penetrate the northern region, and send a letter to the New Mexican friars; but he was unable to reach the Moqui towns as he wished, and returned by a different route from that followed by Anza and the rest, arriving at his mission of Bac in July.[30]

About this time Apache depredations were more frequent and deadly than usual; and the friars, counting on the renewed interest felt in northern affairs, deemed the opportunity favorable for securing some needed reforms—such as an escolta and a second missionary for each mission—in Pimería Alta as a necessary preliminary to the proposed advance; but though the viceroy issued a favorable preparatory decree, nothing was effected in the direction of increased protection for the southern establishments. As to the new ones proposed, Captain Anza, having gone to Mexico, and being called on for a report, advised that they should be founded, not on the Gila, where they would be exposed to Apache raids, but on the Colorado, and there only after new explorations and under the protection of a strong presidio to furnish a guard for each mission. At the same time came orders from Spain to send reënforcements to California. It was therefore decided that Anza should conduct the Californian expedition by the Colorado route, and that in connection with his expedition the required explorations should be made. A letter of Inspector Oconor to Father Garcés also shows that the proposition to transfer the presidios of Horcasitas and Buenavista to the Gila and Colorado, respectively, had been ap-

[30] *Arricivita*, 455–6. At S. Simon or Oparsoitac (called Upasoitac by Anza, 38 l. above the junction, and below the big bend) Garcés proposed to visit the Yavipais and Niforas, but the Ind. would not guide him nor carry the letter. Then he travelled 30 l. to a large laguna of the Jalchedunes, and thence to another, seeing farther up many people, and large fields; but having reached the frontier of the Quilmurs, a hostile tribe, said to be 5 or 7 days from the people who made the 'mantas prietas,' he deemed it unsafe to go farther up the river (Colorado or Sta María) for lack of water, left the letter, and was guided by a Jalchedun, back to the Cocomaricopas, who escorted him in turn to the Gileños, and thence he went by a new route to Bac, arriving July 10th.

proved. At the same time the Querétaro college
resolved to turn over the missions of Pimería Baja to
the bishop, in order to have missionaries to spare for
the new service. Thus the prospects seemed bright
again.[31]

I have before me a report of December 1774, addressed to the viceroy by Governor Crespo of Sonora,
who had been requested to give his views on the proposed expedition. His chief recommendations were,
that Anza should march, not through Papaguería, but
by way of Bac, or better still, down the San Pedro and
Gila; that instead of going down to the Colorado
junction he should cross over to the Jalchedunes country, crossing the river there, and proceeding directly
to Monterey, thus avoiding the southern California
desert; and above all, that in connection with this
expedition, steps should be taken to explore a way to
New Mexico and the Moqui towns, which the writer
believed to be easily accessible from the south-west.[32]
It was in this connection, also, that the government
called upon the New Mexican authorities and friars
for their views on the best way of reaching the Moquis from Sonora or California. This phase of the
subject has been presented earlier in this volume as a
part of New Mexican annals.[33] Father Escalante was
the leading spirit in resulting efforts. He not only
visited the Moquis, counting 7,494 souls, and earnestly
advocated their subjection by force of arms, but he
gave in detail his views as to the best routes of approach. He thought the way from the south and the
Gila would present no very serious difficulties, but was
sure that from the west and Colorado would be found
impracticable, and had no doubt that the best route

[31] *Arricivita*, 456–61.

[32] *Crespo (Francisco Antonio), Informe que hizo al Virrey el gobernador de Sonora acerca del descubrimiento de N. Mexico para Monterey.* MS., in *N. Mex.,
Doc. Hist.*, 802–28. The writer favors a presidio at the mouth of the S. Pedro,
and a mission among the Gileño Pimas. He also encloses a letter of Inspector
Oconor, who recommends as sites for the three frontier presidios S. Bernardo
Xaguionar, Sta Cruz, and Junta de los Rios. As we have seen, the only
change made was that of Tubac to Tucson a little later.

[33] See chap. xii., this volume.

of all was one from Monterey, directly east and then
south-east to Santa Fé. The zealous padre had the
courage of his convictions, and soon started with Padre
Dominguez on an exploring tour to the north-west,
bent on reaching Monterey; but he had to turn back
from Utah Lake, returning by way of Moqui, only to
learn that another Franciscan had successfully traversed the central route which he had declared the
most difficult of all.

Anza, now lieutenant-colonel, left Tubac on his second expedition the 23d of October, 1775. Besides
the California party of 207, he had twenty-five men—
including ten soldiers and Padre Pedro Font as chaplain—who were to return to Sonora, and also two
friars, Garcés and Tomás Eixarch, with six servants
and interpreters, who were to be left on the Colorado.
His route was by Tucson to the Gila, and down that
river to the Colorado, which he forded at the end of
November; and early in December, leaving the two
friars, he went on to California.[34] On the return, Anza
crossed the river on May 14, 1776. Padre Eixarch,
whose experience among the Yumas had been most
satisfactory, here rejoined the party, but Garcés had

[34] See *Hist. Cal.*, chap. xii., this series. The original authorities are *Anza,
Diario*, MS., *Font's Journal*, MS., and *Garcés, Diario;* with also an extended
account in *Arricivita*, 461 et seq. The diary through Arizona was as follows:
Oct. 23d, Tubac to La Canoa, 4 l.; 24th, to Llano Grande or Punta de los
Llanos, 4 l.; 25th, to Bac, 5 l.; 26th, to a point 1 l. past Tucson, Tuison, or
Tuquison, 5 l.; 27th, to Tutuetac, or Frente Negra Mts, or Llano del Azo-
tado, 5 l.; 28th, to Ditt-pax, pueblo viejo, or Oytapayts, or Oitapars, 6 l.;
29th, to Bajio de Aquituno, Quitcac, Ttacca, or Mt Taceo, 5 l.; 30th, to Ca-
mani, or La Laguna, on the Gila, 10 l.; 31st, devoted to rest and to an examination of the Casa Grande; Nov. 1st, down the river to Tutunitucan, or S.
Juan Capistrano de Ulurituc, or Utilltuc, 4 l.; 2d, to Encarnacion Sutaquison,
last of the Pimas (other Pima rancherías were S. Andrés, Tubuscabors, Atison,
and S. Serafino del Napcub), 2 or 4 l.; 3d, to Laguna del Hospital, not far
above the junction of the Asuncion, 2 l.; 4th, 6th, detained by illness of a
woman; 7th, s. w., to cut off the bend, to Puerto de los Cocomaricopas, 6 l.;
8th, to S. Simon y Judás de Opasoitac, or Uparsoitac, or Posociom, 7 l.; 11th,
to rancherías de S. Martin of the Opas, 1½ l.; 12th, to S. Diego on the river,
4 l.; 13th, to Rinconada, or Aritoac, across the river, 4 l.; 14th, to Agua Caliente, 4 l.; 16th, to S. Bernardino, 7 l.; 17th, to El Pescadero, in Yuma
country, 1½ l.; 18th, to S. Pascual, recrossing the river, 3 l.; 22d, to hill of
Sta Cecilia, or Metate, 5 l.; 25th, to Laguna Salada, 4 l.; 26th, to cerros del
Cajon, 4 l.; 27th, to Los Cerritos, 3 l.; 28th, to junction of the Gila (which
was crossed) and Colorado, 4 l. The distances are from Anza; Font often
makes them greater.

gone up the Colorado and could not be found.   Palma,
the Yuma chief, also joined the Spaniards for a trip
to Mexico; and the return march was through Papaguería to Caborca and Altar, where they arrived on
the 1st of June.[35]   Though the diaries of Anza and

PADRE FONT'S MAP OF 1777.

[35] May 14th, ford of the Colorado below the Gila; 15th, up the Gila to
Cerros del Cajon, 5 l. (or 7); 16th ditto to Laguna Salada, 7 l. (or 4); 17th,
leaving the river for the s. E., to Pozos de Enmedio, or Zacatal Duro, 8 l. (or
11); 18th, E. S. E. past Tinajas de Candelaria, to Puerto Blanco, or Llano del
Fuzal, 9 l. (or 18); 19th, s. E. to Arroyo del Sonoitac, or Carrizal, 8 l. (or 10);
20th, past the ruined mission of S. Marcelo de Sonoitac, 12 l. (or 18); 21st, past S.
Luis Quitobac to S. Juan de Mata, 14 l. (or 17); 22d, past S. Eduardo de
Aribacpía, to S. Ildefonso, 11½ l. (or 15); 23d, to Caborca, 9 l.

Font, and doubtless the report of Eixarch, contained much information about the Yumas and other tribes, there was no real exploration, such as had been suggested in the preliminary correspondence, except that accomplished by Garcés.

Left by Anza on the Colorado, Father Garcés immediately set out on his exploring tours, leaving his companion at Palma's ranchería to prepare the Yumas for mission life. In December he went down to the mouth of the Colorado, and in February 1776, up the river to the country of the Yamajabes, or Mojaves; crossed the country westward to San Gabriel in March, explored the great Tulares valley in April and May, and returned to the Colorado. Details of these Californian wanderings do not belong here.[36] Though in receipt of Anza's letter, the explorer resolved to visit the Moqui towns, and set out from the Mojave region on the 4th of June. This journey, as the second through this region, and the first of which we have a detailed account, is a most interesting and important one, to which nothing like justice can be done in the appended résumé of the diary, which, however, as a record cannot be omitted.[37] The starting-point was

[36] *Garcés, Diario y Derrotero,* 244–309; see also *Hist. Cal.,* i. 273–7. Padre Font's map I take from *Hinton's Hand-book,* with some changes of names to correct blunders.

[37] *Garcés, Diario y Derrotero,* 309–48. June 4th (104th day's journey), 2 l. N. w. up the Colorado to place in lat. 34° 1'; 5th, 1. l. N., ½ l. s., 3 l. E. N. E.; 6th, E. N. E. over Sierra de Santiago, 1½ l. E. S. S. E. to Aguage de S. Pacífico, 2 l. S. S. E., 1 l. E.; 7th, 4 l. E. to the Jaquallapais (Hualapais), on a little stream; 8th, 3½ l. N. E. by the skirt of the Sierra Morena, 2½ l. N. E. to a ranchería; 9th, 5 l. E. to Arroyo de S. Bernabé, 1 l. on the stream to an abandoned ranchería, where many Ind. soon gathered and new guides were obtained; 15th, up the arroyo N. E. and N. past Pozos de S. Basilio to a ranchería, 4½ l.; 16th, 4 l. N. E. and N. over pine hills, 5 l. N. to a sierra of red earth, said to be near the Colorado, deep cajones; 17th, 2½ l. N. E. over a rough sierra to a ranchería, where there was a junta of Ind. and much festivity. From here he might have gone more directly to Moqui, but turned off to see more people; 19th, 1 l. E. to Pozo de la Rosa, 2 l. N.; 20th, 5 l. E., 2 l. N. E., over a bad wooded country, with deep cañons, to a r. on the Rio Cabezua, or Jabezua, named S. Antonio, through a deep cañon pass. Here were a few cattle and horses from Moqui, also iron implements. This seems the largest r. of the Yavipais. The river runs w., N. w., and N. into the Colorado near by, water used for irrigation; 25th, 2 l. s. to summit of a sierra, 3 l. s. E. and N., through forest, to a Cabezua r.; 26th, 4 l. s. E. and s. to a place in sight of the deep gorges, through which flows the Colorado, through a cut in the blue sierra named Bucareli Pass, toward the E. N. E., but difficult

probably in the region of the later Fort Mojave, or latitude 35°, and the winding and complicated route corresponded in a general sense with that of Oñate in 1604–5, and the line of the modern Atlantic and Pacific railroad. Garcés was most kindly treated everywhere on the way, but on the Moquis even he could make no impression. They would have nothing to do with him, and took no interest in his picture of hell and heaven. Some visiting Zuñis offered to guide

to reach; also saw in N. smoke of the Payuchas N. of the river. From the sierra stretching W. the Rio Asuncion is thought to rise, 4 l. S. E. to a pinal; 27th, 4 l. S. E. and E.; 28th, 3½ l. S. E., S., and E. to Rio Jaquevila, or S. Pedro, which runs W. N. W. into the Colorado a little above the Puerto de Bucareli, through a deep cañon cut in living rock, 8 l. N. by another cajon to a r. of Yavipais, where two Moquis were seen.

July 1st, 1½ l. E. S. E. to a river that seemed to be the S. Pedro de Jaquesua, and a ruined pueblo said to be of the Moquis, 6 l. across treeless plains; 2d, 3 l. E. S. E., 3 l. E. and S. to the Moqui town of Oraive, called by the Yavipais Muca; much descriptive matter; 3d, 3 l. toward another pueblo, but returned; 4th, started on return, 12 l. E. N. W. to Rio S. Pedro Jaquecila. The names of the Moqui towns in Yavipais language are Sesepaulabá, Masaqueve, Janogualpa, Muqui, Concabe, and Muca, called Oraive by the Zuñis; 5th, 1½ l. E. N. W. to Yavipais r.; heard of the Guamua, Guañavepe, Gualliba, and Aguachacha, also different tribes of Yavipais, including the Yavipaistejua in the sierras of the Rio Asuncion; also on the Colorado the Yutas, Chemeguabas, Payuchas, Japul, Gualta, and Baquiyoba, probably only r. of one nation; 6th, 4 l. S. W. to Rio S. Pedro again; 7th, 2 l. N. W. and W. to near a cave; 8th, over the Sierra and past the Bajío, 4 l. W. and S. W. to Pozo de Sta Isabel; 9th, 5 l. N. W., 3 l. E. N. W. to r. in the cajones of the Jabesua, staying 6 days; 15th, 5 l. W. and S. by the new Canfran, though the natives wished him to go by the Escalera route; 16th, 6 l. W. to Pozo de las Rosas; 17th, S. W. past Sierra de Pinales and S. Diego to Arroyo de S. Alejo at a Yavipais r., leaving the former route; 18th, 1½ l. down the arroyo N. W. over hills to valley of Lino with much wild flax, 3½ l. W. to a r.; 19th, ½ l. N. to Aguage de Sta Margarita, over the Sierra Morena, 2 l. W. to Pozo de Avispas into a valley 4 l. wide, and 4 l. more to a r.; 23d, 2 l. S. W. to a pozo and r.; 44th, up the Sierra E. 2 l., 1 l. N. to r. with 2 pozos, in sight of a valley near the river, 4 l. to a r. of the Cueromaches. 25th, 2 l. S. W. to Sierra of Santiago, W. to Aguage de Sta Ana, 1½ l. S. W. to Rio Colorado, 2 l. S. down the river to Punta de los Jamajabs; 26th, 2½ l. S. down river to r. of S. Pedro; 27th, 1 l. S. to another r.; 28th, 3 l. S. E. to r. de la Pasion. The Ind. here said he could safely go through the country of the Yavipaistejua to the Cocomaricopas, but he preferred to keep on; 31st, 2 l. S. S. W. to r.

Aug. 1st, 2 l. S. to Sierra de S. Ildefonso, at end of the Jamajab country, a good place for 2 missions; 2d–5th, down the river S. 14 l. to Rio Sta Maria (now so named, Bill Williams Fork); 6–8th, 14 l. S. to r. of the Jalchedumes, before named S. Antonio; 11th, 2 l. W. S. W. to r. Sta Coleta near the river; 12th, 2½ l. S. W. to r. near laguna de Trinidad; 14th, crossed the Colorado on a balsa to r. de Asuncion (on the California side); 16th–21st, 7 l. down river; 22d, recrossed the river and went 1 l. S.; 23d, 1½ l. S. to last r. of the Jalchedumes; 24th, 4 l. S. S. W.; 26th, crossed the river, 1½ l. S. W. to a great pool, 5 l. S.; 4 l. S. E. to Puerte de la Concepcion. Returned to Bac by the same route Anza's exped, had come, arriving Sept. 17th. Diary dated Tubutama Jan. 30, 1777.

him to New Mexico, but he deemed it unsafe to make the trip, fearing also that his coming might be deemed by the authorities an intrusion; and so, having passed two nights in a corner of the court-yard at Oraibe, and having written a letter to the padre at Zuñi, he left this inhospitable tribe, and found his way back to the Colorado, down that river to the Yumas, and thence back to his mission of San Javier del Bac in September.

Padre Garcés supplemented his diary with extensive information respecting the geography of the country and the disposition of the different native tribes, adding also his views as to the methods by which the new spiritual conquest might best be effected. Though differing on some details, Anza and all the friars agreed that missions should be established on the California side of the Colorado, under the protection of a strong presidio. The natives were eager for such establishments, Palma, the Yuma chief, visiting Mexico to advance the cause; the government was favorably disposed; promises were freely made; and it was supposed there would now be no delay. Yet for various reasons, including the departure of Anza for New Mexico, the Apache warfare and consequent difficulty of obtaining men and money, and divers controversies in Mexico, nothing whatever was done for three years. Then Garcés went again to the Colorado in 1779, and was soon joined by another friar and a guard of twelve soldiers. Meanwhile the Yumas had become tired of waiting and were disgusted by the petty nature of the mission enterprise in comparison with promises of the past; other tribes were hostile to the Yumas; and Palma had lost something of his authority. In 1780 the formal founding of two mission pueblos was ordered; but the idea of a presidio was abandoned, and a new system was devised, under which each mission was to have ten soldiers and ten settlers. Friars and officials qualified to judge in the matter protested against the system as suicidal, and the result fully justified their fears. In July 1781, the two missions of San Pedro y San Pablo and Concepcion were destroyed and about fifty Spaniards were killed, including Padre Garcés with three other friars, and Captain Fernando Javier Rivera y Moncada, on his way to California with reënforcements and supplies. The missions were on the California side of the river, and all needful details of this disaster, with its causes and results, have been presented in another part of my work.[38]

After the military expeditions sent from Sonora to avenge this massacre, expeditions which practically accomplished nothing, there were no further definite efforts to found Spanish establishments on the Gila and Colorado; the whole region was left to the aborigines; indeed, the viceroy's instructions of 1786 required that the Yumas should be let alone until the Apaches were conquered, no attempt to be made meanwhile to open communication with California by land. A project for such communication with the peninsula, to be protected by one or more presidios near the head of the gulf, was indeed discussed in 1796–7, but nothing more.[39] Lieutenant-colonel José Zúñiga is said to have explored in 1794 a route from Sonora to New Mexico by way of Tucson and Zuñi, but of particulars nothing is known.[40] The meagre record of developments at the Moqui towns after the visit of Garcés has already been presented. In 1779–80, Anza, now governor of New Mexico, learning that the Moquis were in great trouble, made an earnest effort to effect their submission. Visiting the pueblos he learned that by drought, resulting in famine and pestilence, supplemented by raids of Navajos and Yutas, this brave people had been almost annihilated, only 800 surviving of the 7,500 counted in 1775. The

[38] See *Hist. Cal.*, i., chap. xvii., for 'pueblo missions on the Colorado,' *Arricivita*, 491–514, being the chief authority, with many additions from divers original sources on several phases of the subject.

[39] See *Hist. North Mex. States*, i., chap. xxvi., this series.

[40] *Z'ñiya (Iynacio), Rapida Ojeada*, 16.

proud chief at Oraibe still declined to submit to the
Spanish king or a foreign god, or to accept aid for his
afflicted subjects; but he permitted such as might
desire it to depart, and thirty families were brought
out to be settled in New Mexico. Nothing more is
known of the Moquis in Spanish or Mexican times.[41]

Another matter demanding brief mention here, as
pertaining to Arizona annals of the century, is the
Peralta grant of Gila lands. It is claimed that by
cédula of December 20, 1748, the king, Fernando VI.,
in reward for services to the crown conferred on Don
Miguel Peralta de Córdoba the title Baron de los
Colorados, and ordered the viceroy to grant him 300
leagues of land in the northern regions. On October
10, 1757, officials of the inquisition recommended the
grant, and certified on the testimony of Padre Paver
of Bac, of Padre García, and of Bishop Tamaron, that
to the lands selected in Pimería Alta, the missions
had no conflicting claims. On Junuary 3, 1758, Viceroy Amarillas accordingly granted the tract north of
San Javier mission, including the Gila River, and extending ten leagues north and south by thirty leagues
east and west. In a document dated 'El Caudal de
Hidalgo, Pimería Alta,' May 13, 1758, Peralta, Caballero de los Colorados certifies that he has surveyed
the grant and formed the required map. The documents were recorded in the audiencia office at Guadalajara, as shown by a certificate of June 23, 1768.
On August 1st of the same year, Peralta applied to
Cárlos III. for a confirmation granted by indorsement
December 2, 1772, and by a formal approval of January 22, 1776. By his will of 1788, Peralta bequeathed
the estate to his son Miguel Peralta, who in 1853, residing at San Diego, California, obtained from President Santa Anna a certified title, that is, copies of all
records in the case from the Mexican archives, with
the president's assurance of its validity and sufficiency.
From the younger Peralta, the title passed in 1864 to

[41] See chap. xii. of this volume.

George M. Willing, Jr, and from the latter in 1867 to James Addison Reavis, the present owner.[42] This immense grant of over 2,000 square miles extends from the region of the Pima villages eastward, for some seventy-five miles up the Gila valley, including valuable portions of three counties. Respecting its validity, depending on the genuineness of the documents and on various legal technicalities, I have of course no opinion to express. In a sense the title is plausible enough on its face; but it is somewhat remarkable that the annals of the province, as recorded, contain no allusion to Peralta, to the caballero de los Colorados, or to the Caudal de Hidalgo.

Of mining operations in Arizona, during any portion of the Spanish or Mexican period, nothing is practically or definitely known. The records are barely sufficient to show that a few mines were worked, and that the country was believed to be rich in silver and gold. In several districts have been found traces of these early workings; and these, with traditions arising from the Planchas de Plata find at Arizona proper just south of the line, are for the most part the only foundation for the many 'lost mines' of which much has been vaguely written, and more said. I have already remarked that modern writers have greatly exaggerated the country's former prosperity in mining and other industries, and it may be added that they have as a rule given the wrong date to such prosperity

[42] Reavis, 'El Caudal de Hidalgo' (Peralta Grant), Before U. S. Surveyor-general of Arizona, etc. Brief and argument of petitioner. S. F., 1884. Mr Reavis has also shown me his MS. documents in the case, including photographic copies of the original papers, diseño, etc., from the Mex. archives, furnished by authority of the governor of Jalisco and a Guadalajara court in 1881 and 1883; also photographs of doc. from the archives of S. Javier del Bac. According to the original survey of 1758, the initial point or centre of the western boundary line was fixed in the current of the Gila, the line extending thence south by the base of the Maricopa mountain on the east of the Sierra Estrella, bearing to the west of the Sta Cruz valley, a distance of 5 leagues to a point in the south boundary line; and from the same initial point north, across the Gila and Salt rivers, 5 l. north to a point in the north boundary line. I understand Mr R. to say that artificial corner marks have also been found.

as did exist, by assigning it to the earlier years of the Jesuit period. Contrary to what has been a some-what prevalent impression, there are no clear indica-tions of prehistoric mining, that is, by the Pueblo In-dians, when their towns extended over a large part of the territory; and there is no proof either that the Jesuits ever worked any mines, or that in their time there were carried on any mining operations except on a very limited scale near the Tubac presidio, though in occasional prospecting tours it is probable that some discoveries were made. In Franciscan times for over two decades the same state of things continued. But from 1790 for twenty or thirty years, the period of comparative peace with the Apaches, the veritable era of Arizona's early prosperity, there can be no doubt that many mines were opened from time to time, and that some were profitably worked, though we have no definite record of particulars, and though there is no reason to believe that there were any very extensive or wonderfully rich developments. It is to this period almost exclusively that we must trace the old work-ings discovered in later years, and also all the tradi-tions of lost mines that have any other than a purely imaginary foundation. I append a few items of in-terest in this connection, without attempting to repro-duce or analyze the many newspaper reports on the ancient mines.[43]

[43] From the report of 1777 on the Tubac region, *Yuma Sentinel*, April 13, 1878, I quote as follows: 'There are many mines of very rich metals to the west, in the vicinity of Aribac, at a distance of seven leagues; there are three particularly in the aforesaid vicinity, one of which yields a silver mark from one arroba of ore, the other 6 marks from a load, and the 3d a little less.   Three leagues beyond, in the valley of Babocomori, there are fine gold placers examined by D. José de Toro and this whole population.   After three visits, which these people made with D. José at great risks, and by remaining over 3 days at each trip, it was verified by their having brought away and spent with two traders, who at this time have it, as much as $200 in gold. In Sta Rita mountain and its environs, which is distant from Tubac 4 l., there have been examined 5 silver mines—two have been tried with fire, and 3 with quicksilver, and with tolerable yield.   All this is notorious among this entire population, and they do not work them because there are Apaches in all these places.'   Anza, *Descubrimiento de 1774*, MS., also says that in the Aribac valley there were gold and silver mines worked till 1767.   Nuggets of considerable size had been found.   In the Ures *Estrella de Occidente*, Nov. 9, 1860, it is stated that the Arizpe archives show an investigation at Tucson

What has been said in this chapter, though relating mainly to the eighteenth century, also includes nearly all that can be known of the country's annals down to 1845   There are no data on which to found anything like a chronologic record of events from 1800, and the few items of local interest that are accessible have already been presented.   The prosperity that began in 1790 may be regarded as having continued to about 1820, but as having disappeared entirely with the end of Spanish rule in 1822.   During these three decades the Apaches were for the most part at peace under treaties which by gifts and rations it was made their interest to observe.   Many of them came to live in rancherías near the presidios.   At the same time the presidial garrisons were vigilant, and with the aid of friendly Pimas and Pápagos had little difficulty in protecting the country from the occasional raids of the distant and hostile bands.   It was the golden era of

in the time of Viceroy Galvez in the case of a man accused of having bought a gold nugget of 15 marks 2 oz. for a presidio horse. 'Las arenas del Rio Colorado son un placer perenne de arenas de oro de buenos quilates, sea que por sí mismo las cria ó que desciendan con las corrientes que nacen de la sierra en donde tiene su orígen.' *Frejes, Hist. Breve*, 7.   The existence of quicksilver deposits in the Moqui region, as reported in ancient times, was verified by expeditions of the comandantes of Tucson and Tubac about 1840–5. *Retes, Portentosas Riquezas; Hall's Sonora*, MS., 251–2.   Enormous masses of virgin iron in the Madera Mt., between Tucson and Tubac. *Velasco, Not. Son.*, 221.   Of the 'Arizona' mine, of especial interest on account of the name, Anza says in 1774, *Descub.*, MS.: 'De esta mision (Saric) á la Arizona hay 8 leguas al Norte.   No se ha descubierto la veta madre.'   And Zúñiga, *Rápida Ojeada*, 32, writing in 1835, says that about 1833 he obtained from Arizona, or the Planchas de Plata, a silver brick of 6 marks 5½ oz., almost pure, which he presented to the museum.   He recommends moving the Altar presidio to the Arroyo de Arizona, so that new discoveries and settlements might follow.   In *Hinton's Hand-book*, 72–4, 192, 195–7, and *Arizona History*, 191–4, 202, 207, are some remarks on early mining discoveries.   These writers show a tendency to subdivide the Planchas de Plata discovery into several lost mines.   The former mentions an expedition of Dionisio Robles in 1817, into the Sta Rita Mts, in search of the old mines.   Much pure silver was found in old prospect holes.   'Quaint old chronicles' and 'musty records' are cited, but not named.   The other work notes the evidences of former placer workings near the Quijotoas.   In many Cal. and Ariz. newspapers of 1872 or thereabouts were published articles about mines in Northern Ariz., in the region west of the Mojaves, whose traditions of Spaniards and Jesuits from Upper California, who used to cross the Colorado into the mountains and return with loads of silver, are corroborated—so we are gravely told—by records of S. Juan Capistrano mission, and also by records at S. Javier del Bac of annual expeditions in the olden time to a wonderfully productive mine some 200 l. north of the Gila !

Pimería history, though only so in comparison with past and future misfortunes. Naturally under these circumstances, not only were the missions somewhat prosperous, as shown particularly by the magnificent church structure at Bac, but mines were worked as before explained, and stock-raising ranchos and haciendas were built up in the region extending from Tucson to the south-east and south-west. The ruins of these establishments are yet to be seen at many points.[44]

Then during the last years of the war for independence—which, however, in itself produced no direct developments in connection with the history of this far north—and especially in the early years of Mexican rule, all this was changed and all prosperity vanished; the Apaches resumed their depredations, the garrisons became demoralized, and all other establishments were practically abandoned. The causes of this radical change must apparently be sought, not in any modification of policy in treating the savages nor in any new feeling of hostility on the part of the Apaches, but simply in the neglect of the presidios by the government. Hitherto strict discipline had been enforced, soldiers and officers had been promptly paid, experience had taught the best methods of management, and the military organization was in every way effective. But from 1811 money and food began to be inadequately and irregularly supplied; credits, discounts, and paper money began to do their work of demoralization; official peculations and speculations became rife; and discipline and vigilance began to be relaxed. The Apaches, hostile as ever at heart, as soon as their rations ceased to be furnished liberally and regularly went on the war-path as the second best way of making a living; the friars, from feelings of loyalty to Spain and disgust at independence, gradu-

[44] Especially in and near the S. Pedro valley, not occupied in earlier Spanish nor in later Mexican times. Indian outbreaks in 1802 and 1827 are mentioned in the *Ariz. Hist.*, 27, with no details or sources. See *Hist. North Mex. States*, ii., for Apache wars in general, 1813–19, with references to the meagre sources.

ally lost interest in the presidios that had protected the existence of their missions; and the settlers, harassed by the savages, deprived of protection, and burdened by taxes, failed to give a hearty support to the soldiers, and gradually abandoned their ranchos. Finally all was desolation and disaster. This fatal neglect of the presidial organizations has been more fully set forth, so far as details are concerned, in the annals of California, where, however, in the absence of formidable foes, the results were much less disastrous.

Don Ignacio Zúñiga, who had served for years as commander of northern presidios, writing in 1835 on the condition of Sonoran affairs, gives an excellent idea of the Pimería disasters and their causes, though it is probable that he somewhat overrates the preceding prosperity. He declares that since 1820 no less than 5,000 lives had been lost; that at least 100 ranchos, haciendas, mining camps, and other settlements had been destroyed; that from 3,000 to 4,000 settlers had been obliged to quit the northern frontier; and that in the extreme north absolutely nothing was left but the demoralized garrisons of worthless soldiers, though in the most recent years, for lack of anything worth plundering and on account of the hostility of the Pimas and Pápagos, Apache raids had been somewhat less frequent than before.[45] This writer's plan was to restore everything as nearly as possible to the old condition. The presidial companies must, he thought, be discharged and new ones organized, to be paid and disciplined as in Spanish times; control of the temporalities must be given again to

[45] Zúñiga, Rápida Ojeada al estado de Sonora, dirigida y dedicada al Supremo gobierno de la nacion, por el C. Ignacio Zúñiga, natural del mismo estado. Mexico, 1835, 8vo, 66 p. Says Hamilton, Resources of Ariz., 20: 'During the régime of the mission fathers many prospecting and exploring parties penetrated southern Arizona, and a number of settlements were established. Besides the presidios of Tucson and Tubac there were flourishing haciendas at S. Bernardino, Barbacomari, S. Pedro, Arivaca, and Calabazas. These settlements possessed large flocks of sheep and herds of cattle. Mining was also prosecuted vigorously, especially at Arivaca and Cababi. After the breaking-up of the missions (1828) these prosperous colonies were despoiled by the savages and abandoned by those who escaped the tomahawk and the torch.'

the friars; colonists of good character must be sent to occupy the deserted northern ranchos; some of the presidios should be moved to better positions; and finally the Colorado and Gila establishments should be founded as proposed in the past century.[46] As a matter of course, no such reforms were carried out.

The Sonora record shows a period of general warfare against the Apaches in 1832–6, ending in some kind of a patched-up peace; also troubles with the Pápagos in 1840–1; and a little later serious revolts of the Yaquis and Mayos.[47] Unfortunately political and revolutionary controversies introduced new complications into Indian affairs, Gándara and other partisan leaders being accused of trying to advance their own interests by inciting the Yaquis and Pápagos to revolt. Moreover this political warfare was most disastrous in its effects on the frontier presidios, the commandants being often called from their proper duties to aid in sustaining the state government. For the period of 1842–5 I have a large number of detached fragmentary records, which, while not sufficing for a complete chronologic narrative, give a very satisfactory idea of the general condition of affairs on the frontier. There is no indication that in Arizona any Mexican settlement existed, except at Tucson and Tubac, where under protection of soldiers a few settlers still managed to live. From the two presidios complaints of inadequate force, arms, horses, and other supplies are frequent. In 1842–3 the Pápagos and Gila tribes were concerned in hostilities at the instigation of

[46] In 1795, 1801, and 1823–6, there had been some slight agitation of the project of establishing communication between Cal. and N. Mex. guarded by a presidio on the Colorado. *Hist. Cal.*, i. 573; ii. 3–4, 507–8; *Borica, Informe sobre comunicacion con N. Mexico, 1796; Borbon, Parecor sobre el proyecto de abrir via....y establecer un presidio á la entrada de Rio Colorado, 1801; Nava, Informe, 1801; Romero, Doc. relativas á la expedicion del capilan R. para abrir camino, 1823–6*. All these being MSS. in the *Arch. Cal.* Capt. José Romero actually made the trip from Tucson to Cal. and back; and in connection with his trip Gen. Figueroa also visited the Colorado. The corresp. is bulky, but we have no diaries. The result was that all schemes of land communication were abandoned. In later years, however, small well-armed parties not infrequently made the trip to and from Cal. by the Gila and Colorado route.

[47] See *Hist. North Mex. States*, ii.

Gándara as was charged, but they became repentant and were pardoned in May 1843. There were still rancherías of friendly Apaches at Tucson and Tubac, who even served as allies of the Mexicans in various campaigns; and some of the distant Apache bands were generally well disposed; but others were constantly on the war-path. Not much damage was done in Arizona because there were no ranchos left to be plundered, but farther south disasters to life and property were unceasing. On hearing of one of these raids, Captain Comaduran of Tucson generally started to cut off the retreating foe; several such campaigns are recorded, including one on a larger scale under Colonel Narbona in June 1843; and results at best were a few Apaches killed. a few women and children captured, a few cattle recovered, or perhaps the chief of some band forced to sue for peace, with a never-ending supply of plausible reasons why no more could be accomplished. The reports are strikingly similar to those we read in the newspapers of 1886 respecting Apache warfare in the same region. In April 1845 Colonel Elias Gonzalez made a full report on the condition and needs of the frontier presidios, showing no improvement in the general state of affairs; and at the same time he presented a plan for a grand campaign with over 1,000 men in August. In September, when the forces had been united and all was nearly ready for the start, Colonel Elias was summoned to the south with his troops to support the governor in suppressing a revolution. It was decided in a council of war at Tucson to disobey the summons and go on with the Apache campaign; but we have no record of results, except that Comaduran in December, with a force of 155 men, succeeded in killing six Apaches.[48]

[48] *Pinart, Doc. Hist. Son.*, MS., iii., passim, including extracts from the *Voto de Sonora* and other newspapers of the period. Col Elias Gonzalez' report and plan of April 30, 1845, is a MS. on p. 231–44. The Tucson Council of Sept. 11th is recorded in the *Centinela de Sonora*, Oct. 10, 1845. See also *Pinart, Col. Doc.*, MS., and print, no. 11, 45, 57, 62, 147; *Velasco, Not. Son.*, 256–7. In connection with raids of 1845 the Apache chief Mangas Coloradas, famous in late years, is mentioned.

Of the missions and visitas down to 1827, there is nothing to be added to the few local items already presented, except to note the visit of Bishop Bernardo del Espíritu Santo in 1821;[49] and after 1827 there is nothing to show the existence of the Arizona establishments. Hamilton states that they "were finally abandoned by a decree of the government in 1828;"[50] and though I have not found the original record, I have no doubt that such was practically the truth. The order of expulsion against Spaniards probably caused the departure of some of the friars in 1827–8, the management of the temporalities was taken away from them, and some of the establishments—including all in Arizona—were abandoned. South of the line, however, the Queretaranos still remained at several of the missions in charge of spiritual interests for many years; and even in the north the Pimas and Pápagos continued to live more or less continuously in communities at Bac, Tumacácori, and perhaps some of the other pueblos.[51]

The only explorations of Arizona in Mexican times, besides those effected by the military detachments in pursuit of Apache raiders, were those of foreign trappers, chiefly Americans from New Mexico. The adventures of some of these parties, as described by James O. Pattie in a published narrative, have already been noticed. The Patties first trapped on the Gila and its branches in the autumn of 1825, again visiting the region in 1826, and in the same year going down to the junction and up the Colorado in the track of Garcés. In the autumn of 1828 they again followed

---

[49] *Tubac, Lib. Mis.*, MS.

[50] *Hamilton's Resources*, 20; also *Ariz. Hist.* (Elliott & Co.), 52.

[51] In 1828 P. Gonzalez at Caborca asks the ayuntamiento of Altar if it is true the padres must go at once as ordered by the com.-gen., or await orders of civil authorities. *Pinart, Doc. Hist. Son.*, MS., i. 122. In 1844 a padre speaks of the missions having been destroyed, and the temporalities taken by the govt. *Id.*, iii. 181. Zúñiga, as we have seen, in 1835 recommended that the missions be restored to the padres; and there are other such allusions. Still the mission books of most of the establishments of Pimería Alta show the friars still in charge, perhaps practically as curates. In 1843 there was a decree permitting the Jesuits to establish missions in Sonora.

the Gila down to the Colorado, and made their way to California.[52]   The narrative is devoted mainly to personal adventures and encounters with bears and Indians, having more fascination than real value.   Of the few trapping parties which may have preceded those with which Pattie was connected, and the many that followed them, very little is known; but there were few of the later years in which the Arizona streams were not trapped to some extent.   Pauline Weaver was a famous pioneer who traversed the country as early as 1832, as did Kit Carson perhaps still earlier.   In 1829–32 the parties of Ewing Young and David Jackson crossed Arizona to California, as did a party of New Mexicans under José Antonio Vaca; and many of the early trapping and trading pioneers mentioned in the annals of California had visited this country sooner or later, though the regular route for trading parties and immigrants from Wolfskill's trip of 1831 was by a route north of the Colorado.[53]   Down to about 1836 the Apaches are said to have been friendly to the Americans; but about that time the famous chief Juan José was treacherously killed with many of his people by one Johnson, and the Apaches immediately attacked and killed Charles Kemp's party of 22 trappers on the Gila, as well as other parties farther east in New Mexico.[54]

[52] *Pattie's Personal Narrative;* see also this vol., p. 337–8, and *Hist. Cal.,* iii. 162–72.

[53] See *Hist. Cal.,* iii. 172–5, and chap. xiv.

[54] Benj. D. Wilson, *Observations,* MS., 2–18, gives the most complete account, having been encamped on the Gila at the time.   His party was also attacked, and several men were killed, Wilson being captured and barely escaping with his life.   James Johnson did not get the reward from the Mexicans that he had hoped for, and came to Cal., where he died in great poverty. His accomplice was a man named Glisson.   Gregg, *Com. Prairies,* i. 295–8, also mentions this affair.   An exploration of the Colorado mouth by Lieut. Hardy in 1825–8 is mentioned in *Bartlett's Pers. Narr.,* ii. 170–1; and in *Victor's River of the West,* 153, we are told that in 1834 a trapping party of 200 men of the Rocky Mt Fur Co. crossed from Bill Williams Fork to the Moqui towns, where several trappers plundered the gardens and shot 15 or 20 peaceful Moquis who objected to such treatment.

CHAPTER XVII.

AMERICAN OCCUPATION OF NEW MEXICO.

1846–1847.

The Mexican War—Kearny's Army of the West—The March—Mission of Cooke and Magoffin—Plans for Bloodless Conquest—Armijo's Preparations and Flight—From Bent's Fort to Las Vegas—Santa Fé Occupied—Kearny's Proclamation—Tour in the South—Doniphan in Command—Turbulent Volunteers—Price and the Mormons—Navajo Treaty—Chihuahua Campaign—Civil Government and Kearny Code—Plots of Ortiz and Archuleta—Grounds of Complaint—Revolt of 1847—Murder of Governor Bent—Disasters at Taos, Arroyo Hondo, and Mora—Price's Campaign—Fights at Cañada, Embudo, and Taos—Further Troubles with Insurgents and Indians—Executions.

In 1846 the United States began a war against Mexico for the acquisition of territory. This war and its causes are treated fully in other parts of this series devoted to the history of Mexico, of Texas, and of California. New Mexico and Arizona, except in the mere fact of being parts of the territory to be acquired, figured very slightly, if at all, in the preliminaries of the proposed conquest. There was, it is true, a claim that Texas extended south and west to the Rio Grande, by which shallow pretence the government of the northern republic managed to afford some comfort to the national conscience, on the plea that the defence of this 'disputed' tract by Mexico was the first act of war. It should be remarked, however, that the field of the first hostilities—of the Mexican invasion!—was not on the New Mexican frontier, but farther south-east.[1]

[1] I have the *Confidential Circular* of May 13th, with the autograph of James Buchanan, containing the declaration that war 'exists.' 'The truth is, that

War, or its 'existence,' having been declared, an army of the west was organized at Fort Leavenworth in June. Its commander was Colonel Stephen W. Kearny, its mission the occupation of the broad territory stretching from New Mexico to California, and also if practicable coöperation with other branches of the army in operations farther south. The advance division of this force consisted of 300 regulars of the first United States dragoons under Major Edwin V. Sumner, a regiment of mounted volunteers called out by Governor Edwards of Missouri for this campaign, and commanded by Colonel Alexander W. Doniphan, and five additional companies of volunteers, including one of infantry and two of light artillery, or a total of nearly 1,700 men. The second, or reserve division, comprised another regiment of Missouri volunteers under Colonel Sterling Price, a battalion of four companies under Lieutenant-colonel Willock, and the Mormon Battalion, in all about 1,800 men. The advance, or army of conquest, left Fort Leavenworth late in June; the long supply train of over 1,000 mules was soon augmented by the 400 wagons of the annual Santa Fé caravan; and all the companies, except the artillery, were encamped at the beginning of August near Bent's Fort on the Arkansas, after a tedious but uneventful march of some 650 miles across the plains.[2] An advance guard of four com-

we had endured so many insults and grievous wrongs from Mexico, with such unexampled patience, that at the last she must have mistaken our forbearance for pusillanimity. Encouraged, probably by this misapprehension, her army has at length crossed the Del Norte—has invaded the territory of our country—and has shed American blood upon the American soil.' *Larkin's Doc. Hist. Cal.*, MS., iv. 121. Prince, *Historical Sketches of New Mexico*, 290–327, devotes two chapters to the 'American Occupation' and 'Revolt of 1847.' His treatment of the subject is excellent, and in almost every respect satisfactory; but I can hardly agree with his preliminary statement, 'suffice it to say that the origin of the hostilities'—that is, of the Mexican war as shown by the context—'was found in the dispute as to the ownership of the territory between the Rio Grande and the Nueces River.' This is also affirmed on p. 240.

[2] *Hughes' Doniphan's Expedition; containing an account of the Conquest of New Mexico; General Kearney's overland expedition to California; Doniphan's campaign against the Navajos; his unparalleled march upon Chihuahua and Durango; and the operations of General Price at Santa Fé. With a sketch of the life of Col Doniphan. Illustrated with plans of battle-fields, a map, and fine*

panies had made an unsuccessful attempt to overtake a party of traders believed to have in their possession arms and ammunition for the enemy.

From Bent's Fort, Lieutenant Decourcy was sent with twenty men to Taos to learn the disposition of the people, rejoining the army later with some prisoners and a report that resistance might be expected at

engravings. *By John T. Hughes, A. B., of the First regiment of Missouri cavalry.* Cincinnati, 1850, 12mo. I have also ed. of Cin., 1849, 8vo; and there are ed. of Cin., 1848, and apparently 1847. This work is a standard authority on the campaign, written in a clear and pleasing style, and with an accuracy that has not, I believe, been questioned, though the author, like others of his time and class, takes an ultra-American view of most questions, and has no doubt of the entire righteousness of the war against perfidious Mexicans.

There were apparently 5 companies of the 1st U. S. dragoons. I have found no record of the company organization, but the officers were captains Edwin V. Sumner (act. major), Philip St George Cooke, Thomas Swords (asst. Q. M.), Benj. D. Moore, John H. K. Burgwin, Henry S. Turner (adj. gen.), Abraham R. Johnston, and Philip R. Thompson (some of whom were probably lieutenants at the start); and lieut. Patrick Noble, Thomas C. Hammond, Rufus Ingalls, John W. Davidson, Joseph McElvain, C. J. L. Wilson, and Oliver P. H. Taylor. I take this imperfect list from the *U. S. Official Register*, 1845-7, and from occasional mention in the different narratives.

Officers of the 1st Mo. volunteers, Col Alex. W. Doniphan (a lawyer who had enlisted as a private, elected colonel June 18th); lieut.-colonel, C. F. Ruff; major, Wm Gilpin (both of whom were elected from the ranks); captains of the 8 companies (856 men rank and file) each enlisted in a county of Mo., Waldo, Walton, Moss, Reid, Stephenson, Parsons, Jackson, and Rodgers; sutler, C. A. Perry; adjutant, G. M. Butler; surgeon, Geo. Penn; asst surgeons, T. M. Morton and I. Vaughn.

A battalion of light artillery, under Major Clark, consisted of two companies from St Louis, under captains Weightman and Fischer, about 250 men. A battalion of infantry had 145 men in two companies, commanded by captains Angney and Murphy. There was also a troop of volunteer cavalry from St Louis; the Laclede Rangers, 107 strong, under Capt. Hudson, attached to the dragoons. Also lieutenants Wm H. Emory, W. H. Warner, J. W. Abert, and W. B. Peck of the U. S. topographical engineers, Warner commanding the artillery on the march to Sta Fé.

The 2d regiment of Mo. volunteers was mustered into the service at Ft Leavenworth, about the 1st of August. Its officers were Sterling Price colonel, D. D. Mitchell lieut.-colonel, Edmondson major. It numbered about 1,000 men. There was also a separate battalion under Lieut.-col Willock, 300 men in four companies, captains Smith, Robinson, Morin, and Hendley; and a small artillery detachment under officers of the regular army.

The Mormon Battalion consisted of about 500 Mormons, who entered the service as a means of reaching California, where, according to the terms of their enlistment, they were to be discharged. It was organized at Council Bluffs in June, by Capt. James Allen of the 1st dragoons, who was to command the battalion as lieut.-colonel, but died before departure. Lieut. A. J. Smith commanded on the march to Sta Fé, and Lieut.-colonel P. St Geo. Cooke on that to Cal. The captains of the 5 companies were Jefferson Hunt, Jesse D. Hunter, James Brown, Nelson Higgins, and Daniel C. Davis; Adjutant Geo. P. Dykes, and later P. C. Merrill; surgeon Geo. B. Sanderson. For a full history of the Mormon Battalion, see *Hist. Cal.*, v., chap. xviii., this series; also *Tyler's Mormon Battalion*.

every point. Similar reports had previously been received from Major Howard and the mountaineer Fitzpatrick. From Bent's Fort, also, Captain Cooke, with twelve picked men, was sent in advance, nominally as a kind of ambassador to treat with Governor Armijo for the peaceful submission of eastern New Mexico,[3] but really to escort James Magoffin, the veritable ambassador, intrusted with a secret mission at Santa Fé. To send an army of 1,700 men, mainly composed of undisciplined volunteers, on a march of a thousand miles over a desert occupied by hostile savages, to conquer, by force of arms, so populous an interior province, and one so well defended, at least by nature, as New Mexico, was on its face a very hazardous enterprise. It was a radically different matter from the proposed occupation by naval forces of a coast province like California. In the annals of the latter country we have seen, however, what agencies were relied on by the government, acting through Consul Larkin as a confidential agent, to insure a bloodless victory, though the success of the plan was seriously impaired by the blundering and criminal disobedience of another and subordinate agent. These complications of the farthest west are now well known in every particular.[4] That the policy respecting New Mexico was similar in its general features, there can be no doubt, though most details have never come to light. During the past years, the Santa Fé traders, both American and Mexican, had done much to make the condition and disposition of each people well known to the other, to convince the New Mexicans

---

[3] 'My mission...was in fact a pacific one. The general had just issued a proclamation of annexation of all the territory *east of the* Rio Grande; the government thus adopting the old claim of Texas' (the procl. of July 31st, as given in *Cutts' Conq.*, 42, the only one I have found, contains no such proposition), 'and thus manifestly, in a statesman's view, a bloodless process would lead to its confirmation in the treaty of peace; and the population would be saved from the bitterness of passing *sub jugum*. The difficulty of a half-measure remains; it cuts the isolated province in two! There must be an influential Micawber in the cabinet. At a plaintive compliment, that I went to plant the olive, which he would reap a laurel, the general endeavored to gloss the barren field of toil to which his subordinates, at least, were devoted.' *Cooke's Conq.*, 7.

[4] See *Hist. Cal.*, v., this series.

how futile must be any attempt to resist the United States, and the Americans how easy would be the occupation of Santa Fé. Doubtless, certain prominent traders had been at work virtually as secret agents of the government at Washington, which from their reports had come to believe that no serious opposition was to be expected to the change of flag. It was understood that the New Mexicans, after long years of neglect and so-called oppression, had retained but a nominal allegiance to Mexico; that many influential citizens, from motives of personal interest as traders or land-owners, desired the downfall of Mexican rule; that many others were convinced that resistance would be useless, and more than half convinced that the change would be a benefit; that prominent officials were already disposed, or might be influenced by certain appeals to their love of gain, or ambition for office, to submit without a struggle to the inevitable; that the masses might be controlled for the most part through the leaders; and that finally, any opposition based on pride, patriotism, or prejudice of race or religion, must be more than counterbalanced by lack of unity, of leaders, of arms, and other resources. Thus Kearny's army of the west was sent to occupy, not literally to conquer, New Mexico. Nevertheless, the enterprise was one attended with many risks.

Magoffin, or Don Santiago, was an Irish Kentuckian, long in the Santa Fé trade, a man of wealth, with unlimited capacity for drinking wine and making friends, speaking the Spanish language, and on friendly terms with most of the leading men in New Mexico and Chihuahua. At Washington he was introduced by Senator Benton to the president and secretary of war, and at the request of the three agreed to accompany the expedition, professing his ability to prevent any armed resistance on the part of Governor Armijo and his officers.[5] Cooke's party, without adventures

---

[5] *Benton's Thirty Years' View*, ii. 682–4. In the *Cal. and N. Mex., Mess. and Doc., 1850*, p. 240–1, are letters of June 18th, from Sec. Marcy to Kearny and to the commandant of the Chihuahua expedition, introducing Magoffin

requiring notice, arrived the 12th of August at Santa
Fé, where he was hospitably received by Armijo, who,
although he "seemed to think that the approach of
the army was rather sudden and rapid," concluded to
send a commissioner in the person of Dr Connelly,
with whom the captain set out next day on his return
to meet the army.[6]   Meanwhile, according to Benton,
our only authority, and as there is perhaps no reason
to doubt, Magoffin easily prevailed on the governor to
promise that no defence should be made at Apache
Cañon, a point on the approach to Santa Fé which
might have been held by a small force.   He had more
difficulty with Archuleta, the second in command, but
by appealing to his ambition, and suggesting that by
a pronunciamiento he might secure for himself western
New Mexico, on which Kearny had no designs, he at
length overcame that officer's patriotic objections, and
thus secured an open road for the army.[7]

as a man regarded by the president as one who could render important services.   Magoffin was accompanied by a friend, Gonzalez, a trader of Chihuahua; and after accomplishing his purpose at Sta Fé, he went south to prepare
the way for Gen. Wool as he had done for Kearny.   Here, however, he was
suspected, and kept a prisoner for a long time.   After the peace he returned
to Washington, where Benton, in a secret session of the senate, obtained for
him an appropriation of $50,000 for secret services, of which sum a new ad-
ministration, after much haggling, paid $30,000, a sum barely covering M.'s
expenses and losses.   Says Benton: 'The paper which he filed in the war office
may furnish some material for history—some insight into the way of making
conquests—if ever examined.   This is the secret history of Gen. Kearny's
expedition, given because it would not be found in the documents.'   In the
Cal. and N. Mex., Mess., p. 236, is another letter of Sec. Marcy of May 27th
to Kearny, announcing that the president has determined to send a catholic
of good standing, able to speak Spanish, to serve as a kind of chaplain, with
a view of allaying religious prejudices of the New Mexicans against the U. S.
I have no record that such a man was sent.

[6] *The Conquest of New Mexico and California; an historical and personal narrative.   By P. St Geo. Cooke, brigadier, brevet major-general U. S. A.*, author
of '*Scenes and Adventures in the Army; or, Romance of Military Life,*' etc.   N. Y.,
1878, 12mo.   The diary of this advance trip is found on p. 6–34, and there
follow good accounts of later events, the march to Cal., etc.

[7] While, as I have said, there may be no reason to question the general
accuracy of Benton's version, or to doubt that Magoffin really obtained these
promises from Armijo, Archuleta, and others, yet it is probable that there is
much exaggeration in the implied opinion that the U. S. relied mainly on, or
that Kearny's success was due mainly to, M.'s negotiations at this time.   M.'s
efforts were rather the supplement or conclusion to a long chain of investigations and negotiations by himself and others.   Kearny's immunity from armed
opposition of a serious nature rested on something more than Magoffin's ability to manage the N. Mexican leaders.

Unfortunately we have no definite information from New Mexican sources respecting Armijo's preparations, real or pretended, for defence; and the fragmentary rumors that found their way into current narratives are meagre, contradictory, and of no value. The governor understood perfectly his inability to make any effective resistance; and all that he did in that direction was with a view merely to 'save his responsibility' as a Mexican officer, even if he did not, as is probable, definitely resolve and promise not to fight. The people were called upon, as usual in such cases, to rise and repel the invader; and a considerable force of militia was organized and joined the two or three hundred soldiers of the army. These auxiliaries were, however, but half in earnest and most inadequately armed. If any considerable portion of them or their officers ever thought seriously of fighting the Americans, their patriotic zeal rapidly disappeared as the numbers and armament of the invaders became more clearly known from returning scouts, who, in many instances, were captured and released by Kearny. With perhaps 2,000 men—though American reports double the number—Armijo seems to have marched out to Apache Cañon with the avowed intention of meeting the enemy; but on the last day, in consequence of differences of opinion between the general and his officers, the former dismissed the auxiliaries to their homes, and with his presidial troops retreated to the south by way of Galisteo, near which point he left his cannon. Armijo was blamed by the many who were hostile to the invaders and who were ashamed to see their country thus surrendered without a struggle. Doubtless the governor, had he desired it, might have waged a guerilla warfare that would have given the foe much trouble; and there is much cause to believe that his reason for not doing so was not a praiseworthy desire to prevent the useless shedding of his subjects' blood.[8]

[8] In *Bustamante, Nuevo Bernal Diaz*, ii. 103–5, is an account of the N. Mex. affair made up from newspaper articles founded on information from Chihua-

Kearny's army left Bent's Fort on the 2d of August. The route was nearly identical with the later line of stage travel, and differed but slightly from that of the modern Atchison, Topeka, and Santa Fé railroad. The march was a tedious one, there being many cases of fatal illness among the volunteers. Through some miscalculation or mismanagement of the supply trains, the men were on short rations for a larger part of the way; and it was besides a season of drought. The advance was in several divisions, by slightly different routes from day to day, in order to utilize the scanty water and grass. Fitzpatrick was the guide, Robidoux the interpreter, while Bent commanded a company of spies. After the settlements were reached, American residents, such as Towle, Bonney, Wells, and Spry, were met, and gave information respecting the state of things at Santa Fé and Taos. Small parties of Mexican scouts were also frequently captured, or came voluntarily into camp, where they gave vague and contradictory accounts of Armijo's preparations for defence, and whence, being set at liberty, they carried back exaggerated reports of the American force and cannon, with copies of Kearny's proclamation. On the 14th, 15th, and 16th, respectively, the army reached Las Vegas, Tecolote, and San Miguel del Vado. At each of these places, Kearny—now brigadier-general by a commission received at Las Vegas—made a speech from a housetop, absolving the people from their allegiance to

hua. With several blunders it contains very little definite and accurate information. Kearny's force is put at 3,000, with 1,000 in the rear, guarding a caravan whose goods amounted to $1,000,000. Armijo retreated because he could not control his men, who showed a disposition to pass over to the enemy, though the people blamed him. He had gone to El Paso, where a stand would be made, as 400 men from Chih. had started too late for the protection of N. Mex. At the Cañon de Pecos, on Aug. 14th, he had 2,000 men, of whom 270 were regular troops, with 7 guns. On the 15th, disputes with the auxiliary officers caused him to dismiss the force. The guns were spiked near Galisteo, and A. went south with only 60 men. Kearny had made Magoffin gov. at Sta Fé. Connelly, in the name of the new govt, had written to invite Armijo to return to his post as gov. with guaranties, but the offer was not accepted. The caravan will proceed south to El Paso, with troops to seize the custom-house. There are also brief notices in *El Tiempo*, April 19, 1846; and *Iris de España*, Dec. 12, 1846.

Armijo, and promising protection to the life, property, and religion of all who should peaceably submit to the new order of things; and the alcalde, and in some cases the militia officers of each town, being induced more or less willingly to take an oath of allegiance to the United States, were continued in office. A letter was received from Armijo, making known his purpose to come out to meet Kearny; but whether as friend or foe, the vague wording did not clearly indicate. Cooke and Connelly were met at Tecolote, but the message brought by the latter is not known to the chroniclers. Among the men and subordinate officers, there was an expectation of having to encounter from 2,000 to 10,000 foes in the mountain defile; but the general is said to have borne himself as coolly as as if on parade, as indeed well he might, knowing how slight was the danger of a conflict. At San Miguel a Mexican officer was captured—Salazar, son of the officer with whom the Texans had to do in 1841—who reported the flight of Armijo. On the 17th the army passed the ruins of Pecos; and on the 18th, marching without the slightest opposition through the famous cañon, the Americans entered Santa Fé at 6 P. M., being accorded a friendly reception by Juan B. Vigil, the acting governor. The flag of the United States was raised at sunset, and saluted with thirteen guns. General Kearny slept in the old *palacio*, and the army encamped on an adjoining eminence. Thus was the capital of New Mexico occupied without the shedding of blood.[9]

[9] If General Kearny ever made a detailed report of this campaign I have not found it. A brief statement is found in his letter of Aug. 24th, on p. 59–60 of Cutts' *The Conquest of California and New Mexico, by the forces of the United States, in the years 1846 and 1847. By James Madison Cutts, with engravings, plans of battle, etc.*, Phil., 1847, 12mo. This is an excellent narrative en résumé of the whole conquest, the earliest published, and supplemented with many original documents, a few of which I have not found elsewhere. The most complete original record of the march to Sta Fé is to be found on p. 15–32 of Emory's *Notes of a Military Reconnoissance, from Fort Leavenworth, in Missouri, to San Diego, in California, including part of the Arkansas, Del Norte, and Gila rivers. By Lieut.-col W. H. Emory. Made in 1846–7, with the advance guard of the 'Army of the West.'* Wash., 1848, 8vo (*U. S. Govt Doc.*, 30th cong. 1st sess., H. Ex. Doc. 41, Sen. Ex. Doc. 7). This is a

On the day following his entry into the capital, General Kearny caused the people to be assembled in the plaza, where through an interpreter he made a speech.   Then the acting governor, secretary, alcaldes, and other officials took the required oath of allegiance, Governor Vigil also delivering a brief address and reading the general's earlier proclamation.   The exercises were similar, if somewhat less hurried, to the earlier ones at Las Vegas and San Miguel.   The New Mexicans as subjects of the United States from this time were assured of full protection for their lives, property, and religion, not only against American depredators, but against the Mexican nation, Governor Armijo, and their Indian foes.   Three days later Kearny's position was fully explained in the formal proclamation which is appended.[10]

diary day by day down to and including the march to Cal. It is largely devoted to a scientific description of the country visited, and contains drawings. *Emory's Journal* (unofficial), extending from Aug. 2d to Sept. 5th, was published in the newspapers, and I find it in *Niles' Register*, lxxi. 138–40, 157–9, 174–5. In *Id.*, 90–2, is a fragment of the journal of some officer not named, covering the period of Aug. 13th–23d. Cooke's diary, *Conquest*, 34 et seq., also includes the march of the main army from the 15th of Aug., and of course it is described by Hughes and the rest. Says Cooke: 'I commanded the advance guard, and held to the main road, not receiving orders to take the obscure route, known to the general, which turned the position at the cañon. As I passed it I concluded that important information had been received in the night. So it proved, and I found at the rocky gorge only a rude breastwork of large trees felled across it. It had evidently proved impossible to give coherence to the wretched mass of our opponents who were now for the first time assembled together. They became panic-stricken at once on the approach of such an imposing array of horsemen of a superior race, and it appeared, overestimated our numbers, which the reports of ignorance and fear had vastly magnified.'

[10] 'Proclamation ! As by the act of the republic of Mexico, a state of war exists between that government and the U. S., and as the undersigned, at the head of his troops, on the 18th took possession of Sta Fé, . . . he now announces his intention to hold the department, with its original boundaries (both sides of the Del Norte)'—so it seems the original boundaries were on both sides !— 'as a part of the U. S., and under the name of the territory of New Mexico.' The undersigned has come to N. Mex. with a strong military force, and an equally strong one is following close in his rear. He has more troops than necessary to put down any opposition that can possibly be brought against him, and therefore it would be folly and madness for any dissatisfied or discontented persons to think of resisting him. The undersigned has instructions from his govt to respect the religious institutions of N. Mex., to protect the property of the church, to cause the worship of those belonging to it to be undisturbed, and their religious rights in the amplest manner preserved to them. Also to protect the persons and property of all quiet and peaceable inhabitants within its boundaries, against their enemies the Utes, Navajos, and others. And while he assures all that it will be his pleasure as well

From the 9th for many days representatives of other towns, of the Indian pueblos, and in some cases of Navajo, Yuta, and even Apache bands, came to listen to the general's explanations of United States policy, and to offer peaceful submission to his authority. Many among the ignorant populace had been led to believe that they would be robbed, outraged, or murdered by the Americanos; and many of a higher class had left the city with their families in fear of insults from a lawless soldiery; but these fears were to a considerable extent removed by the general's words and acts, and many of the fugitives returned to their homes. A flag-staff to bear the stars and stripes was raised in the plaza. Captain Emory on the 19th selected a site for a fort, and four days later work was begun on Fort Marcy, an adobe structure commanding the city from an adjoining hill. The animals were sent to the region of Galisteo to a grazing camp guarded by a detachment under Lieutenant-colonel Ruff. On the 23d and following Sundays the general and staff attended church; an express for the states was despatched on the 25th; and in the evening of the 27th

as his duty to comply with those instructions, he calls upon them to exert themselves in preserving order, and in promoting concord, and in maintaining the authority and efficiency of the laws; to require of those who have left their homes, and taken up arms against the troops of the U. S., to return forthwith to them, or else they will be considered as enemies and traitors (!), subjecting their persons to punishment and their property to seizure and confiscation for the benefit of the public treasury. It is the wish and intention of the U. S. to provide for N. Mex. a free govt, with the least possible delay, similar to those in the U. S., and the people of N. Mex. will then be called on to exercise the rights of free men in electing their own representatives to the territorial legislature; but until this can be done, the laws hitherto in existence will be continued until changed or modified by competent authority; and those persons holding office will continue in the same for the present, provided they will consider themselves good citizens and willing to take the oath of allegiance to the U. S. The undersigned hereby absolves all persons residing within the boundary of N. Mex. from further allegiance to the republic of Mexico, and hereby claims them as citizens of the U. S. Those who remain quiet and peaceable will be considered as good citizens and receive protection. Those who are found in arms, or instigating others against the U. S., will be considered as traitors (!), and treated accordingly; Don Manuel Armijo, the late gov. of this department, has fled from it. The undersigned has taken possession of it without firing a gun or shedding a drop of blood—in which he most truly rejoices; and for the present will be considered as governor of this territory. Given, etc., Sta Fé, Aug. 22, 1896. By the Governor, S. W. Kearny, Brigadier-General.' The copy in *Cutts* reads S. W. Kearny, brig-gen. U. S. A., by the governor, Juan Bautista Vigil y Alarid.'

Kearny gave a grand ball to officers and citizens. Minor military movements, such as the arrival of small parties that had lagged on the way and the stationing of local detachments, need not be noticed in detail. There were unfounded rumors of hostile preparations in the south, and that Colonel Ugarte was approaching with a Mexican force from Chihuahua, which caused Kearny to march down the river with nearly half his army. This tour extended to Tomé, occupied the time from the 2d to the 13th of September, and revealed no indications of hostility among the abajeños.

Back at Santa Fé, the general sent strong detachments under Major Gilpin and Lieutenant-colonel Jackson, who had succeeded Ruff by election of the volunteers—to Abiquiú and Cebolleta on the Navajo frontier; and gave his attention to the organization of a civil government put in operation on the 22d of September. Then on the 25th, he set out on the march to California by the Gila route, with his 300 dragoons, two thirds of which number, however, were presently sent back, when Kit Carson was met with the inaccurate news that the conquest of California had already been accomplished.[11] Orders left were to the effect that the Mormon Battalion should follow the general to California, and that Doniphan's regiment, on the arrival of Price's to take its place, should march south to join General Wool at Chihuahua. Among the volunteers of both regiments there was much sickness, caused to a considerable extent by indulgence in the various dissipations of the New Mexican metropolis. Some 300 of the Missourians are said to have been buried at Santa Fé. There was also a great scarcity of supplies, the commissary department of the army of the west being grossly

[11] See *Hist. Cal.*, v., for the conquest of Cal., including Kearny's march across the continent, and disaster at S. Pascual. *Emory's Notes* is the most complete narrative of the march. Carson was met on Oct. 6th, and 3 of the 5 companies were sent back. It was on Oct. 15th that Kearny left the Rio Grande, in about lat. 33° 20', to strike off westward to the Gila, which river he followed down to the Colorado. I shall say more of his march across N. Mex. and Ariz. a little later.

mismanaged, as it appears. Provisions must be bought from fellow-citizens, not seized, as in an enemy's country; and even the money furnished the troops was not apparently of a kind that could be utilized, to say nothing of exorbitant prices. The men were profoundly disgusted with the country and its people, and their complaints were doubtless somewhat too highly colored. Moreover, the restraints of military life were irksome to the Missourians. They were willing to fight the Mexicans, but could not understand their obligation as soldiers to work on the fort, wear their coats under a hot sun, observe petty regulations, or obey orders against the propriety of which, as American citizens, they could present strong arguments. The popularity of the officers was therefore in inverse ratio to their knowledge and enforcement of discipline. Brawls and arrests for insubordination were of not infrequent occurrence. Yet amusements were not wanting, among which were theatrical performances by a company of military amateurs.[12]

Colonel Price with his 2d Missouri volunteers arrived at Santa Fé about the 1st of October.[13] The

[12] In *Niles' Register*, lxx.–iii. passim, are many items from various sources on all phases of the N. Mex. campaign, including many complaints from the volunteers. The disorders and insubordination are also narrated by Hughes and others, who often defend the volunteers and condemn the officers. Lieut.-col Ruff was much disliked, and the qualities that made him unpopular procured him a captain's commission in the regular army. A private was elected to fill his place over the major. Geo. F. Ruxton, *Adventures in Mexico and the Rocky Mountains*, N. Y., 1848, p. 178–90, an English traveller who wrote from personal observation, pronounced the volunteers 'the dirtiest, rowdiest crew I have ever seen collected together;' and he gives a much more unfavorable account of their lack of discipline in camp and lawless conduct in town, than any other writer—probably too unfavorable; yet he admits they were good fighters. Cutts, *Conquest*, 220–1, gives a programme of the theatrical performance on Christmas evening.

A Campaign in New Mexico with Colonel Doniphan. By Frank S. Edwards, a volunteer. With a map of the route, and a table of the distances traversed, Phil., 1847, 12mo. This is an interesting though brief narrative of the campaign in N. Mex. and Chihuahua, though more attention is given to the country and people than to the historic sequence of events. Another anonymous narrative is *The Conquest of Santa Fé and subjugation of New Mexico,* Phil., 1847, 8vo.

[13] Perhaps a little earlier, as the arrival was made known to Kearny on his march Oct. 2d or 3d. I have found no narrative or report devoted especially to the movements of Price's regiment.

Mormon Battalion under Lieutenant Smith arrived in two divisions on the 9th and 12th. On account of illness about 150 of the men with most of the families were detached and sent to winter at Pueblo, in what was later Colorado, from which point they found their way the next year to Salt Lake. The rest of the battalion, 340 strong, was put under the command of Lieutenant-colonel Cooke, and started on the 19th to follow Kearny and open a wagon-road across the continent. Meeting the returning dragoons on the 23d and turning off from the Rio Grande November 13th, they found it impracticable to find a way for their wagons toward the west, and accordingly directed their course farther southward to the San Bernardino rancho on the later frontier, and thence marched by Tucson to Kearny's route on the Gila. The adventures of the battalion from its organization pertain to the history of California rather than to that of New Mexico.[14]

Orders came back from Kearny that Doniphan before starting for Chihuahua should undertake a campaign in the Navajo country. In September, as we have seen, Lieutenant-colonel Jackson with three companies had been sent to Cebolleta on the frontier; and from this point, apparently before Kearny's last orders were known, Captain Reid, with thirty volunteers and a chief called Sandoval as guide, starting the 20th of October, had in twenty days made a somewhat remarkable entry far to the west and north into the heart of the Navajo country. He met the head chief Narbona, found the Indians well disposed toward the Americans, made arrangements for a treaty council at Santa Fé, and returned to Cebolleta. Major Gilpin, who had been stationed at Abiquiú in September, had made an expedition into the Yuta country, and had brought some 60 leading men of that nation to Santa Fé, where a treaty was made on October 13th. Un-

---

[14] See *Hist. Cal.*, v., chap. xviii., this series. For the march the authorities are *Tyler's History; Bigler's Diary*, MS.; *Cooke's Journal; Id., Report; Id., Conquest.*

der the new orders, Gilpin left Abiquiú on the 22d
with his two companies, reënforced by 65 pueblo and
Mexican allies; went up the Chama, crossed to the
San Juan, descended that river, reached the Chelly
cañons, thence apparently turned eastward and by
way of the Laguna Colorada reached a place called
Ojo del Oso, or Bear Spring, on the 20th of November.[15]   Meanwhile Doniphan left Santa Fé on October 26th, but from Alburquerque sent most of his
force down the river to Valverde to protect the caravan of traders and make prepartions for the march to
Chihuahua.[16]   With a small party he then went to
Covero, whither Jackson had moved his force from
Cebolleta.   From this point, having received a de-
spatch from Gilpin on the San Juan, and sent in reply
orders to assemble as many Navajos as possible at
Ojo del Oso, Doniphan with Jackson and 150 men
started on the 15th toward the headwaters of the
Puerco and thence north-westward, toiling through
the deep snows and over the mountains, and joining
Major Gilpin on the 21st.   There were about 500
Navajos present, including the chiefs of many bands.
They professed friendship and admiration for the
Americans, but had much difficulty in comprehending
why the new-comers should interfere with their war-
fare against the detested Mexicans.   At last, however,

---

[15] I do not find this spring on the maps, but suppose it was not far from
Red Lake, N. E. from Ft Defiance, in the later Navajo reservation.   Doniphan's report states that Gilpin reached the Little Colorado; and Hughes'
narrative indicates a limit very far west for both Gilpin and Reid; but in the
absence of original diaries I suppose that neither went much farther west
than the Chelly, from which the Ojo del Oso was 1 day's march possibly west
but probably east.

[16] The Valverde detachment of 3 companies was under Capt. Walton, starting south on Nov. 2d from a point opposite Alburquerque.   Capt. Burgwin
with his dragoons also went to the relief of the traders.   There was a rumor
of a Mexican force advancing from the south.   The Navajos had also been
raiding Isleta and the southern towns, and Lieut. Grier pursued one party,
killing 3, and recovering captives and live-stock.   Walton reached Valverde
on Nov. 24th.   All kinds of rumors were current; sheep and cattle were repeatedly run off by Indians and others; and two volunteers were killed by
the savages.   An Englishman came as ambassador to induce the traders to
dismiss all American teamsters and guards, trust the Mexicans, pay 13 cents
per lb. on their goods, and enter Chihuahua unmolested.   Some were inclined
to accept this proposition; but Walton sent a force to Fra Cristóbal to prevent the passage of any part of the caravan.

after a day of speech-making, they consented to a treaty, which was formally signed on the 22d by Doniphan, Jackson, and Gilpin on the one side, and fourteen chieftains on the other.[17]   Its terms included "a firm and lasting peace" between the Navajos and Americans—the latter to include New Mexicans and Pueblos; mutual free trade, including visits for trading purposes; mutual restoration of all captives, and of all property taken since the 18th of August.   Gifts were exchanged, and then the parties separated.   The Americans returned by different routes, one division with the three regimental officers and a few native chieftains going by way of Zuñi, where on the 26th a treaty was concluded between the Zuñis and Navajos. All were reunited at Valverde about December 12th. The treaties, like dozens of earlier ones with the same tribes, had but slight practical effect; but the journals of the different branches of this complicated campaign if extant would doubtless furnish many interesting and valuable items of geographical information.[18]

Before the colonel's return from the Navajo campaign James Magoffin with Dr Connelly and a few others ventured southward, but were arrested at El Paso and carried as prisoners to Chihuahua; the traders also started in advance of the army, by which they were overtaken on the way; and a company of volunteers known as the Chihuahua Rangers left Santa Fé on December 1st under Captain Hudson, with the idea of opening communication with General Wool, but they also turned back to join the army before reaching El Paso.   Finally Doniphan's army of about 900 men left Valverde in three divisions on the 14th,

---

[17] The treaty of Ojo del Oso is given in *Hughes' Doniphan's Exped.*, 188–9.
[18] There is a very brief undated report of the campaign by Col Doniphan in the documents accompanying the president's message of Dec. 7, 1847. *U. S. Govt Doc.*, 30th cong. 1st sess., Sen. Ex. Doc. i., p. 496.   A detailed report is promised, but I have not found it.   The most complete narrative, and a very satisfactory one except in certain geographic respects, is that in *Hughes' Doniphan's Exped.*, 143–94.   The subject is also recorded more or less fully in the other narratives already cited in this chapter.   Collins, in *Ind. Aff. Report*, 1858, p. 188, tells us that the conditions of the treaty were not observed by the Indians, who continued to murder and steal as before.

16th, and 19th of December.   After passing the
Jornada del Muerto all were reunited on the 22d at
Doña Ana, including Hudson's company and the traders.   Two Mexican scouts were killed with one bullet
on the 24th; and at El Bracito, some 30 miles below
Doña Ana, on Christmas afternoon a force of the
enemy, estimated at about 600 regulars—Vera Cruz
dragoons, with cavalry and infantry from Chihuahua
—and 500 El Paso militia, was encountered.   These
troops, commanded by an officer named Ponce de
Leon, made a charge upon the Americans, but being
met by a volley of rifle bullets at short range were
forced to retreat, pursued for a short distance, and losing perhaps thirty men killed.[19]   No further opposition was encountered, and on December 27th, Doniphan took possession of El Paso, the citizens having
come out to meet him with a white flag, offering
surrender and asking for clemency and protection.
After a stay of forty-two days, and being reënforced
by 117 men of the artillery batallion under Clark and
Weightman from Santa Fé, the army marched on
February 8, 1847, for Chihuahua, which city they
occupied at the beginning of March, after a brilliant
victory over four times their own number of Mexican
troops at Sacramento.   General Wool was not here,
and after holding the town about two months to await
orders and protect the traders in the sale of their
goods, Doniphan marched on to Saltillo, presently
returning by water via New Orleans to Missouri as
the time of the volunteers had expired.   The expedi-

[19] Semi-official report of Lieut. C. H. Kibben of the artillery in *Cutts'
Conq.*, 77; *Brooks' Campaign*, 169–71.   K. says 'the number of their dead is
said to be at least 30; that of their wounded was slight so far as ascertained.'
Brooks, p. 87, says the Mexican loss in killed and wounded was about 200
men! Hughes, *Doniphan's Exped.*, 266, puts the loss at 71 killed, 5 prison-
ers, and not less than 150 wounded including their general, Ponce de Leon.
The Mexicans also lost a cannon.   The American loss was 7 or 8 wounded.
   Some additional references for the N. Mex. campaign in general are *Rip-
ley's War with Mexico*, i. 270–80; *Furber's Twelve Months' Volunteer*, 247–63,
437, et seq.; *Jenkins' Hist. Mex. War*, 135–40; *Mansfield's Mex. War*, 78–83;
Davis' El Gringo, 93 et seq.; *Miller*, in *Sta Fé, Centennial*, 24–6; *Brackett's
Hist. U. S. Cavalry*, 69–71, 104–7; also mention in many other works on Mex.,
N. Mex., and the war.

tion of the regiment had been a remarkable one, in some respects almost without parallel, though its most brilliant features do not pertain directly to the annals of New Mexico.

General Kearny's original instructions of June 3, 1846, from the secretary of war, included the following: "Should you conquer and take possession of New Mexico and California, or considerable places in either, you will establish temporary civil governments therein —abolishing all arbitrary restrictions that may exist, so far as it may be done with safety. In performing this duty it would be wise and prudent to continue in their employment all such of the existing officers as are known to be friendly to the United States, and will take the oath of allegiance to them. You may assure the people of these provinces that it is the wish and design of the United States to provide for them a free government with the least possible delay, similar to that which exists in our territories. They will then be called upon to exercise the rights of free men in electing their own representatives to the territorial legislature. It is foreseen that what relates to the civil government will be a difficult and unpleasant part of your duty, and much must necessarily be left to your own discretion. In your whole conduct you will act in such a manner as best to conciliate the inhabitants, and render them friendly to the United States."[20] Kearny's proclamation of August 22d, more or less in accordance with these instructions, though going in certain respects far beyond their letter, has already been presented in this chapter. From the first day of occupation, Captain Waldo, of the volunteers, was set at work translating all the Spanish and Mexican laws that could be found at Santa Fé; while Colonel Doniphan, a lawyer by profession, aided by Willard P. Hall— elected to congress during this absence—busied him-

[20] These instructions may be conveniently consulted in *Cutts' Conquest*, 246–7, though often repeated elsewhere.

self with the preparation of a code of laws founded in part on Waldo's fragmentary translations, but mainly on the laws of Missouri and Texas. Finally, on the 22d of September, the general published this code— still in force in New Mexico down to 1886—printed in English and Spanish with the old press and type found at the capital, and at the same time his appointment of governor and other officials, thus organizing the civil government deemed necessary.[21] With the code was submitted to the government at Washington an "organic law of the territory of New Mexico," which provided for a permanent territorial organization under the laws of the United States, naming the first Monday in August 1847 as the day for electing a delegate to congress.[22]

It was noticeable that Kearny's proclamations ignored the old theory that eastern New Mexico belonged to Texas. A still more notable feature was the clearly announced intention of retaining the country as a permanent possession of the United States. This was the first open avowal of the administration's real purpose to make this a war for the acquisition of territory, and not, as had been pretended, for the pro-

[21] Sept. 22, 1846, Kearny's report on the code and its publication; also his appointment of officers, in *Cutts' Conquest*, 64–5. The latter reads: 'Being duly authorized by the pres. of the U. S. of America, I hereby make the following appointments for the government of N. Mex., a territory of the U. S. The officers thus appointed will be obeyed and respected accordingly.' Governor, Charles Bent, part owner of Bent's Fort, married to a native of Taos; secretary, Donaciano Vigil, a native of New Mexico, of long official experience in various civil and military positions; marshal, Richard Dallam, an American mining operator at Los Placeres; district attorney, Francis P. Blair, Jr, in later years somewhat famous as congressman and politician; treasurer, Charles Blumner; auditor, Eugene Leitzendorfer, a Sta Fé trader, married to a daughter of the former governor, Santiago Abreu; judges of the superior court, Joab Houghton, a lawyer of later prominence in the territory, Antonio José Otero, of a prominent and influential Spanish family, and Charles Beaubien, a pioneer of 1827, married to a native wife. The biographic items are from *Prince's Hist. Sketches*, 367–8. The Kearny code, with the precedent bill of rights issued on the same date, may be found in *New Mexico, Compiled Laws*, Sta Fé, 1885, p. 82–129.

[22] *U. S. Gov. Doc.*, 29th cong. 2d sess., H. Ex. Doc. 19. I have not seen this document in its original form. Most of the papers are reprinted in *Cutts' Conq.*, and elsewhere, but not the organic law, which was not approved at Washington. *Cooke, Conquest*, 66, gives the date fixed for the election; also in *Niles' Reg.*, lxxii. 48, where it is stated that the whole doc. as printed filled 115 pages.

tection of Texan boundaries, the avenging of past wrongs, and the obtaining of indemnity for just claims. This brought the subject before congress, which body called on the president for all the instructions that had been given respecting civil government in New Mexico and California. In the debates this subject was utilized chiefly as a basis for attacks on the administration and denunciations of the war for conquest. Nobody cared what was done at Santa Fé except as it could furnish material for arguments on one side or the other of the great and complicated national struggle for political supremacy between the north and south. Belligerent rights were, however, pretty thoroughly discussed; and it was clearly shown that a temporary civil government might be, if the people were submissive and friendly, a legitimate and proper feature of a conqueror's military rule. This whole subject and others closely connected with it have been somewhat fully presented in the *History of California*, and repetition is not deemed necessary here.[23] General Kearny as a conqueror had absolute power, limited only by the requirements of humanity and justice, or international usage. He might enforce strict martial law, or protect the people's rights and interests by civil methods, as he saw fit. He had no power to make New Mexico a territory of the United States, or the people citizens, or non-submissive enemies traitors, nor could he in a sense exact an oath of allegiance to the United States. All these matters would be settled by the final treaty closing the war. But he might perhaps promise or threaten these things, or almost any others, and he might exact from officials any oath they could be induced to take. His promises the government at Washington, if the treaty should cede the territory, would be in equity under obligation to fulfil; but it would have no right to carry out his threats.

[23] See *Hist. Cal.*, v., chap. xxii., especially pp. 601 et seq. with ref. to *U. S. Govt. Doc.* and *Cong. Globe.* Cal. and N. Mex. were in precisely the same position, since the pretended rights of Texas were at this time practically ignored.

The president in his reply of December 22d, furnishing the desired information, declared that Kearny's
acts, so far as they purported to establish a permanent
territorial government, and to give the inhabitants
political rights as citizens, under the constitution of
the United States, had not been recognized or approved;
but that otherwise his acts, and the instructions on
which they were based, "were but the amelioration of
martial law, which modern civilization requires, and
were due, as well as the security of the conquest, to
the inhabitants of the conquered territory;" and moreover, "it will be apparent that if any excess of power
has been exercised, the departure has been the off-
spring of a patriotic desire to give to the inhabitants
the privileges and immunities so cherished by the people of our own country, and which they believed calculated to improve their condition and promote their
prosperity.   Any such excess has resulted in no practical injury, but can and will be early corrected in a
manner to alienate as little as possible the good feelings of the inhabitants of the conquered country."[24]
As I have remarked, congress paid very little atten-
tention to the matter, except as indicating the intention
of permanent occupation, which the president did not
pretend to deny.   Respecting the actual operations of
the civil government in 1846–7, practically nothing is
recorded; probably there was very little to record.

From the first there had been occasional rumors of
intended revolt among the natives as well as of attack
by forces from the south, but such rumors could be
traced to no definite foundation, and at the time of
Doniphan's departure no danger was apprehended.
Price had nearly 2,000 men with whose aid to keep
the province in subjection, though many of them were
on the sick-list.   The main force was stationed at
Santa Fé, but detachments were posted at other
points, including the dragoons under Captain Burg-

[24] *U. S. Govt. Doc.*, and *Cutts' Conquest*, as in note 22.

win at Alburquerque, a company under Captain
Hendley in the Mora valley, and another near
Cebolleta on the Navajo frontier. Soon after Doniphan left the capital, disquieting rumors again became
prevalent, and in December these became of so definite a nature that many arrests were made. The
result of an investigation is affirmed to have been the
disclosure of a carefully devised plot to regain possession of the country by killing the Americans and all
natives who had espoused their cause. The leaders
were Tomás Ortiz and Diego Archuleta, who under
the new régime were to be governor and comandante
general respectively; several of the priests were
prominent in the plot, notably padres Juan Felipe
Ortiz and José Manuel Gallegos; and many leading
citizens of the northern sections were involved.
Meetings were held at the house of Tomás Ortiz;
plans were minutely discussed and arranged; parts
were assigned to the leaders, who secretly visited
the different towns to incite the lower classes of
Mexicans and pueblo Indians; and the 19th of December was fixed for the rising. This date was subsequently changed to Christmas night, when the town
would be crowded with natives, and the Americans,
by reason of the festivities, would be off their guard.
Before this time, however, the plot was revealed,
perhaps by the mulatto wife of one of the conspirators, and many of the alleged leaders were arrested
by order of Colonel Price, though Ortiz and Archuleta escaped to the south.[25]

[25] This version is given with a few unimportant variations in all the general narratives that have been cited. Among the best is that in *Prince's Hist.
Sketches*, who, however, mainly follows Davis and Hughes. Prince says: 'It
was agreed that on the night of the appointed day those engaged in the conspiracy in Sta Fé were to gather in the parochial church, and remain concealed. Meanwhile friends from the surrounding country under the lead of
Archuleta were to be brought into the city, and distributed in various houses
where they would be unobserved. At midnight the church bell was to sound,
and then the men within the church were to sally forth, and all were to rendezvous immediately in the plaza, seize the cannon there, and aim them so as
to command the leading points, while detachments under special orders were
to attack the palace and the quarters of the American commandant, and
make them prisoners. The people throughout the whole north of the territory had been secretly notified, and were only awaiting news of the rising

From the meagre details of testimony extant, as
repeated in substance by the different writers, from
the fact that no positive evidence could be found against
the parties arrested, and from the confidence felt by
the authorities that all danger ended with the revela-
tion of the plot, it would appear that not very much
was brougth to light by the investigation, or rather
that the conspiracy had not assumed any very formidable proportions.   There is no reason to doubt,
however, from this testimony and later developments
that Ortiz and Archuleta had really plotted a rising,
and had found many adherents, though nothing like a
general consent of the leading men of different sections
and different classes had been secured.   Perhaps the
only wonder under the circumstances is, that the movement was not more wide-spread.   No blame or taint
of treason could be imputed to the New Mexican people—except to individual officials who had promised

at Sta Fé to join in the revolt and make it a sure success.' Says Col Price,
in his report of Feb. 15, 1847: 'About the 15th of Dec. last I received information of an attempt to excite the people of this territory against the American govt.   This rebellion was headed by Thomas Ortiz and Diego Archuleta.
An officer, formerly in the Mexican service, was seized, and on his person
was found a list of all the disbanded Mex. soldiers in the vicinity of Sta Fé.
Many other persons supposed to be implicated were arrested, and a full investigation proved that many of the most influential citizens in the northern
part of this territory were engaged in the rebellion.   After the arrest above
mentioned and the flight of Ortiz and Archuleta, the rebellion appeared to be
suppressed; but this appearance was deceptive. *Sta Fé, Conq.*, 27–8.   On
Dec. 26th, Gov. Bent writes: 'On the 17th inst I received information from
a Mexican, friendly to our govt, that a conspiracy was on foot among the
native Mexicans....I immediately brought intu requisition every means in
my power to ascertain who were the movers in the rebellion, and have succeeded in securing 7 of the secondary conspirators.   The military and civil
officers are now both in pursuit of the two leaders and prime movers....So
far as I am informed, this conspiracy is confined to the 4 northern counties
of the territory, and the men considered as leaders cannot be said to be men
of much standing.'   After securing information, etc., the gov. turned the
the matter over to the military authorities. *N. Mex. and Cal., Mess. and
Doc.*, July 24, 1848; *U. S. Govt Doc.*, 30th cong. 1st sess., H. Ex. Doc. 70,
p. 17.   The only definite and literally preserved testimony of the time is that
of José María Sanchez.   He says that on Dec. 15th (from other sources it
appears that the 1st meeting had been held on the 12th) he was summoned
by Miguel Pino to a meeting at the house of Ortiz.   He found there Tomás
Ortiz, Diego Archuleta, Nicolás and Miguel Pino, Santiago Armijo, Manuel
Chavez, Domingo Vaca, Pablo Dominguez, and Juan Lopez.   Tomás Vaca,
Blas Ortega, and the priest Leiva are also named.   (Prince says that several
of these men proved their innocence, notably Chavez and the Pinos.)   Then
he narrates the plottings substantially as given above in this note. *Sta Fé
Conq.*, 27.

allegiance—had they chosen to rise in a body against the American invaders. The temptation for such a rising was strong. The national pride of many leading citizens had been deeply wounded by Armijo's disgraceful surrender of their country without a struggle. High officials might naturally feel that in Mexico they would be regarded as implicated in the general's actions and regarded as traitors. The American occupation had as yet brought no benefit to the country. The natural bitterness of the lower and middle classes had been aggravated rather than appeased by recent occurrences. The situation was somewhat similar to that in southern California just before the Flores revolt. We have no positive evidence of gross outrages or oppression of the natives; indeed, in a sense, the efforts of the American authorities were constant and generally effective to protect them in their legal rights; but the volunteers were overbearing, abusive, and quarrelsome, taking no pains to conceal how much they despised all that was Mexican; and instances of individual insult and outrage were frequent. The natives were naturally revengeful, many of them vicious, ignorant, and ready to listen to the exaggerated charges and promises of the few reckless characters, who from motives of ambition or resentment were bent on stirring up a revolt. Moreover, the New Mexicans noted the inroads of sickness among their invaders, their difficulty in obtaining supplies, their comparatively small number, and their distance from reënforcements. Again, they probably received false news respecting Mexican successes and prospects in the south; and it is not unlikely that they heard of the Californian revolt. There was much jealousy against those natives who had been given office on the part of those who had lost their old positions; and it was asserted by Senator Benton that Archuleta's hostility arose from the fact that the Americans had not kept their promises of leaving the western country to his control. Yet notwithstanding all this, so strong was the influ ence of those who had directly or indirectly espoused the American cause, of those whose interest required a continuance of the new régime, and of those who realized the impossibility of a revolt that should be permanently successful, that the masses of the people looked with little favor on the movement, and it was practically abandoned, as I have no doubt, on the flight of Ortiz and Archuleta.

But the embers of revolt were left smouldering among the Indians of Taos, and they were fanned into flame by a few reckless conspirators, who trusted that once begun the revolt would become general. Governor Bent—having on January 5th issued a proclamation in which he announced the discovery of the plot, the flight of the leaders, and also the victory of Doniphan at El Bracito[26]—believing that all danger was past, went on the 14th with Sheriff Lee and others to Taos, his home. On the 19th, the Indians came from their pueblo to demand the release of two prisoners. On this being refused, they killed the sheriff and prefect; then attacked the governor's house, killing and scalping Bent and two others.[27] Messengers were at once despatched in all directions to announce that the first blow had been struck, and to urge a general rising. It does not clearly appear that the Taos outbreak had been definitely planned in advance, though most writers state that such was the case, as indeed it may have been. Many Mexicans at once joined the Indians. At Arroyo Hondo, some twelve miles away, eight men were attacked on the same day at Turley's mill and distillery, and seven of them killed after a desperate resistance of two days.[28] Two

[26] In *Cutts' Conq.*, 218.

[27] The victims were Charles Bent, gov.; Stephen Lee, sheriff; James W. Leal, circuit attorney; Cornelio Vigil, prefect; Narciso Beaubien, son of the judge; and Pablo Jaramillo, brother-in-law of Bent.

[28] The victims were Simeon Turley, Albert Turbush (or Cooper), Wm Hatfield, Louis Tolque, Peter Robert, Joseph Marshall, and Wm Austin. John Albert, though wounded, escaped, and reached a camp on the Arkansas. Ruxton, *Adven.*, 203, 227–30, was encamped there at the time, and gives the most complete account of the fight as related by Albert. The two killed at Rio Colorado were Mark Head and Wm Harwood; at Mora, Waldo, Benj. Prewitt, R. Culver, Noyes, and others not named.

other Americans were killed at Rio Colorado; and at Mora, eight traders who had just arrived in a wagon from Las Vegas, including L. L. Waldo, brother of Captain Waldo of the volunteers. At Las Vegas the alcalde not only fulfilled his oath of allegiance, but induced the people to remain quiet.

Through intercepted letters from the rebels, calling for aid, Colonel Price at Santa Fé heard of the revolt on the 20th. Ordering reënforcements from Albur- querque, he marched northward on the 23d with 353 men, including Angney's infantry and a company of Santa Fé volunteers under Captain St Vrain,[29] and four howitzers under Lieutenant Dyer. The enemy, 1,500 strong, as was estimated, and commanded by Jesus Tafoya, was encountered on the 24th near La Cañada, or Santa Cruz, and put to flight with a loss of 36 killed, including General Tafoya. Price lost two men.[30] Four days later, at Los Luceros, reën- forcements came up under Captain Burgwin; on the 29th the foe was again driven from a strong position at the pass of El Embudo, with a loss of twenty killed; and the 3d of February, after a hard march through deep snow, the army reached the pueblo of Taos, within whose ancient structures the rebels had forti- fied themselves. A hard day's fighting on the 4th, marked by a continuous cannonade and several as- saults, put the Americans in possession of the church and that part of the pueblo west of the stream. About 150 of the Indians are said to have been killed, including one of their leaders, Pablo Chavez; while the American loss of seven killed and 45 wounded—many of them fatally—included Captain Burgwin. Next morning the Indians sued for peace,

[29] Prince gives the muster-roll of this company. Capt. Ceran St Vrain, Lieut. Charles Metcalf and George Peacock; rank and file 65 men. There are several Spanish names.

[30] Price's report of the campaign, dated Feb. 15th, as given in *Cutts' Con- quest*, 223–31, and in several of the narratives, is the best authority. In *N. Mex. and Cal., Mess.*, July 24, 1848, pp. 18 et seq., are several reports and proclamations of Acting Gov. Vigil during the campaign. Prince, *Hist. Sk.*, 319, tells us that the S. Juan Indians, who had joined the rebels under com- pulsion, surrendered before the fight.

HIST. ARIZ. AND N. MEX. 28

which was granted on their giving up Tomás, one of the leading conspirators, who was soon killed in the guard-house by a private. Pablo Montoya, another leader, also fell into the hands of Price, and was hanged on the 7th, after which only one of the chief conspirators, Manuel Cortés, survived. The army returned to the capital, where, on the 13th, occurred the funeral cere-monies of Governor Bent and Captain Burgwin.[31]

[31] Price's report is found in *Niles' Reg.*, lxxii. 121; and there is also another diary of the campaign in *Id.*, 119–20. I have plans of the three battles of La Cañada, Embudo, and Taos, in *Mex. War Col.*, v. no. 26. Rosters of troops in 1846–7, with losses, etc., in *U. S. Govt Doc.*, 31st cong. 1st sess., H. Ex. Doc. 24. Also lists of casualties in *Niles' Reg.*, lxxii. 128. The remains of Burgwin, Hendley, and other officers were later in the year removed from Sta Fé to their homes in the states. *Hughes*, 397.

Unfortunately on the revolt as on the American occupation we have practically nothing of real value from Mexican sources. Most items in Mexican newspapers and other publications are mere inaccurate references to the fact that a revolt had taken place. Others dwell on and perhaps exaggerate the oppressive conduct of the Americans provoking the revolt; and generally exaggerate its success throughout the year 1747. Says Busta-mante, *Invasion de los Americanos*, MS., 66: ' Con bastante temor estoy respecto de N. Mex., donde se frustró un alzamiento que estaba á punto de realizarse y lo evitó un nuevo-mexicano denunciante; habian ya tomado dos cañones y tuvieron que devolverselos. Han cometido crímenes horribles exigiendoles tambien una contribucion de 80,000 pesos. El alma de esta sub-levacion fue el cura Ortiz de Sta Fé. Aquel pueblo ha recibido un tríste disengaño de lo que son y deben prometerse de tales malvados, á quienes tenian afecciones por un comercio proveyendose de cuanto necesitaban, y que no son lo mismo comerciantes que conquistadores orgullosos.' Notice of Gov. Bent's death in *Id.*, *Mem. Hist.*, MS., March 11, 1847. In *Id.*, 207, Apr. 13th, it is announced that the N. Mexicans had killed 1,200 of the Americans. 'Este es el verdadero modo de recobrar la libertad.' In *Id.*, vii. 11–12, May 4th, the outbreak is said to have originated in the killing by a N. Mex. of his wife whom a Yankee had seduced and carried to the cuartel. A mob formed to support the native; the troops brought out 2 cannon, but did not fire them from fear of killing Amer. in the crowd, and made a charge; then a by-stander fired the cannon in their rear into the crowd of friends and foes; and the *cíbolos* took advantage of the slaughter and fright to enter the cuartel, seize the arms, and kill 'á cuanto pintaba en Yankee.' 'It is added that Padre Ortiz is marching on Chihuahua with 4,000 Ind. and N. Mexi-cans'! In *Id.*, May 8th, it is said that the Yankee invaders of Chih. (Doni-phan's army) are retreating on account of the news of a general slaughter in the north. The N. Mex. were aided by the Navajos. And on July 28th, *Id.*, 164, more of the *triunfo en N. Mexico*, where only 300 Amer. were left who would soon be exterminated. The *Sonorense* of March 5, 1847, copies from the *Registro Oficial* of Durango an account of the failure of the 1st plot, revealed by a friend of the 'infamous' Vigil y Alarid. However, a new movement was daily expected, which would wipe out the Yankees, who had lost their horses and wagons, and had no money. Conflicts are frequent, caused by the outrages of the soldiers, who, except 300 veterans (the dragoons), are chiefly Irish and Italians! The N. Mexicans are very sad at being deemed allies of the Yankees, whom they detest. They carried off 2 cannon from the plaza, but had to give them up. See also *Id.*, May 28th, Aug. 20th, Nov. 12th; *El Razonador*, Oct. 30th, Dec. 11th; *Iris Español*, May 8th, June 12th; *Arco Iris*, Aug. 7th.

With the exception of Price's report of this campaign, there does not exist, and cannot be formed, anything like a continuous record of the insurrection, or of the subsequent annals of the year. After the defeat at Taos, it was only east of the mountains, and chiefly under the direction of Manuel Cortés, that hostilities were continued. At the first, as we have seen, Waldo and party had been killed at Mora, but Las Vegas had been kept in subjection by the efforts of the alcalde, and the presence of Captain Isaac R. Hendley with his company. He occupied Las Vegas on January 20th, concentrated his grazing guards, and on the 24th appeared with 225 men before Mora, where he attacked several hundred insurgents, killing 25 or 30 and capturing fifteen prisoners, but was himself killed with a few of his men, and the party was repulsed. A little later Captain Morin renewed the attack, and drove the inhabitants into the mountains, destroying the town and a large supply of grain. In May a grazing party and also a wagon train were attacked, one or two men killed, and a large number of horses and mules driven off. Following the marauders' trail, Major Edmonson overtook them, 300 or 400 strong, in a deep cañon of the Red River, but after a fight of several hours, in which he killed many of the Mexicans and Indians, and lost only one man, he was forced to retire. Next morning the enemy had fled. Late in June there was trouble at Las Vegas. Lieutenant Robert T. Brown and three men, pursuing horse-thieves, were killed; whereupon Edmonson made an attack, killed ten or twelve men, found indications of a new revolt, captured the town, and sent some fifty prisoners to Santa Fé, also burning a mill belonging to the alcalde, who was charged with complicity. In July a party of 31 soldiers was attacked at La Ciénega not far from Taos, Lieutenant Larkin and five others being killed. On the approach of reënforcements, however, the enemy fled. In the same month, Edmonson is said to have destroyed the town of Las

Pias (?) with considerable loss to the foe, and to have marched by way of Anton Chico to La Cuesta, where were some 400 insurgents under Cortés and Gonzalez. Fifty captives were taken, the rest fleeing to the mountains, and many horses were recovered. After July we have no definite record of hostilities.

Of the prisoners brought to the capital by Price, and sent in later by his officers, some fifteen or twenty, perhaps more, were tried by court-martial, sentenced to death, and executed. These included six of the murderers of Brown, who were hanged on the 3d of August. Many others are said to have been flogged and set at liberty. Others accused of complicity in the original plot were turned over to the civil authorities. In March four of these were indicted by the grand jury for treason, 25 being discharged for want of evidence, and one of the four convicted and sentenced to death. This was Antonio María Trujillo, father-in-law of Diego Archuleta, an infirm old man of high standing, in whose behalf a petition for pardon was sent to Washington by Governor Vigil and others. At the same time District Attorney Blair asked for instructions, since the accused had pleaded lack of jurisdiction on the part of the court. In reply the secretary of war for the government took the ground that, while the New Mexican insurgents might properly be punished even with the death penalty for their offence against the constituted authorities, they could not be prosecuted for treason against the United States, since they were not yet citizens. For similar reasons the president declined to pardon Trujillo, but counselled mercy in his case. Apparently, he and others convicted at the May term were discharged or pardoned by Price or the governor; but not, as is stated by some writers, by the president.[32]

While Indians from some of the pueblos were aiding the insurgent Mexicans in their guerilla warfare

---

[32] Corresp. in *N. Mex. and Cal.*, *Mess.*, July 24, 1848, p. 26–34. Prince states that 15 were executed in all, 8 Mexicans and 7 Indians.

against the Americans, with aid from various bands of Apaches and others, the tribes of the plains—the Comanches, Pawnees, and Arapahoes, incited and aided, as the Americans believed, by Mexicans—became troublesome from April to August on the Santa Fé trail. Hardly a party, large or small, traders or soldiers, crossed the plains without suffering from their depredations. Many were killed, and large numbers of horses, mules, and oxen were lost. Lieutenant Love, with a company of dragoons escorting government funds, had five of his men killed, and lost his animals in June. Later in the year comparative security was restored by the stationing of troops at different points; and then the Indians, in their turn, were made the objects of outrage, as when a party of Pawnees were treacherously massacred at Fort Mann. In the west and north-west the Navajos had paid no heed to their treaty with Doniphan, but continued their raids for plunder on the settlements of the Rio Grande.[33]

[33] On Indian troubles, which I make no attempt to present in detail, see *Cutts' Conquest*, 234–5, 240–3; *Hughes' Doniphan's Exped.*, 403–5; *Niles' Reg.*, lxxii.-iii.; passim; *Honolulu Polynesian*, iv. 89; *Arco Iris*, July 5, 1847; *Ind. Aff. Rept*, 1858, p. 188. Gov. Bent had been ex-officio superintendent of Ind. affairs; and his report on the various tribes and means to keep them in subjection, dated Nov. 10, 1846, is given in *Cal. and N. Mex.*, *Mess. and Doc.*, 1850, pp. 191 et seq. He estimates their number as 36,950, but this includes tribes whose range extended far beyond N. Mex. proper.

Some additional references for the U. S. occupation, and the revolt in 1876–7, are as ·follows: *Patton's Hist. U. S.*, 738–41; *S. F. Californian*, May 29, 1847; *Frost's Mex. War*, 217, 219, 285–90; *Taos Co. Herald*, Aug. 22, 1884; *Honolulu Polynesian*, iv. 43; *Mayer's Mex. Aztec*, i. 343, 353; *Frost's Ind. Wars*, 291–3; *Young's Hist. Mex.*, 287, 436–40; *Arny's Centen. Oration*, 24–7; *Spaniards in N. Mex.*, MS., 13; *Bancroft's New Mex., Miscel.*, MS., 16; *S. F. Cal. Star*, Apr. 24, May 22, 29, Oct. 9, 16, 1847; *Harper's Mag.*, July 1880, p. 191–2; *Murray's Pict. Hist. U. S.*, 474–5; *Oswald, Californien*, 82; *Amer. Quar. Reg.*, i. 14; *Harrison's Battlefields*, 435–7, 446–8; *Sta Fe Centen.*, 24–6; *Lossing's Hist. U. S.*, 486–7; *Watts' Sta Fé Affairs*, MS., 11–14; *Peterson's Mil. Heroes*, ii. 66–73.

CHAPTER XVIII.

MILITARY RULE IN NEW MEXICO.

1847–1850.

AT Santa Fé and in the settlements generally for
six months after the revolt, the state of affairs was
far from satisfactory, worse in every respect than
before.   For a time, indeed, a greater degree of vigilance and discipline was observed; but the former,
with its accompaniments of severe punishments, habitual distrust, and oppressive regulations, rapidly destroyed the confidence and friendliness before shown
by large portions of the native population; while the
latter soon became relaxed, and the soldiers more
turbulent and unmanageable than ever.   The New
Mexicans were regarded as at heart deadly foes, and
were treated accordingly.   Sickness continued its
ravages; supplies were still obtained with difficulty;
the Indians constantly attacked the caravans on the
plains; Navajo raids on the settlements never ceased,
there being some reason to believe that they were not
discouraged by the Americans so long as directed

against the natives; and the situation was still further
complicated by disagreements between military and
civil authorities, and by serious dissensions among military officers, there being much dissatisfaction with
Colonel Price's management.[1]

The volunteers' terms of enlistment expired at
different dates from June to August, causing fears that
the country would be left without sufficient protection
against a new revolt. At the same time, however, a
new volunteer force was organized in Missouri for
this service. On the 6th of August a company of the
1st Dragoons, Lieutenant Love, reached Santa Fé
with $350,000 of government funds. On the 17th
Colonel Price, leaving besides the three dragoon
companies a battalion of reënlisted volunteers under
Lieutenant-colonel Willock, started with his men for

---

[1] It is fair to state that there was a strong political element, and therefore
presumably more than one side in the Price controversy. 'The soldiery
have degenerated into a military mob, are the most open violators of law and
order, and daily heap insult and injury upon the people.' No protection
against Indians as promised by Kearny. 'One half the captains do not know
the number of their men nor where they are to be found; and they themselves
are to be seen nightly in fandangos and even less reputable places of dissipation. The soldiers are never drilled or mustered; all is insubordination, misrule, and confusion. About one fifth of the whole command have died from
the effects of dissipation...The want of ability and military knowledge in
the commander, added to his inability to control his officers or soldiers, can
only produce the strongest feelings of disgust and hatred, and desire to rebel
among the native inhabitants...It is certain that if such a state of things
were to be found in any of the territories of the U. S., neither the civil nor
military govt would exist for a week.' Letter in *Niles' Reg.*, lxxii. 252.
Since the suppression of the revolt, 'I regret to say, nearly the whole territory has been the scene of violence, outrage, and oppression by the volunteer
soldiery against all alike...The civil authorities find themselves utterly
powerless...The mil. authorities are incapable of controlling this lawless
soldiery or are entirely indifferent.' By the Navajos over '50 citizens have
been killed or carried into captivity, and more than 60,000 head of horses,
mules, and sheep carried off from the Rio Abajo.' The Amer. therefore appear to the N. Mex. as practically allies of their savage foes. *Id.*, lxxiii. 155.
'All is hubbub and confusion here; discharged volunteers leaving, drunk;
and volunteers not discharged remaining, drunk.' Another letter in *Id.* New
Mex. under neither U. S. nor Mex. laws; 'los caprichos, los rencores, y el
aguardiente estan posesionados del gobierno civil y militar.' *Sonorense*, Nov.
12, 1847, from *El Faro* of Oct. 26th. Hughes, *Doniphan's Exped.*, 399–400,
tells us that the Mex. could no longer carry arms or ride about the country
with impunity. The soldiers 'scarcely spared the innocent and unoffending,'
though there were no acts of violence (!) and a 'suspicious quietude' prevailed.
June 26th the sec. of war writing to Price alludes unofficially to rumors of
lax discipline, which of course are not believed; still it would be well for P.
to 'brace up' somewhat and be very careful. *N. Mex. and Cal., Mess.*, July
24, 1848, p. 34.

the states, meeting on the way various bodies of the new troops. These included two regiments of volunteers, one of infantry under colonels Newby and Boyakin, the other of cavalry under Ralls and Jones; also an infantry battalion under Lieutenant-colonel Easton, and later another battalion of cavalry and artillery under Lieutenant-colonel Gilpin, known as the Indian Battalion, and at first stationed on the plains to keep hostile tribes in order. There is nothing of importance recorded respecting military affairs at Santa Fé after August; but in December Price came back as a brigadier-general to resume the command. The force was now nearly 3,000 men, with a part of which the general marched south, and in March 1848 fought the last battle of the war at Santa Cruz de Rosales near Chihuahua.[2] On their return north and the announcement of peace, the volunteers, except two companies, went home to the states, starting in August or September. At the same time the force of regulars was slightly increased by reënforcements from Chihuahua. In 1849 the force was still further increased till it numbered 885 men, including a garrison at El Paso. Four companies of volunteers were also called into service in March 1849; and a company of Mexicans and pueblo Indians served in a Navajo compaign. During Price's absence the military command had been held by Colonel E. W. B. Newby in 1847, and by Major Benjamin L. Beall in 1848. Major John M. Washington assumed the command in September of that year, and in October 1849 was succeeded by Lieutenant-colonel John Monroe.[3]

[2] On military movements and distribution of troops, see *N. Mex. and Cal., Mess.*, July 24, 1848, p. 28; *Niles' Register*, lxxii. 375; lxxiii. 76–7, 155, 246, 256, 305; *Hughes' Doniphan's Exped.*, 398, 405–7; *Cutts' Conq.*, 240; *Brackett's U. S. Cavalry*, 122; and especially, on the Chihuahua campaign and Maj. Gilpin's operations against the Indians, *U. S. Govt Doc.*, 30th cong. 2d sess., H. Ex. Doc. 1, p. 113–51.

[3] We have but few details of military matters in 1848–9, except certain Ind. campaigns and explorations to be noted later. One comp. of horse artill. and one of 2d dragoons came with Washington from Chih. in Sept. 1848. Co. C 1st dragoons, Lieut. Whittlesey, was stationed at Taos in Oct. In

We have seen that the government at Washington, while not ostensibly recognizing General Kearny's acts so far as they made New Mexico a territory—and its people citizens—of the United States, did recognize his right to establish a temporary civil government for the management of territorial affairs. Charles Bent as governor, and other officials as already named, were appointed in September 1846, the native prefects, alcaldes, and other local authorities being for the most part continued in office on taking the oath of allegiance. During the last months of 1846 very little for good or bad was done by the new civil authorities; and after the revolt their powers were still further subordinated to those of the military, a state of things causing many complaints on the part of the people. On the death of Governor Bent in January 1847, Secretary Vigil became acting governor. He desired the appointment of a successor, recommending Céran St Vrain, but the authorities at Washington disclaimed all powers in the matter, and in December Vigil himself was appointed governor by General Price. In the same month a legislative assembly met at Santa Fé, accomplishing and attempting nothing of importance, so far as can be

Nov. the force was 3 comp. 1st dragoons, 1 comp. 2d dragoons, and 1 battery 3d artillery. In 1849, 4 comp. 3d inf., and 2 comp. 2d artill., arrived in June; 1 comp. 2d dragoons came from Ft Leavenworth July 11th; 2 comp. of the same left Cal. to relieve the 1st dragoons; 4 comp. 3d infantry and 2 comp. 2d artill., Lieut.-col Alexander, came from Ft Leavenworth July 23d; and 6 comp. 3d inf., Maj. Van Horn, arrived at El Paso Sept. 8th. Thus in Nov. 1849, there was a force of 885 men stationed at 7 posts, as follows: Sta Fé 1 comp. 2d artill.; Taos 1 comp. 2d drag.; Alburquerque, ditto; Doña Ana, ditto; Socorro part of 1 comp., ditto; El Paso, 6 comp. 3d inf.; for posts to be established 1 comp. 2d artill., and 4. comp. 3d inf. N. Mexico formed the 9th military department. Adj.-gen.'s reports, etc., in *U. S. Govt Doc.*, 30th cong. 2d sess., H. Ex. Doc. i., 161-2, 165, 225; *Id.*, 31st cong. 1st sess., H. Ex. Doc. 1, pt i., p. 182, 184; *Id.*, 31st cong. 2d sess., H. Ex. Doc. 1, pt ii., p. 291-301; also Maj. W.'s reports 1848-9, in *Id.*, 31st cong. 1st sess., H. Ex. Doc. 5, p. 104-16. Oct. 13, 1848, sec. war to Maj. Washington, presumes the volunteers will have departed; cannot send more regulars before June 1849. *Id.*, 31st cong. 1st sess., H. Ex. Doc. 17, p. 263. The payment of volunteers' claims for services against Ind., etc., in N. Mex. in '48 et seq., was still before congress in '60-3. *Id.*, 36th cong. 1st sess., H. Com. no. 537; 37th cong. 3d sess., H. Com. no. 52; also in 1870-1. *Cong. Globe*, 1870-1, p. 633; and in '74, 43d cong. 1st sess., H. Ex. Doc. 272. See also military items in *Niles' Reg.*, lxxiv.-v., passim.

known.[4] Vigil's rule seems to have continued nominally until October 11, 1848.   A newspaper, the Santa
Fé *Republican,* was published from the 4th of September.

By the treaty of Guadalupe Hidalgo, finally ratified
on May 30, 1848, and proclaimed at Santa Fé in
August, New Mexico became part of United States
territory, the boundary on the south being the Rio
Grande, the Upper Gila, and a line—of which more
will be said later—uniting these rivers just above the
latitude of El Paso.   The people were given a choice
of citizenship between the two republics, and pending a
decision were assured of full protection for their persons, property, and religious faith.   News of the treaty
produced practically no immediate changes in the territory, except the departure of the volunteer troops.
In the matter of civil government, the new status of
the country involved some perplexing questions, which
seem, however, not to have greatly troubled the New
Mexican mind at first.   The military régime was
properly at an end, and the civil government organized as a temporary phase of the military occupation,
strictly speaking, ended with it; but the position
assumed by the administration at Washington, and
carried out by the military commanders, was that
"the termination of the war left an existing govern-

---

[4] Ritch, *Legislative Blue-book of the Territory of N. Mexico,* Sta Fé, 1887—an
excellent compendium of official annals—gives on p. 98–9 the members of the
assembly which met on Dec. 6th, and an extract on educational matters from
Gov. Vigil's message.   Of the council Antonio Sandoval was president, Henry
Henrie, clerk, and James Hubble, doorkeeper.   Members, central district,
José Fran. Vaca, J. A. Sandoval, Juan Tullis; northern district, Nicolás
Lucero, Pascual Martinez; southern district, Ant. Sandoval, Juan Otero;
house-speaker, Wm Z. Angney; clerk, James Giddings; doorkeeper, E. J.
Vaughan; members, Sta Fé county, Manuel Álvarez, Angney, Ant. M.
Ortiz; Sta Ana co., Tomás Vaca, Jesus Sandoval; S. Miguel co., Miguel
Sanchez, Ant. Sais, Levi J. Keithlay; Rio Arriba co., José R. Vigil, José
Ant. Manzanares, Mariano Lucero; Taos co., José Martin, Geo. Gold, Ant.
José Ortiz; Bernalillo co., Juan Perea, Rafael Armijo; Valencia co., Wm
Skinner, Juan Cruz Vaca, Juan C. Chavez, Rafael Luna, Juan Sanchez.   Ac-
cording to *Id., Chron. Annals,* 19, Gov. Vigil's appointment was on Dec.
17th, and P. José Ant. Martinez headed a petition for U. S. citizenship.
According to *Niles' Reg.,* lxxiii. 305, a bill was passed to authorize the elec-
tion of delegates to consider annexation to the U. S.   In the *Sta Fé New
Mexican,* Aug. 28, 1877, is a synopsis of Gov. V.'s message.

ment, a government de facto, in full operation; and this will continue, with the presumed consent of the people, until congress shall provide for them a territorial government." Accordingly, Governor Vigil ruled for a few months, and after him the commandants Washington and Monroe, there being no attempt to appoint a purely civil successor to Vigil. The state of things was like that in California, in the history of which country the reader will find some additional matter on the general subject.[5] This solution of the difficulty was, perhaps, as satisfactory as any that could have been devised; and the New Mexicans did well in following the advice of the president "to live peaceably and quietly under the existing government" for a "few months," until congress should attend to their civil needs. Senator Benton, however, took it upon himself to give contrary advice.[6] Declaring all that had been done by the military authorities to be null and void, he counselled the people "to meet in convention—provide for a cheap and simple government—and take care of yourselves until congress can provide for you." And they did hold a convention at the call of Governor Vigil on October 10th; which body, however, contented itself with sending a memorial, or petition, to congress, asking for the "speedy organization by law of a territorial civil government;" and at the same time protesting against dismemberment in favor of Texas, and against the introduction of slavery.[7]

[5] See *Hist. Cal.*, v., chap. xxii., this series. In Cal., however, the treaty found the military governor already in possession of the civil power. I have found no definite orders or reasons assigned for not having continued Vigil in power, or appointed a successor; but I suppose there were orders similar to those sent to Kearny and Mason in Cal., but of later date.

[6] Benton's letter of Aug. 28, 1848, to people of Cal. and N. Mex., in *Niles' Reg.*, lxxiv. 244-5.

[7] Record of the convention in *Ritch's Blue-book*, 99-100. Ant. José Martinez was pres., J. M. Giddings clerk, Henry Henrie interpreter, and Thos White doorkeeper. Ex-gov. Fran. Sarracino, Gov. Vigil, J. H. Quinn. and Juan Perea were appointed as a committee to prepare a memorial, which was signed Oct. 14th, by A. J. Martinez, Elias P. White, Juan Perea, Ant. Sais, Santiago Archuleta, James H. Quinn, Manuel A. Otero, Don. Vigil, Fran. Sarracino, Gregorio Vigil, Ramon Luna, Chas Beaubien, and José Pley. The mem. was sent to Benton and John M. Clayton, with a request to repre-

The expenses of the civil government were partly paid during the military régime by the duties on imports; and after February 1848, General Price ordered a duty of six per cent to be still collected on imports from the United States. The citizens and traders held meetings in August to protest against such illegal exaction on goods introduced from one part of the United States to another. Price declined to modify the order, which he regarded as a measure of absolute necessity, the only source of revenue; but the government at Washington sustained the people, and in October ordered the refunding of all duties collected since the 30th of May. Consequently, salaries and other expenses went for the most part unpaid, and in 1851, when the old régime came to an end, there was a debt of $31,562.[8]

sent the territorial interests at Washington. It was received in the senate Dec. 13th, evoking a little storm of comment, especially from southern men who were astounded at the 'insolence' of the N. Mexican claim. *Niles' Reg.*, lxxiv. 407. Nov. 8th, Maj. Washington to sec. of war, mentioning the convention, stating that the Kearny code was still in force, and representing the importance of fixing a permanent system as soon as possible. *U. S. Govt Doc.*, 31st cong. 1st sess., H. Ex. Doc. 5, p. 104. Davis' version, *El Gringo*, 109, is as follows: 'In the fall of 1848, Wm Z. Angney, a lawyer of very considerable talent, and late a captain in the army,...returned from Missouri full of the idea set forth in Mr Benton's letter, and endeavored to induce the people of N. Mex. to follow the course he recommended. Col Washington, ...finding that an excitement was growing up on the subject, issued a proclamation, dated the 23d of Nov., 1848, commanding the inhabitants to abstain from "participating in or being movers of seditious meetings;" after which public meetings ceased for a time, and all things went on quietly. In Dec. of the same year' (the dates must be wrong) 'a convention...assembled in Sta Fé, and memorialized congress for a territorial govt, but none was granted during that session....N. Mex. not having a repres. in Wash....the people resolved to send an agent there. A movement to this effect was put on foot in May 1849, which resulted in Hugh N. Smith being sent,...his expenses being borne by an association of private individuals. This begat an opposition on the part of certain gentlemen who coveted the position for one of their own number,...mainly Maj. Weightman and Mr Angney, who stirred up the public mind, and held several meetings at Sta Fé.' Then followed Beall's proclamation, and the convention which elected Smith as a delegate, as narrated a little later in my text.

[8] Meetings, etc., at Sta Fé. *Niles' Reg.*, lxxiv. 259–60, from *St Louis Republican* and *Sta Fé Republican*. Order of sec. war, Oct. 12th, in *Cal. and N. Mex., Mess.*, 1850, p. 261. In his message of July 24th, the president said the civil govt had been supported out of military exactions and contributions from the enemy. 'No part of the expense has been paid out of the treasury of the U. S.' Gov. Washington on Nov. 8th wrote that there would be no govt funds unless Price's order was enforced. A report of the sec. war, May 5, 1852, is devoted to the matter of civil expenses and the debt. *U. S. Govt Doc.*, 32d cong. 1st sess., Sen. Ex. Doc. 71. It contains several communications

In September 1849 another convention assembled
at Santa Fé, consisting of nineteen delegates elected
by the people under a proclamation issued by Lieutenant-colonel Beall, acting as governor in Major
Washington's absence. This body proceeded to elect
Hugh N. Smith as a delegate to congress, to adopt a
plan, or basis, for the territorial government, the establishment of which he was to urge at Washington,
and to prepare a series of instructions for his guidance. A notable feature of these documents, as distinguished from the petition of 1848, was the absence
of protests against slavery and Texan encroachments.
The territory was simply to be bounded on the east
by Texas.[9] Governor Washington, it appears, de-

on the subject, including a tabular statement extending from Sept. 22, 1846,
to March 31, 1850. The amount already paid to Dec. 22, 1850, was $12,098;
amount due $26,504, or with estimate to March 22, 1851, $81,562. The official
list seems worth preserving, and is as follows: Gov.—salary $2,000—Charles
Bent from Sept. 22, '46, Donaciano Vigil from Jan. 19, '47, J. M. Washington
from Oct. 11, '47, John Monroe from Oct. 23, '49; judges of supreme court
—salary $1,500—Joab Houghton, Ant. J. Otero, and Charles Beaubien from
Sept. 22, '46; secretary—salary $1,200—Donaciano Vigil from Sept. 22, '46;
auditor—salary $250—Eugene Leitensdorfer from Sept. 22, '46; Joseph Naugle
from June 1, '49, Richard Owens from July 20, '50; treasurer—$250—Chas
Blumner fr. Sept. 22, '46; attorney-general—$250—Hugh N. Smith fr. Oct.
1, '46, Murray F. Tuley fr. June 25, '49, Merrill Ashurst fr. Oct. 2, '50; attorney of southern dist.—$125—James H. Quinn fr. Oct. 19, '46, Elias P.
West fr. Aug. 21, '49, M. F. Tuley fr. Nov. 29, '49, M. Ashurst fr. Oct. 2,
'50; attorney of north dist.—$125—James W. Leal fr. Dec. 10, '46, Theo. D.
Wheaton fr. Mar. 29, '47; U. S. attorney—$500—F. P. Blair and R. Dal-
lam fr. Sept. 22, '46, to June 22, '47; prefects—$200—Sta Fé, Lucien F.
Thurston fr. Aug. 18, '46, Fran. Ortiz fr. Feb. 18, '48; Sta Ana, Fran. Sando-
val fr. Dec. 1, 46, Miguel Montoya fr. Sept. 22, '48; S. Miguel, Manuel A.
Vaca fr. Dec. 1, '46, Herman Grolman fr. Sept. 22, '48; Rio Arriba, Salvador
Lucero fr. Dec. 1, '46, José P. Gallegos fr. Sept. 2, '48; P. José A. Manza-
nares fr. Apr. 29, '49. Salv. Lucero fr. Aug. 12, '50; Taos, Cornelio Vigil fr.
Dec. 1, '46, Vicente Martin fr. Feb. 10, '47, José M. Valdés fr. Sept. 22, '48,
S. H. Quinn fr. Apr. 10, '49, Robt Carey fr. June 19, '49, J. M. Valdés fr.
Feb. 15, '50; Valencia, José M. Sanchez fr. Jul. 16, '47, James L. Hubbell
fr. Sept. 22, '48, Manuel A. Otero fr. June 15, '49, Ramon Luna fr. Apr.
15, '50; Bernalillo, Fran. Sarracino fr. Sept. 22, '46. The terms end Dec.
22, '50. The salaries are as fixed by the Kearny code.

[9] *New Mexico, Journal of the convention of the Territory, 1849*, in *U. S.
Govt Doc.*, 31st cong. 1st sess., H. Ex. Doc. 17, p. 93–104. Rather
strangely Mr Ritch does not mention this convention at all. *Ritch's Legis.
Blue-book*, 100. The meetings were held Sept. 24–26th. The members were,
from Bernalillo co., Manuel Armijo, Ambrosio Armijo, Rio Arriba, Jos.
Naugle, Salv. Lucero; S. Miguel, Greg. Vigil, Manuel A. Vaca; Sta Ana,
Miguel Montoya, Fran. T. Vaca; Sta Fé, Manuel Álvarez, E. V. Deroin, W.
Z. Angney; Taos, Ceran St Vrain, Ant. J. Martin, Ant. Leroux; Valencia,
Juan J. Sanchez, Wm C. Skinner, Mariano Silva, Ant. J. Otero, Manuel A.
Otero. The president was the cura, Ant. José Martinez, sec. J. H. Quinn,

clined to recognize officially the acts of this convention; but Smith soon started for Washington, where,
in July 1850, the house, by a vote of 92 to 86, after
a long discussion, refused to admit him as a delegate.[10]
But even before Delegate Smith's failure to secure
recognition for New Mexico as a territory, yet
another experiment had been tried in the form of an
attempted organization as a state, this being in accordance with advice from Washington.[11]   By proclamaion

doorkeeper E. J. Vaughn. The com. to report a plan, etc., was composed
of W. Z. Angney, Jos. Naugle, Wm C. Skinner, F. T. Vaca, and A. J. Otero.
Gov. Washington, Justice Houghton, and Sec. Vigil accepted seats in the
convention. On plan there was a majority report by Skinner and a minority
report by Naugle, both of which are given. Fran. Sarracino was chosen as
substitute delegate to congress. The final 'instructions,' as adopted, took
the form of a series of modest requests for-aid and protection.

[10] Oct. 16th, J. S. Calhoun, Ind. agent, to sec. interior. *Cal. and N. Mex.*,
Mess., 1850, p. 90–1; debate in *Cong. Globe*, 1849–50, p. 1376–1408. A delegate from Utah, or Deseret, was refused admission.

[11] Nov. 19, 1849, Sec. War Crawford to Lieut.-col Geo. A. McCall, on his
way to join his regiment in N. Mex., in *Cal. and N. Mex.*, *Mess.*, 1850, p.
280–1. 'Since their annexation these territories, in respect to their civil
govt, have in a great measure depended on the officers of the army there in
command; a duty it is considered as falling beyond their appropriate spheres
of action...This condition has arisen from the omission of congress to provide suitable governments, and in regard to the future there is reason to
believe that the difficulties of the past are still to be encountered...It is not
doubted that the people of N. Mex. desire and want a govt organized...The
question readily recurs, how that govt can be supplied. I have already
adverted to past and still existing difficulties that have retarded and may
continue to retard the action of the U. S. in respect to this necessary
and first want. To remove it may, in some degree, be the part of the duty
of officers of the army, on whom, on whom the necessities of the case, has been
devolved a partial participation in their civil affairs. It is therefore deemed
proper that I should say that it is not believed that the people of N. Mex.
are required to await the movements of the Federal govt, in relation to a plan
of govt for the regulation of their own internal concerns. The constitution
of the U. S. and the late treaty with Mexico guarantee their admission into
the union of our states, subject only to the judgment of congress. Should
the people of N. Mex. wish to take any steps toward this object,...it will
be your duty, and the duty of others with whom you are associated, not to
thwart but to advance their wishes. It is their right to appear before congress and ask for admission into the union.' Doubtless similar instructions
were sent to other officers.

Davis, *El Gringo*, 111–12, gives the best connected narrative of political
events of this period in N. Mex. He says: 'About this time two opposite
parties sprang up, one in favor of a state, and the other a territorial govt,
which engendered a deal of excitement and ill feeling. Several large public
meetings were held by the respective parties in Sta Fé...At one of these
meetings the excitement ran so high that it almost led to bloodshed' (on
account of Texan complications, of which more presently). 'The agitation
of the question of a state govt originated with the national administration...
In the spring of 1849, James S. Calhoun went to N. Mex. as Ind. agent, but
upon his arrival he declared that he had secret instructions from the govt at
Wash. to induce the people to form a state govt. For a time the plan received

of Governor Monroe, issued in April 1850, a convention assembled at Santa Fé the 15th of May, under the presidency of James H. Quinn, and after sessions of ten days framed a constitution for the state of New Mexico. This document prohibited slavery, and fixed as the eastern and western boundaries the 100th and 111th meridians respectively.[12]

It was submitted to the people by the military governor's order of May 28th, requiring an election to be held on the 20th of June, at which the electors were to vote on a separate ballot "for governor, lieutenant-governor, representatives to congress, and for senators and representatives to a state legislature to convene at the capital on Monday, the 1st day of July next. It being provided and understood that the election of all officers can only be valid by the adoption of the constitution by the people, and otherwise null and void; and that all action of the governor, lieutenant-governor, and of the legislature shall remain inoperative until New Mexico be admitted as

but little support, but in the course of the summer and fall an excitement was raised, and both parties, state and territorial, published addresses to the people, the former being headed by Calhoun, Álvarez, and Pillans, and the latter by St Vrain, Houghton, Beaubien, and others. The matter continued to be discussed without much effect in favor of the state until the spring of 1850, when Col Geo. A. McCall arrived from the states, upon a like mission as Calhoun. He informed the people that no territorial govt would be granted by congress, and that Pres. Taylor was determined that N. Mex. should be erected into a state govt, in order to settle the question of slavery, and also that of boundary with Texas. The delegate in congress, Mr Smith, wrote home to the same effect.' In view of the neglect of congress, threats of Texas, and disgust of military rule, 'the territorial party at last yielded and joined in the advocacy of a state govt. Accordingly, resolutions to that effect were adopted at a meeting at Sta Fé, Apr. 20th, and also requesting Col Monroe to issue a proclamation, calling upon the people to elect delegates to a convention to be convened on the 15th of May.' The proclamation is found in *U. S. Govt Doc.*, 31st cong. 1st sess., Sen. Ex. Doc. 60.

[12] This constitution in its essential parts is given in the *Amer. Quart. Register*, iv. 582 et seq. I have not found the journal or list of members, but in number and personnel this convention was probably similar to that of 1849. The constitution was dated May 25th. The boundary as defined was as follows: From the irrigating dam of the Rio Grande just above El Paso, east to 100th parallel, north to Arkansas River, up the river to its source, thence by a straight line to where the Rio Colorado is intersected by the 111th parallel, south to the Gila, up the Gila to the intersection of the west line of N. Mex. as it shall be determined by the boundary com., along the national boundary to the Rio Grande, and down that river to the place of starting. Davis tells us that the constitution was drafted by Joab Houghton and M. F. Tuley.

a state under said constitution, except such acts as may be necessary for the primary steps of organization and the presentation of said constitution properly before the congress of the United States. The present government shall remain in full force until, by the action of congress, another shall be substituted."[13] At the election of June 20th, the constitution was adopted by a vote of 8,371 to 39; while Henry Connelly and Manuel Álvarez were elected governor and lieutenant-governor by a large majority over the opposing candidates, Vaca and St Vrain. William S. Messervy was chosen as representative to congress.[14]

The newly elected legislature assembled at Santa Fé at the beginning of July, Álvarez acting as governor in the absence of Connelly. Francis A. Cunningham and Richard H. Weightman were elected United States senators; appointments were made; and elections for local officials were ordered for August. The intention at once became apparent to put the state government into immediate and full operation, without waiting for approval from Washington; to put an end to the existing régime, without regard to the conditions clearly expressed in Monroe's proclamation. This led to a controversy, into the developments and merits of which it is not necessary for us to enter minutely. The military governor declared the election proclamation, and any others emanating from the new authorities, to be null and void, instructing prefects that "the state government of New Mexico has no legal existence, until New Mexico shall be admitted into the union as a state by the congress of the United States; and that, until otherwise determined by competent authority, the present government continues and will

---

[13] Gov. Monroe's procl. of May 28, 1850, in *N. Mex., Corresp. on Civil Affairs*, 1850, p. 93–4. In Cal. the date and manner of the election were fixed in the schedule of the constitution itself, and Gov. Riley in his proclamation clearly announced his intention to surrender his powers to the new governor if the constitution should be ratified. *Cal. and N. Mex., Mess.*, 1850, p. 858–9.

[14] *U. S. Govt Doc.*, 31st cong. 2d sess., Sen. Doc. 26, p. 16; *Ritch's Legis. Blue-book*, 100.

be sustained." And this position he successfully maintained to the end, notwithstanding the protests and arguments of his adversaries, who rather forcibly cited as a precedent for Monroe the submission of Riley in California under similar circumstances.[15]

Respecting the civil status of the newly acquired territories after the treaty and before congressional action, there were substantially three theories, in some phases tolerably distinct, in others perplexingly interlaced. First, that the treaty put an end to the Mexican system and to the temporary system of the military régime, leaving no government at all, but a right on the part of congress to impose a government,

[15] *New Mexico, Correspondence on the su'ject of civil affairs,* 1850, in 31st cong. 2d sess., Sen. Ex. Doc. 1, p. 92–109. This collection includes, 1st, Monroe to adj.–gen., July 16th, a report of the whole matter; 2d, M.'s procl. of May 28th; 3d, M. to legisl., July 4th, has no communication to make; 4th and 5th, notes of M. and Álvarez, July 11th, 12th; 6th, Álvarez to M., a long defence of his course, or of the state govt. He claims the people had a right to organize a civil govt without consulting the mil. gov.; that any private citizen might have issued the proclamation; that in the absence of congressional legislation, the people of N. Mex. had as good a right to form or remodel their old system, or establish a new one, as the people of N. Y. or Va; that Monroe's civil power could be no greater than that of the president; and that the president had never pretended to have the power to make a govt for N. Mex., or insist on the old one; but that the president's instructions and all others from Wash. simply advised temporary submission to the old govt as existing by presumed consent of the people. That consent had been withdrawn, and a new govt organized; which must be recognized, until congress should refuse to sanction it. 7th, M.'s reply to A., July 12th, insisting on adherence to the terms of his original procl., and on a continuance of the old régime pending congressional action; 8th, A. to M., July 12th, deploring the controversy, but asserting that the people cannot surrender their dearest rights, etc.; 9th, mem. of legislative action, on a state seal, county of Socorro, census in 1852, election of alcaldes, etc., election of senators, memorial to congress, etc. A sec. state, 4 judges, auditor, and treasurer were nominated and confirmed by both houses. 10th, M. to adj.-gen., July 31st, enclosing doc.; 11th, M. and Calhoun to local Indian authorities, assuring them that no change is to be made, June 29th; 12th, M. by Sec. Vigil to prefects, July 23d, directing that no attention be paid to Álvarez' orders, etc.; 13th, A.'s procl. of July 20th for elections; 14th, extract of the legislature's law on elections; 15th, M. to adj.-gen., Aug. 26th, transmitting the following papers; 16th, resolutions of the house and senate, signed by W. Z. Angney, speaker, and Joseph Mangle, speaker, July 15th, approving the position taken by Álvarez; 17th, Lewis D. Shutz, sec. state, July 17th, transmitting the preceding to Monroe; 18th, Álvarez to people, Aug. 8th, no officer elected or appointed under the state govt will attempt to exercise any jurisdiction until after Nov. 1st, or until duly commissioned to act as such. (This is by a joint resolution of the legislature, and may indicate a kind of compromise.) 19th, M. by Vigil to prefects, Aug. 9th, no obstruction to be offered to, and no part to be taken in, the state elections of the 12th Aug., but officials elected are not to be recognized; 20th, sec. war to M., Sept. 10th, in reply to M.'s letter of July 16th, the difficulty removed by act of congress.

and on the part of the people, pending congressional
action, to organize one for themselves. This was the
settlers' theory. Second, that the laws of New Mexico,
that is, the Mexican laws, not inconsistent with the
constitution and treaties of the United States, were
still in force, and must still continue in force till
changed by competent authority; that is, by that of
congress; meanwhile the military commandant was
civil governor. This was the position assumed for a
time by Governor Riley of California.[16] Third, that
the temporary system of the military interregnum,
virtually the Mexican law as modified by necessity,
remained in force as a de facto government with the
consent of the people, a consent presumed as an alter-
native of a state of anarchy, and could be changed
only by congress. This theory, in a practical sense
not differing much from the second, was that held by
the administration at Washington, and inculcated in
various instructions to officers in New Mexico and
California, and it was virtually the one maintained to
the end in the former territory. Respecting the merits
of these conflicting theories no final decision was ever
rendered by competent authority. In a practical sense,
most differences were slight. No one seems ever to
have seriously questioned the right of the people to
organize a government and submit it to congress for
approval. The administration at first simply advised
them to submit to the de facto government resting on
their presumed consent, but a later administration
favored the withdrawal of that consent and the application for admission as states. In both sections
of the new territory this was done. As to the real
status of the new governments as organized before
approval or disapproval by congress, the only important
practical question at issue, there was no decision.
Riley in California, under instructions from Washington, though expressing grave doubts on the legality

---

[16] Royce, *California*, 246 et seq., the best treatment of the whole subject
extant, is 'advised by good authority that Riley's position, in so far as he
consistently held to it, was no doubt sounder than the opposing views.'

of this course, surrendered his civil authority, and permitted the new government to go at once into operation, as indeed he had promised to do in his order for the election; this being in a sense approved by the admission of California as a state. Monroe in New Mexico, more consistently but also under instructions, inserted in his election order a condition which was subsequently enforced. The people as represented by Álvarez made out a very plausible case, but the Washington plans must not be disturbed, and any change from a state government in full operation to a territorial system might have been awkward. For it must be understood that the whole matter was manipulated by a few men at Santa Fé. In California, the gold-seeking new-comers included a multitude of politicians, with 'a right smart sprinkling' of men who believed themselves statesman, so that there was a strong public sentiment on various matters; but in New Mexico the masses took little or no interest in theories as to civil government. They had a degree of prejudice against the existing military rule, and partially realized the desirability of a permanent civil system; but the various conventions and petitions and plans in no sense emanated from the New Mexicans, being the work of a few Americans who acted for their own personal interest or that of their party or section in the states, and aroused popular enthusiasm only slightly by false appeals to native fears—notably that of Texan encroachment. A few of those politicians thought they saw an opportunity to serve themselves by interfering with the plan and putting the state government into immediate operation, as had been done in California; but their attempt was not successful.

Turning from Santa Fé to Washington, I find it by no means necessary to follow congressional debates, or even to chronicle the many successive measures proposed for the government of the new territories. Even a brief résumé would extend far beyond the

space at my disposal here, and the subject does not
properly belong to New Mexican history at all.
Somewhat more attention is given to it in other
volumes of this series on California;[17] but the whole
matter belongs to the great national controversy; and
nothing that was done or left undone in New Mexico,
nothing in the needs or wishes of the people, had any
real weight in congress. The territory belonged to
the United States, and the necessity, or at least propriety, of providing for it a regular system of government was obvious to all. Neither was the task in
itself a difficult or complicated one. The south proposed simply to extend national laws over the new
territories by the organization of territorial governments. This was on its face a natural and proper
course, and under ordinary circumstances all details
might have been readily arranged. But a controlling
element in the north refused to admit the territories
under any system, except with conditions prohibiting
slavery. The south had made the war expressly to
gain new southern territory, and consequent extension
of southern power in the national councils. The north
had opposed the war mainly because of the geographic
position of the territory to be acquired. This opposition had failed, as had the attempt to make the acquisition of territory conditional on the Wilmot proviso
prohibiting slavery; but now the north was stronger
and more fully aroused, and was resolved to take a
firm stand against the extension of the peculiar institution. Southerners maintained their right under
the constitution of holding slaves in the territories,
though many doubted that any considerable portion
of the country in question would naturally become in
the end slave territory; they held, moreover, that if
there was any doubt respecting their position, or
respecting particular points—such as the effect of old
Mexican laws abolishing slavery—the question should
be decided by the courts; they favored compromise,

[17] See *Hist. Cal.*, v., chap. xxii.; vi., chap. xiii.

founded on mutual concessions, such as the admission of free and slave states in equal numbers, or a geographic line like that of the Missouri compromise; and they protested against an aggressive and offensive policy on the part of the northerners, who would listen to no compromise, and would give southern institutions no standing whatever in the newly acquired domain. And indeed, the northern position was radically aggressive; but if on the face of the matter and on the points immediately at issue there was a degree of unfairness, it was believed to be justified by the political trickery on the other side that had led to the present complication, by the irrepressible nature of the great sectional conflict that had begun, and especially by the great moral question at issue between slavery and freedom. The fight in congress was a long and bitter one, most ably fought on both sides; but, as I have said, the record of its details and the discussion of its merits do not belong in this work.[18]

There was, however, one phase of this controversy that did directly affect New Mexico, and in which her people took a real interest, though their wishes had very little weight in congress; and this was the question of eastern boundary. As we have seen, Texas had claimed since 1836 the Rio Grande from its mouth to its source as her western bound, relying, so far as it was deemed necessary to rely on anything but repeated asseverations, on the treaty signed by Santa Anna as a prisoner—a treaty never confirmed but always repudiated by Mexico, and never entitled to the slighest consideration from any point of view. For two centuries and a half New Mexico had been ruled continuously as a Spanish and Mexican province, and Texas had never for a day exercised any sort of jurisdiction over any portion of the province, but had, on the contrary, been disastrously defeated in her only

[18] See *Congressional Globe*, 1845–50, 29th to 31st cong., as per index headings, N. Mexico, California, Utah, Texas, Slavery in the Territories, Compromise Bill, etc.

attempted invasion. As I have before stated or implied, the claim of Texas as against Mexico or New
Mexico never had any real foundation in fact or justice. But against the United States after the treaty
of 1848, the claim assumed in some respects a different
aspect. In annexing Texas the United States had in
a sense taken her side in the boundary dispute against
Mexico;[19] and they had still more definitely assumed
that ground by regarding the crossing of the Rio
Grande by the Mexicans as an invasion and declaration of war. Again during the military occupation,
while from motives of policy the Texan claim was
virtually ignored by Kearny and his successors, yet
in reply to the complaints, or inquiries, of Texas, the
president explained that the civil government organized as a temporary expedient at Santa Fé was by no
means to be considered as interfering with the ultimate rights of Texas;[20] and the military governor was
a little later instructed definitely not to interfere with
the exercise of Texan authority east of the Rio
Grande.[21] Thus while the administration gradually
assumed the ground that there was a question to be
settled by congress and the state, yet in an important
sense the national government was committed to the
justice of the Texan claim. Meanwhile the Texans
at home and at Washington constantly asserted their
claim with an earnestness that almost leads the reader

[19] True, in the act of annexation there was an adjustment of boundaries
left to congress; but this adjustment might naturally and properly be regarded as affecting the rights of Mexico only. It furnished, however, a somewhat plausible basis for a different view.
[20] N. Mex. and Mess., July 24, 1848.
[21] 'With respect to that portion of the instructions which is in the following words: "In regard to that part of what the Mexicans called N. Mexico,
lying east of the Rio Grande, the civil authority which Texas has established
or may establish there is to be respected, and in no manner interfered with by
the military force in that department, otherwise than to lend aid on proper
occasions in sustaining it," I have to remark that it is not expected Texas
will undertake to extend her civil government over the remote region designated; but should she do so, you will confine your action, under the clause
above cited, to arranging your command in such a manner as not to come into
conflict with the authorities so constituted. On the claim of Texas to any or
the whole of N. Mexico east of the Rio Grande, it is not necessary to give an
opinion, as congress and that state alone have the power of adjusting it.' Sec.
war. to com. N. Mex. March 26, 1849, in *Cal. and N. Mex., Mess.*, 1850, p. 272.

to think they really believed it a just one; and the state had also contracted a debt, based on the 'full extent' of its domain, so that the interests and rights of 'innocent third parties' became involved. To dismember New Mexico would be an outrage; still, something was due to Texas.

I find no very definite record of what occurred in this connection at Santa Fé; but it appears that the Texan legislature went so far as to organize a county government for New Mexico, to give that county a right to one representative, to pass acts regulating the militia, to establish a judicial circuit, and to appoint a judge to hold court in the Rio Grande valley.[22] Says Davis: "Early in the spring of 1850 Texas sent a commissioner, Robert S. Neighbors, into New Mexico, with instructions to divide the country east of the Rio del Norte into several counties of that state, and to hold elections in them for county officers. Upon the mission of Neighbors being known, it was loudly denounced in public meetings throughout the territory, and a very strong opposition was raised against him and the objects he had in view. He issued a proclamation fixing time and places for an election, but nobody went to the polls, and the matter fell to the ground.[23] In congress, while Texan repre-

[22] See *Niles' Reg.*, lxxiv. 211, 224, with references to the *Sta Fé Republican*, which journal thinks Texas would do well to go slow if she wishes to avoid a coat of tar and feathers for her representatives. The judge who started for Sta Fé to hold court is called Beard.

[23] *Davis' El Gringo*, 110–11. He adds that the state party favored Neighbors and the Texan scheme, while the territorial party took the opposite view; but this seems hardly possible, as there was nothing west of the river to make a state of. Probably the territorial party tried to make capital against their opponents by charging them with secret favor to Texas. Acc. to Ford in *Creuzbaur's Route to Cal.*, 4, Maj. Neighbors was accompanied by D. C. Sullivan, A. D. Neal, and Dr John S. Ford, with a party of Indians, starting in March 1849. Says Thrall, *Hist. Texas*, 360: 'In 1847 Gov. Henderson had called the attention of the legislature to our claim to Sta Fé; and in 1848 a bill passed the legislature extending the laws of Texas over that portion of N. Mex. east of the Rio Grande River, and Judge Beard was sent there to hold district court. Col Munroe paid no attention to the Texas judge, and proceeded to order an election of a territorial delegate to the U. S. congress. Gov. Wood requested the legislature to put the whole military power of the state under his control, that he might enforce the claim; but in a corresp. with the state dept at Washington he was notified that if Texas attempted a forcible possession of Sta Fé the Texans would be treated as

sentatives never lost an opportunity of declaiming on the unquestionable validity of their claim, there was much difference of opinion, even among southern members, on its original merits; but in this, as in every phase of the whole matter, all was merged in the slavery issue.   Texas was a slave state, and eastern New Mexico, if decided to be a part of Texas, would be an immense territory gained at once for the south, whatever might be the final result farther west.   This was the only real strength of the Texan claim in congress beyond the zealous efforts of the Texans themselves, among whom, however, as we shall see, a new motive soon became potent in the matter.   This phase of the slavery question also caused northern members to favor a territorial government in New Mexico, as a choice of evils, even if slavery could not be prohibited.

Early in 1850 the great battle in congress reached its height, and so hot and bitter had the struggle become that conservative leaders on both sides were seriously alarmed at the possibility of a sectional conflict, which might disrupt the union.   Therefore the idea of compromise gradually gained ground, even among northern members.   A new and wonderful industrial development and growth of population, resulting from the discovery of gold, had not only fitted California for immediate statehood, but had made it apparent that slavery could never exist in the north, though the south still made a struggle for a possible slave state of the future in southern California.   In Texas, the idea of relinquishing the claim to New Mexico for a money consideration from the United States rapidly grew in favor, being powerfully supported at Washington by a lobby representing the

intruders.   In the heat of the controversy some of our writers contended that if the delegate from N. Mex. was admitted to his seat in congress, the Texas delegates should withdraw, and the state resume her separate nationality. This question, like that of the settlement of the public debt, was left for the next administration.'   In the 2d sess. of the 30th cong. there was considerable discussion of this Texan matter without definite results. *Cong. Globe,* 1848–9.

state creditors. In January Mr Clay introduced in the senate a series of compromise resolutions, the contents of which, in variously modified forms, afforded matter for a complicated and exciting debate of six months. These resolutions were not adopted, and various compromise bills, embodying provisions of a somewhat similar nature, were, as a whole, defeated; but nevertheless the ideas involved became firmly rooted, and enough conservative votes on each side were gained to adopt separately the compromise measures, which became laws in September.

By this action the south gained a more satisfactory fugitive slave law than had before existed; while the north secured the prohibition of slave trade in the District of Columbia. California was admitted as a free state. New Mexico and Utah, embracing all the rest of the newly acquired domain, were admitted as territories, without conditions prohibiting slavery. And finally, Texas was paid $10,000,000, about half of which amount may be regarded as having gone to pay for her New Mexican claim. Thus each portion of the region wrested from Mexico got the government best suited to its condition, and so far as local interests, rights, and needs were concerned, the solution was eminently a satisfactory one. It was hardly less so as a temporary compromise of the great sectional struggle. The south won the main point at issue by defeating all measures designed to prohibit slavery in the territories, but lost a possible chance of making southern California a slave state; while the north, though forced to recede from its original uncompromising position, gained a free state, and made no permanent concession to slavery, since the great question of the right to hold slaves in the territories was left open— to be fought out, to the ultimate triumph of freedom, in the greatest war of modern times.

The senate passed the Texas boundary bill on the 7th, and the bill providing a territorial government for New Mexico on the 15th of August; the two bills

were joined by the house, came back to the senate on
September 9th, and were signed by the president on
the same day. The act was not, however, to go into
effect until the general assembly of Texas should have
formally accepted the boundary, which was done on
the 25th of November.[24] The territory, as thus organized in 1850, included substantially the New Mexico
and Arizona of later years,[25] with a small part of Colorado. Congress reserved the right to divide the
territory, or to attach any portion of it to any other
territory or state. When admitted as a state, New
Mexico was to be received with or without slavery as
her constitution might prescribe. The new government did not go into actual operation at Santa Fé
until March 1851; and it may be noted here that a
memorial of the legislature, received in congress after
the passage of the territorial bill, excited some fears,
real or pretended, of an attempt on the part of the
north to admit the state after all; also that Senator-
elect Weightman made his appearance, and vainly
tried to collect his mileage of $2,000 on the plea, sup-
ported by several in the senate, that his position, so
far as mileage was concerned, was identical with that
of the senators from California.[26]

[24] I take this date from *Thrall's Hist. Texas*, 367. In *U. S. Govt. Doc.*,
31st cong., 2d sess., H. Ex. Doc. 8, is the message from Texas, formally announcing the agreement.

[25] The boundary was as follows: 'Beginning at a point in the Colorado River
where the boundary line with the republic of Mex. crosses the same; thence
eastwardly with the said boundary line to the Rio Grande; thence following
the main channel of said river to the parallel of the 32° north lat.; thence
east with said degree, to its intersection with the 103° long. west of Green-
wich; thence north with said degree of long. to the parallel of 38° north lat.;
thence west with said parallel to the summit of the Sierra Madre; thence
south with the crest of said mountains to the 37° north lat.; thence west with
said parallel to its intersection with the boundary line of the state of California; thence with said boundary line to the place of beginning.' That part
lying west of long. 109° was detached in 1863 to form Arizona; and that part
above lat. 37° in 1867 was attached to Colorado. There was also a large addition in 1854 by the Gadsden purchase, most of which was detached with
Arizona. Utah as organized in 1850 included the later Nevada, Utah, and
those parts of Colorado and Wyoming which lie south of lat. 42° and west of
the mountains. There was a little strip of the territory acquired from Mexico, lying between lat. 38°, the mountains, and the Arkansas River, that does
not seem to have been provided for in the final settlement of 1850.

[26] *Cong. Globe*, 1849–50, p. 1808, 1828, 1933–5, 1948–9. See also, on the
general subject of the debate and final settlement, *Benton's Debates*, xvi. 592

The treaty brought within the limits of the United States about 120,000 Indians as was estimated at the time, over one fourth of which number were in New Mexico, or a still greater proportion if all on the frontiers were included. The government had assumed the obligation of protecting the province from the incursions of hostile tribes, an obligation it could by no means fulfil, especially in the first years. The military force was altogether inadequate, the local authorities had little skill or experience, and the failure of the Americans was even more complete than that of the Mexicans in earlier times. Never had the condition of the province in this respect been worse than in 1848–50. Doubtless this unfortunate state of things was due largely to unavoidable results of the late war, to the presence and acts of the Missouri volunteers in 1846–7, to delays in substituting a proper force of regulars in 1848–9, and especially to bitterness, dissensions, and lack of confidence between the Americans and Mexicans growing out of the revolt of 1847. The Navajos and Apaches were as always the country's chief terror, and their raids for murder and plunder were unceasing. The Navajos, who were rich and prosperous at home as well as valiant warriors, made the stealing of live-stock a regular business by which to increase their wealth, openly declaring that they would long ago have exterminated the Mexicans had it not been deemed more profitable to use them as shepherds. The Apaches came to regard their raids as a legitimate occupation, their only means of gaining a livelihood; and they were generally on friendly terms with a disreputable gang of Mexican and American traders, through whom they carried on a profitable trade in stolen articles, including women and children captured in the Sonora towns, they being sometimes at peace with Chihuahua, and drawing regular supplies at Janos. The pueblo Indians were peaceable and

5; *Amer. Quar. Register*, iv. 54–60; v. 9–31, 86–7, 537–9; *North Amer. Review*, lxxi. 221–51; *Lossing's Hist. U. S.*, 499; *Cluskey's Pol. Text-book*, 117–19.

well disposed toward the Americans, but their status involved many perplexing problems to be solved under conditions that were far from favorable.

James S. Calhoun arrived at Santa Fé in July 1849, with a commission as Indian agent for the territory. He seems to have been a zealous and intelligent official, who, while he could do little toward putting an end to the depredations of savages, performed well his duty of reporting to the government the exact state of affairs, and the measures and means required for the country's protection. His correspondence of 1849–51 contains a large amount of valuable information respecting the numbers and disposition of the different tribes, advice as to the appointment of subagents and stationing of garrisons, earnest appeals on the most urgent necessity of immediately increasing the military force, and a mention of many events of Indian warfare.[27] Besides Calhoun's correspondence,

[27] *Calhoun's Reports of an Indian agent at Sta Fé, 1849–51.* The corresp. of 1849 is found in 31st cong. 1st sess., H. Ex. Doc. 17, p. 191–228; that of 1849–50, in 31st cong. 2d sess., Sen. Ex. Doc. 1, p. 125–43, and that of 1850–1, in 32d cong. 1st sess., H. Ex. Doc. 2, p. 448–67. These references also include Calhoun's instructions, etc., and a few communications from other men on Ind. affairs. He was appointed April 7, 1849, at a salary of $1,500, the whole expense of the agency not to exceed $3,800. Gov. Bent's report of 1846 was furnished as a sort of base on which to build up information. He arrived at Sta Fé July 22d. In his report of Oct. 4th he gives the Pueblo population as 6,524 above 5 years of age, not including the Moquis, as per census of 1847; and in this and other reports he dwells on the importance of protecting and improving these superior natives, both as a matter of justice and of policy. The Pueblos, by reason of their thrift, were favorite victims of the savage raids. Oct. 5th, Bent's Fort has been burned by the owners; Ind. more troublesome than ever; 'this whole country requires a thorough purging, which can be accomplished only by a thorough exploration of every hole and corner in it...Military roads should be opened, and posts and depots established.' Oct. 13th, 'But a short time since a band said to be commanded by an Englishman, well known in Sta Fé, ordered, in the name of the U. S., the pueblo of Laguna to furnish them with 25 horses and to call upon the quartermaster in Sta Fé for payment. The order was promptly obeyed, and the Ind. do not yet understand the contrivance by which they lost their horses.' Oct. 15th, the Zuñis are confident of their ability to form a combination of Pueblos which can defeat the Navajos and Apaches if arms are furnished by U. S., and especially if the operations of the roving traders, who sell arms and circulate false reports, etc., can be stopped. Calhoun has much to say of the harm done by these traders who are never molested by the savages; and he thinks there is a class of Mexican citizens, including some priests, who stir up trouble deliberately with a view of keeping American settlers out of the country. Difficulties arising from the fact that the Apaches live on both sides of the Mex. boundary are also noted. 'Expend your *million* now, if necessary, that you may avoid the expenditure of *millions*

the records on this subject, if far from complete, are
somewhat voluminous, and not without interest; but
it is almost impossible to make any adequate use of
them here, since I have no space for a chronologic
catalogue of depredations and resulting campaigns.
Indeed, the history of Indian warfare in these countries for centuries is made up of items, for all of which
one record might almost suffice if blanks were left to
be filled in with dates, names, and localities. Watching for an opportunity, the savages attack some rancho
or settlement, kill few or many of the inhabitants,
according to the resistance offered, and run off as many
stolen animals as possible. The alarm is given at the
nearest post, and a party of regulars, generally reënforced by volunteers, sets out in pursuit. Often the
savages cannot be overtaken before the horses of the
pursuers are worn out or their supplies exhausted. If
overtaken, they lose part or all of their plunder, and
generally a few lives; but they also kill a few soldiers,
and charge the difference to profit and loss, hoping for
better luck next time. Occasionally, by a combined
movement of troops, or a rapid succession of move-

hereafter.' The Ind. should be confined to certain limits, and made to realize
the strength of the U. S. If allowed to roam, they will never keep their
treaty promises. Agencies should be established at Taos, to include the
Yutas, at Zuñi for the Navajos, and at Socorro to look after Apaches and
Comanches. For a year, at least, there should be a subagent in every pueblo.
Nov. 17th, suggestions on amendments of the act of congress on trade, etc.,
with Ind. March 29, 1850, explanation of a map showing Ind. tribes and
pueblos. March 30th, plans and financial estimates. March 31st, four returned captives and their stories. In Oct. the Moquis sent a deputation to
learn the views and purposes of the govt toward them, complain of Navajo
depredations, claim that their pueblo of Oraibe can turn 100 warriors. In
the autumn of 1850 the savages were somewhat less troublesome, but in the
spring of 1851 were worse than ever. The losses of live-stock in Sta Ana and
Bernalillo counties in 1846–50, exclusive of govt animals, are given as 150,231
sheep, 893 horses, 761 mules and asses, and 1,234 cows. (In *Bartlett's Pers.
Narr.*, ii. 386, the total losses in 1846–50 are given as 453,293 sheep,
12,887 mules, 7,050 horses, and 31,581 cattle. See also 35th cong. 1st sess.,
H. Ex. Doc. 123.) There is much complaint from natives respecting the in-
efficient manner in which the troops pursue the raiders. In 1851 Calhoun
was governor, but continued to report many details of Ind. affairs, and on
Aug. 31st writes: 'Without a dollar in our territorial treasury, without
munitions of war, without authority to call out our militia, without the co-
operation of the military authorities of this territory, and with numberless
complaints and calls for protection, do you not perceive I must be sadly embarrassed and disquieted?'

ments in some particular direction, a tribe is forced to make a treaty, which is observed as long as the interest of the Indians seems to require it. It must be added that outrage and bad faith were by no means confined to the Indians; but were frequent on both sides, so far as individuals and small parties were concerned, neither side having to go far back for plausible pretexts. The Americans had better arms than the Mexicans of earlier times, and there was less red tape in the fitting-out of their expeditions; but for some years they had less experience in this kind of warfare, their movements were slower and more in accordance with military rules, they did not know the country so well, and their general success, as compared with that of their predecessors, was not remarkable.[28]

[28] *Washington's Reports*, 1849, 31st cong. 1st sess., H. Ex. Doc. 5, p. 104 –14, give many items. On May 30th the Apaches killed 10 persons in Abiquiú valley, and Capt. Chapman pursuing killed 20, losing two. Also *Id.*, pt i., p. 91, 93–4, rept of sec. war; *Id.*, pt iii., p. 951–4, 994–1102; *Id.*, acts and resol., 222–9. A campaign of Maj. Steen in July is described in *Rodenbough's Everglade to Cañon with the 2d Dragoons*, 163–4. Some items of 1848 in *Niles' Reg.*, lxxiv. 68, 224, 251; lxxv. 340. Inspector-general Geo. A. McCall's *Letters from the Frontiers*, Phil., 1868, p. 490 et seq., contains two very valuable reports of July and Dec. 1850 on the general condition of the country, including much information respecting the Indians, and the best methods of controlling them. The author believes that the future prosperity of N. Mex. 'will depend in great measure on the impression now to be made on these Indians. It may be apprehended that if they are not in the beginning impressed with the ability and the settled purpose of the U. S. to chastise those who plunder and murder its citizens, if acts of this kind, now of almost monthly occurrence, and utterly beyond the power of the present military force to check, are continued longer unpunished, the Ind. will hold us in the contempt with which they now look upon the Mexicans, whom they have wantonly robbed and murdered for two centuries. And the inevitable consequences will be sooner or later a war with the surrounding tribes.' Toward the Pueblos, 10,000 in number, a mild and conciliatory and helpful policy should be shown, to inspire them with confidence and make them friends and allies. The Navajos, 10,800, the richest of all and most civilized, except the Moquis, might probably by a strong military force in their country, to show that a treaty is something more than idle talk, be induced to settle permanently like the Pueblos, and thus in time be controlled, in which case they would be invaluable as allies. The Moquis, thought to number 2,450, are friendly, and their friendship should be cultivated in every way. The Yutas, 4,000 or 5,000, do not extend their raids far south, though they often aid the Jicarilla Apaches. They might easily be held in check if the Navajos were friendly. The Comanches, over 12,000, rarely commit depredations in N. Mex., but join the Apaches in raids for live-stock and captives in Chihuahua, also trading their plunder with N. Mexicans. The Apaches, some 4,000 exclusive of the Gila bands, seem to be incorrigible robbers, and have no other means of living. Possibly they may be improved, but it will take time, and at first they must be fed while some scheme is being devised and put in practice. The least force that can suffice for the present protection of the country

Colonel Doniphan's treaty with the Navajos in 1846, a treaty which had no effect whatever, has been noted in the preceding chapter. Colonel Newby made a similar expedition and treaty in 1848.[29] In 1849 Major Washington repeated the operation, starting from Jemes on August 22d with 350 men, and being accompanied by Indian-agent Calhoun. On the 30th at Tunicha several hundred Navajos were met who professed a willingness to submit to the United States, attributing recent depredations to bad and uncontrollable men of their tribe. They gave up some animals and began the negotiation of a treaty; but there was a dispute about a horse, and when Washington ordered its seizure the Indians ran away and were fired at, losing several men, including their great chief Narbona. On the 6th of September the army reached the Chelly Cañon, where on the 9th a treaty of 'lasting peace' was signed. The Indians gave up three captives and some property, agreeing to surrender the rest at Jemes a month later. The return march was by way of Zuñi, Laguna, and Alburquerque. The Navajos, it is needless to add, did not appear at Jemes as agreed, but they had a good excuse, having been informed, as they said, by Mexican traders—after they had collected the plunder and set out for the rendezvous— that the Americans were coming to attack them.[30] Among the most notable of Indian outrages was the killing of White and party of seven or eight at Point of Rocks on the way from the states to Santa Fé, in

is 2,200 men, of whom at least 1,400 should be mounted. Stations are suggested for the detachments, including 450 men in the Navajo country, 450 among the eastern Apaches, and 300 on the Gila. See also on Ind. affairs of 1850, reports of sec. int. and com. ind. affairs in 31st cong. 2d sess., H. Ex. Doc. 1, p. 28–30, 423; *Id.*, pt ii. 67–75, 292–300; *Id.*, Sen. Doc. 26, p. 5, 10–19; 36th cong. 1st sess., Sen. Mis. Doc. 45; *Hayes' Scraps, Ind.*, iii. no. 45, 47; iv. 14–16; v. 5–6, 10–14; *Brackett's U. S. Cav.*, 127–8; and *Cremony's Life among the Apaches*, passim. This author spent some 6 months at the Copper mine near the Gila, with the boundary commission.

[29] *Ind. Aff. Rept*, 1858, p. 188.

[30] *Washington's Reports*, 111–15, including the treaty; *Calhoun's Reports*, 202–10; and especially *Simpson's Journal*. In the *Ind. Aff. Rept*, 1858, p. 188, it is stated that after this treaty the Navajos reached the settlements before the soldiers, and stole mules almost in sight of the Sta Fé flag-staff.

October 1849.   Mrs White and daughter of ten years were at first spared by the Apaches, but the former was soon killed.   Calhoun made every possible effort, and congress voted $1,500, to effect the girl's rescue, but without success.[31]

The annals of New Mexico in the early years of American occupation would not be complete without mention of the geographical and other scientific information about the country acquired and published at this period—or rather of the various explorations by which this information was gained and of the books where it may be found, for obviously my space will permit nothing more.   A. Wislizenus left Independence in May 1846, with Speyer's trading caravan, and from Santa Fé went to El Paso and Chihuahua, finally joining Doniphan's army as physician.   His tour was mainly scientific in its purposes, and the resulting memoir contains a considerable amount of original and valuable data on New Mexico as well as the regions farther south.[32]   In all the narratives that have been cited on the conquest and following events, there is more or less matter of a descriptive nature, but particularly in Emory's diary of the march from Fort Leavenworth by Bent's Fort to Santa Fé and thence down the Rio Grande and to California by the Gila.[33]   Captain Abraham R. Johnston's printed journal also covered the march from Santa Fé to the California frontier.[34]   Philip St George Cooke described the march to Santa Fé and the later one to

[31] Calhoun's Repts, 226; McCall's Letters, 493–4; U. S. Govt Doc., 31st cong. 2d sess., H. Ex. Doc. 1, p. 29–30, 42–3.

[32] Memoir of a Tour to Northern Mexico, connected with Col Doniphan's expedition, in 1846 and 1847. By A. Wislizenus, M. D. [with a scientific appendix and three maps]. Wash., 1848, 8vo, 141 p. (30th cong., 1st sess. Sen. Miscel., no. 26.) Also translation, Denkschrift über eine Reise nach Nord-Mexiko, etc. Aus dem Englischen übertragen von George M. von Ross, etc. Braunschweig, 1850, 8vo, 211 p.

[33] Emory's Notes of a Military Reconnoissance, Wash., 1848, with plates, scientific appen., and tables; also Abert's notes of the journey as far as Bent's Fort, as a brief note by Maj. Cooke.

[34] Johnston's Journal, attached to Emory's Notes as part of 30th cong. 1st sess., Ex. Doc., no. 41. It contains some cuts of antiquities.

California, in which, with the Mormon Battalion, he opened a wagon-road by a route farther south than Kearny's. His writings, however, contain somewhat less of scientific description, if more of philosophy, than those of the other officers.[35] Lieutenant J. W. Abert, of the topographical engineers, was left ill at Bent's Fort by Kearny and Emory at the end of July, 1846. The first part of his report includes the results of his observations at the fort, on the journey to New Mexico, and in the vicinity of Santa Fé, where he arrived on the 27th of September.[36] Kearny had left instructions for a survey of the country to be made by Abert and Peck, which was made between October 8th and the 23d of December, with results constituting the second part of the report. The route was south-westward to the junction of the Jemes and Rio Grande, San Felipe, Santo Domingo, and Santa Ana being visited; thence down the main river past Alburquerque, and westward to the Puerco and to Cebolleta. After exploring the Laguna group of pueblos, including Acoma, they returned to the Rio Grande and went down to the Isleta region, and eastward to Chilili and Tajique, thence southward to Quarra and Abó, and back to the river, down which they went to Valverde and returned to Santa Fé. The third part of the report is the diary of the return from New Mexico to Fort Leavenworth, December 28th to March 1st.[37] The author added to his text valuable engravings of towns, ruins, landscapes, and native types; and he also gave attention to the fauna and

[35] *Cooke's Report of his march from Santa Fé, New Mexico, to San Diego, Upper California*, 1846. Attached to *Emory's Notes*, p. 549 et seq., with a map of the route; *Cooke's Journal of the march of the Mormon Battalion*, etc., in *U. S. Govt Doc.*, 30th cong. special sess., Sen. Doc. 2, 85 p.; *Cooke's Conquest of New Mexico and California.* Some descriptive matter is also to be found in the other narratives of the march of the Mormons, *Tyler's Hist.* and *Bigler's Diary*, MS.

[36] This part includes also a tour to the gold placers and the notes of Lieut. Peck on the region north of Sta Fé to Taos, examined by P. and Warner before Abert's arrival.

[37] *Report of Lieut. J. W. Abert of his examination of New Mexico in the years 1846-47.* With *Emory's Notes*, 417-548. Also a résumé in *Warren's Memoir*, 53-4.

flora of the country, and to native vocabularies and traditions with other ethnographic matter, producing on the whole a most excellent report.

The campaign of Doniphan and the others against the Navajos, though involving the first American exploration of a broad region, has left in print but little of geographic or descriptive value; and the same may be said of the campaigns resulting from the insurrection of 1847. In this connection may be mentioned a report of Thomas Fitzpatrick, describing a trip from Fort Leavenworth to Santa Fé in the summer of 1847, though it is mainly devoted to Indian affairs.[33] For 1848 we find very little of recorded exploration, but may note the narrative of an overland trip with Kit Carson from Los Angeles to Taos and Santa Fé, the author being perhaps Lieutenant Brewerton of Stephenson's regiment, and the story of slight value.[39] It was also in the winter of 1848–9 that Captain Frémont, in his fourth exploration, attempting to cross the mountains at the head of the Rio Grande, in what is now Colorado, met his great disaster, attributed by him to the incompetence of his guide, the famous Bill Williams, losing eleven of his men by cold and starvation. With the rest he succeeded in reaching Taos, where the company was broken up, and himself proceeded early in 1849 to California by a southern overland route.[40] In 1849–50 the reports of Calhoun, the Indian agent, as already cited, contained a limited amount of general information not pertaining directly

---

[38] Dated Bent's Fort, Sept. 18th. The author was with Lieut. Love's party when attacked by the Indians. *U. S. Govt Doc.*, 30th cong. 1st sess., Sen. Ex. Doc. 1, app. p. 238–49.

[39] *Van Tramp (John C.)*, *Prairie and Rocky Mountain Adventures, or Life in the Far West, etc.* St Louis, 1860. This is a somewhat trashy collection of material from various sources. Brewerton's narrative is on p. 172–236, but it is not quite clear how much of it is B.'s work, nor is it stated from what source it was obtained. It is called an abridgment. The route was by the regular Sta Fé trail north of the Colorado.

[40] Mrs Frémont's *Year of Amer. Travel*, 69 et seq., contains the captain's letters from N. Mex. narrating this disaster. See also *Bigelow's Mem. Frémont*, 357–78. The diaries of the 3d and 4th expeditions have not been published, though probably included in *Frémont's Memoirs of my Life*, the early publication of which is announced as I write, in June 1886.

to the author's special subject;[41] and the same may be said of the correspondence of governors Washington and Monroe, and of other officials in the same years. In April 1849, Lieutenant James H. Simpson made an exploring tour from Fort Smith, Arkansas, westward to Santa Fé; and later in the year Captain Marcy, coming from Fort Smith by the same route, went down the river to Doña Ana, and thence crossed an unexplored country eastward to Preston, Texas.[42] But by far the most notable and valuable of the exploration records to be mentioned in this connection is that of Lieutenant Simpson's tour to the Navajo country and Chelly Cañon, returning by way of Zuñi. The author accompanied Governor Washington's expedition of 1849, and his journal is filled with the most interesting and valuable descriptions of physical features of the country, towns, natives, and relics of antiquity, being illustrated with excellent drawings, which are especially important as showing the wonderful ruins of the Chaco and Chelly and the records at Inscription Rock.[43] It should be added that in 1849–50 the California immigrants crossed New Mexico in considerable numbers, both by the old Santa Fé trail and by the new southern routes.

The survey of a boundary line between the United States and Mexico under the treaty of Guadalupe

[41] *Calhoun's Reports*, passim. In Oct. 1849 he sent to Washington Major H. L. Kendrick's *Table of marches made in the summer of 1849, from Ft Leavenworth to Santa Fé*, in *Cal. and N. Mex.*, *Mess.*, 1850, p. 91–2.

[42] *U. S. Govt Doc.*, 31st cong. 1st sess., Sen. Ex. Doc. 12, and H. Ex. Doc. 45, with maps; also *Warren's Memoir*, 56–7. In the spring of 1849 Dr John S. Ford accompanied Maj. Robert S. Neighbors, the Texan commissioner, from Austin, Texas, to El Paso, by a partially new route. *Ford*, in *Creuzbaur's Route to Cal.*, 4–5. See also reports of routes from Texas to El Paso in 31st cong. 1st sess., H. Ex. Doc. 5, pt 1, p. 281–93; 31st cong. 2d sess., H. Ex. Doc. 1, pt ii., p. 302–23; also Lieut. Michler's report on route from Sta Fé north in 31st cong. 1st sess., H. Ex. Doc. 67; and a reconnoissance of the Rio Pecos in 1850 by R. H. Kern, in *Warren's Mem.*, 62.

[43] *Simpson (James H.), Journal of a military reconnoissance, from Santa Fé, New Mexico, to the Navajo, made with the troops under command of Brevet Lieutenant-colonel John M. Washington, etc.*, in *1849. By James H. Simpson, A. M., first lieutenant corps of topographical engineers.* Phil., 1852, 8vo, 140 p., plates. Also in *U. S. Govt Doc.*, 31st cong. 1st sess., Sen. Ex. Doc. 64, with map; résumé in *Warren's Memoir*, 56–7.

Hidalgo is properly noticed here, so far as it affects New Mexico, though it extends chronologically beyond the limits of the chapter. In the west, from the Pacific to the Colorado the line was surveyed before February 1850.[44] In November of the same year the new commissioner, John Russell Bartlett, arrived with his party at El Paso, having crossed Texas from the coast; General Pedro García Conde, the Mexican commissioner, soon made his appearance; and before the end of the year several meetings were held at which the initial point and other preliminaries were decided. Active operations in the field began early in 1851; the American party had its headquarters for several months at the Santa Rita copper mines, Colonel Craig commanding an escort of 85 men; and though there were some vexatious delays and controversies, resulting in part from the tardy arrival of Gray and Graham, by September the region from El Paso to the San Pedro had been explored and the boundary line partly surveyed—to its full extent, indeed, by the Mexicans. Then Bartlett went to Sonora and California, returning east to publish his narrative in 1854.[45] Lieutenant Whipple went down the Gila;

[44] John B. Weller was the first U. S. commissioner, and the Cal. survey was made from June 1849 to Feb. 1850 by Andrew B. Gray as surveyor and Wm H. Emory as astronomer. The commission then adjourned to meet at El Paso in Nov. John C. Frémont was appointed to succeed Weller, but resigned, and John Russell Bartlett was appointed in June. Under Bartlett Gray was still surveyor till succeeded by Emory in Nov. 1851; Col John McClellan was astronomer—succeeded by Lieut.-col J. D. Graham in Oct. 1850, and he by Emory in Oct. 1851—and Lieut. A. W. Whipple assistant astronomer.

[45] *Personal Narrative of Explorations and incidents in Texas, New Mexico, California, Sonora, and Chihuahua, connected with the United States and Mexican boundary commission, during the years 1850, '51, '52, and '53. By John Russell Bartlett, United States commissioner during that period. In two volumes, with map and illustrations,* N. Y., 1854, 8vo, 2 vol. This has always been regarded as a standard work, containing in pleasing form much original and valuable information on the countries visited as well as the author's personal adventures and a history of the survey. Bartlett became the author of several other works of good repute especially some of a bibliographic nature. He was for many years in charge of the famous Carter Brown collection of Americana, and as I write, in June 1886, news comes of his death at an advanced age. John C. Cremony was interpreter for the U. S. commissioner, and his *Life Among the Apaches*, S. F., 1868, is devoted to a considerable extent to his experiences in this exploration, which, however, he erroneously dates 1849–50 instead of 1850–1.

García Conde died in Sonora; and the survey was suspended for a time, to be resumed and completed, on the Rio Grande at least, in 1852–3 by Robert H. Campbell as commissioner and W. H. Emory as astronomer and surveyor.[46] Particulars, whether of exploration or adventure, can of course find no place here. Still less is it possible or necessary to chronicle the complicated series of quarrels between Bartlett, McClellan, Graham, Gray, and others, which seriously retarded practical operations, and the record of which fills the larger part of two volumes published by the government.[47] There was, however, one question respecting the boundary itself that merits further notice.

By the terms of the treaty of Guadalupe Hidalgo of 1848, the line was to follow the Rio Grande up "to the point where it strikes the southern boundary of New Mexico; thence westward along the whole southern boundary of New Mexico (which runs north of the town called Paso) to its western termination; thence northward along the western line of New Mexico until it intersects the first branch of the river Gila (or if it should not intersect any branch of that river,

[46] *U. S. and Mex. Boundary Survey (1854–5). Report of Wm H. Emory*, Wash., 1857, 4to, 3 vol. This is a report of a later survey under a new treaty; but in his 1st chapter Emory gives an outline history of operations under the treaty of 1848, with severe criticisms of Bartlett's acts. He says that when he arrived in the field, Nov. 1851, 'the commissioner was absent on an expedition into Sonora, the commission was in debt, and not one cent was at my disposal to prosecute the survey. Beyond running an erroneous line a degree and a half west of the del Norte, and starting a party with limited means under Lieut. Whipple to survey the Gila, and another to survey the Rio del Norte, nothing had been accomplished.' After his arrival, surveys seem to have been confined to the Rio Grande, and I find no record of any subsequent survey under the old treaty between that river and the Gila.

[47] *Mex. and U. S. Boundary Survey. Report of the Secretary of the Interior*, etc., July 1852, in *U. S. Govt Doc.*, 32d cong. 1st sess., Sen. Ex. Doc. 119, 8vo, 515 p., with maps. See also an earlier report and doc. of 1850 in 31st cong. 1st sess., Sen. Ex. Doc. 34. In 32d cong. 1st sess., Sen. Ex. Doc. 121 (250 p.), is a report of Aug. 1852, containing *Graham's Report on Boundary Line between the U. S. and Mexico*, with a mass of accompanying doc. Graham gives a diary of proceedings after Bartlett's departure till the survey was suspended. See also *Warren's Memoir*, 82 et seq. The quarrel was a disgraceful one, growing mainly out of jealousies between the military, civil, and scientific branches of the commission; also to some extent founded on unfit appointments by political influence. Bartlett blames Graham chiefly, and vice versa. I do not meddle with the merits of the matter. The volumes cited contain also, if life were long enough to search out the items, a tolerably complete record of exploring operations.

then to the point on the said line nearest to such branch,
and thence in a direct line to the same); thence down
the middle of said branch and said river until it empties
into the Rio Colorado." The southern boundary of New
Mexico had indeed been somewhat definitely fixed at
one point as just above El Paso, leaving that town in
Chihuahua; but I have found no evidence that any
western boundary had ever been fixed at all, or even
thought of. There may have been, however, a kind
of tacit agreement, as on a matter of no practical importance, that the line between Chihuahua and Sonora,
that is, a line between Janos and Fronteras in about
longitude 108° 30', extended northward indefinitely.
In no other sense had New Mexico a western boundary;
and in equity, had the treaty gone no further, this
should have been the line adopted. But the treaty
contained an additional provision that "the southern
and western limits of New Mexico, mentioned in this
article, are those laid down in" Disturnell's map of
Mexico, edition of New York, 1847.[48] This map shows
an irregular dotted line extending westward from the
river just above El Paso about 180 miles, and thence
northward. To locate this line was therefore the only
duty of the boundary commission; but in locating it,
should its latitude and longitude be considered, or its
distance north of El Paso and west of the Rio Grande?
This was the question, and an important one, for on
the treaty map the town was some 30 minutes too far
north and the river some two degrees and a half too
far west. The complication will be more clearly understood from the appended map. García Conde of
course claimed the determination by parallels as most
favorable to his nation, while Bartlett for like reasons
favored the other basis of settlement. I think there
can be no doubt that the latter was technically in the
right; but he yielded one point by consenting to fix the
initial monument in latitude 32° 22' on the river; while

[48] A copy of part of this map is included in the volume cited in note 45;
also in various editions of the treaty.

the Mexican commissioner yielded the other by consenting to the extension of the line 180 miles westward
from the river. Bartlett's concession was severely

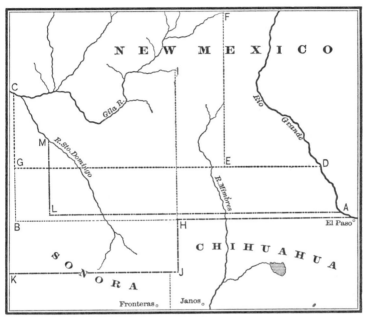

THE BOUNDARY QUESTION.

A B C is the line as determined by distances from the town and river, the
extreme claim of the U. S. commissioner. D E F is the extreme Mexican
claim, or the line as fixed by lat. and long. D G C is the line adopted as a
compromise. A H I would have been the equitable boundary if Disturnell's
map had not been mentioned in the treaty. A L M is the line said to have
been finally fixed by the U. S. surveyor, under the treaty of 1848. A H J K is
the boundary under the later treaty of 1853 and survey of 1854–5.

criticised; but if his solution of the difficulty is regarded
as a compromise it was a wise one, since the territory
gained would have been more valuable than that lost.
But Bartlett's line is said to have been rejected by
his government and a new line adopted on latitude
31° 54′ 40″ from the Rio Grande west to longitude 109°
37′, and on that meridian north to the Santo Domingo

River, though I have not been able to find the record
of such an agreement or survey.[49]

Under the treaty, citizens of New Mexico might
leave the territory or remain either as citizens of the
United States or of Mexico, but such as should not
within one year make known their choice were to
become citizens of the United States. Although I
find no very definite records on the subject, it appears
that many declared their intention of retaining their
Mexican nationality, some of these departing and
others formally withdrawing the declaration, while of
those who departed some came back. It was estimated that in 1848-9 the territory thus lost only
about 1,200, though in 1850 a considerable number
of wealthy hacendados withdrew with their peones and
possessions to Chihuahua.[50] The Mexican government made an appropriation to aid its migrating citizens, and in 1849 Padre Ramon Ortiz and Manuel
Armendariz were sent as commissioners to promote
the movement. Ortiz claimed that in the first county
visited, that of San Miguel del Vado, 900 out of 1,000
families eagerly agreed to go, and that the whole
number of emigrants was likely to reach 80,000; but
that the territorial authorities, frightened at the prospect, threw obstacles in the way. For this reason,
or because of financial difficulties, or because the people became on reflection less desirous of quitting the
land of their birth—to say nothing of the possibility
that the honest presbítero greatly exaggerated the

[49] It is so stated in *Warren's Memoir*, 84, a good authority, but without the
author's usual reference to his sources; and Emory, *U. S. and Mex. Bound.*,
16, also says that Bartlett's line was 'finally repudiated by the government.'
Later records connected with the new treaty of 1853-4 simply show a dispute
but no settlement. I think that Bartlett's opponents may have surveyed the
new line and reported it to the govt, which did not perhaps formally approve
either. Besides the survey of a boundary line, the commissioners were to
explore the country for a railroad within one league north or south of the
Gila, this railroad to be the subject of subsequent agreement between the two
republics. Neither of the lines considered, however, would have given the
U. S. a railroad route. Bartlett's work, published in 1854, seems to imply
that his line was the one approved.
[50] *McCall's Letters*, 496.

original enthusiasm—very little was actually accomplished.[51]

[51] Ortiz' letter of June 9, 1849, to Gov. Más of Chih., in *Pino, Not. Hist.*, 92–8, with other corresp.; *Mexico, Mem. Rel.*, 1849, p. 14; *Id.*, 1850, p. 22. The proceedings were under the colonization law of Aug. 19, 1848 *Mexico, Col. Leyes y Decretos, 1848*, p. 309. It appears that the governor obliged Ortiz to suspend his personal visits to the different counties, alleging that there was danger of a revolt or popular tumult. He consented at first to the appointment of subagents, but suspended also this privilege as soon as it became clear that the desire for emigration was so general. These orders are given in Pino's work as cited. Ortiz also claims that previous to his visit, unfair means had been taken to prevent the citizens from making the formal declarations required by the treaty. I am inclined to think there is much truth in his statements, as well as a degree of exaggeration. Mexico had appropriated $200,000, of which only $25,000 was available, and Ortiz estimated that $1,653,342 would be needed! The allowance was $25 for an adult, and $12 for children. There was also some trouble about the transfer of property, and about Ortiz' official status. In 1850 a Mexican consul was sent to attend to this and other matters.

CHAPTER XIX.

ANNALS OF ARIZONA.

1846-1854.

Affairs in Pimería Alta — Apache Raids — Tubac Abandoned — The Mexican War—Explorations—Kearny's March—Cooke and the Mormons—Wagon Road—Graham's Dragoons—Treaty and Boundary—Whipple and Bartlett—Sitgreaves—Railroad Surveys—Parke's Explorations—Overland Emigration to California—Hayes' Diary—Indians—The Oatman Massacre—Colorado Ferry and Camp Calhoun—Glanton's Outrages—Fort Yuma Established—Colorado City—Navigation of the River—Derby's Survey—The First Steamers.

That part of the country known later as Arizona remained a Mexican possession down to the signing of the treaty of Guadalupe Hidalgo in 1848, and all south of the Gila, the only portion inhabited by any but Indians, for five years longer, or until the signing of the treaty of December 1853, or its approval in 1854. The annals of this southern region, the ancient Pimería Alta, might almost be disposed of by adding 'et cetera' to the chapter in which the record has been brought down to 1845.[1] That is, the Mexicans under the Sonora government barely maintained a precarious possession of Tucson and a few other establishments in the Santa Cruz valley. The Apaches continued their raids, sometimes driving off live-stock from under the very walls of the presidios. Retaliatory raids of the soldiers became less and less effective, though the Pápago allies were somewhat more successful in repelling and pursuing the savages. There was a constant diminution of the population,

[1] See chap. xvi., this volume.

and most of the few remaining ranchos were abandoned. A census report of September 1848, gave Tucson 760 inhabitants, and Tubac 249.[2] In December of the same year, after an attack in which nine persons were killed, Tubac and the adjoining settlement of Tamacácori were abandoned, the people transferring their residence to Tucson.[3] Between this presidio and that of Santa Cruz south of the line it does not clearly appear that a single Mexican establishment of any kind remained, though before 1852 a small garrison had reoccupied Tubac.[4] In the meagre and fragmentary record of Mexican annals down to 1854, I find only an occasional complaint of impending ruin, as in earlier times, with appeals for aid, mention of a few Apache depredations and campaigns, and the names of a few officials, but nothing from which to form anything like a continuous narrative, or to form any more definite idea of the general condition of affairs than that expressed in this paragraph.[5]

[2] *Pinart, Col. Doc.*, print, no. 980. This is a list furnished by Gov. Gándara for election purposes.

[3] *Sonorense*, Feb. 21, 1849. Some details of Apache wars in these years are found in *Hist. North Mex. States*, ii., this series. The Mexicans believed that the Indians were incited by Americans. Doubtless the unfortunate state of affairs in N. Mex., and the acts of disreputable American and Mex. traders, had much to do with Indian troubles.

[4] *Bartlett's Pers. Narr.*, ii. 302 et seq., where a very good account of the state of things in the Sta Cruz valley is given.

[5] I give some items, chiefly from the *Sonorense* and MS. records of the Pinart collection, omitting many more of similar nature but of even less importance. In Sept. 1847 the Pinaleño Apaches pretended to desire peace at Tuscon, but continued their attacks on Tubac. A combined exped. from the three presidios, consisting of 77 soldiers and a force of 133 citizens, Pimas, and friendly Apaches, marched against them, killing 17 and capturing 14, with a loss of two men. *Son.*, Oct. 8th. A year later Capt. Comaduran reports a successful exped. of the Pápagos, bringing in the ears of many Apaches. *Id.*, Dec. 1st. In March 1849 the inhab. appealed for aid to the Sonora congress, declaring their purpose if not aided to go and live among the Gila tribes ! *Id.*, Sept. 28th. Congress promised arms and ammunition, and the com.-gen. assured the people of his desire and power to afford full protection. *Pinart, Col. Doc.*, MS., 113. Sept.–Oct., Col Elias made a successful campaign to the Gila. *Id., Doc. Hist. Son.*, MS., 166–70, with many details. Jan. 1850, over 100 cattle driven off from Tucson. *Son.*, Feb. 1st. Feb. 7th, decree of gov. fixing bounds for the presidios of the 'Colonias militares de Occidente,' including Tubac and Tucson. *Id.*, Feb. 15th. The abandonment of Tucson in March 1850 was reported in the Cal. papers, but doubtless without foundation. Aug., the paymaster with funds for the colonists at Tucson from Arizpe was attacked and lost several men, but saved his money. *Son.*, Sept. 20th. In Dec. the presidio was assaulted in the daytime,

The war of 1846–8, except in the treaty that ended it, had but slight bearing on the history of Arizona. The plans of the United States did not include the occupation of the Pimería towns south of the Gila, and north of that river there were no towns to be occupied, though in a certain sense the conquest of California on the west and New Mexico on the east may be regarded as having included that of the broad region lying between the two. The war also led to the crossing of this region in the southern parts by several parties, thus involving its first exploration by Americans but for the previous exploits of Pattie and other trappers and traders. In August, 1846, General Castro, driven from California, found his way by the Colorado and Papaguería to Altar in Sonora, accompanied by a small party;[6] and at the end of the same month Kit Carson went east by the Gila route as the bearer of despatches from Commodore Stockton,

all the live-stock outside the walls carried off, and 3 or 4 persons killed; then the foe sued for peace (!), offering to give up all their booty, and asserting that there was a division in their ranks as to peace or war. While negotiations were in progress Pápago reënforcements arrived, and the Apaches were attacked and driven off. *Son.*, Jan. 10, 1851. June 1851, mil. comandante acc. to instruc. of this date had no authority over vecinos except in case of an attack. *Id.*, June 27th. July, friendly Apaches attacked by hostiles, and 59 either killed or carried off. *Id.*, Oct. 24th. Pay of the colony for Oct.–Nov., $2,077; paymaster, José M. Elias Carrillo. *Id.*, Nov. 14th. Feb.–April 1852, campaign of Luguez with Pimas and Pápagos. *Pinart, Doc. Hist. Son.*, MS., v. 21–2. In March an exped. from Tubac was defeated by the Ind. *Id.*, 14–15. June, Tucson again attacked and cattle driven off, but by the prompt action of Capt. Agustin Romanos, now com., aided by the juez de paz and his vecinos, and also by Apaches and Pápagos, and by 20 French settlers, the plunder was recovered. In following the foe, tracks of 'American shoes' were found, perhaps not on the feet of Americans. *Id.*, v. 37–41. The French settlers were 57 in number, who this year became citizens, probably with a view of coöperating with Raousset de Boulbon in his filibustering project in Sonora, as most of them joined his party. *Id.*, 60–9, 99. In Nov. Capt. Andrés Zenteno was put in command. *Id.*, 34–6. In 1853 similar items on Apache warfare appear; no indication of any radical change. In July there were 112 friendly Apaches living at Tubac. *Pinart, Col. Doc.*, MS., 118. See items of 1853–4, in *Pinart, Doc. Hist. Son.*, MS., chiefly from *El Sonorense*, v. 176–8, 180–1, 186–90, 192, 212–13, 252–3. José Paredes was com. at Tubac in Sept. 1853. *Id.*, *Col. Doc.*, MS., no. 130. Americans join the Mex. against Apaches in Oct. 1854, killing 21.

[6] *Hist. Cal.*, v. 277–8, this series. The crossing of Arizona between Cal. and Sonora, both by the Tucson and Sonoita routes, was in this and the preceding years not a very unusual or dangerous matter, the Indians being generally well disposed.

announcing somewhat prematurely the conquest of the coast province.[7]

Meeting Carson and inducing him to turn back as guide, General Kearny, with a force of 200 dragoons, left the Rio Grande in the middle of October, reaching the Gila by way of the copper mines, and on the 22d crossed what was later the Arizona boundary. The march of some 400 miles across the entire width of the territory, following the river—except at the big bend—down to the Colorado junction, occupied exactly a month. The journey was marked by no startling adventures or hardships, except the exhaustion of the mules and horses. The few Apaches met were suspicious and would sell no mules; the Pimas farther down the river were altogether friendly and eager for trade, but had no animals for sale; but near the Colorado the army's needs in this respect were supplied from a band of horses that a party of Mexicans under Captain Segura were driving from California to Sonora. The narratives, especially that of Captain Emory, contain a good description of the country traversed, with its plants and animals; and relics of the ancient inhabitants, in the form of ruins, pottery, and rock-inscriptions—now for the first time examined by Americans—attracted much attention. This may be regarded as the first in the series of scientific transcontinental surveys in the south.[8]

Following Kearny, but taking a more southern route that a way might be found for wagons, came Lieutenant-colonel Cooke with the Mormon battalion, arriving on the 2d of December at the rancho of San Bernardino near the south-eastern corner of what was later Arizona. Cooke's route from this point to the intersection with Kearny's, also a new one to any but

[7] *Id.*, 286, 336. There were several subsequent crossings of Arizona in 1847-9 by bearers of despatches, which I do not deem it necessary to record in this volume, as not belonging properly to Arizona annals.

[8] *Emory's Notes of a Military Reconnoissance*, 63-94; *Johnston's Journal; Griffin's Journal*, MS. Names used by Emory, and apparently applied at this time on the upper Gila, were Night Creek, Steeple Rock, Mt Graham, Mt Turnbull, Saddle-back Mt, and Mineral Creek.

Indians and Mexicans, was west to the Rio San Pedro, down that river northward some fifty miles, thence across to Tucson by the line of the later railroad, and north-westward, still not far from the railroad route, to the Gila. The march of the Mormons, by reason of their duty of opening a wagon road and their character as infantry, was much more difficult than that of the dragoons; but they were under a special divine protection presumably not accorded to the less saintly branch of the service. Their only active foes were a herd of wild bulls on the San Pedro, with which they had a battle on the 11th of December, several men being wounded, one of them Lieutenant George Stoneman, since governor of California. Six days later the army camped at Tucson. Captain Comaduran had sent a request to the Americans not to pass through the town, as he had orders to prevent it; and Cooke had in turn proposed the turning-over of a few arms as a token of surrender, binding them not to fight during the war. This was declined, and the comandante with his garrison abandoned the presidio, as did most of the inhabitants. Accordingly, Cooke left a friendly letter for Governor Gándara, reminding him of Sonora's wrongs at the hands of Mexico and the Indians, and suggesting that "the unity of Sonora with the states of the north, now her neighbors, is necessary effectually to subdue these Parthian Apaches;"[9] then he marched on, reaching the Gila on the 21st and the Colorado on January 9, 1847. The wagon road thus opened was not only utilized by the California emigrants in the following years, but as a possible railroad route it was a potent element in prompting the later purchase by the United States of territory south of the Gila.[10]

[9] Dec. 17th, Capt. Comaduran wrote to the com. gen. of Sonora that an Amer. force of 500 men had arrived at Tucson. Dec. 28th, the com. gen. issued a circular stating that on receipt of the news he began organizing a force to repel the invaders, but soon heard that the enemy had evacuated Tucson and marched 'precipitately' for Alta California. *Sonorense*, Jan. 1, 1847. There was in the night of the 17th a false alarm of attack from the Mexicans, which caused much excitement in camp.

[10] *Cooke's Journal*, in *U. S. Govt Doc.*, 30th cong. spec. sess., Sen. Doc. 2; *Id.*, *Report*, in *Emory's Notes*, 549-62, with maps of route; *Id.*, *Conquest*, 138-72,

During the war there were no more explorations or marches across Arizona to be noticed here; but in 1848, after the treaty of peace, a battalion of dragoons under Major Lawrence P. Graham marched from Chihuahua to California. Coming from Janos this party reached San Bernardino the 4th of October, but instead of following Cooke's trail, Graham kept on south of the line to Santa Cruz presidio, and thence followed the river down to Tucson. The Gila was reached at the end of the month, and the Colorado on the 22d of November. The Americans were delighted, as had been those under Kearny and Cooke, with the hospitality of the Gila Pimas, and the thrift displayed at their villages exceeding anything elsewhere seen in the transcontinental journey. Owing to the drunkenness and consequent incompetence of the leader, this party endured greater hardships than either of the preceding. No narrative of this march has ever been published, but I have Captain Cave J. Coutts' manuscript diary, which contains an excellent account of adventures on the way, and many valuable notes on the country.[11]

The treaty of 1848 adopted the Gila as the international boundary, so far as Arizona is concerned, except that the Bartlett line on latitude 32° 22' and longitude about 109° 50'—and the corrected line on latitude 31° 54', longitude 109° 20', and the Santo Domingo River—gave the United States a small tract south of the Gila. The survey in 1851, under commissioners Bartlett and García Conde, has been recorded in the preceding chapter.[12] The river, as a natural boundary, hardly required a formal survey,

with map; *Tyler's Hist. Mormon Battalion*, 211–40; *Bigler's Diary of a Mormon*, MS. Leroux and Charbonneaux were the principal guides; Stephen C. Foster served as interpreter. Says Tyler, when at the Pima villages on the Gila: 'Colonel Cooke very kindly suggested to our senior officers that this vicinity would be a good place for the exiled saints to locate. A proposition to this effect was favorably received by the Indians.' The Mormons take much pride in having thus been the pioneer surveyors of the Southern Pacific Railroad, while their companions at Salt Lake were 'paving the way for the Union Pacific.'

[11] *Coutts' Diary of a March to California in 1848*, MS., p. 62–98.
[12] See p. 467 et seq., this volume, and maps.

especially after Emory's reconnoissance of 1846; still
the most complete possible exploration of the region
for general purposes, and particularly the search for a
railroad route, were deemed essential. So far as can
be learned from the confused records, the results were
not very important. Mr Bartlett, departing from the
copper-mine region in September 1851, for Sonora,
and not returning on account of illness, left on the
San Pedro a party under Gray and Whipple to complete the survey of the Gila. Gray, with two men,
subsequently crossed the country to Tucson, went up
the river, and met Bartlett again at Santa Cruz,
returning to the San Pedro on the 2d of October.
Next day the whole party started for the Gila, reaching
it on the 9th at a point just below the San Cárlos
junction; and by December 24th the survey had
been completed to a point within about 60 miles of
the Colorado, when it was suspended for want of supplies, and the explorers found their way to San Diego
in January 1852. Here they met Bartlett again,
who in May, with Whipple and party, started for
the Gila to complete the survey. Before reaching
the Colorado, Colonel Craig, commanding the escort,
was killed by deserters whom he was trying to arrest.
The Yumas were found to be hostile, but an escort
to the Pima villages was furnished from the garrison
at Fort Yuma. The journey through Arizona, up
the Gila and Santa Cruz, was accomplished between
June 18th and July 24th. This seems to be all that
is necessary, or possible in the space at my command,
to say about the boundary survey under the treaty of
Guadalupe Hidalgo, so far as it effects the subject of
this volume, though there were many complications
of some interest. It should be added that Bartlett's
narrative contains an excellent description of the
country visited, with notes on early history, and the
aborigines, and views illustrating physical features,
and especially ruins and relics of antiquity.[13]

[13] *Bartlett's Personal Narrative*, i. 355-405, from copper mines to Sta Cruz;
map of the regions surveyed; ii. 156-313, return from Ft Yuma in 1852,

It was in 1851 that the first government explora-
tion was made across northern Arizona.   Captain L.
Sitgreaves was ordered to follow the Zuñi, Colorado
Chiquito, and Colorado rivers down to the gulf.
With a party of twenty he left Zuñi in September,
but did not attempt to follow the river through the
great cañons, turning off to the west on the 8th of
October, crossing the country just above the parallel
of 35°, approximately on the route followed by Padre
Garcés in 1776, reaching the Mojave region on the
Colorado, November 5th, and following the main
river south to Fort Yuma, where he arrived at the
end of November.   The condition of the animals and
lack of supplies had not permitted this expedition to
accomplish all that had been expected of it, but the
result of this first exploration was an interesting itinerary, a map of the route, and various scientific reports
on a new region.[14]

Sitgreaves' exploration was followed in 1853–4 by
the 35th parallel Pacific Railroad survey under Lieutenant A. W. Whipple.   With Lieutenant J. C. Ives
as chief assistant in a corps of twelve, and an escort
of the 7th U. S. infantry under Lieutenant John M.
Jones, Whipple, having completed the survey from
Fort Smith across New Mexico, left Zuñi on November 23, 1853.   His route was for the most part somewhat south of that followed by Sitgreaves, though

and p. 597–602, Lieut Whipple's report of the trip down the Gila.   Another
report of Whipple is attached to *Graham's Report*, 32d cong. 1st sess., Sen.
Ex.'Doc. 121, p. 221–5.   See also, on the killing of Craig, Webb's report, etc.,
in *U. S. Gov't Doc.*, special sess., 1853, Sen. Doc. 129, p. 125–36.   See also
Mex. and U. S. Boundary Survey, 32d cong. 1st sess., Sen. Ex. Doc. 119,
passim, especially reports of A. B. Gray, on p. 267–9, 305–7, and that of
Thos H. Webb, sec. of the commission, p. 465–8.   Gray states that monuments were erected all along the line.

[14] *Sitgreaves, report of an Expedition down the Zuñi and Colorado rivers, by
Captain L. Sitgreaves, corps topographical engineers.   Accompanied by maps,
sketches, views, and illustrations.*   Wash., 1853, 8vo, 198 p., 80 pl. and map.
The appendices are *Woodhouse (S. W.), Report on the Natural History*, with
chapters on zoölogy, botany, etc., by different men; and *Woodhouse, Medical
Report.*   The plates are many of them colored.   The party consisted of Capt.
Sitgreaves, Lieut. J. G. Parke, Dr S. W. Woodhouse, physician and naturalist,
R. H. Kern, draughtsman, Antoine Leroux, guide, 5 Americans, and 10
Mexicans, packers, etc.   An escort of 30 men of the 2d artill. was com-
manded by Maj. H. L. Hendrick.

HIST. ARIZ. AND N. MEX. 31

his survey covered the same region. Descending the Zuñi, and Colorado Chiquito, and later the Santa María and Bill Williams fork, this party reached the Colorado the 20th of February, followed that river up to latitude 34°, 50', and thence in March continued the survey across California. The resulting report as published by government, though of similar nature, is very much more elaborate and extensive than that of Sitgreaves, containing an immense amount of the most valuable descriptive, geographic, and scientific matter on northern Arizona, profusely illustrated by fine colored engravings and maps.[15]

The Mexican government having permitted, a little in advance of the new treaty, the survey for a railroad route south of the line, Lieutenant John G. Parke with a party of about 30 and an escort under Lieutenant George Stoneman left San Diego January 24, 1854, and began his survey at the Pima villages on the Gila. He reached Tucson the 20th of February, thence proceeding to the San Pedro and eastward by a route somewhat north of Cooke's wagon road for a part of the way, known as Nugent's trail. Coming again into Cooke's road on March 7th, he followed it to the Rio Grande.[16] Again in May 1855 Lieuten-

---

[15] *Whipple, Report of Explorations for a railway route, near the thirty-fifth parallel of north latitude, from the Mississippi River to the Pacific Ocean, by Lieutenant A. W. Whipple, corps of topographical engineers, assisted by Lieutenant J. C. Ives, etc., 1853–4.* Wash., 1856, 4to, being vol. iii. of the *Pacific Railroad Reports*, 33d cong. 2d sess., Sen. Ex. Doc. 78. There is an introduction consisting of extracts from Whipple's preliminary report, 36 pages; then Part i., Itinerary, 136 p. (the Arizona matter being on p. 67–120); Part ii., Report of Topographical Features, 77 p.; Part iii., *Whipple, Ewbank, and Turner, Report upon the Indian Tribes,* 127 p., a standard authority on the subject, with many colored plates, résumés of aboriginal traditions and Spanish history, etc.; Part iv., Report on the geology of the route, 175 p., maps. Whipple's preliminary report may be found in 33d cong. 1st sess., Ex. Doc. 129, with maps. Also in *Pac. R. R. Repts,* i. 1–134, passim, is some information on this route in doc. attached to the report of the sec. war, Feb. 27, 1855. Excellent résumés of this and other surveys may be found in *Warren's Memoir.* The principal members of the corps were J. M. Bigelow, surgeon and botanist, Jules Marcou, geologist, C. B. R. Kennerly, physician and naturalist, A. H. Campbell, railroad engineer, H. B. Möllhausen, topographer and artist. The *Tagebuch einer Reise von Mississippi nach den Küsten der Südsee von Baldwin Möllhausen,* Leipzig, 1858, 4to, 499 p., colored plates, map, is an excellent narrative of the same exploration.
[16] *Parke, Report of Explorations, etc., between Doña Ana and Pimas Villages on the Gila,* in *Pac. R. R. Repts,* ii., no. 6, 28 p.

ant Parke with another party started from San Diego
for the Pima villages, and made a more careful survey
by several routes of the country stretching eastward
from the San Pedro.[17]

After the discovery of gold in California, emigrants
in large numbers began to cross southern Arizona,
from Sonora and other Mexican states in 1848, and
from the eastern United States in 1849. Of this
movement, which continued for many years, we have
naturally no records except for a few parties. The
route followed was by the Santa Cruz and Gila valleys, though some Mexican parties preferred to cross
Papaguería; and the Americans reached Tucson from
the Rio Grande for the most part by Cooke's wagon
road of 1846, though various cut-offs were likewise
attempted. It was a journey of much hardship
always, and especially so in seasons of drought, though
not more difficult apparently than on other routes.
The experiences of the gold-seekers on any of the
great lines of travel to California would supply material for a fascinating volume, but only a few of the
diaries are extant, and not even one of them can be
closely followed here. The journal kept by Benjamin
Hayes in 1849 is the most complete that I have seen,
minutely describing the events of each day's progress
of his large party from the end of October, when they
left the Rio Grande, to the end of December, when
they crossed the Colorado into California. The tedious
march, novel features of the country and its products
noted, the search for grass and water, petty accidents
to men and mules, occasional meeting with Indians,

---

[17] *Parke, Report of Explorations from the Pima Villages to the Rio Grande,*
1854-5, in *Pac. R. R. Repts,* vii., pt ii. pp. 19-42, with maps. Description
of the country and colored plates of scenery. See also *Warren's Memoir,*
80-1. In *El Nacional,* March 24, 1854, is a communication from Ayud. Inspector Bernabé Gomez at Tucson, dated March 2d, reporting Parke's
arrival to survey boundaries.

In *Brown's Apache Country,* 18-19, is a mention of exploring expeditions
in these years, which is repeated substantially in *Hinton's Hand-book,* 32-3,
Hamilton's Resources, 21, *Arizona Hist.* (Elliott & Co.), 62-3, and in other
works. This would seem to be a carelessly prepared record, omitting some
explorations and adding others that did not reach Arizona.

the frequent and careful perusal of records left on trees and rocks by preceding parties, delays caused by illness and occasional deaths, passing the graves of earlier emigrants, discussions on the route and speculations on the prospects offered by the land of gold, and the thousand and one petty items that make up this journal and hundreds of others written and unwritten—all give a strong fascination to the monotonous record, but all resist condensation, or if condensed show simply that an emigrant party once on a time passed that way. The parties numbered hundreds, and the emigrants tens of thousands, but details must and may safely be left to the imagination.[18]

Both exploring and emigrant parties had occasional troubles with the Apaches, who could not always resist the temptation to steal animals, though their chief fury was directed against the Mexicans, and they often professed friendship for the Americans, and even aided them for compensation. Large parties with due vigilance had no serious difficulty in Apachería, but small and careless companies were sometimes less fortunate;[19] and after 1854 depredations seem to have increased. The most notable, or at least the best recorded, of their outrages before that date was the Oatman massacre of 1851. Roys Oatman, with his wife and seven children, left Independence, Missouri, in August 1850, with a party of about 50 emigrants, part of whom remained at Tucson and the rest at the

---

[18] *Hayes (Benj.), Diary of a journey overland from Socorro to Warner's Ranch, 1849–50.* Autograph MS. presented by the author. There are many scattered items in books and newspapers about individuals and parties who crossed the plains by the southern route, but none of these seem to require notice in connection with Arizona history. Information about the country is better derived from the official surveys. The journals of the explorers, however, often note the meeting with an emigrant party.

[19] In *Bartlett's Pers. Narr.*, and *Cremony's Life among the Apaches*, as well as in the journals of other railroad and boundary surveyors, are found many items of Indian affairs; others are given in such works as *Cozzens' Marvellous Country*; and many more in newspaper records, though the latter are often indefinite in respect of date and other details. Arizona was in these years a part of New Mexico, and much that is recorded of Indian affairs in the annals of that territory as given in government reports may be applied to this western region. April 11, 1849, John C. Hays is appointed sub-Indian agent for the Gila tribes. *Cal. & N. Mex., Mess.*, 1850, p. 230–1.

Pima villages, while Oatman and his family went on alone in February 1851. He was passed on the 15th by John Lecount, by whom he sent a letter to Major Heintzelman at Fort Yuma, asking for aid.[20] A few days later while encamped on the Gila just below the big bend, at a place since known by his name, he was visited by a party of Indians who seemed friendly at first but soon attacked the family, and killed father, mother, and four children, leaving one son, Lorenzo, aged 14, stunned and presumably dead, and carrying off as captives two daughters, Olive aged 16, and Mary Ann a girl of 10. The Indians are said to have been Tonto Apaches, though there was some doubt on this point not yet entirely removed, I think. Lorenzo Oatman recovered and found his way back to the Pima villages, thence going with the other emigrant families to Fort Yuma, and to San Francisco. The commandant of the post, on the receipt of the letter, sent two men with supplies; but on hearing of the disaster did not feel at liberty to pursue the savages or attempt the captives' recovery, because the massacre had been committed on Mexican soil.[21] The captive girls were carried northward into the mountains, and after a time sold to the Mojaves. The younger died after a year or two, but Olive was kept as a slave until 1857, when, chiefly by the efforts of a

[20] I have this original letter, furnished by Capt. G. C. Smith, U. S. A., at Camp Grant, A. T., in 1877. *Misel. Hist. Pap.*, MS., 18; also a letter of Heintzelman of March 27th in which he says he has heard from a party of emigrants that O. had been killed on Feb. 18th, probably by Maricopas; also the testimony of Lorenzo D. Oatman on the occurrence.

[21] The excuse seems to me insufficient under the circumstances. Stratton and young Oatman bitterly complained of Heintzelman's refusal to succor the emigrants or pursue the murderers, stating that he brutally disregarded the entreaties of his men and others. There is probably much exaggeration in the charges. It seems that Hewitt and Lecount wrote to the newspapers on the subject, but Heintzelman answered in the S. F. *Alta* of July 24, 1851, claiming that he could not have prevented the disaster, since it occurred two days before he received Oatman's letter, giving his reasons as in my text for not pursuing the Indians, and stating that Hewitt and Lecount were acting in a spirit of revenge because he had refused to furnish an escort for their gold-hunting operations. Bartlett, *Pers. Narr.*, ii. 203–4, who was at the fort in 1852, says: 'The major immediately despatched a party of soldiers with provisions for those still behind, and with orders to scour the country, and endeavor if possible to recover the missing girls. But they saw no Indians, nor has it yet been ascertained by what tribe the outrage was committed.'

Mr Grinell, she was ransomed, brought to the fort, and joined her brother, the two soon going east to live in New York. Her sufferings as a captive had of course been great, though her fate was in some respects less terrible than might have been expected. A volume founded on her statements and those of her brother had a very wide circulation.[22]

The number of emigrants crossing the Colorado near the Gila junction before the end of 1851 has been probably overestimated at 60,000, but they were very numerous.[23] They and the Indians and the soldiers made this the most bustling point in the country for several years. The Indians were not at first openly hostile, though they required constant watching, and the different tribes were often at war with each other, but rendered the emigrants some aid in crossing. Lieutenant Cave J. Coutts, commanding an escort to the boundary surveyors under Whipple, established Camp Calhoun on the California side at the end of September 1849, and for two months greatly aided the worn-out and hungry gold-seekers,

[22] *Stratton, Captivity of the Oatman girls; being an interesting narrative of life among the Apache and Mohave Indians; containing also an interesting account of the massacre of the Oatman family by the Apache Indians in 1851; the narrow escape of Lorenzo D. Oatman; the capture of Olive A. and Mary A. Oatman; the death by starvation of the latter; the five years' suffering and captivity of Olive A. Oatman; also, her singular recapture in 1856; as given by Lorenzo D. and Olive A. Oatman, the only surviving members of the family, to the author, R. B. Stratton.* S. F., 1857, 12mo, 231 p., portraits, map, and cuts. Also the same, 3d ed., 26th thousand, N. Y. (1858), 12mo, 290 p. The subject was a most fascinating one, as shown by the large sale; but the intrinsic interest was, or should have been, wellnigh destroyed by the dress of literary fustian in which it pleased the Rev. Stratton to present the narrative of the captive woman. The Oatman massacre is mentioned in nearly all Arizona books and articles. Conklin, *Picturesque Arizona*, 195–6, says that Olive Oatman died in a N. Y. insane asylum before 1877. I have a daguerreotype likeness taken just after her release, belonging to the Hayes' collection. In the *S. Diego Union*, April 25, 1856, is a narrative founded on an interview with the released captive. See also a letter of Capt. Nauman to Capt. Jones, in *U. S. Govt Doc.*, 34th cong. 1st sess., Sen. Doc. 66, p. 67–8; act of relief by Cal. legislature. *Cal. Jour. Ass.*, 1856, p. 923; *Jour. Sen.*, 906; *Hayes' Scraps, Ind.*, ii. 75–81: *Id., Angeles*, xviii. 11–15.

[23] An excellent guide-book for emigrants by this route was the *Route from the Gulf of Mexico and the Lower Mississippi Valley to California and the Pacific Ocean, illustrated by a general map and sectional maps; with directions to travellers. Compiled by Robert Creuzbaur, 1849.* N. Y., 1849, 16mo, 40 p. This book is made up chiefly of extracts from official diaries of the explorers; hence its comparative excellence.

whose arrival is noted almost every day.[24] The 1st of November there arrived a flat-boat which had made the voyage down the Gila from the Pima villages with Mr Howard and family and two men, a doctor and a clergyman, on board. During this voyage, also, a son was born to Mrs Howard, perhaps the first child of American parents born in Arizona, and named, as Coutts tells us, Gila. The lieutenant is understood to have purchased the craft, which plied as a ferry-boat during the remainder of his stay, and was then transported to San Diego, where it was used on the bay. Such was the history of the first Colorado ferry.[25] After the departure of Coutts, the Mexican surveying party remained till the end of the year, and the ferry service—perhaps with another boat —was continued by the officer commanding the escort.[26]

Early in 1850, Lincoln seems to have engaged in the business of running the Colorado ferry, soon form-

[24] *Coutts' Diary*, MS., 128–67, extending from Sept. 14th, when he left S. Diego, to Nov. 22d, not long before he left the Colorado on his return, the diary terminating abruptly. It is a very interesting and amusing narrative of the officer's experience in attending to the complicated wants of the scientists, the emigrants, and the various bands of Indians. Several parties of U. S. officials, in different branches of the service, also passed that way, and one of these, Capt. Thorn, was drowned with three companions on Nov. 16th, by the upsetting of a canoe.

[25] *Coutts' Diary*, MS., 165. The author does not mention the purchase or any ferry; but many pioneers remember crossing the river on his ferry. E. H. Howard, in the *S. F. Bulletin*, July 8, 1885, gives the most complete record. He says the boat, 16 ft long by 5 ft 6 in. wide, was built for the trip, and first launched on Lake Michigan, being mounted on wheels for land service, but used to cross rivers on the way. The writer sailed in her later on S. Diego Bay; and he says the boy born on the Gila is still living in Lake Co., Cal. See other letters, in *Id.*, July 10th and Aug. 24th. One writer thinks the institution was not properly a ferry, because skiffs and canoes had been used at the crossing before. Some writers imply that Coutts' boat remained at the Colorado for the next season. I think there may be some doubt about its having been carried that year to S. Diego.

[26] *Hayes' Diary*, MS., 143–6. H. crossed on Dec. 31st. He found a rope stretched across the river, by which the boat (not described) was guided. The charge was $2 for a man or mule, which caused some swearing among the Missourians; but Iturbide (son of the ex-emperor), who was interpreter for the boundary commission, had been educated at the same school as Hayes, and obtained a reduction in the ferry rates. Col Carrasco estimated the emigrants of the season at 12,000. It was complained that Coutts had collected a tax from all Mexican emigrants. C. in his diary mentions that he was advised to do so, but does not tell us if he followed the advice. It was understood that the Indians had a ferry for emigrants farther down the river.

ing a partnership with one John Glanton, described as
leader of a gang of cutthroats, who had been engaged
in hunting Apaches for a scalp premium in Sonora
and Chihuahua, but had been driven out by the government, when it was discovered that they brought
in the scalps of friendly Indians or even of Mexicans.
On the Colorado these villains continued their evil
ways, plundering emigrants and attributing their depredations to the Indians.   The Yumas were at first
friendly, but soon became hostile, especially when the
manager of their opposition ferry—said to have been
a deserter from the army—was killed by Glanton;
and they attacked their white rivals, killing about a
dozen, including the leaders.[27]   A little later, in July
of the same year, we are told that another party under
Jaeger and Hartshorne reëstablished the ferry, bringing lumber from San Diego for the construction of
their boat, and continuing the business profitably for
over a year.   On November 27, 1850, Heintzelman
arrived from San Diego to establish a garrison and
protect the emigrants.   His post was called at first
Camp Independence, but was transferred in March
1851 to the site of the old Spanish mission, and was
soon named Fort Yuma.   There was much trouble
about supplies, but the Indians were not hostile, and
in June the fort was left in charge of Lieutenant L.
W. Sweeney with ten men.   Soon the Yumas became
troublesome, killing some immigrants and even attacking the post; the scurvy also became prevalent and
supplies exhausted; Captain Davidson took command
in November; and in December fort and ferry were
abandoned.   Heintzelman came back in February
1852 to rebuild the fort and permanently reëstablish

[27] *Yuma Sentinel*, Aug. 11, 1877; *S. Diego World*, Feb. 1, 1873; *Ariz. Hist.*
(Elliott & Co.), 245; *Hamilton's Resources*, 85.   It is generally implied that all
this occurred in 1849, which is hardly possible.   Three men are said to have
escaped, C. O. Brown, Joe Anderson, and another.   In the *Ariz. Hist.*, 60-1,
John Galantin is named as leader of the scalp-hunters, and is said to have
been engaged in driving sheep from N. Mex. to Cal., being killed by the Yumas with all his gang, and 21 other American sheep-drivers.   There is evidently some confusion here.

the garrison. Complicated Indian hostilities, chiefly on the California side, continued until late in the same year, when a treaty was made, though the Yumas and Cocopas still fought occasionally among themselves.[28]

Fort Yuma was in California, and across the Colorado there seems to have been no permanent settlement until 1854, though temporary structures may have stood there at times in connection with the ferry. In 1854 a store was perhaps built, and a site for Colorado City was formally surveyed; but in 1861 there were still only one or two buildings, which were washed away in the flood of 1862; and the real growth of the place, later called Arizona City and finally Yuma, seems not to have begun until about 1864.[29] The early navigation of the Colorado is a subject demanding notice in this connection. When Major Heintzelman was ordered to establish a military post at Yuma, an exploration of the river was determined on with a view to the furnishing of supplies by that route. Lieutenant George H. Derby, of later fame as a humorist under the name of John Phœnix, was put in charge of the survey, and sailed from San Francisco, November 1, 1840, on the schooner *Invincible*, Captain A. H. Wilcox. The month of January 1851 was spent in the river, up which the schooner,

[28] The early annals of Ft Yuma are given with apparent care and accuracy in a series of articles published in the *Yuma Sentinel*, May 4, 11, 18, 25, 1878. In Oct. 1852, the Yumas are said to have numbered 972. Oct. 26th, a fire destroyed most of the buildings. In Dec. an earthquake made some changes in the river. In 1853 there was much fighting between the Indian tribes. In April 1854 some of Walker's filibusters arrived from the mouth of the Colorado. In July Capt Geo. H. Thomas took command. In Jan. 1855 a new treaty with Yumas and Cocopas. Changes in commanders, etc., down to 1861 are given. It should be noted that in Jan. 1851 the proprietors of the ferry are named by Lieut. Derby, who met them on the river, as Ogden and Henchelwood. *Derby's Report*, 18.

[29] See references in two preceding notes. Also *Los Angeles Star*, Nov. 16, 1854; *Hayes' Scraps, Ariz.*, v. 109; *Id.*, *S. Diego*, i. 18; *Hinton's Hand-book*, 247. Pumpelly, *Across America*, 60, found but one house in 1861. He heard from a friend (C. D. Poston) that the town survey in 1854 had been simply a device to pay ferry charges. The friend and party were bound to California and had no money; the engineer (Ehrenberg) was set to work on the survey, and the German ferry-man (Jaeger) became so enthusiastic over the prospective rise of his property that he gladly took city lots for ferriage. Lieut. Michler, in *Yuma Sentinel*, Feb. 16, 1878, also mentions the city on paper in 1854.

drawing eight or nine feet of water, could only ascend
some 25 miles to latitude 30° 50', but in his boat
Derby went up 60 miles farther, meeting Heintzelman
and a party from Yuma.[30]   It appears that also in the
spring of 1851 George A. Johnson arrived at the
river's mouth on the schooner *Sierra Nevada* with
supplies for the fort, and lumber from which were
built flat-boats for the trip up the Colorado.   In 1852
the first steamer, the *Uncle Sam*, was brought by
Captain Turnbull on a schooner to the head of the
gulf, and there put together for the river trip.   She
reached Fort Yuma at the beginning of December,
but had been obliged to land her cargo of supplies
some distance below.   After running on the river for
a year or two, the *Uncle Sam* grounded and sank,
being replaced in January 1854 by the *General Jesup*,
under Captain Johnson, the new contractor, but exploding in August.   The *Colorado*, a stern-wheeler
120 feet long, was put on the route in the autumn of
1855, and from this time the steam navigation, with
an occasional opposition line, seems to have been continuous.[31]

[30] *Derby (Geo. H.), Reconnoissance of the Gulf of California and the Colorado
River, 1850–1*.   Wash., 1852, 8vo, 28 p., cuts and maps, being report of sec.
war, June 15, 1852, 32d cong. 1st sess., Sen. Ex. Doc. 81.
[31] *Yuma Sentinel*, May 4, 25, 1878; J. A. Mellen, in *Ariz. History*, 318–19,
245; *Hinton's Hand-book*, 247–8.   In *Hayes' Scraps, Mining*, v. 60–2, I find
the articles of incorporation of the Gila Mining and Steam Navigation Company, organized at S. Francisco in Nov. 1853.

CHAPTER XX.

THE GADSDEN PURCHASE.

1853-1863.

TREATY OF 1853—SOUTHERN ARIZONA ADDED TO THE UNITED STATES—NEW
BOUNDARY SURVEY—BEALE'S ROAD—IVES ON THE COLORADO—SOUTHERN
ROAD AND OVERLAND STAGE—MILITARY POSTS—MINING DEVELOPMENTS
—FORT YUMA—GILA PLACERS—INDIAN AFFAIRS—APACHE RAIDS—
COCHISE ON THE WAR-PATH—CRABB AND THE FILIBUSTERS—SONORAN
VAGABONDS—OUTLAWS FROM TEXAS AND CALIFORNIA—POLITICS—EF-
FORTS FOR A TERRITORIAL ORGANIZATION—COOK AND MOWRY AT WASH-
INGTON—BILLS IN CONGRESS—CONSTITUTIONAL CONVENTION—THE FIRST
BOOK—ARIZUMA—FINAL SUCCESS—WAR OF THE REBELLION—SECESSION
OF ARIZONA—TROOPS WITHDRAWN—TRIUMPH OF APACHES—CONFEDER-
ATES TAKE TUCSON—BUT RETREAT BEFORE THE CALIFORNIA COLUMN—
BIBLIOGRAPHY OF THE PERIOD.

ON December 30, 1853, James Gadsden, United
States minister to Mexico, concluded a treaty by which
the boundary line was moved southward so as to give
the United States, for a money consideration of
$10,000,000, all of modern Arizona south of the Gila,
an effort so to fix the line as to include a port on the
gulf being unsuccessful.[1] The treaty was first concluded on the 13th of December, but in consequence

[1] Text of the Gadsden treaty in *New Mexico, Compiled Laws*, 38–44; *U. S.
Govt Doc.*, 33d cong. 1st sess., H. Ex. Doc. 109; 47th cong. 2d sess., H. Mis.
Doc. 45; *Mexico, Legislacion Mejicana*, June–Dec. 1854, 117–32; *Dublan* and
Lozano, Legislacion Mej., vii. 261–4; *Ariz., Howell Code*, 482–5; and elsewhere
often repeated. The boundary as fixed by this treaty was the Rio Grande
up to lat. 31° 47', due west 100 miles; south to lat. 31° 20'; west on that
parallel to long. 111°; thence in a straight line to a point in the Colorado
River 20 miles below the Gila junction; up the middle of the Colorado to the
intersection of the former line (that is, to mouth of the Gila); and thence on
the former line to the Pacific. This is the line as it still exists in 1887. Besides the boundary changes, the U. S. gained by this treaty two important
advantages: 1st, by art. 11, a release from the responsibility for outrages by
U. S. Indians in Mex. territory, art. 12 of the former treaty being abrogated;
and 2d, by art 8, free railroad transit across the isthmus of Tehuantepec.

of new instructions from Washington was modified
on the 30th. Again it was changed—notably by reducing the price from twenty to ten millions—by the
United States senate. In June 1854 it came back
with Mexican approval to Washington; on the 28th
and 29th, after much debate in the house, a bill appropriating the money was passed by congress;[2] on the
30th the treaty was published by President Pierce,
and by President Santa Anna on the 20th of July.
Of the preliminary negotiations and the successive
modifications of terms, not much is definitely known;
but the latter may probably have included, not only
the reduction of price and the introduction of the
Tehuantepec concession, but also a reduction of territory—perhaps involving the cession of a gulf port—
and the omission of an article making the United
States responsible for filibustering expeditions across
the line.[3]

On the face of the matter this Gadsden treaty was
a tolerably satisfactory settlement of a boundary dispute, and a purchase by the United States of a route
for a southern railroad to California. Under the
treaty of 1848, the commissioners, as we have seen,
had agreed on latitude 32° 22′ as the southern boundary of New Mexico, but the United States surveyor
had not agreed to this line, had perhaps surveyed
another in 31° 54′, and the New Mexicans claimed

[2] See debates in *Cong. Globe*, 1853–4, p. 1466, 1476, 1519–68, passim.
The treaty had to be ratified before June 30th, and as it was presented to
congress on the 21st the appropriation bill had to be passed in a hurry.
Friends of the measure would not permit the passage of a resolution calling
on the president for instructions to Gadsden and correspondence on the
treaty; and opposition was based—nominally at least—on unwillingness to
vote money for a treaty whose true inwardness was not known, especially as
many mysterious rumors were current of stock-jobbing schemes and far-reaching political intrigues of the administration and of the south. The bill was
passed in the house by a vote of 103 to 62, and in the senate by 34 to 6.

[3] In *Rivera, Hist. Jalapa*, iv. 418–19, 458–9, 487–9, 499, is given what pur-
ports to be a résumé of the treaty in its original form. Art. 4 provided for
a junta to decide on Mex. claims not in the final treaty; art. 8 bound both
governments to prevent filibustering, replaced finally by the Tehuantepec
clause. The original boundary is not given. Santa Anna, however, *A sus
Compatriotas*, April 12, 1858, in a defence of his policy, says that the boundary was modified, and that he rejected Gadsden's propositions for a cession
of Baja Cal. and parts of Chih. and Sonora.

the Mesilla valley between the two lines as part of their territory. The United States were, to some extent, bound by the act of their commissioner; but Mexico, besides being wrong on the original proposition, was not in condition to quarrel about so unimportant a matter. On the other hand, the northern republic could afford to pay for a railroad route through a country said to be rich in mines; and Mexico, though national pride was strongly opposed to a sacrifice of territory, was sadly in need of money, and sold a region that was practically of no value to her.[4] In both countries there was much bitter criticism of the measure, and a disposition to impute hidden motives to the respective administrations. I am not prepared to say that there were not such motives; but I find little support for the common belief that the Gadsden purchase was effected with a definite view to the organization of a southern confederacy, though this theory was entertained in the north at the time. It is a remarkable circumstance that in Mexico, both by the supporters and foes of the measure, it was treated as a cession of the Mesilla valley in settlement of the boundary dispute, though that valley was, in reality, but a very small and unimportant portion of the territory ceded.

William H. Emory was appointed United States commissioner and surveyor to establish the new boundary line, José Salazar Ilarregui being the Mexican commissioner, and Francisco Jimenez chief engineer. The commissioners met at El Paso at the end of 1854, and the initial monument was fixed on January 31, 1855. In June the survey had been carried

---

[4] As to the abrogating of art. 11 of the treaty of 1848, Santa Anna declared—*A sus Comp.*, 8–11—that he had never for a moment expected the U. S. to keep their agreement by paying for damages done by the Indians; while in the U. S. this was held out as a great gain in view of immense prospective claims on the part of Mexico. It was at least a release from embarrassing promises which never would have been kept. On the Gadsden treaty, see also *Zamacois*, *Hist. Mej.*, xiii. 776; *Domenech*, *Hist. Mej.*, ii. 262–6; *Mex.*, *Mem. Relac.*, 1870, p. 410–11, 433; and most other histories of Mexico; also mention in most works on Arizona and New Mexico, including *Johnson's Hist. Ariz.*, 24.

westward to Los Nogales, or longitude 111°. Meanwhile Lieutenant N. Michler arrived at Fort Yuma at the end of 1854, and was occupied until May 1855, with Salazar, in fixing the initial monument on the Colorado and surveying the line for a short distance eastward toward Sonoita; but they were obliged to suspend operations for lack of water, and proceeded by the Gila and Tucson route to Nogales, where they met Emory in June, and before the end of August completed the survey westward. There were no controversies in connection with the operations under Emory and Ilarregui, the Mexicans and Americans working in perfect harmony for a speedy and economical termination of the work, and all being in marked contrast to the disgraceful and costly wranglings of the former commissions. There was nothing in the personal experiences of the surveying parties that calls for notice here. The published report contains an excellent description of the country with various scientific appendices of great value.[5]

Besides the boundary survey, there are but few official explorations to be noted, though by prospectors and Indian fighters the whole country was pretty thoroughly explored in these years. In 1857 Edward F. Beale opened a wagon road on the 35th parallel, following nearly the route of Whipple and Sitgreaves. He left Zuñi in August, and reached the

[5] *United States and Mexican Boundary Survey. Report of William H. Emory, Major first cavalry and U. S. commissioner.* Wash., 1857, 4to, 3 vol., many fine engravings and colored plates. The narratives of Emory and Michler, with other matter directly connected with the geographic survey, fill 252 p. of vol. i., the rest of the work being devoted to the geology, botany, and zoology of the expedition. Along the line as surveyed, monuments of stone or iron were erected at frequent stations, from each of which careful sketches of the topography in different directions were made, in order that the sites of the monuments, if destroyed by the Indians—as they often were—might be easily found without a repetition of the complicated observations and calculations. The Mexicans were eager to complete the work, because $3,000,000 of the purchase-money was payable only on such completion. At the beginning of 1855 there was some complaint in Mexico that the U. S. had taken possession at one or two points without waiting for a formal survey or transfer, and it was feared they might delay operations to prevent payment of the money. *Correo de España,* Jan. 17, 1855. There was also much trouble about the collection and disposition of the funds; but this does not concern us here.

Colorado in January 1858.   The steamer *General Jesup* was waiting in the Mojave region to carry this party across the river, but Beale with twenty men returned to New Mexico, thus proving the practicability of his road for winter travel.[6]   Another important exploration was that of Lieutenant Joseph C. Ives.   In November 1857, he arrived at the head of the gulf on a schooner from San Francisco, which also brought an iron stern-wheel steamer fifty feet long, built for the trip in Philadelphia, and named the *Explorer*.   On this craft, launched the 30th of December, Ives left Fort Yuma on January 11, 1858, and on March 12th had passed through the Black Cañon of the Colorado and reached the mouth of Virgin River.   Returning from this point to the Mojave villages, he sent the boat down to the fort, and with part of his scientific corps, being joined also by Lieutenant Tipton with an escort of twenty men, he started eastward by land. His route after a little was to the north of that followed by earlier explorers, including the cañons of the Colorado Chiquito and other streams, and also, for the first time since the American occupation, the Moqui pueblos.   Ives reached Fort Defiance in May, and his report, illustrated by fine engravings of new scenery, is perhaps the most fascinating in all the series of government explorations.[7]   Besides the Beale

[6] *Beale (Edward F.), Wagon Road from Fort Defiance to the Colorado River. Report of the Superintendent*, April 26, 1858, in *U. S. Govt Doc.*, 35th cong. 1st sess., H. Ex. Doc. 124, with map showing route, with those of Sitgreaves and Whipple.   Beale used camels on this trip, and declared them better adapted than mules to the service.

In *Cincinnatus' Travels on the western slope of the Mexican Cordillera*, 336–51, is an account by H. S. Washburn, deputy U. S. surveyor, of a trip from Ft Yuma up the Gila to Tucson, and back by way of Altar and Sonoita in 1856.

[7] *Ives' Report upon the Colorado River of the West, explored in 1857 and 1858 by Lieutenant Joseph C. Ives, corps of topographical engineers under the direction of the office of explorations and surveys, A. A. Humphries, captain topographical engineers, in charge.   By order of the Secretary of War.*   Wash., 1861, 4to, 131, 154, 30, 6, 32 p., with plates and maps. *U. S. Govt Doc.*, 36th cong. 1st sess., H. Ex. Doc. 90; see also 35th cong. 2d sess., Sen. Ex. Doc. 582; *Id.*, H. Ex. Doc. 2, p. 608–19; 34th cong. 1st sess., H. Miscel. Doc. 86; Sen. Miscel. Doc. 39.   Mölhausen, *Reisen*, i. 116–443, ii. 1–139, 144–5, map, who had been with Whipple, was also with Ives as artist, etc., and gives a full narrative.   Capt. A. D. Byrd, for seven years a pilot on the Colorado, published in 1864 a new chart of that river. *Browne's L. Cal.*, 47.   In the *S. F. Call* of April 9, 1877,

road in the north, another was opened in the south by Superintendent James B. Leach and Engineer N. H. Hutton. This corresponded largely with the Cooke road of 1846, but led down the San Pedro to the Arivaipa, and thence to the Gila, 21 miles east of the Pima villages, thus saving 40 miles over the Tucson route, and by improvements about five days for wagons. The work was done by Leach and Hutton from the Rio Grande to the Colorado, between October 25, 1857, and August 1, 1858.[8] Over this road ran in 1858–60 Arizona's first stage, the Butterfield overland line from Marshall, Texas, to San Diego, carrying the mails and passengers twice a week, until the service was stopped by Indian depredations.[9]

It was not until 1856 that the United States took military possession of the Gadsden purchase by sending a detachment of four companies of the First Dragoons, which force was stationed at Tucson and later at Calabazas. In 1857 a permanent station was selected, and Fort Buchanan was established on the Sonoita about 25 miles east of Tubac. The site was afterward deemed to have no special advantages, and no buildings worthy the name of fort were erected. There were various other temporary camps occupied in the following years according to the demands of the Indian service, the force being from 120 to 375

is an account by Capt. John Moss of his voyage down the Colorado through all the cañons on a raft in 1861. If performed as described, it was a most extraordinary exploit.

[8] *Campbell (Albert H.), Report upon the Pacific Wagon Roads, 1859,* p. 9–12, and *Hutton's Report, El Paso and Fort Yuma Wagon Road,* in *Id.,* 77–100, with map; 35th cong. 2d sess., H. Ex. Doc. 108.

[9] Under act of congress of March 3, 1857, bids were received for an overland mail service, and that of John Butterfield for a semi-weekly service by the southern route at $600,000 per year was accepted, the contract being signed Sept. 16th. Many particulars in *Overland Mail Service to Cal.* (n. p., 1857), 8vo, 45 p.; *Overland Mail Co., Memorial,* 1860, 7 p.; *Id., Observations,* 5 p. See also *Hayes' Scraps, Ariz.,* v. 247, 251, 277, 299; S. F. papers of 1858–60. According to *Ariz. Hist.* (Elliott & Co.), 316–17, Burch and Woods ran the stage for a year before Butterfield began; and from the newspapers of the time it appears that for a time two lines were running. There was in 1859 a branch stage from Ft Buchanan to Tubac, and there were probably several others on short routes in the territory. Fred Huselman, P. M. at Tubac, made arrangements in 1859 for a weekly mail to and from Sonora. See *Estrella de Occidente,* Dec. 30, 1859.

men, besides that of parties from abroad occasionally engaging in campaigns.   In some years only two companies are mentioned.   Late in 1858 Fort Mojave near Beale's crossing of the Colorado was established with three companies of infantry; and late in 1859 Fort Breckenridge at the junction of the San Pedro and Arivaipa with part of the garrison from Fort Buchanan.   The soldiers did much good service and had many hard fights with the Apache foe; but the force was of course utterly inadequate for the protection of the country.   On the outbreak of the war in 1860–1, all the forts were destroyed and abandoned, and the troops removed.[10]

The territory of the Gadsden purchase was believed to be rich in precious metals.   Americans had long been more or less conversant with Mexican traditions of immensely rich mines discovered in Jesuit times and abandoned in consequence of Apache raids—traditions for the most part false in their details, and so far as the Jesuits were represented as miners, but well founded to the extent that prospectors had actually found many rich deposits of silver.   Reports of the various government explorers, who had in all directions noted indications of mineral wealth, corroborated the current traditions, and made Arizona a most attractive country for adventurers, and all the more so because of the recent successes of gold-seekers in California.

[10] I have followed the U. S. adj.-general's reports of 1856–61 attached to the messages of the president in the 1st volumes of Ex. Doc. of each session. *U. S. Govt Doc.*   Maj. E. Steen was in command at Ft Buchanan in 1857; Capt. E. H. Fitzgerald in 1858; Capt. J. D. V. Reeve in 1859; Capt. R. S. Ewell in 1860.   Lieut. J. R. Cooke commanded 67 men at Ft Breckenridge in 1860. In 1861 the report mentions no troops in Arizona, though Ft Mojave, established by Col Hoffman, is said not to have been abandoned till May 1861. In the south Col Morrison is said to have succeeded Ewell in 1860, and infantry to have been substituted for the cavalry, though I find nothing of this in the military records.   See also on forts, with many dates and names not agreeing with the original reports, *Hamilton's Resources*, 22–3, 110; *Hinton's Hand-book*, 308–18; *Ariz. Hist.*, 209, 221; *Hayes' Scraps, Mining*, v. 16–17; *Id.*, *Ariz.*, v. 259–307.   In *Id.*, *Angeles*, viii. 179, is mentioned a Ft Floyd, changed to Ft McLane in 1861; and in *U. S. Surgeon-general's Circular*, 8, p. 552, a Camp Verde is mentioned in 1861.   In Sept. 1855 the Mex. garrison at Tucson. 26 men, was commanded by Capt. Hilarion García. *Pinart, Col. Doc.*, MS., no. 153–4.

The Ajo copper mines in the Sonoita region, which
had been discovered by Mexicans, was worked by a
San Francisco company from 1855.[11]   Charles D.
Poston with Herman Ehrenberg, after a preliminary
tour in 1854–5 from the gulf coast, formed a company
in the east, and in 1856 began the development on a
large scale of silver mines near Tubac.   Half a dozen
other companies in this and the following years undertook similar operations in the same region, that is, in
the mountain ranges on both sides of the Santa Cruz
valley in the southern part of the territory.   The
garrison at Fort Buchanan afforded protection to a
certain extent, and the laborers employed were chiefly
Sonorans from across the line.   Fuel and water were
scarce, apparatus and supplies of all kinds were obtained only at an excessive cost by reason of the long
and difficult routes of transportation, and the Indians
were troublesome; but many of the mines were rich
and even under such unfavorable circumstances yielded
a large amount of bullion.   Developments extended
over a wide region, including mines of copper and gold
as well as silver, especially in the east on the New
Mexican border; and prospecting operations, often
with great success, were extended to the upper and
lower Gila and even into the unexplored regions farther north.   Tucson recovered something of its old-
time prosperity; Tubac became a flourishing little town
of some 500 inhabitants, where the first Arizona newspaper was published in 1858–60;[12] a few ranchos were
established, including several in the Gila valley on
the stage route; and the American population increased to several thousands.   Emigrants continued,
though in diminished numbers, to cross Arizona by

[11] In the *Yuma Sentinel*, March 30, 1878, is an account by one of the party,
fitted out to search for the famous Planchas de Plata in Sonora, some of whose
members turned aside to take possession of the Ajo mines.
[12] The weekly *Arizonian*, often cited in Cal. newspapers of these years.
See *Barton's Directory of Tucson*, 1881, p. 10; *Tucson Star*, Dec. 4, 1879; *S. F.
Bulletin*, March 22, 1850; *Hinton's Hand-book*, 40, 186; *Ariz. Hist.*, 260.   The
paper was moved to Tucson in 1860, and suspended in 1861, the office furniture—two derringers—being advertised for sale.

the southern route, and many of them remained here for a while before going on to California.[13]

Fort Yuma, on the Colorado side of the Colorado, was occupied continuously by United States troops, affording much better protection to this part of Arizona than was enjoyed in the south-east. Steamers continued to ply on the Colorado; the ferry did a prosperous business; the overland stage had a station here; and much teaming was done in the transportation of supplies and ores to and from the copper mines in Papaguería and the silver mines by the Gila route. The settlement on the Arizona side known as Colorado City and Arizona City is often mentioned as a thriving town, as under the circumstances it should have been; but the more definite of current items reduce it to a very few buildings, mostly destroyed in the flood of 1861–2.[14] In 1858 gold placers were discovered on

[13] On Arizona mining before 1863, including companies, districts, particular mines, colonization and prospecting parties, with naturally much on Indian troubles, the cataloguing of the complicated and often vaguely recorded details being obviously impracticable here, see *Hayes' Scraps, Mining,* v., passim; *Id., Ariz.,* i. v., passim; California newspapers, especially the *Sac. Union,* March 22, Oct. 12, 1854; April 25, May 29, June 13, 17, Aug. 12, Nov. 28, Dec. 15, 1857; March 31, Oct. 22, Nov. 1, 3, 8, 11, 12, 16, Dec. 11, 20, 28, 29, 30, 1858; Jan. 3, 20, March 14, April 15, May 11, 14, 16, June 10, 1859; Feb. 24, May 23, June 28, July 9, 14, Nov. 3, 17, 1860; April 17, May 13, 21, June 27, 1861; Feb. 10, 1862; *S. F. Alta Cal.,* March 6, Aug. 21, 1854; Aug. 25, Oct. 14, 1856; May 29, Aug. 21, Sept. 6, 1857; Jan. 18, March 12, 27, April 15, 27, May 11, 21, June 3, Nov. 2, 6, 7, 12, 25, Dec. 21, 24, 27, 31, 1858; Jan. 11, 19, 24, 26, Feb. 6, 11, March 1, 10, 21, April 3, 4, 8, 13, 15, 21, May 11, 17, 22, June 3, 28, July 8, 23, 25, 31, Aug. 8, Sept. 12, Dec. 12, 31, 1859; June 17, 1860; March 18, June 27, July 17, 1861; July 30, Oct. 14, 1862; *S. F. Bulletin,* March 14, 1856; April 13, May 11, 12, Sept. 15, Oct. 30, Nov. 6, 11, 13, 17, 26, Dec. 9, 17, 18, 1858; Jan. 3, 10, 11, 26, Feb. 4, 11, 12, 14, 28, March 12, April 7, 8, 27, May 9, 12, 14, 23, 27, June 5, 8, 24, July 18, 28, Aug. 20, 27, 1859; May 24, June 10, 16, 18, July 9, 14, 18, 21, 22, 28, Aug. 1, 28, Sept. 3, 10, 26, Oct. 10, Nov. 21, 1862; *Yuma Sentinel,* Jan. 12, March 30, 1878; Jan. 7, 1883; *Poston's Arizona,* in *Id.,* May 7, 1873; *Mining Magazine,* i. 1–15, 243, 321–2; ii. 83; ix. 383–4; x. 335–6; *Harper's Mag.,* xxix. 557–60, 690–2; *Hamilton's Resources,* 22, 145–7; *Hunt's Merch. Mag.,* xxxiv. 759–60; xlii. 117; xliv. 242–3; *Dublin* and *Lozano, Legis. Mex,* vii. 521–2; *Hinton's Hand-book,* 32–42, 185; *Arizona, Hist.* (Elliott & Co.), 63, 201, 207–10, 220–2, 244, 301–2; *Arizona Scraps,* passim; *Hodge's Ariz.,* 61–5, 69, 124–9; *U. S. Census,* 9th, p. 665; *Box's Adven.,* 317–34; *Conklin's Pict. Ariz.,* 186; *Browne's Min. Resources,* 136, 142, 156–9, 466; *Id., Apache Country,* passim; *Ind. Aff. Rept,* 1862, p. 327; *Sonora, Doc. Hist.,* MS., iv. 174–7; *Niles' Reg.,* lxxv. 348; *Hall's Sonora,* MS., 72–3; and *Mowry's Works on Ariz.,* passim.

[14] The most definite and most flattering statement that I have seen is that in the *S. F. Bulletin* of Aug. 9, 1859, which states that Colorado City had but one house, of adobe, and used as a custom-house; Arizona City had half

the Gila some twenty miles above the junction, but extending for several miles along the river; and a new town of shanties sprang into existence, under the name of Gila City. Five hundred miners or more were at one time at work here, some of them very successfully; but there was great difficulty in getting water, the richest diggings being several miles from the river, and before 1862 the glory of these placers had departed, and the city was destroyed by the flood.[15] There was no settlement north of the Gila, though prospecting was carried on in different directions, a few emigrants came over the Beale wagon road, and Fort Mojave, as we have seen, was garrisoned from 1858.[16]

For five or six years after the American occupation, the Indians caused comparatively little trouble, though constant vigilance was required, and petty depredations never ceased entirely. The Yumas, not a numerous tribe, were kept in control by the garrison and rarely molested Americans except as pilferers, though

dozen adobe buildings, including 2 stores, 2 saloons, and a post-office; while at the ferry, a mile below the Gila junction, was the stage station, 2 stores, 2 blacksmith shops, a hotel, and several houses, the three 'cities' being all within the space of a mile. Most items, except those that simply speak of a flourishing town, mention only one or two buildings, but perhaps refer only to that portion known as Colorado City. See *Id.*, Oct. 13, Nov. 17, 1857; Nov. 8, 1858; *Hayes' Scraps, Angeles*, iv. 33; *Id., S. Diego*, i. 192-200; *Yuma Sentinel*, May 23, 1878; *Hinton's Hand-book*, 246; *S. F. Alta*, Aug. 25, 1857; May 27, 1859; Feb. 11, 1862; *Sac. Union*, April 9, 1856; *S. F. Herald*, Dec. 18, 1857; *Arizona, Hist.*, 245. The receipts of the ferry in 1857 are given as $2,000 a day.

[15] The references in note 13 include the Gila mines. See also on Gila City, *Hayes' Scraps, Mining*, v. 78; *S. F. Alta*, Dec. 27, 1858; *Sac. Union*, Feb. 12, 1862, according to which Gila City was also destroyed by the flood. Conklin, *Pict. Ariz.*, 84-5, describes the city—which had had 1,200 inhab. in 1861—as being in 1877 a stage station, with stable, corral, 'Gila Hotel,' and kennel, and containing by a census made at the time 9 inhabitants, including 3 dogs, squaw, and papoose.

[16] Here may be noted that in 1862 Maj. D. Fergusson made a reconnoissance of a route from Tucson to the gulf, with a view to opening a shorter and cheaper way for the transportation of supplies to the Arizona mines. He found no serious impediment to travel, and pronounced the ports of Libertad and Lobos well fitted for the purpose. *Fergusson's Report on the country, etc., and the route between Tucson and Lobos Bay, 1862.* Letter of sec. war in *U. S. Govt Doc.*, 37 cong., spec. sess., Sen. Ex. Doc. 1, 22 p., maps. In 1860, Gov. Pesqueira had, by decree, permitted the transit of U. S. merchandise through Sonora. *Hayes' Scraps, Ariz.*, v. 311-12; *Id., Angeles*, viii. 24; *Estrella de Occidente*, Jan. 25, 1861; *S. F. Alta*, Mar. 8, 1861.

often in trouble with their neighbors. In 1857, with Mojave, Cocopa, and Tonto allies, they attacked the Pimas and Pápagos up the river, and in a great battle were almost annihilated. The Mojaves were more hostile and treacherous, committing many depredations on emigrants and others in 1858; but during this year and the next were brought into subjection by Colonel Hoffman's efforts, and by the establishment of the fort. The Pimas, numbering about 4,000, the Maricopas 500, and the Pápagos 3,000, were uniformly friendly, and of great assistance in keeping hostile tribes in check. From 1859 John Walker was Indian agent for these Indians, residing at Tucson, being succeeded by Abraham Lyons in 1862. By act of congress, February 28, 1859, a sum of $1,000 was appropriated for a survey of the Pima and Maricopa lands on the Gila, and $10,000 for gifts in the form of implements and clothing. The survey was made by Colonel A. B. Gray, and the presents were distributed by Lieutenant Sylvester Mowry before the end of the year. As to the Apaches, estimated at about 10,000 in number, under the care of M. Steck as agent, and after a campaign by Colonel Bonneville in 1857, they were for a time, comparatively speaking, at peace, though continuing their raids across the line, attacking Mexicans wherever they could be found, and often committing petty depredations against small parties of Americans. Agents reported some progress in inducing the Mescalero Apaches to till the soil and refrain from hostilities; and it was urged by all familiar with the subject that all the Apaches must be induced to settle north of the Gila, there to be instructed, aided, and watched, while the southern passes must be guarded by garrisons at several points. Nothing was done, however, except the division of the military force, and the establishment of Fort Breckenridge on the San Pedro. In 1860 hostilities became more frequent and general, and were greatly aggravated by bad management and injustice on the part of the officers, by which Cochise, a prominent chieftain, was made the life-long foe of the Americans. Soon all were on the war-path, murders and robberies were of daily occurrence, and even the soldiers were hard pressed. Then in 1861, when for other reasons the stage line was abandoned, and the troops recalled from Arizona, the Indians naturally regarded this as their triumph, redoubled their efforts, and for over a year were masters of the territory, having killed or driven out all the white inhabitants except a few hundred who took refuge within the walls of Tucson.[17]

In 1856–7 Henry A. Crabb of California had attempted a filibustero conquest of Sonora under the

[17] *Ind. Aff. Reports,* 1857–63, reports of agents and others in N. Mexico and Arizona. 'The arrival of the Cal. column under Gen. Carleton in June 1862 found the country between the Colorado and Rio Grande a desolation marked by new-made graves.' *Poston,* in *Id.,* 1863, p. 383–4. The California and Sonora papers of 1861–3 contain many items; also *Hayes' Scraps, Ariz.*; and each of the general works on Arizona narrates a few of the disasters, though not much reliance can be placed in details, which I do not attempt to catalogue. See *Pumpelly's Across Amer.,* 1–67, for an excellent account of Arizona affairs in these years; also *Ross Browne's Adventures in Apache Country,* chap. i. Says Hinton, *Hand-book,* 41–2: 'A few American miners held on to their locations in the Cerbat and Hualapai mountains. In the Salt River valley there was a ranch or two; and elsewhere, except at Tucson and Yuma, there was nothing to be found except a few Mexicans, the Pimas and Pápagos, with the hostile Indians at every turn.' And Hamilton, *Resources,* 23: 'The Apache marauders swept down from their mountain strongholds, and carried death and destruction throughout southern Arizona mines; ranches and stock-ranges were abandoned, and the few whites left in the country took refuge within the walls at Tucson. The savages indulged in a saturnalia of slaughter, and the last glimmer of civilization seemed about to be quenched in blood. The horribly mutilated bodies of men, women, and children marked nearly every mile of the road to the Rio Grande. This frightful condition of things existed for nearly a year after the withdrawal of the troops.' In the *S. F. Alta,* Dec. 16, 1872, is an article by Gov. Safford giving a history of Cochise's career. Besides Cochise, Mangas Coloradas was the most famous of Apache chiefs. It should be noted that in all these years a remnant of the tame Apaches continued to live near Tucson, taking no part in the hostilities of their people. Hamilton, *Resources,* 108–9, gives a good account of the beginning of the war in 1860. Lieut. Bascom, a young West Point graduate, was sent to Apache Pass to recover some live-stock which a settler had lost. Cochise, the chief, said his tribe had not taken the property, but he would try to find and return it. Next day Cochise and his warriors were invited to a 'big talk,' and having assembled were surrounded and told they would be held as hostages till the cattle and a captive were restored. A desperate struggle ensued, in which several were wounded and six warriors captured, including the chief's brother; but Cochise escaped though badly wounded. He declared life-long war on the Americans, and kept his threat. The troops had a narrow escape, and the six captives were hanged.

guise of colonization, counting on the support of one of the two contending factions. With an advance party of 100 men he crossed Arizona from Yuma to Sonoita and Caborca, but was defeated and shot with all his companions. A party of thirty went from Tucson to his rescue, but were too late and barely escaped sharing his fate.[18] Crabb's ill fortune prevented later attempts of a similar nature; but the spirit of filibusterism was potent in Arizona, and the Sonoran authorities were always fearful and suspicious. Sonoran laborers of a vicious class were employed in the mines, and were accused of many robberies and murders, being hardly less feared than the Apaches. Another prominent and but little better element of the population was that of outlaws and desperados from California and Texas, who looked with contempt after the manner of their class on all of Mexican blood. There were public meetings held to urge the expulsion of the hated 'greasers' from the mines and from the country. A war of races at times seemed impending. Even before the withdrawal of troops enabled the savages to take possession of the country, broils, murders, robberies, duels, and outrages perpetrated in the name of vigilantes were of constant occurrence, and created perhaps a more disgraceful and disastrous condition of affairs than is elsewhere revealed in western annals. After the abandonment of the country, Sonoran marauders are said to have crossed the line to steal or destroy any petty remnant of property left by the Apaches.[19]

Arizona, besides its Apaches and outlaws, had during ing this period its politics and politicians, though not much government. From 1851 to 1854 it was a part of the territory of New Mexico, and was theoretically divided into five or six counties; that is, the boundaries

[18] For details of the Crabb affair, see *Hist. North Mex. States,* ii., this series.

[19] I follow Cal. and Sonora newspaper items, besides the general accounts given in works that have been cited. All authorities agree in the outline and coloring, though not many particulars are clearly recorded. One of the most famous duels was that between Lieut. Mowry and Editor Cross at Tubac in 1859. It was fought with rifles, and nobody hurt.

of the New Mexican counties extended west to California;[20] but as Arizona—north of the Gila, the only part belonging then to New Mexico or the United States— had no settlements, there existed hardly the semblance of county jurisdiction. By act of congress, August 4, 1854, the Gadsden purchase was added to New Mexico; and by act of the legislature, January 18, 1855, it was attached to Doña Ana county, a part of which it remained till 1863.[21] In records of the time, however, the only indication of county rule is the occasional sending of a criminal to Mesilla for trial. There were also justices of the peace at Tucson and perhaps elsewhere. From the first, there was much complaint that the country was not and could not be properly governed from Santa Fé, with corresponding petitions for a separate territorial organization, the Mesilla district making common cause in this matter with Arizona proper, being separated from the capital by the Jornada del Muerto.

A convention was held at Tucson on August 29, 1856, which resolved, not only to send a memorial to congress urging the organization of a territory of Arizona, but to send a delegate to Washington. The memorial was signed by some 260 names, and Nathan P. Cook was in September elected delegate.[22] He was not admitted to a seat, but his mission was brought before the house in January 1857. The committee on territories reported against a territorial organization, because of the limited population, but recognized the unfortunate condition of the people, and recommended

[20] See *New Mex., Comp. Laws*, secs. 242 et seq., for the county lines. Doña Ana county included a small area of Ariz. south of the Gila.

[21] *Cong. Globe*, 1853–4, p. 2207; *N. Mex., Comp. Laws*, sec. 277. On Feb. 3, 1855, an act divided the Mesilla valley into three precincts, *Id.*, sec. 254; but there is no mention of the Arizona settlements proper.

[22] The president of the convention was Mayor M. Aldrich of Tucson; vice-pres. James Douglas of Sopori, José M. Martinez of S. Javier; sec. G. K. Terry and W. N. Bonner; N. P. Cook, G. H. Oury, H. Ehrenberg, Ign. Ortiz, and I. D. L. Pack were the committee on resolutions and memorial. The white population was estimated at 10,000 (!). Oury was elected member of the N. Mex. legislature. Cook arrived at S. Diego Sept. 22d, and soon sailed for Washington. *Hayes' Scraps, Ariz.*, v. 244–5; *S. F. Alta*, Oct. 27, 1856; *Sac. Union*, Oct. 16, 30, 1856; *Arizona Scraps*, 445.

a bill to organize a judicial district south of the Gila,
to appoint a surveyor-general, and to provide for rep-
resentation at Santa Fé as well as for the regulation
of land claims and mining titles. Such a bill was
passed by the senate in February, but was not acted
upon by the house.[23] The president, in his messages
of 1857–8, recommended a territorial government;
Senator Gwin in December 1857 introduced a bill to
organize such a government for the Gadsden purchase,
under the name of Arizona; the legislature of New
Mexico in February 1858 passed resolutions in favor
of the measure, though recommending a north and
south boundary line on the meridian of 109, and also
the removal of all New Mexican Indians to northern
Arizona; several favorable petitions were received
from different parts of the union; and in an election
held at Tucson in September 1857, the people had
prepared a new petition and chosen Sylvester Mowry
as a delegate to congress. The delegate was not admitted, and Gwin's bill was not passed.[24] In the following years Mowry continued his efforts with much
zeal and no success, being reëlected as delegate; other

[23] *Cong. Globe*, 1856–7, p. 815–21, 830; 34th cong. 3d sess., H. Rept 117;
H. Jour. 515; 35th cong. 1st sess., H. Jour. 137, 210. The bill passed the
senate Feb. 21st, and was still before the house in Jan. 1858. It was a long
and complicated bill, dealing with the many complications of Mexican land
titles, etc.; and this seems to have been the chief ground of opposition in the
senate, led by Mr Crittenden. There was no discussion on its merits in the
house. Mowry, *Mem.*, 25, says the bill passed both houses, but owing to
minor differences and the lateness of the session, failed to become a law.
[24] Gwin's bill included, not only the Gadsden purchase, but Doña Ana
county in N. Mex., extending east to Texas. It was introduced Dec. 17,
1857; reported with an amendment by the com. on territories Apr. 8, 1858;
postponed on June 14th to Dec.; recommitted Dec. 13th; and adversely reported Feb. 8, 1859. *U. S. Govt Doc.*, 35th cong. 1st. sess., Sen. Jour. 47, 329,
719; *Cong. Globe*, 1857–8, p. 13, 62, 1531, 3042; 1858–9, p. 48, 103. Also on
N. Mex. memorial and other preliminaries, Sen. Miscel. Doc. 208; H. Miscel.
Doc. 101; Sen. Jour. 41, 52, 245, 296; H. Jour. 524, 271; president's messages, in H. Ex. Doc. 2, p. 26; 35th cong. 2d sess., H. Ex. Doc. 2, p. 19. I find
no authority for the statement in *Ariz., Jour. 1st Legis.*, 11, that Gwin's bill
'was defeated by a decided vote.' Of the election in Arizona I find no more
definite record than the statement in a letter of S. Warner from Tucson,
Mowry's Mem., 22, that it was held on the 1st Monday in Sept. 1857. Mowry
was already at Washington, whither his certificate of election was sent. This
document was presented to congress in Jan. 1858, and excited some debate,
though on purely parliamentary points. *Cong. Globe*, 1857–8, p. 312. See also
S. F. Alta, Feb. 8, Mar. 23, May 13, Aug. 15, 1858.

bills of similar nature were introduced but defeated;
and the people of Arizona held other meetings, and
sent more memorials, to which little attention was paid.[25]
As a rule, there was no debate on these bills, so that
the ground of opposition is not very clearly indicated;
but it was doubtless founded mainly on the old sectional quarrel growing out of the slavery question,
though the exact force of the slavery issue in Arizona
is not very apparent, or the proper time to raise that
issue would seem to have been in 1854, when the Gadsden purchase was attached to New Mexico.   But the
purchase had been a southern measure, the country was in southern hands, and it was felt that the
territorial organization must be in some way a scheme
for southern aggrandizement.   Moreover, the population—represented as from 8,000 to 10,000—and the
country's need of a government were thought to be
exaggerated, and it was feared the whole project was
that of a few office-seeking speculators in mines or
lands; so that the measure could not command the
full support even of the democratic party, while of
course the north was not strong enough to organize
the territory with any kind of Wilmot proviso.

In 1860, from the 2d to the 5th of April, there was

[25] On Dec. 10, 1858, a bill was introduced in the house by McKibben,
and another by Stephens Jan. 20, 1859. This was laid on the table by a vote
of 121 to 79, on Feb. 16th.   During the debate, an amendment was offered
by Grow to the effect that slavery remain abolished as per Mex. laws.   *Cong.
Globe*, 1858–9, p. 657, 1063; 35th cong. 2d sess., H. Jour. 58, 223, 278, 419;
Sen. Jour. 50–1, 284.   In his message of Jan. 1858, the gov. of Cal. recommended action in favor of Arizona as a territory. *Cal. Jour. Ass.*, 1858, p. 56.
On June 19, 1859, a convention met at Mesilla, presided over by Jas A. Lucas
with S. W. Cozzens as sec.; and in its resolutions reaffirmed the resolutions
of a similar convention of Sept. 3, 1858, complained that no court had been
held south of the Jornada del Muerto for 3 years, declared that the south
would take no part henceforth in N. Mex. elections, favored an election for
delegate on Sept. 1st, approved the acts of Mowry (who addressed the meeting) and nominated him for reëlection, and sent representatives of each town
to a convention to be held at Tucson on June 27th. *Hayes' Scraps, Ariz.*, v.
253–4.   The Tucson meeting was held July 3d, John Walker president, J. H.
Wells sec., was addressed by Mowry, and adopted resolutions similar to
those of the Mesilla convention.   Mowry thought the prospects good if he
were reëlected. *Id.*, 264–5.   He was reëlected almost unanimously, receiving
2,164 votes at the Sept. election. *Id.*, 269–71.   See also *Sac. Union*, May 20,
1859; *S. F. Bulletin*, Jan. 31, May 18, June 7, 1859; *S. F. Alta*, May 22,
June 23, 1859.

held at Tucson a constitutional convention composed
of 31 delegates, which proceeded to "ordain and establish" a provisional constitution to remain in force
"until congress shall organize a territorial government
and no longer." The new territory included all of
New Mexico south of latitude 33° 40′, and was divided
by north and south lines into four counties. A governor was elected in the person of Dr L. S. Owings
of Mesilla; three judicial districts were created, the
judges to be appointed by the governor, as were also
an attorney-general, lieutenant-governor, and other
officials; a legislature of nine senators and eighteen
representatives was to be elected and convened at the
governor's order; provision was made for organizing
the militia; an election of county officers was called
for May; the general laws and codes of New Mexico
were adopted; and the records of the convention,
schedule, constitution, and governor's inaugural address were printed at Tucson in what was, so far as I
know, the first book ever published in Arizona.[26] If
anything was done under this soi-disant government
beyond the election and appointment of officials, I
have found no record of the fact. In November,
Edward McGowan, district judge under the new
régime, and somewhat notorious in California annals,

[26] *Arizona, The Constitution of the Provisional Government of the Territory of
Arizona, and the proceedings of the convention held at Tucson.* Tucson, J. Howard Wells, publisher, 1860, 12mo, 23 p. James A. Lucas was president, and
the sec. were G. H. Oury and T. M. Turner. The places represented were
Mesilla, Sta Rita del Cobre, Las Cruces, Doña Ana, La Mesa, Sto Tomás,
Picacho, Amoles, Tucson, Arivaca, Tubac, Sonoita, Gila City, and Calabazas.
Capt. R. S. Ewell, U. S. A., occupied a seat by invitation. Thanks were
voted to Mowry, and to Ewell and the military officers; and a protest was
adopted against the removal of any part of the troops. The counties were,
1, Doña Ana, all east of the Rio Grande; 2, Mesilla, from the river west to
the Chiricahui Mts.; 3, Ewell, from the mts west of a line crossing the Little
Desert, near the centre; and 4, Castle Dome, all west of Ewell county. See
also newspaper records of the convention and matters connected therewith in
Hayes' Scraps, Ariz., v. 205–320, passim. The governor's appointments were
as follows: Lieut.-gov., Ignacio Orantia; sec. state, James A. Lucas; con-
troller, J. H. Wells; treasurer, M. Aldrich; marshal, Sam. G. Bean; district
judges, G. H. Oury (chief justice), S. H. Cozzens, and Edward McGowan;
district attorneys, R. H. Glenn, Rees Smith, Thos J. Mastin; major-general,
W. C. Wordsworth; adj.-gen., Palatine Robinson. See also S. F. newspapers of the year; *Barter's Directory of Tucson*, 1881, p. 11–12.

was elected delegate to congress to succeed Mowry.[27]
The New Mexican legislature this year passed new
resolutions in favor of a division; and also by act of
February 1st created a new county called Arizona,
from the western portion of Doña Ana county, with
Tucson as county seat; but no attention was paid to
this act, and it was repealed two years later.[28] In
December a bill to organize the territory came up
again in congress, but without success, even though
the proposed name was changed to Arizuma to suit
the whim of some theorist. There was some debate,
but all on the slavery question, and without definite
reference to Arizona, as was indeed natural enough at
this time of secession acts.[29]

Finally, in March 1862, the Arizona bill was again
introduced and discussed in congress. The southern
element being eliminated, the measure was now a republican one, containing a proviso against slavery,
though it met opposition from members of both
parties. Unlike former bills, this adopted a north
and south boundary on the meridian of 109°, and
named Tucson as the capital. Watts, the New Mexican delegate, and Ashley, of Ohio, were its chief
advocates in the house, and Wheeler of New York
the opposition spokesman. On the one side it was
argued that Arizona's white population of 6,500 and
4,000 civilized Indians were entitled to a protection
and a civil government as citizens of the United
States, which they had not received and could receive
under the territorial rule of New Mexico, the vast
mineral wealth of the country amply justifying the
necessary expenditure. On the other side, it was
claimed that the population had never been sufficient

[27] *Hayes' Scraps, Ariz.*, v. 283, 286, 310.
[28] *U. S. Govt Doc.*, 36th cong. 1st sess., Sen Miscel. Doc. 21; *N. Mex.,
Comp. Laws*, sec. 267. The law is not given, but only the repealing act. It
is mentioned also in congressional debates.
[29] *Cong. Globe*, 1860–1, pp. 195 et seq. Jefferson Davis was the author of
this bill. *Id.*, 1861–2, p. 2027. I have found no indication of McGowan's
presence at Washington, except a reference, *Ib.*, to three delegates having
been sent—that is, Cook, Mowry, and McGowan. Nor is there any allusion
in congress to the provisional govt.

for a territory, that the 6,500 of the census included Mexicans and half-breeds unfit for citizens, that the American population had now been driven out, and the territory was in possession of rebels and hostile Indians. It was alleged that under such circumstances a civil government would be no real protection, and would be indeed a mere farce; that in the midst of a great war, with an overburdened treasury, congress had no right to appropriate money for the benefit of territorial office-seekers; but that the money should be spent, if at all, in efforts to protect the country by military methods from its rebel and savage foes. There was also an idea that the measure was favored by a certain element, not because of its propriety or necessity, but solely because the territory could now be organized with an anti-slavery proviso. But it passed the house by a small majority on the 8th of May. In the senate, after a similar debate, the bill was postponed from June to December; but came up finally in February 1863, when, under the championship of Senator Wade, the clause fixing Tucson as the capital being removed, it was passed by a vote of 25 to 12 on the 20th, becoming a law on the 24th.[30]

[30] *Cong. Globe*, 1861-2, p. 1341-2, 2023-30, 2569-72, 3093; *Id.*, 1862-3, p. 1125-9, 1306. Senator Trumbull led the opposition, and McDougal of Cal. was an earnest advocate of the bill. See text of the act in *U. S. Govt Doc.*, 37th cong. 3d sess., Acts and resol., 46-7; *Id.*, Public Laws, 664-5; *Ariz., Comp. Laws*, 13; *Id., Jour. Legis.*, 1864, p. 3-4. Charles D. Poston, *Reminiscences*, gives the following account of the preliminary wire-pulling of 1862 at Washington: 'At the meeting of congress in Dec. 1862 I returned to Washington, made friends with Lincoln, and proposed the organization of the terr. of Arizona. Oury' (who I suppose had been elected delegate in '62 to succeed McGowan) 'was in Richmond, cooling his heels in the ante-chambers of the confederate congress without gaining admission as a delegate from Arizona. Mowry was a prisoner in Yuma, cooling his head from the political fever which had afflicted it, and meditating on the decline and fall of a West Point graduate. There was no other person in Washington, save Gen. Heintzelman, who took any interest in Arizona affairs. They had something else to occupy their attention, and did not even know where Ariz. was. Old Ben Wade, chairman of the senate com. on territories, took a lively and bold interest in the organization of the territory, and Ashley, chairman of the com. in the house, told me how to accomplish the object...He said there were a number of members of the expiring congress, who had been defeated in their own districts for the next term, who wanted to go west and offer their political services to the "galoots," and if they could be grouped and a satisfactory slate made, they would have influence enough to carry the bill through congress. Consequently, an "oyster supper" was organized, to which the

Having thus recorded the acquisition from Mexico in 1853-4 of southern Arizona, or the Gadsden purchase, and the boundary and railroad surveys immediately following; having noted the establishment of military posts, the influx of seekers for precious metals, the rapid development of mining industry, the opening of wagon roads, the establishment of the overland stage line, the journeyings of immigrants to California, the Yuma ferry, and navigation of the Colorado; having chronicled in a general way the depredations of hostile Indians, filibuster outrages, troubles with vicious Sonoran laborers, the lawless proceedings of adventurers from Texas and California, and their oppression of the native or Mexican population; having given somewhat more minute attention to the country's politics, to the people's well-founded complaints of neglect by the government at Santa Fé and Washington, to the successive efforts to secure a territorial organization from congress, and to the final success of those efforts; and having mentioned incidentally in connection with all these topics the disastrous happenings of 1861-2, which involved the withdrawal of the troops, the suspension of the overland mail, the ruin of mining and other industries, the triumph of the bloodthirsty Apaches, and the murder or flight of most of the white inhabitants—it only remains, in order to complete the annals of Arizona as a part of New Mexico, to notice more particularly the immediate cause of the country's misfortunes; that is, the war of the rebellion, or the confederates in Arizona. Records on the subject I have found extremely meagre.

Confederate plans respecting the south-west belong

"lame ducks" were invited, and then and there the slate was made, and the territory was virtually organized...So the slate was made and the bargain concluded, but toward the last it occurred to my obfusticated brain that my name did not appear on the slate, and in the language of Daniel Webster I exclaimed, "Gentlemen, what is to become of me?" Gourley politely replied, "O, we will make you Indian agent." So the bill passed, and Lincoln signed all the commissions, and the oyster supper was paid for, and we were all happy, and Arizona was launched upon the political sea.'

in their general scope to the history of California, which country was the chief prize in view;[31] and in details of actual operations to that of New Mexico, as recorded in a later chapter of this volume. Here it suffices to say that those plans, in which the Texans were especially enthusiastic and active, included the occupation of all the southern frontier regions to the Pacific. It was hoped that California, or at least southern California, might decide to unite its destinies to the confederacy; otherwise, the western movement was not prospectively of much permanent importance. Arizona in itself had no special value to the south except by reason of its geographic position. There were, however, some military stores worth capturing; an open line of communication would encourage prompt action on the part of Californian secessionists; the occupation of so broad a territory could be made to appear at Richmond and in Europe a great achievement; and it presented no difficulties whatever.

Public sentiment in Arizona was almost unanimously southern and disunion, and no secret was made of the feeling in this respect, the few union men having little or nothing to say. In 1861 a convention at Tucson seems to have formally declared the territory a part of the confederacy, and in August of that year Granville H. Oury was elected delegate to the southern congress.[32] It was openly asserted that the country's misfortunes were due to neglect of the government, and that this neglect arose from Arizona's well-known and patriotic devotion to the southern cause. Most officers serving at the south-western posts were

---

[31] See *Hist. Cal.*, vii., this series.

[32] *Tucson Arizonian*, Aug. 10, 1861, in *S. F. Alta*, Sept. 2d. The election took place the preceding Monday. There were only 68 Amer. voters at Tucson, when the 'eleven starred banner' was then waving. Tubac had been abandoned on the 3d. Violent deaths since 1857 had numbered 111 Amer. and 57 Mex. out of an average population of 750. It is said that McGowan, elected delegate in 1860, had instructions to apply for admission to the southern congress, should secession be effected; but I have no proof of that, and I have found no definite record of the convention which resolved on secession. Evidently there was such action, else no delegate would have been openly elected.

southerners who made haste to join the confederate army, though the privates are said to have remained faithful to their government almost without exception. Captain Ewell, commanding in Arizona, became prominent as a confederate general.

In July 1861 Lieutenant-colonel John R. Baylor, with a Texan force, entered the Mesilla valley, and took possession for the confederacy. In a proclamation of August 1st, he declared the territory of Arizona to comprise all that part of New Mexico south of latitude 34°; that all offices under the laws of 'the late United States' or of the territory were vacant; continued in force all laws not inconsistent with those of the confederate states; made Mesilla the capital; and organized a military government with himself as governor. The next day he appointed territorial officials, including James A. Lucas as secretary, M. H. McWille attorney-general, and E. Angerstein treasurer.[33] On Baylor's approach the officers in command at forts Buchanan and Breckenridge were ordered to abandon those posts, destroying the buildings with all military stores that could not be removed, and march eastward to the Rio Grande. This order was obeyed, and, all military protection being withdrawn, the Apaches, as already related, took posses-

[33] See more details of Baylor's operations in chap. xxvii., this vol. He created two judicial districts, the 1st including all east of Apache Pass. His appointments were for the 1st district, H. C. Cook being judge, Frank Higgins probate judge, and J. A. Roberts sheriff. The proclamations are given in *Hayes' Scraps, Angeles*, vi. 104, 107.

I find no definite information as to the source of the order to evacuate the Arizona posts. It doubtless came through Maj. Isaac Lynde, commanding the southern district of N. Mex. at Ft Fillmore near Mesilla. Before the arrival of the Arizona troops, some 400 in number, Lynde made a most disgraceful surrender of his 700 men as prisoners of war to Baylor, the confederate commander, leaving the whole district in rebel possession. The Arizona troops, hearing of this on the march, destroyed most of their impedimenta and marched to Ft Craig. It was believed at Tucson that the country was abandoned to the Apaches because of the people's southern sympathies, and this idea possibly had some foundation in fact; on the other hand, the order may have been legitimately, if not very wisely, given with a view to reenforce Lynde and repel the Texan invaders; or again it may have been simply a part of Lynde's scheme to surrender the united force and leave the whole country open to the invaders. The stage service was suspended at this time, or perhaps a few months earlier, several writers stating that the route was changed by act of congress.

sion of the country, killing all who could not either escape from the country or take refuge at Tucson. Sonoran adventurers are said to have crossed the line to supplement the work of plunder and devastation. Early in 1862 a force of two or three hundred Texans, under Captain Hunter, marched westward from Mesilla, and in February took possession of Tucson for the confederacy. There was of course no opposition, union men, if there were any left, fleeing across the line into Sonora.[34] Not much is really known of Hunter's operations in Arizona so far as details are concerned, even the date of his arrival being doubtful.[35] Besides holding Tucson, driving out men suspected of union sympathies, confiscating a few mines belonging to northerners, and fighting the Apaches to some extent, he sent a detachment to the Pima villages, and possibly contemplated an attack on Fort Yuma. But —to say nothing of the recent floods, which had greatly increased the difficulties of the route, destroying Gila and Colorado cities—the news from California was not reassuring, and Hunter deemed it best to retire.[36]

This news was to the effect that California troops were on the march eastward. These troops, about 1,800 strong, consisted of several volunteer regiments or parts of regiments organized at the beginning of

[34] It seems there had been some effort to induce Gov. Pesqueira to throw off the allegiance of Sonora to Mexico and join the confederacy; indeed, many believed all the filibustering projects of late years to have been really part of the great southern scheme. In 1861 there had been corresp. between the U. S. and Mex. respecting the transit of U. S. troops through Sonora. *U. S. Govt Doc.*, 39th cong. 1st sess., Sen. Doc. 17. Gen. Wright, com. in Cal., had also recommended the temporary seizure of Guaymas to prevent the rebels doing so. *Vega, Doc.*, MS., 788–98. The exploration by Maj. Fergusson of the route to gulf ports in 1862 has already been noted.

[35] Feb. 27th is given as the date by Browne and those who have followed him. As early as Nov. 1861, the report reached Yuma that the rebels had sent 300 men to take Tucson; and in Jan. 1862 it was reported that the town had been taken by 900 Texans under Baylor. *S. F. Alta*, Dec. 8, 1861; Feb. 11, 1862. In *Id.*, Sept. 8, 1861, Nov. 19, 1862, are found general accounts of Lynde's operations on the Rio Grande, one of them from the *Mesilla Times* of Aug. 10, 1861. See also *Hayes' New Mex. Campaign of 1862*, p. 172.

[36] I have found no definite original records beyond a few newspaper items. The narrative given by Ross Browne, *Adventures in Apache Country*, 24–6, agreeing with that of the newspapers, has been followed in substance by Hinton, Hamilton, and other recent writers.

the war, and which, on receipt of intelligence that
Arizona had been invaded, were ordered to Yuma and
Tucson, constituting what was known as the California column, under the command of Colonel James H.
Carleton.[37] The main body of this army in detachments, whose exact movements now and later I do
not attempt to follow in detail, left Los Angeles and
was concentrated at Yuma in April, and in May followed the Gila route to Tucson. But previously
Lieutenant-colonel West, commanding the advance,[38]
had sent out some parties from Yuma, and these were
the only troops that came in contact with the confederates.   Jones, in February, was sent with despatches
to Tucson and fell into the hands of Hunter, who released and sent him back by another route, bearing
the first definite news that Tucson had been occupied.
Captain William McCleave of company A, first cavalry,
being sent out to look for Jones, was captured with
three men at the Pima villages on the 6th of April,
and was carried to Mesilla, where he was soon exchanged.   Captain William P. Calloway was next
sent up the Gila with a stronger force to rescue Mc-
Cleave.   At the Pima villages he heard of a confederate detachment of 16 men under Lieutenant Jack
Swilling, and sent Lieutenant James Barrett with 12
men to cut them off.   Pursuing the enemy into a
chaparral Barrett was killed with two of his men,
one or two of the foe being also killed and three
taken prisoners.   This was the only skirmish of the
campaign with confederates, and it occurred on the
15th of April at a spot known as El Picacho.

[37] For more details of the organization of Cal. regiments, see *Hist. Cal.*,
vii., this series; also *Cal., Adj.-general's Reports*, 1861 et seq.   The so-called
California column consisted of the 1st regiment infantry, 10 companies, Col
Carleton, Lieut.-col Joseph R. West; battalion of 1st cavalry, 5 companies,
Lieut.-col Edward E. Eyre; 5 or 6 companies of the 5th infantry, some of
which did not go beyond Ft Yuma; Col Geo. W. Bowie, Co. B, 2d cavalry,
Capt. John C. Cremony; and Lieut. Shinn's light battery belonging to Co.
A, U. S. artillery.

[38] West was at Yuma in Nov. 1861, guarding the ferry and keeping a
sharp lookout for rebel messengers and correspondence; for it appears that
the Texans were in constant communication with sympathizers in Cal., who
sent not only information but aid and men.

It seems to have been on May 20th that Lieutenant-colonel West with the advance of the California
column raised the stars and stripes again over Tucson.
Captain Hunter had retreated to the Rio Grande,
losing several men and much property on the way in
a fight with the Apaches. The Californians left a
garrison at the Pima villages, naming the post Fort
Barrett in honor of the only officer killed by confederate bullets in Arizona. Forts Buchanan and
Breckenridge were reoccupied, the latter being renamed Fort Stanford, but both positions were presently abandoned, as the sites were undesirable and
the buildings had been destroyed. A post was also
established at what was later called Camp Lowell
seven miles from Tucson. There was a hard fight
with the Indians at Apache Pass in the east, and
there Fort Bowie was established. Early in June
Colonel Carleton arrived at Tucson, where in an order
of the 8th he proclaimed the news of a territorial
organization by congress, and declared the territory
under martial law. Good order was easily preserved,
the most violent rebel partisans having departed with
Hunter, all being required to take the oath of allegiance, turbulent and undesirable characters being
easily driven away by threats of arrest for disunion
sentiments, and a few union men finding their way
back from Sonora. Some 20 political prisoners were
arrested and sent to California, one of the number
being no less a personage than Sylvester Mowry, captured at his Patagonia mine, which was confiscated.
He was accused of having given aid and encouragement
to the rebels; but probably certain personal jealousies
and the spirit of the time, requiring reprisals for some
of Hunter's acts, were the real causes of his arrest;
at any rate, after a long imprisonment he was acquitted
on trial, and his property seems to have been at least
nominally restored to him.

Carleton was made brigadier-general, and a little
later put in command of the department. From June

to August a large part of the California troops were transferred to New Mexico, where they did good service in the following years in garrison and Indian service. A part of the force was left to garrison the Arizona posts under Major David Fergusson, who was made commandant of the western district, Major Theodore Coult also serving for a time in that capacity. During this and the following years the soldiers fought the Apaches and prospected the country for precious metals, but there was nothing in their adventures requiring special notice here.[39]

[39] No complete and detailed narrative of the operations of the Cal. column has ever been published so far as I know, though such a work would have much interest as a contribution to the history of the war as well as to that of Cal., Ariz., and N. Mex. I have prepared my résumé mainly from correspondence in the San Francisco and Los Angeles newspapers, most of which is collected in *Hayes' Scraps, Ariz.*, i., v., passim, especially v. 325–84. Capt. Cremony's *Life among the Apaches* contains some details of adventures with the Indians in this campaign; and I think C. was also the correspondent of the *Alta.* See also *Arizona Hist.* (Elliott & Co.), 74–9, 251–2. On the Mowry mine confiscation, see also *U. S. Govt Doc.*, 38th cong. 1st sess., Sen. Doc. 49.

Among the works relating wholly or mainly to the Gadsden purchase in 1854–63, the most important are those written by Sylvester Mowry, who went to the country as a lieut. in the U. S. A. in 1855, became an enthusiast in all pertaining to the territory's advancement, purchased and worked the Patagonia or Mowry silver mine, was twice elected delegate to congress, but was finally arrested on account of his southern proclivities. The first of his published works was the *Memoir of the Proposed Territory of Arizona, by Sylvester Mowry, U. S. A., délegate elect*, Wash., 1857, 8vo, 30 p., and map. It contains a description of the country with its mineral wealth and other resources drawn from the author's personal knowledge and from the explorations of Col A. B. Gray of the boundary survey; an argument on the territory's need of protection and government; extracts from the corresp. of such men as Poston, Douglas, Oury, Warner, Fitzgerald, and Ehrenberg; and a petition signed by 500 citizens. Next was *The Geography and Resources of Arizona and Sonora; An Address before the American Geographical and Statistical Society. By Hon. Sylvester Mowry, of Arizona. New York, February 3, 1859. Published by the Society.* Wash., 1859, 8vo, 47 p. This covers in a sense the same ground as the *Memoir*, but gives more information on early history, on the Indians, and on the state of Sonora, containing as an appendix extracts from the speech of Jefferson Davis in the U. S. senate, Jan. 1859, on the Pacific Railroad bill, favoring the 32d parallel route. *The Geography, etc. By Sylvester Mowry, of Arizona, graduate of the U. S. military academy at West Point, late lieutenant third artillery, U. S. A., corresponding member of the American Institute, late U. S. boundary commissioner, etc....A new edition with appendix.* S. F. and N. Y., 1863, 8vo, 124 p. The title is self-explanatory. This edition contains besides the original address a preface written after congress had passed the territorial bill. The new appendix gives, 1st, the history of the country and its mines since 1859, including the author's arrest and release after six months, with severe criticism of Gen. Carleton's course throughout the campaign; 2d, 'the mines of Arizona,' by F. B(iertu), Feb. 1861, a description of the various mines and their prospects; 3d, about 50 p. on the mines of Sonora and Chihuahua; 4th, a note on the Apaches, 'devils,' or 'wolves.' The author says 'the Apaches are not a serious obstacle to the working of mines in Arizona. The danger to be apprehended is on the roads; and this can be avoided by ordinary caution...There is only one way to wage war against the Apaches. A steady, persistent campaign must be made, following them to their haunts—hunting them to the "fastnesses of the mountains." They must be surrounded, starved into coming in, surprised, or inveigled—by white flags or any other method, human or divine—and then put to death. If these ideas shock any weak-minded individual, who thinks himself a philanthropist, I can only say I pity without respecting his mistaken sympathy. A man might as well have sympathy for a rattlesnake or a tiger;' and 5th, letters from S. W. Inge, C. E. Bennett, Joseph Lane, John C. Hays, John Nugent, and Miguel A. Otero, on the wealth, population, and needs of the country. A 3d edition is entitled *Arizona and Sonora; the geography, history, and resources of the silver region of North America. By Sylvester Mowry of Arizona, etc. Third edition revised and enlarged.* N. Y., 1864, 12 mo, 251 p. Besides new notes by the author, this ed. contains a chapter from Ross Browne's work, and an extract from *Ward's Mexico.* It also includes as one of its chapters a reprint of the following pamphlet: *The Mines of the West. Shall the government seize them? The mining states. How shall they be taxed? By Sylvester Mowry of Arizona.* N. Y., 1864, 8vo, 16 p., from the *N. Y. Herald.* In the form of this final 3d edition *Mowry's Arizona* is doubtless the best work published down to 1864, and hardly excelled by any published since.

Charles D. Poston was another prominent pioneer, whose writing on historical subjects have not, however, the book form. *Poston's Narrative,* forming chap. xxiv. of *Browne's Adventures,* is an extract from his original MS. journal, describing his first tour through Arizona in 1854. *Poston's Reminiscences,* covering in a sense the period from 1854 to 1864, was an article contributed to the *Tucson Citizen* of April 15, 1884, and reproduced in *Arizona History,* 207–10. These brief sketches have much interest and value, but it is unfortunate that we have no more complete record of this pioneer's recollections. The author is an intelligent, active, and somewhat eccentric man. The *Speech of Charles D. Poston, of Arizona, on Indian affairs, delivered in the House of Representatives, Thursday, March 2, 1865,* N. Y., 1865, 8vo, 20 p., is explained by the title. In later years he published *The Sun-worshipers of Asia. By Charles D. Poston. Reprinted from the London edition.* S. F., 1864, 16mo, 106 p., the materials for which 'lecture were collected during an official visit to India, China, Japan, etc., accredited by the govt of the U. S.' Still later appeared *Apache-land. By Charles D. Poston, of Arizona.* S. F., 1878, 12mo, 141 p., with portrait. This is a poem not without merit, though some of the rhymes and measures would make an Apache's hair stand on end.

Adventures in the Apache country: a tour through Arizona and Sonora, with notes on the silver mines of Nevada. By J. Ross Browne, author of, etc. Illustrated by the author. N. Y., 1871, 12mo, 535 p. (292 p. on Arizona), is a work which, though describing a visit in 1863–4, belongs historically here, since it describes the country's condition as it was after the disasters described in this chapter, and before the work of regeneration had made much progress, besides narrating incidentally many events of the preceding years. The work was first published in *Harper's Magazine,* xxix.–xxx., 1864–5. The author accompanied Poston in his tour as Indian agent; his skill as a writer is too well known to require notice here; and though his ridicule and sarcasm, as applied to certain matters, have been regarded by some as injurious to the interests of Arizona and Nevada, yet no other work gives so vivid and interesting or more accurate account of the country as it actually was. Of it, in conclusion, he says: 'I believe it to be a territory wonderfully rich in minerals, but subject to greater drawbacks than any of our territorial possessions. It will be many years before its mineral resources can be fully and fairly developed. Emigration must be encouraged by increased military protection; capital must be expended without the hope of immediate and extraordinary

returns; civil law must be established on a firm basis, and facilities of communication fostered by legislation of congress. No country that I have yet
visited presents so many striking anomalies. With millions of acres of the
finest arable lands, there was not a single farm under cultivation; with the
richest mines, paper money is the common currency; with forts innumerable,
there is scarcely any protection; with extensive pastures, there is little or no
stock; with the finest natural roads, travelling is beset with difficulties; with
rivers through every valley, a stranger may die of thirst. Hay is cut with a
hoe, and wood with a spade or mattock. In January one enjoys the luxury
of a bath as under a tropical sun, and sleeps under double blankets at night.
There are towns without inhabitants, and deserts extensively populated;
vegetation where there is no soil, and soil where there is no vegetation.
There are Indians the most docile in North America, yet travellers are murdered daily by Indians the most barbarous on earth. The Mexicans have
driven the Pápagos from their southern homes, and now seek protection from
the Apaches in the Pápago villages. Fifteen hundred Apache warriors,
beaten in every fight by the Pimas, Maricopas, and Pápagos, keep these and
all other Ind. closed up as in a corral. Mines without miners and forts without soldiers are common. Politicians without policy, traders without trade,
store-keepers without stores, teamsters without teams, and all without
means, form the mass of the white population.'

   *Across America and Asia. Notes of a five years' journey around the world
and of residence in Arizona, Japan, and China. By Raphael Pumpelly, professor in Harvard University, and sometime mining engineer in the service of the
Chinese and Japanese governments. Third edition revised,* N. Y., 1870, 8vo,
454 p. (67 p. on Arizona), illustrations and maps. The author went to Arizona in 1860, to take charge as mining engineer of the Sta Rita silver mines,
and was driven out by the Apaches in 1861, many of his companions being
killed. As a description of the country visited, as a narrative of personal
experiences, and as a philosophic view of topics connected with Indian affairs,
social conditions, etc., Pumpelly's work merits high praise. On the Indian
question he writes: 'One cannot but look upon the history of our intercourse
with the original owners of our country as a sad commentary on the protestant civilization of the past two centuries...The example of duplicity set by
the early religious colonists of New England has been followed by an ever-
growing disregard for the rights of the Indian...While our forefathers made
at least a show of paying the natives for the land taken from them, there is
now not even a pretence of such compensation...As by far the greater
number are solely hunters, the area necessary to their support is out of all
proportion to that required for the subsistence of an equal number of agriculturists. With the influx of a mining population, the Indians, unable to
encroach upon the territory of neighboring tribes, are gradually driven to the
most barren parts of the mountains, and with the disappearance of game are
reduced to the verge of starvation. Whether they oppose bravely at first
the inroads of the whites, or submit peacefully to every outrage until forced
by famine to seek the means of life among the herds of the intruder, the result is the same. Sometimes hunted from place to place in open war; sometimes their warriors enticed away under peaceful promises by one party,
while a confederate band descends on the native settlements, massacring
women and children, old and young; they are always fading away before the
hand of violence. No treaty or flag of truce is too sacred to be disregarded,
no weapons too cruel or cowardly to be used or recommended by Americans.
Read the following quotation from a late work [Mowry as quoted in this
note]. I have quoted this passage because it expresses the sentiment of the
larger part of those directly interested in the extermination of the Indians,
who are exercising a constant pressure on the govt, and making healthy and
just legislation in the matter impracticable. If it is said that the Indians are
treacherous and cruel, scalping and torturing their prisoners, it may be answered that there is no treachery and no cruelty left unemployed by the
whites. Poisoning with strychnine, the wilful dissemination of the small-

pox, and the possession of bridles braided from the hair of scalped victims and decorated with teeth knocked from the jaws of living women—these are heroic facts among many of our frontiersmen.'

The Marvellous Country; or, Three Years in Arizona and New Mexico, the Apaches' home. Comprising a description of this wonderful country, its immense mineral wealth, its magnificent mountain scenery, the ruins of ancient towns and cities found therein, with a complete history of the Apache tribe, and a description of the author's guide, Cochise, the great Apache war chief. The whole interspersed with strange events and adventures. By Samuel Woodworth Cozzens. Illustrated by upwards of one hundred engravings. Boston, etc. (1874), 8vo, 532 p. The author visited the country in 1858–60, being interested in mines and taking some part in politics. He seems, however, to have drawn much of his matter from other sources, and the book is of a somewhat sensational type, written mainly to sell, though not grossly inaccurate.

American Pioneering, an address before the Travellers' Club. By E. E. Dunbar (N. Y.), 1863, 8vo, 45 p. The author was interested in the Ajo copper mine from 1855–6. 'I escaped out of Arizona, a territory teeming with the precious and other metals, in the spring of 1858, and came to Washington, believing in my verdancy that I should be able to excite some interest for that most important but suffering and neglected frontier. I encountered a member of congress from one of the eastern states. He was puffing a cigar and toasting his feet before a good fire at Willard's Hotel. I approached this member of congress in my most bland and winning manner, and after begging his pardon. . .recounted to him in thrilling tones and impressive manner the trials, difficulties, and dangers we were encountering in opening the new territory to civilization. The member of congress quietly heard what I had to say, and then coolly turning to me, inquired: "What the devil did you go to such a God-forsaken country for?" This tells the whole story of my Washington experience in attempting to excite an interest on behalf of Arizona.'

CHAPTER XXI.

POLITICAL ANNALS OF ARIZONA.

1864–1887.

Origin of the Name Arizona—Territorial Organization—A Migrating Government—At Navajo Spring—Governor Goodwin and Congressman Poston—First Legislature—Seals—Political Affairs—Rulers—The Capital Question—Prescott versus Tucson—Original Counties—Map—Boundary Dispute at Yuma—Statistics of Population — Immigration — Mormons — Powell's Exploration of the Colorado—Wheeler's Surveys—Floods and Earthquakes—Lists of Federal and Territorial Officers—Members of Council and Assembly—Résumé of Legislative Proceedings.

Now that we have at last reached a period when our territory has legally a name of its own, it is well to devote a few lines to that name, mainly for the purpose of correcting prevalent errors respecting its origin. Arizona, probably Arizonac in its original form, was the native and probably Pima name of the place—of a hill, valley, stream, or some other local feature—just south of the modern boundary, in the mountains still so called, on the headwaters of the stream flowing past Saric, where the famous Planchas de Plata mine was discovered in the middle of the eighteenth century, the name being first known to Spaniards in that connection and being applied to the mining camp, or real de minas. The aboriginal meaning of the term is not known, though from the common occurrence in this region of the prefix *ari*, the root *son*, and the termination *ac*, the derivation ought not to escape the research of a competent student.[1] Such

---

[1] Prof. Alphonse Pinart told me that he had discovered the derivation of the name, but I am not acquainted with his conclusions.

guesses as are extant, founded on the native tongues, offer only the barest possibility of partial and accidental accuracy; while similar derivations from the Spanish are extremely absurd.[2] The oft-repeated assertion that the original Spanish form was Arizuma has no other foundation than a misprint in some old book or map. The name should properly be written and pronounced Arisona, as our English sound of the *z* does not occur in Spanish. Suggestions for the legal name were Arizuma, Arizonia, Pimería, and Gadsonia. Pimería would have been in some respects more appropriate than Arizona—as being of provincial and not merely local application—and quite as euphonious.

The territorial act having been passed by congress in February 1863, and officials appointed by President Lincoln in March, the whole party of emigrant statesmen, headed by Governor John N. Goodwin of Maine,[3] started in August for the far west, leaving Leavenworth on September 25th, Santa Fé November 26th, and Alburquerque December 8th, under the escort of troops from Missouri and New Mexico. It was on the 27th that the party crossed the meridian of 109° into Arizona, and two days later in camp at Navajo Spring, the government was formally organized in the wilderness. The flag was raised and cheered; a prayer was said by H. W. Read; the oath

[2] Of the former class may be mentioned the following: *ari,* 'maiden,' and *zon,* 'valley,' from the Pima; *ara* and *sunea,* or *urnia,* the sun's beloved, from the Mojave; *ari,* 'few,' and *zoni,* 'fountains;' *ari,* 'beautiful,' and the Spanish *zona: Arizuma,* Aztec for 'silver-bearing;' *Arezuma,* an Aztec queen; *Arizunna,* 'the beautiful;' *Arizonia,* the maiden queen or goddess who by immaculate conception gave being to the Zuñi Indians; also the meaning 'little creek' is given. Of the second class we may note *arrezafe,* a country covered with brush-wood; *árida zona,* or an arid zone or region; and *narizona,* a big-nosed woman ! Accurate results are rarely, if ever, reached by the favorite method of seeking for similar sounds in various languages.

[3] See official list at the end of this chapter. Of the original appointments, John A. Gurley of Ohio was governor, but died Aug. 18th, and Goodwin was appointed on the 21st, Goodwin being succeeded as chief justice by Turner. John Titus of Penn. was the original district attorney, his place being taken by Gage before starting. The surveyor-gen., Bashford, was appointed May 26th.

of office was taken by the officials; and a proclamation of Governor Goodwin was read, in which the vicinity of Fort Whipple, established only a month earlier by Major Willis of the California column, was named as the temporary seat of government; and here all arrived on January 22, 1864. In May the fort was moved some 20 miles to the south-west, and near it by July a town had been founded on Granite Creek to become the temporary capital. It was named Prescott, in honor of the historian.

Meanwhile the governor made a tour of inspection in the south, and other parts of the territory; by proclamation of April 9th three judicial districts were created, and the judges assigned;[4] the marshal was instructed to take a census; and an election proclamation was issued on the 26th of May. Accordingly, at the election of July 18th, there were chosen a council of nine members, and a house of eighteen;[5] also a delegate to congress in the person of Charles D. Poston.[6] The legislature was in session at Prescott from September 26th to the 10th of November. Besides attending to the various routine duties, and passing special acts, some of which, for this as for other sessions, will be noticed elsewhere, this body adopted a mining law, and a general code of laws, prepared by Judge Howell, and called in his honor

[4] The 2d district included all west of long. 114°; Allyn, judge, court at La Paz; 1st district, all east of 114°, and south of the Gila; Howell, judge, court at Tucson; 3d district, all east of 114°, and north of the Gila; Turner, judge, court (fixed a little later) at Prescott. On May 11th the gov. at Tucson appointed municipal officers for that town.

[5] See note at end of this chapter for members of this and later legislatures.

[6] Poston, as supt ind. affairs, had not come to Ariz. with the rest, but by way of California, whence in company with Ross Browne—see *Adven. in Apache Country*—he made a tour for the inspection of the friendly Indian tribes, and the distribution of supplies furnished for the govt, subsequently continuing his tour for electioneering purposes. Poston seems to have been nominally a union candidate, and Charles Leib was another, W. D. Bradshaw being the democratic candidate. The customary charges of trickery and rascality, of secessionists masquerading as union men, of rebels, Sonorans, and Pápagos allowed to vote, while loyal teamsters and soldiers were denied the right, etc. There was also much hostility to the new government, the garrison at Ft Whipple in April signing a set of resolutions in which the territorial officials were accused of various shortcomings, such as selling for their own profit stores furnished by the govt. *Hayes' Scraps, Cal. Politics*, vi. 150; *Id., Ariz.*, i., passim.

the Howell Code, being based mainly on the codes of New York and California.[7] It also divided the territory into four counties under the aboriginal names of Pima, Yuma, Mojave, and Yavapai;[8] and adopted a territorial seal, though for nearly 20 years a different seal appears to have been in use. Both are shown in the annexed cut.[9]

It is not my purpose to attempt any minute résumé or analysis of legislative proceedings. Much of the most important legislation was connected with Indian affairs, mining, and other subjects that will be noticed in other chapters; and at the end of this will be found a note, in which a few of the more notable measures adopted at the successive sessions are cited. In the same note is given a list of all federal and territorial officials from the beginning to 1885, together with the names of members and officers of both branches of the legislature at its thirteen consecutive sessions.[10]

[7] *The Howell Code, Adopted by the first Legislative Assembly of the Territory of Arizona. Session begun, etc.* Prescott, 1865, 8vo, 4J1 p. *Arizona, Mining Law of the Territory of.* Prescott, 1864, 8vo, 18 p. In the title an 'N' with the side lines cut out was made to do duty for a 'Z,' which was apparently lacking in the font.

[8] *Arizona, Comp. Laws*, 31, where, however, the date, Oct. 11, 1864, is not given. Pima co., capital Tucson, included all east of long. 113° 20', and south of the Gila (subsequently divided into 5 counties or parts of counties); Yuma co., capital La Paz, all west of long. 113° 20' and south of Bill Williams fork, and the Sta María (never changed); Mojave co. (officially but incorrectly written *Mohave*), capital Mojave City, all west of 113° 20' and north of Bill Williams fork and the Sta María (as it still exists but for the loss of the part joined to Nevada, and an addition from Yavipai, north of the Colorado in 1883; see map); and Yavapai, capital Prescott, all east of 113° 20' and north of the Gila (subsequently divided into 6 counties and parts of counties). See county map and annals in chap. xxiv., this volume.

[9] The seal described in the act of 1864—*Arizona Compiled Laws*, 542—is the upper one in the cut. I find it used for the first time—in print—in the *Laws* of 1883. The earlier seal, the lower of the cut, of origin unknown to me, is printed in the *Journals* and *Acts* as late as 1879. For humorous comments on this seal, see Ross Browne, in *Harper's Mag.*, xxix. 561.

The best authority on the organization of the territorial govt in 1863–4 is the introduction and appendix of the *Arizona, Journals of the First Legislative Assembly*, Prescott, 1865, 8vo, 250, xviii., p., to the contents of which the various writers have added nothing. The *Arizona, Message of the Governor, 1864*, Prescott, 1864, 12mo, 9 p., was separately published, as were later messages, which will not be specially noticed, as they are contained in the journals.

[10] The authorities are, of course, the *Arizona, Journals*, 1864–85; and *Arizona, Acts, Resolutions, and Memorials of the First (second, etc.) Legislative Assembly*, Prescott, 1865 (et seq.), 8vo, 79 p., with some slight supplementary information from other sources. After 1868 the sessions were biennial.

If we credit the statements of political and personal foes, the members of council and house, like territorial and federal officials, were for the most part a sad set of rogues and fools; but judging by the record

SEALS OF ARIZONA

of their acts, they compare favorably, in respect of honor, ability, and patriotic devotion to their country's needs, with representatives of other territories and states in the west and east.

Arizona has been ruled by a line of eight governors.

appointed at Washington, as the custom is, more through political influence than a consideration of the country's needs, yet as a rule with fairly good results, as follows: John N. Goodwin in 1863–5, Richard Mc-Cormick in 1865–9, A. P. K. Safford in 1869–77, John P. Hoyt, acting, in 1877–8, John C. Frémont in 1879–81, John J. Gosper, acting, in 1881–2, F. A. Tritle in 1882–5, and C. M. Zulick from 1885. The last, appointed by President Cleveland, is a democrat; all the rest have been more or less republican in politics. Governors McCormick and Safford, ruling for the longest terms, were more fully identified than the others with the real interests of the territory, and perhaps were more efficient rulers; but the rest seem to have been for the most part honorable and intelligent men. In a general way their acts call for no further criticism, favorable or otherwise. One of the number should be well enough known to readers of my history of California; but Frémont was appointed merely that his chronic poverty might be relieved; and in Arizona he seems to have done nothing worse than neglect his duties. Delegates in congress were not less zealous and intelligent men, being in politics union, or republican, to 1874, democratic to 1884, and then republican again.[11] Though working with due zeal at Washington, the delegates, as is true for most territories, have been able to accomplish but little for the advancement of Arizona, since congress contented

[11] The vote and politics of the 12 elections for delegate were as follows: 1st, 1864, Poston, union; Bradshaw, democrat; Leib, un.; vote not found. 2d, 1864, Goodwin, un., 707; Allyn, un., 376; Poston, un., 260; total, 1,343. 3d, 1866, Bashford, republican, 1,009; Poston, rep., 518; Sam. Adams, indep., 168; total, 1,695. 4th, 1868, McCormick, rep., 1,237; John A. Rush, dem., 836; Adams, indep., 32; total, 2,105. 5th, 1870, McCormick, 1,882; Peter R. Brady, dem., 832; total, 2,714. 6th, 1872, McCormick, 2,522; total, 2,522. 7th, 1874, Stevens, indep. dem., 1,442; Bean, rep., 1,076; John Smith, rep., 571; total, 3,089. 8th, 1876, Stevens, 1,194; W. H. Hardy, rep., 1,099; Oury, dem., 1,007; total, 3,250. 9th, 1878, Campbell, dem., 1,452; A. E. Davis, rep. and granger, 1,097; Stevens, dem., 1,090; K. S. Woolsey, indep. dem., 822; total, 4,461. 10th, 1880, Oury, dem., 4,095 (or 4,176); Stewart, rep., 3,606 (or 3,778); total, 7,701 (or 7,954). 11th, 1882, Oury, 6,121; Porter, rep., 5,141 (or 5,243); total, 11,262 (or 11,364). 12th, 1884, Bean, rep., Head, dem. The figures are from *Hamilton's Resources*, 102–5, and *Ariz. Hist.* (Elliott & Co.), 315.

itself for the most part with the annual appropriations
for routine expenses.[12]

On the question of a permanent capital the legislatures of 1864–5–6 could not agree. Representatives
of the first district were not quite strong enough to
decide in favor of Tucson, to which town undoubtedly
at that time the honor belonged; but they were able
to defeat the pretensions of Prescott. It was a barren
victory, however, since by the governor's proclamation
from year to year the legislature was convened at
Prescott as the temporary seat of government. In
1867, however, the tables were turned, and by a majority of one vote Tucson was made the capital, five
sessions of the legislature being held there; until in
1877 the northern combination was in turn trium-
phant, and Prescott has been the capital ever since.
Agitation on the subject is by no means at an end,
but Tucson is thought to have but slight chance of
regaining its old position, though a change in favor of
Phœnix or some other town of the central region
seems not unlikely in the future.[13]

[12] See *U. S. Acts*, etc., for congressional action; also *Cong. Globe* (through
index under ' Arizona ') and *Journals* of senate and house for discussions and
unsuccessful efforts. The appropriation for ordinary expenses of the govt
down to 1868 was $33,500 per year; with $5,000 extra in 1866, besides $5,000
for compiling the laws, and $4,160 for a census. After 1868 the amount was
from $33,500 to $40,000 for years when the legislature met, and $13,500 to
$23,000 in other years. For the Indian service, that is, for Ind. on reserva-
tions and friendly tribes, there was a varying but increasing appropriation of
$10,000 to $172,000 (in 1881 as high as $346,000 apparently); besides a yearly
amount from $150,000 to $425,000 for the reservation Apaches after 1872, this
including, however, part of the N. Mex. Apaches. For surveys, besides the
expenses of the office for Cal. and Ariz., there was an appropriation of $5,000
to $10,000 down to 1870; and later $20,000 or less, sometimes nothing; besides $6,000 to $9,500 for the surveyor-gen. and his office. Some of the special acts of congress will be noted in other connections. A few not thus noted
are as follows: 1867, internal revenue of 1866–8, devoted to the building of a
penitentiary; 1869, sessions of the legislature to be biennial; 1870, salaries of
justices to be $3,000, and $2,000, appropriated for a law library; 1878, council
not to exceed 12 and house 24 members at $4 per day.

[13] In the original bill, as introduced in congress, Tucson was named as
capital, but on final passage that clause was removed, and thus the gov. was
left to select a temporary and the legislature a permanent capital. Why
Goodwin selected a spot so far away from the settlements is not clearly explained. Possibly he thought Prescott likely to become the centre of population, or was influenced by certain personal interests of his associates, and
probably the secession proclivities of Tucson had much to do with his choice.
The Tucson people were disappointed and angry. Poston, *Reminiscences*, 210,

As we have seen, four counties were created in 1864. In 1865 Pah-Ute county was organized from northern Mojave; but the next year congress attached the north-western corner of Arizona—all north and west of the Colorado and longitude 114°—to Nevada; and the legislature, after vain protests against this change, finally in 1871 repealed the act creating Pah-Ute, and restored what was left of that county to Mojave, which in 1883 was extended eastward, north of the Colorado, from longitude 113° 20′ to Kanab Wash. Utah also tried in 1865 to get a slice of northern Arizona, without success; while Arizona's effort of 1877 to annex Grant county, New Mexico, was equally unsuccessful. Maricopa county was created in 1571; Pinal in 1875; Apache in 1879; Cochise, Graham, and Gila being organized in 1881. Thus the number of counties was increased to ten, a tier of four being created in the central or Gila region, while Yavapai in the north and Pima in the south were each divided by a north and south line. Boundaries as they now stand are shown on the map.

says Prescott was selected by influence of Carleton, and against his own advice. In the legislature representatives of the 1st district voted solid against Prescott, trying to gain a vote or two from the opposition by favoring successively La Paz, Walnut Grove, and a town to be called Aztlan, at the junction of the Verde and Salado; but they had lost one of their members of the house by death, and the members from the 2d and 3d district gave 9 votes to 8 in favor of Prescott. In the council, however, there was a vacancy in the 2d district, so that the vote was a tie, 4 to 4. In the session of 1865 the council voted 4 to 1 in favor of Prescott, but in the house the matter was indefinitely postponed, vote not given. As 3 members of the council and 8 of the house were not in attendance, this action may indicate magnanimity on the part of Yavapai—perhaps. In 1866 the bill in favor of Prescott was defeated in council by a tie vote of 4 to 4, Yuma and Pah-Ute joining Pima in the fight. In 1867 it was Yavapai against the field, but the best this county could do against Tucson was to gain one Yuma vote for La Paz, Mojave and Pah-Ute in the house deserting their northern allegiance, and Prescott was defeated 9 to 7, and 5 to 4 in council where Mojave voted for Prescott. At this session a minority report opposed Tucson on the ground that a majority of the population lived outside of Pima co.! On this basis it would be hard to locate a capital in any of the U. S. Poston, *Remin.*, 210, says that McCormick by his influence gave the capital to Tucson on a promise of support for delegate. In 1875 there was a vote for Tucson, which is not quite intelligible (see note on 8th sess., p. 541, this vol.). In 1877 the northern population had considerably increased, and by united action gave 12 votes to 6 for Prescott in the house, and 5 to 4 in the council. If later or intermediate agitation ever took the form of bills introduced and not passed, such bills have escaped my notice.

Yuma alone has retained its original extent, yet not
without a boundary dispute. It had doubtless been
the original intention that the Colorado should be
the boundary between Arizona and California, but

COUNTIES OF ARIZONA.

owing to a peculiar bend of the river, the line as correctly surveyed from the Gila junction toward San
Diego left a small area south and west of the Colorado opposite Fort Yuma, technically in California.
On this area was a considerable amount of taxable

property, including the ferry buildings. The Arizona legislature rather indiscreetly asked congress for the land in 1864–5; California took the hint; the property was taxed by both Yuma and San Diego counties; and a spirited controversy was carried on from about 1867, each claimant ridiculing the other's absurd pretensions. In 1871 there seems to have been some kind of a decision at Washington in favor of Arizona, and after 1873 I find no trace of the dispute.[14]

The white population of Arizona—that is, of Arizona county, New Mexico—according to the somewhat doubtful census of 1860, was 2,421, or perhaps 6,481, including all Mexicans and mixed breeds. During the disasters of 1861–3, the number was perhaps reduced to 500 or 600.[15] After the organization of the government, the first territorial census of 1866 showed a total—excluding Indians—of 5,526; and the second, 7,200 in 1867.[16] The United States census of 1870 shows a population of 9,658;[17] and the figures in 1872 and 1874 were 10,743 and 11,480, respectively, with a notable increase to 30,192 in 1876.[18] The federal census of 1880 raised the figures to 40,440.[19] For later years we have no accurate

[14] See governor's message, in *Ariz., Jour.*, 1871, p. 55; *Id.*, 1867, passim; *Id.*, 1868, p. 189–92; also, not only on this controversy, but particularly on all the county boundaries and their successive changes, note on legislative proceedings at end of this chapter, and local annals in chap. xxiv. On July 28, 1873, the com. of pub. lands at Wash. informed the surv.-gen. of Ariz. of a decision in favor of the territory. *Yuma Sentinel*, Sept. 13, 1873.

[15] Hinton, *Hand-book*, 44, gives the pop. in 1863 as 581. Mowry, *Arizona*, 71, grossly overestimates the number in 1864 as 20,000.

[16] Governor's report in *Ariz., Journal*, 1866, p. 264–5; *Id.*, 1867, p. 259.

[17] *U. S. Census*, 9th. The total included 26 negroes, 20 Chinamen, and 31 Indians; no. of citizens (males above 21 years) 3,397; native (U. S.) born 3,845, of whom 1,221 born in Ariz.; foreign born 5,809, of whom 4,339 in Mexico; males 6,887, females 2,771; families 2,290; dwellings 2,822. Engaged in agric. 1,285; in professional and personal service 3,115; in trade and transportation 591; in mining, manuf., and mechanical industries 1,039.

[18] *Ariz., Jour.*, 1874, p. 78; *Id., Acts*, 1876, p. 123; *Hinton*, 44, 377; *Ariz., Hist.* (E. & Co.), 30.

[19] *U. S. Census*, 10th. Of the 40,440, there were 155 negroes, 1,630 Chinese, and 3,493 Indians. Citizens 18,046; native born 24,391, of whom 8,166 in Ariz.; foreign born 16,049, of whom 9,330 in Mexico; males 28,202, females 12,238; families 9,536; dwellings 9,033. Engaged in agriculture 3,435; in profession and personal service 8,210; in trade and transportation 3,252; in mining, manuf., and mechanical industries 7,374.

statements; but the population in 1886 should not be less than 75,000.[20]

In former years, immigration to Arizona depended mainly on the varying prospects of the mines, though by no means all immigrants were miners. Of late, however, it has been clearly demonstrated that the country possesses a great variety of resources, and is capable of supporting a large miscellaneous population, though here, as elsewhere, attempts at colonization have met with indifferent success.[21]   It is certain that the land possesses in abundance two of the three great sources of wealth—mining and agriculture—and to develop them only the industry of man is needed. Together with her large area of grazing and arable lands, the territory contains nearly every variety of mineral, and in her valleys can be raised all kinds of cereals, vegetables, and fruit, the citrus belts of southern Arizona being destined at no very distant day to rival those of California.

Among the early settlers were the Mormons, who in 1868 had a settlement at St Thomas, in Pah-Ute county, a region later attached to Nevada.   In 1873 the authorities in Utah formed a plan of colonization, and a pioneer party of 700 men was sent south, intending to get a start by working on the Texas Pa-

[20] Gov. Tritle's estimate was 75,000 for 1884, acc. to *Ariz., Hist.* (E. &. Co.), 30.   Hamilton, *Resources,* 97, gives a pop. of 82,976 in 1882, and that from a census; but I suppose there can be no real authority for so large a figure.   Perhaps the fact that in 1882 Ariz. was seeking admission as a state had some influence on this report.

[21] In 1871 is mentioned a scheme to introduce as colonists the better classes of the French communist prisoners at govt expense, C. D. Poston being interested in the project, with much encouragement, it is said, from the French ministry. *S. F. Call,* Aug. 21, 1871.   Again, in 1873, a French colony is mentioned as having a large grant, and proposing to build a railroad from Guaymas. *S. F. Bulletin,* Feb. 27, 1873; *Hayes' Scraps, Ariz.,* v. 131.   In 1876–8 we hear of the Arizona Colonization Company of Boston, under the presidency of Cozzens, author of the *Marvellous Country,* I suppose, which enlisted over 200 colonists for the Colorado Chiquito region.   The first party of 45 arrived in May of this year, but they soon became disgusted and scattered to seek employment at the towns.   Another party is said to have been on the way, but I find no definite record that any colony was established. *Conklin's Pict. Ariz.,* 352–3; *Anaheim Gazette,* May 20, 1876.   In 1882 G. W. Webb is named as the agent of a company which had constructed a ditch and proposed to found a kind of Arizonian Riverside in the Gila valley. *Yuma Sentinel,* Jan. 28, 1882.

cific Railroad, but became discontented with the prospect and went home.[22] The project was revived in 1876-7, and a beginning was made in two districts—on the Upper Colorado Chiquito and on Salt River. At a meeting held at Salt Lake City, in January 1876, missionaries were present from different parts of Utah, and an organization was effected under Lot Smith as president. The first party arrived in March at the Sunset crossing, and soon the camps of Sunset, Allen, Ballinger, and Obed were established. Progress was slow, the first season's crop not sufficing for the colony's needs, and teams having to be sent to Utah for supplies; but the pioneers were resolute men, and though many, first and last, abandoned the enterprise, at the end of 1877 the mission numbered 564 souls, and a year later 587. In 1884 the population is given by the newspapers as 2,507, the chief settlements being Sunset, St Joseph, and Brigham City.[23]

[22] *Ladd's Little Colorado Settlements*, MS., 1; *Hayes' Scraps, Ariz.*, vi. 126; *S. F. Bulletin*, Feb. 4, July 14, 1873.

[23] The original leaders, each at the head of saints from some neighborhood in Utah, were Lot Smith, Geo. Lake, Wm C. Allen, and Jesse O. Ballinger. Smith's camp was called Sunset, but was moved the 1st year 2 miles north. Allen's camp was renamed St Joseph in 1878. Lake's camp was called Obed, about 2 m. west of Allen, but was abandoned in 1877 on account of fever and ague. Ballinger's camp was named Brigham City in 1878. Woodruff was founded in 1877, 25 m. above St Joseph. Moan Coppy, in Yavapai co., 36° on the road to Lee's ferry, was founded by Lamanites in 1877; also in that year Forest Dale in the south. Taylor, near Brigham City, was founded in 1878, but soon abandoned, and a new settlement estab., which was later known as Snowflake. In 1876 much damage was done by floods; but forts of logs and stone were built, and a steam saw-mill was started in the Mogollon Mts, 40 m. w. of Sunset, sometimes called Millville. A tannery was later in operation here, but the mill was sold in '81, and removed to the eastern stake. In 1877 a grist-mill was built near Ballinger's, horse-power having been used before, and a reënforcement from the southern states, under A. P. Beebe, arrived. In 1878 occurred another flood; the Little Colorado 'stake of Zion' was organized, with Smith as pres., Jacob Hamilton and L. H. Hatch as councillors, and bishops Geo. Lake, L. M. Savage, John Bushman, and John Kaitchum. Also the stake of eastern Ariz. was set off, the dividing line being the Berado rancho on the Col. Chiq. 1879 was a year of good crops, and dairying was carried on in Pleasant valley, 40 m. w. of Sunset; a woollen factory at Moan Coppy; Wilford Woodruff at work as missionary, and extending his efforts to the Laguna and Isleta Ind. in N. Mex. 1880 was a bad year, with poor crops; Brigham City was nearly abandoned, and the saints regarded themselves as cheated in the count of votes at election. In 1881 crops were also bad in many places, and a flood destroyed dams, also carrying away the bridge at Sunset. Brigham City was nearly abandoned by the Mormons, the site being turned over to the church, and sold to Adams, Whiting, and Company; yet this was the headquarters of the Mormon con-

The settlements of this region were in 1878 organized
into the Little Colorado stake of Zion; and at the
same time an eastern Arizona stake was organized in
the region about St John, but I have no details on
the annals of this stake.

The Salt River settlements, later Maricopa stake,
above Phœnix, were begun in March 1877 by nine
families from Utah, organized at St George by Brigham Young, under Daniel W. Jones as president.
There were 71 persons in the colony, the settlement
being called successively Camp Utah, Utahville, Jonesville, and finally Lehi. The Utah ditch was constructed
by the incorporated Utah Irrigating and Farming
Company. Elder Jones had some troubles with his
flock, the site of the village seems to have been slightly
changed once or twice, and in 1884 the population
was less than 200.[24] In January 1878 there arrived
from Salt Lake City—part of the members coming
from Idaho—another colony of 77 saints, including
the Sirrines, formerly of Brannan's California colony.
They declined to join Smith in the north, failed to
make a satisfactory arrangement with Jones, and so
founded Mesa City, four miles from Jonesville, incorporating a new company for the construction of a
ditch, by which at a cost of $43,000 about 5,000 acres
have been reclaimed from the desert. The population
was about 600 in 1884. Jesse H. Perkins was presiding elder from October 1878, and A. F. McDonald

tractors on the A. & P. R. R. Here ends my only detailed authority, the
Settlements of the Little Colorado, Arizona, MS., prepared for my use by S. G.
Ladd. See also, on these settlements, *Yuma Sentinel*, Mar. 18, 1876; Nov.
17, 1877; Nov. 2, 1878; *Anaheim Gazette*, Dec. 16, 1876; *Hinton's Hand-book*,
296; *Prescott Miner*, Sept. 19, 1879; June 25, 1880; *Salt Lake Herald*, Dec. 1,
1877. Elliott & Co. state that in the latest years the Col. Chiq. farms have
proved a failure, on account of alkali, and possibly the pop. given in my text
from newspaper authority may be too large. It includes, however, the eastern stake.

[24] *Maricopa Stake*, MS., by Chas J. Robson, one of the pioneers. The
original company consisted of D. W. Jones, P. C. Merrill, Henry C. Rogers,
Thos Biggs, Joseph McRae, D. J. Merrill, Isaac Turley, Geo. E. Steel, and
——Williams, all with families. F. E. Robson taught the 1st school at Lehi
in 1878. See also *Salt Lake Herald*, May 5, 1877; Aug. 12, 1880; *Phœnix
Herald*, July 30, 1880; *Prescott Miner*, Oct. 19, 1877; *Los Ang. Express*, April
14, 1877; *S. Luis Ob. Tribune*, July 28, 1877; *Ariz., Hist.* (E. & Co.), 284.

president from February 1880, the Maricopa stake being permanently organized in December 1882.[25]

In 1878 P. C. Merrill and four families left the Jones colony and founded St David on the San Pedro. In 1879 Joseph K. Rogers with four families came from the eastern Arizona stake and settled at Smithville—called Pima from 1883—on the upper Gila in Graham county. Other settlements formed in 1881–4 were Curtis, Graham, Thatcher, Central, Layton, and McDonald on the San Pedro. All those south-eastern establishments were organized in February 1883 into the stake of St Joseph under Christopher Layton as president. Pima is the chief town, and had in 1885 about 600 inhabitants.[26]

The Mormons have always been regarded as among the best of Arizona settlers, being quiet, industrious, and economical in their habits, and not disposed to intrude their religious peculiarities. As a rule polygamy has not been practised, though there are many exceptions. Their neat adobe houses, orchards, gar-

[25] *Robson's Maricopa Stake*, MS. The original colony consisted of F. M. Pomeroy, E. Pomeroy, John H. Pomeroy, Wm Newell, C. J. Robson, G. W., W. L., L. C., and P. P. Sirrine, Chas Mallory, Wm Schwartz, J. H. Smith, Chas Crismon, J. D. Hobson, Wm Crismon, and J. H. Blair, most of them with families. H. C. Rogers and G. W. Sirrine were councillors; and from 1882 E. Pomeroy and Thos C. Jones bishops. In 1884 the Tempe branch was organized with Sam. Openshaw as bishop, Mesa being divided into 2 wards, with O. M. Stewart as bishop of Alma. 1st Sunday school 1880, under C. J. Robson; Mutual Improvement Assoc. 1880, C. J. Robson pres.; Relief Soc. 1880, Sarah Phelps pres.; 1st school taught by Miss Ursula Pomeroy. In *Ariz., Hist.* (E. & Co.), 282–4, is an account of the Mesa colony, with view on p. 168, and sketch of Pres. McD. on p. 299–300. See also *Prescott Miner*, Feb. 1, 1878; *S. F. Chronicle*, Aug. 6, 1883.

[26] James H. Martineau's *Settlements in Arizona*, MS. The St David pioneers were the 4 or 5 Merrills, Geo. E. Steel, Jos. McRae, and A. O. Williams. It was named for David Patten, the martyr. The bishops have been D. P. Kimball, H. J. Horner, W. D. Johnson, and M. H. Merrill. The Pima pioneers were Rogers, Teeples, Haws, Welch, and Dall, Rogers being the bishop to 1885. Curtis was founded in 1881 by 3 Curtis families, Moses M. Curtis being the bishop. Graham in 1881 by Jorgenson, Skinner, Anderson, and Wilson, with Jorgenson as bishop. Thatcher in 1882 by Moody, Pace, and others, Moody being succeeded by Sam. Clearidge as bishop. Central in 1882 by Bishop Jos. Cluff, Clemons, Young, and Witbeck. McDonald was made a ward in 1883, H. J. Horner bishop, Hill, Hoops, and other settlers. Layton, near Safford, in 1884 by John Welker bishop, A. Welker, B. Peel, etc. A settlement in Sulphur Spring valley, founded by Elder Wm Fife in 1882, has been nearly abandoned. There are good schools and churches; grist-mill at Curtis, saw-mill at Mt Graham. Central and St David have each about 250 inhab., the others 50 to 150 each.

dens, and well-tilled fields form veritable oases in the desert. Their lands are held by the community, work and trade are carried on for the most part on the coöperative plan, and they even live in community houses, eating at a common table, though each family has its separate rooms. It has been their aim to produce all that they eat and wear, sugar-cane and cotton being among their crops. Notwithstanding their community system, much freedom is conceded to individuals, who may in most respects live as they please and mingle freely with the gentiles. Less despised and persecuted than in Utah, they are naturally less clannish, peculiar, and exclusive. In politics they are nominally democratic, but often divide their vote on local issues, or put their united vote where it will do most good for their own interests. As a rule, they are prosperous but not yet wealthy farmers. Polygamy has led them into trouble, as it has others of their faith, and in 1884-5 several of their prominent members have been sent to prison.[27]

Of the Salt River valley a brief description may here be inserted; further mention will be made in a later chapter. It contains one of the largest bodies of agricultural land between the states of California and Kansas. It is walled in by mountains, and watered by a stream which has its source in one of the loftiest ranges, and is fed by the melting snows and by a hundred tributaries. Near the river is found a dark alluvial mold, with a depth of from six to fifteen feet, adapted to cereals and grasses; back from this is a belt of rich loam of remarkable fertility, and near the foothills the surface is of a light and porous nature, suited to the cultivation of fruit.

As the average rainfall of Arizona does not exceed ten inches, the people depend largely on irrigation for the watering of their farms and orchards. In this

[27] *S. F. Chronicle*, Nov. 28, Dec. 5, 1884; *Sac. Record-Union*, Apr. 8, 13, 1885; *Tucson Star*, Dec. 4, 1880.

valley alone eight main canals had been constructed
up to 1887, at an expense of nearly $1,000,000, with
a water-way of about 160 miles, and a total carrying
capacity of 70,000 miners' inches, these being the
largest and most expensive works of the kind in the
entire territory. At that date the area reclaimed
was estimated at 168,000 acres.

In 1887 not more than 50,000 acres were under
cultivation, of which about 12,000 were in wheat,
16,500 in barley, 15,000 in alfalfa, 5,600 in fruit, and
1,000 in miscellaneous crops. Of cereals, grasses,
fruits, and vegetables, nearly every variety can be
raised; of textile plants, there are cotton, hemp, jute,
and flax; while tobacco and the sugar-cane are also
cultivated, the latter being equal to the best products
of Louisiana. Of fruit, the yield is almost unprece-
dented, from the fig-tree being gathered two and even
three crops a year; while few portions of this coast are
better adapted to the cultivation of grapes, the product
of which reached six or seven tons to the acre. For
cattle-raising the valley is also well adapted, beeves
fattened on the alfalfa pastures being little inferior to
the stall-fed animals of the eastern states. Thus, by
means of irrigation and by the enterprise and ingenu-
ity of man, has a lifeless solitude been transformed
into one of the fairest valleys of the Pacific slope.

Among Arizona explorations of later years, Major
J. W. Powell's adventurous trip down the Colorado
deserves especial mention. With a party of ten, in
four boats built expressly for the purpose, Powell left
the railroad and started down Green River, late in
May 1869. In the early days of August he crossed
the Arizona line, and for about a month was whirled
by the torrent through the tortuous channel of the
great cañons, whose precipitous sides towered to a
height of several thousand feet—sometimes over a
mile—above the voyagers' heads. The river proved
a succession of rapids and whirlpools; each days' advance brought its new perils and toil; hairbreadth

escapes from destruction were of frequent occurrence;
one of the boats was lost; and the supply of instru-
ments, food, and clothing gradually disappeared in the
never-ending series of accidents.   On the 27th three
of the party resolved to scale the cliffs and make an
attempt to reach the settlements.   It is believed that
they were killed by Indians.   The rest continued their
voyage in two of the boats, and in three days found
succor and reached the mouth of the Rio Vírgen.
From this point three men went on down the Colorado, while Powell and the rest found their way
to Salt Lake City.   In this connection also should
be mentioned the surveys of Captain George M.
Wheeler and his corps in 1871–8, by which a large
portion of Arizona was for the first time accurately
mapped.[28]

[28] (*Powell*), *Exploration of the Colorado River of the West, and its Tributaries,*
explored in 1869, 1870, 1871, and 1872, under the direction of the Secretary of
the Smithsonian Institution.   Wash., 1875, 4to, xi., 291 p., with illustrations and
maps.   See also *Scribner's Monthly*, vol. ix.; *Appleton's Journal*, xi.; *Popular*
Science Monthly, xl. 385–99; xlii. 670–80; *U. S. Govt Doc.*, 42d cong. 1st sess.,
H. Mis. Doc. 37; 42d cong. 2d sess., no. 173; 42d cong. 3d sess., no. 76; 43d
cong. 1st sess., no. 265.   Wheeler's explorations are recorded in *U. S. Geog.*
Survey West of 100th Meridian, Annual Reports, 1871–8, 8vo, with atlas, maps,
and 4to vols on scientific branches.
    A bill for the admission of Arizona as a state was introduced in congress
by delegate Oury in 1871.   Not many years should be required to raise the
population to the required figure; whether political obstacles can be as
quickly removed, is another question.
    Notwithstanding the territory's general characteristic of extreme dryness,
floods are of not infrequent occurrence, especially in the Gila and Salt River
valleys.   The inundations are caused by heavy rains and so-called cloud-bursts
in the mountains, subsiding rapidly, but often doing considerable damage to
settlements and farms on the river banks.   The flood of Sept. 1868 was perhaps the most destructive ever known, destroying three of the Pima villages
and a large amount of property on the lower Gila.   1872 was also a season of
heavy rains, during which the levee at Yuma City was broken.   1876 was
another year of high water.   In 1883 cloud-bursts did much damage at Silver
King, Florence, and near Tombstone.   Yuma was again flooded in 1884, the
R. R. bridge being carried away.   No severe earthquakes have been known
in Arizona, though shocks are reported at Prescott in March 1870, at Yuma
in 1872, and at Indian Wells in 1874.

ARIZONA OFFICIAL LIST.

    Governor, 1863–5, John N. Goodwin; 1865–9, Richard C. McCormick;
1869–77, A. P. K. Safford; 1877–8; John P. Hoyt (acting); 1879–81, John C.
Frémont; 1881–2, John J. Gosper (acting); 1882–5; F. A. Tritle; 1885–7, C.
M. Zulick.
    Secretary, 1863–5, R. C. McCormick (H. W. Fleury, asst in 1865–7);
1866–9, James P. T. Cartter; 1870–6, Coles Bashford; 1876–8, John P. Hoyt;

1879–81, John J. Gosper; 1883–5, H. M. Van Arman (asst H. P. Garthwaite); 1885–7, James A. Bayard (asst T. E. Farish).

Justices, 1863–4, Wm F. Turner (C. J.), Wm T. Howell, Jos. P. Allyn; 1865–6, Turner (C. J.), Henry T. Backus, Allyn; 1867–70, Turner (C. J.), Backus, Harley H. Cartter; 1870–2, John Titus (C. J.), Isham Reavis, C. A. Tweed; 1873–4, Titus (C. J.), Tweed, Deforest Porter; 1875, E. F. Dunne (C. J.), Tweed, Porter; 1875–8, C. G. W. French (C. J.), Tweed. Porter; 1879–80, French (C. J.), Porter, Chas Silent; 1881, French (C. J.), Porter, W. H. Stilwell; 1882, French (C. J.), Stilwell, W. W. Hoover; 1883–5, French, and later Sumner Howard, (C. J.), D. H. Pinney, A. W. Sheldon, and later W. S. Fitzgerald; 1885–8, J. C. Shields, W. W. Porter, and W. H. Barnes.

MEMBERS OF THE LEGISLATURE.

1st session, 1864. Council, 1st district: Coles Bashford, Francisco S. Leon, Mark Aldrich, Patrick H. Dunne; 2d dist: Geo. W. Leihy, José M. Redondo; 3d dist: King S. Woolsey, Robert W. Groom, Henry A. Bigelow. President, Bashford; sec., Almon Gage. House, 1st dist: W. C. Jones, John G. Capron, Gregory P. Harte, Henry D. Jackson, Jesus M. Elias, Daniel H. Stickney, Nathan B. Appel, Norman S. Higgins, Gilbert W. Hopkins; 2d dist: Luis G. Bouchet, Geo. M. Holaday, Thos H. Bidwell, Ed. D. Tuttle, Wm Walter; 3d dist: John M. Boggs, James Garvin, James S. Giles, Jackson McCrackin. Speaker, Jones; clerk, Jas Anderson; chaplain, H. W. Fleury; translator, W. C. Jones.

2d session, 1865. Council, Yavapai co., K. S. Woolsey, R. W. Groom, H. A. Bigelow; Mojave co., Wm H. Hardy; Yuma, Manuel Ravena; Pima, Coles Bashford, F. S. Leon, P. H. Dunne; pres., Bigelow; sec., Jas Anderson. House, Yavapai, Jas S. Giles, J. McCrackin, Daniel Ellis, Jas O. Robinson; Mojave, Octavius D. Gaso, Converse W. Rowell; Yuma, Peter Doll, Alex. McKey, Wm K. Heninger; Pima, D. H. Stickney, and 8 members who did not attend. Speaker, Giles; clerk, J. E. McCaffry; translator, McKey.

3d session, 1866. Council, Yavapai, John W. Simmons, Dan. S. Lount, Lewis A. Stevens; Mojave, Wm H. Hardy; Pah-Ute, O. D. Gass; Yuma, Alex. McKey; Pima, Mark Aldrich, Mortimer R. Platt, Henry Jenkins; pres., Aldrich; sec., John M. Rountree. House, Yavapai, John B. Slack, Dan. Ellis, Hannibal Sypert, Wm S. Little, Underwood C. Barnett; Mojave, Alonzo E. Davis; Pah-Ute, Royal J. Cutter; Yuma, Marcus D. Dobbins, Robert F. Piatt, Wm H. Thomas; Pima, G. H. Oury, Wm J. Osborn, Henry McWard, Jas S. Douglas, Oscar Buckalew, Michael McKenna, S. W. Chambers, Thos D. Hutton. Speaker, Oury; clerk, J. S. Giles and H. A. Bigelow; chaplain, Chas M. Blake; translator, O. D. Gass.

4th session, 1867. Council, Yavapai, John W. Simmons, D. .S. Lount, Lewis A. Stevens; Mojave, W. H. Hardy; Pah-Ute, O. D. Gass; Yuma, Alex. McKey; Pima, D. H. Stickney, M. R. Platt, H. Jenkins; pres., Gass; sec., Gage. House, Yavapai, J. S. Giles, John A. Rush, John H. Matthews, Ed. J. Cook, Allen Cullumber, John T. Dare; Mojave, Nathaniel S. Lewis; Pah-Ute, Royal J. Cutler; Yuma, Oliver Lindsey, John Henion; Pima, Chas W. Lewis, John B. Allen, Marvin M. Richardson, U. C. Barnett, Francis M. Hodges, S. W. Chambers, Philip Drachman. Speaker, Lindsey; clerk, Follett G. Christie; chaplain, Thos H. Head.

5th session, 1868. Council, Yavapai, John G. Campbell, John L. Alsap, F. M. Chapman; Mojave and Pah-Ute, O. D. Gass; Yuma, Jos. K. Hooper; Pima, Estévan Ochoa, Hen. Jenkins, D. H. Stickney, Alex. McKey; pres., Alsap; sec., G. W. Pierce; chaplain, A. B. Salpointe. House, Yavapai, Thos W. Brooks, F. G. Christie, Wm S. Little, John Smith, E. Lumbley, G. R. Wilson; Mojave, U. C. Doolittle; Pah-Ute, Andrew S. Gibbons; Yuma, Jas P. Lugenbul, Thos J. Bidwell, Oliver Lindsey; Pima, J. M. Elias, Francis H. Goodwin, Hiram S. Stevens, John Owen, John Anderson, Sol. W. Chambers, Robt M. Crandal. Speaker, Bidwell; clerk, J. E. McCaffry.

6th session, 1871.   Council, Yavapai, J. T. Alsap, H. H. Carter, Andrew J. Marmaduke; Yuma, John H. Philips; Pima, H. S. Stevens, D. H. Stickney, E. Ochoa, F. S. Leon; pres., Stickney, and after his death Carter; sec., John Anderson; chaplain, Antonio Jouvenceau.   House, Yavapai, J. H. Fitzgerald, John L. Taylor, Wm J. O'Neill, G. A. Wilson, Jos. Melvin, James L. Mercer; Yuma, Marcus D. Dobbins, C. H. Brinley, T. J. Bidwell; Pima, J. W. Anderson, F. H. Goodwin, Wm Morgan, W. L. Fowler, Ramon Romano, Juan Elias, Rees Smith.   Speaker, Dobbins; clerk, Wm J. Boyd, and J. E. McCaffry; chaplain, Peter Bernal.

7th session, 1873.   Council, Yavapai, J. P. Hargrave, A. O. Noyes; Y. and Maricopa, K. S. Woolsey; Yuma, Thos J. Bidwell; Y. and Mojave, W. F. Henning; Pima, H. S. Stevens, Mark Aldrich, Juan Elias, Levi Ruggles. Pres., Hargrave; sec., J. T. Alsap; chaplain, Rev. G. A. Reeder.   House. Yavapai, John H. Behan, Wm Cole, Fred. Henry, Thos Stonehouse, Henry Wickenberg; Maricopa, G. H. Oury; Yuma, C. W. C. Rowell, J. M. Redondo, C. H. Brinley; Yuma and Mojave, Geo. Gleason; Pima, John B. Allen, Wm C. Davis, Lionel M. Jacobs, J. S. Josberg, F. M. Larkin, John L. Smith, John Montgomery, John W. Sweeney.   Speaker, Oury; clerk, Hyler Ott; chaplain, Rev. Ant. Jouvencean.

8th session, 1875.   Council, Yavapai, J. P. Hargrave, John G. Campbell, L. S. Stevens; Maricopa, K. S. Woolsey; Mojave, A. E. Davis; Yuma, J. M. Redondo; Pima, Wm Zeckendorf, S. R. Delong, P. R. Brady.   Pres., Woolsey; clerk, E. S. Penwell.   House, Yavapai, C. P. Head, Hugo Richards, A. L. Moeller, Levi Bashford, W. J. O'Neil, Gideon Brook; Maricopa, J. T. Alsap, G. H. Oury; Yuma, H. Goldberg, Sam. Purdy, Jr, R. B. Kelly; Mojave, S. W. Wood; Pima, F. M. Griffin, John Montgomery, Geo. H. Stevens, Alphonso Stevens, S. H. Drachman, J. M. Elias.   Speaker, Alsap; clerk, Andrew Crouly.

9th session, 1877.   Council, Yavapai, John A. Rush, Geo. D. Kendall, Lewis A. Stevens, A. L. Moeller; Maricopa, K. S. Woolsey; Yuma, J. M. Redondo; Pinal, Levi Ruggles; Pima, F. H. Goodwin, F. G. Hughes.   Pres., Woolsey; clerk, Alsap.   House, Yavapai, W. W. Hutchinson, C. B. Foster, S. C. Milles, G. Hathaway, Hugo Richards, John H. Marion, Wm S. Head, Ed. G. Peck; Maricopa, J. A. Parker, M. H. Calderwood; Yuma, J. W. Dorrington; Mojave, James P. Bull; Pinal, Geo. Scott; Pima, D. A. Bennett, Wm Ohnesorgen, Estévan Ochoa, M. Samaniego, Geo. H. Stevens.   Speaker, Calderwood; clerk, Crouly.

10th session, 1879.   Council, Yavapai, C. C. Bean, W. S. Head, W. A. Rowe, E. W. Wells; Maricopa, E. H. Gray; Yuma, F. D. Welcome; Pinal, P. Thomas; Pima, F. G. Hughes, J. M. Kirkpatrick.   Pres., Hughes; clerk, Hinson Thomas.   House, Yavapai, W. M. Buffum, John Davis, Thos Fitch, Pat Hamilton, P. McAteer, E. R. Nicoles, J. A. Park, Jas Stinson; Maricopa, J. T. Alsap, J. D. Rumburg; Yuma, Sam. Purdy, Jr; Mojave, John H. Behan; Pinal, W. K. Meade; Pima, A. E. Fay, C. P. Leitch, Jas Speedy, M. W. Stewart, Walter L. Vail.   Speaker, Stewart; clerk, B. A. Fickas.

11th session, 1881.   Council, Yavapai, Murat Masterton; Apache, S. Barth; Maricopa, A. C. Baker, R. S. Thomas; Yuma, J. W. Dorrington; Mojave, A. Cornwall; Pinal, J. W. Anderson; Pima, B. H. Hereford, B. A. Fickas, Geo. H. Stevens, W. K. Meade, H. G. Rollins.   Pres., Masterton; clerk, Jos. C. Perry.   House, Yavapai, Geo. E. Brown, R. B. Steadman, L. Wollenberg; Apache, J. Barton, G. R. York; Maricopa, N. Sharp, P. J. Bolan, J. R. McCormack; Pinal, D. Robb, A. J. Doran; Mojave, D. Southworth; Yuma, G. W. Norton, J. F. Knapp; Pima, H. M. Woods, J. K. Rodgers, M. G. Samaniego, John Roman, John McCafferty, Thos Dunbar, E. H. Smith, John Haynes, E. B. Gifford, M. S. Synder, M. K. Lurty.   Speaker, Knapp; clerk, Richard Rule.

12th session, 1883.   Council, Yavapai, E. W. Wells, M. Goldwater, M. Masterton, F. K. Ainsworth; Apache, H. E. Lacy; Maricopa, A. D. Lemon; Pinal, J. W. Davis; Yuma and Mojave, L. S. Welton; Pima, J. F. Knapp, F. G. Hughes; Cochise co., E. H. Wiley; C. and Graham, P. J. Bolan.

Pres., Wiley; clerk, J. A. Carpenter; chaplain, E. G. Fowler. House, Yavapai, C. A. Randall, A. Allen, R. McCallum, R. Connell, E. H. Gobin, John Ellis, Chas Taylor, W. A. Rowe; Apache, C. A. Franklin; Maricopa, J. P. Holcomb, S. F. Webb; Pinal, J. W. Anderson; Yuma, J. W. Dorrington; Mojave, L. J. Lassell; Pima, R. C. Brown, E. B. Gifford, Moye Wicks, J. H. Fawcett; Cachise, W. H. Savage, D. K. Wardwell, J. F. Duncan; Graham, A. Solomon, D. Snyder; Gila co., Wm Graves. Speaker, Rowe; clerk, A. E. Fay; chaplain, U. S. Truett.

13th session, 1885. Council, Yavapai, W. G. Stewart; Apache, E. S. Stover; Maricopa, R. B. Todd; Pinal, Thos Weedin; Mojave, John Howell; Pima, R. N. Leatherwood; Cochise, W. A. Harwood; Graham, W. G. Bridwell; Gila, Alonzo Bailey; Yuma, J. W. Dorrington; northern district, F. K. Ainsworth; southern district, C. C. Stephens. President, Ainsworth; clerk, A. E. Fay; chaplain, Nathan Guthrie. House, Apache, J. D. Houck, Luther Martin; Cochise, W. F. Frame, T. T. Hunter, W. F. Nichols, Hugh Percy, D. K. Wardwell; Gila, W. C. Watkins; Graham, James Sias; Maricopa, J. S. Armstrong, Deforest Porter; Mojave, Wm Imus; Pima, E. W. Aram, G. W. Brown, S. M. Franklin, E. W. Risley, H. G. Rollins; Pinal, Levi Ruggles; Yavapai, D. J. Brannan, J. A. Brown, R. Connell, L. P. Nash, W. H. Robbins; Yuma, S. Purdy. Speaker, Rollins; clerk, Morris Goldwater; chaplain, J. M. Greene.

14th session, 1887. Council, Yavapai, C. B. Forster; Apache, J. H. Breed; Pinal, J. W. Anderson; Maricopa, L. H. Goodrich; Yuma, Isaac Lyons; Mojave, E. L. Burdick; Pima, C. R. Drake; Cochise, L. W. Blinn; Graham, G. H. Stephens; Gila, R. C. Robertson; at large, north, A. Cornwall; at large, south, W. C. Watkins. President, Cornwall; clerk, Charles Driscoll; chaplain, J. G. Eberhart. House, Yavapai, A. G. Oliver, W. H. Ashurst, J. J. Fisher, H. T. Andrews, O. C. Felton; Apache, J. Q. Adamson, James Scott; Pinal, A. J. Doran; Maricopa, J. Y. T. Smith, Samuel Webb; Yuma, Charles Baker; Mojave, P. F. Collins; Pima, R. N. Leatherwood, J. B. Scott, A. A. Bean, C. R. Wores, A. McKey; Cochise, F. W. Heyne, J. M. Bracewell, Scott White, B. L. Peel, Michael Gray; Graham, D. H. Ming; Gila, Eugene Trippel. Speaker, Webb; clerk, Richard Rule; chaplain, J. C. Houghton.

ACTS OF THE LEGISLATURE.

1st session, 1864. Acts, incorporating 6 road companies and two railroad companies—the Castle Dome R. R. Co. and Arizona R. R. Co., granting exclusive ferry rights at Mojave and La Paz; incorporating the Hualapai Min. Co. and Arizona Hist. Soc.; providing for a territorial map; giving $1,500 to certain schools; authorizing the raising of rangers and a loan to pay expenses of an Apache campaign; allowing soldiers to vote and hold mining claims; providing for government expenses; protecting possessory titles in lands; and for the benefit of several individuals, including a divorce. The resolutions included thanks to most territorial officials; invitations for the delivery of lectures; instructions to the delegate in congress on mails, arms, and surveys; publication of laws, etc., in Spanish; the purchase of books for a territorial library; and a protest against the recent expulsion of Sylvester Mowry by Gen. Carleton. The memorials asked for the tract of land in the Colorado bend opposite Ft Yuma; for an increase of salaries; for $150,000 for placing the Colorado Ind. on a reservation; $250,000 for Apache warfare; and $150,000 to improve the navigation of the Colorado.

2d session, 1865. Acts, creating county of Pah-Ute from Mojave (later for the most part attached to Nevada); repealing a previous act for stay of proceedings on foreign indebtedness; creating boards of supervisors for the counties; securing liens to mechanics, etc. Resolutions, on national affairs; on the importance of surveying territorial boundaries, with a view of getting for Ariz. the Yuma land, and perhaps the Rio Vírgen settlements of Utah; on the library; on C. D. Poston's attempt to contest Goodwin's seat in congress. Memorials, for improvement of the Colorado; for the land at Yuma; for a separate land district and surveyor-general; for Ind. reservations on the lower Gila; for an increase of military force. This year Utah tried to obtain a part of northern Ariz. *Utah, Acts*, 1865, p. 91–2.

3d session, 1866. Acts, creating the offices of district attorney and auditor; providing for the location and registration of mines. Resolutions, of thanks to Ariz. volunteers and to several officials. Memorials, against the cession of Pah-Ute to Nevada; for new mail routes; and urging the importance of a southern Pac. R. R.

4th session, 1867. Acts, permanently locating the capital at Tuscon (see *Ariz., Compiled Laws*, 1871, p. 564); moving the county seat of Pah-Ute to St Thomas; authorizing the digging of wells on desert lands; providing for public schools. Resolution, asking that Ariz. be separated from the com. of Gen. McDowell, and made a separate mil. department. Memorials, for a separate customs district; for the construction of military roads; and against the cession of Pah-Ute to Nevada. On the dispute about taxes, involving the ownership of the land opposite Ft Yuma by Cal. or Ariz. See, for this year, *Cal., Jour. Sen.*, appen., no. 53, 70; also, for original corresp. and doc., *Savage, Doc. Hist. Cal.*, MS., iv. 81–98, 115.

5th session, 1868. Acts, locating the territorial prison at Phœnix; creating offices of attorney-general and county surveyor; and establishing public schools. Resolutions, asking for mail routes; recommending a U. S. depository in Ariz.; instructing the officials of Yuma co. to assess all property within the limits as fixed by the Howell Code (that is, to disregard the claim of Cal.); and in favor of artesian wells. Memorials, asking appropriations for capitol buildings, territorial library, and codification of the laws; also the appointment of a surveyor-gen., and an appropriation for surveys. On the boundary question there is a full report of a com. against the pretensions of Cal. in the *Journal*, p. 189–92.

6th session, 1871. Acts, changing county seat of Yuma to La Paz; divorcing several couples; creating county of Maricopa from that part of Yavapai south of lat. 34° and west of the S. Cárlos, county seat at Phœnix; repealing the act to create Pah-Ute co., and attaching what was left of it in Ariz. to Mojave; providing for biennial sessions from Jan. 1873; authorizing the publication of information to attract immigration; establishing schools; providing for roads, bridges, and ferries; and for the revision and printing of the laws. Memorials, asking protection from Ind.; and a modification of excise laws. In the *Journal* are several reports relating to outrages by Mexicans, and attempts to arrest the offenders. On the Yuma boundary dispute, see *S. Diego Union*, Apr. 14, 1870; *Hayes' Scraps, Ariz.*, v. 167. This year was published *The Compiled laws of the Territory of Arizona, including the Howell Code and the session laws from 1864 to 1871 inclusive...Compiled by Coles Bashford*. Albany, N. Y., 1871, 8vo, 607 p. (A later edition of the *Compiled Laws* was that prepared by John P. Hoyt, and published at Detroit 1877.)

7th session, 1873. Acts, to divorce several persons, including the governor, and changing the names of others; changing the name of Arizona City to Yuma; authorizing a levee on the Gila and Colorado; encouraging the sinking of artesian wells; prohibiting the sale of liquor to Indians; providing for the incorporation of religious, social, and benevolent societies; and adding to Maricopa co. that part of Pima north of lat. 32° 34′ and west of about long. 112° 6′ (as it still exists south of the Gila). Resolutions, expressing satisfaction with Gen. Crook's methods of fighting Apaches. Memorials, asking for a reduction of the White Mt Ind. reservation; for a donation of land for artesian wells; and for school lands. On Cal. boundary dispute, see *Hayes' Scraps, Ariz.*, v. 175; *Ariz. Sentinel*, April 12, 1873.

8th session, 1875. Acts, creating county of Pinal, with county seat at Florence, from Pima, Maricopa, and Yavapai (boundaries complicated but about the same as on map, except in the N. E. corner, including Globe); taxing net product of mines; on fences and trespassing animals; on compulsory education; abolishing office of attorney-gen.; transferring Mojave to 3d judicial district; providing for a census; and to locate the capital permanently at Tucson. (Approved Feb. 12th, acc. to *Acts*, p. 121, but vetoed acc. to *Jour.*,

301–2. The gov. says he has received three acts, one fixing the capital at Prescott, and another at Phœnix. It is not clear why an act was needed in favor of Tucson.) Resolution, thanking Gen. Crook. Memorial, on Pima and Maricopa Ind., and on mail service. An appendix to the *Acts* contains U. S. and Ariz. mining laws, treaties, and rules of the supreme court.

9th session, 1877. Acts, to permanently locate the capital at Prescott; to transfer Maricopa to 2d jud. district; to make Mineral Park the county seat of Mojave; to define the boundaries of Maricopa (extending it on the east from the S. Cárlos to long. 110°; and slightly changing the central parts of the N. line, as still existing; see map); to incorporate the city of Tucson; to authorize a comp. of volunteer Ind. fighters; to extend the W. boundary of Pinal co. (so as to include a small isolated tract in the N. W. which had apparently been left in Pima by the act creating Pinal); to provide for the revision and publication of the laws; and to divorce many couples. Memorials, for an increase of the council to 13 and the house to 27 members; for the annexation of Grant co., N. Mex.

10th session, 1879. Acts, creating Apache co. (all of Yavapai east of long. 119° 45', as it still exists, except that the portion south of Black River has been added to Graham co.), county seat at Snowflake (moved to Springerville the next year); authorizing lotteries to raise funds for various public purposes; and 64 other acts, none of which can be singled out as of especial importance. Memorials, asking for a mint at Florence, an assay-office at the capital, and a special mail agent.

11th session, 1881. Acts, to fix county seat of Apache at St Johns; to create the county of Cochise from eastern Pima (boundaries as still existing; see map), county seat at Tombstone; to create the county of Graham from Pima and Apache (boundaries as in map), county seat at Safford; to create the county of Gila from Maricopa and Pinal (boundaries as in map, except that the south-eastern line was a northern continuation of the Pinal line instead of the S. Cárlos), county seat at Globe; to incorporate the cities of Tombstone, Phœnix, and Prescott; to restrict gambling; to provide for a census; to redistrict the territory (1st district, Pima, Pinal, and Cochise (and Graham?); 2d dist, Yuma, Maricopa, and Gila; 3d dist, Yavapai, Mojave, and Apache; to create the office of geologist. Memorials, against extension of the Navajo reservation; for privilege of mining on Mex. border; for opening parts of the S. Cárlos reservation to settlers. At this and later sessions the council had 12 members and the house 24.

12th session, 1883. Acts, to locate county seat of Graham at Solomonville; to transfer Cochise from 1st to 2d district; to change boundary of Mojave co. (so as to include that part of Yavapai north of the Colorado and west of Kanab Wash, as per map); to provide for funding debt and issuing bonds; to aid construction of several railroads; to create the office of attorney-general; to thank the president of the U. S. for suppressing lawlessness; to prevent export of timber. Memorials, for an investigation of matters at the Pápago reservation; aid for the public schools; improvement of the Colorado; and removal of the Apaches. From this sess. the title of the *Acts*, etc., is changed to *Laws of the Territory of Arizona. Twelfth (etc.) Legislative Assemby; with Memorials and Resolutions.* Prescott, 1883 et seq.

13th session, 1885. Acts, creating county courts for the different counties; for an election to permanently locate the county seat of Mojave; authorizing a railroad and telegraph from Fairbanks to Tombstone, from Phœnix to the S. P. R. R., from Prescott to the A. & P. R. R., from Globe to the A. & P. R. R. at or near Flagstaff, and from Phœnix of Wickenburg; creating the office of commissioner of immigration; to promote breeding of live-stock; to build a levee on the Gila at Yuma; to establish a public school system; to change the eastern boundary of Gila co. (to the S. Cárlos on the east, as per map); to transfer Cochise co. to 1st judicial district, and Pinal to 2d district; to organize the university of Arizona; and to incorporate the Ariz. Industrial Exposition Assoc. Resolutions, inquiring into imprisonment of Americans at Magdalena, Sonora; and thanking Gen. Crook for Apache operations.   Memorials, to change the southern boundary of the White Mt Ind. reservation so as to open the coal mines; to urge the payment of old claims for Ind. depredations; against interference with the silver coinage; for the restoration to settlement of S. P. R. R. land claims; for a fourth judge and increase of salary from $3,000 to $5,000; for improvement of Colorado navigation; for the purchase from Mexico of that part of Sonora west of long. 111° and north of lat. 30°, so as to give Ariz. a post; for the appointment of residents as territorial officials; against the projected leasing of U. S. grazing lands; for authority to control and dispose of school lands; for the removal of the Apaches and throwing open the reservation to settlement; and for an appropriation of $160,000 to dig artesian wells.

CHAPTER XXII.

INDIAN AFFAIRS OF ARIZONA.

1864–1886.

The Friendly Tribes — Superintendents and Agents—The Yumas—
Mojaves — Hualapais — Yavapais — Suppai — Moquis — Pimas and
Maricopas—Pápagos—The Apaches—Early Hostilities—Errors of
the Government—Forts and Camps—A Thousand Victims—Carle-
ton's Campaign—General Mason —Wallen, Lovell, Gregg, and
Crittenden—Devin and Wheaton—Popular Indignation—A Mili-
tary Department under Stoneman—Camp Grant Massacre—Crook
in Command—Peace Policy—Colyer and Howard—More War—
Peace in 1873-4—The Apaches on Reservations—Concentration--·
Kautz, Willcox, and Crook again—Raids of Renegade Chiricahuas—Exploits of Gerónimo—General Miles—Success at Last—
Prospects—Crime and Lawlessness.

THE aborigines of Arizona in 1863–4 numbered
about 25,000, slightly less than two thirds belonging
to the friendly tribes as distinguished from the
Apaches. In 1886 there are left about 18,000, not
including in either estimate the Navajos, treated in
this volume as a New Mexican tribe, though their
home has always been partly in Arizona.[1] I may
state at the outset that it is not my purpose to attempt any index or classification of the sources for
Indian affairs. The principal of these are named in
the appended note; and only for special purposes shall
I make more minute references or cite additional
authorities.[2] In considering modern annals of the

[1] The primitive condition of all the tribes has been treated in another work
of this series. For manners and customs, geog. distrib., etc., see *Native
Races*, i. 471–555, 591–603, on Apache and Pueblo families; for myths, etc.,
iii., first half, passim; languages, iii. 680–705; material relics, iv. 680–805.
[2] The chief sources are the annual *Ind. Aff. Repts*, 1863 et seq.; *U. S. Govt
Doc.* of the different classes by congress and session, especially military re-

Arizona Indians, let us first glance at the friendly tribes.

When the territory was created, Charles D. Poston came as superintendent of Indian affairs in 1864, making a tour with Ross Browne, but supplementing his report with his resignation in September. George W. Leihy then held the office until November 1866, when he was killed by Indians. G. W. Dent served in 1867–9; George L. Andrews in 1869–70; and H. Bendell in 1871–2. After 1872 the office was abolished, agents reporting directly to the commissioner at Washington. Special inspectors were, however, sent by the government from time to time to visit the agencies.[3]

The Yumas were formerly a numerous and powerful tribe, of fine physique and war-like nature. My readers will remember their old-time thirst for Christianity, and their massacre of the padres and settlers in 1781. Their home was about the Gila junction on both sides of the Colorado. In Spanish and Mexican times they were alternately hostile and friendly, but suffered much in wars with other tribes. Later the tribe was kept in order by the American garrison at Fort Yuma, but its strength was broken in 1857, when its grand 'army' was almost annihilated in a war with the Pimas. Since that time the Yumas have been worthless but harmless vagabonds, though cultivating small patches of ground in the Colorado bottoms, catching fish, and doing odd jobs for the whites. Pascual has been their most famous chief; and their number is now about 1,000. They have never been

ports in those of the sec. of war for each year; the governor's annual messages and other legislative matter in *Ariz., Jour.*, 1864 et seq.; files of Cal. newspapers, notably the *S. F. Bulletin, Alta, Chronicle,* and *Sac. Union*; and especially *Hayes' Scrap-books, Ariz.*, i.–vi., containing classified clippings from the journals of southern Cal. and Arizona. The leading modern works, *Hinton's Hand-book, Ariz. Hist.* (E. & Co.), and *Hamilton's Resources,* like most other works on Ariz. named in these chapters, contain much on Ind. affairs. It will be understood that all have been utilized, but space does not permit repeated citation or a pointing-out of discrepancies.

[3] Before 1864 an agent at Mesilla had merely nominal control of the Arizona Ind.

willing to settle at the up-river agency, but in late years a reservation has been set apart for them on the California side at Fort Yuma.[4] The Mojaves—Yamajabs or Amajabas of early times—living originally on both sides of the Colorado above Williams fork, a people whose intercourse with Padre Garcés in 1774–6 will be recalled, and who sometimes appear in the Spanish annals of California, were also a brave tribe, whose good qualities have for the most part disappeared. Their hostility to Americans ended with their defeat and the founding of Fort Mojave in 1858–9. In 1864 Poston selected a reservation on the river bottom at Half Way Bend, in latitude 34°, and the land was set apart by act of 1865. It was intended for all the river tribes, and for the Hualapais and Yavapais; but only the Chemehuevis and half of the Mojaves could ever be induced to occupy it permanently. Agriculture depended on the annual overflow of the river, and crops often failed. A canal was dug in 1867–74 for nine miles at a cost of $28,000, but was not a success; and a system of water-wheels proved likewise a failure. The Indians took much interest in these experiments,' and even did a large amount of hard work; but the outside tribes, gradually losing their confidence in the white man's ability to control the elements, declined to come in; and the Mojaves—about 800, under Iriteba down to his death in 1874—learned to depend chiefly on government aid.

[4] *Hamilton's Resources*, 299. I have seen no original record of this reservation. A school at the old fort in 1884 is mentioned in *Ariz., Hist.* (E. & Co.), 244. In 1864 Francis Hinton was employed by Supt Poston as agent for the Yumas, but later they were nominally in charge of the Mojave, or Colorado, agency. Forty years of intercourse with white men has had a most pernicious effect on this people, especially through the prostitution of the women and indulgence in strong drink. Except some slight and irregular gifts, they have received no aid from the government. The Cocopas are a tribe living on the Colorado below the Yumas, whom they resemble somewhat in character and modern history. They live mainly in Mexican territory, though coming in contact more with Americans. The Chemehuevis and Pah-Utes are Shoshone tribes, both frequenting north-western Arizona to some extent in early times. The former in later years live, about 300 in number, on the Cal. side of the Colorado; while the latter belong mainly to Nevada and Utah, though still found to some extent in Ariz. north of the Colorado. These tribes require no further notice here.

The rest lived near Fort Mojave and fared somewhat
better, a crowd of them being still seen at the Atlantic
and Pacific railroad stations in this region. In all
they number from 1,000 to 1,200, addicted to gambling and intoxication, nearly all tainted with syphilitic
diseases, a hopelessly wretched and depraded race, or
at least past regeneration by any methods yet applied;
yet they are peaceful, and in a sense honest and industrious.   A school was in operation at times from 1873,
and a native police from 1881.   No real progress has
ever been made, though the agents have occasionally
reported encouraging features, generally not visible to
their successors.[5]

The Hualapais, or Apache-Yumas, and Yavapais,
or Apache-Mojaves, were, before 1864, tribes of 1,500
and 2,000 souls, allied in race and character to the
river tribes on the west and the Apaches on the east.
For some years, during the flush times of the Colorado placers, they were friendly, living at times on the
reservation; but in 1866-8, being suspected of certain
depredations, they were the victims of several disgraceful outrages, and went on the war-path until
1871-2.   The Yavapais became identified with the
Apaches, and with them were transferred to the San
Cárlos reservation in 1874.   The Hualapais, after
submission, did good service against the Apaches, were
gathered at Beale Spring, and were moved against their
will to the Colorado agency in 1874.   Running away

[5] The Colorado agency was in charge of Herman Ehrenberg and John C.
Dunn in 1864-6, John Feudge in 1866-9, Helenas Dodt in 1870, J. A. Tonner
in 1871-5, W. E. Morford in 1876-7, John C. Mallory in 1877-8, Henry R.
Mallory in 1878-80, Jonathan Biggs in 1880-2.   Ehrenberg, an engineer, reported against the selected reservation at the first, and his objections proved
well founded.   For executive orders of Nov. 22, 1873, Nov. 16, 1874, and
May 15, 1876, extending and defining the boundaries, see report sec. int. in
U. S. Govt Doc., 47th cong. 1st sess., H. Ex. Doc. 1, pt 5, p. 304.   Its area in
1874 is given as 200 sq. miles; in 1884 by Hamilton and others as 600 sq.
m.   It extends from a point four miles above Ehrenberg some 45 miles up the
river, including a tract occupied by 200 Chemihuevis on the Cal. side.   Com-
fortable adobe buildings were constructed from 1867.   In 1882 the Ind.
were reported as living on govt rations, on agric. labor, and on natural products of the soil in about equal proportions.   They owned a few horses, used
only for racing, and of no advantage.   At Camp Colorado, near the agency,
was posted a small garrison at times.

the next year, but professing friendship, they were permitted to live in their old haunts, living on the country's natural products, and more than once saved from starvation by the charity of settlers. A tract of 2,000 square miles on the Grand Cañon bend of the Colorado was set apart for them in 1881–3, and there they now live, 600 to 800 in number, mustering in force at Peach Spring at the passage of each railroad train. Though superior to the reservation Mojaves, they are a destitute and vicious lot of beggars, wholly non-progressive.

The Suppai, or Ava-Supies, 200 or 300 in number, of whom little is known, but probably renegades originally from other tribes, have, since 1880, a reservation of 60 square miles on Cataract Creek, just above latitude 36°, a fertile tract on the creek bottom between precipitous cliffs, accessible only at two points by a narrow trail. Here they raise fruits, grain, and vegetables, trading with the Moquis and Hualapais, prosperous and contented, but rarely visited by white men.[6]

Of the Moquis much has been recorded in this volume. The Mexicans had little if any intercourse with them; but several American explorers visited their towns, beginning with Ives in 1858. An agency was maintained from 1869, the agent living at Fort Defiance down to 1875, but later at buildings erected fifteen miles east of the first town. These peculiar, superstitious, and childishly variable Indians were always friendly, except that the Oraibe chief was sometimes, as of old, reserved and sulky. There was a school in several years, and in 1882 a missionary was preparing to get ready to begin his teachings. The Moquis were always temperate, chaste, and industrious, tilling their barren lands, where crops often failed for want of water, keeping a few sheep and cattle, gladly accepting the meagre government pittance, and some-

[6] Orders of 1880–2 on the reserv., in rept sec. interior, 1883, p. 306–7. In *Arizona Scraps*, 133, is an account of a visit in 1880 by Beckman and Young.

times disposed to the theory that the 'great father' at Washington should and perhaps would support his Moqui children in idleness.   They would never listen to proposals of removal from their cliff homes of so many centuries, but they were sometimes induced to cultivate fields at some distance; they farmed on shares with the Colorado Chiquito Mormons; and it is even said that the saints have made some Moqui converts. Their reservation of 4,000 miles was set apart in 1882, adjoining that of the Navajos; and their numbers since 1869 have perhaps increased from 1,500 to 2,000. There is no more interesting aboriginal people in United States territory.[7]

Turning again to the south, we find the Pimas living on the Gila, where their home has been for centuries, and on a reservation set apart for them and the Maricopas in 1859.   They have always been foes of the Apache and friends of the American, it having been their boast for years that they had never killed a white man.   They are an industrious agricultural people, producing a large surplus of grain for sale. Living in a dozen villages of conical willow huts, they have never changed materially their manner of life, but there is no improvement, except that some children have learned to read; and in many respects there has been a sad deterioration during forty years of contact with civilization, notably by acquiring habits of intemperance, prostitution, and pilfering; yet they are still vastly superior to most other tribes.   For several

[7] Agents were A. D. Palmer in 1869–70, W. D. Crothers in 1871–2, W. S. Defrees in 1873–4, W. B. Truax in 1875–6 (agency abandoned in Oct. '76 to Feb. '78), Wm R. Mateer in 1878–9, John H. Sullivan in 1880–1, J. D. Flemming in 1882.   In 1864 the Moquis are said to have sent to Salt Lake City for aid against the Navajos.   Poston named John Moss as agent.   Kit Carson made a visit in 1864, and Vincent Colyer in 1869, both overestimating the pop. as 4,000.   In 1866, the gov. says, the Moquis had sent delegates to Prescott, and were willing to be removed to the Tonto Basin.   It was understood that in 1855–6 and in 1866–7, the towns were temporarily abandoned on account of small-pox and drought; but there is no foundation for the oft-repeated statement that the name *moqui* means death, and was of modern application. Among the recent descriptions of Moqui manners and customs may be mentioned Capt. John G. Bourke's *The Snake-dance of the Moquis of Arizona, Being a narrative of a journey from Santa Fé*, etc.   N. Y., 1884, 8vo, xvii., 371 p., plates.

years, from 1868, serious troubles with them seemed imminent. Presuming on their military services and past immunity from all restraint, they became insolent and aggressive, straying from the reservation, robbing travellers, refusing all satisfaction for inroads of their horses on the settlers' fields, the young men being beyond the chiefs' control. Swindling traders had established themselves near the villages to buy the Indians' grain at their own prices, and even manipulate government goods, the illegal traffic receiving no check, but rather apparently protection from the territorial authorities. Whiskey was bought at Adamsville or from itinerant Mexicans; the agents were incompetent, or at least had no influence, the military refused support or became involved in profitless controversies. Worst of all, white settlers on the Gila used so much of the water that the Pimas in dry years had to leave the reservation or starve. General Howard deemed the difficulties insurmountable, and urged removal. Had it not been for dread of the Pima numbers and valor, the Apaches still being hostile, very likely there might have been a disastrous outbreak. But from 1874, for reasons only partially apparent, there was a marked improvement. Copious rains for several years prevented clashing with the settlers; several chiefs visited the Indian territory and talked favorably of removal; there was less friction between authorities. In 1876–82 the Pima reservation was considerably extended, and a new tract on Salt River below Fort McDowell was finally set apart, making the whole extent about 275 square miles. A school has been kept up with some success, a little missionary work was done, and a native police, until disorganized by whiskey, did something to prevent disorder. Yet the old troubles are sleeping rather than dead. There is still much popular dissatisfaction on various phases of the matter; and in view of the non-progressive nature of the Indians, the large extent of their lands, the growing white population, and the agricul-

tural prospects of the Gila and Salt valleys under an
extensive system of irrigation, there can be little doubt
that difficulties will increase, and the Pimas sooner or
later will have to quit their old home.[8]

The Pápagos have been regarded as the best Indians
of Arizona. They were of the same race and language
as the Pimas; but there is no foundation for the theory that they were simply Pima converts to Christianity, *pápago* meaning 'baptized.' They were, however, converts, retaining a smattering of foreign faith,
with much pride in their old church at Bac. They
differ but little from Arizona Mexicans, if of the latter
we except a few educated families and a good many
vicious vagabonds. More readily than other Indians
they adapt themselves to circumstances, tilling the
soil, raising live-stock, working in the mines, or doing
anything that offers. As the reader knows, they sometimes had trouble with the Spaniards and Mexicans,
but they have always been friends of Americans and
deadly foes to Apaches. Without having escaped the
taint of vice, they are not as a rule addicted to drink,
gambling, or licentiousness. They have received very
little aid from the government. In 1874 a reservation
was set off for them at San Javier, and in 1882 another
at the Gila bend, 200 square miles in all. From 1876
their agency was consolidated with that of the Pimas.
Their number has remained at about 5,000, some 2,000

[8] Pima agents: A. M. White to 1865, Levi Ruggles in 1866–9 (C. H. Lord
deputy in 1867), F. E. Grossman in 1869–70, J. H. Stout in 1871–5, 1877–8;
Charles Hudson in 1876, A. B. Ludlam in 1879–80, E. B. Townsend in 1881,
R. G. Wheeler in 1881–2, A. H. Jackson in 1882. In number the Pimas have
increased slightly, between 4,500 and 5,000. The Maricopas are a small fragment from farther down the river, allied in race to the Yumas, but for many
years living with the Pimas, whom they resemble in habits. The Pimas make
some rude pottery. They have received comparatively little aid from the
govt, and often complain that the Apaches are treated much better. Mormons have favored the Ind. more than other settlers. Rusling, *Across America*, 369–72, describes the villages in 1867. In 1870 the agent surveyed an
extension, which, through the legislature's influence, was not approved. By
order of Aug. 31, 1876, additions were made on the s. E. In 1877 the legislature tried to have the Ind. removed from Salt River, but Inspector Watkins
in 1878 reported against this as inhuman. An order of Jan. 10, 1879, extended
the reserve E. to that of White Mt, but this was cancelled by the order of
July 14th, setting apart the Salt River tract and making other additions, still
further increased by order of May 5, 1882.

living on the reservations or near Tucson, while the
rest are scattered through Papaguería or live across the
Mexican line.[9]

INDIANS OF ARIZONA.

[9] Agents for this tribe were M. O. Davidson in 1864–5, Levi Ruggles and
C. H. Lord in 1866 et seq., R. A. Wilbur in 1871–4, and John W. Cornyn
in 1875. A school has been kept up at S. Javier, with good success, under
the sisters of St Joseph, though sectarian attacks on the Catholics have not
been wanting. The principal fault of the Pápagos has been their possession
of so much valuble land near the city. There were many encroachments by
wood-cutters, and many settlers held on to their farms till 1882, when they
were forcibly ejected by the Ind. under Agent Wheeler. This led to appeals
from the legislature on behalf of the settlers, and to much controversy. In
1885 a sheriff attempting to serve a writ was forcibly resisted by the military;

The Apache country proper was that part of Arizona lying east of the Santa Cruz in the south, and of the Verde in the north. In 1864 the Apaches had for several years waged war upon the whites, hostilities being for the most part confined to the south-east, because the north was not yet occupied by Americans. From 1862, however, the Colorado gold placers drew a crowd of miners, who pushed their operations eastward to the Prescott region. They were not much troubled by the Indians at first; but from 1865, as Apache land was penetrated by prospectors, and the frontier became settled, the war was transferred, or rather extended, to the north-west; and with the disaffection of the Hualapais and Yavapais, mainly caused by outrages of the whites, the field of hostilities was widened to a considerable distance west of Prescott. For about ten years this warfare was continuous and deadly. During this period about 1,000 men, women, and children were murdered by the Apaches, of whom perhaps 2,000 were killed, with a loss of probably not over 150 soldiers. The loss of live-stock and destruction of other property was of course great, and all real progress in the territory was prevented. The Apaches did not fight battles, except when cornered; their idea being primarily to steal, and then to kill without being killed. They attacked individuals or small parties from ambush, and fled to their mountain strongholds, often inhumanly torturing their captives. By nature and the education of centuries, they were murderous thieves; and they looked forward to a life-long struggle with the whites as a natural and their only means of subsistence. The people of Arizona, feeling that they were entitled to protection, but appealing for it

and the same year there was a threatened war with the Pápagos, in consequence of a quarrel about the possession of a spring. The Ind. rescued a prisoner from the sheriff, and a force of volunteers marched out from Tucson, but an amicable settlement was finally reached. *Ariz., Laws*, 12th sess., 291–2; *S. F. Chronicle*, May 9, 1883; *Sac. Record-Union*, March 9, May 18–20, 1885. I have seen no original record of the Gila reserv. of 1882, but it is shown on govt maps, and mentioned in *Ariz., Hist.* (E. & Co.), 179, where is given a list of the 15 Pápago rancherías, with a pop. of 2,925. A few Pápagos have always lived with the Pimas, and a few Apaches Mansos with the Pápagos.

in vain, became excited and desperate as the years passed by, doing and countenancing many unwise and even criminal acts. The government at Washington, vaguely aware that there were Indian troubles in Arizona, which were very expensive, and not realizing any difference between Apaches and other hostile Indians, simply furnished from 1,000 to 3,000 troops to garrison the posts, made imperfect arrangements for supplies, with an occasional change of commander or military organization, ignored for the most part all appeals, and left the problem to solve itself. Officers and soldiers did their duty well enough, striking many hard blows, which after a long time became in a cumulative sense effective. If any of these parties is to be blamed on the whole, it is not the citizens, the military, the Apaches, or even the newspapers and Indian agents, but the government, for its half-way measures, its desultory warfare, and its lack of a definite policy, even that of 'extermination,' which is sometimes attributed to it. True, a somewhat consistent policy was developed in the end; but I cannot think there was any need of so long and bloody and costly a process of evolution. From the first there was no real difference of opinion among men with practical knowledge of the Apaches respecting the proper policy to be adopted. The Apache must first be whipped into a temporary or partial submission, then made to understand that it was for his interest to keep the peace, and finally watched and taught, if possible, better methods of life. The result might have been effected, so far at least as it ever has been effected, in two years.

I shall not here chronicle the series of Apache atrocities, name the victims, or even summarize the record for places or periods. Neither is it proposed to detail the military record of campaigns, or deal minutely with annals of companies, commanders, or posts. Still less shall I find room for the many controversies that continuously arose from one phase or another of this unfortunate Apache business. To treat all these matters in such a manner as to utilize fully the mass of evidence before me with justice to all interests involved, would require a whole volume. Yet though compelled by limitation of space to avoid particulars, especially in relation to persons, I hope to present all the general aspects of the subject in a clear and impartial manner.[10]

We left the Arizona posts, as part of the department of New Mexico, garrisoned in 1863 by the California volunteers. In 1864, having had much success in fighting eastern Apaches and the Navajos, General James H. Carleton turned his attention to the west, confidently expecting to subdue the foe and remove

[10] My general authorities are cited in note 2. Additional references are mainly to other and special sources. Here should be mentioned *Massacres of the Mountains. A History of the Indian Wars of the Far West. By J. P. Dunn, Jr, M. S., LL. B. Illustrated.* N. Y., 1886, 8vo, ix., 784 p., map. Chap. xii., 'death to the Apache,' and xxi., 'cruelty, pity, and justice,' relate to my present subject. This book is the latest, best, and indeed almost the only connected view of the Apache wars extant. Both in matter and manner it merits high praise.

Military commanders in Ariz. were: Gen. J. H. Carleton, 1864–5; Gen. John S. Mason, 1865–6; Col H. D. Wallen in the north, and Col C. S. Lovell in the south, 1866–7; Gen. J. I. Gregg and Gen. T. L. Crittenden, 1867–8; Gen. T. C. Devin, 1868–9; Gen. Wheaton, 1869–70; Gen. Geo. Stoneman, 1870–1; Gen. Geo. Crook, 1871–5; Col A. Kautz, 1875–7; Gen. O. B. Willcox, 1877–82; Gen. Geo. Crook, 1882–6; Gen. Nelson Miles, 1886.

The principal or permanent forts and camps in Arizona are as follows: Ft Whipple, named for the explorer, in Yavapai co. near Prescott, established in 1863 in Chino valley, over 20 m. farther north, but transferred in 1864, and later made headquarters of the department. Ft Verde, named for the river, in Yavapai co., was estab. in 1864 as Camp Lincoln, the site being slightly changed in 1871. Here was an Ind. reserv. for several years. Camp Date Creek, in s. w. cor. of this co., was estab. as C. McPherson in 1866, the name being changed in 1868. Here also was a temporary asylum for Ind., and when the Ind. were moved in 1879 to Verde the post was abandoned. Ft McDowell, named for the general, in Maricopa co., was estab. in 1865. Ft Apache, in Apache co., was estab. in 1870, and was known as C. Mogollon, C. Ord, and perhaps C. Thomas. This fort was on the Ind. reserv. estab. in 1870, the agency being later moved to S. Cárlos. Ft Mojave, in Mojave co., was estab. in 1858, being abandoned for a time in 1861–3. Camp Thomas, named for the general, in Graham co., was estab. in 1875, on the Gila, above the site of old Camp Goodwin of earlier years. Fort Grant, in Graham co., was originally from 1862 at the junction of the S. Pedro and Arivaipa, where Ft Breckenridge had been estab. since 1859. It was transferred to its present site in 1873. Camp Lowell, in Pima co., named for Gen. C. R. Lowell, was the Tucson post from 1862, permanently estab. and named in 1866. Ft Huachuca, Cochise co., named for the mountain range, was estab. in 1876, but had been preceded by C. Wallen since 1874, a little farther north; that by C. Crittenden farther west, in Pima co., in 1867–74; and that by the old Ft Buchanan of 1855–61. C. Rucker was a post farther east after 1880. Fort Bowie, in Cochise co., named for the colonel of a Cal. regiment, was estab. by the volunteers in 1862, becoming a permanent post from 1863.

the humbled survivors to the Pecos reservation of Bosque Redondo. The people were equally hopeful, and for nearly a year active war was waged in different directions. The result was over 200 Apaches killed, but very slight perceptible progress toward permanent success. The general was, of course, severely criticised, and his grand campaign declared a failure; yet there is really little fault to be found with Carleton's policy or his general management. The radical error was that the means were not supplied for properly following up his blows.[11]

The great war between north and south was now ended, but instead of sending 10,000 troops to Arizona with authority to raise two or three regiments of native volunteers, the government transferred the territory from the military department of New Mexico to that of California. General McDowell sent General John S. Mason to take command, with a reënforcement of California volunteers, raising the force to about 2,800 men. Four companies of Arizona volunteers, two of them composed of Pimas and Pápagos, were also mustered in, doing excellent service. Mason took command in June 1865, but for want of supplies, and by reason of various blunders connected with the change of departments and commanders, preparations were not complete till November; and the following campaign, though including several effective expeditions, was on the whole perhaps even less successful than that of Carleton. Mason was not a very brilliant Indian fighter, and did not escape abuse, yet it does not clearly appear how any

[11] A company of volunteers under King S. Woolsey took a prominent part in this campaign, beginning operations before Carleton arrived, and being warmly commended by the legislature. *Ariz., Jour.*, 1864, p. 44, 127, 244; *Id., Acts*, 1864, p. 68-9. One of the Woolsey's achievements, the 'Pinole treaty,' has been condemned as an outrage. Fifty Tontos, being assembled in what is now Gila co. for a big talk, were attacked at a signal and 31 (or 19 as some reports have it) were killed. W. claimed to have knowledge of intended treachery on the part of the Ind. A few days later Capt. Tidball and his Californians killed 63 of the same tribe. For memorial to congress for aid against the Apaches, see *U. S. Govt Doc.*, 38th cong. 2d sess., H. Mis. Doc. 18, 19. See also *Poston's Speech*, in H. of R., Mar. 2, 1865.

officer could have done much better in his place.   In
April 1866 he reported 900 Apaches on a temporary
reservation at Camp Goodwin, and believed that by
offering on the one hand food and protection, and on
the other incessant attack from all directions, permanent success might be achieved.   But the campaign
was interrupted by the gradual withdrawal of the volunteers; and in May or June Mason was removed.[12]

Mason's successors were Colonel H. D. Wallen in
the north and Colonel Charles S. Lovell in the south.
They were succeeded by General J. I. Gregg and
General T. L. Crittenden, respectively, early in 1867.
The volunteers had been replaced by regular troops
to the number of 1,500 or 2,000, soon considerably
increased.   In October Arizona was formally declared
a military district by order of General Halleck.   Mc-
Dowell visited this part of his department in December.   In 1868 General T. C. Devin assumed the
command, being succeeded apparently for a time in
1869–70 by General Wheaton.   General Ord, the
new department commander, visited Arizona in 1869.

[12] During this period there was comparative security in the S. E.; but
in the Prescott region the Apaches were worse than ever, the Yavapais
and Hualapais being also on the war-path.   Of the Cal. volunteers, all
mustered out in 1866, a good account is given in the *S. F. Call*, Aug. 3,
1886.   The reënforcements of 1865 included the 7th inf. Cal. vol., Col
Charles H. Lewis, and the 1st battalion Native Cal. cavalry, Maj. Salvador Vallejo, and later John C. Cremony.   On the Ariz. volunteers, also mustered out before Oct. 1886, see report of adj.-gen. in *Ariz. Jour.*, 1866, p.
250–4.   Gov. Goodwin went to Cal. to work for the interests of his territory,
returning with Gen. Mason.   In Dec. '65 a comp. of rangers killed 23 Apaches
85 miles E. of Prescott.   In Feb. '66 Lieut. Gallegos with his Ariz. vol. killed
30 or 40 in a three-days raid from C. Lincoln.   In March Lieut. Cervantes in
the same region killed 22, and the Pimas in a raid from their villages killed
25.   In July the settlers were ordered by the Ind. to quit Skull valley, and
at a ' big talk ' on the subject, Lieut. Hatton having arrived with reënforcements, and the Ind. making a treacherous attack, 32 were killed.   In '66
there was a false report widely circulated that 2,000 Ind. had taken Ft Goodwin and killed all the garrison.   It was in Nov. '66 that Supt Leihy and his
clerk, W. H. Everts, were killed by Ind. at Bell's Cañon.   For tabular statement of Ind. depredations 1865–75, see *U. S. Govt Doc.*, 43d cong. 2d. sess.,
H. Ex. Doc. 65; 43d cong. 1st sess., Sen. Rept 12; H. Mis. Doc. 16.   Gen.
C. A. Whittier made a tour of inspection in the spring of 1866; and Gen.
James F. Rusling in the winter of 1866–7.   The latter's report is found in
U. S. Govt Doc., 40th cong. 2d sess., H. Mis. Doc. 153, 36 p.   The narra-
tive portion was expanded into *Across America; or, The Great West and the
Pacific Coast.   By James F. Rusling, late Brevet Brigadier-General U. S. A.*
N. Y., 1874, 12mo, 503 p., with cuts.   Pages 355–424 relate to Arizona.

Meanwhile the war continued much as before in 1866–70, there being no cessation of Apache hostilities, and the troops, though in some respects less efficient than the volunteers, engaging in many expeditions that were by no means without results. I cannot entirely agree with the idea of Dunn and others that the experience of these years was a trial and failure of the 'extermination' policy. It seems to me that while none of these officers was the equal in skill or experience of him who finally achieved success, yet their policy did not differ very radically from his, and their efforts contributed in the aggregate very largely to his success. Moreover, Carleton's efforts to remove the Indians to a New Mexican reservation, and the protection and feeding of hundreds of Apaches at Camp Goodwin and elsewhere under Mason and his successors, show the germs of later success in this direction also. Indeed, as I have said before, in both branches of the matter was success being slowly evolved, where no evolution was really necessary, could the government have been persuaded to do its duty.[13]

[13] Gen. Devin's report for 1868 shows that in the northern districts in 46 expeditions 114 Ind. had been killed, 61 wounded, and 35 captured. In the south little had been done, though Cochise had promised to keep the peace. Much work had been done at the forts, and several new posts had been established. The force this year was two regiments of infantry, and 9 comp. of cavalry. Gen. Halleck thought a larger force was needed, that negotiations were useless, and that Ariz. should be made a separate department. The inspector favored concentration of forces and the abandonment of small posts, which was not approved by Gen. McDowell. In 1869, according to report of Inspector Jones, the Camp Goodwin temporary reserv., estab. by Gen. McDowell in 1866, was broken up at the end of 1868, Gen. Devin stopping rations because the Ind. would not surrender murderers or agree to settle permanently; there had also been a temporary reserv. at Camp Grant, where many Pinal Apaches were fed in 1867–8, but this was also abandoned, the Ind. refusing to agree to proposed terms. At Camp Reno in 1869, however, Delche's band of Tontos and others were at peace, and doing some work for whites. In Pima co. for the year ending July 17, 1869, 52 whites were killed and 18 wounded by Apaches; and in the next year 47 killed and six wounded, besides the destruction of property worth $10,000 according to lists pub. in the papers. In 1870 Delegate McCormick presented in congress a list of 144 murdered recently by Apaches, stating that this was not over half the real number of victims. In 1870 special efforts were made without much success to organize and arm the militia. A member of the legisl., A. M. Erwin, was among those killed in 1868. *Ariz. Jour.*, 1868, p. 269, *Powell's Explor.*, 126–31, and *Tyler's Posts and Stations*, 3, contain some information for 1869 et seq. See also *Overland Monthly*, i. 202–9; *Clifford's Overl. Tales*, 309;

In these years the people of Arizona became discouraged, not to say exasperated, and clamorous for
various reforms. They declared the force utterly inadequate, and regular troops unfit for Indian service;
complained that they were not permitted to raise volunteers and finish the war in their own way; desired
Arizona to be made a separate department; were indignant at the suggestion of any policy but that of
incessant warfare; and protested against all half-way
measures. They regarded the temporary reservations
and feeding-stations as so many depots of supplies
where the Apaches could recruit their strength for
new atrocities. Newspapers of Arizona and California reëchoed the popular outcry. Governor and legislature were in full sympathy with the people. There
was much difference of opinion between military inspectors and other officers as to what should be done.
It was a period of excitement and exaggeration, of
intemperate expression, of unreasonable views, of numerous outrages perpetrated upon the Indians. And
the people as a whole are not to be blamed. It is not
easy to be calm and philosophical while one's relatives
and friends are being butchered from week to week.

As a result of this agitation, or at least in the midst
of it, in 1869 Arizona and southern California were
formed into a military department with headquarters
at Fort Whipple; and in the middle of 1870 General
George Stoneman assumed command. The war went
on as before, and mainly because the change failed to
bring any immediate relief, the new general was censured even more severely than his predecessors.   He

Hobbs' Wild Life, 316–39. A memorial of the legisl. to congress in 1870,
Ariz., Acts, 1871, p. 142–3; *U. S. Govt Doc.*, 42d cong. 1st sess., H. Mis. Doc.
16, was published in pamphlet form as *Arizona, Memorial and Affidavits showing
outrages perpetrated by the Apache Indians in the Territory of Arizona, during
the years 1869 and 1870. Published by authority of the legislature of the Territory of Arizona.* S. F., 1871, 8vo, 32 p. The affidavits show 178 murders,
and 3,768 head of cattle and horses stolen. See also McCormick's speeches
in congress Feb. 28 and July 11, 1870, in *Hayes' Scraps, Ariz.*, iii. 136; *Cong.
Globe*, 1869–70, app. 615–18. Gov. Safford's *Narrative*, MS., 42–7, contains a
study of the Ind. troubles; *Conklin's Pict. Ariz.*, passim, contains much on the
subject; as does the *Arizona Resources*, etc., S. F., 1871, pub. by authority of
the legislature.

was thought to spend too much time in red-tape details of military organization, in establishing new posts and improving the old ones; while he also looked with too much favor on the feeding-stations where the Indians continued to assemble in increasing numbers. At the same time Stoneman was blamed in the east for his excessive severity in attacking all Apaches for the offences of a few! I find in his theory and practice little ground for censure. He believed that by furnishing rations and blankets to a few he could induce others to come in and thus advance the work of subduing all. The temporary reservations proved that progress had been made, being an essential link in the evolutionary chain; but the people feared, with some reason, such apparent success as might result in a patched-up peace, a suspension of campaigns, and a reduction of force, to be followed inevitably by a new and more disastrous outbreak.

Unfortunately, the popular feeling led to the commission of a gross outrage. In the spring of 1871 a band of Apaches surrendered to Lieutenant R. E. Whitman at Camp Grant, and being unwilling to go to the White Mountain reservation recently set apart temporarily by Stoneman, they were allowed to live near the post on the Arivaipa, rationed as prisoners of war, performing some useful work, especially in the cutting of hay, behaving well so far as could be known to the officers in charge, and increasing in number to about 300. The citizens were indignant at this feeding of the Apaches, refused to believe that they had submitted in good faith, and found satisfactory evidence that the unceasing depredations in the south-east were committed by these very Indians. At the end of April 40 citizens and 100 Pápagos from Tucson and vicinity marched out to the camp and killed 85, all women and children but eight, and captured some 30, who were sold by the Pápagos as slaves. The perpetrators of this crime to the number of 108 were tried for murder later in the year and acquitted.

Whether the Arivaipa Apaches were guilty of the
thefts and murders imputed to them it is impossible
to know, strong evidence being produced by the citizens on one side and by the officers on the other; but
in any case the massacre of women and children was
a crime in justification of which nothing can be said.[14]
In June 1871 General George Crook succeeded Stoneman in command of the department. His reputation
as an Indian-fighter gained in other fields, his openly
expressed condemnation of the vacillating policy and
desultory warfare of the past, his idea of a reservation
as a place where the Apache must be forced to remain
and work for a living, and above all his energetic
preparations for an effective campaign against the
hostiles, won for him at once the confidence and admiration of the people. For three months Crook
carried on his preliminary operations to culminate in
a general aggressive movement from which the greatest results were expected by all, when the good work
was interrupted in a manner that was most exasperating to all but the Apaches.

In 1867 a board of peace commissioners for the
management of Indian affairs had been appointed at
Washington, being made permanent in 1869, and the

[14] The act was generally excused and defended by the Arizona press and
people. Lieut. Whitman, though a worthless fellow in several respects,
seems to have had remarkable tact in gaining the confidence of Indians, many
of whom, persuaded that the military had no part in the outrage, were induced to return under their chief Eskimenzin; but soon one of the returning
parties, by some blunder not clearly explained, was fired upon by a squad of
soldiers, and the Indians fled to the mountains more hostile than ever. The
trial of the C. Grant murderers is reported in the *S. F. Alta*, Feb. 4, 1872.
Whitman's report is in *Ind. Aff. Rept*, 1871, p. 69; and a good account of the
whole affair is found in *Dunn's Massacres*, 719 et seq. The *Prescott Miner* of
Oct. 14, 1871, gives a list of 301 persons killed by the Apaches since 1864.
In May Lieut. H. B. Cushing was killed in a fight with the foe. In Nov. the
Wickenburg and La Paz stage was attacked, and six men were killed, including Fred. W. Loring, a young man of literary and scientific attainments
connected with Wheeler's survey, whose fate made a sensation in the east,
doing much to call attention to the real state of affairs. I met him in S. F.
earlier in the year. The day before his departure for Ariz. he had his hair
cut very short, jocularly remarking in my Library that the Apaches would
find it difficult to take his scalp. The gov. in his message of this year presented a very gloomy picture of the prospects. There had been reports in
Feb. about abandoning many posts and reducing the force; indeed, such
orders seem to have been issued.

movement being warmly supported by President
Grant and many other prominent military men and
civilians throughout the nation.   The feeling that led
to this movement, and that actuated the board in its
operations, namely, the desire to protect the Indian
from injustice, and to establish a uniform and benevolent policy for his improvement, was worthy of all
praise, and of the hearty support it received from all
Americans of the better class.   The movement resulted, moreover, in great good throughout the Indian
country of the far west.   Yet in some phases of its
practical application, and notably in the theory that
the Arizona Apaches could be subdued by kindness or
influenced by other motives than those of fear and
self-interest, the new 'peace policy' was a sad mistake.[15]   The commission had exerted an influence in
the setting-apart of temporary reservations during
Stoneman's command; but its first direct interference
in Arizona was marked by unfortunate blunders on

[15] In 1867 a joint special committee of congress, appointed by act of 1865,
had made an elaborate report on the condition of the tribes and their treatment by civil and military authorities, though this report contained very
little on Arizona. *Ind. Aff. Rept Joint Spec. Com.*, 1867, 8vo, 532 p.   Says
Dunn, *Massacres*, 717, referring to the operations of the later commission:
'Unfortunately for the Indian, the feeling in his favor wandered off into the
channel of abstract compliment.   From a demon, he was raised to the position of a temporal deity by the extremists, who were now given an opportunity to aid him.   The gentlemen who wrote the reports of the commissioners
revelled in riotous imaginations and discarded facts as a part of the old and
offensive régime which was henceforth to be abandoned.'   I think that Dunn,
however, is inclined to draw too sharp a distinction between the 'extermination' policy of 1864-9 and the 'peace' policy of later years.   Instead of any
sudden change of policy in which the people of Arizona and the military were
compelled to acquiesce somewhat unwillingly, there was simply a gradual
awakening on the part of the government and people of the U. S. to the
truth, as realized in Ariz. from the first, that the Apaches must be forced
upon reservations and then protected.   The 'extermination' talk of certain
classes, and the ultra 'persuasion' rot of certain others, were mere excres-
cences that never had much real weight with practical men of any class.
And indeed, Dunn wisely remarks of the earlier period: 'Although extermination was not being satisfactorily accomplished in Arizona, the legitimate
object of war was being obtained.   The Apaches were gradually being brought
to a realization that peace was a better mode of life than war.   They were
learning that their enemies could invade their homes, destroy their property,
and keep them in constant apprehension of death.   Some of them were ready
to live peaceably at places where they could be protected, but for this result,
which ought to have been the primary object of the war, there had been no
adequate preparation.'

both sides, at a time when prospects were brighter than ever before. On the one side was the Camp Grant massacre; on the other—though prompted largely by that outrage—the sending of Vincent Colyer of the commissioners, an ultra fanatic, with full powers to settle the Apache question.

Colyer, who had visited New Mexico, and even reached the Moqui towns in 1869, arrived in August 1871. Cook, in obedience to his orders, suspended military operations, and Governor Safford issued orders for the commissioner's protection, with a view to restrain the popular fury. Colyer came fully imbued with the belief that the Apaches were innocent victims of oppression, and the whites wholly to blame for past hostilities; and he would listen to nothing not confirmatory of his preconceived views, scorning to seek information from the rascally citizens, the bloody-minded officers, or anybody else who knew anything about the real state of affairs. Protected by an escort, he visited the posts and met several bands of Apaches, just then disposed by the destitution arising from past reverses to come in, make peace, and be fed. From them he got all the testimony he desired on their peaceful and harmless disposition. He approved or selected temporary reservations or asylums at camps Grant, Apache, Verde, McDowell, Beale Spring, and Date Creek; then he went on to California in October, followed by the curses of Arizonans, but fully convinced that the Apache question was settled. If let alone, the Indians would gladly come upon the reservations, eager for peace and civilization. Should there be new troubles, the whites might quit the country, or, staying, comfort themselves for the murder of their families and loss of their property with the thought that all these evils were due to ancient or modern aggressions of their own race. Colyer's mission did perhaps some good by calling attention in the east to Arizona; its harm was the suspension of Crook's operations for a long time, and the encourage-

ment of Apache hopes that a new era of protection
for their great industry of plunder had dawned.[16]

Within a year from Colyer's arrival, the Apaches
are known to have made 54 raids, and killed 41 citizens. The absurdities of his report were somewhat
apparent even at Washington; and though his acts
were approved, orders were sent to Crook through
General Schofield in November 1871, not only to enforce strict measures on the reservations, but to wage
war on all who refused to submit. February 1872
was fixed as the date before which all must come in,
or take the consequences. In April, however, General
O. O. Howard came as a special commissioner to protect the Indians, persuade them to submit, and advance the reservation work in general. While he
was not to interfere directly with Crook's operations,
his mission had practically the effect to postpone the
campaign till late in the year. Remembering Colyer,
the Arizonans were prejudiced against Howard; but

[16] Colyer's preliminary report of 1869 is found in *Ind. Aff. Rept*, 1870, p.
70 et seq.; and that of 1871 in *Id.*, 1871, p. 41-95, with much matter bearing
on the general subject in other parts of the same vol. Dunn, *Massacres*, 726,
thinks that while Colyer 'was notoriously ultra in his peace theories, and
evidently did not understand the situation in Ariz.,' yet 'he was quite as
correct as his assailants.' 'His changes of the location of the Ind. were
rather extensive, and none of them produced good results.' The reference is
mainly to the change from Cañada Alamosa to the Tularosa val. in N. Mex.,
where some of the Mimbreños and Chiricahuas went unwillingly, the latter
soon returning to their old home. The rest were later moved to Ojo Caliente,
whence the name Hot Spring Apaches.

Notwithstanding my slighting allusions to Colyer's mission, it must be
understood that I do not deny the truth of his allegations that the Apaches
had often been grossly wronged. Many such instances have been recorded
by me. Much may be urged, moreover, against the right of a foreign race to
take from the Indians their country, and very little in defence of Spanish or
English treatment of the aborigines from the beginning. A white man's
reservation, under Apache control, would be somewhat more in accordance
with the eternal principles of justice than the present state of affairs. I do
not blame the Apaches for defending their homes and liberties in their own
way. But as there was no proposition or possibility in the case of Arizona to
turn back to the first page and begin a new record, I am disposed to doubt
that a consideration of the ancient or modern short-comings of their race required the Arizona settlers to submit to plunder and murder, or even to quit
the country, to believe that they were entitled to the protection of their government, and to deny that there was ever a time, in this century at least,
when the Apaches could be controlled by kindness and justice. As Dunn
says, 'no warlike Indians ever submitted to reservations until he had been
whipped.' There was ample room for the application of our limited supply
of benevolence and fair treatment after forcing the Indians to submission.

the latter was a very different man, his peace theories
being strongly tinged with common sense. He consulted the people freely, and found them reasonable, if
not very strong in faith, respecting reservation and
treaty success. Mutual respect, if not entire agreement of opinion on certain phases of the Apache question, was developed by the intercourse. Howard
visited the posts; did much to encourage the submissive bands; made treaties between Apaches and their
Pima and Pápago foes; changed the Camp Grant
reservation to the Gila, naming it San Cárlos; and
carried away some chiefs on a visit to Washington.
In the autumn he came back to complete his work,
making several changes. He abolished the asylums
at McDowell, Date Creek, and Beale Spring, permitting the Indians to choose homes at the other reservations. But his principal achievement, though as it
proved an unfortunate one, was to visit Cochise at his
mountain home, receive that chief's submission, and
establish the Chiricahua reservation in the south-
eastern corner of the territory.

Then, in 1872–4, General Crook waged a continuous
and effective war on the hostiles. For the first time
all departments were working in harmony under a
definite policy. As the governor put it in his message,
Howard had offered the olive-branch, and Crook, with
the sword, was enforcing its acceptance. Half-sub-
dued bands often left their reservations to resume their
raids, but such were hard pressed, not only by the
troops, but by Apache warriors, whose submission was
evidently not all pretence, and whose services were
most profitably utilized. As before, I attempt no
record of the campaign in its complications. By the
middle of 1873, the last of the Tontos, Hualapais, and
Yavapais had submitted; and in 1874, with the defeat
of several renegade bands, the war was regarded as at
an end. In a sense, and for large portions of the territory, the peace proved lasting. The great mass of
the Apaches was now under military control on the

reservations. The people and territorial authorities regarded Indian troubles as practically at an end. General Crook was deservedly the hero of the time.[17]

Notwithstanding this peace, which in a sense, as already remarked, was permanent in the north and west, the south-eastern frontier region in Arizona and New Mexico, after a few years, was for another decade to be the scene of Apache warfare, several times devastated with deadly results by renegade bands from the reservations. ' This result was due, not only to the savage instincts and ineradicable hostility of some of the worst Apache tribes, but also and largely to mismanagement. An outline of reservation annals is given in the appended note, including brief mention of the principal outbreaks.[18] In 1874 control of the

[17] Some details respecting the final campaigns, for which I have no space, may be found in Hamilton's work and others of recent years. Crook's merits, which were very great, have doubtless been exaggerated in view of his success by those who have forgotten the similar if less brilliant efforts of his predecessors. He was the best Indian-fighter of all, but by no means the only one. He had a firm grasp of both branches of his task. His energy and skill in carrying on a military expedition were not more marked than his tact in managing Indians in council, and gaining their confidence, or his earnest efforts in behalf of justice and fairness on the part of both races. He fully understood the Indian character, exercised practical good sense in all he undertook, being unaffected by sickly sentimentalism on one side, or exterminating vengeance on the other. Yet in earlier years his success might have been much less complete; and for a comparative failure on one later occasion, he was condemned by Arizonans much as other commanders had been in earlier times.

[18] Apache reservations. The White Mountain reserv. had its origin when Maj. John Green in 1869 found a band of friendly Coyoteros there. In June 1870 he established Camp Ord (later called Ft Apache), and gathered 1,043 Ind. His favorable reports led to a corresp. between the peace com. and mil. authorities; and in April 1871 the reserv. was set apart by Gen. Stoneman, being approved by Colyer, and confirmed by exec. order of Dec. 14, 1872, which also added a tract s. of the Gila, and abolished the C. Grant reserv., thus creating the S. Cárlos agency. (There were thus two agencies, S. Cárlos and Ft Apache on the White Mt reserv., but as the northern agency was later discontinued, the name S. Cárlos came to be commonly applied to the whole reserv.) In 1872 Gen. Howard found and caused to be recalled an order suspending rations, and appointed Dr Milan Soulé to succeed Maj. Dallas in charge. In 1873–4 James E. Robert was agent, and the population increased to 1,800. The Ind. behaved and worked well, being apparently content and showing some interest in their fields and ditches. In Oct. came an order for their removal to S. Cárlos, which was effected much against their wishes, but without the use of force, in July 1875. A considerable number, however, remained behind; and in 1881 some 500 were living on Cibicu Cr. in the extreme N. w. of the reserv. The arrest of a medicine-man who professed to bring dead warriors to life caused an outbreak in June, 10 soldiers and 8 citizens being killed, and Ft Apache being once attacked. The friendly scouts joined the foe, for which three were hanged and two sent to Cal. as prisoners.

reservations passed from the war department to the
Indian bureau, with unfortunate results.   General

Before Sept. 21st, the hostiles came in and surrendered in small parties.   (See
notes on S. Cárlos below.)

At Camp Date Creek in July 1870, there were gathered 225 Ind., mostly
Yavapais, who for a year were allowed to get a living by hunting, etc., but
from June 1871 were given rations, though not subject to much control so
long as they kept the peace.   In Sept. 1872 the number had increased to
750, including some rather turbulent characters.   Lieut. F. H. E. Ebstein in
charge was succeeded, in July 1872, by Dr Josephus Williams.   At the end
of 1872, by advice of the agent and others, Gen. Howard discontinued this
feeding station, and the Ind. were transferred in May 1873 to the C. Verde
reserv., which had been set apart by Colyer in 1871, and where a large number of Tontos had been gathered.   Williams became agent at Verde, and the
highest number of Ind. in 1873 was 2,000, 900 running away in Aug., but
400 returning in Sept.   W. S. Schuyler succeeded Williams; there was much
sickness, and the site of the agency was changed more than once; in Feb.
1874 there were 1,078 Ind., but the soldiers brought in more till in June
there were 1,544.   Later in the year much progress had been made in agric.,
buildings, etc.; the Ind. seemed well disposed, and prospects were considered
good.   But to the great displeasure of the natives and against the protest of
Gen. Crook they were removed in March 1875, in charge of Special Commissioner Dudley to the S. Cárlos reserv., the Tontos and Yavapais having on
the way a fight among themselves, in which five were killed.

The Chiricahua reserv., including approximately that portion of Cochise
co. lying east of the Dragoon Mts, was estab. in Oct. 1872 by Gen. Howard,
on the conclusion of a treaty with the chief Cochise, and the failure of all
attempts to induce this tribe to leave their old homes.   The reserv. was set
apart by exec. order of Dec. 14th, and by the end of the year over 1,000
Apaches were being fed according to the report of the agent, Thos T. Jeffords.
The agency was at Sulphur Spring, Ciénega de S. Simon, Pinery Cañon, and
Apache Pass successively.   Cochise remained faithful to his death in June
1874, and was succeeded by his son Taza, though neither had full control of
all the bands.   There was no farming land, but the Chiricahuas were not
farmers, and did not care to learn the business.   The reserv. being on the
Mexican border, there was much raiding across the line; but Agent Jeffords
insisted that these depredations were committed by Ind. from S. Cárlos and
Hot Spring, and Mexico, and never by his Chiricahuas, a statement not implicitly believed outside the reserv.   Jeffords admitted, however, some slight
troubles with visiting and renegade Apaches and Mex. traders and soldiers.
Supt L. E. Dudley of N. Mex. endeavored to have the Chiricahuas removed
to Hot Spring, but they refused to go.   Finally, in April 1876, serious trouble
arose from the sale of whiskey by one Rogers at Sulphur Spring station, the
drunken Ind. fighting among themselves, killing the liquor-dealer and his
assistant, going on the war-path, and committing many depredations.   Accordingly, by the influence of Gov. Safford and against the advice of Gen.
Kautz then in command, the removal of all the Ind. was ordered.   A band
of 140 went to Hot Spring; 325 under Taza were sent to S. Cárlos in June;
and the rest—400 according to Jeffords' figures, the accuracy of which has
been questioned—ran away to commit depredations on the frontier.   The
reserv. was restored to the public domain by exec. order of Oct. 30, 1876.

The S. Cárlos division of the White Mt reserv. originated in 1872 with
the abolishment of the C. Grant reserv. (which also seems to have been moved
to the region of the mouth of the S. Pedro at first).   Records of the change,
which was not completed till Feb. 1873, are not very clear.   The successive
agents in 1872–4 were Ed. C. Jacobs, Geo. H. Stevens, H. R. Wilbur, C. F.
Larrabee, W. H. Brown, J. E. Roberts, and John P. Clum.   There were from
900 to 1,800 Ind. on the rolls, but from some mismanagement or frequent
change of agents there were constant troubles, desertions, and recaptures.

Crook should have been left for several years at least in full control. From 1875 the policy of concentrat-

In May 1873 there was a plot to kill all the whites. It was discovered in time, but Lieut. Almy was shot, and three chiefs with their bands fled to the mountains. These Ind. were harassed for a year, and not permitted to return till they had killed the three chiefs. In Jan. 1874 other serious troubles occurred, resulting in the flight of several bands, and in six months of war before all submitted. Still considerable progress in agric. was reported. There were 1,000 of the original S. Cárlos Ind. in Sept. 1875, besides 1,400 who had come from C. Verde in March, and 1,800 from Ft Apache in July, or a total of 4,200, who got no rations except in payment for labor. In June 1876 the Chiricahuas, 325 strong, were brought in from the south; from Oct. the troops were removed, and reliance was placed on the native police, not only to preserve order, but also to pursue renegades; and Clum took 25 of his Apaches east to the centennial fair. In May 1877 the renegade Chiricahuas having joined the Hot Spring Ind. in depredations, it decided to break up the Hot Spring reserv., and 453 Ind were transferred to S. Cárlos, Victorio and 40 warriors escaping to avoid the transfer, and 300 of the 453 escaping in Sept., though about 190 of them were perhaps brought back before the end of the year. The renegades did bloody work in N. Mex. Clum claimed that no depredations were committed by his reserv. Ind. proper, and that all was prosperous, but his reports may have been somewhat highly colored. Meanwhile the exec. order of Dec. 14, 1872, creating the reserv., was supplemented by several new orders. That of Aug. 5, 1873, cut off all the Gila valley above old C. Goodwin, or about 110° 5′, and that of July 21, 1874, all east of long. 109° 30′ (the reserv. had at first extended to the N. Mex. line). That of April 27, 1876, cut off a strip on the east; that of Jan. 26, 1877, a tract of 7,421 acres in N. E. corner; and that of March 31, 1877, the S. W. corner S. of the Gila. *Rept Sec. Int.*, 1882, p. 309-11. As left, the reserv. contains 4,440 sq. miles. H. L. Hart was agent in 1877-8, Adna R. Chaffee in 1879-80, J. C. Tiffany in 1880-1, Phil. P. Wilcox in 1882-3, G. Ford in 1884. Though the presence of many different and mutually hostile bands necessitated their separation to some extent into distinct camps, there were no serious troubles with the masses; the native police rendered good service; and fair progress was reported in agriculture. In 1878 about 400 Apaches were absent, working in the mines, etc., and giving no cause for complaint. In the same year mining discoveries in the N. W. at McMillan's caused some complaint of encroachment on the reserv. In 1879 the pop. was 4,652; there were 2,000 cattle and horses; and 5,000 lbs. of barley were sold. The taking of water from the Gila above the reserv. caused some fears. The Apaches were generally disarmed, and the use of *tiswin*, the native liquor, was prevented. Apache women were as a rule chaste, but habits of prostitution, with resulting disease, had been brought to some extent by the Colorado River bands. In 1880 the renegade chiefs Juh and Gerónimo, with 108 Chiricahuas, were brought in from Mexico. Another chief, Victorio, continued his raids on the border until killed by the Mexicans. In 1881 Nané, Victorio's associate, continued his depredations; and Juh and Nachez with a party of Chiricahuas ran away from the reserv. in Sept., and after a fight were driven into Mexico. Petty disturbances increased somewhat; whiskey sellers at Globe caused some trouble; but notwithstanding a flood, goods crops were raised, live-stock increased, good buildings were completed, and a school was taught by A. B. Ross and wife. The discovery of rich coal deposits this year introduced new complications for which no solution has yet been found, though there has been much discussion of the subject in Ariz. and in congress. The people are eager to have the mining tract restored to the public domain; while on the other hand is advocated either the working of the coal mines by the Ind., or a lease for their benefit. It should be stated, however, that serious doubts were finally thrown on the accuracy of Agent Tiffany's favorable reports on

ing all the Apaches at San Cárlos was enforced.
Those of forts Verde and Apache were transferred in
March and July; the Chiricahuas in June 1876; and
the Hot Spring bands in May 1877.   While in a general way this policy of concentration may have been
well founded, while some changes were probably necessary—notably at the Chiricahua reservation on the
Mexican border—and while no policy would have entirely prevented the subsequent troubles, yet there
can be no question that nearly all the later outbreaks
and disasters may be traced directly to these transfers.
The Indians were naturally unwilling to quit the regions in which they had been born or which they had
chosen, which, as they understood it, the government
had given them for permanent homes, and where in some
instances they were making progress; many of them
objected particularly to the San Cárlos tract; besides
their aversion to any change and their special objections to the new home, there was much fear of their
new neighbors; and the mingling or near approach of
so many distinct and hostile bands—which had never
agreed on any proposition except that of hostility to
the whites—was sure to make serious trouble.   With
the special reasons assigned for the change, the mis-
conduct of certain renegade bands or turbulent characters, the masses of the Apaches at each point had
little to do; and in some cases the influence of whites
coveting the reservation lands was a controlling motive.   General Crook protested earnestly against the
first transfer, that of the Verde Indians; but he was
removed to another department to fight the Sioux,
and was succeeded in March 1875 by General August
V. Kautz.   This officer also opposed the changes, and
in connection with the removal of the Chiricahuas and
resulting depredations of renegades, he became involved in serious controversies with Governor Safford,

the condition of affairs.   From 1882 the reservation was practically under
control of the military commander; and the condition of affairs was for the
most part satisfactory, but for the escape of renegade bands in 1885, and
their depredations on the border.

which finally led to his removal in 1878, his successor being General O. B. Willcox.[19]

On the transfer of the Chiricahuas in June 1876, a considerable number escaped, went on the war-path, and in four months killed 20 persons. On the transfer of the Hot Spring bands in May 1877, Victorio and party escaped to Mexico; and in September 300 escaped from San Cárlos. The ensuing pursuits, fights, surrenders, and reëscapes are too complicated for detailed record here; but large numbers of the renegades, while sometimes submitting in New Mexico, refused to be removed to San Cárlos, and ran away every time it was attempted. Resulting depredations, sometimes exaggerated by the citizens and newspapers, and perhaps underrated by the military, were constant and serious on the border, especially in New Mexico; and for years the warfare was almost as deadly as ever. From this time the Indians were well armed with repeating rifles, and pursuits by the troops were generally fruitless. In 1879 Victorio came from the south, was reënforced by various renegade bands, and killed 73 victims before he could be driven back into Mexico. He was killed in 1880 by Mexicans, while Juh and Gerónimo, with 110 Chiricahuas, were brought in to the reservation. In 1881 occurred the Cibicu Creek outbreak, as mentioned elsewhere; Nané, Victorio's successor, made a bloody raid from across the line, and part of the Chiricahuas, under Juh and Nachez, ran away from San Cárlos. In April 1882 these were followed by Gerónimo and the rest of the renegade Chiricahuas, with Loco and his Hot Spring

---

[19] The gov. accused Kautz of inefficiency in Ind. warfare against the renegades, and in his message of 1877 called on the legisl. to raise a force of militia or Ind. scouts to protect the country, since the military were doing nothing. *Ariz. Jour.*, 1877, p. 233–4. Both parties wrote severe letters for the newspapers, and Safford made an effort to have Kautz removed. The general defends himself at length in his regular report of Aug. 15, 1877. *U. S. Govt Doc.*, 45th cong. 2d sess., H. Ex. Doc. ii. 133–49. Hoyt, *Leading Events*, MS., 15 et seq., says that Kautz was a little later court-martialed and reprimanded for publishing a pamphlet reflecting on Judge-advocate-gen. Dunn. Though the north was generally spoken of as being at peace, Kautz' report shows several expeditions in the C. Verde region, in which 38 Ind. were killed and 42 captured.

band.   Further trouble occurred on the reservation,
and the general outlook was very discouraging.   Military men were nearly unanimous in the opinion that
all these later troubles were due to the disturbance of
Crook's plans, the turning-over of the reservations to
the Indian bureau in 1874, the unwise concentration
of the Apaches at San Cárlos, and subsequent mismanagement on the part of civil agents with the resulting controversies.   It is clear that this view of the
matter is to a considerable extent well founded.

In 1882 General Crook came back to relieve General Willcox, to whom, however, no special fault was
imputed.   A treaty was made by which Indians might
be pursued across the boundary by United States and
Mexican troops, respectively.   And with Crook's return there came about rather mysteriously, as Dunn
remarks, "a reasonable harmony between representatives of the Indian bureau and war department in
Arizona."   He found the reservation Indians sullen,
suspicious, and discontented, complaining of wrongs at
the hands of their late agent, distracted with rumors
of intended attack, disarmment, and removal, and disposed to go again on the war-path as a choice of evils.
With his old tact the general made them understand
that war was just what their enemies desired, and
peace their only means of saving their reservation.
The old system of strict discipline, metal tags, and
frequent roll-calls was restored, and the native police
reorganized.   Confidence being restored, Crook permitted a large number of the Indians to leave the
river agency and live in the northern part of the reservation without rations.   They succeeded so well
that about 1,500, or one third of the whole number,
were soon living in the north and almost self-sustaining.

Meanwhile, Gerónimo and the rest were raiding in
Mexico; and in March 1883, Chato with fifty Indians
crossed the line and killed a dozen persons in Arizona,
including the family of Judge McComas.   With about

50 soldiers and 200 Apache scouts, having fortunately secured the services as guide of a chief who had deserted from the foe, and having made arrangements for the coöperation of the Mexican forces, Crook marched in May to the Apache stronghold in the Sierra Madre—a place never reached by troops before, and which could not have been reached without the services of the guide. A complete surrounding and surprise of the foe was prevented by the hasty firing of the scouts; but Chato's band was defeated with a loss of nine killed and five captives; and the rest entered into negotiations. Finally, they offered to surrender on the condition that past offences should be forgotten, and all be settled on the reservation. Because a successful prosecution of the campaign at this time and in this country was impossible, because to withdraw and await a more convenient opportunity of surprising the foe would involve renewed disaster to the scattered settlers, and because the Chiricahua outbreak had been caused to a considerable extent by unfair treatment, Crook accepted the terms and brought back to San Cárlos nearly 400 renegades, including Gerónimo, Chato, Nachez, Loco, and all the chiefs except Juh, who had escaped. For two years these Indians under military management behaved well, and it was hoped that the Apache question had been at last settled.[20]

[20] *Annual Report of Brigadier-general George Crook, U. S. Army, commanding department of Arizona, 1883,* n. p., 12mo, 17, 1, 2, 3, 12, 1, 3 p.; *Id.,* 1884, 12mo, 10 p. In *Ariz. Laws,* 1883, p. 292–6, is a memorial of the legisl., explanatory of the situation and asking that all the Apaches be removed. *An Apache Campaign in the Sierra Madre; an account of the expedition in pursuit of the hostile Chiricahua Apaches in the spring of 1883. By John G. Bourke, Capt. Third Cavalry, etc.,* N. Y., 1886, 12mo, 112 p., furnishes also a good narrative of Crook's campaign. Crook says: 'From my experience of late years I can state, unhesitatingly, that since the Ind. have learned the strength of our people, in almost every Ind. war which I have known anything about, the prime cause has been, either the failure of our govt to make good its pledges, or the wrongs perpetrated upon them by unscrupulous whites. That Ind. are often robbed of their rations, goods, etc.,...by rascally agents and other unscrupulous white men, is a fact within the knowledge of any one having relations with them. These are the men who are responsible for this unsettled state of affairs. Public sentiment in frontier communities does not consider the malicious killing of an Ind. murder, nor the most unblushing plundering theft...I have no knowledge of a case on record where a white

Yet once more in the early summer of 1885, Gerónimo and Nachez, with a part of their Chiricahua
warriors, fled from the reservation, and resumed their
deadly raiding on the settlers on both sides of the line.
No definite reason for the outbreak is known, though
the chief's detection in the illicit manufacture of *tiswin*, the native liquor, has been suggested; and later
Gerónimo has talked vaguely of plots against his life.
This occurrence, while not affecting the wisdom of
Crook's general policy, or proving that past troubles
had not been largely due to reservation changes and
mismanagement, or even justifying the suspicion that
the general had been so far carried away by his theories as to become a dupe of Apache cunning—yet
shows clearly enough that even with just and careful
treatment under military auspices the Apache could
not be trusted, that the problem had not been so near
an easy solution as Crook had believed, and that past
outbreaks were due in part to inherent savagism.
Again, with his accustomed vigor, and with the aid
of Apache scouts, under Captain Crawford—who was
killed in an unfortunate encounter with Mexicans—
Crook pursued the renegades into Sonora, and in

man has been convicted and punished for defrauding an Indian. I am not
an apologist for the Chiricahuas—they are bad Ind., probably the very worst
on the continent.' 'An Ind. in his mode of warfare is more than the equal
of the white man, and it would be practically impossible with white soldiers
to subdue the Chiricahuas in their own haunts.' He thinks the Ind. should
own their lands in severalty, as most of them desire. To disarm them he
believes impossible and undesirable; they must have arms for protection
against lawless whites. 'Their removal would bring on the bloodiest Ind.
war this country has ever experienced.' But the general goes much too far
in urging that the ballot should be given the Ind. In his report of 1884,
after a year of peace, Crook expresses great satisfaction with the progress
made, and the prospects, notwithstanding certain obstacles—notably the ex-
tortions of traders. One chief, for making warlike speeches, was arrested,
tried, and convicted—all by natives—and sent to Cal. for imprisonment.
Gerónimo and Nachez are among the most successful farmers. Crops of the
season were 3,850,000 lbs. corn, 550,000 lbs. barley, 54,000 lbs. beans, 20,000
lbs. potatoes, 50,000 lbs. wheat, 200,000 pumpkins, and 90,000 melons, in spite
of some bad luck caused by freshets.
   It should be noted here that there is extant in Arizona a theory that in
the campaign of 1883 Gen. Crook, through placing too much confidence in
his scouts, found himself really in the power of the Chiricahuas, and was
obliged to accept Gerónimo's terms. I have not attached much importance
to this theory, though the events of 1885-6 tend somewhat to give it plausibility.

March 1886 forced them to promise surrender. But before entering Arizona, not obtaining satisfactory guaranties of restoration to reservation life, and fearing the punishment his crimes deserved, the wily Gerónimo and his companions effected their escape to ravage the frontier with death and desolation for five months more. This misfortune, or blunder, brought upon Crook a storm of abuse which resulted in his removal; and General Nelson Miles was appointed to take his place. Under the new commander and his subordinates, notable among whom was Captain Lawton, the campaign was continued; and after various delays and contretemps that did not fail to arouse a clamor of popular criticism, the Chiricahua band of some 20 warriors was in August forced to surrender without conditions.

As I write, not only these captives, but all the Chiricahuas and Hot Spring Indians at San Cárlos have been sent to Florida. Arizona is again joyful in the belief that her Indian troubles are forever at an end. General Miles is the hero of the day, naturally, and justly to the extent that he has well performed his duty, but unfairly in so far as his service of a few months is made to outweigh the still more valuable work of Crook for years. Whether Gerónimo will be hanged, as he should be, is not yet settled, and for the welfare of Arizona it is immaterial. There is no reason to doubt that there will be other troubles with the Apaches; but they should not be very serious, especially if the policy of exiling all renegades shall be strictly enforced.

As to the general prospects of the reservation Indians of all tribes, they cannot be said to be encouraging. A mountainous mining country on the national frontier, where white men can hardly be made to behave themselves, is not fit for an Indian reservation. It would be better for Arizona that all should be removed; and better for the Indians, if there be any region where success with other tribes is at all en-

couraging.   Yet the removal would be very difficult,
perhaps impossible.   Though no real progress has as
yet been made, reservation annals furnish many items
to indicate seemingly that the seeds of advancement
might easily be made to take root.   The Indians often
show traits of docility, patience, industry, and ambition to improve, of which it would seem advantage
might be taken; but with these traits are inextricably
mingled others of stupid perversity and savagism that
practically bar the way to all improvement; and the
monumental capacity for blundering, the rascality, the
bigotry, the lack of skill, the fondness for controversy
on the part of agents, teachers, missionaries, and all
who undertake the management of Indians, have thus
far coöperated most effectually against success.   Probably no radical change is to be expected in either red
men or white; probably a foreign civilization cannot
be ingrafted on aboriginal stock; apparently the Indians, non-progressive savages, ever the victims of
injustice, must dwindle in numbers and finally disappear; or, at best, the germs of civilization be planted
in a few individuals surviving the tribal annihilation.
Yet the line of our nation's duty is clear in the matter.   The Indians must be fully protected in their
rights.   Outrages upon them must be promptly and
severely punished.   Every attempt at improvement
must be encouraged.   As fast as possible the tribal
relation must be broken up.   Lands must be given in
severalty to all who are capable of utilizing them.
Government aid must be mainly in the form of implements and instruction and protection.   Primary
schools must be liberally supported; but religion must
be made a secondary matter.   Above all, earnest,
honest, practical men must be put in charge and paid
for their services.   The survival of the fittest must
be encouraged.   If any must perish, let it be the
good-for-nothing; if any are to be helped, let it be
those who are disposed to help themselves.

Apaches have not been the only outlaws who have afflicted Arizona. Acts of lawless violence, including murders, robberies, and lynchings, have been but too common throughout the territory's history. Yet such irregularities have not been greater but rather much less than was to be expected under the peculiar circumstances, in consideration of which Arizona's record is not worse than that of the other western regions. The Indian wars in themselves, during which every citizen's life was in constant danger, tended strongly to establish the habit of reliance on force rather than legal forms for protection from other foes. Desperadoes might always commit outrages with a fair chance of their being attributed to Indians. The geographic position of the territory contributed to the same result. Mexican outlaws of a peculiarly vicious class frequented the frontier districts, easily escaping after the commission of crimes into Sonora, where their punishment, by reason of endless complications of international red tape, was generally impracticable. These Mexicans, bad as they were, had like the Indians to bear the responsibility for hundreds of offences they never committed. The native population of Spanish race, here as in other border regions of the United States, has often been the object of most unfair treatment. Too often has there been a popular clamor for the expulsion of all Mexicans from some mining camp, innate race prejudice being aggravated by the acts of a few outlaws, and the result being utilized by designing desperadoes or politicians of another race for the carrying-out of their various designs. A sparsely settled mining country is never a favorable field for the proper enforcement of law; and Arizona for many years, by reason not only of its Indian troubles, but of its undeserved reputation as a desert unfit for homes, was chiefly attractive to the least desirable class of adventurers from California, Nevada, Colorado, and Texas. Again the long and unprotected stage

and express routes over which rich bullion prizes were
carried, have furnished especial temptations and facilities for highway robbery. And it must be admitted
that the combination of national and territorial authority has not always been favorable to the administration of justice; and that locally the qualities of energy
and bravery required in officers of justice have been
too often sought in men more or less identified with
the criminal element. It is not my purpose to present a chronicle of Arizona crimes and criminals,
though I append some items and references in a note.
While it can hardly be hoped that troubles of this
class are at an end, yet constant progress in the right
direction and growth of proper public sentiment are
to be noted. With railroads, agricultural development, and increase of law-abiding population, scenes
of violence will be more and more confined, as they
have been for the most part in late years, to new
mining districts and isolated frontier settlements.[21]

[21] Some items on Ariz. committees of vigilance, etc., may be found in my
Popular Tribunals, i. 722 et seq. In his message of 1868 the gov. compli-
ments the Mex. pop. for their obedience to law and general good character.
Down to this time there have been no special complaints of lawlessness
except before 1864. In '68, however, the gov. offers a reward of $300 for the
arrest of a murderer. *Ariz. Jour.*, 1868, p. 272. From '70 murders and robberies attributed to Mex. became frequent on the Gila. Three Amer. were
killed at Mission Camp. A reward of $1,000 was offered, and an agent sent
to Sonora, but Gov. Pesqueira declined to give up the criminals. *Id.*,
1871, p. 53–4, 157–9, 163–4, 222–8, 234–8; *Hayes' Scraps, Ariz.*, iii. 101.
Baker and family were murdered at Blue Water Station in Dec. '71. *Id.*, iii.
289–91, 312, 315; *U. S. Govt Doc.*, 42d cong. 3d sess., H. Ex. Doc., i. 383–6,
411–12; and many newspaper articles. Four or five murders are noted in
'72. There were also complaints on the Sonora side of outrages on Mex.
Estrella de Occid., Mar. 29, 1872; *Mex., Mem. Rel.*, 1875, annex 1, p. 3–13.
In 1873 there were several vigilance organizations, and also the 1st legal execution—that of one Fernandez at Yuma. *Hayes' Scraps, Ariz.*, v. 165, 169, 188,
199, 210; vi. 160, 167–8, 172, 193; *Ariz. Scraps*, 165. In 1877 the gov. announced that for 2 years but slight troubles had occurred; yet predicted that
with increasing wealth the temptation for robbery would increase; and advised the legislature to continue its appropriations for the arrest of criminals,
and to make highway robbery a capital offence. And indeed, from 1878 murders and robberies are frequently catalogued in the newspapers each year.
The Mex. do not seem to have been prominently accused in these years,
but some corresp. on the subject is found in *Mex. Corresp. Diplomática*, i.
779–84; *U. S. Govt Doc.*, 46th cong. 2d sess., H. Ex. Doc., i. 734. In '79 the
Phœnix stage was robbed 4 times in as many months; Gov. Gosper offered
$500 for the killing and $300 for the arrest of a stage robber; and several
lynchings are recorded. *Ariz. Scraps*, 129; *Phœnix Herald*, June 25, '80;
Prescott Miner, Dec. 3, '80; *S. F. Bulletin*, Aug. 22, '79; *S. F. Chronicle*, Aug.

23, '79. In '80-2 matters assumed their worst aspect, stage robbers were
lynched, cowboys attacked some of the towns, sheriffs and their posses were
often resisted, bloody affrays occurred between Amer. and Mex., an emigrant train was attacked by robbers, and several legal executions are
recorded. Tombstone was a centre of lawless operations, the U. S. marshal
was shot, and several bloody fights took place between the desperadoes and
scarcely less desperate officers of justice. The citizens were at last fully
aroused; money was contributed, and a volunteer force raised; the president
of the U. S. issued a proclamation; and in '83 quiet was restored, and the
prisons were full. See files of Tombstone and other newspapers in these
years; also *Ariz. Jour.*, 12th legis. ass. 30-2; *U. S. Govt Doc.*, 47th cong. 1st
sess., H. Ex. Doc. 188. The last serious trouble was at Bisbee in Dec. '83,
when five armed men deliberately and openly robbed a store and killed 5
citizens in cold blood. The 5 culprits were speedily convicted and hanged at
Tombstone in March '84; while another accomplice, being condemned to imprisonment for life, was lynched by citizens in Feb. See *Ariz. Hist.* (E. &
Co.), 154-5; and the newspapers.

HIST. ARIZ. AND N. MEX. 37

CHAPTER XXIII.

ARIZONAN INDUSTRIES AND INSTITUTIONS.

1864–1886.

MINING—EARLY OPERATIONS—THE GOLD PLACERS—EFFECT OF APACHE WARS—OTHER OBSTACLES—FINAL SUCCESS—STATISTICS—SILVER AND GOLD BELT—THE FOUR GROUPS, MOJAVE, YAVAPAI, GILA, PIMA, AND COCHISE—SOME LOCAL ITEMS—FAMOUS MINES—TOMBSTONE—COPPER MINES—DIAMOND HOAX—MODERN WORKS ON ARIZONA—AGRICULTURE—CLIMATE AND PRODUCTS—STOCK-RAISING—GOVERNMENT LANDS—MEXICAN GRANTS—MANUFACTURES AND TRADE—ROADS, STAGES, AND MAILS—RAILROADS AND TELEGRAPHS—EDUCATION—LIBRARY—HISTORICAL SOCIETY—CHURCHES—NEWSPAPERS.

FROM the time when it first became known to Europeans, Arizona has been especially noted for its mineral wealth. There is no evidence that its mines were ever worked by the aborigines; but by the Spaniards its treasure of precious metals was much talked of, even before being found. It was enough to know that the country was in the mysterious north, and occupied by savage tribes; its wealth was taken for granted. On its partial exploration, however, and the establishment of missions and presidios on its borders early in the eighteenth century, abundant indications of gold and silver were found in all directions. Yet so broad and rich was the mineral field farther south, and so feeble the Spanish tenure in Alta Pimería by reason of Indian hostility, that not even the wonderfully rich 'planchas de plata' at the Arizona camp, giving name to the later territory though not within its limits, led to the occupation of the northern parts by miners. As I have already explained, the current traditions of extensive mining in Spanish

(578)

times are greatly exaggerated. The Jesuits worked no mines; and in their period, down to 1767, nothing was practically accomplished beyond irregular prospecting in connection with military expeditions and the occasional working of a few veins or placers for brief periods, near the presidios. It is doubtful that any traces of such workings have been visible in modern times. Later, however, in about 1790–1815, while the Apaches were comparatively at peace and all industries flourished accordingly, mines were worked on a small scale in several parts of what is now Pima county, and the old shafts and tunnels of this period have sometimes been found, though the extent of such operations has been generally exaggerated. With Mexican independence and a renewal of Apache raids, the mining industry was entirely suspended, only to be resumed in the last years, if at all, on a scale even smaller than before 1790.

Still the fame of hidden wealth remained and multiplied; and on the consummation of the Gadsden purchase in 1854, as we have seen, Americans like Poston and Mowry began to open the mines. Eastern capital was enlisted; several companies were formed; mills and furnaces were put in operation; and for some six years, in the face of great obstacles —notably that of expensive transportation—the southern silver mines were worked with considerable success and brilliant prospects, until interrupted by the war of the rebellion, the withdrawal of troops, and the triumph of the Apaches in 1861. The mining properties were then plundered and destroyed, many miners were killed, and work was entirely suspended, not to be profitably resumed in this region for many years. During this period the Ajo copper mines in Papaguería were also worked with some success; and on the lower Gila from 1858 gold placers, or dry washings, attracted a thousand miners or more, being somewhat profitably worked for four years, and never entirely abandoned. In 1862 the placer excitement was trans-

ferred northward across the Gila, and up the Colorado
to the region where La Paz, Olive City, and Ehrenberg soon came into existence. For several years
these Colorado placers attracted a crowd of Californians, and a large amount of coarse gold was obtained;
but as a rule the dry washing processes were too
tedious for the permanent occupation of any but Mexicans and Indians; and the Americans pushed their
prospecting north-eastward, under the pioneers Pauline
Weaver and Joseph Walker, for whom new and rich
districts in what is now Yavapai county were named
in 1863. Not only was the placer field thus extended,
but rich gold and silver bearing veins were found, giving promise of a permanent mining industry for the
future.[1]

Such was the state of affairs in 1864–5, when the
territory of Arizona was organized; and the mining

[1] The Cal. papers of 1862–3 are full of corresp. on the Colorado placers,
and there is a large col. of this corresp. in *Hayes' Scrap-books, Ariz.*, i., passim.
The number of miners in 1862 is estimated from 500 to 1,500. Reports are
contradictory; but nobody seems to be making much money. There is much
discussion of the best routes from Los Angeles, the number of miners returning in disgust being apparently about equal to those starting out in high hopes.
In 1863–4 the La Paz fields are comparatively deserted for the north and east;
and we hear more and more of veins and lodes of gold, silver, and copper.
Olive City was then called Olivia. Many discoveries are mentioned in Mojave
co., and we hear much of the Moss lode, Eldorado Cañon, and Hardyville.
The placer excitement ended about 1864, though the deposits continued to be
worked, and often with profit. According to Raymond's rept of 1870, the
placer gold of the Gila and Colorado fields is of local origin from small gash-
veins in slates and greenstone. The gravel is angular and not rounded by
water, having little or no earth with it. Only coarse gold had been saved,
and there was more left than had been taken out. From 1870 there was a
revival of interest in the placers, though they had never been wholly abandoned. A machine for dry washing was used on the Colorado; and on
the Gila a company pumped water into a reservoir on the hills. Hamilton
says the Yuma co. placers have yielded over $2,000,000. The census report
and King give the placer yield of 1880 as $30,000. Lynx Creek and the
Weaver district in Yavapai are said to have produced over $1,000,000 each
from gravel; and there were several other rich districts, the placer yield of
1873 being put at $40,000. Richmond Basin, Gila co., was a most remark-
able placer, over $100,000 in nuggets being picked from the surface, and
there being 10 feet of gold-bearing mud on the bed-rock. In the Quijotoa
region, Pima co., dry placers have been worked by Mexicans and Pápagos.
Extensive placers are mentioned in the Sta Rita Mts. In Graham co., on S.
Francisco River, is a broad tract of gravel which is thought to promise well
for hydraulic work. Hardly a year has passed without a placer discovery in
some part of Ariz., chiefly in Yavapai; and work has been continuous and in
a small way profitable, though interrupted often in one section or another by
drought. Statistics of production in this branch of mining are naturally
very meagre and unreliable

excitement in Yavapai doubtless had much influence in making Prescott the capital. This excitement continued for years, new and rich discoveries being frequent; but the richest lodes were always those to be discovered a little farther on in the Apache country. The Apache war soon made mining and even prospecting extremely perilous in most regions, at the same time preventing the influx of capital from abroad; and in many of the mines that could be worked it was soon found that the ores were too refractory for reduction by the crude processes and with the imperfect machinery of the pioneers. One or two mines of extraordinary richness were continuously profitable; a few others paid well at times; many men gained a living by working placers and small veins; and some mines near the Colorado made a profit by sending selected ores at enormous cost to San Francisco. Meanwhile every military expedition was also a prospecting tour; and the attitude of the people was one of most impatient waiting for the time when, with the defeat of the Apache and the return of peace, the development of mineral wealth might begin in earnest. Enthusiasm over the country's prospects was unbounded; the local newspapers were full of rose-colored predictions; the governor and legislature were strong in the faith; and the government commissioners of mining statistics, Ross Browne and R. W. Raymond, gave some prominence to Arizona in their reports.[2]

[2] See annual messages of the gov. in *Ariz., Journals*, 1865 et seq. *Reports upon the Mineral Resources of the United States, by special commissioners J. Ross Browne and James W. Taylor* (for 1866). Wash., 1837. This contains on Ariz. only Gov. McCormick's message, and the mining law, p. 135, 249. *Report of J. Ross Browne on the Mineral Resources of the States and Territories west of the Rocky Mountains* (for 1867). Wash. and S. F., 1868; also published as *Resources of the Pacific Slope*, etc., S. F., 1869. This report, p. 443–81, contains a good account of Ariz. mines, made up in part from the author's observations, but mainly from notes of various writers, especially those furnished by Gov. McCormick. *Statistics of Mines and Mining in the States and Territories west of the Rocky Mountains; being the first (eighth) annual report of Rossiter W. Raymond, United States commissioner of Mining Statistics* (1837–75). Wash., 1869–77, being published in the House Ex. Doc., from the 40th cong. 3d sess. to 44th cong. 1st sess. The report of 1870 is founded mainly on the personal observations of Prof. A. Eilers, a deputy commissioner, and is very complete in its account of the geology of Ariz., and the various districts and mines. The last

With the end of Apache war in 1874 came the expected revival and development of mining industry, old mines being worked with profit, and many new lodes being brought to light, notably in the central region of Gila and Pinal counties. The revival extended to the old districts of Pima county in the south, where the mines had been practically abandoned for thirteen years. While, however, there was marked progress in discoveries and workings, and in the influx of population, the output of bullion beginning also to assume proportions, yet the grand 'boom' was hardly so immediate or complete as Arizonans, in their long pent enthusiasm, had hoped for. Capital was still somewhat timid and tardy in its approach; the Indians became again to a certain extent troublesome; and above all, the cost of transportation was enormous. The railroad then became the prospective panacea for all the territory's ills. It reached the Colorado border in 1878, and five years later two lines extended completely across the country from east to west. The railroad, with its policy of demanding "all the traffic will bear," by no means put an end to excessively high rates, yet it afforded some relief; and meanwhile the discovery of the Tombstone bonanzas, aided by the failure of the Comstock lode as a paying property, gave to Arizona in 1880–4 a very high and previously unexcelled degree of prosperity. In 1884–6, however, the extremely low price of silver and copper bullion, together with labor troubles and a disastrous fire in the south-east, and the bursting of the Quijotoa bubble, have thrown over the country's progress a cloud, which it is hoped will soon disappear.

The total gold and silver product of the Arizona mines has been perhaps about $60,000,000. For the decade ending in 1869 it was estimated, on no very

report, of 1875, is also extensive. The others are shorter, being made up from information derived from residents.

For mining laws of Ariz., see *Ariz.*, *Mining Law*, Prescott, 1864, 12mo, 21 p.; *Id.*, *Acts.*, 1875, p. 152–5; *Id.*, *Compiled Laws*, 532–4; *U. S. Govt Doc.*, 38th cong. 2d sess., H. Mis. Doc. 14; *Hinton's Hand-book*, app. 1–12; *Shinn's Min. Camps*, 282.

secure basis, at $1,000,000 per year on an average.
Then it fell off to $800,000, to $600,000, and in 1873–4
to $500,000, being $750,000 in 1875.   For the next
four years it averaged about $2,000,000.   For 1880
the amount is given as $5,560,000; for 1881 it was
$8,360,000; and for 1882 over $8,500,000.   In 1883–4
the production fell off to about $6,000,000, and to a
still less figure probably in 1886.   Down to the end
of the Apache war the amount of gold largely exceeded that of silver, but later was only about one
sixth, though exceeding $1,000,000 in 1881–2.[3]

The most notable general characteristics of the Arizona lodes would seem to be the great extent of mineral-bearing lands, the extremely varied and complicated nature of the deposits, and their extraordinary
richness, especially on and near the surface.   No
description even en résumé is possible within my
limits.   Arizona resembles a kind of laboratory where
nature has tried experiments preliminary to a general
distribution of minerals in the Pacific states.   The
experienced miner from abroad is puzzled by the array

[3] For statistics, besides the reports of Browne and Raymond already cited,
see Horatio C. Burchard's *Report of the Director of the Mint upon the Statistics
of the production of the precious metals in the United States* (for 1880 et seq.),
Wash., 1881 et seq.   For 1878-9-81, between the reports of Raymond and
Burchard, the condition of the mines was treated in reports of the governor.
U. S. Govt Doc., 45th cong. 3d. sess., H. Ex. Doc., ix., pt 5, p. 1089–90; 40th
cong. 2d sess., H. Ex. Doc., x., pt 5, p. 390–6; 47th cong. 1st sess., H. Ex.
Doc., x. 929–32 (report of Patrick Hamilton); *Id.*, xi., pt 5, p. 354, pl.
xlviii.-ix. (King's Geol. Report); also mint statistics in the annual reports of
the sec. treasury.   Alex. Delmar's *History of the Precious Metals from the
earliest times to the present*, Lond., 1880, contains, p. 168, a table of production
for Ariz. in 1869–78, based on the *U. S. Monetary Commission, Report*, 1876,
or on the estimates of Valentine, supt of Wells, Fargo, & Co.'s express. See
also 9th and 10th *U. S. Census Reports*, the former for 1870 containing nothing
of any value.   The Arizona newspapers contain some valuable estimates.
Among the states and territories in 1880 Ariz. ranked in the production of
gold 9, silver 5, total 7; or in prod. per sq. mile 8, per capita 4.   In '81 there
were 56 mills running, with 590 stamps, in 75 districts; 123 districts in 1882.
Down to 1876 the no. of mines recorded was 11,605. *Hinton.* About '630 are
named in the index of Burchard's report of 1883.   Hinton gives for 1877–8
long lists of mines for the different counties.   As an instance of varying estimates may be noted those of 1875.   That of Wells, Fargo, & Co. is $109,093;
that of Surv.-gen. Wasson $1,500,000; a newspaper estimate $2,000,000; and
that of Raymond $750,000.   Clarence King and the census give the yield of
1880 as $2,399,211 in bullion, but the assay value as $4,723,638.   As Burchard's figures are $5,566,601, this suggests uncertainty as to what is meant
by the figures for other years.

of new combinations and strange geologic conditions, though he generally finds, sooner or later, all that he has known in other states. To a greater extent than in other regions, rich veins near the surface have been worked on a small scale, but profitably, by individuals with limited capital; but the prospects for deep mining in the future are understood to be encouraging on the whole. The natural facilities for mining, in the supply of wood and water—except in a few sections, and for placer mines—and especially in climate for continuous working, are excellent in comparison with those of other states; while agricultural resources more than suffice for the support of a dense mining population. Of the whole area, about 72,000,000 acres, nearly one half is described as mineral-bearing. Ores producing from $1,000 to $20,000 per ton in gold and silver have been of frequent occurrence; but here, as elsewhere, such are not the deposits that promise the greatest permanent results. Nowhere has more money been wasted in blundering mismanagement; and even rascality in certain directions has not been wanting; yet Arizona has not been famous as the field of stock-board swindles; and her record has been for the most part one of dividends rather than assessments.

In the north-eastern section of the territory, the region tributary to the Colorado, above the big bend, an area of about 40,000 square miles out of the entire 100,000, including northern Mojave, about three fourths of Yavapai, and nearly all of Apache counties, no rich deposits of the precious metals have been found; yet the extreme north-east, beyond the Colorado Chiquito, with the region of Fort Defiance and the Moqui towns as a centre, contains immense coal-fields that can hardly fail to assume great importance in time.[4]   All the rest of the territory, except a broad

---

[4] On these Apache co. coal-beds, see *Hinton's Hand-book*, 85-7; *Hamilton's Resources*, 243-5; and *Ariz., Hist.* (E. & Co.), 204-5. The coal is bituminous, and said to be of good quality, having been tested by use on the A. & P. R. R., and considerable quantities shipped to Cal. Petroleum, according to Hamilton, has been found near the coal-fields, which extend into Utah and N. Mex.,

tract of the Gila valley, and adjoining deserts, is dotted with mines; but the great silver and gold belt may be described as a tract from 60 to 70 miles wide, and 400 miles long, adjoining the non-metallic region above described on the south-west, extending from the Colorado, just below the big bend, south-eastward to Gila county, and thence south to the Mexican boundary. The principal mines of this belt may be noticed briefly in four groups.

The first group in the north-west includes the mines of Mojave county explored to some extent from 1858, and worked in considerable numbers from 1863, though operations were much interrupted in 1866–70 by Hualapai hostilities. The number of claims recorded down to 1882 was about 2,700. All the mountain ranges are rich in minerals, promising discoveries have been made each year, and the county has often seemed on the verge of great developments, which from one cause or another—mainly the great cost of transportation preventing the working of ores producing less than $500 per ton—have never come. The completion of the railroad in 1883, however, seems to have removed the worst of Mojave's disadvantages.[5]

being perhaps second in extent only to those of Pennsylvania. In the *Los Angeles Star* of Feb. 6, 1864, and *News* of Feb. 5th, is noted the discovery of valuable coal-beds by Tyson, in the La Paz region. Five lodes were explored and named, and fine specimens sent to Los Angeles and S. Francisco, one of the papers pronouncing the coal anthracite; but I find nothing more about this Yuma co. coal. In his message of 1871, the gov. mentions the discovery of extensive coal deposits in the White Mts, near C. Thomas; and in 1879 he recommends a survey of the coal-fields as most important in connection with R. R. developments. Coal discoveries on the S. Pedro and Arivaipa are occasionally mentioned from 1878, some of the coal being described by Hinton and the newspapers as anthracite. The deposits discovered in 1881, on Deer Creek, Pinal co., on the S. Cárlos reservation, have been mentioned in the preceding chapter. In 1885 the secretary of the interior recommended the segregation of these lands, and by fair means or foul the coal will doubtless be made available.

[5] The product of the Mojave mines in 1880–3 is given as, gold $20,000, $25,000, $15,000, and $20,000; silver, $210,000, $75,000, $50,000, and $150,000. Hinton gives the product in 1887 as $200,000 per month. Hamilton, 1884, says that 3,000 tons of silver ore are shipped at Kingston on the R. R. each month. In 1864-7, the Eldorado Cañon mines in the extreme north are much talked of in the newspapers. The Cerbat, or Hualapai, district in the region around Mineral Park, with the country eastward to Hackberry in the Maynard district, was the chief silver-producing district before 1875. The Moss gold mine near Hardyville was one of the earliest discoveries, and with

Off the main belt, and not included in the four groups, are the Yuma county mines of gold, silver, lead, and copper. The gold placers of the Gila and Colorado, which caused great excitement in 1858–64, and have been worked with some profit ever since, have been noticed elsewhere. The silver lodes near the junction of the two rivers, though the ores are of low grade, have had the advantage of comparatively cheap river transportation, are near the railroad, and in recent years are attracting renewed attention.

The second group, hardly separated from the first, includes the mines of southern Yavapai and northern Maricopa, in the region south of Prescott, on the head-waters of the Hassayampa and Agua Frio. These mines were discovered during the placer 'rush' of 1863–4, and have been the chief gold-producers of Arizona. Down to 1876 there had been recorded 7,300 mines. Gold was found everywhere; the placers yielded richly for years, and are still worked with profit in wet seasons; immensely rich gold veins were worked near the surface; but with increasing depth the lodes became chiefly silver-bearing. Apache raids, and ores that proved refractory under the rude process in vogue, were the earlier obstacles to perfect success; and in

its great body of free-milling gold-bearing ore was for years regarded as the coming bonanza. Much money was spent on mills, tunnels, etc.; and for final failure or abandonment no other reason is assigned than unwise management. The McCracken and Signal silver mines in the south were discovered in 1874, and became the largest bullion producers, the total yield being over $1,000,000, and the ore running from $60 to $600 per ton in silver and lead. The mills were at Greenwood and Virginia. But work on these mines was suspended about 1880.

Southward across the Bill Williams River in Yuma co. are the Planet copper mines, and others, which have since 1863 sent over 8,000 tons of ore, yielding 20 to 60 per cent of copper, to S. Francisco. Wood and water are very scarce in this district. The Castle Dome mines in the south were discovered in 1863 and supposed to be immensely rich, but were abandoned when it was learned that the ore was chiefly lead. Large quantities of lead were subsequently shipped to S. F.; and from 1869–70 the mines were profitably worked. The ore yields 50 to 70 per cent of lead, and $23 to $190 per ton of silver, the cost of working being $40 and of freight $28. Before 1881 the district had produced $2,000,000. The Silver district, just north of Castle Dome, has been very prominent in late years, and there are many other somewhat prosperous districts. The bullion product of Yuma co. in 1874 is given, as gold $50,000, silver and copper $138,500; 1880, about $60,000; 1881, gold $30,000, silver $105,000; 1882, gold $20,000, silver 250,000; 1883, gold $30,000, silver $75,000.

later years remoteness from the railroad has been a serious drawback, soon to be remedied now. The leading districts are Weaver, Hassayampa, Lynx Creek, Turkey Creek, Humbug, Peck, and Martinez or Date Creek. But the most famous mine of all was the Vulture in Maricopa county, discovered in 1863 by Henry Wickenburg—for whom the town near by was named —and in the next ten years producing over $3,000,000 in gold, though the ore had to be hauled some 15 miles to mills on the Hassayampa. Large quantities of low-grade ore were left when work was suspended; and from 1879, with water brought in iron pipes for an 80-stamp mill, the mine started on a new career of prosperity.[6]

Still farther south-east, across the Verde, in Gila and Pinal counties, between the Gila and Salt rivers, is the third group of the belt; the leading districts being Pioneer and Globe, and the veins being remarkable for their variety and richness in silver, gold, and copper. Development began in 1875 with the discovery of the famous Silver King, and the equally

[6] The gold product of Yavapai in 1873 is put at $103,600; 1880, gold $5,000, silver $265,000; 1881, gold $50,000, silver $450,000; 1882, gold $30,000, silver $400,000; 1883, gold $25,000, silver $800,000. Product of Maricopa, 1880, gold $120,000, silver $280,000; 1881, gold $240,000, silver $75,000; 1882, gold $250,000, silver $75,000; 1883, gold $330,000, silver $25,000. An average assay from 10 mines in the Humbug dist was over $1,000 per ton. Lynx or Walker Creek was perhaps the richest stream in Ariz., yielding over $1,000,000 from gravel. The ores were base, and mills stopped running in 1870. Tiptop from small rich veins produced $2,000,000, giving fortunes, as Hamilton observes, to many small chloriders. Turkey Creek district, without surface indications, gave almost pure silver at a slight depth, sometimes in 'chunks' worth $14 a pound. Here the Goodwin mine was the oldest, and the Hidden Treasure, Wonder, and Pine Spring have been prominent in late years. Rich Hill, in Weaver dist, yielded $500,000 in nuggets from an acre on the summit 4,000 ft high, and $500,000 more from gulches on its sides. The Peck lode produced in 1875-8 $1,200,000, some ore running from $10,000 to $17,000 per ton; depth, 312 ft. In 1879-82 work was suspended through legal complications, but has since been resumed. The Vulture produced $254,110 in 1868, the ore yielding $24 per ton. In 1870 the cost is given as $4.12 for mining, $8 for freight, and $2.81 for milling. In 1881 the product was $240,000, but involving, acc. to Burchard, a loss, the cost being $2.81 and yield $2.69 per ton; Hamilton puts the cost at $2.50, and yield at $4 to $6. The Tiger, adjoining the Vulture, also produced a large amount of gold; and there are several other districts, including the Myers dist, south of the Gila, with the Gunsight and Burro Burro mines. In late years Maricopa, in the production of gold, is second only to Cochise.

wonderful lodes at Richmond Basin and McMillan-ville. The Silver King lode differs from any other known, being a circular chimney of ore, with thousands of veins centring in it. The mine has reached a depth of over 800 feet, and though the ores are refractory, the production has been over $6,000,000 in silver, and nearly $2,000,000 have been paid in dividends. The Mack Morris mine, in Richmond Basin, and the Stonewall Jackson, at McMillanville, are among the best of other mines, but the mountains in all this region abound in rich lodes, and the prospects are most encouraging, though railroad facilities are sadly needed. The product of this Gila and Pinal group in 1884, when work at Tombstone was partially suspended, is said to have been greater than that of any other in the territory.[7]

Southward across the Gila, and past the Casa Grande and Arivaipa, or Defreese, districts, we find the fourth and final group in Pima and Cochise counties, mainly in the ranges bordering on the Santa Cruz and San Pedro valleys. This was the exclusive field of all Spanish and Mexican mining down to 1854, and but for the lower Gila placers, of all American operations down to 1861. From that date to 1873-4 the mines were for the most part abandoned, but in later years have been worked in great numbers with constantly increasing profits, producing more bullion than all others in Arizona combined. The Tombstone mines, the most productive of all, having yielded about $30,000,000, were discovered in 1878 by Ed.

[7] Product of Pinal, 1880, $1,404,380; 1881, gold $25,000, silver $1,250,000; 1882, gold $20,000, silver $900,000; 1883, gold $20,000, silver $700,000. Product of Gila, 1882, gold $50,000, silver $570,000; 1883, gold $15,000, silver $120,000. The Silver King was first discovered by Stoneman's soldiers in 1871, and on their reports rediscovered by four farmers in 1875; 1,500 lbs., broken off the croppings as a sample, were sold for $800. Ore assays, acc. to Hinton, $1,000 to $20,000 per ton. Product in 1880, $505,642; in 1883, $592,504. Dividends to Jan. 1884, $1,309,000; depth, 814 ft. In the Globe dist, says Hinton, 'such a mine as the Comstock would not be looked at'! Nine tons from the Stonewall sent to S. F. yielded $200,000 in silver, acc. to Hamilton. The Mack Morris, to 1881, yielded $300,000. The Silver Nugget is another rich mine. The Golden Eagle is the chief gold mine of Globe dist. South of the Gila is the Casa Grande dist, the Vekol being the chief silver mine, and not far off the Copperosity, a copper mine.

Schieffelin, and named from the dismal forebodings of his friends on his departure from Fort Huachuca. The first stamps began to run in 1879, and from 1880 bullion in large quantities was produced. The veins are larger than elsewhere, and the ore is easily worked, yielding, in one of the principal mines, $73 in silver and $4 in gold per ton on an average. There are over 3,000 locations in the district, the most famous mines or companies being the Contention, Grand Central, and Tombstone. The depth reached is over 750 feet, and extensive pumping machinery for working below the water level was completed in 1883. Little doubt is entertained respecting the future productiveness of the lodes at greater depths. The Bisbee copper mines of Cochise county produced, in 1881, over $3,000,000; and other prominent districts of the county are the California, Turquoise, and Swisshelm. The Quijotoa silver mines of Papaguería, Pima county, were discovered by Alexander McKay in 1883, and passing into the hands of the great 'bonanza firm' of California, were confidently expected to become the richest in all Arizona. Respecting the results of extensive workings, not much is definitely known; but the general impression is, that Quijotoa has proved a complete failure, though many still believe that vast treasures will be uncovered when silver shall be restored to its legitimate value, or when the public shall be deemed ripe for plunder by a stock 'boom.' Other districts in Pima county, as the Empire, Arivaca, Harshaw or Patagonia. Silver Belt, Oro Blanco, and Aztec, rival the famous lodes discovered by Schieffelin.[8]

---

[8] Edward Schieffelin, a Pennsylvanian by birth, came with his family to Cal. in 1857, being then only 10 years of age. At 17 we find him working a mining claim in Jackson, Or. Thenceforth he engaged in sundry occupations, principally mining and prospecting, until 1878, almost by accident, he discovered the Tombstone district. In 1880 he disposed of his interest and settled at Los Angeles, removing in 1884 to Alameda, where he has since resided, though making occasional trips for pleasure, health, or profit from Arizona northward to Alaska.

Product of Pima co. in 1880. $3,012,222; 1881, gold $15,000, silver $750,000; 1882, gold $70,000, silver $150,000; 1883, gold, $85,000, silver $250,000. Product of Cochise co., 1881, gold $645,000, silver, $4,065,000;

Arizona is almost as famous for its copper mines as for its deposits of silver and gold. The ores are widely distributed and of high grade, often yielding from 60 to 80 per cent of metal. Production on a large scale began in 1881, from which date the total product per year was about six, seventeen, twenty-five, and perhaps thirty-five million pounds in 1884. Leading mines, or groups, are the Planet, Centennial, and Copper King of Bill Williams River in northern Yuma; the United Verde Company's mines in the Black Hills of Yavapai; the Globe district lodes of Gila; the old Ajo mines in western Pima; and the Copper Queen and others of Bisbee in southern Cochise. But at the head of all stand the wonderful copper deposits near Clifton in Graham county, where rich ore is quarried rather than mined, and whence a railroad has been built to carry the product to the main line of the Southern Pacific.[9]

1882, gold $600,000, silver $5,200,000; 1883, gold $410,000, silver $3,050,000. Product of Graham co., 1882, gold $10,000, silver $5,000; 1883, gold $15,000, silver $30,000. The Tombstone mills were at first on the S. Pedro; but later some of them at the mines, supplied with water from the mines and by pipes from the Dragoon and Huachuca Mts, 8 and 25 miles away. The ores are said to yield 90 per cent of assay value by stamping process. The Contention produced $1,676,000 in 1882; and down to May 1883, with a depth of 600 ft, had produced $5,000,000 and paid $2,475,000 in dividends. The cost of working is about one third that of the Comstock ores. The pumps cost $350,000. The Grand Central in 1883 had reached a depth of 750 feet and produced $3,000,000. The Tombstone, including 11 mines, down to 1883 had produced $2,870,000, and paid in dividends $1,650,000. The Bronkow mine in this region was discovered as early as 1858, and relocated in 1880. A gold mine at Apache Pass is mentioned by the gov. in 1869 as just starting with a 10-stamp mill and good prospects; but the superintendent, Stone, was killed by Apaches in Oct. The Empire district, with the Total Wreck as the principal mine, is described in 1882 as having $4,000,000 in sight and a 20-stamp mill nearly ready. In 1883 the mill in a run of 5 months had produced $450,000; depth, 360 ft.; assay value, $60 per ton. The Arivaca dist is described by Hamilton as not very prosperous on account of bad management; but the Cerro Colorado mine had produced $2,000,000. The Hermosa is the principal mine of the Harshaw dist, producing $700,000, but the mill being idle in 1883-4. The famous Mowry mine is not successful in late years. Hinton says that 975 mines were recorded in Pima co. down to 1876.

[9] The copper product in 1883 was worth about $4,000,000. Twenty furnaces were running, with a capacity of 1,000 tons per day. Leading items of this year's production are given by Elliott & Co. as follows: Arizona Co. (Clifton), 4,106,000 lbs.; Detroit Co. (Clifton), 4,035,000; Copper Queen (Bisbee), 7,950,000; Old Dominion (Globe), 4,590,000; Un. Verde Co. (Yavapai), 1,763,000. Many new comp. to begin operations in 1884, with good prospects. Discov. of copper in 1863. S. F. Alta, Sept. 2, 1874. The Ajo mines, though rich, were abandoned from 1870, on account of expensive freight

In 1872 the alleged discovery of diamond-fields in Arizona created a great excitement throughout the nation. Arnold and Slack were the discoverers; splendid diamonds and rubies were exhibited in New York and San Francisco; Harpending, Lent, Roberts, Dodge, and other capitalists became sponsors for the great find; Henry Janin visited the fields as an expert, reporting them rich in diamonds; a company with a capital of ten millions was formed, with such men as Latham, Selby, Ralston, Sloss, Barlow, and General McClellan as directors; a title to 3,000 acres was obtained; large sums were paid for interests in the scheme; and all was made ready, not only to work the claim, but to offer the stock to a credulous and excited public. Meanwhile the papers were full of the matter, though there was less excitement in Arizona than elsewhere; a dozen parties visited the fields, some connected with the Harpending Company, and others not; and most of them, finding the spot without difficulty, brought back a variety of beautiful stones. All agreed that the place was in the region of Fort Defiance, some locating it across the line in New Mexico, but most in the extreme north of Apache county, near the junction of the Chelly and San Juan, where the inscription Diamond Fields is to be seen on modern maps. Arnold, however, said the spot was south of the Moqui towns near the Colorado Chiquito.

through a waterless desert. Work was resumed after 1880. The Globe mines, down to 1883, yielded 12,000 tons, and in 1883-4, 2,508 tons of 98 per cent bullion. The Planet mine sent 6,000 tons of 20 to 60 per cent ore to S. Francisco, work beginning in 1863. The United Verde, in a run of 230 days, produced 2,000 tons, besides 225,000 oz. of silver, paying $97,500 in dividends. The Bisbee mines were discov. in 1875-6. The Copper Queen, located in 1878, and worked from 1880 at a depth of 300 ft, had an ore body 150 by 80 ft, and sold for $1,250,000. It produced in 1881-4 $3,368,000, and paid $1,225,000 in dividends. Average yield of ore 13.5 per cent; average yield of bullion 98 per cent. Down to April 1, 1885, acc. to the statement of Supt Williams, the Copper Queen has produced 15,929 tons of black copper, worth $5,000,000. The leading mines of the Clifton group are the Longfellow, Coronado, Metcalf, and Queen. They were discovered in 1871, and were somewhat profitable, when the copper, costing 5 cents per lb., was shipped to Baltimore at a cost of 6 cents. The R. R. to Lordsbury, N. Mex., was completed in 1883. The mines have produced 20,000,000 lbs. of copper down to 1882, and are mainly owned by a Scotch company.

Finally, Clarence King, United States geologist, visited the fields, and discovered that the claim had been artfully 'salted' with rough diamonds from Africa, Brazil, and other parts of the world. Fortunately, the exposure came in time to prevent the swindling of the general public. Of the capitalists involved, who were victims and who culprits was never exactly known. The point of the whole matter, however, lies in the fact that, while in all that was written, it was the Arizona diamond-fields that were described, and the 'Arizona diamond swindle' that was denounced, not only were there no diamonds in Arizona, but the salted claim was in north-western Colorado, hundreds of miles from the Arizona line![10]

In closing what I have to say of mining industries in Arizona, it is proper to acknowledge my indebtedness to the works of Hinton, Elliott, and Hamilton, who have treated the subject more minutely than I have had space to do. And not only on the subject of mining, but on all others pertaining to the history of late years, and to the country's resources and condition, do these works deserve much praise, comparing very favorably with such works of the better class

---

[10] The S. F. papers of 1872 are full of this matter; and a good collection of clippings is found in *Hayes' Scraps, Ariz.*, iv. 258–90. Arnold's version first appeared in the *Laramie Sentinel* in Aug. 1872. The gov., in his message of 1873, expresses satisfaction that the Arizona press and people, much as they desired immigration, had not encouraged the diamond excitement. *Ariz., Jour.*, 1873, p. 38. And this was true as a rule; yet there was much searching for precious stones in different parts of the territory; and even in Yuma Co., near Arizona City, the finding of diamonds—one of them by a judge—was reported. A party from Prescott claimed to have found the Harpending co.'s notices posted in the northern part of Apache co., and it is possible that such notices were posted there with intent to mislead treasure-seekers. Obviously, it was desirable to conceal the real locality of the 'salted' grounds, as the diamond 'salt' cost many thousands of dollars in London; the Ariz. field was too distant for the safety of such operations; but it was well fitted for the false location, because it abounded in a variety of pretty stones, crystallized quartz, petrifactions, garnets of slight value, etc. Even after the exposure of the fraud, one Stanton seems to have made an effort to renew the Arizona excitement by exhibiting a fine collection of alleged rubies, emeralds, etc. The diamond company was called the S. F. & N. Y. Mining and Commercial Co.; additional directors being A. Gansl, Wm F. Babcock, Maurice Dore, and W. M. Lent, with D. D. Colton as manager. It is probable that most of the directors were innocent victims; that there may have been one or two such among the original capitalists—Harpending, Roberts, Lent, Dodge, etc.; and that Arnold and Slack were willing tools of the swindlers.

relating to other parts of the country. Of the three, Hinton's work is the earliest, and on many points is followed by the others; Elliott's folio is the largest, and has perhaps the greatest percentage of defects, resulting mainly from its class rather than from any fault of its editors; and Hamilton's book is the most compact and readable presentment of the subject. On aboriginal, Spanish, and Mexican annals these works, as I have already had occasion to point out, are very faulty, the author who has least to say being the least inaccurate; but their defects in this respect were to a large extent unavoidable, since the writers had no access to the veritable sources.[11]

[11] *The Hand-book to Arizona: its resources, history, towns, mines, ruins, and scenery. Amply illustrated. Accompanied with a new map of the territory. By Richard J. Hinton.* S. F., 1878, 12mo, 431, c. p. The author was a prominent journalist of S. Francisco, who had spent some time in Arizona. The book is an excellent one of its class. *History of Arizona Territory, showing its resources and advantages; with illustrations descriptive of its scenery, residences, farms, mines, mills, hotels, business houses, schools, churches, etc., from original drawings. Wallace W. Elliott & Co., publishers.* S. F., 1884, fol., 323 p. The writers or editors are not named; but it is stated that 'we visited every county, village, and mining camp of importance, and by personal examination were enabled to give statements about all localities in Arizona, which we think are substantially correct.' These pictorial subscription books of the 'county-history' variety, notwithstanding their peculiar blending of literature and business, contain a good deal of useful information, and deserve in some respects a better repute than they enjoy. *The Resources of Arizona. Its mineral, farming, grazing and timber lands; its history, climate, productions, civil and military government, prehistoric ruins, early missionaries, Indian tribes, pioneer days, etc. Third edition, revised and enlarged, with a new map and illustrations. By Patrick Hamilton.* S. F., 1884, 12mo, 414 p. I have also the ed. of Prescott,, 1881, 8vo, 120 p. This work was originally a report embodied in that of the gov. on the condition of the country. The author has been long a resident of Ariz., and is an intelligent, observant man, enthusiastic in admiration of his territory. Hiram C. Hodge's *Arizona as it is; or, The Coming Country, compiled from notes of travel during the years 1874, 1875, and 1876.* N. Y., 1877, 12mo, 273 p.; and E. Conklin's *Picturesque Arizona. Being the result of travels and observations in Arizona during the fall and winter of 1877.* N. Y., 1878, 12mo, 380 p., illust.—are pleasing and useful little works, by travelling newspaper men, sufficiently described by their titles, the former being much the more valuable of the two.

On mining topics, other references—besides the *Hayes' Scrap-books, Ariz.*, passim, and files of Cal. and Ariz. newspapers—are as follows: *Silliman's Journal*, xxxvi. 152; xl. 388; xli. 289; *Ind. Aff. Reports* and *Land Office Reports*, 1864 et seq., passim; *Mowry's Arizona; The Miner*, i., passim; *Wheeler's Surveys; Pacific Coast Directory*, 1871–3; *Anderson's Silver Country*, 46–7, 69–75; *Hoyt's Arizona*, MS., 17–26, 31–4; *The Mining Review*, 1876 et seq.; *The Californian*, July 1881, p. 50–3; *Mining Industry*, ii. 22; *Disturnell's Business Directory*, 1881, p. 23–70; *Atlantic & Pac. R. R. Co. Prospectus; Silver King Min. Co. Report*, 1880; *Hall's Great West*, 74–88; *Rand, McNally, & Co.'s Overl. Guide*, 135–61; and especially Wm R. Balch's *Mines, Miners, and Mining Interests of the United States*, Phil., 1882, fol., 1191 p., illust.

HIST. ARIZ. AND N. MEX. 38

Several tribes of aborigines in Arizona were found by the Spaniards in the sixteenth century, supporting themselves wholly or in part by tilling the soil. These tribes occupied but a limited area, but widely scattered groups of ruins prove that in earlier centuries all the principal valleys were inhabited by a numerous people who could have lived only by agriculture; and indeed, in many districts clear traces of their irrigating canals are still to be seen. From the eighteenth century, the Spaniards irrigated and tilled small tracts in the Santa Cruz valley, producing such grain, vegetables, and fruits as were required for home consumption; and they also introduced the new industry of stock-raising. During the period of peace with the Apaches in 1790–1815, many flourishing farms and haciendas were established in the southern region; and meanwhile the Indians, from the southern Pápagos and Pimas to the Moquis of the north, including some bands of the Apaches, continued to depend to greater or less extent on their crops. Some of the tribes raised cattle and sheep on a small scale after the Spaniards came; other tribes preferred to steal their livestock.

To Americans in the earliest years, Arizona seemed, except a small portion of the later acquired Gadsden purchase, an utterly barren and worthless waste of sandy deserts and rocky mountains, probably rich in minerals, but of no agricultural value whatever. There was no thought of seeking farms in Arizona; but having come there in search of silver and gold, they began to till the soil in spots to supply their necessities, and found it wonderfully productive wherever water could be obtained. Progress has been constant if not very rapid from the first; the press never tired of exalting the country's advantages in soil and climate; the governor and legislature often called attention to the subject; the Mormons came in as agricultural immigrants; and finally, about 100,000 acres have been brought under cultivation with the most encouraging results. The climate, agreeable in winter and in the mountains, the mean temperature at Prescott ranging from 30° in January to 72° in July, though disagreeably hot in the lower valleys and in summer, frequently over 100° from May to September at Phœnix and Tucson, and over 115° for the same period at Yuma, is remarkably healthful, and altogether favorable to farming operations. The soil, a sandy loam with rich adobe on the banks of streams, is easily worked; and its strength and recuperative power are shown by the undiminished yield in spots cultivated by the Indians for centuries. All the cereals, vegetables, and fruits of temperate and semi-tropic climes are successfully produced; cotton has always been raised in small quantities; in recent years the culture of oranges, grapes, and olives has passed far beyond the stage of experiment; and sugar-cane is produced in considerable quantities for the manufacture of syrup.

Still the area of farming lands, as limited by the supply of water for irrigation, without which practically nothing can be produced, does not probably exceed 2,000,000 acres out of a total of 72,000,000; though in the distant future, with constant cultivation lessening the amount of water required, with the planting of trees, with artesian wells and other devices for irrigation, a surprising encroachment on what is still regarded as a desert may be expected. In the Colorado bottoms of Yuma and Mojave counties is a broad tract of land that in time, with the construction of expensive reclamation works on a large scale, bids fair to produce large quantities of sugar, rice, tobacco, cotton, and other crops. The largest body of available land, however, is found in the Gila and Salt River valleys of Maricopa and Pinal counties, about Phœnix and Florence as centres. Here also have been made the greatest improvements, though only about 50,000 of the 500,000 acres have been brought under cultivation. A dozen canals have been constructed to take water from the rivers, and their number and extent are being constantly increased. Here we have already a prosperous agricultural community, which must grow rapidly.   In Pima county, the field of early Spanish and Mexican cultivation, the lands lie chiefly in the Santa Cruz, Sonoita, and Arivaca valleys.   Cochise has a limited but fertile area in the San Pedro, Sulphur Spring, and San Simon valleys.   Pueblo Viejo valley in Graham has some 40,000 acres of excellent land in a body.   Yavapai's largest body is on the Rio Verde, but here many small tracts are cultivated without irrigation.   Apache has a fertile tract of 13,000 acres on the Colorado Chiquito, nearly all taken up by the Mormons.   Other agricultural tracts are scattered in small pieces.

A large portion of the agricultural area is still government land, and open to settlement; though part of it in the south was burdened down to 1885 by a doubtful railroad title to the alternate sections, other parts are included in Indian reservations, and still others held in grants not yet confirmed.   Wild lands in private ownership are sold at five to ten dollars per acre, and improved lands at $15 to $40, prices that are rapidly increasing.   Limited as they are in extent, it will be seen that Arizona's lands, if the water supply is properly utilized, are amply sufficient for the requirements of a population ten or twenty times that of the present.   A country of mining camps, such as Arizona promises to be for many years, affords the best possible market for small farmers.   In the export of agricultural products—pending wide-spread reclamation of the Colorado bottoms—not much can be expected from grain and the other ordinary crops; but fruits ripen nearly a month earlier than in California, and if the industry of fruit-shipping in the latter state proves as successful as it promises, there is no apparent reason why Arizona should not receive a rich share of the profits.   The country also is admirably fitted for the production and curing of raisins; and the export of olive-oil may yet prove profitable.[12]

[12] Agric. statistics from the 10th U. S. census, showing increase from 1870 to 1780, and supplemented in some items by figures from the U. S. agric. rept of 1882, are as follows: no. of farms 172–767; acres 21,807–135,573,

Stock-raising was for many years unprofitable, on account of Apache hostilities; but the country's natural advantages for this industry have long been known, and since 1875 flocks and herds have increased rapidly. Over half of Arizona's area, or nearly 40,000,000 acres, is available for grazing lands of a superior quality, the native gramma, bunch, and mezquite grasses affording an abundance of the most nutritious food, the climate being peculiarly favorable, both to the healthful development and inexpensive care of animals, and their various diseases being as

acres improved 14,585-56,071, value $161,340-$1,127,946; persons engaged in agric. 1,285-3,435; product of barley 55,077-239,051-327,500 bush.; wheat 27,052-136,427-220,000 bush.; corn 32,041-34,746-57,000 bush.; oats 25-504 bush.; hay 109-5,606-12,500 tons; tobacco 100-600 lbs.; potatoes 575-26,249-72,750 bush.; sweet potatoes 16-5,300 bush. The acreage and value in 1882 was, corn 2,709, $62,700; wheat 15,500, $308,000; barley 17,366, $311,125; potatoes 970, $80,025; hay 12,000, $231,250; total 48,515, $993,100. Hamilton's statement of acres cultivated in 1883 is, Maricopa 35,000, Apache 13,000, Pinal 7,000, Graham 7,000, Yavapai 6,500, Cochise 4,000, Pima 3,000, Gila 1,500, Yuma 1,500, Mojave 1,000, total 79,500, besides about 5,000 by Indians. His estimates of lands that might be cultivated seem to foot up less than 1,000,000 acres. Hinton puts the area irrigable by surface water at 2,800,000 acres, and thinks there are 10,000,000 or more to be reclaimed for agric. by artesian wells. Farming by white men in Maricopa dates from 1868; 32,000,000 lbs. of grain produced in 1883, 25 bush. per acre; 8 tons of alfalfa per acre in 4 crops; 4 irrigations on an average; planting Nov. to March, harvest June to July; average profit per acre $8.50; 500 acres with 50,000 fruit-trees, chiefly peaches; 400,000 vines. The Arizona Canal on Salt River will be 40 miles long, and reclaim 100,000 acres, costing $500,000, and furnishing also a fine water-power. Several canals projected near Gila Bend. Pinal co. in 1883 produced 450,000 lbs. of grain, two crops per year being raised. In Yavapai corn is the chief crop, which does not flourish so well in the south. Some of the best land in Pima co., including 10,000 acres at Arivaca, is held under Spanish grants. In Cochise co. water is very near the surface, and some flowing wells have been found. In Mojave co. 1,000 acres are cultiv. in Big Sandy valley. Hemp is cultivated on the Colorado Chiquito, the old Rio del Lino. In 1883 an act was passed to encourage the cultivation of cotton. *Ariz., Laws,* 149. The gov. gives attention to agric. in his biennial messages. *Ariz., Jour.,* 1864 et seq. In 1875 he complains of a surplus product after all demand, has been supplied. See also *Land Office Reports,* 1864 et seq.; *Agric Reports,* 1869 et seq.; *Hamilton's Resources,* 81-90, 307-46, 361-70; *Hinton's Hand-book,* 168-243, passim, 273-307, appen. 49; *Wheeler's Surveys,* iii. 573-4, 583-603; *Id., Reports,* 1875, p. 121-9; *Id.,* 1876, p. 42-6; *Porter's The West, Census of 1880,* p. 460; *Hodge's Arizona,* 42-56; *Conklin's Pict. Ariz.,* 116-28, 179-80; *Ariz., Hist.* (E. & Co.), 127-38, 270-4; *Goddard's Where to Immigrate,* 134-5; *Beadle's Western Wilds,* 123-6; *Roberts' With the Invader,* 107-9.

On irrigation, especially the efforts to encourage the sinking of artesian wells, for which the legislature offers premiums, see *Ariz., Acts,* 1868, p. 60; 1873, p. 61, 176-7; 1875, p. 21; *Id., Jour.,* 1873, p. 42-3; 1875, p. 36; *Id., Comp. Laws,* 501-4; *U. S. Gov't Doc.,* 43d cong. 1st sess., H. Miscel. Doc. 57; *Hinton's Hand-book,* 68-9; *Ariz., Hist.* (E. & Co.), 32, 282-4.

yet for the most part unknown. Considerable progress has already been made in the introduction of improved breeds of cattle, sheep, and horses. The best ranges, with natural water supply, are already occupied, but by means of an artesian supply, for which the conditions are favorable, and of surface wells and windmills, nearly the whole extent of grazing land may be utilized; and it is believed that in most sections agricultural operations can never encroach greatly on the ranges. As in all countries where alfalfa flourishes, the fattening of cattle and hogs on the valley farms also promises to become profitable. Apparently the exportation of meat and wool must increase rapidly, becoming, after—perhaps eventually before—mining, the territory's leading industry.[13]

A surveyor-general for Arizona was appointed in 1863, and made a report on the country's resources; but in 1864 the territory was attached to the New Mexico land district, whose surveyor-general made a tour with some estimates and suggestions, selecting an initial point on the Gila opposite the mouth of Salt River, finally adopted as fixing the base line and meridian of Arizona surveys. In 1867 a land-office was created at Prescott, but the territory was attached to

[13] The 10th U. S. census gives the increase of live-stock in 1870–80 as follows: value $143,996–$1,167,989, cattle 3,607–34,843, sheep 803–76,524, horses 335–6,798, mules and asses 401–891, oxen 567–964, milk-cows 938–9,156, swine 720–3,819, product of wool 679–313,698 lbs., butter 800–61,817 lbs., cheese 14,500–18,360 lbs. Hamilton's statistics for 1883 are as follows: Yavapai co., cattle 75,000, horses 6,000, mules 2,000, swine 1,000, sheep 50,000; Pima, c. 75,000, h. 6,000, m. 2,000, sw. 1,100, sh. 5,000; Cochise, c. 70,000, h. 4,000, m. 3,000, sw. 500, sh. 5,000; Apache, c. 43,000, h. 3,000, m. 1,500, sw. ——, sh. 600,000; Graham, c. 20,000, h. 4,000, m. 1,000, sw. 500, sh. 10,000; Pinal, c. 25,000, h. 2,000, m. 1,000, sw. 600, sh. 3,500; Gila, c. 15,000, h. 1,000, m. 800, sw. 300, sh. 3,000; Maricopa, c. 8,000, h. 5,000, m. 1,500, sw. 7,000, sh. 1,500; Mojave, c. 10,000, h. 1,000, m. 500, sw. 200, sh. 2,000; Yuma, c. 5,000, h. 800, m. 300, sw. 200, sh. ——; total, cattle 346,000, horses 31,800, mules 13,600, swine 11,400, sheep 680,000; value, cattle, at $25 per head, $7,200,000, sheep about $2,380,000, wool for year 5,440,000 lbs., worth $1,196,800 (not including the wool product of the Navajos). *Hamilton's Resources*, 256–88; *Arizona Scraps*. 11–20, 222; Gov.'s mess., etc., in *Ariz., Jour.; Surv.-gen. Reports; Ariz., Hist.* (E. & Co.), 139–46; *Wood Brothers, Live-stock Movement; Nat. Conven. of Cattlemen, Proc.*, 12–13; *Hoyt's Ariz.*, MS., 26; *Thompson's Law of the Farm*, 82; *Porter's West Census*, 460–1. The gov., in 1879, notes Hardy's success in raising Angora goats in Mojave.

the California surveying district. It was not until 1868 that a beginning of surveys was made, and the work was continued somewhat slowly from that year. In 1870 a separate district was created, and John Wasson appointed surveyor-general, holding the office for twelve years. The Gila district was created in 1873, with office at Florence, removed in 1882 to Tucson. The total area of public land surveyed down to 1883 was a little over 8,000,000 acres, and that disposed of by the various methods of sale, homestead, timber-culture entry, etc., was about 270,000 acres.[14]

Mexican land grants in Arizona are much less numerous than in California and New Mexico, being all in Pima county and in the territory ceded to the United States in 1853. Troubles resulting from these claims are similar to those arising in California, though on a much smaller scale. Most of the claims are doubtless equitably valid and will eventually be confirmed, though some are fraudulent. Not much is known of them in detail, though since 1879 the sur-

[14] *Land Office Reports*, 1864 et seq., including annual reports of the surveyor-general. In *U. S. Govt Doc.*, 47th cong. 2d sess., H. Ex. Doc. 72, p. 146, is a statement of the lands disposed of from 1872 to 1882 as follows: 3,857 acres in '72, 6,790 in '73, 7,124 in '74, 9,034 in '75, 8,862 in '76, 52,560 in '77, 63,585 in '78, 28,281 in '79, 17,067 in '80, 19,203 in '81, 21,156 in '82, and (acc. to Elliott & Co.) 33,878 in '83. Under the timber-culture act in 1877-9, the entries were 7,320 acres. Possibly the total of surveys should be over 9,000,000, as there are in each set of annual reports two or three conflicting totals which might perhaps be understood if life were a little longer. It was said in 1880 that the 5,800,000 acres surveyed included nearly all the irrigable agricultural land; 13 military reservations in 1881 included 197,052 acres, acc. to a newspaper résumé of the land-office report in 1886, 534,139 acres were disposed of in that year. The peculiar situation of large portions of the farming lands in narrow strips along the streams added greatly to the practical difficulties of surveying by the rectangular system, one instance being mentioned in which one claim included 44 corners! The lack of a law, by which the grazing lands—valueless in tracts of 160 acres—could be surveyed and sold, has been the subject of constant complaint. The timber lands have also caused some trouble. The territory contains a broad extent —perhaps 15 or 20 thousand square miles—of magnificent forests, but these grow on mineral and mountain land useless for agriculture, and not subject to purchase or entry under the laws. In 1878, after much urging, congress passed an act permitting the cutting of timber for home use, except by railroads, on U. S. mineral lands in Ariz.; and in 1873 the legislature forbade the shipping of such lumber out of the territory. *Ariz., Acts*, 1873, p. 262. The A. & P. R. R. grant, however, opens a vast lumbering region; and there can be no doubt that the country's forests are to be an important element of its natural wealth.

veyor-general has investigated fourteen of them or more, and recommended them for approval or rejection. This delay on the part of the government has been entirely inexcusable, as the matter might have been easily settled fifteen years ago. Since that time lands have increased in value; conflicting interests have come into existence; probably fraudulent schemes have been concocted; and even a hope has been developed that all the Mexican titles might be defeated. Owners have no real protection against squatters, cannot sell or make improvements, and in fact have no other right than that of paying taxes; while on the other hand the rights of settlers are jeopardized by possibly invalid claims, and a generally unsettled and unsatisfactory system of land tenure is produced.[15]

[15] The *Land Office Reports* contain nearly all that is known about this subject, though the newspapers have something to say about it. In 1865 the legislature passed a law, apparently inoperative, requiring all claims to be recorded in the county recorder's office before Jan. 1, 1866. There was no national law on the subject until 1870, when the surveyor-gen. was required by act of congress to investigate the titles and report to congress for the final issuing of patents. But no definite instructions were issued or means furnished until 1877, and the investigation was not begun till 1879, though the surveyor-gen. constantly urged the importance of the matter, at the same time declaring his inability to do justice to the subject, and recommending the creation of a commission, or the devising of some other means of prompt action. In 1875, however, an act was passed, on the governor's recommendation, authorizing patents for small tracts occupied by Mex. claimants in the Sta Cruz valley, on proof before the register and receiver of the land-office that these tracts had been occupied for 20 years by claimants or their ancestors. *Zabriskie's Land Laws*, suppl. 1877, p. 75; *Governor's Mess.*, 1873. I suppose that some of these patents were issued, though I have found no record of the fact. Meanwhile also, in 1873-4, corresp. was had with Mex. national authorities, and R. C. Hopkins was sent to Mex. and Guadalajara, with a view to find records of the Arizona grants; but none were found—in Mexico because Ariz. had belonged to the Provincias Internas, and in Guadalajara because most of the records had been destroyed by fire. *U. S. Govt Doc.*, 43d cong. 2d sess., Sen. Doc. 3. The claims favorably reported by Surv.-gen. Wasson in 1879-82 were as follows: S. Rafael del Valle, 4 leagues, Camon brothers; Tumacácori and Calabazas, 11 l., Sykes and Currey; S. José Sonoita, 1¾ l., Alsua; S. Ignacio de la Canoa, 4 l., Maish et al.; Arivaca, 2 l., Poston and Ainza; S. Juan Boquillas y Nogales, 4 l., Howard and Hearst; Los Nogales de Elías, 2 l., Camon and Elías; unnamed small tracts of 4-500 acres, Otero et al.; Buena Vista, 4 l., Maish and Driscoll; Rancho de Martinez, small tract, Martinez et al. Those rejected as fraudulent were Paso de Algodones, 5 l., Colorado comp.; and El Sopori, 31 l., Sopori Land Co.; while S. Ignacio Babocomari, 8 l., Perrin et al.; and S. Rafael de la Zanja, 16 l., Romero et al., were cut down from the area claimed to that granted. In the report of 1882 it is stated that most claims were not presented at all, holders of valid ones being confident they must be finally confirmed, and others not desiring investigation. Probably more have been investigated

Manufacturing industries in Arizona call for no special mention in an historical work, being confined to a few establishments, chiefly flouring and lumber mills, for the partial supply of territorial needs. Future developments will naturally be limited for a long time by home requirements, most of which may eventually be supplied; yet with the growth of stock-raising it would appear that tanning and the manufacture of leather goods should assume larger proportions; and doubtless other industries will in time produce articles for export.[16] Commerce may be disposed of for the most part as summarily. The territory's trade has consisted of the bringing from abroad and the distributing to towns and camps of the various supplies required. Each settlement has its shops for the supply of local demands, and each of the dozen larger centres its wholesale establishments, whence goods are hauled in all directions. In these establishments, some of them doing business on a large scale, many a fortune has been made. There are no available statistics of value or interest, except in local phases of the subject, for which I have no space. The great question has always been one of transportation routes and rates, and the latter have been invariably high, with the natural result of excessive prices. Before the building of the transcontinental railroads of the south, a considerable amount of freight was brought in at

since 1882. A search of the archives in Son. and Chih. is recommended, not only on account of the Ariz. grants, but in view of 'manifest destiny' farther south. No patents have been granted so far as I know, and difficulties will probably be permitted to assume still larger proportions before the matter is settled. Hinton, *Hand-book*, 303, points out the facts that while sec. 5 of the Gadsden treaty reënacts the provisions of the treaty of Guadalupe Hidalgo, yet sec. 6 provides that no titles shall be valid unless recorded in the Mex. archives. Also, that a Mex. law of 1853, repealed in 1855, declared invalid all grants by states and territories. Therefore, the Ariz. grants must, he thinks, be defeated. Evidently there are legal quibbles enough on which to found such action if the U. S. govt cares to engage in that kind of business.

[16] Statistics of manuf. showing increase in 1870–80, from 10th U. S. census: no. of estab. 18–66, capital $150,700–$272,600, employés 84–220, wages $45,580–$111,180, products $185,410–$618,365, raw material $110,090–$380,-023. Of the estab., 13 were saw-mills, 8 flour-mills, 2 butter and cheese, 1 brickyard. There are also some distilleries and breweries, and tobacco and cigar factories.

times by mule-teams from the terminus of the Denver railroad, from Austin, Texas, by way of Mesilla, and to a slight extent from Salt Lake City and through Sonora from Guaymas; while there was frequent agitation of a project to open a route from Tucson to the nearer port of Libertad on the gulf; but the bulk of all freight came in teams across the desert from San Francisco via Los Angeles, or by the gulf and Colorado River in boats. But the railroads gave the wholesale trade mainly to the eastern cities, and destroyed, for the most part, the prominence of Yuma as a distributing centre in favor of Tucson and other inland stations. It should also be noted that a flourishing branch of Arizona commerce has been an extensive contraband trade with Sonora, a large part of that territory's supply of dry goods being smuggled across the line from Tucson. According to the census, 591 persons in Arizona were engaged in trade in 1870, and in 1880 the number had increased to 3,252.[17]

[17] Hinton gives the most complete details on routes of trade and transportation. In the early years there was much agitation of projects for improving the navigation of the Colorado; but very little was ever done. The beginning of steam navigation has been noted elsewhere. Down to 1871–2 sailing vessels plied irregularly to the head of the gulf, and freight was towed in barges by small steamers up to Yuma and Hardyville. Subsequently, the Col. Steam Nav. Co. ran a line of steamers regularly from S. F. to Yuma. Hodge, *Ariz.*, 210, gives the amount of freight brought to Yuma in 1875 as over 4,500 tons, and exports as over 10,000 tons, the largest item being hides. On the efforts and explorations of 1864–70, including the operations of Capt. S. Adams, see *Ariz.*, *Acts*, 1864, p. 79; 1865, p. 73, 77–8; 1866, p. 61; *Id.*, *Jour.*, 1864, p. 161–2; 1865, p. 43; *U. S. Govt Doc.*, 38th cong. 2d sess., H. Mis. Doc. 17, 142, 153; Rept Sec. War, 865–6; 41st cong. 2d sess., H. Ex. Doc. 281; Sen. Mis. Doc. 17; 41st cong. 3d sess., H. Mis. Doc. 12; 42d cong. 1st sess., H. Mis. Doc. 37; 42d cong. 2d sess., H. Ex. Doc. 166; 43d cong. 1st sess., H. Jour., p. 1257; H. Ex. Doc. 154; 44th cong. 2d sess., Sen. Rept 624; 56th cong. 3d sess., vol. xvi., pt 1, p. 842; *U. S. Rept Chief of Engin.*, 1868, p. 1188–96; *Hayes' Scraps, Ariz.*, i. 105–6, 120, 125, 239, 268; v. 141; *Id.*, *S. Diego*, i. 203–10, 213; ii. 193; *Ariz. Scraps*, 437–43; *S. F. Times*, Nov. 6, 17, 1866; March 23, April 15, May 11, Sept. 28, Oct. 15, 16, 18, Nov. 2, 18, 1867.

In large partions of the territory the natural roads are excellent, so far at least as grade is concerned, stage routes being practicable wherever watering-places can be found. Many good mountain roads have also been constructed from time to time, as mining and military needs have demanded. The legislature from year to year incorporated many road companies; but only comparatively few of the enterprises were carried out. At each session of congress also various mail routes were opened; but for a long time the mails were carried on horseback. In his message of 1866 the gov. states that there is not a stage running in the territory. Indian hostilities naturally interfered

With two of the great transcontinental lines passing through the territory from east to west, and a connecting line to Guaymas on the gulf, Arizona is in a sense, for so new a region, well supplied with railroads. Branch roads in several directions are urgently needed, and some of these have been or are being constructed. The complicated history of the main lines pertains but very slightly to Arizona, though the military necessities and prospective resources of that territory may be supposed to have had some little influence in favor of their construction. Therefore that history is not given here, nor is any attempt made to chronicle the hopes and fears and rumors respecting routes current for many years among the people on this vital matter. Early surveys, by which the practicability of the routes by the 25th and 32d parallels was ascertained, have been recorded. From 1864 the subject was always under discussion, and various projects took more or less definite shape ; but there was a broad region to be crossed before the iron road should even approach Arizona. In 1866 the Atlantic and Pacific was chartered with a land grant on the 35th parallel, but no western progress was made. In 1870–1 this company was reorganized, making some show of active work ; and the Texas and Pacific was

seriously with the mails and stages; but progress was constant, if not so rapid as the people desired, and before 1870 the service was tolerably complete. The main stage line corresponded with the overland route of 1859–61 from Los Angeles, via Yuma and Tucson to Mesilla, N. Mex. Another line was from Yuma to Wickenburg and Prescott, connecting with others to Alburquerque in the east and Mojave in the west. At times, however, the Prescott stage left the Cal. route west of the Colorado, crossing at Ehrenberg. A line from Tucson afforded communication with Sonora. As the railroads approached, of course the stage lines were constantly changed, until the system became one of comparatively short routes from R. R. stations to the various towns and districts. The most important have been those from the A. & P. to Prescott, from the S. P. to Phœnix, Florence, Globe, and Graham Co. in the north, and to Tombstone in the south. B. C. Truman was sent to Ariz. as mail agent in 1867. The subject of mails and stages was naturally in all years, and especially in early times, one of great popular interest to Arizonans, and therefore I find in public doc., newspapers, etc., a bulky mass of data; but I have no space to chronicle details, and do not deem it necessary to present even the latest catalogue of routes, mail statistics, etc. The annual reports of the P. M. general contain most that is essential on this matter.

organized to reach San Diego by the Gila route, with a land grant like that of the Atlantic and Pacific, including the alternate sections for a width of 80 miles throughout the whole extent of Arizona from east to west. For a few years from 1872 Arizonans believed their railroad future assured from this source; but financial obstacles proved insuperable, and Scott's line never reached the eastern line of the territory. In 1877, however, the Southern Pacific from California was completed to the Arizona line at Yuma, and in the following years, not without some serious complications with the rival company, was rapidly continued eastward, reaching Tucson in 1880, and in 1881 effecting a junction with the Atchison, Topeka, and Santa Fé road at Deming, New Mexico. Practically by the latter company the Sonora road, connecting Guaymas with the Southern Pacific at Benson, was completed in 1882; and the company is accredited with the intention of securing a through-line to Guaymas, by building a new road from Deming to Benson or Fairbanks. Meanwhile the completion of the Atchison line down the Rio Grande valley enabled the Atlantic and Pacific to resume operations in the west, and in 1880–3 this road was completed from Isleta to the Colorado at the Needles, connecting there with the California Southern. As all these roads were built, so they have been operated without any special regard to the interests of Arizona; yet they have necessarily—even as masters instead of servants of the people, as they should be—been immensely beneficial to the territory.[18]

[18] *Mowry's Ariz. and Sonora*, 217–31, gives a good idea of the R. R. situation in 1863–4. In the governor's messages to the legislature may be found a résumé of progress and prospects from time to time. Newspaper files of Arizona and Cal., many clippings from which are found in *Hayes' Scraps*, contain a large amount of R. R. information and rumor. For incorporation and subsidies to railroads in the territory, with some slight attempts by the legislature to regulate fares and freights, see *Ariz., Acts*, 1864, p. 25–7, 51–3; 1865, p. 45–7, 78; *Id., Jour.*, 1865, p. 49–50, 216–17; *Id., Acts*, 1879, p. 42–60; *Id., Laws*, 1881, p. 80, 118, 133; 1883, p. 61–5, 137, 150–5, 160–71, 221–3, 244–51, 423–6.

On most of the branch roads incorporated, no work has ever been done. The Ariz. Copper Co. has built a narrow-gauge road of 71 miles from Lords-

The importance of education has been realized in
Arizona from the beginning. In early years, the
sisters of St Joseph maintained a small but useful
school at Tucson. The first legislature of 1864 not
only provided in the code for the establishing of common schools when needed, but appropriated small
sums for the mission school at Bac, and for public
schools at the larger towns. Prescott alone took advantage of this appropriation, maintaining a private
school in 1865. But no progress was made for years.
In 1871 the governor announced that with 1,923 children Arizona had not a single public school, though
1868 is generally given as the date when the first was
founded, because in that year was passed an "act to
establish public schools," levying a tax of ten cents on
each hundred dollars, and creating a board of edu-

burg, N. Mex., on the S. P. R. R., to their mines at Clifton. On a road from
Tucson to Globe a few miles have been graded, the line receiving a subsidy of
$200,000 from Pima co. A road is also projected from Tucson up the Sta
Cruz to Calabazas, connecting the S. P. R. R. by a direct line with the Guay-
mas road; and another from Tucson to Port Lobos on the gulf in Sonora.
Roads from Maricopa to Phœnix, and from Casa Grande to Florence and Silver
King, are talked of and needed. A line to connect Tombstone with one of the
main lines is among the probabilities of the near future; or perhaps the
Atchison extension may touch Tombstone on its way to Fairbanks. In the
north the Central Ariz. R. R. Co. is building a road from the A. & P. at a
point near Ash Fork southward. Some 30 miles have been completed, and
the road is expected to reach Prescott early in 1887. A branch is to be built
to Jerome; and the road is to be continued down the Agua Fria to Phœnix.
Among other possibilities are a road from Flagstaff on the A. & P., through
the lumber region to Globe and Benson, and an extension of the Cal. Southern
from the Needles to Wickenburg, Phœnix, and Florence. Predictions respecting these projected roads are very hazardous; but if the county is to
prosper, many branch roads must and will be built.
   The telegraph was talked of from 1866, but nothing was done until 1873,
when with an appropriation from congress, and primarily for military purposes,
a line was constructed from S. Diego to Yuma, and thence to Prescott and
Tucson, being in a few years extended to all the military posts and to Sta Fé.
Three successive appropriations amounted to $120,000; and before the R. R.
reached Yuma in 1877 there were about 1,000 miles of wire in operation
within the territory. This military telegraph was regarded as an especial
benefit to Ariz., as the rates were much lower than on corporation lines.
Western Union wires were however added, and to some extent substituted,
on the completion of the R. R.; and there are some private or mining co.
lines in operation. See gov.'s messages, 1864–71, 1875, 1877; *U. S. Govt Doc.*,
42d cong. 2d sess., Sen. Jour. 305, 445; Sen. Doc. 14; 3d sess., Sen. Doc.
12; 43d cong. 1st sess., H. Ex. Doc. 204, 232, 270; 2d sess., Rept Sec. War,
i. 195–6; 47th cong. 1st sess., H. Ex. Doc., vol. vii., p. 217–27, being a statistical table; see also Ariz. and Cal. newspapers, especially of 1873; *Hamilton's Resources*, 129; *Hinton's Hand-book*, 318–19; *Hodge's Ariz.*, 213–14; *Elliott
& Co.*, 317.

cation, with the governor and probate judges as ex-officio territorial and county superintendents. Governor Safford, particularly, distinguished himself by his efforts in this direction; a good beginning had been made by 1873; and from the close of the Apache wars, progress was rapid. A new act was passed in 1875, increasing the tax to 15 cents, and requiring a county tax of 35 cents—subsequently increased to 50 cents—and making school attendance compulsory, though this proved for the most part a dead letter. Various supplemental acts were passed from session to session; and in 1883 a new school law was framed, under which M. H. Sherman became superintendent. Still another law, with no very radical changes, was enacted in 1885, and in that year R. L. Long became superintendent. The system seems fully equal to that in other states and territories, and the schools are reported as prosperous. As in all new territories, children in the more remote districts are inadequately provided for; but in all the towns there are commodious school buildings and competent teachers.[19]

[19] School statistics of 1882 show 98 districts, 126 teachers, 10,283 school children, and value of school-houses $116,750. The average salary of teachers is $75 per month. The territorial apportionment of 1884 was $8,096, or 86 cents for each of 9,376 scholars. County taxes for schools amount to about $100,000. A uniform series of text-books has been used since 1882. The percentage of persons unable to read, .135 in 1880, is large, but this is largely due to the Mex. population. There are as yet no institutions for a higher education, though there are a dozen private schools. In 1864–5 provision was made for a university and regents were appointed, but nothing was accomplished. In 1881 congress granted 72 sections of govt land for a univ., which were selected in the timber region of the S. Francisco Mountains. Finally, in 1885, an act was passed by the legislature to organize such an institution at or near Tucson, with 6 regents, including the gov and supt ex officio. A loan of $25,000 was authorized on condition of Pima co. giving 40 acres of land. What prospects of success this enterprise may have, I do not know. The school law in its final form may be found in *Ariz., Laws*, 13th sess., 138–70. Complete information on the progress of schools, etc., is given in the governor's messages, in *Ariz., Jour.*, 1864 et seq.; *Ariz., Acts* (and *Laws*), 1864 et seq.; *U. S. Commissioner of Educ. Reports*, 1869 et seq.; *U. S. Census*, 9th and 10th, 1870–80; *U. S. Statutes*, 46th cong. 3d sess., 326; *U. S. Govt Doc.*, 43d cong. 1st sess., H. Mis. Doc. 83; see also *Ariz , Hist.* (E. & Co.), 147–9; *Hamilton's Resources*, 247–51; *Hinton's Hand-book*, 378; *Hodge's Ariz.*, 196–9; *Hoyt's Ariz.*, MS., 5–7; *Safford's Arizona*, in *S. F. Spirit of the Times*, Dec. 25, 1877; *Ariz. Scraps*, 57; *Hayes' Scraps, Ariz.*, v. 10; vi. 91, 206.

Provision was made by the first legislature in 1864 for a territorial library at the capital, to contain miscellaneous as well as law books; through the influence of McCormick, a considerable quantity of books was obtained from the east, as a beginning; and the journals of the early sessions contain catalogues of the collection. According to the governor's message of 1877, the library then contained 2,200 vols, worth $8,200. Respecting the status of this institution in recent years, I have found no information.

The library was to have a 'historical department' for the especial preservation of all written and printed matter pertaining to the territory. Whenever the accumulation of MS. was sufficient for a vol. of 200 p., it was to be published at the public expense. At the same time an Historical Society was organized and chartered. A few years later this society and a Pioneer Association had united and opened a library and reading-room at Prescott; but in the bloody ordeal through which Ariz. was called to pass, all these praiseworthy enterprises come to naught. At the beginning of 1884, however, a new Pioneer Society was organized, which, I think, still exists, with some prospects of usefulness. *Ariz. Hist. Soc., Charter, etc.*, Prescott, 1864, 12mo, 16 p.; *Id., Comp. Laws*, 541; *Howell Code*, 171; *Hayes' Scraps, Ariz.*, ii. 38–9, 120; *Hoyt's Ariz.*, MS., 3–4; *Sac. Record-Union*, Feb. 2, 1884.

The various secret and other societies of Masons, Odd Fellows, etc., are firmly established in most of the Arizona towns; and a very good account of such organizations is found in the work of Elliott & Co. Hamilton, *Resources*, p. 251–3, and E. & Co., p. 151–3, give church statistics, from which it appears that there are 25 churches in the territory, of which the catholics—under J. B. Salpointe as bishop of Tucson—have 8, the methodists—with G. H. Adams as president of the mission—6, baptists 4, presbyterians 3, congregationalists 2, and episcopalians 9, besides the Mormon churches on the Colorado Chiquito, Gila, and Salt River. The figures given represent church buildings, but the different associations do some missionary, charitable, and Sunday-school work in other settlements. There are also some religious exercises—both Christian and aboriginal—on the different Ind. reservations. According to the census of 1870, there were only 4 churches, worth $24,000. The finest edifice is the old mission church at Bac, where services are held every Sunday.

A list of Arizona newspapers in 1884 is given by Elliott & Co. as follows: Phœnix (D. and W.) *Ariz. Gazette*, from '80, H. H. McNeil, editor. Phœnix (D. and W.) *Herald*, from '79, N. A. Morford, ed. Phœnix (W.) *Union*, from '83, Aguirre & Célis, ed. Phœnix (W.) *Mercurio*, from '84, F. T. Dávila, ed. Clifton (W.) *Clarion*, from '83, D. L. Sayre, ed. Tucson (D. and W.) *Citizen*, from '70, W. W. Hayward, ed. Tucson (W.) *Mining Index*, from '83, G. W. Barter, ed. Tucson (D. and W.) *Star*, from '77, L. C. Hughes, ed. Tucson (W.) *Live Stock Journal*, from '84, Cameron, ed. Tucson (W.) *Fronterizo*, from '78, C. I. Velasco, ed. Tucson (W.) *Ariz. Methodist*, from '81, Geo. H. Adams, ed. Quijotoa (W.) *Prospector*, from '84, H. Brook, ed. Globe (W.) *Ariz. Silver Belt*, from '78, A. H. Hackney, ed. Prescott (D. and W.) *Ariz. Journal*, from '72, J. C. Martin, ed. Prescott (D. and W.) *Courier*, from '82, J. H. Marion, ed. Prescott (D. and W.) *Ariz. Miner*, from '64, W. O. O'Neil, ed. Flagstäff (W.) *Champion*, from '83, A. E. Fay, ed. Tombstone (D. and W.) *Epitaph*, from '80, C. D. Reppy, ed. Benson (W.) *Herald*, from '83, W. A. Nash, ed. Florence (W.) *Ariz. Enterprise*, from '80, L. F. Weedin, ed. St John (W.) *Orion Era*, from '83, M. P. Romney, ed. St John (W.) *Apache Chief*, from '84, Geo. A. McCarter, ed. Mineral Park (W.) *Mojave Co. Miner*, from '82, J. J. Hyde, ed. Yuma (W.) *Ariz. Sentinel*, from '71, J. W. Dorrington, ed. Holbrook (W.) *Times*, from '84, H. Reed, ed. Wilcox (W.) *Sulphur Val. News*, from '84, Montague, ed. Several other papers, suspended before '84, have been incidentally mentioned elsewhere. The oldest was the *Arizonian*, pub. at Tubac and Tucson, in 1858-9. The pioneer press used for this paper was later used for the Tombstone *Nugget*, and was rendered worthless by one of the fires, acc. to E. & Co. The *Mineral Park Miner* of Aug. 30, '85, mentions the Casa Grande *Voice of Ariz.*, Phœnix *Territorial Chronicle*, one at Kingman, and another at Nogales, making 28 at that date. See also *Pettingill's Newsp. Dir.*, 197 et seq.; *Barter's Dir. Tucson*, 1881, p. 38–9; *Pac. Coast Dir.*, 1871–3, p. 154–5; *Tucson D. Citizen*, Oct. 14, 1880; *S. F. Bulletin*, Feb. 6, 1882.

CHAPTER XXIV.

A MAP showing the county boundaries, as accurately
as is possible on a small scale, is given on the next
page. Apache county, so named from the Indian
tribe, or perhaps immediately from the fort, has an
area of 20,940 square miles, ranking second in extent.
It was created from Yavapai by act of 1879 and curtailed in 1881 by the cutting-off of that part of Graham between the Black and Gila rivers. The county
seat was originally at Snowflake, but was moved to
Springerville in 1880, and to St John in 1881. That
portion north of latitude 35°, or of the railroad, is a
region of plateaux and mesas from 4,000 to 7,000 feet
above the level of the sea, with peaks rising to nearly
twice those heights. The few streams run in deep
cañons and are dry in summer, and though the plateau
produces good grass, the country is for the most part
valueless for agricultural purposes. Here, however,

are immense coal deposits, which are sure to assume great value in time. The northern portion is covered by the Moqui and Navajo Indian reservations, having

COUNTIES OF ARIZONA.

practically no white inhabitants. The Moqui towns and the ruins of Chelly Cañon are among the most interesting relics of antiquity to be found in the United States; Fort Defiance is the oldest post in the county; and the famous 'diamond-fields,' of 1872 are to be found—on the maps—in the extreme north. South

of the railroad the county is well watered by the
Colorado Chiquito and its branches, supporting a
population of nearly 6,000, a prominent element being the Mormons, numbering about 3,000, and whose
occupation dates from 1876–7.   Besides the grazing
and farming lands, there are valuable forests of pine.
The extreme south, about Fort Apache, is included
in the San Cárlos, or White Mountain, Indian reservation.   St John, the county seat, is a thriving village
of over 1,000 inhabitants, with two newspapers; and
Holbrook on the railroad, with a population of about
500 and one newspaper, is the distributing point for
all the county.[1]

Yavapai county, so named from the Indian tribe,
was one of the four original counties created by the
first legislature of 1864.   At that time it included over
half of the whole territory—all north of the Gila and
east of the meridian of 113° 20′; and it still comprises
more than one fourth, with an area of about 28,000
square miles.[2]   North of latitude 35°, or of the rail-

[1] The successive county changes have been noticed in chap. xxi., in connection with legislative proceedings; so also the Ind. reservations, coal-fields,
Mormons, and some other topics in other chapters.   Census statistics of 1880
are as follows: pop. 5,283; by towns, St John 546, Springerville 364, Snowflake 275, Brigham City 191, Walker 165, Sunset 161, Woodruff 66; no. of
farms 96, value $62,596, implements, etc., $4,384, produce $63,960; crops,
barley 20,761 bush., wheat 11,075, corn 4,368, oats 564; improved land 5,389
acres; horses 665, mules and asses 72, oxen 440, cows 1,693, cattle 3,857,
sheep 30,606, swine 96; wool 86,681 lbs., butter 5,742 lbs., cheese 94,85 lbs.,
value of live-stock $123,992; assessment $600,000, tax $15,570.   Hamilton's
stat. for 1882–3 are, pop. 6,816, St John 1,200, Holbrook 500 (200 acc. to E.
& Co.); land under cultivation 13,000 acres, cattle 43,000, horses 3,000, mules
1,500, sheep 600,000; assessed valuation of all property in 1884 $1,090,000.

The stock industry is rapidly increasing in late years.   E. & Co. state that
the Mormon settlements have been nearly abandoned on account of alkali in
the soil.   The St John papers are the *Apache Chief* and *Orion Era*, the latter
a Mormon organ; at Holbrook is published the *Times*.   Near Holbrook are
extensive petrified forests.   Winslow is a new railroad town in the east, corresponding nearly to the old Brigham City.   Eben Stanley of Ia, a soldier in
the war of 1861–4, first came to Ariz. with a drove of govt cattle in 1866,
returning in 1869.   For seven years he was a chief of scouts under Gen. Crook,
and since 1879 has been raising stock near Springerville.   He has a wife,
Mary Stickard, and two children.   R. C. Kinder, engaged in sheep-raising,
is a native of Ill., who came from Cal. in 1876.

[2] A part of Maricopa was cut off in 1871 and 1877, part of Pinal in 1875,
Apache in 1879, part of Gila in 1881, and finally a part of Mojave in 1883.
See legisl. acts in chap. xxi.   Hamilton gives the area as 30,015 sq. m., but
he seems not to have accounted for the loss of the N. W. corner.   E. & Co.
make the area 37,000 m.

road, is the Colorado plateau, cut to a depth of 1,000 to 6,000 feet by the grand cañon of the great river, and by the hardly less wonderful cañons of the Colorado Chiquito and other branches. This region has some fine forests and extensive grazing lands, but as a rule little water available for agriculture; and it is for the most part unoccupied, except by the Hualapai and Suppai Indians, and by a few Mormons on the Utah frontier. South of latitude 35°, the country is mountainous, but has many fertile valleys, of which that of the Verde is most extensive. It is well timbered, and has in most parts plenty of water, the climate being the most agreeable to be found in the territory. Here the lands are tilled to some extent without irrigation. All the mountains are rich in the precious metals; but most of the mines, as of the population, about 10,000 souls—perhaps considerably more[3]—are in the southwestern corner of the county. Prescott, founded in 1864 on Granite Creek, at an altitude of about 5,500 feet, is delightfully situated, and has many fine buildings of wood, brick, and stone. More than others in Arizona, it is described as resembling an eastern town. In 1864–7, Prescott was the temporary seat of government, and since 1877 has been the permanent capital; it has many large mercantile establishments; is well supplied with banks and with public buildings; and has three daily newspapers, including the *Arizona Miner*, the oldest journal of the territory. Its population is about 2,000. Flagstaff, with perhaps 500 inhabitants, is the leading railroad town, and the centre of an active lumbering and mercantile industry. The Arizona Central Railroad to connect Prescott with the Atlantic and Pacific in the north, and with Phœnix in the south, is expected to accomplish great things for the capital and for the country.[4]

[3] Hamilton gives the pop. in 1882 as 27,680, which is doubtless a great exaggeration, though I have no means of determining the correct figures. Acc. to the U. S. census of 1880, Yavapai had a pop. of 5,013, and Prescott 1,836. Hodge gives the county pop. as 13,738 in 1876. Hinton, 15,000 in 1878. All this is very confusing.

[4] Census statistics of 1880 are as follows: no. of farms 244, extent 45,013 a., average size 184 a., improved 11,239 a., value $337,950, val. implements

Mojave, named from the Indian tribe, was another of the four counties organized in 1864.   At that time

$20,352; horses 2,685, mules 267, oxen 286, milk-cows 1,936, cattle 12,034, sheep 34,680, swine 570, value of live-stock $435,502; wool clip 201,320 lbs.; milk sold 27,376 gal., butter 31,895 lbs., cheese 7,050 lbs.; crop of barley 16,944 bush., corn 14,841, wheat 5,070, value of farm produce $149,872, assessment $1,808,402, debt $152,570, tax $69,202.   Hamilton's stat. for 1883 are, cattle 75,000, horses 6,000, mules '2,000, swine 1,000, sheep 50,000; land cultiv. 6,500 a.; assessment for 1884, $3,785,131.   Vote in 1882, 2,171.

Prescott is also the military headquarters of the territory, Ft Whipple being situated at a distance of only one mile, and Camp Verde about 50 m. east. It has two territorial libraries, law and miscellaneous.   There is a fine brick school-house and 5 churches.   The newspapers are the *Miner* (estab. by Gov. McCormick in 1864), *Journal*, and *Courier*.   Some of the *first* things are as follows: 1st house of logs Fleury's, still standing; 1st clergyman Wm H. Reid, who estab. a Sunday-school in '64; 1st marriage J. H. Dickson to Mary J. Ehle, Nov. 17, '64, by Gov. Goodwin; first child born Molly Simmons Jan. 9, '65; 1st ball Nov. 8, '64; 1st Masonic lodge '65, Odd Fellows '68; 1st and only earthquake '71; telegraph '73.   Town incorporated 1881 and 1883.   *Ariz., Acts*, 11th sess., 136; 12th sess., 66–107.   See also on Prescott, especially its earlier history, besides Hinton, Hamilton, and Elliott & Co., *Hayes' Scraps, Ariz.*, i. 197, 200, 269; ii. 120–2; *Hodye's Ariz.*, 14, 148–51; *Hoyt's Ariz.*, MS., 27–8; *U. S. Govt Doc.*, 39th cong. 2d sess., H. Miscel. Doc. 24; *Ind. Aff. Rept*, 1864, p. 155; *Land Off. Rept*, 1865, p. 120; *McCormick's Oration*, July 4, 1864, 12mo, 15 p; *Rusling's Across Amer.*, 397–418; *Ariz. Scraps*, 120–4; *Prescott Miner*, Jan. 26, Mar. 9, June 29, July 20, Dec. 21, 1877; Dec. 27, 1878; June 11, 1880; *Truman*, in *S. F. Bulletin*, May 3, 1867; *Prescott Arizonian*, Aug. 17, 1879; *Tucson Star*, Mar. 6, 1879.

Other towns of Yavapai are simply mining camps, one of the most flourishing being Jerome, at the United Verde Co.'s copper mines, with about 400 inhab.   Mines of this and other counties have been briefly noticed in the preceding chapter.   Flagstaff is noted for its stone quarry, its elevation of 6,500 ft, and fine climate, its forests, mills, game, and farming lands.   A trail leads to the wonderful Grand Cañon, but Peach Springs is the R. R. station nearest to that most wonderful natural attraction, and also to the Hualapai Ind. reservation.

Pauline Weaver, one of the earliest Americans who visited Ariz., perhaps before 1830, certainly as early as 1832, was a native of Tenn., about whose life in detail very little is known.   He was a famous trapper and explorer, acquainted with all the broad interior and its Ind. tribes.   He discovered in 1862 the Colorado placers, and the next years the Hassayampa mines, in the district bearing his name.   In 1865 he was tilling a patch of land on the same stream.   I have not found the date or circumstances of his death.   Joseph R. Walker crossed Ariz. between 1830 and 1840, was captain of the prospectors of 1861–3, and discoverer of many mines in Yavapai.   For a biog. sketch of this famous guide and mountaineer, see Pioneer Register, in *Hist. Cal.*, v. A. E. Fay of N. Y. came to Ariz. in 1876, and for two years edited the Tucson *Star;* was clerk of the 10th legisl.; established the Tombstone *Nugget* in 1879; was clerk of the house, 12th legisl.; and in 1883 started the *Arizona Champion* at Flagstaff, where he now resides as proprietor and business editor of the paper.   His wife was Amanda Hicklin.   Edmond W. Wells, a lawyer of Prescott, is a native of Ohio, who came to the territory in 1864.   He was for a time clerk in the Q. M. dept, and has been three times a member of the council.   His wife was Rosa Baughart, and they have four children.   Wm Wilkerson of Mo. crossed the plains to Cal. in 1853, and came to Ariz. in 1869, mining for a time at Lynx Creek.   He was for many years clerk of the district and supreme courts, and was four times elected county recorder.   He resides at Prescott with his wife, who was Hattie Skinkle.   S. C. Dickenson, a native of N. Y., came to the territory in 1875, and is a farmer at Date Creek, with a wife and several children.   Joseph R. Walker, born in Mo.

it included all that part of Nevada south of latitude 37,° the county seat being Hardyville. In 1865 all north of Roaring Rapid, or about 35° 50', was set off as Pah-Ute county, with the county seat at Callville, moved the next year to St Thomas. In 1866 that part of both counties lying west of the Colorado and longitude 114° was attached to Nevada; in 1871 what was left of Pah-Ute was reattached to Mojave; in 1877 the county seat was moved to Mineral Park;

1832, was one of the famous party of prospectors under his uncle, Capt. Joe Walker, in 1861–3. Ind.-fighter and miner for many years, he was sheriff of Yavapai in 1878–80, and since has raised stock and carried on a butchering business at Prescott. Portrait in E. & Co. s *Hist.*, 60. W. J. Mulomon of Mass. came in 1875 from N. Mex. He has been a miner; also deputy sheriff and sheriff of Yavapai, residing at Prescott. Wm Powell of Ill. came from Nebraska in 1875, and is a stock-raiser at Cherry Creek. His wife was Julia A. Allen, and he has a family of six children. Charles B. Rush of Mo. came overland via Cal. in 1877. He is a lawyer and stock-raiser of Prescott, having held the office of district attorney. He married Mary Givens in 1880, and has two children.

Charles L. Spencer, a merchant of Prescott, is a native of Ohio, born in 1852. He was in Ariz. 1870–3, and came back in 1875. W. W. Hutchinson, a wealthy cattle-man of Prescott, came to Ariz. in 1870. He was born in Mo., came across the plains to Cal. in 1850, and was subsequently a miner at Frazer River and in Idaho. He was married in 1877 to Mary Hawkins, and in 1885, while on a pleasure trip in the east with his wife and adopted daughter, died suddenly at N. Orleans. He had been member of the legislature and county supervisor. James L. Hall of N. H. was a soldier in the 5th U. S. inf., serving in the Navajo wars of 1860–1 in N. Mex. Later he was a miner, trader, and butcher in Id., Or., and Cal., until he came to Ariz. in 1877. He is a butcher at Prescott, having also held the positions of mayor and probate judge. His wife was Catharine Odell of Canada, who has borne him five children. He sends me some items about Navajo customs.

James M. Baker, a Missourian who came overland to Cal. in 1853, and travelled over the Pac. territories from 1861, came to Ariz. with Dr Jones from Salt Lake in 1866, married Sarah Ehle in 1870, and has been engaged in stock-raising near Prescott.

Frank Kenly Ainsworth, M. D., was born in Vt, and came to Ariz. in 1880. His wife is Nellie H. Trowbridge. He has been member of the council, surgeon-general of the territory, and president of the Medical Soc., residing at Prescott.

John Goulder Campbell is a Scotchman, aged 60, who came to Cal. overland by way of Mexico and Mazatlan in 1849. In 1864 he came to Arizona, becoming a prominent merchant and stockman at Prescott. He was twice a member of the legislature, county supervisor in 1871–2, and delegate in congress in 1879. He married in Cal. 1857, and again at Washington in 1880, having three children. I. N. Berry sells liquor at Flagstaff. He came from Indiana, and spent some years in N. Mex.; wife, Mary Parker.

Charles S. Black, from Maine, drove a band of cattle from Cal. in 1873, having a farm and stock ranch in Kirkland valley.

Robert Connell, a liquor merchant of Prescott, and member of the legislature in 1883, is a native of Ark., who came from Col. in 1874. He went to Ill. for a wife in 1878, and has several children.

John Chartz raises cattle in Thompson valley. He is a Canadian, age 30, who has been a sailor, and came from Cal. in 1873.

and in 1883 the county north of the Colorado was extended east some 50 miles to Kanab Wash. The present area is about 12,500 square miles. The region is traversed from north to south by a succession of mineral-bearing mountain ranges, separated by narrow valleys, fertile, but for the most part without water, though prospectively valuable for grazing purposes with the aid of artesian wells. The most valuable agricultural lands are embraced in the Colorado bottom. The county has many rich mines of gold, silver, copper, and lead, and from the beginning has been the field of frequent excitements, alternating with periods of depression. The railroad, however, has brought the promise of increased prosperity. Its population is about 1,500, of which Mineral Park, the county seat, contains nearly one third. It is built chiefly of adobe, and is the distributing point of supplies for the different mining camps. Kingman is the principal railroad town.[5]

[5] Statistics from the 10th census are as follows: pop. 1,190, at Mineral Park 318, Ft Mojave 78; no. farms 41, average size 84 ac., extent 3,430 a., improved 1,557 a., value $39,670; implements, etc., $1,925; value of farm products $19,998; horses 388, mules 66, oxen 18, milk-cows 248, cattle 3,483, swine 161; value of live-stock $62,555; crop of barley 5,817 bush., corn 430, wheat 320; milk 712 gal., butter 1,565 lbs. Assessment $470,943, tax $13,731, debt $23,253. Hamilton's stat., pop. 1,910, assessed val. of property $1,756,000, land cultivated 1,000 a., cattle 10,000, horses 1,000, mules 500, swine 200, sheep 2,000.
The region north of the Colorado is for the most part uninhabited, and but partially explored. A portion of the Mojave Ind. live near the fort, and not on the reservation farther south, frequenting the station at the Needles, where the R. R. crosses the river. Ft Mojave dates from 1858. Hardyville, so named from Wm H. Hardy, a prominent pioneer, is at the practical head of navigation on the Colorado, was formerly county seat, and was in early mining excitements a bustling place, but is now nearly deserted. Aubrey Landing, at the junction of the Colorado and Williams fork, is a point of distribution for the southern mining districts of Mojave. Large quantities of ore are shipped at Kingman station both east and west. The *Mojave Miner* is published at Mineral Park.
Wm or 'Bill' Williams, for whom a branch of the Colorado was named, was a famous mountain man, who in early years visited most parts of Ariz. as of other regions in the great interior. He is said to have been in Mo. a Methodist preacher, and was finally killed by the Ind. I find no reliable dates or details respecting his Ariz. explorations. Adamson Cornwall, a native of Oregon, and sometime teacher in Cal., resides since 1875 near Signal as a ranchero. He has been a member of the legislative assembly.
Robert Steen, of N. Y., came to Nev. in 1859, served as sheriff of Nye co., and came to Ariz. in 1873. He was a miner until 1882, and since that time has been sheriff of Mojave co., residing at Mineral Park.

Yuma is another of the original counties, named like the rest from its chief aboriginal tribe; and it is the only county whose boundaries have never been changed. It has an area of 10,138 square miles, and is for the most part an arid desert, marked in the west by parallel north and south ranges, and in the east by detached spurs. The chief characteristic of its climate is extreme heat. It will never do to publish a work on Arizona without repeating John Phœnix' old story of the wicked Yuma soldier, who, after death, was stationed in a region reputed to be hot, yet was obliged to send back for his blankets. The heat, however, is much less oppressive than the thermometer would indicate, the air being pure and healthful. Agricultural possibilities depend mainly on the reclamation of Colorado bottoms by extensive irrigation works, and there are also broad tracts of grazing lands that may be utilized by means of wells. With these artificial aids, it is by no means improbable that in time Yuma may take a very prominent rank among the counties of the territory. Its placers on the Gila and Colorado were the foundation of several 'rushes' from 1858 to 1864, and are still worked to some extent, the sands in many places being rich in gold if water could be obtained for washing. Deep mines, as elsewhere noted, have yielded rich treasures of silver, lead, and copper, the mining industry here having been less disastrously affected than elsewhere by Indian hostilities, and by transportation difficulties. Yuma, or the region about the Gila and Colorado junction, figures prominently in the early Spanish annals, as already presented in this volume, though the ill-fated missions were on the California side, where also in later emigrant and ferry times Fort Yuma, now abandoned, was the centre of desert life. A remnant of the Yuma Indians, a once powerful tribe of the Gila valley, has now a reservation on the California shore at the old fort. Arizona City, since called Yuma, opposite the fort, came into existence with the old ferry establishment, and though encountering many obstacles, including several partial destructions by flood, it prospered exceedingly from 1864–5, as the principal distributing point for all the military posts, towns, and mining camps in the territory. The coming of the railroad in 1877—and Yuma had the honor of a first visit from the iron horse—took away much of its commercial glory; but it is still a town of about 1,000 inhabitants, site of the territorial prison, with a brisk local trade, and an excellent newspaper in the *Arizona Sentinel;* and its position on the railroad and the great river gives promise of permanent prosperity within somewhat narrow limits. The county seat has been here since 1871, being removed from La Paz, a town which rose and fell with the Colorado mining excitement of 1862–7. Ehrenberg, founded—as Mineral City—in 1863, a few miles below on the river, flourished with the decay of La Paz from 1867–9, and became an active trade centre, though losing for the most part its prominence when the stage gave way to the locomotive. The Colorado Indian reservation above La Paz, where a part of the Mojave tribe have their home, has been noticed in another chapter.[6]

[6] Yuma co. statistics of the 10th census: pop. 3,215, Yuma city 1,200, Ehrenberg 248, Raw Hide 40, Plomosa 39; farms 2, average size 965 a., extent 1,930 a., improved 500 a., value $6,500, implements $900; horses 39, mules 3, cows 7, cattle 25, sheep 100, swine 35, val. of live-stock $1,100; wool 300 lbs., barley 3,000 b., corn 1,251 b., wheat 400 b., value of farm products $9,000; assessment $419,397, tax $12,802, debt $60,000. Hamilton's stat., pop. 3,922, assessment $1,000,000; cattle 5,000, horses 800, mules 300, swine 200; acres cultiv. 1,500. Hodge puts the pop. at 2,212 in 1876, and of the city 1,500, Ehrenberg 300. For sketch of Yuma co. and its history, see *Yuma Sentinel,* Nov. 10, 1877; Apr. 19, 1879. Name of Arizona city changed to Yuma city in 1873. *Ariz., Acts,* 1873, p. 39. See also, on the town, *Hayes' Scraps, Ariz.,* iv. 182, 188, 193, 272; v. 37, 109–10, 150; *Ariz. Scraps,* 122–5, 133; *Prescott Miner,* July 13, 1877; *Disturnell's Dir.,* 1881, p. 199–200. On Ehrenberg, *Conklin's Pict. Ariz.,* 168; *Ariz. Scraps,* 124. On La Paz, *Id.,* 500; *S. F. Times,* Sept. 18, 1868.

Herman Ehrenberg, a German engineer, after an adventurous career in Texas and in Cal. from 1847, came to Ariz. in 1854, and was one of the territory's most notable pioneers and prospectors. He gave his name to the town, and was killed by Ind. on the Cal. side of the Colorado. He was a writer as well as adventurer. See Pioneer Register in *Hist. Cal.* J. W. Dorrington is a prominent newspaper man of Yuma, being editor and proprietor of the *Arizona Sentinel,* a paper which next to the *Prescott Miner* furnishes more items on territorial annals than any other. Dorrington was born in N. Y., 1843, and came via Cal. in 1869. Serving as clerk in the district court at La Paz

Pima county, bearing like the others the name of its aboriginal inhabitants, included at the time of its organization in 1864 all south of the Gila and east of Yuma, or nearly all of the Gadsden purchase. A part of Maricopa was cut off in 1873, of Pinal in 1875, Cochise and a part of Graham in 1881. Its present area is about 10,500 square miles. Tucson has always been the county seat, and in 1867–77 was also the territorial capital. Western and northern Pima, the former known as Papaguería, is an arid plain sparsely covered in spots with grass and shrubs; not without fertility, but having for the most part no water, and dotted here and there with isolated mountains and short ranges. The south-eastern portion in and adjoining the valley of the Santa Cruz, the county's only stream of importance, but sinking in the sand before reaching the Gila, is a fertile and agreeable region, though not well wooded or watered, and bordered by lofty mountain ranges. Here were the only Arizona settlements of Spanish and Mexican times, the presidios and missions of the Apache frontier dating from early in the eighteenth century. This early history has been as fully presented as the fragmentary records permit, and need not be even outlined here. The prosperity and antiquity of these establishments have always been exaggerated by modern writers, but their very existence under the circumstances was re-

and Yuma to 1876, he was later several times a member of the legislature and council.

Charles Baker, a butcher at Yuma, is a New Yorker, who came overland to Cal. in 1858, and to Ariz. in 1862. Wife Concepcion Rodriguez, 2 children.

Abraham Frank, of German birth, came to the U. S. in 1854, and to Ariz. in 1867. He opened a store at Ehrenberg, which he still owns, having also a store at Yuma, and being also a contractor for govt supplies. He married Tomasa Sortillon in 1883, and has one child. Has been member of the legislature and supervisor of Yavapai.

Geo. E. Bateman, whose P. O. address is Yuma, is interested in the Blythe colony on the lower Colorado. He is a native of Mass., who came to Cal. in 1849, and has lived and travelled much in Mex. Has a Mex. wife and a son.

Geo. M. Thatcher of Me, a liquor merchant at Yuma, was a miner in W. T., also visiting Australia, until he came to Ariz. in 1866 by way of Utah and down the Colorado in a boat. He has been supt of the penitentiary and county supervisor. His wife was Aurora Santoya, and they have two children.

markable.   Their nearest approach to real prosperity
was in 1790 to 1815.   The north-eastern and south-
eastern parts of the county are traversed by the
Southern Pacific and Guaymas railroads, respectively.
With about 15,000 inhabitants, Pima is the most
populous of all the counties, and many of its mining
districts, as elsewhere noted, give good promise of
future wealth.   Tucson, founded in 1776, having at
times in the old régime a population of over 1,000,
but greatly reduced in the last days of Mexican and
first of American rule, gained something by the disasters of 1861, which depopulated the rest of the county,
still more by the renewal of mining industry following the peace of 1873–4, and received its last and
greatest impetus on the completion of the railroad.
With 10,000 inhabitants or a little more, about one
third being of Mexican race, Tucson is and is likely to
remain the territorial metropolis and centre of trade.
Large portions of the city have still the characteristics of a Spanish American town with its adobe buildings; but recent improvements have been marked and
rapid, brick and wood replacing to a considerable extent the original building material.   Its schools,
churches, and other public buildings are not dis-
creditable to an American town of the century, while
many merchants transact wholesale business on a
large scale.   The other old settlements of the valley,
such as Bac, Tubac, Tumacácori, and Calabazas, must
still seek their glory in the remote past or future.
At San Javier still stands the famous old church of
mission times, which constitutes the county's most
notable relic of modern antiquity.   Here also is the
reservation set apart for the Pápagos, an interesting
portion of Pima's population, and in many respects
Arizona's most promising aboriginal tribe.   At Quijotoa in the west two new towns sprang into existence,
Logan and New Virginia, but their future, depending
on that of the mines, is at present problematic or even
doubtful.   Nogales is the frontier custom-house town

on the railroad, part of it being in Sonora. With Pima county's position on the Mexican border, its strong element of foreign and Indian population, its old-time history and traditions, its bloody Indian wars perhaps finally ended in 1886, its peculiar political and secession experiences of 1861–2, and its successive periods of excitement and depression in mining industry, it must be regarded as the representative county of Arizona in the past; and in the future, with its metropolis, its undeveloped mineral resources, its fertile though limited farming lands, and its existing and projected railroad facilities, Pima is not unlikely to retain its prominence.[7]

[7] Pima statistics of the 10th census of 1880, including Cochise and Graham at that time, as must be noted: pop. 17,006, Tucson 7,007, Smithville 148, Maxey 145, Harlowville 55, Ft Lowell 227; no. farms 137, average size 175 a., extent 23,986 a., improved 9,205 a., value $220,900, implements $18,695; horses 1,328, mules 208, oxen 218, cows 3,171, cattle 8,353, sheep 11,125, swine 636, value of live-stock $295,373; barley 33,511 b., corn 9,486 b., wheat 9,890 b., wool 25,360 lbs., milk 6,280 gal., butter 8,390 lbs., cheese 1,000 lbs., value of farm products $88,837, assessment $2,851,212, tax $117,325, debts $65,284. Hamilton's stat. of 1882–3: assessment $5,000,000, pop. 17,425, cattle 75,000, horses 6,000, mules 2,000, swine 1,100, sheep 5,000, cultivated land 3,000 a. For sketches of the county, see *Arizona Scraps*, 123; *Yuma Sentinel*, March 15, Nov. 16, 1878; Jan. 18, 1879; *Tucson Star*, Jan. 9, 1879.

Tucson was incorporated in 1877, extended in 1881, and reincorporated in 1883. *Ariz., Acts*, 1877, p. 52–63; *Id., Laws*, 1881, p. 20; 1883, p. 181–211. Hamilton says the Pimas pronounce Tucson *Chookson*, and that it means 'black creek.' I question the first part of this statement, or at least that such was the original Pima pronunciation. The city has fine public buildings, cathedral, 4 churches, 5 hotels, public and high school, opera house, two flourmills, R. R. shops, 8 newspapers—2 of them daily and 2 Spanish—electric lights, and water brought in pipes 7 miles from the river. Hotel arrivals in 1882 were over 40,000. On Tucson, besides Hamilton, Hinton, and Elliott & Co., see *Barter's Directory*, 1881, p. 9–13; *Disturnell's Bus. Dir.*, 1881, p. 184–7; *Californian*, Apr. 1880, p. 370–1; *Hodge's Ariz.*, 153–5; *Rusling's Across Amer.*, 374–5; *Washburn*, in *Cincinnatus' Trav.*, 343; *Hayes' Diary*, MS., 45–9; *Hughes' (Law), Pima Co. and Tucson MS.*; *Ariz. Scraps*, 37–8, 92, 123, 230, 502; *Hayes' Scraps, Ariz.*, iii. 153, 164–5, 312–13; iv. 70, 111–12, 146–7, 301–2; v. 349–50; *Tucson Star*, W., Feb. 13, 1879, Jan. 1, Aug. 20, 1880; *D.*, Jan. 20, 1880; *Id., Citizen*, W., March 7, 1879; June 26, 1880; *D.*, Aug. 11, 1880; *Yuma Sentinel*, Sept. 22, 1877; *Phœnix Herald*, June 12, 1882; *Prescott Miner*, Feb. 5, 1875; *S. F. Bulletin*, Nov. 19, 1858; Mar. 1, 4, 1879; *S. F. Alta*, Aug. 31, 1867; June 5, 1880; *S. F. Herald*, Jan. 18, 1858; *S. F. Times*, Oct. 24, 1868; *S. F. Chronicle*, Mar. 14, 1881; *S. F. Call*, Apr. 2, 1881; *S. F. Post*, Jan. 4, 1881.

Many Pima co. pioneers have been mentioned in connection with territorial annals. Samuel Hughes was born in Wales, 1829, coming to the U. S. in 1838, and overland to Cal. in 1850. In Cal. and Or. he had a varied experience as fisherman, cook, miner, cattle-trader, and Indian-fighter. In 1858 he came to Ariz. and settled at Tucson, where he has become a wealthy owner of live-stock and real estate. He has furnished many items for my

Cochise county, named for the famous chief of the Chiricahua Apaches, lies east of Pima, from which it was cut off in 1881, forming the south-eastern corner of the territory, and having an area of 5,925 square miles. The county seat is at Tombstone. It is a region of wooded mountains and grassy valleys, affording a considerable area of grazing lands, but only slight agricultural promise, for lack of water. The San Pedro is the only permanent stream, carrying but little water in summer; but artesian wells have proved successful in Sulphur Spring, one of the county's eastern valleys. The stock-raising industry promises well; but it is to the wonderful metallic wealth of its hills that Cochise owes its world-wide

use respecting early times in Pima and the growth of Tucson. Solomon Warren, according to Elliott, came from Yuma in 1856, and opened the first American store at Tucson. Teodoro Ramirez, a native and formerly an official during the Mex. régime, died at Tucson in 1871, at the age of about 94. Amasa B. Sampson is a native of Mass., who went to Kansas in 1855, serving with Gen. Lane's free-state forces, and later going to Pike's Peak, where he was sheriff. In 1861–5 he served with the Col. volunteers in N. Mex., and was subsequently a merchant at Helena, Mont., and at S. Francisco, Coming to Tucson in 1879 he has since carried on a large tobacco business. and was elected county recorder in 1884. He married Anna Gallagher in 1885. He seems to be a deservedly popular man. Chas Tozer, a well-known mining expert, was speaker of the 1st legislature. He came to Tucson about 1856, and commanded the party that attempted to rescue Crabb and his filibusters in Sonora. R. H. Paul, for several terms sheriff of Pima co., is a native of Mass., who was a sailor in early life, coming to Cal. in 1849. There he was a miner in 1849–54 and 1861–72; constable and sheriff in Calaveras co. in 1854–61; and from 1872 an employé of Wells, Fargo, & Co., in which capacity he came to Ariz. in 1878. He married Margaret Coughlan in 1862, and has three children. Portrait in E. & Co.'s *Hist.*, 244. Geo. J. Roskruge, a prominent surveyor and Freemason of Tucson, was born in England 1845, coming to the U. S. in 1870, and to Ariz. from Col. in 1872. He came in a party seeking timber lands, and had at the start some exciting adventures with Indians. Joining a surveying party as cook and packer, he became chief draughtsman in the surv.-gen.'s office, deputy surveyor of Ariz. and N. Mex., and city and county surveyor. He was also supt of irrigation, member of the board of education, and grand sec. of the Masons. H. E. Lacy, an Englishman, came to the U. S. in 1864, and served with the Cal. volunteers in Ariz. 1865–6. He came back to Ariz. in 1866, and was a trader at Ft Goodwin and Camp Apache, representing Apache co. in the council of 1883, and now living at Tucson as a money-lender. Gilbert W. Hopkins, one of the early pioneers, was a member of the 1st legislature, and regent of the university. He was killed by Apaches near Ft Buchanan in Feb. 1865. B. H. Hereford, a native of Miss., went to Chih. in 1849, and to Cal. in 1853, being for seven years clerk for his brother who was district attorney of Sacramento co. From 1863 he was county clerk, deputy sheriff, and book-keeper for the Bonanza firm in Nev., coming to Ariz. in 1876, and there practising law. He was a member of the council and district attorney of Pima, residing at Tucson. His son Frank was Gov. Tritle's private secretary.

fame, and particularly to developments in the Tombstone lodes, which have proved by far the most extensive and productive in the territory. This region has been the field of the most bloody and longest continued Indian atrocities; and it has suffered much in later years from the pest of border outlaws; but it is hoped that its pioneer troubles and youthful irregularities are for the most part at an end. Tombstone, where the first house was built in 1879, and which has been twice nearly destroyed by fire, has been the most flourishing mining camp in the territory, and is now a town of nearly 4,000 inhabitants, chiefly built of adobe, but having many fine brick structures. An ample and excellent supply of water is brought from the Huachuca mountains, over 20 miles distant; and the city is well supplied with newspapers, schools, churches, and mercantile establishments, to say nothing of saloons and other adjuncts of civilization. Bisbee, in the extreme south, is a town of nearly 500 inhabitants, built up at the works of the Copper Queen Company, and the prospective centre of a rich mining district. Benson is at the junction of the Guaymas railroad with the main overland line, and the centre of a large grazing district, having large smelting-works, a newspaper, and a population of 500. Fairbanks, on the Guaymas railroad, is the point of departure of stages for Tombstone. Willcox, with about the same population, is a railroad station in the north-east, the point of departure for places in Graham and Gila counties, having also its newspaper.[8]

[8] The 10th census has no statistics for Cochise, then a part of Pima, except the pop. of the following towns: Tombstone 973, Charleston 350, C. Bowie 184, Contention 150, Dos Cabezas 126. Hamilton's statistics are: pop. 9,640, assessed value $4,263,684, cattle 70,000, horses 4,000, mules 3,000, swine 500, sheep 5,000, cultivated land 4,000 a. Mining stat. have been given in another chapter. Elliott & Co.'s stat.: cattle 52,000, horses 4,000, mules 2,200, swine 1,000, sheep 5,000, value of live-stock $2,180,000. 5,000 of the 5,925 sq. m. are agricultural lands! Something of the growth of Tombstone has been recorded in connection with mining. The destructive fires were in 1881-2, but the excellent water supply has now greatly reduced the danger, though it did not prevent the destruction of the pumping-works in 1886. The public buildings include a county court-house of brick, costing $43,000, a fine city hall, and school building. There are 4 churches, 2 hotels, theatre, and bank. The

We now come to the four new counties along the
Gila, cut off at different dates since 1871 from Yavapai
on the north and Pima on the south.   The eastern-
most is Maricopa, created in 1871, increased from Pima
in 1873, losing part of Pinal in 1875, extended in the
north-east to longitude 110° in 1877, and losing northern Gila in 1881.   Its present area is 9,354 square
miles, and its county seat has been Phœnix from the
first.   The name, like those of all the counties before
mentioned, is that of the principal aboriginal tribe.
The extreme western portion does not differ much in
its natural features from Yuma, having in the north
the famous Vulture mines and in the south the Myers
district.   Above the big bend, however, on the Gila,
Salt, and Verde rivers, the plain is favorably situated
for irrigation from the streams; and this eastern portion
of Maricopa, especially the Salt River valley, forms
the largest and most available body of farming land
in the territory.   By canals that have been and are
being constructed, large areas of the desert are being

newspaper is the *Epitaph.*   For several years the city has been under a cloud,
but there seems to be no permanent foundation for depression.   The city was
incorporated in 1881. *Ariz., Acts*, 11th leg. ass., 39–78.   The files of the Tombstone *Epitaph, Nugget,* and *Record* contain of course much information about
the town, as also the San Francisco papers.   See also *Californian*, July 1881,
p. 53–7; *Disturnell's Bus. Dir.*, 1881, p. 171–5; *Ariz., Scraps*, 431; and of
course full descriptions in Hamilton and Elliott.
    Ed Schieffelin and Richard Gird, both residents of Cal. in later years,
were the discoverers of the Tombstone mines.   W. H. Savage, county and city
attorney at Tombstone, is an Irishman who came to the U. S. in 1847.   In
the war of 1861–5 he enlisted four times in the navy, cavalry, and infantry,
reaching the rank of lieut.   J. V. Vickers is a real estate and insurance
agent at Tombstone, also interested in mining and stock-raising.   He came
to Ariz. in 1880, being a native of Pa, and a merchant in N. Y. city in 1874–
80.   Benj. Williams, a native of England, came to the U. S. in 1855, to Cal.
in 1874, and from Nev. to Ariz. in 1878.   He has furnished interesting and
useful information about the town and its mines.   Among other prominent
citizens of Tombstone are the following: Judge W. H. Stilwell, in 1880 associate judge of the supreme court; E. C. Dunn, M. D., who settled at Tombstone in 1881; F. L. Moore, the vice-president and manager of the Cochise
Hardware and Trading Company; P. B. Warnekros, a general merchant; S. C.
Bagg, proprietor of the *Tombstone Prospector;* J. P. McAllister, a foundry-
man; B. S. Coffman, superintendent of the Water Vail Mining Company;
J. E. Durkee, the largest freighter in Arizona; J. J. Patton, who is in the
harness and saddlery business; J. S. Robbins, manager and half owner of the
Whitbeck Land and Cattle Co.; S. L. Hart, a dealer in hardware and fire-
arms; and L. W. Blinn, a lumber merchant, and president of the Tempe
Land Improvement Company.

transformed into grain-fields, orchards, vineyards, and gardens. Apparently the county must always maintain its agricultural supremacy. Here is one of the Pima Indian reservations, and here the Mormons have their most prosperous settlements. The county's great need is additional facilities for transportation, which will be afforded by a railroad connecting the Atlantic and Pacific and Prescott in the north with the Southern Pacific—which traverses Maricopa from east to west, south of the Gila—and Tucson in the south. The population is about 6,000. The first settlement was at Wickenburg in the extreme north in 1863; but the valley settlement, the digging of canals, the raising of crops, and the building of houses date from 1867-8; and the founding of Phœnix—so called from the new civilization that was expected to rise here from the ashes of the past—from 1870. This is a thriving town of some 3,000 inhabitants, built largely of adobe, but with many structures of brick and wood, on an open plain formerly classified as desert but now distinguished among Arizona towns for its wealth of shade trees and attractive homes. Excessive heat is the only drawback to comfort in this favored region. The city is reached by a stage route of about 30 miles from Maricopa station on the Southern Pacific, but railroad connection with the north and south cannot be long delayed.[9]

[9] Maricopa (including northern Gila) statistics of the 10th census: pop. 5,689, Phœnix 1,708, Seymour 258, Mesa City 151, Tempe 135, Utahville 123, Wickenburg 104, Wheatfield 72; no. of farms 171, average size 205 a., extent 35,011 a., improved 19,447 a., value $287,180, implements $24,465; horses 1,151, mules 192, oxen 13, cows 1,623, cattle 2,954, sheep 8, swine 1,904, value of live-stock $161,406; wool 24 lbs., milk 4,600 gal., butter $7,800 lbs.; barley 125,138 b., corn 2,165, b., wheat 87,315; value of farm products $210,785, assessment $915,131, tax $27,575, debt $76,394. Hamilton's stat. of 1882-3: pop. 6,408, assessed value $2,078,147, cattle 8,000, horses 5,000, mules 1,500, swine 7,000, sheep 1,500, land cultivated 35,000 a. Elliott & Co.'s stat. of 1883: assessment $1,939,231, acres of alfalfa 3,973, vines 213,420, fruit-trees 30,260; product of wheat 13,686,780 lbs. or 24⅔ b. per acre, barley 18,792,091 lbs. or 26½ b. per acre, wheat raised by Ind. 2,000,000 lbs., cotton 3,390 lbs. on 5 a. These stat. were taken from the Phœnix *Gazette*. On the organization of the county and successive changes in the boundaries, see *Ariz.*, *Acts*, 1871, p. 53-4; 1873, p. 87; 1877, p. 12. On Maricopa co. and Salt River valley, see, besides the references given below for Phœnix, *Yuma Sentinel*,

Farther east on the Gila is Pinal county, named for its pine groves, or perhaps directly from the Pinal Apaches, created in 1875 from Pima and Yavapai, slightly extended westward in 1877 to correct an error of boundary, and losing the Globe district of southern Gila in 1881. Its present area is 5,210 square miles, and its county seat Florence. The southern portion of the county is largely a desert, traversed in the west by the railroad and the underground channel of the Santa Cruz, and in the east by the San Pedro and several ranges of mineral-bearing mountains. In the northern hills are several mining districts grouped around the famous Silver King as a centre. Along the Gila, which traverses the county from east to west, is a body of fine irrigable land, similar to that in Maricopa, though of less extent. In the west, lying along the river, is the Pima reservation, parts of which have been cultivated for centuries with undiminished yield; while farther up the valley eastward is a tract irrigated and utilized by settlers in recent years, and closely resembling in most respects that on Salt River. The lower San Pedro also contains a limited amount of good farming land.

April 21, 1877; April 12, 1879; *Prescott Miner,* Nov. 2, 9, 1877; *Tucson Citizen,* May 30, 1879; *S. F. Call,* Feb. 16, 1879; *Arizona Scraps,* 19, 123.

Phœnix has 5 churches, 2 of adobe, 2 of brick, and one of wood; a two-story brick school-house; fine brick court-house; 4 newspapers, the *Herald, Gazette, Mercurio,* and *Union*; an ice-factory, brewery, and flouring mill which in 1883 turned out 3,000,000 lbs. of flour. The city was incorporated in 1881. *Ariz., Acts,* 105–16. On the history and condition of Phœnix, the *Phœnix Herald* file contains a large amount of information; see also *Hayes' Scraps, Ariz.,* vi. 110; *Ariz. Scraps,* 19, 133; *Prescott Arizonian,* July 19, 1879; *Cal. Agriculturist,* ii. 10. Jonesville, the oldest Mormon settlement, dates from 1877, and has a pop. of about 150; Mesa City was founded in 1878; Tempe is a pleasant village with a large flouring mill.

John Y. T. Smith is named as the 1st settler in Salt River valley, and J. W. Swilling as the originator of the 1st irrigating canal. Henry Wickenburg, for whom the town was named, came from Cal. in 1862, and discovered the famous Vulture mine. He was still living in 1875, and perhaps 10 years later. James Stinson resides at Phœnix, and has a stock ranch in the Tonto Basin. He is a native of Maine, came to Cal. in 1855, and after extensive wanderings in the northern territories, to Ariz. from Colorado in 1873. His wife was Melissa Bagley, and they have two children. M. H. Sherman of N. Y. came in 1873 as principal of the Prescott schools. He was elected supt of public instruction in 1880, and appointed adj.-gen. in 1883. He is president of a bank at Phœnix.

The railroad extends about 70 miles across the south-
western part of the county; and in this region stands
also the famous Casa Grande, an adobe structure
which was probably seen by the Spaniards in 1540,
and was certainly built at a much earlier date.   Florence, on the Gila, is the county seat and metropolis,
and has a population of over 1,000, in many respects
resembling the town of Phœnix.   Casa Grande station, with nearly 500 inhabitants, is the principal
railroad town, and Silver King and Pinal are the
most flourishing settlements of the mining region.
By reason of its situation and varied resources, this
county bids fair to be permanently one of the most
prosperous in Arizona.   The Deer Creek coal-field, of
great prospective value, is on the eastern frontier of
Pinal, within the Indian reservation.   A large portion of the county is included in the Reavis land
grant.[10]

[10] Pinal statistics of the 10th census: pop. 3,044, Florence 902, Pinal 166;
Maricopa 96, Miami 53, Sanford 39, Casa Grande 33. no. of farms 76, average
size 215 a., extent 16,337 a., improved 7,841, value $173,750, implements $13,-
000, horses 542, mules 83, oxen 9, cows 478, cattle 3,537, sheep 5, swine 417,
value of live-stock $88,061, wool 14 lbs., milk 3,650 gal., butter 9,425 lbs.,
cheese 825 lbs., barley 33,800 b., corn 2,205 b., wheat 22,357, value of farm
products $71,875, assessments $2,205,129, tax $36,831.   Hamilton's statistics:
pop. 3,362, assessed value $1,753,000, cattle 25,000, horses 2,000, mules 1,000;
swine 600, sheep 3,500, cultivated land 7,000 a., not including the Indian
farms.   Assessed value in 1883, acc. to E. & Co., $1,898,142.   Florence was
founded in 1869, the 1st house having been built in 1866.   Its buildings are of
adobe, and a large element of the pop. is Mexican.   There are 2 hotels, 2
schools, catholic church, court-house, brewery, flouring mill, and many stores,
shops, etc.   The newspaper is the *Enterprise*.   Elliott notes Primrose Hill,
near the town, where Poston proposed to built a temple to the sun for the
Parsee worship, spending several thousand dollars in grading a spiral road to
the summit.   Another of Poston's schemes was to establish an ostrich farm.
Pinal was formerly called Picket Post.   It has a church and school, and a
pop. of nearly 400.   Here are the mills of the Silver King Co.   Its newspaper
is the *Drill*.   Silver King, with 500 inhab., is at the mine.   It has 2 hotels,
and a fine hall.   The mine was located in 1875.   Casa Grande is an adobe
town, and is the principal shipping point and stage station for Florence,
Globe, and Quijotoa.   Adamsville on the Gila is now abandoned.   Levi Ruggles, the founder of Florence, where he resides as a merchant, came to Ariz.
in 1866 as Ind. agent.   He was a member of the council in 1873 and 1877,
also registrar and receiver of the land-office.   He is a native of Ohio, and his
wife was Cynthia M. Tharp.   Arthur Macy, born in N. Y. city, 1852, and
graduate of the school of mines, was R. R. and mining engineer, and expert
in N. Y., N. C., Col., and Id. down to 1883, when he came to Ariz. as supt
of the Silver King Mining Co.   He has furnished an excellent account of the
discovery and history of this most famous of all Ariz. mines.

Gila county, named for the river, was created from Maricopa and Pinal in 1881, being extended eastward to the San Cárlos in 1885. Globe City is its county seat, and it is the smallest of Arizona counties, having an area of 3,400 square miles, and a population of about 1,500. Gila is essentially a mining county, its settlement dating from the discovery of the Globe district lodes in 1876, and all its many mountains and ranges being rich in gold and silver, as noted in another chapter. The mountains are also well timbered, and the valleys, small but numerous, are fertile, with abundance of grass, and some of them well watered by the Salt River and its tributary creeks. Much of the best land is, however, within the limits of the San Cárlos reservation, and thus closed to settlers. Globe City, the chief town and county seat, is a flourishing place on Pinal Creek, in the centre of the southern part of the county, a town of wood and brick buildings, having nearly 1,000 inhabitants. The great need of Globe, and of all the Gila camps, is railroad communication with the outer world, the distance at present to railroad stations, Willcox in the south-east or Casa Grande in the south-west, being over 100 miles.[11]

Graham county, so called probably from the mountain peak of that name,[12] was created in 1881 from

Thomas F. Weedin, editor and proprietor of the Florence *Enterprise*, is a native of Mo., born in 1854, who learned his trade as printer at Kansas City, first coming to the Pac. coast in 1875. He was a member of the 13th legislature, and is a man enthusiastically devoted to the interests of his town and county.

[11] In the 10th census Gila is included in Maricopa and Pinal. The pop. of Globe is given as 704. Hamilton's statistics of 1882–3: pop. 1,582, assessed value $1,115,000, cattle 15,000, horses 1,000, mules 800, swine 300, sheep 3,000, cultivated land 1,500 acres. Globe may have been named from a globe, or bowlder, of silver weighing 300 lbs., found here at the beginning. The town has an altitude of over 4,000 ft, with an agreeable and healthful climate. It has 2 churches, school, hotel, two newspapers—the *Silver Belt* and *Chronicle*—bank, brewery, 12 stores, and all the usual establishments of a mining camp and distributing point for other camps. Hamilton and Elliott have but little to say in detail of the other camps, except in connection with the mines, on which their existence depends. By reason of expensive transportation, with unwise and extravagant management, most of the mines have been under a cloud in late years. Here, as in most other regions of Arizona, a railroad is projected.

[12] The name Mt Graham is used by Emory in the report of his reconnois-

Pima and Apache, the county seat being at first Safford, but moved to Solomonville in 1883. In 1885 a
small tract west of the San Cárlos was cut off and
added to Gila, the remaining area being about 6,475
square miles. Its population is about 4,000. In the
north, west, and south are large tracts of excellent
grazing land, the half-dozen ranchos of H. C. Hooker,
and especially the Sierra Bonita of 500 square miles,
with its thoroughbred horses and cattle, being famous
throughout the territory; but a very large part of the
north-western region, about one fourth of the whole
county, is within the White Mountain Indian reservation. In the central portion of the Gila is a fine tract
of fertile and irrigable land, notably the Pueblo Viejo
valley, once inhabited by Pueblo tribes, as is indicated
by traces of aboriginal structures. This region is as
yet but sparsely settled, but is being gradually occupied by Mormon and other settlers. In the east,
adjoining New Mexico on the tributaries of the San
Francisco, are the copper mines, which are among the
most productive in the world, this region being connected by a narrow-gauge railroad with the Southern
Pacific at Lordsburg, New Mexico. Solomonville,
named for a pioneer family, is an adobe town of nearly
400 inhabitants, in the centre of the Pueblo Viejo
valley. Clifton, the metropolis, with a population of
about 1,000, is built in a cañon of the San Francisco
River, where are the reduction-works of the Arizona
Copper Company, and is the terminus of the railroad.
Fort Grant and Camp Thomas are the county's military posts, Smithville and Central are Mormon villages
on the Gila.[13]

sance of 1846, its origin not being stated. Otherwise, I should suppose it to
have been named for Graham, who was prominent in the boundary survey of
1850–2. The facts have escaped my search.
   [13] Statistics of the 10th census: pop. of Solomonville 175, San José 186,
Safford 173, C. Thomas 112, C. Grant 243. Hamilton's stat.: pop. 4,229,
assessed value $1,181,064, cattle 20,000, horses 4,000, mules 1,000, swine 500,
sheep 10,000, cultivated land 7,000 acres. A large part of the pop. is Mexican. Clifton has a newspaper, the *Clarion*, a school, 2 hotels, 8 stores, and
saloons more than sufficient for its needs. The town has all the characteristics of a prosperous mining camp. Solomonville has a fine adobe court-house,

school, hotel, and the necessary stores and shops.   It will doubtless become the metropolis in time, being in the centre of a rich agricultural and grazing region.   Safford, farther down the Gila, is a pleasant village, with a hotel, flouring mill, and two stores.   Fruits promise well in this region.   The Mormon settlements are below Safford.   Thomas is a town of 10 stores, 2 hotels, shops, etc., supported mainly by the adjacent military post.

Geo. H. Stevens, county recorder, was born in Mass. 1844, and came to Ariz. in 1866.   He served as Indian agent at Camp Grant and S. Cárlos, serving with Gen. Crook's scouts, being employed to remove the White Mt Apaches in 1875, and being post-treasurer at S. Cárlos till 1878, being also the owner of Eureka Springs rancho, and later of the Eagle Creek rancho, till driven out by Ind. in 1880, when he settled in Pueblo Viejo valley.   He was three times a member of the legislature, clerk of board of supervisors, and sheriff.   Was at one time the only resident of the county.   He resides at Solomonville.

The following residents of Arizona, who have kindly furnished me with dictations, are also deserving of mention.   In Tucson, M. G. Samaniego, in 1881 a member of the legislature, and in 1888 county assessor; G. N. Tichenor, a manufacturer and mining man; H. B. Tenney, editor and manager of the *Arizona Citizen;* A. Steinfeld, one of the leading merchants in Arizona; A. Goldschmidt, a wholesale grocer; M. S. Snyder, a member of the legislature; C. A. Shibell, clerk and recorder of Pima county; G. H. Barnhart, a mining man; F. L. Proctor, a stock-raiser; C. R. Wores, the owner of sampling works; Major F. W. Smith, a native of Virginia; W. K. Meade, U. S. marshal; H. D. Underwood, a commission, mining, and real estate man; Gen. T. F. Wilson, a lawyer, and formerly U. S. consul to Brazil and elsewhere; F. A. Austin, a merchant and mining man; Judge J. H. Wright, chief justice of Arizona.   In Prescott, S. C. Miller, a stock-raiser; C. S. Hutchinson, a druggist; J. Lawler, a mining man; T. J. Eaman, a stock-raiser; J. Dougherty, a general merchant; F. Q. Cockburn, manager of the Arizona Sampling Works; Judge S. Howard, in 1884 chief justice of the territory, and in 1887 mayor of Prescott; T. W. Boggs, a mining man and ranchowner.   In Phœnix, A. L. Meyer, in 1888 its mayor; O. L. Mahoney, M. D., superintendent of the insane asylum; W. J. Murphy, a contractor; H. E. Kemp, whose business is in hardware and agricultural implements; E. Ganz, a wholesale liquor merchant; A. C. Baker, the city attorney; J. W. Evans, a real estate agent; C. Eschman, a druggist; J. Campbell, probate judge; L. H. Chalmers and Judge W. Street, lawyers; F. Cox, district attorney; F. M. Scofield, a ranch-owner; Col W. Christy, cashier, and E. J. Bennett, assistant cashier, of the Valley Bank of Phœnix; C. Churchill, formerly attorney-general of Arizona; Dr J. E. Wharton, county physician, etc.; S. E. Patton, a contractor and builder.   In Nogales, G. Christ, a mine, ranch, and hotel owner; J. T. Brickwood, a ranch and city real estate owner; J. J. Chatham, proprietor of the *Sunday Herald,* and member of the legislature; Major H. A. Read, a mining man; Capt. John J. Noon, a native of Ireland, an experienced and successful mining man, having travelled extensively in the territories of the Pacific coast, discoverer of the well-known Noon mine in Nogales; Louis Proto, a substantial merchant and mining man.   In Mayer, G. E. Brown and J. Miller, and in Stoddard, Roberts and Wells, cattle-raisers. Mention is also required of W. C. Land, a member of the well-known cattle firm of Tevis, Perrin, Land, & Co., whose interests are in Cochise and Pima counties.   To this gentleman I am indebted for a valuable dictation on the cattle interests of Arizona and her adjoining territories.

CHAPTER XXV.

TERRITORY OF NEW MEXICO.

1851–1863.

ORGANIC ACT — LIST OF GOVERNORS AND OTHER OFFICIALS — CIVIL VERSUS MILITARY AUTHORITY—SUMNER'S SUGGESTIONS—LEGISLATIVE ASSEMBLIES—MEMBERS AND ACTS—SYSTEM FOLLOWED—CAPITAL AND CAPITOL — ARCHIVES AND HISTORICAL SOCIETY — COUNTIES — POPULATION — FINANCE—EDUCATION—INDUSTRIES—TRADE—FAIRS—AGRICULTURE AND STOCK-RAISING—STATISTICS FROM CENSUS REPORTS—PUBLIC LANDS— PRIVATE LAND CLAIMS—PUEBLO GRANTS—MINING INDUSTRY—NEW MEXICO IN CONGRESS—CONTESTED SEATS—APPROPRIATIONS—DISPUTED BOUNDARY—THE MESILLA VALLEY—EXPLORATIONS.

IN an earlier chapter the history of New Mexico has been brought down to the organization of a territorial government by act of congress in 1850, and in certain matters, notably the Mexican boundary controversy and survey, has been carried somewhat further.[1] The organic act of September 9, 1850, was similar to those by which other territories were created, and need not be analyzed here, so far as minute details are concerned. By its provisions the president was to appoint for four years a governor at a salary of $1,500, a secretary at $1,800, attorney at $250, marshal at $200 and fees, and three justices of the supreme court at $1,800 each. The governor was to act also as superintendent of Indian affairs for a compensation of $1,000 per year. The secretary was to act as governor in the absence or disability of that officer. A legislative assembly, consisting of a council of thirteen members elected for two years, and house of 26 representatives elected for one year, was to hold annual

[1] See chap. xviii. of this volume.

sessions of 40 days at a compensation of three dollars
per day for each member, and mileage at the rate of
three dollars for 20 miles.   All acts must be submitted
to congress, to be null and void if disapproved.   The
supreme court was to consist of a chief justice and
two associates, appointed by the president for four
years at a salary of $1,800, each to reside and hold
district court in one of the three judicial districts
assigned him, besides an annual session of the whole
court at the capital.   A delegate to each congress was
to be elected by the people.   The choice of a temporary seat of government, apportionment of representatives, time and places of election, and the appointment
of local and subordinate officials were left at the beginning with the governor, but were subsequently to
be regulated by territorial law.[2]

The officials appointed by the president in 1851
were James S. Calhoun as governor, already in New
Mexico for some years as superintendent of Indian
affairs; Hugh N. Smith, not confirmed by the senate,
and replaced by William S. Allen, as secretary;[3]
Grafton Baker as chief justice, with John S. Watts
and Horace Mower as associates;[4] Elias P. West as
attorney; and John G. Jones as marshal.   Governor
Calhoun was inaugurated on the 3d of March, and
thus, very quietly so far as the records show, the
territorial government went into operation; an election was held by the governor's order, and the new
legislature was ready to begin work in June.   I ap-

[2] See *N. Mex., Compiled Laws*, 45–54, for the organic act, followed, pp. 55
et seq., by organic acts common to all the territories.   The legislature was
prohibited from interfering with the primary disposal of lands, from taxing
U. S. property, and from taxing the property of non-residents higher than that
of residents; otherwise, it might pass any acts not inconsistent with the
organic act or the constitution of the U. S.

[3] Delegate Weightman opposed the nomination of Smith and defeated him,
but could not secure the appointment of Manuel Álvarez as he desired. *Cong.
Globe*, 1852–3, app. 108.   Allen did not reach N. Mex. till June, and D. V.
Whiting acted as sec. by appointment of the gov. from April 5th to June 20th.
Corresp. about his claim for pay in *U. S. Govt Doc.*, 32 cong. 1st sess., H. Ex.
Doc. 81.

[4] Acc. to list in *N. Mex., Reports*, i., these justices were appointed in 1852;
but Ritch, *Blue-Book*, has it 1851, which I have no doubt is accurate.   I have
found no original records of these early appointments.

pend a list of the territorial officials in 1851–63, the limits of this chapter.[5] These early officials were for

[5] See, besides miscel. records in U. S. and N. Mex. documents, *Ritch's Legislative Blue-Book*, which is the best and most comprehensive list; for perhaps that in *McCarty's Statistician*, 1884, from material furnished by Ritch; also *Amer. Almanac*, 1851–63; and *Camp's Year Book*, 1869, p. 69. The dates given in the following lists are those of appointment or election. I have in most cases found no original records of exact dates, and as to the years there is some discrepancy, especially respecting the judges of the sup. court, the dates of the list in *N. Mex. Reports*, i., being apparently inaccurate in this respect.

Governors, 1851–2, James S. Calhoun; 1852, Col E. V. Sumner, mil. com., acting as gov. for a few months; 1852, John Greiner, sec., acting as gov. for 2 months; 1852–3, Wm Carr Lane; 1853–4, Wm S. Messervy, sec., act. gov. for 4 months; 1853–7, David Merriwether; 1854–7, W. H. H. Davis, sec., act. gov. for 11 months; 1857–61, Abraham Rencher; 1861 et seq., Henry Connelly.

Secretaries, 1851, D. V. Whiting, acting for a time by gov.'s appointment; 1851–2, Wm S. Allen; 1852–3, John Greiner; 1853–4, Wm S. Messervy; 1854–7, W. H. H. Davis; 1857–61, A. M. Jackson; 1861, Miguel A. Otero; 1861–2, Jas H. Holmes; 1862 et seq., W. F. M. Arny.

Delegates in congress, 32d cong., 1851–2, R. H. Weightman; 33d cong., 1853–4, José M. Gallegos; 34th to 36th cong., 1855–60, Miguel A. Otero; 37th cong., 1861–2, John S. Watts.

Chief justices, 1851–3, Grafton Baker; 1853–8, Jas J. Davenport; 1858 et seq., Kirby Benedict. The chief justice was assigned to the 1st district residing at Sta Fé. Associate justices of 2d and 3d districts respectively (but the districts were changed from 1860), John S. Watts 1851–4 and Horace Mower 1851–3; Perry E. Brocchus 1854–9 and Kirby Benedict 1853–8; W. F. Boone 1859–61 and Wm G. Blackwood (preceded by L. L. Nabers and followed by W. A. Davidson, who were apparently appointed but did not serve) 1858–61; Sydney A. Hubbell and Jos. S. Knapp 1861 et seq. Clerks of sup. court, 1852–4, Jas M. Giddings; 1854–6, Lewis D. Sheets; 1856–9, Augustine Demarle; 1859 et seq., Sam. Ellison.

Attorney-generals, 1852–4, Henry C. Johnson and Merrill Ashurst; 1854–8, Theo. D. Wheaton; 1858–9, R. H. Tompkins; 1859–60, Hugh N. Smith (died in office); 1860–2, Spruce M. Baird; 1862, Chas P. Cleaver and Sam. B. Elkins; 1863 et seq., C. P. Cleaver.

Treasurers, 1851–4 (from '46?), Chas Blumner; 1854–7, Chas L. Spencer; 1857, Hezekiah S. Johnson (resigned); 1857 et seq., Chas Blumner.

Auditors, 1851, Jas W. Richardson; 1851–2, Robert T. Brent; 1852–3, Lewis D. Sheets; 1853, J. W. Richardson (but named in laws of '51–2 as appointed in place of Sheets, resigned); 1853–6, Horace L. Dickenson; 1856–61, Aug. Demarle; 1861 et seq., Demetrio Perez.

U. S. attorneys, 1851, E. P. West; 1853, W. H. H. Davis; 1855, Wm C. Jones; 1858, R. H. Tompkins; 1860, T. D. Wheaton.

U. S. marshals, 1851, John G. Jones; 1853, Chas L. Rumley; 1854, Chas H. Merritt; 1856, Chas Blumner (but named in laws of '54–5); 1860, Chas P. Cleaver; 1861, Abram Cutler.

Surveyor-generals, 1854–60, Wm Pelham, with C. B. Magruder as clerk and D. V. Whitney as translator; 1860, Alex. P. Wilbar, with D. J. Miller clerk and trans.; 1861 et seq., John A. Clark, with Miller.

Register of Sta Fé land-office, 1858, W. A. Davidson; 1860, O. P. Richardson; 1861 et seq., Joab Houghton. Receiver, 1858 et seq., W. A. Stout.

Adjutant-general, 1861 et seq., C. P. Cleaver. Assessor of internal revenue, 1862, J. M. Vaca (did not qualify); 1862, Vicente St Vrain. Collector int. rev., 1862 et seq., Chas Blumner. In charge of U. S. depository, 1858 et seq., Wm A. Stout. Librarian, 1852–4, John Ward; 1854–7, Juan C. Tapia; 1857 et seq., vacant.

the most part men of fair ability and honesty, though not as a rule appointed with any special view to their fitness. Governor Calhoun was a politician of considerable executive ability, honorable in his intentions, popular, but intemperate, who was for some time unfitted by illness for his official duties, and died in June 1852 on his way to the states. Colonel E. V. Sumner, the military commander, in the absence of the secretary, took charge of civil affairs until Governor Lane arrived in September. This act of Sumner, particularly his dealings with certain criminals, led to a controversy. The people, or the little clique of politicians masquerading as the people, claimed the right to choose their temporary rulers in the absence of the appointees, and some public meetings were held to protest against military despotism. On the other hand, anarchy and even intended revolt were talked of, all apparently without any real foundation. All was indeed an outgrowth of the old quarrel of 1849–50 between the advocates of state, territorial, and military government, which for several years did not wholly disappear. The masses knew but little and cared less about the matter. Colonel Sumner in his report of May took a very unfavorable view of the country and its prospects. No civil government emanating from the United States could be maintained without the army, making it virtually a military government, costly and burdensome to the nation, without helping the New Mexicans, who would become only the more worthless the more public money was spent in the country. "Withdraw all the troops and civil officers," was his advice, "and let the people elect their own civil officers, and conduct their government in their own way under the general supervision of our government. It would probably assume a similar form to the one found here in 1846; viz., a civil government but under the entire control of the governor. This change would be highly gratifying to the people. There would be a pronunciamiento every month or two, but these would be of no consequence, as they are very harmless when confined to Mexicans alone." The secretary of war went a step further, and suggested the buying of all New Mexican property, either for money or in exchange for other lands, and abandoning the territory as much cheaper than employing a military force at an annual cost of nearly half the total value of real estate. And indeed, it would have been cheaper in dollars if humanity, civilization, and treaty rights might have been disregarded. But Delegate Weightman spoke eloquently in defence of the character of his constituents and their claim to protection; and presumably there was no danger that congress would seriously entertain so remarkable a proposition.[6] Nearly every prominent official became involved in controversies and the object of divers accusations, into the merits of which, with the often meagre and one-sided evidence at my command, I cannot enter with any hope of doing justice to the parties interested. Governor Lane was highly esteemed as a man of superior ability, and his rule ended in his attempt to be elected delegate and his defeat by Padre Gallegos. Governor Merriwether had his foes, and was even burned by them in effigy.[7] Secretary Davis has become famous for his books on New Mexico elsewhere noticed, in one of which he describes to some extent his experiences in these years. Governor Rencher was a lawyer who had been member of congress and minister to Portugal. Governor Connelly was an old resident and trader on the Santa Fé trail, a man of good intentions, of somewhat visionary and poetic temperament, of moderate abilities and not much force. All these rulers performed their routine

[6] Sumner's reports in *U. S. Govt Doc.*, 32d cong. 2d sess., i. pt ii. 23–6; Weightman's speech in *Cong. Globe*, 1852–3, app. 103 et seq. Another speech of W. *Id.*, 1851–2. App. 323–36, contains an interesting narrative of political wrangles for the past few years, but far too complicated to be utilized here. *Ellison's Hist. N. Mex.*, MS., contains notes on the character of the early governors and other officials.

[7] *Wingfield's Defence*, 9, which work also contains many petty details of prevalent complications.

duties with commendable zeal and skill; and their annual messages are filled with expressions of patriotic and intelligent interest in the welfare of the territory.[8] The first legislative assembly convened at Santa Fé on June 2, 1851. A large majority of the members of council and house were naturally native New Mexicans. I append a list of members of this and the later assemblies down to 1863.[9] About twenty

[8] The governor's messages are printed in the *N. Mex. Journal* of each session, and many, perhaps all, of them were also separately published in pamphlet form.

[9] The names are to be found in the successive *Laws* and *Journals;* and a satisfactory list is also given in *Ritch's Legis. Blue-Book.*

1st assembly, 1851. Council: president Ant. J. Martinez (2d sess. Juan F. Ortiz), sergt-at-arms Robt Cary, clerk Fern. Pino; members, 1st dist (Taos and Rio Arriba co.), Pablo Gallegos, Geo. Gold, Ant. J. Martinez, Vicente Martinez, Ant. Ortiz; 2d dist (Sta Fé and S. Miguel co.), José Fran. Leiva, Juan F. Ortiz, Hugh N. Smith; 3d dist (Bernalillo and Sta Ana co.), Tomás C. Vaca, José M. Gallegos; 4th dist (Valencia and Socorro co.), Florencio Castillo, Juan C. Chavez, Fran. A. Otero. House: speaker Theo. Wheaton, clerk Robt A. Johnson (2d sess. Thos D. Russell), sergt John M. Clifford; members, Taos co., Raimundo Córdova, Dionisio Gonzalez, Pascual Martinez, Miguel Mascarena, Theo. Wheaton; Rio Arriba, Gerónimo Jaramillo, José Ant. Manzanares, Diego Salazar, Celedonio Valdés, Ramon Vigil; Sta Ana, José A. Sandoval; Sta Fé, Cándido Valdés, Palmer J. Pilans, Merrill Ashurst, Robt T. Brent; S. Miguel, Hilario Gonzalez, M. Sena y Quintana, M. Sena y Romero; Bernalillo, Juan C. Armijo, Spruce M. Baird, José L. Perea; Valencia, Juan C. Vaca, Juan J. Sanchez, Wm C. Skinner; Socorro, Juan Torres, Esquipala (?) Vigil.

2d assembly, 1852-3. Council: pres. Juan F. Ortiz, clerk Tomás Ortiz, sergt Fran. Vaca; members, 1st dist, Pablo Gallegos, Geo. Gold, Ant. J. Martinez, Ant. Ortiz, Vicente Martinez; 2d dist, José F. Leiva, H. N. Smith, Juan Fel. Ortiz; 3d dist, Tomás C. Vaca, José M. Ortiz; 4th dist, Fran. Castillo, Juan C. Chavez, Fran. A. Otero. House: speaker Wheaton, clerk Russell, sergt Fran. Ortiz; Taos, Wheaton, P. Martinez, Fran. Gonzalez, José G. Gallegos, Bibiano Sisneros; Rio Arriba, G. Jaramillo, José L. Gallegos, José M. Chavez, C. Valdés, Fran. Martinez; Sta Fé, José E. Ortiz, C. Ortiz, Donaciano Vigil, Fern. Pino; S. Miguel, H. Gonzalez, Mig. Sena y R., Juan M. Varela; Sta Ana, Jesus Silva; Bernalillo, J. C. Armijo, Juan Perea, Murray F. Tuley; Valencia, Raf. Chavez, Mig. Otero; Socorro, José A. Vaca, Romualdo Vaca; Doña Ana, John C. Craddock.

3d assembly, 1853-4. Council: pres. Jas H. Quinn, clerk Elias T. Clark, sergt J. B. Edelen; members, Taos, J. H. Quinn, Geo. Gold, José M. Martinez, V. Martinez; Rio Arriba, José A. Manzanares; Sta Fé, Tomás Ortiz; Sta Ana, Fran. Sandoval; S. Miguel, José Ulibarri, Bernalillo, Hen. Connelly; Valencia, Juan C. Vaca; Socorro, José A. Vaca, Ant. M. Vaca. House: speaker Wheaton, clerk D. V. Whiting, sergt García Necibio; members, Taos, Albino Chacon, P. Martinez, Inocencio Martinez, José M. Valdés, Wheaton, Rio Arriba, Diego Archuleta, Lafayette Head, José A. Roibal, Cel. Valdés, Ger. Jaramillo; Sta Fé, José Vaca y Delgado, Facundo Pino, Chas L. Spencer, Caleb Sherman; S. Miguel, Faustino Vaca, Juan N. Gutierrez, Juan M. Vaca; Sta Ana, J. Sandoval; Bernalillo, Man. Armijo, Serafin Ramirez, Morris (?) F. Tully (?); Valencia, Dámaso Chavez, José Jaramillo; Socorro, José Apodaca, Andrés Romero.

4th assembly, 1854-5. Council: pres. José A. Vaca y Pino, clerk Clark,

family names include a very large majority of the
membership for the whole period; and indeed, a few

sergt Aniceto Valdés; members, Taos, Quinn, Gold, J. M. Martinez, Vic.
Martinez; Rio Arriba, Manzanares; Sta Fé, Anastasio Sandoval; S. Miguel,
Ulibarri, Ant. Vaca y Sisneros; Sta Ana, Sandoval; Bernalillo, Connelly;
Valencia, Vaca; Socorro, Vaca y P., Vaca. House: speaker Facundo Pino,
clerk Jesus M. Sena y Vaca, sergt Sebastian Abria; members, Taos, Juan
Bernadet, Guad. Lujan, Fel. Sanchez, Pas. Martinez, Santiago Valdés; Rio
Arriba, Pablo Gallegos, Diego Archuleta, J. A. Roibal, Ger. Jaramillo, Fran.
Martinez; Sta Fé, F. Pino, Cand. Ortiz, J. Vaca y D., Mig. E. Pino; S. Mi-
guel, Man. Varela, Faust. Vaca, Juan Gutierrez; Sta Ana, Man. Vizcarra;
Bernalillo, S. Ramirez, Sidney A. Hubbell, Narciso Santístévan; Valencia,
Man. Sanchez, Ant. Chavez; Socorro, Rom. Vaca, Celso C. Medina.

5th assembly, 1855-6. Council: pres. Facundo Pino, clerk Clark, sergt
Ant. J. Salazar; members, Taos, José A. Ortiz, Juan B. Valdés, Pas. Mar-
tinez; Rio Arriba, J. A. Martinez, Pablo Gallegos; Sta Fé, F. Pino, Simon
Delgado; S. Miguel, Man. D. Pino; Sta Ana, Fran. Sandoval; Bernalillo,
Connelly; Valencia, José Salazar; Socorro, Anast. García; D. Aña, Domingo
Cuberco. House: speaker Celedonio Valdés, clerk Whiting, sergt Fran. Sa-
lazar; members, Taos, Juan A. Vaca, Julian Solis, José D. Giron, Domingo
Mendez (or Montes); Rio Arriba, D. Archuleta, Jesus Trujillo, Man. Trujillo,
Man. Valdés; Sta Fé, Man. Vaca y D., Vic. García, Cand. Ortiz, Anast.
Sandoval; S. Miguel, Ant. Vaca y B., José Gonzalez, José G. Gallegos; Sta
Ana, Jesus M. C. Vaca; Bernalillo, Hubbell, S. Ramirez, Juan Montoya;
Valencia, Demesio Chavez, Juan Vigil; Socorro, Candelario García, Pedro
Torres; D. Ana, Raf. Ruelas.

6th assembly, 1856-7. Council: pres. Pino, clerk Clark, sergt José Ta-
foya; members, Taos, Ant. J. Ortiz, Pas. Martinez, L. Head; Rio Arriba, J.
A. Manzanares, P. Gallegos; Sta Fé, F. Pino, S. Delgado; S. Miguel, M. D.
Pino; Sta Ana, F. Sandoval; Bernalillo, Connelly; Valencia, Salazar; Socorro,
García; D. Ana, Cubero. House: speaker José S. Ramirez, clerk Chas B.
Magruder, sergt Fran. Sandoval; members, Taos, Santiago Vaca, Jesus Ve-
lasquez, Man. Martinez, Juan A. Romero, José D. Duran; Rio Arriba, D.
Archuleta, J. Trujillo, M. Trujillo, Man. Valdés, Jesus M. Vigil; Sta Fé,
Sam. Ellison, Victor García, Jas J. Webb, José Vaca y Delgado; S. Miguel,
M. Sena y Romero, Juan M. Vaca, J. M. Gutierrez; Sta Ana, José Molera,
Lorenzo Montaño; Bernalillo, Juan José Luero (?), José S. Ramirez; Valencia,
José Pino, Juan C. Chavez; Socorro, Rom. Vaca, José A. Torres; D. Ana,
Cesario Duran.

7th assembly, 1857-8. Council: pres. Donaciano Vigil, clerk C. P.
Cleaver, sergt Seb. Gonzalez; members, Taos, Albino Chacon, L. Head, José
B. Martinez; Rio Arriba, Ger. Jaramillo, Pedro Salazar; Sta Fé, Nasario
Gonzalez; S. Miguel, Don. Vigil, Miguel Sena y R.; Sta Ana, J. M. C. Vaca;
Bernalillo, Connelly; Valencia, Juan J. Sanchez; Socorro, Mariano Silva; D.
Aña, C. Duran. House: speaker Merrill Ashurst, clerk R. H. Tompkins,
sergt Max. Montoya; members, Taos, Sant. Valdés; R. Arriba, Jesus M.
Herrera, Fran. A. Salazar, Gervasio Ortega; Sta Fé, Fran. Ortiz y Delgado,
M. Ashurst; S. Miguel, Man. Pino; Bernalillo, Juan Perea, Juan C. Armijo;
other counties.

8th assembly, 1858-9. Council: pres. L. Head, clerk Nic. Quintana,
sergt Jesus Sandoval; members, Taos, J. B. Martinez, A. Chacon, Head; R.
Arriba, Ger. Jaramillo, Pedro Salazar; Sta Fé, Nasario Gonzalez; S. Miguel,
D. Vigil, M. Sena y R.; Sta Ana, J. M. C. Vaca; Bernalillo, Connelly; Va-
lencia, J. J. Sanchez; Socorro, M. Silva; D. Ana, C. Duran. House: speaker
José G. Gallegos, clerk J. M. Sena y B., sergt Lorenzo Martin; members,
Taos, Felipe Sanchez, Mateo Romero, Pedro Valdés, Raf. Vigil, Pedro
Marles (?); R. Arriba, Pedro Aragon, Ant. G. Córdova, Fran. E. Salazar,
Man. Jaramillo; Sta Fé, Bonifacio Romero, O. P. Hovey, J. H. Herrera, Juan

wealthy and influential families in each county, in connection with the few American residents, natural-born
politicians, controlled the election of representatives
and all other matters of territorial government, with
only the slightest interest or action on the part of the
masses. Yet the legislators were as a rule intelligent
and patriotic men, but rarely accused of corruption,

Benavides; S. Miguel, A. R. Aragon, J. G. Gallegos, Man. Herrera; Sta Ana,
Nic. Lucero; Bernalillo, Mig. Gonzalez, José Lueras, Fran. Perea, Fran.
Lopez, José Vigil; Socorro, Apodaca; D. Ana, Mig. Salazar.

9th assembly, 1859-60. Council: pres. J. G. Gallegos, clerk J. M. Sean
y B., sergt Fel. Sandoval; members, Mora co., Fel. Romero; Taos, A. J.
Ortiz, Sant. Valdés; R. Arriba, Ant. M. Pacheco, Pedro B. Gallegos; Sta Fé,
M. Ashurst; S. Miguel, J. G. Gallegos, Fran. Lopez; Sta Ana, T. C. Vaca;
Bernalillo, S. M. Baird; Valencia, Joaq. A. Bazan; Socorro, J. A. Torres; D.
Aña, Ignacio Orrantia. House: speaker Levi Keithly and C. C. Medina,
clerk Louis Felsenthal, sergt Clemente Ortiz; members, Mora, Agapito Vigil;
Taos, Matias Medina, José V. García, Mig. Ortiz, N. Gallegos; R. Arriba,
Man. S. Salazar, José M. Chavez, Vicente Trujillo, Agustin Sisneros, José
A. Martinez; Sta Fé, F. E. Kavanaugh, Pablo Delgado, Ramon Sena y
Rivera; S. Miguel, L. Keithly, Teod. Vaca, Ant. Tafoya; Sta Ana, Juan
Torres; Bernalillo, Fern. Aragon, Mig. Ant. Cobato; Valencia, J. A. Chavez;
Socorro, Caudel. García, C. C. Medina; D. Ana, ——.

10th assembly, 1860-1. Council: pres. J. G. Gallegos, clerk R. H. Tompkins, sergt J. M. Bazan; members, same as in '59-60, except S. A. Hubbell
in Bernalillo. House: speaker J. M. Gallegos, clerk Facundo Pino, sergt
Man. Gonzalez; members, Mora, José Mestas; Taos, Wheaton, Sabino, Mondragon, Fel. Sanchez, José A. Martinez; Rio Arriba, Juan A. Roibal, Ger.
Jaramillo, Pablo Gallegos, Fran. Salazar, Man. Trujillo; Sta Fé, J. M. Gallegos, Mig. E. Pino, Vic. Valdés; S. Miguel, L. Keithly, John Whitlock, Elen-
terio Rael; Bernalillo, José A. García, Mig. A. Lobato, Vic. Chavez; Sta Ana,
Hermenegildo Sanchez; Socorro, Rom. Vaca, Candel. García; Valencia, D.
Ana and Arizona, ——.

11th assembly, 1861-2. Council: pres. F. Pino, clerk Sant. Vaca, sergt
Andrés Salazar; members, Mora, Tomás Lucero; Taos, Pas. Martinez, Ant.
J. Martinez; Rio Arriba, Fran. Salazar, Fran. A. Mestas; Sta Fé, F. Pino;
S. Miguel, Prudencio Lopez, Ant. Vaca; Sta Ana and Bernalillo, Tom. C.
Vaca, Diego A. Montoya; Valencia, Man. Sanchez y Castillo; Socorro, J. A.
Torres; D. Ana and Arizona. House: speaker J. M. Gallegos, clerk Ant.
Sena, sergt Ramon Ortega; members, Mora, Fel. Tafoya, J. M. Bernadet;
Taos, J. D. Gallegos, Juan A. Zamora, Man. A. Sanchez, Estévan García; R.
Arriba, Luciano Herrera, Pablo Valdés, Man. Jaramillo; Sta Fé, J. M. Galle-
gos, Vicente García, O. P. Hovey; S. Miguel, Man. Gonzalez, Rómulo Lucero,
Pascual Vaca, Faustino Vaca; Bernalillo, Pablo Perea, Pablo Vaca, José A.
García; Sta Ana, Patricio Silva; Valencia, Perfecto C. Hidalgo, Juan Mon-
toya; Socorro, Rom. Vaca, J. J. García; D. Ana and Ariz., ——.

12th assembly, 1862-3. Council: pres. F. Pino, clerk Nic. Quintana,
sergt Crescencio Torres; members, same as in '61-2, except Meliton Vigil for
Sta Ana and Valencia. House: speaker J. M. Gallegos, clerk J. M. Sena,
sergt Canuto Torres; members, Mora ——; Taos, Sant. Valdés, Pedro Sanchez
Man. Atencio, José Tafoya; R. Arriba, D. Archuleta, Diego Salazar, Ant. M.
Vigil; Sta Fé, Fel. Delgado, J. M. Gallegos, Mig. E. Pino; S. Miguel, Valentine Vasquez, J. J. Herrera, M. G. Montoya, Jesus G—— y Vigil; Bernalillo
and Sta Ana, John A. Hill, Wm H. Henrie; Valencia, Fran. A. Chavez, Cresc.
Chavez; Socorro, Candel. García, Rom. Vaca.

and probably superior in respect of honesty to representatives of later years. All proceedings were carried on in the Spanish language, the acts and journals being printed in that language and also in English translations. In session the members puffed their cigarettes and indulged in other peculiarities of conduct unknown to American assemblies; but the results will I think compare favorably in most respects with those of early legislative efforts in other territories.

In a note I give a résumé of legislative acts for the successive sessions.[10] To a large part of these acts no

[10] *New Mexico, Laws of the Territory of* ——, *passed by the first (et seq.) Legislative Assembly, etc.* [*Id., Leyes*, etc.,—same title in Spanish], Sta Fé, 1852, et seq., 8vo. The Span. laws and Engl. translations are printed on alternate pages. The first vol. has 412 p., containing as a prefix the constit. of the U. S. and the organic act of 1850, Kearny code, etc.; and as an appendix the acts of 1847. Succeeding volumes to 1861-2 vary from 71 to 148 p. each. The 1st vol. contains both sessions of the 1st legislature. The early sessions are numbered from 1st to 5th, but when the numbering is again resumed in '71-2 that session is called the 20th instead of 21st, one of the two sessions of '51-2 being thus ignored. Mr Ritch in his *Blue-Book* has carried this numbering back to the beginning, and I have found it most convenient to follow him, applying the numbers to the assembly rather than to the sessions as printed. The acts of the 1st sess. are also printed in *U. S. Govt Doc.*, 32d cong. 1st sess., H. Mis. Doc. 4.

1st assembly, 1851-2 (1st sess., June–July '51); acts declaring a bill of rights; making Sta Fé the capital; appropriating $20,000 for expenses of govt; providing that existing laws not repugnant to those of the U. S. and the organic act be still in force, except the registry of lands under Kearny code; for publication of laws in Engl. and Span. 500 copies; for a board of com. to compile the code; the legisl. to meet 1st Monday in Dec.; the gov. to appoint a translator at a salary of $2,000; approp. money for a territorial census; incorporating city of Sta Fé; incorp. order of Odd Fellows; organizing the militia; regulating contracts between master and servant; defining judicial districts as follows: 1st dist, under chief justice, counties of Sta Fé, S. Miguel, and Sta Ana; 2d dist, Taos and Rio Arriba; 3d dist, Bernalillo, Valencia, Socorro, and Doña Ana; and an election law providing for election of delegate to congress and 13 councilmen, on 1st Monday in Sept. from '53 every two years, of 26 representatives yearly from '52, and of county officers yearly from '51; voters must be white men, and not connected with the army. Joint resolutions authorizing loan of $20,000 against U. S. approp.; asking for protection of wood and timber, salt marshes, etc., and perpetuation of Mex. mining law. Memorials asking for a road from Taos to Sta Fé, and for a geol. and min. survey of the territory.

1st assembly, 1851-2 (2d sess., Dec.–Jan. '51-2); acts dividing N. Mex. into 9 counties (see *Compiled Laws*), providing that former bounds remain, except a change between Socorro and Doña Ana, changing seat of Valencia to Tomé, Rio Arriba to S. Pedro Chamita, and Sta Ana to Peña Blanca, and apportioning numb. of legisl. as follows: for council, Taos and Arriba 5 memb., Sta Fé and S. Miguel 3, Sta Ana and Bernalillo 2, Valencia, Socorro, and Doña Aña 3; house of rep., Taos 5, Rio Arriba 5, Sta Fé 4, S. Miguel 3, Sta Ana 1, Bernalillo 3, Valencia 2, Socorro 2, Doña Ana 1. Acts suspending and repealing incorp. of Sta Fé; establishing an annual fair of 8 days from

justice can be done in such a résumé.   Many of them
at each session relate to the subdivision of counties

Aug. 8th at Las Vegas; repealing ad valorem tax of ¼ of one per cent on
merchandise (Kearny code) to all who pay the present license tax; making
occupation and improvement on public land a transferable interest; providing for public acequias and retention of the old regulations; regulating wills
and inheritance; estab. justices' courts; making 6 per cent legal interest;
providing for a mechanics' lien; and licensing gambling-houses at co. seats at
$600.   Joint resol. asking for 2 volunt. regiments and other aid against In-
dians; for legalization of this sess. of the legisl.; for extension of sess. to 90
days; providing for spending the $20,000 approp. for public buildings; and
protesting against any treaty with the Navajos not including a restoration
Mex. captives and indemnity for past injuries.

2d assembly, 1852–3, acts amending the act on masters and servants; forbidding sale of liquor to Ind., except Pueblos; enabling owners to obtain
property recovered from Ind. by traders, paying not less than 10 per cent;
changing seat of Doña Ana co. to Las Cruces; estab. an annual fair of 8 days
from Feb. 2d, at Doña Ana; on robbery and its punishment; on punishment
of drunkards, etc.; pimps to get 30 lashes in public, and ride on an ass on a
feast day accomp. by the town-crier; for management of the ter. library,
librarian to get $100 per year; authorizing erection of pub. buildings; and an
act against vagrants.   Joint resol. in favor of a regt of rangers, asking permission to use for ter. unexpended balance of U. S. approp.; complimenting
deceased gov. Calhoun, and approp. $300 for a tablet; claiming the right to
hunt buffalo, etc., on the plains adjoining N. Mex., lately interfered with by
the mil. in behalf of the Ind.   Memorials, asking that judges be men familiar
with the Span. language; asking for a penitentiary to cost $50,000, for a
yearly approp. for education, for roads to other states and ter., especially
the Mo. line, for mail facilities, and for wells on the *jornada*.

3d assembly, 1853–4.   Acts establishing annual fairs at Las Cruces, Alburquerque, and Socorro; changing seat of Bernalillo co. from ranchos to
town of Alburquerque, and seat of Socorro co. to town of Socorro; incorporating Sta Fé Artesian Well Co., N. Mex. Mining Co., and order of Masons;
and authorizing gov. to appoint a person to revise the laws.   Memorials on
roads, geological survey, artesian wells in the jornada, archives, Indians,
Mex. land grants, public buildings, and Fort Atkinson.   Resolutions on mail
route from Independence to California, and bridges across the Rio Grande.

4th assembly, 1854–5.   Acts estab. annual fairs at Mesilla, 8 days from
March 1st, at Tomé 12 d. from Sept. 1st, and at Sta Fé 8 d. from July 4th;
changing seat of Rio Arriba co. from S. Pedro to Los Luceros; authorizing
gov. to call out 1,000 volunteers for Ind. service when expedient; attaching
the Gadsden purchase to Doña Ana co.; providing for govt of territ. prison;
and permitting probate judges to issue gambling licenses in and out of co.
seats.   Joint resol. to choose a territ. printer; to appoint a com. to correct
and amend criminal law; thanking Lieut Sturgis for service in an Apache
campaign; recom. Céran St Vrain as col of a vol. regiment; calling for the
organiz. of more volunteers.   Memorials for payment of post Ind. claims, for
further protection, 1,000 stands of arms, active campaigns, etc.   Memorials
asking aid for schools.

5th assembly, 1855–6.   Acts changing seat of Doña Ana co. to Mesilla;
creating office of public recorder; abolishing office of territorial translator;
organizing Atlantic & Pac. R. R. Co.; and establishing means of education.
Memorials for pay of volunteers and militia, mails, bridges, roads, and Indian
depredations.   Resolutions for removal of Justice Brocchus, thanking the
army and volunteers, asking for establishment of forts and on Indian depredations.

6th assembly, 1856–7.   Acts changing seat of Socorro co. to Limitar; re
pealing acts permitting annual fairs, and act providing means of education;
restraining gambling, and closing stores on Sunday; on free negroes; incor-

into precincts and other local matters which are here
altogether omitted.   Another large class, also omitted,

porating Alburquerque Academy, and N. Mex. Mining & R. R. Co.
Memorials for mil. roads, $50,000 to complete public buildings, and for pay-
ment of volunteers.

7th assembly, 1857–8.   Acts authorizing election of a public printer; repealing act establishing a penitentiary; incorporating N. Mex. Min. Co.
Resolutions on the Palacio and its grounds, Judge Brocchus, and school
lands.

8th assembly, 1858–9.   Acts 'to provide for the protection of property in
slaves;' for arrest of runaway servants; to require justices of the peace to
keep a record of all Ind. depredations; to create office of attorney-general,
salary $1,500 and fees; that owners of unfenced orchards, etc., cannot claim
damages in winter; assigning Justice W. F. Boone to 3d jud. district;
authorizing publication of decisions of sup. court at U. S. expense (no reports
were pub., I think, till 1881); to estab. a market in Sta Fé at county expense;
to appoint a com. for revision of the laws.   Joint resol. to print 1,000 copies
of Gov. Rencher's mess., and the resol. of the legisl. on the Navajo war (not
given).

9th assembly, 1859–60.   Acts providing for education of children; authorizing any man to raise 200 or 250 volunteers and engage in Ind. campaigns;
forbidding Ind. to leave animals within a league of any cultiv. field, under
penalty of having to pay damages and $2 besides to recover the animal; to
prohibit the pasturing of cattle, etc., in considerable numbers, within 3 l. of
the settlements, creating Arizona co. from the Gadsden purchase, seat at Tubac; also creating co. of Mora, with seat at Sta Gertrudis de Mora; changing
seat of Rio Arriba co. to Plaza del Alcalde, and that of S. Miguel to lower
plaza of Las Vegas, qualifying those who formerly signed the declaration to
remain Mex. citizens, but have since decided to become citizens of U. S. to
serve on juries; forbidding sale of liquor to officers and soldiers; prohibiting
the carrying of weapons, with strict rules for fandangos; providing that no
man shall hold two offices of honor or profit; incorporating the N. Mex.
R. R. Co., Henry Connelly et al., the Rio Grande Co. to build a bridge near
Mesilla, the Mesilla Min. Co., and the Historical Soc. of N. Mex.   Joint
resol. asking for a reëstablishment of the overland mail route via Alburquerque; asking information as to whether the Navajos have complied with
the conditions of the treaty of '59; urging the organiz. of volunteers, and an
approp. by congress, also of a mil. post in the Navajo country, one on the
Pecos, and others out on the plains.

10th assembly 1860–1.   Acts requiring Ind. agents to make their distrib.
of goods at least 10 miles from any settlement; extending act of '60 on damages by animals of Ind. so as to include the Pueblos; prohibiting gambling,
and apparently doing away with the license system; to investigate means of
increasing water supply of Sta Fé; amending election law in details; to incorporate Pious Fraternity of the Co. of Taos, Mining Co. of the North, N.
Mex. Wool Manuf. Co., S. Miguel Feather Manuf. Co., S. Miguel Wool Manuf.
Co., Abiquiú, Pagosa, & Baker City Road Co., Sta Fé Fire Co., Montezuma
Copper Min. Co., Rio Arriba Bridge Co., and Rio del Norte Bridge Co.; to
change seat of Arizona co. from Tubac to Tucson; to create co. of S. Juan
in extreme N. w., seat at Baker City.   Joint resol. calling for reports on Ind.
depredations.   Proclam. of gov., Feb. 6, '61, apportioning the representatives
which the legisl. had failed to do, as follows: council, Taos, S. Miguel, and
Rio Arriba 2 memb. each; Mora, Sta Fé, Sta Ana, Bernalillo, Valencia, and
Socorro, 1 each; Doña Ana and Arizona, 1 together; repres. Taos and S.
Miguel, 4 each; Rio Arriba and Sta Fé, 3 each; Mora, Bernalillo, Valencia,
Socorro, and Doña Ana, 2 each; Sta Ana and Arizona, 1 each.

11th assembly 1861–2.   Acts authorizing the gov. to call into service the
whole force of the territory to aid U. S. troops in repelling invasion (by
Texan rebels; repealing act of '61 to create S. Juan co., and also adding the

is that relating to court sessions and legal methods in
civil and criminal practice. Of acts of still another
class,.that bearing on the agricultural, stock-raising,
mining, and other industrial interests of the territory,
an analysis would seem desirable from certain points
of view, but is found to be absolutely impracticable
within the space at my command. The general method
observed in these matters was to continue the ancient
usages and the Mexican laws in respect of irrigating
ditches, herding, fencing, etc. The laws passed were
as a rule special and local, such as seemed to be called
for by the needs of the time and district. Though
this plan led to the accumulation of a mass of special
laws, complicated and even contradictory, which in
later years had to be replaced by general legislation,
yet it is probable that under the peculiar circumstances
no system likely to be adopted would have led to better results. With the exception of the classes here
referred to, all important acts of the legislature are
mentioned in the note.

Among the acts thus mentioned in my résumé, there
are many bearing upon a few special topics so clearly
historical in their nature that they may properly receive brief additional attention in my text, with further information in some cases from other sources.
At the first session, the capital was fixed at Santa Fé,
where it had always been, and has since remained
without controversy. Congress had appropriated in
1850, for the erection of public buildings, $20,000,
with which the foundations of a grand capitol were
laid on a lot adjoining the old *palacio*. A new appropriation of $50,000 was obtained in 1854, and with it
the walls of the awkward and ill-planned structure

remaining parts of Arizona co. to Doña Ana; changing seat of S. Miguel co.
to S. Miguel; repealing the act for protection of slave property; calling for
reports of Ind. depred.; declaring all public lands fit for grazing to be reserved as public pastures for common use; repealing act of '57 which prohibited keeping stores open on Sundays; repealing act of '60 which prohibited
one man from holding more than one office; providing for vaccination; incorporating the Union Min. Co. A manifesto of the legislature is alluded to in
a joint resol. to print 1,000 copies, but its purport is not given.

were raised a story and a half in height to stand in the same condition for over 30 years.[11] Meanwhile, the adobe palacio served for all public purposes, frequent efforts to obtain funds for proper repairs being unsuccessful. The importance of preserving the Spanish archives was more or less fully realized, and often urged; but there was no money, and these invaluable records of the past were left for the most part uncared for, to be exposed in later years, as we shall see, to still more disastrous neglect. An historical society was organized in 1859–60, but practically nothing was accomplished.[12]

The first legislature at its second session divided New Mexico into nine counties—Taos, Rio Arriba, Santa Fé, San Miguel, Santa Ana, Bernalillo, Valencia, Socorro, and Doña Ana—with names and bounds substantially as in earlier times. In 1854–5 the Gadsden purchase was added to Doña Ana county, but in 1859–60 was organized into a new county of Arizona with county seat at Tubac, and a little later at Tucson. At the session of 1861–2, on the organization of Arizona territory, the county act was repealed, and all of Arizona remaining in New Mexico was restored to Doña Ana. In 1860 the county of Mora was created in the north-east, with seat at Santa Gertrúdis de Mora. In 1861 was created the county of San Juan in the north-west, with seat at Baker City; but the next year this act was repealed.

[11] An approp. of $60,000 was made in '60, but it was soon offset by a war tax, and the money was never expended, or even raised. The governor's message of 1871 contains a sketch of capitol history, and the subject is often mentioned in other messages.

[12] W. J. Howard, John B. Grayson, D. V. Whiting, C. P. Cleaver, Dr Sloan, and others are named in the act of incorporation. See also mention in *Historical Mag.*, ix. 77–8, 142–3. Ellison, *Hist. N. Mex.*, MS., and Watts, *Sta Fé Affairs*, MS., have much to say on the early neglect of the archives. On some efforts in congress, see *U. S. Govt Doc.*, 33d cong. 2d sess., H. Jour. 245; 34th cong. 1st sess., H. Mis. Doc. 138. In response to the gov.'s urging, a law was passed in '63 for the custody and preservation of the archives. *N. Mex., Revised Laws*, 674. Congress approp. $500 for a territorial library in '50, and with this sum a beginning was made, but the librarian's salary was only $100 per year, for which no competent person could be employed, and the post was much of the time vacant. The census of 1860 shows 15 public and 2 church libraries, with a total of 10,670 volumes.

Changes of county seats will be mentioned in a later chapter on local matters, and a map will indicate the boundaries as finally fixed.

In 1850, according to the United States census, New Mexico had a population of 61,547, exclusive of Indians, and in 1860 the number had increased to 80,567. Of these numbers respectively, 58,415 and 73,856 were natives of the territory, 772 and 1,168 being natives of other parts of the United States, while 2,151 and 5,479 were of foreign birth. I append some details, deducting as accurately as possible the figures for Arizona.[13] Financially, as the salaries of territorial officers and legislature were paid by the United States, the burden of taxation was not heavy. The total valuation of property, which was $5,174,471 in 1850, had in 1860, according to the census reports, increased to $20,838,780, of which sum $7,015,260 is given as the value of real estate; $2,361,070 should be deducted for Arizona. The total taxation in 1860 was $29,790, or $9,255 for territory, $12,485 for counties, $3,550 for towns, and $4,500 miscellaneous. A direct war tax of $62,648 per year was imposed in 1861, but this was offset a little later by the capitol and road appropriations, and was never collected. The territorial debt in 1860 was $3,673, which was constantly diminished, until in 1863 there was a surplus of $3,080, in the treasury.

[13] *U. S. Census Reports*, 7th and 8th census, the figures being repeated in various other works. Pop. by counties, the double numbers throughout representing the two years 1850 and 1860: Bernalillo, 7,749, 8,574; Rio Arriba, 10,667, 9,329; Sta Ana, 4,644, 1,505; Sta Fé, 7,699, 7,995; S. Miguel, 7,070, 13,670; Taos, 9,507, 13,479; Valencia, 14,189, 8,482; new counties in '60, Doña Ana, 6,239; Mora, 5,524; Socorro, 5,706; total of whites 61,525, 80,503; males, 31,725, 42,001; females, 29,800, 38,502. Free colored pop. 22, 64; slaves, ——. Natives of N. Mex., 58,415, 73,856; natives of U. S., 772, 1,168; foreign, 2,151, 5,479; unknown, 209. Occupation: bakers, 11, 39; butchers, 4, 23; carpenters, etc., 215, 287; clerks, 60, 201; clergymen, 24, 37; coopers, 22, 6; drivers, 3, 37; farmers, 7,889, 5,922; goldsmiths and silversmiths, 30, 37; hatters, 43, 6; herdsmen, 65, 412; hunters, 1, 55; laborers, 6,128, 13,821; lawyers, 11, 23; mechanics, 44, 175; miners, 9, 917; masons, 14, 101; merchants, 134, 363; musicians, 41, 68; officials (local), 22, 13; officials (U. S.), 184, 56; physicians, 9, 14; printers, 6, 15; servants, 1,264, 2,560; soldiers, 655, ——; smiths, 132, 181; seamstresses, ——, 211; students, 5, 19; traders, 12, 34; teachers, 8, 59; tailors, 97, 98; teamsters, 72, 551; weavers, 59, 50; all employments, 17,478, 28,933. Some deductions should be made for a part of the territory finally added to Colorado.

Nowhere in the United States was popular education in so lamentable a condition as in New Mexico during this period. Of the population in 1850 the census showed a total of 25,085 adults, and in 1860 of 32,785, who could not read or write; and the correct figures would doubtless have been considerably larger. The reports of 1860 show that 600 pupils, though one table makes the total attendance 1,466, were being educated in four colleges, academies, or private schools, and 17 public schools, with 33 teachers and a revenue of $13,149. There were practically no public schools at all. The priests, though in theory friends of education and somewhat awakening from their apathy of centuries sufficiently to regret that they had no funds to establish catholic schools, practically used their influence against any common-school system. Territorial officials and leading citizens realized the importance of educating the masses; and several memorials were sent to congress asking for money aid in place of the usual land appropriations, which as yet could not be utilized.[14] At the session of 1854–5 was passed an act establishing a system of schools to be supported by a tax; but in four counties this proposition was submitted to the people, with the result of 5,016 votes against to 37 in favor of the tax.[15] In 1859–60 an act of the legislature provided for a school in each settlement, to be supported by a tax of fifty cents for each child, the justice of the peace to employ a teacher and require attendance from November to April, and the probate judge to act as county superintendent. This was the system for many years with but very slight modification.

All industries were at a standstill in those years. There were no modifications of method worth noticing, and it is not my purpose to present here the slight available statistics and details of non-progressive mo-

[14] *N. Mex., Acts*, 1854–5, p. 125; *U. S. Govt Doc.*, 33d cong. 2d sess., H. Jour. 323; Sen. Jour. 208; 34th cong. 3d sess., H. Mis. Doc. 40.
[15] *U. S. Govt Doc.*, 43d cong. 1st sess., Rept Sec. Int., ii. 326–8; *Davis' El Gringo*, 193–5.

notony.   Some statistics of 1860 may be utilized later
for purposes of comparison.   Indian depredations, as
we shall presently see, were worse than ever, effectually preventing all progress in the old industries of
commerce, agriculture, and stock-raising as well as
the development of mining and other new industries.
Merchandise to supply the needs of the people was
still brought in wagon trains from the Missouri over
the old Santa Fé trail.   We have few details of the
business, but Davis estimated the amount at from
$750,000 to $1,000,000 per year, the freight costing
nine or ten cents per pound.   The trains arrived in
August, after a trip of 45 to 60 days.   The circulating
medium was gold from California and silver from
Mexico, the merchants making their remittances to
the states in drafts obtained from United States officials.   Merchants paid a license for transacting business,
and by the act of 1852 were relieved of the ad valorem
tax of the Kearny code.   In 1862 Acting-governor
Arny had high hopes of being able to take advantage
of the United States and French blockades of Texan
and Mexican ports to supply large portions of Mexico
with goods by way of New Mexico and restore the
past glories of the Santa Fé trade.   The old-time
annual fairs were still a prominent feature of trade,
and the legislature in 1852–5 legally established these
fairs for eight or twelve days at Las Vegas, Doña Ana,
Mesilla, Tomé, Las Cruces, Alburquerque, Socorro,
and Santa Fé.   Trading at these periods was free from
all taxation, and gambling was permitted by payment
of a small license; at Santa Fé, indeed, all the prohibited
games might be played free of license, and the occasion was to be marked by an oration and other literary
exercises, the pueblo Indians being invited to come
in and indulge in their characteristic dances.   But the
acts establishing these fairs were repealed in 1856–7.

There was a marked increase in the number, size,
and value of farins in the decade of 1850–60, though
the census reports show a diminution in the acreage

of improved lands, the increase being in grazing farms. Several acts bearing on irrigation, fencing, and other matters connected with these leading industries are mentioned in my résumé of legislative proceedings, and many more of a local nature are omitted. The presence of the United States troops afforded an improved market for many products; but at the same time the money spent by the government gave an opportunity for many to live with less exertion than before, and that seems to have been now as ever the main purpose of the masses. Seasons of drought were thought to be of more frequent occurrence than in earlier times. The boring of artesian wells for an increased water supply was often urged, and sometimes discussed in government reports. In 1858-9 a well was bored near Galisteo, as an experiment, to the depth of 1,300 feet, but though it showed the practicability of wells for the supply of travellers, it did not bring water to the surface, and so far as irrigation was concerned, was deemed a failure. Horses and mules increased during the decade from 13,733 to 21,357; cattle from 32,977 to 88,729; and sheep from 377,271 to 830,116, notwithstanding the constant depredations of Indians, which were commonly asserted to have paralyzed stock-raising. A large number of sheep were driven from New Mexico to California, especially in 1858-9.[16]

[16] Statistics from the census of 1850 and 1860: no. of farms 3,750, 5,086; average acreage, 77,278; land improved 166,201, 149,274 ac.; unimproved 124,370, 1,265,635 ac.; value of farms $1,653,922, $2,707,386; value of implements, etc., $77,960, $192,917. Farm products, wheat 196,516, 434,309 b., corn 365,411, 709,304 b., tobacco 8,467, 7,044 lbs., beans and pease 15,688, 38,514 b., wine 2,363, 8,260 gal., garden produce $6,679, $17,664, fruits $8,231, $19,651, wool 32,901, 492,645 lbs., butter 111, 13,259 lbs., cheese 5,848, 37,240 lbs., molasses 4,236, 5,419 gal. Horses 5,079, 10,066, mules and asses 8,654, 11,291, cows 10,635, 34,369, oxen 12,257, 25,266, other cattle 10,085, 29,094, sheep 377,271, 830,116, swine 7,314, 10,313. Value of livestock $1,494,629, $4,499,746; value of stock slaughtered $82,125, $347,105. Davis' *El Gringo* is the best work on the condition of N Mex. in 1851-7, and on p. 195–207 he gives an excellent account of the condition and methods of agriculture and stock-raising. See also *U. S. Govt Doc.*, 31st cong. 2d sess., Sen. Doc. 26, p. 4–9; 32d cong. 2d sess., H. Ex. Doc. 65, p. 345–52; *Sumner's Report*, in *Id.*, Sen. Ex. Doc., i., p. 25; *Pat. Office Reports*, 1851, ii., p. 478–92, 495–511; 1852, ii. 345–52; *McCall's Letters*, 510; *Beadle's Great West*, 514–15; *Porter's West Census of '80*, p. 451; *N. Mex., Revised Laws*, per index

Closely connected with agricultural interests in a new territory should be the disposal of public lands; but as in New Mexico nearly all the available, that is, irrigable, lands had long been reduced to private ownership, and as there was practically no immigration, the matter did not of itself assume any very important phases in this period. The legislature in 1851–2 passed resolutions in favor of reserving mineral and timber lands for public uses, and provided that a claim or improvements on public lands should be a transferable interest, and valid against all parties but the United States. In accordance with the president's recommendation of 1853, congress, by act of July 22, 1854, provided for the appointment of a surveyor-general,[17] extended the operation of the land laws over the territory, and gave to every citizen residing there before 1853, or settling before 1858, a donation of 160 acres, to be patented after four years' occupation. The usual grant of two sections in each township, 16 and 36, for schools and two townships for a university was made. Surveyor-general Pelham arrived in December, and in the following April established an initial point for base and meridian lines at a hill on the west bank of the Rio Grande, in latitude 30° 19′. From this beginning the surveys were slowly advanced from year to year, appropriations being small, the authorities at Washington not deeming a rapid or extensive survey desirable until private and Indian claims could be settled, and the remoteness of the public lands from the settlements rendering operations in the field often dangerous. Down to 1863 there had been no sales, though a land-office was opened at Santa Fé in 1858.[18] About 100 donation claims were filed, but only a few

on irrigation. On artesian well boring by govt, see *U. S. Govt Doc.*, 35th cong. 2d sess., H. Ex. Doc. 2, p. 590–608; 36th cong. 1st sess., Sen. Ex. Doc., ii. 544–9; *S. F. Bulletin*, Sept. 6, 1859. The well was bored by Capt. John Pope, U. S. Top. Engineers. On the driving of sheep to Cal., see *Brevoort's Sta Fé Trail*, MS., 7–8; *Sac. Union*, Nov. 8, 1858; *S. F. Alta*, Nov. 6, '58; Jan. 18, '59; *S. F. Bulletin*, Nov. 24, '58; Jan. 26, Mar. 4, '59.

[17] *Dunlop's Digest U. S. Laws*, 427–9.

[18] *U. S. Stat.*, 1857–8, p. 292.

patented. The total area surveyed was 2,293,142 acres, the area of the territory being 77,568,640 acres, or 121,201 square miles.[19]

New Mexico being an old province, settled for two centuries and a half by an agricultural community, the best portions of the territory along the rivers and susceptible of irrigation had naturally long been reduced to private ownership under Spanish and Mexican grants, protected in theory by the treaty of 1848. In a general way, these New Mexican private claims, and the problems arising in connection with them, were the same as in California. There was the same careless informality in respect of title papers, and the same vagueness in boundaries; the grants were, however, more numerous, much more complicated by transfers and subdivisions, more varied in their nature as originating from different national, provincial, sectional, and local officials; and the archives were much less complete; but on the other hand, there was no influx of settlers and speculators to foment controversy and fraud, and to create an active demand for the segregation of public lands. The proper policy of the United States was or should have been clear enough. Commissioners and surveyors should have been promptly sent to examine titles, take testimony on possessory rights, and define boundaries, that patents might be issued—all at government expense. There would have been a certain amount of error and injustice; many personal and local controversies would have been encountered, to be settled by arbitration, by the awarding of other lands, or by litigation in territorial courts; but the great question of land tenure in its essential features would have been easily and inexpensively solved, and the country left in a proper condition for future development. Otherwise serious troubles, including the success of fraudulent claims and defeat of just ones, were sure to result. The government did nothing until

[19] *U. S. Land Com. Repts*, 1855–63, containing annual reports of the surveyor-gen.

1854, and then instructed the surveyor-general to investigate the private and town claims, and report them to congress for confirmation.   That official had no facilities for this work, clerical assistance and appropriations being entirely inadequate; but he searched the archive records at Santa Fé to some extent, finding some thousands of documents bearing on about 200 claims; and he notified claimants to present their titles. Many in their ignorance were timid about surrendering their papers, feeling moreover secure in their long possession, and noting presently how tardy was action on the claims presented.   Moreover, by the law of 1862, they had to bear all the expense of investigation and survey, which temporarily put an end to the presentment.   Down to 1863, however, out of 60 or more claims filed, about 30 had been examined, and most of them approved by the surveyor-general.   He had also approved the Indian pueblo claims, which to the number of 17 were confirmed by congress in the act of December 22, 1858.   By this act and the later one of June 21, 1860, congsess also confirmed 19 private and town claims.   In 1861, there had been surveyed 25 claims of both classes covering an area of 2,070,094 acres.   In 1862–3 there had been examined of all classes 48 claims, and approved by congress 38.   The surveyor-general constantly protested his inability to do justice to this work, urging the appointment of some kind of a commission, and congressional committees fully realized the impossibility of founding correct decisions on the meagre data furnished, predicting much more serious difficulties in the future; but no change was made in the system, and matters were allowed to drift.[20]

[20] The pueblo claims confirmed by act of '58 were Jemez, Acoma, S. Juan, Picurí, S. Felipe, Pecos, Cochití, Sto Domingo, Taos, Sta Clara, Tezuque, S. Ildefonso, Pojuaque, Cia, Sandía, Isleta, and Nambé.   The private and town claims confirmed by this act and that of '60 were: 1 Preston Breck Jr, 2 Town of Tomé, 3 Man. Martinez, 4 Chas Beaubien, 5 Town of Casa Colorado, 6 Hugh Stevenson et al., 7 Town of Tecolote, 8 Donaciano Vigil, 9 John Scolly et al, 10 John Lany, 11 Town of Chilili, 12 Ant. Sandoval, 13 Town of Belen, 14 Serafin Ramirez, 15 Chas Beaubien and Guad. Miranda, 16 José L. Perea, 17 C. St Vrain et al., 18 Alex. Valle, not numbered E. W.

The period of 1851–63 was in no sense one of mining development. That the country was rich in mineral resources was not doubted, but such items and statements as are extant on the subject deal almost exclusively with mining successes of the remote past, generally exaggerated as the reader of earlier annals is aware, and with predictions of future successes resting on a much more solid foundation. On account of the slight immigration, and especially of constant Indian hostilities, the conditions were most unfavorable for mining; yet the soldiers and others accomplished much work incidentally in the way of prospecting, some discoveries being made in different sections, and the prospects, as is customary in a country of hostile Indians, being as a rule too highly colored. In the last years of the period some actual work was done in the south. The census reports of 1860 mention only one silver and three copper mines, all in Doña Ana county, employing 390 workmen, and producing $212,000; but the governor in his message of 1861–2 alludes to 30 gold lodes at Pinos Altos, employing 300 miners and paying $40 to $250 per ton, to rich gold placers near Fort Stanton, and to work at Placer Mountain near Santa Fé, besides the copper mines at Santa Rita and Hanover. There are other items of information on these and other mines, but I have not deemed it necessary to compile the meagre data, though some items may be utilized in later mining annals. All work was suspended during the confederate invasion of 1861–2, but from 1863 the industry was in a small way revived.[21]

Eaton. A few claims were limited by congress in extent; in a few cases, not confirmed, the claimants were authorized to select other public lands; and J. B. Vigil might bring suit for his rejected claim within two years. On the subject of land claims, see *U. S. Land Com. Reports*, 1855–63; and also a large amount of corresp. and documents in *U. S. Govt Doc*, 34th cong. 3d sess., H. Ex. Doc. 36, 37, 73; H. Mis. Doc. 25; 35th cong. 1st sess., H. Ex. Doc. 57, 89, 261; H. Rept, i. 457; H. Mis. Doc. 37; Sen. Rept 4; 35th cong. 2d sess., H. Mis. Doc. 37; 36th cong. 1st sess., Sen. Rept 228; H. Rept 321; H. Ex. Doc. 14; 36th cong. 2d sess., H. Ex. Doc. 28, 57, 58; 37th cong. 2d sess., H. Ex. Doc. 112; 40th cong. 1st sess., H. Ex. Doc. 13.

[21] On mining in 1851–63, see *N. Mex., Mining Co., Preliminary Report*, N. Y., 1864; *Id., Messages of governor*, 1855–63; *U. S. Govt Doc.*, 31st cong.

The New Mexican delegates to congress have been
named in this chapter.   In some cases, the elections
were contested and charges of fraud freely made, but
evidence is much too meagre for impartial investigation of these contests on their merits.[22]   The struggle
was largely one between two factions of the catholic
church, one headed by Bishop Lamy—of French origin—and his new clergy, and the other by the Mexican priests, who regarded the new-comers as intruders.
Gallegos elected in 1853 was a priest.   His election
was contested unsuccessfully by Ex-governor Lane,
who claimed among other things that the votes of
pueblo Indians for him had been illegally rejected.
This appears to have been the main point, but congress
decided practically against the right of the Indians to
vote.[23]   Gallegos was again elected, according to the
governor's certificate, in 1855; but his seat was successfully contested by Otero.   The chief ground of
this contest was the voting of men who, after the treaty
of 1848, had chosen—not in due legal form as was
claimed—to remain citizens of Mexico, but had now
changed their minds.   Congress was not disposed to

2d sess., Sen. Doc. 26; 42d cong. 1st sess., H. Ex. Doc. 10, p. 284; *U. S.
Land Office Repts*, 1855 et seq.; *Ind. Aff. Rept Spec. Com.*, 110 et seq.; *Hunt's
Merch. Mag.*, xxvi.; xxviii. 763; xxx. 260; *Whitney's Metallic Wealth*, 134;
Mining Mag., i. 79; *N. Mex. Scraps*, 21, 35; *Domenech's Deserts*, 192–5; *Möllhausen, Tagebuch*, 237; *U. S. Census*, 8th, Manuf., 666–7; *Hall's Great West*,
105–8; *Hittell's Wash. Scrap-book*, 117, 119; *National Almanac*, 1864, p. 456–
7; *Mayer's Mex. Aztec*, ii. 356–7; *S. F. Herald*, June 19, 1851; Sept. 23, Oct.
12, 1853; March 9, '54; *S. F. Alta*, Sept. 24, '53; Feb. 27, '54; Sept. 7, Oct.
5, Nov. 13, Dec. 20, '56; July 11, '61; *S. F. Bulletin*, Jan. 16, 28, Feb. 3,
March 24, April 9, 10, May 23, Sept. 12, '63; *Sac. Union*, Jan. 17, March 11,
19, Sept. 5, '63.
[22] According to a convenient list in *Porter's Directory of Las Vegas*, 46,
Weightman was elected in '51 over Messervy and A. W. Reynolds; Gallegos
in '53 over Wm C. Lane; Otero in 1855 over Gallegos, in '57 over S. M. Baird,
and in '59 over Gallegos; and Watts in '61 over Diego Archuleta.   In the
election of '59, Judge Watts made in a speech at Mesilla some remarks on the
family of Otero which led to a bloodless duel between the two. *Hayes' Scraps,
Ariz.*, v. 269.
[23] See *U. S. Govt Doc.*, 33d cong. 1st sess., H. Rept 121; *Cong. Globe*,
1853–4, p. 490, etc.   There were also charges of frauds in voting and counting,
which the committee found to be nothing more serious than the irregularities
of form natural in a new territory; also that the votes of Mex. citizens had
been received, but the com. held that this was not proved, and that if so the
number was not sufficient to change the result.   The original vote for Gallegos
was 4,971 to 4,526 for Lane; cut down by rejecting votes to 2,806 against
2,267.   The Ind. vote was 262 at Laguna and Taos.

recognize these men as citizens of the United States, but the controversy lasted many years.[24] The delegates seated were men of fair abilities, and perhaps did as much for their constituents as anybody could have done, which was very little. Congress took but slight interest in New Mexican affairs, and was content for the most part with making the annual appropriations called for by the organic act, with grudging concessions of other small sums for special purposes, and with much larger payments of Indian and military expenses. A résumé of congressional action is appended in a note.[25]

In an earlier chapter I have recorded the national boundary survey, and noted the fact that the United

[24] On Otero vs Gallegos, see *U. S. Govt Doc.*, 34th cong. 1st sess., H. Mis. Doc. 5, 15, 114; H. Rept 90, with voluminous testimony, arguments, and lists of voters. The vote was 6,914 to 6,815, making G.'s majority 99. The com. reported that O.'s majority was 290. There were about 1,400 of the disputed Mex. votes. O. alleged, among many other frauds, that in one precinct the priest of S. Juan received and read all the votes, rejecting all that were not for G. On the other hand, the bishop and his French clergy worked for O. In 1862 a committee reported against extending citizenship to some 2,000 Mexicans of the class alluded to.

[25] See *U. S. Statutes*, 1850 et seq., per index; 1850, acts organizing territory and approp. $20,000 for public buildings and $5,000 for library; 1851, acts approp. $34,700 for ter. govt, $18,000 for Navajo Ind., and $135,530 for volunteers of 1849; 1852, acts approp. $31,122 for govt; 1853, acts approp. $32,555 for govt, and $10,000 for Ind service; authorizing legisl. to hold extra session of 90 days; authorizing employment of translator and clerks, sessions of 60 instead of 40 days, payment of code commissioners; 1854, approp. $31,620 for govt, $50,000 for public buildings, roads $32,000, and Ind. service $45,000; appointing surveyor-gen. and donating lands to settlers; increasing salary of gov. to $3,000, and judges to $2,500; attaching Gadsden purchase to N. Mex.; authorizing payment of civil salaries for 1846–51 under Kearny code; and establishing a collection district; 1855, approp. for govt $36,500, includ. $2,000 for archive vaults, Ind. service $52,500, surveys $30,000, Texas boundary $10,000, raising gov.'s salary to $3,000 (?); 1858, approp. for govt $33,000, Ind. service $85,000, road $150, creating a land district confirming pueblo land grants, 1859, approp. for govt $17,000, Ind. $75,000; 1860, approp. for govt $23,500, Ind. $50,000 capitol $50,000, confirming private and town land grants; 1861, approp. for govt $20,500, Ind. $50,000, roads $50,000; act attaching all north of lat. 37° to Colorado; 1862, approp. for govt $33,500, includ. $5,000 to print laws; Ind. $50,000; 1863, approp. for govt $31,500, Ind. $25,000, U. S. depository $2,800; reestablishing collection dist and facilitating col. of revenue. There are some slight appropriations for deficiencies, etc., and for surveyor-gen.'s office, not mentioned in this note; also some additional Ind. approp. which pertain to N. Mex. in connection with other territories; and largest of all the military expenditures not given with the territorial appropriations. In the *Cong. Globe*, and house and senate *Journals* of the successive sessions, through the index, may be found some congressional discussion, etc., on bills passed and defeated.

States and Mexican commissioners agreed upon an initial point on the Rio Grande, which gave the Mesilla valley to Mexico. Before this agreement, it appears that a few settlers from Doña Ana, a little farther north, had entered the valley; and after it a Chihuahua colony under Rafael Ruelas had colonized the district in 1849–50 as Mexican soil. While I find no evidence, as I have before stated, that any other line was ever agreed upon down to the date of the Gadsden treaty, which settled the whole matter in 1853–4, yet there was a senate report against the Bartlett line, and the appropriation bill forbade the expending of money on the survey until it should appear that the line was not farther north of El Paso than it was laid down on Disturnell's map, the president accordingly declining to authorize the expenditure.[26] In New Mexico there was much feeling on the subject, involving a popular determination not to give up Mesilla. Governor Lane, who it seems also engaged with Bartlett in some written controversy, by a proclamation of March 13, 1852, asserted the jurisdiction of New Mexico over the disputed tract. I must confess that I have not been able to find any satisfactory original evidence as to what ensued. Lossing, the historian, says that "in 1854 Chihuahua took armed possession of the disputed territory. For a time war seemed inevitable between the United States and Mexico." Newspapers of the time also contained some warlike rumors, with very little definite information. We have seen that Bartlett was probably wrong in the original concession; but obviously Mexico could not be blamed for regarding the agreement of the commissioners as final; and while there was a question whether the United States was bound by the agreement—especially in view of the refusal of the surveyor to sign it—it was clearly a matter to be settled by national negotiation as it was settled by the final treaty. The only troublesome

<hr>

[26] *U. S. Govt Doc.*, 32d cong. 2d sess., H. Ex. Doc., i., pt i., p. 50–5.

point left in later years was respecting the validity of the Mexican colony grants made after 1848, and therefore not protected by the treaty of Guadalupe Hidalgo.[27]

The explorations of this period for railroad and other purposes, such as those of Sitgreaves in 1851, Whipple in 1853–4, Parke in 1854–5, Beale in 1857, and Ives in 1858, though pertaining more or less to New Mexico, have been sufficiently noticed with references to the authorities in the annals of Arizona.[28] In 1851 Captain John Pope made a reconnoissance from Santa Fé to Fort Leavenworth by the Cimarron and Cedar Creek.[29] The Texan explorations of captains Marcy and McClellan in 1852 involved some matters pertaining to different parts of New Mexico, and the routes leading to that territory from the east.[30] In December 1853 Major J. H. Carleton, with a detachment of 100 men, made an exploring expedition from Alburquerque to Casa Colorada, Abó, Quarra, and Gran Quivira.[31] The railroad survey of the thirty-second parallel from the Red River to the Rio Grande was accomplished by Captain Pope in 1854.[32] Secretary

[27] The most important record of the whole matter that I have seen is *A Review of the Boundary Question; and a vindication of Governor Lane's action in assuming jurisdiction over the Mesilla Valley. By Fernandez de Taos.* Sta Fé, 1853, 8vo, 32 p. See also *Lossing's Hist. U. S.*, 515; *Cozzens' Marvellous Country*, 47–8; *S. F. Alta*, Dec. 31, '52; Jan. 7, 53; *S. F. Herald*, Apr. 29, July 8, 31, '53; *Eco de España*, Sept. 10, '53. In the *Review*, p. 21–2, are noted certain acts of the Mex. govt bearing on the boundary before 1848, not cited in my earlier chapter, as follows: July 6, 1824, act of Mex. cong. creating state of Chihuahua, and making the northern boundary lines drawn east and west from El Paso; 1836, official rept of Gen. Conde, and map making the line cross the river at 32° 30′ and thence N. w. to 32° 57′, so as to include the copper mines; 1847, amendment of constitution of Chih., making the bound 32° 57′ 43″. These acts, as will be seen, furnish some testimony on both sides, though the right of Chih. to change its boundaries was with much reason denied.

[28] See chap. xix.-xx. of this volume.

[29] *Warren's Memoir*, 63. Parke's map of N. Mex. ordered printed in 1852. *U. S. Govt Doc.*, 32d cong. 1st sess., Sen. Jour. 295. See *Frœbel, Aus Amerika*, ii. 138–88, 369–403, for a descriptive narration of 1852–3.

[30] *Marcy (R. B.) and McClellan (G. B.), Exploration of the Red River of Louisiana in the year 1852.* Wash., 1853, 8vo, 320 p., illust., maps, and tables, in *U. S. Govt Doc.*, 32d cong. 2d sess., Sen. Ex. Doc. 54. Also *Pac. R. R. Repts*, xi. 64.

[31] *Smithsonian Report*, 1854, p. 296–316.

[32] *Pope (John), Report of exploration of a route for the Pac. R. R. near the 32d parallel of north lat. from the Red River to the Rio Grande, by Brevet Capt.*

Davis' book contains an interesting narrative of his journeyings to and in New Mexico in 1854–5, though these are not in the nature of explorations.[33]   In 1859 Captain Macomb made an important exploration of the north-western portions of the territory, and of the adjoining parts of Colorado and Utah.[34]

John Pope, 1854, in *Pac. R. R. Repts*, ii. no. 4, 5, 4to, 185, 50 p., with diary and scientific appendices.   See also *Warren's Memoir*, 79–80.   In *U. S. Govt Doc.*, 34th cong. 3d sess., H. Ex. Doc. 2, p. 212–16, is Capt. Humphreys' report of 1856 on Capt. Pope's survey of the Pecos country and Llano Estacado, with a view to boring artesian wells.

[33] *Davis' El Gringo*, passim.

[34] *Macomb (J. N.), Report of the exploring expedition from Santa Fé, New Mexico, to the junction of the Grand and Green rivers of the great Colorado of the West.   In 1859, under the command of Capt. ——.   With geological report by Prof. J. S. Newberry, geologist of the expedition.*   Wash. 1876, 4to, 147 p., plates, and fine map.   A new map of N. Mex. by Surv.-gen. Clark in 1862 is noticed by the newspapers as superior to any of earlier date.

CHAPTER XXVI.

INDIAN AND MILITARY AFFAIRS.

1851-1863.

NINTH MILITARY DEPARTMENT—COMMANDERS—FORCE—FORTS—GOVERN-
MENT POLICY—LACK OF SYSTEM—NUMBER OF INDIANS—WARFARE—
PLUNDERING AS A PROFESSION—SUMNER'S EFFORTS—TREATIES BY LANE
AND MERRIWETHER—LATER CAMPAIGNS—CARLETON'S POLICY AND SUC-
CESS—SUPERINTENDENTS AND AGENTS—CONGRESSIONAL ACTS—RESERVA-
TION EXPERIMENTS—UTES AND JICARILLAS—AGENCIES AT ABIQUIÚ,
TAOS, AND CIMARRON—SOUTHERN APACHES—MESCALEROS AT FORT
STANTON—THE MIMBRES—CONFEDERATE INVASION—THE PUEBLOS—
LAND GRANTS—THE NAVAJOS—THEIR WARFARE ON NEW MEXICANS—
TREATIES MADE TO BE BROKEN—CHRONOLOGIC SKETCH—THE WAR OF
1858-63—CARSON'S CAMPAIGN.

NEW MEXICO in 1851-63 was the ninth military
department of the United States. It was commanded
in 1851 by Colonel John Monroe; in 1851-2 by Colonel
E. V. Sumner, 4th artillery; in 1852-4 by Colonel
Thomas J. Fauntleroy, 1st dragoons; in 1854-8 by
General John Garland, 8th infantry; in 1858-9 by
Colonel B. L. E. Bonneville, 3d infantry;[1] in 1859-60
by Fauntleroy again; in 1860-1 by Colonel W. H.
Loring; in 1861-2 by Lieutenant-colonel E. R. S.
Canby, 10th infantry; and in 1862-3 by General James
H. Carleton, 6th infantry and California volunteers.

The force under these commandants down to 1858
was from 1,400 to 1,800 men; and later from 2,000 to
4,000, distributed generally at from twelve to fifteen
posts or forts, of which the most important were forts
Union, Marcy, Defiance, Craig, Stanton, Fillmore,
Bliss, and Sumner. The military headquarters was

[1] Who also commanded temporarily in '56. See *Ritch's Legis. Blue-Book*,
and the miscel. records on which this chapter rests.

successively at Santa Fé, Fort Union, Alburquerque, and again at Santa Fé from 1852. The troops in the first years were the 1st and 2d dragoons, nine companies; 3d infantry, ten companies; and 2d artillery, two companies. In 1856–7 a regiment of mounted riflemen was transferred from Texas for a time, and two companies of the 8th infantry were added to the force. In 1860–1 other companies of the 5th and 10th infantry were added, and three regiments of New Mexico volunteer cavalry were called into service. There were 58 companies in 1861, and in 1862–3 the California volunteer regiment served in New Mexico, some of the other troops, however, having been withdrawn.[2]

The duty of the army, maintained at a cost of about three million dollars a year on an average, was—except during the Texan invasion connected with the war of the rebellion in 1861–2—to afford to the New Mexican people that protection from their Indian foes

[2] See annual reports of the sec. war, with tabular statements of posts and distribution of forces. Ft Union, Mora co., was established by Col Sumner in '51, as headquarters of the dept. At the same time a military farm was attempted on Ocate Creek, which after a few years proved a failure. *Ancient Sta Fé*, MS., a col. of items from late N. Mex. newspapers. Forts Union and Marcy, at Sta Fé, were continuously garrisoned, though sometimes by a small detachment, especially Ft Marcy. Cantonment Burgwin at Taos and Alburquerque are mentioned in all the reports. Col Sumner in '51 found the southern troops posted at Socorro, Doña Ana, El Paso, and S. Elizario; but he moved them to two new posts, Ft Conrad—later called Ft Craig—being established near Valverde, and Ft Fillmore some 40 miles above El Paso. In '58, 634 citizens of Doña Ana protested against the proposed abandonment of Ft Fillmore. It is named in the report of '60, but not in that of '61. Ft Webster, at the copper mines, was abandoned in '54, though three comp. were stationed there in '53. *Parke's Report*, 12. Rayado, 40 m. from Taos, and Abiquiú were garrisoned in the early part of '51, also Cebolleta in that year, all temporarily. A post in the Navajo country was estab. in '51, and from '52 was known as Ft Defiance, just across the line in Arizona. At Las Lunas on the Rio Grande was a garrison in '53–7. Ft Massachusetts in '53 was some 85 m. north of Taos, beyond the limits of N. Mex.; and at or near the same site stood Ft. Garland from '56. Ft Stanton on the Rio Bonito, and Ft Bliss near El Paso, figure in the reports from '54–5; and Ft Thorne, at the upper end of Mesilla valley, established at the same time, was abandoned in 1859. Old Ft Wingate is said by Ritch to have been estab. in '57 and moved in '60. Camp Loring on Red River is mentioned in '58. In '59–60 Hatch's rancho on the Gallinas, and Beck's rancho, as well as the copper mines, were military stations. Ft Lyon, Ft Wise, and Camp Cameron are new names of '61, there being also a force at Abó Pass and Hubbell's rancho, and Ft Fauntleroy being mentioned in the Navajo country. And in 1862 were established Ft Wingate on the Gallo, Ft Sumner at Bosque Redondo on the Pecos, and Ft West at Pinos Altos.

which had been promised by General Kearny in 1846, and by the treaty of 1848. No such protection was in reality afforded, and Indian depredations were as constant and disastrous, or more so, as was claimed by many, as in any corresponding period of the Mexican régime. Though the commanders were for the most part competent men, and the soldiers fought bravely in hundreds of toilsome campaigns, the force was inadequate, and no definite consistent policy was adopted by the government at Washington. In general terms there was no radical difference of opinion as to the course that should be taken. The savage tribes must be exterminated, which would require a large military force, and which nobody really favored; or they must be fed at government expense, which would cost a large amount of money, though less for some years than the policy of extermination; or a combination of the two methods should be adopted, including the employment of an adequate military force to chastise the hostile bands, forcing them to make treaties and settle on reservations, together with strict vigilance and a proper supply of food, until the Indians could be made to understand the advantages of peace. The merits of this last plan, though there were minor variations of opinion respecting details, were clear enough to all in the territory and at the national capital; there were no very formidable obstacles in the way if men and money could be supplied; but the government preferred to let matters drift in the old way, spending its money in driblets, and accomplishing practically nothing until the last years of this period. The system, so far as any definite plan was followed, was to send out detachments from the different posts in pursuit of marauding bands, often unsuccessful, but often killing a few Indians and recovering all or part of the plunder. Occasionally an expedition was organized on a larger scale, to wage war on some tribe or district, generally resulting in a treaty, kept by the foe for only a very brief period. Hardly anything was done

to remove the Indians' idea of past years and centuries, that warfare for plunder, with occasional intervals
of peace and gifts and recuperation, with alternate
victory and defeat, was to be the main industry of
themselves and their descendants, as it had been of
their ancestors.   And practically, the Mexican population was to a considerable extent under the influence
of the same idea.   Outrages perpetrated upon the
Indians were hardly less frequent than depredations
upon the people.   Civil authorities, the military, and
the citizens were often at variance on almost every
phase of Indian affairs, these differences being the
natural result of the prevailing policy, or lack of policy, and no party, white or Indian, except the national
government, being much to blame.   The people on
several occasions furnished volunteers to aid in the
military campaigns; sent out, with partial authority
from the legislature and sometimes against the wishes
of federal and military officers, many badly managed
and ineffective private expeditions; and were always
clamorous for more soldiers, especially for license to
organize volunteer troops for the United States service.   They also urged congress in frequent memorials
to pay for the past services of volunteers, and for
property stolen and destroyed by the Indians since
1846; but no attention was paid to these demands,
founded in right, though often exaggerated as to
amount, during the period covered by this chapter.

The number of wild Indians—that is, excluding the
7,000 peaceful and friendly Pueblos—in New Mexico
was about 17,000; that is, 10,000 Navajos in the
north-west, 2,000 Utes in the north, and 5,000 Apaches
occupying the rest of the territory, though these numbers were usually overstated in reports of the earlier
years, and though it must be noted that hostile bands
from abroad—Apaches from the west and south, Utes
from the north, and especially Comanches, Kiowas,
and other natives of the plains from the east—often
extended their raids into New Mexico.   There were

three or four years of the thirteen covered by this chapter which were regarded as years of peace, though none which were entirely free from depredations; but in the other years, all or part, especially of the Navajos and Apaches, were on the war-path. Much that has been said of Indian warfare in Arizona may be applied to that in New Mexico; but here the Indians as a rule did not kill for the sake of killing, as did the Apaches of Arizona and of southern New Mexico in later years, but only incidentally in the prosecution of their profession as plundering raiders. Women and children captured became servants or practically slaves, many of those taken by the Indians being sold to distant tribes. In this constant warfare the Indians were believed to be more successful than their adversaries in their capture of live-stock, while in the matter of captives the citizens had the best of it. There are no definite or trustworthy records of casualties except for brief periods, but the number of whites killed was probably from 200 to 300, and the property lost may have amounted to a million dollars. I make no attempt to catalogue depredations or campaigns, since I have neither space, nor in most cases sufficient data, for a complete record. I shall first present a general and brief view of military operations, then a similar résumé of Indian affairs in the territory as managed by the civil authorities; and finally the different tribes and sections will be treated successively, with somewhat more of detail in certain phases of the subject.

Colonel Sumner assumed command in July 1851, with instructions to select new sites for military posts, to act in concert with the superintendent of Indian affairs, to inflict severe punishment on the savage foe, and to effect a reduction in military expenditures. In all these things he was successful to a certain extent, if one or two of the usual Navajo campaigns and temporary treaties may be regarded as the severe chas-

tisement ordered. In the latter part of 1852 the
country was reported at peace, the Indians for the
most part friendly, and, particularly the Navajos and
Apaches, 'completely overawed.'[3] This state of comparative peace lasted a little more than a year, during
which time a little progress was made by the civil
department. But this progress cost too much;
methods were not approved, and promises not kept;
so that in 1854–5 almost all the bands were again on
the war-path. General Garland and his subordinates
made active campaigns in all directions, especially
against the Mescaleros, Jicarillas, and Utes; a volunteer force was called into the service; treaties were
made by Governor Merriwether—not destined to be
approved; and thus for 1856–7 a kind of precarious
peace was patched up.[4] Then in 1858 serious troubles
arose with the Navajos, and the war, with its many
campaigns under the direction of Garland, Bonneville, Fauntleroy, and Canby, was continuous in 1859
–61, as will be more fully recorded a little later. At
the same time the southern Apaches took advantage
of the occasion to renew their raids; the Mormons

[3] Rept sec. war, and *Ind. Aff. Rept*, 1852; Sumner's reports and other
corresp., in *U. S. Govt Doc.*, 32d cong. 1st sess., H. Ex. Doc., ii., pt i., p. 125–
36; 2d sess., H. Ex. Doc., i., pt ii., p. 25–7. The corresp. on Ind. depred.
and minor expeditions indicates that many of the latter were based on false
or exaggerated reports, very little being really accomplished by this desultory
warfare. The establishment of new posts has already been noticed; also
Sumner's discouraging view of future prospects, prompting a recommendation,
adopted by the sec. war, to abandon the territory for economic reasons. The
reduction of expenses did not please the people, not only because it indicated
less earnest operations against the Ind., but because the disbursement of
military funds was in a sense the country's main dependence. The Sonorans
accused the Americans of waging war on the Mex. territories through the
Indians, selling them arms and ammunition and buying captives. *Sonorense*,
March 28, Dec. 5, 1851.

[4] *Brackett's U. S. Cavalry*, 133–8, gives some details of campaigns made by
Sturgis, Ewell, Walker, Bell, Davidson, and Fauntleroy. See also reports of
Gen. G. and other officers, in *U. S. Govt Doc.*, 34th cong. 1st sess., H. Ex.
Doc., i., pt ii., p. 56–72; and Merriwether, in *Ind. Aff. Rept*, 1854, p. 166–8.
The treaties were made in June–Sept. 1855. Casualties in '54 were estimated
at 50 killed or captured, and $112,000 worth of property lost. A memorial
of the legislature asked for payment for these losses, and also for $20,000 to
pay the volunteers. Though in '56–7 most of the bands were reported as
observing the treaties, the Navajos gave much trouble, and Brackett, p. 171
et seq., mentions several expeditions, chiefly in the extreme south. Claims
before congress in '58 for property lost in past years amounted to $516,160.

were thought to be tampering with the Utes; troops were brought in from abroad; and the volunteers were somewhat irregularly reorganized for active service.[5]

In 1861, when affairs were in this condition, and the war still in progress, an invasion of the territory by Texan confederates, an episode of New Mexican annals to be treated in the following chapter, caused the troops to be withdrawn from their Indian campaigns for other service deemed more urgent; and for over a year, while the Utes and Jicarillas remained friendly, the Navajos and other Apache bands were left free to devastate the settlements, without opposition except such as the citizens in small parties could offer. It was alleged that the southern Apaches and Texan tribes were incited and aided by the confederates; and however this may have been, the latter certainly had no motive for affording protection to their foes. In 1862, when the invaders had been driven out, and fears of further confederate operations had for the most part disappeared, General Carleton, succeeding Canby in September, his army being composed largely of Californian and New Mexican volunteers, turned his attention most energetically to the Indian foe. For the first time a definite policy was adopted. Carleton's idea, and a very sensible one, was to chastise the savages thoroughly, and show them that there was to be no more trifling. No treaties were to be made, and no terms accepted except unconditional surrender as prisoners of war. In the field no quarter was to be shown except to women and children. At Bosque Redondo, on the Pecos, Fort Sumner was established, and here all the Navajo

[5] See military reports and correspondence of 1858–60, in *U. S. Govt Doc.*, 35th cong. 2d sess., H. Ex. Doc., ii., pt ii., p. 278–329; Sen. Ex. Doc., ii., p. 278–329; 36th cong. 1st sess., Sen. Ex. Doc., ii., p. 256–354; H. Ex. Doc., ix., no. 69; 2d sess., Sen. Doc., ii., 51–69, with catalogue of exped., p. 199–205; report of sec. war, 1860; *Brackett's U. S. Cavalry*, 194 et seq. The S. F. newspapers also contain some news of Ind. troubles in 1858–9. The official reports here cited contain a large and complicated mass of details, mainly on the Navajo war, but also giving much information on Apache expeditions and depredations. See later note of this chapter for additional authorities.

and Apache prisoners were to be brought as fast as taken, to await later decisions as to their fate, but with a plan of making this a permanent reservation for those tribes. The general's force was not sufficient for the full accomplishment of his plans; but he went to work in earnest, and effected much. First the Apaches were taken in hand, and by the spring of 1863 about 400 Mescaleros had submitted, and were living in peace at the Bosque, while the other bands had been forced to suspend for a time their raids, Fort West having meanwhile been garrisoned at Pinos Altos. Then began the campaign against the Navajos, carried on with such energy that by the end of the year a considerable number of that tribe were either at Fort Sumner or on the way thither, and the prospect was encouraging for complete success in the near future, though conflicts were still occurring in many parts of the territory, and various obstacles were yet to be encountered.[6]

In 1848–51 James S. Calhoun was general agent for the New Mexican Indians. On the organization of the territory, the governor became ex-officio superintendent of Indian affairs, and the position was held successively by Calhoun in 1851–2, Lane in 1852–3, and Merriwether in 1853–7. Then the offices were separated, and James L. Collins, an old resident of New Mexico, served as superintendent in 1857–63, being succeeded by Michael Steck in 1863. These superintendents appear to have been earnest and capable men, but their actions were so hampered by lack of means, conflicting or insufficient instructions, lack of a definite policy, and—especially in the early years— misunderstandings with the military authorities, that

[6] *Carleton's Correspondence of 1862–4,* in *Ind. Aff. Rept Spec. Com.,* 1867, p. 98 et seq., containing an immense mass of details. On p. 247–57 is a chronologic list of fights with Indians, with a tabular statement showing that in 1863–4 there were killed, in 143 encounters, 664 Ind.; wounded 227, and captured 8,793; officers and men killed 24; wounded 50; live-stock taken by Ind., 28,587 sheep, 47 horses, 359 mules, 432 cattle; taken from Ind., 36,550 sheep, 2,622 horses, 267 mules, 246 cattle, 35 asses.

they could accomplish but little. They were instructed to accompany in person or by agents all expeditions, and to make treaties with the Indian tribes; but Calhoun in 1851 complained much of the difficulties that surrounded him, of lack of support and coöperation by the military, of increasing depredations, and of the efforts of designing men, his enemies, to prevent his success, and even draw the Pueblos into hostility; yet he made some kind of a treaty with the eastern Apaches.[7] Congress in February 1851 extended over New Mexico all existing laws on trade and intercourse with the Indians, at the same time providing for the appointment of four agents at a salary of $1,500 each.[8]

The four agents appointed in April 1851 were R. H. Weightman, soon elected to congress; John Greiner, stationed for a time at Taos, and later territorial secretary; Abram R. Wooley, of whom nothing more appears; and Edward H. Wingfield, who was stationed in 1852-3 at Fort Webster, was dismissed in 1853, and who published a pamphlet in defence of his conduct.[9] In 1852 Michael Steck and Spruce M. Baird were appointed in place of Weightman and Wooley; and in 1853 a new corps, consisting of Kit Carson, Henry L. Dodge, James M. Smith, and Edmund A. Graves. Subsequent changes are given

[7] See *Ind. Aff. Reports*, 1851-63. The report of '51 contains Calhoun's corresp. and complaints. There was evidently a strong feeling of antagonism between the civil and military authorities. Sumner was inclined, as we have seen, to regard the Ind. depredations and other prospective troubles as of slight importance, though his view of the territory's prospects was in some respects more discouraging than that of the governor. This antagonism partially disappeared in later years.

[8] *U. S. Statutes*, 1851 et seq. Congressional appropriations, not including salaries of agents, also excluding certain amounts to be expended for N. Mex. in connection with other territories, and omitting some small amounts for deficiencies and other miscellaneous purposes, were as follows: 1851, $18,000 for Navajo treaty of '49; 1852 (not found); 1853, $10,000; 1854, $30,000, plus $5,000 (continued in '55-6) for Navajo treaty, plus $10,000 for the Pueblos; 1855, $25,000; '56, $47,500; '57 (not found); '58, $85,000; '59, $95,000; '60, '61, '62, each $50,000; '63, $25,000.

[9] *Wingfield, E. H., Defence of his Acts as Indian Agent.* Wash., 1854, 8vo, 16 p. After reaching N. Mex. he was sent to Wash. on a mission by Gov. Calhoun. He was accused of excessive expenditures, and of absence from his post, having great difficulty in collecting his pay. One or two of the others seem also to have been in trouble and dismissed, but I find no particulars.

in a note or in a later portion of this chapter in the annals of the different agencies.[10]

Superintendent Lane in 1852-3 was a believer in the policy of keeping the Indians quiet by feeding them, as cheaper and more effective than fighting. Accordingly, he made provisional treaties with some of the north-eastern and south-western Apache bands, agreeing to furnish food for five years, and some other aid to all who would work. A considerable number in the north were induced to settle on a farm west of the Rio Grande, and a like experiment was tried at Fort Webster. We know but little of details, except that, without waiting for approval of the treaties, Lane spent about $20,000 in the execution of the plan; and when the rations were suspended for want of funds, the Apaches became worse than ever. Superintendent Merriwether from 1853 found the Indians for the most part hostile. His theory was that the Indian title to all lands near the settlements should be purchased, to be paid for in annuities, from which the amount of depredations should be deducted. Before the end of his term in 1857 he made several treaties with different tribes, which were never approved. There was a general agreement in these and later years that the Indians must be induced to settle on reservations, and aided to a considerable extent for some time, but the government was very slow to act. Efforts to promote such settlement were, however, recommended, appropriations were increased, and some attention was paid to the various agencies, where goods

[10] See, besides, *Ind. Aff. Reports*, 1851 et seq.; the *American Almanac*, 1851-61; and *National Almanac*, 1863-4. Several of the names are not mentioned in the official reports, and some of the appointees probably did not serve. The list of '54-6 is Carson, Dodge, Steck, Lorenzo Labadi, and Sam. H. Montgomery, replaced by A. G. Mayers. In '57-9 we have, besides Carson and Steck, W. R. Harley (replaced by Silas F. Kendrick in '59), Diego Archuleta, S. M. Yost (temporarily replaced by R. S. Cowart in '58), and J. Walker. In '61 John T. Rnssell appears instead of Yost. In '63-4 Carson's name disappears; José A. Manzanares and John Ward take the places of Archuleta, Kendrick, Russell, and Walker, the number being reduced to four; and Fernando Maxwell takes the place of Steck, who became supt. For acts of the legislature from session to session on Ind. affairs, see the résumé in the preceding chapter.

were distributed each year. Under superintendents
Collins and Steck there was no change of a general
nature to be noted. It was, for the most part, a period of constant warfare. The Texan invasion caused
most of the agencies to be abandoned for a time in
1861–2. The people, legislature, and all officials became extremely impatient. Various views on details
of policy were expressed, various petitions and protests
made; the necessity of a definite reservation system
became more and more apparent; and there were few
who did not approve, in a general way, General Carleton's energetic measures of 1862–3, though some of
his acts and views led to bitter controversy.[11]

The northern part of the territory, outside of the
Navajo country, was occupied or ranged over by the
Jicarilla Apaches—so named in early times from
the pottery made in small quantities by their women
—about 900 in number, and by three bands of Utes
—also written Utahs, and in earlier times by the
Spaniards, Yutas—numbering 2,000 or more. The
Jicarilla country was properly east of the Rio Grande,
and the Mohuache Utes also came to regard this
region as their home, the agency for both tribes being
at Taos, and later at Cimarron, or Maxwell's rancho.
The Ute country was west of the river, stretching
north-westward into Colorado and Utah, where most
of the tribe lived, and the agency for the Capotes and
Pauches, or Tabuaches, as the New Mexican bands
were called during this period, was at Abiquiú. The
Utes and Jicarillas were, to some extent, related by
intermarriage, and in disposition and habits had much

[11] See acts of the legislature, governors' messages, repts of supt and agents,
etc. In *U. S. Govt Doc.*, 35th cong. 1st sess., H. Ex. Doc., xi., p. 82, is Supt
Collins' report of '58, on taking a deputation of different tribes on a visit to
Washington. An effort was made by the legislature to obtain full reports of
depredations for use in congress. The raising of volunteers also caused much
excitement. There was much complaint of the evil effects of selling liquor to
the Ind., and much declamation against the 'sickly sentimentality' of eastern
people. It was often pointed out that the Ind. were as bad and the people
less protected than when the U. S. took possession, notwithstanding the
large expenditure of money.

in common, being roving tribes, who were naturally averse to restraint, settlement, or civilization. Both were always ready to be fed by the government, and equally disposed to steal such supplies as were not otherwise obtainable without much work. The Utes were brave, warlike, better armed than other tribes, and skilful hunters; bold in the assertion of their right to the broad tract over which they ranged, wholly opposed to farming or reservation life, but willing to be friendly and abstain from depredations if liberally supplied with food. Their ideal was to retain their hunting-grounds, periodically visiting an agency to receive their gifts—which must not be less than other tribes received—and having free access to the settlements, where whiskey could be procured. The Jicarillas were equally fond of whiskey, somewhat more treacherous and cruel, less brave and energetic as warriors and hunters, making pottery, and sometimes planting on a small scale, and regarding theft as a natural means of supporting themselves if no easier way could be found. A large reservation near the settlements, where they could lead an easy, vagabond, drunken life, would have pleased them well enough.

At the beginning, both tribes were engaged in constant raids for plunder, and the Jicarillas were regarded as among the worst of Apaches. Yet Governor Calhoun made some kind of a treaty with them in 1851; they were pleased with the distribution of goods at Taos, and in 1853 Governor Lane induced 250 of them to settle on a farm west of the Rio Grande, on the Rio Puerco. But when Merriwether was obliged to announce that Lane's treaties were not approved, and to suspend the distribution of supplies, both Jicarillas and Utes in their disgust went on the war-path. The former, after an active campaign by troops under lieutenants Bell and Davidson, in one battle of which over 20 dragoons lost their lives, were conquered, and made a treaty in July 1854; while the latter were defeated by Colonel Fauntleroy in a campaign of March to May 1855.[12] From this time these tribes were friendly, though committing occasional thefts, or even worse depredations, and sometimes accused of other offences of which they probably were not guilty. The frequent raids of other tribes from the west and east made it difficult in many cases to identify the real culprits. The Indians did not live at or generally near the agencies, and were only in the slightest degree under the agents' control. They came in to get their irregular allotments of goods, which were generally exchanged as soon as possible for liquor. They became, naturally, more and more a horde of drunken, pilfering, destitute, and mendicant vagabonds. At certain times and places they showed indications of a tendency to industry and good behavior, but the abominable lack of system prevented any of these rare exceptions being utilized as the nucleus of real improvement. There was no progress, but constant deterioration. Reports on their condition and prospects varied with the point of view. Some agents, considering their past history and present circumstances, wondered that they were no worse, and wrote encouragingly; others, looking at the Indians as they were, and unmindful of the environment, could see no gleam of hope. The Jicarillas and Utes were, however, the only 'union' Indians, except the Pueblos, during the war of 1861–2, which fact—in view of their holding, as foes of the Navajos and tribes of the eastern plains, a kind of balance of power—with the additional circumstance that the Utes resisted the Mormon efforts of 1858, made them in these and later years the recipients of many complimentary allusions. All agreed, however, that these Indians should be put on reservations, which should be far from the settlements. Indeed, the suggestion was often made, as followed

[12] Gov. Merriwether's report of Sept. '54, in *Ind. Aff. Rept; Brackett's U. S. Cav.*, 135–8; *Frost's Ind. Battles*, 393–8; Fauntleroy's reports of April–May '55, in *U. S. Govt Doc.*, 34th cong. 1st sess., H. Ex. Doc., i., pt ii., 56–72. Lieut. Maxwell was killed in June '54. A memorial of the legislature for a Jicarilla reservation is mentioned in *Id.*, 33d cong. 1st sess., H. Miscel. Doc., no. 45.

later, that the Jicarillas should be joined to the southern Apaches, and the Utes to the Colorado bands.[13]

Respecting the northern agencies, agents, and native bands in charge of each, there is some confusion, the reports of early years being vague or altogether lacking. In 1851–3 John Greiner seems to have been stationed at Taos; then in 1853–9 Christopher Carson had charge of this agency.[14] In 1860–1 special agents A. H. Pfeiffer and Henry Mercure were in charge; in 1861 the agency was moved from Taos to Cimarron, or Maxwell's rancho, W. F. M. Arny being made agent, and his successor in 1862–3 was Levi Keithly. At the Abiquiú agency of the Capote and Pauche Utes, E. A. Graves appears as agent in 1853, Lorenzo Labadi in 1855–6, Diego Archuleta in 1857, Lafayette Head in 1859–61, and José A. Manzanares in 1862–3. Agent Head had his headquarters at Conejos in 1860, and special agent Henry Mercure was in charge of the Pauches in 1862, on the Rio Chama, and in 1863 at Tierra Amarilla.

Of the southern Apaches during this period it is difficult to present a definite and connected record. The bands belonging properly to New Mexico were the Mescaleros of the east, between the Pecos and Rio Grande, and the Mimbres and Mogollones— sometimes grouped as Gila Apaches—of the west. The number of these three bands at the first could not have exceeded 4,000, was perhaps considerably less—estimates of the time being very confusing—and

[13] There was a special appropriation of $5,000 for the Utahs in '58. In '59 there were troubles between the Tabuaches and Pike Peak 'miners. According to reports of '62, there were 566 Mohuaches, 960 Jic., and 2,500 Capotes and Pauches; but there is in different reports and estimates a wide discrepancy. In '63 the Utes are reported as behaving much worse than the Jicarillas.

[14] *Carson Papers*, MS. This is a collection of Kit Carson's original papers, furnished for my use by Thomas O. Boggs, the administrator of the Carson estate. The papers relate chiefly to C.'s accounts as Indian agent, and though bulky, the matter cannot be fully utilized here; but there are a few papers which have furnished information of some value on other topics. Carson's skill in the management of Indians and his official integrity were never called in question; but he was a clumsy accountant, and he was often complained of, and once even suspended for irregularities in this respect.

constantly diminished before 1863; but the adjoining bands of Arizona and Chihuahua frequently entered New Mexico, as the lines were often crossed by the New Mexicans. There were few years in which some of these bands or parts of bands were not committing ravages in one section or another, and few in which other parties were not showing encouraging signs of a willingness to abandon their raiding habits. In disposition they were not unlike the Arizona Apaches, though not so bad as the worst of that territory. They often extended their raids into Mexican territory, carrying on a constant trade in plunder and captives with Mexicans, New Mexicans, and Navajos. In these early years they rarely molested the scattered herders of the frontier regions, holding also free intercourse with a disreputable class of traders, who kept them supplied with whiskey and ammunition. They were generally willing to abstain from theft on condition of being fed, and in several instances engaged in farming; but they were of variable temperament, impatient of all restraint, the victims of mismanagement and of frequent outrage.

In the first years but little appears about the Apaches, but from the boundary survey and overland mail and immigration records I infer that their hostilities were not very continuous or serious.[15] In 1852-3 a considerable number of the Gila bands was collected at Fort Webster, and under the care of Agent Wingfield they were induced, under a promise of supplies for a term of years—the arrangement being similar to that made with the Jicarillas in the north—to promise peace and make a beginning of farming. It was a costly though somewhat successful experiment, but naturally, when the treaty was not confirmed and the supplies were stopped the Indians became worse than ever. E. A. Graves is named as agent at Doña Ana in 1854, resigning in June. At this time the Mescaleros began to give much trouble, and campaigns were

---

[15] *Cremony's Life among the Apaches*, 217-322, contains many items.

made against them by Lieutenant Sturgis and Captain Ewell, with such success that in March 1855 they were suing for peace,[16] and in June a treaty was made by Governor Merriwether, by which a reservation was designated near Fort Stanton, a new post established at this time and named for a captain killed in the campaign. The treaty was not approved, but an agency was from this time maintained at the fort under Michael Steck as agent, and the Mescaleros, or a considerable part of them, kept the peace, received their goods, and in most seasons tilled the soil, for six years. There were some drunken quarrels, troubles with other Indians, and petty thefts. Once in 1856 they all ran away to the mountains on Steck's refusal to give them their supplies until stolen property had been returned. The governor disapproved the agent's action, but the Indians returned after a few months. Agent Steck had great faith in the possibility of reforming the Apaches under a proper system, and he went to Washington in 1860 in their interest, leaving W. A. Sapp in charge at Fort Stanton.

Governor Merriwether also made a treaty in 1855 with the Mimbres, and they behaved nearly as well as the Mescaleros, planting and keeping the peace, though much demoralized by liquor and cheated by citizens. The Mogollones were somewhat less tractable, and by Colonel Bonneville's campaign through their country against the Coyoteros and other bands of the Gila in 1857, an unfortunate movement in the opinion of Agent Steck, both they and the Mimbres were scattered, and rendered to a considerable extent hostile.[17] In 1858, however, many of both bands had resumed their friendly attitude, planting on the Rio

[16] On military operations of '54–5, see *U. S. Govt Doc.*, 34th cong. 1st sess., H. Ex. Doc., i., pt ii., 56 et seq.; *Brackett's U. S. Cav.*, 137–9; *Brevoort's Sta Fé Trail*, MS., 12–13. Sturgis received the thanks of the legislature for his services, as did the volunteers who aided his force. *N. Mex., Laws*, 1854–5, p. 99, 101, 103, 105, 111.

[17] For reports of Bonneville's campaign, see *U. S. Govt Doc.*, 35th cong. 1st sess., H. Ex. Doc., ii., pt ii., 135–41; 2d sess., H. Ex. Doc. no. 2, p. 20 et seq; *Wilhelm's Eighth U. S. Infantry*, ii. 47–8, and *Ind. Aff. Repts.* Agent H. L. Dodge was killed by the Mogollones at this time.

Palmas and Santa Lucía in 1857–8. From this time a reservation on the Upper Gila for all the Apaches was strongly recommended, and in 1860 such a reservation was authorized and surveyed near the Arizona line.

In 1861 the confederate invasion put an end to all efforts of the civil department in behalf of the Apaches, and all—including the Mescaleros on the abandonment of Fort Stanton—threw off every restraint, and gave themselves up to hostile raids, the agencies being broken up. This state of affairs continued until 1863, though Agent Labadi at Anton Chico made some fruitless efforts to regain control of the Mescaleros, who, in August 1862, killed forty men and six children, besides taking some captives and a large amount of live-stock. Before the end of the year they asked for peace, but no faith was felt in their sincerity. In 1863 General Carleton's active operations resulted in bringing about 400 of this tribe together at Fort Sumner, or the Bosque Redondo, where they behaved well, according to Agent Labadi's reports, though the general regarded them as a band of murderous vagabonds, in whose promises no reliance was to be placed. The other Apaches were kept quiet, a garrison being stationed at Fort West. Fernando Maxwell this year appears as agent for the Southern Apaches at Mesilla.[18]

The Pueblos now, as before and later, led a quiet and industrious life in their twenty communities, with about 7,000 inhabitants.[19] They never cost the United States a dollar of warlike expenditure, and they received much less aid from the civil department than any of the hostile tribes. This was often noted by

[18] *Carleton's Correspondence*, and *Ind. Affairs Reports.* See also *Hayes' Scraps, Los Ang.*, vi. 113–16; *N. Mex. Scraps*, 19, 23; *Overland Monthly*, v. 222–32; *Newlin's Prop. Ind. Policy*, 43–5.

[19] See *U. S. Govt Doc.*, 40th cong. 2d sess., rept sec. int., p. 213, for abstract of different censuses from 1770 to 1864; also the successive *Ind. Aff. Reports.* The number was frequently given as 8,000 or more, and was perhaps somewhat more than 7,000.

them and others as an injustice, yet it was perhaps
only apparently so, since it was also remarked that a
man will surrender all his money to a highway robber
more readily than he will give a small sum to a deserving applicant for charity.   In New Mexico and
at Washington, among officials and others, the high
merit of the Pueblos was constantly remarked, but
there were other more urgent appeals for money.
The only aid they got was $5,000 in 1855 and $10,000
in 1857 for the purchase of implements, only a small
portion of which was of any real use to them.   Their
agents were A. G. Mayers in 1856, S. M. Yost from
1857, S. F. Kendrick in 1860, and John Ward in
1861-3.   Reverend Samuel Gorman, a baptist clergyman, worked as a missionary among them from 1854,
having a school at Laguna at times.[20]   In 1851 Governor Calhoun expressed fears that these Indians
would be drawn into hostility, but his fears had apparently very slight foundation.   In 1853, according to
Whipple's report, the small-pox carried off many of
the people, especially in the west.   As a rule, there
was but slight change in condition during these years.
The Indians with their docility retained all their old
superstitions, even putting to death several persons
accused of witchcraft at Nambé in 1854.   They were
nominally catholics, but the church did nothing for
their education, only a few pueblos having resident
priests, and the rest being but rarely visited.   Yet
they were sufficiently under priestly control to give
protestants a chance to bewail their ecclesiastical
bondage.   Politically each pueblo ruled itself in its

[20] *Gorman, Sam., Address before the Historical Society of N. Mex.*, N. Y.,
1860, 8vo, 25 p.   This treats of the early history, manners, and customs, etc.,
of the Pueblos; and the same is true of most reports and other writings of the
period in which they are mentioned.   With this subject my readers are already fully acquainted.   Meline, *2,000 Miles*, 222, gives a table for 1863,
showing that the Pueblos had 671 horses, 64 mules, 818 asses, 2,143 cows, and
783 oxen.   See also, in *U. S. Land Off. Rept*, 1861, p. 125-6, list of pueblos,
with location, population, extent, and wealth.   The total of personal property
in 18 pueblos was $518,496.   Most of them had about 17,500 acres of land;
Picurí had 34,766, Pecos 18,763, Cochití 24,256, Sto Domingo 74,743, Pujuaque 13,520, Sandía 24,187, Isleta 110,080, and Nambé 13,586.

own way, but as Indians the people were, to a certain extent, under control of the department, and there was some clashing with territorial authority. The legislature about 1855 declared the pueblos corporate bodies, capable of suing and being sued, which led to much vexatious litigation, and to the danger of all property being eaten up in legal expenses. The Indians in some cases voted for delegate to congress, but their votes were rejected. Indeed, in not being citizens to be ruled by the civil laws, or Indians in the sense of adaptability to regulations of the interior department, or hostiles to be taken in hand by the military, their position was anomalous and perplexing. Yet in many respects they were the best people in the territory. They were jealous of interference, especially with their lands, sometimes even declining to receive gifts from the government for fear of incurring a debt that might lead to a loss of their titles. In this matter, however, the government acted with comparative promptness and wisdom, and most of the pueblo titles—some of them resting on written grants, and others on testimony of long possession, with loss of papers—being examined and approved by the surveyor-general, were confirmed by congress in 1858, and many of them surveyed for patent before 1863. The grants contained generally about 17,500 acres, some being much larger, and a few smaller. The necessity of schools, and especially of industrial education, was often urged, but nothing was practically accomplished till a later period.

Of all the New Mexican tribes, the Navajos—Navajóes in the original form—caused the most trouble and expense to people and government during these thirteen years; but in their case, also, was finally made the greatest progress toward a final settlement. The Navajos, about 10,000 in number, occupying a broad tract in the north-west in this territory and what became Arizona, were somewhat similar to the Apaches in their predatory habits, though superior to them in every respect except the immorality of their women, but also like the Pueblos in their stock-raising, cultivation of the soil, and manufacture of blankets.   Conscious of their strength, they paid little heed to the rights of other tribes, by all of whom they were hated. For many years plundering raids on the Mexican flocks and herds had been their leading though not their only industry.   In this warfare they had lost more captives—to become slaves of the New Mexicans— than they had taken, but in the taking of live-stock the advantage had been largely in their favor.   On the merits of the long struggle, except that it had originated in the predatory instincts of the Indians, each party was about equally to blame, instances of treachery and outrage being frequent on both sides for a century past.   To the Americans, on their taking possession of the territory, the Navajos professed friendship, but, as we have seen, could hardly understand why that should interfere with their warfare on the Mexicans; and presently they came to class the Americans with their old foes, and to regard chronic war with the United States as their normal occupation for the future.   Having no realization of their new enemy's power, they deemed the conditions of the struggle about equal.   Regarding the proffer of peace as an indication of weakness or fear, they were willing when hard pressed at any point to make a treaty, which they broke just as soon as their interest seemed to require it.   Treaty-making was simply an incidental feature of their business, like treaty-breaking; and had plausible pretexts been deemed essential, the New Mexicans, continuing like the Indians their raids as of old, rarely failed to furnish them.   Another complicating circumstance was the fact that the Navajos were much less completely than other tribes under the control of their chiefs, so that one portion of the nation often made war when the rest deemed it not wrong but unwise.   No tribe was more in need of or likely to be so much benefited by a sound whipping.

The Navajos having broken, not only the treaty made by Washington in 1849, but a new one made at Jemes by Calhoun and Sumner in confirmation of the former, Colonel Sumner in the winter of 1851–2 made an expedition with his dragoons, and even penetrated eight or ten miles into the famous Chelly Cañon stronghold, but was obliged to retire without having accomplished anything. Fort Defiance, however, was established about this time, just across the later Arizona line, and not without some restraining effect.[21] H. L. Dodge was put in charge as agent at the fort, holding the position until his death in 1856; and some distributions of goods were made; but only by a portion of the tribe were depredations suspended. In 1853, on their refusal to surrender a murderer, Sumner prepared for a campaign; but by the new commander and governor these preparations were suspended, and all past offences were pardoned, including the murder. Presently, in 1854, a soldier being killed, the Navajo chiefs gained much credit by hanging the murderer in presence of the troops. It was known later that they had hanged a Mexican captive instead of the real culprit! In 1855 Governor Merriwether formed a treaty with this as with other tribes, respecting which not much is known, except that, like the rest, it was never approved. The distribution of goods continued, and though no successor to Dodge was immediately appointed, comparative peace lasted through 1857.[22]

In July 1858 occurred another murder, that of a negro servant at Fort Defiance. A prominent Navajo killed him simply because he had trouble with his wife,

[21] Carson, Carleton, and Allison, in *Ind. Aff. Rept, Joint Spec. Com.*, 1867, 97, 323–4, 335; *Brackett's U. S. Cav.*, 129–30; *Hayes' Scraps, Angeles*, vii. 39. The legislature protested against any treaty not providing for restitution (by the Navajos!) of captives and payment of indemnity for past wrongs.

[22] Collins, in *Ind. Aff. Rept*, 1858, p. 189 et seq. One band under the chief Sandoval remained faithful to the Americans now and later, and the wealthier Navajos were often apparently in favor of peace; but there was always an element that could not be controlled.

and the usages of his tribe required that somebody must die.   In order to force the Indians to surrender the murderer—which they never did—a constant warfare was waged from August by Colonel D. S. Miles, the new commander at the fort; captains McLane, Hatch, and Lindsay, with Major Brooks, being the officers prominent in the campaigns.   The Navajos did not fight so well as usual, a fact due, it was thought, to their use of fire-arms instead of the customary bows and arrows.   It was alleged, with some show of supporting testimony, that the guns had been supplied by the Mormons of Utah.   There were several fights, resulting in the death of some fifty Indians and seven or eight soldiers, with the serious wounding of Captain McLane; but the Indians lost a large amount of sheep and other live-stock, and in December were suing for peace.   An armistice was made on the 4th, and a treaty of peace, involving indemnification in live-stock for all depredations committed since August, the liberation of all captives who might desire it, and the fixing of bounds beyond which the Indians were not to pass, was signed on the 25th.[23]

As usual, the Indians failed to comply with the conditions of this treaty, which had been made by Colonel Bonneville, the successor of General Garland; and in 1859 Major Simonson made an unsuccessful expedition to enforce compliance, depredations continuing as before.   Alexander Baker was this year put in charge of the agency, and was succeeded in September by Silas F. Kendrick.[24]

[23] Reports of the campaigns, in *U. S. Govt Doc.*, 35th cong. 2d sess., H. Ex. Doc., ii., pt ii., 293–399; 36th cong. 1st sess., Sen. Ex. Doc., ii. 256–354; Gov. Renchero's reports, disapproving the war and also the armistice. *Id.*, 36th cong. 2d sess., H. Ex. Doc., vi., no. 24.   Capt. Elliott and Lieut. Averill are also named; and Capt. Blas Lucero with his native company of spies did good service.   Dunn, *Massacres of the Mountains*, chap. ix., gives an excellent account of the Navajos, and a narrative of this war of 1858. See also testimony of Collins and Kennon, in *Ind. Aff. Rept, Joint Spec. Com.*, 1867, p. 330–4. Kennon thinks the killing of the negro to have been only a pretext of Gen. Garland for yielding to the great pressure from citizens for a war for plunder and captives; or at least he says that Gen. G. resisted that pressure until the killing of the boy.

[24] *Ind. Aff. Rept*, 1859–60.   The agents and the citizens regarded the treaty

In 1860 the Navajos became so bold as to attack
Fort Defiance in April, though they were repulsed
without serious loss on either side.[25]   An active campaign was ordered from Washington, and was made
by Colonel Canby in the winter of 1860–1, the regular troops being aided by a large force of volunteers,
including many Pueblo and Ute Indians.[26]   So far as
fighting was concerned, not much was effected by
Canby, but by losses of live-stock the Indians were
led to sue for peace in February 1861, when an armistice of three months, later extended to twelve, was
agreed upon.   In July all the troops were withdrawn,
except two companies at Fort Fauntleroy.   Depredations were by no means suspended, and in September
the Navajos were rendered still more hostile by an
outrage at Fort Fauntleroy, where, in a dispute about
a horse-race, the Indians were fired upon, and a dozen
or more killed, the rest, with many wounded, taking to flight.[27]   The confederate invasion made it
impossible to send regular troops to the north-west,
and the governor's call on the militia for a campaign

as a blunder. The legislature passed resolutions asking the gov. for information about the treaty, especially desiring to know if the Navajos had complied with the conditions; also urging the organization of volunteers and a
new post in the Navajo country.

[25] Report of Capt. Shepherd, in *U. S. Govt Doc.*, 36th cong. 2d sess., Sen.
Doc., ii. 51–63 et seq., with mention of many hostile acts.

[26] There was much confusion and controversy about the employment of
this volunteer force. At the beginning of the year Gov. Rencher called on
Col Fauntleroy for arms, etc., for volunteer companies organized under an
act of the legislature for raids on the Navajos; but F. declined. Later, when
troops had come from Utah, and the expedition was being organized, the people, in a meeting at Sta Fé, called on the gov. to raise a regiment of volunteers. He refused, and at another meeting they resolved to take the matter
into their own hands, and did so, in spite of a warning proclamation issued
by the gov. in August. Gov. R. disapproved this independent action, and
blamed the delegate in congress for having in a silly speech declared the N.
Mexicans fully capable of taking care of themselves. *U. S. Govt Doc.*, 36th
cong. 2d sess., H. Ex. Doc., vi., no. 24.

[27] Testimony of Capt. Hodt, in *Ind. Aff. Rept, Joint Spec. Com.*, 1867, p.
313–14. Lieut.-col Chavez was in command, and gave the order to open fire
with the artillery. Some women and children were killed with the bayonet.
Supt Collins, in *Ind. Aff. Rept*, 1861, p. 124, says that nearly 300 citizens
had been killed in the past 18 months, which is doubtless an exaggeration.
Agent Head, in *Id.*, p. 162, says that the Navajos had compelled the abandonment of the S. Juan and Rio Animas mines, killing 40 Americans and 15
Mexicans on the road.

in October had no effect, though the governor, general, and superintendent had a talk with the Navajo chiefs, and obtained many assurances of friendly intentions.[28]

There was no change in 1862, except that the Navajos became somewhat bolder in their raids, which extended to all parts of the country. There were no campaigns by regular troops, though the establishment of Fort Wingate moved the Indians in December to send in one of their petitions for peace. Some raids were made by New Mexican companies, but all efforts to organize a general movement by the militia were unsuccessful. General Carleton took command in September, but his attention for the rest of the year was devoted mainly to the Apaches. In 1863 operations were carried on by Colonel Carson in the north-west, the plan of removing all the Indians to Fort Sumner on the Pecos was developed, July 20th was fixed as the date after which every Navajo was to be treated as hostile, and orders were repeatedly issued to kill every male Indian capable of bearing arms. While there were no great fights or victories from a military point of view, and while there was but slight diminution in the frequency and extent of depredations, yet, by continuous and active operations in all parts of the country, and by prompt refusal to entertain any proposition of peace or the old-time treaties, very great progress was made in the essential task of showing the Indians that their foe was at last in earnest, and that they must yield or be exterminated. A beginning was also made at the Bosque Redondo, where over 200 Navajo prisoners were gathered, or were at least en route at the end of the year. At the beginning of 1864 Carson and his forces marched to the Chelly Cañon, and while the direct result of the campaign was only 23 killed, 34 captured, and 200 surrendered, and while there were continued hostilities in other regions, yet from this time

[28] *N. Mex., Governor's Message*, 1862; *Dunn's Massacres*, 451.

the Indians began to surrender in large numbers, and before the end of the year the Navajo wars were practically at an end, and over 7,000 of the tribe were living at Bosque Redondo. Their reservation life, and the controversies arising from their transfer, will be recorded in a later chapter.[29]

[29] *Carleton's Correspondence,* ; *Dunn's Massacres,* 447–64, including some details from Carson's MS. report, which has not been printed; *Ind. Aff. Repts,* 1862–4.

CHAPTER XXVII.

CONFEDERATE INVASION OF NEW MEXICO.

1861–1862.

SOUTHERN SYMPATHIES—SLAVERY IN THE TERRITORY—PEONAGE—INDIAN SERVANTS—LAWS ON SERVITUDE—IN CONGRESS—NEW MEXICANS NOT SECESSIONISTS—HATRED OF TEXANS—SOUTHERN PLANS—CAUSES OF FAILURE—AUTHORITIES—PLOTS OF LORING AND CRITTENDEN—FLIGHT OF SOUTHERN OFFICERS—BAYLOR AT MESILLA—LYNDE'S SURRENDER—SIBLEY'S EXPEDITION—CANBY'S EFFORTS—OPPOSING FORCES—HUNTER'S ARIZONA CAMPAIGN—TEXAN ADVANCE—DEFEAT OF THE FEDERALS AT VALVERDE—CONFEDERATE OCCUPATION OF ALBURQUERQUE AND SANTA FÉ—ARRIVAL OF COLORADO VOLUNTEERS AT FORT UNION—TWO BATTLES IN APACHE CAÑON—PIKE'S PEAKERS AGAINST TEXANS—RETREAT OF THE CONFEDERATES—FIGHT AT PERALTA—FLIGHT OF SIBLEY—ARRIVAL OF THE CALIFORNIANS—END OF THE WAR.

IN a general way, so far as they had any knowledge or feeling at all in the matter, the New Mexicans were somewhat in sympathy with the southern states as against those of the north in the questions growing out of the institution of slavery. Their commercial relations in early times had been chiefly with southern men; the army officers with whom they had come in contact later had been largely from the south; and the territorial officials appointed for the territory had been in most cases politicians of strong southern sympathies. Therefore most of the popular leaders, with the masses controlled politically by them, fancied themselves democrats, and felt no admiration for republicans and abolitionists. Yet only a few exhibited any enthusiasm in national politics, apathy being the leading characteristic, with a slight leaning on general principles to southern views.

There were no negro slaves in the territory, except a few body servants, brought in from time to time by military and other officials. Yet two other forms of slavery were prevalent; namely, that of peonage, or voluntary servitude for debt, involving no loss of civil rights, no sale or transfer of service, and no legal obligation on the part of the children of peons;[1] and that of the practical enslavement of Indian captives, who were bought and sold, one or more serving in the family of each citizen of the wealthier class. There were few military or civil officials who did not own captive slaves, and they were found even in the service of the Indian agents.[2] This enslavement of Indians seems to have rested alone on long custom, and not on law, except that no laws were invoked to prevent it. It was abolished by the president's emancipation proclamation of 1865, and orders issued in consequence of that measure. The actual freeing of the servants, whose condition had been in most instances bettered by their servitude, which was in a sense largely voluntary, was probably effected very slowly, but I have no definite records.[3]

[1] Emory, *Notes*, 52, mentions an instance which clearly shows the nature of peon slavery; that of an arriero serving a sutler in Kearny's army of 1846. He owed his master $60, and was paying the debt by serving at $2 per month, out of which he had to feed and clothe himself. Thus $60 was the price of a man's labor for life, without any expense of maintenance on the part of the employer. Davis, *El Gringo*, 231-3, gives a good account of the system, showing that the negro slave's only practical disadvantage, as compared with the peon, is in his being bought and sold; otherwise he has the advantage of maintenance and better care. The peon's master is required by law to treat him well and furnish food, etc., at reasonable prices; but the law is generally disregarded. Practically, his family is also reduced to servitude, the sons in all Mexican provinces feeling themselves under obligation to pay their father's debts.

[2] Benedict, in *Ind. Aff. Rept, Joint Spec. Com.*, 1867, p. 326, testifies on this subject, noting that besides captives, orphans and children of the destitute were also sold into slavery by their relatives. A healthy, intelligent girl of 8 years was worth $400 or more. Their children were not regarded as salable property, but treated as citizens. The number of these servants was estimated at from 1,500 to 3,000. Under the laws these Ind. were entitled to their freedom, there being several decisions in their favor; but the Ind. did not seek the aid of the courts. "Those who hold them are exceedingly sensitive of their supposed interest in them, and easily alarmed at any movements in the civil courts, or otherwise, to dispossess them of their imagined property."

[3] *N. Mex., Message of Gov.*, 1862, 1866. In 1862 the gov. thinks that congress should pay for the freedom of the captives, estimated at 600; since the

Peonage, on the contrary, was sanctioned by territorial law, as well as by the usage of Mexican provinces. An act of 1851 regulated contracts between masters and servants, preventing the latter from quitting the former's service while in debt; an amendment of 1853 made the regulations yet more stringent, authorizing the sheriff in certain cases to contract the debtor's services to the highest bidder; and in 1859 an act provided for the arrest of fugitive servants, and prohibited the courts from interfering in the correction of servants by their masters, unless administered "in a cruel manner with clubs or stripes."[4] This system was not affected by the emancipation proclamation, not being regarded as 'involuntary servitude;' but it was abolished by act of congress in 1867.[5]

The New Mexicans, as I have said, had no negro slaves, and they desired none. As Mexicans they had a strong feeling against the institution; and it was well understood, not only by the natives, but by all acquainted with the territory, that it was not a promising field for the introduction of slave labor. The organic act, however, as an enforced concession to the south, had provided that New Mexico should eventually be admitted as a slave or free state, as its people in their constitution might decide, thus permitting, in the view of all but partisan northerners, the holding of slaves under the territorial organization; at least, until congress and the courts should definitely decide the great national question of slavery in the territories. Thus, New Mexico was more or less a thorn in the flesh of northern politicians, and was often

people could hardly be expected to lose their value, and at the same time add them to the unmanageable Ind. population. And in 1866 he thinks there is a question if their servitude is not really voluntary, and that it would be inhuman to remove them from the protection of the families for whom they have worked. At any rate, N. Mex. cannot afford to stand the expense of their release.

[4] *N. Mex., Acts*, etc., 1851–2, 1852–3, 1858–9.

[5] Act of March 2, 1867. *Cong. Globe*, 1866–7, appen. 238. In 1868 the gov. reports that the law has been very generally and successfully enforced. The penalty was a fine of $1,000 to $5,000, and imprisonment of one to five years. The same penalty, with dismissal from service by court-martial, was prescribed for military officers obstructing the execution of the law.

mentioned in the endless congressional debates on slavery. This, perhaps, had some reflex influence in the territory on the politicians if not on the people, and a kind of mild southern partisanship was developed. In 1857 a law was enacted, prohibiting, under penalty of fine and hard labor in the penitentiary, the residence of free negroes or mulattoes in the territory for a period exceeding thirty days.[6] And in 1859 was passed an act "to provide for the protection of property in slaves in this territory." It punished the enticing-away or aiding to escape of a slave, like stealing him, with imprisonment from four to ten years; prohibited the furnishing or sale of arms to slaves, and all trade with them except with the masters' written consent; provided stringent and detailed regulations for the return of fugitive slaves, including his sale if not claimed; forbade masters giving their slaves the use of their time; permitted stripes for insolence and disorderly conduct, and branding for crime; declared that slaves could not testify in court against free persons; prohibited and annulled all marriages between whites and blacks; forbade emancipation; required slaves to have passports when absent from their masters' premises; and expressly provided that this law should not apply to peonage, but only to African slavery.[7] There was no need of any such ultra pro-slavery measure, and its enactment was brought about for political effect by a few men. In congress it brought out a resolution to annul all acts of the New Mexican legislature authorizing involuntary servitude except for crime, which passed the house, but not the senate. On the governor's suggestion that it was too severe in some respects, however, the act was repealed in December 1861. In 1865–6 the act of 1857 against free negroes was repealed; and in 1866–7

[6] Act of Jan. 29, '57. *N. Mex., Revised Laws,* 456. The act did not apply to actual residents, except in requiring them to give bonds for good behavior. The marriage of a negro or mulatto, free or slave, to a white woman was prohibited. Any owner of a slave who might free him was required to transport him beyond the territory within 30 days.

[7] *N. Mexico, Acts,* 1858–9.

an act was passed abolishing all involuntary servitude in the territory.[8]

In view of the circumstances that have been noted, and of the facts that New Mexico had so recently been added by conquest to the United States, and that the territory had not received from the government at Washington the protection that had been promised, it might naturally have been expected, as indeed it was expected by the south, that the people would favor the secession movement. But when the test came, even in the height of apparent confederate success, they did nothing of the kind, the masses favoring the union cause, and furnishing five or six thousand troops, volunteers and militia, to resist the invasion. A few prominent natives, including some branches of the Armijo family and even the delegate in congress, used their influence and money against the union, but without avail, most of the wealthy and influential families being pronounced union men.[9] While this sentiment of loyalty was undoubtedly real, reflecting credit on the New Mexicans, yet its fervor should not be exaggerated, apathy in national questions being a characteristic of the people; and it should be understood that their sentiment resulted largely from the fact that the confederate invasion came from Texas, the old hatred of the Texans being the strongest popular feeling of the natives, far outweighing their devotion to either the south or north.

[8] *U. S. Govt Doc.*, 36th cong. 1st sess., H. Rept 508; Sen. Miscel. Doc. 12, including an elaborate minority report of the house com. against the right of congress to interfere with slavery in N. Mex.; *N. Mex., Message*, 1861; *Id., Laws*, 1861–2, p. 6; 1865–6 and 1866–7.

[9] Lossing and others mention an address of Delegate Otero, published in Feb. 1861, which incited the New Mexicans to rebellion. I have not seen the document. Ritch, *Legis. Bluebook*, app. 11, names as among the natives who distinguished themselves on the union side: Facundo Pino, José M. Gallegos, José A. Martinez, Donaciano Vigil, Trinidad Romero, Pedro Sanchez, Francisco P. Abreu, Miguel E. Pino, J. F. Chavez, Francisco Perea, Manuel Chavez, Rafael Chacon, José D. Sena, and Manuel D. Pino. Says Gov. Wallace, *N. Mex., Message*, 1880: 'I have yet to hear of one native born of a Mex. mother who refused to support the old flag.' In his report to the sec. interior in '81 the gov. states that N. Mex. furnished over 6,000 volunteers, who did good service. See militia lists in *U. S. Govt Doc.*, 37th cong. 2d sess., H. Ex. Doc. 58.

As my readers well know, the acquisition of frontier territory by the Mexican war of 1846–8, and by the negotiations resulting in the Gadsden purchase of 1853–4, had been a southern measure. It has been often asserted by northern writers, and denied by those of the south, that the acquisition was made with a direct view to ultimate secession, and a southern confederacy of the future to stretch from ocean to ocean, and eventually to include still larger tracts of Mexican territory. Doubtless, the territory was acquired with a view to the extension of slave-state power within the union, and it is wellnigh certain that there were men who even in the early years looked forward to a separation. I am not disposed to attach too much importance to the partisan assertions of later years, or to be overmuch indignant at the alleged iniquity of early southern plans, respecting which I have no definite opinion to offer, since these matters are beyond the field of my special research.

In 1861, however, whatever might have been the nature and scope of earlier schemes, the confederates intended to occupy all or a large portion of the territory accquired in 1846–54. This is shown by their acts, as well as by statements in such documents as are extant, though I cannot claim to have made any original research in this phase of the matter, or, indeed, to have examined all that has been made public in the voluminous war histories. It was hoped, as is shown in another work of this series,[10] that California, or at least southern California, would be brought by inclination and intrigue into the confederacy. It was thought that the strong southern element would be able to control Colorado. Some reliance was probably placed in the hostility of the Mormons to the government, so far as Utah was concerned. Arizona was known to be controlled by secessionists. The native New Mexicans were confidently expected to espouse the southern cause as soon as there might be a show of

[10] See *Hist. Cal.*, vii.; also *Hist. Colorado*.

success.   And the Apaches and Navajos were looked
upon, not exactly as partisans of the south, but as a
potent factor in the defeat of union forces.   Troops
in the territory were barely sufficient for defensive
warfare against the Indians, and New Mexico was a
long way from Washington, even if there had not been
a need of all available forces nearer the national capital.
Moreover, there were military stores in the New
Mexican forts worth capturing, to say nothing of the
opportunity for a display of exuberant Texan patriotism, even if the Californians and Coloradans, by failing
to perform their part of the contract, should render it
impossible to carry out the scheme in its grander
phases and extend the confederacy to the Pacific
shores.   The project was a grand, and from a southern
point of view a legitimate, one, with good apparent
prospects of success.   It failed, not only because the
confederate forces in general were as fully occupied
in the east as were the federals, so that the enterprise
had to be intrusted to the Texans alone, whose resources
were limited, but because New Mexican sympathy for
the south and animosity for the national government
proved less potent than their union proclivities, prejudice against African slavery, and hatred of Texas;
because California not only remained true to the union,
but sent a column of volunteer troops to drive the
rebels out of Arizona; and above all, because Colorado
under energetic union management, not only was able
to control the strong secession element within her borders, but to send a regiment which struck the decisive
blow in ridding her southern neighbor of invaders.

My chief authorities for the subject-matter of this
chapter are mentioned in a note; and it must be confessed that in respect of originality and conclusiveness
on details of some phases they are less satisfactory
than would be desirable, such being necessarily the
case in most attempts to chronicle a minor topic of
the great national struggle.[11]

[11] The first place in national aspects of the matter and in respect of original research must be given to A. A. Hayes, Jr, in whose *New Colorado and*

It is stated, on authority not very clearly defined, that attempts were made in the autumn of 1860 and spring of 1861 by Colonel W. H. Loring of the mounted rifles, of later fame in Egypt as Loring Pasha, temporarily in command of the department, with the aid of Colonel George B. Crittenden, commanding an expedition against the Apaches, both officers having been sent to the territory for that special purpose, to attach the New Mexican troops through the influence of southern officers to the confederate cause; also, that this plan was defeated by the efforts of Lieutenant-colonel B. S. Roberts. However this may have been, the rank and file remained true to their allegiance, with the exception of a single soldier, and even he is not known to have joined the enemy. Many of the officers, however, made haste to espouse the confederate cause, including Loring— succeeded by Canby in the command—Crittenden, and Major H. H. Sibley. This was in June 1861; about the same time the territorial secretary, Alex-

the Santa Fé Trail, N. Y., 1880, 8vo, 200 p., chapter xii., p. 160–73, of which is *An unwritten episode of the late war;* and who contributed to the *Magazine of American History,* of Feb. 1886, p. 170–84, an article entitled *The New Mexican campaign of 1862. A stirring chapter of our late civil war.* The writer has consulted original records to a considerable extent, including several MS. journals, and has conversed with many participants in the campaign, evidently making a careful use of his material, though often unable to reconcile discrepancies of testimony. J. M. Chivington, the fighting parson, major, and later colonel of the Colorado troops, has furnished me, in his *First Colorado Regiment,* MS., a concise and straightforward narrative of the campaign in which he was the leading figure. Ovando J. Hollister's *History of the First Regiment of Colorado Volunteers,* Denver, 1863, 8vo, 178 p., gives in the form of a diary an interesting statement of events as witnessed by himself as a soldier of the regiment, together with additional matter from other sources. To the same subject is devoted chapter xiv., p. 72–89, of the *History of the City of Denver, Arapahoe County, and Colorado,* published by Baskin & Co., at Denver, 1880, which is also inserted in other local histories of the same firm. Lossing, in his *Pictorial History of the Civil War,* ii. 184–8, records the invasion of New Mexico, giving some information not found by me elsewhere, and falling evidently into some errors. The *Civil war in Arizona,* including events in New Mexico, is treated with some completeness on p. 69 et seq. of Elliott & Co.'s *Arizona History.* It is to be regretted that we have no consecutive narrative from the confederate side, and very slight information from N. Mexican sources, most pertaining to the doings of the Colorado troops. See also testimony before cong. committee on the invasion, in *U. S. Govt Doc.,* 37th cong. 3d sess., Sen. Rept 108, p. 364–72; *Overland,* xiii. 337–9; *Hayes' Scraps, Angeles,* vi. 101–20; *Porter's West, Census,* 448; *Sta Fé, Centen. Celeb.,* 27–8; *Meline's 2,000 Miles,* 115–16; *S. F. Alta,* Nov. 19, 1862; *Morris' Address before Soc. of Cal. Volunteers,* S. F., 1866.

ander M. Jackson, resigned his office to go south; and
the project of invasion began to assume definite shape.[12]
Major Sibley was made brigadier-general, and
ordered to Texas in July to organize and command
the expedition; Ex-secretary Jackson became his
assistant adjutant-general of the army of New Mexico; and the order for the brigade to advance from
San Antonio was given on November 16th. Before
Sibley's arrival, however, operations had been begun.
Lieutenant-colonel John R. Baylor, second mounted
rifles, C. S. A., occupied Fort Bliss on the Texas side in
July, crossing into New Mexico and occupying Mesilla
on the 25th. On the 1st of August he issued a proclamation as governor, taking possession in the name
of the confederate states.[13] Major Isaac Lynde, of
the seventh infantry, in command of the southern
district of New Mexico, had a force of about 700 men
at Fort Fillmore. He was a northern man, whether
a traitor or a coward is not quite clear; but in a few
days, perhaps on July 27th, he surrendered his whole
force as prisoners of war to Baylor.[14]   A little earlier,

[12] Hayes quotes briefly some original correspondence. Sibley writes from
El Paso, June 12th: 'We are at last under the glorious banner of the confederate states...I regret now more than ever the sickly sentimentality by
which I was overruled in my desire to bring my whole command with me. I
am satisfied of the disaffection of the best of the rank and file in N. Mex.'
June 30th, 'chief-justice' M. H. McWille wrote from Mesilla: 'Now, might
it not be well, secretly, of course, and at an early moment, to fit out an expedition to N. Mex.?...The stores, etc., in N. Mex. and Ariz. are immense,
and I am decidedly of the opinion that the game is worth the ammunition...
The exped. would relieve Texas, open communication to the Pacific, and
break the line of operations...designed to circumvallate the south...One
regiment of Cherokees or Choctaws would inspire more wholesome terror in
the N. Mex. population than an army of Americans.' It is charged that Sec.
Floyd, besides sending Loring and Crittenden to win over the troops, had
taken pains to send immense quantities of military stores to N. Mex., with a
view to their falling into confederate hands. To say nothing of the somewhat
threadbare nature of this charge, there is little in the prevalent complaints of
preceding years to indicate any marked excess in the quantity of such stores.

[13] The territory of which Baylor took possession was Arizona, to comprise
all south of lat. 34°. He declared all offices vacant, organized a military government, fixed the capital at Mesilla, divided the territory into two judicial
districts, and in a proclamation of Aug. 2d appointed civil officials, including
Jas A. Lucas as secretary, M. H. McWille as attorney-gen., E. Angerstein
as treasurer, and Geo. M. Frazier as marshal; with H. C. Cook and Frank
Higgins as judges, and J. A. Roberts as sheriff of the 1st, or eastern, judicial
district. The proclamations are in Hayes' Scraps, Angeles, vi. 104, 107.

[14] There are few reliable details on record respecting this disgraceful surrender. It appears that Lynde sent a party toward Mesilla, which had a

orders had been sent to the Arizona commandants to abandon forts Buchanan and Breckenridge, which they did, destroying all property that could not be removed. On the march these garrisons heard of the surrender of Lynde, and directed their course, about 450 strong, to Fort Craig. In December Baylor's confederate force was estimated by Canby at 800 Texans, besides 200 or 300 volunteers from the floating Mexican population of Mesilla valley.

About the middle of December General Sibley with his brigade of Texan rangers arrived, and issued his proclamations, declaring martial law and taking possession of the territory.[15] Meanwhile, Colonel Canby was striving to organize his forces and provide means for defence. His reports show that he was greatly embarrassed by the lack of military supplies. He reported the people loyal but apathetic, and doubted the possibility of raising a sufficient force within the territory, placing but very slight reliance on the volunteers or militia. But the legislature authorized the governor to call into service the whole force of the territory to resist invasion, volunteers were rapidly

slight skirmish with the Texans and retired to the fort. Then orders were received to march the garrison to Ft Craig or Alburquerque, and soon after starting, when, as is stated, the men had been given all the whiskey they wanted, and were mostly drunk, they met a Texan force, to which the major, after a council of officers, surrendered. It is said that the more sober of the officers and men protested and wished to fight. The paroled prisoners were allowed to go to Alburquerque, suffering intensely on the march. For this act Maj. Lynde was dismissed from the army; and Capt. A. H. Plummer, the commissary, who turned over to the enemy $17,000 in drafts, was merely reprimanded and suspended for six months. The most detailed account of the affair and of Baylor's operations is found in an article from the *Mesilla Times* and other clippings in *Hayes' Scraps, Angeles*, vi. 101 et seq. It appears that there was some fighting and loss of life at the taking of Mesilla, or its attempted retaking by Lynde's force on July 25th; also that 14 federal soldiers refused parole.

[15] In *Miscel. Hist. Papers*, 23, I have an original copy of Sibley's procl. of Dec. 16th, at Ft Bliss, declaring martial law, 'anticipating a sincere and hearty coöperation and firm support from the inhabitants.' From another procl., of Dec. 20th, Hayes quotes as follows: 'To my old comrades in arms, still in the ranks of the usurpers of their govt and liberties, I appeal in the name of former friendship. Drop at once the arms which degrade you into the tools of tyrants, renounce their service, and array yourselves under the colors of justice and freedom. I am empowered to receive you into the service of the confederate states, the officers upon their commissions, the men upon their enlistments.'

enrolled, and Governor Connelly in his message con-
gratulated the people on their patriotism, announcing
that the confederates had not come north of the jornada, and that the federal force was sufficient for their
expulsion.[16]   At the beginning of 1862 Canby established his headquarters at Fort Craig, where he had a
force of about 4,000 men, of whom, however, 1,000
were useless militia, and less than 1,000 regular troops.
Sibley, on the other hand, had about 2,500 men,
Texan rangers, accustomed to Indian warfare, and
good fighters.[17]

That branch of the confederate campaign pertaining to Arizona has been recorded in another chapter
of this volume,[18] and may be briefly disposed of here.
Captain Hunter with a few hundred Texans of Sibley's army was despatched to the west, and in January
or February occupied Tucson. There was no opposition, union men—if there were any such in southern
Arizona—fleeing into Sonora. Hunter sent a detachment to the Pima villages on the Gila, and awaited
developments in the farther west, which developments,
from a Texan point of view, were most unsatisfactory.
The 'California column,' of 1,800 federal volunteers
under Colonel Carleton, advanced eastward from Fort
Yuma, and the little confederate band had to retire
to the Rio Grande. A captain and three men of
Carleton's advance were captured by Hunter's men on

[16] *N. Mex., Message of Gov.*, 1861; *Id., Acts*, 1861-2. A manifiesto of the
legisl. to the people is also alluded to. The *Ariz., Hist.* (E. & Co.), 72, tells us
that in Oct. there were two minor skirmishes near Ft Craig, in one of which
Capt. Mimk's comp. of N. Mex. volunteers was defeated by a party of
Texans, themselves routed in turn by regulars from the fort.

[17] Canby, according to Hayes, gave his aggregate force as 3,810, and Sib-
leys as 2,600. Sibley gave his own force (on the march northward, some
being naturally left in garrison) as 1,750, while he attributed to Canby 5,000.
A letter from a Texan volunteer, published by Hollister, represents the confederate force leaving Ft Fillmore as 3,800 men. Canby's army was made up
of 11 comp. of the 5th, 7th, and 10th U. S. inf.; 7 comp. of the 1st and 3d
U. S. cavalry; McRae's battery, manned by 2 comp. of 2d and 3d cavalry;
Capt. Dodd's comp. B, 2d Col. volunteers; Lieut.-col Kit Carson's 1st regt
N. Mex. vol.; 17 comp. of 2d, 3d, 4th, and 5th N. Mex. vol.; a spy comp.;
and 1,000 militia. Sibley had the regiments of colonels Reilly and Green;
5 comp. of Steele's regt; 5 comp. of Baylor's regt; and Teel's and Riley's battery.   Lossing, p. 186, gives a portrait of Gen. Sibley.

[18] See chap. xx.

the Gila; and on the 15th of April, in a skirmish between small parties under lieutenants Swilling and
Barrett, the latter with two men was killed on the
federal side, while the confederates lost one or two
killed and three prisoners. In May, Tucson was occupied by the Californians. The Apaches kept the
troops busy enough for a while; but in July and August they advanced to the Rio Grande, too late to aid
in expelling the invaders, but in time to do much
good service against the Indians in this and the following years.

In February 1862 Sibley advanced up the Rio
Grande on the western side by way of Mesilla and
Fort Thorn. On the 18th his army appeared before
Fort Craig,[19] and a cavalry force was sent out by
Canby to defeat the apparent intention of the foe to
pass to the west of the fort; but the Texans had no
idea of going in that direction or of attacking the
garrison. They were manœuvring to protect their
crossing of the river, which was effected at the Panadero ford, several miles below. Next day Canby sent
an artillery force supported by volunteers to occupy
the bluff on the eastern bank, and here on the 20th
there was some firing. As in this skirmish the volunteers behaved badly, as no harm could be done to
the Texans, and as the latter's purpose was clearly to
turn and not attack the position, the troops were withdrawn at night, and Major Roberts with an infantry
force and two batteries was sent to occupy the upper,
or Valverde, ford, some seven miles above.[20] The

[19] According to Hollister, whose account, though made up from hearsay
after the Col. troops reached this region in April, is most detailed and clear-
est, the approach of the Texans was known some days earlier, when Grayden's
party was driven in from a scout and Wingate with an infantry battalion was
sent down to the ford opposite Panadero. Subsequently, Canby came down
with his whole force, but soon returned to the fort, leaving the ford to the
enemy.

[20] On his way 200 mules were captured, which greatly embarrassed Sibley's
transportation service. Hollister represents the march on both sides to have
been made in the night; but Hayes implies that it was in the morning of the
21st. It is said that in the skirmish of the 20th Col., Pino's 2d regiment N.
Mex. vol. was thrown into confusion, while Carson's 1st regt stood firm; but
such is the prevalent confusion of testimony that I attach little importance to
such distinctions.

confederates on the other side made for the same point; and at the ford a fight occurred early on the 21st, in which Roberts had the advantage, crossing the river, posting his batteries, and repulsing the confederate advance.[21]   Canby arrived on the field soon after noon, and an advance was ordered, the batteries were pushed forward, and fire was opened.   One division of the Texans charged Hall's battery and was repulsed; but the movement was apparently intended as a feint to draw off supporting troops from the other battery. This latter was then attacked most furiously by 1,000 Texans; the struggle was desperate; Captain McRae was killed on his guns, and his gunners were wellnigh annihilated; the supporting troops acted very badly; the guns were lost; and Canby's army was driven in some disorder across the river to retire to the fort, leaving the northern route open to the foe.

This fight of Valverde, as it is known, reflected little credit on the federal arms.   Many individuals and a few companies fought bravely, but such is the discrepancy of testimony that I make no attempt to point out cases of bravery or cowardice, blunders or wise management.   The Texans, though victorious, lost probably more than the federals, whose loss was about 90 killed and mortally wounded and 100 wounded.[22]   The confederates marched on up the river without opposition to Alburquerque, leaving their sick and wounded at Socorro.   We have no details respecting Sibley's movements in these days, or those of a detachment sent to occupy Santa Fé, which was apparently accomplished without resistance.

[21] The Colorado company is accredited with having had a desperate fight in this affair with two comp. of Texan lancers, killing a large part of their opponents and having 40 per cent of their own force put hors du combat.   The forces engaged in this preliminary conflict were about 700 men on each side.   Hollister says Canby arrived at 1 P. M.; Hayes says it was 2.45.

[22] Hollister gives the federal loss as 64 killed, 26 mortally wounded, 100 wounded; Texans 200 killed, 200 wounded.   Lossing says the federals lost 62 killed and 142 wounded; Texans about the same.   Hayes gives no figures. Acc. to *Ariz.*, *Hist.* (E. & Co.), there were about 60 killed and 140 wounded on each side.

The main force directed its march toward Fort Union, where there were stores worth about $300,000, and where Major Donaldson arrived on the 10th of March with a train of 120 wagons from Alburquerque, where he had destroyed such federal stores as could not be removed. The Texan advance under Major W. R. Scurry reached Apache Cañon on the 25th. The garrison at the fort was entirely inadequate for its defence; but aid had most opportunely arrived from the north.

Colorado's experience in the civil war has been else-where recorded in the volume devoted to that terri-tory. Here it must suffice to state that by the energetic efforts of Governor Gilpin and his asso-ciates a union force was raised, which not only defeated all confederate hopes at home, but was also able to go abroad and turn the scale in New Mexico. Two companies, which later became A and B of the second Colorado volunteers, were mustered in December 1861, going to New Mexico in January 1862. Company B, Captain T. H. Dodd, served un-der Canby at Valverde, as we have seen;[23] and Com-pany A, Captain J. H. Ford, remained at Fort Union. The first regiment of Colorado volunteers was com-manded by Colonel J. P. Slough, S. F. Tappan being lieutenant-colonel, and J. M. Chivington major. The regiment was composed largely of ' Pike's Peakers,' the best of fighting material, intensely loyal to the union, always eager to go to the front, but not taking kindly to the restraints of military discipline when there was no fighting to be done. Whole companies were often under arrest for mutiny; and an order to march to the relief of Canby—obtained by Major Chivington from General Hunter mainly with a view to prevent the disintegration of the regiment—was welcome to all. The troops left Denver in February; the different divisions united March 7th at the foot of the Raton

[23] This company lost 5 killed and 38 wounded, killing 72 of Lang's Texan lancers. *Denver Hist.*

Pass; a march of 64 miles was once made in 24 hours, and the regiment arrived at Fort Union on the 11–13th of March. Major G. R. Paul, colonel of New Mexico volunteers, was in command of the post, but was ranked by Colonel Slough, who assumed command of the united forces.[24]

On March 22d Colonel Slough's army of 1,342 men, including 300 regular troops,[25] marched from Fort Union toward Santa Fé, encamping at Bernal Spring on the 24th. On the 25th the advance of 400 men, half of them mounted, encamped near the old Pecos ruins; and a scouting party under Lieutenant Nelson captured four men of the enemy's picket, five miles farther west at Pigeon's rancho. Next morning Major Chivington advanced with all his force, and about a mile beyond the rancho, at the mouth of the Apache Cañon proper, found a Texan battery posted, which opened fire.[26] This was about 2 P. M. The federal infantry, deployed to the cañon slopes as skirmishers, advanced ·to the attack, the cavalry remaining behind a spur in the ravine, with orders to charge when the battery showed signs of retreating. The battery presently fell back a mile or more, but Captain Howland failed to charge as ordered. The new position of the Texan guns was at a bend in the cañon, across a dry arroyo-bed, supported by the infantry, strongly posted among the rocks and on the summits. Chivington repeated his former manœuvre, but dismounting Howland's and Lord's men to strengthen the infantry on the flanks, he left the cavalry charge to 100 Colorado horsemen under Captain Cook. After a sharp fight on the flanks the battery yielded, and Cook dashed forward, his horsemen leaping the arroyo

[24] Chivington in his MS. narrative says that the famous forced march of 64 miles in 24 hours ended at Maxwell's rancho, and was prompted by messages from Fort Union that the post was in great danger. He also states that Maj. Paul had mined the fort and made preparations to destroy all public property on the coming of the confederates, and then march to meet the Coloradans.

[25] These troops included two companies of the 5th infantry and two light batteries under captains Ritter and Claflin. *Denver Hist.*

[26] Chivington says that before this his force met the Texan advance guard and captured a lieut. and 30 men before a gun was fired.

with a yell, and charging through and through the enemy's ranks. Cook fell, severely wounded, but Lieutenant Nelson took his place. The infantry, under captains Downing and Wyncoop, coöperated most effectively; the Texans were driven from the field, and the fight of Apache Cañon was won. Statements of casualties are conflicting; but the federals seem to have lost from five to fifteen killed, and the confederates from 20 to 40, with nearly 100 prisoners. Chivington before night fell back to Pigeon's rancho to bury his dead, care for the wounded, and send back the prisoners, with a message to Colonel Slough and the main army. That night or the next morning he retired four or five miles farther, to Kolosky's rancho, where the water supply was better; and here he was joined by Slough and his troops in the night of the 27th.[27]

[27] Chivington and Hollister give tolerably clear accounts of the fight in which they took part. C. in his MS. does not give a statement of casualties; but acc. to Hayes he reported a loss of 5 killed and 14 wounded, the enemy's loss being 32 killed, 43 wounded, and 71 prisoners. Hollister says the federals lost 5 killed, 13 wounded, and 3 missing; and the confed. 16 killed, 30–40 wounded, and 75 prisoners, including 7 officers. The *Denver Hist.* has it 13 fed. killed, 13 wounded; confed. 40, 75, and 108 respectively. Hayes, who regards this affair as a drawn fight and gives few details, says that the reports of Scurry and Sibley give no figures. Perhaps the Coloradans exaggerate their victory, and it would seem that Hayes may have found some evidence to this effect in the confed. reports, which he does not specify. The Frenchman, Alex. Vallé, known as 'Pigeon'—whence the name Pigeon's rancho—described Chivington's operations to Hayes as follows: "'H poot 'is 'ead down and foight loike mahd bull.' Hollister prints a letter from a Texan to his wife, found at Mesilla, which gives a very vivid description of the fight, and of their surprise when 'instead of Mexicans and regulars' they saw 'they were regular demons, that iron and lead had no effect upon, in the shape of Pike's Peakers from the Denver gold mines.' After the first retreat of the battery and the forming a line of battle at the new position, 'up came the cannon, with the enemy at their heels; but when they saw us ready they stopped, but only for a short time, for in a few moments they could be seen on the mountains jumping from rock to rock like so many sheep. They had no sooner got within shooting distance than up came a comp. of cavalry at full charge, with swords and revolvers drawn, looking like so many flying devils. On they came, to what I supposed certain destruction, but nothing like lead or iron seemed to stop them, for we were pouring it into them from every side like hail. In a moment these devils had run the gauntlet for half a mile and were fighting hand to hand with our men in the road.' Behind the ditch 'we felt safe, but again we were mistaken, for no sooner did they see us than some of them turned their horses, jumped the ditch, and like demons came charging on us.... We expected to shoot the last one before they reached us, but luck was against us, and after fighting hand to hand with them, and our comrades being shot and cut down every moment, we were obliged to sur-

On March 28th Slough pushed forward with his full force; but Chivington, with 400 or 500 men under the guidance of Lieutenant-colonel Manuel Chavez, was detached to cross the mountains and attack the enemy's rear. His success will be noted presently. The rest of the army, 700 or 800 strong, met the Texans, sooner than Slough expected, half a mile beyond Pigeon's rancho, about 9 A. M. From the first the federals were outnumbered, acted on the defensive, and though fighting bravely for about five hours, were forced back to the rancho, to a new position half a mile farther east, and finally to Kolosky's. Had the enemy known the number of the troops opposed to them, or had they not been somewhat overcautious as a result of the former battle, the federal repulse might have been a disastrous defeat. The federal loss is given as from 20 to 50 killed, 40 to 80 wounded, and 15 to 20 prisoners; that of the confederates 36 to 150 killed, 60 to 200 wounded, and 100 prisoners, the last figure apparently, however, including both battles.[28] Scurry, the Texan commander, instead of following up his success, sent a flag of truce, asking an armistice for the purpose of burying his dead, and caring for his wounded. This was granted by Slough, and the Texans took advantage of the opportunity to fall back to Santa Fé, which position they presently abandoned and retreated down the Rio Grande.

The cause of Sibley's retreat, notwithstanding his apparent victory, must be sought in the operations of

render. Now, who do you suppose it was that came charging and nearly running over me, with a revolver pointed at my head, etc.? It was Geo. Lowe....You know him well....How one of the men that charged us ever escaped death will ever be a wonder to me....About 80 of us were taken prisoners and marched off toward Ft Union. How many were killed and wounded I don't know, but there must have been a large number.'

[28] Hayes gives the federal losses as 29 killed, 42 wounded, and 15 prisoners; confederate 36 killed and 60 wounded, as admitted by Scurry. Lossing says the federals loss 23 k. and 50 w.; confed. same as Hayes. Gov. Connelly reported the confed. lost as 400 k., w., and prisoners. Hollister puts the fed. loss at 46, 64, and 21; confed. 281, 200, 100 (prob. including both battles). The *Denver Hist.* has it 134 k. and w. on the fed. side; and 151, 200, and 100.

Chivington. This officer, on the 28th, with 370 Colorado volunteers and 120 regulars, had been guided by Chavez over the mountains to the rear of the enemy, where they arrived about noon. Descending the precipitous cliffs in single file, they drove off the Texan guard, capturing several of their number, spiked the cannon, killed the mules, burned 64 wagons, and destroyed all the enemy's supplies, thus rendering it impossible for the confederates to continue their offensive operations. This virtually ended the campaign; the 'Pike's Peakers' had proved more than a match for the 'Texan rangers,' saving New Mexico for the union; and Chivington, presiding elder of the methodist church in Colorado, had made himself the hero of the war.[29]

Orders now came from Canby to Slough to protect Fort Union at all hazards; and, very much against the wishes of the Coloradans, the army fell back to the fort, arriving on the 2d of April. On the 5th, under new orders, the army marched for the south, under the command of Colonel Paul, Slough having resigned his commission. Galisteo was reached on the 10th, details of movements in these days having very slight significance,[30] and here was met an adjutant from Canby. This officer, leaving Fort Craig garrisoned by volunteers under Carson, had marched northward on April 1st with 860 regulars and 350 volunteers. The confederates, or a part of them, had fallen back on Alburquerque; and against this town, on the 8th, Canby's troops made a demonstration,

[29] Chivington's own narrative is most satisfactory, besides agreeing in most respects with others. His officers were captains W. H. Lewis and A. B. Carey of the regulars, and Wyncoop of the volunteers. Chivington says that they bayoneted 1,100 mules. On their return they reached the camp at Kolosky's at midnight, entering it prepared to fight, with the idea that it was a camp of the enemy.

[30] Hollister and the *Denver Hist.* give many such details. Slough seems to have resigned in his disgust at not being permitted to pursue the retreating Texans. On the 9th, according to Hayes, Col Paul marched from Bernal Spring toward Sta Fé, meeting on the way Maj. Jackson and party, with a flag of truce, and soon learning that Sta Fé had been evacuated. On the 12th he wrote from Galisteo that the Union troops had been cheered on entering the capital.

with but slight effect,[31] thence turning to the right,
and joining Paul's force at Tijeras on the 13th.   The
next day, Chivington having been appointed colonel
of the Colorado regiment, the united army marched
to the Rio Grande, and down that river to Peralta,
where the confederates were posted in the adobe town,
having abandoned Alburquerque.   It was to some
extent a surprise, and a few pickets were captured.
Chivington was eager to take the town by assault, but
Canby would not permit it.

On the 15th a belated Texan train coming in sight
from Alburquerque was captured by 30 mounted
Coloradans, who lost one man and killed four, taking
one gun, a dozen prisoners, 70 mules, and 15 horses.
Presently the confederates opened fire with their artillery, which was answered, the firing being continued
to some extent all day, with but slight and unrecorded
effect.   The Colorado troops retired to the river, and
planned an attack under cover of the banks, but Canby
forbade the movement.   He is accused of an unwillingness to kill his old comrades, of jealousy toward
the volunteers, and even of cowardice.   Hayes, however, states that the reason for inaction was that he
"had no desire to capture men whom he could not
feed."   The Texans took advantage of a tempestuous
night to ford the river and escape.   On the 16th and
17th the armies advanced slowly southward in sight
of each other on opposite sides of the river,[32] the
Texans burning some of their baggage on the way,
to La Joya; but on the 18th the confederates had
disappeared, to be seen no more, leaving, however,

[31] Hayes says that in this engagement, respecting which no details are
given, Maj. Duncan, 3d cavalry, was seriously wounded.   Chivington says:
'They fought all day at long range, and at night Canby took a side route and
attempted to form a junction with us, and Sibley escaped down the Rio
Grande with his force.'

[32] Chivington says: 'They disputed our crossing for 4 days and nights
whenever we attempted to cross; and we tried to get sufficiently far in advance to cross without being subject to their artillery fire.   On the 4th night
they burned their transportation, and abandoned everything except some
light vehicles, packed their provisions, and took to the mountains.'   There is
no other evidence that Canby's force attempted to cross at all.   See account
of fight at Peralta, in *Las Vegas Chronicle*, Feb. 21, 1885.

some of their sick and disabled, with a few wagons, which were found by Captain Grayden on a trip to the western side. A day or two later Sibley destroyed the rest of his baggage, and followed a trail over the mountains far to the west of Fort Craig, and thence to the Mesilla valley and to Fort Bliss, where he arrived early in May.[33] In killed, wounded, prisoners, and stragglers, they had left nearly half their original force in New Mexico.[34]

The federals advanced much at their leisure in three columns under Paul, Chivington, and Captain Morris, crossing the river at Limitar, just above Socorro, on the 20th, and there learning definitely of the enemy's flight.[35] On the 22d they reached the old battle-field of Valverde, where the volunteers encamped, and the regulars took up their quarters at Fort Craig. There was no thought of further pursuit, General Canby returning to Santa Fé, and leaving Colonel Chivington in command of the southern district, which position he held until succeeded by Colonel Howe. Some Texan rangers still remained in the Mesilla valley, and in May a party of them appeared at the Panadero, below the fort, but there was no fighting. On July 4th the Californian advance reached the Rio Grande, and two days later the last of the invaders left the territory. It does not seem necessary to record the movements of the Colorado companies in garrison at different posts and in a few Indian expeditions during the following months. Before the end of the year the last of them had left New Mexico for home and other service, their places being taken by the California volunteers, and General Carleton assuming command of the department in September.

[33] May 4th, according to Lossing; but on the 18th Canby, acc. to Hayes, reported the confed. as scattered along the valley from Doña Ana to El Paso.
[34] Canby's report, as quoted in *Ariz.*, *Hist.* (E. & Co.). A prisoner 'tells me that out of the 3,800 men and 327 wagons that were with us when we left Ft Fillmore, only 1,200 men and 13 wagons remained together when they were obliged to flee to the mountains.' Letter of a Texan quoted by Hollister.
[35] Hollister says that 30 prisoners came into camp on the 19th, and were paroled, one of them being Ex-surveyor-gen. Pelham. At Limitar 75 sick and stragglers were taken.

The legislature at the session of 1862–3 passed resolutions thanking "the brave California and Colorado troops for their timely aid in driving the traitors and rebels from our soil," with an additional paragraph especially complimentary to General Carleton and the Californians, whose march across the desert was regarded as "one of the most remarkable achievements of the age." This paragraph brought out a letter from Governor Evans of Colorado, who, in view of the fact that the Californians had not arrived until the campaign was over, complained of injustice done to the Coloradans, who had really expelled the invader. Accordingly, at the next session, the legislature attempted to set the matter right, solemnly affirming, in a resolution respecting the Colorado troops, that "it is not the intention to place these brave soldiers second to none"![36]

[36] *N. Mex., Acts*, 1862–3, 1863–4; *Colorado, House Journal*, 3d sess., p. 72–7. In 1865 Kit Carson was promoted to brigadier-general of volunteers for his gallantry at Valverde and other services. *Carson, Papers*, MS. These papers contain a few documents bearing on details of this campaign, including correspondence showing that Canby and Carson had some doubts about the loyalty of the militia and some of the volunteers. Claims for damages done by rebels were filed by citizens, and the subject was often agitated; but down to 1880 at least none of these claims had been paid. *N. Mex., Mess., of Gov.*, 1880.

CHAPTER XXVIII.

CHRONOLOGIC AND OFFICIAL.

1864–1886.

Chronologic Résumé—Governors—List of Officials—Members and Officers of the Legislature for Each Session—Summary of Legislative Acts—Changes in Sessions and Rules—Delegates in Congress—Contested Seats—National Legislation—Public Buildings —Historical Society—Finances—Claims against the United States —Revised Laws—Supreme Court—Lawyers—Efforts to Secure Admission as a State—Surveys and Boundaries—Crime and Disorder—Statistics of Population.

In the history of New Mexico after 1863 chronologic annals have but small part. The government record, Indian affairs, industries and institutions, and local matters will be treated in four successive chapters. All these, and especially the first, will be devoted for the most part, not to a consecutive narration of events, but to classified records and statistical matter showing the territory's condition and development, a large part of which matter may be presented most profitably in fine-print notes. I begin, however, by appending a chronologic summary of the most important happenings of 1864–86, embracing many topics to be noted more fully in the following pages and chapters. And the completeness and utility of this summary are increased by extending it backward, so far as leading events are concerned, to the American occupation in 1846; and even farther, in the briefest of outlines, to the beginning of New Mexican annals.[1]

---

[1] Chronological summary of New Mexican history: Discovery and exploration, 1540–97: see chap. i.–v. of this vol. 1535–6, Cabeza de Vaca, passing through Texas and Chihuahua, hears of the N. Mex. pueblos. 1540–2, Coronado's army enters via Sin., Son., and Ariz., spending two winters in the Rio

The territory was ruled from 1864 by a succession of eight governors: Henry Connelly from 1864, Robert

Grande valley. 1581, Fr. Agustin Rodriguez enters N. Mex. from Chih. 1582–3, entrada of Espejo. 1583–95, several projects of conquest, without results. 1590–1, illegal entry of Castaño de Sosa from N. Leon via Texas. 1594–6, expeditions of Bonilla and Humaña.

Spanish conquest and occupation: see chap. vi.–x. 1598–9, conquest by Juan de Oñate. 1601–5, Oñate's exped. to Quivira and mouth of the Colorado. 1615, Sta Fé founded about this date. 1630, from 50 to 100 missionaries serving in from 90 to 150 pueblo missions. 1640, beginning of dissensions between govt and missionaries. 1650, beginning of serious troubles with the Indians. 1664 et seq., Penalosa's filibustering schemes. 1670 et seq., Apaches begin their raids; Navajóes mentioned; Span. pop. about 2,400, converted Ind. 20,000. 1680, revolt of Pueblos, expelling Span., and killing 400; El Paso founded. 1681–2, Otermin's vain efforts to reconquer the province. 1692–6, reconquest by Diego de Vargas.

Spanish rule continued: see chap. xi.–iii. 1706, founding of Alburquerque. 1709, first important war and treaty with the Navajos. 1712 et seq., efforts to conciliate or conquer the Moquis, who refused to submit. 1716 et seq., first troubles with Comanches. 1730–42, controversies of Franciscans with the church and with the Jesuits. 1730, first visit by the bishop. 1750, Span. pop. 4,000, Ind. converts 12,000. 1760, tour of Bishop Tamaron. 1760–1800, a period of dissension, rascality, and decadence. 1774–6, active efforts for exploration in west, and for conversion of the Moquis; exped. of Dominguez and Escalante to Utah. 1776–7, organization of Provincias Internas, including N. Mex. 1780–1, ravages of small-pox, leading to consolidation of missions. 1786, new Apache policy. 1800, Span. pop. 18,000, Ind. 9,700. 1803, Luisiana ceded to U. S. 1804–5, beginnings of Sta Fé trade; working of Sta Rita copper mines. 1806–7, Pike's exploring exped. 1810, Pino sent to Span. córtes from N. Mex. 1819, boundary treaty with U. S. 1821, N. Mex. supports Iturbide. 1822, Span. pop. 30,000, Ind. 10,000.

Mexican rule: see chap. xiv. 1822, N. Mex. becomes a Mexican province. 1824, a territory of the Mex. republic; beginning of the legal Sta Fé trade. 1828, expulsion of Spaniards and partial secularization of missions; discovery of the gold placers. 1833, visit of the bishop. 1835, first printing-press and newspaper. 1836, N. Mex. a department under a governor. 1837–8, rebellion of Gonzalez and accession of Gov. Armijo. 1839, N. Mex. a separate comandancia; discovery of the 'new' placers. 1841, Texan Sta Fé invasion. 1844, department divided into districts and partidos. 1845, pop. about 70,000, Ind. 10,000; Texas annexed to U. S.

Rule of the United States: see chap. xvii., xxv.–vii. 1846, Mex. war; occupation of N. Mex. by Gen. Kearny. 1847, revolt of the New Mexicans; first legislature and first newspaper in English. 1848, treaty between U. S. and Mex., the latter ceding N. Mex.; territorial convention. 1849–50, state convention; debates in congress on slavery and Texan boundary. 1850, N. Mex. admitted as a territory; pop. 61,547; vicarate of Sta Fé estab., Lamy honorary bishop. 1850–1, Mex. boundary survey. 1851, organization of territorial govt, and meeting of 1st legislature. 1851–9, several R. R. and other explorations. 1853–4, dispute with Mex. for possession of the Mesilla valley. 1854–5, Gadsden purchase annexed to N. Mex.; Ind. wars. 1855, surveyor-general's office estab. 1858–60, pueblo, private, and town land claims confirmed by congress. 1858–63, Navajo wars, ending with exped. of '63–4 by Carleton and Carson. 1861, Cimarron Ind. agency estab. 1861–2, confederate Texan invasion; territory of Colorado cut off. 1863, Arizona cut off; Fort Sumner and Bosque Redondo reservation estab.

Chronologic annals of 1864–86: see for details this and the three following chapters. 1864, also *Ritch's Blue-Book.* 1864, gov. Connelly; gen. Carleton; Ind. supt Steck; Navajos at Bosque Redondo. 1865, publication of revised statutes; Ind. supt Delgado. 1866, gov. Mitchell; Ind. supt Norton; re-

B. Mitchell from 1866, William A. Pile in 1869–71, Marsh Giddings in 1871–5, Samuel B. Axtell in 1875–8, Lewis Wallace in 1878–81, Lionel A. Sheldon in 1881–4, and Edmund G. Ross from 1885. I append a list of all territorial and federal officials for the period.[2] **Most of**

pairs on the palacio; Mescaleros quit the Bosque Redondo reservation. 1867, gen. Sykes and Getty; Ind. supt Webb; discovery of Moreno mines; peonage abolished; death of Padre Ant. J. Martinez; decision of sup. court that Pueblos are citizens; soldiers' monument dedicated at Sta Fé. 1868, Grant co. created; 1st daily mail from east; Navajos removed from Bosque Redondo to their old home in the N. W.; 1st mil. telegraph in operation; death of Kit Carson; Chavez, contestant, seated as delegate in congress; Fort Sumner abandoned.

1869, gov. Pile; Ind. supt Gallegos and Clinton; Colfax and Lincoln counties created; archives sold for waste paper; complaints against Justice Houghton; earthquakes. 1870, Ind. supt Pope; population, 90,573; forts Cummings and McRae garrisoned; sale of the Maxwell rancho; Apaches at Cañada Alamosa moved by Colyer to Tularosa; 1st national bank at Sta Fé. 1871, gov. Giddings; gen. Granger (also 1875); biennial sessions of legislature; water found by Martin in the Jornada del Muerto; filing of land claims resumed. 1872, Ind. supt (the last) Dudley; state constitution formed; new public school law. 1873, gen. Gregg; Jesuit school at Alburquerque. 1874, gen. Devin; Mescaleros on reserv. at Fort Stanton; Apaches moved to Hot Springs; new land district in south at Mesilla; prot. episcopal missionary diocese. 1875, gov. Axtell; mil. telegraph, Sta Fé to Mesilla; archdiocese of Sta Fé created; Rev. Tolby murdered in Colfax co.; Jesuit schools at Las Vegas and La Junta. 1876, col Wade and gen. Hatch; telegraph to Tucson; R. R. at Trinidad, Col.; prefect system of co. govt abandoned; murder of Hon. Louis Clark in Rio Arriba; Ft Selden abandoned. 1877, Apaches removed to S. Cárlos, Ariz.; telegraph to S. Diego; survey of land claims resumed; grand lodge of masons organized. 1878, gov. Wallace; R. R. crosses N. Mex. line at Raton Mt.; war of stockmen begins in Lincoln co.; act incorporating Jesuits annulled by congress in '79; Sta Fé academy incorporated; Jicarillas moved to a reserv. in N. W.; Utes removed to Col.; Apache raids of Victorio, '78–82. 1879, beginning of a 'boom' in mines; White Oaks mines discovered; Los Cerrillos camps; R. R. reaches Las Vegas; Hot Springs hotel opened; 1st prot. epis. church in N. Mex. dedicated at Las Vegas; Alburquerque academy incorporated.

1880, R. R. reaches Sta Fé, Alburquerque, and Isleta; narrow-gauge R. R. from north enters the territory; general incorporation act; Bureau of Immig. and Historical Soc. organized; founding of New Alburquerque; Victorio killed in Mexico; visit of Gen. Grant and Pres. Hayes; Maxwell Grant co., organized under laws of Holland; Rio Arriba co. enlarged; gas at Sta Fé; street R. R. at Alburquerque; Las Vegas academy; fire at Las Vegas; pop. of the territory 109,793. 1881, gov. Sheldon; gen. Bradley and Mackenzie; R. R. completed to Deming, El Paso, and Cal.; also D. & G. R. R. in the north, and A. & P. to the Arizona line; 1st territorial fair, and congregational church at Alburquerque; educational assoc. organized; Ind. school at Alburquerque; 1st vol. of N. Mex. sup. court reports published; telephone at Sta Fé. 1883, tertio-millennial celebration at Sta Fé; A. & P. R. R. reaches Colorado River; Jicarilla Ind. removed to the Mescalero reservation. 1884, Sierra co. created; Navajo reserv. extended and consolidated with that of the Moquis; $200,000 approp. for completing public buildings; wrangle about organization of the legislature. 1885, gov. Ross; publication of *Compiled Laws*. 1886, fire at Socorro; population probably 150,000.

[2] New Mexico official list 1863 et seq. See *Laws* and *Journals;* also *Ritch's Legislative Blue-Book; National Almanac; Tribune Almanac,* etc.

the rulers managed New Mexican affairs with commendable tact and honesty, taking some pains to ac-

Governors: Henry Connelly 1861-5; W. F. M. Arny, acting, 1865-6; Robert B. Mitchell 1866-9; Wm A. Pile 1869-71; Marsh Giddings 1871-5; Wm G. Ritch, acting, 1875; Samuel B. Axtell 1875-8; Lewis Wallace 1878-81; Lionel A. Sheldon 1881-5; Edmund G. Ross 1885-6.

Secretaries (often acting as gov., especially Arny and Ritch): W. F. M. Arny 1862-7, 1872-3; H. H. Heath 1867-70; Henry Wetter 1870-2; Wm G. Ritch 1873-85; Sam. A. Losch 1885; Geo. W. Lane 1885-6.

Delegates: 38th congress, 1863-4, Francisco Perea; 39th to 41st cong., 1865-70, José Francisco Chavez (though C. P. Clever receiving the certificate of election held the seat in 1867-8); 42d cong., 1871-2, José Manuel Gallegos; 43d and 44th cong., 1873-6, Stephen B. Elkins; 45th cong., 1877-8, Trinidad Romero; 46th cong., 1879-80, Mariano S. Otero; 47th cong., 1881-2, Tranquilino Luna, 48th cong., 1883-4, Francisco A. Manzanares; 49th cong., 1885-6, Anthony Joseph (reëlected to 50th cong.).

Chief justices: 1858-66, Kirby Benedict; 1866-8, John P. Slough; 1868-9, John S. Watts; 1869-76, Joseph G. Palen; 1876-8, Henry L. Waldo; 1878-9, Charles McCandloss; 1879-82, L. Brandford Prince; 1882, Samuel B. Axtell, Wm A. Vincent 1885, E. V. Long 1885-6.

Associate justices, 2d district, 1861-4, Sydney A. Hubbell; 1864-9, Perry E. Brocchus; 1869-76, Hezekiah S. Johnson; 1876-7, John I. Redick; 1877-8, Samuel B. McLin; 1878-85, Joseph Bell; 1885-6, Wm H. Brinker; 3d district, 1861-5, Joseph G. Knapp; 1865-9, Joab Houghton; 1869-70, Abraham Bergen; 1870-1, Benj. J. Waters; 1871-2, Daniel B. Johnson; 1872-85, Warren Bristol; 1885, Wm B. Flemming; 1885-6, Wm F. Henderson.

Clerks of sup. court: 1859-66, 1868-9, Sam. Ellison; 1866-7, Wm M. Guynnf; 1867-8, Peter Connelly; 1869-73, Wm Breeden; 1873-7, Rufus J. Palen; 1877-80, John H. Thompson; 1880-2, Frank W. Clancy; 1882-5, Charles W. Philips; 1885, R. W. Webb; 1885-6, R. M. Johnson.

Attorney-generals: 1863-7, C. P. Clever; 1867-9, Merrill Ashurst; 1869-72, Thos B. Catron; 1872-80, Wm Breeden; 1880, Henry L. Waldo; 1880, Eugene A. Fiske (not confirmed); 1881-6, Wm Breeden.

Treasurers: 1863-5, Wm Osterton and Anastasio Sandoval; 1865-6, Felipe Delgado and A. Sandoval; 1866-9, Simon Delgado; 1869-72, Felipe and Pablo Delgado; 1872-80, Antonio Ortiz; 1880-2, Juan Delgado; 1882-6, Antonio Ortiz.

Auditors: 1863-5, Miguel E. Pino; 1865-7, Epifanio Vigil; 1867, Anastasio Sandoval; 1867-9, Epifanio Vigil; 1869-72, A. Sandoval; 1872-86, Trinidad Alarid.

U. S. attorneys: 1860-7, T. D. Wheaton; 1869-71, S. B. Elkins; 1871-2, S. M. Ashenfelter; 1872-8, Thos B. Catron; 1878-82, S. M. Barnes; 1882-5, Geo. W. Prichard; 1885, Thos Smith.

U. S. marshals: 1861-6, Abram Cutler; 1866-76, Thos B. Catron; 1876-82, John Sherman, Jr; 1882-5, A. L. Morrison; 1885-6, Rómulo Martinez.

Surveyor-generals: 1861-8, John A. Clark; 1868-9, Benj. C. Cutler; 1869-72, T. R. Spencer; 1872-6, James K. Proudfit; 1876-85, Henry M. Atkinson; 1885-6, Geo. W. Julian, clerk and translator; 1860-84, David J. Miller.

Registers land-office Sta Fé: 1861-8, Joab Houghton; 1868-70, Ed. D. Thompson; 1870-2, Eben Everett; 1872-5, Abram G. Hoyt; 1875-8, José D. Sena; 1878-81, John C. Davis; 1881-4, Max Frost. Receivers: 1858-64, W. A. Street; 1864-6, John Greiner; 1866-70, J. L. Collins; 1870-6, E. W. Little; 1876, Geo. R. Smith, C. M. Howard; 1876-7, A. G. Hoyt; 1877-81, Elias Brevoort; 1881-5, W. H. Bailhache; 1885-6, C. F. Easley. Registers at Mesilla land-office: 1876-82, Geo. D. Bowman; 1882-5, John R. McFie. Receivers: 1876-8, Lawrence Lepoint; 1878-80, Mariano Varela; 1880-4, S. W. Sherfey.

Adjutant-generals: 1861-5, C. P. Clever; 1865-7, John Gwin; 1867-8,

quaint themselves with the territory's needs, so far as
can be determined from their messages, from the praise
of friends and censure of foes, and from the various
records of their official acts, though not appointed with
any special view to their fitness or the people's de-
sires, and having but slight opportunity for useful
service. Connelly, as we have seen, was a weak man,
of good intentions, who, notwithstanding his loyal
sentiments, made no very brilliant record as a 'war'
governor. He died in office, and was succeeded temporarily by W. F. M. Arny, the secretary, a man
prominent in Indian affairs and other public matters,
involved in many controversies, but of good repute.
Governor Mitchell incurred the enmity of the legislature to such an extent as to call out from that body
a resolution for his removal. He was accused of having absented himself during the session, removing on
his return the officials appointed by Secretary Heath,
and refusing to sanction a memorial passed in his absence. He even had the audacity to appoint a delegate to congress to fill a vacancy! It was resolved
to send laws not approved by him to congress for confirmation, at the same time asking for an abrogation of
the governor's absolute veto power, which was granted
by an amendment of the organic act in 1868. There
was a controversy between the governor and secretary,
the latter being denounced in public meetings at the
capital but sustained by two resolutions of the assembly. Of Governor Pile, but little appears beyond the
stupid blunder by which half the old Spanish archives
were lost, as noticed elsewhere. He was later United
States minister in Venezuela. Governor Giddings
died in office in 1875, and was succeeded temporarily
by Secretary Ritch, a man who as secretary, acting

Clever and John T. Russell; 1868–70, Geo. W. Cook and James M. Wilson;
1870–1, Wm L. Rynerson; 1871, A. Sandoval; 1871–3, W. M. Giddings;
1873–80, Thos S. Tucker; 1880–1, J. H. Watts; 1881–2, Max. Frost; 1882–3,
Louis Felsenthal; 1883–6, E. L. Bartlett.

Librarians: 1869–71, Ira M. Bond; 1871–8, James McKenzie; 1878–80,
Aniceto Abeitia; 1880, R. H. Tompkins; 1880–6, Sam Ellison.

governor, president of the Immigration Society, author, and citizen has been since 1873 one of the most active and successful workers for the benefit of his territory. Governor Axtell was later chief justice; Governor Wallace, famous as a general and as an author; and Sheldon, a most efficient and popular governor.

Next is appended a full list of the members of the legislative assemblies from the thirteenth to the twenty-sixth sessions.[3] It will be noted that the pre-

[3] Members of the legislatures, 1864 et seq. See *N. Mex. Laws; Id., Journals;* and *Ritch's Legisl. Blue-Book.*

13th assembly, 1863–4. Council: president Diego Archuleta, clerk Pedro Valdés, sergt José Duran y B.; members, Mora, Severiano Martinez; Taos, Gabriel Vigil, Matias Medina; Rio Arriba, D. Archuleta, Man. Trujillo; Sta Fé, Anastasio Sandoval; Sta Ana and Bernalillo, Serafin Ramirez, Nicolás Lucero; Valencia, Clemente Chavez; Socorro, Dionisio Jaramillo; Doña Ana and Arizona, Cristóbal Sanchez. House: speaker Vicente García, clerk Fran. Salazar, sergt J. A. Martinez; members, Mora, Apol. García, J. J. Gallegos; Taos, Ventura Herrera, José Duran, Ramon Arellano, Cris. Mares; Rio Arriba, José Salazar, Jesus M. Herrera, José M. Vigil; Sta Fé, Vicente García, Simon Delgado, Jesus M. Ortiz; S. Miguel, Desiderio Gallegos, Regino Ulibarri, José Aragon y P., Celso Vaca; Sta Ana, Patricio Silva; Bernalillo, H. L. Johnson, Tomás C. Gutierrez; Valencia, Greg. N. Otero, Filomeno Sanchez; Socorro, ———; Doña Ana and Arizona, Frank Higgins.

14th assembly, 1864–5. Council: pres. D. Archuleta, clerk Nic. Quintana, sergt Pelagio Ortiz; members, same as preceding session, except J. A. Vaca for Medina in Taos; S. Miguel, Don. Vigil, Man. Herrera; Socorro, vacant. House: speaker Pedro Valdés, clerk Sant. Valdés, sergt Juan M. García; members, Mora, Felipe Sanchez, Nestor Martinez; Taos, Pedro Valdés, Felipe Archuleta, Buenaventura Lobato, Nicanor Vigil; Rio Arriba, Fran. Salazar, Jesus Lujan, M. Lucero; Sta Fé, Felipe Delgado, Man. Rodriguez, Theodore S. Greiner; S. Miguel, Arthur Morrison, Ed. Martinez, Trinidad Romero, Desiderio Romero; Sta Ana, Fran. Vaca; Bernalillo, Wm H. Henrie, W. P. Strachan; Valencia, Filomeno Sanchez, Roman Vaca; Socorro, Candelario García, José A. Vaca y Pino; Doña Ana, Stephen B. Elkins.

15th assembly, 1865–6. Council: pres. Miguel E. Pino, clerk Fran. Salazar, sergt José Sena; members, Mora, vacant; Taos, Pascual Martinez, Rafael Chacon; Rio Arriba, Ant. G. Córdoba, Vicente Aragon; Sta Fé, M. E. Pino; S. Miguel, Tomás D. Vaca, Man. Herrera; Sta Ana and Bernalillo, Jesus M. Silva, Guadalupe Perea; Valencia, Man. Sanchez; Socorro, José A. Torres; Doña Aña, ———. House: speaker Samuel Ellison, clerk J. M. H. Alarid, sergt Estévan García; members, Mora, Fel. Sanchez, José Mestas; Taos, Fel. Montoya, Juan B. Cola, Ant. A. Mondragon, Juan N. Sanchez; Rio Arriba, Tomás Salazar, Tomás Montaña, Fran. Salazar; Sta Fé, Sam. Ellison, C. B. Ortiz, Man. Vaca y Delgado; S. Miguel, Man. Flores, Pedro Archiveque; Sta Ana, Nic. Valencia; Bernalillo, Vicente Chavez, Mateo Luna; Valencia, Man. Salazar, Greg. N. Otero; Socorro, Jesus M. Chavez; Doña Ana, Cesario Duran, Ignacio Orrantia.

16th assembly, 1866–7. Council: pres. M. E. Pino, clerk Fran. Salazar, sergt Pedro Sanchez; members, same as before, except Ant. M. for Mora; Man. Herrera and M. Mestas for S. Miguel. House: speaker R. M. Stevens, clerk Nic. Quintana, sergt José D. Tafoya; members, Mora, José Gallegos,

ponderance of Spanish names is even more marked than in the assemblies of earlier years.   Indeed, until

Trinidad Lopez; Taos, Pedro García, Santos Muñiz, José A. Martinez y Medina, Buen. Lobato; Rio Arriba, Man. Jaramillo, Pablo Jaramillo, José R. Ortega; Sta Fé, R. M. Stevens, Vicente García, Juan Gonzalez; S. Miguel, Benigno Jaramillo, Matias Rivera, Man. Vaca, José M. Martinez; Sta Ana, Sam. Ellison; Bernalillo, Benj. Stevens, Fran. Perea; Valencia, Pedro Torres, Filomeno Sanchez; Doña Ana, Frank Higgins.

17th assembly, 1867–8.   Council: pres. Anastasio Sandoval, clerk Rafael Chacon, sergt José Montoya; members, Mora, Felipe Sanchez; Taos, J. B. Valdés, Jesus M. Pacheco; Rio Arriba, D. Archuleta, Juan A. Martinez; Sta Fé, A. Sandoval; S. Miguel, Severo Vaca, Celso Vaca; Sta Ana and Bernalillo, Fel. Sandoval, Andrés Romero; Valencia, Juan Salazar; Socorro, Candelario García; Doña Ana, Wm B. Rynerson.   House: speaker José M. Gallegos; members, Mora, Fernando Nolan, Fel. Tafoya; Taos, Pedro Gallegos, Rómulo Martinez, Juan P. Romero, Juan I. Pacheco; Rio Arriba, Gerónimo Jaramillo, Fran. Jaramillo, Teodoro Esquibel; Sta Fé, J. M. Gallegos, Michael Steck, Vicente García; S. Miguel, Fran. P. Abreu, Aniceto Salazar, Leandro Sanchez, Julian Aragon; Sta Ana, Simon Sandoval; Bernalillo, Wm H. Henrie, Vicente Chavez; Valencia, Greg. N. Otero, Pedro Torres, Rómulo Sanchez; Doña Ana, Ignacio Orantía, Pablo Melendrez.

18th assembly, 1868–9.   Council: pres. Severo Vaca, clerk Raf. Chacon, Ricardo Gallegos; members, same as before.   House: speaker R. M. Stevens, clerk Fran. Salazar, sergt Greg. Jaramillo; members, Mora, Fern. Nolan, Lorenzo Romero; Taos, José G. Fernandez, A. D. Torres, S. H. Simpson, Fran. Montoya; Rio Arriba, Man. García, Mariano Larragoitia; Sta Fé, R. M Stevens, Juan García, Benito Vaca; S. Miguel, Aniceto Salazar, Donaciano Serrano, Dom. Trujillo, Desiderio Romero; Sta Ana, Esquipula Romero; Bernalillo, Benj. Stevens, Henry Hilgert, Julian Sanchez; Socorro, Jesus M. Chavez, Saturnino Vaca; Doña Ana and Grant, Ign. Orantía.

19th assembly, 1869–70.   Council: pres. Nic. Pino, clerk Nicanor Vigil, sergt Man. E. Pino; members, Mora and Colfax, Jesus M. Pacheco; Taos, Sant. Abreu, Juan A. Vaca; Rio Arriba, D. Archuleta, Pablo Gallegos; Sta Fé, Nic. Pino; S. Miguel, Benigno Jaramillo, Cris. Sanchez; Bernalillo, Sant. Gonzalez; Sta Ana, Jesus-M. Vaca; Socorro and Lincoln, Candelario García; Valencia, vacant; Doña Ana and Grant, Wm L. Rynerson.   House: speaker Greg. N. Otero, clerk Jesus M. Sena, sergt Juan Ortiz; members, Bernalillo, Andrés Romero, Wm H. Henrie; Colfax, H. S. Russell; Doña Ana, Apolonio Varela; Grant, John D. Bail; Lincoln, ——; Mora, José Mestas; Rio Arriba, Donaciano Montoya, Ramon Aragon; Sta Ana, Nepomuceno Silva; Sta Fé, R. M. Stevens, Vicente García, José B. Ortiz; S. Miguel, José M. Vaca, Sacramento Montoya, Isidro Pino, Leandro Sanchez; Socorro, Jesus M. Chavez; Taos, José D. Tafoya, José D. Mondragon, Pedro García, Greg. Velarde; Valencia, Greg. N. Otero, Lauriano Jaramillo.

20th assembly, 1871–2.   Council: pres. Severo Vaca, clerk Fran. Salazar, sergt L. Jaramillo; members, Bernalillo, Juan J. Gonzalez; Doña Ana and Grant, Joseph F. Bennett; Mora and Colfax, Vicente St Vrain; Rio Arriba, D. Archuleta, Dionisio Vargas; Sta Ana, J. M. Silva; Sta Fé, Nazario Gonzalez; S. Miguel, Severo Vaca, Benigno Jaramillo; Socorro and Lincoln, Cand. García; Taos, Nicanor Vigil, Pedro Sanchez; Valencia, Bonifacio Chavez.   House: speaker Milnor Rudolph, and after Jan. '72 Greg. N. Otero, clerk J. M. Sena, sergt Pablo Pino; members, Bernalillo, Juan C. Chavez, Vicente Chavez; Colfax, H. S. Russell; Doña Ana, Eugenio Moreno, Man. Nevares; Grant, J. R. Johnson; Lincoln, Wm Brady; Mora, Alex. Branch; Rio Arriba, Evaristo Mestas, Isidoro Martinez; Sta Ana, Florencio Sandoval; Sta Fé, Juan C Romero, José A. Romero, Luis Griego; S. Miguel, Pascual Vaca, Ladislas Gallegos, Julian Cisnero, M. Rudolph; Socorro, Julian Montoya; Taos, Juan A. Sanchez, Buen. Lobato, Ant. J. Gallegos, Raf. Martinez; Valencia, Julian Sanchez, Greg. N. Otero, Silvestre Abeitia.

the last sessions, almost the whole membership was
made up of native New Mexicans, all business being

21st assembly, 1873–4. Council: pres. Pedro Sanchez, clerk Ant. Salazar,
sergt Luciano Herrera; members, Bernalillo, Benj. Stevens; Doña Ana and
Lincoln, John D. Bail; Mora and Colfax, Vicente Romero; Rio Arriba, Fran.
Salazar; Sta Fé and Sta Ana, Nic. Pino, Nepomuceno Silva; S. Miguel, Fran.
P. Abreu, Sant. Vaca; Socorro, Pablo Padilla; Taos, Pedro Sanchez, Marcelo
Vigil; Valencia, Juan Salazar, Bonif. Chavez. House: speaker Greg. N.
Otero, clerk Amado C. Vaca, sergt Apolonio Gutierrez; members, Bernalillo,
W. H. Henrie, J. C. Chavez; Colfax, Melvin W. Mills; Doña Ana, Lincoln,
and Grant, Wm T. Jones, Jacinto Armijo; Mora, Bernardo Salazar, Pablo
Mares; Rio Arriba, J. M. Herrera, Perfecto Esquibel; Sta Ana and Sta Fé,
Anast. Sandoval, Ramon Sena, Ant. Abreu, David C. Vaca; S. Miguel, J. M.
Gallegos, Donaciano Serrano, Agustin Vigil, Candelario Ulibarri, Rodrigo
García; Socorro, Cand. García, John M. Shaw; Taos, Luis Gallegos, Lorenzo
Lobato, J. M. Lesser; Valencia, Greg. N. Otero, José G. Chavez, Luciano
Trujillo.

22d assembly, 1875–6. Council: pres. Pedro Sanchez, clerk José D. Sena,
sergt Benj. Stevens; members, Bernalillo, José Armijo; Colfax and Mora, A.
J. Calhoun; D. Ana, Lincoln, and Grant, Jacinto Armijo; Rio Arriba, Louis
Clark; Sta Fé and Sta Ana, Wm Breeden, Esquipula Romero; S. Miguel,
Fran. P. Abreu, Romualdo Vaca; Socorro, Ant. Abeitia; Taos, Pedro San-
chez, Tricanor Vigil; Valencia, J. F. Chavez, Juan Salazar. House: speaker
Roman A. Vaca, clerk Amado C. Vaca, sergt Estévan Vaca; members, Ber-
nalillo, José Chavez, Alej. Sandoval; Colfax, M. W. Mills; D. Ana, Grant,
and Lincoln, John M. Ginn, Eugenio Moreno; Mora, Sixto Chavez, Pedro J.
Gallegos; Sta Fé and Sta Ana, Anast. Sandoval, Aniceto Abeitia, Jesus Sena,
Agustin Quintana; S. Miguel, Hermenejildo Lucero, Man. Gonzalez, Jesus
C. Vaca, Ed. Martinez, Agustin Quintana (?); Socorro, Cand. García, José A.
Romero; Valencia, Roman A. Vaca, Pablo García, Eufemio Romero.

23d assembly, 1878. Council: pres. Sant. Vaca, clerk Jesus M. Sena,
sergt Gabriel Vigil; members, Bernalillo, Sant. Vaca, Fel. García; Colfax and
Mora, Fern. Nolan; D. Ana, Grant, and Lincoln, John S. Crouch; Rio Arriba,
D. Archuleta; Sta Fé, Nic. Pino; S. Miguel, Lorenzo Lopez, Gabriel Rivera;
Socorro, Tomás Gonzalez; Taos, Juan G. Martin, Juan A. Sanchez; Valencia,
Greg. N. Otero, J. F. Chavez. House: speaker J. B. Patron, clerk Amado
Chavez, sergt Julian Vaca; members, Bernalillo, José M. Montoya, Jesus
Armijo, Man. Gonzalez; Colfax, Wilson L. South; D. Ana, Lincoln, and
Grant, John K. Houston, J. B. Patron; Mora, Raf. Romero, Alex. Branch;
Rio Arriba, José M. Sanchez, Perfecto Esquibel; Sta Fé, J. J. Padilla, Cris-
tino Montoya, Anast. Sandoval; S. Miguel, Roman Lopez, Atanasio García,
Ramon Ulibarri, Benito Romero, Ant. J. Gallegos; Socorro, José J. García,
José V. Padilla; Taos, Sant. Abreu, José L. Martinez, Matias Ortega; Va-
lencia, Julian P. Connelly, Man. Sanchez, Policarpio García.

24th assembly, 1880. Council: pres. J. F. Chavez, clerk Amado Chavez,
sergt Jesus M. Lucero; members, Bernalillo, Jesus M. Perea, Florencio San-
doval; Colfax and Mora, Frank Springer; D. Ana, Lincoln, and Grant, S. B.
Newcomb; Rio Arriba, Pedro I. Jaramillo; Sta Fé, Wm Breeden; S. Miguel,
Pedro Valdés, Ed. Martinez; Socorro, Tomás Gonzalez; Taos, Sant. Valdés,
Man. A. Sanchez; Valencia, J. F. Chavez, Greg. N. Otero. House: speaker
Raf. Romero, clerk Marcos C. Vaca, sergt Blas Chavez; members, Bernalillo,
Juan E. Varela, Melquíades Chavez, Feliciano Montoya; Colfax, W. L. South;
D. Ana, Lincoln, and Grant, Robert Black, Man. Nevares; Mora, Raf. Ro-
mero, Macario Gallegos; Rio Arriba, Fran. Salazar, Teodoro Esquibel; Sta
Fé, Bernard Seligman, Atanasio Romero, Felipe Delgado; S. Miguel, Pablo
Aragon, Eugenio Gallegos, Fran. Lucero, T. C. Vaca, Raf. Rail (?); Socorro,
Nestor Gonzalez, Luciano Chavez; Taos, José G. Griego, Fel. Montoya, Salomé
Jaquez; Valencia, Jesus H. Chavez, Teófilo Chavez, Man. Sanchez.

25th assembly, 1882. Council: pres. Severo Vaca, clerk Ant. Ortiz, sergt

transacted in the Spanish language, so that the journals and laws had to be translated into English for publication. A few prominent families in each county still
controlled the elections, though perhaps in somewhat
less degree than formerly. In politics the legislature
was generally and nominally republican, though political considerations were always secondary to those of
a local and personal nature. There were a few petty
wrangles over organization; notably in 1884, when
the councilmen from Bernalillo and Santa Fé were refused their seats on allegations of fraudulent election,
and the contestants without certificates were sworn in
by the secretary, on a vote of the other members that
they were entitled prima facie to the seats. This led

J. M. Martinez; members, Bernalillo, Wm C. Hazeltine, Sant. Vaca; Colfax
and Mora, Anastasio Trujillo; D. Ana, Grant, and Lincoln, John A. Miller;
Rio Arriba, Man. García; Sta Fé, W. T. Thornton; S. Miguel, Severo Vaca,
José Raf. Martinez; Socorro, José M. Apodaca; Taos, Anthony Joseph, Juan
P. Romero; Valencia, J. F. Chavez, Narciso Pino. House: speaker Pedro
Sanchez, clerk Amado C. Vaca, sergt Ant. J. Martinez; members, Bernalillo,
Andrés C. Vaca, Esquipula Romero, Fran. Chavez; Colfax, Narciso Valdés;
D. Ana, Grant, and Lincoln, D. M. Easton, Greg. Miranda; Mora, Norberto
Saavedra, Macario Gallegos; Rio Arriba, L. M. Ortiz, Ant. Vargas; Sta Fé,
Fran. Montoya, Sam. Bonner, N. B. Laughlin; S. Miguel, Pedro L. Pinard,
José L. Rivera, Fern. Vaca, Miguel Segura, Juan Jaramillo; Socorro, Jacinto
Sanchez, José A. Gallegos; Taos, Pedro Sanchez, Juan Santistévan, José P.
Sanchez; Valencia, Demas Provencher, Jesus Sanchez, Casimiro Sais.
    26th assembly, 1884. Council: pres. José Armijo, clerk Benj. M. Read,
sergt W. F. Hogan; members, Bernalillo, C. C. McComas, J. M. Montoya;
Colfax and Mora, José I. Valdés; D. Ana, Lincoln, and Grant, John A. Mil-
ler; Rio Arriba, José P. Gallegos; S. Miguel, Andrés Sena, W. H. Keller;
Sta Fé, T. B. Catron; Socorro, José Armijo; Taos, ——; Valencia, ——.
House: speaker Amado Chavez, clerk David Martinez, sergt Juan D. Ro-
mero; members, Bernalillo, W. H. Whiteman, Raf. Chavez, Marcos C. Vaca;
Colfax, O. P. McManes; Doña Ana and Lincoln, Nicolás Gallés, Florencio
Gonzalez; Grant, Ed. E. Furman; Mora, A. L. Branch, Macario Gallegos;
Rio Arriba, D. Archuleta, Juan N. Jacqués; S. Miguel, Juan Gallegos, Atana-
sio Sanchez, T. B. Mills, Dionisio Martinez; Sta Fé, J. L. Jenks, Librado
Valencia; Socorro, M. Cooney, R. E. McFarland; Valencia, Amado Chavez,
José R. Salazar, Teófilo Chavez.
    27th assembly, 1886-7. Council: pres. J. F. Chavez; members, Berna-
lillo, Thos Hughes, Pedro Perea; Doña Ana, James P. Booth; Grant, John
J. Bell; Mora, Rafael Romero; Rio Arriba, Thos D. Burnes; S. Miguel, Lor-
enzo Lopez, Geo. W. Prichard; Sta Fé, N. B. Laughlin; Socorro, Candelario
García; Taos, Pedro Sanchez; Valencia, J. F. Chavez. House: speaker M.
C. Vaca, clerk A. C. Vaca, sergt J. Gallegos, chaplain M. Rolly; members,
Bernalillo, Wm Kuchenbecker, Jr, Z. Sandoval, Alej. Sandoval; Colfax,
Russell Marcy; Doña Ana, C. H. Armijo; Grant and Sierra, E. P. Fest; Lin-
coln, C. H. Slaughter; Mora, S. E. Tipton, Desiderio Romero; Rio Arriba,
F. P. Chavez, Juan García; S. Miguel, L. C. Fort, J. P. Rivera, M. C. Vaca,
Leandro Sanchez; Sta Fé, W. J. Davis, W. E. Dame; Socorro, E. V. Chavez,
J. A. Gallegos; Taos, Gavino Vigil; Valencia, J. L. Teller, Casimiro Sais.

to the organization of a rival council under the management of J. F. Chavez, and to much controversy; but I have found no record of the final decision as to the legality of the acts of the legislature thus informally organized.

A résumé of legislative proceedings is given in a note.[4] General remarks in an earlier chapter may be

[4] *New Mexico, Laws of the Territory*, 12th to 26th sessions, 1863–86. Sta Fé, 1863 et seq. From 1873, the title is *Acts of the Legislative Assembly*. Also *Id., Journals*, 1863 et seq. The *Message of the Governor* is included in the *Journals*, and is separately printed for most sessions. A *Report of the Governor to the Secretary of the Interior* is also separately published in pamphlet form in the later years. I have several of them from 1879. For a résumé of proceedings, 1st to 11th sessions, 1851–62, see chapter xxv., this volume.

12th assembly, 1862–3. Acts incorporating 'N. Mex. Wool Manuf. Co.' and 'Bank of N. Mex.;' creating a board of education, and incorporating an 'Industrial College of N. Mex.' at Sta Fé. Resolutions, accepting 30,000 acres of school lands granted by congress; recommending Capt. A. F. Garrison for promotion; asking that Conejos, Costilla, and Culebra be restored to N. Mex. from Col.; thanking volunteers of Cal. and Col. (see chap. xxvii.); and calling a public meeting in each county to provide for strengthening forts Union and Craig, in fear of another Texan invasion.

13th assembly, 1863–4. Acts incorporating 'Kansas, N. Mex., & Cal. R. R. & Telegraph Co.' and the 'Gold & Copper Min. Co. of N. Mex.:' providing for militia and volunteer expeditions against the Indians, and for obtaining reports of depredations; declaring Mex. titles with occupation since 1846 to be valid, and providing for the obtaining of certified copies of records respecting the Mesilla colony; changing seat of S. Miguel co., adding Sta Ana co. to 1st jud. district, and modifying boundaries of Sta Fé co.; providing for further efforts to obtain water for Sta Fé, and regulating the market built by act of 1859. Resolutions, thanking the Col. volunteers and correcting injustice done them in a former resolution. Memorials, asking for $105,000 to complete public buildings; for a survey of lands to induce settlement, also a geol. survey; and for a road, Sta Fé to Taos, $150,000. *U. S. Govt Doc.*, 38th cong. 1st sess., H. Miscel. Doc. 69, 70, 72. The gov. vetoed an act for revision of the laws.

14th assembly, 1864–5. Acts regulating pay of jurors and court officials; concerning public pastures; and preventing fraudulent sales of animals; providing for the punishment of Ind.; adopting the revised laws; concerning mining claims, and amending incorp. of 'Gold & Copper Min. Co.;' incorp. co. to make a road from Taos over the mts via Piedras Coloradas, and the 'Alburquerque Bridge Co.;' opening road from Las Cruces to Mesilla; and regulating the Sta Fé market.

15th assembly, 1865–6. Acts modifying act of '65 on mining claims; incorp. 'Bay State Pinos Altos Min. Co.,' 'Market Gold Min. Co.,' 'Montezuma Min. & Manuf. Co.,' 'Pinos Altos Min. Co.,' and 'Mesilla Ferry Co.;' on fences for special localities; repealing act of '57 on free negroes, and modifying peonage regulations; and authorizing gov. to call a state convention. Memorials, on public works, governor's veto power, and courts. *U. S. Govt Doc.*, 39th cong. 1st sess., H. Miscel. Doc. 58–61.

16th assembly, 1866–7. Acts providing for incorp. of debating, literary, scientific, industrial, and benevolent societies; providing for a monument over soldiers' graves, and approp. $1,500 ($1,800 more in '67–8 to complete the monument); approp. $40 for shelves for the library; incorp. 'Nacimiento Cop. Min. Co.,' 'La Tijera Cop. Min. Co.,' 'Hanover Cop. Min. Co.,' 'N. Mex. Telegraph Co.,' and the Presbyterian church; for public schools; changing seat of So-

applied to the proceedings during this later period;
and now, as before, there is a large mass of legislation,

corro co.; and declaring the Cañada Alamosa hot spring to be a public spring,
free to all, for baths.   Memorials, for additional mil. posts, for a commission
to examine claims for damages by rebels, for telegraph lines, an approp. for
schools, and increased pay for legislature and territorial officials.

17th assembly, 1867–8.   Acts creating a general incorporation act; providing for registration of voters; creating county of Grant; and changing
boundary between Taos and Mora counties.   Resolutions, condemning Gov.
Mitchell's usurpations of power, etc.; that the election of delegate to congress was fraudulent; to send all acts not approved by gov. to congress for
approval; expressing confidence in Sec. Heath; defending Gen. Getty; and
complimenting Arny, who goes to Wash. on Ind. business.   Memorials, for an
approp. of $70,000 to complete the capitol, to aid education of Ind. at Bosque
Redondo, to aid 'U. S. & Mex. Telegraph Co.,' and an approp. of lands
outside of N. Mex. for schools in the territory; against the proposition to
attach Moreno mining district to Col.; for authority to raise vol. regiments
for Ind. service; for a railroad; to take away the absolute veto power of the
gov.; and for a road from Sta Fé to Taos.   For the various resol. and mem.
in congress, see *U. S. Govt Doc.*, 39th cong. 2d sess., H. Ex. Doc. 101, p. 1–4;
40th cong. 1st sess., H. Miscel. Doc. 12, 14, 15, 18, 19, 22; 40th cong. 2d sess.,
H. Miscel. Doc. 25, 33, 94.

18th assembly, 1868–9.   Acts changing seat of Grant co., creating counties of Lincoln and Colfax, and extending limits of Sta Fé co.; repealing act
of '60 which prohibited sale of liquor to soldiers; paying members of legisl.
$5 per day in addition to U. S. pay; providing that no person not a citizen
can hold land, that abandoned lands—except Mex. grants—may be occupied
by another, and that no person can hold Mex. colony lands unless the title
was registered before U. S. possession; imposing a tax on horned cattle
brought into the territory; fixing a sliding scale of prices for merchants'
licenses.   Resolutions, on death of the Jesuit father Billanqui; and reaffirm-
ing confidence in Sec. Heath.   Memorials, for mail service, for more troops
and posts; for an increase of councilmen from 13 to 18, representatives from
26 to 36, and justices from 3 to 4; for govt aid to the railroad, protection of
rights under Mex. grants, and for the removal of Justice Houghton.

19th assembly, 1869–70.   Acts changing name of seat of Lincoln co., uniting Lincoln to Socorro for senatorial purposes, changing bound between
Socorro and Doña Ana, also bet. Bernalillo and Valencia, and estab. seat of
Colfax at Elizabethtown; adopting a new revenue system; providing for the
legitimatizing or adoption of children; and changing dates of election, etc., for
biennial sessions.   Resolutions, to ask for an approp. for the Jicarilla and Ute
Ind.; and to appoint a com. to draft a state constitution,   Memorials, for
annulling the treaty with the Utes, putting U. S. lands on the market as in
other states and territories, for increased mil. force, especially two regiments
of volunteers, and for a settlement of the war claims.

20th assembly, 1871–2.   Acts restricting divorce; fixing bound bet.
Socorro and Doña Ana counties, changing seat of Grant co., also of Colfax
and Valencia; providing for a bridge over the Pecos at Anton Chico upper
ford, and a road from Agua Negra to Taos; providing that foreigners may
hold real estate like natives; authorizing mortgaging or consolidation of
R. R. lines, counties to aid in construction of R. R., and providing for appaise-
ment of R. R. lands; amending the revenue law; providing for a school
board in each county; amending mining-claim act of 1865; and providing for
an election on state constitution.   Memorials, for a reservation for the Mescaleros, removal of Jicarillas and Utes, settlement of land grants and military
claims, and a recompilation of the laws.

21st assembly, 1873–4.   Acts amending the revenue law; incorp. college
of Christian brothers, and the sisters of Loreto; and changing seat of Valencia co.   Memorials, for annual sessions or an extra session, for various tele-

important in a sense, which cannot be satisfactorily summarized in the space at my disposal. It is not,

graph lines, speedy settlement of land claims, including those of citizens who or whose ancestors bought of pueblo Ind., aid for the Jicarillas and Utes, and admission as a state.

22d assembly, 1875-6. Acts annexing Colfax co. to Taos for judicial purposes, abolishing co. of Sta Ana and annexing to Bernalillo, fixing bound bet. Mora and Colfax, and changing seat of Valencia; amending revenue law; imposing a license of $450 on merchants employing drummers; fixing salaries of attorney-gen. at $600, district attorney $400, treasurer $1,000, auditor $1,000, adj.-gen. $250, librarian $150; providing for observance of Sunday; regulating manner of locating mining claims; providing that sessions of the legisl. begin 1st Monday in Jan. instead of Dec.; appointing a com. to revise the laws; and authorizing owners of two land grants to keep records, etc. Memorials, for admission as a state, payment of claims, revision of the laws, military road, mail routes, and artesian wells.

23d assembly, 1878. Acts providing for the incorporation of R. R. companies; permitting the occupation of 320 acres of U. S. lands, with title good against all but govt; establishing district courts in each county; approp. funds to complete capitol; incorporating 'Society of Jesus,' 'Incorporation of Mesilla' or holders of the Mesilla grant, and town of Silver City; repealing act to join Colfax to Taos, fixing bound between Doña Ana and Lincoln, authorizing an election to change seat of Bernalillo; aiding S. Vicente hospital at Sta Fé; and providing for indexing real estate records. Resolution, to appoint a com. to reapportion the legislature. Memorials, for settlement of land titles, selling land to settlers who shall find or store water for grazing, telegraph to forts Stanton and Wingate against reduction of tariff on wool, Navajos to be kept on their reservation, and for defence of town of Lincoln against a land claim.

24th assembly, 1880. Acts for incorp. of cities, societies, and giving foreign corporations the same privileges as local; for revision of laws; prohibiting sale of liquor on election days; organizing a bureau of immigration; protecting fish and game; selecting university lands; authorizing gov. to call out volunteers for Ind. service; paying Lincoln mounted rifles for service in keeping order in 1879; fixing bound bet. Sta Ana and Socorro counties, changing bound of Grant co., changing seat of Rio Arriba, and changing bound of Rio Arriba and Taos. Memorials, for survey of public lands and settlement of private land claims, for increased mail facilities, for roads, for a cession of public buildings by U. S. to the territory, and against enlargement of the Navajo reservation. Resolutions, on early completion of Prince's revision of the laws, on completion of the R. R. to Sta Fé, and thanking Gen. Hatch for his management of mil. affairs.

25th assembly, 1882. Acts estab. 'N. Mex. board of charities and industrial schools' (repealed in '84); providing that sessions begin 1st Monday in Jan. of odd years, 1883, '85, etc. (but this was not done); regulating the library; protecting coal mines and miners; regulating R. R. fares and rates; defining a system of revenue; taxing cattle owned in other states and territories; authorizing ransom of Apache captives; approp. $3,000 in aid of sisters of charity at Sta Fé; changing seat of Colfax, bound bet. Colfax and Mora, bet. Mora and S. Miguel, Sta Fé and S. Miguel, and S. Miguel and Valencia, and fixing seat of Doña Ana at Las Cruces. Memorials, for settlement of land claims, for cession of the adobe palace to the Hist. Society, for opening to settlement a part of the Mescalero reservation, for a special post-office inspector, and for repeal of U. S. law of '78 forbidding troops to act as posse comitatus.

26th assembly, 1884. Acts changing date of opening sessions to last Monday in Dec. 1886-8-90, etc.; repealing gen. incorp. act of '80 and passing a new one; preventing the introduction of diseased cattle; estab. public schools; estab. orphan home and industrial school at Sta Fé under sisters of charity;

moreover, my purpose to present in any sense a compilation of the laws, but only an outline of the more
important acts from session to session.   Several topics
of interest in this connection will be noticed later in
this chapter.   Down to 1869–70 the sessions were
annual.   In 1866–7 a bill was passed by the house
amending the organic act and providing for biennial
sessions; this became a law for all territories in 1869;
and from 1871 the assembly met biennially, though
in 1873–4 and again in 1876 memorials in favor of
yearly sessions were sent to Washington.   By act of
congress in 1871 the legislature was authorized to
meet on the first Monday in December; but in 1876
this date was changed to the first Monday in January,
and the assembly met accordingly in 1878–84.   The
same body again changed the date from the even to
the odd years, beginning with 1883, and members
were elected accordingly; but for want of an appropriation from congress no change was made.   Very
nearly the same effect, however, was accomplished by
an act of 1884 changing the date from January to
December; and the 27th assembly met in December
1886.   A memorial of 1866–7 called for increased pay
for legislators and other officials; and an act of 1869
added five dollars a day to the pay received from the
federal government, which in 1878 was fixed by congress at four dollars, with six dollars for president and

providing for erection of capitol; creating office of county assessor; providing
for a new compilation of the laws; aiding the Hist. Society; prohibiting higher
rate of interest than 12 per cent; requiring cultivated land to be fenced in a
part of the territory; incorp. the 'Colonial Grant' (Vaca) and 'Colony of Re-
fugio' grant in Rio Arriba co.; and creating the new co. of Sierra.   Memorials,
protesting against unjust discrimination of mil. auth. against N. Mex. in
the purchase of supplies; asking that N. Mex. be made a mil. department.
Resolution, denouncing charges against Chief Justice Axtell as 'malicious,
scandalous, and false.'
    Dav. J. Miller was translator of the *Laws* of the 12th assemb., Chas Lieb,
of the *New Mexican*, being printer, and the work much better than in earlier
years.   Theodore S. Greiner translator, 13th assemb.; printer H. S. Johnson,
Alburquerque.   14th assemb. title missing.   15th to 19th assemb., Manderfield
& Tucker public printers, Sta Fé; no translator named; English and Spanish
in separate volumes from the 18th assemb.   20th assemb., A. P. Sullivan
pub. printer.   21st to 23d assemb., M. & F. pub. printers; José D. Sena
translator for 21st; Sam. Ellison translator from 22d to 26th.   R. W. Webb
printer 24th; Chas W. Green 25th; and N. Mex. Printing Co. 26th.

speaker. At the same time the number of councilmen was limited to twelve and of representatives to
24, though an increase from 13 to 18 and from 26 to
36 had been asked for in 1868–9. In 1880 the sessions were limited to 60 days. Congress passed a
special act legalizing the laws of 1866–7 signed by an
acting governor; and also legalized the election of
November 1882, which had been held with a view to
a session in 1883.

Congressional action on New Mexico is epitomized
in another note.[5] It did not extend far beyond the

[5] Congressional appropriations for N. Mex.: 1864, govt $36,480, Ind. ser-
vice $75,000; 1865, govt $33,500, Ind. $150,000; 1866, same; 1867, govt
$33,000, Ind. $250,000, survey of N. boundary $19,000, census of 1860, $784;
1868, govt $33,000, Ind. $462,000; 1869, govt $14,000, Ind. $282,250; 1870,
govt $28,500, Ind. $50,000; 1871, govt $36,000, Ind. $166,000; 1872, govt
$14,500, Ind. $116,000; 1873, govt $36,950, Ind. $116,000, survey of E. bound.
$1,400, mil. road $25,000; 1874, govt $19,000, Ind. $230,000; 1875, govt
$41,878, Ind. $228,675, survey w. bound. $27,350, survey of private land claims
$10,000; 1876, govt $16,000, Ind. $129,175; 1877, govt $33,200, Ind. $221,840;
1878, govt $15,400, Ind. $100,840; 1879, govt $19,483; Ind. $78,000, survey
of private land cl. $10,351; 1880, govt $20,600, Ind. $46,000; 1881, govt
$33,279, Ind. $43,000, land claims $8,000; 1882, govt $15,500, Ind. $6,000;
1884, govt $35,815, Ind. $45,000, land claims $16,000. See *U. S. Statutes*,
1864 et seq. The annual approp. for the land-office, N. Mexico's part of the
military approp., and some minor approp. for deficiences are not included in
this note.

Résumé of congressional action in behalf of N. Mexico, excluding approp.
bills and a large number of bills that were simply introduced and referred to
committees, as well as mention of memorials, etc., received, as noted in legislative proceedings, and action on contested elections, noted elsewhere. 1864–5,
joint resol. to facilitate commun. with N. Mex.; joint commun. of delegates
of N. Mex. and other territories approving the constit. amendment abolishing
slavery; act estab. post-roads (later acts on this subject not noted). 1865–6,
bill to confirm land claim of J. S. Ramirez passed by senate. 1866–7, bill to
abolish peonage, passed sen. and house; bill to amend organic act so as to
prohibit restriction of suffrage on account of race or color, passed sen. and
house after much discussion; bill to provide for biennial sessions of the legisl.
passed the house. 1867, act legalizing acts of the legisl. at session of 1866–7;
bill to settle private land claims referred to com. (as were many other bills
earlier and later on this subject, as also on the war and Ind. claims, not mentioned in this note). 1867–8, resol. for relief of Navajo captives held as peons
passed by sen. and house; several bills on lands, railroads, claims, and other
subjects introduced by delegate Clever, but not finally acted on; bill for relief and reservation of Navajos at Bosque Redondo, passed by house and
amended in sen. 1868–9, act on the Vigil and St Vrain land grants, for benefit of settlers; act confirming 5 land claims; act providing for biennial sessions of the legisl.; also amending organic act on the passing of bills over the
governor's veto by a ⅔ vote; also making gov. supt of public buildings, at a
salary of $1,000; also making salary of sec. $2,000 from '67. 1869, act repealing acts of legisl. to impose a capitation tax on bovine cattle introduced
from other states and territories. 1869–70, bill to annul part of a N. Mex.
law on execution and mortgages, passed house and sen., bill to authorize a
state constitution referred to com.; act on details of Vigil and St Vrain land

granting of the annual appropriations for government expenses, which, in years when the legislature met, were from $33,000 to $40,000, and about half as much in other years, besides much larger amounts for Indian affairs and the military department. Bills relating to this distant territory were, as a rule, referred to committees, and never heard of again; but occasionally, acts were passed, chiefly of a routine nature, some of which have been mentioned in connection with legislative proceedings, and others I shall have occasion to notice in treating other topics.

Delegates to congress have been named in the official list.[6] They did, apparently, all that territorial delegates might do for their constituents, which was very little.

grant; act increasing salary of justices to $3,000. 1870-1, bill to authorize state constitution under the name of Lincoln, reported by sen. com (but again referred to com. in sen. of '71); bill to pay volunteers' claims, tabled in house; bill to confirm Rio Grande land claim, passed house and sen., apparently (but referred to house com. in '71); act to sell mil. reservation at Ft Sumner. 1871, act to authorize legisl. to meet on 1st Monday in Dec., and authorizing an election. 1871-2, bill to enable land claimants to test the validity of their claims ref. to sen. com.; state of Lincoln bill tabled in house; act to pay salary of sec. as supt of public buildings to June '72, but repealing the act of '68 which gave that salary; act appointing A. P. Sullivan and C. P. Clever corporators of Centen. Board of Finance; act granting right of way to N. Mex. & Gulf R. R. 1872-3, act for completing mil. road, Sta Fé to Taos; bill to survey private land grants at govt expense ref. to house com.; bill to donate 10 sections of land for finding water in the desert, tabled; bills to extend time of voting on state constit. and to create a new land district, ref. to com. 1873-4, bill for state constit. passed by house, referred by sen.; act creating a new land district. 1874-5, bill for state constit. passed by sen. with amendments. 1876, bill for a state passed by sen., referred by house. 1876-7, house bill to pay Ind. depredation claims, tabled. 1877, bill to attach Grant co. to Arizona ref. to house com. 1877-8, bill to annul act of the legisl. incorporating society of Jesuits, passed by sen., ref. by house; bill for relief of mounted volunteers, passed by sen., ref. by house. 1878, act providing that the legislature is not to exceed 12 councilmen and 24 representatives, at $4 per day, the president and speaker getting $6. 1878-9, act annulling the act of the legisl. incorporating soc. of Jesuits. 1880-1, act limiting sessions of the legisl. to 60 days. 1881-2, act legalizing election of legisl. of Nov. '80. 1883-4, act legalizing legisl. elected Nov. '82 to meet in Feb. '84. See *U. S. Statutes*, Senate and House *Journals*, *Cong. Globe*, and *Cong. Record*, 1864 et seq.

[6] Perea, democrat, was elected in 1863 over Gallegos by a vote of 7,231 to 6,425; in 1865 Chavez, republican, over Perea, 8,511 to 6,180; in 1867 Clever, dem., over Chavez, 8,891 to 8,794; in 1869 Chavez over Vicente Romero; in 1871 Gallegos over Chavez and José D. Sena; in 1873 Elkins over Gallegos; in 1875 Elkins over Pedro Valdés; in 1877 Romero over Valdés; in 1879 Otero over Benito Vaca; in 1881 Luna over Miguel A. Otero; in 1883 Manzanares, dem., over Luna, 13,376 to 12,287; in 1885 Joseph, dem., over L. B. Prince and W. L. Rynerson, 12,271 to 9,930, and 5,192; in 1887 Joseph over J. W. Dwyer.

The seat of Perea in 1863–4 was unsuccessfully contested by Gallegos. For the congress of 1867–8 there was no election in New Mexico at the proper time, and Governor Mitchell took the liberty of appointing John S. Watts as delegate ad interim, but he was not admitted, all agreeing that the governor had no such power. At the September election C. P. Clever had a majority of 97 votes, his election being certified by the governor, and pro forma by the secretary, and the delegate taking his seat. But Secretary Heath sent a separate certificate, to the effect that the election was fraudulent, which was supported by a resolution of the legislature; and after a long discussion Chavez, the contestant, was seated in February 1869, so that Clever was virtually the delegate in the fortieth congress.[7] Again, in 1883, though Luna received the certificate of election, Manzanares, the contestant, was seated by a unanimous vote of the house.

On the public buildings, capitol and penitentiary, no progress was made after 1857, when about $100,000 had been expended on the foundations, though there were frequent appeals to congress for appropriations to complete the structures. Meanwhile, the old adobe 'palace' was used for all public purposes. On this building repairs to the extent of $5,000 were made in 1866–7; but nothing more was done; the roof was leaky, the exterior was unplastered, and the rooms were small and inconvenient. "It is safe to say no other legislative body in the United States, outside of New Mexico, ever met inside of such disgraceful surroundings," wrote Secretary Ritch in 1875. In 1877–8, however, $2,260 was expended, of which $1,680 was paid by the national government, and the balance provided for by act of the legislature. In 1880 congress was asked to cede the site and foundations of the new structures to the territory, and the legislature of

---

[7] *U. S. Govt Doc.*, 40th cong. 2d sess., H. Mis. Doc. 154; 3d sess. H. Mis. Doc. 14; H. Rept 18; *Cong. Globe*, 1867–8, p. 499–500, 778; *N. Mex. Laws*, 1867–8, p. 148–50.

1884 appropriated $200,000 in 20-year seven-per-cent bonds for their completion.[8]

Meanwhile, despite an appropriation of $40 in 1866-7 for shelves, the territorial library and the archives were in a fearful condition of neglect. Many books were scattered, lost, or stolen; and the rest were left in disorder and dirt. The sale of the old Spanish archives for wrapping paper in the time of Governor Pile, 1869-71, has been elsewhere noted. Governor Giddings boxed up about five cords of such remnants as could be rescued, to protect them from the weather and further loss.[9] In 1880 the Historical Society of New Mexico was reorganized, and this society, or rather Ritch, Prince, and a few other individuals acting in its name, has accomplished something toward the preservation of relics and records and awakening interest in historical matters.[10] Since 1882, under the care of Samuel Ellison as librarian, the archives and library have been kept in order, and the former to some extent classified.

The territory was never in very desperate straits financially. In 1864 there was reported in the treasury a surplus of $5,416, which, however, dwindled to $15 in 1867, becoming a debt of $17,029 the next year, and of $70,000 in 1871. The debt diminished to $15,181 in 1880, was $25,372 in 1883, and was apparently wiped out in 1884.[11] The assessed value of

[8] See full reports of condition in 1867, in *U. S. Govt Doc.*, 40th cong. 2d sess., H. Ex. Doc. 33. Mem. of legisl. for $70,000 to complete the work. *Id.*, 39th cong. 2d sess., H. Ex. Doc. 101, p. 1-4. Mem. of the legisl. for $105,000 in 1864. *Id.*, 38th cong. 1st sess., H. Mis. Doc. 69. In 1868-9 the sec. was made ex-officio supt of public buildings, at an additional salary of $1,000; but the salary clause was repealed in 1872. *Id.*, 42d cong. 2d sess., H. Ex. Doc. 128; *U. S. Stat.*, 1868-9, 1871-2. Estimates for repairs in 1875. H. Ex. Doc. 10, 44th cong. 1st sess.

[9] See *N. Mex., Message of Gov.*, 1871.

[10] *N. Mex. Hist. Soc., Charter, By-laws, etc.*, Sta Fé, 1881; *Ritch's Inaugural Address*, Sta Fé, 1881. In '82 the legisl. sent a memorial asking that the adobe palace, as a relic of antiquity, be ceded to the Hist. Soc., and in '84 voted to permit the society to occupy rooms in the palace, besides appropriating $400 for the purchase of relics, etc. In '82 an act was passed regulating the territorial library; and the librarian's report of 1883 contains a catalogue of 1,810 volumes, and mentions 144 pasteboard boxes containing the classified archives. *N. Mex., Official Reports*, 1882-3, p. 31-5.

[11] *M. Mex., Reports of Auditor and Treasurer*, in *Journals*, and some of them printed separately; also messages of gov. and reports to the sec. inte-

property, which had been $20,000,000 in 1860, before
the cutting-off of Arizona and Colorado, was about
$18,000,000 in 1870, in 1880 apparently several mil-
lions less—though there is no agreement between
different reports—and in 1884 about $29,000,000.[12]
The rate of taxation was never excessively high, the
total rate in 1884, according to the governor's report,
being eleven and one fourth mills on the dollar, of
which five were for the territory, three for schools,
two and one half for the counties, and the rest for
interest, the poll tax of one dollar being for the benefit
of schools.[13]

Claims of New Mexican citizens against the United
States were of several different classes, including those
for losses in the revolt of 1847, for Indian depredations in the later years, for militia service against the
Indians, for similar service against the confederates,
and for the destruction of property by the latter.
Almost every legislature in memorials, and the governors in their messages, urged the payment of these

rior. The financial condition of '81 as given by Ritch, *Blue-Book*, 87, seems
less satisfactory than is indicated by the other reports, since, while it shows a
surplus of $13,415, besides delinquent taxes to the amount of $96,881, it also
mentions militia warrants outstanding to the amount of $527,170, which I
suppose had not been paid in 1884. In 1871 territorial bonds were selling
for 40 cents. County finances were not in so satisfactory a condition generally as those of the territory. The *U. S. Census Report* of 1870 gives the
debt as $7,560.

[12] *U. S. Census Reports;* governor's reports; *Ritch's Blue-Book;* auditor's
reports; differing widely in their figures in most years. The gov. in '84
notes an increase of $16,000,000 in three years, also stating that $4,000,000
of R. R. property would become taxable in '86, and $10,000,000 in 5 years.
Taxes amounted to 29 m. in '60, 61 m. in '70, 91 m. in '80, and 126 m. in '83.
See also *Porter's West. Census '80*, p. 454; *N. Mex., Business Directory*, 1882,
p. 227. Internal revenue taxes seem to have been $34,380 in 1871-2 and
$44,021 in 1881-2.

[13] See résumé of legislative acts for various revenue acts. The act of 1869-
70 was long and elaborate, imposing a tax of 20 cents on the $100 for territory,
and 5 cents for counties; exempting property to value of $500, and $100 for
provisions for family for one year, and certain implements, live-stock, etc.
In 1871-2 licenses were abolished for many kinds of business; all property
was to pay one per cent; and the poll tax was fixed at one dollar. A law
exempting debts on real estate was declared by the gov. in 1873 to work
badly. In 1873-4 and 1875-6 the revenue law was also amended; and the
revenue system was defined in 1882. *N. Mex., Revenue Law.* Sta Fé, 1882,
8vo, 33 p.; *N. Mex., Business Directory*, 1882, p. 198-204. In '83 the gov.
states the tax to be 1 per cent, ½ for territory, ¼ for counties, ¼ for schools,
besides poll tax and small licenses on a few trades. *Rept to Sec. Interior.*
The office of co. treasurer was created in '69, and that of co. assessor in '84.

claims; and the subject came up at nearly every session of congress after as well as before 1864; but I cannot learn that any of the demands were ever paid.[14]

A "Revised Code of New Mexico" had been prepared in 1856, but not published, so far as I know. In 1862 the governor, authorized by an act of 1859, appointed Kirby Benedict, C. P. Clever, and Facundo Pino as commissioners to codify the laws; but their work was delayed by Pino's death and other causes. In 1864 the legislature authorized the secretary to appoint a commission, and Justice Houghton and four others were appointed; but Governor Connelly vetoed the act, and apparently filled the old board or appointed a new one, since the result was published in 1865.[15] A new revision was urged by governor and legislature in 1871-2 and again in 1875-6, an act of the latter year authorizing the appointment of five commissioners; but nothing was accomplished, apparently   In 1880 a similar act was passed, and a joint resolution rejoiced in the early completion of Judge Prince's compilation, at the same time asking for funds for its publication;

[14] On the claims, see, 1854, *U. S. Govt Doc.*, 33d cong. 2d sess., H. Rept 38; 1855, *Id.*, H. Jour. 323, Sen. Jour. 208; *N. Mex.*, *Laws*, 1854-5, p. 113-19; gov.'s rept to sec. int., 1858, 35th cong. 1st sess., H. Ex. Doc. 123; H. Jour. 235, 314, 1199; H. Mis. Doc. 38; 1859-60, H. Rept 122, 537; Sen. Mis. 45; 1862, 37th cong. 3d sess., H. Rept 52; 1866-7, laws and memorials; message of gov., *Ind. Aff. Rept*, 1866, p. 136, the amount of Ind. depred. being $1,377,329; 1869-71, mem. of the legisl.; bill tabled in cong. *Globe*, 1870-1, p. 633; mess. of gov., 1871 (the war claim of $100-$200,000 is said to have been fraudulently magnified to $800,000; a commission recommended); 1871-2, *Laws*, p. 72-4; 1873-4, 43d cong. 1st sess., H. Ex. Doc. 272; bills referred in cong.; unfavorable rept of sec. war; 1874-5, 43d cong. 2d sess., H. Ex. Doc. 65; H. Rept 333, incl. tabular statement of Ind. depred., and a favorable report on war claims; 1875-6, mem. of legisl. for payment of a special claim for horses sent by Gen. Canby from Ft Craig to Bosque Redondo and captured by Texans in '62, 45th cong. 2d sess., Sen. Rept 495; 44th cong. 1st sess., H. Mis. Doc. 88; 1876-7, bill for Ind. depred., tabled; 1877-8, bill for relief of mounted volunteers passed the senate; 1879, claims of N. Mex. volunteers to be presented to court of claims; 1880, nothing yet paid. Mess. of gov.

[15] *Revised Statutes of the Territory of New Mexico, in force at the close of the session of the Legislative Assembly ending February 2, 1865. Published by authority.* St Louis, 1865, 8vo, 856 p. English and Spanish text on alternate pages. The commissioners are not named, but the secretary certifies that the work was done by a commission appointed by the gov., and that the work was approved by the legisl. act of Jan. 24, 1865. Gov. C.'s veto message of the earlier act is in *N. Mex.*, *Journal*, 1863-4, p. 196.

but we hear no more of this work.[16]   Finally, under
an act of 1884, a new compilation was published in
1885.[17]

From 1861 there were frequent efforts to secure
the admission of the territory of New Mexico into the
union as a state; and in 1872 a constitution was
formed by a convention formed for that purpose.
The population was sufficient, much larger than that
of some other states at the time of their admission,
but the prospective politics of the new state was generally not encouraging to the administration or the

[16] *Ritch's Legislative Blue-Book* of 1882 contains a most useful compilation
of fundamental law, rules, etc.
[17] *Compiled Laws of New Mexico.   In accordance with an act of the legislature,
approved April 3, 1884.   Including the constitution of the Unit 1 States, the
treaty of Guadalupe Hidalgo, the Gadsden treaty, the original act organizing the
territory, the organic acts as now in force, the original Kearny code, and a list of
laws enacted since the compilation of 1865.   Edward L. Bartlett, Charles W.
Greene, Santiago Valdez, commission; Ireneo L. Chaves, secretary.*   St.. Fé, 1885,
8vo, 1706 p.   Same title in Spanish, with English and Spanish text on alternate pages.
The justices of the supreme court have been named in the official list.
The legislature often asked for an increased number of judges, and for increased pay.   The salary was fixed at $3,000 by act of congress in 1870.   In
1869 there was a memorial asking for the removal of Judge Houghton and
the appointment of John Bail in his place.   Non-residence, neglect of duties,
engaging in private practice of law, partisanship for Andrew Johnson, and
illegal decisions were the alleged grounds for removal.   There was occasional
trouble about the apportionment of justices, efforts being made to change the
judges from one district to another on account of local interests or prejudices.
In 1872 an effort was made to send the chief justice to a remote district and
an associate to Sta Fé; but the act was vetoed by the gov.   R. H. Tompkins
was recommended for chief justice by the legislature of 1878.   A volume of
reports was published in 1881, *Reports of Cases argued and determined in the
Supreme Court of the Territory of New Mexico, from January term, 1852, to
January term, 1879, inclusive.   Reported by Charles H. Gildersleeve, Counsellor at
Law.*   San Francisco, 1881, 8vo, xii., 879 p.   I think a 2d volume has since
been published.   This 1st vol. contains a list of the judges, and also of the
attorneys practising in the court, as follows: Sam. T. Allen, Merrill Ashurst,
John D. Bail, Spruce M. Baird, Sidney M. Barnes, Marshall A. Breeden,
Thos B. Catron, Edgar Caypless, J. F. Chavez, W. B. Childers, Frank W.
Clancy, Thos F. Conway, W. W. H. Davis, Francis Downs, Edmund F.
Dunne, Eugene A. Fiske, Jos. E. Gary, C. H. Gildersleeve, John M. Ginn,
Jesse C. Goodwin, Wm C. Graves, Wm C. Hasledine, Joab Houghton, Abram
G. Hoyt, Sidney A. Hubbell, Henry C. Johnson, John H. Knaebel, Geo.
Lemon, Ira E. Leonard, Chas C. McComas, Melvin W. Mills, S. B. New-
comb, Palmer J. Pillians, G. G. Posey, Ed. S. Price, Geo. W. Prichard, Jas
H. Quinn, Jas R. Reynolds, John P. Risque, Wm G. Ritch, Wm L. Ryner-
son, José D. Sena, Jas M. Shaw, Wm C. Skinner, Andrew Sloan, Hugh N.
Smith, Frank Springer, Benj. Stevens, Louis Sulsbacher, Wm C. Terrill, Wm
T. Thornton, R. H. Tomkins, L. S. Trimble, Murray F. Tuley, Hanson Wait-
man, Henry L. Waldo, Milton J. Warner, W. W. Watson, Elias P. West,
Theodore D. Wheaton.

dominant party in congress; and moreover, there was a valid objection to the character of the native inhabitants, whose language was foreign, and who had but slight knowledge respecting the principles of American government. The subject was somewhat complicated with Indian affairs and frontier controversies; and it was feared that the admission of such a people might establish a bad precedent for the future if new territory should ever be acquired on the south. Therefore, New Mexico's legitimate ambition for statehood has not been gratified. But the matter is still agitated, and it is not unlikely that, under new political exigencies and the aims of a democratic administration, the desire of the people may be gratified at no very distant day. For a time it was proposed to call the new state Lincoln. I append a few details.[18]

[18] Efforts of 1861. *U. S. Govt Doc.*, 36th cong. 2d sess., Sen. Mis. Doc. 11; H. Journal 534, 560; *Hayes' Scraps, Angeles*, vi. 100. 1863, Sen. Journal 260, 293, 37th cong. 3d sess.; *S. F. Bulletin*, May 28, '63. 1866, act of legisl. authorizing gov. to call a convention, to be elected 1st Mond. in March, to meet at Sta Fé 5th Mond. in April, and the constit. to be voted on 4th Mond. in June. *Laws*, 1865–6; H. Mis. Doc. 57, 39th cong. 1st sess., with proclamation. 1869–71, efforts to secure admission as state of Lincoln. *Laws*, 1869–70, p. 190–5, append. 4; *Id.*, 1871–2, p. 54–6; bills in congress referred and reported. *U. S. Acts*, 41st cong. 2d and 3d sess.; *Cong. Globe*, 1869–71, as per index, including a speech by Delegate Chavez in favor of the measure, in the *Globe* of 1870–1, app. 244; Sen. Journal, 41st cong. 3d sess., 500; *Id.*, 42d cong. 1st sess. 203, H. Jour. 237. Meanwhile, a convention was held at Sta Fé, and a constitution formed. *N. Mex., Constitution of the State of.* Sta Fé, 1872, 12mo, 47 p. This was approved by the gov. Feb. 1st, and an act of the legisl. ordered an election for 1st Mond. in June, state officers to be elected, if the constit. was adopted, on 1st Mond. in Sept. See also *N. Mex., Journal*, 1871–2, appendix. But the vote was not received in time to be legally counted before the period expired, and the movement came to naught. *N. Mex., Mess. of gov.*, 1873, p. 17–18. The house bill on state of Lincoln was tabled in the senate, *Cong. Globe*, 1871–2, p. 2950; and presently a bill to extend the time of voting was referred in the house. In the legisl. session of 1873–4 a new memorial was sent, and in congress a bill was passed by the house, but referred by the senate. *Cong. Globe*, 1873–4; H. Rept 561, 43d cong. 1st sess. There were many newspaper articles on the subject in 1874, the *Mesilla News*, as quoted by the *S. Diego Union*, Jan. 22d, opposing the movement. See also *S. F. Examiner*, June 4th; *S. F. Alta*, June 5th; *S. F. Call*, April 9th; *Sac. Union*, June 6th; *N. Mex., Scraps*, 18. In 1875 the house bill was passed by the sen. with amendments; a new resolution being received from the legisl. 44th cong. 1st sess., Sen. Rept 69; H. Mis. Doc. 63. In 1876 there was another memorial and another bill, which passed the senate after much discussion, but did not go beyond reference to a com. in the house. 43d cong. 1st sess., H. Mis. Doc. 190; *Globe*, 1875–6, per index; 43d cong. 2d sess., H. Jour. 577, 645; 44th cong. 1st sess., H. Rept 503. The report of the com. was favorable, but I find no record of later agitation, except a few newspaper articles of 1885. See *S. F. Bulletin*, July 16, 1885.

The geologic and geographic surveys of the western United States territories, executed under the charge of Professor Hayden and Captain Wheeler in 1869–78, included a considerable portion of New Mexico, the reports and maps containing a vast amount of valuable information, which cannot be even summarized here.[19] The southern boundary having been fixed by the national or treaty survey, the northern, eastern, and western lines were successively surveyed under appropriations of congress made in 1867, 1873, and 1875, the work being simply the determination of the different meridians and parallels, but furnishing, naturally, considerable geographical and other information.[20] There were unsuccessful attempts to restore the tract containing Conejos, Costilla, and Culebra from Colorado to New Mexico; to attach the Moreno mining district to Colorado; and to set off Grant county in the south-west as part of Arizona.

In the matter of crime and disorder the territory presents a record that is by no means unfavorable, considering the circumstances of position on the Mexican frontier, constant ravages of Indian foes, defective organization of the courts, lack of suitable jails, the ignorance and primitive character of the people, and the presence of miners, soldiers, and liquor-traders in remote parts of the country. Of course, there were many irregularities and lawless acts, the record of which is very imperfect and cannot be presented in detail here even so far as it exists; but the New Mexicans proved themselves to a much greater extent than has generally been believed abroad a peaceful and law-abiding people. From 1878 to 1882 the state of affairs in most districts, particularly in the south,

[19] *U. S. Geol. and Geog. Survey, Hayden,* especially the report of 1867–9, p. 106–7, 157–73; *Bulletin,* ii., no. 4, p. 279–308; iv., no. 1; *U. S. Geog. Survey, Wheeler,* iii. 505–67, 603–16, 623–7, 638–61; Report for 1875, p. 40–150; Report for 1876, p. 126–47; 1876, p. 199–202; 1877, p. 1273–8, 1295–1303; 1878, p. 103–6, 131–9; also maps in atlas. See also *Daly's Address before Amer. Geog. Soc.,* 1873, p. 14–15; *Galaxy,* xxi. 429–30.

[20] The survey of the northern or Colorado boundary is described in the *U. S. Land Office Rept,* 1869, p. 37–41; also later surveys in the report of 1872.

was much worse than at other periods.[21] The population of New Mexico in 1860, with some imperfectly estimated deductions for the territory detached later, has been given as 80,567, exclusive of Indians. In 1870 the figures had increased to 90,573, and in 1880 to 109,793. Of these numbers, in the two years respectively, 180 and 1,015 were colored; and in 1880 there were also 57 Chinese. The number born in New Mexico was 82,193 and 92,271; born in other parts of the United States 2,760 and 9,471; born in Mexico 3,903 and 5,173; born in other foreign countries 1,717 and 2,878. The governor's[22] estimate in 1883 was

[21] Corresp. with Mex. on entry of Mex. troops in pursuit of robbers, 1864. *U. S. Govt Doc.*, 39th cong. 1st sess., Mex. affairs, ii. 266–75. 1868, killing of Chief Justice Slough. *N. Mex., Scraps*, 82; *S. F. Times*, Jan. 17, 1868; June 21, 1869. Lynching in 1870. *S. F. Bulletin*, Nov. 9, 1870. Election riot at Mesilla Sept. '71, in which 7 persons were killed. *S. F. Alta*, Sept. 21, '71; *Independence Indep.*, Oct. 14, '71. On sale in N. Mex. of live-stock stolen in Mex. *Mex., Informe Pesquisador*, 1874, p. 26, 101–2. 1874–8, murders in Lincoln co., U. S. troops called out; mob destroys a newspaper at Cimarron; riot at El Paso. *N. Mex., Scraps*, 16, 82; *S. F. Bulletin*, Oct. 24, '77; *S. F. Alta*, Oct. 22, '78. Troops crossing frontier in pursuit of trespassers. 45th cong. 1st sess., H. Ex. Doc. 13, p. 116–31, 227–8. 1879, lynching at Las Vegas. *N. Mex. Scraps*, 2. Disposition of criminals. *N. Mex., Mess. of gov.*, 8–9. 1880, troubles with cowboys and outlaws, lynching in Lincoln co. and Las Vegas, killing an editor at Socorro, etc. *Denver Tribune*, June 19, July 15, Nov. 18, Dec. 26, 28, '80; *Tucson Star*, Feb. 12, Jan. 15, May 27, '80. Similar items for 1881, including the killing of 'Billy the Kid' by the sheriff. *S. F. Chronicle*, April 1, '81; *Tombstone Epitaph*, June 16, '81; *Pinal Drill*, Aug. 6, '81; *Sac. Record-Union*, July 27, '81; *N. Mex., Acts*, 1882, p. 191. Items of 1882. *S. F. Bulletin*, Jan. 25, Feb. 13, Nov. 11, '82. Items of 1883, including the 'rustler' war in Doña Ana co. *N. Mex., Offic. Repts*, 1882–3, pt iii., 64–84; *S. F. Chronicle*, Feb. 10, '83. 1884, see governor's message. 1885, lynching, and riot at Springer. *S. F. Bulletin*, March 17, '85.

[22] Lionel A. Sheldon, in 1881 appointed governor of New Mexico, is of Norman descent, his ancestors settling in Yorkshire, England, about the time of the conquest, one of them being afterward appointed lord mayor of London, another bishop of Canterbury, and a third lieutenant-general. In 1646 three brothers of this family emigrated to America, and from one of them Lionel is descended, his birthplace being Worcester, New York, and his birthday the 30th of August, 1831. After receiving a thorough legal training, at the age of 21 he was elected justice of the peace, and soon afterward probate judge for Lorain county. At the expiration of his term he practised law, and took an active part in political and military affairs. In 1858 he was appointed brigadier-general of militia, and at the outbreak of the war joined the Union army as captain of a cavalry company, soon afterward being promoted to a colonelcy and brevet brigadier-general, and taking part in a number of engagements. In 1868, and again in 1870 and '72, he was chosen for congress from New Orleans, and later was attorney for the government in the Alabama claims. In 1880 he was member of the Chicago convention which nominated Garfield for the presidency, and for several weeks was his guest at the White House. During his career as governor he thoroughly cleared the territory of its lawless element, promoted industries and education,

150,000, and the population may have reached that figure in 1886.

and brought peace and prosperity to the land.   Afterward he rendered good service in putting an end to the great labor strike on the Texas and Pacific Railroad, and as receiver for that line handled $15,000,000 without a single discrepancy in his accounts.   In January 1888 he settled at Los Angeles, where he became interested in the Centinela-Inglewood Company. A man of strong character and of great physical strength, a thorough lawyer, and a ripe scholar, perhaps his strongest trait is his cool and unflinching determination, as is displayed in his war record, and in many incidents of his eventful career.

SEAL OF NEW MEXICO.

CHAPTER XXIX.

INDIAN AND MILITARY AFFAIRS.

1864-1887.

MILITARY COMMANDERS—FORCES—FORTS—INDIAN POPULATION—SUPERIN-
TENDENTS — APPROPRIATIONS — CHRONOLOGY — THE NAVAJOS — BOSQUE
REDONDO--CARLETON'S EFFORTS—CONTROVERSY—THE RESERVATION A
FAILURE—REMOVED TO THEIR OLD HOME—AGENTS—PROSPERITY IN THE
NORTH-WEST—COMANCHES—JICARILLAS AND UTES—AGENCIES AT CIMAR-
RON, ABIQUIÚ, AND TIERRA AMARILLA—FINAL REMOVAL—THE PUE-
BLOS—LIST OF AGENTS AND CHRONOLOGIC SUMMARY—PRESBYTERIAN
SCHOOLS—THE MESCALEROS—AT FORT SUMNER AND FORT STANTON—
AGENTS AND ANNALS—SOUTHERN APACHES—HOSTILE BANDS—RESERVA-
TIONS—CAÑADA ALAMOSA, TULAROSA, AND OJO CALIENTE—VICTORIO'S
RAIDS—APACHES REMOVED TO ARIZONA.

THE military commanders in New Mexico from
1864 were as follows: General James H. Carleton,
1864-6; General George Sykes, 1867; General George
W. Getty, 1867-71; General Gordon Granger, 1871–
3 and 1875-6; General J. I. Gregg, 1873-4; General
Thomas C. Devin, 1874-5; Colonel James F. Wade,
1876; General Edward Hatch, 1876-81; General
Luther P. Bradley, 1881; General R. S. Mackenzie,
1881-3.[1] All seem to have been faithful and efficient
officers, if we may credit the annual reports of General Pope, commanding the division of the Missouri,
which included New Mexico. Most of them, however, as was inevitable, antagonized at one time or
another the Indian agents or some clique of citizens.

[1] Carleton was major 6th inf. and brevet maj.-gen. volunteers; Sykes col
20th inf. and brevet maj.-gen. U. S. A.; Getty col 37th inf. and ditto;
Granger col 15th inf. and ditto; Devin lieut.-col 8th cavalry and brevet
brig.-gen. U. S. A.; Wade maj. 9th cav. and brevet col U. S. A., temporarily
in command; Hatch col 9th cav. and brevet maj.-gen. U. S. A.; Bradley
col 13th inf. and brevet brig.-gen. U. S. A.; Mackenzie col 4th cav. and
ditto; *Ritch's Blue-Book*, 125-6.

For instance, Getty in 1867 and Hatch in 1880 were denounced in public meetings, but sustained by resolutions of the legislature. Details of these controverses are not fully recorded, and if they were, would hardly be worth reproducing.

The California volunteers were mustered out in New Mexico on the expiration of their terms of enlistment in 1865–6,[2] and their places were taken by regular troops. The force in 1867 was over 1,500 men, but was gradually diminished, until in 1875 it was less than 600. Next year, however, it was 1,200, and was increased until 1883, when it was nearly 1,600, and in 1884 perhaps 2,300.[3] These troops, maintained at an annual cost of nearly three millions, were distributed, according to the varying exigencies of the Indian service, at forts Bascom, Bayard, Craig, Cummings, McRae, Marcy, Selden, Stanton, Sumner, Union, and Wingate. The military headquarters was at Santa Fé; several of the older forts do not appear in the records of this period; and some of those named were new, and others abandoned before 1884.[4] The legis-

[2] *Low (F. F.) and Gen. J. H. Carleton, Correspondence*, in *Cal., Journals*, appen., 16th sess. There was some dissatisfaction among the men about the place of discharge, mileage, delays in getting pay, and the supply of rations. See also 39th cong. 1st sess., H. Ex. Doc. 138.

[3] 2,356, according to *N. Mex., Acts*, 1884, p. 236. I have no regular reports after 1883.

[4] Reports of the general of the army in reports of sec. war, 1864, etc., containing tables of the troops and their distribution from year to year. I have no space to record garrison changes and commanders. Ft Bascom was on the Canadian Riv., in S. Miguel co., and was abandoned in 1871, declared a mil. reserv. in 1869; area 8,840 acres; apparently on the Montoya grant, as was Ft Butler, near by, occupied as a post before Bascom, and never declared as a reserv. Ft Bayard, at Pinos Altos, corresponding to the former Ft West; name changed before 1867; having one of the largest garrisons in the territory, especially in the Apache troubles of '80 et seq.; no mil. reservation. Ft Craig, on the Rio Grande, garrisoned throughout the period; built on leased land claimed as part of a Span. grant, and the claim causing much controversy in 1870. *U. S. Govt Doc.*, 41st cong. 2d sess., H. Ex. Doc. 73; declared a reserv. in 1869; area 24,805 acres. Ft Cummings, at Cook Spring, garrisoned in 1870, and again in 1881–3; reserv. declared in 1870; area 2,500 acres; abandoned by war dept, and sale recommended in 1875. Ft McRae, on the Rio Grande, garrisoned from 1870 to 1876; reserv. declared in 1869; area 2,500 acres; like Craig, on the claimed Armendáriz grant. Ft Marcy, at Sta Fé, occupied by a small detachment, acc. to the reports of most years; reserv. declared in 1868; area 17 acres. Ft Selden, near Doña Ana; aband. as a post after 1876, but again garrisoned in 1881–3; reserv. declared 1870; area 9,613 acres. Ft Stanton, Lincoln co., continuously garrisoned; reserv. 1859; re-

lature now, as before, made frequent appeals for increased force, and especially for authority to raise volunteer regiments; with occasional requests for military posts at certain exposed points; but there is no indication that these efforts ever produced any results. Something was, however, accomplished in the way of organizing the militia force.[5]

The Indian population of the territory in 1864–86 may be put at 26,000 to 28,000, with but little variation.[6] The superintendents in charge down to 1874, when the office was abolished, were Michael Steck in 1864, Felipe Delgado in 1865–6, A. B. Norton in 1866–7, Luther E. Webb in 1867–9, José M. Gallegos in 1869, William Clinton in 1869–70, Nathaniel Pope in 1870–2, L. E. Dudley in 1872–4.[7] For the general Indian service, congress made an annual appropriation, which was $75,000 in 1864, about $50,000 a year in 1865–75, $18,000 to $30,000 in 1876–81, and

duced in 1872 from 12 miles sq. to 10,240 acres. Ft Sumner, on the Pecos, in S. Miguel co., abandoned in 1868, when the Navajos were removed; and reserv. sold in 1871; but the cemetery, 320 acres, reserved by order of May 22, 1871. Ft Thorn, in Mesilla Valley, not garrisoned; reserv. never declared; but surveyed in 1857; recom. in 1870 to be restored to public domain. Ft Union, continuously garrisoned, and generally regarded as headquarters; reserv. declared in 1868; area with timber reserves 66,880 acres; on the Mora grant (also another reserv. of 5,120 acres on Mora Riv., declared in 1870). Ft Wingate, near R. R. south of Navajo reserv.; continuously garrisoned (Ft Defiance being abandoned); reserv. declared in 1870; area 64,000 acres. On the mil. reservations and propositions for their sale. see *Cong. Globe*, 1870–1, appen. 341; *U. S. Govt Doc.*, 43d cong. 1st sess., H. Ex. Doc. 43, p. 103; 46th cong. 3d sess., H. Ex. Doc. 47, p. 1180; pt v., vol. ix., p. 459; 47th cong. 1st sess., H. Ex. Doc., ix., pt v., p. 784; 2d sess., H. Ex. Doc. 45, p. 1180; H. Mis. Doc. 45, p. 252.

[5] On the militia regulations and organization, with something of their services in suppressing lawlessness, see *N. Mex., Rept of Adj.-gen.*, 1882–3, in *Id., Official Reports*, p. 61–144; *Ritch's Blue-Book*, 71–3.

[6] That is, after 1880 there were 16,000 Navajos, 9,000 Pueblos, and 3,000 Apaches. In the early years the general estimates from different sources were 19,000 or 20,000, which were too small, the Navajos especially being underestimated at about 11,000; there were also 1,500 to 1,800 Utes. The Pueblos increased somewhat, and the Navajos considerably; but the Apaches steadily decreased, and the Utes were removed from the territory. See estimates of the different tribes and bands later in this chapter.

[7] *Ind. Aff. Reports*, 1864 et seq. Subsequently, however, B. M. Thomas, the Pueblo agent, was a kind of special agent for all tribes. In '66 J. K. Graves is named as a special agent; and in '68 N. M. Davis was acting supt. Besides certain differences with the mil. authorities on points to be noted in connection with annals of the tribes, there is nothing requiring special notice in the administration of the successive superintendents.

$1,000 to $5,000 later; besides special appropriations, chiefly for the Navajos and Apaches, amounting to about $2,000,000 in 1864–84.[8] The military expenditure, as we have seen, was about $3,000,000 per year.

Respecting the subject of Indian affairs in New Mexico since 1864 as a whole—that is, as distinct from the history of the separate tribes and sections, to be presented a little later—there is not much to be profitably said. In all the general phases of its development, including obstacles, controversies, and results, nearly all that has been said on Indian history in Arizona and other territories for the corresponding period, and in this territory for the preceding period, might be repeated without essential modification. I append some general notes in chronologic order.[9] As a rule,

[8] *U. S. Statutes.* See also résumé of congressional action earlier in this chapter.

[9] 1864. The gov. reports depred. much less frequent and serious than in former years, though the Apaches are hostile. The supt. declares that depred. have been frequent, and might have been prevented by more liberal supplies of food. The com. of Ind. affairs notes no improvement under mil. management, but thinks some experience is being gained for future guidance. A mem. of the legisl. gives losses at the hands of Ind. in the past 15 months at 99 killed, 47 wounded, 18 captured; and property stolen to the value of $448,683. In *Morris' Address* are given statistics, etc.

1865. Supt complains of want of funds; commissioner, that most agents cannot speak English. Gov. in a procl. of May 4th forbids exped. by citizens, and all trade in captives.

1866. Special agent Graves makes a report, generally adopted by the com. and supt. The settlement of the claims of citizens for Ind. depred., breaking-up of peonage and captive slavery, and suspension of raids by citizens are urged. Agents should be Americans, and their salary not less than $2,500 (instead of $1,500); a special com. should select reservations; and whites should be strictly excluded. A few bad Ind. spoil the reputation of a whole tribe. The Apaches may be made self-sustaining in 3 years by liberal approp. and good management. The gov. says the Ind. must, 1st, be conquered; 2d, their claimed right to roam taken away by treaty; 3d, reserv. defined, at a distance from settlements; 4th, Ind. must be kept on and whites off the reserv.; 5th, the U. S. must aid liberally in cloth, seeds, implements, etc., for 10 years; 6th, education must be enforced in an industrial school on each reserv. A mem. of the legisl. and the gov.'s mess. give the losses since 1846 as 90 killed, 31 wounded, 20 captured (123, 32, and 21, acc. to *Ind. Aff. Rept*); and property to value of $1,377,329.

1867. Report of joint spec. com., devoted mainly to earlier annals and to Carleton's corresp. Expend. since U. S. occupation $4,000,000 per year. It would have been much cheaper to buy the whole territory and turn it over to the Ind.

1868. Report, chiefly devoted to an argument against turning over Ind. affairs to the war dept. Army was sent to Wash. on a mission connected with Ind. affairs. Cong. com. report against an increased and deficiency approp. Gov. is bitter against the U. S. for not sending more troops, now that the war of rebellion is over, also against the peace com.; complains of

while petty depredations never ceased entirely, the loss of life and property was never serious after the Navajos had been settled on their north-western reservation, and before the southern Apache outbreaks of 1880 and the following years. Finally, all the natives were gathered on reservations or in their pueblos, and Indian wars have become, perhaps, a thing of

constant depred.; and says the settlements must defend themselves, as it is not best to call out the militia. Utes peaceful, Jicarillas ditto, but 'constitutionally dishonest,' other Apaches hostile, and but little to hope for the Navajos.

1869. Com. disapproves treaties with Ind. as sovereign powers; no decided improvement. Supt says nothing can be done till congress furnishes means to carry out policy of feeding as cheaper than fighting Ind. 1870. Nothing notable. Report on missionary work, in *U. S. Govt Doc.*, 41st cong. 3d sess., Sen. Ex. Doc. 39, p. 98–113.

1871. Bigger approp. needed. Com. thinks Grant's peace policy has improved the character of agents, etc. List and statistics of reservations, in *Ind. Aff. Rept*, 683. Collyer, in his report of Dec., says that for 15 years the Apaches have desired peace, but the agents have had no means of feeding them.

1872. Some general progress; but all rules fail when applied to Apaches. It is better to feed than fight them, but neither will control them, though a combination of the two in the hands of a discreet man will accomplish much. The supt should have authority to investig. all claims. Reports on Ind. and operations of troops, in *U. S. Govt Doc.*, 42d cong. 3d sess., H. Repts, iii. Discussion on Ind. aff., *Cong. Globe*, 1875–6, p. 2607–11.

1873. Supt reports things generally in a satisfactory condition. Better agents should be secured by higher salary. Prompt approp. would secure lower prices for all goods. The com. thinks the plan of appointing agents on recom. of religious bodies is working well. Gov. says Ind. depred. no longer amount to anything, a false impression having gone abroad on that matter. *Ritch's Hist. N. Mex.*, MS., 4–6, gives some information about Ind. affairs from 1873.

1874. Supt Dudley at Wash. reports that not a single white had been killed during his term. Official rept on education, in 43d cong. 2d sess., H. Ex. Doc., viii., pt v., p. 515.

1875. Agents' reports show no troubles. Petition of citizens for removal of Ind., noted in 43d cong. 2d sess., H. Jour. 270.

1876. Com. urges in general concentration, allotment of lands in severalty, extension of U. S. court jurisd. over Ind., and the removal of N. Mex. Ind. to Ind. Territory. *Rideing's A-Saddle*, 83–6, contains some information on the mismanagement of reserv. 1877–9. Nothing new, but southern Apache troubles began at the end of '79. Nothing of general interest in 1880.

1881. The com. says: 'To allow the Ind. to drag along year after year and generation after generation in their old superstitions, laziness, and filth, when we have the power to elevate them, would be a lasting disgrace.' No change to be expected as long as the Ind. are simply fed. All the Ind. of southern N. Mex. should be moved north, away from the frontier. On this latter proposition the mil. authorities were agreed. Nothing of general importance in 1882–3.

1884. The gov. thinks no more raids like those of 1880–2 in the south are likely to occur. The legisl. protests against discrimination against N. Mex. in the purchase of supplies, and asks that N. Mex. be made a mil. department, with headquarters at Sta Fé.

the past.　In New Mexico, as in the other territories, however, the problem of educating and civilizing the aborigines, of protecting their rights as well as those of the citizens, remains to be solved, with but slight prospects of success.　Elements and conditions of the problem are substantially the same here as elsewhere; though certain qualities of the Pueblos and Navajos should offer more than ordinary encouragement.

In a former chapter we left the Navajos, or over 7,000 of them, at the Bosque Redondo reservation, on the Rio Pecos, where they had been brought in by the campaigns of Carson and other officers, under the direction of General Carleton, where they were kept as prisoners of war under military management and under guard of the garrison at Fort Sumner, and where were also 400 Mescalero Apaches under Agent Labadi.　Subsequently, more Navajos were brought in, and the greatest number at the Bosque was 8,491 in 1865.　It was supposed by Carleton and others that not more than 2,000 remained in their old home; but it later appeared that not much more than half the whole number, and these not the most troublesome, had been removed.　Finally, for want of accommodations and means of subsistence, orders had to be given to send no more prisoners to Fort Sumner.　At the end of five years the number had been reduced by deaths and escapes to 7,304; but the greater part of the decrease was in 1864–5, when there were several outbreaks and pursuits.[10]

As a military measure, to gain complete control of the Navajos, to show them the power of the government, to make them appreciate the value of their old home, to prepare the way for a treaty, and to teach the Indians their true interest in keeping the treaty, General Carleton's policy of removal, as compared with

[10] On the Bosque Redondo experiment of 1864–8, see *Ind. Aff. Reports,* especially *Rept Joint Com.,* 1867, including *Carleton's Correspondence. Dunn's Massacres of the Mountains,* 447–76, has an excellent chapter on the subject.

any other likely to have been adopted at the time, must be considered a wise one; and too much praise cannot be accorded him for his energy in carrying out his plans. But the Bosque Redondo as a reservation had no merits whatever; and as a means of civilizing the Indians, the project proved a total failure. Carleton was disappointed in his belief that he had captured nearly all of the Navajos, and in his hope that their removal would open up a rich mining district in the north-west. Still more was he disappointed in his expectation that when the Indians had been conquered, removed, and supported for a year or two at a cost of over a million dollars, the government would be ready with funds and a settled policy to take them off his hands, and proceed in earnest with the work of teaching them to be self-supporting. The government, as usual, did nothing promptly or definitely.

Moreover, a bitter opposition to the scheme was aroused from the first. Nobody in New Mexico desired the raiding Navajos to remain permanently on the Pecos, especially under the lack of control which experience had taught the people to expect; though the governor and others favored somewhat the Bosque Redondo as a possible stepping-stone to the ultimate removal of the Indians from the territory. Superintendent Steck was a leader in the opposition, finally going to Washington to urge his views; and the controversy between Carleton and his opponents became very hot, leading to much exaggeration on both sides.[11]

[11] 1864. Preliminary discussion on the reserv. in Wash. *U. S. Govt Doc.*, 38th cong. 1st sess., H. Ex. Doc. 65, 70; Sen. Doc. 36; Sen. Mis. Doc. 97; Gov. Connelly's ideas in his mess. of '63–4. Petition for Carson's appt as supt at B. R. signed by gov. and many citizens. *Carson, Papers*, MS. There was an approp. of $100,000 soon expended. T. W. Woolson was appointed a com. to investigate. Supt declared the scheme would cost $2,678,000 per year. Much inform. in *Carleton's Corresp.* for 1864–5. C. says that Steck favored the B. R. plan before he went east. The reserv. was 40 miles sq. C. promised the Ind. that the reserv. should be permanent; and he favored neglecting all other Ind. in favor of the Navajos. 1865. In April a board under Maj. McCleave made a report on the management at B. R. A board of com., J. R. Doolittle pres., took much testimony, which is given in the report of '67, p. 323–62. The commissioner at Wash. took no decided position in the controversy, but says the Ind. seem to be doing well and cultivating 3,500 acres. Delgado, Steck's successor as supt, approved Carleton's ideas.

Meanwhile, on the reservation matters went on from bad to worse. The Navajos were not farmers, and from lack of skill, ravages of the corn worm, and various other causes, the crops failed year after year. Most of their flocks and herds had been lost, and the grazing was not sufficient for the animals left. There was the greatest difficulty in keeping them from starvation. They were once or twice attacked by the Comanches and other Indians of the plains. They quarrelled with the Mescaleros, who ran away in 1866, after their agent had been driven off on a charge of irregular dealings in cattle. Under the new conditions the health of the Indians was much impaired, and the ravages of syphilitic disease became alarming.

Finally, in May 1868, when the condition of affairs had become hopelessly bad, the peace commissioners, General Sherman and Colonel Tappan, arrived, and on the 1st of June made a treaty for the removal of the Navajos to a reservation of 5,200 square miles in their old country, in the north-western corner of the territory. Each Indian was to receive five dollars in clothing per year, and each one engaged in farming or any trade was given ten dollars. The head of a family could select 160 acres of land if he chose, and was in that case given $100 in seeds and implements the first year, and $25 for the second and third years. 15,000 sheep and 500 cattle were to be purchased for the tribe; buildings were to be erected at a cost of $11,500; and a school-house and teacher were to be

1866. Spec. agent Graves favored B. R. as a permanent reserv. It was the intention to turn over the Ind. to the interior department. Theodore H. Dodd acted as a kind of agent from June. There were only 1,050 horses and 1,100 sheep at B. R. 1867. Approp. of $200,000, but no rations to be served after July 1st, except in case of extreme necessity. Speech of Delegate Chavez in congress protesting against refusal to make approp. for B. R. *Cong. Globe*, 1866–7, app. 149. Bill to authorize a treaty for removal of the Navajos from B. R. and an approp. of $150,000, passed by house and amended by senate. The legisl. asked for an approp. for education at B. R., favoring the views of Father Bleick. Five soldiers killed in a fight with the Ind. Reports on unsuitable nature of the B. R. reserved. *U. S. Govt Doc.*, 40th cong. 2d sess., H. Ex. Doc. 248, 308. 1868, More approp. urgently demanded. *Id.*, H. Ex. Doc. 185. Howsley's claim for damages to his farms by Navajos. *Id.*, 42d cong. 2d sess., H. Ex. Doc. 99. Treaty and removal.

provided for each 30 pupils, the Indians binding themselves to compel the attendance of all children from
six to sixteen years of age. An appropriation of
$150,000 was made by congress to pay the cost of
removal, and make a beginning of reservation work
under the treaty.[12]

The removal was immediately effected, 7,304 Navajos arriving at Fort Wingate, where the new agency
was temporarily established, on the 23d of July,
under the care of Agent Dodd. I append a list of
agents in later years.[13] From this date the Navajos
have lived more or less quietly on their reservation,
and with the exception of occasional misdeeds of
renegades for a few years, their old-time raids for
plunder and their broken treaties were at an end.
They have grown rich as a tribe in flocks and herds,
and from a military point of view have given the
government no trouble. Over 16,000 in number, and
constantly gaining, they fully understand, as they
did not in earlier times, that war is likely to prove
fatal to all their interests. Their reservation annals
have been similar in most respects to those of other
tribes. Some details are appended.[14] The Navajos

[12] The total of approp. for the Navajos in 1864–84 was about $2,000,000,
the largest amount being $422,000 in 1868, and the smallest $5,000 in 1882.

[13] Navajo agents: Theo. H. Dodd 1866–8, J. C. French 1868–9, F. T. Ben-
nett 1869–71 (with —— Ford, succeeded by J. A. Manley, as spec. agents in
1870), James H. Miller 1871–2, W. F. Hall 1872–3 (Kearnes in charge from
June to Sept. '72, between Miller's death and Hall's appointment), W. F. M.
Arny 1873–5, (I. D. Gould spec. agent in '73), Alex. Irvine 1875–8, J. E.
Pyle 1878–9, Galen Eastman 1879–83 (T. T. Bennett acting in '80), D. M.
Riordan 1883–4.

[14] 1869. Census for distrib. of goods 8,181: 2,000 or more roving or with
other tribes. Survey of reserv. being made by Capt. E. W. Darling. Complaints of depred. caused Gov. Mitchell in Aug. to issue a procl. declaring the
whole tribe outlaws; but Gov. Pile in Sept. modified this so as to include
only the marauding bands.

1870. Survey completed; area given as 6,120 sq. m. Count 8,234. Agency
estab. at mouth of the Cañon Bonito, 48 m. N. W. of Ft Wingate, and across
the Ariz. line (old Ft Defiance); 14,000 sheep and 1,000 goats distrib. in Nov.
'69 and doing well. Trouble in getting the money approp. Much planting
on widely scattered farms, but failure of crops and prospective destitution.
Many outrages by Mex. and Utes; a few slight depred. by Navajos. There
should be 5 subagencies. Miss Charity A. Gaston kept a school of 30 pupils
for several months, aided by Rev. J. M. Roberts. The Ind. have fully kept
the treaty.

1871. Continued failure of crops; 30,000 sheep, 8,000 horses, and a few

were more intelligent and industrious than the Indians
of most other tribes, but their great advantage, or

cattle; more sheep needed.   Great need of buildings.   Only 1 acre in 50 of
the 3,916,800 acres of the reserv. tillable.   Rev. Roberts and John Menaul
acting as missionaries, without much progress.   Mrs (Charity Gaston) Menaul's
school has 40 pupils.   Treaty with the Moquis and Zuñis.   Some disease contracted at Bosque Redondo.

1872.   Crops look well, but not enough raised for support.   New farming
district in the S. Juan valley.   130,000 sheep, 10,000 horses.   Census 9,114.
100 captives restored by Mex. settlers.   School not very prosperous, on acct
of irregular attendance; industrial school needed.   Mounted native police
did good service, 100 strong.   Agent Miller killed by Utes in Sept.

1873.   Crops bad again; reserv. not fit for agric., but half of it good for
stock; 175,000 sheep; $50–75,000 needed for food till next harvest.   No school.
Arny favors an indust. school on S. Juan, but the supt disapproves this.
Seed and tools needed.   The reserv. should be extended on the south.   Police
disbanded.   Supt thinks the Ind. will be self-supporting on expiration of
treaty.

1874.   Good prospects.   New police force of 200.   Force of employés reduced by act limiting expense to $6,000.   School taught by Prof. Freise, Mrs
C. A. Stowe matron; new school-house for 28 pupils; 85 taught in all.   Census 9,068.   Many sheep killed by cold; crops generally suffice to Dec. 1st.
Bill to reduce reserv. in north and extend it in south approved by house com.
43d cong., 1st sess., H. Rept 638.

1875.   Agent Arny and the teachers involved in a quarrel, and driven off,
as he says, by influence of the 'squaw men.'   He is very bitter against the
military for refusing aid, favoring prostitution, etc.   Hand-looms introd., with
prospects of success, which were not realized.

1876.   Grasshoppers destroyed the wheat crop.   The agency should be
moved to the S. Juan, where extensive farming would be done but for the hostility of the Utes.   The southern extension asked for proves to be on R. R.
lands.   The agency is close to the line and traders do much harm.   No progress in schools.   Mormons making advances.   An Ind. being killed by a
herder, a herd of sheep was seized, and the mil. permitted 450 sheep to be
retained.

1877.   All going well.   200,000 lbs. of wool sold, besides blankets and
skins.   The horses a detriment.   Most of the good land utilized.   Chiefs object to a census for distrib. of goods.   Whiskey-selling does much harm.
School not prosperous.   Steam saw-mill procured.

1878.   Ind. prosperous and industrious, but best land on the S. Juan not
utilized for fear of the Utes.   Only half the Ind. on the reserv., which is too
small.   Little or nothing accomplished for educ., because the govt has not
fulfilled the treaty obligations.   Buildings in a bad condition.   Rations
should be stopped.   Treaty about to expire; but no danger, because of property interests.   Legisl. demands that the Ind. be kept on the reserv., which,
by order of Oct. 29th, was extended westward in Ariz. to 110° long. north of
36° lat.

1879.   Count of 11,400 Ind., but many never visit the agency.   500,000
sheep, 22,500 horses, 1,600 cattle.   Only ¼ crop, on acct of drought; 40,000
bush. corn.   Only 11–15 children attending school, but they learn well.
Presbyt. missionary expected.   Ind. have partially adopted dress of civilization—also taste for whiskey and cards.

1880.   Agent Eastman incurred the hatred of the Ind. by his efforts to
regulate their amusements, keeping Sunday, etc.   To avoid an open rupture,
Gen. Pope put Capt. Bennett in charge, and quiet was restored.   Pope
deemed E. an unfit man by reason of his fanaticism, and his view was sustained at Wash. *Rept Sec. War*, p. 85.   Only 7 per cent of subsistence furnished by govt.   40,000 horses, 500 mules, 1,000 burros, 500 cattle, and
700,000 sheep; 800,000 lbs. of wool sold, 10,000 acres of land cultivated.

that of those attempting to control them, was their inclination to raise live-stock. In 1884 they had a million sheep and 35,000 horses, though the latter were practically of no use to them. The possession of so much wealth made them fear war. In agriculture they were not so successful, though showing commendable industry under adverse circumstances, cultivating at times over 10,000 acres. The farming lands were, however, of limited extent and scattered in small patches; the water supply was inadequate and irregular; frosts and various pests were frequent obstacles; and the crops were usually more or less complete failures. Their chief disadvantages were the gross immorality of their women; their addiction to strong drink, though some progress was made in checking this evil; the inability of the chiefs and rich men to control the masses; their living in widely scattered bands from the necessities of farming and con-

Windmills and pumps introduced. Fine building being erected for a boarding-school. Rev. A. H. Donaldson died in April, soon after arrival. No police organization, on acct of small pay allowed. Whiskey does much harm; and some of the young men getting restless. Legisl. protests against order of Jan. 6th, which added to the reserv. a strip 15 m. wide on the east and 6 m. on south.

1881. Pop. estim. at over 16,000. Agent Eastman restored, and complaining of mil. interference and pretexts. Crops ruined by drought and flood. No increase in stock since '79. Approp. much too small. The R. R. brings some evils. Homestead acts of '75 and '80 will enable Ind. to keep their farms off the reserv. School not thriving, but Mr and Mrs Perkins have done all they could. Arms are illegally sold to Ind.; and illicit sexual relations with whites are increasing. 5 per cent of subsistence from hunting and 5 per cent from govt. Gen. Pope thinks there is great danger of trouble since E.'s restoration. The tribe is very powerful, and must be carefully treated. He expressed the same views later, also disapproving the extension of the reserv., but he was finally pleased with Riordan's appointment.

1882. A good season until the frosts came. $5,000 an absurdly small approp. School-house nearly done. No missionary work. 54 pupils. The R. R. creates a market for blankets. Of the treaty approp. there was an unexpended surplus of $156,651, and an effort was made to secure this for the Ind.

1883. Gen. Pope deems the Mormons dangerous, and says there is no doubt they incite the Ind. to hostility. No. of sheep said to be 900,000. Native work in jewelry described in *Matthews' Navajo Silversmiths*. Wash., 1883, fol., p. 171–8. Some troubles by roaming bands.

1884. Reserv. extended westward to long. 111° 30′, and consolidated later with the Moqui reserv.; on the north the boundary was made the S. Juan and Colorado rivers; but 46,000 acres were thus cut off in N. Mex., leaving the area 8,159,360 acres. Estim. pop. 17,000; 15,000 acres of land cultiv.; crops 220,000 bush. corn and 21,000 bush. wheat; 35,000 horses and 1,000,000 sheep; 50 men induced to build houses; 25 able to read.

venience of grazing; and their habit of burning every
house in which a person had died, preventing the
wealthy Indians from building permanent homes.
Except in the partial adoption of the white man's
dress, there was no modification of their old customs.
Toward their civilization no progress whatever was
made. A school was in existence much of the time,
but the attendance was very small, the tribe not com-
pelling attendance, as promised in the treaty, and the
government not fulfilling its treaty obligation to build
school-houses and furnish teachers. The old buildings
at Fort Defiance were always in a dilapidated condition; and the agency was so near the reservation lines
that outside whiskey-traders were given too great
facilities. The reservation was several times extended,
until it covered an area, for the most part sterile, of
over eight million acres. The railroad along their
southern border brought both good and evil to this
people. The Navajos still live, in the old way, where
they have lived for centuries; and while their prosperity in some respects has been remarkable, it is to
be noted that all is due to their own original and
inherent qualities, and nothing to their contact with a
superior race. Here, as elsewhere, prospects for the
future are not encouraging.

The Comanches, Kiowas, and other tribes of the
eastern plains were somewhat troublesome in 1864–6,
and several expeditions under Carson, McCleave, and
others were sent against them from Fort Bascom as a
base by General Carleton; but later, so far as New
Mexico was concerned, there were no hostilities, though
complaints of trading in stolen goods occasionally
appear.[15]

The Jicarilla Apaches, from 750 to 950 in number,

[15] *Carleton's Corresp.*, 268–9; *Carson, Papers*, MS.; *Hayes' Scraps, Angeles*,
viii. 443; *Ariz.*, i. 274; *S. Cal., Wilmington*, 59. Carson had a fight in Nov.
'64, and in May '65 was ordered to estab. a post at Cedar Bluffs or Cold
Spring to protect the Cimarron route. An agency at Ft Bascom was proposed in '65, and all trading licenses were revoked. Some complaints in
'70–1.

and the three bands of Utes, numbering from 1,500 to 1,800, continued to live for the greater part of the period under consideration in the northern portions of the territory, with agencies at Cimarron, east of the Rio Grande, and at Abiquiú, or finally at Tierra Amarilla, in the west. I append lists of agents successively in charge at the two agencies.[16] What has been said in an earlier chapter respecting the character and conduct of these Indians requires no modification or supplement here. They were always nominally at peace, though committing many petty thefts, and accused of many depredations of which they were probably not guilty; they were worthless, drunken vagabonds, especially the Jicarillas, visiting the agencies only to receive their annual allowance of goods, and spending their time in hanging about the settlements, where they were a great nuisance, or— especially the Utes—in hunting expeditions; and they were always averse to settlement, work, or removal, preferring and claiming the right to roam at will, and to receive liberal annuities on condition of abstaining from depredations.

In the chronologic record of Ute and Jicarilla affairs there is nothing requiring notice except the efforts to effect their removal and final settlement. There was no improvement in their condition, and no effort was made to improve or educate them. They were simply

[16] Cimarron agents, Jicarillas and Mohuache Utes: Levi J. Keithly 1864–5 (Ferd. Maxwell spec. agent in '64), Lorenzo Labadi 1865–6, Manuel S. Salazar 1866, E. B. Dennison 1866–70, W. P. Wilson 1870, Charles F. Roedel 1870–2. The agency was now abolished, but the Ind. remained, and were in charge of R. H. Longwell 1872–3, Thos A. Dolan 1873–4, Longwell 1874, Alex. G. Irvine 1874–5, John E. Pyle 1875–6, and B. M. Thomas (Pueblo agent) 1876–83, when the Ind. were finally removed.

Abiquiú and Tierra Amarilla agents, Capote and Payuche Utes, also some Jicarillas at times: Head or Pfeiffer (?) 1864–5, Diego Archuleta 1865–7 (Manuel García spec. agent), W. F. M. Arny 1867–8, James C. French 1868–9, John Ayers 1869, J. B. Hanson 1869–71 (Capt A. S. B. Keyes also named in '69), John S. Armstrong 1871–2 (agency transf. from Abiquiú to Tierra Amarilla), W. S. Defrees 1872–3, W. D. Crothers 1873–4 (C. Robbins and F. Salazar also named as being in charge in '74), Sam. A. Russell 1874–8. The Utes were removed and agency abolished in '78, but the remaining Jicarillas were in charge of B. M. Thomas, the Pueblo agent, in 1878–83, and the farmers in charge were J. M. Roberts 1878–9, J. B. Holt 1879–80, W. B. Jones 1880–2, and F. W. Reed 1882–3.

given a small annual supply of goods, and thus induced to keep the peace.   Their homes were on private lands, and it was understood by all that they must
go elsewhere.   They were generally unwilling to
make any change; when they were favorably disposed
the government failed to act promptly until the
Indians had changed their mind, or perhaps selected
some destination that had never been favored by them.
The Utes at Abiquiú pretended at times a willingness
to settle on a reservation in the San Juan valley, but
this was not acceptable to the government, though
often recommended by agents.   It was deemed desirable to move them to the reservation of their tribe in
Southern Colorado; and in 1868 a treaty was made
to that effect; but the Utes refused to go, alleging
that the treaty had been fraudulent, and dissatisfied
because an agency site had not been chosen on Los
Pinos Creek, as promised.   Their view of the matter
was sustained by many, including the legislature.   In
1872 the agency was moved from Abiquiú to Tierra
Amarilla, farther north.   In 1873, by another treaty,
the Utes promised to go to Colorado 'after a while;'
but again became disgusted with the choice of an
agency site, and with having to go north for their
goods before final transfer.   By several acts of congress, however, of 1877–8, and by abolishing the
southern agency, they were finally removed to the Colorado reservation in April to July 1878; and New
Mexico was thus rid of them.

The Jicarillas it was at first desired to remove to
Bosque Redondo, but they were unwilling to go there,
and General Carleton was unwilling to receive them.
In 1870 the Maxwell rancho was sold, and this still
further complicated matters, as the Indians had an
idea that they were the real owners.   The suspension
of annuities in 1871, a measure adopted for effect on
the Utes, greatly disgusted the Jicarillas.   In 1872
the Cimarron agency was nominally abolished, and an
effort was made to move the Indians south to Fort

Stanton or Tularosa, but most of them were permitted to go to Tierra Amarilla, though rations were still distributed in the east. In 1874 a reservation of 900 square miles was set off east of the Navajo reserve and north of the river; but nothing further was done toward moving the Indians, who seem to have been willing, though refusing to go south. There was an act of 1878 requiring them, on the departure of the Utes, to be sent to Fort Stanton, and 32 of those at Cimarron went there; but the rest refused, and on the suspension of supplies committed many thefts. In 1880 they desired a home in the north; five chiefs visited Washington; the act of 1878 was repealed; and in July a new reservation on the Rio Navajo was selected, to which they were removed in December. Here they lived until 1883, when, against the views of the military authorities, they were again transferred to Fort Stanton, where they have since remained.[17] (On April 13, 1887, the day that this page goes into type, the newspapers announce that they are to be returned to the northern reservation.)

A list of agents in charge of the pueblos is given in a note,[18] to which is added a brief chronologic

[17] In a recent article in the *Century* (1887), it is stated that 100 Jicarillas have left the reserv. and bought lands north of Sta Fé, paying in horses, and founding a colony. Besides the annual *Ind. Aff. Repts*, see *U. S. Govt Doc.*, 41st cong. 2d sess., Sen. Mis. Doc. 97; 43d cong. 1st sess., H. Ex. Doc. 130; 2d sess., H. Ex. Doc. 138; 45th cong. 2d sess., Sen. Doc. 8, 21; *N. Mex., Laws*, 1869–70, appen. 6–10; *Id.*, 1870–2, p. 68–9; *Dead Men's Gulch*, MS., 4; *Dixon's White Conquest*, i. 215, etc.; *Sac. Rescue*, June 13, 1872.

[18] Pueblo agents: John Ward 1864–8 (Toribio Romero also in '66), Charles L. Cooper 1869–71 (Geo. E. Ford spec. agent in '69), W. F. M. Arny 1871–2, John O. Cole 1872–3, Ed. C. Lewis 1873–4, B. M. Thomas 1874–83, Pedro Sanchez 1883–4.

1864. Pueblo grants patented, all but two, amounting to 687 sq. miles. Retrograde in education since '46. In 10 years but one charge of theft against a Pueblo Ind. in 1st district, embracing half of the pueblos. Pop. 7,066. Grants of 15 towns cover 434,864 acres.

1865. Crops largely lost by flood and grasshoppers. All the grants but those of Laguna and Acoma patented.

1866. Supt urges that the sale of liquor be prohibited; also sales of lands, past sales being annulled; and that suits against Ind. be brought only in U. S. courts. None of the younger Ind. can read or write, nor do they learn to speak Spanish or English. Catholic efforts for schools meet no encouragement from Ind. or govt. Gov. says pop. is 7,066, families 1,282, children 2,084; only 49 can read and write. 1867. Decision of Justice Slough that the Ind. are citizens.

summary of their record for these years, as drawn from agents' reports and other sources.   Their number was

1868.   Ind. complain that so much is done for others and nothing for them.   No resident priests except at S. Juan and Isleta.   Some encroachment on Ind. lands; and some damage by floods.   Report in favor of Sta Ana land claim.   *U. S. Govt Doc.*, 40th cong. 2d sess., H. Rept 70.

1869.   Ind. much imposed on under the citizenship decision of '67, subsequently confirmed by Chief Justice Watts; case carried to U. S. sup. court; agents oppose the decision, and Ind. do not wish to be citizens.

1870.   Approp. of $5,000, and some implements distrib.   Some Ind. declined them because there were not enough for all.   The gov.'s message contains statistics.

1871.   Approp. of $5,000.   Arny's report contains full statistics, as follows: Ind. pop. 7,310, white pop. on pueblo grants 5,543; able to read and write 57; teachers 13 (but really no schools in actual operation).   Zuñi is not included in the report.   Zuñi and Sta Ana had no grants of land; while those of Laguna and Acoma were not surveyed.   As to the white residents, the Ind. were generally willing to let old settlers remain, and A. opposes their removal, but would prohibit further sales and require each settler to prove 5 years' residence, no family to have over 160 acres.   Yet there were many disputes about land and water, and many complaints of illegal trade and trespass.   Pop. by pueblos as follows: Acoma 344, Cia 121, Cochití 243, Isleta 768, Jemes 344, Laguna 927, Nambé 78, Pecos 35 (living at Jemes), Picurí 127, Pujuaque 32, S. Felipe 482, S. Ildefonso 156, S. Juan, Sandía 186, Sta Ana 1,530, Sta Clara 189, Sto Domingo 735, Taos 397, Tesuque 98.

1872.   Pop. 7,683.   Some controversy on relig. matters.   Citizenship question still pending.   Ind. have served on juries.   All teachers not able to teach English discharged; 5 or 6 schools doing fairly well.   Arny went east and made arrangements for teachers for 14 pueblos, paid half by govt and half by religious bodies.

1873.   Failure of crops.   No drunkenness.   No justice in Mex. courts. Confirmation of the citizenship decision by U. S. sup. court feared, as it would deprive the Ind. of all protection.   Priests hinder all educational efforts, not favoring instruction in English.

1874.   Crops good.   8 schools with 298 pupils (or 6 with 170).   Opposition to educ. decreasing.   1875.   7 schools, 139 pupils.   Women's industrial school at Cochití.   Some pueblos need more land.   1876.   Presbyterian mission at Laguna under Rev. Menaul and wife.

1877.   Numbers slowly decreasing (?).   Six schools, 155 pupils; attendance irregular.   Mission at Laguna has 50 pupils and a printing-press.   Bad crops. Land set apart for Zuñi.   Jemes in the courts succeeded in ejecting settlers. Boundary troubles between Acoma and Laguna, caused by interference of settlers.

1878.   Good progress in schools.   School at Jemes opened and doing well. Zuñi school under Rev. H. K. Palmer and wife opened, but had to be closed. Llewellin Harris, Mormon missionary, claims to have cured many of small-pox, exciting jealousy of the presb. at Zuñi.   Near Z. was a Mormon settlement of Savoya (Sevilla or Cebolla).   *Spencer's Labors in the Vineyard*, 61–4.

1879.   Zuñi school under Rev. T. F. Ealy, M. D., 44 scholars, many of whom died of small-pox.   20–30,000 sheep.   Pop. 9,013.   School at Jemes under Dr Shields and 2 young women from Pa.

1880.   The railroads cut several pueblo grants, causing much trouble about right of way.   Schools at Laguna, Zuñi, and Jemes prosperous.   10 children, half from Zuñi, sent to Carlisle, Pa, for education.   A witch executed at Zuñi.

1881.   Exact census 9,060.   School at Zuñi, S. A. Bentley and Miss Hammaker; at Laguna Rev. Menaul and Miss Perry; at Jemes J. M. Shields and Miss Harris; average attendance at the 3 schools 81.   In Jan. a boarding and industrial school opened at Alburquerque by presb., 40 pupils.   10 more

given as from 7,000 to 9,000; but in the earlier estimates and counts the Zuñis seem to have been omitted, and the real number may be regarded as having increased from about 8,500 to somewhat over 9,000. They are still the same peaceable and inoffensive, industrious, simple, credulous, and superstitious people that they have always been. In their character and primitive manner of life there has been no essential change. They were neglected during this later period by the priests, and the work of protestant missionaries has but slightly affected them; though at Laguna a body of so-called protestants became strong enough to engage in certain controversies. Except in paying an agent's salary, appropriating $10,000 in 1871–2 for implements, and paying a part of teachers' wages, the government did nothing for them, and they have given the military and civil authorities no trouble. Their land grants were patented and surveyed, though a few boundary disputes occurred later, and the Indians have been often imposed upon by trespassing settlers. For some seven or eight years from 1867 a decision of the supreme court that the Pueblos were entitled to the privileges of citizenship caused much trouble, because, while they did not desire these privileges, a way was opened to great wrong to them in suits with settlers tried before local courts. I have not found the final decision, if there was one, by the United States courts; but there seems to have been no com-

children sent to Pa. Map showing location of pueblo grants, in *U. S. Govt Doc.*, 47th cong. 1st sess., H. Mis. Doc., xx., 319.

1882. Trouble with R. R. at Sto Domingo, the Ind. refusing right of way and land for station. Schools somewhat prosperous, though the priests work against them, and Ind. do not wish the children to be anything but Ind. City of Alburquerque gave 65 acres of land for the school under J. S. Shearer, and later R. W. D. Bryan. A reader printed in Laguna language. 18 children at Carlisle, Pa, school when 5 Ind. went to visit them, and were much pleased.

1883–4. Good progress under Agent Sanchez, but the leasing of lands by Ind. as at Acoma is bad. On the Alburquerque school, which had as high as 114 pupils of different tribes besides the pueblos, see *N. Mex. Indian School*, a collection of printed sheets, from newspapers, etc.; also *Bryan's Alburquerque Ind. School*, MS. I might add many references to descriptive matter on the Pueblo manners and customs, language, origin, traditions, and early annals; but these have properly no place in connection with my present subject.

plaint since 1875.   In education, from about 1873,
earnest efforts were made by the presbyterians, aided
by the government; and schools were established at
several pueblos with considerable success, especially
at Laguna, Zuñi, and Jemes.   Some 20 children were
also sent to Carlisle, Pennsylvania, to be taught; and
in 1881 an Indian boarding-school was founded at
Alburquerque, where in later years over 100 pupils
from all the tribes were gathered; and at latest accounts the results were most encouraging.   This is
almost the only ray of light penetrating the blackness
of prospective Indian affairs in New Mexico.

Of the Apaches, the Mescaleros are the only band
besides the Jicarillas whose annals can be presented
separately.   I append a list of their agents, and a
chronologic résumé.[19]   The Mescaleros were in many

[19] Mescalero agents: Lorenzo Labadi 1864–9 (though at times there was
practically no agent), A. G. Hennisee 1869–71, A. J. Curtis 1871–3, S. B.
Bushnell 1873–4, W. D. Crothers 1874–6, F. C. Godfroy 1876–9, S. A. Russell 1879–81, W. H. H. Llewellyn 1881–4.
    1864. At Bosque Redondo much dissatisfied with the presence of the Na-
vajos, of whom they killed 64 in two fights.   Behaved well in other respects,
selling $4,000 worth of fruit and vegetables, but lost most of their corn crop.
Pop. 427.
    1865. Pop. 472. No change.   1866. Did well until Nov. 3d, when all but
9 left the reserv. on account of troubles with the Navajos, going more or less
on the war-path.   The agent was accused of stealing cattle, or at least of irregularities in trading, and was sent off by Gen. Carleton. 1867. No change.
    1868. Agency nominally at Agua Negra, but the Ind., 525 strong, never
visited it, and continued their depred.   No approp. for several years.   They
would probably accept a reserv. at Ft Stanton, but never at the Bosque.
    1869. No change. Ind. not seen except by Lieut. Stanwood on a scout.
Agency at Ft Stanton, where a reserv. with 500 acres of good land seems to
have been set off (probably the mil. reserve). 1870. No change, except that
the Mescalero and southern agencies are said to have been consolidated in
July.
    1871. Agent Curtis found 27 Ind. on the reserv. and soon had 325, ex-
pecting the rest of the 760.   Prospects good if means are supplied.
    1872. Mescal. over 800 and other Apaches over 1,000 at Ft Stanton.   Prom-
ises not kept by govt. Great need of clothing and of mil. protection, as the
Navajos have made some raids (?).   Whiskey causes much trouble. Reserv. to
be chosen this winter. Legisl. recommends a reserv. s. E. of the fort.   300
Apaches from Tularosa came in, but the Mescal. were opposed to their remaining.
    1873. Reserv. set off, but not surveyed. Ind. roving and committing many
depred.   In Sept. all but 200 ran away on account of the arrest of certain
Ind. as hostages for the return of stolen property. Traders too influential,
but Bushnell attempted reforms.
    1874. Reserv. of 675 sq. m. by order of Feb. 29, '73, and Feb. 2, '74.

respects similar to the Jicarillas. They sometimes, however, engaged in farming, and they also at times joined the other Apache bands in their raids. Their number was between 600 and 800. About 400 were gathered at the Bosque Redondo until November 1866, when, on account of their quarrels with the Na-

From 300 to 700 on or near the reserv.; disposed to roam, but few depred. Not much agric. land, and no disposition to engage in farming.

1875. Ind. accused of depred. and attacked by settlers in Jan. They ran away and were again attacked and a few killed. They were brought back in a starving condition. Inspector McNulta reported that the Ind. were not to blame. A school-house ready.

1876. Reserv. extended by order of Oct., but not yet suitable. Whiskey and the proximity of 2 Mex. settlements do much harm. Ind. work well; have 597 horses and 122 mules. Some feuds with Hot Spring Ind. Mescal. can be made self-supporting in 3 years; they have been grossly misrepresented

1877. Reserv. unfit; agency or settlers must be removed. No buildings. Agent has selected a site at Elk Spring, 15 m. east. Ind. behave well. Would do better in stock-raising than agric. Work interrupted by smallpox. Reserv. raided by Texans in July, and 13 horses driven off. Much illegal traffic. On account of disorders, agent will have to remove his family.

1878. Settlers of two factions engaged in murderous warfare. Ind. much alarmed. Two bands have quit the reserv. Agency must be moved from the main road, and out of the way of Amer. and Mexicans. School doing well, considering circumstances.

1879. Very little planting and only 600 acres fit for cultivation. Ind. kill their horses to eat at feasts. No school; no proper buildings. Victorio and his band came in from S. Cárlos, Ariz. Gen. Pope thinks the Mescaleros do no more harm than other reserv. Ind., but still the reserv. is useless, and serves as a scapegoat for all Ind. troubles, real and imaginary.

1880. Victorio left the reserv. soon after the last report, and induced over 200 Mescaleros to join him in his depredations. In April the rest were alarmed by the coming of troops, and an attempt to disarm them, by Gen. Pope's orders—the agent blaming Col Hatch—caused an affray in which several were killed. Before this it had been proposed to move the Mescal. to Hot Spring.

1881. All in confusion; contradictory reports. Lincoln co., 'under control of thieves and cutthroats,' is no place for the Ind., who should be moved north, which Gen. Pope also urges, as it is impossible to discriminate between the hostile and peaceful. Agency 40 m. s. w. of the fort; reserv. 30 by 36 miles, the 'garden spot of N. Mex.' Ind. quiet; marked improvement (!); school only moderately prosperous; Ind. falsely accused of taking part in raids.

1882. The agencies of Mescal. and Jicarillas had been consolidated with intention of moving Mescal. to north; but Inspector Howard decided to let them remain, but to give up certain lands to miners, etc.; hence the change in reserv. Ind. doing fairly well; 85 acres cultivated; Ind. police of 20 successful in preventing thefts and arresting renegades. They arrested emissaries from Hot Spring, and saved the agent's life in a fight in which several Ind. were killed. Day-school well attended, and some children sent to Alburquerque, but Apache mothers will not part with their girls. The change of reserv. at petition of the legisl. restored five townships to public domain in favor of the Nogal mining district, and disposed of all private claims but two; Ind. consented to the change.

vajos, they left the reservation, and became roving
and hostile.   In 1871 over 300 were reunited at Fort
Stanton, and the number increased to about 800 in
1872.   Here a reservation was set off in 1873-4, and
the Indians were kept under control more or less, and
a little progress was made in farming and education;
though there were almost continuous feuds with settlers, miners, and other Indian bands.   The reservation boundaries were several times changed.   In
1879-81 many of the Mescaleros joined the southern
Apaches in their raids; and many serious complications
resulted, it being difficult or impossible to distinguish
between the guilty and innocent, and there arising
many controversies between the agents and the military on these points.   The location of the reservation
so near the frontier, where the Indians were exposed
to the raids and solicitations of the renegade bands,
was most unfortunate, and a change was often urged,
but never effected.   From 1882 there was a slight renewal of good conduct and comparative progress; in
1883 the Jicarillas were brought to this reservation;
and from that time neither band has caused any
serious trouble.

The southern Apaches of New Mexico, exclusive of
the Mescaleros, consisting chiefly of the Mimbreños
and Mogollones—together known as the Gileños—but
including at times a portion of the Arizona Chiricahuas, numbered from 1,500 to 1,800.   Their annals are
much less definite than those of other tribes, as they
were generally more or less beyond the control of
agents, and spent a part of the time in Arizona and
Mexico.   The list of agents and a summary of annals
are appended.[20]   In 1864-9 these bands were gener-

[20] Southern Apache agents: John Ayres 1868-9 (at Sta Fé), Charles E.
Drew 1869-70 (at Ft McRae), A. G. Hennisee 1870-1 (at Ft Craig), O. F.
Piper 1871-3 (Ayres in charge '72), B. M. Thomas 1873-4, John M. Shaw
1874-6, James Davis 1876-7.   Ind. nominally removed to S. Cárlos, Ariz., in
1877.
    1864.   Gen. Carleton's mil. operations extending through this and the fol-
lowing years.   1865.   Interview of Gen. Davis with Victorio, Nané, etc., at

ally hostile, but were hard pressed by the troops.
Depredations were constant, but the loss of life was

the copper mines, and efforts to induce the Apaches to go to Bosque Redondo.
The chiefs gave some encouragement; but depred. continued. Carleton declined to permit Supt Steck to go for a talk with the Mimbres, who must
surrender without conditions.

1866. Intention to make a campaign against the Mimbres and estab. a
post. A Gila reserv. spoken of, but no Ind. on it. 1867. No change, but
continued hostilities. 1868. Agency at Limitar; constant depredations.

1869. Ind. thought to be tiring of war. Chiefs interviewed by Agent
Drew and willing to go on a reserv. at Hot Spring, which is recommended.
1870. Over 500 Mimbres and Mogollones, with a few Mescaleros, being fed at
Cañada Alamosa. Gen. Pope has no hope of estab. the Apaches on a reserv.,
but agent thinks differently. Agency consolidated with that of the Mescaleros in July, but there is no further trace of this change.

1871. From 1,200 to 1,900 Ind. at Cañada Alamosa, who, however, ran off
when Colyer's escort appeared. Cochise and his Chiricahuas submitted this
year, and came in to the Cañada. Colyer, the peace com., decided to fix the
reserv. farther north-west, at Tularosa, because of the unsuitableness of the
Cañada for agric., and the proximity and opposition of the settlers, who at a
public meeting complained of thefts of cattle and crops, and made preparations to use forcible measures.

1872. About 450 Ind. removed in April, much against their wishes, to the
new reserv. at Tularosa. The rest, including Cochise's band, had run away
to avoid removal. About 1,000 went for a time to the Mescalero reserv., and
many resumed their raids.

1873. From 600 to 700 on the reserv. very discontented; depred. frequent.
The efforts of Maj. Price to enforce the return of stolen cattle caused all to
run off, but 700 were caught and brought back.

1874. Ind. transferred, in accordance with their wishes, to the vicinity of
the Cañada, and a new reserv. of 750 sq. m. set off at the Ojo Caliente, or Hot
Spring, where they behaved better, and even worked a little. Cochise died
this year, and a Chiricahua reserv. was estab. in s. e. Arizona.

1875. Apaches quiet; 1,700 on the Hot Spring reserv., receiving their
rations and committing no depred. A little farming. Whiskey causes some
trouble. Settlers ejected, and new buildings being erected.

1876. General peace and a little progress. A slight trouble in April was
promptly quelled by military. About 250 Chiricahuas came to Hot Spring,
when their reservation was broken up, a part of the tribe being removed to
S. Cárlos, and the rest going on the war-path.

1877. Ind. acc. to agent 'idle, dissolute, and drunken,' yet some encouraging results in agric. Gen. Pope pronounces them 'squalid, idle vagabonds,
utterly worthless and hopeless.' In April–May 450 of the Hot Spring Ind.
were forcibly transferred to S. Cárlos in accordance with the policy of concentration, the rest running off before the removal, the 450 soon escaping from
S. Cárlos, and all resuming their raids. There were many fights, Victorio being in command of the hostiles. About 200 surrendered in Oct., and were
returned to Hot Spring, but part of them ran off again. A party also came
in to the Mescalero reserv.

1878. Victorio in Feb. surrendered, but on the attempt to remove them
from Hot Spring ran away again. In June they came in voluntarily to the
Mescal. reserv., and it was decided to let them remain; but were frightened
off by the coming of county officials, the chiefs being under indictment for
murder, and fearing arrest. After a destructive raid they were driven into
Mexico.

1879–80. Congress decided against a proposition to move the Apaches to
the Ind. territory. Down to Sept. 1879, acc. to Gen. Pope's report, there
were no very serious troubles, though petty depred. never ceased; but then
Victorio with 60 Ind. came from Mex., and attacked the herders at Ojo Cali-

slight.   Then in 1870–1 about 1,800 of the savages,
tiring somewhat of war, were fed at Cañada Alamosa,
in the region of Fort Craig.   By Vincent Colyer a
reservation was selected at Tularosa, where about 500
—the rest going on the war-path—were transferred
against their will, and lived in discontent and trouble
during 1872–3.   In 1874 they were returned to near
their former home, and a reservation was set off at
Ojo Caliente, and here they lived in comparative quiet,
though without any real progress until 1877.   Then
the unwise concentration policy caused the Hot Spring
reservation to be broken up, and 450 of the Apaches
were forcibly removed to San Cárlos in Arizona.
From this time until 1882 southern New Mexico was
for the most part a bloody battle-ground.   The successive outbreaks and raids of Victorio, Nané, Loco,
Chato, Gerónimo, and others are mentioned in my
note, and more details are given in the chapter on
Indian affairs in Arizona.   Since 1882, though the
renegades from Arizona have several times raided the
frontier district, there has been comparative peace.
The management of the southern Apaches has been
a difficult problem; but the Indian department has
much to answer for in the disasters of the last decade,
since most of these may be traced to unwise removals
against the wishes of the Indians, in disregard of

ente, killing several and driving off 46 horses.   He was joined by 100 from
Mex. and by a large party of Mescaleros, and a bitter warfare ensued.   Col
Hatch took command and killed about 100 Ind., driving Victorio into Mex.
Hitherto the scattered Mex. herders in southern N. Mex. had been spared by
the Chiricahuas, to whom they rendered much aid; but now their Mescalero
and Comanche allies spared nobody, and from 70 to 100 settlers were killed.
Victorio twice recrossed the frontier and was driven back, being finally killed
in Mexico.   The newspapers in these years are full of items respecting these
raids.   A volunteer force was organized by the legisl.
    1881–2.   In July 1881 and April 1882 the renegades, now under Nané,
made bloody raids across the border, and were driven back.   They had been
largely reënforced by the Mescaleros and by Chiricahuas from S. Cárlos, under
Loco.   The Hot Spring reserv. was now abolished, and all Apaches not at S.
Cárlos or on the Ft Stanton reserv. were treated as hostiles.   In 1882 an
arrangement was made by which the hostiles could be pursued across the
line.
    1883–5.   No troubles except with the renegades from Arizona under Geró-
nimo and Chato, who committed many atrocities on the southern border, notably the killing of Judge McComas and family in April '83.

promises made, and against the protests of the military authorities.   Of the Apaches, only the remnants of the Jicarillas and Mescaleros remain in New Mexico, and these under control on their reservation. Serious outbreaks are probably at an end.   The problem of ultimate improvement remains unsolved.

CHAPTER XXX.

INDUSTRIES AND INSTITUTIONS.

1864–1887.

Mineral Wealth — Mining Notes of 1864–79 — Great Prospects and Small Results—Statistics of Production—The Mining Districts—Gold, Silver, Copper, Coal, and Iron — The 'Boom' from 1880 — Authorities — Résumé of Developments — General Results and Prospects—Spanish and Mexican Land Grants—List of Claims—Public Lands and Surveys—Agriculture—Statistics—Slight Progress—Stock-raising—Cattle and Sheep — Monopoly and Other Obstacles—Manufactures—Trade—Railroads—Telegraph Lines—Stage and Mail Routes—Bureau of Immigration—Schools—Publications of the Jesuit College—Newspapers—Church Affairs.

From the earliest times New Mexico's prospective mineral wealth has been recognized, and there has hardly ever been a year, perhaps never a decade, in which a few mines of some sort have not been worked. The early Spanish workings, never successful on a large scale, have left traces at many points; but, as elsewhere fully explained, have been habitually and grossly overrated in modern times. Practically, nothing but prospecting was ever done by the Spaniards or Mexicans, and very little more by the Americans for many years after their occupation of the territory. Their small numbers, isolation, and lack of capital, the general apathy of the native population, the heavy cost of transportation, and frequent Indian troubles, afford sufficient explanation of the slight progress made, while each year's operations furnished additional foundation for faith in ultimate success.

Such work as had been previously undertaken was for the most part suspended, on account of the confederate invasion of 1861–2 and the ensuing Indian wars; though at Pinos Altos, in the south-west, a nucleus for future operations still remained; in Santa Fé county preparations for active work were being pressed forward at the Old and New Placers; and each year the natives washed out a considerable quantity of gold in the wet season at many different points. The annals of New Mexican mining in 1864–79 would consist of a long series of detached items, not without interest in themselves, but entirely too bulky for presentation here. I append some general notes and references.[1] The yield of gold and silver has been

[1] See *N. Mex.*, *Acts*, 1864 et seq., as per résumé already given, for legislative action on mines, including the incorporation of many companies. For mining laws of the territory at different periods, see *N. Mex.*, *Revised Laws*, 726–32; *Mills' Hand-book of Min. Laws, and Guide to N. Mex.* Las Vegas, n. d., 12mo, 35 p.; *Raymond's Silver and Gold* (1873), p. 453–9; *Rand's Guide to Colorado*, 85; *Avery's Hand-book of N. Mex.*, 95–7; *Rand & McNally's Overland Guide*, 236–7; *N. Mex.*, *Business Directory*, 1882, p. 185–97; *Ritch's Blue-Book*, 127–8. For mining information in the successive years, see the annual reports of the surveyor-gen. of N. Mex., in *U. S. Land Office Reports*, 1864 et seq.; also *Raymond's Reports* on statistics of mines and mining, 1869 et seq.

1864. *N. Mex. Mining Comp., Preliminary Report.* N. Y., 1864, 8vo, 21 p. This comp. had been organized in '53, and incorporated in '58, to work the Old Placer mines, having purchased the Ortiz grant. This pamphlet contains by-laws, act of incorp., extracts from Gregg, etc., and corresp. intended to 'boom' the company's enterprise. Operations continued for several years, with no very great success, so far as this comp. was concerned. Not much done anywhere this year, on account of the Indians.

1865. Quartz-mill being built at the Ortiz mine. Furnaces at Las Cruces at work on ore from the Organos Mts; 2–300 miners at work at Pinos Altos, with good prospects. *Owen (Richard E.) and E. T. Cox, Report on the Mines of N. Mex....Published by John S. Watts.* Wash., 1865, 8vo, 59 p. This is a report of a geologist and chemist, including an examination of several mines; published in the interests of some comp., and showing everything in somewhat bright colors.

1866. Much prospecting and many discov., including the Moreno mines, Colfax co. N. Mex. Min. Co. at work; another comp. organized to work the mines farther south in same district. Little progress in smelting at Las Cruces, for want of capital. Machinery en route to Pinos Altos. Gold deposited at U. S. mint, $3,155. Gov. Arny's *Message* treats of 'mineral resources,' indicating that nothing much is being done. Copper discov. near Ft Union. *Meline's 2,000 Miles*, 170–9, has a chapter on mines, with something of personal observation. *Clifford's Overland Tales*, 367–83, has a chapter on 'my first experience in N. Mex.' in '66, a pleasing sketch of life at Ft Bayard, and some information on the mines. Sir Morton Peto's *Resources*, N. Y., 1866, p. 170–1, mentions the copper mines of the s. w.

1867. *Browne and Taylor's Report*, 324 et seq., contains Com. J. W. Taylor's report on N. Mex. mines, chiefly made up from old auth., and Gov. Arny's message of '66. It is also found in *Hunt's Merch. Mag.*, lvi. 208, and *Goddard's Where to Emigrate*, 143. Much development at Pinos Altos; 1,000 men at work; 600 lodes within 6 miles; 15-stamp mill. Gold found near

estimated at $125,000 to $250,000 per year down to
1868, $500,000 annually in 1869–74, and $400,000 in

Taos, and 400 men at work.   Ore at Old Placers yields $27.   Many discov.
of silver, but no work.   Fifty silver mines in the Organos Mts.
 1868.   Moreno mines produced about $200,000 in placer gold.   Some in-
form., especially on the Ortiz mine, in the gov.'s message.   The S. F. newspapers of '68–9 have many items.
 1869.   Gold product, $500,000; no silver.   The Moreno mines in 3 districts
—Ute Cr., Willow Cr., and Elizabethtown—yielded $200,000, of which
$100,000 was from the Aztec mine.   Hydraulic machinery at work in the
gulches; 270 lodes registered at Pinos Altos and Central City; product from
quartz, $60–70,000.   Mills at Old and New Placers badly managed; chief
mines, the Cunningham, Ortiz, and Brahm.   Coal being mined at the Placers.
Ditch projected from the Pecos.   Gold and silver lodes on the Arroyo Hondo,
in north.   Gold-washing near Abiquiú.   Carson lode in Manzano Mts very
rich.   Lincoln co. mines, gold placers and quartz—Sierra Blanca, Carriza, and
Jicarilla—showing well.   Recent discov. of copper and silver in the Magdalena Mts, Socorro co.   The Organos Mts yield 80 per cent lead and $50 silver.
Prof. Hayden, *U. S. Geol. Survey*, 1st, 3d rept, visited and described several
min. districts, and has much to say on coal and other minerals.
 1870.   Chief excitement at Ralston (Shakespeare), and Ciénega, Grant co.,
where the silver lodes proved rich and numerous.   Increased production of
the Moreno mines, the Aztec paying $62,000 in 3 months.   In Sta Fé the N.
Mex. Min. Co. had suspended operations.   Large deposits of iron, but as yet
no smelting.   On anthracite and other coal beds, see *Raymond's Report;* and
McFarlane's Coal Regions, 72–6; *S. F. Scientific Press*, April 29, 1871.   Mining
stat., in *U. S. Census Reports*, 9th, Industries.   Items and corresp. on the
Burro mines, or Virginia dist (Ralston), in *Hayes' Scraps, Mining*, iii. 206–9,
212–14, 217–26.
 1871.   Increased yield from Moreno quartz and placers; Maxwell rancho
sold to an English co.   Artesian well of 300 ft at the Sta Fé placers not successful.   Details of Pinos Altos region in report of R. Sturenburg, in *Land
Off. Rept;* prospects good, but no true fissure veins yet discovered.   Some
silver development in the Corona del Pueblo dist, Socorro co., but mines badly
managed and results exaggerated.   Hayden's *U. S. Geol. Surv. Rept* has information on coal deposits.
 1872.   No material improvement or important discov.   Gold yield of
Moreno and the Placers $100,000; Aztec mill suspended.   Grant co. pros-
perous, but operations stopped at Ralston for want of machinery.   Prod. of
the co. $350,000.   Silver City lively, with 4 mills which produced $6,990 in a
week.   Richness of Socorro co. mines confirmed.   Ruby dist, in Rio Arriba
co., shows some activity; includes the reported diamond-fields; many precious
stones exhibited by Ayres and Buckley.   For 1872–4, see *Raymond's Statistics; Id., Silver and Gold; Id., Mining Industry;* all being his annual reports,
separately published.
 1873.   Encouraging success at Silver City.   Among the claims surveyed
are many in Ruby and Spring Hill dist.   Wheeler's *U. S. Geog. Survey*, iii.
632–6 and passim, contains much on the anthracite coal and other minerals.
Partly reproduced in *Ritch's Illust. N. Mex.*, 118–23.
 1874.   Eleven mining claims surveyed.   Not much new development; but
great activity in the old districts, especially in Grant and Socorro.
 1875.   Eleven claims surv.   Wheeler, *U. S. Geog. Surv. Rept*, 1876, p. 66–7,
143–4, 201, describes the Aztec dist in Colfax, said to have yielded $1,000,000
since '68; 12 veins; greatest depth 180 ft; yield per ton $60; formerly a mill,
now only arrastras.   Also the Sta Fé placers, where only a little rude washing is done; nothing on the rich veins.   An article on the copper mines in
Coast Review, vii. 375–7.
 1876.   Nothing new of importance.   Many claims surveyed.   Capital much
needed.   Wheeler, in his report of 1877, p. 1295–1303, describes the northern

1875–80.   The total deposit of gold in United States mints and assay offices down to 1867 was only $85,459. The chief developments during this period were in the districts of western Colfax and Taos counties, where gold placers were profitably worked whenever water could be obtained, where ditches were constructed and hydraulic methods introduced to some extent, and where, at intervals, stamp mills were running after 1868; in Sta Fé and Bernalillo counties, at or near the old and new placers, where the customary washing operations were supplemented by several not very successful experiments in quartz-mining, though the veins were rich, where a mica mine was worked to some extent, and where a bed of pure anthracite coal was opened; in the Sandía and Manzano ranges of Bernalillo and Valencia, where nothing beyond prospecting was practically effected; in the Magdalena Mountains of Socorro, where rich deposits of silver and lead were found; in the region of Fort Stanton, or the Mescalero reservation, Lincoln county, where were rich gold placers and numerous quartz veins; in the Organos Mountains of Doña Ana, the silver ores from which were smelted without much real success at Las Cruces; and above all, in the counties of Grant and the later Sierra in the south-west, where the old copper mines were for the most part unworked, but where gold was washed from many gulches, and where

minerals, quoting from a work by De Groot and Leembruzzen, pub. in Dutch in 1874.   See also *Sta Fé, Centennial Celeb.*, 30–4.

1877.   Fine deposits of mica worked 75 m. N. W. of Sta Fé.   Rich placers near Ft Stanton, in Sierra Blanca, but great lack of water.   The prod. of the year is estimated by the surv.-gen. as $304,000 gold, chiefly from placers; $496,000 silver, chiefly from Grant co.; 2,010,000 lbs. copper, chiefly from Grant; and 850,000 lbs. lead, chiefly from Socorro.

1878.   Increased yield.   New impetus expected from early completion of the R. R.   Mica mines flourishing.

1879.   The gov. in his report takes a very favorable view of the prospects, declaring that the era of prosperity has begun in earnest.   Las Animas Peak gold dist, in Doña Ana, is a recent discov. of rising repute.   Other new developments are at Hillsborough, Ft Stanton, in the Sandía and Manzano mts, near Alburquerque, Los Cerrillos in Sta Fé, near Taos, and in Moreno district.

For statistics of production to 1879, chiefly founded on the estimates of Valentine, of Wells, Fargo, & Co., see *Balch's Mines, Miners, etc.*, 512; *Del Mar's Hist. Prec. Metals*, 168; *Las Vegas Min. World*, 149; *U. S. Sec. Treas.*, Rept on Finances, 1866–7.

many silver mines were developed and many more discovered, especially in the districts of Pinos Altos, Silver City, Burro Mountains, Hillsborough, and Lone Mountain. This was the most prominent section, having several mills at work and producing more silver bullion than all the rest of the territory.

From 1879–80 there was a veritable 'boom' in the New Mexican mines, the railroad bringing a large influx of prospectors, and, what was still more essential, of capitalists, from abroad. So numerous and complicated were the new developments that only the briefest résumé can be presented here.[2] Numerous

[2] Leading authorities are the *Las Vegas Mining World*, 1880 et seq., a paper devoted to the mining interests of N. Mex., and full of useful information, especially in 1880–2, later articles being of a more general and less valuable nature; *Burchard, H. C., Report of the Director of the Mint upon the production of the precious metals in the U. S.*, Wash., 1880–3; *U. S. Land Office Reports*, 1880 et seq.; *Balch (Wm R.), The Mines, Miners, and Mining Interests of the U. S. in 1882*, Phil., 1882, 4to; *N. Mexico, Scraps*, a collection of newspaper clippings; *N. Mexico, A Complete Business Directory and Gazeteer of the Territory*, Sta Fé (1882), containing a description of the mineral resources by counties; *Santa Fé Trail*, 1881 et seq.; *Ritch, Wm S., Illustrated New Mexico* (Sta Fé), 1883; *Id., Aztlan*, Boston, 1885, a later ed. of the same work; *N. Mex. Bureau of Immigration Report on Bernalillo Co.*, by Wm C. Hasledine (on Doña Ana by A. J. Fountain; Grant by W. H. Lawrence; Lincoln by J. J. Dolan; Mora by Wm Krœnig; Rio Arriba by Sam. Eldodt; S. Miguel by G. W. Prichard; Sta Fé by C. W. Greene; Socorro by M. Fischer and Ant. Abeitia; and Taos by L. C. Camp). All or most of these were published as separate pamphlets in 1881–2; and all together in *N. Mex. the Tourist's Shrine*, Sta Fé (1882), which contains also *Ritch's N. Mex. and its Resources*, all with much mining matter; *Avery's Hand-book of New Mexico*, Denver, 1881, 16mo; *Arizona History* (Elliott & Co.).

1880. Total prod. of bullion: gold $677,499, silver $626,078; total of ore raised from deep mines $861,309; worked $441,691; average yield of gold ore $6.62, silver $52.65. *Balch*. Valentine's estimates of total prod. in '80, $711,300; '79, $622,800. More discov. than in the past 20 years. Southern placers at Pinos Altos, Hillsborough, Nogal, and Jicarillas doing well, but lacking water. At the New Placers a pipe line nearly completed. Rich placers found on the Rio Grande in north, and on Rio Hondo and Colorado. Prof. Silliman reports that the region from Embudo north contains very extensive deposits of gold gravel for hydraulic mining, 600 feet thick—the most important gold discov. made since Cal. and Australia. The Old Placers or Ortiz grant sold to a N. Y. and Cal. co., and in this region hydraulic min. to be done on a large scale. Grant co. mines booming; only one smelter at work outside of Grant. Good results in Socorro mines. Other districts, most of them new, which promise well are Silver Buttes, near New Placers, Placitas in Sandía Mts, S. Simon, Shakespeare, Cook's Peake, and McEvers in Grant co., White Oaks and Nogal in Lincoln, S. Agustin in Doña Ana, Picuríes in Taos, Las Vegas, or S. Cárlos dist, in S. Miguel, Hell Cañon, east of Alburquerque, Black Range, in Socorro and Sierra, with many mines, and Los Cerrillos in Sta Fé. *Hayward, J. L., The Los Cerrillos Mines*, South Framingham, Mass., 1880, contains a brief history of the Cerrillos and Galisteo districts, with regulations, list of mines, and maps showing hundreds of

as they are, these developments are confined for the most part to the old regions, which, however, cover a

claims. Prof. Silliman also describes these mines, only a few of which were developed. The ores were rich and the situation on the R. R. and near coal-beds excellent. Here was a turquoise mine, and somewhat extensive old Spanish workings. The *Shakespeare Mining Journal* was published at St Louis to boom the Burro mines. The Homestake mine, White Oaks dist, is mentioned as the richest gold mine in N. Mex. Coal was found in several new places, one of them near Alburquerque. The Cooney dist and gold mines of Cañon del Agua are described in *Tucson Star*, Nov. 24–5, '80.

1881. Wonderful development and almost daily discoveries, though private land grants and Ind. are great obstacles. 40 claims surveyed, of which Cooney, Encarnacion, and Mimbres districts are new. Product of the year, Valentine's estimate, $814,944, of which $705,000 was ore and base bullion, exported; the local prod. being $32,944 gold and $77,000 silver. Mint deposits to June '81, $54,940 gold, $262,212 silver. Coal area on U. S. lands 1,080 acres, sold 720 acres. The coal mines at Amargo, Rio Arriba, yield 225 tons per day. There is no other min. development in this co. Taos has many rich mines; hydraulic operations on Rio Hondo, Bernalillo districts, Hell Cañon, Tijeras Cañon (copper, silver, and lead); New Placers, where water has been brought 15 m. from Sandía mts; and Nacimiento, copper, in the Jemes region. Mora co. believed to have much min. wealth, but undeveloped on account of the land grant. S. Miguel has Mineral Hill, S. Cárlos, Sweepstakes, and Blue Cañon; but only slight development. Socorro's prominent mines are Socorro Tunnel, Torrence, and Merritt; the richest in Central N. Mex.; 3,000 locations in past 6 months; bullion shipped to date $1,067,834; R. R. of 8 m. to the coal-beds to be completed this year. In Grant co. Silver City ranks 1st and Georgetown 2d for the whole territory in prod. of bullion. One mine at Silver City has yielded $1,200,000. The Lake Valley dist (Sierra co.) is wonderfully rich, perhaps the greatest deposit in the world, chlorides yielding $5,000 to $20,000 per ton. 4 groups and comp., each with a capital of $5,000,000; smelters and mills being built. The copper mines of the south-west not worked. New copper discov. in the Oscuras mts, Socorro, said to be the best yet found.

1882. Total prod. of N. Mex. mines: gold $150,000, silver $1,800,000. Of the total of 1,950,000, Sierra, Grant, and Socorro produced $1,820,000. Bernalillo prod. $5,000 silver. The Sandía mts gold and silver and Nacimiento copper mines promise well. In the N. W. are very extensive coal-beds, from 4 to 11 ft thick. Doña Ana (excluding what later became Sierra), prod. very small, but fair prospects in Organos dist at Memphis, Merrimac, Modoc, Iron King, Little Buck, and Copper Duke mines; also copper, gold, and silver in Jarilla dist. Colfax, prod. $20,000 gold. Copper mines on Poñil Cr. 600,000 acres of coal-fields, extensively worked, at Raton. Grant, prod. $425,000 silver, $35,000 gold (but including, apparently, part of what was later Sierra co.). Leading districts: Percha, about Kingston; Silver City, where the Seventy-six mine has prod. in 10 years $1,500,000; Pinos Altos, with much placer and arrastra working, prod. $27,900; Central City, including the Sta Rita Copper and Iron Co.'s mines, greatest depth in the Romero 330 ft; Hanover, copper, silver, iron, lead, and gold; Georgetown, extensive workings in many mines, prod. $287,898 in silver; Lone Mountain, rich chloride silver ores, less worked than formerly; Burro mt. mines, including Oak Grove, Paschal, Bullard's Peak, and Cow Springs dist; Cook's Peak, Tres Hermanns, Victorio, Virginia, S. Simon, Telegraph, Eureka, Steeple Rock, Gillespie, Florida mt., and Carizillo; nearly all having extensive developments, much too complicated for mention here. Lincoln, prod. $40,000 gold, $25,000 silver; co. particularly rich in free gold, with also silver, copper, iron, and coal; not much development of deep mines; leading district White Oaks; others, Gullimas, Jicarilla, Nogal, Rio Bonito, and Vera Cruz; great expec-

very large part of the territory's area. Every county
has proven rich in mineral wealth, and in only a few—

tations and preparations for work. Mora, rich prospects in gold, silver, copper, iron, and coal; but no development, on account of the land grant. Rio
Arriba, great resources, but practically no work done; districts, Bloomfield,
Aztec, and the coal mines of Amargo. San Miguel, some progress at Mineral Hill and Blue Cañon; but generally nothing but prospecting, with good
results. Sta Fé, prod. $25,000 gold, $15,000 silver; numerous mines in Los
Cerrillos and New Placers dist; prod. of the S. Pedro works $20,000 gold,
$10,000 silver, 400,000 lbs. copper; 15,000 acres of anthracite coal; 400 tons
mined for Sta Fé market. Sierra (included in Doña Ana), prod. $900,000
silver, $20,000 gold; chief district Lake Valley, where the Lincoln mine has
prod. $838,958 in bullion in '82; also the Hillsborough dist, with extensive
preparations for hydraulic mining. Socorro, prod. $430,000 silver, $10,000
gold; silver and copper deposits very extensive, but development hindered
by lack of capital and Ind. hostilities; districts, Socorro, Magdalena, Water,
Mogollon or Cooney, Black Range, Apache, Cuchillo Negro, Palomas S.
Cristóbal, Mound Springs, Ladrones, Iron mt., Pueblo, Gallinas, Limitar,
Pittsburg, S. Andrés, Oscuras, Taos, no product; some rich developments of
gold, silver, and copper, especially in Picuríes, Arroyo Hondo, and Rio Cristóbal dist, besides placer mines. Valencia: Spiegelberg, La Joya, and Ladrones
dist; much low-grade ore in these new dist not yet worked.
    1883. Prod. $2,845,000 silver, $280,000 gold, total $3,125,000, of which all
but $99,000 was prod. in Grant, Sierra, and Socorro counties; Valentine's estim.
$3,413,519. A 'Permanent Territorial Mineral Exhibit' estab. at Sta Fe
after the Tertio-millenial celebration The districts were mainly as before;
in the following résumé by counties, from Burchard, only new and important
items are noted. Bernalillo, old Span. mine opened in Las Huertas Cañon;
gold found in old bed of the Rio Grande, near Alburquerque; promising discovery in Tijeras Cañon. Colfax, prod. of gold $25,000. Doña Ana, great
activity in the Organos, especially in the Memphis copper and lead mines;
also discov. in the Sacramento range. Grant, prod. $1,200,000 silv., $110,000
gold; rich discov. in Bald mt. and Bear mt. dist; Silver City is the centre
of mining activity in N. Mex.; much progress in Steeple Rock gold mines;
Carroll is a new dist; Monument dist rich in copper and lead; Florida dist
rich in lead. Lincoln, prod. $24,000 gold, $10,000 silv.; still much activity
in White Oaks and the other dist. Mora, strike in Poverty Hill mine, near
Ocate. Rio Arriba, good promise in gold quartz and placers of the Headstone dist. S. Miguel, great excitement over gold discov. at Las Vegas.
Sta Fé, prod. $15,000 gold, $10,000 silver; new discov. of gold, silv., and
copper in the north; Pecos dist in east, copper and silv.; Sta Fé gold dist
3 m. from the city, and Thayer Camp copper mines 8 m. Sierra co. (with
Doña Ana), prod. $1,225,000 silv., $85,000 gold; Lake Valley, including
Sierra Grande, Sierra Bella, and Apache, still flourishing and prod. $100,000
per month; Hillsborough, with the Bobtail mine, also productive. Socorro,
prod. $400,000 silv., $6,000 gold; many discov., more systematic working, decreased production; Iron Reef, new dist. Taos, $15,000 gold.
    For 1884 the gov. reports prod. greater than ever before, though no statis-
tics are obtainable. Prod. according to the newspapers $3,660,614. Ritch's
Aztlan, of 1885, presents a view of mining progress by counties, showing encouraging progress in most districts. This work has also a chapter on 'the
coal-fields of New Mexico.' Immense copper deposits in Bernalillo are described. Colfax, from its placers and gold quartz, has yielded $2–3,000,000
since '68, having also an unlimited extent of bituminous coal, worked only at
Raton. The Doña Ana, or Organos, mines promise great things, and rich
prospects are found in the Potrillas Range. Grant is still the banner county,
with its many districts and thousands of rich mines. In Lincoln the White
Oaks, with its famous Homestake mine, is still the central district; Red Cloud

Rio Arriba, Mora, Valencia, and San Miguel—has this wealth not been extensively developed. The south-western counties of Grant, Sierra, and Socorro have produced nine tenths of all the bullion, and have to some extent drawn attention from the northern region; though Santa Fé county mines are very numerous. The bullion product of gold and silver is given as $1,300,000 in 1880, $815,000 in 1881, $1,950,000 in 1882, $3,125,000 in 1883, and $3,660,-000 in 1884, most of which was produced in a few districts and a few mines of those districts. The results seem small in view of the rosy-hued reports of 1880–2, after which years there was a noticeable reaction from the somewhat extravagant boom. There was much exaggeration of mining values in most sections, for speculative purposes, much mismanagement, and especially much effort to work mines without sufficient capital. The surface deposits were wonderfully rich and complicated; and much expensive machinery proved useless when more rebellious ores were reached. Very few mines reached a depth of over 300 feet. The low price of copper and lead, with which the gold and silver were largely mixed, had a very depressing effect. While the Lake Valley mines and some others have shown large bodies of ore whose richness has rarely, if ever, been equalled, it must be confessed that no deep mines at all comparable to the Comstock, Leadville, or Tombstone have been developed. Yet there is nothing, so far as I know, to

and Bonito are other districts. Rio Arriba has had no boom, but has illimitable mineral wealth, millions (!) having been taken out by former inhabitants. The Amargo coal mines prod. 17,240 tons of coal in '83. Headstone dist has rich placers and veins, with considerable development. Sta Fé mines still increasing in number, with good prospects of tin, rich gold discov. at Jumbo, close to the city, and the invaluable beds of anthracite. S. Miguel shows little development, but fine ore at Rociado, near Las Vegas. Sierra has Lake Valley, the best district in the territory, and several other rich districts. At Lake Valley $15,000,000 in sight, ore running $100 to $27,000 per ton. In the 'Bridal Chamber' pure silver may be melted off with a candle; and Gov. Safford offered $50,000 for the ore that he could extract unaided in 10 hours. The Percha and Hillsborough dist hardly less rich. Socorro prod. $1,228,266 in '84; 53 districts; smelters of 240 tons per day capacity and 15 stamps. Taos camps prosperous. In Valencia, rich mineral deposits, undeveloped.

indicate that such developments may not be confidently expected. New Mexico among the states and territories in 1880 ranked eighth in the production of silver and thirteenth in gold, being tenth in production of the precious metals in the aggregate, per square mile, and per capita of population. There are no definite statistics of the copper and lead production, though these metals are found in immense quantities in many parts. There is hardly any metal or mineral not found in the territory. Mica and turquoise are mined successfully not far from Santa Fé. Coal deposits extend in all directions, though extensively worked only at Amargo and Raton in the north; and near the capital are the only beds of anthracite to be found west of Pennsylvania. Iron ore is reported as abundant, and in close proximity to iron and limestone, a fact that cannot fail to have a deep significance for the future. Gravel deposits of gold are found in most of the counties, so rich that they have paid fair returns to miners who brought water in barrels or carried the dirt long distances in a dry season; and while hydraulic mining has not yet been largely remunerative in the few trials that have been made, there can be little doubt of ultimate success. No country has a climate better adapted to the mining industry; wood and water are amply sufficient in most districts for deep mining; ores are rich and widely distributed; practically, what has been done in the past is mere prospecting; and there seems to be no good reason to doubt that in the future, when land-grant difficulties are settled, the best methods ascertained, transportation facilities secured, and capital invested, this territory will rank among the first in the production of gold, silver, copper, iron, lead, and coal.

The whole number of private land claims filed in the surveyor-general's office down to 1886, exclusive of the earlier pueblo Indian claims, was 205. Of these 13 were originally rejected and 141 approved,

leaving 51 not acted upon.   Of the approved claims
46 were confirmed by congress, leaving 95 still pending before that body; while patents were issued for
only 15 of the confirmed claims.   By instructions from
the land-office, dated July 23, 1885, however, 35 of the
claims originally approved were re-examined by Surveyor-general Julian before March 1887; and of these
23 were disapproved, six approved as equitable, three
approved in part, two fully approved, and in one case
a new survey ordered; so that of approved cases only
62 are now pending before congress.   Meanwhile, all
the approved claims but 13 have been surveyed, and
found to embrace an area of 13,128,581 acres, the
pueblo claims containing in addition 1,092,266 acres.
I have thought it best to append a complete list of
the grants, showing all desirable data.[3]

[3] See p. 758.   My authority for the list is the statements in the surveyor-
general's annual reports, in *U. S. Land Office Reports*, 1864 et seq. (also a
MS. letter of Surv.-gen. Julian, dated March 3, 1887, on transactions subsequent to July 1883), but a large portion of the same data from the same
source is found also in a table in *Ritch's Legisl. Blue-Book*, 129 et seq., prepared
by Dav. A. Miller; also in *Mills' Hand-Book*, Las Vegas, n. d., 8vo, 35 p.   See
also résumé of legisl. proceedings for successive acts on matters connected
with Span. and Mex. grants.   Many congressional bills on the subject are
recorded in the *Globe* and *Journals*, which, as they did not become laws, I
have not cited.   Additional ref. in chronologic order, chiefly made up of the
surv.-gen.'s reports and congressional action on the same, are as follows:
1865.   *U. S. Govt Doc.*, 39th cong. 1st sess.; *Mex. Aff.*, ii. 7, on the claim for
the site of Ft Craig.   1866.   One claim confirmed.   1868.   *Id.*, 40th cong. 2d
sess., H. Rept 71.   1869.   Five claims confirmed by act of March 3d; mem.
of legisl. and rept of com. on other claims.   *Id.*, 40th cong. 3d sess., Sen.
Rept 198; Sen. Miscel. Doc. 2; *Globe*, 1868–9, appen. 304–5; *U. S. Statutes.*
1870.   One claim conf.   1871.   Reports on various claims, with doc. *U. S. Govt
Doc.*, 41st cong. 3d sess., H. Ex. Doc. 106; 42d cong. 2d sess., H. Ex. Doc.
296; H. Mis. Doc. 181; discussion, chiefly on the R. Grande claim, see *Cong.
Globe* and *H. and Sen. Journals*, per index.   1872.   Reports and doc., including a petition of citizens on the Maxwell (Beaubien & Miranda, No. 15) grant,
42d cong. 2d sess., Sen. Jour. 344, 562; H. Mis. Doc. 181; 3d sess., H. Ex.
Doc. 68; Sen. Doc. 37, 40, 45, 50.   1873.   Reports and doc., 42d cong. 3d
sess., H. Ex. Doc. 37, 40, 128; 43d cong. 1st sess., H. Ex. Doc. 148–9, 206,
213, 258, 280; Sen. Doc. 3, 35, 58.   1874.   Ditto, 1st sess., H. Ex. Doc. 239;
Sen. Doc. 43, 56; 2d sess., H. Ex. Doc. 62; Sen. Doc. 2, 3, 35, 38.   Brevoort,
N. Mex., 124, says that as yet no fraudulent claims have been discovered and
few are believed to exist.   *N. Mex., A Voice from, on Private Land Claims*,
Wash., 1874, 12mo, 7 p., is a defence of the grants, particularly of the
Maxwell grant, assailed by Sen. Sargent in debate.   See also *Catlin's Maxwell Dynasty*, MS., 1875, 44th cong. 1st sess., H. Rept 50; Sen. Doc. 31.
1876.   Discussion. *Cong. Globe*, 1873–6, per index.   1877.   *Id.*, 1876–7, 44th
cong. 2d sess., H. Rept 110–11.   1878.   45th cong. 2d sess., H. Rept 149, 222,
463.   1879.   45th cong. 3d sess., H. Rept 59.

TABLE OF NEW MEXICAN PRIVATE LAND GRANTS.—Grants, the numbers of which are marked *, have been reëxamined since July 1885, and disapproved by the surveyor-general. Those marked † have been on reëxamination approved only as

No.	TRACT.	GRANTEE.	CLAIMANT.
1	Ojito del R. Gallinas.....	Juan E. Pino........	Preston Beck, Jr..
2	Tomé, town.............	J. Varela et al.......	....
3	Tierra Amarilla..........	M. Martinez & sons..	....
4	Sangre de Cristo.........	Lee & Beaubien......	....
5	Casa Col., town..........	R. Gutierrez et al....	....
6	Bracito.................	J. A. García et al.....	....
7	Tecolote, town...........	S. Montoya et al.....	....
8	Los Trigos..............	F. Trujillo et al......	....
9	La Junta...............	John Scolly et al.....	....
10	Nra Sra de la Luz........	C. Herrera...........	Bishop Lamy.....
11	Chilili, town.............	S. Padilla et al.......	....
12	Agua Negra.............	Ant. Sandoval.......	....
13	Belem, town.............	D. T. Salazar et al....	....
14	S. Pedro...............	J. Miera et al........	J. S. Ramirez.....
15	Cimarron or Rincon......	Beaubien et al.......	....
16	Los Esteros.............	P. J. Perea..........	....
17	Las Animas.............	Vigil & St Vrain.....	....
18	Cañon de Pecos..........	J. D. Peña et al......	{ Alex. Valle...... / J. Estévan et al..
19	S. Cristóbal.............	Dom. Fernandez.....	E. W. Eaton......
20	{ Vaca Location 1.........	L. M. C. Vaca.......	Heirs of Vaca.....
	" " 2.........	L. M. C. Vaca.......	Heirs of Vaca.....
	Vegas Grandes........	L. M. C. Vaca.......	Heirs of Vaca.....
20	Las Vegas, town.........	J. D. Maese et al.....	....
21	Tajique, town............	M. Sanchez et al.....	....
22	Torreon, town...........	N. A. Montoya et al..	....
23	Manzano, town..........	J. M. Trujillo et al...	....
24	S. Isidro, town..........	Armenta et al........	....
25	Cañon de S. Diego........	García de Noriega et al.	....
26	Jornada del Muerto.......	A. J. Rivera et al....	....
27	Las Trampas, town.......	J. Argüello et al.....	....
28	S. Joaq. Nacimiento......	S. Martin........	....
29	Anton Chico, town.......	S. Tapia et al........	....
30	Laguna tracts............	....	Rep. V. Duran et al.
31	....	V. Duran de Armijo..	G. Ortiz..........
32	Mora, town.............	J. Tapia et al........	....
33	Valverde & Fr. Cristóbal..	P. Armendariz.......	Heirs of A........
34	....	P. Armendariz.......	Heirs of A........
35	Bosque del Apache.......	A. Sandoval........	....
36	Chamita, town..........	A. Trujillo	....
37	Tejon, town.............	S. Barreras et al.....	....
38	....	P. Sanchez..........	Ramon Vigil......
39	Cañoncito or Sta Clara....	Gerv. Nolan.........	....
40	Cañon del Agua..........	J. S. Ramirez........	....
41	....	P. Montoya..........	....
42	Gallinas................	Ant. Ortiz...........	....
43	Ortiz Mine..............	Ortiz & Cano........	E. Whittlesey et al.
44	Espirito Sto Spr..........	L. M. C. Vaca.......	....
45*	Añil Spr................	J. Sutton............	....
46	Cebolleta, town..........	F. Aragon et al.......	....

equitable claims. Those marked ‡ have been approved for a part of the claim; and those marked §, fully approved. The material for these and other late additions to March 1887 have been kindly furnished me by Surv.-Gen. Geo. W. Julian.

No.	Date	County	Filed	Appro.	Conf.	Surv.	Pat.	Acres
1	1823	S. Mig....	1855	1856	1860	1860	......	318,699
2	1739	Valencia..	1856	1856	1858	1859	1871	121,594
3	1832	Taos	1856	1856	1860	1877	......	594,515
4	1843	Taos	1855	1856	1860	....	......	(In Col.)
5	1823	Socorro...	1856	1856	1858	1877	......	131,779
6	1823	D. Ana ...	1856	1856	1860	1878	......	10,612
7	1824	S. Mig....	1855	1856	1858	1859,'83–4	......	21,636
8	1815	S. Mig....	1855	1857	1860	1860, 1877	......	9,646
9	1846	Mora.....	1856	1857	1860	1877	......	108,507
10	1820	Sta Fé....	1856	1857	1860	1861	1874	16,546
11	1841	Bern......	1857	1857	1858	{ 1877 1859 1883 }	......	{ 23,626 38,435 ...... }
12	1824	S. Mig....	1856	1857	1860	1877	......	17,361
13	1740	Valencia..	1857	1857	1858	1859	1871	194,463
14	1839	Sta Fé....	1857	1857	1860	1866	1875	35,594
15	1841	Colfax	1857	1857	1860	1878	1879	1,714,764
16	1825	S. Mig....	1857	1857	1860	1871	1877	17,712
17	1843	(Colorado).	1857	1857	1860	....	......	....
18	1815	S. Mig....	1857	1857	1860	1877	......	574
19	1827	Sta Fé....	1855	1857	1860	1860	1880	{ 81,032 27,854 }
20	(1860)	Bern......	1855	1858	1860	1877	......	99,289
	(1860)	S. Mig. ...	1855	1858	1860	1861	......	99,289
	1835	S. Mig. ...	1855	1858	1860	....	......	....
20	1835	S. Mig. ...	1855	1858	1860	1860	......	496,446
21	1834	Valencia..	1857	1859	1860	1877	......	7,185
22	1841	Valencia..	1856	1859	1860	1877	......	14,146
23	1829	Valencia..	1856	1859	1860	1877	......	17,360
24	1786	Bern......	1857	1859	1860	1877	......	11,476
25	1798	Bern......	1859	1859	1860	....	1881	116,286
26	1846	Socorro...	1859	(rej.)	......	....	......	......
27	1751	Taos	1859	1859	1860	1877	......	46,461
28	1712	R. Arriba .	1859	1859	1860	1877	......	51,387
29	1822	S. Mig	1859	1859	1860	{ 1883–4 1878 1860 }	......	{ 383,856 ...... 389,662 }
30	......	Valencia..	1857	1859	1860	....	......	101,510
31	1739	Sta Fé....	1859	1859	1860	1877	......	57
32	1835	Mora.....	1859	1859	1860	1860	1876	827,621
33	1820	Socorro....	1859	1859	1860	1872	......	397,235
34	1820	Socorro....	1859	1859	1860	1872, 1878	1878	95,030
35	1845	Socorro ...	1859	1859	1860	1871	1877	60,117
36	1724	R. Arriba .	1859	1859	1860	1877	......	1,636
37	1840	Bern......	1856	1859	1860	1877	......	12,801
38	1742	S.F.&Bern.	1856	1859	1860	1877	......	31,802
39	1845	S. Mig. ...	1855	1860	......	1883	......	575,968
40	1844	Sta Fé....	1859	1860	1866	1866	1875	3,501
41	1824	S. Mig. ...	1856	1860	1869	1872	1877	655,468
42	1819	S. Mig. ...	1857	1860	1869	1877	1877	163,921
43	1833	Sta Fé....	1856	1860	1861	1862	1876	69,458
44	1815	Bern......	1856	1860	1869	1877	......	127,875
45*	1838	Val.......	1858	1861	......	1877	......	69,445
46	1807	Bern......	1859	1861	1869	{ ...... 1878 1877 }	......	{ 199,567 224,770 200,848 }

No.	TRACT.	GRANTEE.	CLAIMANT.
47	Los Luceros	P. Vigil de S. et al...	Ant. Leroux
48	Rio Don Cárlos	G. Nolan	
49	S. Fern. & S. Blas	B. M. Montaño et al..	
50*	Cañada de Apaches, or Alamos	A. Sedillo	
51*	Middle Spr	N. A. Montoya	
52		Roque Lobato	
53	Cañada de Alamos or Apaches	L. Marquez	
54	Cuyamunque	B. Sena et al	
55*	Encinas.	J. B. Valdés	
56	La Gotera	J. D. Peña et al	
57	Cañada S. Francisco	J. F. Vaca et al	
58	R. Rio Grande	J. Mirabal et al	
59	Los Cerrillos	J. M. Peña et al	
60	Galisteo, town	F. Sandoval et al	
61	Cebolla	J. C. Santístivan et al..	
62†	Cieneguilla..	J. Sanchez et al	
63	Caja del Rio	N. Ortiz	
64	Mesita de T. Lopez	D. Romero et al	
65	Cajon de R. Tesuque	J. Gabaldon	
66*	S. Joaq. Nacimiento	J. Luna et al	
67*	S. Clemente	Ana Sandoval	
68⫟	Chamigos Hill	L. Armenta	
69	Alamitos	J. Salas et al	
70*	Estancia	A. Sandoval	
71†	Cañon de Chama	F. A. Salazar et al...	
72	Apache Spr	V. Trujillo	
73	Piedra Lumbre	P. Martin	
74	Chamizos Arr	Marquez & Padilla...	
75*	Sierra Mosca	I. L. Ortiz	
76⫟	S. Ant. Rio Col., town	R. Archuleta et al	
77	Ojo Caliente, town	L. Duran et al	
78	S. Miguel Spr	B. Fernandez	
79*	S. Lorenzo Arr	A. Chavez	
80		J. Mestas	
81	Cuyamunque, pueblo	A. R. Aguilar	
82*	Cerros Negros	S. Gonzalez	
83	Bernalillo, town	F. Gutierrez	
84	Angostura	J. J. Gonzalez	
85	Ancon de D. Ana	Colonists	
86	Mesilla	Colonists	
87*	Sierra Mosca	V. Duran de Armijo..	G. Ortiz
88	Sta Fé, city	City	
89	Talaya	M. Trujillo	
90	Refugio	Colonists	
91*	Alameda, town	F. M. Vigil	
92	Jacona, town	Roibal et al	
93*	Cañon del R. Col	A. E. Armenta et al..	
94	Uña de Gato	Bernal & Lopez	
95	Sevilleta	C. Gabaldon et al	
96*	Chaco Mesa	I. Chavez et al	
97	Sta Teresa de Jesus	I. Mestas	
98*	Cañada de Alamos	Miera y Pacheco et al..	
99*	Nra Sra del Pilar	F. Tafoya et al	

No.	DATE.	COUNTY.	FILED.	APPRO.	CONF.	SURV.	PAT.	ACRES.
47	1743	Taos......	1857	1861	1869	1877	......	126,024
48	1843	(Colorado).	1860	1861	1870	....	......	......
49	1753	Bern......	1869	1870	......	1877	......	151,056
50*	1769	Bern......	1871	1871	......	1877	......	88,079
51*	1831	Val.......	1863	1871	......	1877	......	3,546
52	1785	Sta Fé....	1871	1871	......	1877	......	1,619
53	1785	Sta Fé....	1856	1871	......	1877	......	13,706
54	1731	Sta Fé....	1871	1871	......	1877	......	1,086
55*	1814	R. Arriba .	1871	1871	......	....	......	6,583
56	1830	Sta Fé....	1871	1871	......	{ 1879 1877 1883 }	......	{ 479 2,571 789 }
57	1840	Sta Fé....	1871	1871	......	1877	......	1,589
58	1795	Taos......	......	1872	......	1877, '79-80	......	109,043
59	1788	Sta Fé....	1871	1872	......	1877	......	2,287
60	1814	Sta Fé....	1871	(rej.)	......	....	......	......
61	1845	Taos......	1872	1872	......	1877	......	17,159
62†	1795	Taos......	1872	1872	......	1878	......	43,961
63	1742	Sta Fé....	1871	1872	......	1877	......	62,343
64	1782	Sta Fé....	1872	1872	......	1877*	......	{ 42,022 43,022 }
65	1752	Sta Fé....	1872	1872	......	1877	......	11,619
66*	1769	R. Arriba .	1871	1872	......	1879	......	131,725
67*	1716	Val.......	1855	1871	......	1877	......	89,403
68.	1732	Sta Fé....	1872	1872	......	1879	......	444
69	1840	Sta Fé....	1872	1872	......	1877	......	436
70*	1845	Val.......	1855	1873	......	1877	......	415,036
71†	1806	R. Arriba .	1861	1872	......	1877	......	472,736
72	1842	S. Mig. ...	1872	(rej.)	......	....	......	......
73	1766	R. Arr....	1872	1873	......	1877	......	48,336
74	1742	Sta Fé....	1872	1873	......	1880	......	637
75	1846	Sta Fé....	1872	1873	......	1879	......	33,250
76.	1842	Taos......	1872	1874	......	1880	......	18,955
77	1793	R. Arr....	1873	1874	......	1878	......	38,590
78	1767	Bern......	1873	1874	......	1877	......	25,176
79*	1825	Soc.......	1873	1874	......	1877	......	130,138
80	1699	Sta Fé....	1872	1874	......	1878	......	1,686
81	1699	Sta Fé....	1872	1874	......	1878	......	36
82*	1742	Sta Fé....	1873	1874	......	1879, 1882	......	103,959
83	1701	Bern......	1874	1874	......	1878	......	11,674
84	1745	Bern......	1874	1874	......	1879	......	2,319
85	1839	D. Ana ...	1874	1874	......	1878	......	19,323
86	1853	D. Ana ...	1874	1874	......	1878	......	33,960
87*	1806	Sta Fé....	1873	1874	......	1879	......	......
88	......	Sta Fé....	1874	1874	......	1878	......	17,361
89	1731	Sta Fé....	1874	1874	......	1879	......	1,003
90	1852	D. Ana ...	1874	1874	......	1878	......	26,130
91*	1710	Bern......	1872	1874	......	1879	......	106,274
92	1702	Sta Fé....	1874	1874	......	1878	......	46,341
93*	1836	Taos......	1872	1874	......	1878	......	42,939
94	1839	Colfax....	1874	1874	......	1878	......	......
95	1819	Soc.......	1874	1874	......	....	......	224,770
96*	1768	Bern......	1874	1874	......	1879	......	243,046
97	1768	Bern......	1874	1874	......	1877	......	3,632
98*	1768	Bern......	1874	1874	......	1879	......	148,862
99*	1767	Bern......	1874	1874	......	1877	......	22,578

No.	TRACT.	GRANTEE.	CLAIMANT.
100	Bosque Grande...........	M. & S. Montoya....	....
101	Lagunitas.	Ant. Vaca...........	....
102	S. Mateo (Marcos) Spr....	A. U. Montaño......	....
103*	Agua Salado.............	L. Jaramillo.........	....
104	Encinal.....	B. Vaca & sons......	....
105†	Petaea.....	J. J. Martinez et al...	....
106*	Goat Spr................	J. Otero............	....
107†	Socorro, town............	J. García et al......	....
108*	Vallecito de Lobato......	J. R. Zamora........	....
109	Rancho Taos.............	F. A. Gijosa........	....
110	S. Cristóbal.............	S. & A. Martinez	....
111*	Sta Teresa..............	F. García...........	....
112	{ Mesilla...............	J. Trujillo...........	....
	{ Arroyo Seco...........	J. Trujillo..........	....
113*	Cañ. Pedernales..........	J. B. Valdés........	....
114	Sta Bárbara.............	V. Martin et al......	....
115‡	Cieneguilla..............	F. A. Almazan......	....
116	Lucero de Godoy.........	A. Martinez........	....
117	Orejas del Llano.........	J. J. Lucero........	....
118	Ojo de Borrego...........	N. A. Montoya......	....
119§	S. Mig. del Vado........	L. Marquez et al.....	....
120	....	J. Dominguez.......	....
121	Maragua	Vaca et al..........	....
122	Cañon de S. Diego.......	F. & J. A. García....	....
123	S. Isidro.................	I. S. Vergara.......	....
124	Peña Blanca............	J. M. Vigil.........	....
125	S. Fern. de Taos........	Inhabitants.........	....
126	Torreon	B. Vaca............	....
127	....	B. E. Edwards......	....
128	Las Truchas.............	F. M. Vigil.........	....
129	....	J. M. Sanchez......	....
130	Alburquerque	Inhabitants.........	....
131	Polvadero	J. P. Martin........	....
132†	Hermosa Estrella........	C. Ant. Salazar.....	....
133	....	....	Ant. R. Lujan.....
134	S. Mateo Spr	S. Duran y Chavez...	....
135	Cañ. de Cochití.........	Ant. Lucero........	...---...........
136	La Madera..............	S. Ramirez.........	....
137†	Arroyo Hondo...........	Seb. Vargas........	....
138‡	Cañ. Sta Clara..........	Indians of pueblo.....	....
139*	Sto Tomás Iturbide......	Colonists...........	....
140	Abiquiú, town...........	Inhab..............	....
141	....	Dom. Valdés........	....
142	Sto Dom. & S. Felipe.....	Inhab..............	....
143	Ocate..................	Man. Álvarez.......	....
144	Las Huertas.............	A. Aragon et al......	....
145	Atrisco	Inhab..............	....
146	El Tajo.................	D. Padilla..........	....
147	....	J. A. Lucero........	....
148	Plaza Blanca............	Man. Bustos........	....
149	Plaza Colorada...........	R., J., & J. Valdés...	....
150	Cañ. de Carnué	J. A. Lafoya et al....	....
151	El Rito.................	Town..............	....
152	Guadalupita	P. A. Gallegos et al..	....
153	....	{ P. Gallegos & J. M. } { Maes .... }	....

No.	Date.	County.	Filed.	Appro.	Conf.	Surv.	Pat.	Acres.
100	1766	Bern.	1874	1874	......	1879	......	3,253
101	1762	Bern.	1874	1874	......	1878	......	{ 46,643 / 43,643 }
102	1754	Sta Fé	1873	1874	......	1878	......	1,890
103*	1769	Bern.	1874	1874	......	1870	......	18,046
104	1768	Bern.	1874	1874	......	1879	......	12,207
105†	1836	Taos	1875	1875	......	1878	......	186,977
106*	1845	Val.	1875	1875	......	1879	......	4,340
107†	1846	Soc.	1875	1875	......	1878	......	843,259
108*	1824	Taos	1875	1875	......	1878	......	
109	1715	Taos	......	1878	......	1880,'83–4	......	114,400
110	1815	Taos	......	(rej.) '79	......	......	......	
111*	1790	D. Ana	......	1879	......	1883–4	......	
112	1700	Sta Fé	......	{ 1879 }	......	1880	......	
112	1707	Sta Fé	......	{ 1879 }	......	......	......	5,999
113*	1807	R. Arr	......	1879	......	1883–4	......	
114	1796	Taos	......	1879	......	1880	......	18,489
115‡	1693	Sta Fé	......	1879	......	1880	......	{ 43,244 / 45,244 }
116	1716	Taos	......	1878	......	1880	......	67,480
117	1826	Taos	1877	r.'79,'85	......	......	......	
118	1768	Bern.	......	1880	......	1880	......	60,214
119	1794	S. Mig	1857	1880	......	1880	......	315,300
120	1702	Taos	......	(rej.) '80	......	......	......	
121	1826	Sta Fé	......	1880	......	1883–4	......	
122	1788	Bern.	......	1880	......	1880	......	9,752
123	1809	Bern.	1857	1881	......	1883–4	......	
124	1754	Bern.	......	1881	......	1883–4	......	
125	1799	Taos	......	1881	......	1883–4	......	
126	1819	Val.	......	(rej.) '82	......	......	......	
127	......	Val.	......	1882	1882	1883–4	......	
128	1754	R. Arr	1882	1882	......	1883–4	......	
129	1853	D. Ana	1856	1882	......	1883–4	......	
130	......	Bern.	1882	1883	......	1883–4	......	
131	1766	R. Arr	......	1883	......	1883–4	....	
132†	1835	Mora	......	1883	......	1883–4	......	
133	......	Mora.	......	1883	......	1883–4	......	
134	......	Mora.	......	1883	......	1883–4	......	
135*	1728	Bern.	1882	1883	......	1885	......	104,554
136	1744	Sta Fé	1857	1883	......	1885	......	6,165
137†	......	Sta Fé	1882	(rej.) '84	......	....	......	....
138‡	1763	R. Arr	1882	1885	......	....	......	....
139*	1853	D. Ana	1885	1885	......	....	......	....
140	1754	R. Arr	1883	1885	......	....	......	....
141	1742	Sta Fé	1885	(rej.) '85	......	....	......	....
142	1770	Bern.	1884	1885	......	....	......	....
143	1837	Mora	1855	(rej.) '85	......	....	......	....
144	1767	Bern.	1862	(rej.) '85	......	....	......	....
145	1768	Bern.	1881	1886	......	....	......	....
146	1718	Bern.	1872	1886	......	....	......	....
147	1732	Sta Fé	1885	1886	......	....	......	....
148	1739	R. Arr	1861	1886	......	....	......	....
149	1739	R. Arr	1861	1886	......	....	......	....
150	1819	Bern.	1871	1886	......	....	......	....
151	......	R. Arr	1883	1886	......	....	......	....
152	1837	Mora	1885	(rej.) '86	......	....	......	....
153	1790	Sta Fé	1886	1886	......	....	......	....

Claims Pending before the Surveyor-General.

FILE No.	FILED.	TRACT.	GRANTEE.	COUNTY.	DATE.
4	1855	Ciénega	City of Sta Fé	Sta Fé	1715
5	1855	....	J. Ortiz	Sta Fé	1840
7	1855	Chaperito, town.....	S. Martin et al........	S. Miguel..	1846
23	1856	Angostura de Pecos .	J. M. Sanchez et al....	S. Miguel..	1842
26	1856	Cubero, town.......	Settlers	Valencia ..	1834
35	1856	Mora tract	E. Sandoval et al......	Mora......	1835
37	1856	Sta Rosalía.........	I. Cano..............	Sta Fé	1833
59	1859	Vallecito, town	Settlers	Bernalillo .	1777
71	1859	Rio Picuríes	R. Fernandez et al.....	Taos......	1832
72	1859	Macho Bend........	F. Gonzalez et al.....	S. Miguel..	1846
75	1861	Arquito	R. Archiveque........	Bern	1840
76	1860	Angostura..........	Jer. Gonzalez	S. Miguel..	1843
77	1860	S. Antonito........	C. Jaramillo	Bern	1826
79	1861	Rito de S. José.....	P. Gonzalez et al......	Valencia ..	1847
80	1861	Conejos	J. M. Martinez........	(Colorado).	1833
81	1861	Arroyo Hondo	N. Sisneros et al......	Taos	1815
82	1861	Cañ. de Mesteñas....	V. Trujillo et al.......	Taos	1828
86	1861	Talaya	J. M. Tafoya et al.....	Sta Fé.....	1825
90	1858	Cardillal	J. Chavez et al........	Sta Fé	1846
91	......	S. Ant. Embudo	J. Marquez et al.......	Taos	1725
92	1860	....	G. Dávalos et al.......	D. Ana....	1846
94	1866	Guadalupita	G. Gold et al.........	Mora	1837
98	1871	Rio Tesuque........	Settlers	St Fé	.....
99	1872	Ranchos and towns..	Settlers	Bern......	.....
100	1870	Arkansas colony	Royuela et al.........	(Several)..	1832
101	1870	Lo de Vasquez......	J. Ortiz	Bern......	.....
103	1872	Sta Cruz	L. M. Vaca..........	Bern......	.....
104	1872	....	A. R. de Aguilar......	Sta Fé	1744
105	1872	Guadalupe, town....	Settlers	Taos	1854
106	1872	Frijoles	A. Montoya..........	Bern......	1814
107	1872	Sta Rita del Cobre ..	F. M. Elguea	Grant.....	1804
108	1873	Sta Teresa.........	....	....	.....
109	1876	....	C. D. Serna.........	Taos	1710
110	1876	S. Jerón. de Taos ...	F. A. Luejosa........	Taos	1715
112	1876	Rio del Oso........	J. A. Valdés.........	R. Arriba..	1840
113	1871	Peña Blanca, town ..	J. Pelaez...........	Bern......	1695
114	1863	Mesilla Val.........	M. Guerra et al.......	D. Ana....	1851
183	.....	Vallecito	J. G. Mora et al.......	R. Arriba..	1807
185	1881	S. José Spr........	P. Montoya et al......	Bern......	1768
186	1881	La Naza............	M. Lucero	R. Arriba..	.....
190	1882	S. Mateo Spr	....	....	.....
191	1882	....	A. Salazar...........	....	.....
192	1883	....	A. Jacques et al.......	....	.....
194	1883	Elguea.............	....	....	.....
195	1883	Sitio de Navajo	....	....	.....
197	1883	El Rito............	Joaq. García.........	R. Arr....	1780
198	1884	Pueblo Colorado	J. J. Lobato..........	R. Arr....	1740

It will be noticed that only eight claims were confirmed during the whole period, and only one after
1870; that down to that date only five claims were
filed and one approved; and that down to 1876 only
four had been surveyed. From 1871 many claims
were filed and approved, and from 1877 surveys were
pressed forward, the law that required claimants to
pay the cost of survey having been repealed. Of the
128 claims surveyed, however, only 46 have been confirmed by congress.

On the general subject there is little to be added to
what has been said in an earlier chapter. All the
claims should have been confirmed and surveyed long
before 1864. Then, and for ten years later, there was
no fraud or serious temptation to fraud. The claims
were perfectly valid under the treaty and laws. The
urgent necessity of a prompt settlement was continuously urged by the people, the legislature, the
governor, and the surveyor-general; but always in
vain, for the government did nothing, neglecting even
to fix a limit date for filing claims. No change was
made in the system. The surveyor-general was con-
fessedly and obviously unable to do justice to the
investigation, taking as a rule only ex parte testimony
and forwarding it to Washington, where congress had
even less facilities for an impartial examination. The
claimants, confident in the validity of their claims, and
noting the slow action of the government, were apathetic about filing their titles. From about 1874
frauds began to be discovered and suspected; and the
danger of fraud constantly increased with delay.
Twenty-three claims, originally approved, have recently
been rejected on reëxamination. I have neither space
nor data for a fair presentment of special cases; but
that many spurious claims or genuine ones fraudulently
changed or extended have been presented successfully,
there can be no question. One reason, and perhaps
the only intelligible one—beyond a vague feeling that
providence might one day show some way to annul

all such iniquities as rights under Mexican or Spanish grants—for the inaction of congress, was the fact that minerals, not originally included with the land, could not under United States laws be reserved after a patent or quit-claim had been issued.   As to the validity of the Mexican colony grants made after the treaty of 1848, I am not aware that any final decision has been made.   One of them—the Santo Tomás de Iturbide—has been rejected by the surveyor-general, though new evidence has since changed his opinion.

In the early years of Indian troubles and slight immigration, there was no demand for public lands, and no surveys were made in 1864–6; but from 1867 the work of surveying was carried on as fast as the small appropriations would permit, the amount being greatly increased from 1874.   The fact that the irrigable—and therefore the only desirable—land lay in narrow strips along the streams caused the regular township surveys to cover many unsalable tracts, prompting many demands for a change of system, which were not heeded.   These surveys also extended over more than a million acres of unsurveyed or unfiled private grants.   Another difficulty was the custom of the natives to live in settlements for protection, which custom interfered with the requirement of actual residence on homestead or preëmption claims.   Down to 1882 there had been surveyed about 21,000,000 acres of public lands, making the total surveys, including private and pueblo grants, with Indian and military reservations, nearly half of the territory's whole area of 77,568,640 acres.   For later years I have no exact figures, but the increase in public lands has been very large.   Sales and entries of public lands under the different acts amounted to about 415,000 acres, besides the mineral claims.   A second land district was created for the south at Mesilla in 1874.[4]

[4] See surv.-gen.'s annual reports, and tables connected therewith.   The approp. were $5–10,000 down to 1873, but later $30,000, more or less.   A bill for a change in system to accommodate settlers failed in congress 1866.   For bill of 1874 creating new land district, see *Zabriskie's Land Laws*, suppl ,

Agricultural progress has been slight in comparison with that of other regions. All the valley lands susceptible of irrigation will produce in fair quantity and excellent quality nearly all the crops of temperate and semi-tropical latitudes; and there are limited tracts in the mountain parks that are productive without irrigation; but the quantity of agricultural land in proportion to the whole area is much smaller than in most other states and territories. Statistics from the census reports of 1870 and 1880 are appended, requiring no explanation or comment.[5] Experience in

1877, p. 59. On homestead laws, see *Smyth's Law of Homesteads and Exemptions*, S. F., 1875, p. 45, 467. Wheeler's maps, in *U. S. Geog. Surv.*, contain a classification of lands in parts of N. Mex. For desert land act of 1877, see *U. S. Stat.*, 49th cong., 2d sess., 377. 89 entries of desert lands were made in 1878–82. The unsurveyed irrigable lands were estimated in 1878 at 8,000,000 acres. In 1878 there was an act of the legisl. authorizing the occupation of 320 acres, with title good against all but the U. S.; and a memorial for the privilege of buying 1–5,000 acres by a bona fide settler. In his message of 1883 the gov. notes that the homestead and preëmption laws result in the worst kind of monopoly, since, with 160 acres about a spring, a vast tract was controlled free from taxation. For table of sales in 1872–82, see 47th cong. 2d sess., *H. Ex. Doc. 72*, p. 146.

[5] See *U. S. Census Reports*, 9th and 10th census. The 1st figures in each case are for 1870, the 2d for 1880, and the 3d for 1882, from the *U. S. Agric. Report*, 47th cong. 2d sess., H. Ex. Doc., vol. xxv.–vi. Improved land 143,007 acres, 237,392 a. Unimpr. 584,259 a. + 106,283 a. of wood land, 393,739 a. + 219,224 a. wood. No. of farms, 4,480, 5,053. Average size 186 a., 125 a. Value $2,260,139, $5,514,349 (assessment in '82, land $7,100,744, improv. $4,300,265; '83, land 6,659,669, improv. $5,751,- 370). Value of implements, etc., $124,114, $255,162. Amt of wages paid $523,888, ——. Value of farm products $1,905,060, $1,897,974, $2,716,682. Value of orchard prod. $13,609, $26,706. Market and garden prod. $64,132, $42,679. Forest prod. $500, $77,468. Wheat 352,822 b., 706,641 b., 767,000 b. (wheat yields 12–50 b. per acre). Corn 640,823 b., 633,786 b., 965,000 b. (40–60 b. per acre). Oats 67,660 b., 156,527 b., 185,000 b. (35–45 b. per acre). Barley 3,876 b., 50,053 b., 53,557 b. Rye 42 b., 240 b. Beans and pease 28,856 b., 21,268 b. Potatoes 3,102 b., 25,100 b., 40,500 b. Hay 4,209 tons, 11,025 t., 13,000 t. Tobacco 8,587 lbs., 890 lbs. Wine 19,686 gal., ——. Flax seed ——, 834 lbs. Sorghum molasses 1,765 gal., 251 gal. Butter 12,912 lbs., 44,827 lbs. Cheese 27,230 lbs, 10,501 lbs. Milk 813 gal., 10,036 gal. Eggs ——, 238,858 doz. Honey ——, 450 lbs.

The rainy season is from June to September. On climate, with tables of temperature, rainfall, etc., see *Smithsonian Inst. Rept*, 1877, p. 323 et seq.; *N. Mex., Governor's Report*, 1872 et seq.; *U. S. Govt Doc.*, 45th cong. 2d sess., H. Ex. Doc., vi. 90–1, 145–6, and passim, with charts; 3d sess. H. Ex. Doc., vii. pt ii., 83, 114–19; 46th cong. 2d sess., H. Ex. Doc., vii., pt ii., 128–34, 251–8; 47th cong. 1st sess., H. Ex. Doc., vii. 92, 475, 586; *Schott's Precipitation*, 70–3, 115; *Id., Distribution and Variations*, 54–5; *Wheeler's U. S. Geog. Surv.*, ii. 533, 568 et seq.; *U. S. Surg.-Gen.*, Circular 8, p. 294–8, 302–6, 313. 1865. No probable increase in prod. since 1860. 1866. Meline, *2,000 Miles*, 158–61, describes Maxwell's farm of 5,000 acres as the model and largest in N. Mex. 1868. Gov. urges the great prospects of grape culture. 1869. Sugar-beet, long-staple cotton, and tobacco do well; as silk

the period of 1864–86 has done little more than confirm what was well enough known in past centuries respecting the country's fertility. Farming is still conducted for the most part by the old methods of irrigation and tillage; and practically nothing has been done to increase the water supply or prevent waste. Floods occur occasionally, but the climate is remarkably healthful and well adapted to agricultural pursuits. A living is easily gained, and that is all that the natives desire. There has been little or no exportation of products, and such will perhaps always be the case, unless wine, grapes, and certain fruits—in the production of which New Mexico seems to have some advantages over California—may prove an exception; yet the home market furnished by the mining camps and towns is, and is likely to be, excellent for a vastly increased production; and with the settlement of land titles, storing and proper use of water, and adequate tillage of small farms, agriculture in the future should be a remarkably prosperous industry.

A very large part of the territory, consisting of dry mesa and mountain land unfit for farming, is available for grazing, producing in large quantities the most

and tea ought to do. 1871. Many new vineyards coming into bearing. 1872. Bill to donate 10 sections of land to John Martin for finding water in the desert, tabled in congress. 1873. Govt aid for irrigation urged by surv.-gen. 1874–5. Many destructive floods. 1878. Cotton successfully raised in the south. 1879. Much testimony in *U. S. Pub. Lands Com. Rept* (46th cong. 2d sess., H. Ex. Doc. 46), p. 441–64, 619–22. Wine prod. 240,000 gal. 1880. Severe drought. 1884. Floods.

The *U. S. Dept Agric. Reports* contain nothing on N. Mex. until 1869, when a good sketch from a pamphlet by C. P. Clever is given; and the later reports contain more or less information. The *U. S. Land Office Reports*, 1864 et seq., give the condition of agric. from year to year in the surv.-gen.'s reports; so do many of the governor's messages. *Ritch's Illust. N. Mex.*, and *Id.*, *Aztlan*, passim, are useful authority for the late years; and the *N. Mex. Bureau of Immig.*, *Report of Bernalillo Co.* (and other counties), 1881–2, may be cited as especially valuable. See also *Wheeler's U. S. Geog. Surv.*, iii. 573–83, 601–3; Reports 1875–7, passim, and maps; *N. Mex., Scraps*, passim; *N. Mex. Business Directory*, 1882; *McKenney's Bus. Dir.*, 308; *Hayden's Great West*, 190–3; *N. Mex., A Political Problem; Palmer's Colonization in Colorado*, 22–52, 59–79; *Brevoort's N. Mex.*, 57–68; *New Mex. and the New Mexicans*, 24–5; *Goddard's Where to Emigrate*, 146–7; *Owen's Mines of N. Mex.*, 32–4, 45–7; *Beadle's West Wilds*, 228–9; *Porter's The West, Census of 1880*, 450–1; *N. Mex., Pointers on the S. W.*, 58–9; *Rand, McNally, & Co.'s Overl. Guide*, 84–8; *Roberts' With the Invader*, 25–9, 84–7; *Copley's Kansas*, 68–9; *Hayden, in U. S. Govt Doc.*, 42d cong. 2d sess., H. Ex. Doc. 325.

nutritious of wild grasses; while the climatic and other conditions are all favorable for stock-raising. This industry has therefore, as shown by the appended statistics,[6] far excelled that of agriculture or any other, except perhaps mining, and is likely to retain its precedence in the future. Yet success in raising cattle and sheep has by no means been commensurate with the country's natural advantages. Here the land laws have worked against the industry. The land is worthless for farms, but cannot be sold in tracts sufficiently large for grazing. By owning 160 acres about a spring a few men have control each of an immense range, thus monopolizing the business, very much to the disadvantage of the territory. If the government would permit the taking-up of 'pastoral homesteads' of 1–5,000 acres, sufficing for the support of a family as 160 acres are supposed to suffice as a farm; if it would offer liberal areas for the finding of water by wells, with the privilege of buying more; or if the grazing lands were simply offered for sale at reasonable prices in large

[6] *U. S. Census Reports*, 1870, 1880. Statistics for later years from other sources are very contradictory. Value of animals slaughtered $224,765,——. Value of live-stock, $2,389,157,—— (in '83, $18,159,465, *Cattlemen, Proc. 1st Nat. Conv.*, 12–13; abt $20,000,000 invested in '79, *U. S. Pub. Lands Com. Rept*, 441–64, 619–22; assessment in '82 $5,272,644; in '83 $9,335,299. *Auditor's Reports*). Horses 5,033, 15,557 (in '82, 12,149, in '83, 19,672, *Auditor;* in '83, 16,640, *Cattlemen*). Mules and asses 6,141, 9,063 (in '82, 5,221; in '83, 8,440, *Auditor;* in '83, 10,082, *Cattlemen*). Milch cows 16,417, 12,955. Oxen 19,774, 16,432. Other cattle 21,343, 137,314 (cattle in '82, 267,200; in '83, 471,121, *Auditor;* in '79, 500,000, *Gov. and Surv.-gen.;* in '83, 547,113, *Cattlemen;* in '84, 1,000,000, *Gov.;* in '85, 800,000, *Ritch*). Sheep 619,438, 2,088,831 (in '79, 5,000,000, *Gov.;* 10,000,000, *Surv.-gen.;* in '82, 1,339,718; in '83, 1,757,948, *Aud.;* in '83, 3,960,000, *Cattlemen;* in '84, 1,000,000 and decreasing, *Gov.;* in 85, 5,000,000, *Ritch;* in '83, 25,000,000 (!), *N. Mex. Review*, July 10, 1883). Swine 11,267, 7,857 (in '82, 3,740; in '83, 4,044, *Aud.;* in '83, 19,300, *Cattlemen*). Goats (in '82, 27,692; in '83, 34,003, *Aud.*—probably included with sheep in other figures). Product of wool 684,930 lbs., 4,019,188 lbs. (in '84, 26,610,000 lbs., *Ritch*).

Cattle and sheep have no diseases except as introduced from abroad; and in '84 an act was passed to prevent the introd. of diseased animals from Texas, etc. There was always a conflict between cattle and sheep men, as cattle and horses will not thrive where sheep are grazed; and in the later years it has been thought that sheep must go to the wall; yet it is thought that with careful attention sheep-raising is more profitable, though cattle require much less care. 30 acres will support a beef or 5--6 sheep. Sheep have been worth $1 to $1.50; cattle $15; and horses $20–35. The authorities cited in the preceding note on agric. contain also information on stock-raising; see also *Watts' Sta Fé Affairs*, MS., 17–18; *N. Mex., Its Resources and Advantages*, 8; *Wood Brothers' Live Stock Movement; Stone's Gen. View*, MS., 8–9.

tracts—many of the obstacles to a grand success would apparently be removed, and at least the lands would pay their part of territorial taxes.   But all the numerous efforts to secure these reforms have thus far failed.

New Mexico can hardly be said to have as yet any manufacturing industry; that is, the only establishments of this kind in existence, as shown in statistics of the census in 1870–80,[7] are the few and ordinary ones that naturally spring up in any community to supply in part local needs and furnish a livelihood to those engaged.   Flouring and lumber mills take the lead, followed by the carpenter and blacksmith shops, which can hardly be rated as manufacturing establishments at all.   It will be noted that the list includes no woollen mills, though one was in operation in 1870, and one or more have, I think, been established since 1880.   And there were then no tanneries, notwithstanding the abundance of cattle and the existence of a native plant, the *canaigre*, thought to be well adapted to take the place of oak and hemlock.   It would seem that the manufacture of woollen fabrics and leather

[7] Estab. in '70, '80, 192, 144.   Capital $1,450,695, $463,275.   Hands employed 427, 559.   Wages $167,281, $218,731.   Value of materials $880,957, $871,352.   Products $1,489,868, $1,284,846.
Statistics of 1880:

	Estab.	Capital.	Hands.	Wages.	Material.	Product.
Blacksmith........	11	$4,950	17	$5,944	$6,675	$20,550
Boots....	6	5,300	6	3,650	3,500	11,430
Carpenter........	22	40,250	136	90,075	205,250	336,790
Carriage.	1	20,000	12	9,500	39,000	48,000
Clothing..........	1	500	2	2,100	1,000	3,600
Furniture........	1	3,500	4	3,600	7,000	18,000
Jewelry..........	2	13,000	16	11,000	14,000	35,000
Distilleries........	1	1,000	1	40	350	535
Breweries.........	3	6,000	2	410	1,772	3,290
Wine....	1	1,300	3	800	1,500	4,000
Masons....	2	700	4	2,000	3,300	7,000
Harness..........	5	7,000	11	5,900	6,500	15,800
Tin and Copper....	2	30,000	12	10,100	22,000	40,000
Tobacco....	1	1,000	1	550	500	2,000
Wheelwrights.....	6	3,450	16	12,800	15,000	34,250
Flour-mills.......	51	240,250	134	35,416	435,450	529,179
Saw-mills.	26	74,675	172	24,240	117,055	173,930
Brick.............	1	800	8	600	500	1,500

should assume some importance; and the possibilities of future developments in the extensive working of iron have already been noted.

New Mexican trade consists, as in Arizona, of the bringing-in and distribution of merchandise required for the supply of mining camps and towns, and for the consumption of the people generally, no satisfactory statistics being obtainable, and no comment on methods needed. The advent of railroads put an end to the famous old Santa Fé trade, carried on by wagon-trains across the plains, a trade which amounted in 1876 to over $2,000,000. There is no exportation of products, except those of the mines and flocks; the immense quantities of freight carried through the territory to the Pacific states and Mexico form, of course, no element of New Mexican trade proper; and I find nothing in the distribution of goods from railroad centres or the operations of the ordinary mercantile establishments of the different settlements that calls for remark.

Of railroads the territory has over 1,200 miles, built in 1878–85. They were not built with any view to the benefit or business of New Mexico, but to complete transcontinental connections between the east, the Pacific, and Mexico. Therefore, I do not deem the annals of the various companies, projects, and complications as belonging in any important sense to the history of New Mexico, even if there were space in this chapter for such matter. I append, however, a few miscellaneous notes.[8] The first passenger train

[8] 1855–6. Act of legisl. incorp. A. & P. R. R. Co. 1856–7. Id., incorp. N. Mex. Min. & R. R. Co. 1863–4. Id., incorp. Kansas, N. Mex., Ariz., & Cal. R. R. Co. 1864–5. Bill for R. R. and tel. through N. Mex. and Ariz. tabled in congress, joint resol. to facilitate communication passed. 1866, etc. Laws on A. & P. R. R. in rept sec. int., 1882, p. 596–602. 1867. R. R. projects. *Copley's Kansas*, 68–70; *Sac. Union*, Nov. 2d. 1868. Mem. of legisl. for R. R., as best means of settling Ind. troubles and giving N. Mex. the protection promised by the treaty, often repeated; rept of cong. com. *U. S. Govt Doc.*, 40th cong. 2d sess., H. Rept 43. 1871. Kansas Pac. R. R. now within 3 days' staging; other roads approaching. *N. Mex., Mess. of gov.;* later messages record progress and prospects. 1872. Acts of legisl. giving right of way to N. Mex. & Gulf R. R. (also act of congress); authorizing county aid to R. R.; and mortgage or consolidation; and appraisement of

entered the territory in February 1879, bringing the Colorado legislature to Otero over the Atchison, Topeka, and Santa Fé line; work was rapidly pushed forward, and for the most part completed in five years. The Atchison, Topeka, and Santa Fé line, known also as the New Mexico and Southern Pacific, enters the territory at the Raton tunnel, sending out a short branch to the coal-beds; in 1879 reached Las Vegas, whence a branch extends to the Hot Springs; in 1880 reached Santa Fé by a branch of 95 miles from Lamy; and in 1881, branching at Rincon, reached Deming and El Paso. It has short branches in Socorro county to the mines of Magdalena and Carthage; a narrow-gauge extension of 46 miles from Deming to Silver City; and has in all 680 miles of track. The Atlantic and Pacific line, virtually a part of the Atchison, Topeka, and Santa Fé, began building at Alburquerque in 1880, on the completion of the former line to that point, and was rapidly pushed westward until in 1883 it reached the Colorado River, opening a new and favorite route to California. This road has 179 miles in New Mexico, including a five-mile siding to the Gallup coal mines. The Southern Pacific from Cali-

R. R. lands; cong. bill to incorp. N. Mex. R. R. and Central R. R. 1874 et seq. Surv.-gen. reports progress and prospects. 1878. Act of legisl. for incorp. of R. R. companies; Raton Mt. being tunnelled; D. & Col. R. R. graded to north line of N. Mex. 1879. A. T. & Sta Fé R. R. completed to Las Vegas in July. 1880. Completion of N. Mex. & South R. R. branch to Sta Fé in Feb.; A. & P. R. R. has 9 m. of track westward from Alburquerque; D. & R. G. R. R. graded to Peña Blanca, track to near Embudo; see statistics, etc., in *U. S. Govt Doc.*, 46th cong. 3d sess., H. Ex. Doc., xvi., pt ii., p. 227; Id., 47th cong. 2d sess., H. Ex. Doc., xiii., pt iv., p. 56–9. 1881. A., T., & Sta Fé R. R. completed to junctions with the S. Pac. R. R. at Deming and El Paso; trains running to Ariz. and Cal. from May; S. Pac. R. R. has 155 m. in N. Mex. D. & R. G. R. R. compl. to Española, 80 m., and 60 m. west on S. Juan division. A. & P. R. R. extends 212 m. w. from Alburquerque. See repts of gov. and surv.-gen. See *N. Mex., Railroad Laws, compiled by Catron and Thornton*, Sta Fé, 1881, 8vo, 61 p. 1882. Total miles R. R. in Jan. 1,096; built during the past year 913 m. Act of legisl. to regulate R. R., prohibit discrimination, and fix passenger rates at 6 cts per mile; also authorizing Silver City to subsidize a R. R. See *Ritch's Blue-Book*, 139–45, for details, stations, distances, etc. 1883. Narrow-gauge R. R. compl. from Deming to Silver City, 46 m.; and from Lordsburg to Clifton, 30 m. in N. Mex.; some work done on a line to join Sta Fé and Española. See gov.'s rept and *Ritch's Ill. N. Mex.*, 23–5. 1884. Mex. Central R. R. completed. See details in *McKinney's Bus. Directory*, 308; *Mills' S. Miguel Co.*, 20–1. 1885. See excellent summary in *Ritch's Aztlan*, 13–18, 25–6.

fornia and Arizona has 232 miles in New Mexico, including 50 miles of the Lordsburg and Clifton narrow-gauge road; joins the Atchison, Topeka, and Santa Fé line at Deming and El Paso; and thence extending eastward through Texas forms another overland line. The Denver and Rio Grande road from Colorado in the north enters New Mexico near Antonito, whence one division extends southward 79 miles to within 28 miles of Santa Fé, and another division 60 miles west through the San Juan country to the Amargo coal mines, and thence northward into Colorado. This road has 164 miles of track. Some work has been done on an extension of the road from Española to Santa Fé, and an extension to the Pecos and to Galveston is projected. Other prominent projects are the Gulf, Colorado, and Santa Fé road, and an extension of the Atlantic and Pacific eastward to Indian Territory. Numerous branch lines are projected and will be built in time; meanwhile, the territory, most fortunate in its position on the great overland lines, must be regarded as well supplied with railroads.

A military telegraph line from the north-east was in operation from 1868; and ten years later the line had been extended to all the forts except Wingate and Stanton, and telegraphic communication was opened with California by way of Tucson. Subsequently, telegraph construction progressed with that of railroads, until all the more important settlements are in communication with the east and west.[9]

[9] 1866-8. Act incorp. N. Mex. Tel. Co. and memorials for U. S. aid; as there were mem. for increased facilities in later years. 1868. Gov. in his mess. announces the opening of tel. communication. 1875-8. Items on construction and projects. *N. Mex., Scraps*, 6-7. 1878. Western Union line from Sta Fé via Las Vegas, Ft Union, Cimarron, and Trinidad, Col.; U. S. mil. line to Alburquerque, Las Lunas, Belen, Ft Craig, Las Cruces, Mesilla, Silver City, Tucson, and S. Diego. *Surv.-gen. Rept.* 1879. 1st tel. despatch from N. Mex. received at San Francisco. *S. F. Bulletin*, Aug. 21st. Statistics '81-2. *U. S. Govt Doc.*, 47th cong. 1st sess., H. Ex. Doc., vii. 212-25.

All parts of the territory are tolerably well provided with stage and mail routes from the R. R. stations, though there have been frequent petitions from different sections for increased facilities. The *U. S. Govt Doc.* contain from year to year the records of such petitions, with the opening of new routes, etc. There is also quite a quantity of matter relating to military and other

A bureau of immigration, established by an act of
the legislature in 1880, is an institution, which, under
the presidency of Prince and Ritch, has done much
to attract settlers, by the publication of information
respecting the country's resources and attractions.
The county reports of 1881–2, as published in pamphlet form, have already been noticed; and of Ritch's
work on the resources of New Mexico some 27,000
copies, in six editions, under different titles, have been
issued, and widely circulated from the central office
through the railroad companies and at various fairs
and expositions in the eastern states. It is estimated
that nearly 20,000 immigrants have been drawn to
the territory since 1880; and doubtless the bureau
has exerted a beneficial influence.[10] An annual territorial fair, or exposition, has been held at Alburquerque
since 1881.

Education, respecting which some statistical and
other items are given in a note,[11] has remained in a

roads; but I have not thought it necessary to reproduce these items, even in
a brief résumé. Several incorporations of road and bridge companies are
mentioned in the résumé of legisl. proceedings.

[10] *N. Mex., Bureau of Immig., Report,* 1883; *Id.,* County reports, 1881–2,
as noted earlier in this chapter; *N. Mex., Acts,* 24th sess., p. 74–5; *Ritch's
Illust. N. Mex.* (4th ed.), 1883; *Id., Aztlan* (6th ed.), 1885, with lists of officers
and members, of which there was one commissioner for each county and 5 to
9 com. at large; the gov. being a com. ex officio. The bureau was 'investigated' by the legisl. in 1884, and was warmly praised in the committee's report, all charges of extravagance and inefficiency being refuted. *N. M. Journals,* 26th sess., pt ii., 38–42, 64–8. I have a pamphlet entitled *N. Mex., Premium list of the N. Mex. Exposition and Driving Park Assoc. Third annual
fair,* Alburquerque, 1883; also, *N. Mex. Resources, prepared under the auspices
of the Bureau of Immig. for the territorial fair.* Sta Fé, 1881.

[11] School statistics from the census of 1880: no. of pub. schools 162,
school buildings 46, seats in same 5,580, value of property $13,500, receipts
for year $32,171, expenditures $28,973, teachers 164 (males 128, females 36);
average salary $30.67, average months of school 5.55, pupils 4,755 (males
2,484, females 2,271), average attendance 3,150, inhab. over 10 years of age
unable to read 52,994 (percentage 60.2), unable to write 57,156 (percentage
65).

1863. Act of legisl. creating a board of educ. and estab. a system of
schools; incorp. 'Industrial College of N. Mex.' at Sta Fé. 1866. The
various statutes have no effect, but some activity in private schools. *Meline's
2,000 Miles,* 192–3. 1866. Not a single free public school; an approp. by the
U. S. urged by gov. and legisl. in this and other years. 1867. Act amending
and perfecting school system; probate judges to act as county superintendents. 1868. Still no schools and no school tax collected, acc. to gov.'s message. 1871. In 4 counties, out of 5,053 votes, only 37 were in favor of a law
to support schools by taxation. 1870. Total school attendance acc. to census,

backward condition, notwithstanding the advanced views and earnest efforts of territorial officials and of many citizens. In 1880 there were only 162 schools, with an attendance of 3,150 pupils. By acts of the legislature a public school system was created and perfected at different dates from 1863 to 1884, when it assumed a tolerably effective form, in theory at least. One fourth of all taxes is devoted to education, but in the collection and application of the funds there have been great irregularities, on account of the apathy of the native population. The mixture of language and religion, with a great preponderance of Spanish and the catholic faith, have been the great obstacles; and the cause of education has been retarded also by all the causes that have hindered progress in other directions. With the increase of immigration, however, there is noted a constant though slow growth

1,889. 1872. Act providing for county boards of 4 supervisors. 1875. 8 counties report 138 schools, 47 teachers, and 5,151 pupils, under law of '71 giving the schools $\frac{1}{4}$ of tax and the poll tax. 1880. Act to select university lands. 1881. Educ. compulsory for 5 months per year. 1883. Gov. reports not much progress under the system. 1884. Act establishing public schools, with an elective county superintendent, one or more schools in each district, under 3 directors, and a tax of 3 mills per dollar, with poll tax; school fund this year to be $100,000, or $\frac{1}{4}$ of all taxes.

On educational matters, see *N. Mex., Message of gov.*, from year to year; *U. S. Educational Reports*, containing some details down to 1877, but not much later; *Brevoort's N. Mex.*, 105, showing statistics of 1873, when there were 133 public and 26 private schools; *Mills' S. Miguel Co.*, 19-20; *Ritch's Illust. N. Mex.*, 58-60; *Id., Aztlan*, 78-9; *N. Mex., Business Direct.; N. Mex., Scraps*, 81.

I have before me *Alburquerque Academy, 5th Annual Report*, etc., Alb., 1883-4, 8vo, 15 p.; *University of New Mexico, 1st Annual Catalogue* (Sta Fé), 1882, 8vo, 18 p., containing act of incorporation, officers, etc.; *Las Vegas Jesuit College, Prospectus and Catalogue*, Las Vegas, 1882, 58 p., 1884, 68 p. This latter institution has published *Spelling Book for the Use of Public Schools of N. Mex.*, Alburquerque, 1874, 16mo, 47 p.; *Elementos de Aritmética*, Las Vegas, 1876, 16mo, 146 p.; *Herrainz y Quiroz, Elementos de Gramática Castellana*, Las V., 1877, 16mo, 124 p.; and besides these educational works, the following of a religious and general character: *Balmes, La Religion Demostrada*, Alb., 1873, 16mo, 110 p.; *Los Protectores de la Juventud*, Alb., 1874, 16mo, 151 p.; *Lamy, Constituciones Eclesiásticas para la Diócesis de Sta Fé*, Alb., 1874, 8vo, 37 p.; *Franco, Benjamina, Novela Contemporanea*, Las V., 1877, 12mo, 140 p.; *Id., Los Corazones Populares, Novela*, Las V., 1878, 12mo, 167 p.; *Id., La Pobrecilla de Casamari, Novela Histórica*, Las V., 1879, 12mo, 293 p.; *Centelas, Diálogos y Cartas*, Las V., 1883, 12mo, 156 p.; *Ambert, El Heroismo en Sotana*, Las V., 1883, 12mo, 128 p.; *Los Jesuitas*, n. p., n. d., 16mo, 51 p.; *Coleccion de Cánticos Espirituales*, Las V., 1884, 16mo, 198 p.; *Ripalda, Catecismo*, Las V., 1884, 16mo, 87 p.; and *Classic English Poetry*, Las V. (college press), 1884, 12mo, 139 p. All, with one exception, bear the mark of 'Imprenta del Rio Grande,' from which press is also issued the *Revista Católica*.

of a healthful sentiment in favor of schools; and encouraging progress is looked for in the future.   There is, besides, a considerable number of fairly prosperous private institutions in the larger towns, including several catholic colleges under the direction of the Jesuits, Christian Brothers, Sisters of Loretto, and Sisters of Charity, supported largely by public school funds; and a few others under other religious denominations, supported by tuition fees and private contributions.   The Jesuit college at Las Vegas, that of the Christian Brothers at Santa Fé, and the academies at Alburquerque and Las Vegas may be named as the most prominent educational institutions.

Newspapers in 1850 were two in number, with a circulation of 1,150; in 1860 the figures had not changed; in 1870 there were five journals, but the circulation had only increased to 1,525; while the census of 1880 shows 18, with a circulation of 6,355. In 1885 the number was 39, of which eight were dailies, two semi-weekly, 27 weekly, and two monthly. A list of those published in 1882, not much changed since that date, is appended.[12]   Several of these news-

[12] *U. S. Census Reports; Ritch's Blue-Book*, 96–7; *Id., Aztlan*, 82; *Las Vegas Min. World*, Jan. 1881, p. 147, of 1882; *Pettingill's Newsp. Directory*, 185; *Fisher's Newsp. Agency*, 10; *Brown's Advert. Agency*, 2–5.

List of N. Mex. newspapers in 1882: Alburquerque, *Journal*, daily and weekly; *Review*, w. (pub. from '70 as *Repub. Review*); *Revista*, w.; *Miner and Manufacturer*, w. (another *Miner* susp. in '80). Bernalillo, *News*, w. (*Native* susp. in '80). Raton, *News and Press*, w. (at Cimarron '78–80); *Guard*, w. Mesilla, *News*, w. Las Cruces, *Rio Grande Republican*, w. (also *Thirty-four* in '80). Lake Valley (*Herald* in '84).   Silver City, *New Southwest*, w.; *Mining Chronicle*, w.; *Telegram*, s.-w. (*Grant Co. Herald*, in '78–80; *Sentinel* in '84). Lordsburg (*Advance* in '84). Georgetown, *Silver Brick*, w. Deming, *Headlight*, w. (and *Tribune* in '84). White Oaks, *Golden Era*, w. Tiptonville, *Mora Co. Pioneer*, w. Santa Fé, *New Mexican*, d. and w.; *Mining News*, w.; *Nuevo Mexico*, w.; *Christian Advocate*, monthly; *Democrat*, w.; *Military Review*, s.-monthly (*Rocky Mt. Sentinel* in '80).   Golden, *Retort*, w. S. Pedro, —— w. Las Vegas, *Gazette*, d. and w.; *Optic*, d. and w.; *Revista Católica*, w.; *Mining World*, s.-monthly (*N. Mex. Advertiser* in '78). S. Lorenzo, *Red River Chronicle*, w.; *Crónica*, w. Mineral Hill, *Min. City News*, w.

The following notes respecting newspaper history are chiefly from *Ritch's Blue-Book*. The Taos *Crepúsculo*, 1835, was the 1st paper, published for only 4 weeks. The Sta Fé *Republican*, 1847, was the 1st paper in English. The 1st Sta Fé *New Mexican* was pub. in 1847; the 2d was started in 1863. The Mesilla *News* was pub. in 1860–1; the later *News* from 1873. The Sta Fé *Gazette* was pub. between 1851 and 1860, on the press brought by Gen. Kearny in 1846. The Alburquerque *N. Mex. Press* of 1863 was changed to the *Republican*. The Elizabethtown *Lantern* of 1869; changed to *Railway Press*;

papers are published in Spanish, and several others in English and Spanish. In quality they will compare favorably with similar publications in other territories. A Press Association was organized at Las Vegas in 1880.

The religion of the territory is naturally for the most part Roman Catholic. In 1870 that denomination had 152 of the 158 churches, with church property valued at $313,321. The census of 1880 contains no church statistics. In 1882 there were 72 priests, serving a catholic population of 126,000. New Mexico, with Arizona and Colorado, forms an archbishopric under John B. Lamy since 1865. The Jesuits—an act incorporating which society was annulled by congress in 1878—are active, especially in educational matters, as are the Christian Brothers and Sisters of Charity and Mercy. There has been some clashing between the old native priests and the new-comers introduced by Lamy, but under the bishop's energetic management there has been a notable improvement in the tone of ecclesiastical affairs, and an almost complete weeding-out of the old-time laxity of morals that was remarked by early visitors. Here, as elsewhere, the church is slow to adopt sweeping reforms, and does not often favor educational advancement that it cannot entirely control; but a good work has been slowly accomplished, and there is a tolerably strong tendency to improvement, many of the catholic institutions of education and charity being

consol. in 1875 with *News and Press* at Cimarron. Las Vegas, *N. Mex. Advertiser*, 1870–8, 1st paper in S. Miguel co. Cimarron, *Press*, 1870, absorbed the *News* in 1875. Las Vegas, *Mail*, 1870, changed to *Gazette*. Silver City, *Mining Life*, 1873; suspended 1875; later revived as *Herald*. Las Cruces, *Eco del Rio Grande*, 1874, transferred to Globe, Ariz. Las Vegas, *Revista Católica*, started in 1875; *Revista Evangélica*, 1876–9. Mesilla, *Valley Independent*, 1879–9. Santa Fé, *Illust. Monthly*, Jan.-May 1878. Laguna, *La Solona*, 1878. Taos, *Espejo*, 1878; trans. to Bernalillo, and to Alburquerque 1879; changed to *Mirror;* merged in *Miner;* suspended. Sta Fé, *Rocky Mt Sentinel*, 1878–9. Las Cruces, *Thirty-four*, 1878; Newman's *Thirty-four*, 1881. Silver City, *Silver Record*, 1879; suspended. Otero, *Optic*, 1879; trans. to Las Vegas. *N. Mex. Herald*, 1879; trans. to Sta Fé in 1880 as *Era Southwestern;* ch. to *Democrat*. *Los Cerrillos Prospector*, at Carbonateville, 1879. Alburquerque, *Advance*, 1880; trans to Socorro as *Sun*. Alb., *Golden Gate,* 1880; ch. to *Republican*. White Oaks, *Golden Era*, 1880.

well managed and effective. The Mormons, respecting whose proselyting schemes there has been some excitement, especially in 1875–7, as shown by the newspapers, have a few churches on the eastern border, but I find no definite information or statistics. Of protestant denominations the episcopalians seem to have the lead, with six clergymen under George Kelly as primate in 1882, and three churches as early as 1870. The presbyterians and methodists are reported as having a dozen or more clergymen and 700 communicants; while the baptists, congregationalists, and southern methodists have each two or three clergymen. protestant influence is, however, weak, and is confined for the most part to the new and thriving towns, most of which have one or more church edifices.

CHAPTER XXXI.

COUNTIES AND TOWNS OF NEW MEXICO.

1886.

County Map—Colfax—Area and Annals—Stock-raising—Raton and Springer—Dictations of Prominent Citizens—Mora—Fort Union —Taos—A Garden-spot—Old Pueblo—San Fernando—Rio Arriba—San Juan Indians—Coal—Tierra Amarilla—Oñate's Capital — Bernalillo — A Flourishing County — Tiguex — Pueblos— Alburquerque—Santa Fé—Antiquity and Mines—The Capital— Statements of Citizens—San Miguel—Farms and Ranchos—Las Vegas—Testimony of Residents—Valencia and Las Lunas—Lincoln and White Oaks—Socorro—Mining Activity—Grant—Silver City and Deming—Doña Ana—Mesilla Valley—Las Cruces— Sierra—Hillsborough and Lake Valley.

Boundaries of the thirteen counties of New Mexico are shown on the appended map. Eight of them date back to Mexican times; one was added soon after the territorial organization;[1] and four have since been created.

Colfax county occupies an area of 7,000 square miles in the north-eastern corner of the territory, its altitude being from 5,500 to 8,000 feet, with some lofty peaks. It was created by act of 1869, its boundaries being modified in 1876 and in 1882. The county seat was first at Elizabethtown, which town was incorporated in 1870, but was moved to Cimarron in 1872, and finally to Springer in 1882. In 1876–8 the county was attached to Taos for judicial purposes. About half the area is mesa or prairie land, affording

---

[1] For the counties and boundaries as organized by the legislature of 1852, see *N. Mex., Compiled Laws*, 252 et seq. The county areas as given by me are computed from the map. The authorities differ so greatly, and in some cases are so clearly wrong, that I have hesitated to give their figures, though not very confident that my own are always accurate.

excellent grazing, and supporting in 1880 about 29,000
cattle and 65,000 sheep, the numbers having greatly
increased since that date, 187,000 and 86,000 being

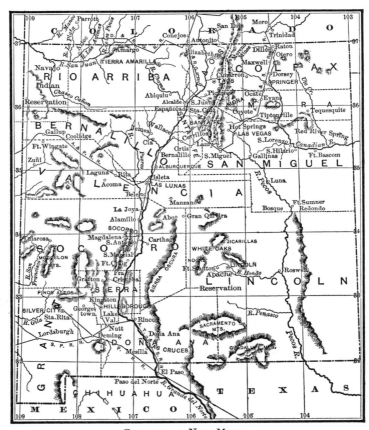

COUNTIES OF NEW MEXICO.

the figures in 1883. Along the watercourses are
numerous narrow tracts, successfully cultivated by irrigation. There are over half a million acres of coal-
fields, and the coal is somewhat extensively worked
in the region of Raton. The mountains are covered
with pine, affording lumber of fair quality in consider-

able quantities. Of gold from the Moreno placers and Ute Creek and other quartz mines several millions of dollars have been produced since 1868, and copper is also found. Over half the county is included in the famous Maxwell rancho, or land grant of Beaubien and Miranda, and here the Jicarilla Apaches and Ute bands had their homes for many years, as related in an earlier chapter. The Atchison, Topeka, and Santa Fé Railroad, the first to enter the territory, crosses Colfax from north to south, and on its line are the leading towns. The population in 1880 was 3,398, and is now perhaps 5,000. The total assessed value of property in 1883 was $5,437,640, the largest item being that of livestock. Raton, with over 2,000 inhabitants, is the largest town, being of modern or railroad origin. Its prominence arises from the proximity of the coal mines, to which a branch road extends, and from the location of the railroad shops here. The town has good water-works, good schools, two newspapers—the *Guard* and *News and Press*—the only ones published in the county, and it aspires to future prominence as a manufacturing centre. Springer, the county seat, had but 34 inhabitants in 1880, but is now a thriving village, with a fine court-house and a cement factory, being also the shipping point for a large territory east and west. Elizabethtown and Cimarron, formerly honored as county seats, had respectively 175 and 290 inhabitants in 1880. The former is a mining town in the Moreno districts; and the latter, formerly known as Maxwell's rancho, may be considered the oldest settlement in the county. Colfax has a smaller proportion of native, or Mexican, population than most parts of the territory.[2]

[2] Among the publications of recent years which contain more or less descriptive matter on the counties and towns are Ritch's *Aztlan*, his *Illust. N. Mex.*, and the various other editions of the same work; the county reports of the *N. Mex.*, *Bureau of Immig.*; *N. Mex.*, *Business Directory*; *McKenney's Business Directory*; *N. Mex.*, *Pointers on the South-west: Rand, McNally, & Co.*, *Overland Guide*; *Id.*, *Guide to Col.*; *N. Mex.*, *Real Estate*, Sta Fé, 1883; *Avery's Hand-Book and Travellers' Guide of N. Mex.*, Denver, 1881, 16mo; *Berger's Tourists' Guide to N. Mex.*, Kansas City, 1883. This last book has

Mora county, lying south of Colfax, with an area of 3,700 square miles, was created in 1860, being cut off from Taos, and including Colfax down to 1869. There were slight changes of boundary in 1868, 1876, and 1882. The county seat has been Mora, or Santa Gertrudis, from the first. The population was 9,751 in 1880, and may be nearly 12,000 now, a majority being of Spanish origin. The average elevation is 4–7,000 feet, the mountainous parts being in the western fourth, while the mesa lands occupy three

a brief treatise on 'Pronunciation of Spanish Names,' which has the unusual merit of being accurate. All the common errors are indicated as errors, and not given, as is too common, for the correct pronunciation. The author, however, is wrong in attributing these errors to N. Mex. especially, or to the uneducated; for they are almost universal in Spanish America, and very common in many provinces of Spain.

The following stock men of Colfax county have given for my use interesting *Dictations* or *Statements* in MS., containing biographic items and information respecting the county's chief industry, the separate MSS. being mentioned under the authors' names in my list of authorities: Thomas O. Boggs, of Springer, is a son of Gov. L. W. Boggs of Mo., a man well known in the annals of Cal. He came to N. Mex. in 1844, and later served as scout in the Ind. wars. He furnished also the *Carson Papers* for my use, having been the executor of Kit Carson's estate. J. B. Dawson, of Vermejo, is a native of Ky, and first came with a herd of cattle from Tex. in 1866. For a long time he was engaged in the purchase of cattle for the Colorado market. He has 5,000 acres in his home rancho, and is a partner in several large cattle companies. He has a large family at his home, including his aged father and mother. Stephen Dorsey, a native of Vt, rose from private to colonel in the war of 1861–5, was U. S. senator from Ark. from 1873, came to N. Mex. in 1877, and became the owner of many ranchos. He has U. S. patents for 4–5,000 acres, including springs and streams, which give him control of immense grazing ranges. He owns about 50,000 head of Durham and Hereford cattle, being connected in the past with several companies, but gradually severing this connection, with the idea of doing business for himself alone. He is one of the most prominent stock-raisers in the territory. Joseph W. Dwyer is the owner, with J. S. Delano, of the Uña de Gato rancho, which grazes 12,000 cattle. He is a native of Ohio. Mrs S. C. Lacy, a native of Ark., and widow of I. W. Lacy, who died in 1881, leaving 5 children, has a rancho at Vermejo, where she raises grain and vegetables, having also a range in Colorado, with 12,000 cattle. John Love, born in Pa, came in 1880 as secretary of S. W. Dorsey, a position which he still held in 1885. He is also the owner of 1,000 cattle. Geoffrey McCroham is foreman of the Cimarron Cattle Co., at Blue Water Hole Springs, where the co. has 26,000 cattle. He has also a farm at Wagon Mound. He is an Englishman who came here from Texas. Russell Marcy has been since 1873, when he came from Cal., a cattle-raiser on Palo Blanco Creek. He is also a banker at Raton, a representative business man of the territory, and has served as constable and county commissioner. Taylor F. Maulding, a native of Tenn., came in 1866, and has a large rancho on the Vermejo. James E. Temple, of Chico Springs, has a home ranch of 2,000 acres. He is an Irishman who, after many wanderings in America, came to N. Mex. in 1867, engaging unprofitably in mining at the Moreno placers, and later, with much success, in the dairy business down to 1882. Since that date he devotes himself to raising cattle.

fourths in the east. These grazing lands resemble those of Colfax in a general way, but are more cut up by ravines and timbered belts affording good protection from the winds. Thirty-eight thousand cattle and 78,000 sheep are noted by the assessor in 1883, but these figures are more than doubled by other authorities. The census of 1880 gives 576 farms, with an average extent of 101 acres, not only cereals but small fruits and sugar beets being successfully produced. In agricultural products for 1880 Mora, with $301,190, stood second in the list of counties. The total assessment in 1883 was $1,540,451. Mineral resources, known to be considerable, have been but very slightly developed, because the deposits are all on the unsettled Mora grant of some 800,000 acres. The railroad crosses the county from north to south, the principal stations being Ocate, Evans, Wagon Mound, Tiptonville, and Watrous. The latter has about 500 inhabitants, a newspaper—the *Pioneer*, formerly published at Tiptonville—and is the point of distribution for stock-men in most parts of the county. Mora, the county seat and the oldest town—dating from the issue of the land grant in 1835—had a population of 915 in 1880, probably scattered over a considerable area. Fort Union is one of the best known military posts of the territory, having been much of the time the military headquarters. The reader will recall the unsuccessful attempt of the confederates to capture this fort in 1861–2.[3]

Taos county covers a tract of about 1,400 square miles in the upper Rio Grande valley, directly west of Colfax and Mora. It was one of the original Mexican counties, including, as bounded by the act of 1852,

[3] The population of other towns in 1880 was, Coyote (upper and lower) 554, Ft Union 164, Guadalupita 428, Sirhuela (?) 179, Tiptonville 128, Watrous 100. A woollen mill, shut down and for sale, is reported in 1883. The raising of horses is named as a prominent industry of the future. Wells are more needed than in many parts, a large part of the grazing lands being available only in the wet season. Ft Union is described in *Worthington's Woman in Battle*, 601, and there is a plan in Wheeler's *U. S. Geog. Surv.*, ii. 491. Wm Krönig's *Report as to Mora County*, Las Vegas, 1881, is the source of most that appears about the county in other works.

all of the present counties of Colfax and Mora, a wide strip of Rio Arriba extending westward to the Arizona line, and all that part of the territory since annexed to Colorado. Thus, from being one of the largest it has become one of the smallest counties. It takes its name from the pueblo of Taos, one of the grandest found by Coronado's expedition of 1540, and still standing as the chief attraction of the region for visitors of to-day. Another of the ancient pueblos, that of the Picuríes, still stands as in the past centuries. The chief town is also Taos—known as Fernandez de Taos or Don Fernandez de Taos, a corruption, I suppose, of San Fernando de Taos—situated several miles from the old pueblo, having a population of about 2,000, and having always been the county seat. The average altitude of the county is 6,000 feet, and it is one of the best watered and timbered regions of the territory, having always been famous for its agricultural excellence. That very much greater progress has not been made in this direction is due chiefly to the fact that four fifths of the 12,000 inhabitants are of Mexican origin, and cling to their primitive methods of cultivation; yet Taos produced $386,283 in agricultural products in 1880, standing first in the list of counties. The assessment was $583,810 in 1883, when there were about 2,000 cattle and 83,000 sheep. There were in 1880, 888 farms, averaging 73 acres in size. The Taos mines have been more fully developed than others in the north, with good results from both quartz and placers, as elsewhere noted. The Denver and Rio Grande narrow-gauge railroad extends through the county, or along the western border, from north to south, affording easy access to what has been a comparatively isolated region; and the result in respects of immigration from Colorado has already been felt. Taos seems destined to be in the future as in the past one of the garden-spots of the territory. There are no towns of much importance, outside of the county seat, not mentioned in the census of 1880; but among the small hamlets may be mentioned Ranchos de Taos, with a fine flouring mill, Arroyo Seco, Arroyo Hondo, San Antonio Cerro, Castilla, Ojo Caliente, Red River Town, and Calabria.[4]

Rio Arriba, or 'Up the River,' county occupies an area of about 12,500 square miles in the north-western corner of the territory, lying west of Taos. It was one of the old Mexican counties, but originally and as organized in 1852 it did not include the northern strip along the San Juan. This strip was in 1861 cut off from Taos and organized as the county of San Juan, with the seat at Baker City; but the act was repealed in 1862; and in 1880 the tract was added to Rio Arriba. (In 1887, as this goes into type, San Juan has been again created.) The county seat was in 1852 fixed at San Pedro Chamita; but moved to Los Luceros in 1855, to Alcalde in 1860, and finally, in 1880, to Las Nutrias, which was renamed Tierra Amarilla. The average altitude is nearly 7,000 feet. In the south-eastern parts, near the Rio Grande, this county resembles Taos, and has all the agricultural advantages of its neighbor in respect of soil, water, and productions. Another fine agricultural tract, which in recent years is rapidly being filled up with settlers, is that in the valleys of the San Juan and Las Animas, in the north-west. In 1880 the county had 915 farms —heading the list—averaging 67 acres in size, and yielding $176,641 of farm products. In 1883, according to the assessor's report, its 80,054 acres were

---

[4] *Theo. C. Camp's Report on Taos Co.*, Sta Fé, 1881, contains nearly all that appears in modern publications on the subject. See also an article in the Las Vegas *Revista Católica*, 1881, p. 534 et seq. The county has no newspaper. The reader will find Taos often mentioned in the country's early annals. At Taos was, for many years, the home of Kit Carson, and here lie his remains. His career has been given in my *History of California*. No man was better known or more respected in N. Mex. than this famous scout and Indian-fighter, who became brevet-colonel of U. S. volunteers, and served also as Indian agent. He died in 1868 at Ft Lyon, and his wife, Josefa Jaramillo, the same year. He left 7 children living, and a considerable amount of property, as shown by his will and other documents among the *Carson Papers*, MS. Santiago Valdés, born and educated at Taos, gave me in 1884 a brief statement on *Public Affairs in New Mexico*, MS. He has been county clerk, many times member of the legislature, and probate judge. He names the famous Padre Martinez as his father as well as teacher.

valued at $87,282; there were 13,791 cattle and 171,107 sheep, not including the extensive flocks of the Navajos; and the total assessment was $788,180. Natural advantages for farming and stock-raising are excellent, but only to a comparatively slight extent utilized; while the mineral resources, known to be large, have been still less developed, though in late years mines are successfully worked in several districts. In the extreme west the Navajos have their immense but somewhat barren reservation, as recorded in other chapters; while in the eastern regions, about Abiquiú and Tierra Amarilla, the Jicarillas and Utes formerly roved and had their agencies. The narrow-gauge railroad from Colorado has its terminus at Española; while another branch extends through the northern borders to and beyond Amargo, where coal mines are worked. Tierra Amarilla, the county seat, is but a small village, and the county has as yet no towns of any special importance, or of more than a few hundred inhabitants, except Santa Cruz, which is said to have had 1,000 in 1883. The total population in 1880 was 11,023, but the number has since been considerably increased by immigration. It will be remembered by the reader that Rio Arriba has played a prominent part in the country's early annals. Here are seen the wonderful cliff dwellings, built by the Pueblo tribes long before the Spaniards visited the province. Here are the aboriginal pueblos of San Juan, Santa Cruz, and Santa Clara. Here Oñate in 1599 fixed his capital, at San Juan de los Caballeros, at the junction of the Rio Grande and Chama; and here he proposed to build the great city of his province, though circumstances required a change of plan, and the town was built at Santa Fé. Under Spanish rule Santa Cruz de la Cañada was a more or less prosperous villa, ranking among the first, with Santa Fé and Alburquerque, in population.[5]

---

[5] The pop. of Rio Arriba towns is given in the census of 1880 as follows: Cañoncito 147, Chimallo 175, El Cerro 228, Embudo 249, La Joya 347, Las

Bernalillo county lies south of Rio Arriba, having an area of some 6,500 square miles, a width of over 70 miles in the great valley, extending westward to the Arizona line, and eastward in an absurd little strip, far enough to make an entire length of about 250 miles. This was one of the original counties of 1852 and earlier, but its boundaries were changed in 1870. The county seat in 1854 was changed from the ranchos to the town of Alburquerque, where it has since remained, though in 1878 an election for a change was authorized. The north-eastern portion was formerly Santa Ana, with seat at Santa Ana and later Peña Blanca; but this little county—also one of the original ones—was merged in Bernalillo by act of 1876. In wealth and population this has always been one of the leading sections of the territory. The rich alluvial lands of the Rio Grande bottom, having for 80 miles an average width of five miles, furnish unsurpassed advantages for agricultural operations; and the region is especially noted for its grapes and small fruits. In 1880 there were only 112 farms, with 3,821 acres of improved land, producing $94,730. In 1883 the acreage is given as 116,037, valued at $1,160,370. Thus the farming lands have not yet been very fully utilized. Back from the river are the mesa tracts, from ten to twenty miles in width, on which, in 1883, grazed 475,000 sheep and 41,700 cattle, this county heading the list in the item of sheep. Mines are successfully worked, especially in the Sandía Mountains, at the New Placers on the Santa Fé borders, and in the Nacimiento or Jemes district. The total assessed value of property in 1883 was $4,328,605. The population in 1880 was 17,225,

Truchas 220, Los Sirceros (Luceros?) 155, Alcalde 168, Puente 195, Sta Cruz 196. Figures of 1883 are: Aztec 200, Española 150, Sta Cruz (1,000), Chama 300, Chamita (500), El Rito (1,000), Embudo (1,500), Porter City (Bloomfield) 300, Tierra Amarilla (1,200); but in case of the larger figures, including Sta Cruz, I suppose the pop. is that of the township, and includes the scattered farmers. Samuel Eldodt's *Report as to Rio Arriba County*, Sta Fé, 1881, is the foundation which other writers have for the most part followed. See also Las Vegas *Revista Católica*, 1881, p. 488 et seq.

but has considerably increased in later years. Here, in that part of the great valley adjoining the town of Bernalillo, was Coronado's Tiguex, where he spent the winter of 1540–2. Of the ancient pueblos, the county contains Jemes, Cia, Santa Ana, Cochití, Santo Domingo, and Isleta; and the most of the towns of the great valley are settlements with which the reader is familiar from Spanish times, very slight improvement being noted in modern times, notwithstanding their exceptional advantages. Alburquerque, the county seat, is, however, a notable exception. It was founded in 1706, named for the viceroy of Mexico, and was in Spanish times a flourishing town, often mentioned in the earlier chapters of this volume. New Mexicans usually write the name Albuquerque, incorrectly, claiming the duke as governor, and being greatly at sea respecting the early annals of the villa. The modern city is of very recent growth, though adjoining the old one, dating from 1880, when the first locomotive arrived over the Atchison, Topeka, and Santa Fé Railroad. Its growth has been remarkable, the population in 1880 being 2,315, in 1883 about 3,500, and now claimed to be 10,000, making this the metropolis of the territory. It is at the junction of the two main lines of railroad, is looking for the arrival of divers other lines, and bases its faith in future greatness on its position as a railroad centre, as well as on the surrounding country's resources. The new town has many solid brick blocks, good hotels, fine residences, several manufacturing establishments, besides the railroad shops; and it takes especial pride in its schools, including the Alburquerque Academy and the Indian school, and above all in its clearly manifested spirit of progress. The second town is Bernalillo, with some 1,800 inhabitants; and the third Golden, with about 1,000.[6]

[6] The pop. of towns by the census of 1880 was: Alameda 570 (650), Alburquerque 2,315 (10,000), Algodones 376 (500), Barelas 350 (400), Bernalillo 1,273 (1,800), Cañon de Jemes 196, Casa de Salazar 200 (400), Corrales 664 (600), El Rancho 400 (300), Guadalupe 161, La Ventura 122 (400), Los Griegos

Santa Fé county, lying east and north of Bernalillo, has an area of 1,250 square miles. It is one of the old counties, with seat of government always at the city of Santa Fé, though the boundaries were slightly changed by acts of 1864, 1869–70, and 1882. It is the smallest subdivision of the territory, of broken and mountainous surface, with a limited area of farming lands and still more limited supply of water; yet, like most other parts of New Mexico, blessed with a most productive soil, with great agricultural possibilities in proportion to its extent. In 1880 there were 313 farms, of 42 acres average size, farm products being estimated at $59,107. In 1883 its 55,425 acres were valued by the assessor at $389,265; there were 3,415 cattle and 22,250 sheep; and the total assessment of property was $2,993,049. The population was 10,867 in 1880, and has since been largely increased. Mining has been more actively prosecuted here than in any other northern county, both in early and later times, the Old and New Placers, Los Cerrillos, and the turquoise mines being famous, as elsewhere recorded. Manufacturing industry here, as everywhere, is yet dormant; but the invaluable beds of anthracite coal, with other natural advantages, promise to make Santa Fé a manufacturing centre of the future. The Atchison, Topeka, and Santa Fé Railroad crosses the county from east to west, sending out a branch from Lamy station northward to the capital. The old Indian pueblos are Nambé, Tesuque, Pujuaque, and

San Ildefonso.   The towns outside of the capital are small but flourishing villages in the mining districts, including Los Cerrillos, Bonanza, Carbonateville, and San Pedro.

The city of Santa Fé—or San Francisco de Asis de la Santa Fé—the county seat and territorial capital, has been from the first the centre of the historical happenings recorded in this volume; and no retrospect is needed here.   The town was founded shortly—perhaps several years—before 1617.   Its oft-repeated claim to greater antiquity, or to be considered the oldest town in the United States, can rest only on the possibility that it was founded on the site of a small aboriginal pueblo, and is not a legitimate claim.   The city is old enough and interesting enough without such exaggeration.   In Spanish, Mexican, and American times it has been the capital, metropolis, and commercial centre of the territory; though in the past few years it has, as is claimed, been surpassed in population by Alburquerque, its chief rival in the past. It had 6,635 inhabitants in 1880, and the population is now about 8,000.   During the past decade its quaint old, Mexican, one-story adobes have given way to a considerable extent to brick blocks and residences of modern style.   It has gas and water works, good hotels, and fine churches and schools.   The town is the archbishop's residence, and the catholics have three churches besides the cathedral, with the San Miguel college of the Christian Brothers, the convent and academy of Nuestra Señora de Luz.   Other educational institutions under protestant auspices are the Santa Fé academy and the university of New Mexico.   At Fort Marcy, in the city, are the military headquarters.   Among relics of antiquity the old adobe *palacio* holds the first rank, while the old foundations of the more modern capitol and penitentiary are also interesting ruins.   The town has an altitude of 7,044 feet, and is noted as a sanitarium.   With this advantage, its fascinating reminiscences of past centuries, its central position, its modern spirit of thrift, its extensive mercantile establishments, and its half-dozen newspapers, Santa Fé looks forward to a future of prosperity, and has not the slightest idea of ceding its supremacy, political, commercial, or in any respect, to either Alburquerque or Las Vegas, its most ambitious rivals.[7]

[7] The census of 1880 names besides Sta Fé only Galisteo, with 506 inhab. In 1883 Los Cerrillos is said to have a pop. of 1,800, and Golden of 300. The Sta Fé newspapers are the *New Mexican, Mining News, Nuevo Mejicano, Christian Advocate, Democrat,* and *Military Review;* while at Golden is published the *Retort,* and S. Pedro has a weekly, the name of which is not given. Ritch's *Aztlan* gives the best sketch of Sta Fé; but there is hardly a work cited by me in these chapters that does not devote much space to the description of this old city.

Major John Ayers, often named in other chapters as Indian agent, is a New Yorker, who after 10 years of sailor life went to Cal. in 1849. In 1861 he enlisted in the Cal. volunteers, and came to N. Mex. with Gen. Carleton, being promoted in the service to lieut. and quartermaster. He dates the real improvement of the native population from the coming of the soldiers; and in his *Soldier's Experience in N. Mex.,* MS., 1884, he gives many valuable items on military and Ind. affairs, land grants, and events generally. The decoration of Sta Fé with trees began in 1866 at his instigation and under his direction. Hon. Elias Brevoort is a native of Mich., who came in 1850, after a long experience as trader among the Indians; and he has since travelled extensively in this and other territories and in Mexico. He takes pride in having ridden 300 miles from Doña Ana to Sta Fé in three days on one horse. A printed work from his pen is noted elsewhere; he has given me much aid in obtaining original material; and his *Sta Fé Trail,* MS., is an interesting narrative of his experience and observations. Judge Francis Downs, a prominent lawyer of Sta Fé since 1880, is a Canadian by birth, who served four years in the union army during the war of 1861–5, subsequently practising law in Arkansas, being twice elected to the bench, and also a member of the constitutional convention of 1874. He takes a deep interest in the early annals of New Mexico; gave me a brief *Dictation* in 1885; and has otherwise been of great service to me in obtaining items of information on various subjects. Samuel Ellison, territorial librarian, is another who has given me important aid in my researches, and has been named often in this volume. He is a Kentuckian, who went to Texas as a lieut. in 1837, served in the Mex. war as quartermaster, and came to this territory from Mex. in 1848 with Col Washington. Later he was secretary, interpreter, translator, legislator, and held various other positions before being made librarian and keeper of the archives in 1881. His *History of N. Mex.,* MS., 1884, is not only a sketch of his own life, but contains his important testimony on early events and officials. Geo. W. Hickox is a native of Ohio, who came in 1880 and is engaged in the manufacture of the famous Sta Fé gold and silver filagree jewelry, employing 8 to 15 hands, and making annual sales of $75–110,000. Wm G. Ritch has also been frequently named in a variety of connections. He came as territorial sec. in 1873. He is a native of N. Y. For biog., see Chicago *Inter-Ocean,* June 2, 1883. No man has worked more actively or efficiently for the territorial welfare, especially in the cause of education, and in making known the country's resources. As secretary, acting gov., and president of the Historical Society and Bureau of Immig., he has played an important part from the first. His *Hist. N. Mex.,* MS., contains some hasty notes of much interest and covering a wide range of topics. Lehman Spiegelberg, a prominent merchant of Sta Fé, is a Prussian, who came in

San Miguel county lies east of Santa Fé and Bernalillo, extending eastward to the Texas line, with an area of 10,600 square miles. It was one of the old organizations, the boundaries being slightly modified in 1882, and the county seat being changed from San Miguel to Las Vegas and back again in 1860–2, but finally fixed at Las Vegas from 1864. San Miguel had a population of 20,638 in 1880, which has been largely increased. Not only is it the most populous and one of the largest counties, but it is probably in most important respects—except that of mineral resources, which exist but have not been much developed —the best and richest. It is watered by the Pecos and Canadian, with their branches, and contains a large amount of the richest soil, well situated for irrigation, while certain considerable tracts will produce crops without artificially supplied water. In 1880 there were 622 farms, averaging 283 acres in size, and yielding $155,286 in products. In 1883 the valuation of farm property was $362,443. The mesas of the east and south furnish the best of grazing ranges, and stock-raising is the county's industry. In 1883 there were assessed 47,295 cattle and 385,799 sheep, San Miguel taking second rank in each item; but in later years there has been a very great development, and now this county probably heads the list. The western mountains are well wooded, and the lumber business has assumed comparatively large proportions. In climate and scenery this region is unsurpassed by any in the territory. The abandoned pueblo of Pecos —the Cicuye of Coronado in 1540—is an object of historic interest, and there are many older ruins; the

1858, being preceded by four brothers in 1844–54, and followed by another in 1861. His *Commerce of Sta Fé*, MS., is a sketch of his journey across the plains, and of his observations of trading matters in early times, and a general idea of the country's progress in other respects. J. H. Watts is a son of John S. Watts, one of the original justices of the supreme court. He is a native of Ohio, and came in 1857 at the age of 18. He has had much experience as translator and surveyor in the military and land offices. His *Sta Fé Affairs*, MS., 1878, is devoted largely to pointing out the sources of historical information; also in part to his own observations in the country, and to his father's services.

route of the old Santa Fé trading caravans was nearly
identical with that of the modern railroad; here were
fought the battles of the confederate invasion of
1861–2. Las Vegas, the county seat, though its history dates back only to 1835, has grown steadily and
become the third town in New Mexico, with a population of about 6,000, and with unlimited aspirations
for the future. It is in all respects a 'live' town in
its commerce and industries, and perhaps the most
agreeable of all New Mexican towns as a place of
residence. It has several good newspapers, fine public buildings and hotels, gas and water works, a street
railroad, several churches, and exceptionally good
educational institutions, headed by the Jesuit college.
The city expects to be a railroad centre when divers
inevitable lines shall have been built, is as well situated
as any other town for business, is the distributing
point for an immense stock and farming region in the
east, has enterprising merchants, who already do a
large trade, and will by no means yield the palm as
commercial metropolis of the future either to Santa
Fé or Alburquerque. Six miles away, with a branch
railroad, are the Las Vegas Hot Springs, with fine
and constantly increasing accommodations for pleasure-
seekers and invalids. The waters are claimed to be
unsurpassed, like the climate, and the property is fortunately controlled by the railroad company, which
has the means and disposition to make this the great
resort of the south-western interior. Outside of Las
Vegas the villages are as yet of small population and
of no special importance. One of the smallest and
least important of these is San Miguel del Vado,
which in Spanish and Mexican times was the place
most frequently mentioned, and which gave a name
to the county.[8]

[8] The pop. of towns by the census of 1880 is as follows: Agua Zarca 128,
Cañon del Agua 186, El Bruno 139, La Cinta 117 (150), Las Colonias 148, S.
Lorenzo 249, Nietos 382, Pecos 241, Romero 159, Sabinosa 169, S. José 277,
Sapello 182, Tewlotenos (?) 176, Vigilias 123. In 1883 are mentioned Anton
Chico 500, Gallinas Spr. 900, Glorieta 300, Liberty 200, Los Alamos 600,

Valencia county lies south of Bernalillo, having the same length from east to west, and covering an area of about 7,500 square miles. Its southern boundary with that of San Miguel forms a dividing line between northern and southern New Mexico. This is one of the old counties, its boundaries having been modified by acts of 1870 and 1882. The county seat was in early times at Valencia, but in 1852 was moved to Tomé, to Belen in 1872, back to Tomé in 1874, and finally to Las Lunas in 1876. The population in 1880 was 13,095, ranking third in the list of counties. There were 239 farms, of 97 acres average size, and farm products were valued at $102,701. In 1883 the

Puerto de Luna 600, Red River Springs 23, S. Hilario 600, most of these figures including townships rather than villages. The newspapers are the Las Vegas *Gazette, Optic, Revista,* and *Mining World;* and the S. Lorenzo (or S. Hilario) *Red River Chronicle, Crónica,* and Mineral City *News. G. W. Prichard's Report of San Miguel County* was published at Las Vegas, 1882. See also *H. T. Wilson's Historical Sketch of Las Vegas,* Chicago, n. d., an excellent work; *Porter's Directory of Las Vegas,* 1882-3; *N. Mex., Climate of, and Las Vegas Hot Springs,* Chicago, 1885; *Las Vegas Hot Springs,* 3d ed., Springfield, O., 1883; *Alburquerque and Las Vegas Directory,* 1883.
     The following residents of S. Miguel co. have given me MS. *Dictations* or *Statements,* as noted in the list of authorities, on stock-raising and other interests of their region: Frank W. Dale, from Ohio, has since 1883 been in the cattle business at Carpenter's rancho, near Ft Bascom, where he is constantly increasing his herd of Durhams. Henry Dold, of Las Vegas, is the son of Andrew D., a German, who came in 1851 and became a prominent merchant and govt contractor, being the owner of the Hot Springs property, which he sold to the R. R. for $41,000. Dr E. C. Henriques, a practising physician of Las Vegas since 1878, has also a large stock range in Valencia co. He is a native of Conn. James C. Leary, a native of Mass., came in 1879, and was for 6 years foreman for S. W. Dorsey. Later he organized the Wagon Mound Cattle co., of which he is still secretary, being also largely interested in other companies, besides doing a live-stock commission business at Las Vegas. Francisco Lopez, a native of Sta Fé, was the founder of S. Lorenzo in 1862. He was also in the sheep and later the cattle business. W. H. McBroom, a Canadian, came to the territory in 1876, and lived at Sta Fé for 9 years. Then he engaged in cattle-raising near Ft Sumner, where, by owning water-rights, he controls a range of 800,000 acres. He is also interested in breeding fine horses. Benigno Romero, born at Sta Fé, is a merchant at Las Vegas, in partnership with his brother, Don Hilario. To his *Dictation* is appended a newspaper biog. of his mother, Doña Josefa Delgado de Romero. Michael Slattery, a New Yorker, formerly engaged in freighting in Col. and Montana, came to N. Mex. in 1867, and is manager of the Waddingham Ranges and Cattle-raising Assoc., which controls 100,000 acres near Ft Bascom, the Montoya rancho of 655,000 acres, and the P. P. range of 36,000 acres. Napoleon B. Stoneroad, residing with his family at Las Vegas, is a member of the firm of S. Brothers, who raise cattle on a large scale at the Cabra Springs range of 318,000 acres, having abandoned sheep as less profitable. He is a native of Ala. and a '49er of Cal., coming to N. Mex. with a drove of sheep in 1876.

land was assessed at $2,209,323, and all property at $3,834,200, there being 12,066 cattle and 217,778 sheep. These figures would indicate a good showing as compared with those for other parts of the territory; though most current descriptions point to a lack of development. The agricultural land is for the most part confined to the Rio Grande valley, whose length in Valencia is limited, but the grazing lands are of great extent, though standing in greater need of wells than many other sections. Mineral resources are almost entirely undeveloped, though several districts, notably the Manzano, Ladrones, La Joya, and Spiegelberg, have shown good prospects. There are broad coal-fields and fine deposits of salt. Las Lunas, the county seat and chief town, has a population of about 2,000, and is a distributing point of some importance. Belen, or Bethlehem, has nearly 1,500 inhabitants. Fort Wingate, in the north-west, is near the Navajo reservation, and is intended to keep the Indians in subjection. Zuñi and Acoma are the aboriginal pueblos, both famous in early annals. Coronado's route in the sixteenth century led him past Zuñi, or Cíbola, and the peñol town of Acoma to the great valley, and the Atlantic and Pacific Railroad follows nearly the same route. The fall of Acoma was the deciding event of Oñate's conquest, and has been graphically narrated in Villagrá's epic. Laguna, by its situation, gives the overland passenger by rail his best view of a pueblo, though it is of comparatively modern origin.[9]

Lincoln county, lying south of San Miguel and Valencia, and occupying the south-eastern corner of the territory, is the largest of the counties, with an area of 20,000 square miles, and has the smallest population, only 2,513 in 1880. It was created in 1869, being

[9] The census of 1880 gives Las Lunas a pop. of 876, S. Mateo 311, and Cubero 253. In 1883, according to the *N. Mex. Bus. Directory*, Las Lunas had 2,000, Belen 1,500, Manzano 600, Peralta 1,000, S. Mateo 411, Zuñi 2,000, Laguna 1,200, Cubero 400. The R. R. stations have as yet assumed no importance as towns. The county has no newspaper, and the settlements still retain for the most part their old Mexican characteristics.

cut off from Socorro, and the boundaries being defined by act of 1878. The seat was fixed at Rio Bonito, formerly called Las Placitas, and renamed Lincoln in 1870. The county was for a time attached to Socorro for judicial purposes. It is watered by the Rio Pecos, the old Rio de las Vacas, and its branches; and the great valley is thought to possess great agricultural possibilities for the future. In the east, adjoining Texas, the plains are arid and largely unfit for grazing except by means of wells. In the western plains and mountain valleys the grazing is excellent. In 1883 Lincoln headed the list with 81,053 cattle, and stood sixth with 137,013 sheep. The assessed value of property was $2,053,176; and 18,283 acres of land were valued at $60,628. In 1880 there were 60 farms, averaging 224 acres in size, and producing $38,749. Rich mines have been worked in the districts of White Oaks, Nogal, Bonito, Red Cloud, and others in the western mountains. Among the impediments to progress the most serious have been Indian troubles, the disorderly character of the population, and the lack of means of transportation. Here, under the protection of Fort Stanton, is the Apache reservation, and the field of countless raids in former years. Here have been the most serious disturbances and 'rustler' wars between Texan, native, and Mexican stock-men, miners, and desperadoes. And this is the only county that has no railroad, though several are projected. Lincoln, the county seat, with 500 inhabitants, has no special importance, except in being the county seat. White Oaks, a mining town, has a population of about 1,000, and is the county metropolis. Roswell is regarded as the prospective site of an important agricultural centre.[10]

[10] Population by census of 1880: Ft Stanton 118, Lincoln 638, South Fork 196, White Oaks 268. The *Guadalupe Mountains*, n. p., n. d., is a pamphlet of 8 pages of descriptive matter. *Garrett (Pat. F.), The Authentic Life of Billy the Kid*, Sta Fé, 1882, 137 p., is a biog. of Wm H. Bonney, a famous outlaw and murderer, by the sheriff who finally killed him. The book contains much information about the 'Lincoln Co. War' of stock-men in 1878, etc.

Socorro county covers an area of about 12,000 miles west of Lincoln and south of Valencia. It originally included all of southern New Mexico; but Doña Ana was cut off in 1852 and Lincoln in 1869; and the boundaries were otherwise somewhat changed in 1870, 1872, and 1880. The county seat was removed to Limitar in 1854, but restored to Socorro in 1867. With its long stretch of fertile alluvial soil in the main valley, and its 4–6,000,000 acres of grazing lands, this county is believed to have unexcelled advantages for agriculture and stock-raising, though both industries, and especially the former, have hitherto been too much neglected. In 1880, nevertheless, there were 728 farms, averaging 53 acres each, and producing $217,295. In 1883 the assessment was $330,793 on 393,170 acres; there were 20,430 cattle and 66,615 sheep; and the total valuation of property was $2,450,-193. According to Ritch, in 1882–4 cattle increased from 9,000 to 70,000, while sheep decreased from 300,000 to 100,000. Mining activity dates from about 1881, and in the yield of silver, gold, and copper Socorro has become one of the leading counties, with over 50 districts and many remarkably productive mines. With the growth of this great mining industry the others retrograded at first, but in recent years there are indications of revival; and a prosperous future seems assured. Socorro, the county seat, is a flourishing town of over 3,000 inhabitants, with every sign of becoming a commercial centre of great importance; and doubtless other settlements will eventually enter the race of progress, though hitherto all have been content with mere existence. The railroad down the Rio Grande traverses the county from north to south, two short branches extend to the mines at Carthage and Magdalena, and here, as everywhere, several cross-county roads are looked for in the early future. In a certain sense Socorro may be regarded as the oldest Spanish name in New Mexico, though it is not quite certain that the pueblo or spot so named in the sixteenth century by Oñate is exactly the site of the present town. In this region was the southern-most group of pueblos, noted by all the early explorers coming from the south, or in the case of Coronado from the north; and the name Nuestra Señora del Socorro was given in 1598, in recognition of the succor there found after crossing the southern deserts. Span-ish and Mexican annals deal for the most part only with the line of settlements along the river, where the early pueblos have long since disappeared; but in the north-east were several flourishing mission pueblos, eventually destroyed by Apaches, the ruins of which are still seen at Abó, Gran Quivira, and other places.[11]

Grant county occupies the south-western corner of the territory, with an area of about 7,000 square miles, being bounded on the west by Arizona and on the south by Mexico. It is a new county, organized by act of 1868. It was then cut off from Doña Ana, and a small portion of its territory was included in the Arizona county of 1860–1, before Arizona was or-ganized as a territory. There was in 1877 an un-successful attempt to attach it to Arizona; and the boundary was slightly changed in 1880. The county seat was originally at Central City, but was moved to Pinos Altos in 1869 and to Silver City in 1872. This region does not figure in the early records, except as the Santa Rita copper mines were worked to some ex-tent in Mexican and Spanish times. It is essentially a mining county, the development of which began at Pinos Altos in 1866, and the yield of which in 1872–81 was about $5,000,000. In this industry, as elsewhere recorded, it heads the list of New Mexican counties. Here was the home of the Apaches, and the scene of many a bloody combat. The population was 4,539 in

[11] Socorro, with a population of 1,272, is the only town noted in the census of 1880. S. Marcial and Chloride are mentioned in 1883; also as post-offices Beaver, Ft Craig, Horse Springs, Magdalena, Paraje, S. Antonio, S. Fran-cisco, Cherryville, and Clairmount. Ft Craig is a place of historical interest, as is Valverde, the battle-field of 1862. *Magdalena, Prospectus of the Town*, is a pamphlet pub. at Sta Fé, 1885, 12mo, 24 p. M. Fischer and A. Abeytia are the authors of the *Report as to Socorro Co.*, Soc., 1881.

1880, and has been doubled since. The native or Mexican element is comparatively small. There are excellent agricultural tracts, especially in the valleys of the Mimbres and Gila, where about 10,000 acres are cultivated, the mining camps affording an advantageous market. In 1880, 68 farms, with an average extent of 144 acres, are noted as producing $145,167. In 1883 the assessment was $64,350 on 5,052 acres; total valuation of property $2,960,874. Grazing lands are extensive, of good quality, and somewhat more fully utilized than in other parts of the territory. In 1883 there were 15,871 cattle and 328,400 sheep. The Southern Pacific Railroad crosses the county from west to east, with a narrow-gauge branch from Lordsburg to Clifton in Arizona; while the Atchison, Topeka, and Santa Fé road comes to Deming and has a branch to Silver City. The county seat, Silver City, is the mining centre, and though a new town, incorporated in 1878, has a population of 3,000, with solid brick buildings and all the characteristics of a thriving modern city. Deming, at the junction of the two great railroad lines, and noted as the only competing railroad point in the territory, has sprung up since 1880, and has a population of nearly 2,000, with well-founded aspirations to the position of county metropolis in the early future. Georgetown, Pinos Altos, Santa Rita, Lordsburg, Shakespeare, and Carlisle are the most prominent of other settlements.[12]

Doña Ana county covers an area of about 6,700 square miles on the southern frontier, between Grant on the west and Lincoln on the east. It comprises a considerable portion of the Gadsden purchase of 1853-4. The county was cut off from Socorro in 1852, and then included all of southern New Mexico. Besides

[12] The census figures of 1880 were: Central City 126, Georgetown 540, Pinos Altos 150, S. Lorenzo 284, Silver City 1,800. This county produced 15,222 lbs. of butter in 1880, more than double the product of any other. *W. H. Lawrence's Report as to Grant County*, Silver City, 1881, contains nearly all the information extant in other works. The newspapers are the Silver City *New South-west*, *Mining Chronicle*, and *Telegram;* the Lordsburg *Advance;* Georgetown *Silver Brick;* and Deming *Headlight.*

the cutting-off of the other southern counties, as elsewhere recorded, the boundary was modified by acts of 1870, 1872, and 1878. The county seat was originally Doña Ana, but was changed to Las Cruces in 1853, to Mesilla in 1856, and finally to Las Cruces again in 1882. The population in 1880, including most of Sierra county, was 7,612; and is now, alone, probably much more. The lower Rio Grande valley is known as the Mesilla valley, and is a veritable garden-spot, famous not only for its general crops of grain, but for its vegetables—especially onions—small fruits, and above all, for its grapes and wine. Its soil is fertile and easily irrigated; two crops in a year are often raised, and hay can be cut on the mesas any day in the year. In 1880 there are noted 431 farms, averaging 107 acres, and producing $175,005. In 1883 the assessment was $474,817 on 36,584 acres; and the total valuation of property was $1,417,354. Back from the river the mesas furnish the same advantage for grazing that are found in other regions; but in 1883 only 7,248 cattle and 24,853 sheep are reported. Rich mines have been worked, especially in the Organos, Jarillas, and Potrillas mountains. The county is traversed by the Southern Pacific Railroad from Deming to El Paso, and by the Atchison road from Deming to Rincon, and from Rincon down the Rio Grande to El Paso, so that no region is better supplied with railroads. Las Cruces, the county seat, has about 1,500 inhabitants, a newspaper, the *Rio Grande Republican*, and is the business centre. Mesilla, with a population of 1,200, and another paper, the *News*, is a close rival. Rincon and Nutt are railroad junction stations. This section has no early history, except that it was traversed by all the explorers and travellers between new and old Mexico. I have not even been able to learn from what particular Doña Ana the settlement derived its name; probably from the wife of one of the early explorers or governors. The first settlement of the Mesilla valley was by a Chihuahua colony, after the boundary survey had left this tract in Mexico, and before the Gadsden treaty restoring it to the United States.[13]

Sierra county is a new creation of 1884, when it was formed from portions of Doña Ana, Grant, and Socorro, with county seat at Hillsborough. It has an area of about 2,100 miles, as I estimate it from the map, though different figures are given by Ritch and others. On account of its recent origin no statistics are accessible. It is a mountainous region, with considerable grazing ranges, which have been comparatively well utilized, and many fertile though small valleys, which may in time be cultivated. The main industry is, however, mining, in which the county takes the highest rank in proportion to its size, and very nearly so without reference to area. Only a few mines have been developed, notably those of the Lake Valley district,.but these have proved by far the most productive of the territory. Hillsborough, the county seat, Lake Valley, and Kingston are connected with the main railroad by a branch from Nutt station, and are thriving mining centres, of small population as yet; and the northern settlements are Palomas, Fairview, Grafton, Robinson, and Chloride. The Cañada Alamosa is known to the reader as the site of a former Indian reservation; and in the main Rio Grande valley, now traversed by the Atchison, Topeka, and Santa Fé Railroad, is the famous Jornada del Muerto, an object of terror in early times to all who were compelled to make the trip between old and new Mexico.

[13] La Luz and Tularosa, with pop. of 249 and 549, are the only towns named in the census of 1880. The post-offices named in 1883 are Colorado, near Hatch Station, 500, Doña Ana 600, Ft Selden, S. Agustin, Tularosa, Chamberino, La Mesa, Thorne, and Victoria. *A. J. Fourtain's Report on Doña Ana Co.*, 1882, corresponds with the other county reports cited, and is quoted by Ritch and others.

INDEX.

NOTE.—Attention is called to the heading 'Lists' and to other general or inclusive headings, such as 'Statistics,' 'Pueblos,' 'Towns,' 'Forts,' Landgrants,' 'Governors,' 'Officials,' 'Military Commanders,' 'Mines,' 'Legislature,' etc., the separate items of which are not as a rule entered alphabetically in this index; that is, in looking for a particular governor, or fort, or town, see, in addition to the references here given, the general heading that includes it.

A

Abeitia, Antonio, 752, 798.
Abert, J. W., 465.
Abiquiú, 249, 258, 307, 340, 419, 421–2, 462, 665 et seq., 737 et seq.
Abó, 129, 138, 161, 170, 653, 798.
Abreu, gov. Santiago, 313, 318, 426.
Acebedo, Fr., 72.
Acha, 64.
Acoma, 42, 50–1, 54, 56, 86, 97, 138–45, 160–1, 182, 195, 200, 202, 207, 216–7, 221–2, 226, 229, 231, 274.
Acts of Legislature, Ariz., 539–42.
Acts of Legislature, N. Mex.. 637–40, 710 et seq.
Acuco, 45, 50, see 'Acoma.'
Acuña, Fran., 355.
Acus, 31, see 'Acoma.'
Acuye, 53.
Adams, G. H., 107.
Adams, Whiting & Co., 531.
Agents, see 'Ind. Affairs.'
Agin, 53.
Ago, 51.
Agriculture, Ariz., 530, 534–5, 545, 572, 594 et seq., 596–7.
Agriculture, N. Mex., 275–6, 302–3, 644–5, 766–8.
Agua Caliente, 366–7.
Agua Fria, 586, 605.
Agua Negra, 742.
Aguas Calientes, 63.
Aguas Zarcas, 77.
Aguato, 87.
Aguatuvi, 201, 222, 225, 238, 249, 363–4, see 'Moqui.'
Aguilar, Alonso R., 236.
Aguilar, Pablo, 128, 133, 143.
Ahacus, 31, 41.

Aijados, 149.
Aijaos, 163.
Ainsworth, F. K., 613.
Ajuico, 170.
Ajo mines, 498, 579, 590.
Alameda, 188.
Alamillo, 181.
Alarcon, Hern., 9, 32, 35–6.
Albert, John, 432.
Alburquerque, 79, 168, 170, 188, 228, 231, 234, 239, 274, 296, 422, 428–9, 433 692–3, 697–8, 740–3, 774, 787–9.
Alcalde, plaza, 785.
Alcaldes, see 'government.'
Alchedomas, see 'Halchedumas.'
Aldrich, M., 504, 507.
Alegre, authority, 80.
Alencaster, Joaq. Real, gov., 284, 295–6, 300.
Alexander, lieut-col, 441.
Allande, gov. Pedro M.,284, 298.
Allen, Alf., 298.
Allen, Wm. C., 531.
Allyn, judge, 522.
Almanza, Ant., 296–7.
Almazan, Fran. A., 209.
Almy, lieut, 567.
Alona, 202–234.
Aloqui, 185, see 'Moqui.'
Alpuente, Juan, 205, 210.
Altar, 378, 393, 406.
Alvarado, Hern., 50 et seq.
Alvarado, Pedro, 35.
Alvarez, Juan, 227–8.
Alvarez, Manuel, 447–9.
Alvarez, Sebastian, 306.
Amacavas, 155, 348, see 'Mojaves.'
Amajavas, see 'Mojaves.'
Amales, 507.
Amargo, 786.

THIS is the third volume to be published by Calvin P. Horn and William S. Wallace with the Horn & Wallace imprint. In keeping with a policy of producing "books worth collecting," the publishers retained the services of one of the outstanding book designers in the United States, Roland F. Dickey, of Albuquerque, to design and direct through its manufacture this edition of Bancroft's History of Arizona and New Mexico. The publishers are indebted to Senators Clinton P. Anderson and Barry Goldwater for their generous and thoughtful contributions to this volume.

Beginning with the title on page iii, the present edition reproduces by direct facsimile the pages of the 1889 edition in their original sequence except for the large map which preceded page 1 of the first edition and has been enlarged and printed on the end papers of the present volume. The new title is handset in De Roos type, and the new fore matter is set in Linotype Electra — type faces chosen for intrinsic beauty and harmonious relation to the entirely hand-composed typography of the original edition. The book is printed by offset on Maxwell Offset paper. Binding is Bancroft's Buckram.

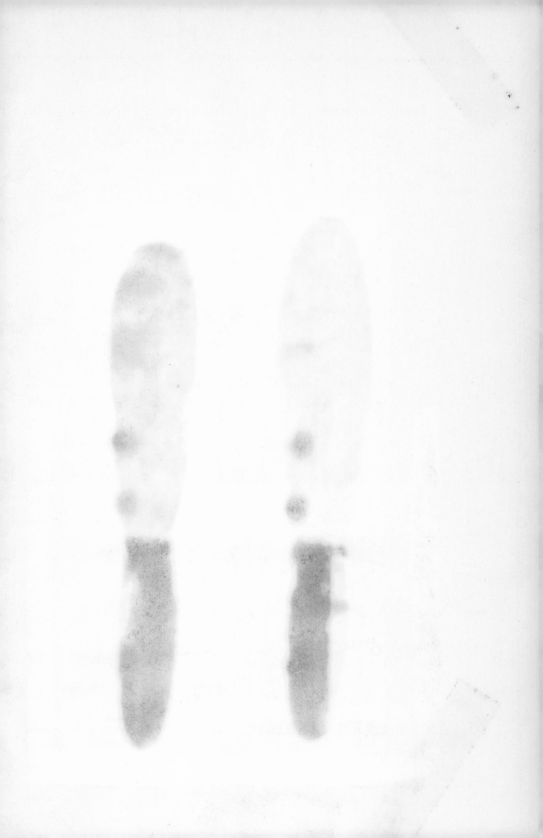

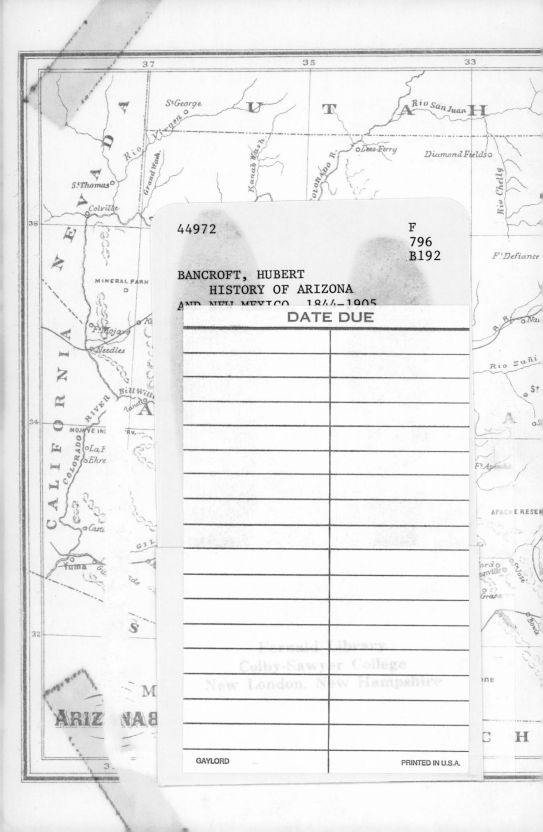